University Casebook Series

LAW

OF

MASS COMMUNICATIONS

FREEDOM AND CONTROL OF PRINT
AND BROADCAST MEDIA

By

DWIGHT L. TEETER, JR., Ph.D.
Professor and Dean, College of Communications
University of Tennessee

DON R. LE DUC, JD., Ph.D.
Professor and Chairman, Department of Mass Communication
University of Wisconsin—Milwaukee

EIGHTH EDITION

Westbury, New York
THE FOUNDATION PRESS, INC.
1995

COPYRIGHT © 1969, 1973, 1978, 1982, 1986, 1989, 1992 THE FOUNDATION PRESS, INC.

COPYRIGHT © 1995 By THE FOUNDATION PRESS, INC.

615 Merrick Ave.
Westbury, N.Y. 11590–6607
(516) 832–6950

Library of Congress Cataloging-in-Publication Data

Teeter, Dwight L.
    Law of mass communications : freedom and control of print and
broadcast media / by Dwight L. Teeter, Jr., Don R. Le Duc. — 8th
ed.
        p.   cm.
    Includes index.
    ISBN 1–56662–245–X (hardcover)
    1. Telecommunication—Law and legislation—United States.   I. Le
Duc, Don R.   II. Title.
KF2750.N4   1995
343.73099'8—dc20
[347.303998]   95–5869

 TEXT IS PRINTED ON 10% POST
CONSUMER RECYCLED PAPER

 PRINTED WITH
SOY INK

FOR TISH AND ALICE

*

PREFACE TO EIGHTH EDITION

A wise historian once noted that the present is only the cutting edge of the past. That's a comforting phrase when one searches for continuities in a time of cataclysmic changes in society and in communication devices, techniques and industries. If, however, you seek reality instead of comfort, it will become apparent that onrushing change is outracing much of the American legal order. For the most part, law *reacts*, it does not guide.

As American mass media continue to merge and to converge at a rate far faster than the ponderous pace of judicial review, mass communication law textbooks must have the capacity to examine legal implications of such changes in media systems or services wherever they may occur. The traditional communication law "case book," heavily dependent upon judicial opinions for its legal analysis, can furnish only limited guidance in an era when many of this field's most significant issues have not yet been reviewed by the courts.

Fortunately, **Law of Mass Communications** never has been constrained by this narrow "case book" view of mass communication law. For the past quarter century, this text's heritage of broadly based legal analysis has freed its authors to trace communication law issues to their sources. In this Eighth Edition, with the courts still in disarray over a wide range of communication law questions, it is necessary once again to venture beyond conflicting judicial opinions in search of answers traditional case law is as yet unable to provide.

From such a perspective, for example, it is possible to see how private negotiations among publishers, broadcasters, cable operators and telephone carriers are beginning to redefine the mass communication roles of each medium. This approach offers a useful vantage point from which to observe how Congress, the courts and federal regulatory agencies are responding to such media policy maneuvers.

The book continues to serve four purposes for students of mediated communication:

First, gaining added appreciation for (or dismay over) the workings of the legal process.

Second, surveying areas of law essential for those mass communications practitioners who hope to "stay out of legal trouble," areas including—to name three examples—libel, invasion of privacy, and copyright.

Third, discussing and suggesting ways of coping with growing problems of getting access to governmental records and meetings.

Fourth, acquainting students with some of the emerging contours of our information environment. To that end, this textbook considers the convergence of information delivery systems and studies eddying patterns in regulation and deregulation.

The authors thank those who have helped us in the preparation of this Eighth Edition. Special thanks go to librarians at the University of Wisconsin-Milwaukee and to Professor (and Acting Dean) Steven M. Barkan, Director of the Marquette University Law Library; to William J. Beintema, Director of Law Library and to Jean E. Moore, Instructor in the Law Library, both of the University of Tennessee. Special mention goes to Peggy R. Goodman, Assistant to the Dean, and to Dean Richard S. Wirtz of the Tennessee College of Law.

Particularly helpful to Dwight Teeter were Tennessee colleagues, Professors Dorothy A. Bowles, Herbert H. Howard, and Barbara A. Moore, and Dean Emeritus Kelly Leiter. The values and enduring scholarship of Dr. Harold L. Nelson, a founding author of this text, are gratefully acknowledged. Thanks also go to Knoxville attorney Richard L. Hollow, a superb advocate for the First Amendment.

DWIGHT L. TEETER, JR.
DON R. LE DUC

SUMMARY OF CONTENTS

SUMMARY OF CONTENTS

APPENDICES

TABLE OF CONTENTS

xi

*

LAW

OF

MASS COMMUNICATIONS

FREEDOM AND CONTROL OF PRINT
AND BROADCAST MEDIA

*

Part I

HISTORICAL AND CONSTITUTIONAL FOUNDATIONS OF FREE EXPRESSION

Chapter 1

FREEDOM AND CONTROL

Sec.
1. The Worth of Freedom.
2. The Constitutional Guarantees.
3. "The Intent of the Framers."

A major test of a nation's freedom is the degree of liberty its people have in speaking, writing, and publishing. The hand of authority rests lightly on speech and press at some places and times, heavily at others. But its presence is felt everywhere, including the nations of the Western World which generally consider themselves the most freedom-loving of all.

Some degree of legal control over expression has been in place even in the freest societies through history. Although values of free speech and press may be considered paramount and exalted, there are circumstances where other values may take priority and win in a conflict over rights. The individual's right to a good reputation limits verbal attacks through the law of civil libel. In wartime, assertions of national security may be given precedence over press freedom. Multitudes of laws regulating business, industry and trade apply fully to the commercial press, to advertising, to public relations, and to broadcasting and newer communication technologies.

The goal of this textbook is to serve students in a first or survey course in communication law. A major reason for this book is to help communicators try to "stay out of trouble," to learn something about the pitfalls of libel and slander, invasion of privacy, and copyright infringement. Perhaps the examples and discussion offered here can serve, as legal historian James Willard Hurst has suggested of his field, like training for wrestlers: to help keep their balance, to avoid being upset by sudden and unexpected

1

onslaughts.[1] And on many occasions, of course, attention to ethical behavior will prevent legal questions from arising at all.

This book will provide students with some "how to" information, especially in chapters dealing with access to information.[2] It also tries to give students some understanding of the legal systems of the United States, especially as they interact with the sweeping field vaguely called "communication law." The law of mass communications can *not* be taught as if it is some compartmentalized area marked off by logical boundaries. Of necessity, this book cuts across most areas covered in a law school curriculum:

Constitutional Law deals with the basic governmental framework, as with a state constitution or the federal Constitution. The federal Constitution—the highest law of the land—divides government powers into the legislative, executive, and judicial branches. Powers of government are apportioned among those branches, and the document also lists, in the First Ten Amendments, powers that the U.S. government may *not* bring to bear on its citizens.

The federal Constitution is one of many constitutions in the United States. There are, after all, fifty-one legal systems—the federal system plus fifty state systems. In addition, there are charters governing the organization and operation of cities and counties. Keep in mind that the federal Constitution is the highest law of the land: state constitutional provisions in conflict with it are not enforceable.

By their nature, as basic or "organic" law, constitutions are not easily changed. As spelled out in the federal Constitution, it takes the vote of three-fourths of the states (via states' legislatures or called constitutional conventions) to amend the Constitution.

The First Amendment guarantee of freedom of speech and press is of central importance to this book. If a law or state or lower federal court decision is declared "unconstitutional" by the Supreme Court of the United States, that law or decision is null and void.

Most of the nation's law is *statutory:* made by legislatures, from Congress to state legislatures to county boards and city councils. If the meaning of a statute is at issue in a legal case or controversy, the meaning of the statute can be interpreted by courts. This search for meaning, called *statutory construction,* tries to define vague terms in the statute, often by digging back into the statute's *legislative history.* What did the legislature intend to do when it passed the measure?

---

[1] James Willard Hurst, Introductory Lecture, course on Legal History, University of Wisconsin–Madison, Spring, 1961.

[2] See Chapters 14 and 15.

There are abundant examples of statutes directly affecting the communication media. Consider, for example, the basic federal anti-obscenity law, 18 U.S.C.A. § 1461 [Title or Volume 18, United States Code, at Section 1461.] That statute, passed more than a century ago, forbids sending obscene material through the mails or in interstate commerce. But what is obscene? The statute is unclear. As discussed in Chapter 8, U.S. courts have devoted much energy trying to define "the obscene."

Statutory law was not always the most important branch of law in the United States. Well into the nineteenth century, *common law*—law "found" or "discovered" by judges—was the most important point of growth. Actual judge-made law-making involving an entire area has been rare during the past century. It has been suggested that because of the rarity of common-law creation in this century, there has grown up considerable scholarly fascination with the law of privacy. Privacy law is largely common-law, made by courts instead of legislatures.

Equity is an area which originated in England centuries ago. The Chancellor devised a court—called a Court of Chancery or a Court of Equity (based on what was fair or equitable)—to decide disputes which did not fit into the ordinary framework of the regular or "law" courts. Courts in the United States have combined the functions, and now are said to "sit in both law and equity." Pieces of "equity" remain and are sometimes in the news. For example, in some situations the monetary award remedy available by winning a lawsuit would not be appropriate. Sometimes, what is "equitable" is to have a court order someone to do something (as in a writ of "mandamus," which is Latin for "we demand"), or not to do something (as by a court granting an injunction or "cease and desist" order).

One of the most famous First Amendment cases featured in this book—the "Pentagon Papers" to be discussed in Chapter 2— involved the Supreme Court's overturning a lower court's injunction forbidding *The New York Times* from publishing a series of secret documents on the Viet Nam conflict.

Administrative law has grown rapidly in the past century. As the nation grew more complex, Congress found itself overmatched by commercial and industrial growth involved in the industrial revolution and the nation's westward expansion. Beginning in 1890 with the Interstate Commerce Commission (to regulate railroads), Congress delegated some of its power to an agency. Similar agencies followed; two having particular applicability to the mass media are the sometime regulator of advertising, the Federal Trade Commission (FTC), established in 1914, and the Federal Communications Commission (FCC, established in 1934 but actually following a pattern set by the Federal Radio Commission Act of 1927).

Additionally, the federal Executive branch has the power to make a kind of law through *executive orders*. For example, the "Confidential," "Secret" and "Top Secret" document classifications were established in 1951 by a Presidential executive order by Harry S Truman, and remain in effect today.

Another way of classifying legal actions is as *criminal* and *civil* actions. *Black's Law Dictionary* (Rev. Fifth Ed.) defines a crime as an offense against the state. A crime can be accomplished by *omission,* failing to perform a legally commanded duty (e.g. failure to register for the draft) or *commission* (e.g. killing someone on purpose with a blunt instrument). The latter example could lead to a charge of murder, or wrongful taking of another's life. Crimes are variously classified as *misdemeanors* (minor crimes, usually carrying a jail term of less than a year) and *felonies* (major crimes, generally defined as carrying a jail term of more than a year).

Crimes to be taken up in this book include obscenity, seditious libel, and some aspects of copyright infringement.

Civil Law includes personal damage actions ("lawsuits") in which a person asks for "the establishment, recovery, or redress of private and civil rights." If a publication hurts your reputation by printing a false and harmful statement about you, you could bring a legal action ("sue"), asking for "damages" (see "money"). Much of this book is taken up with discussion of damage actions in the areas of libel, invasion of privacy, and copyright infringement.

Another term which is a staple area in law school curricula is *tort*. It is simply a French word meaning "wrong," and the law assumes that if persons have serious wrongs done to them, they ought to be able to sue for compensation. Libel is a tort. Invasion of privacy is a tort.

For a further exposure to legal terminology, please see Appendices B and C of this book.

SEC. 1.   THE WORTH OF FREEDOM

Major values underlying free speech and press include society's need for maximum flow of information and opinion, and the individual's right to fulfillment.

Freedom to speak, to write, to travel—and to criticize governments and government officials—now seems as natural as breathing to most residents of the United States. Late in the Twentieth Century, North Americans generally take for granted systems of representative self-government, with legislative and executive officials—and some judges as well—selected at regular intervals via secret ballots.

Taking freedoms for granted can be the world's most dangerous complacency. Particular concern should be directed at official efforts to discourage dissent or to push for some particular orthodoxy. If dissenters' freedoms are not protected, then all freedoms are in danger. Sometimes, individuals will find that they hold views that are widely despised, and will take risks in speaking out, especially in times of great social or political tension. And if there is no dissent, the results may be disastrous. Consider the words of Martin Niemoeller, haunted by the millions of Jews killed in Hitler's Holocaust: [3]

> First they came for the socialists, and I did not speak out— because I was not a socialist. Then they came for the trade unionists, and I did not speak out—because I was not a trade unionist. Then they came for the Jews, and I did not speak out—because I was not a Jew. Then they came for me—and there was no one left to speak for me.

One test of freedom is the ability to go unpunished after venting severe criticism of those holding political power. And, if a government official can check over what you've written and deny you the right to publish it, that's pre-publication censorship. More than three hundred years ago, the now-legendary poet John Milton (*Paradise Lost*) argued against pre-publication censorship by church authorities, who then had power inseparable from government. Writing in 1644, Milton declared that because religious truth was so essential to the fate of mankind the authorities should open up the arena for debate. Truth was the only safe basis for a society's life, he said: [4]

> And though all the winds of doctrine were let loose to play upon the earth, so truth be in the field, we do injuriously, by licensing and prohibiting, to misdoubt her strength. Let her and falsehood grapple; who ever knew Truth put to the worse, in a free and open encounter?

Those words from John Milton—expressing what is often called the "diversity principle"—still resound in 20th Century American law, in key court decisions on the scope of freedom.[5]

---

[3] Martin Niemoeller, Exile in the Fatherland, ed. by H.G. Locke (Grand Rapids, MI: Eerdmans, 1986), p. viii.

[4] John Milton, Areopagitica (Chicago, 1953). See Thomas I. Emerson, The System of Freedom of Expression (New York: Random House, 1970), Chap. 1, for discussion of social and individual values of free expression. See also Vincent Blasi, "The Checking Value in First Amendment Theory," 1977 Am.Bar Found.Res.J. 523.

[5] See, e.g., the dissent by Justice O.W. Holmes, Jr., in Abrams v. United States, 250 U.S. 616, 40 S.Ct. 17 (1919) and Justice Hugo L. Black's opinion for the Court in Associated Press v. United States, 326 U.S. 1, 65 S.Ct. 1416 (1945). See also

In 1988, for example, New York Times columnist Anthony Lewis quoted from a Miltonian-sounding expression of the diversity principle written by Supreme Court Justice Robert H. Jackson in 1943: After referring to the United States as a country of "individualism and rich cultural diversities," Justice Jackson wrote for the Court in support of a freedom to differ.[6]

> If there is any fixed star in our constitutional constellation, it is that no official, high or petty, can prescribe what shall be orthodox in politics, nationalism, religion or other matters of opinion ...

It is not always easy to separate society's need and the individual's right as the two grounds for freedom of expression. If the individual's right is thoroughly protected, the social good in the confrontation of ideas presumably follows. The English writer John Locke, often called the philosophical father of the American Revolution, argued persuasively late in the 17th Century in favor of the individual's rights. In words which later echoed in the Declaration of Independence, Locke wrote of the "natural right" of every person to life, liberty, and property. His ideological descendants included speech and press as among those liberties, equally applicable to all men in all times and situations.[7]

In the Twentieth Century, social good arguments have been more compelling than natural rights as a basis for freedom and control of expression. Society's stake in free speech and press is plain in the structure and functioning of a self-governing people. Only through a "clash of ideas in the open marketplace" [8] can working truths be reached. The social good argument runs that the widest diversity of opinion and information must flow through channels of debate and discussion to arrive at worthwhile solutions to problems adding up to sound public policy. Although Milton's pleas for freer debate were couched in terms of seeking religious truth, Twentieth Century theorists and judges have found the confrontation of idea against idea and fact against fact essential to all kinds of "truth," whether in social relations, politics, economics or art.

Over the years, the range of rationales for the practice of open debate in the United States and the Western World has expanded.

discussion in Zechariah Chafee, Jr., Free Speech in the United States (Cambridge, Mass., 1964 [6th printing of 1941 ed.]), pp. 3, 29, 298, 316, 325, 559–561.

[6] West Virginia State Board of Education v. Barnette, 319 U.S. 624, 63 S.Ct. 1178 (1943). Justice Jackson wrote for the Court in a 7–2 decision that children of Jehovah's Witnesses could not be compelled to salute the flag because this ceremony conflicted with their religious beliefs.

[7] John Locke, Second Treatise of Government, ed. Thomas P. Peardon (N.Y., 1952); Leo Strauss, Natural Right and History (Chicago, 1953).

[8] Cf. Holmes, supra note 5.

Both the individual and society benefit from free interchange of ideas, and rationales for such benefits include goals of sound public policy, fulfillment of the potential of human beings, and creation of societies where—with openness—individuals need not distrust each other.[9]

Both judges and lawyers have based their arguments for freedom on both the social and the individual good. Barrister Francis L. Holt, whose early Nineteenth Century book on libel was one of the English texts relied on in developing American law, put primary emphasis on freedom of the press. Holt called that freedom one of the "rights of nature * * * that is to say, of the free exercise of our faculties." But press freedom was more than an individual natural right, for it produced a common good. He declared the English system of liberty which overcame feudal anarchy and monarchial despotism as being "the fruit of a free press." [10]

Some important Twentieth Century judges have spoken similarly, linking individual and societal freedom. The late Justice Hugo Black of the United States Supreme Court pointed out in Braden v. United States (1961) [11] that "There are grim reminders all around this world that the distance between individual liberty and firing squads is not always as far as it seems." [12] Twenty years earlier, in Bridges v. California (1941), he wrote of society's stake. He warned that contempt of court citations—judge-imposed fines and jail terms—against newspapers for commenting on trials in progress would "produce their restrictive results at the precise time when public interest in the matters discussed would naturally be at its height." [13]

It should not be suggested that the worth of freedom to the individual and to society goes unchallenged. Freedom is always a risk, and in any society, some hate and fear the expression of ideas contrary to their own. Is it permissible to denigrate races, nationalities or religions? Should pornographers be allowed to "subordinate" women in demeaning or violent depictions? Should a socialist newspaper be allowed to publish in times of threat from "alien ideologies"? Even today, after almost two centuries under

[9] For discussion of the range of values making up the worth of freedom of expression, see Blasi, 544–567.

[10] Francis L. Holt, The Law of Libel ... in the Law of England, ed. Anthony Bleecker (New York: 1818), quoted in H.L. Nelson, Freedom of the Press from Hamilton to the Warren Court (New York, 1967), pp. 19–20. The individual right claimed emphasis anew in the 1970s. See Thomas I. Emerson, First Amendment Doctrine and the Burger Court, 68 Calif.L.Rev. 422, 424–7; Ronald Dworkin, Is the Press Losing the First Amendment?, New York Review, Dec. 4, 1980, 49–57.

[11] 365 U.S. 431, 445–446, 81 S.Ct. 584, 593 (1961).

[12] See also Branzburg v. Hayes, 408 U.S. 665, 92 S.Ct. 2646, 2668 (1972).

[13] 314 U.S. 252, 268, 62 S.Ct. 190, 196 (1941). See also Robert O'Neill, "Second Thoughts on the First Amendment," 13 N.Mex.L.Rev. 577, Summer 1983.

the First Amendment to the Constitution proclaiming freedom of speech and press, many Americans would answer that *true freedom* protects only virtuous or responsible communication.

But who is to say what is responsible? Suppose that the Constitution of the United States were to be amended to make the press both free and responsible. Perhaps the wording might say something like this: [14]

> In accordance with the interest of the people and in order to strengthen and develop the ... system ... citizens ... are guaranteed freedom of speech, of the press, and of assembly, meetings, and of street processions and demonstrations.

That is a quotation from an actual 1977 constitution of another nation, one which then had little freedom. It is printed with only a few words deleted: the words "socialist," "working people," and "of the U.S.S.R." Even though it proclaimed "freedom," it was apparent that in the now-defunct Soviet Union, speech could be "free" only as rulers interpreted speech and press as operating responsibly in support of an existing order, "to strengthen and develop the system." [15]

There is also the related view that true "liberation" of societies is not possible as long as toleration of aggression in national policies is practiced, or if racial, religious, or class hatred may be stirred up. Following this position, some ideas and policies must be forbidden, for to permit them to be expressed is to tolerate conditions that perpetuate servitude and misery.[16]

If a society has free expression, that very freedom may lead to its destruction. The right to challenge the very principle of free expression is, of course, a good indicator of the extent of freedom in a society. " * * * Man can *seem* to be free in any society, no matter how authoritarian, as long as he accepts the postulates of the society, but he can only *be* free in a society that is willing to allow its basic postulates to be questioned." [17]

SEC. 2.   THE CONSTITUTIONAL GUARANTEES

Federal and State Constitutions all guarantee freedom of expression but some State Constitutions declare that citizens are responsible for the abuse of that right.

[14] See F.J.M. Feldbrugge, ed., The Constitutions of the USSR (The Netherlands, 1979), see Art. 50, p. 101.

[15] Ibid.

[16] Robert P. Wolff, Barrington Moore, Jr. and Herbert Marcuse, A Critique of Pure Tolerance (Boston, 1965) p. 87ff.

[17] John B. Wolfe, in Wilbur Schramm, Responsibility in Mass Communication (New York, 1957) p. 106.

Protection for the dissenters as well as the advocates of the status quo is part of the basic, organic law of the United States. The Federal and State constitutions unanimously give free expression a position of prime value.

The Americans who wrote and in 1791 adopted the Bill of Rights of the United States Constitution followed a theme in Anglo–American liberty. Those Americans who had seen the breaking of the ties connecting them to Britain in 1776 with the Declaration of Independence drew on a long history of struggle against arbitrary power. With their lively knowledge of their past, they knew of the Englishmen who in 1215 forced King John to sign the Magna Charta—the "large charter" of rights promising lawful rule by duly constituted authority and trial by jury. They knew also of the Englishmen who passed the Habeas Corpus Act in 1679 saying that persons could not be imprisoned except by lawful authority, and of the English Bill of Rights of 1689.[18]

This sense of history doubtless impelled Americans, after the War for Independence, to set down the framework of government—first of the emerging states after the Declaration of Independence, and later the Articles of Confederation and Constitution—*in writing*. Government's powers were to be made explicit.[19]

The Constitution of 1787, adopted after weeks of meetings *in secret* by the Constitutional Convention in Philadelphia, proposed much more centralization of power in the national government than did the nation's first constitution, the Articles of Confederation. Although the Constitution of 1787 is much revered today, and was elevated virtually to the level of Divine inspiration by the 1987 Bicentennial Celebration, it should be kept in mind that the Constitution was—and is—a practical political "frame of government" document.[20]

Although much rhetoric has flowed over the Bill of Rights and the First Amendment, the practical political fact remains that the Bill of Rights—and the First Amendment—were political afterthoughts, compromises. Strong Antifederalist opposition led supporters of the Constitution to conclude that the required nine (of thirteen) states would never ratify the Constitution as written.[21] The Antifederalists pushed a boisterous campaign to prevent adoption of the Constitution, claiming it would create a tyrannous, monolithic national government that would trample liberties then

[18] Winston Churchill, The Birth of Britain (New York, 1956), pp. 252–254; Leonard W. Levy, Emergence of a Free Press (Oxford, 1985), Chs. 1 and 2.

[19] Sanford Levinson, Constitutional Faith (Princeton, N.J., 1988) pp. 30–31.

[20] Jackson Turner Main, The Antifederalists: Critics of the Constitution (Chapel Hill, 1961), *passim*.

[21] Ibid., 158–161.

enjoyed by the people under the Articles of Confederation. Supporters of the Constitution defused their opposition enough to secure ratification in the states by pledging to add a Bill of Rights to place explicit limits on the national government, providing a list of rights that the United States could not infringe.[22]

After initial reluctance to see a Bill of Rights added, James Madison—as a representative to the First Congress from Virginia—served as a major draftsman and the prime mover in getting the Bill of Rights passed for submission to the states. Madison, although staunchly for civil liberties, had questioned whether a national Bill of Rights would be effective. Later, evidently seeing both substance and political usefulness, Madison finally managed—after several months—to get Congress to consider drafting proposed amendments. Such delay suggests that Congress found other matters more pressing than the promised Bill of Rights. (Although some boosterish renditions of journalism history of the after-dinner speech variety claim the First Amendment was listed first because it was considered most important, it seems to have become the first merely because a couple of early draft amendments were edited out.) On the last day of 1791, state ratification of the Bill of Rights gave force to these words making up the First Amendment: [23]

> Congress shall make no law respecting an establishment of religion, or prohibiting the free exercise thereof; or abridging the freedom of speech, or of the press; or the right of the people peaceably to assemble, and to petition the Government for a redress of grievances.

The meaning of the First Amendment was by no means clear. The noted Constitutional historian Leonard Levy once contended that a long and bitter civil war—called by Americans the War for Independence—was hardly a good time for the birth or nurturing of civil liberties. In an inspired phrase, Levy asserted in 1960: "There is even reason to believe that the Bill of Rights was more the chance product of political expediency on all sides than of principled commitment to personal liberties." [24]

In the late Eighteenth Century, and even today, "freedom of speech and press" was an ill-defined and much-debated phrase. But however unsettled the nation's founders were about expanding the reach of free expression beyond that in England, they stated a broad principle in firmly protective terms, and left it to future generations to interpret.[25]

[22] Ibid.

[23] U.S. Constitution, Amendment 1.

[24] Levy, Legacy of Suppression (Cambridge, Mass., 1960), pp. vii–viii.

[25] Levy, Emergence, pp. 348–349.

The states adopted their own constitutions, some beginning as early as 1776 and then revising the documents over the years. Freedoms of speech and press evidently were not seen as "absolutes;" this was recognized, over time, by most states' constitutions. Nearly all agreed that freedom of expression could be "abused," although that "abuse" was not defined. Typically, the sentence in the state constitution that started with the guarantee of free expression ended with a qualification. The Constitution of Pennsylvania of 1790 said: "The free communication of thoughts and opinions is one of the invaluable rights of man, and every citizen may freely speak, write and print on any subject, being responsible for the abuse of that liberty." [26]

As the Federal Constitution's First Amendment left the "freedom of speech and press" to future interpretation, the state constitutions tended to leave "abuse" to later definition. The principle resembled that expressed by Sir William Blackstone, prestigious English legal authority whose famed *Commentaries,* published in 1765–1769, amounted to a kind of legal Bible for the lawyers of the emerging United States. Blackstone's definition of press freedom declared: [27]

> The liberty of the press is indeed essential to the nature of a free state: but this consists in laying no *previous* restraints upon publications, and not in freedom from censure for criminal matter when published. Every freeman has an undoubted right to lay what sentiments he pleases before the public: to forbid this, is to destroy the freedom of the press: but if he publishes what is improper, mischievous, or illegal, he must take the consequences of his own temerity.

Blackstone's formulation had great force as state legal systems emerged. In times before law schools, when would-be lawyers "read law" as assistants to experienced lawyers, a law practice would often be started with two books: the Bible and a copy of Blackstone. Note that Blackstone's definition of freedom guaranteed little beyond no pre-publication censorship. As will be discussed in later sections, criticism of government which Blackstone likely would have considered illegal "abuse" of press freedom now is fully protected as courts interpret the Constitution.

Gitlow v. New York (1925)

Each state's power to define what it considered abuse of free expression long went unchallenged before the Federal courts. But

[26] Constitution of Pennsylvania, Art. 1, § 7.

[27] 4 Blackstone Commentaries 151, 152.

in 1925, the United States Supreme Court in effect *nationalized* the First Amendment.[28]

A hapless radical, Benjamin Gitlow, had been charged with violating the criminal anarchy law of the state of New York. That statute defined criminal anarchy as the doctrine " ' . . . that organized government should be overthrown by force or violence, or by assassination of the executive head or of any of the officials of government, or by any other means.' " The state's statute also made it a crime to advocate, advise or teach such a doctrine. Gitlow and friends had circulated "The Left Wing Manifesto," which advocated "revolutionary mass action" to establish Communist Socialism.[29]

Ironically, even though the Supreme Court of the United States found that a New York jury was warranted in finding Gitlow guilty of advocating governmental overthrow, it also held that the protections of the First Amendment were applicable to the states through the Fourteenth Amendment, which had been adopted in 1868 to protect the rights of slaves freed by the Civil War. The Fourteenth Amendment declares that *no state* shall "deprive any person of life, liberty or property, without due process of law * * *."[30] In the Gitlow case, the Supreme Court for the first time held the "liberty" mentioned in the Fourteenth Amendment. Until Gitlow v. New York (1925), state courts' rulings on freedom of expression cases were allowed to stand without review by the U.S. Supreme Court. In the Gitlow decision, however, Justice Sanford wrote for the seven-man majority of the Court that:[31]

> * * * we may and do assume that freedom of speech and of the press—which are protected by the First Amendment from abridgment by Congress—are among the fundamental rights and "liberties" protected by the due process clause of the Fourteenth Amendment from impairment by the States.

These words did not help Ben Gitlow; since the Supreme Court had upheld his conviction, he went to jail. Two members of the Supreme Court—Justices Oliver Wendell Holmes and Louis D. Brandeis—dissented, saying that the "Manifesto" posed little threat of doing harm, let alone a "clear and present danger"[32] from the small minority who shared Gitlow's views. In later years, when the Supreme Court of the United States tended to be more tolerant and supportive of expression than many state courts, the

[28] 268 U.S. 652, 666, 45 S.Ct. 625, 630 (1925).
[29] Chafee, op. cit., pp. 318–325.
[30] U.S. Constitution, Amendment 14.
[31] 268 U.S. 652, 672, 45 S.Ct. 625, 630 (1925).
[32] 268 U.S. 652, 672, 45 S.Ct. 625, 632 (1925).

1925 decision in Gitlow v. New York proved to be the case which opened the door to the Supreme Court review of state courts' actions involving speech and press. After the Gitlow case the Fourteenth Amendment took its place with the First Amendment as a major protection for expression. By helping to"bring the First Amendment home to the states," the Gitlow decision made possible the landmark case limiting pre-publication censorship, Near v. Minnesota ex rel. Olson (1931),[33] and the famous decision protecting the news media against libel suits by public officials, New York Times Co. v. Sullivan (1964).[34]

The Fifth Amendment

One other amendment to the Federal Constitution also applies to expression. This is the Fifth Amendment, which has language similar to part of the Fourteenth Amendment.[35] The Fifth Amendment says "No person shall be compelled in any criminal case to be a witness against himself, nor be deprived of life, liberty, or property, without due process of law." [36]

When those words are taken together with the First Amendment's command protecting "the freedom of speech, or of the press," the Fifth Amendment may be read as helping guarantee the liberty to speak or write. The Fifth Amendment also provides protection for a witness against self-incrimination. The right against self-incrimination stems from a revolting practice, common in England until the Seventeenth Century, of forcing people—often through torturing them—to testify against themselves. Again, knowledge of history by the men who wrote and adopted the Bill of Rights no doubt come into play. One person who became a symbol to that generation was "Freeborn John" Lilburne, one of the most contentious figures in the history of England's freedoms. Brought before the secret Court of the Star Chamber in 1641 for his alleged importation of anti-government and heretical books, Lilburne was whipped and pilloried because he refused to take an oath to testify against himself. He then petitioned Parliament for compensation for the wrongs he had suffered. Parliament declared Lilburne's sentence "illegal and against the liberty of the subject," and voted him an indemnity of 3,000 pounds. Lilburne had won the day for the "right not to accuse oneself," a right given constitutional status in the U.S. when the Fifth Amendment was ratified 150 years later, in 1791.[37]

[33] 283 U.S. 697, 51 S.Ct. 625 (1931).

[34] 376 U.S. 254, 84 S.Ct. 710 (1964).

[35] U.S. Constitution Amendment 14.

[36] Ibid., Amendment 5.

[37] Erwin N. Griswold, The First Amendment Today (Cambridge, 1955) pp. 3, 4.

Think again about the wording of the First, Fifth and Fourteenth Amendments to the Constitution as discussed in the preceding pages. The First Amendment says, with no limiting words that
"Congress shall make no law ... abridging the freedom of speech,
or of the press...." On the other hand, both the Fifth and the
Fourteenth Amendments, say that persons *can* be deprived of life,
liberty, or property through due process of law. Further, many
State constitutions state that although there is freedom of speech
and press, those freedoms can be abused, and the abusers of those
freedoms held responsible. Even in a Constitution granting freedoms, certain boundaries for speech and press were suggested.

Boundaries For Freedom

As the final authority on what the Constitution means, it has
fallen to the Supreme Court of the United States to say what
expression is protected—or "constitutional" and what is not protected. Although the First Amendment says "Congress shall make
no law * * * abridging freedom of speech, or of the press * * *,"
the nation's courts have been unable to draw an exact, ruler-
straight line between the permissible and the punishable. American theorists, courts, legislatures, and laymen have stated the
boundaries of expression in various ways. If a scale could be made
with "freedom" at one end and "restraint" at the other, many
Americans would cluster toward "freedom."

Of all American spokesmen, the late Justice Hugo L. Black
most flatly stated the position for a right of unlimited expression,
interpreting the First Amendment as an "absolute" command
forbidding any restraint on speech and press: [38]

> I believe when our Founding Fathers * * * wrote this
> [First] Amendment they * * * knew what history was
> behind them and they wanted to ordain in this country
> that Congress * * * should not tell the people what reli-
> gion they should have or what they should believe or say
> or publish, and that is about it. It [the First Amendment]
> says "no law," and that is what I believe it means.

> * * *

> I have no doubt myself that the provision, as written
> and adopted, intended that there should be no libel or
> defamation law in the United States.

Although such ringing statements made Justice Black a hero to
many journalists and civil libertarians, such words might also cause
consternation among legal historians. Many legal scholars, writing

[38] Edmond N. Cahn, "Justice Black and First Amendment 'Absolutes': A Public
Interview," 37 N.Y.U.L.Rev. 548 (1962).

before and after Justice Black, have contended that such historical assertions were flawed by one-sidedness, ignoring abundant contrary evidence of libel actions brought by the generation that adopted the First Amendment.[39]

The late philosopher Alexander Meiklejohn also favored a kind of "absolute" freedom, but only in the realm of expression of political ideas. Speaking in the mid–1950s, when anti-Communism had reached heights known as McCarthyism and efforts to curb Communists' freedom were powerful, Meiklejohn declared: [40]

> The first amendment * * * admits of no exceptions. It tells us that the Congress, and by implication, all other agencies of Government are denied any authority whatever to limit the political freedom of the citizens of the United States.

Such "absolute" positions, however, although theoretically appealing to some, have never found official acceptance or support in the United States. Perhaps the myths of history still cling to ideas of freedom. Even though Twentieth Century courts are still quoting John Milton's plea against censorship from roughly three and one half centuries ago, Milton's expanded concept of freedom did not include those whose religion and morals he could not accept.[41] And only a few years after writing the famed *Areopagitica,* Milton himself had official employment ... as a censor. Ever since Milton, the case for freedom of expression has been qualified and limited in various ways as efforts are made to define the boundaries of legal control.

Written about 1765, Sir William Blackstone's vastly influential commentaries expounded the doctrine that government shall lay no restraint on writers *before* publication, but may punish them *after* publication of anything violating the law. (The problem here, of course, is that if it is against the law to criticize government, going to jail or being executed after publication is likely to discourage other dissident speakers or writers.)

Briefly, here are some other concepts to keep in mind as you consider efforts to define freedom of expression:

[39] See, e.g., Paul Murphy, "Time to Reclaim: The Current Challenge of American Constitutional History," 69 Amer.Hist.Rev. 64–654 (1963); Dwight L. Teeter and MaryAnn Yodelis Smith, "Mr. Justice Black's Absolutism: Notes on His Use of History to Support Free Expression," in Everette Dennis, et al., eds., Justice Hugo Black and the First Amendment (Ames, Iowa, 1978).

[40] Alexander Meiklejohn, Testimony of Nov. 14, 1955, U.S. Senate, Committee on Judiciary, Sub–Committee on Constitutional Rights, "Security and Constitutional Rights," pp. 14–15.

[41] See, e.g., Court's opinion by Black, J., in Associated Press v. United States, 326 U.S. 1, 8–10, 65 S.Ct. 1416, 1419 (1945).

Liberty v. License: This old distinction line that rolls easily off the tongue but has little operational content is often heard. It is said, "Liberty is not the same as licentiousness." (Beyond personal predilections, it is impossible to say where one notion begins and the other leaves off.)

Bad Tendency: "Intent"—or presumed intent—was and is used as a gauge for testing whether someone would have to be legally responsible for a communication. For example, individuals accused of opposing or disrupting the United States war effort during World War I were often convicted and jailed for words which in more recent years would be regarded as innocent expression.

Consider the case of Jacob Abrams. He and some other Russian immigrants were convicted of violating the Espionage Act of 1917, as amended in 1918. The 1918 amendment, since repealed, made punishable (among other things) any false statements harmful to the war effort. The statute went further, forbidding [42]

" . . . any disloyal, profane, scurrilous or abusive language about the form of government of the United States, or the Constitution . . . or the military or naval forces of the United States, or the flag . . . or the uniform of the United States . . . "

Jacob Abrams and his friends were convicted of violating that statute by throwing leaflets out of a manufacturing building in New York. One leaflet, headlined "THE HYPOCRISY OF THE UNITED STATES AND HER ALLIES" did not criticize the war efforts of the U.S. against Germany. Instead, it protested United States taking part with other nations in sending an expeditionary force into Russia, calling for workers in munitions factories to strike so bullets made by them would not strike down Russians.[43] There was no proof that such pamphleteering had any harmful effect or caused one less bullet to be made in a munitions factory. But World War I was a time of war hysteria and freedoms taken for granted in peacetime were cast aside. The pamphlet's fervent language, denouncing President Woodrow Wilson and "the plutocratic gang in Washington" was then enough to convince a jury to convict Abrams and three others.[44]

The U.S. Supreme Court upheld the conviction, basing its decision not on any demonstrable harm from the pamphlets, but on their "bad tendency." Writing for the Court, Justice Clarke declared that [45]

[42] U.S. Stats. at Large, vol. XL, p. 553ff.

[43] Abrams v. United States, 250 U.S. 616, 40 S.Ct. 17 (1919); see also Zechariah Chafee, Jr., Free Speech in the United States (Cambridge, 1941 ed.) 114ff.

[44] Chafee, p. 109ff.

[45] 250 U.S. 616, 621, 40 S.Ct. 17, 19 (1919).

It will not do to say, as is now argued, that the only intent of these defendants was to prevent injury to the Russian cause. Men must be held to have intended, and to be accountable for, the effects their acts were likely to produce.

Marketplace of Ideas: That prosecutor's delight, the "bad tendency" test, was enough for a majority of the Supreme Court to uphold Abrams' conviction. In dissent, Justice Oliver Wendell Holmes presented a moving expression of the "marketplace of ideas" philosophy. He built on the ideas of John Milton, and those of the Nineteenth Century British philosopher John Stuart Mill. In *On Liberty,* Mill wrote that members of society needed access to many kinds of ideas, false as well as true, to discern the truth. Mill declared that government had no legitimate power to suppress opinions: [46]

> If all mankind minus one were of one opinion, and only one person were of the contrary opinion, mankind would be no more justified in silencing that one person, than he, if he had the power, would be justified in silencing mankind.

In the *Abrams* dissent, Justice Holmes wrote: [47]

> In this case sentences of twenty years imprisonment have been imposed for the publishing of two leaflets that I believe the defendants had as much right to publish as the Government has to publish the Constitution now vainly invoked by them.

> * * *

> Persecution for the expression of opinions seems to me perfectly logical. If you have no doubt of your premises or your power and want a certain result with all your heart you naturally express your wishes in law and sweep away all opposition. * * * But when men have realized that time has upset many fighting faiths, they may come to believe even more than they believe the very foundations of their own beliefs that the ultimate good desired is better reached by free trade in ideas—that the best test of truth is the power of the thought to get itself accepted in the competition of the market, and that truth is the only ground upon which their wishes safely can be carried out. That at any rate is the theory of our constitution. It is an experiment, as all life is an experiment. Every year if not

---

[46] Mill, On Liberty (New York: Appleton–Century, 1947) p. 16.
[47] 250 U.S. 616, 629, 40 S.Ct. 17, 22 (1919).

every day we have to wager our salvation upon some prophecy based upon imperfect knowledge.

Expression v. Action—In 1919, shortly before the *Abrams* case, Justice Holmes wrote for the Court's majority in Schenck v. United States.   Schenck and his co-defendants had mailed circulars in violation of the Espionage Act of 1917, urging men who had been called to military service to resist the draft.   Writing for a unanimous Court, Holmes created some famous, flashing phrases which seemed to offer promise to protect some kinds of anti-government expression, even in wartime.   Justice Holmes then stated the famous *clear and present danger test.*[48]

> We admit that in may places and in ordinary times the defendants in saying all that was said in the circular would have been within their constitutional rights.   But the character of every act depends upon the circumstances in which it is done.   The most stringent protection of free speech would not protect a man in falsely shouting fire in a theatre and causing a panic.   * * * The question in every case is whether the words used are used in such circumstances and are of such a nature as to create a clear and present danger that they will bring about the substantive evils that Congress has a right to prevent.   It is a question of proximity and degree.   When a nation is at war many things that might be said in time of peace are such a hindrance to the effort that their utterance will not be endured . . .

The clear and present danger test did not free Schenck, nor was it to be used by Supreme Court majorities in support of free expression for two decades to come.[49]   Although this test was a minority view, its development by Justices Holmes and Brandeis in later dissents—as in Abrams v. United States (1919)—served as a rallying point for libertarians for years.[50]

The clear and present danger test asked judges to assess the *likelihood* that dissident speech would be transmitted into illegal action.   At what point, however, does "expression" become so dangerous that it creates a "clear and present danger?"

A major formulation by Thomas I. Emerson, one of the nation's foremost First Amendment scholars, was expressed this way in 1970: [51]

[48] 249 U.S. 47, 52, 39 S.Ct. 247, 249 (1919).

[49] See Bridges v. California, 314 U.S. 252, 62 S.Ct. 190 (1941), for use of that test in a contempt case.

[50] See Chafee, *passim.*

[51] Emerson, The System of Freedom of Expression, p. 17.

The central idea of a system of freedom of expression is that a fundamental distinction must be drawn between conduct which consists of "expression" and conduct which consists of "action." "Expression" must be freely encouraged. "Action" can be controlled.

SEC. 3. "THE INTENT OF THE FRAMERS"

"Law office history"—assertions by judges, lawyers and politicians that they know the "intent of the Framers"—sometimes makes law affecting First Amendment rights.

Statements continue to be heard about the "intent of the Founding Fathers" or the "Framers" on the true meaning of the national constitutional provision on freedom of the press. This is a cautionary note for readers of court decisions or legal arguments which purport to offer *the* meaning of The First Amendment or some other facet of the Constitution of the United States. If you believe such legal arguments, the authors of this book have some real estate and a bridge they'd like to sell you.[52]

First, there's what might be called the journalistic fallacy, talking about the First Amendment as if it contained only guarantees for freedom of speech and press. But read what that Amendment says: it is a group of rights protecting religion, speech, press, assembly, and petition ... mentioned in that order, for whatever order of mention is worth. The exact words say:

ARTICLE I

Congress shall make no Law respecting an establishment of religion, or prohibiting the free exercise thereof; or abridging the freedom of speech, or of the press; or the right of the people peaceably to assemble, and to petition Government for a redress of grievances.

Obviously, the First Amendment is not just about speech and press. As civil libertarians frequently observe, it is a bundle of rights, and whatever affects one part of that Amendment almost certainly will have repercussions for the other rights it lists.

When you hear a politician assert that "all history proves," brace yourself for a whopper. And be similarly skeptical about lawyers' and judges' use of history-as-argument or history-as- precedent. The legal process in this nation, after all, is an adversary

[52] See, Levy, Original Intent and the Framers' Constitution (New York: 1988) pp. xii–xiii, 377.

system, and selective perception of evidence—especially historical evidence—is not infrequent in the judicial system.[53]

Many of the following pages will contain assertions made by judges, lawyers, and journalists about the intent underlying the First Amendment as it applies—to name just a few examples—to criticism of government, or prior restraint, access to information, defamation, or invasion of privacy.

If communicators, lawyers, judges or scholars talk about "the First Amendment intent of the Framers," regard their words skeptically. Face it, the Framers were the men who met in secret, behind closed doors—so much for their intent concerning access to information?—in Philadelphia during the spring and summer of 1787. If someone insisted that their true intent on free speech or press or religion could be found in that document, then what? The body of the Constitution mentioned nothing at all about the rights guaranteed by the First Amendment. Members of the Constitutional Convention signed the document they produced in 1787. Although the Constitution was ratified by the necessary nine states in 1788, and although the new government began in the spring of 1789 the Bill of Rights was not adopted by the states until the end of 1791.

It has been said that the War for Independence and the troubled early years of the struggling new United States of America, instead of securing rights for speech and press, came close to eradicating them.[54] As historian Leonard W. Levy once argued, the First Amendment and the Bill of Rights were "chance products of political expediency," created to overcome the objections of the Antifederalists who were seeking another constitutional convention to undo the document aiming toward a centralized, truly national government. Under that analysis, the Bill of Rights was drafted out of pragmatism, to overcome Antifederalist charges that freedom of speech, press, assembly, and religion would be taken away under a monolithic new government. Other charges included taking away of right to trial by jury and that a heartless national government would torture people until they confessed to crimes they had not committed. Pay specific attention to the language of the First Amendment: it does *not* say that freedoms of speech and press shall not be abridged. It says that Congress (not the states) "shall make no law." True, the Federalists argued that the various states had their own free speech and press guarantees, but the Antifederalists anti-ratification arguments dealt with what the new national government *might* do.

[53] Charles Miller, The Supreme Court and the Uses of History (Cambridge, Mass. Belknap Press, 1969).

[54] Levy, Legacy of Suppression (Cambridge: Belknap/Harvard, 1960) p. 182; Jackson Turner Main, op. cit., pp. 160–161.

Anthony Lewis has written that a meaningful understanding of "original intent" would have to include posthumous reading of the minds of the different groups of men who drafted the Constitution, and the men who were voting in the ratifying conventions of each state. The intent behind the Bill of Rights is even harder to discern: there is hardly any record of the legislative history of what members of the First Congress meant in offering the Amendments in 1789.[55]

The Constitution and the Bill of Rights have not remained frozen in time. It is likely that this nation was able to celebrate 200 years under its Constitution because it is a brief, broadly stated "frame of government." And it may be asserted with safety that the First Amendment has been changed, over time, as courts— however haltingly or imperfectly—interpreted new meanings into the document. And the Framers' intent? As David A. Anderson has argued, " ... [M]ost of the Framers perceived, however dimly, naively, or incompletely, that freedom of the press was inextricably related to the new republican form of government and would have to be protected if their vision of government by the people was to succeed." [56]

[55] Anthony Lewis, review of Leonard W. Levy's Original Intent and the Framers' Constitution (New York: Macmillan, 1989), New York Times Book Review, Nov. 6, 1988, p. 11.

[56] David A. Anderson, "The Origins of the Press Clause," 30 UCLA L.Rev No. 3 (February, 1983), p. 537.

Chapter 2

THE FIRST AMENDMENT AND THE PRINT MEDIA: HISTORICAL BACKGROUND AND TODAY'S LAW

Sec.
4. Seditious Libel: Ancient Enemy of Freedom.
5. Prior Restraint.
6. Prior Restraint: Licensing.
7. Forcing Communication to Occur.
8. Criminal Libel.
9. Taxation.
10. The Contempt Power and Criticizing Courts.

It has been said that the present is only the cutting edge of the past. This is especially true in law, with courts for the most part looking to earlier decisions, "following precedent." In studying struggles for freedom of expression, it is easy to wonder if there is much that is new. Old patterns of control—ancient enemies of freedom—may be traced to authoritarian philosophies hundreds and hundreds of years old. Major controls over the press well known in Seventeenth and Eighteenth Century England and America set the pattern for battles for freedom of expression which have continued into the last decades of the Twentieth Century.[1] Patterns of control continue, and so do the fights against them.

SEC. 4. SEDITIOUS LIBEL: ANCIENT ENEMY OF FREEDOM

Sedition—defined roughly as expression attacking government's form, laws, institutions, or officers—is a criminal charge many centuries old. In the United States of the Twentieth Century the crime has been restricted by court rulings.

The crime of seditious libel or "sedition" has a long and bloody history. Generally, sedition has been defined as attacking government (its form, laws, institutions) or government officers (includ-

---

[1] Fredrick S. Siebert, Freedom of the Press in England, 1476–1776 (Urbana: Univ. of Illinois Press, 1952). This is the classic treatment of the instruments of control. See also Norman L. Rosenberg, Protecting the Best Men: An Interpretive History of the Law of Libel (Chapel Hill: Univ. of North Carolina Press, 1986), and Leonard W. Levy, Emergence of a Free Press (New York: Oxford, 1985).

ing, in Seventeenth Century England, members of the Royal family).

Consider the case of William Prynn, a prude who advocated strict Puritanism. In his book, *Histrio–Mastix,* he denounced such popular pastimes as dancing, hunting, Christmas-keeping, and play-going. How did this attack government? The attack was inferred from Prynn's assertion that lewd women and whores acted in plays: It seems the Queen of England had taken part in a pastoral play at Somerset House. Prynn was fined £10,000 and given life imprisonment. In addition, he was pilloried (made to "stand in the stocks," held in a frame in a public square where passers-by could revile him) and had his ears cropped off.[2] A year later, in 1637, Dr. John Bastwick and Henry Burton were treated similarly by the infamous Court of the Star Chamber for their attacks on the Pope. Mob demonstrations against authority followed Prynn's sentencing. He was released from prisons by the Long Parliament in 1641 after Puritan forces had gained ascendancy in England and after the abolition of the Court of the Star Chamber.[3]

Today, treason is thought of as betraying a nation to an enemy, and conjures up visions of spying or sabotage or of the notorious "Tokyo Rose" who made pro-Japanese broadcasts to American military forces during World War II. Treason is a crime punishable by death. It had been defined very broadly in England since 1352, in the time of Edward III. Treason then meant not only making war against the King or giving aid and comfort to enemies, it also included "compassing the death of the king," or imagining his death. (Put this concept in a Twentieth Century form: How many times have citizens heard and read comments "imagining the death of the President of the United States?" What about comments on candidates for Vice President of whom it is asked, "Do you want this person only a heartbeat away from the Presidency?")

Consider the case of John Twyn, who printed a book called *A Treatise on the Execution of Justice.* Writing was included in "compassing the death of the king," and at a 1663 session of the Old Bailey court in London Twyn was indicted for treason. The book contended that a ruler is accountable to the people, and that the people may take up arms against and even kill a king who refuses accountability. Although Twyn had not written the book, he refused to say who did. And as the printer, he then received the full weight of the law's brutality. The judge pronounced the sentence of guilty: [4]

[2] 3 Howell's State Trials 561 (1632–3).

[3] Siebert, pp. 123–125.

[4] Howell's State Trials 513 (1663).

... "that you be ... drawn upon a hurdle [sledge] to the place of execution; and there you shall be hanged by the neck, and being alive, shall be cut down, and your privy-members shall be cut off, your entrails shall be taken out of your body, and you living, the same to be burnt before your eyes; your head to be cut off, your body to be divided into four quarters.... And the Lord have mercy upon your soul."

Martyrs to the principle of free expression had their impact as spokesmen for a new philosophy such as John Milton and John Locke had theirs. But the legal principle of seditious libel remained in force: if people criticized government, they did so at their peril. Seditious libel soon was transported to the English colonies in America, although punishments for the crime never descended to the level of cruelty inflicted on the drawn-and-quartered John Twyn.

Sedition in America: The Zenger Trial

At least four colonial Americans faced sedition prosecutions for printed words before the most celebrated criminal trial of the colonial period took place in 1735. The outcome of that famous trial—involving *New York Weekly Journal* printer John Peter Zenger—still symbolizes press struggles for freedom to criticize government, even late in the Twentieth Century.

Zenger became a hero of press freedom by getting into the middle of a bitter factional dispute in New York colony politics. New York Governor William Cosby, a greedy and autocratic man, was opposed by lawyer James Alexander, a leader of the powerful Lewis Morris faction. Alexander wrote anonymous attacks labeling Governor Cosby a tyrant and oppressor of the colony. Those attacks were published in John Peter Zenger's *New York Weekly Journal*.[5]

The colony's attorney general tried, unsuccessfully, to get a grand jury to indict the printer. Thwarted in that direction the attorney general brought charges of sedition on his own, filing an "information" with the New York court. Zenger was jailed, and remained there for eight months awaiting trial for seditious libel. While Zenger sat in jail, Alexander—as the behind-the-scenes political agitator—kept the *Journal* printing and the campaign against Governor Cosby simmering. Wearing his lawyer's hat, Alexander prepared to defend Zenger. He was unable to do so, however, because Chief Justice De Lancey, who had been appointed by

[5] Stanley Nider Katz, A Brief Narrative of the Case and Trial of John Peter Zenger (Cambridge: Harvard, 1963); Harold L. Nelson, "Seditious Libel in Colonial America," 3 Am.Jour.Legal History 160 (1959).

Cosby, disbarred Alexander from practicing law. Alexander then turned to Andrew Hamilton of Philadelphia to plead Zenger's case.

The original "Philadelphia lawyer," Hamilton had built a reputation as the ablest attorney in the colonies. The dignity of age, his utter confidence, and his bold advocacy that the court discard old patterns of thinking about sedition came to bear in an irresistible way with jurors already sympathetic to Zenger's cause. The law of sedition had long held that the defendant was not to be permitted to plead that his offending words against government were true; the truth, it was held, only aggravated the offense, for it was more likely than falsehood to cause the target to seek violent revenge and breach the community's peace. Furthermore, the law had given the jury only a minor role in a sedition trial: its job was to decide whether the accused had, indeed, printed the words. It was up to the court to decide whether they were illegal words.

Jockeying with Chief Justice De Lancey, Hamilton urged the jury to recognize truth as a defense for Zenger, and argued that the jury should decide "the law"—whether the words were libelous—as well as the fact of printing. Blocked by the judge from expanding on these points, he shifted his tactic and went to the importance of permitting men to criticize their governments: [6]

> Men who injure and oppress the people under their administration provoke them to cry out and complain, and then make that very complaint the foundation for new oppressions and prosecutions. I wish I could say there were no instances of this kind. But to conclude, the question before the Court and you, gentlemen of the jury, is not of small or private concern; it is not the cause of a poor printer, nor of New York alone, which you are trying. No! it may, in its consequences, affect every freeman that lives under a British government, on the main of America. It is the best cause; it is the cause of liberty; and I make no doubt but your upright conduct, this day, will not only entitle you to the love and esteem of your fellow citizens, but every man who prefers freedom to a life of slavery, will bless and honor you as men who have baffled the attempts of tyranny; and by an impartial and uncorrupt verdict, have laid a noble foundation for securing to ourselves, our posterity, and our neighbors, that to which nature and the laws of our country have given us a right—the liberty—both of exposing and opposing arbitrary power in these parts of the world at least, by speaking and writing truth.

Hamilton ended his plea in an emotion-charged courtroom; De Lancey delivered a confusing charge to the jury, which retired to

[6] Stanley Katz (ed.), A Brief Narrative ... pp. 2–9.

deliberate. In a short time the jury emerged with a "not guilty" verdict. There were celebrations in the streets that night; there were printings and re-printings of the Hamilton plea for years to come, more even in England than in the colonies. The court trial for seditious libel was finished for the colonial period as an instrument for control of the press. Not for 40 years or more would seditious libel be used again in America by a court.[7]

It was the elected Assembly, or lower house of the colonial legislature, that was the most successful and most active force in official control of Eighteenth Century colonial printers. Jealous of its powers under the view that it was Parliament in miniature, and unwilling to have its acts criticized, this agency of government disciplined printer after printer. Even as it emerged as the main check on the powers of the Crown's governors, even as it showed itself as the seat of government support for the movement for independence, the Assembly demonstrated its aversion to popular criticism. Its instrument for control was the citation for contempt ("breach of privilege"), and it haled a long line of printers before it for their "seditious" attacks on its performance. The legislative contempt citation was a legislative sedition action.

Historian Leonard Levy has demonstrated the relative power and activity of the Assemblies in respect to the press. Up and down the seaboard, printers were brought to the legislative bar and there were forced to kneel and beg the pardon of the stern lawmakers, swear that they meant no harm by their writings, and accept rebuke or imprisonment. Printer James Franklin's irony put him in jail in 1722; he had speculated that the Massachusetts government might get around to outfitting a ship to pursue a pirate "sometime this month, wind and weather permitting." New Yorkers James Parker and William Weyman were jailed for an article on the poverty of Orange and Ulster counties; the Assembly construed it as a reflection upon its stewardship. These were only a few actions among many, and they continued to the eve of the Revolutionary War in some colonies.[8]

The great article of faith that heads America's commitment to free expression was adopted in 1791 by men who had not yet thought through all that "free speech and press" implies. The

[7] Harold L. Nelson, "Seditious Libel in Colonial America," 3 Am.Journ.Legal History 160 (1959).

[8] Levy, Emergence of a Free Press, 71–84. No other historian has stimulated others to study 18th-Century American press freedom as has Levy, whose thesis that the First Amendment was not intended by the Framers to end the British common law of seditious libel in America has aroused many to dissent. Revising his early, provocative Legacy of Suppression (1960) in Emergence of a Free Press (1985), and conceding some errors and misinterpretations in Legacy, he responds directly to many of the protestors but concedes nothing central to his main thesis. See Emergence of a Free Press, passim, for many of the confrontations.

First Amendment to the Constitution states that "Congress shall make no law * * * abridging freedom of speech, or of the press * * *." Although some then argued over precisely what they meant by the words, none spoke doubts about the importance of the principle. They were deeply aware of the lasting symbolic power of the courageous Zenger in accepting prison in the cause of free press. They knew well the spirited, soaring arguments for free press by England's famed "Cato," printed and re-printed in the little colonial newspapers. Behind them lay the great pamphleteering and newspapering that had raised sedition to an art in bringing the colonies to revolt against the Mother country, printed words indispensable in bringing down the most powerful nation on earth.

Yet in the searing newspaper debates of the nation's first years, with Federalists and anti-Federalists indulging in political vitriol seen by many as seditious and thus criminal, the axioms of centuries were with them. It still seemed to many that no government could stand if it could not at some point punish its critics, if their new government was meant to last. Some words surely were illegal. Not, perhaps, in the realm of religion, where James Madison, among others, argued an unlimited freedom to speak and write; but could sedition be given such scope? It was the party of Thomas Jefferson that gave an answer, in the debates over and sequel to the Alien and Sedition Acts of 1798–1800.

The Alien and Sedition Acts, 1798–1800

In the complex story about the reluctant retreat of the crime of sedition through more than 150 years of American history, no episode stands out more than the controversy of 1798–1800 over the Alien and Sedition Acts. It was only seven years after the adoption of the Bill of Rights and its First Amendment that the Acts were written, at a time of high public and official alarm. With France and England in conflict through the 1790s, America had been pulled by both toward war. The Republicans—Jefferson's party—had favored France, while the Federalists sided with England. Angered at Jay's Treaty of 1794 with England, which she felt placed America on the side of her enemy, France had undertaken the raiding of American shipping. America's envoys, sent to France to negotiate a settlement, were faced with a demand for an American war loan to France, and a bribe of a quarter-million dollars. This unofficial demand as a price for negotiations was revealed to Americans as the notorious "X, Y, Z Affair." Now most of America was incensed; President John Adams called for war preparation, which his Federalist Congress set about in 1797.[9]

---

[9] James M. Smith, Freedom's Fetters (Ithaca: Cornell Univ.Press, 1956), Chap. 2. This is the leading work on the Alien and Sedition Acts.

The Republicans, although they suffered heavy political losses because of the nation's war fever, did not abandon their support of France. Stigmatized in the refusal to do so, associated by the Federalists with the recent French Revolution and its Terror, and beleaguered on all sides for their continued opposition to Britain, the Republicans were in deep trouble. And in this context, the Federalist Congress passed the Alien and Sedition Acts as measures to control opposition to America's war policy and to the Federalist majority party.

It was the Sedition Act that struck most lethally at opposition and at the Republicans. The Act made it a crime to publish or utter false, scandalous, and malicious criticism of the President, Congress, or the government with the intent to defame them or bring them into disrepute.[10]

Fourteen indictments were brought under the Act, all against Republican newspapermen and publicists, and all 14 resulted in convictions.[11] The first action put Rep. Matthew Lyon in jail for four months and cost him a fine of $1,000. He had claimed that under President Adams, the Executive Branch showed "an unbounded thirst for ridiculous pomp, foolish adulation, and selfish avarice," and that the public welfare was "swallowed up in a continual grasp for power." Anthony Haswell, Republican editor of the (Bennington) *Vermont Gazette,* came to Lyon's defense while the latter was in prison. He wrote that Lyon was held by "the oppressive hand of usurped power," and said that the federal marshal who held him had subjected him to indignities that might be expected of a "hard-hearted savage." Haswell's fine was $200 and his term in federal prison two months.[12]

Its back to the wall under the attempt of the Federalists to proscribe it as a party of disloyalty and subversion, the Republican Party put forth spokesmen who declared that the idea of sedition was odious to a self-governing society, and denied that the federal government had any kind of power over the press. The Acts, the Jeffersonian Republicans said, were unconstitutional in making it a crime to criticize the President and government. No matter that the Acts permitted the defenses for which Andrew Hamilton had argued in defending Zenger: truth was of little use in defending opinions (how to prove the truth of an opinion?), and jury power to find the law could be circumvented by judges in various ways. A people, they argued, cannot call itself free unless it is superior to its government, unless it can have unrestricted right of discussion. No natural right of the individual, they contended in Philosopher John Locke's framework, can be more important than free expres-

10 Ibid., Chap. 6.

11 Ibid., p. 185.

12 Each trial is treated in Smith, Chaps. 11–17.

sion. The Jeffersonians rested their case on their belief in reason as the central characteristic of men, and on the people's position of ascendancy over government.[13] The radical Thomas Cooper dissected one by one the arguments for permitting a sedition power in government.[14] Calmly and systematically, lawyer Tunis Wortman worked out philosophical ground for freedom in the fullest statement of the group.[15] James Madison, St. George Tucker, and others drove home the arguments.

The unpopularity of the Alien and Sedition Acts and outrage at the prosecutions of Republican printers helped defeat the Federalist Party and President John Adams in 1800. President Jefferson was committed to letting the Acts lapse, and they died in early 1801. The nation would see no federal peacetime sedition act again for 140 years. Furthermore, the alternative route of using the common law as a basis for federal sedition actions was closed to the government only a few years later. The Supreme Court ruled in cases of 1812 and 1816 that federal courts had been given no authority over common-law crimes by the Constitution, and that whatever question there had been about the matter had been settled by public opposition to such jurisdiction.[16]

The fear and hatred of French revolutionary doctrine had been real factors in the passage of the Alien and Sedition Acts. Different fears, different hatreds led to suppressive laws in the South about a generation later, when states began passing laws to silence Abolitionists. The anti-slavery drive, coupled with incidents such as Nat Turner's slave rebellion, caused paroxysms of fear among Southerners that their "peculiar institution" and the shape of society and government would be subverted and destroyed. Laws were passed—sedition laws, though not labeled as such in statute books—making it a crime to advocate the abolition of slavery or to argue that owners "have no property" in slaves, and denying abolitionist literature access to the mails.[17] The suppression of anti-slavery argument became almost total in most of the South by 1850.

Sedition in World War I

Sedition actions surfaced again in the early Twentieth Century when both state and federal lawmakers acted to check criticism of

[13] Levy, Chap. 10. And see Chap. 9 for evidence that several Jeffersonians had no objection to a sedition power in *state* governments.

[14] Political Essays (Phila.: Printed for R. Campbell, 1800), pp. 71–88.

[15] Treatise Concerning Political Enquiry, and the Liberty of the Press (New York: Printed by George Forman, 1800).

[16] United States v. Hudson and Goodwin, 11 U.S. (7 Cranch.) 32 (1812); United States v. Coolidge, 14 U.S. (1 Wheat.) 415 (1816).

[17] Three Virginia laws passed between 1832 and 1848 are in Nelson, Freedom of the Press from Hamilton to the Warren Court, pp. 173–178.

government in response to alarm at the rise of socio-political protest. Prosecutions to punish verbal attacks on the form of government, on laws, and on government's conduct, found new life at the federal level some 100 years after they had been discredited by the Alien and Sedition Act prosecutions of 1798–1800. The actions focused on a new radicalism, flourishing in the poverty and sweat-shop conditions of industrial cities and in the lumber and mining camps of the West. Whether seeking an improved life for the deprived, driving for power, or fostering revolution, socialists, anarchists, and syndicalists advocated drastic change in the economic and political system. Laws and criminal prosecutions rose to check their words.[18]

In the aftermath of the assassination of President William McKinley in 1901, the states of New York, New Jersey and Wisconsin passed laws against anarchists' advocating the destruction of existing government. Congress passed the Immigration Act of 1903, barring from the country those who believed in or advocated the overthrow of the United States government by violence. Industrial turbulence, the growth of the Industrial Workers of the World, the surge of right- and left-wing socialism, contributed to alarm in the nation. And as the varied voices of drastic reform and radical change rose loud in the land, the coming of World War I increased their stridency: This, they insisted, was a "Capitalists' war," fostered and furthered for industrial profit. By 1918, national alarm was increased by the victory of revolutionary communism in Russia.[19]

World War I brought a wave of legislation across the states to make criminal the advocacy of violent overthrow of government. Yet it was the federal government's Espionage Act of 1917 and its amendment of 1918 to include sedition that put most muscle into prosecution for criminal words. Foremost among forbidden and prosecuted statements were those that were construed to cause insubordination or disloyalty in the armed forces, or to obstruct enlistment or recruiting.[20] Some 1,900 persons were prosecuted for speech, and possibly 100 newspapers and periodicals were barred from the mails.[21] Polemics in pamphlet form, as well as books, also were the cause of prosecutions.

[18] William Preston, Jr., Aliens and Dissenters, Federal Suppression of Radicals, 1903–1933 (Cambridge: Harvard Univ.Press, 1963).

[19] Ibid.; Paul L. Murphy, World War I and the Origins of Civil Liberties in the United States (New York, 1979); H.C. Peterson and Gilbert C. Fite, Opponents of War, 1917–1918 (Madison: Univ. of Wis.Press, 1957).

[20] 40 U.S. Statutes 217. For state laws, see Zechariah Chafee, Jr., Free Speech in the United States (Boston, 1941), pp. 575–597.

[21] Chafee, p. 52.

The best-known of the Socialist newspapers prosecuted under the Espionage Act were the *New York Call,* the *Masses,* also of New York, and the *Milwaukee Leader.* In the last of these, editor Victor Berger had denounced the war, the United States government, and munitions makers. Postmaster General Albert Burleson considered this the kind of opposition to the war forbidden by the Espionage Act, and excluded it from the mails as the Act provided. Further, he said, the repeated attacks on the war effort in the Leader were evidence that it would continue doing the same in the future, and on these grounds, the Leader's second-class mail permit should be revoked. He was upheld in his revocation of the permit by the United States Supreme Court, and the Leader was thus denied the low-rate mailing privilege from 1917 until after the war.[22]

Pamphleteers of the left were convicted under the Espionage Act and under state anarchy and sedition acts. The famous case of Schenck v. United States, in which Schenck was prosecuted for polemics that actually went to the matter of resisting the draft, brought Justice Oliver Wendell Holmes' articulation of the clear and present danger test:[23]

> We admit that in many places and in ordinary times the defendants in saying all that was said in the circular would have been within their constitutional rights. But the character of every act depends upon the circumstances in which it was done * * *. The question in every case is whether the words used are used in such circumstances and are of such a nature as to create a clear and present danger that they will bring about the substantive evils that Congress has a right to prevent. It is a question of proximity and degree. When a nation is at war many things that might be said in time of peace are such a hindrance to its effort that their utterance will not be endured * * *.

As noted earlier, this new test did not free Schenck, and it did not protect radicals seen as illegally opposing the war; they went to jail. Its plain implications, however, were that old tests were too restrictive for the demands of freedom under the First Amendment. As elaborated and developed in subsequent opinions by Holmes and Justice Brandeis against restrictive interpretations of free expression,[24] the test helped force the Court to think through the meaning

[22] United States ex rel. Milwaukee Social Democratic Pub. Co. v. Burleson, 255 U.S. 407, 41 S.Ct. 352 (1921).

[23] 249 U.S. 47, 39 S.Ct. 247 (1919).

[24] Notably Abrams v. United States, 250 U.S. 616, 40 S.Ct. 17 (1919); Gilbert v. State of Minn., 254 U.S. 325, 41 S.Ct. 125 (1920); Gitlow v. People of State of New

of the First and Fourteenth Amendments, and served as a rallying-point for libertarians for decades to come.

As noted on page 12, above, another milestone in the Supreme Court's consideration of sedition cases was reached in a post-war case, Gitlow v. People of New York.[25] Here the 1902 New York statute on anarchy was invoked against the publication of the "left Wing Manifesto" in a radical paper called *Revolutionary Age.* It advocated and forecast mass struggle, mass strikes, and the overthrow of the bourgeoisie after a long revolutionary period. Convicted, business manager Benjamin Gitlow appealed to the Supreme Court. It upheld his conviction under an old test of criminality in words—whether the words have a tendency to imperil or subvert government.

But even as it upheld conviction, the Court wrote a single short paragraph accepting a principle long sought by libertarians: It said that the Fourteenth Amendment's barrier to states' depriving citizens of life, liberty, or property without due process of law protected liberty of speech and press against invasion by the states. Before *Gitlow,* the Supreme Court had tightly restricted the scope of the "liberty" protected by the Fourteenth Amendment; it had left it up to each state to say what liberty of speech and press was. After *Gitlow,* the Supreme Court would review state laws and decisions on free expression.[26]

The Smith Act of 1940

Immediately after World War I, the thrust of revolutionary communism had spurred the Attorney General of the United States to urge the passage of a federal peacetime sedition act. His call for such a peacetime measure (the Espionage Act of 1917 had applied only to war) brought concerted opposition; the move was stopped although widespread deportation of Russians and other aliens for their ideas and words was accomplished. But 20 years later, similar fears engendered with the coming of World War II and the activity of domestic communists brought success for a similar bill. This was the Alien Registration Act of 1940, known as the Smith Act for Rep. Howard W. Smith of Virginia who introduced it.[27] For the first time since the Alien and Sedition Acts of 1798, America had a federal peacetime sedition law. The heart of its provisions, under Section 2, made it a crime to advocate forcible or violent overthrow of government, or to publish or distribute material advocating violence with the intent to overthrow government.

York, 268 U.S. 652, 45 S.Ct. 625 (1925); Whitney v. People of State of California, 274 U.S. 357, 47 S.Ct. 641 (1927).

[25] 268 U.S. 652, 45 S.Ct. 625 (1925).

[26] Ibid., at 666, 45 S.Ct. at 630.

[27] 54 U.S. Statutes 670.

The Act was to have little or no impact upon the mass media of general circulation. They advocated the *status quo,* not radical change or revolution. But for speakers, teachers, and pamphleteers of the Communist Party, the Smith Act came to mean a great deal. Fewer than 20 persons had been punished under the Alien and Sedition Acts of 1798–1801; it is estimated that approximately 100 persons were fined or imprisoned under the Smith Act between 1940 and 1960.[28] In one sense, however, the Smith Act was less suppressive than its ancestor: The Alien and Sedition Acts had punished criticism of government officials, Congress, and the laws, an everyday exercise of the press, but the Smith Act limited the ban to advocating violent overthrow.

The government made its first move in 1943. Leaders of a revolutionary splinter, the Socialist Workers Party which followed Russia's banished Trotsky, were the target. They were brought to trial in Minneapolis and convicted for the advocacy of violent overthrow in their printed polemics. The Court of Appeals sustained the conviction, and the United States Supreme Court refused to review the case.[29]

But the Communist Party was much more the target of government prosecution than the little group of Trotskyites. In the context of the cold war between the United States and the U.S.S.R. following World War II, almost 10 years of prosecution took place. The first case, Dennis v. United States, brought major figures in the Communist Party to trial and convicted 11 of them.[30] The charges were that they had reconstituted the American Communist Party in 1945, and conspired to advocate violent overthrow of the government.

For almost nine months the trial went on in federal district court under Judge Harold Medina. The nation was fascinated and bored in turn as the defense introduced complex legal challenges to the trial and the prosecution introduced exhibit after exhibit. Newspapers, pamphlets, and books were employed as evidence of the defendants' intent, from the *Daily Worker* to *The Communist Manifesto.* Scores of pages were read into the record, as the government sought to show conspiracy by publishing and circulating the literature of revolutionary force. Judge Medina followed the doctrine of the *Gitlow* case in instructing the jury that advocacy or teaching of violent overthrow of the government was not illegal if it were only "abstract doctrine." What the law forbade was

[28] Don R. Pember, The Smith Act as a Restraint of the Press, Journalism Monographs # 10, May 1969; Zechariah Chafee, Jr., The Blessings of Liberty (Phila., N.Y.: J.B. Lippincott Co., 1954), p. 22.

[29] Dunne v. United States, 138 F.2d 137 (8th Cir.1943).

[30] 341 U.S. 494, 71 S.Ct. 857 (1951).

teaching or advocating "action" to overthrow the government.[31] The jury found that the 11 did, indeed, conspire to advocate forcible overthrow. The Court of Appeals upheld the conviction and the case was accepted for review by the Supreme Court of the United States.

The justices wrote five opinions, three opinions concurring in conviction and two dissenting. Chief Justice Vinson wrote the opinion that carried the most names (three besides his). He said that free expression is not an unlimited or unqualified right, and that "the societal value of speech must, on occasion, be subordinated to other values and considerations."[32] But a conviction for violation of a statute limiting speech, he said, must rest on the showing that the words created a "clear and present danger" that a crime would be attempted or accomplished. Thus he went to the famous Holmes rule first expressed in the *Schenck* case in 1919, and interpreted it as follows:[33]

> In this case we are squarely presented with the application of the "clear and present danger" test, and must decide what that phrase imports. We first note that many of the cases in which this Court has reversed convictions by use of this or similar tests have been based on the fact that the interest which the State was attempting to protect was too insubstantial to warrant restriction of speech. * * * Overthrow of the Government by force and violence is certainly a substantial enough interest for the Government to limit speech. Indeed, this is the ultimate value of any society, for if a society cannot protect its very structure from armed internal attack, it must follow that no subordinate value can be protected. * * * Certainly an attempt to overthrow the Government by force, even though doomed from the outset because of inadequate numbers or power of the revolutionists, is a sufficient evil for Congress to prevent.

Having thus rejected the position that likelihood of success in committing the criminal act is the criterion for restricting speech, Chief Justice Vinson adopted the statement of the Court of Appeals in interpreting the clear and present danger test. Chief Judge Hand had written: "In each case [courts] must ask whether the gravity of the 'evil,' discounted by its improbability justifies such invasion of free speech as is necessary to avoid the danger."[34]

[31] United States v. Foster, 80 F.Supp. 479 (S.D.N.Y.1948). Upon appeal, this case became United States v. Dennis et al., 183 F.2d 201 (2d Cir.1950).

[32] Dennis v. United States, 341 U.S. 494, 71 S.Ct. 857 (1951).

[33] Ibid., at 508–509, 71 S.Ct. at 867.

[34] Ibid., at 510, 71 S.Ct. at 868, from 183 F.2d at 212.

Vinson was arguing that the danger need not be immediate when the interest (here, self-preservation of government) is important enough.

Deep disagreement in the Court over thus limiting the scope of free expression appeared in the dissents of Justices Black and Douglas. The latter could see no clear and present danger to the government and state in the words and papers of the 11 Communists. Neither as a political force nor as a disciplined corps of poised saboteurs did Justice Douglas see them as a threat: [35]

> Communists in this country have never made a respectable or serious showing in any election * * *. Communism has been so thoroughly exposed in this country that it has been crippled as a political force. Free speech has destroyed it as an effective political party. It is inconceivable that those who went up and down this country preaching the doctrine of revolution which petitioners espouse would have any success.
>
> * * *
>
> * * * Free speech—the glory of our system of government—should not be sacrificed on anything less than plain and objective proof of danger that the evil advocated is imminent.

Through most of the 1950's, cases under the Smith Act continued to move through the courts. But in the wake of the decision in Yates v. United States in 1957, prosecutions dwindled and died out. In this case, the Supreme Court reversed the conviction of 14 Communist Party leaders under the Smith Act. Its decision turned in large part on the difference between teaching the need for violent overthrow as an abstract theory or doctrine, and teaching it as a spur to action.[36] Since the trial court had not required the jury which found the defendant guilty to make the distinction, the conviction was reversed. There was no reference to the famous clear and present danger doctrine.

The Warren Court—so called for chief Justice Earl Warren who had been appointed in 1953—had grown less and less willing to uphold convictions under the Smith Act, and with the *Yates* decision, charges against many other defendants in pending cases were dismissed in lower courts. The Smith Act soon lapsed into disuse, and in the several versions of a bill for the broad reform of the federal Criminal Code that labored toward adoption by Congress

[35] Dennis v. United States, 341 U.S. 494, 588, 71 S.Ct. 857, 906–907 (1951).
[36] Yates v. United States, 354 U.S. 298, 77 S.Ct. 1064 (1957).

beginning in 1977, the Act was omitted and thus scheduled for repeal.[37]

Yates had found that the trial judge's instructions had allowed conviction for mere advocacy without reference to its tendency to bring about forcible action, and overturned the convictions. In 1969, the Supreme Court was presented with the appeal of a Ku Klux Klan leader who had been convicted under the Ohio Criminal Syndicalism statute for advocating the duty or necessity of crime, violence or unlawful methods of terrorism to accomplish political reform. The leader, Brandenburg, had been televised as he made a speech in which he said the Klan was "not a revengent [sic] organization, but if our President, our Congress, our Supreme Court, continues to suppress the white, Caucasian race, it's possible that there might have to be some revengeance taken." He added that "We are marching on Congress * * * four hundred thousand strong."

The Supreme Court reversed the conviction. Citing precedent since *Dennis,* it said: [38]

> These later decisions have fashioned the principle that the constitutional guarantees of free speech and free press do not permit a State to forbid or proscribe advocacy of the use of force or of law violation except where such advocacy is directed to inciting or producing imminent lawless action and is likely to incite or produce such action. * * * A statute which fails to draw this distinction impermissibly intrudes upon the freedoms guaranteed by the First and Fourteenth Amendments.

The "inciting" or producing imminent lawless action clause has been called merely a version of the "clear and present danger" test.[39] It has continued to serve a protective role. Words challenging the authority of the state have brought criminal conviction at trial, but under the test have continued to find protection upon appeal to the Supreme Court.[40] Less than an absolute barrier to government's control of expression, the *Brandenburg* test is a

[37] For other controls on news media embraced by the Act (S.1437), see Reporters Committee for Freedom of the Press, News Media Alert, Aug. 1977, pp. 4–5.

[38] Brandenburg v. Ohio, 395 U.S. 444, 89 S.Ct. 1827 (1969).

[39] Gerald Gunther, Cases and Materials on Constitutional Law, 9th ed., Mineola, N.Y.1975, p. 1128; Thomas I. Emerson, "First Amendment Doctrine and the Burger Court," 68 Univ. of Calif.L.Rev. 422, 445–46, feels the "incitement" test is subject to "serious objections," including its permitting government to interfere with expression "at too early a state."

[40] Hess v. Indiana, 414 U.S. 105, 94 S.Ct. 326 (1973); Healy v. James, 408 U.S. 169, 92 S.Ct. 2338 (1972).

strong element in the heavy crippling of the sedition action.[41]

Symbolic Speech: U.S. v. O'Brien (1968) as a "Gift" to Communications Law

"Mass communications law" is not an island unto itself. It often is affected—and buffeted—by winds of change touching other parts of American law and society. Take the example of a 1968 conviction of a young man who violated federal law by burning his draft card. Daniel James O'Brien claimed that his act was "symbolic speech" to protest the Vietnam War and thus was protected by the First Amendment. Seeking a rationale for upholding O'Brien's conviction, the Supreme Court of the United States hit upon a rather complicated formula which has showed up as pivotal to the reasoning in cases far removed from draft cards on fire.

In particular, this decision has been used by courts in cases upholding regulation of advertising[42] and of cable television.[43] The crucial terminology in United States v. O'Brien was found in Chief Justice Earl Warren's opinion for the Court: [44]

> This court has held that when "speech" and "nonspeech" elements are combined in the same course of conduct, a sufficiently important governmental interest in regulating the non-speech elements can justify incidental limitations on First Amendment freedoms. * * * [W]e think it clear that a government regulation is sufficiently justified if it is within the constitutional power of the government; if it furthers an important or substantial governmental governmental interest; if the governmental interest is unrelated to the suppression of free expression; and if the restriction on alleged First Amendment freedom is no greater than is essential to the furtherance of that interest.

Those factors listed in United States v. O'Brien have been turned to repeatedly as the Supreme Court has tried to craft constitutionally acceptable rationales for regulating both cable TV

[41] See Harry Kalven, "The New York Times Case: a Note on The Central Meaning of the First Amendment", 1964 Sup.Ct.Rev. 191.

[42] See, e.g., Chapter 11's treatment of the four-part test in Central Hudson Gas & Electric Co. v. Public Service Comm'n., 447 U.S. 557, 100 S.Ct. 2343 (1980); Posadas de Puerto Rico v. Tourism Co., 478 U.S. at 340, 106 S.Ct. at 2976 (1986), and Board of Trustees of the State University of New York v. Fox, 492 U.S. 469, 109 S.Ct. 3028 (1989).

[43] See, e.g. Chapter 10's discussion of key cable TV regulation decisions, including Home Box Office v. FCC, 567 F.2d 9 (D.C.Cir.1977); Quincy Cable TV, Inc. v. FCC, 768 F.2d 1434 (D.C.Cir.1985); Century Communications Corp. v. FCC, 835 F.2d 292 (D.C.Cir.1987); Turner Broadcasting v. FCC, 810 F.Supp. 1308 (D.C.D.C. 1992); Turner Broadcasting v. United States, 114 S.Ct. 244 (1994), 22 Med.L.Rptr. 1865.

[44] United States v. O'Brien, 391 U.S. 367, 376, 88 S.Ct. 1673, 1678–1679 (1968).

(see Chapter 10) and advertising/commercial speech (see Chapter 11).

SEC. 5.   PRIOR RESTRAINT

Despite authoritative statements that the chief purpose of the First Amendment guarantee is to prevent previous restraints upon publication, prior restraints have continued to be exerted into the late Twentieth Century.

In perhaps the most influential First Amendment decision by the Supreme Court of the United States, Chief Justice Charles Evans Hughes wrote that it is generally considered " . . . that it is the chief purpose of the [First Amendment] guarantee to prevent previous restraint on publication." [45]   Journalists and civil libertarians have long counted pre-publication censorship as the most despised of all controls.   Prior restraint's origins may be traced back virtually as long as there has been printing.   It was tied in Sixteenth and Seventeenth Century England to requiring printers to get permission or license from government to publish.   And then censors often pored over every word, to make sure that nothing harmful to those in authority would be printed.

Obviously, if government can stop publication before it occurs, that is the ultimate in repressiveness.   Although it is true that a person may be deterred from publishing by the threat of post-publication punishment (as in the case of libel, invasion of privacy, or obscenity), that is not the issue here.   As the U.S. Supreme Court has said: "If it can be said that a threat of criminal or civil sanctions after publication 'chills' speech, prior restraint 'freezes' it . . . " [46]

The power in government to approve who might publish, or to order non-publication—under threat of punishment—has a long and oppressive history.   In revolutionary America, the leaders and printers considered that whatever the quicksilver phrase "freedom of the press" meant, it meant an end to prior restraint.[47]   If the press were to act as a check on government or to aid society by spreading knowledge and opinion needed for a self-governing society, prior restraint could not be tolerated.   Society's chief weapon against the institution which possessed the power of guns and police was words.

Government attempts to use prior restraint have taken place, with almost predictable regularity, when some form of crisis occurs.

[45] Near v. Minnesota ex rel. Olson, 283 U.S. 697, 713, 51 S.Ct. 625, 630 (1931).

[46] Nebraska Press Ass'n v. Stuart, 427 U.S. 539, 559, 96 S.Ct. 2791, 2803 (1976), 1 Med.L.Rptr. 1064.

[47] Levy, Emergence of a Free Press, Chaps. 6, 8.

During pre-Civil War days when Abolitionists' agitating threatened "the peculiar institution" of slavery, the South often used prior restraint as a weapon. Postmasters regularly refused to deliver mailings from Northern anti-slavery societies. And during the Civil War, Northern generals would occasionally shut down pro-South ("Copperhead") publishers. President Abraham Lincoln himself ordered the closing of newspapers on one occasion.[48] Later in the Nineteenth Century, heavy restrictions on publishing and distributing of materials discussing sex were extensively used, and prior restraint was part of the control. Postal and customs officials' use of prior restraint, in peacetime to control materials labeled "obscene" and in wartime to stop "sedition," was vigorous and frequent through the first third of the Twentieth Century.[49]

The area of prior restraint expanded in the Twentieth Century in matters not related to governmental acts of self-protection. As discussed in Chapter 3—and still ordained by the number of frequencies available—there is the governmental licensing of all broadcasters to prevent overcrowding the airwaves. There are also many areas in which courts can issue injunctions against speaking, publishing, or distributing words or symbols—and those are prior restraints. For example, the Federal Trade Commission can issue "cease and desist" orders against anticompetitive or deceptive ads, and can order advertisers to publish corrective statements.[50] Copyright law provides for court-issued injunctions to restrain illegal use of copyrighted materials.[51]

The U.S. Supreme Court has approved prohibition of newspaper publication of material from pre-trial "discovery" proceedings.[52] During the 1970s, in fact, a striking extension of prior restraint burst out as courts across the nation forbade publishing of accounts of part or all of the records in pre-trial hearings and even in trials. No phase of prior restraint has been more alarming to the media in recent years (see Chapter 11).

Later chapters will detail aspects of prior restraint. In this chapter, the special concern goes to government's claims to suppress, on its own behalf, attacks on its personnel and structure, or words constituting danger to national security.

[48] Russel Blaine Nye, Fettered Freedom (East Lansing: Michigan State, 1951).

[49] Vincent Blasi, Toward a Theory of Prior Restraint, 66 Minn.L.Rev. 11, 14–15 (Nov.1981).

[50] Anon., The FTC's Injunctive Authority Against False Advertising of Food and Drugs, 75 Mich.L.Rev. 745 (March 1977).

[51] 17 U.S.C.A. §§ 502, 503.

[52] E.g. Seattle Times Co. v. Rhinehart, 467 U.S. 20, 104 S.Ct. 2199 (1984), 10 Med.L.Rptr. 1705.

Near v. Minnesota

Mr. Chief Justice Hughes' majority opinion in Near v. Minnesota, a case of 1931, established groundwork that may be seen as a watershed which turned United States Supreme Court majorities in the direction of expanded press freedom.[53]

That decision grew out of scruffy origins. Howard Guilford and J.M. Near were publishing partners in producing *The Saturday Press,* a Minneapolis "smear sheet" which charged that gangsters were in control of Minneapolis gambling, bootlegging and racketeering, and that the city law enforcement and government agencies and officers were derelict in their duties. It vilified Jews and Catholics. And it published the articles that eventually required the Supreme Court of the United States to make one of its most notable descriptions of the extent of freedom of the press in America.

Publication of *The Saturday Press* was halted when a Minnesota statute authorizing prior restraint of "nuisance" or "undesirable" publications was invoked. That statute declared that any person publishing a "malicious, scandalous and defamatory newspaper, magazine or other periodical" could be found guilty of creating a nuisance and could be enjoined from future wrongdoing.[54] Near and Guilford were indeed brought into court after a temporary injunction ordered cessation of all activity by their paper. After the hearing, the injunction was made permanent by a judge, but with the provision that *The Saturday Press* could resume publication if the publishers could persuade the court that they would run a newspaper without objectionable content described in the Minnesota "gag law" statute.[55]

Near and Guilford appealed to the Supreme Court, which found in their favor by the margin of five votes to four. Speaking for the Court, Chief Justice Charles Evans Hughes noted the importance of this case: "This statute, for the suppression as a public nuisance of a newspaper or periodical, is unusual, if not unique, and raises questions of grave importance transcending the local interest involved in the particular action." Hughes declared of this prior restraint, "This is the essence of censorship."[56]

Hughes then turned to history-as-precedent to answer the question of whether a statute authorizing such proceedings in

[53] Near v. Minnesota ex rel. Olson, 283 U.S. 697, 51 S.Ct. 625 (1931); Paul L. Murphy, Near v. Minnesota in the Context of Historical Developments, 66 Minn. L.Rev. 95 (Nov.1981); Fred W. Friendly, Minnesota Rag (N.Y., 1981).

[54] Chapter 285, Minn.Sess.Laws 1925, in Mason's Minn.Stats., 1927, Secs. 10123–1 to 10123–3.

[55] Near v. Minnesota ex rel. Olson, 283 U.S. 697, 702–707, 51 S.Ct. 625, 628 (1931).

[56] Ibid., at 707, 713, 51 S.Ct. at 627, 630.

restraint of publication was consistent with the concept of liberty of the press, declaring here that the chief purpose of the constitutional guaranty is to prevent previous restraints.

He embarked upon a two-fold modification of the old English authority, Blackstone. Blackstone would have had *no prior restraint,* period. The Chief Justice, however, conceded that such a prohibition against all prior restraint might be "stated too broadly," and said that " * * * the protection even as to previous restraint is not absolutely unlimited." In a few exceptional cases, limitation of the principle of "no prior restraint" could be recognized: [57]

> No one would question but that a government might prevent actual obstruction to its recruiting service or the publication of sailing dates of transports or the number and location of troops. On similar grounds, the primary requirements of decency may be enforced against obscene publications. The security of the community life may be protected against incitements to acts of violence and the overthrow by force of orderly government. The constitutional guaranty of free speech does not "protect a man from an injunction against uttering words that may have all the effect of force."

Although Blackstone's "no prior restraint" was thus modified, another aspect of Blackstone was liberalized. Blackstone had approved punishing the publication of criticisms of government or government officials. But Hughes said that the press had a right— and perhaps even a duty—to discuss and debate the character and conduct of public officers.[58]

> ... [T]he administration of government has become more complex, the opportunities for malfeasance and corruption have multiplied, crime has grown to most serious proportions, and the danger of its protection by unfaithful officials and of the impairment of the fundamental security of life and property by criminal alliances and official neglect, emphasizes the primary need of a vigilant and courageous press, especially in great cities.

> The fact that the liberty of the press may be abused by miscreant purveyors of scandal does not make any the less necessary the immunity of the press from previous restraint in dealing with official misconduct. Subsequent punishment for such abuses as may exist is the appropriate remedy, consistent with constitutional privilege.

[57] Ibid., at 716, 51 S.Ct. at 631.
[58] Ibid., at 719–720, 51 S.Ct. at 632–633.

Despite the four dissenting votes, Near v. Minnesota has stood since 1931 as one of the most important decisions of the Supreme Court. *Near* was the first case involving newspapers in which the Court applied the provisions of the First Amendment against states through the language of the Fourteenth Amendment.[59] And it was to serve as important precedent for protecting the press against government's demands for suppression.

It was 40 years before the press again collided with government bent on protecting its own interest and functions through prior restraint. On June 30, 1971, the United States Supreme court cleared the confrontation with a decision hailed by many news media with such headlines as "VICTORY FOR THE PRESS" and "The Press Wins and the Presses Roll." [60] These triumphant headlines were tied to the "Pentagon Papers" case. Early in 1971, *New York Times* reporter Neil Sheehan was given photocopies of a 47–volume study of the United States involvement in Vietnam titled *History of the United States Decision–Making Process on Vietnam Policy.* On Sunday, June 13, 1971, the *New York Times—* after a team of reporters had worked with the documents for three months—published a story headlined: "Vietnam Archive: Pentagon Study Traces 3 Decades of Growing U.S. Involvement." Within 48 hours after publication, Attorney General John Mitchell sent a telegram to the Times, urging that no more articles based on the documents be published, charging that the series would bring about "irreparable injury to the defense interests of the United States." [61] The Times chose to ignore Attorney General Mitchell's plea, and columnist James Reston angrily wrote: "For the first time in the history of the Republic, the Attorney General of the United States has tried to suppress documents he hasn't read about a war that hasn't been declared." [62]

After the Times' refusal to stop the series of articles, the Department of Justice asked U.S. District Court Judge Murray I. Gurfein to halt publication of the stories. Judge Gurfein, who was serving his first day as a federal judge, issued a temporary injunction on June 15, putting a stop to the Times' publication of the articles. But silencing the Times did not halt all publication of the "Pentagon Papers." *The Washington Post*—and a number of other major journals—also weighed in with excerpts from the secret report. The Justice Department likewise applied for—and was

[59] William A. Hachten, The Supreme Court on Freedom of the Press: Decisions and Dissents (Ames, Ia.: Iowa State Univ. Press, 1968), p. 43.

[60] Newsweek, Time, July 12, 1971.

[61] Don R. Pember, "The Pentagon Papers Decision: More Questions Than Answers," Journalism Quarterly 48:3 (Autumn, 1971) p. 404; New York Times, June 15, 1971, p. 1.

[62] New York Times, June 16, 1971, p. 1.

granted—a temporary restraining order against *The Washington Post*.[63]

After two weeks of uncertainty, the decision by the Supreme Court of the United States cleared the papers for publication. *New York Times* Managing Editor A.M. Rosenthal was jubilant: "This is a joyous day for the press—and for American society." *Time* added, "Certainly the Justice Department was slapped down in its efforts to ask the courts to enjoin newspapers, and will not likely take that route again." [64] Despite such optimism, some observers within the press were disturbed by the outcome of the *"Pentagon Papers"* case. Not only were there three dissents against lifting the injunction among the nine justices, there was also deep reluctance to do so on the part of two of the majority justices. Furthermore, federal court injunctions had now, for the first time in American history, been employed to impose prior restraint upon newspapers, and the courts had preserved those injunctions intact for two weeks.

The Court's decision was short. It refused to leave in effect the injunctions which the Justice Department had secured against the Times and the Post, and quoted Bantam Books v. Sullivan: [65]

> "Any system of prior restraints of expression comes to this Court bearing a heavy presumption against its constitutional validity." Bantam Books, Inc. v. Sullivan, 372 U.S. 58, 83 S.Ct. 631 * * * (1963); see also Near v. Minnesota ex rel. Olson, 283 U.S. 697, 51 S.Ct. 625 * * * (1931). The Government "thus carries a heavy burden of showing justification for the imposition of such a restraint." Organization for a Better Austin v. Keefe, 402 U.S. 415, 91 S.Ct. 1575, 1578 (1971).

With those words, a six-member majority of the Court ruled that the government had not shown sufficient reason to impose prior restraint. Of the six, four found nothing in the facts of the case to qualify their positions. Justices Hugo L. Black and William O. Douglas expressed abhorrence for prior restraint, Douglas saying "uninhibited, robust and wide-open debate" on public questions was essential, and "The stays in these cases that have been in effect for more than a week constitute a flouting of the principles of the First Amendment as interpreted in Near v. Minnesota * * * " [66]

[63] For a clear account of the cases' journeys through the courts, see Pember, pp. 404–405.

[64] Time, July 12, 1971, p. 10.

[65] New York Times Co. v. United States, 403 U.S. 713, 714, 91 S.Ct. 2140, 2141 (1971).

[66] Ibid., at 724, 91 S.Ct. at 2146.

Justice William J. Brennan, Jr., although not subscribing to an absolutist position about prior restraint, nevertheless declared that it was permissible in only a "single, extremely narrow" class of cases, as when the nation was at war or when troop movements might be endangered. For all the government's alarms as to possible dangers of nuclear holocaust if secrecy were breached, it had not presented a case that publication of the Pentagon Papers would cause such an event. Therefore:[67]

> * * * every restraint issued in this case, whatever its form, has violated the First Amendment—and none the less so because the restraint was justified as necessary to examine the claim more thoroughly.

With reluctance, Justices Byron White and Potter Stewart joined the majority. Stewart approved secrecy in some contexts, and said he was convinced that the Executive branch of government was correct in attempting to suppress publication of some of the documents here. But he voted with the majority, he said, because he could not say that disclosure of any of the Pentagon Papers "will surely result in direct, immediate, or irreparable damage to our Nation * * *."[68] White said that if any of the published material proved, after publication, to be punishable under the Espionage Act of 1917, the newspapers now stood warned: "I would have no difficulty in sustaining convictions under [the Espionage Act] on facts that would not justify * * * the imposition of a prior restraint."[69]

Justice Marshall declared that Congress had twice rejected proposed legislation that would have given the President war-time powers to prohibit some kinds of publication. And, he said, it would be inconsistent within the concept of separation of powers for the Court to use its contempt power to prevent behavior that Congress had specifically declined to prohibit.[70]

Dissenting, Justice Harlan wrote that disputes about matters so grave as the alleged contempt and publication of the Pentagon Papers needed more time to resolve, and he voted to support the injunctions.[71] He found that the Court had been almost "irresponsibly feverish in dealing with these cases" of such high national importance in only a few days' time. Justice Blackmun agreed with Harlan, and added a shrill indictment of the press:[72]

[67] Ibid., at 727, 91 S.Ct. at 2148.

[68] Ibid., at 730, 91 S.Ct. at 2149.

[69] Ibid., at 735–738, 91 S.Ct. at 2152–2154.

[70] Ibid., at 746, 91 S.Ct. at 2157.

[71] Ibid., at 753, 91 S.Ct. at 2161.

[72] Ibid., at 763, 91 S.Ct. at 2165. Blackmun was quoting the dissent of Judge Wilkey in the Pentagon Papers case involving the Washington Post in the Court of

If, however, damage has been done, and if, with the Court's action today, these newspapers proceed to publish the critical documents and there results therefrom "the death of soldiers, the destruction of alliances, the greatly increased difficulty of negotiation with our enemies, the inability of our diplomats to negotiate," to which list I might add the factors of prolongation of the war and of further delay in the freeing of United States prisoners, then the Nation's people will know where the responsibility for these sad consequences rests.

It should be recognized that no new legal course was charted by the *Pentagon Papers* case. After a delay of two weeks—a prior restraint imposed by lower federal courts at the insistence of the Department of Justice—the Supreme Court allowed the press to resume publication of the documents. By a 6–to–3 margin, the Supreme Court adhered to Near v. Minnesota, that classic case which, by a 5–to–4 margin, forbade prior restraint except in time of war, or when the materials involved were obscene, or when there was incitement to violence or to the overthrow of the Government.

The *Pentagon Papers* case underlines the important truth that no freedom is ever won, once and for all. Consider this statement:

> Some people may think that leaders of the free press would perhaps accomplish more if their claims of constitutional right were less expansive. I do not agree with this. I say it is their duty to fight like tigers right down to the line and not give an inch. This is the way our freedoms have been preserved in the past, and it is the way they will be preserved in the future.

No editor, publisher, or reporter said that. The quotation is from a statement by U.S. Senior Circuit Judge for the Second Circuit Harold R. Medina. Judge Medina's words emphasize an obvious but necessary history lesson. Each freedom has to be won anew by each succeeding generation. And sometimes, as is apparently true during the latter third of the Twentieth Century, freedom has to be fought for again and again within one generation.

Doom for national security had been forecast by officials of the State Department as they testified against permitting the Times to continue publishing the Pentagon Papers, one of them declaring that further publication would "irreparably harm the United States." But, as Times columnist Anthony Lewis remarked some five years later, "the Republic still stands," and "Today, hardly

Appeals for the Second Circuit, United States v. Washington Post Co., 446 F.2d 1327 (D.C.Cir.1971).

anyone can remember a single item of the papers that caused all the fuss." [73]

A multi-volume history of policy-making in the Vietnam War was not the publication at issue, however, when at the end of the decade the federal government learned that *The Progressive,* a magazine of Madison, Wis., was about to print an article titled "The H–Bomb Secret: How We Got It, Why We're Telling It." The manuscript, the U.S. Attorney charged, carried the deepest of technical secrets relating to the security of our weapons. Publication would endanger national security and that of the world, and in the process would violate the U.S. Atomic Energy Act of 1954 by making public "restricted data" about thermonuclear weapons. The government sought and got a temporary injunction against publication of the article by journalist Howard Morland. [74]

Morland swore that everything in the article was in the public domain, that he had in no way been forced to secret sources for the information; the government denied that this was the case. While the trial was in mid-course, it also came to light that similar information had been available to the public by accident, for a time, in a government science laboratory. [75] Federal District Judge Robert Warren was fully aware of the Supreme Court's rule that "any prior restraint on publication comes into court under a heavy presumption against its constitutional validity." Warren found the revelation of secret technical details about the H-bomb quite different, however, from revealing a secret history of war-policy making. He found that publication offered the possibility of "grave, direct, immediate and irreparable harm to the United States," and said: [76]

* * * because the government has met its heavy burden of showing justification for the imposition of a prior restraint on publication of the objected-to technical portions of the Morland article ... the Court finds that the objected-to portions of the article fall within the narrow area recognized by the Court in Near v. Minnesota in which a prior restraint on publication is appropriate.

Yet Warren's deep concern at the possible outcome of publication ("I'd want to think a long, hard time before I'd give a hydrogen bomb to Idi Amin.") was questioned in the national

[73] "Congress Shall Make No Law," New York Times, Sept. 16, 1976, p. 39.

[74] United States v. Progressive, Inc., 467 F.Supp. 990 (W.D.Wis.1979), 4 Med. L.Rptr. 2377. Major prior restraint cases are discussed by U.S. Circuit Judge J.L. Oakes in "The Doctrine of Prior Restraint Since the Pentagon Papers," 15 U.Mich. Journ.L. Reform 497 (Spring, 1982).

[75] United States v. Progressive, Inc., 486 F.Supp. 5 (W.D.Wis.1980), 5 Med.L.Rptr. 2441.

[76] United States v. Progressive, Inc., 467 F.Supp. 990 (W.D.Wis.1979), 4 Med. L.Rptr. 2377, 2380.

debate and discussion which surged over the case. The government, it was asserted, had not shown that publication would result in "direct, immediate, or irreparable damage to the Nation" that the Pentagon Papers decision had insisted was necessary to justify prior restraint. The field of journalism was divided in its support.[77]

The Progressive and Morland, seizing on implications of the Atomic Energy Act that conceivably rendered even innocent conversations about nuclear weapons subject to classification ("classified at birth") insisted that no real secrets had been told. They appealed, and prior restraint held through six months of court process. Suddenly intruding into the matter was the publication on Sept. 16, 1979, of a long letter in the Madison, Wis. *Press Connection*, a daily of 11,000 circulation, from an amateur student of the nuclear bomb. A copy of a letter from computer programmer Charles Hansen to Sen. Charles Percy of Illinois, it included a diagram and list of key components of an H–bomb. Other newspapers which had received copies had not yet published it when, on the following day, the government moved to drop its court action to bar publication of the Morland article. A U.S. Justice Department spokesman said that the Hansen letter had exposed three "crucial concepts" that the government was trying to protect from publication.

Morland's article was published. *The Progressive* set about trying to raise $200,000 from the public, which was the cost, it said, of defending. No prosecution of the *Press Connection* or other newspapers that published the Hansen letter materialized. Judge Warren dismissed the case against *The Progressive* on Sept. 4, 1980.[78]

Not only the security of the United States' war effort and the provisions of the Atomic Energy Act have made a groundwork for the government's demand for prior restraint. Rules of administrative agencies can furnish the same.[79] The CIA is experienced in the matter. Its employee Victor L. Marchetti resigned from the agency and, with John Marks, wrote *The CIA and the Cult of Intelligence.* This, the CIA charged upon learning of its existence in manuscript form, violated the secrecy contract Marchetti had signed when first employed, promising not to divulge any classified information without specific permission from the CIA.[80] It obtained an injunction in

---

[77] Civil Liberties, No. 328, June 1979, p. 1; Ben Bagdikian, "A Most Insidious Case," Quill, 67:6, June 1979, pp. 21, 22; "Editors and Lawyers Share Mixed Views on Story Ban," Editor & Publisher, March 17, 1979, p. 13.

[78] Milwaukee Journal, Sept. 4, 1980, Part 2, pp. 1, 10.

[79] Ithiel de Sola Pool, "Prior Restraint," New York Times, Dec. 16, 1979, p. E19, portrays unintended prior restraint on research publication through elaborate funding rules of the U.S. Dept. of Health, Education, and Welfare—"a nightmare of bureaucracy run wild, producing results that no one intended."

[80] United States v. Marchetti, 466 F.2d 1309 (4th Cir.1972).

federal district court, the judge ordering Marchetti to submit all writings about the CIA or intelligence work to the Agency for review as to whether it contained classified information that had not been released to the public. As the case proceeded (the Supreme Court of the United States denied certiorari),[81] the CIA's scrutiny of the manuscript resulted in its demand that 339 deletions be performed. "It was the Devil's work we did that day," said Marchetti's attorney, Melvin L. Wulf, after he and the authors spent hours literally cutting out passages of the manuscript— perhaps as much as 20 per cent.[82] Resisting all the way, Marchetti finally won agreement from the court that all but 27 of the 339 deletions would be restored.[83] The book was finally published with blank spaces and the prominent, repeated notation: DELETED.

Frank Snepp, strategy analyst for the CIA in Vietnam, succeeded in getting his case against the CIA to the Supreme Court. He, too, had resigned from the agency and written a book—*Decent Interval*—about his experiences. He, too, had signed an agreement not to publish without first submitting the manuscript to the CIA, and the agency brought legal action. The Supreme Court, by a 6–3 vote, ruled that Snepp had broken his contract, approved an injunction requiring Snepp to submit future writings for publication review, and ruled that he must give all profits from the sale of the book to the CIA through a "constructive trust" imposed on him by the court.[84] He had a fiduciary obligation to the CIA and had breached his trust by publishing.

The government had not alleged that classified or confidential information was revealed by the Snepp book. Rather, it alleged "irreparable harm" in his failure to clear the material with the CIA, and the Supreme Court approved the lower courts' finding that publication of unreviewed material "can be detrimental to vital national interests even if the published information is unclassified." [85]

If the agent published unreviewed material in violation of his fiduciary and contractual obligation, said the court, the constructive trust remedy simply "required him to disgorge the benefits of his faithlessness * * *." Snepp "disgorged" about $138,000, the proceeds from *Decent Interval*.[86]

[81] Marchetti v. United States, 409 U.S. 1063, 93 S.Ct. 553 (1972).

[82] Melvin D. Wulf, Introduction to Victor Marchetti and John D. Marks, The CIA and the Cult of Intelligence (New York: Alfred A. Knopf, 1974), p. xxv.

[83] Ibid., p. xxiv.

[84] Snepp v. United States, 444 U.S. 507, 100 S.Ct. 763 (1980), 5 Med.L.Rptr. 2409.

[85] Ibid., 2411.

[86] Herbert Mitgang, "Royalties to the Treasury," New York Times Book Review, Aug. 31, 1980.

The Snepp case was more than just a case of prior restraint applied through the administrative machinery, law reporter Anthony Lewis of the *New York Times* found. For the fiduciary, constructive-trust formulation was a far-reaching legal theory: [87]

> * * * one that could apply to hundreds of thousands of federal government employees. For Snepp * * * had no greater access to secrets than do vast numbers of people in the State and Defense Departments * * *. Any one of them, under the theory of the Snepp case, can now be enjoined from talking to a reporter—or have his profits seized if he writes a book.

Non-disclosure agreements similar to that which Snepp and Marchetti had signed so appealed to President Ronald Reagan that in 1983, he issued a directive requiring them of all persons who had access to classified government information, numbering—declared protesting media—more than 100,000 employees. The President withdrew the directive in the face of congressional and media protest.[88]

If the emergence of non-disclosure agreements in the decade beginning with Marchetti appeared as one more example of government creativity in devising prior restraints in the name of national security, predictably enough that newly minted instrument was not the end of invention in prior restraint. In 1982, the Secretary of State's denial of a passport to former CIA agent Philip Agee was upheld by the United States Supreme Court: Agee had asserted his purpose of exposing CIA agents abroad, driving them out of the countries where they operated, and obstructing the operations and recruitment efforts of the CIA, and had taken measures to do so. These statements and actions, the Court said, were no more protected by the First Amendment than those prohibited in Near v. Minnesota half a century earlier.[89] By 1982, Congress and the President had effected a law making it a crime for news media to make public the names of secret U.S. intelligence agents or their sources.[90]

Prior Restraint and the High School Press

As was evident from the discussion of Near v. Minnesota (1931), the key case on prior restraint, not all pre-publication censorship is unconstitutional. Early in 1988, in Hazelwood School

---

[87] New York Times, Feb. 25, 1980.

[88] Directive on Safeguarding National Security Information, 9 Med.L.Rptr. 1759 (1983).

[89] Haig v. Agee, 453 U.S. 280, 101 S.Ct. 2766 (1981), 7 Med.L.Rptr. 1545.

[90] News Media and the Law, Sept./Oct. 1982, 39.

District v. Kuhlmeier,[91] the U.S. Supreme Court held that public school officials have the power to impose pre-publication censorship on student newspapers. The newspaper involved in this case, *Spectrum,* was published at Hazelwood High School near St. Louis, Mo.

The newspaper was to be six pages long in its 1983 school-year-end edition as produced by the school's Journalism II class. On May 10, 1983, Principal Robert Reynolds was shown proofs for the edition due to appear on May 13. The proofs were taken to the principal by an interim newspaper adviser; the regular Journalism II instructor had left Hazelwood East for another job just 12 days earlier.

After Principal Reynolds was shown page proofs, he objected to publication of two stories. One described three Hazelwood East students' experiences with pregnancies; the other discussed the effect of divorce on students at the school. Although the pregnancy story used fictitious names to mask identities, the principal decided that the masking was insufficient. Evidently he also thought that the article's references to sex and birth control were not appropriate for some of the younger students in the school. Finally, he was concerned that a student was identified by name in the divorce story, and that the student's parents had not been given the opportunity to respond.

Apparently believing that there was no time for redoing the stories—and that the paper could not appear at all at school year's end if delays occurred—Principal Reynolds deleted two entire pages containing the stories he found offensive. The deleted pages contained other articles—on teen marriages, runaways, juvenile delinquency, and a general article on teenage pregnancy. Principal Reynolds later testified that he had no objection to those articles; they were deleted only because they were on the same pages with the articles that troubled him.[92]

Cathy Kuhlmeier and two other former Hazelwood East students who had been newspaper staffers claimed Reynolds' action violated their First Amendment rights, and sought injunctive relief and monetary damages in a Federal district court.

The trial court upheld the principal's actions. Deletion of the divorce article on invasion-of-privacy grounds was held reasonable, as was the principal's desire to avoid younger students' exposure to "unsuitable material." Further, the district court concluded that the principal was justified in having a " 'serious doubt that the article complied with the rules of fairness which are standard in the

---

[91] 484 U.S. 260, 108 S.Ct. 562 (1988), 14 Med.L.Rptr. 2081.

[92] 484 U.S. at 264, 108 S.Ct. at 566 n., 14 Med.L.Rptr. at 2082–2083, 2083 n.

field of journalism and which were covered in the textbook used in the Journalism II class.' " [93]

The Eighth Circuit Court of Appeals, however, reversed the district court, holding that the newspaper was both a part of the school's curriculum *and* public forum, " 'intended to be operated as a conduit for student viewpoints.' " Since the newspaper was a public forum, the appeals court held, school officials could not censor its contents except when necessary " ' . . . to avoid material and substantial interference with school work or discipline . . . or with the rights of others.' " [94]

The Court of Appeals thus found no evidence in the trial court's record to indicate that the principal could have predicted reasonably that the articles would be disruptive or cause disorder. Also, the court added that the articles could have caused no tort liability for libel or privacy, and concluded that school officials had violated the students' First Amendment rights.

The U.S. Supreme Court granted certiorari and reversed the Court of Appeals, thus upholding the principal's prior restraint of the newspaper. Justice White wrote for the majority in this 5–3 decision. He outlined circumscribed freedoms available to students in public high schools. Although quoting from the famous language of the Vietnam war armband protest case—Tinker v. Des Moines Independent Community School District [95]—public school students do not " 'shed their constitutional rights at the schoolhouse gate' "—Justice White then took a restrictive tack. He declared that "the First Amendment rights of students in the public schools 'are not automatically co-extensive with the rights of adults in other settings.' " [96]

Student rights must be applied " 'in the light of special characteristics of the school environment.' " Quoting Bethel School District No. 403 v. Fraser (1986), he wrote that a school need not tolerate speech that is inconsistent with its educational mission, even though government could not censor such speech outside the school. (The Bethel case involved disciplining a student who had made a campaign speech in behalf of a student politician; the speech was replete with sexual double entendres.) [97]

Justice White's majority opinion declared that the *Spectrum* was not a forum for public expression: It was a part of the school's curriculum, a regular educational activity. He also interpreted the

[93] Hazelwood School Dist. v. Kuhlmeier, 484 U.S. 260, 264, 108 S.Ct. 562, 566 (1988), 14 Med.L.Rptr. 2081, 2083.

[94] Ibid., at 265, 108 S.Ct. at 567, 14 Med.L.Rptr. at 2083.

[95] See Tinker, 393 U.S. at 511, 89 S.Ct. at 739, quoted in Ibid.

[96] Ibid.

[97] 478 U.S. 675, 106 S.Ct. 3159 (1986).

school board's policy statement supporting free expression for school-sponsored publications as suggesting "at most that the administration will not interfere with the students' exercise of those First Amendment rights that attend the publication of a school-sponsored newspaper. It does not reflect an intent to extend those rights by converting a curricular newspaper into a public forum." [98]

The majority opinion also said that a school in its capacity of publisher may " 'disassociate itself' " from speech which is disruptive, or which sets a bad example in terms of speech that is "ungrammatical, poorly written, inadequately researched, biased or prejudiced, vulgar or profane, or unsuitable for immature audiences."

This meant, the Court said, that educators

> ... do not offend the First Amendment by exercising editorial control over the style and content of student speech in school-sponsored expressive activities so long as their actions are reasonably related to legitimate pedagogical concerns.

In dissent, Justice William J. Brennan, Jr., joined by Justices Marshall and Blackmun, said that when the students enrolled in that Journalism II course, they expected a civics lesson. They argued that only substantially disruptive speech should be censored, conceding that poor grammar, writing or research would disrupt or subvert the school's curricular purpose.[99]

> The same cannot be said of official censorship designed to shield the *audience* or dissociate the *sponsor* from the expression. Censorship so motivated ... in no way furthers the curricular purpose of a student *newspaper,* unless one believes that the purpose of the school newspaper is to teach students that the press ought never to report bad news, express unpopular views, or print a thought that might upset its sponsors.

* * *

The young men and women of Hazelwood East expected a civics lesson, but not the one the Court teaches them today.

At least two kinds of fallout can now be seen from the bombburst unleashed by *Hazelwood.* On the one hand, censorship of high school (and some college) papers increased dramatically after that decision. Director Mark Goodman of the Student Press Law Center (SPLC) reported that as the 1988 *Hazelwood* decision began

---

[98] 484 U.S. at 270, 108 S.Ct. at 569, 14 Med.L.Rptr. at 2085, 2086.

[99] 484 U.S. at 290, 108 S.Ct. at 580, 14 Med.L.Rptr. at 2091, 2094.

to be put to use, calls to the SPLC (mostly about threatened or actual censorship) doubled in the first half of 1990.[1] On the other hand, all was not bleak. By the fall of 1991, four states—California, Colorado, Iowa, and Massachusetts—had passed statutes providing student journalists with protection for free expression, and adoption in New Jersey was expected. Efforts to pass similar legislation continues in a number of other states.

State-by-state action now seems the student journalists' best chance to overcome *Hazelwood*. As Justice Brennan and others have suggested, the more expansive among state constitutions may offer help. That is, some state charters may provide leverage to overcome mechanical application of the *Hazelwood* rule that if high school journalism is embedded in a class setting, it is not a First Amendment-protected public forum.[2]

SEC. 6. PRIOR RESTRAINT: LICENSING

When licensing power over expression amounts to prior censorship, it is constitutionally forbidden. Broadcasting, however, has long been a "special case," outside some First Amendment protections of the print media.

Licensing is one aspect of that most hated of all controls over the media: prior censorship. And—as is discussed in Chapter 3, licensing is still alive in the United States. That chapter discusses the Federal Communications Commission's system of allocating broadcast frequencies "in the public interest, convenience, or necessity." [3]

Past forms of licensing, as in England in the Sixteenth and Seventeenth Centuries, meant that only licensed printers—persons who had the approval of the government—were allowed to print. Late in the Twentieth Century, licensed broadcast stations—or the braver ones among them—seem to find the intestinal fortitude to criticize government from time to time, knowing full well that broadcast re-licensing largely has become a routine matter.

If licensing broadcasting stations seems a comparatively benign form of that ancient control—although it has its vociferous critics—other kinds of licensing raise sharper-edged issues. Consider the American Nazis decision to march, displaying swastikas, through a mostly Jewish neighborhood in Skokie, Illinois, in 1977. Nazi leader Frank Collin asked a number of Chicago suburbs for permits (licenses) for demonstrations in their parks or on their streets.

[1] Student Press Law Center Report, Fall, 1990, p. 3.

[2] SPLC Report, Fall, 1991, pp. 3, 11.

[3] See Chapter 3 on the matter of broadcast station licensing.

Skokie officials responded that the Nazis would have to post an insurance bond of $350,000 as a hedge against property damage.[4]

The American Civil Liberties Union (ACLU), which lost many Jews from its membership over this issue, was cast in the ironic role of defending the Nazis' right to march and to demonstrate. The Illinois Supreme Court supported the ACLU position and struck down the licensing attempt by the Village of Skokie. The court said: [5]

> The display of the Swastika, as offensive to the principles of a free nation or the memories it recalls may be, is symbolic political speech intended to convey to the public the beliefs of those who display it. It does not, in our opinion, fall within the doctrine of "fighting words," and that doctrine cannot be used here to overcome the heavy presumption against the constitutional validity of prior restraint.

So it may be seen that licensing battles reoccur. England's authoritarian licensing system was allowed to expire in 1695, but no battle for freedom ever seems to be won once and for all.[6] Major weapons against licensing in the Twentieth Century were hammered out by repeated battles by Jehovah's Witnesses. The struggles of the Jehovah's Witnesses were noteworthy: Time and again they fought their cases all the way to the Supreme Court of the United States and ultimately won. This religious group, as Professor William A. Hachten noted, endured great suffering. "The ACLU reported, for example, that in one six-month period of 1940, 1488 men, women and children in the sect were victims of mob violence in 355 communities in 44 states." [7] Professor J. Edward Gerald wrote that the Witnesses made themselves unpopular with their refusal to salute the American flag and with their disdain for most if not all organized religion, including denunciations of the Catholic Church. Likewise, their persistent street sales of literature and doorbell ringing for their causes often irritated non-believers.[8]

The Jehovah's Witness cases are useful reminders that the right of freedom of expression belongs not only to media corpora-

[4] See Areyeh Neier, Defending My Enemy: American Nazis, the Skokie Case, and the Risks of Freedom (New York: E.P. Dutton, 1979).

[5] Village of Skokie v. National Socialist Party of America, 69 Ill.2d 605, 14 Ill.Dec. 890, 373 N.E.2d 21 (1978).

[6] Fredrick S. Siebert, Freedom of the Press in England, 1476–1776 (Urbana, Ill: University of Illinois Press, 1952), pp. 260–263.

[7] William A. Hachten, The Supreme Court on Freedom of The Press (Ames, Iowa: Iowa State University Press, 1968), p. 73.

[8] Hachten, p. 74; Lovell v. City of Griffin, Georgia, 303 U.S. 444, 58 S.Ct. 666 (1938).

tions but to the people.   Furthermore, a landmark case won by the Witnesses—Lovell v. City of Griffin, Georgia[9]—is crucially important because it explicitly gives constitutional protection to *distribution* of literature as well as to publication.

Alma Lovell, a Jehovah's Witness, was convicted in a municipal court in Griffin, Ga., and sentenced to 50 days in jail when she refused to pay a $50 fine.   Her crime?   She had not received advance permission from the City Manager of Griffin to pass out literature, as required by a municipal ordinance.

Alma Lovell simply could not be bothered with such technicalities.   She regarded herself as a messenger sent by Jehovah and believed that applying to the City Manager for permission would have "been 'an act of disobedience to His commandments.' "   The Supreme Court, however, regarded the city ordinance as far more than a mere technicality.   Speaking for a unanimous Court, Chief Justice Charles Evans Hughes denounced the ordinance.[10]

> We think that the ordinance is invalid on its face. Whatever the motive which induced its adoption, its character is such that it strikes at the very foundation of the freedom of the press by subjecting it to license and censorship.

> The liberty of the press is not confined to newspapers and periodicals.   It necessarily embraces pamphlets and leaflets.   These indeed have been historic weapons in the defense of liberty, as the pamphlets of Thomas Paine and others in our own history abundantly attest.   * * *

> The ordinance cannot be saved because it relates to distribution and not to publication.   "Liberty of circulating is as essential to that freedom as liberty of publishing; indeed, without circulation, the publication would be of little value."   Ex parte Jackson, 96 U.S. 727, 733, 24 L.Ed. 877.

Since the ordinance of the City of Griffin was not limited to " 'literature' that is obscene or offensive to public morals or that advocates unlawful conduct," the ordinance could not be upheld. In Schneider v. New Jersey, the Supreme Court reviewed four cities' ordinances.   Three of these anti-littering ordinances in effect punished distributors should the recipient of a leaflet throw it to the ground.   The Supreme Court held that such ordinances were unconstitutional.[11]

[9] 303 U.S. 444, 58 S.Ct. 666 (1938).

[10] Lovell v. City of Griffin, 303 U.S. 444, 451–452, 58 S.Ct. 666, 669 (1938).   Mr. Justice Cardozo took no part in this decision.

[11] 308 U.S. 147, 60 S.Ct. 146 (1939).

"Time, Place and Manner"

Such cases, of course, do not mean that advocates can distribute anything they want at any time or place. What the courts call "time, place and manner" restrictions may be upheld as lawful if they are administratively even-handed and do not favor some kinds of content over others.

As Justice Owen Roberts wrote for the Court in deciding the Town of Irvington Jehovah's Witness case (above): [12]

> We are not to be taken as holding that commercial soliciting and canvassing may not be subjected to such regulation as the ordinance requires. Nor do we hold that the town may not fix reasonable hours when canvassing may be done . . .

Jehovah's Witnesses were to have many other days in court, defending freedoms of religion, speech and press guaranteed by the First Amendment and protected from state encroachment by the Fourteenth Amendment. The persistence of this religious group, annoying to some, has resulted in some of the Supreme Court's most sweeping language in support of the First Amendment.[13]

In writing the words used to decide that another city license was unconstitutional in Jones v. City of Opelika (1942), Justice Harlan Fiske Stone asserted a favored position for the First Amendment, a "preferred position" view generally out of judicial favor by the 1980s. He wrote: [14]

> The First Amendment is not confined to safeguarding freedom of speech and freedom of religion against discriminatory attempts to wipe them out. On the contrary the Constitution, by virtue of the First and Fourteenth Amendments, has put those freedoms in a preferred position.

Lowe v. SEC (1985)

A licensing effort by the Securities and Exchange Commission (SEC) was slapped down in the spring of 1985 by an 8–0 vote of the Supreme Court of the United States. The SEC, concerned about regulating many things affecting the health of the nation's financial communities, set about licensing financial news media.[15]

---

[12] Ibid.

[13] See also other Jehovah's Witness cases: Jones v. Opelika, 316 U.S. 584, 62 S.Ct. 1231 (1942); Martin v. Struthers, 319 U.S. 141, 63 S.Ct. 862 (1943); Douglas v. Jeannette, 319 U.S. 157, 63 S.Ct. 877 (1943); Murdock v. Pennsylvania, 319 U.S. 105, 63 S.Ct. 870 (1943).

[14] "SEC Attacks Financial Press," The News Media & The Law, November/December 1984, p. 4.

[15] Ibid.

Take the case of Christopher Lowe, operator of the "Lowe Investment & Financial Letter." He ran afoul of SEC contentions that it had the power to require permission to publish, plus the power to get injunctions to stop publications if SEC dictates were not obeyed. Lowe had been a licensed investment adviser, operating within the provisions of the Investment Advisers Act of 1940, and founded his newsletter in 1974.[16]

Lowe, however, fell on hard times. He was convicted of stock fraud, of check kiting, and of tampering with evidence.

Until 1981, he had been registered with the S.E.C., but that registration was withdrawn in 1981 after Lowe's convictions in New York for securities law violations, fraud, and bad checks. As News Media & the Law reported, "Lowe stopped giving individual advice on investments after his license was revoked, but continued to publish the newsletters."[17] In 1981, the S.E.C. issued an order, revoking Lowe's registration as an investment adviser, and forbidding him to associate with any investment advisers.[18] As the U.S. Court of Appeals reported as it upheld the S.E.C. action in trying to halt Lowe's newsletters,[19]

> No contention is made that any of the information published in the [Lowe] advisory services has been false or materially misleading. Nor is it alleged that Lowe himself * * * has profited through personal or corporate investments from the investment advice offered.

Saying that it believed that the Lowe case added up to permissible regulation of economic activity, the court added: "we believe that the Investment Advisers Act withstands constitutional scrutiny under the First Amendment doctrine relating to commercial speech as well."[20]

The Supreme Court disagreed, finding—without reaching constitutional analysis—that the SEC had overreached its authority. Writing for the Court, Justice John Paul Stevens said that Congressional legislation creating the S.E.C. gave the regulatory body no jurisdiction over investment publications.

The New York Times noted that the Supreme Court did not rule out all S.E.C. control over investment newsletters. If a newsletter's publishers had an interest in some stock they were recommending—or if the publication contained information that was

[16] "Publisher Elated By S.E.C. Victory," The New York Times, June 12, 1985, p. 30.

[17] News Media & the Law, November/December, 1984, p. 4.

[18] Ibid.; see also "Newsletter Setback for S.E.C.," The New York Times, June 11, 1985, p. 33.

[19] SEC v. Lowe, 725 F.2d 892 (2d Cir.1984), 10 Med.L.Rptr. 1225, 1226.

[20] Ibid., at p. 1231.

purposely misleading or false—then the S.E.C. could have power over the situation under the Investment Advisers Act of 1940.[21]

Other Forms of Prior Restraint

Government pre-publication censorship continues to be discouraged by courts, but—as discussed earlier—it can occur. In addition, prior restraint may occur in other contexts, cropping up in connection with topics covered in following chapters of this book. Courts are petitioned for prior restraint orders—injunctions against publication—in areas of law including defamation,[22] privacy,[23] copyright,[24] obscenity,[25] access to government information,[26] and advertising/commercial speech.[27] Although courts, in general, grant prior restraint orders grudgingly, the issue lives on. In libel, for example, courts usually will not halt defamatory publications via injunction. In copyright law and other areas dealing with business relationships, pre-publication injunctions may be found frequently enough that they are not aberrations. Prior restraint assumes so many guises that it can not safely be said that battles against pre-publication controls are ever won, once and for all time.

SEC. 7.   FORCING COMMUNICATION TO OCCUR

The other side of prior restraint (preventing communication in the first place) is forcing communication to occur. Except for the broadcast media, forcing communication to occur generally is forbidden.

Forcing communication to take place is closely connected with—is often the "flip side" of—a system of prior restraint. As Fredrick Siebert showed in his pathbreaking study of the develop-

[21] Lowe v. S.E.C., 472 U.S. 181, 105 S.Ct. 2557 (1985); "Newsletter Setback for S.E.C.," The New York Times, June 11, 1985, p. 33.

[22] For an annotated listing of prior restraint cases in general, see Floyd Abrams, "Prior Restraints," in James C. Goodale, chairman, Communications Law 1993 (New York: Practising Law Institute, 1993), Vol.3, pp. 799–1079. See Chs. 4 and 5, below, on defamation. Libel decisions refusing to grant injunctions to plaintiffs include Dworkin v. Hustler Magazine, Inc., 634 F.Supp. 727 (D.Wyo.1986), and Lothschuetz v. Carpenter, 898 F.2d 1200 (6th Cir.1990).

[23] Similarly to defamation, courts have been reluctant to issue injunctions to plaintiffs in privacy cases. See Abrams, op. cit., p. 484. See Organization for a Better Austin v. Keefe, 402 U.S. 415, 91 S.Ct. 1575 (1971).

[24] See Ch. 13, above, and Abrams, op cit., pp. 515–531. Injunctions occur more frequently in trademark disputes, although they are occasionally granted—temporarily—in copyright cases. See, e.g., Rosemont Enterprises, Inc. v. Random House, Inc., 256 F.Supp. 55 (S.D.N.Y.1966), reversed at 366 F.2d 303 (2d Cir.1966).

[25] See Ch. 7, above.

[26] See Ch. 9, above.

[27] See Ch. 11, above. See especially Posadas de Puerto Rico Associates v. Tourism Co., 478 U.S. 328, 106 S.Ct. 2968 (1986).

ment of freedom of expression in England from 1476 to 1776, printers who did not publish what they were told to print by government often put themselves in real peril.[28] Similarly, in the early years of Britain's American colonies, printers—who needed government subsidies to survive—had to display "Published by Authority" on their newspapers. Such printers often learned that they dared not deviate from printing only the official accounts— edited for public consumption—of the meetings (held in secret) of colonial legislatures of Governor's councils.[29]

After the War for Independence and the creation of the United States, the development of strongly competing political factions— and later, political parties—helped distribute "official printing" business while criticizing government raucously.[30] Later, in the first four decades of the Nineteenth Century, the rise of mass circulation newspapers supported primarily by advertising helped free the press from government.[31]

Over time, the libertarian ideas borrowed from England evolved, with arguments taken from John Milton from the Seventeenth Century and from "Country Whig" philosophers of the Eighteenth Century.[32] Those ideas developed in the crucible of American politics into the ideas that government should keep hands off the press, allowing criticism of government through a "free marketplace of ideas," assuming that truth would win over falsehood in the process of argumentation.

This "marketplace of ideas" philosophy became a kind of received truth, cited with the force of binding precedent by the Supreme Court of the United States in important Twentieth Century decisions.[33] But when major riots occurred after the assassination of Martin Luther King, law professor Jerome Barron articulated a troubling and persistent viewpoint. He argued that lack of access to media of communication by disadvantaged minorities showed that government should intervene to give the voiceless a

[28] Siebert, Freedom of the Press in England, 1476–1776; Clyde A. Duniway, The Development of Freedom of the Press in Massachusetts (Cambridge: Harvard Univ. Press, 1906), pp. 104–05.

[29] Jean Folkerts and Dwight L. Teeter, Jr., Voices of a Nation (New York: Macmillan, 1989), pp. 18–23.

[30] See, e.g., Jackson Turner Main, The Antifederalists: Critics of the Constitution (Chapel Hill: Univ. of North Carolina Press, 1961); Teeter, "Press Freedom and the Public Printing: Pennsylvania, 1775–1783," Journalism Quarterly XLV (Autumn, 1968), p. 445.

[31] Folkerts & Teeter, op. cit., pp. 129–149.

[32] See Chapter 1, Sec. 1; see also Norman L. Rosenberg, Protecting the Best Men (Chapel Hill: Univ. of North Carolina Press, 1985).

[33] See, e.g., the classic newspaper antitrust case of Associated Press v. United States, 326 U.S. 1, 28, 65 S.Ct. 1416, 1418 (1945).

voice. Otherwise, people left voiceless were going to "take it to the streets," violently.[34]

In an age of mass communication, Barron asserted, the members of the public must have access to the columns and airwaves of the mass media. Barron elaborated the position that for many decades the high cost of ownership had barred countless voices from a part in the "marketplace of ideas." The media—giant in size and cost, relatively few in number, and owned by largely like-minded entrepreneurs devoted to the economic and political *status quo*—have the power to deny citizens the right to have their message communicated widely.

The media themselves, in Professor Barron's view, are crucial barriers to a diversity of opinion and fact in the marketplace. "At the very minimum," Barron wrote, "the creation of two remedies is essential—(1) a nondiscriminatory right to purchase editorial advertisements in daily newspapers, and (2) a right of reply for public figures and public officials defamed in newspapers." [35]

Professor Barron's "right of access to the press" ideas were tested—and found wanting—in a famed 1974 decision by the U.S. Supreme Court. In Miami Herald v. Tornillo, the Supreme Court took on a case that had arisen in Florida under that state's "right of reply" statute. The Miami Herald had refused to print a reply by a political candidate, Pat L. Tornillo, Jr., to a Herald editorial criticizing his candidacy for the Florida legislature. When Tornillo asked for his right of reply in the columns of the newspaper, he was refused access, so he sued.

The Florida Supreme Court upheld Tornillo's arguments, and said he should have a right of reply to the print media similar to the right granted under the equal opportunities and fairness doctrines to persons attacked by broadcast media and cable. (See Chapter 9.) At this writing the "equal opportunities" ["equal time"] law for political candidates is still in force, as is the "personal attack" portion of the Federal Communications Commission's fairness doctrine. Other portions of that doctrine, however were repealed by the FCC in 1987.) The First Amendment, said the Florida Court, "is not for the benefit of the press so much as for the benefit of us all," and added: [36]

> The right of the public to know all sides of a controversy and from such information to be able to make an enlightened choice is being jeopardized by the growing

[34] Jerome A. Barron, "Access to the Press—a New First Amendment Right," 80 Harv.L.Rev. 1641 (1967).

[35] Barron, Freedom of the Press for Whom? (Bloomington: Indiana Univ. Press, 1973), p. 6.

[36] Tornillo v. Miami Herald Pub. Co., 287 So.2d 78 (Fla.1973).

concentration of the ownership of the mass media into fewer and fewer hands, resulting ultimately in a form of private censorship.

The Supreme Court of the United States, however, reversed the Florida court.[37]

In so doing, the nation's highest court conceded the dangers of concentration of media ownership, cross-channel ownership and chains and syndicates all of which focused great power to inform and to influence public opinion in the hands of a few. However valid those arguments, the Court said, government coercion by a remedy such as a right of reply "brings about a confrontation with the express provisions of the First Amendment."

Chief Justice Warren Burger wrote for a unanimous court in rejecting the arguments advanced by Pat Tornillo and Jerome Barron. Reviewing past decisions of the Court, the Chief Justice declared: [38]

> The clear implication has been that any such compulsion to publish that which " 'reason' tells them [editors] should not be published" is unconstitutional. A responsible press is an undoubtedly desirable goal, but press responsibility is not mandated by the Constitution and like many other virtues it cannot be legislated.

The Florida statute, the Court said, penalized on the basis of the content of a newspaper. The penalty is increased cost of production, and taking up space that could go to other material the paper may have preferred to print. Infinite expansion of its size to accommodate replies that a statute might require is not to be expected of a newspaper.

But cost aside, the Florida statute failed "to clear the barriers of the First Amendment because of its intrusion into the function of editors." The functions of choosing content, determining size of the paper and treatment of public issues, may be fair or unfair, said the Chief Justice. He added that "[i]t has yet to be demonstrated how governmental regulation of this crucial process can be exercised consistent with First Amendment guarantees of a free press . . ."

The Tornillo decision developed no reasoning as to why newspapers were exempt, but broadcasting need not be, from the requirements of furnishing opportunities to reply. Once again, as in

---

[37] Miami Herald Pub. Co. v. Tornillo, 418 U.S. 241, 94 S.Ct. 2831 (1974).

[38] Ibid. Quotes and paraphrases following are from Chief Justice Burger's majority opinion at 2838–2840.

other circumstances, the First Amendment's shield proved stronger for printed journalism than for broadcasting.[39]

SEC. 8. CRIMINAL LIBEL

Control of words critical of officials and other citizens was provided by criminal libel law in the states the nation's early years, almost disappearing in the years after World War II.

Like the vampire legend, criminal libel never quite seems to die out. Even though it was conventional wisdom late in the Twentieth Century to assert that criminal libel is dead in the United States, you could not make South Carolina newsman Jim Fitts believe that in 1988. He spent two days in jail on criminal libel charges in 1988 for his newspaper's denunciations of two state legislators. Twenty-four states still had criminal libel statutes on their books in that year[40], although it is evident that if criminal libel is not dead, it is barely breathing.

In 1991, Mr. Fitts won a measure of vindication, when a U.S. District Court held that South Carolina's criminal libel statute unconstitutional. The statute was declared overbroad in that it did not stipulate that the publisher had to know information published to be false or published with reckless disregard for truth.[41]

In origins, criminal libel overlaps the old crime of sedition: laws making verbal attacks on government applied also to words that assailed government officials. That may be seen earlier in this chapter in Section 4's discussion of the Alien and Sedition Acts of 1798. After the death of the Alien and Sedition Acts in 1801, statutes making libel a crime began to proliferate in the states.

Keep the phrase *criminal libel* in mind, distinguishing it from *civil libel*. A *criminal* charge or case is brought by an official or agency of government; if a defendant is convicted at trial he or she is subject to imprisonment, payment of a fine, or possibly both. *Civil* libel—dealing with publications (including broadcasts) which are false and which harm a person's *reputation*—do not involve criminal penalties. The person winning a civil libel case can receive "damages" (money) for reputational damage caused by the defendant.

The Jeffersonians who successfully ended the Federalists' Alien and Sedition Acts had a limited sense of freedom themselves. The Jeffersonians, hating the *national* sedition law when brought to

[39] See below, Chapter 9.

[40] "Column Puts Publisher in Jail," The News Media & The Law,: Summer, 1988, pp. 3–4.

[41] Fitts v. Kolb, 779 F.Supp. 1502 (D.S.C.1991), 20 Med.L.Rptr. 1033, 1045–1046.

bear on their newspapers and editors, nevertheless accepted the power to punish political speech when it was held by the states.[42] Supposedly, citizens could control their local-state affairs and check tendencies toward oppression close to home more easily than they could check a remote, centralized national government.

Laws of the new states provided that libel could be a crime whether it was aimed at plain citizens or government men. That the laws went under the name "criminal libel" laws instead of under the hated term "seditious libel" made them no less effective as tools for prosecution of those who attacked officials.

Under the British common law tradition for criminal libel, truth was not a defense. The old reasoning was that the truer the disparaging words, the more likely the insulted person to seek violent revenge, breaching the peace. Thus the legal aphorism of the Eighteenth Century: "the greater the truth, the greater the libel."

The states drew up safeguards against some of the harshest features of the old English law of libel. The principles that Andrew Hamilton pleaded for in defending Zenger emerged as important ones early in the Nineteenth Century as states embarked upon prosecutions. Truth slowly was established as a defense in criminal libel actions, and juries were permitted to "find the law" (rule whether the words were defamatory) under growing numbers of state constitutions and statutes as the century progressed.

A celebrated early case in New York encouraged the spread. It stemmed from a paragraph reprinted by Federalist editor Harry Croswell from the *New York Evening Post* attacking President Thomas Jefferson: [43]

> Jefferson paid Callender [a Republican editor] for calling Washington a traitor, a robber, and a perjurer; for calling Adams a hoary-headed old incendiary, and for most grossly slandering the private characters of men who he well knew to be virtuous.

The great Federalist leader, Alexander Hamilton, in 1804 took the case after Croswell had been convicted of criminal libel in a jury trial in which he had not been permitted to show the truth of his charge. Hamilton argued that "the liberty of the press consists of the right to publish with impunity truth with good motives for justifiable ends though reflecting on government, magistracy, or individuals." This, of course, made the intent of the publisher crucial. He also urged that the jury be allowed to find both the law and the facts of the case. He lost, the appeals court being evenly

[42] Levy, Emergence of a Free Press, Chaps. 9 and 10; Berns, pp. 89–119.

[43] People v. Croswell, 3 Johnson's Cases at 337 (N.Y.1804).

divided. The result, however, was so repugnant to people and lawmakers that the New York Legislature in 1805 passed a law embracing the principles that Hamilton urged.[44]

Other states adopted Hamilton's formula, and a few, indeed, made truth a defense no matter what the intent of the writer. But Nineteenth Century American courts were reluctant to give truth a protected position in the law, even though statutes seemed to endorse

But Nineteenth Century American courts were reluctant to give truth a protected position in the law, even though statutes seemed to endorse the position that the public needs to know the truth. As legislatures adopted truth as a defense in libel statutes during the Nineteenth Century, courts nevertheless clung tenaciously to the old idea that if the truth produced a breach of the peace, it could be punished.[45] Although few statutes or constitutions retained words' "tendency to breach the peace" as a basis for criminality in libel in the Twentieth Century, judges who wanted to employ it found it readily accessible in common law principles.

Criminal libel actions were few through most of the Nineteenth Century. They surged in number in the 1880s and held at some 100 reported cases per decade for 30 years or more. Not all, by any means, were brought for defamation of public officials in the pattern of seditious libel actions.[46] But criticism of police, governors, mayors, judges, prosecutors, sheriffs, and other government officials was the offense in scores of criminal libel cases.

Famous criminal libel charges arose from President Theodore Roosevelt's attempt to punish the *New York World* and the *Indianapolis News* for charging deep corruption in the nation's purchase of the title to the Panama Canal from France. President Roosevelt was so enraged at the *World* and its publisher, Joseph Pulitzer, that he delivered a special message to Congress. He charged that Pulitzer had libeled the U.S. Government, individuals in government, and the "good name of the American people." He called it "criminal libel," but his angry words carried his accusation deep into the realm of sedition.[47]

[44] An Act Concerning Libels, Laws of the State of New York, Albany, 1805.

[45] Elizabeth Goepel, "The Breach of the Peace Provision in Nineteenth Century Criminal Libel Law," (Univ. of Wis.1981), unpublished Master's thesis.

[46] John D. Stevens, et al., Criminal Libel as Seditious Libel, 43 Journalism Quar. 110 (1966); Robert A. Leflar, The Social Utility of the Criminal Law of Defamation, 34 Texas L.Rev. 984 (1956). Stevens et al. found that about one-fifth (31) of the 148 criminal libel cases reported in the half-century after World War I grew out of charges made against officials.

[47] House of Rep.Docs., 60 Cong., 2 Sess., § 1213 (Dec. 15, 1908), pp. 3–5.

For whatever reasons, criminal libel actions dropped after World War I from about 100 per decade to much smaller numbers.[48] Courts increasingly held that civil libel suits to recover damages were much to be preferred to criminal libel prosecutions, which more and more seemed inappropriate to personal squabbles between citizens. Duelling, that extreme breach of the peace, was out of favor as a means of settling personal differences or avenging verbal insults, as in centuries past. Also, the defamed person ordinarily had more to gain through a civil judgment for money damages than through a criminal conviction.

In the mid–1990s, criminal libel seemed to have little in the way of constitutional support, but there are occasional signs that criminal libel is not yet buried. As Robert Sack has noted, a 1991 Colorado Supreme Court decision held that state's criminal libel statute invalid "only insofar as it reaches constitutionally protected statements about public officials or public figures on matters of public concern." The Colorado Supreme Court found that "where one private individual has disparaged the reputation of another private individual," the Colorado statute remains valid.[49]

Criminal Libel of Groups

Perhaps adding tenacity to the shrinking offense of criminal libel was a highly unusual case of 1952 that claimed the attention of much of the world of civil liberties. It involved a special and rarely employed version of the ancient criminal libel law—that under some circumstances, *groups* could be libeled and the state could bring criminal action against the libeler. Beauharnais v. Illinois was decided in 1952 with a finding of "guilty."[50] It involved a leaflet attack on the African Americans in Chicago, at a time when the memory of Hitler Germany's mass killing of Jews was fresh in the minds of the nation. Migration of blacks from the south into northern cities was swelling. Beauharnais, president of the White Circle League, had organized his group to distribute the leaflets, and they did so in downtown Chicago. Among other things the leaflet called for city officials to stop "the further encroachment, harassment, and invasion of the white people * * * by the

[48] Stevens, op. cit.

[49] People v. Ryan, 806 P.2d 935 (1991), 19 Med.L.Rptr. 1074, 1078, cited in Sack, op. cit., at p. 174n. This case involved a fake "wanted poster" distributed to several bars and businesses in Fort Collins, Colo., by a disgruntled former date, falsely accusing a woman of being wanted for a number of crimes and falsely warning that she had sexually transmitted diseases.

[50] 343 U.S. 250, 72 S.Ct. 725 (1952). See also People v. Spielman, 318 Ill. 482, 149 N.E. 466 (1925). Also "Knights of Columbus" cases: People v. Turner, 28 Cal.App. 766, 154 P. 34 (1914); People v. Gordan, 63 Cal.App. 627, 219 P. 486 (1923); Crane v. State, 14 Okl.Cr. 30, 166 P. 1110 (1917); Alumbaugh v. State, 39 Ga.App. 599, 147 S.E. 714 (1929). And see Joseph Tannehaus, "Group Libel," 35 Cornell L.Q. 261 (1950).

Negro * * * ", and predicted that "rapes, robberies, knives, guns, and marijuana of the negro" surely would unite Chicago whites against blacks.

Beauharnais was prosecuted and convicted under an Illinois law making it unlawful to exhibit a publication which "portrays depravity, criminality, unchastity, or lack of virtue of a class of citizens, of any race, color, creed or religion which said publication * * * exposes the citizens of any race, color, creed or religion to contempt, derision, or obloquy or which is productive of breach of the peace or riots." [51]

The charges against Negroes, said the Court, were unquestionably libelous; and the central question became whether the "liberty" of the Fourteenth Amendment prevents a state from punishing such libels when they are directed not at an individual, but at "designated collectivities." The Court said that only if the law were a "wilful and purposeless restriction unrelated to the peace and well-being of the State," could the Court deny a state power to punish utterances directed at a defined group.

Justice Frankfurter found that for more than a century, Illinois had been "the scene of exacerbated tension between races, often flaring into violence and destruction." He cited the murder of abolitionist Elijah Lovejoy in 1837, the "first northern race riot"— in Chicago in 1908—in which six persons were killed, and subsequent violence in the state of Illinois down to the Cicero, Ill. race riot of 1951. He concluded that "In the face of this history and its frequent obligato of extreme racial and religious propaganda, we would deny experience to say that the Illinois legislature was without reason in seeking ways to curb false or malicious defamation of racial and religious groups." [52]

Four members of the court delivered strong dissents to the majority opinion that sustained Beauharnais' conviction. Justice Hugo Black stated much of the case against the concept of group libel as an offense acceptable to American freedom. Calling the law a "state censorship" instrument, Black said that permitting states to experiment in curbing freedom of expression "is startling and frightening doctrine in a country dedicated to self-government by its people." [53]

By 1992, hate-crime legislation was adopted in most states: All but four states—Alaska, Nebraska, New Mexico and Wyoming—had hate crime statutes. Thirty-one states' laws closely followed a model of the Anti–Defamation League of B'nai B'rith calling for

[51] Beauharnais v. Illinois, 343 U.S. 250, 251, 72 S.Ct. 725, 728 (1952).

[52] Ibid., at 258–261, 72 S.Ct. at 731–733. Illinois dropped this statute in 1961, but later enacted a hate-crime law.

[53] Ibid., at 270, 272, 273, 72 S.Ct. at 737, 738, 739.

both criminal sanctions and civil penalties. But in 1992, the U.S. Supreme Court was decided R.A.V. v. St. Paul, a test of a city ordinance's application to a 17–year-old accused of cross-burning in a black family's fenced yard.[54]

The 17–year-old—identified as R.A.V.—was accused of violating a St. Paul, Minnesota, "Bias–Motivated Crime Ordinance." That ordinance made it misdemeanor disorderly conduct for anyone to place, on public or private property, any symbol, object or graffiti "including, but not limited to, burning a cross or placing a Nazi swastika, which one knows . . . arouses anger, alarm, or resentment in others on the basis of race, color, creed, religion or gender. . . ." [55] The Minnesota Supreme Court upheld the ordinance, saying it merely made illegal speech of the "fighting words" variety, words long held to be beyond constitutional protection.[56]

Writing for five members of the Court, Justice Antonin Scalia declared the ordinance unconstitutional because "it prohibits otherwise permitted speech solely on the basis of the subject it addresses." He wrote: [57]

> Let there be no mistake about our belief that burning a such behavior without adding the First Amendment to the fire.

Although the other four members of the Court concurred, they took aim on the majority's reasoning. For example, Justice White argued that by equating fighting words with political expression, the Court's majority showed disrespect for the latter: [58]

> Fighting words are not a means of exchanging views, rallying supporters, or registering a protest: they are directed against individuals to provoke violence or to inflict injury. Therefore, a ban on all fighting words or on a subset of the fighting words category would restrict only the social evil of hate speech, without creating the danger of driving viewpoints from the marketplace.

* * *

> Indeed, by characterizing fighting words as a form of "debate," the majority legitimizes hate speech as a form of public discussion.

---

[54] Mary Deibel, "Hate Crimes," Scripps–Howard News Service, Knoxville News–Sentinel, Dec. 1, 1991, p. F–1, and see Hadley Arkes, "Civility and Restriction of Speech: Rediscovering the Defamation of Groups," 1974 Sup.Ct.Rev. 281–335; City of Chicago v. Lambert, 47 Ill.App.2d 151, 197 N.E.2d 448 (1964).

[55] R.A.V. v. St. Paul, 112 S.Ct. 2538, 2541 (1992).

[56] Ibid., citing Chaplinski v. New Hampshire, 315 U.S 568, 62 S.Ct. 766 (1942).

[57] 112 S.Ct. 2539, 2550 (1992).

[58] Ibid., p. 2554.

Effects on Campus Hate Speech Codes?

Trying to curtail racist or ethnic hate speech, a number of colleges and universities have ladled good intentions into their student conduct codes. However, as Tim England wrote in 1992, speech codes of universities have been found unconstitutional when subject to court challenges.[59]

William Celis 3d reported in The New York Times that the R.A.V. case appeared to weaken if not invalidate some speech codes. He pointed out in 1992 that this was no small matter because perhaps as many as 100 universities had instituted codes to punish discriminatory or intimidating name-calling or symbolic acts based on racism or other prejudices: ethnic, religious, sex, sexual orientation, national origin, or handicap.[60]

Such codes collide with traditional ideas of free expression on campus. For example, if a sociology class discussed racial slurs, might that not violate a hate speech regulation? Because of such "overbreadth," codes at the University of Michigan and the University of Wisconsin–Milwaukee were found unconstitutional.[61]

William Celis found that such constitutional concerns have caused some university officials and lawyers to take another tack: looking toward language prohibiting one-on-one incidents of violation or intimidation. He wrote that such an approaches "are considered more likely to survive legal challenge because they closely follow state and Federal anti-discrimination laws." [62]

Criminal Libel of Officials

In 1966, the Court focused on breach of the peace in common law criminal libel, and found that it did not square with the First Amendment. Merely to say that words which tend to cause breach of the peace are criminal, is too indefinite to be understandable, the court said. The case, Ashton v. Kentucky,[63] involved a pamphlet in which Ashton charged a police chief with law-breaking during a strike of miners, a sheriff with attempts to buy off a prosecution, and a newspaper owner with diverting food and clothing collected for strikers to anti-strike workers. Ashton was convicted under a definition of criminal libel given, in part, by the judge as "any

[59] Tim England, "Racist Speech: A First Amendment Issue on College Campuses," Southwest Colloquium of the Association for Education in Journalism and Mass Communication, 1992.

[60] William Celis 3d, "Universities Reconsidering Bans on Hate Speech," The New York Times, June 24, 1992, p. A11.

[61] England, op. cit. Cases discussed by him included Doe v. University of Michigan, 721 F.Supp. 852 (E.D.Mich.1989) and The UWM Post v. Board of Regents, University of Wisconsin, 774 F.Supp. 1163 (E.D.Wis.1991).

[62] Celis, op. cit.

[63] 384 U.S. 195, 86 S.Ct. 1407 (1966).

writing calculated to create disturbances of the peace." The Supreme Court said that without specification that was too vague an offense to be constitutional: [64]

In the second case, the Supreme Court's 1964 ruling in the civil libel action New York Times Co. v. Sullivan produced a heavy impact on the decaying bastions of criminal libel as applied to criticism of public officials. The *Sullivan* decision said that critical words must be used with actual malice if they were to be the object of a *civil* libel action against officials, and now the Supreme Court moved the same rule into the field of *criminal* libel. The case was Garrison v. Louisiana.[65] Here Garrison, a prosecuting attorney for the State of Louisiana, gave out a statement at a press conference attacking several judges of his parish (county) for laziness and inattention to their official duties. He was convicted of criminal libel, and his case ultimately reached the Supreme Court.

The Court cited the Times v. Sullivan rule defining actual malice—that a public official might recover damages as a remedy for civil libel only if it could be shown that there was knowing falsity or reckless disregard for truth.[66]

> The reasons which led us so to hold * * * apply with no less force merely because the remedy is criminal. The constitutional guarantees of freedom of expression compel application of the same standard to the criminal remedy. Truth may not be the subject of either civil or criminal sanctions where discussion of public affairs is concerned. And since " * * * erroneous statement is inevitable in free debate * * * " only those false statements made with the high degree of awareness of their probable falsity demanded by New York Times may be the subject of either civil or criminal sanctions. For speech concerning public affairs is more than self-expression; it is the essence of self-government.

The Louisiana court's ruling that Garrison's criticism of the judges constituted an attack on the personal integrity of the judges, rather than on their official conduct, was not accepted. The state court had said that Garrison had imputed fraud, deceit, and dishonesty to the judges and malfeasance in office. But, said the United States Supreme Court: [67]

---

[64] Ibid., at 198, 86 S.Ct. at 1409–1411.

[65] 379 U.S. 64, 85 S.Ct. 209 (1964); Harry Kalven, "The New York Times Case: a Note on the Central Meaning of the First Amendment," 1964 Sup.Ct.Rev. 191.

[66] Ibid., at 74, 85 S.Ct. at 215. Mr. Garrison was famous again in 1992 because of his depiction as a seeker after truth in Oliver Stone's "JFK," a movie about the President's 1963 assassination.

[67] Ibid., at 77, 85 S.Ct. at 217.

Of course, any criticism of the manner in which a public official performs his duties will tend to affect his private, as well as his public, reputation. The New York Times rule is not rendered inapplicable merely because an official's private reputation, as well as his public reputation, is harmed. The public official rule protects the paramount public interest in a free flow of information to the people concerning public officials, their servants. To this end, anything which might touch on an official's fitness for office is relevant. Few personal attributes are more germane to fitness for office than dishonesty, malfeasance, or improper motivation * * *.

As criminal libel cases arose on rare occasions during the decade after *Garrison,* several state statutes were found in violation of the Constitution—Pennsylvania's,[68] Arkansas',[69] and in 1976, California's. In the last of these, an action was brought against the publisher of the *L.A. Star,* a weekly tabloid of southern California, by the Los Angeles city attorney. The Star had published a photo superimposing a picture of a well-known actress' face on an unidentified nude female body in "a sexually explicit pose."[70] At trial and on appeal, the California criminal libel statute was held unconstitutional. For one thing, it provided that truth was a defense to a charge of criminal libel only if it were published with good motives and for justifiable ends, and since the *Sullivan* case, that had been an unconstitutional limitation on the truth defense. Further, the law provided that an injurious publication is presumed to be malicious if no justifiable motive is shown, and malice may not be presumed but must be alleged and proved. Burdened with these rules out of the past which now were rejected under an outlook in the Supreme Court of the United States that over a 50–year period had slowly freed the press from ancient restrictions of English origin and American adoption, the criminal libel statute of California was shredded by the decision. The Supreme Court of the state said that "any attempt at draftsmanship on the part of the court to save the remainder of the statute would transgress both the legislative intent and the judicial function and would be a flagrant breach of the doctrine of separation of powers."[71] Broken and impotent,

---

[68] Commonwealth v. Armao, 446 Pa. 325, 286 A.2d 626 (1972).

[69] Weston v. State, 258 Ark. 707, 528 S.W.2d 412 (1975). See also Williamson v. State of Georgia, 249 Ga. 851, 295 S.E.2d 305 (1982), 9 Med.L.Rptr. 1703, striking down the state's criminal libel statute.

[70] Press Censorship Newsletter No. VI, Dec.-Jan. 1974–75, p. 31.

[71] Eberle v. Municipal Court, Los Angeles Judicial District, 55 Cal.App.3d 423, 127 Cal.Rptr. 594, 600 (1976). For a suggestion that criminal libel may not be dead, see Keeton v. Hustler Magazine, 465 U.S. 770, 104 S.Ct. 1473 (1984), fn. 6, 10 Med.L.Rptr. 1405.

the law was an unlikely candidate for salvage by the state's legislature.

Criminal libel continues to be rare, but the impulse behind such law—to punish dissidents, to silence criticism, by no means is gone. As Norman L. Rosenberg has noted, although the means for suppression or intimidation may vary, the end remains the same.[72] Over time in the United States, when those in power could no longer use seditious or criminal libel effectively to muzzle or to punish dissent, they switched to lawsuits for civil libel.[73] The key question, then, revolves around the concept of *political* libel, regardless of the label the particular legal action may carry.[74]

SEC. 9.   TAXATION

The mass media are constitutionally protected from discriminatory or punitive taxation.

Taxation has long been a fighting word to the press. Taxes on the press instituted in England were called "taxes on knowledge" because they raised the purchase price of pamphlets and other printed materials beyond the means of most persons. Taxation also came to be a hated symbol of control and oppression in American history. The British Stamp Act of 1765 imposed great hardships on printers in colonial America, taxing newspapers, advertisements, pamphlets and many legal documents and became a great rallying cry for colonists who resisted British authority.[75] Such a storm of protest arose in the colonies, reflected in angry writings in newspapers and pamphlets and, ultimately, in mobs which forced British stamp agents to resign. Faced with such furious opposition, Parliament repealed the Stamp Taxes as they affected printer-editors.

If American colonists hated the Stamp Act taxes and argued against them in terms of "freedom of the press," American memories also were very short. In 1785, only two years after the War of Independence officially ended, the state of Massachusetts passed a newspaper stamp tax.

Howls of protest echoing the Stamp Act disturbances soon resounded from the Massachusetts newspapers. One writer calling himself "Lucius" declared that the tax on newspapers was a "*stab to the freedom of the people.*" He acknowledged that the tax of a

[72] See Norman L. Rosenberg, Protecting the Best Men: An Interpretive History of Libel (Chapel Hill: University of North Carolina Press), p. 6.

[73] Ibid., Chapter 4 and 5.

[74] Ibid., p. 7.

[75] Arthur M. Schlesinger, Prelude to Independence: The Newspaper War on Britain, 1763–1776 (New York: Knopf, 1958), p. 68.

penny on each copy seemed small, but "Lucius" added that "tyranny begins small:" a tax of even a half-penny an issue could be a precedent for a tax of £100 on each issue.[76] Such protests quickly led the to the repeal of the Massachusetts stamp tax on newspapers later in 1785, although the state's legislature soon enacted a tax on newspaper ads.[77] The advertising tax was repealed in 1788.[78]

Newspapers and other units of the mass media of communications are businesses. As such, the media are not immune from taxation just like other business enterprises, as long as the taxes fall with a more or less even hand upon the press as well as other businesses. *Discriminatory* or *punitive* taxation, however, raises quite different issues. The classic case in United States constitutional law occurred during the 1930s and involved the flamboyant Huey "Kingfish" Long, the political boss and governor of Louisiana who entertained dreams of someday becoming President. The Supreme Court decision in Grosjean, Supervisor of Accounts of Louisiana v. American Press Co., Inc.[79] effectively halted a Huey Long-instigated attempt to use a punitive tax to injure newspapers which opposed Long's political regime.

During the 1930s, Louisiana's larger daily newspapers were increasingly expressing opposition to Long's political machine. Louisiana's larger newspapers' sniping at Governor Long's dictatorial posturings soon brought about retaliation. The Louisiana legislature passed a special two per cent license tax on the gross receipts of all newspapers, magazines, or periodicals having a circulation of more than 20,000 copies per week.[80] Of Louisiana's 163 newspapers, only 13 had circulations of more than 20,000 per week. Of these 13 newspapers to which the tax applied, 12 were opponents of Long's political machine.[81] This transparent attempt to silence newspaper critics was challenged in the courts by nine Louisiana newspaper publishers who produced the 13 newspapers then appearing in the state which had circulations of more than 20,000 copies a week.

In declaring the Louisiana tax unconstitutional, a noted conservative—Justice George Sutherland—spoke for a unanimous Su-

[76] Massachusetts Centinel, May 28, 1785.

[77] Ibid., July 6, July 30, 1785.

[78] Clyde Augustus Duniway, Freedom of the Press in Massachusetts (New York, 1906), p. 137.

[79] 297 U.S. 233, 56 S.Ct. 444 (1936).

[80] Grosjean v. American Press Co., 297 U.S. 233, 240, 56 S.Ct. 444, 445 (1936).

[81] J. Edward Gerald, The Press and the Constitution 1931–1947 (Minneapolis, University of Minnesota Press, 1948) p. 100; William A. Hachten, The Supreme Court on Freedom of the Press: Decisions and Dissents (Ames, Iowa: Iowa State University Press 1968) p. 77; Grosjean v. American Press Co., 297 U.S. 233, 56 S.Ct. 444, 445 (1936).

preme Court. Justice Sutherland, a man not revered for his felicity of expression, may indeed have had some able assistance in writing what has come to be known as "Sutherland's great opinion in *Grosjean*." It has been asserted that Sutherland's opinion included a proposed concurring opinion which had been drafted by the famed liberal Justice Benjamin Nathan Cardozo, and which the Court wished to add into Justice Sutherland's opinion.[82]

Whether assisted by Cardozo or not, the Sutherland opinion in Grosjean remains noteworthy. Justice Sutherland began with a historical overview of government-imposed dangers to freedom of expression, including reference to John Milton's 1644 "Appeal for the Liberty of Unlicensed Printing" and to the end of the licensing of the press in England in 1695. As Sutherland noted, "mere exemption from previous censorship was soon recognized as too narrow a view of the liberty of the press." Sutherland wrote that taxes in Eighteenth Century England were quite commonly characterized as "taxes on knowledge." [83]

Justice Sutherland asserted that if taxes had been the only issue, many of England's best men would not have risked their careers and their lives to fight against them. The issue in England for many years, however, involved discriminatory taxation designed to control the press and silence criticism of government. The *Grosjean* opinion added: [84]

> The framers of the First Amendment were familiar with the English struggle, which had then continued for nearly eighty years and was destined to go on for another sixty-five years, at the end of which time it culminated in a lasting abandonment of the obnoxious taxes. The framers were likewise familiar with the then recent [1785–1788] Massachusetts [stamp tax] episode . . .

Justice Sutherland rejected the State of Louisiana's argument that the English common law in force when the Constitution was adopted forbade only prior restraints on the press and said nothing about forbidding taxation.[85] In reply, Sutherland's opinion quoted from a great 19th century American constitutional scholar, Judge Thomas Cooley, and declared that Cooley had laid down the test to be applied.[86]

[82] Irving Brant, The Bill of Rights: Its Origin and Meaning (New York: Bobbs–Merrill, 1965) pp. 403–404.

[83] Grosjean v. American Press Co., 297 U.S. 233, 249, 56 S.Ct. 444, 449 (1936).

[84] Grosjean v. American Press Co., 297 U.S. 233, 247–248, 56 S.Ct. 444, 448 (1936).

[85] Grosjean v. American Press Co., 297 U.S. 233, 249, 56 S.Ct. 444, 449 (1936).

[86] Grosjean v. American Press Co., 297 U.S. 233, 249, 56 S.Ct. 444, 449 (1936), quoting 2 Cooley's Constitutional Limitations (8th ed.) p. 886.

The evils to be prevented were not the censorship of the press merely, but any action of the government by means of which it might prevent such free and general discussion of public matters as seems absolutely essential to prepare the people for an intelligent exercise of their rights as citizens.

Application of this test led Justice Sutherland to rule that the Louisiana gross receipts tax on its larger newspapers was an unconstitutional abridgement of the First and Fourth Amendments. Sutherland declared: [87]

It is not intended by anything we have said to suggest that the owners of newspapers are immune from any of the ordinary forms of taxation for support of the government. But this is not an ordinary form of tax, but one single in kind, with a long history of hostile misuse against the freedom of the press.

* * *

The tax here involved is bad not because it takes money from the pockets of the appellees. If that were all, a wholly different question would be presented. It is bad because, in the light of its history and of its present setting, it is seen to be a deliberate and calculated device in the guise of a tax to limit the circulation of information to which the public is entitled in virtue of the constitutional guaranties. A free press stands as one of the great interpreters between the government and the people. To allow it to be fettered is to fetter ourselves.

Despite these ringing words, it should be noted again that the communications media are not exempt from paying non-discriminatory general business taxes. A case in point involved *The Corona Daily Independent,* a California newspaper which challenged a $32–a–year business license tax imposed by the City of Corona. The newspaper, which had paid the tax in a number of previous years, in 1951 refused to pay the tax. The newspaper went to court, arguing that the tax violated freedom of the press as guaranteed by the First and Fourteenth Amendments. However, the California Appellate Court ruled: [88]

[87] Grosjean v. American Press Co., 297 U.S. 233, 250–251, 56 S.Ct. 444, 449 (1936). Accord: See City of Baltimore v. A.S. Abell Co., 218 Md. 273, 145 A.2d 111, 119 (1958). It was held that Baltimore city ordinances imposing taxes on advertising media were unconstitutional in that they discriminatorily taxed newspapers and radio and television stations. About 90 per cent of the impact of the taxes was on those businesses.

[88] City of Corona v. Corona Daily Independent, 115 Cal.App.2d 382, 252 P.2d 56 (1953), certiorari denied 346 U.S. 833, 74 S.Ct. 2 (1953). See also Giragi v. Moore, 44 Ariz. 74, 64 P.2d 819 (1937) (general sales tax law placing a one per cent tax upon

There is ample authority to the effect that newspapers and the business of newspaper publication are not made exempt from the ordinary forms of taxes for the support of local government by the provisions of the First and Fourteenth Amendments.

Grosjean v. American Press Co. remains the leading case for the proposition that the mass media are constitutionally protected from discriminatory or punitive taxation. The *Grosjean* case, as seen on earlier pages, dealt with a garish fact situation, a transparent attempt by Louisiana Governor Huey "Kingfish" Long and his allies to silence newspaper critics.

Unlike the *Grosjean* situation, the State of Minnesota was operating out of more defensible motives during the 1970s when it enacted a "use tax" on paper and ink consumed applicable to newspapers. This apparently was only a revenue measure, not an attempt to control or to punish the press. Even so, the Supreme Court of the United States voided the tax by an 8–1 margin. The tax was held unconstitutional because it singled out the press for special treatment.

"Use taxes" are imposed by states to discourage their citizens from purchasing items in other states which have lower sales taxes. Minnesota's newspapers were exempted from use taxes until 1971, when the state began taxing the cost of paper and ink used in producing a publication.[89] In 1974, another change in the tax law exempted a publication's first $100,000 of ink and paper consumed from the 4% use tax.[90]

The $100,000 exemption meant that only the largest of Minnesota's publishers were liable to pay the tax. Only 11 publishers, producing 14 of the state's 388 paid-circulation newspapers, had to pay the tax in 1974. The Minneapolis Star and Tribune Company was the major revenue source from the tax. Of $893,355 collected in 1974, $608,634 was paid by the Star and Tribune.[91]

The Star and Tribune Company sued, asking a refund of the use taxes paid from January 1, 1974, to May 31, 1975. The company contended that the use tax violated freedom of the press and equal protection of the laws as guaranteed by the First and Fourteenth Amendments.[92] The Minnesota Supreme Court ruled

businesses' sales or gross income not unconstitutional as applied to newspapers); Arizona Publishing Co. v. O'Neil, 22 F.Supp. 117 (D.Ariz.1938), affirmed 304 U.S. 543, 58 S.Ct. 950 (1938).

[89] Minn.Stat.Ann. §§ 297A.14, 287A.25i.

[90] Minn.Stat.Ann. § 297A.14.

[91] Minneapolis Star and Tribune Co. v. Minnesota Commissioner of Revenue, 460 U.S. 575, 103 S.Ct. 1365, 1368 (1983), 9 Med.L.Rptr. 1369.

[92] Ibid.

the use tax constitutional,[93] and the Supreme Court of the United
States then noted probable jurisdiction.[94]

Justice Sandra Day O'Connor wrote for an 8–1 Supreme Court
in declaring the Minnesota tax unconstitutional on its face because
it singled out publications for unique treatment under the state's
law. She declared that there is evidence that differential taxation
of the press would have troubled the Framers of the First Amendment. "A power to tax differentially, as opposed to a power to tax
generally, gives government a powerful weapon against the taxpayer selected." [95] Her opinion also suggested the threat of burden-
some taxes might operate as a form of censorship, making the press
wary of publishing the critical comments which often allow it to
serve as an important restraint on government.

Even though the media are protected from discriminatory or
punitive taxation by the First Amendment, a 1987 Ad Tax dispute
in Florida was a sign of things to come. In 1987, Florida passed a
5% business service sales tax which included taxes on mass media
advertising. That tax on services cast a wide net: other services
declared taxable included accounting, legal services, and pest control.[96]

Although that clumsily designed tax on services quickly fell
under its own weight and a barrage of media complaints, that
Florida episode symbolizes federal and state governments' ceaseless
hunt for new revenues. Because governments are exhausting traditional sources of money, various aspects of the media industry
present inviting possibilities for taxation which could well be held
to be constitutional.

Small wonder that Florida's legislature repealed that tax within a matter of months. USA Today gave examples of the unwieldi-
ness of the Florida tax as it would have applied to advertising: [97]

> IBM might pay $200,000 for a 30–second commercial
> during NBC's St. Elsewhere. If Floridians are 5% of the
> nationwide TV audience, IBM theoretically would pay $10,-
> 000 to reach them. So IBM's tax liability for that commer-
> cial would be 5% of $10,000, or $500.

[93] Minneapolis Star and Tribune Co. v. Commission of Revenue, 314 N.W.2d 201
(Minn.1981).

[94] Minneapolis Star and Tribune Co. v. Minnesota Commissioner of Revenue, 457
U.S. 1130, 102 S.Ct. 2955 (1982).

[95] Ibid., at 586, 103 S.Ct. at 1372. Justice—later Chief Justice William H.
Rehnquist was the sole dissenter.

[96] Marilyn Marks, "Florida Ends Tax on Services . . .", Governing, January, 1988,
p. 57; "Governor Acts to End Florida Tax," The New York Times, Sept. 19, 1987, p.
21.

[97] James Cox, "Big advertisers balk at new Florida sales tax," USA TODAY, p. B1,
June 23, 1987.

Although that services tax died in Florida in 1987, it was evident in the 1990s that legislatures all over the nation were in hot pursuit of new sales revenues. The New York Times and Presstime magazine reported in 1992 that a tax on circulation was under consideration in California, and that other states might soon follow that approach. In addition, as of 1992, there were 14 states, including California, taxing newspaper sales, with sales taxes proposed in seven other states.[98]

In Leathers v. Medlock, the Supreme Court took up the kind of issue that could make it the High Court of Taxation for some years. In *Leathers,* the Court whittled on the Court framed to the issue as "whether the First Amendment prevents a State from imposing its sales tax on only selected segments of the media." This case involved a complaint by Arkansas cable TV operators that a state sales tax applied to cable TV but excluded or exempted newspapers, magazines and satellite broadcast services.

The U.S. Supreme Court held that cable operators' rights were not violated because the Arkansas tax did not apply just to the media but was a tax generally applicable to businesses. Furthermore, unlike the Minnesota use tax on print and ink, applying to only 16 of 374 newspapers in that state, the Arkansas tax applied to all 100 cable TV operations in the state.[99]

In California, Sacramento Cable Television (SCT) and a cable subscriber challenged a city ordinance including cable TV under a city utility user's tax along with gas, electric, and telephone services. The California Court of Appeals, Third Circuit, agreed with the prevailing view that cable TV is speech protected by the First Amendment. Even so, that appellate court held it constitutional for Sacramento to tax cable TV because cable logically could be categorized along with other utilities.[1]

What of a tax applied to newspapers but not magazines? In Florida Department of Revenue v. Magazine Publishers of America (1992), the Florida Supreme Court ruled that a state sales tax imposed upon magazines but not upon newspapers did not pass muster under the First Amendment.

[98] Alex S. Jones, "Newspapers See A Threat of Spreading Sales Taxes," The New York Times, Sept. 19, 1991, p. C6, using a graphic from Presstime magazine. States shown with sales taxes on newspapers: Alabama, Arizona, California, Delaware, Florida, Hawaii, Georgia.

[99] 111 S.Ct. at 1443, 18 Med.L.Rptr. at 1956 (1991).

[1] Sacramento Cable Television v. Sacramento, 234 Cal.App.3d 232, 286 Cal.Rptr. 470 (1991), 19 Med.L.Rptr. 1532, 1533, 1536. See also Cox Cable Hampton Roads Inc. v. Norfolk, 242 Va. 394, 410 S.E.2d 652 (1991), 19 Med.L. Rptr. 1656, holding that although cable TV may be taxed as a utility, the case should be returned to the trial court for consideration of Cox Cable's Equal Protection claim.

The Florida Supreme Court found that the state's sales tax was not "content neutral" in exempting newspapers. Although some of the requirements publications had to meet to be termed "newspapers" were content-neutral (usually published weekly or daily, intended for general circulation to the public), one requirement was a problem. One provision called for the Department of Revenue to determine whether publications—to be "newspapers" and thus exempt from the sales tax—contain " 'reports of current events and matters of general interest which appeal to a wide spectrum of the general public.' " [2] That criterion added up to an impermissible content-based judgment which invalidated the Florida tax exemption of newspapers under the First Amendment.

The magazine publishers—which hoped to join newspaper publishers in Florida in a tax exemption—were disappointed. Ironically, instead of invalidating the tax on magazines, the Florida Supreme Court invalidated the newspapers' exemption. If misery loves company, it now has more of it.

The basic rule remains: the press may not be singled out for "differential treatment" when being taxed. That does not mean the press will pay less in taxes than other kinds of businesses.

SEC. 10. THE CONTEMPT POWER AND CRITICIZING COURTS

Criticism of judges while cases were pending was long considered an interference with justice, and was punishable as contempt of court.

The offense known as "constructive contempt of court"—notably, contempt shown toward judges in newspaper criticism—had a long and sometimes troublesome life in the United States. This nation had been in existence almost 150 years before the U.S. Supreme Court issued decisions virtually demolishing that word crime.

Judges had—and still have—power to control what goes on in their courtrooms, or to punish persons who are under their jurisdiction and disobey court orders. That is the "direct contempt" power. If a person stands up in a courtroom and screams obscenities at a judge, the judge can use his or her "summary" power—can declare that person in contempt of court, and can sentence that individual *on the spot* to pay a fine, serve a jail term, or both. And journalists, as discussed in Chapter 13, sometimes run afoul of the contempt power when they defy court orders to reveal sources for stories or information gathered in the course of reporting.

[2] Florida Department of Revenue v. Magazine Publishers of America, 604 So.2d 459 (Fla.1992), 20 Med.L.Rptr. 1502, 1503.

The constructive contempt control over the press lay in the power of judges to punish their critics while cases were pending in court. Even though English precedent for such a power was weak, the American judiciary took this power unto itself and extended it.[3]

Judges taking such power upon themselves proved upsetting, and Pennsylvania and New York both passed statutes early in the Nineteenth Century to curb judges' power over published criticism. And in 1831, Congress passed a similar law. The reason for the Congressional action came from an attorney, Luke Lawless, who had been found in contempt by Federal Judge James H. Peck. Lawless, who had published newspaper articles critical of the judge's handling of land claims, had sought the impeachment of Judge Peck. Judge Peck retaliated by finding the lawyer in contempt and suspending him from the practice of law for eighteen months.

The House of Representatives ultimately impeached (brought charges) against Judge Peck, but the Senate ultimately found Peck not guilty by the narrowest of margins.[4]

But Congress wanted no more punishment for criticism of judges in the press. Only a month after the impeachment proceedings against Judge Peck, Congress passed an act in 1831 saying that federal judges might punish only misbehavior taking place "in the presence of the courts * * * or so near thereto as to obstruct the administration of justice." [5]

Many states' judges, however, were not ready to permit criticism. The main line of cases from the mid-Nineteenth Century until 1941 found judges asserting their "immemorial power": to cite and punish for newspaper criticism taking place far from their courtrooms.[6]

Two rules emerged: "pendency" and "reasonable tendency." The pendency rule meant that criticism of courts and judges could not be published while a case was still pending. That included attempts to influence judges or participants in cases or publishing false or inaccurate reports of trials. "When a case is finished," said Justice Oliver Wendell Holmes, Jr., in a federal case in 1907, "courts are subject to the same criticism as other people ..." Published criticism could then be labeled as interference with the

[3] Walter Nelles and Carol Weiss King, Contempt by Publication in the U.S., 28 Col.L.Rev. 401–431, 525–562 (1928).

[4] Arthur J. Stansbury, Report of the Trial of James H. Peck (Boston: Hilliard Gray & Co., 1833).

[5] Nelles and King, op. cit. at p. 430, citing Act of Mar. 2, 1831, c. 98, 4 Stat. 487.

[6] Ronald L. Goldfarb, The Contempt Power (New York, 1963).

judicial process and punished as contempt.[7]

The "reasonable tendency" judicial concept meant that there did not have to be any proof of harm to the judicial process from published criticism. A "tendency" to create such harm would be enough to cite for contempt, the U.S. Supreme Court said in a 1918 decision.[8]

Note that Justice Holmes, who wrote for the majority in the 1907 Patterson v. Colorado decision involving criticism of pending cases, valued the role of a free press more when he dissented from a 1918 decision involving "reasonable tendency." He declared that the Court's majority erred in upholding a contempt citation against a Toledo newspaper. His dissent invoked the 1831 federal statute, so long forgotten. Holmes wrote, "so near thereto" means so near as actually to obstruct justice, and misbehavior means more than unfavorable comment or disrespect.[9]

Then in a series of decisions in the 1940s, the Supreme Court yielded up its long-standing power, telling the entire judicial branch to do the same. In Bridges v. California,[10] Justice Hugo Black's majority opinion shredded both the pending case rule and the reasonable tendency test. In *Bridges*, trial-court judges had convicted Californians for contempt by publication for admonishing courts about pending cases. Black said that such contempt orders silence discussion when public interest would be at its height, and that any moratorium on public discussion—which could last for years during a case's "pendency" was not an insignificant abridgement of freedom of expression. Black also said that neither a reasonable tendency nor an "inherent tendency" of words to interfere with courts was enough to support a contempt order. A "clear and present danger" to the administration of justice had to be shown.[11] The clear and present danger rule was used in other cases to overturn contempt by publication convictions. The rare contempt conviction for criticizing courts now is almost certain to be overturned on appeal.[12]

[7] Patterson v. Colorado ex rel. Attorney General, 205 U.S. 454, 27 S.Ct. 556 (1907).

[8] Toledo Newspaper Co. v. United States, 247 U.S. 402, 421, 38 S.Ct. 560, 564 (1918).

[9] Ibid., at 422, 38 S.Ct. at 565.

[10] 314 U.S. 252, 62 S.Ct. 190 (1941).

[11] 314 U.S. at 268–269, 62 S.Ct. at 196–197.

[12] See Pennekamp v. Florida, 328 U.S. 331, 66 S.Ct. 1029 (1946); Craig v. Harney, 331 U.S. 367, 67 S.Ct. 1249 (1947); Wood v. Georgia, 370 U.S. 375, 82 S.Ct. 1364 (1962), and Cooper v. Rockwood Nsprs., 34 Ill.App.3d 645, 339 N.E.2d 477 (1975).

Chapter 3

THE FIRST AMENDMENT AND
ELECTRONIC MEDIA

The constitutional history of American broadcasting is neither as impressive nor as extensive as that of the American press. Yet nothing in the language of the Constitution itself denies to broadcasting any of those free speech rights now being exercised by the press. Why, then, should American broadcasting have its own distinctive and less expansive body of constitutional law? What prevents a broadcaster from simply claiming that full legacy of First Amendment protections already won for American mass media by the press?

The answers to these questions can be found in the earliest days of radio regulation in the United States, when the federal government began to draw those legal distinctions that would isolate broadcasting from all other forms of American mass communication, restricting it to a much narrower range of constitutionally protected free speech rights.

SEC. 11. FROM RADIOTELEGRAPHY
TO BROADCASTING

Broadcasting began in the United States as a service regulated by laws designed for an entirely different form of communication.

It all began with Guglielmo Marconi, who never wanted to be known as the "father of radio"; and in reality—wasn't. Marconi was interested only in discovering some way to transmit telegraphic code through space, so he could offer the owners of the world's great merchant fleets a global communications system capable of delivering messages directly to their ships at sea.[1] In 1901, Marco-

---

[1] Because Marconi attempted to design a "closed" communication system, not intended for the general public but only those using his equipment, he could be

ni demonstrated the effectiveness of his new "radiotelegraphy" device, and immediately began building "wireless" stations to relay telegraphic messages to vessels following every major trade route of the world.

Marconi expected to profit from his invention by selling or leasing the equipment he manufactured to all the large shipping companies of Europe and North America. It soon became apparent, however, that in freeing the telegraph from the constraints of its wire, he had created a *public* communications network, accessible to anyone possessing a transmitter or receiver obtained from any source. To discourage ship owners from building their own wireless devices or buying them from a growing number of competitors, Marconi instructed his own operators not to acknowledge or relay any radio message from a vessel known to be using non-Marconi radiotelegraphy equipment.

International reaction to Marconi's decision was both prompt and hostile. What might have been viewed as a sensible business policy for a land-based communications service seemed brutal and barbaric at sea, where refusal to relay a distress signal could easily imperil the lives of innocent ship passengers and crews.

The first radio law enacted in the United States, "The Wireless Ship Act of 1910," [2] dealt only with this single issue in the field of maritime radiotelegraphy, requiring every large ocean-going vessel leaving an American port to have a wireless transmitter and receiver aboard, and making it unlawful for any ship wireless operator to refuse to acknowledge or to relay a wireless message from any other radiotelegraphy operator on sea or shore.

As the number of radio-equipped vessels increased with each passing year, interference caused by the growing volume of ship-to-shore transmissions became a serious problem. International maritime radiotelegraphy conferences were held in Berlin in 1903 and 1906, and in London in 1912 to negotiate treaty arrangements for the supervision of these radio communications that each country would be expected to enforce though its own national laws.[3]

described more accurately as the father of "narrowcasting," forerunner of modern pay–TV services, rather than broadcasting.

[2] Public Law 262, 61st Congress June 24, 1910. This requirement was imposed only on vessels carrying 50 or more people, and travelling more than 200 miles between ports.

[3] These international negotiations took on a special urgency after the sinking of the Titanic in April 1912. The ship rammed an iceberg in the north Atlantic, and sank three hours later. Some 700 of her 2,200 passengers and crew were saved, but a nearby ship that might have been able to save many more lives failed to respond to her distress call because no wireless operator was on duty during the early morning hours when the Titanic was sinking.

The United States complied with these international obligations by enacting the "Radio Act of 1912" [4], requiring all wireless companies operating within the United States to transmit only on those frequencies approved for their use by the Commerce Department. This law authorized stations engaged in maritime communication to select and use two separate channels of radio frequencies, while all other operators were restricted to a single channel. In addition, those not engaged in either business or maritime radio communication message delivery service were relegated to a less effective frequency band, and were limited to a maximum of one kilowatt of transmission power.

American radio experimenters who attempted to "broadcast" to anyone who might be listening, rather than directing their messages to a specific receiver, were placed in this miscellaneous category of communication service by the Radio Act.

Reginald Fessenden, an early radio experimenter, designed the first wireless equipment capable of transmitting the sound of the human voice in 1906. But Fessenden, as Marconi, had no interest in "broadcasting" to the general public. His "radiotelephone", as the name suggests, was developed only to allow voice as well as telegraph messages to be delivered by wireless transmission anywhere in the world.[5]

In reality, of course, there was no American broadcast audience of any size to serve in 1906, because the complicated and expensive radio receivers of this era were still being designed and produced only for business use, while the inexpensive "crystal" detector receiver that had recently been developed was still crude and unreliable and required some degree of skill to assemble and operate.

From 1906 through 1917, the only broadcast service available anywhere in the United States was being provided by a rather small band of amateur radio operators in various parts of the country who enjoyed spending an evening or two each week transmitting a blend of recorded music and commentary to an equally small group of amateur radio enthusiasts who had assembled the reception equipment necessary to hear their broadcasts.

During this same period, the continuing expansion in the volume of private radio communications began to overcrowd that band of frequencies that had originally been allocated in 1912 to maritime and business service. But although the Department of Commerce was urged by several radio industry leaders to reclaim

[4] Public Law 264, 62nd Congress, August 13, 1912.

[5] For a more complete account of this early history of broadcasting, see Christopher H. Sterling and John M. Kittross, Stay Tuned: A Concise History of American Broadcasting (Belmont, CA: Wadsworth Publishing, 1977), pp. 16–46.

for business radio those spectrum assignments that had been made to amateur broadcast operators, the Department refused to do so, deciding that such experimentation would continue to be tolerated as long as it did not interfere in any way with the more important and useful communication functions of private radio.

That era of toleration ended in 1917, when the United States entered World War I, and the only important radio communication function suddenly became support of the nation's war effort. In April 1917 all radio transmission equipment not under government control was ordered dismantled, and the United States Navy was granted emergency power to develop the most effective radio equipment possible by requiring all American radio manufacturers to pool their existing radio patents and to cooperate in future research efforts.

The immediate effect of this wartime control was to transform radio equipment manufacturing in the United States into a growth industry. The U.S. Navy alone had purchased 10 million dollars of radio equipment from these suppliers by the end of 1917, and the government imposed "patent pool" stimulated more technological advances during two years it remained in effect than the industry itself had been able to achieve during the previous decade of fierce competition.

But then, with the American radio equipment manufacturers producing transmitters and receivers at a record pace, the war came to an end in November 1918, ending at the same time the massive military market for radio equipment. Soon afterward the Navy announced its intention to abandon its program protecting radio manufacturers from patent infringement claims, setting off an incredibly complex series of mergers and cross-licensing agreements to maintain those conditions that had permitted the industry to develop so rapidly during the war-time era.

By June 1921 these corporate maneuvers created a patent pooling, cross-licensing combination among General Electric, Westinghouse, the newly formed Radio Corporation of America (RCA) and American Telegraph and Telephone (AT & T) that made them the dominant force in the field of American radio equipment manufacturing and marketing.[6] At the same time, these corporate giants entered into a formal agreement granting to General Electric and Westinghouse exclusive rights to manufacture radio receivers that RCA would market as sales agent for the two companies.

RCA, General Electric and Westinghouse each realized that to create public demand for their radio receivers, they would have to

---

[6] For a much more detailed discussion of these corporate negotiations, including a description of AT&T's important role in this trade combination, see Sterling–Kittross, op.cit, pp. 53–58.

provide regular broadcast service themselves. By the end of 1920, KDKA, a Westinghouse station, was providing such a service and in 1921 the Department of Commerce began to issue licenses to broadcast applicants.

Yet, even before the first of these new stations went on the air, this two-decade history had already begun to determine the future status of broadcasting as a mass medium in the United States. The Radio Act of 1912 had been designed for communication common carriers; services that did not communicate themselves, but merely served as channels to deliver the messages of others.[7] As a very secondary service within this regulatory scheme, broadcasting was tolerated but never recognized as having any unique rights of its own as a communications medium.

The Act made access to the electromagnetic spectrum a privilege, subject to governmental approval. Those private radio services regulated under its provisions had no legal basis for challenging this type of federal control because as common carriers, they were already subject to other similar regulatory constraints on their operations.[8] Since experimental broadcasting was authorized under the same law, it was simply assumed that its privilege of operation was also dependent upon government approval, an assumption that no small and disorganized band of radio amateurs was in a position to challenge.

Thus, as the radio era was beginning in the United States, a precedent had already been established for making the broadcaster's right to communicate a conditional one, dependent on the willingness of government to grant the applicant a license. At this point, however, the decision of whether or not to issue such a license was still being made solely on the basis of engineering criteria; determining in each case whether the broadcast license

[7] This vital distinction between the rights and obligations of *communication common carriers*, such as telephone and telegraph companies on one hand, and broadcasters on the other, would not be drawn until 1927, when the Federal Radio Commission was granted authority to regulate *broadcasting*, while the Department of Commerce continued to regulate common carriers under an entirely different set of standards. Today, the Federal Communications Commission regulates both types of communication services, but under those distinctly different standards established for each in 1927.

[8] A "communications common carrier" at law is one who provides message delivery facilities for public use. Because most carriers, such as local telephone companies, exercise at least limited monopoly power over the service they offer, they are subject to regulation to ensure that they furnish this public access in a nondiscriminatory manner, provide all necessary services, and establish reasonable rates for those services. In contrast, a broadcaster has no general obligation to provide either free or paid public access to the station's facilities. Instead, the broadcast licensee has complete editorial control over the content of each message transmitted and is legally responsible for the content of every message delivered to the public. These distinctions are reflected in the Communications Act of 1934, at Sections 153(b) and 153(h) that declare "a person engaged in radio communication shall not ... be deemed to be a common carrier."

requested could be approved without creating an unacceptable level of interference with other existing radio services in the area in which it would operate. This single criterion for licensing did not pose any threat to the free speech rights of the broadcaster, but the precedent of licensing itself would soon serve as the basis for a much broader range of government controls.

SEC. 12. SPECTRUM SPACE: FROM CRISIS TO CONTROL

Unprepared for rapid growth of broadcasting, Congress was forced to react with regulatory legislation outdated by the time it was enacted.

RCA, Westinghouse and General Electric each applied for broadcast licenses in 1921, as did a number of other smaller radio manufacturers and retailers. By 1923, nearly half (46%) of the radio stations on the air were being operated by radio manufacturers, dealers, or department stores selling radio receivers.[9] Except for its promotional value in marketing radio receivers, there was as yet no other financial incentive for providing broadcast service, because at the time it was still considered to be improper and unethical to use the broadcast spectrum to transmit advertising messages.

As Secretary of Commerce Herbert Hoover told industry representative at the Third National Radio Conference in 1924,

> I believe that the quickest way to kill broadcasting would be to use it for direct advertising. The reader of the newspaper has an option whether he will read an ad or not, but if a speech by the President is to be used as the meat in a sandwich of two patent medicine advertisements, there will be no radio left.[10]

By 1926, however, this opposition had become less intense and stations were permitted to begin broadcasting commercials; although they were still discouraged from accepting advertising that detailed the qualities of a specific product or mentioned its selling price.

During this same period, another significant change was taking place in American broadcasting. When radio began in 1921, there were an estimated 60,000 radio receivers in the United States, or approximately one radio for every 500 American households. This broadcast audience of 1921 was still primarily one of radio experi-

[9] Sydney W. Head, Broadcasting in America, 2nd ed. New York, Houghton Mifflin, 1972, p. 137.

[10] Herbert Hoover at the Third National Radio Conference, October 6–10, 1924 as quoted in Sterling–Kittross, op. cit, p. 49.

menters, testing the sensitivity of their homemade receivers each evening by attempting to "pull in" as many different static-laden signals as possible from stations in distant states. By 1926, the typical household radio came encased in a handsome wooden cabinet for display and use in the family living-room. The set's storage battery had been replaced by a convenient wall plug, and its speaker allowed the entire family to enjoy its favorite radio programs together every evening. By this time there were already 4.5 million radio households and by 1928, eight million, or more than 25% of all homes in the United States.[11]

Unfortunately, as the number of new American broadcast stations increased proportionately during this same era, it soon became impossible to prevent one station's transmissions from interfering with those of other radio stations using the same or an adjacent frequency channel. When the Secretary of Commerce began issuing broadcast licenses in 1921, only two different frequency channels were assigned to be used by every broadcast station in the nation.[12]

In 1922, the Department of Commerce hurriedly added a third channel for broadcast service, and the following year, developed a far more comprehensive frequency allocation plan that set aside 73 new frequency channels exclusively for broadcast use. Yet, even though this new license assignment plan seemed well designed from an engineering standpoint to protect against future broadcast band interference, the Commerce Department's power to enforce its plan was dependent upon that very narrow base of regulatory authority it had been granted by the Radio Act of 1912.

Although the 30 radio stations using the broadcast spectrum in 1921 had swelled to 530 stations by 1924, Congress continued to disregard annual requests of the Secretary of Commerce to provide him with that broader authority he needed to deal with this ever increasing problem of broadcast interference. As one scholar in this field suggests, Congress may have been reluctant to act because

> the nature of broadcasting had not yet been clearly defined, and it was difficult to pass a law to regulate an unknown quantity.[13]

Whatever the reason for this reluctance, the failure of Congress to revise the antiquated radiotelegraphy legislation soon placed the Commerce Department in a difficult position. When the Secretary

[11] Sterling and Kittross, op.cit., p. 533.

[12] In September 1921, 833.3 Khz was the frequency to be used for all regular news and entertainment broadcast stations, while 618.6 Khz was set aside for broadcast of special government weather or crop information reports.

[13] Head, op.cit, p. 158.

of Commerce tried to enforce the Department's new broadcast frequency allocation plan by denying a license on the grounds of insufficient spectrum space to accommodate it, a federal court could find nothing in the Radio Act of 1912 that gave him the right to make such a regulatory judgment.[14]

Despite the fact that this decision suggested quite clearly that the Department's license assignment plan was not legally enforceable, most major broadcast organizations continued to comply voluntarily with its provisions, realizing that it was in their best interests to do so. As Commerce Secretary Hoover pointed out to industry leaders at each of the National Radio Conferences held between 1921 and 1925, broadcasting could continue to avoid direct governmental control only as long as self-regulation maintained an orderly, interference free broadcast service.

Unfortunately, self-regulation gave the radio industry no legal authority to compel any of its more than 500 licensed broadcasters to comply with Commerce Department directives, as Congress had given the Department no legal power to punish such noncompliance. As a result, the entire broadcast licensing and frequency assignment structure during this period had to rest upon the fragile hope that no broadcaster would ever force the Commerce Department to rely upon the Radio Act of 1912 again to enforce those regulatory policies the Department had adopted to solve the industry's interference problems.

That hope ended in 1926, and the voluntary licensing plan collapsed within a matter of months. Zenith Radio Corporation, a receiver manufacturer, had grown dissatisfied with the two hours a week it was authorized to broadcast on a frequency channel it was compelled to share with several other stations in the Chicago area. Believing that it deserved the same type of broadcast license privileges that Westinghouse, General Electric, RCA and other radio industry competitors had been granted, Zenith ignored the Commerce Department's refusal to grant it another channel and began to transmit its programs on that channel without authorization. Although Secretary Hoover was reluctant to have the Commerce Department's licensing authority tested in federal court, this challenge left him no alternative. The frequencies Zenith was using without permission had been reserved for Canadian stations by international agreement, an agreement that legally obligated the Department to protect these Canadian interests. In addition, after Zenith had defied the Commerce Department in this way, other stations soon announced their intention to follow its example.

As expected, when the Commerce Department tried to enforce its frequency assignment decision in federal court, the court found

[14] Hoover v. Intercity Radio Company, 52 App.D.C. 339, 286 Fed. 1003 (1923).

nothing in the Radio Act of 1912 that authorized its enforcement, or that permitted the Secretary of Commerce to do anything more than issue broadcast licenses upon request.[15] Required from this point onward simply to grant each broadcast application as it was received, the Department was forced to issue more than 200 new licenses during the remainder of 1926, creating an even more intolerable level of broadcast interference in urban areas throughout the United States.

Realizing that radio service under these conditions could not survive for long, leaders of broadcast industry themselves began demanding that broadcasting be regulated by the federal government. As the year 1926 was ending, even President Calvin Coolidge, never an ardent supporter of government control, was urging Congress to enact legislation to regulate broadcasting, justifying his position by pointing out that

> ... many more stations have been operating than can be accommodated within the limited number of wave lengths available; further stations are now in the process of construction; many stations have departed from the scheme of allocation set down by the Commerce Department and the whole service of this most important public function has drifted into such chaos as seems likely, if not remedied, to destroy its great value.[16]

In March of the following year, Congress passed the Radio Act of 1927.[17] A new agency, the Federal Radio Commission, was created to administer the Act. Having failed in the past to provide the Commerce Department with the authority needed to protect the technical quality of broadcast transmissions, Congress now seemed to lurch in the opposite direction, granting the new Commission power not only over the engineering aspects of radio, but over the "public interest" qualities of broadcast programming as well. As the one of the co-authors of the new Radio Act declared at the time:

> We have reached the definite conclusion that the rights of our people to enjoy this means of communication can be preserved only by the repudiation of the idea underlying the 1912 law that anyone who will may transmit and by the assertion in its stead of the doctrine that the right of the public is superior to the right of any individual to use the airwaves.[18]

[15] United States v. Zenith Radio Corporation, 12 F.2d 614 (D.C.Ill.1926).

[16] As quoted in Frank J. Kahn (ed.) Documents of American Broadcasting (3d ed.) Englewood Cliffs, NJ; Prentice Hall, 1978, pp. 15–17.

[17] Public Law 632, 69th Congress.

[18] Senator Wallace H. White, as quoted by Commissioner Robert T. Bartley in FCC mimeo. 1336 (January 29, 1934).

Although the Act expressly prohibited censorship of broadcasting, it did officially empower an agency of the federal government to grant or revoke the right to communicate by radio on the basis of the quality of that communication.[19] While not as severe a constraint upon freedom of expression as actual censorship, this unique degree of governmental influence authorized over broadcast free speech during the past six decades has resulted in all electronic mass media being relegated to a less privileged status in terms of constitutional protections, unable to assert that full range of First and Fourteenth Amendment rights recognized by the courts as properly belonging to the American press.

In the last analysis, broadcast self-regulation had failed primarily because Congress itself had failed to sense the growing popularity and importance of the broadcast medium until the problem of chaotic interference compelled immediate legislative action. If Congress had simply revised the obsolete Radio Act of 1912 to give the Secretary of Commerce the broadcast licensing authority he had requested, it seems quite likely that the interference crisis of 1926 could have been averted.

In that sense, then, self-regulation actually may have worked too well, because in cooperating as effectively as it did with the Department of Commerce's licensing plan to reduce the degree of broadcast interference through the years, the radio industry permitted Congress to postpone and delay consideration of the federal government's proper role in the field of broadcast communication until it was too late for such a profound and complex question to be raised, much less answered.

SEC. 13.   RATIONALIZING GOVERNMENT REGULATION

Although a number of arguments have been advanced to justify federal broadcast regulation, the judiciary has relied upon only one in affirming this right of government control, the rationale of spectrum scarcity.

The Federal Radio Commission began with the assumption that Congress had provided it with sufficient legal authority to regulate broadcast programming. As the agency declared in one of its first annual reports to Congress,

> The radio act specifies that the commission shall exercise no censorship over programs. Nevertheless, the kind

---

[19] Section 29 of the Radio Act of 1927 stated in part, "Nothing in this Act shall be understood or construed to give the licensing authority the power of censorship over the radio communication or signals transmitted by any radio station, and no regulation or condition shall be promulgated or fixed by the licensing authority which shall interfere with the right of free speech by means of radio communication." This statutory provision was incorporated as Sec. 326 of the current broadcast law, The Communications Act of 1934.

of service rendered by a station must be a means of appraising its relative standing and must be considered by the commission in making assignments.[20]

In 1930 the Commission decided for the first time to refuse to renew a broadcast license solely on the basis of what it deemed to be programming not in the public interest. The broadcaster appealed, contending that permitting a federal agency to determine what was proper or permissible broadcast program content constituted a form of censorship clearly prohibited by the Radio Act.

The federal court disagreed, upholding the Commission's action by observing,

> There has been no attempt on the part of the commission to subject any part of appellant's broadcasting matter to scrutiny prior to its release. In considering the question whether the public interest, convenience or necessity will be served by a renewal of the applicant's license, the commission has merely exercised its undoubted right to take note of appellant's past conduct, which is not censorship.[21]

A second FRC denial of license renewal based primarily on inadequate broadcast programming performance was also sustained by a federal court the following year. In appealing the agency's action, the broadcaster invoked First Amendment as well as the non-censorship provision of the Radio Act, arguing that even if a federal licensing decision based upon the quality of broadcast communication was not "censorship" as defined by the Act, it was at least an unconstitutional abridgement of a broadcaster's right of freedom of expression.

Once again the court disagreed, upholding the agency's right to consider a broadcaster's past programming efforts in deciding whether to renew a broadcast license, and declaring that such a review of program content was

> ... neither censorship nor prior restraint, nor is it a whittling away of the rights guaranteed by the First Amendment, or an impairment of their free exercise.[22]

In each of these cases, the Federal Radio Commission's position may have been strengthened by the fact that the broadcasters involved were rather notorious characters with long and well documented histories of using their stations for their own personal

---

[20] Federal Radio Commission, Third Annual Report (Washington: Government Printing Office, 1929) p. 3.

[21] KFKB Broadcasting Ass'n v. Federal Radio Commission, 47 F.2d 670 (D.C.Cir. 1931).

[22] Trinity Methodist Church, South v. Federal Radio Commission, 62 F.2d 850, 853 (D.C.Cir.1932).

benefit. "Doc" Brinkley, owner of KFKB, was a diploma-mill physician who used the airwaves to sell his patent medicines and fabulous "goat gland" operation, guaranteed to rejuvenate the lagging sexual powers of older men, while Reverend Shuler, whose church owned the Trinity Methodist station, seemed to specialize in defaming public officials. Describing Shuler's conduct while on the air, the federal court said: [23]

> On one occasion he announced over the radio that he had certain damaging information against a prominent unnamed man which, unless a contribution (presumably to the church) of a hundred dollars was forthcoming, he would disclose. As a result he received contributions from several persons ... He alluded slightingly to Jews as a race, and made frequent and bitter attacks on the Roman Catholic religion ...

The FRC also may have been benefited to some extent in gaining judicial approval of its authority over broadcast program content from its special relationship with the federal court that reviewed its actions. The Court of Appeals for the District of Columbia was designated by statute to be the court to hear all appeals from FRC actions and during this period it seemed particularly willing to apply the doctrine of "judicial forbearance;" that is, not to substitute its own judgment for that of the regulatory agency unless that agency decision was obviously in error.[24]

It's important to note, however, that during this entire FRC era, the United States Supreme Court had never considered, much less affirmed, the authority of the government agency to evaluate the quality of broadcast programming in deciding whether an applicant would be granted the right to communicate with a broadcast audience.[25] In 1934, Congress replaced the FRC with the Federal Communications Commission, consolidating regulation of both broadcast and communication common carrier services in the same agency, but controlling each separately under different provisions of the Communications Act of 1934.[26]

In 1937, the FCC launched an investigation of broadcast networks to determine whether the virtual monopoly control they exercised over the production and distribution of popular evening radio programming in the United States was in the public interest. In the FCC's view, these networks were using their programming

[23] Ibid, at 852.

[24] See Don Le Duc, Thomas McCain, "The Federal Regulatory Commission in Federal Court: Origins of Broadcast Doctrines," Journal of Broadcasting, Fall 1970, pp. 393–410.

[25] The Trinity Methodist decision had been appealed, but the Supreme Court declined to review the lower court decision. 285 U.S. 599 (1933).

[26] Public Law 416, 73rd Congress, 1934.

power to force stations seeking to affiliate with them to delegate to the networks too much authority over each station's broadcast scheduling decisions.

In order to protect station owners from these network pressure tactics, the FCC adopted rules in 1941 that limited the amount of network broadcast time that any affiliate station could carry, and authorized the agency to revoke the license of any broadcast station that exceeded this limit.[27]

The networks challenged the Commission's new rule, alleging among other things that by establishing limitations in advance upon the amount of time a broadcast station could devote to any specific type of programming, the federal government was encroaching upon the First Amendment protected free speech rights of the broadcaster. Justice Felix Frankfurter, speaking for a unanimous Supreme Court, furnished the first clear expression of the court's willingness to allow the federal government to establish and enforce programming standards in the field of broadcast speech.[28] Frankfurter wrote: [29]

> The question here is simply whether the Commission, by announcing that it will refuse licenses to persons who engage in specified network practices ... is thereby denying such persons the constitutional right of free speech ... The licensing system established by Congress in the Communications Act of 1934 was a proper exercise of its power over commerce. The standard it provided for the licensing of stations was the "public interest, convenience or necessity." Denial of a station license on that ground, if valid under the Act, is not a denial of free speech.

The underlying rationale for this position, Frankfurter explained, was that unlike other mass media, being allowed by government to broadcast was a privilege, not a right because,[30]

> ... its facilities are limited; they are not available to all who may wish to use them; the radio spectrum simply is not large enough to accommodate everybody.

In essence, then, the court held that by accepting the privilege of using the limited and valuable public resource of spectrum space,

---

[27] CFR 47 §§ 3.101–3.108. The FCC was forced to impose these rules upon individual radio stations because the networks used telephone circuits rather than spectrum space to distribute their programming to affiliated stations, and therefore did not require a FCC issued broadcast license to operate.

[28] Although the decision was unanimous, Justices Black and Rutledge took no part in the consideration of this case.

[29] National Broadcasting et al. v. United States et al., 319 U.S. 190, 226–227, 63 S.Ct. 997, 1014 (1943).

[30] Ibid., at 213, 63 S.Ct. at 1008.

each broadcast licensee also assumed an obligation to exercise this privilege for the benefit of the public; an obligation the FCC had the authority to enforce on behalf of the public.

The Supreme Court did not return to this specific broadcast free speech question again for more than a quarter of a century, but when it finally did so in 1969, Justice White, speaking once more for a unanimous court, explained its "spectrum scarcity" justification for broadcast content control even more clearly and forcefully than it had been described in the earlier Supreme Court decision.[31]

> Although broadcasting is clearly a medium afforded First Amendment interest, differences in the characteristics of new media justify differences in the First Amendment standards applied to them ... When there are substantially more individuals who want to broadcast than there are frequencies to allocate, it is idle to posit an unabridgeable First Amendment right to broadcast comparable to the right of every individual to speak, write or publish ... the people as a whole retain their interest in free speech by radio and their collective right to have the medium function consistently with the ends and purposes of the First Amendment. It is the right of the viewers and listeners, not the right of the broadcasters, which is paramount.

Scarcity of broadcast spectrum space remains the only legal justification for federal regulation of broadcast programming in the United States. Following the sensible judicial practice of phrasing exceptions to general legal rules as narrowly as possible, the federal courts have been unwilling to adopt any broader rationalization for this governmental role in media free speech than absolutely necessary, fearing that expanding the basis for media content control might encourage this uniquely threatening power to extend beyond its intended range.[32]

As long as broadcasting remained the dominant electronic mass medium in the United States, there was nothing particularly unfair about all regulatory authority being based upon the legal concept of scarcity of spectrum space. Broadcasters might complain about their "second class" mass communications status in comparison to

[31] Red Lion Broadcasting Co. v. FCC, 395 U.S. 367, 386–390, 89 S.Ct. 1794, 1805–1806 (1969).

[32] A number of other rationales have been suggested through the years for imposing content controls on broadcasting, while protecting other media from similar governmental constraints, including broadcasting's unique pervasiveness and influence upon our society, its unique accessibility to children in the home, and its status as the only medium operating under government license.

the press, but at least all FCC regulations applied equally to every station competing for the same broadcast audience.

All this changed, however, when cable TV began for the first time to pose a serious competitive challenge to broadcasting in the late 1970s. Unlike broadcasting, cable TV systems did not require broadcast spectrum channels to deliver their programming, and so the FCC had no constitutional basis for imposing the same type of regulatory controls on a cable system as it imposed on its broadcast competitor. Now, the issue was no longer simply whether broadcasters should enjoy the same degree of freedom of expression as the American press, but whether within the field of electronic media itself, radio and television should be singled out by law as being the only forms of mass communication that remain subject to government content control.

SEC. 14. SPECTRUM SCARCITY AND EXPANDING NEW MEDIA CHANNELS

The federal government has moved toward deregulation largely because it seems inequitable to impose regulation upon certain forms of electronic media that cannot legally be imposed upon others.

Although the FCC never attempted to license cable TV operators, the agency did use its regulatory authority over those microwave systems cable TV required to import their television signals to dictate cable TV programming policies. The Commission's technique was simply to adopt rules prohibiting the use of microwave relay services by cable systems not conforming to the agency's programming standards. Since virtually every cable system needed those additional television channels from distant markets to attract subscribers, this indirect regulatory influence upon cable programming worked quite effectively.

In 1968 the Supreme Court was asked for the first time to consider whether the FCC could exert this type of influence over a communications medium Congress had not granted it legal authority to regulate directly. The court affirmed this authority, but suggested quite clearly that its scope was limited.[33]

> There is no need here to determine in detail the limits of the Commission's authority to regulate CATV. It is enough to emphasize that the authority we recognize today ... is restricted to that reasonably ancillary to the effective performance of the Commission's various responsibilities for the regulation of television broadcasting.

[33] United States v. Southwestern Cable Co., 392 U.S. 157, 88 S.Ct. 1994 (1968).

Four years later, in reviewing a FCC rule that required all major cable TV systems to originate one channel of television programming themselves, the Supreme Court, in a 5–4 decision, again affirmed the Commission, but with Chief Justice Burger warning that such a cable programming requirement,[34]

> strains the outer limits of even the open-ended and pervasive jurisdiction that has evolved by decisions of the Commission and the Courts.

That limit of judicial toleration was finally reached in 1979, when the Supreme Court reviewed FCC regulations requiring cable TV systems serving more than 3,500 subscribers to set aside certain cable channels for public access programming. The cable operator in this case had argued that by denying the system the right to decide who should be allowed access to these channels, or how these channels should be programmed, the FCC had deprived cable TV of constitutionally protected editorial control over the nature of its programming services.

The Court agreed with this argument, but chose to overturn the cable TV access rules without considering their First Amendment implications. Instead, the Court found the rules to be unenforceable because they treated cable TV systems as communication "common carriers," required to provide access to all, and Congress had not authorized the FCC to impose this type of communication obligation upon either broadcasting or cable.[35]

In 1977, a federal appeals court struck down FCC rules attempting to protect broadcasters from the competitive threat of cable delivered pay–TV services. In Home Box Office, Inc. v. Federal Communications Commission [36], the court found that Commission restrictions imposed upon the type of programming pay–TV could provide were not within the regulatory powers granted the agency by Congress. Although this finding in itself determined the outcome of the case, the court also discussed the broader First Amendment implications of such federal cable TV program regulation.

In essence, it pointed out that while incidental constraints upon cable TV free speech might be permissible to achieve some broader electronic media policy objective, there was no reasonable justification for believing in this situation that pay–TV would siphon away the most popular programs from traditional broadcast

---

[34] United States v. Midwest Video Corp., 406 U.S. 649, 92 S.Ct. 1860 (1972).

[35] Federal Communications Commission v. Midwest Video Corp., 440 U.S. 689, 99 S.Ct. 1435 (1979). A communications "common carrier" is an organization such as a telephone or telegraph company in the business of conveying messages that others pay to have delivered.

[36] 567 F.2d 9 (D.C.Cir.1977).

services. As the court observed, "where the First Amendment is concerned, creation of such a rebuttable presumption of siphoning without clear record support is simply impermissible."

As the 1980s began, it was apparent that the federal courts were no longer sympathetic with FCC efforts to impose content controls of any kind upon cable TV systems. While the courts still chose to overturn Commission cable policies on the basis of these regulations exceeding the authority granted the agency by Congress, it was doubtful that any cable programming legislation Congress might adopt could actually withstand First Amendment challenge in the courts.

At this point, then, the FCC began moving in the opposite regulatory direction. Although as an agency of Congress, the Commission was compelled to continue to enforce all requirements imposed upon broadcasters by the Communications Act of 1934, the FCC started rescinding every radio and television rule of its own that no longer seemed justified by the less active regulatory role in broadcasting it intended to play in the future.

At the same time, the Commission began actively to encourage the development of other new electronic media, authorizing direct broadcast satellite (DBS), low power TV (LPTV) and multi-point, multi-channel distribution systems (MMDS) under standards much less stringent than those traditionally imposed upon broadcast license applicants.[37]

The underlying policy objective of both deregulation and new media system authorization has been to create such a vast electronic media marketplace of viewing and listening alternatives for American audiences that there will be no need for any further intervention on the part of the federal government to protect public interests in electronic mass communication. The Supreme Court has already acknowledged the impact such an electronic marketplace of ideas could have upon the traditional spectrum scarcity justification for broadcast regulation observation. Justice Brennan observed, in a footnote comment, that,[38]

> The prevailing rationale for broadcast regulation based upon spectrum scarcity has come under increasing criticism in recent years. Critics ... charge that with advent of cable and satellite technology, communities now have access to such a wide variety of stations that the scarcity doctrine is obsolete ... We are not prepared, however, to reconsider our long standing approach without

[37] These systems and their regulation will be discussed in more detail in Chapter 10.

[38] Note 11, FCC v. League of Women Voters of California, 468 U.S. 364, 104 S.Ct. 3106 (1984).

some signal from Congress or the FCC that technological developments have advanced so far that some revision of the system of broadcast regulation may be required.

Is the time approaching, then, when all legal distinctions between broadcasting and the press will be abolished? Will the rights of the "fourth" and "fifth" estates eventually merge, creating a single body of constitutionally protected mass communication freedom of expression?

SEC. 15.   THE CONVERGENCE OF "BROADCAST" AND "PRESS" LAW

Technological advances have begun to blur traditional legal distinctions between "broadcast" and "press" mass communication functions.

When broadcast regulation began in the United States during the 1920s, the only obvious similarity between radio news program and the daily newspapers was the teletype machine they both relied upon for their national and international wire service stories. As far as news production and distribution was concerned, while the radio journalist simply read scripted news items transmitted through the electromagnetic spectrum, the press still relied upon the complex "hot-type" publishing process to produce the daily newspaper.[39]

Today, both broadcast and press journalists write their stories on CRT's (cathode ray tube) word processors linked to a central computer, and a newspaper like the *Wall Street Journal* is distributed nationally by satellite transmission of facsimile pages to local printing plants across the nation, where plates of every page are made and each issue of the *Journal* is then published for delivery to subscribers in that area of the country.

But what if these facsimile pages were relayed instead by satellite directly to every television household equipped to reproduce them, eliminating local publishing and distribution costs, and allowing immediate access to each news item in the paper as it was being transmitted? Would such a change in the method of delivering a newspaper also alter its First Amendment status as a communications medium?

Recent federal case law suggests that it could. The Commission has attempted on several occasions to exempt specialized spectrum services similar to this satellite newspaper relay network

---

[39] "Hot type" refers to producing images on paper by the complex and expensive process of setting them in molten lead, rather than recreating them photographically on paper. During that era, newspaper copy was typed, set in print by a linotype operator, proofed, made up into pages, mat molded, and then bundled as it rolled off the press to be shipped by truck for local delivery.

from its full range of traditional broadcast regulatory requirements, but federal courts have had difficulty finding any legal justification for such exemptions.

The problem for the courts is that Congress, through its Communications Act of 1934, has imposed specific regulatory obligations on each class of broadcast spectrum users that the FCC, as an agency of Congress, has no legal authority to modify or reduce.

In 1981, the Commission sought to encourage the growth of teletext service in the United States.[40] To stimulate its development, the FCC decided to minimize the program content responsibilities of those pioneering this service by exempting teletext from most of the political access requirements imposed on regular broadcasters.[41] In Telecommunications Research and Action Center v. FCC,[42] the court rejected this FCC action, finding no justification in the Communications Act for excusing this particular type of broadcast service from those general requirements Congress had imposed on all broadcasters.[43] Similarly, in National Association of Broadcasters v. FCC,[44] the court denied the Commission the right to exempt direct broadcast satellite operators from ownership and political access requirements imposed on all other broadcast licensees.[45]

[40] "Teletext" is an information service TV stations can provide to households with specially equipped receivers. The station transmits a continuing sequence of some 500 pages or frames of different news or information items, using a small portion of its television channel not needed for regular TV service, and each household can select from the index of pages provided the specific pages or frames of information they want to retain and read on their screens.

[41] In the Matter of Amendment of Parts 2, 73 and 76 of the Commission's Rules to Authorize the Transmission of Teletext by TV Stations, 53 RR 2d 1309 (1983). The FCC justified its exemptions by described teletext as being not a regular, but only an "ancillary" broadcast service and therefore not requiring the full range of political content controls applied to broadcasting.

[42] 801 F.2d 501 (D.C.Cir.1986).

[43] The FCC was allowed to exempt teletext from Fairness Doctrine requirements, but that was only because the majority of the court found Fairness not to be a Congressionally imposed obligation.

[44] 740 F.2d 1190 (D.C.Cir.1984). Also see Telecommunications Research and Action Center v. FCC, 836 F.2d 1349 (D.C.Cir.1988) where an attempt by the Commission to exempt Instructional Television Fixed Service (ITFS) licenses from Congressionally mandated broadcast minority preference standards was also struck down by the court.

[45] Recently, however, in National Ass'n for Better Broadcasters v. FCC, 849 F.2d 665 (D.C.Cir.1988), at least one panel of DC Court of Appeal judges did affirm an FCC regulatory finding that broadcast spectrum transmissions not intended for the general public (such as encoded pay-TV transmissions) could be legally classified as "non-broadcast" services, and thereby exempted from regulations that Congress had designed solely for regular broadcasters. See also, Subscription Video, 62 RR2d 389 (1987), the rule-making proceeding in which the Commission first proposed this legal distinction between broadcast transmissions intended for the general public, and those services intended only for that segment of the public willing to pay for them.

At the moment, then, it appears that a newspaper might well be transformed by law into a "broadcaster" by the simple act of deciding to distribute its pages directly to the subscriber through the broadcast spectrum, rather than leaving those identical pages imprinted on paper at the front door of the same household.

While this example might seem to illustrate how illogical law can be at times, what it really demonstrates is the difficulties that legal reasoning faces when distinctions that once were useful and sensible no longer are as significant or logical. During an era when only broadcasters delivered their messages through the spectrum, there may have been valid legal reasons for defining their communication rights differently from those of other media that did not use this public resource. But now as that area is coming to an end, we face a future, as one noted scholar in this field has written, where . . .

> . . . the industries of print and the industries of tele-communications will no longer be kept apart by a fundamental difference in their technologies. The economic and regulatory problems of the electronic media will thus become the problems of the print media too . . . The issues that concern telecommunications are now becoming issues for all communications as they all become forms of electronic processing and transmission.[46]

During the past decade it has been the telephone industry that has spearheaded this movement towards media convergence. When the massive AT&T telephone empire was dismantled in 1981, the Bell Systems newly released from AT&T control soon demanded freedom as well from those regulatory constraints they had been forced to endure as part of that vast empire.

No longer content to operate solely as passive communication common carriers, these Bell Systems sought to expand the scope of their activities far beyond their traditional point-to-point personal communication services to include electronic publishing and video program delivery as well. Both of these demands were met in 1992, when the FCC authorized Bell System distribution of television programming as a federal court was lifting the ban that had prevented these companies from entering the electronic publishing business.[47]

---

[46] Ithiel de Sola Pool, On Free Speech in An Electronic Age: Technologies of Freedom, (Cambridge: Harvard University Press, 1983) p. 42.

[47] Telephone–Cable Cross–Ownership, 7 F.C.C. Rcd 5785 (1992). The federal court decision was United States v. Western Electric Co., 767 F Supp. 308 (D.D.C. 1991) stay vacated sub nom. 1991–2 Trade Cases (CCH) ¶ 69,610 (D.C.Cir.) review denied sub nom. American Newspaper Publishers Assn. v. United States, 112 S.Ct. 366 (1991). See also United States v. Western Electric Co., 900 F.2d 283 (D.C.Cir.

At the same time the FCC was also considering requests from cable TV and broadcast organizations to be allowed to offer communication common carrier services in addition to that video programming they already provided. In September 1992 the Commission began to allocate spectrum space for personal communication service (PSC), a new form of wireless telephone and computer terminal delivery service. These low-cost PCS systems would make it possible for cable operators, among others, to compete directly against existing telephone companies in their own service areas, offering an alternative network for the delivery of point-to-point messages.

In an effort to find some technological solution to these competitive conflicts among rival telecommunication industries, Vice President Gore has advanced a Clinton administration policy proposal to encourage the development of nationwide fiber optic networks capable of delivering a wide variety of divergent communication services within the same system. This policy concept, initially described as the "National Information Infrastructure" but soon rechristened by the press as the *Information Superhighway*, seeks to encourage private development of these fiber optic networks by eliminating every outdated federal regulatory barrier that now prevents head-to-head competition among various telecommunication organizations.[48]

As part of this policy, the administration asked Congress to create a new section of the Communications Act of 1934, Title VII, that would create a simplified, less rigid set of regulatory requirements for any company operating one of these new broadband networks. Several other legislative proposals now being considered by Congress would also repeal many of those legal restrictions that now discourage any tendency towards media convergence because of the different regulatory requirements they impose on broadcasting, cable TV and other telecommunication services.

But even though media technology may in time erode those legal barriers that deny broadcast service many of those rights now enjoyed by the press, that time has not yet come. The American legal system continues to recognize these traditional distinctions, and so broadcasting remains a unique area of mass communication law, still lacking the same level of constitutional protection accorded all other mass media in the United States.

Communication by broadcasting is still dependent on governmental approval, and thereafter subject to continued governmental

1990) cert. denied sub nom. MCI Communication Corp. v. United States, 498 U.S. 911, 111 S.Ct. 283 (1990).

[48] Kim McAvoy, "Al Gore: Directing Traffic onto the Superhighway", Broadcasting, Jan. 10, 1994. p. 10.

approval for its exercise. A federal agency retains the authority to impose conditions upon this right, limiting a broadcaster's freedom of expression, and the government reserves to itself the power to decide whether the quality of that expression merits a continuation of the privilege to communicate.

For this reason, then, while it is important to be aware of that powerful technologically driven movement toward media convergence that is almost certain to exert an ever increasing influence upon basic principles of broadcast and electronic media law in the future, it is at least equally important to understand the actual regulatory environment in which broadcasting and its media competitors still operate today.

Part II

MASS COMMUNICATIONS LAW AND THE CITIZEN

Chapter 4

DEFAMATION: LIBEL AND SLANDER

SEC. 16. DEFAMATION DEFINED

Defamation is communication which exposes persons to hatred, ridicule, or contempt, lowers them in the esteem of others, causes them to be shunned, or injures them in their business or calling. Its categories are libel— broadly, printed, written or broadcast material—and slander—broadly, spoken words of limited reach.

Brace yourselves. The next three chapters are intended to serve as lessons in self-defense for persons working in mass communications fields. These chapters deal with defamation, the term which includes the "twin torts" of libel and slander. Chances are good that if you work in as a journalist that you will be sued for defamation, which the law classifies as a tort, a civil wrong other than breach of contract for which the legal remedy is a court action for monetary damages.[1]

Chances of being sued are substantial, for one thing, because there are so many lawyers in the United States. By 1995, the United States had more than two-thirds of all the lawyers in the

---

[1] William L. Prosser, The Law of Torts (St. Paul: West Publishing Co., 1964) 3d ed., p. 2. For a major study, see Robert D. Sack and Sandra Baron, Libel, Slander, and Related Problems, 2d ed. (New York: Practising Law Institute, 1994).

world, or about 950,000. And lawyers litigate. Back in 1987, Americans filed lawsuits at the rate of 15 million a year, roughly one for every sixteen of us. Understandably, libel and invasion of privacy lawsuits are on the rise. The average cost of defending a libel suit may run as high as $100,000 or even $150,000, and that refers only to legal costs and not to money paid out in a lost lawsuit. And litigation that might sting a large newspaper or radio station or its insurance company could ruin a small media outfit.

Although more attention to fair play and ethical considerations might well stave off many of the libel suits now brought against the media, a free society by its nature is going to allow communication which harms many reputations. Freedom, after all, is a risk. Although society has a strong interest in the free flow of information, there is also a societal stake in allowing protection of one's reputation.

This chapter deals with the basics of libel: It discusses its elements to alert you to situations in which a problem might arise. The next chapter talks about the constitutional defense to libel growing out of 1964's New York Times v. Sullivan landmark and about older, more traditional defenses to libel under state law.

Protecting one's reputation and society's strong interest in providing such protection justify libel suits. As Supreme Court Justice Potter Stewart said, an individual's right to the protection and comfort of his own good name "reflects no more than our basic concept of the essential dignity and worth of every human being—a concept at the root of any decent system of ordered liberty." [2] At the same time, First Amendment values—freedom, an informed citizenry, and media that serve as a check on government—justify strong defenses against the suit. "It is important to safeguard First Amendment rights; it is also important to give protection to a person who is defamed, and to discourage * * * defamation in the future. A balance must be struck." [3]

This "balancing," however, is not an exact process. The late William L. Prosser, long considered America's leading torts scholar, expressed this disenchanted view: [4]

> It must be confessed ... that there is a great deal of the law of defamation which makes no sense. It contains anomalies and absurdities for which no legal writer ever has had a kind word, and it is a curious compound of a strict liability imposed upon innocent defendants ... with

[2] Rosenblatt v. Baer, 383 U.S. 75, 92, 86 S.Ct. 669, 679 (1966).
[3] Maheu v. Hughes Tool Co., 569 F.2d 459, 480 (9th Cir.1977).
[4] Prosser, Law of Torts, 4th ed. (1971), at p. 737.

a blind and almost perverse refusal to compensate the plaintiff for real and very serious harm.

As a distinguished study asserted in 1987, the law of libel aims at one thing and hits another. This study, entitled Libel Law and the Press: Myth and Reality, noted that the law assumes that by suing, plaintiffs whose reputations have been injured can somehow be made whole by receiving money. That study found, however, that plaintiffs tend to be more interested in correction of falsity and in "setting the record straight." [5]

Damages justly termed "staggering" by the Libel Defense Resource Center are often returned by juries, with multi-million-dollar awards to plaintiffs (including $58 million in one Texas case, although it was rumored to be reduced to under $20 million in an out-of-court settlement). Huge jury verdicts against media defendants usually are drastically reduced by judges. Nevertheless libel verdicts which survive appeals are being seen with increasing frequency in millions of dollars.

Losing a libel case, however, is not the only problem. In addition, attorneys' fees and court costs may be even greater than such awards. In one extraordinary case in 1985, costs to *Time* magazine were estimated as $3 million for its successful defense; and in another—arguably the most-publicized libel case in the nation's history—one estimate was $8 million in legal costs for both sides, although the plaintiff dropped his suit before it reached the jury. Such prospects may lead media to avoid the huge costs of defending a drawn-out trial by settling out of court—for $800,000 in case of a 1984 agreement by the *Wall Street Journal*.[6]

Today's defamation law carries with it much ancient historical baggage. If it is hard to understand today, chalk that up to its past. Defamation traced a tortuous course through the medieval and early modern courts of England. Feudal and then ecclesiastical (church) courts had jurisdiction over libel as a crime before libel moved haltingly into the common law courts, where people would sue for "damages" (money) for injury to their reputations. Difficulties arose, for example, when printing became more common. Then it seemed important to separate damage done by the spoken word (slander), which was fleeting, from damage done by the printed word, which might be more harmful because it was permanent and more widely diffused than speech. Rules that made sense several centuries ago turned into confusing anachronisms that lived

[5] Randall P. Bezanson, Gilbert Cranberg, and John Soloski, Libel Law and the Press: Myth and Reality (New York: The Free Press, 1987).

[6] Sharon v. Time, Inc., Time, Feb. 4, 1985, 64; Westmoreland v. CBS, New York Times, Feb. 19, 1985, 1, Feb. 20, 1985, 13; 10 Med.L.Rptr. # 25, 6/19/84, News Notes, citing LDRC Report of July 29, 1984.

on into the age of television and communication satellites.[7]

In bringing defamation substantially under the U.S. Constitution, the landmark *Sullivan* decision was one factor that tended to wipe out a major complicating element in the law as applied to media: the division of defamation into libel (written defamation) and slander (spoken). Because radio broadcasting was speech, some states considered broadcast defamation to be slander; because it relied on written scripts, other states called it libel; because in combining slander and libel rules for broadcasting, one court was persuaded that a new name was called for, a judicial flyer into creative linguistics produced the name "defamacast."[8] *Sullivan*— the New York Times v. Sullivan case discussed in Section 26— treated the matter as libel, and where *Sullivan* applied, states were to follow suit.

Meanwhile, the prestigious American Law Institute (ALI) resolved the question for its followers by emphasizing the extensive harm that a defamatory broadcast to thousands or millions could do to a reputation. It followed, said ALI, that the more severe penalties of libel should result from broadcast defamation, rather than the lesser ones of slander which had been shaped centuries before to compensate for unenhanced oral denigration to small audiences. Thus the ALI said: " * * * defamation by any form of communication that has the potentially harmful qualities characteristic of written or printed words is to be treated as libel."[9]

The ALI pronouncement that libel should encompass broadcasting was by no means the first time that adjustments in the law had attached "libel" to varied media of communication. Before broadcasting, the Twentieth Century had produced motion pictures, and they had rather early been ruled to be libelous, if defamatory. Long before movies arrived—at least as early as the celebrated case of People v. Croswell in 1804—pictures and signs were included within libel.[10]

The most-used definition of libel is that it is a false statement about an individual which exposes him to "hatred, ridicule, or

[7] Prosser, 2nd ed. 754, 769; John Kelly, "Criminal Libel and Free Speech," 6 Kans.L.Rev. 295 (1958); Anon., "Developments in the Law, Defamation," 69 Harv. L.Rev. 875 (1956).

[8] D.H. Remmers, "Recent Legislative Trends in Defamation by Radio," 64 Harv. L.Rev. 727, 1951; Prosser, 2nd ed. 754, 769–81; Grein v. La Poma, 54 Wash.2d 844, 340 P.2d 766 (1959); American Broadcasting–Paramount Theatres, Inc. v. Simpson, 106 Ga.App. 230, 126 S.E.2d 873 (1962).

[9] Restatement, Second, Torts, Vol. 3, 182. Some states have abolished the distinction between libel and slander, e.g. Illinois: Brown & Williamson Tobacco Corp. v. Jacobson, 713 F.2d 262 (7th Cir.1983), 9 Med.L.Rptr. 1936, 1939. But see Nevada Broadcasting Co. v. Allen (Nev.Sup.Ct.1982), 9 Med.L.Rptr. 1770.

[10] Movies: Youssoupoff v. Metro–Goldwyn–Mayer Pictures, 51 L.Q.Rev. 281, 99 A.L.R. 864 (1934); Pictures: People v. Croswell, 3 Johns Cases 337 (N.Y.1804).

contempt, or which causes him to be shunned, or avoided, or which has a tendency to injure him in his office, profession or trade." [11] While that definition takes in a wide reach of words, it is nevertheless probably too narrow.   Courts recognize mental anguish and personal humiliation as the bases of libel.   Prosser pointed out that words which would cause most people to sympathize with the target have been held defamatory, such as an imputation of poverty, or the statement that a woman has been raped.[12]   If a person is lowered in the estimation or respect of the community, he is not necessarily hated, held in contempt, or shunned.

To have definitions such as the above is by no means always to be able to predict what will be held libelous.   The legal axiom which says that "every definition in the law is dangerous" most certainly applies to defamation.   Whether words are defamatory depends, in part, on the temper of the times and current public opinion; "words harmless in one age, in one community, may be highly damaging to reputation at another time or * * * place." [13] While it was probably not defamation to falsely call one a Communist in the 1930s, several later cases have found the appellation libelous.[14]

It must be understood that in a suit where it is shown that the plaintiff has been libeled—money damages are not necessarily awarded.   There are various circumstances in which the law protects media against liability for libeling.   Chapter 5 is devoted to the defenses that furnish these protections.

Anyone who is living [15] may be defamed—unless that person is so notorious as a criminal as to be "libel-proof" and courts will not accept that person's libel action— [16] and so may a corporation or partnership where its business standing or practices are impugned. A voluntary association organized for purposes not connected with profit or the self-interest of the organizers also may be defamed.[17]

[11] Sir Hugh Fraser, Libel and Slander (London: 1936), 7th ed., p. 3; Perry v. Columbia Broadcasting System, Inc., 499 F.2d 797 (7th Cir.1974).

[12] Time, Inc. v. Firestone, 424 U.S. 448, 96 S.Ct. 958 (1976); Prosser, 2nd ed. p. 756.

[13] Mencher v. Chesley, 297 N.Y. 94, 75 N.E.2d 257 (1947).

[14] Spanel v. Pegler, 160 F.2d 619 (7th Cir.1947); Levy v. Gelber, 175 Misc. 746, 25 N.Y.S.2d 148 (1941); Gertz v. Robert Welch, Inc., 418 U.S. 323, 94 S.Ct. 2997 (1974).

[15] For another rejection of a challenge to the general rule that the dead can't sue for defamation (or relatives sue in behalf of a deceased person), see Gugliuzza v. KCMC, Inc., 606 So.2d 790 (La.1992), 20 Med.L.Rptr. 1866.

[16] Cardillo v. Doubleday & Co., Inc., 518 F.2d 638 (2d Cir.1975).

[17] Americans for Democratic Action v. Meade, 72 Pa.D. & C. 306 (1950); New York Society for the Suppression of Vice v. MacFadden Publications, Inc., 129 Misc. 408, 221 N.Y.S. 563 (1927), affirmed 222 App.Div. 739, 226 N.Y.S. 870 (1928); Mullins v. Brando, 13 Cal.App.3d 409, 91 Cal.Rptr. 796 (1970); Friends of Animals,

However, it is not possible for one to be defamed through an insult or slur upon someone close to him, such as a member of his family.[18] Nor can a dead person be defamed,[19] nor in most circumstances a group. A government entity, such as the city of Philadelphia, cannot bring a civil libel action.[20]

Large groups such as business executives in general, or labor, or a political party, or all the Muslims of the world, or an ethnic group of a large city, cannot sue for libel. When, however, a defamatory statement is leveled against a small group, each member may be considered by the law to be libeled, and the individuals may bring separate suits even though no one has been singled out. It is by no means clear what the upper limit of a "small group" might be.

SEC. 17. THE FIVE ELEMENTS OF LIBEL

The plaintiff in a libel suit must plead that there was Publication, Identification, Defamation, Fault and Injury.

Potential libel suit defendants—and that includes all of us—need to know (as do lawyers filing libel suits) that five conditions must be present before a suit can hope to succeed. (This discussion assumes that the action for defamation will have been filed in a timely fashion to conform to the deadline set by the state where the suit is filed: the *statute of limitations*. In half of the states, the statute of limitations for libel is one year after publication, and is two or three years in the remainder.)[21]

Inc. v. Associated Fur Manufacturers, Inc., 46 N.Y.2d 1065, 416 N.Y.S.2d 790, 390 N.E.2d 298 (1979), 4 Med.L.Rptr. 2503.

[18] Gonzales v. Times Herald Printing Co., 513 S.W.2d 124 (Tex.Civ.App.1974); Wildstein v. New York Post Corp., 40 Misc.2d 586, 243 N.Y.S.2d 386 (1963); Security Sales Agency v. A.S. Abell Co., 205 Fed. 941 (D.Md.1913); but "daughter of a murderer" has been held libelous: Van Wiginton v. Pulitzer Pub. Co., 218 Fed. 795 (8th Cir.1914).

[19] McBeth v. United Press International, Inc., 505 F.2d 959 (5th Cir.1974). But see Canino v. New York News, Inc., 96 N.J. 189, 475 A.2d 528 (1984), 10 Med. L.Rptr. 1852, where a libel action filed before death did not abate at death.

[20] City of Philadelphia v. Washington Post Co., 482 F.Supp. 897 (E.D.Pa.1979), 5 Med.L.Rptr. 2221.

[21] Half of the states—any states not listed here plus the District of Columbia—have a one-year statute of limitations. States with two-year statutes include Alabama, Alaska, Connecticut, Delaware, Florida, Hawaii, Idaho, Indiana, Iowa, Maine, Minnesota, Missouri, Montana, Nevada, North Dakota, South Carolina, South Dakota, Virginia, Washington, and Wisconsin. Arkansas, Massachusetts, New Hampshire, and Vermont's limitations are three years. The Arkansas statute of limitations is one year for slander, and three years for libel; the Tennessee statute of limitations is six months for slander but one year for libel. (See Henry R. Kaufman, ed., LDRC 50–State Survey 1993–1994: Current Developments in Media Libel and Invasion of Privacy Law (New York: Libel Defense Resource Center, 1993),

The five necessary conditions for suit are:

1. Publication
2. Identification
3. Defamation
4. Fault
5. Injury

Publication

Publication means circulation of a statement. It may be in printed, written form, or, in the case of broadcasting and movies, oral. Even signs or statues may qualify as a form of publication.

The first of the five allegations the party filing a libel suit must consider is that the derogatory statement was published. Publication can occur only if it is made to the person defamed and one other person. A communication can't harm a reputation unless it is spread to at least one person besides the target. Although the mass media ordinarily publish to huge audiences, it is worth remembering that no more than a "third person" need to be involved for publication to take place. In one case, a man dictated a letter to his secretary accusing the addressee of grand larceny. The secretary typed the letter and it was sent through the mail. The letter's recipient brought a successful libel suit: the court held that publication took place at the time the stenographic notes were read and transcribed.[22]

For the printed media, courts of most states call the entire edition carrying the alleged libel one publication. That is, an over-the-counter sale of back copies of a newspaper weeks or months after they were first printed would not constitute further publication. That is known as the "single publication rule."[23] Where this is not the rule, there is a chance that a plaintiff can stretch the statute of limitations indefinitely, perhaps by claiming a separate publication in a newspaper's selling a February issue the following December. In Tocco v. Time, Inc., it was held that the publication takes place at the time a magazine is mailed to subscribers, or put in the hands of those who will ship the edition to wholesale distributors.[24] That approach, however, is not universally accepted. To the contrary, Osmers v. Parade Publications, Inc., stated that a publication date is when the libel was "substantially and

passim; summarized in Robert D. Sack and Sandra S. Baron, Libel, Slander and Related Problems, (New York: Practising Law Institute, 1993), Appendix 1, p. 835.

[22] Ostrowe v. Lee, 256 N.Y. 36, 175 N.E. 505 (1931). See also Arvey Corp. v. Peterson, 178 F.Supp. 132 (E.D.Pa.1959).

[23] Sack, op. cit., pp. 363–364.

[24] 195 F.Supp. 410 (E.D.Mich.1961).

effectively communicated to a meaningful mass of readers—the public for which the publication was intended, not some small segment of it." [25]

Beyond publication, sometimes media executives need to ponder the occasional perils of re-publication. In Warford v. Lexington Herald–Leader Co. (1990), the 1986 republication of a 1985 series charging an assistant basketball coach with recruiting violations brought a lawsuit. The Kentucky Supreme Court noted that a basketball player who was a source for damaging information published by the newspaper about assistant coach Reggie Warford had promptly denied and retracted his statements, and his denial was published by the Herald–Leader.

The series, which won a Pulitzer Prize, was then republished in 1986, retitled "1985: A Year of Crisis in College Athletics." The 1986 publication, which omitted the athlete's denial, was sent to "the president, athletic director, faculty representative, and head football and basketball coaches at each [NCAA] member university, as well as 100 major newspapers...." [26] Assistant Coach Warford, who asserted that the series had damaged his employment chances, won his lawsuit against the newspaper.

Identification

To bring a successful libel action—once publication has been established—a plaintiff must also demonstrate that he or she was *identified* in the alleged libel. Plaintiffs must show that the statement complained about refers to them.

Most of the time, the identification is obvious. A plaintiff's name or picture is used, right along with the statements claimed to be defamatory. But sometimes identification may occur in a less direct way: in one case, a camera shop answered a competitor's ads with these words:

USE COMMON SENSE * * *
You Get NOTHING for NOTHING!
WE WILL NOT

1. Inflate the prices of your developing to give you a new roll free!

2. Print the blurred negatives to inflate the price of your snapshots!

The Cosgrove Studio sued for libel, claiming that ad implied Cosgrove used dishonest business practices. In upholding a damage award for Cosgrove, a Pennsylvania appeals court made an

[25] 234 F.Supp. 924, 927 (S.D.N.Y.1964).

[26] Warford v. Lexington Herald–Leader Co., 789 S.W.2d 758, 759–760 (Ky.1990).

important point: Identification of the defamed need not be by name. "A party need not be specifically named, if pointed to by description or circumstances tending to identify him," the court held.[27]

Cautious journalists check and double-check identifications and addresses. All too frequently, publication of a typographical error, wrong initials, or an incorrect address may result in a totally unintended identification. Such a slip-up by a careless editor or reporter can falsely link an innocent person with a crime, or immorality, or unethical business conduct that forms the basis for a libel suit.

Some libel cases may instill caution bordering on paranoia. Special care is indicated, for example, in those unusual circumstances where a publication wishes to do a story about a person endeavoring to cope with a socially stigmatized condition such as AIDS or cocaine addiction. It might be the publication decides that the story needs to be told, but that it can be reported only if the source's request not to be identified is honored. If a fictitious name is used to mask identity, ethically that should be made clear in the story. Take care, however, that the "fictitious" identity does not somehow identify some real-life individual.

In a famed English case, E. Hulton & Co. v. Jones,[28] the *Sunday Chronicle* had published a story from a correspondent in France about a supposedly fictitious person named Artemus Jones. He had been seen, the story said, keeping company with a woman who was not his wife. The Chronicle soon learned, through the filing of a libel suit, that there was a *real* Artemus Jones. Jones told the court that some of his friends believed the story was about him. It was found that the identification was sufficient for Jones, a lawyer, to collect damages of £1750.

In a far more recent case in the United States, Springer sued Viking Press for libel, complaining that she was identifiable to friends as the model for a prostitute in a novel written by Tine, a former friend. The book, Ms. Springer claimed, described the prostitute's physical characteristics as highly similar to her own. Both Ms. Springer and the fictional prostitute lived on the same street in Manhattan, she said, and both received gifts of a diamond and a necklace from a boyfriend, both spoke fluent French and dated Iranian men.

[27] Cosgrove Studio & Camera Shop, Inc. v. Pane, 408 Pa. 314, 182 A.2d 751 (1962). See also Grove v. Dun & Bradstreet, Inc., 438 F.2d 433 (3d Cir.1971), and Dictaphone Corp. v. Sloves (N.Y.Sup.1980), 6 Med.L.Rptr. 1114.

[28] A.C. 20, 1909, 2 K.B. 444 (1910).

A New York court said that there was similarity between Ms. Springer and the fictional prostitute, and refused to grant Viking Press's motion to dismiss the libel suit.[29]

Identification cannot be established by a person who says that an attack on a large heterogeneous group libels her because she happens to belong to it. To suggest some examples, derogatory statements about a political party, an international labor union, the Presbyterian Church, or the Rotary Club do not identify individuals so as to allow them to bring a libel action.

If, however, the attack is on a small sub-group of an organization, that's quite different. Suppose a defamatory attack is made on the directors of the Smithjones County Democratic Party, on the officers of a labor union (whether it be a national or local unit), or the presiding elders of a church, or on the civic club's officers. Then, each individual member of the attacked sub-group may be able to establish identification—even though his or her name was not used—and bring suit.

A sleazy book—*U.S.A. Confidential*—resulted in the often cited—and often misinterpreted—case known as Neiman–Marcus Co. v. Lait. That case set down these guidelines:

(1) Where the group or class libeled is large, none can sue even though the language used is inclusive.

(2) When the group or class libeled is small, and each and every member of the group or class is referred to, then any individual member can sue.

(3) That while there is a conflict in authorities where the publication complained of libeled some or less than all of a designated small group, the federal court ruling in the Neiman–Marcus case said it would allow such an action.

Those guidelines were drawn from a garish fact situation. Authors Jack Lait and Lee Mortimer claimed in *U.S.A. Confidential* that swingers looking for a "good time" need look no further in Dallas than that city's famed department store, Neiman–Marcus. The book's chapter on Dallas asserted that all of the store's models (there were nine) were prostitutes, the highest-paid in town. The book also said that the "nucleus of the Dallas fairy colony" was in the Neiman–Marcus men's store (which had 25 salesmen). Finally, these fearless authors declared that the store's "salesgirls" (there were 382) were prostitutes too, cheaper and more fun than the models.[30]

In applying these rules to the facts, the court dismissed the lawsuits of the saleswomen (382 was simply too large a group to

[29] Springer v. Viking Press (N.Y.Sup.1980), 7 Med.L.Rptr. 2040.
[30] 107 F.Supp. 96 (S.D.N.Y.1952); 13 F.R.D. 311 (1952).

have identification take place), but allowed the suits of the models and the salesmen.

But please note what the Neiman–Marcus case did NOT say. It did not say that if a group is larger than 25, you can publish anything you want about that group.   In point of cold legal fact, identification has been held to take place when an unnamed person was a member of defamed groups with memberships as high as 53.[31]   Keep in mind that group size from which an otherwise unidentified libel plaintiff may emerge varies from state to state. And also remember that 25 is not a magic number.

Defamation

Is the publication or broadcast defamatory?   The third necessary allegation asserts that the statement indeed did defame.   That says in effect that the words injured reputation, or, in some circumstances, caused emotional distress.   Plaintiffs must assert that defamation occurred, although—as with the elements of publication and identification—they may not be able to prove defamation at trial.

The court decides whether a publication is libelous *per se* (by itself).   But when the words complained of can have two meanings—one innocent and the other damaging—it is for the jury to decide in what sense the words were understood by the audience. Both judge and jury, in their interpretation of the statement claimed to be defamatory, should give language its common and ordinary meaning.[32]

Fault

A fourth element of libel that the aggrieved person must allege and persuasively demonstrate is "fault" on the part of the publisher or broadcaster.

"Fault" is part of the complex legal geometry which has developed in the aftermath of New York Times Co. v. Sullivan

[31] See Brady v. Ottaway Newspapers, Inc., 84 A.D.2d 226, 445 N.Y.S.2d 786 (1981), 8 Med.L.Rptr. 1671, where a plaintiff policeman who was a member of a group of 53 unnamed policemen was not barred from bring a libel suit.   Courts also have held that members of a jury can be defamed [Byers v. Martin, 2 Colo. 605 (1875)]; all four officers of a labor union [De Witte v. Kearney & Trecker Corp., 265 Wis. 132, 60 N.W.2d 748 (1953)].   Another court, however, has held that a libel action would not work against a magazine which attacked all distributors of the controversial anti-cancer drug laetrile [Schuster v. U.S. News & World Report, Inc., 602 F.2d 850 (8th Cir.1979), 5 Med.L.Rptr. 1773.]   Also, a newspaper was ruled not to have identified individuals when 21 individuals of a town police department sued following publication of a printed rumor about one unidentified officer.   Arcand v. Evening Call Pub. Co., 567 F.2d 1163 (1st Cir.1977).

[32] Peck v. Coos Bay Times Pub. Co., 122 Or. 408, 259 P. 307, 311 (1927); Prosser, 4th ed., p. 746.

(1964).[33] Journalists need to know about courts' renditions of just what "fault" is, but they should also know that this is lawyer's territory. Journalists who don't have law degrees and a real specialty in communication law should not bet their employers' money and their careers on knowing what "fault" means in a given time and place (libel laws do vary from state to state and time to time).

The concept of fault is taken up in depth in Chapter 5. Suffice it to say here that the cases growing out of New York Times v. Sullivan (1964) have added up to some squirmy, stretchy "rules" about determining fault. As will be seen in Chapter 5, "public officials" or "public figures" who claim that they have been injured by a defamatory falsehood have to meet a tough standard of proof called "actual malice."

"Actual malice" as defined in New York Times v. Sullivan meant that public officials (and added later in other cases, public figures) would have to prove that the libel was published " ... with knowledge that it was false or with reckless disregard of whether it was false or not." [34]

It should be evident that such a standard gives the press a very large benefit of the doubt; it is difficult for a public person to prove that the news organization knew something was false, for example. Private persons—that is, people who are not classed as public officials or public figures by a court—have to meet a lesser, easier standard of proof. They have to prove only that the defamation complained of was negligently published, or published without the "due care" that would be used by an "average person of ordinary sensibilities." [35] But as is discussed in some detail in Chapter 5, courts have not sent clear signals about just who is or is not a "public official" or "public figure."

Because clear guidelines are not available, journalists should not take it upon themselves to decide close calls about who is a "public official" or a "public figure." That suggests that deadline-time discussions such as the following hypothetical conversation should not happen.

Rather Nott, Reporter: "It's a great story, but the competition is on to it too. We've got to get it published. I can't get at any other sources until tomorrow."

Molly Typo, Editor: "Let's go with it on Page 1. After all, the persons we're writing about are well known here.

[33] 376 U.S. 254, 84 S.Ct. 710 (1964).

[34] 376 U.S. 254, 279–80, 84 S.Ct. 710, 725 (1964).

[35] See Gertz v. Welch, Inc., 418 U.S. 323, 94 S.Ct. 2997 (1974); see also Black's Law Dictionary.

They're public figures. And two of them used to serve on the school board."

Perhaps the old Associated Press motto should be repeated to Mr. Nott and Ms. Typo: "Get it first, but get it right." Beyond that, the reporter and editor had better get some expert advice—and no doubt the blessing of their bosses—before proceeding to publish. How good are the sources and the evidence assembled so far? And would a court be likely to say that the people to be written about are "public figures?" It takes more than an offhand newsroom guess to make someone into a public figure. A knowledgeable attorney should be able to make a better guess (and it may be just that). In any case, the newsroom folks ought to be aware, for example, that the Texas Supreme Court declared an elected county surveyor to be a private figure.[36] And that a jet-setter with a nationally famous last name was a private figure, said the U.S. Supreme Court, even though she gave news conferences during her divorce trial.[37]

In summary, a public official or public figure must show evidence that the fault of the news medium amounted to *actual malice:* knowledge that the communication was false or reckless disregard as to its truth or falsity. A private individual who sues for libel must bring evidence that the fault amounted at least to *negligence* by the news medium. In the absence of some evidence of the appropriate level of fault, a libel suit will no more "stick" (be accepted for trial) than if there is no publication, identification, or defamation. Many courts have rejected libel suits and discharged them without trial (granted "summary judgment" to the defendant) for this defect. Fault and summary judgment will be treated further in Chapter 5.

"Actual Injury"

Finally, there is the fifth element that needs to be pleaded by a plaintiff in a libel suit: "actual injury." The private-person plaintiff must demonstrate loss or reputational injury of some kind. Actual injury may include a showing in court of out-of-pocket money loss, of impairment of reputation and standing in the community, of personal humiliation, and of mental anguish and suffering, as the Supreme Court of the United States said in Gertz v. Robert Welch, Inc.[38]

---

[36] Foster v. Laredo Newspapers, Inc., 19 TX S.Ct.Jrnl. 390, 541 S.W.2d 809 (1976), cert. denied 429 U.S. 1123, 97 S.Ct. 1160 (1977).

[37] Time, Inc. v. Firestone, 424 U.S. 448, 96 S.Ct. 958 (1976).

[38] 418 U.S. 323, 348–350, 94 S.Ct. 2997, 3011–3012 (1974).

SEC. 18.   LIBELOUS WORDS CLASSIFIED

Five categories or kinds of words may be identified in organizing the field of libel. (Libel also may be classified according to libel *per se,* or words defamatory on their face; and libel *per quod,* or words defamatory when facts extrinsic to the story make them damaging. See Sec. 23.)

Danger signals to help journalists avoid libel can be raised by grouping the kinds of statements and the circumstances which have brought suits into classes. A study of reported libel cases found that the large majority of accusations by plaintiffs were that they had been falsely accused of "crime, moral failings, and incompetence in trade or profession." [39]   In the following pages, five categories are used to help clarify that which can bring hatred, ridicule, contempt, loss of esteem, humiliation, or damage in one's trade or profession.

1. Damage to the Esteem or Social Standing in Which One Is Held

Of the various ways in which a person may be lowered in the estimation in which he is held, none has brought as many libel suits as a false charge of crime. The news media cover the police and crime beat daily; the persistent possibility of a mistake in names and addresses is never absent. And the courts hold everywhere that it is libel to charge one erroneously with a crime.

Thus to print falsely that a person is held in jail on a forgery charge,[40] or to say incorrectly that one has illicitly sold or distributed narcotics,[41] is libelous on its face. To say without legal excuse that one made "shakedown attempts" on elected officers,[42] or committed bigamy,[43] perjury,[44] or murder [45] is libelous.

There is no substitute for the ancient admonition to the reporter: "Accuracy always." [46]   Failure to check one more source

[39] Marc Franklin, Winners and Losers and Why: a Study of Defamation Litigation, Am. Bar Foundation Research Journ. 1980, Summer, 499.

[40] Oklahoma Pub. Co. v. Givens, 67 F.2d 62 (10th Cir.1933); Barnett v. Schumacher, 453 S.W.2d 934 (Mo.1970).

[41] Snowden v. Pearl River Broadcasting Corp., 251 So.2d 405 (La.App.1971).

[42] Bianco v. Palm Beach Newspapers, Inc., 381 So.2d 371 (Fla.App.1980), 6 Med.L.Rptr. 1484.

[43] Taylor v. Tribune Pub. Co., 67 Fla. 361, 65 So. 3 (1914); Pitts v. Spokane Chronicle Co., 63 Wash.2d 763, 388 P.2d 976 (1964).

[44] Milan v. Long, 78 W.Va. 102, 88 S.E. 618 (1916); Riss v. Anderson, 304 F.2d 188 (8th Cir.1962).

[45] Shiell v. Metropolis Co., 102 Fla. 794, 136 So. 537 (1931); Frechette v. Special Magazines, 285 App.Div. 174, 136 N.Y.S.2d 448 (1954).

[46] For a classic mixup in names: Francis v. Lake Charles American Press, 262 La. 875, 265 So.2d 206 (1972).

of information before writing a story based upon a supposedly plausible source has brought many libel suits.

The *Saturday Evening Post* published a story titled "They Call Me Tiger Lil" in its Oct. 26, 1963 issue. The subject was Lillian Reis Corabi, a Philadelphia night club owner and entertainer. The article connected her in various ways with murder and theft, quoting a police captain as saying she and others were responsible for a death by dynamite, and in other ways connecting her with burglary and an apparent drowning. The *Post* argued that the words complained of were not defamatory, but the Pennsylvania Supreme Court upheld the trial judge in his finding some 18 paragraphs of the article "capable of defamatory meaning." It defined defamation as that which "tends so to harm the reputation of another as to lower him in the estimation of the community * * *." [47] The court's decision thus found the elements of libel present in the story, although it agreed with the lower court that because of a grossly excessive award of damages by the jury—$250,000 in compensatory and $500,000 in punitive damages—there should be a new trial. [48]

Nor was the *Post* successful in arguing that libel was not present in a story on Mafia activities on Grand Bahama Island, in which it carried a photo of a group of people including Holmes, a tourist. The photo caption referred to "High–Rollers at the Monte Carlo club," and said that the club's casino grossed $20 million a year with a third "skimmed off for American Mafia 'families'." Holmes, the focal point of the picture and a man in no way connected with Mafia, sued for libel. The *Post,* saying the story was not defamatory, moved for a judgment on the pleadings; but the court held that a jury case was called for and that a jury might find libel. [49]

The failure of a reporter to check the proper source for an address caused an error in identities in a story about a man who pleaded guilty to breaking into business establishments—and the result was a $60,000 libel judgment against a newspaper company. In taking the details of the trial for "breaking" from the court records, the reporter omitted the address of Anthony Liquori of Springfield, the convicted man, and later extracted an address from a telephone book. Unfortunately, the telephone-book address was for a different man of the same name, and, using it, the reporter wrote that Anthony Liquori of 658 Cooper St., Agawam, Mass., had been convicted. The innocent Liquori brought a libel action. The

[47] Corabi v. Curtis Pub. Co., 441 Pa. 432, 273 A.2d 899, 904 (1971).

[48] Corabi v. Curtis Pub. Co., 437 Pa. 143, 262 A.2d 665, 670 (1970). See Sec. 24 of this chapter for a discussion of types of damages awarded in libel cases.

[49] Holmes v. Curtis Pub. Co., 303 F.Supp. 522 (D.S.C.1969).

Massachusetts Appeals Court said that there was negligence in not checking the address with court personnel or the attorney for the accused. The court upheld the jury award of damages.[50]

The news story which states incorrectly that a person has been *convicted* of a crime, as in the Liquori case, may be more dangerous than the one which wrongly suggests or states that he is *accused* of crime. But whatever the difference, the latter can cause libel suits, as we have seen above in the suggestion that Corabi was associated with major crimes.

It should be obvious that one should beware of publishing words imputing sexual acts outside prevailing moral codes, or that falsely state that a woman has been raped. Esteem and social standing, it is plain, are at stake. Courts everywhere regard written or printed statements charging without foundation that a woman is immoral as actionable libel. The charge of indiscretion need not be pronounced; any statement fairly imputing immoral conduct is actionable.[51]

Pat Montandon, author of *How To Be a Party Girl,* was to discuss her book on the Pat Michaels "Discussion" show. *TV Guide* received the show producer's advance release, which said that Montandon and a masked, anonymous prostitute would discuss "From Party–Girl to Call–Girl?" and "How far can the 'party-girl' go until she becomes a 'call-girl'." *TV Guide* ineptly edited the release, deleting reference to the prostitute and publishing this: "10:30 Pat Michaels—*Discussion* 'From Party Girl to Call Girl.' Scheduled guest: TV Personality Pat Montandon and author of 'How to Be a Party Girl'." Montandon sued for libel and won $150,000 in damages.[52]

On the other hand, a woman who posed in the nude for a film maker but later got his agreement not to show the film, was unsuccessful in a libel action following his breaking of the agreement. She charged that his showing of the film to people who knew her caused her shame, disgrace and embarrassment. But the court said that "a film strip which includes a scene of plaintiff posing in the nude does not necessarily impute unchastity", and that it was not libel *per se.*[53]

[50] Liquori v. Republican Co., 8 Mass.App.Ct. 671, 396 N.E.2d 726 (1979), 5 Med.L.Rptr. 2180.

[51] Baird v. Dun & Bradstreet, 446 Pa. 266, 285 A.2d 166 (1971); Wildstein v. New York Post Corp., 40 Misc.2d 586, 243 N.Y.S.2d 386 (1963); Youssoupoff v. Metro–Goldwyn–Mayer, 50 Times L.R. 581, 99 A.L.R. 964 (1934).

[52] Montandon v. Triangle Publications, Inc., 45 Cal.App.3d 938, 120 Cal.Rptr. 186 (1975).

[53] McGraw v. Watkins, 49 A.D.2d 958, 373 N.Y.S.2d 663 (1975). But contra, see Clifford v. Hollander (N.Y.Civ.1980), 6 Med.L.Rptr. 2201, where a photo of a nude woman, identified falsely as that of a woman journalist, was held libelous.

Esteem and social standing can be lowered in the eyes of others by statements concerning political belief and race as well as by those grouped under crime and under sexual immorality in the preceding pages. To take political belief first, many important cases since the late 1940's have largely involved false charges of "Communist" or "Red" or some variant of these words indicating that one subscribes to a generally hated political doctrine. But before these, a line of cases since the 1890's produced libel convictions against those who had labeled others as anarchists, socialists, or fascists.

In the days of Emma Goldman and Big Bill Haywood, it was laid down by the courts that to call one an "anarchist" falsely was libelous; [54] when socialism protested capitalism and America's involvement in World War I, "red-tinted agitator" and "Socialist" were words for which a wronged citizen could recover; [55] In the revulsion against Nazi Germany and Japan during World War II, false accusations of "Fascist" and "pro-Jap" brought libel judgments.[56]

Magazines, columnists, newspapers, and corporations have paid for carelessness indulged in by charging others as "Communist" or "representative for the Communist Party." The "basis for reproach is a belief that such political affiliations constitute a threat to our institutions * * *." [57]

In the famous case of Gertz v. Robert Welch, Inc.,[58] the trial court found that the publication of the John Birch Society had libeled Chicago Attorney Elmer Gertz in charging falsely that he was a "Leninist," a "Communist-fronter," and a member of the "Marxist League for Industrial Democracy." Gertz was awarded $400,000. In another case, where one organization called another "communist dominated" and failed to prove the charge in court, $25,000 was awarded to the plaintiff organization.[59]

Not every insinuation that a person is less than American, however, is libelous. Goodman, a selectman of Ware, Mass.,

[54] Cerveny v. Chicago Daily News Co., 139 Ill. 345, 28 N.E. 692 (1891); Wilkes v. Shields, 62 Minn. 426, 64 N.W. 921 (1895).

[55] Wells v. Times Printing Co., 77 Wash. 171, 137 P. 457 (1913); Ogren v. Rockford Star Printing Co., 288 Ill. 405, 123 N.E. 587 (1919).

[56] Hartley v. Newark Morning Ledger Co., 134 N.J.L. 217, 46 A.2d 777 (1946); Hryhorijiv v. Winchell, 180 Misc. 574, 45 N.Y.S.2d 31 (1943).

[57] Anon., "Supplement," 171 A.L.R. 709, 712 (1947). Grant v. Reader's Digest Ass'n, Inc., 151 F.2d 733 (2d Cir.1945). And see Wright v. Farm Journal, 158 F.2d 976 (2d Cir.1947); Spanel v. Pegler, 160 F.2d 619 (7th Cir.1947); MacLeod v. Tribune Pub. Co., 52 Cal.2d 536, 343 P.2d 36 (1959).

[58] 306 F.Supp. 310 (N.D.Ill.1969); 418 U.S. 323, 94 S.Ct. 2997 (1974).

[59] Utah State Farm Bureau Federation v. National Farmers Union Service Corp., 198 F.2d 20 (10th Cir.1952). See also Cahill v. Hawaiian Paradise Park Corp., 56 Haw. 522, 543 P.2d 1356 (1975).

phoned a call-in radio talk-show of the Central Broadcasting Corp. station, WARE, to explain his opposition to a proposed contract for the local police union, at issue in the town prior to a citizen vote on the matter.   During his extended and agitated discussion, he said that " * * * if we do not get together and stop the inroad of communism, something will happen."   A libel suit was brought by the police local's parent union against Central Broadcasting, and the Massachusetts Supreme Judicial Court held that this fragment of Goodman's statement was "mere pejorative rhetoric," and an "unamiable but nonlibelous utterance." [60]

The law of libel's past is racist.   Where the courts held an incorrect racial identification libelous in the United States, the word at issue was usually "Negro" or some variant thereof and the locale generally below the Mason–Dixon line.   Although it is to be hoped that no American court could issue such a judgment today, at least as far back as 1791 and as recently as 1954, cases in the South allowed whites to recover damages for being called Negro or black. [61]

Finally, there are many words among those lowering esteem or social standing that defy classifying.   Appellations that may be common enough in the excited conversation of neighborhood gossips can turn to actionable libel when reduced to print or writing. It has been held actionable on its face to print and publish that one is "a liar," [62] "a skunk," [63] or "a scandalmonger"; [64] "a drunkard," [65] "a hypocrite," [66] or "a hog"; [67] or to call one heartless and neglectful of his family. [68]   Other actionable epithets include linking a person to a swastika symbol, [69] or calling one a "despicable human being," [70] or a "bitch" (implying a woman is a prostitute). [71]   Name-

[60] National Ass'n of Government Employees, Inc. v. Central Broadcasting Corp., 379 Mass. 220, 396 N.E.2d 996 (1979).   Also McAuliffe v. Local Union No. 3, 29 N.Y.S.2d 963 (Sup.1941); McGraw v. Webster, 79 N.M. 104, 440 P.2d 296 (1968); "pro-Castro," Menendez v. Key West Newspaper Corp., 293 So.2d 751 (Fla.App. 1974).

[61] See, e.g., Eden v. Legare, 1 Bay 171 (1791); Strauder v. West Virginia, 100 U.S. (10 Otto) 303 (1879); Jones v. R.L. Polk & Co., 190 Ala. 243, 67 So. 577 (1915); Natchez Times Pub. Co. v. Dunigan, 221 Miss. 320, 72 So.2d 681 (1954).

[62] Melton v. Bow, 241 Ga. 629, 247 S.E.2d 100 (1978); Paxton v. Woodward, 31 Mont. 195, 78 P. 215 (1904); Smith v. Lyons, 142 La. 975, 77 So. 896 (1917); contra, Bennett v. Transamerican Press, 298 F.Supp. 1013 (S.D.Iowa 1969); Calloway v. Central Charge Service, 142 U.S.App.D.C. 259, 440 F.2d 287 (1971).

[63] Massuere v. Dickens, 70 Wis. 83, 35 N.W. 349 (1887).

[64] Patton v. Cruce, 72 Ark. 421, 81 S.W. 380 (1904).

[65] Giles v. State, 6 Ga. 276 (1848); cf. Smith v. Fielden, 205 Tenn. 313, 326 S.W.2d 476 (1959).

[66] Overstreet v. New Nonpareil Co., 184 Iowa 485, 167 N.W. 669 (1918).

[67] Solverson v. Peterson, 64 Wis. 198, 25 N.W. 14 (1885).

[68] Brown v. Du Frey, 1 N.Y.2d 190, 151 N.Y.S.2d 649, 134 N.E.2d 469 (1956).

[69] Mullenmeister v. Snap–On Tools, 587 F.Supp. 868 (S.D.N.Y.1984).

[70] Smith v. McMullen, 589 F.Supp. 642 (S.D.Tex.1984).

[71] Stone v. Brooks, 253 Ga. 565, 322 S.E.2d 728 (1984).

calling where private citizens are concerned is occasionally the kind of news that makes a lively paragraph, but the alert and responsible reporter recognizes it for what it is and decides whether to use it on better grounds than its titillation value.

2. Damage Through Ridicule

It is pointless to try to draw a narrow line to separate words that ridicule from those that lower esteem and social standing. That which ridicules may at times have the effect of damaging social standing. Yet that which attempts to satirize, or which makes an individual appear uncommonly foolish, or makes fun of misfortune has a quality distinct enough to serve as its own warning signal.

Ridicule must be more than a simple joke at another's expense, for life cannot be so grim that the thin-skinned, the solemn, and the self-important may demand to go entirely unharried. But when the jocular barb penetrates too deeply or carries too sharp a sting, or when a picture can be interpreted in a deeply derogatory manner, ridicule amounting to actionable libel may have occurred.

To sensationalize the poverty of a woman so as to bring her into ridicule and contempt, and to make a joke out of the desertion of a bride on her wedding day [72] have been held libelous. A famed case arose from a photo in an advertisement that accidentally gave the illusion of a "fantastic and lewd deformity" of a steeplechaser holding a riding crop.[73]

Yet there is room for satire and exaggeration. *Boston Magazine* published a page titled "Best and Worst Sports," including the categories "sports announcer," "local ski slopes," and "sexy athlete," some categories plainly waggish, some straightforward and complimentary. Under "sports announcer," the best was named and given kudos; and then appeared: "*Worst:* Jimmy Myers, Channel 4. The only newscaster in town who is enrolled in a course for remedial speaking." Myers sued, lost at trial for failure to establish defamation, and appealed.[74]

The Massachusetts Supreme Judicial Court described the appearance of the magazine's page, with its title, lampooning cartoons, and a mood of rough humor in the words, including "one-liners" and preposterous propositions under such titles as "Sports

[72] Moffatt v. Cauldwell, 3 Hun. 26, 5 Thomp. & C. 256 (N.Y.1874), but "poverty" and "unemployment" have been held not actionable words: Sousa v. Davenport, 3 Mass.App.Ct. 715, 323 N.E.2d 910 (1975); Kirman v. Sun Printing & Pub. Ass'n, 99 App.Div. 367, 91 N.Y.S. 193 (1904).

[73] Burton v. Crowell Pub. Co., 82 F.2d 154 (2d Cir.1936).

[74] Myers v. Boston Magazine Co., Inc., 380 Mass. 336, 403 N.E.2d 376 (Mass.Sup. Jud.Ct.1980), 6 Med.L.Rptr. 1241.

Groupie." It ruled that the statement about Myers made on such a page would not reasonably be understood by a reader to be an assertion of fact. "Taken in context, it can reasonably be considered to suggest that Myers should have been so enrolled," even though the words read "is enrolled." The words stated "a critical judgment, an opinion." And since Myers was himself available to the critic's audience, being often on view, his performances were in line with the rule that facts underlying opinions could be assumed—the performances "furnished the assumed facts from which the critic fashioned his barb." The court said that words such as these are meant to "sting and be quickly forgotten". Although for the plaintiff who "is the victim of ridicule, the forgetting may not be easy," the law refuses to find a statement of fact where none has been uttered. This was opinion, and if such "is based on assumed, nondefamatory facts, the First Amendment forbids the law of libel from redressing the injury." [75]

While a living man whose obituary has mistakenly been printed may feel annoyed and injured, and may attract unusual attention and perhaps a rough joke or two as he walks into his office the next morning, he has not been libeled. As one court said, death "is looked for in the history of every man," and where there is notice of a death that has not occurred, "Prematurity is the sole peculiarity." [76] Yet an erroneous report of death has been held to be the cause of an action for "negligent infliction of emotional distress"—an injury closely related to defamation.[77]

3. Damage Through Words Imputing Disease or Mental Illness

The law has long held that diseases which may be termed "loathsome, infectious, or contagious" may be libelous when falsely attributed to an individual. That which is "loathsome" may change with time and changing mores, of course, but venereal disease, the plague, leprosy, small pox and AIDS to fit this description. Anyone alleged to be at present suffering from any of these diseases is likely to be shunned by associates. And if the disease carries the stigma of immorality, such as venereal disease or alcoholism or addiction, it may be libelous to say of persons that they formerly had it, although they have since overcome it.

To charge without legal excuse that one has leprosy was held libelous in Lewis v. Hayes; the imputation of venereal disease was

[75] Ibid., 1243, 1245.

[76] Cohen v. New York Times Co., 153 App.Div. 242, 138 N.Y.S. 206 (1912); Cardiff v. Brooklyn Eagle, Inc., 190 Misc. 730, 75 N.Y.S.2d 222 (1948).

[77] Rubinstein v. New York Post Corp. (N.Y.Sup.Ct.1983), 9 Med.L.Rptr. 1581. Emotional distress is treated in Sec. 20, below.

held libelous in *King v. Pillsbury*.[78] An incorrect assignment of mental impairment or of mental illness to a person is libel on its face.[79] The magazine *Fact* published in its September–October issue of 1964, an article billed as "The Unconscious of a Conservative: A Special Issue on the Mind of Barry Goldwater." Goldwater was the Republican Party's candidate for president and a senator from Arizona at the time. He was portrayed in one of two articles as "paranoid," his attacks on other politicians stemming from a conviction that "everybody hates him, and it is better to attack them first." A *Fact* poll of psychiatrists, asked to judge whether Goldwater was psychologically fit to serve as president, also was reported on. A jury found libel and awarded Goldwater $1.00 in compensatory damages and $75,000 in punitive damages.[80]

4. Damaging One in a Trade, Occupation, or Profession

So long as one follows a legal calling, he has a claim not to be defamed unfairly in the performance of it. The possibilities are rich for damaging one through words that impugn honesty, skill, fitness, ethical standards, or financial capacity in his chosen work, whether it be banking or basket-weaving. Observe some of the possibilities: that a University was a "degree mill;"[81] that a contractor engaged in unethical trade;[82] that a clergyman was "an interloper, a meddler, a spreader of distrust;"[83] that a schoolmaster kept girls after school so that he could court them;[84] that a jockey rode horses unfairly and dishonestly;[85] that an attorney was incompetent,[86] and that a corporation director embezzled.[87]

By no means every statement to which a businessman, tradesman or professional takes exception, however, is libelous. Thus Frederick D. Washington, a church bishop, sued the *New York Daily News* and columnist Robert Sylvester for his printed statement that Washington had attended a nightclub performance at

---

[78] 165 Cal. 527, 132 P. 1022 (1913); King v. Pillsbury, 115 Me. 528, 99 A. 513 (1917); Sally v. Brown, 220 Ky. 576, 295 S.W. 890 (1927).

[79] Cowper v. Vannier, 20 Ill.App.2d 499, 156 N.E.2d 761 (1959); Kenney v. Hatfield, 351 Mich. 498, 88 N.W.2d 535 (1958). But not in Virginia: Mills v. Kingsport Times–News, 475 F.Supp. 1005 (W.D.Va.1979), 5 Med.L.Rptr. 2288.

[80] Goldwater v. Ginzburg, 414 F.2d 324 (2d Cir.1969).

[81] Laurence University v. State, 68 Misc.2d 408, 326 N.Y.S.2d 617 (1971). Reversed on grounds that State official's words were absolutely privileged, 41 A.D.2d 463, 344 N.Y.S.2d 183 (1973).

[82] Greenbelt Co-op. Pub. Ass'n v. Bresler, 253 Md. 324, 252 A.2d 755 (1969), reversed on other grounds 398 U.S. 6, 90 S.Ct. 1537 (1970).

[83] Van Lonkhuyzen v. Daily News Co., 195 Mich. 283, 161 N.W. 979 (1917).

[84] Spears v. McCoy, 155 Ky. 1, 159 S.W. 610 (1913).

[85] Wood v. Earl of Durham, 21 Q.B. 501 (1888).

[86] Hahn v. Andrello, 44 A.D.2d 501, 355 N.Y.S.2d 850 (1974).

[87] Weenig v. Wood, 169 Ind.App. 413, 349 N.E.2d 235 (1976).

which a choir member of his church sang. The bishop argued that
his church did not approve of its spiritual leaders' attending night-
clubs, and that he had been damaged. The court said the account
was not, on its face, an attack on the plaintiff's integrity, and called
the item a "warm human interest story" in which there was
general interest. This was not libel on its face and the court
upheld dismissal of Bishop Washington's complaint.[88]

Nor did David Brown convince the court that there was libel in
a pamphlet that opposed his attempt to get a zoning change from
the City Council of Knoxville, Tenn. The pamphlet attacked a
change that would have permitted Brown to build apartments in a
residential district, and asked the question: "Have the 'Skids Been
Greased' at City Council?" Brown sued for libel, arguing that the
question suggested he had bribed the City Council and that it had
accepted the bribe. But the court held that the question did not
suggest bribery in its reasonable and obvious meaning; but rather,
that pressure in the form of political influence had been brought to
bear on certain Council members to expedite matters. This was
not libel. Had the pamphlet said that "palms are greased at the
City Council," that would have been libel on its face and actionable.[89]

A margin of protection also exists in the occasional finding by a
court that mistakenly attributing a single instance of clumsiness or
error to a professional man is not enough to damage him. Rather,
such cases have held, there must be a suggestion of more general
incompetency or lack of quality before a libel charge will hold. One
court said: [90]

> To charge a professional man with negligence or uns-
> killfulness in the management or treatment of an individu-
> al case, is no more than to impute to him the mistakes and
> errors incident to fallible human nature. The most emi-
> nent and skillful physician or surgeon may mistake the
> symptoms of a particular case without detracting from his
> general professional skill or learning. To say of him,
> therefore, that he was mistaken in that case would not be
> calculated to impair the confidence of the community in
> his general professional competency.

[88] Washington v. New York News Inc., 37 A.D.2d 557, 322 N.Y.S.2d 896 (1971).

[89] Brown v. Newman, 224 Tenn. 297, 454 S.W.2d 120 (1970). An official who
resigned from a "financially troubled bank" was not libeled: Bordoni v. New York
Times Co., Inc., 400 F.Supp. 1223 (S.D.N.Y.1975).

[90] Blende v. Hearst Publications, 200 Wash. 426, 93 P.2d 733 (1939); November v.
Time Inc., 13 N.Y.2d 175, 244 N.Y.S.2d 309, 194 N.E.2d 126 (1963); Holder Const.
Co. v. Ed Smith & Sons, Inc., 124 Ga.App. 89, 182 S.E.2d 919 (1971). But see Cohn
v. Am–Law, Inc. (N.Y.Sup.Ct.1980), 5 Med.L.Rptr. 2367, where defamation was
found in a magazine story saying an attorney went "unprepared" to a single
hearing.

5. Damage to a Corporation's Integrity, Credit, or Ability to Carry on Business

It is possible to damage the reputation of a corporation or partnership by defamation that reflects on the conduct, management, or financial condition of the corporation.[91]   To say falsely that a company is in shaky financial condition, or that it cannot pay its debts, would be libelous, as would the imputation that it has engaged in dishonest practices.   While a corporation is an entity quite different from the individuals that head it or staff it, there is no doubt that it has a reputation, an "image" to protect.

Publishing or broadcasting casual statements that a business or corporation is "broke" or "going bankrupt" or "has a rotten credit rating" can be risky business indeed unless you are prepared to prove the truth of such statements in court.   When Dun & Bradstreet—which is in the business of giving credit ratings—published erroneous information indicating falsely that a Greenmoss Builders had filed for bankruptcy, that was held to be defamatory.   Both the Vermont courts and the United States Supreme Court agreed that a $350,000 award should be paid to the building firm.[92]

Charging dishonest or unethical behavior by a firm can also result in a successful defamation suit.   Although tobacco companies have received much flak, the Chicago TV station WBBM—owned by the CBS Network—found in 1988 that such a firm could still be libeled.   The Supreme Court denied *certiorari,* leaving intact a $3 million damage award in the case of Brown & Williamson Tobacco Corp. v. Jacobson and CBS, Inc.

Back in 1981, Jacobson had delivered a "Perspective" report denouncing the makers of Viceroy cigarettes for hiring advertising "slicksters" to create an advertising strategy to "hook" the young. The strategy used by Brown & Williamson, Jacobson said, was taken from a report recommending that smoking be portrayed to youth as a kind of rite of passage involving wearing a bra or shaving, or drinking wine or beer.   The broadcast added up to an accusation of unethical youth-oriented advertising by Brown & Williamson for its Viceroy cigarettes, thus endangering the health of the impressionable young.[93]   That huge judgment—one of the

---

[91] Dupont Engineering Co. v. Nashville Banner Pub. Co., 13 F.2d 186 (D.C.Tenn. 1925); Electric Furnace Corp. v. Deering Milliken Research Corp., 325 F.2d 761 (6th Cir.1963); Golden Palace, Inc. v. National Broadcasting Co., Inc., 386 F.Supp. 107 (D.D.C.1974).

[92] Dun & Bradstreet, Inc. v. Greenmoss Builders, Inc., 472 U.S. 749, 105 S.Ct. 2939 (1985).

[93] Certiorari denied 485 U.S. 993, 108 S.Ct. 1302 (1988), upholding the judgment of the United States Court of Appeals, Seventh Circuit. See 827 F.2d 1119 (7th Cir.1987) 14 Med.L.Rptr. 1497.

largest media libel awards to survive appeals—is only part of the story. The case of Brown & Williamson v. CBS provides multiple lessons about things journalists should not do.

This Walter Jacobson report attacking the cigarette manufacturer was said to be based on a "confidential report in the files of the federal government." Such a report did exist in the files of the Federal Trade Commission (FTC); it had been prepared by a research firm working for Ted Bates & Co., an ad agency once employed by Viceroy Cigarettes' parent company, Brown & Williamson.

At one point, a *confidential* FTC report had assumed, evidently erroneously, that Viceroy had adopted a "hook the young" ad strategy. A researcher for the CBS station—Michael Radutzky— had learned of the FTC report from a newspaper article, and even received copies of some pages of that report. However, Radutzky couldn't persuade FTC staffers to send him copies of the confidential report; the staffers would only "confirm that the report and its findings were accurate."

The FTC's ambiguous response to Radutzky, however, was contradicted directly by a Thomas Humber, a spokesman for Brown & Williamson. Humber told Radutzky that Brown & Williamson had rejected the strategy suggested in documents submitted by the Ted Bates ad agency.[94]

> Humber stated [to Radutzky, according to Humber's notes] that the proposals referred to in the FTC report were similar to a proposed libelous story that a young inexperienced reporter might submit to his editors but that it was corrected by a news organization's editors and attorneys. Humber stated that in such a case no legitimate criticism could be leveled at the news organization.

In response to a request from Jacobson, researcher Radutzky had searched unsuccessfully for "pot, wine, beer and sex" ads for Viceroy cigarettes. Radutzky had made lengthy notes as he conducted interviews and read those pages of the FTC report provided to him by a newspaper reporter. Radutzky also made handwritten entries on the margins of the FTC report pages he had, and also developed an 18–page sample script.

The jury, however, never saw this work by Radutzky. Before the trial, Radutzky "destroyed all of his contemporaneous interview notes, five of the ten pages of the FTC report ... and fifteen of the

---

[94] Brown & Williamson Tobacco Corp. v. Jacobson, 827 F.2d 1119, 1123 (7th Cir.1987).

original eighteen pages of the sample script." [95]

Radutzky testified that he had destroyed those materials while "housecleaning" after a district court had dismissed an original Brown & Williamson libel complaint. The lawsuit, however, was later reinstated and, as the Court of Appeals noted, the destruction of materials violated CBS policy. The Court of Appeals concluded that Brown & Williamson had proved "by clear and convincing evidence that the defendants either knew the Perspective [Jacobson's commentary] was false or in fact entertained serious doubts as to its truth," thus allowing the district court jury's verdict against the TV station to stand. Furthermore, "[t]he most compelling evidence of actual malice submitted to the jury was the intentional destruction of critical documents by Jacobson's researcher...." [96]

A number of lessons may be taken from this case, including:

(1) Let a story's facts determine its conclusions, not the other way around.

(2) Try to present "both sides" or "several sides" of a controversy. It is dangerous for a reporter or a commentator to decide that only one side of an issue should be presented.

(3) Publishers and broadcasters need to develop clear policies about preparation of news or commentary reports. In any event, once a legal proceeding has started ... and until it has concluded, beyond possibility of re-filing or appeal—notes, memos, tapes, or videotapes may not be destroyed safely.

SEC. 19.   OPINION AND RHETORICAL HYPERBOLE

In defining "libel," many abusive words arising in heated controversies are treated as statements of opinion, or rhetorical hyperbole, and as such are not libelous.

Courts have increasingly come to rule that the agitated, heated dialogue of encounters such as political controversy and labor dispute deserve strong protection against libel actions when it is reported in the media. Rich name-calling that grows out of spirited and hot argument is protected because it is essentially opinion, or it is "rhetorical hyperbole"—extravagant or fanciful exaggeration.

As for opinion, the rule takes force from the Supreme Court's

[95] Ibid.; see Stuart Taylor, Jr., "Justices Uphold $3 million Libel Award on CBS," The New York Times, April 4, 1988.

[96] Ibid.

statement in Gertz v. Robert Welch, Inc. in 1974: [97] "Under the First Amendment there is no such thing as a false idea." However, as discussed in Sec. 35, the 1990 *Milkovich* case has diluted the opinion defense; opinions not supported by facts can be actionable.

In the *Old Dominion* case of 1974,[98] shortly after *Gertz* was decided, the Supreme Court found that the word "scabs" applied by publications of union letter-carriers against named, non-union letter-carriers was opinion, and not libel. The publications were used in on-going efforts to organize remaining non-union people. In a long statement accompanying the names, the publication used many pejorative terms in defining "scab," including "traitor." The named non-union people brought a libel action and were awarded damages which were upheld by the Virginia Supreme Court. The union appealed, and the United States Supreme Court reversed the verdict, 6–3, Justice Marshall writing the majority opinion. He reviewed the verbal rough-and-tumble of labor organizing dispute, and cited precedent that had refused to consider this language libel. Speaking of the union publication's definition of the word "scab," derived partly from an old description of scabs by the novelist Jack London, he said: [99]

> The definition's use of words like "traitor" cannot be construed as representations of fact.... Such words were obviously used here in a loose, figurative sense to demonstrate the union's strong disagreement with the views of those workers who oppose unionization. Expression of such an opinion, even in the most pejorative terms is protected * * *.

It was opinion that brought a libel suit against reporter Jack Newfield and his publisher, for charges against New York Judge Dominic Rinaldi in Newfield's Book, *Cruel and Unusual Justice*. Newfield called Rinaldi one of New York's 10 worst judges, and in detailed, illustrative cases about the judge's work, said that large-scale heroin dealers and people close to organized crime got lenient treatment from the judge, while blacks and Puerto Ricans received long sentences. Newfield called for Rinaldi's removal from the bench. Rinaldi sued. Newfield and his publisher eventually won a

[97] 418 U.S. 323, 339–340, 94 S.Ct. 2997, 3007 (1974). Opinion is treated in detail in Sec. 35, Chap. 6, below.

[98] Old Dominion Branch No. 496, National Ass'n of Letter Carriers, AFL–CIO v. Austin, 418 U.S. 264, 94 S.Ct. 2770 (1974).

[99] Ibid., at 284, 94 S.Ct. at 2781.

summary judgment (i.e., a decision in their favor without going to trial).[1]

Newfield's attacks on Rinaldi were largely opinion, the New York Court of Appeals found, and the facts supporting them were set forth in the book. The court quoted Gertz v. Welch, "there is no such thing as a false idea", and added that opinions "false or not, libelous or not, are constitutionally privileged and may not be the subject of private damage actions provided that the facts supporting the opinion are set forth." The free flow of information to the people concerning the performance of their public officials is essential. "Erroneous opinion must be protected so that debate on public issues may remain robust and unfettered." [2]

At the same time that Justice Marshall ruled in *Old Dominion* (above, Sec. 18) that statements of opinion in such agitated circumstances were not to be held libelous, he also characterized the words as no more than "rhetorical hyperbole": " * * * Jack London's 'definition of a scab' is merely rhetorical hyperbole, a hasty and imaginative expression of the contempt felt by union members toward those who refuse to join." [3] Hyperbole earlier had been described as not libelous in the *Greenbelt* case, decided in 1970 by the Supreme Court.[4] Real estate developer Charles Bresler was petitioning the Greenbelt, Md., City Council for zoning changes that would allow him to build high-density housing on some of his land. Simultaneously, the city was trying to buy a tract of Bresler's land on which to build a school.

As the Supreme Court said, the situation provided Bresler and the council with much bargaining leverage against each other. Community controversy arose over the matter, and several tumultuous city council meetings were held at which citizens emphatically spoke their minds. The *Greenbelt News Review* reported the meetings at length, including charges by citizens that Bresler's negotiating position was "blackmail," and a case of "unethical trade." Bresler sued and a jury awarded him a total of $17,000 in compensatory and punitive damages. The Maryland Court of Appeals upheld the judgment, and the newspaper took its case to the United States Supreme Court, which reversed the lower courts. The *News Review*, it said, was performing its function as a community newspaper when it published the reports. The reports were

---

[1] Rinaldi v. Holt, Rinehart & Winston, Inc., 42 N.Y.2d 369, 397 N.Y.S.2d 943, 366 N.E.2d 1299 (1977), certiorari denied 434 U.S. 969, 98 S.Ct. 514 (1977), 2 Med. L.Rptr. 2169.

[2] Ibid., at 380; 366 N.E.2d at 2173; see Gertz v. Welch, 418 U.S. 323, 340, 94 S.Ct. 2997, 3007 (1974).

[3] Old Dominion Branch No. 496, National Ass'n of Letter Carriers, AFL–CIO v. Austin, 418 U.S. 264, 2782, 94 S.Ct. 2770, 2782 (1974).

[4] Greenbelt Cooperative Pub. Ass'n v. Bresler, 398 U.S. 6, 90 S.Ct. 1537 (1970).

accurate, full and fair, with Bresler's proposal given proper coverage. The court said: [5]

> It is simply impossible to believe that a reader who reached the word "blackmail" in either article would not have understood exactly what was meant: it was Bresler's public and wholly legal negotiating proposals that were being criticized. No reader could have thought that either the speakers at the meeting or the newspaper articles reporting their words were charging Bresler with the commission of a criminal offense.

To find libel for such rhetorical hyperbole, the Court said, would "subvert the most fundamental meaning of a free press, protected by the First and Fourteenth Amendments."

Numerous decisions following *Greenbelt* and *Letter Carriers* have found words in similar settings to be matters of opinion or hyperbole, and sometimes both as Justice Marshall did in the latter. In the *Myers* decision (above, p. 118), "the only sports announcer enrolled in a course for remedial speaking" was ruled to be opinion and "rhetorical license." In a Missouri case, the Court of Appeals has ruled that "sleazy sleight-of-hand" written by a newspaper of an attorney was opinion and not libelous.[6]

In other cases, however, defendants have asserted that their words were hyperbole or opinion without success. The United States Labor Party published a leaflet opposing a candidate for the Baltimore City Council, charging him with a "SS [Nazi] background" and asserting that he had associations with the Gestapo—charges which, in a libel suit, won $30,000 for the plaintiff. On appeal, the Labor Party argued that its words were merely "rhetorical hyperbole" and so not libelous. But the Maryland Supreme Court said no: Rhetorical hyperbole exists only when a reader could not possibly understand the statement to be a fact—and the general public which saw the leaflet had nothing to prevent its understanding that the words did not mean what they said.[7] Similarly, a California court refused to agree that it was either opinion or hyperbole where the newsletter of a citizens' group charged a councilman with "outright extortion" and "blackmail." [8]

[5] Ibid.

[6] Anton v. St. Louis Suburban Newspapers, Inc., 598 S.W.2d 493 (Mo.App.1980).

[7] U.S. Labor Party v. Whitman, 442 U.S. 919, 99 S.Ct. 2842 (1979).

[8] Good Government Group of Seal Beach v. Superior Court, 22 Cal.3d 672, 150 Cal.Rptr. 258, 586 P.2d 572 (1978); McManus v. Doubleday & Co., Inc., 513 F.Supp. 1383 (S.D.N.Y.1981), 7 Med.L.Rptr. 1475.

SEC. 20.   EMOTIONAL DISTRESS
AND MENTAL ANGUISH

Accompanying libel's damage to reputation is a newer partner whose presence in recent years has become a disagreeable reality for libel defendants, even though it remains an infrequent visitor.[9] Widely termed intentional or negligent "infliction of emotional distress," it refers to the power of words and pictures to carry psychological, rather than reputational harm. A tort separate from defamation in many states, it exists in other states as part of the law of defamation. Thus Justice Powell of the United States Supreme Court said, in discussing harmful components of defamatory falsehood in the 1974 *Gertz* case, that among them are "personal humiliation, and mental anguish and suffering." [10]

Mary Alice Firestone's suit for libel—against *Time* magazine for an erroneous report that her husband had won his divorce action on grounds of adultery—was allowed even though she had withdrawn her claim for harm to reputation before trial. She won a judgment for $100,000, in other words, for emotional anguish.[11] The much-publicized case of Carol Burnett followed, in which she recovered damages in a libel suit against the National Enquirer, almost entirely for emotional distress over the magazine's portrayal of her as "drunk, rude, uncaring and abusive" at a restaurant.[12]

Hustler Magazine v. Falwell (1988)

In the mid–1980s, the emerging separate tort of infliction of mental injury offered a major threat to the press. But in 1988, that threat was lessened by the U.S. Supreme Court's decision in Hustler v. Falwell, which held that the First Amendment protects parodies—even Hustler magazine's mock ad which said Rev. Falwell's first sexual experience had been in an outhouse, with his mother, while she was drunk.

Following what then seemed to be a trend, Rev. Falwell sued Hustler magazine and its publisher, Larry Flynt, for libel *plus* invasion of privacy *plus* intentional infliction of emotional distress.

Not surprisingly, even though the fine print said "ad parody— not to be taken seriously"—a U.S. district court jury was sympathetic to Rev. Falwell. (After all, Flynt had declared, while giving a pre-trial deposition, that his intent in publishing the parody was to

---

[9] Terrance C. Mead, "Suing Media for Emotional Distress," 23 Washburn Law Journ. 24, Fall 1983. Mead found only 18 cases in which emotional distress was part of libel actions, out of 484 against media defendants between 1977 and 1981. See David A. Anderson, Reputation, Compensation, and Proof, 25 William and Mary L.Rev. # 5, 1983–84, 747, 756–64.

[10] Gertz v. Robert Welch, Inc., 418 U.S. 323, 349–350, 94 S.Ct. 2997, 3011–3012 (1974).

[11] Time, Inc. v. Firestone, 424 U.S. 448, 460, 96 S.Ct. 958, 968 (1976).

[12] Burnett v. National Enquirer (Cal.Sup.1981), 7 Med.L.Rptr. 1321.

"assassinate" the minister's reputation.)[13] Sympathetic or not, the jury found that Falwell had not been libeled: "no reasonable person would believe that the parody was describing actual facts about Falwell." The jury also declined to find that his privacy had been invaded. Jurors, however, seized upon the idea of infliction of mental injury and awarded Falwell $200,000: $100,000 in compensatory damages, plus $50,000 in punitive damages against Flynt and $50,000 against his magazine.

The Court of Appeals, Fourth Circuit—like the trial court— concluded that Rev. Falwell was a public figure.[14] That public figure status meant that defendants Flynt and Hustler Magazine were entitled "to the same level of first amendment protection in an action for intentional infliction of mental distress that they would receive in an action for libel."[15] Even so, the Court of Appeals found the ad parody so offensive that it affirmed the trial court's ruling.[16] The U.S. Supreme Court disagreed.

Chief Justice William Rehnquist defined the issue as whether the First Amendment limits a state's authority to protect its citizens from intentional infliction of mental distress. He wrote, "We must decide whether a public figure may recover damages for emotional harm caused to him by an ad parody offensive to him, and doubtless gross and repugnant in the eyes of most."[17]

To the surprise of many, Chief Justice Rehnquist then set about a sweeping re-affirmation of First Amendment principles— principles which he has questioned or derided in other cases.[18] He wrote approvingly of the free flow of ideas and opinions on matters of public interest as being at the heart of the First Amendment. " '[T]he freedom to speak one's mind is not only an aspect of individual liberty—and thus a good unto itself—but also is essential to the common quest for truth and the vitality of society as a whole.' "[19]

Chief Justice Rehnquist wrote that under the First Amendment robust political debate will result in speech critical of public officials or public figures who are " 'intimately involved in the

[13] David Margolick, "Some See Threat in Non–Libel Verdict of Falwell," The New York Times, Dec. 10, 1986, p. 6.

[14] Hustler Magazine v. Falwell, 485 U.S. 46, 108 S.Ct. 876 (1988), 14 Med.L.Rptr. 2281, 2282.

[15] Falwell v. Flynt, 797 F.2d 1270, 1274 (4th Cir.1986), 13 Med.L.Rptr. 1145.

[16] 485 U.S. at 50, 108 S.Ct. at 879, 14 Med.L.Rptr. at 2283.

[17] Ibid.

[18] See, e.g., Rehnquist opinion in Wolston v. Reader's Digest Ass'n, Inc., 443 U.S. 157, 99 S.Ct. 2701 (1979). He there rejected the argument that a person who engages in criminal conduct automatically becomes a limited-purpose public figure. See also his opinion in Time, Inc. v. Firestone, 424 U.S. 448, 96 S.Ct. 958 (1976).

[19] 485 U.S. at 50, 108 S.Ct. at 879, 14 Med.L.Rptr. at 2283.

resolution of important public questions, or, by reason of their fame, shape events in areas of concern to society at large.' " [20]

He emphasized, however, that freedom of expression is not an absolute. The First Amendment does not mean that " ... any speech about public figures is immune from sanction in the form of damages." Although false statements—unknowingly false statements—will be protected to insure breathing space needed to ensure open debate, knowingly or recklessly false statements are valueless and will not be protected.[21]

Rehnquist wrote that the law does not regard an intent to inflict emotional harm with much solicitude. He termed it understandable that most jurisdictions have created civil liability when such conduct is sufficiently outrageous. But Reverend Falwell, powerful individual and sometime candidate for President, was a public figure involved " ... in the world of debate about public affairs, [where] many things done with motives that are less than admirable are protected by the First Amendment." [22]

Chief Justice Rehnquist declared that any system of civil damages that might teach Flynt a lesson would also endanger a long and valued tradition of caustic American political caricatures— verbal and visual—and cartoons. He pointed to the prominent role in political debate played by satire and political cartoons, and to the impact of images enduring over the years: Lincoln's gangly frame, Teddy Roosevelt's glasses and teeth, Franklin D. Roosevelt's cigarette holder and jutting jaw.

Even though Falwell argued that the Hustler magazine parody was so outrageous that it should be deprived of First Amendment protection, the Court disagreed. True, wrote the Chief Justice, "*Hustler* is at best a distant cousin of ... political cartoons ... and a rather poor relation at that." The Chief Justice expressed doubts that a sufficiently precise standard could be found safely to distinguish Flynt's publication from political cartoons in general.[23]

The Falwell case is important. University of Texas law professor David A. Anderson termed it a tremendous victory because it " ' ... cuts off the main avenues of the emotional distress claim' and ' ... because it is such a ringing affirmation of the principles of New York Times v. Sullivan.' " [24]

---

[20] Ibid., quoting Associated Press v. Walker, 388 U.S. 130, 164, 87 S.Ct. 1975, 1996 (1967).

[21] Ibid., 485 U.S. at 52, 108 S.Ct. at 880, 14 Med.L.Rptr. at 2283–2284.

[22] Ibid., 485 U.S. at 52, 108 S.Ct. at 880, 14 L.Rptr. at 2284.

[23] Ibid., 2285.

[24] Margaret G. Carter, "Press Breathes Sigh of Relief after the Falwell Decision," Presstime, April, 1988, p. 34.

Another respected communications lawyer, Robert D. Sack, has written that for there to be a successful emotional distress claim, the conduct must be "extreme and outrageous," [25] must cause severe emotional distress, and must be made with "conscious disregard of a high degree of probability that severe emotional distress will result." [26]

Emotional distress cases that cause trouble for the media often share characteristics of extreme and juror-offending conduct by media employees. And when jurors perceive powerful, arrogant mass media "kicking around" individual citizens, is it any wonder that jury verdicts unfavorable to the media frequently result?

Take the case of Kolegas v. Heftel Broadcasting Co. (1992), a confrontation that arose when two Chicago radio show hosts did a telephone interview with Anthony N. Kolegas. Mr. Kolegas had called station WLUP to promote a cartoon festival he organized, with some of the proceeds to support the Neurofibromatosis Foundation (NF). That foundation works to better the lot of people suffering from the condition commonly called Elephant Man's Disease.

While talking to the hosts, Kolegas mentioned that both his wife and son suffered from NF. The radio show hosts expressed disbelief that there was such a cartoon festival, and one said that Kolegas was "scamming" them. One host then said [27]

"Why would someone marry a woman if she had Elephant Man disease? It's not like he couldn't tell—unless it was a shotgun wedding. * * * If he is producing it [the cartoon festival], he's only producing it part-time. The rest of the time he's too busy picking out their wardrobe ... to make sure they have large hats to cover their big heads ..."

In their lawsuit, Mr. and Mrs. Kolegas said they had not had a "shotgun wedding," nor did Mrs. Kolegas or their son have abnormally large heads. The Illinois Supreme Court held that there was sufficient evidence of conduct not protected by the First Amendment to take this emotional distress case to trial against station WLUP–Chicago.

SEC. 21. THE FORM OF THE LIBEL

Damage may be caused by any part of the medium's content, including headlines, pictures and advertisements.

[25] Sack, p. 676, citing Kolegas v. Heftel Broadcasting Co., 154 Ill.2d 1, 180 Ill.Dec. 307, 607 N.E.2d 20 (1992), 20 Med.L.Rptr. 2105, 2106.

[26] Sack, p. 677.

[27] Kolegas v. Heftel Broadcasting Co., 154 Ill.2d 1, 180 Ill.Dec. 307, 607 N.E.2d 201 (1992), 20 Med.L.Rptr. 2105, 1206.

Whatever is printed or broadcast is disseminated at the peril of the publisher. A picture may be as libelous as words; a headline, in some states, may be libelous even though modified or negated by the story that follows. Libelous copy in an advertisement leaves the publisher liable along with the merchant or advertising agency that furnished it.

A 1956 decision explains how headlines and closing "tag-lines" of a news story can be libelous (even though in this case the newspaper defended itself successfully). One story in a series published by the *Las Vegas Sun* brought a libel suit because of its headline and closing tag-line advertising the next article in the series. The headline read "Babies for Sale. Franklin Black Market Trade of Child Told." The tag-line promoting the story to appear the next day read "Tomorrow–Blackmail by Franklin." The body of the story told factually the way in which attorney Franklin had obtained a mother's release of her child for adoption. Franklin sued for libel and won. But the *Sun* appealed, claiming among other things that the trial judge had erred in instructing the jury that the words were libelous. The *Sun* said that the language was ambiguous, and susceptible of more than one interpretation.

But the Nevada Supreme Court[28] said that the headline and tag-line were indeed libelous. Under any reasonable definition, it said, "black market sale" and "blackmail" "would tend to lower the subject in the estimation of the community and to excite derogatory opinions against him and hold him up to contempt." Then it explained the part the headline played in the libel: [29]

> Appellants * * * contend, the headline must be qualified by and read in the light of the article to which it referred and the tag-line must be qualified by and read in the light of the subsequent article to which it referred.
>
> This is not so. The text of a newspaper article is not ordinarily the context of its headline, since the public frequently reads only the headline * * *. The same is true of a tag-line or leader, since the public frequently reads only the leader without reading the subsequent article to which it refers. The defamation of Franklin contained in the headline was complete upon its face * * *. The same is true of the tag-line.

[28] Las Vegas Sun, Inc. v. Franklin, 74 Nev. 282, 329 P.2d 867 (1958). The *Sun* won the appeal on other grounds.

[29] Ibid., at 869. New York and Louisiana follow the same rule: Schermerhorn v. Rosenberg, 73 A.D.2d 276, 426 N.Y.S.2d 274 (1980), 6 Med.L.Rptr. 1376, Forrest v. Lynch, 347 So.2d 1255 (La.App.1977), 3 Med.L.Rptr. 1187. But in some states, the meaning of headline and story *taken together* govern the finding: Ross v. Columbia Newspapers, Inc., 266 S.C. 75, 221 S.E.2d 770 (1976); Sprouse v. Clay Communication, Inc., 158 W.Va. 427, 211 S.E.2d 674 (1975); Adreani v. Hansen, 80 Ill.App.3d 726, 36 Ill.Dec. 259, 400 N.E.2d 679 (1980), 6 Med.L.Rptr. 1015.

The dangers of libel in advertisements, of course, have been suggested in the case of Cosgrove Studio & Camera Shop, Inc. v. Pane, discussed earlier in Section 17.[30] As for pictures, pictures standing alone, without caption or story with them, would rarely pose danger of defamation. But almost invariably in the mass media, illustration is accompanied by words, and it is almost always the combination that carries the damaging impact. In an issue of *Tan,* a story titled "Man Hungry" was accompanied by a picture taken several years earlier in connection with a woman's work as a professional model for a dress designer. With it were the words "She had a good man—but he wasn't enough. So she picked a bad one!" On the cover of the magazine was the title, "Shameless Love."

The woman sued for libel, and the court granted her claim for $3,000. "There is no doubt in this court's mind that the publication libeled plaintiff," the judge wrote. "A publication must be considered in its entirety, both the picture and the story which it illustrates." [31]

During a program broadcast in Albuquerque, N.M. over station KGGM–TV, the secretary of a Better Business Bureau was speaking about dishonest television repairmen. He held up to the camera a newspaper advertisement of the Day and Night Television Service Company. . . . The speaker said that some television servicemen were cheating the public:

> This is what has been referred to in the trade as the ransom. Ransom, the ransom racket. The technique of taking up the stuff after first assuring the set owner that the charges would only be nominal, and then holding the set for ransom. . . .

The New Mexico Supreme Court pointed up the effect of combining the picture and the words: "Standing alone, neither the advertisement nor the words used . . . could be construed as libel. But the two combined impute fraud and dishonesty to the company and its operators." [32]

The use of the wrong picture in an advertisement may give the foundation for actionable libel, as decided in Peck v. Tribune Co.[33]

[30] 408 Pa. 314, 182 A.2d 751 (1962).

[31] Martin v. Johnson Pub. Co., 157 N.Y.S.2d 409, 411 (1956). See also Farrington v. Star Co., 244 N.Y. 585, 155 N.E. 906 (1927) (wrong picture); Wasserman v. Time, Inc., 138 U.S.App.D.C. 7, 424 F.2d 920 (1970), certiorari denied 398 U.S. 940, 90 S.Ct. 1844 (1970).

[32] Young v. New Mexico Broadcasting Co., 60 N.M. 475, 292 P.2d 776 (1956); Central Arizona Light & Power Co. v. Akers, 45 Ariz. 526, 46 P.2d 126 (1935).

[33] Peck v. Tribune Co., 214 U.S. 185, 29 S.Ct. 554 (1909).

The use of false or unauthorized testimonials in advertisements also may constitute libel.[34]

SEC. 22.   BROADCAST DEFAMATION

Broadcasting's vast audience gives vast potential for harm in defamation, and it is now treated as libel instead of the lesser wrong of slander. Special problems arise in broadcast libel uttered without advance warning by participants in programs.

While defamation suits during the early decades of radio were sometimes brought under the rules of slander—spoken defamation—the offense today is handled as libel. The American Law Institute finds that "defamation by any form of communication that has the potentially harmful qualities characteristic of written or printed words is to be treated as libel." [35]   Broadcasting's wide diffusion of its programs to millions, and its prestige and impact among audiences, makes it potentially much more damaging than the slanderous speech of one to another in a neighborhood gathering, or of one to an audience in a lecture hall. *Media Law Reporter,* the publication that gathers and reprints court decisions from all jurisdictions in the nation, has no "Slander" subtitle in its classification guide.

If there were a rare case in which broadcasting defamation might still be ruled slander, it would be somewhat harder for the offended person to get his case into court than if his case were libel. Ancient rules persist that protect spoken defamation more than written. Thus slander plaintiffs must show precise, special damages—monetary loss—to get many cases into court. That rule applies in all cases except those arising from offending words that impute crime, loathsome or contagious disease, or unchastity or immorality in a female, or injure one in business or calling. And special damages are hard to establish at trial.

That is not to say that broadcasting presents no special libel circumstances different from those of the printed media. For one thing, a study of a three-and-one-half-year period of all defamation decisions reported among the official published court cases, showed that radio and television were the defendants in 32 cases (26 television, 6 radio), compared to 94 for newspapers, 25 for magazines, and 12 for books. For whatever reasons, thus, the raw numbers of reported cases suggest that broadcasters are less frequently confronted with the libel peril than newspapers.[36]

[34] Foster–Milburn Co. v. Chinn, 134 Ky. 424, 120 S.W. 364 (1909).
[35] Restatement Second, Torts, Vol. 3 p. 182.
[36] Franklin, 479, 488.

But even if broadcasters are sued less frequently than print media, that could change. It could mean that the lessened emphasis on broadcast news in recent years—following the Federal Communications Commission's lifting of requirements as it "deregulates"—has cut the amount of news and public affairs content generating lawsuits.[37] Keep in mind, however, that one of the largest libel awards in a mass media setting—$3.05 million—came in Brown & Williamson v. Jacobson and CBS. That case resulted from inaccurate portrayal of the tobacco company's advertising tactics.[38]

Offerings such as CBS's "60 Minutes" and ABC's "20/20" tend to generate libel and privacy actions: they dare to do investigative programs. Also, it is clear that if sued successfully, networks do have the deep pockets to pay large damage awards.

Beyond news or news-related shows, entertainment programming creates what some lawyers term "exposure to suit." Comedic silliness can generate litigation. David Letterman was sued for defamation in 1987 for making a statement parodying an ad featuring "Martha Raye, actress, denture wearer." Letterman said, " 'I saw the most terrifying commercial on television last night, featuring Martha Raye, actress, condom user.' " Ms. Raye's defamation suit failed on grounds that Letterman's quip could not be taken as a statement of fact. Further, Letterman did make a retraction, stating it was "only a joke." [39]

But suppose a defamatory "ad lib" occurs—a spontaneous statement fired off by a gifted comedian in mid-broadcast? A famous old case—Summit Hotel Co. v. NBC (1939) [40]—provides some background. The famed Jazz Singer, Al Jolson, was appearing on an NBC program sponsored by Shell Petroleum; Jolson actually was being paid by the J. Walter Thompson advertising agency, which had been hired by Shell. A golf champion appearing on the show said that his first job was at the Summit Hotel. Jolson blurted an unscripted ad lib: "That's a rotten hotel." Summit sued NBC.

Was NBC to be held to strict accountability for the words, as a newspaper is held strictly accountable for anything it publishes? Or would the nature of the communication process by radio, incompatible with total advance control by the broadcast company, permit a different treatment? The court took into account the

[37] In re Deregulation of Radio, 84 FCC 2d 968, 49 R.R.2d 1 (1981); for TV deregulation of content, see 56 R.R.2d 1005 (1984).

[38] Brown & Williamson Tobacco Corp. v. Jacobson, 827 F.2d 1119 (7th Cir.1987), 14 Med.L.Rptr. 1497.

[39] Raye v. Letterman (Ca.Sup.Ct., L.A. County, 1987), 14 Med.L.Rptr. 2047.

[40] 336 Pa. 182, 8 A.2d 302 (1939).

special character of broadcasting, and held that the rule of strict accountability did not apply: [41]

> Publication by radio has physical aspects entirely different from those attending the publication of a libel or a slander as the law understands them.
>
> * * *
>
> A rule unalterably imposing liability without fault on the broadcasting company under any circumstances is manifestly unjust, unfair and contrary to every principle of morals * * *.
>
> * * *
>
> We therefore conclude that a broadcasting company that leases its time and facilities to another, whose agents carry on the program, is not liable for an interjected defamatory remark where it appears that it exercised due care in the selection of the lessee, and, having inspected and edited the script, had no reason to believe an extemporaneous defamatory remark would be made. Where the broadcasting station's employee or agent makes the defamatory remark, it is liable, unless the remarks are privileged [e.g. as part of a public record]. . . .

Radio Talk Shows

The popular radio format of the call-in talk-show presents a similar problem. Louisiana and Wyoming courts have settled actions against telephoned libel in diametrically opposed ways. The announcer for the call-in program of station WBOX of Bogalusa, La., asked call-ins not to use specific names and places unless they were willing to identify themselves, in fairness to all people. A call-in by an unidentified person associated the Pizza Shanty with narcotics, and said that Dr. Newman "is writing those prescriptions," and "Guerry Snowden [manager of a drug store] is filling them and they are selling them down there." The announcer broke in repeatedly, trying to get the name of the caller, but did not succeed. Snowden, Newman and Blackwell of the Pizza Shanty sued, and a jury awarded them $4,000, $5,000, and $2,500 respectively. The station appealed, and in upholding the judgments, the Louisiana Appeals Court explained in detail why the station's behavior was reckless disregard of truth or falsity: [42]

> The procedure employed amounted to an open invitation to make any statement a listener desired, regardless of

[41] Summit Hotel Co. v. National Broadcasting Co., 336 Pa. 182, 199, 204, 8 A.2d 302, 310, 312 (1939).

[42] Snowden v. Pearl River Broadcasting Corp., 251 So.2d 405 (La.App.1971).

how untrue or defamatory it might be, about any person or establishment, provided only that the declarer identify himself. * * * Such an eventuality was easily foreseeable and likely to occur, as it in fact did. In our judgment, the First Amendment does not protect a publisher against such utter recklessness.

The vastly different outlook of the Wyoming courts was delivered in the case of Adams v. Frontier Broadcasting (1976).[43] Here a caller to a talk-show charged falsely that businessman Adams (a former state official) "had been discharged as Insurance Commissioner for dishonesty," and Adams sued. The trial court ruled that he did not have a suit, because the station did not have "reckless disregard" for truth or falsity in failing to use a delay device to cut dangerous words off the air. Adams appealed, and the Wyoming Supreme Court upheld the trial court. It said that requiring stations to use the delay system would mean that [44]

> * * * broadcasters, to protect themselves from judgments for damages, would feel compelled to adopt and regularly use one of the tools of censorship, an electronic delay system. While using such a system a broadcaster would be charged with the responsibility of concluding that some comments should be edited or not broadcast at all. Furthermore, we must recognize the possibility that the requirement for the use of such equipment might, on occasion, tempt the broadcaster to screen out the comments of those with whom the broadcaster * * * did not agree and then broadcast only the comments of those with whom the broadcaster did agree.

The court said that uninhibited, robust, wide-open debate "must, in the balance, outweigh the * * * right of an * * * official or public figure to be free from defamatory remarks." Reports such as the call-ins, the court added, are a modern version of the town meeting, and give every citizen a chance to speak his mind on issues.

Electronic News Gathering (ENG)

Reported defamation decisions involving Electronic News Gathering (ENG)—the technology for picturing events live! *live!* LIVE! from the scene to the living room—had not appeared by late 1994. With developing areas of law, courts will look to similar fact situations, reasoning by analogy from the past to see whether principles applied previously can be stretched to create rules of law to govern new cases and controversies.

---

[43] 555 P.2d 556 (Wyo.1976), 2 Med.L.Rptr. 1166.

[44] Ibid., 564–567, 2 Med.L.Rptr. at 1173–75.

ENG technology, with small cameras (mini-cams) which journalists use to relay reports instantaneously from a scene—by microwave transmission from a remote truck back to the television studio and onto the air and home TV screens, unedited. So is the television station liable if during an ENG report an interviewee utters—without any warning—a defamatory comment?

If the Wyoming decision just discussed on the preceding page is followed, then broadcasters could relax to some extent about the dangers inherent in using ENG equipment. The Wyoming decision valued free discussion over a system of taped delays that might justify broadcasters in airing only those views agreeable to them.[45]

On the other hand, if the Louisiana court's reasoning is followed—to the effect that using live ENG transmissions with little or no ability to control defamatory blurting or sign-waving is negligent or reckless behavior—then use of ENG technology in spot news situations will become chancy indeed.[46] Perhaps the safest course is to pass up some of the freewheeling, competitively advantageous use of live ENG reports. Instead, the live feed from the scene of a news story could be taped and reviewed by a news producer for possible editing of obviously defamatory material— before sending the pictures on to the television station's viewers. But that course, obviously, dispels the advantage of live broadcasting, and mistakes in failing to remove defamatory material during the "live-delayed" tape editing might also create liability for a television station.

The Candidate for Public Office

A special problem in broadcast defamation grew in the special relationship of the political candidates and the broadcast media. The famous Section 315 of the federal Communications Act of 1934[47] says that if a station decides to carry one political candidate's message on the air, it must carry those of any of his political opponents who may seek air time. The station is specifically barred from censoring the candidate's copy.

For decades, this put the station in a difficult position. If it refused air time to all candidates, it could be criticized for refusing to aid the democratic political process, even though it was within the law in so doing. But suppose that it accepted the responsibility of carrying campaign talks: Then, if it spotted possible defamation in the prepared script of the candidate about to go on the air, it had

---

[45] Ibid. See also Teeter, "ENG and the Law: An Introduction," chapter in Richard D. Yoakam, Charles F. Cremer and Phillip O. Keirstead, ENG: Television News and the New Technology, 3rd ed. (New York: Random House, 1995).

[46] Snowden v. Pearl River Broadcasting Corp., 251 So.2d 405 (La.App.1971).

[47] 48 Stat. 1088, as amended, 47 U.S.C.A. § 315(a).

no way of denying him access to its microphone and no power to censor. The law in effect forced the station to carry material that might very well damage it.

Several cases arose in which campaign talk produced defamation for which stations were held liable.[48] But in 1959, a case from North Dakota reached the Supreme Court of the United States and the problem was settled in favor of the beleaguered broadcasters. A.C. Townley, some 30 years after he had been a major political figure in upper midwest states, returned to the political arena in 1956. He ran for the U.S. Senate in North Dakota. Under the requirements of Section 315, radio station WDAY of Fargo, N.D., permitted Townley to broadcast a speech in reply to two other candidates. In it, Townley accused the Farmers Educational and Cooperative Union of America (FECUA) of conspiring to "establish a Communist Farmers Union Soviet right here in North Dakota." FECUA sued Townley and WDAY for libel. The North Dakota courts ruled that WDAY was not liable and FECUA appealed.[49]

The Supreme Court held that stations did not have power to censor the speeches of political candidates. For with that power, it said, "Quite possibly if a station were held responsible for the broadcast of libelous material, all remarks even faintly objectionable would be excluded out of an excess of caution," and further, a station could intentionally edit a candidate's "legitimate presentation under the guise of lawful censorship of libelous matter."[50] The Court was confident that Congress had intended no such result when it wrote Section 315.

FECUA also argued that Section 315 gave no immunity to a station from liability for defamation spoken during a political broadcast even though censorship of possibly libelous matter was not permitted. The court said:[51]

> Again, we cannot agree. For under this interpretation, unless a licensee refuses to permit any candidate to talk at all, the section would sanction the unconscionable result of permitting civil and perhaps criminal liability to be imposed for the very conduct the statute demands of the licensee.

In ruling that WDAY was not liable for defamation in campaign broadcasts under Section 315, the Supreme Court gave great

[48] Houston Post Co. v. United States, 79 F.Supp. 199 (S.D.Tex.1948); Sorensen v. Wood, 123 Neb. 348, 243 N.W. 82 (1932); Daniell v. Voice of New Hampshire, Inc., 10 Pike & Fischer Radio Reg. 2045.

[49] Farmers Educational and Cooperative Union of America v. WDAY, Inc., 360 U.S. 525, 79 S.Ct. 1302 (1959).

[50] Ibid., at 530, 79 S.Ct. at 1305.

[51] Ibid., at 531, 79 S.Ct. at 1306.

weight to the principle of maximum broadcast participation in the political process. And it relieved stations of an onerous burden that they had formerly carried in the furtherance of that participation.

SEC. 23. EXTRINSIC CIRCUMSTANCES, LIBEL PER SE, AND LIBEL PER QUOD

Facts extrinsic to the story itself sometimes are necessary to make out a defamatory meaning; such "libel per quod" is distinguished from "libel per se" which ordinarily means that the words are defamatory on their face.

In most cases of libel, the hard words that cause a suit are plain to see or hear in the written word or broadcast. They carry the derogatory meaning in themselves: "thief" or "swindler" or "whore" or "communist" is defamatory on its face if falsely applied to a person. Words that are libelous on their face are called libel *per se*.[52]

But on some occasions, words that have no apparent derogatory meaning turn out to be libelous because circumstances outside the words of the story itself become involved. In the classic case, there was no apparent derogatory meaning in a brief but erroneous story saying that a married woman had given birth to twins. But many people who read the story knew that the woman had been married only a month.[53] Facts extrinsic to the story itself gave the words of the story a libelous meaning. Where extrinsic facts turn an apparently harmless story into defamation, it is called by many American courts libel *per quod*.[54]

In a records column in the *Spokane Chronicle,* this entry appeared on April 21, 1961: "Divorce Granted Hazel M. Pitts from Philip Pitts." In these words alone there was no defamation. But the divorce had taken place on Feb. 2, 1960, 14 months earlier, and now Pitts had been married to another woman for several months. Some of his acquaintances and neighbors concluded that Pitts had been married to two women at once and was a bigamist. Extrinsic facts made the story libelous, and the Pittses were awarded $2,000.[55]

---

[52] 33 Am.Jur. Libel and Slander § 5; Martin v. Outboard Marine Corp., 15 Wis.2d 452, 113 N.W.2d 135, 138 (1962); Prosser, p. 782.

[53] Morrison v. Ritchie & Co., 39 Scot.L.R. 432 (1902).

[54] 53 C.J.S. Libel and Slander § 8a; Prosser, p. 781; Electric Furnace Corp. v. Deering Milliken Research Corp., 325 F.2d 761, 764–765 (6th Cir.1963).

[55] Pitts v. Spokane Chronicle Co., 63 Wash.2d 763, 388 P.2d 976 (1964).

In some jurisdictions it is held that where extrinsic facts are involved in making out a libel, the plaintiff must plead and prove special damages. These damages are specific amounts of pecuniary loss that one suffers as a result of libel, such as cancelled contracts or lost wages.

The magazine *Life* published a story on May 20, 1966, dealing with electronic eavesdropping. With it was a picture of Mary Alice Firestone, her estranged husband, and Jack Harwood who had a business in electronic "snooping," especially in connection with divorce suits. The story read: [56]

> TWO–WAY SNOOP. In Florida, where electronic eavesdropping is frequently employed in divorce suits, private eyes like Jack Harwood of Palm Beach shown above with some of his gear, do a thriving business. Harwood, who boasts, "I'm a fantastic wire man," was hired by tire heir Russell Firestone to keep tabs on his estranged wife, Mary Alice. * * * She in turn got one of Harwood's assistants to sell out and work for her and, says Harwood "He plays just as rough with the bugs as I do." * * * A court recently ordered Russell and Mary to stop spying on each other.

Mrs. Firestone brought suit for libel per quod, saying that the story injured her in her pending marital litigation. The trial court dismissed her complaint, but the U.S. Circuit Court of Appeals ruled that she had a case, reversing the trial court. It said: [57]

> We are of the opinion that appellant's allegations of injury to her pending marital litigation constitute allegations of "special damages" for libel per quod which are sufficient to withstand a motion to dismiss. While it may be difficult indeed [for Mrs. Firestone] to prove these damages, we are not convinced that they are so speculative that she could not prove them under any circumstances.

SEC. 24. DAMAGES

Compensatory or general damages are granted for injury to reputation, special damages for specific pecuniary loss, and punitive damages as punishment for malicious or extremely careless libel.

Courts and statutes are not entirely consistent in their labeling of the kinds of damages that may be awarded to a person who is libeled. Generally, however, three bases exist for compensating the injured person.

[56] Firestone v. Time, Inc., 414 F.2d 790, 791 (5th Cir.1969).
[57] Ibid.

The first is that injuring reputation or causing humiliation ought to be recognized as real injury, even though it is impossible to make a scale of values and fix exact amounts due the injured for various kinds of slurs. If such injury is proved, "general" or "compensatory" damages are awarded.

There is also harm of a more definable kind—actual pecuniary loss that a person may suffer as a result of a libel. It may be the loss of a contract or of a job, and if it can be shown that the loss is associated with the libel, the defamed may recover "special" damages—the cost to him. It is plain, however, that some states use the term "actual damages" to cover both pecuniary loss and damaged reputations. Thus it was held in Miami Herald Pub. Co. v. Brown: [58]

> Actual damages are compensatory damages and include (1) pecuniary loss, direct or indirect, or special damages; (2) damages for physical pain and inconvenience; (3) damages for mental suffering; and (4) damages for injury to reputation.

The third basis for awarding damages is public policy—that persons who maliciously libel others ought to be punished for the harm they cause. Damages above and beyond general and actual damages may be awarded in this case, and are called punitive or exemplary damages. Some states deny punitive damages, having decided long ago that they are not justified. For more than a century, Massachusetts, for example, has rejected punitive damages, under a statement by the famed Oliver Wendell Holmes, Jr., then judge of the Massachusetts high court: "The damages are measured in all cases by the injury caused. Vindictive or punitive damages are never allowed in this State. Therefore, any amount of malevolence on the defendant's part in and of itself would not enhance the amount the plaintiff recovered by a penny * * *." [59]

Huge amounts of damage are often claimed, and sometimes awarded although juries' judgments of such astronomical sums as $5,000,000 or $25,000,000 are invariably cut back by trial judges or by appeals courts. Thus not only "private" persons, but also public officials and public figures, even under the requirements of proving actual malice, have in recent years won major damage awards. Some sizable amounts include as $114,000 compensatory plus $100,000 punitive damages (charge of soliciting bribes); [60] $250,000 plus interest (dishonest practices in real estate); [61] $85,000 (sadis-

[58] 66 So.2d 679, 680 (Fla.1953). See, also, Ellis v. Brockton Pub. Co., 198 Mass. 538, 84 N.E. 1018 (1908); Osborn v. Leach, 135 N.C. 628, 47 S.E. 811 (1904).

[59] Burt v. Advertiser Newspaper Co., 154 Mass. 238, 245, 28 N.E. 1, 5 (1891).

[60] Cape Publications, Inc. v. Adams, 336 So.2d 1197 (Fla.App.1976), certiorari denied 348 So.2d 945 (Fla.1977).

[61] Sprouse v. Clay Communication, Inc., 158 W.Va. 427, 211 S.E.2d 674 (1975).

tic, paranoid); [62] $450,000 (fixed a football game); [63] $350,000 plus possible $50,000 court costs (connections with underworld); [64] $400,000, of which $300,000 was punitive damages (false charge of "Communist"), [65] and $3,000,000 (tobacco company accused of ad strategies to "hook" young smokers). [66]

A California court jury in 1981 awarded $1.6 million to America's beloved comedienne, Carol Burnett, who was falsely portrayed by the *National Enquirer,* said the judge in the case, as "drunk, rude, uncaring and abusive" in the Rive Gauche restaurant, Los Angeles. [67] The judge disagreed with the jury only in the amount of damages, which he cut in half to $50,000 compensatory plus $750,-000 punitive, and the punitive total was cut to $150,000 by the California Court of Appeal more than two years after the jury trial. [68]

"Miss Wyoming" of 1978, Kimerli Jayne Pring, won a jury award of $25 million in punitive damages plus $1.5 million in compensatory damages from *Penthouse* magazine in 1981. She alleged that a *Penthouse* story falsely implied that she was sexually promiscuous and immoral. The staggering punitive award was quickly halved by Federal District Court Judge Clarence C. Brimmer, who said that the reduced figure must be one that would exceed *Penthouse's* libel insurance protection of $10 million if the magazine were to be punished. *Penthouse,* of course, appealed the enormous remainder, and after another year received the judgment: the article could be reasonably understood by readers as only a "pure fantasy," not as defamation of Pring. [69]

One of the largest libel judgments on record against a newspaper is $9.2 million granted in 1980 by an Illinois circuit court jury to a builder for words that the *Alton Telegraph* never published. The offending words were in a memo from two Telegraph reporters to a Justice Department task force on crime, alleging connections of Alton citizens with organized crime. The paper filed for bankruptcy to delay the force of the judgment until the outcome of its appeal

[62] Goldwater v. Ginzburg, 414 F.2d 324 (2d Cir.1969).

[63] Curtis Pub. Co. v. Butts, 388 U.S. 130, 87 S.Ct. 1975 (1967).

[64] Alioto v. Cowles Communications, Inc., 430 F.Supp. 1363 (N.D.Cal.1977). Four trials were conducted over eight years before ex-Mayor Alioto of San Francisco won the judgment.

[65] Gertz v. Robert Welch, Inc., 680 F.2d 527 (7th Cir.1982), 8 Med.L.Rptr. 1769.

[66] Brown & Williamson Tobacco Corp. v. Jacobson, 827 F.2d 1119 (7th Cir.1987).

[67] Burnett v. National Enquirer, Inc. (Cal.Super.Ct.1981), 7 Med.L.Rptr. 1321, 1323.

[68] Burnett v. National Enquirer Inc., 144 Cal.App.3d 991, 193 Cal.Rptr. 206 (1983), 9 Med.L.Rptr. 1921, appeal dismissed 465 U.S. 1014, 104 S.Ct. 1260 (1984).

[69] Pring v. Penthouse Intern., Ltd., 695 F.2d 438 (10th Cir.1982), 8 Med.L.Rptr. 2409.

was known, and in May 1982, the U.S. Bankruptcy Court for the Southern District of Illinois approved a settlement reported to be $1.4 million between the Telegraph and the central complainant, realtor James Green.[70] The "chill" induced upon future investigative reporting by a newspaper of modest size by such an award takes meaning from the Telegraph's publisher, who said: "Let someone else stick their neck out next time."[71] Since then, that family-owned newspaper has been sold—to a newspaper group.

Courts—as well as media and their attorneys—find evidence in of hatred and resentment of media in such astronomical awards by juries. Widespread anti-media attitudes in the public are likely to be represented among the cross-section of people that comprises a jury: attitudes that media are over-powerful, arrogant, unfair, immoral, inaccurate, and invaders of privacy.[72] In Guccione v. Hustler Magazine, Inc. the Ohio Court of Appeals looked at a jury award of some $40 million against Hustler. Even though the trial judge had reduced it to about ⅓ of that amount, the Appeals Court said, the jury award was so influenced by passion and prejudice and was so grossly excessive as to indicate the jury's intent to drive *Hustler* out of business. The Court ordered a new trial on the issue of damages.[73]

[70] News Media & the Law, June/July 1982, p. 20.

[71] Carley, How Libel Suit Sapped the Crusading Spirit of a Small Newspaper, Wall St. Journal, Sept. 29, 1983, p. 1; Marc Franklin, What Does "Negligence" Mean in Defamation Cases? 6 Comm/Ent 259, 277 (Winter 1984).

[72] Max McCombs, "Opinion Surveys Offer Conflicting Views as to How Public Views Press," Presstime, Feb. 1983, p. 4; "The Media's Credibility Gap," Washington Post National Weekly, April 29, 1985, p. 38; Rober O. Wyatt, Free Expression and the American Public (ASNE/Chair of First Amendment Studies, Middle Tennessee State University, 1991).

[73] 7 Med.L.Rptr. 2077 (1981).

Chapter 5

THE CONSTITUTIONAL DEFENSE
AGAINST LIBEL SUITS

SEC. 25. THE PUBLIC PRINCIPLE

News media defend against libel suits on grounds of their service to the public interest.

Libel may be an old area of law, but its dangers are exceedingly real today. This chapter deals with defenses to libel both new and old. Sweeping changes in libel law since 1964 have changed not only the law of defamation but also have altered key interpretations of the Constitution of the United States.

The American Constitution was nearly two hundred years old before courts, attorneys, and journalists concluded that it ought to protect speech and press against libel actions. It was in 1964 that the Supreme Court of the United States ruled in New York Times Co. v. Sullivan that public officials who sued for libel would have to clear a First Amendment barrier rather than the long-used lesser barriers of state laws and precedents. The emergence of multiple suits claiming formerly unheard-of amounts of damages threatened losses so high as to turn "watchdog" media into sheep. The public interest in vigorous, unintimidated reporting of the news was endangered. The society could not accept self-censorship on the part of media "chilled" by fear of libel awards. The United States Constitution itself, through the First Amendment, would provide the shield for discussion of public matters that the narrow vagaries of many state libel laws denied and that the public welfare demanded.

Striking as the new application of the Constitution was, it really amounted to an expansion of the "public principle" inherent in centuries-old defenses against libel suits. Defenses had grown in the context of the need of an open society for information. Society

148

needs full discussion in media if its citizens are to participate in decisions that affect their lives, are to have the opportunity to choose, are to maintain ultimate control over government. Those who claimed harm to their reputations might find their suits unavailing if certain public concerns and values were furthered by the publication: Where the hard words were the truth, or were privileged as in news of court proceedings, or were fair criticism of performances by artists and others, the public had a real stake in receiving those words.

The First Amendment protection raised by the Supreme Court in the 1964 *Sullivan* case told public officials they would have to accept more fully the verbal rough-and-tumble of political life. Most notably, they would have to show that the news medium published the offending words with *actual malice*—knowledge of falsity, or reckless disregard for falsity.

Libel suits remain at the forefront of media's legal encounters. Suits do not drop in number, jury awards to plaintiffs are often astronomical and are sometimes found by courts to reflect deep jury prejudice against media, defense attorneys' fees may reach six or seven figures, public hostility toward media is widespread and intense. The self-censorship and "chill" that the *Sullivan* decision was intended to avert nevertheless has penetrated some newsrooms, diluting investigative reporting. Journalists, legal scholars, the American Civil Liberties Union, and others have urged strengthening of the *Sullivan* doctrine.[1] They are of course opposed by some who feel that *Sullivan* has been too protective of media.[2]

SEC. 26. DEFENSE AGAINST PUBLIC OFFICIALS' SUITS

Under the doctrine of New York Times Co. v. Sullivan, the First Amendment broadly protects the news media from judgments for defamation of public officials.

The Supreme Court of the United States handed down a decision in 1964 that added a great new dimension of protection to

[1] Anthony Lewis, "The Sullivan Case," The New Yorker, Nov. 5, 1984, 52; Marc Franklin, "Good Names and Bad Law: a Critique of Libel Law and a Proposal," 18 Univ.S.F.L.Rev. 1, Fall 1983; "Symposium, Defamation and the First Amendment: New Perspectives," 25 William & Mary L.Rev. 1983–1984, Special Issue; Michael Massing, "The Libel Chill: How Cold Is It Out There?," Columbia Journ. Rev., May/June, 1985, 31; Gilbert Cranberg, "ACLU Moves to Protect All Speech on Public Issues from Libel Suits," Civil Liberties, Feb. 1983, 2.

[2] Jan Greene, Libel Plaintiffs Organize Against Media, 1985 Report of Society of Professional Journalists, Sigma Delta Chi, Freedom of Information '84–'85, 4; Bruce E. Fein, New York Times v. Sullivan: an Obstacle to Enlightened Public Discourse * * *, quoted in 11 Med.L.Rptr. #3, 12/18/84, News Notes.

news media in the field of libel. It said that news media are not liable for defamatory words about the public acts of public officials unless the words are published with "actual malice." This defined the word "malice" with a rigor and preciseness that had been lacking for centuries and in a way that gave broad protection to publication. Public officials, it said, must live with the risks of a political system in which there is "a profound national commitment to the principle that debate on public issues should be uninhibited, robust, and wide-open * * *." Even a factual error, it said, will not make one liable for libel in words about the public acts of public officials unless actual malice is present.

The case was New York Times Co. v. Sullivan.[3] It stemmed from an "editorial advertisement" in the Times, written and paid for by a group intensely involved in the struggle for equality and civil liberties for African Americans. Suit was brought by L. B. Sullivan, Commissioner of Public Affairs for the city of Montgomery, Ala., against the Times and four black clergymen who were among the 64 persons whose names were attached to the advertisement.

The now-famous advertisement, titled "Heed Their Rising Voices," recounted the efforts of southern Negro students to affirm their rights at Alabama State College in Montgomery and told of a "wave of terror" that met them. It spoke of violence against the Reverend Martin Luther King, Jr. in his leadership of the civil rights movement: [4]

Heed Their Rising Voices

As the whole world knows by now, thousands of Southern Negro students are engaged in wide-spread, non-violent demonstrations in positive affirmation of the right to live in human dignity as guaranteed by the U.S. Constitution and the Bill of Rights. In their effort to uphold these guarantees, they are being met by an unprecedented wave of terror by those who would deny and negate that document which the whole world looks upon as setting the pattern for modern freedom * * *.

* * *

In Montgomery, Alabama, after students sang "My Country, 'Tis of Thee" on the State Capitol steps, their leaders were expelled from school, and truck-loads of police armed with shotguns and tear-gas ringed the Alabama State College Campus. When the entire student body

[3] 376 U.S. 254, 84 S.Ct. 710 (1964).

[4] Ibid., facing 292, see also Anthony Lewis, *Make No Law* (New York: Random House, 1991).

protested to state authorities by refusing to re-register, their dining hall was padlocked in an attempt to starve them into submission.

* * *

Again and again the Southern violators have answered Dr. King's protests with intimidation and violence. They have bombed his home almost killing his wife and child. They have assaulted his person. They have arrested him seven times—for "speeding," "loitering" and similar "offenses." And now they have charged him with "perjury"—a *felony* under which they could imprison him for *ten years*. Obviously, their real purpose is to remove him physically as the leader to whom the students and millions of others—look for guidance and support, and thereby to intimidate *all* leaders who may rise in the South * * *. The defense of Martin Luther King, spiritual leader of the student sit-in movement, clearly, therefore, is an integral part of the total struggle for freedom in the South.

Sullivan was not named in the advertisement, but claimed that because he was Commissioner who had supervision of the Montgomery police department, people would identify him as the person responsible for police action at the State College campus. He said also that actions against the Rev. King would be attributed to him by association.

It was asserted by Sullivan, and not disputed, that there were errors in the advertisement. Police had not "ringed" the campus although they had been there in large numbers. Students sang the National Anthem, not "My Country, 'Tis of Thee." The expulsion had not been protested by the entire student body, but by a large part of it. They had not refused to register, but had boycotted classes for a day. The campus dining hall was not padlocked. The manager of the Times Advertising Acceptability Department said that he had not checked the copy for accuracy because he had no cause to believe it false, and some of the signers were well-known persons whose reputation he had no reason to question.

The trial jury ruled that Sullivan had been libeled and awarded him $500,000, the full amount of his claim. The Supreme Court of Alabama upheld the finding. But the Supreme Court of the United States reversed the decision, holding that the Alabama rule of law was "constitutionally deficient for failure to provide the safeguards for freedom of speech and of the press that are required by the First and Fourteenth Amendments * * *."

The Court said there was no merit to the claim of Sullivan that a paid, commercial advertisement does not ever deserve constitutional protection.   The Court said the advertisement: [5]

> ... communicated information, expressed opinion, re-
> cited grievances, protested claimed abuses, and sought
> financial support on behalf of a movement whose existence
> and objectives are matters of the highest public concern
> * * *.   That the Times was paid for publishing the adver-
> tisement is as immaterial in this connection as is the fact
> that newspapers and books are sold * * *.   Any other
> conclusion would discourage newspapers from carrying
> "editorial advertisements" of this type, and so might shut
> off an important outlet for the promulgation of informa-
> tion and ideas by persons who do not themselves have
> access to publishing facilities—who wish to exercise their
> freedom of speech even though they are not members of
> the press.   The effect would be to shackle the First
> Amendment * * *.

The Court said that the question about the advertisement was
whether it forfeited constitutional protection "by the falsity of some
of its factual statements and by its alleged defamation of respondent".

The Court rejected the position that the falsity of some of the
factual statements in the advertisement destroyed constitutional
protection for the Times and the clergymen.   "[E]rroneous statement is inevitable in free debate, and * * * it must be protected if
the freedoms of expression are to have the 'breathing space' that
they need to survive, * * * "it ruled.   Quoting the decision in
Sweeney v. Patterson,[6] it added that " 'Cases which impose liability
for erroneous reports of the political conduct of officials reflect the
obsolete doctrine that the governed must not criticize their governors * * *.   Whatever is added to the field of libel is taken from the
field of free debate.' "

Elaborating the matter of truth and error, it said that it is not
enough for a state to provide in its law that the defendant may
plead the truth of his words, although that has long been considered a bulwark for protection of expression: [7]

> A rule compelling the critic of official conduct to
> guarantee the truth of all his factual assertions—and to do
> so on pain of libel judgments virtually unlimited in
> amount—leads to * * * "self-censorship."   Allowance of
> the defense of truth, with the burden of proving it on the
> defendant, does not mean that only false speech will be
> deterred.

[5] Ibid., at 266, 84 S.Ct. at 718.
[6] 76 U.S.App.D.C. 23, 128 F.2d 457, 458 (1942).
[7] New York Times Co. v. Sullivan, 376 U.S. 254, 279, 84 S.Ct. 710, 725 (1964).

This was the end for Alabama's rule that "the defendant has no defense as to stated facts unless he can persuade the jury that they were true in all their particulars." But the decision reached much farther than to Alabama: Most states had similar rules under which public officials had successfully brought libel suits for decades. In holding that the Constitution protects even erroneous statements about public officials in their public acts, the Court was providing protection that only a minority of states had provided previously.

Having decided that the constitutional protection was not destroyed by the falsity of factual statements in the advertisement, the Court added that the protection was not lost through defamation of an official. "Criticism of their official conduct," the Court held, "does not lose its constitutional protection merely because it is effective criticism and hence diminishes their official reputations." [8]

Then Mr. Justice Brennan, who wrote the majority decision, stated the circumstances under which a public official could recover damages for false defamation: Only if actual malice were present in the publication: [9]

> The constitutional guarantees require, we think, a federal rule that prohibits a public official from recovering damages for a defamatory falsehood relating to his official conduct unless he proves that the statement was made with "actual malice"—that is, with knowledge that it was false or with reckless disregard of whether it was false or not.

Malice in the new context was no longer the vague, shifting concept of ancient convenience for judges who had been shocked or angered by words harshly critical of public officials. It was not the oft-used "evidence of ill-will" on the part of the publisher; it was not "hatred" of the publisher for the defamed; it was not "intent to harm" the defamed. Rather, the actual malice which the plaintiff would have to plead and prove lay in the publisher's knowledge that what he printed was false, or else disregard on the part of the publisher as to whether it was false or not.

The old, tort-based libel requirement that the publisher would have to prove the truth of his words disappeared in Brennan's formulation: No longer would the publisher carry the burden; instead, the plaintiff official would have to prove falsity. Further, it would not be enough for the plaintiff to prove knowing or reckless falsity by "the preponderance of evidence". Instead, he would have to prove it "with convincing clarity." Also, to learn whether the

[8] Ibid., at 273, 84 S.Ct. at 722.
[9] Ibid., at 279–280, 84 S.Ct. 725–726.

trial court had properly applied the law in this important case over how expression might be regulated, the appellate courts were to independently review the trial record itself to make sure that there had been no forbidden intrusion on free expression.[10]

As court interpretation and litigation proceeded after these drastic revisions of the libel law of centuries, New York Times Co. v. Sullivan came to be recognized as the most important First Amendment case for decades. Famed attorney Floyd Abrams termed the decision "majestic," and "one of the most far reaching, extraordinary, and beautiful decisions in American history." [11]

The United States Constitution's guarantee of freedom of speech and press—which of course rules in all states as well as in federal courts [12]—protects all that is said about public officials in their public conduct unless there is "actual malice." But did "public official" mean every person who is employed by government at any level? Justice Brennan foresaw that this question would arise, but said in a footnote in the *Sullivan* case: "It is enough for the present case that respondent's position as an elected city commissioner clearly made him a public official * * *." [13]

In 1966, Rosenblatt v. Baer helped the definition. Newspaper columnist Alfred D. Rosenblatt wrote in the *Laconia Evening Citizen* that a public ski area which in previous years had been a financially shaky operation, now was doing "hundreds of percent" better. He asked, "What happened to all the money last year? And every other year?" Baer, who had been dismissed from his county post as ski area supervisor the year before, brought a suit charging that the column libeled him. The New Hampshire court upheld his complaint and awarded him $31,500. But when the case reached the United States Supreme Court, it reversed and remanded the case. It said that Baer did indeed come within the "public official" category: [14]

> Criticism of government is at the very center of the constitutionally protected area of free discussion. Criticism of those responsible for government operations must

[10] Ibid., at 285, 84 S.Ct. 728. Reaffirmed 20 years later by the Supreme Court in Bose Corp. v. Consumers Union, 466 U.S. 485, 104 S.Ct. 1949 (1984), 10 Med.L.Rptr. 1625, 1636–1639, this rule was held to govern all appellate courts in the determination of actual malice under *Sullivan*, rather than a lesser legal standard which provides that trial-court findings of fact are not to be set aside by appellate courts unless they are "clearly erroneous." Appeals courts have usually practiced independent review: LDRC Bulletin #13, Spring 1985, 2.

[11] 10 Med.L.Rptr. #17, 4/24/84, News Notes.

[12] Dodd v. Pearson, 277 F.Supp. 469 (D.D.C.1967); Beckley Newspapers Corp. v. Hanks, 389 U.S. 81, 88 S.Ct. 197 (1967).

[13] New York Times Co. v. Sullivan, 376 U.S. 254, 282 n. 23, 84 S.Ct. 710, 727 n. 23 (1964).

[14] Rosenblatt v. Baer, 383 U.S. 75, 86 S.Ct. 669 (1966).

be free, lest criticism of government be penalized. It is clear, therefore, that the "public official" designation applies at the very least to those among the hierarchy of government employees who have, or appear to the public to have, substantial responsibility for or control over the conduct of governmental affairs.

The Court also said that the *Sullivan* rule may apply to a person who has left public office, as Baer had, where public interest in the matter at issue is still substantial.

Defining "Public Officials"

Discussions of "who is a public official" (or "public figure") all too often come up after a publication or broadcast has been made that looks as if it may result in a defamation lawsuit. Some of the time, it will be apparent that the individual involved is a public official: the President of the United States, a governor, a state legislator. It would be simple if holding a government position automatically gave one the status of public official. But in the famous 1979 decision in Hutchinson v. Proxmire, the U.S. Supreme Court said in a footnote that "public official" is not synonymous with "public employee." [15]

Such uncertainty comes from the legal fact of life that every libel suit is tried on a case-by-case basis. Because, as has been said, courts move with adequate precedent if not with adequate grace, it is not surprising that courts sometimes reach inconsistent and even contradictory conclusions about who is and who is not a public official.

Consider these examples:

—A coach and athletic director at a 130–student Texas high school is a public official,[16] yet a wrestling coach known state-wide in Ohio was held to be a private figure.[17]

—As Robert D. Sack and Sandra S. Baron have noted, "authorities are sharply divided over whether a public school teacher ... is a public official." [18]

[15] 443 U.S. 111, 119 n.8, 99 S.Ct. 2675, 2680 n.8 (1979). See David A. Elder, "The Supreme Court and Defamation: a Relaxation of Constitutional Standards," Kentucky Bench and Bar, Jan. 1980, pp. 38–39.

[16] Johnson v. Southwestern Newspapers Corp., 855 S.W.2d 182 (Tex.App.1993), 21 Med.L. Rptr. 1746.

[17] Milkovich v. News–Herald, 15 Ohio St.3d 292, 473 N.E.2d 1191 (1984), 11 Med.L.Rptr. 1598 (Ohio App., 1986).

[18] Robert D. Sack and Sandra S. Baron, Libel, Slander and Related Problems (New York: Practising Law Institute, 1994) p. 255, citing Basarich v. Rodeghero, 24 Ill.App.3d 889, 321 N.E.2d 739 (1974) (teacher is public figure) and Richmond Nsprs., Inc. v. Lipscomb, 234 Va. 277, 362 S.E.2d 32 (1987), 14 Med.L.Rptr. 1953, and others (teacher not public figure.)

Cases that did not reach the United States Supreme Court have provided some guidance, starting soon after Times v. Sullivan was decided. During 1964, the Pennsylvania Supreme Court applied public figure status to a senator who was candidate for re-election.[19] Shortly, state legislators were included,[20] a former mayor,[21] a deputy sheriff,[22] a school board member,[23] an appointed city tax assessor,[24] and a police sergeant.[25] A state legislative clerk was ruled a public official, in his suit against a former state senator who accused the clerk of wiretapping when he was actually doing his clerk's duty in trying to identify a telephone caller of obscenities.[26]

In some cases, it has been held that one retains public-official status despite lapse of time: A former federal narcotics agent was designated "public official" in his libel suit for a story about his official misconduct, despite the fact that he had left office six years earlier.[27] And since 1971, the Supreme Court's rule has been that a charge of criminal conduct against a present official, no matter how remote in time or place the conduct was, is always "relevant to his fitness for office," and that he must prove actual malice in a libel suit.[28]

Although "public official" would seem to be readily identifiable, many questions remain. Courts and commentators have long taken the view that holding a government position almost automatically gives one the status of public official. But in a case of 1979, Hutchinson v. Proxmire, the Supreme Court said in a footnote that "public official" is not synonymous with "public employee"; that matter remains unsettled.[29] In a Texas case, a county surveyor who brought a libel suit against a newspaper for its criticism of his work as an engineering consultant to a municipality was ruled not to be a public official but a private person in his consultant's

[19] Clark v. Allen, 415 Pa. 484, 204 A.2d 42 (1964).

[20] Washington Post Co. v. Keogh, 125 U.S.App.D.C. 32, 365 F.2d 965 (1966); Rose v. Koch and Christian Research, Inc., 278 Minn. 235, 154 N.W.2d 409 (1967).

[21] Lundstrom v. Winnebago Newspapers, Inc., 58 Ill.App.2d 33, 206 N.E.2d 525 (1965).

[22] St. Amant v. Thompson, 390 U.S. 727, 88 S.Ct. 1323 (1968).

[23] Cabin v. Community Newspapers, Inc., 50 Misc.2d 574, 270 N.Y.S.2d 913 (1966).

[24] Eadie v. Pole, 91 N.J.Super. 504, 221 A.2d 547 (1966).

[25] Suchomel v. Suburban Life Newspapers, Inc., 84 Ill.App.2d 239, 228 N.E.2d 172 (1967).

[26] Martonik v. Durkan, 23 Wash.App. 47, 596 P.2d 1054 (1979), 5 Med.L.Rptr. 1266.

[27] Hart v. Playboy Enterprises (D.C.Kan.1979), 5 Med.L.Rptr. 1811.

[28] Monitor Patriot Co. v. Roy, 401 U.S. 265, 91 S.Ct. 621 (1971).

[29] 443 U.S. 111, 119 n. 8, 99 S.Ct. 2675, 2680 n. 8 (1979). See David A. Elder, "The Supreme Court and Defamation: a Relaxation of Constitutional Standards," Kentucky Bench and Bar, Jan. 1980, pp. 38–39.

work.[30] And in a federal case of 1980, the Court of Appeals for the Fourth Circuit ruled that the Iroquois Research Institute, employed by the Fairfax County (Va.) Water Authority as a research consultant in a county project, was not a public official. Relying on the Rosenblatt v. Baer decision (discussed above), the court said that Iroquois was in the sole role of a scientific factfinder, merely reporting the facts it found to the Water Authority. It had no control over the conduct of government affairs, made no recommendations, was little known to the public, and exercised no discretion.[31] It was private.

Nine major media organizations unsuccessfully urged the United States Supreme Court to review the appeals court decision for Iroquois, asserting that the case "presents perhaps the most significant unresolved issue in the constitutional law of defamation * * *."[32] The Supreme Court denied review and the case went back to trial court with Iroquois confirmed for trial as a private agency.

John B. McCrory and Robert C. Bernius described a good analytical frame for determining when a person could be classed as a public official. If a person is in a position to make policy and has access to the press (presumably for self-defense), that can add up to classification as a public official.[33] That analysis—doubtless making too much sense to apply uniformly to defamation cases—cuts across whether an official is elected or appointed. Such an approach even meant that a receptionist in a public clinic was a public official, because she had sole responsibility for making appointments, making her job performance a matter of undeniable public interest.[34]

SEC. 27. DEFENSE WHERE PUBLIC FIGURES AND PUBLIC ISSUES ARE CONCERNED

The doctrine of New York Times Co. v. Sullivan extends the requirement of proving actual malice to public figures, such as non-official persons who involve themselves in the resolution of public questions.

[30] Foster v. Laredo Newspapers Inc., 541 S.W.2d 809 (Tex.1976), certiorari denied 429 U.S. 1123, 97 S.Ct. 1160 (1977).

[31] Arctic Co., Ltd. v. Loudoun Times Mirror et al., 624 F.2d 518 (4th Cir.1980), 6 Med.L.Rptr. 1433, 1435.

[32] 6 Med.L.Rptr. #31 (Dec. 9, 1980), News Notes; John Consoli, "Consultants to Gov't. Aren't Public Figures," Editor & Publisher, Jan. 17, 1981, 9.

[33] 1993 edition of "Constitutional Privilege in Libel Law," by John B. McCrory and Robert C. Bernius, updated by Robert D. Sack et. al., in James C. Goodale, chairman, Communications Law 1993, Vol. II, p. 259.

[34] Ibid., p. 261, citing Auvil v. Times Journal Co., 10 Med.L. Rptr. 2302 (E.D.Va. 1984).

In the *Rosenblatt* case treated above, Justice William O. Douglas of the Supreme Court wrote a separate concurring opinion. In it he raised the question of what persons and what issues might call for an extension of the *Sullivan* doctrine beyond "public officials." He said: [35]

> * * * I see no way to draw lines that exclude the night watchman, the file clerk, the typist, or, for that matter, anyone on the public payroll. And how about those who contract to carry out governmental missions? Some of them are as much in the public domain as any so-called officeholder. * * *. [T]he question is whether a public *issue* not a public official, is involved.

Back in 1966, the decision in a suit brought by the noted scientist and Nobel Prize winner, Dr. Linus Pauling, indeed said that not only "public officials" would have to prove malice if they were to succeed with libel suits.

Pauling sued the *St. Louis Globe–Democrat* claiming libel in an editorial entitled "Glorification of Deceit." It referred to an appearance by Pauling before a subcommittee of the United States Senate, in connection with Pauling's attempts to promote a nuclear test ban treaty. It read in part: "Pauling contemptuously refused to testify and was cited for contempt of Congress. He appealed to the United States District Court to rid him of the contempt citation, which that Court refused to do." Pauling said that he had not been cited for contempt, that he had not appealed to any court to rid himself of any contempt citation, and that no appeal was expected.

The federal court conceded that Pauling was not a "public official" such as the plaintiff in New York Times Co. v. Sullivan. But it added: [36]

> We feel, however, that the implications of the Supreme Court's majority opinions are clear. Professor Pauling, by his public statements and actions, was projecting himself into the arena of public controversy and into the very "vortex of the discussion of a question of pressing public concern". He was attempting to influence the resolution of an issue which was important, which was of profound effect, which was public and which was internationally controversial * * *.

* * *

[35] Rosenblatt v. Baer, 383 U.S. 75, 89, 86 S.Ct. 669, 678 (1966).

[36] Pauling v. Globe–Democrat Pub. Co., 362 F.2d 188, 195–196 (8th Cir.1966).

Pauling took his case to the United States Supreme Court, but that court denied certiorari, and the lower court's decision stood.[37]

Walker v. A.P. (1967)

While public figure Linus Pauling was thus being embraced within the *Sullivan* rules, another man who had formerly been a general in the United States Army was undertaking a set of "chain" libel suits. This was retired Maj. Gen. Edwin A. Walker, who after a storm of controversy over his troop-indoctrination program had resigned from the Army in 1961. Opposed to the integration of the University of Mississippi, he had in 1962 appeared on the scene there when rioting took place over the enrollment of an African–American, James H. Meredith. An Associated Press dispatch, circulated to member newspapers around the nation, said that Walker had taken command of a violent crowd and had personally led a charge against federal marshals. Further, it described Walker as encouraging rioters to use violence.

Walker's chain libel suits totalled $23,000,000 against the *Louisville Courier–Journal* and *Louisville Times* and their radio station; against *Atlanta Newspapers Inc.* and publisher Ralph McGill; against the Associated Press, the *Denver Post*, the *Fort Worth Star–Telegram* and its publisher, Amon G. Carter, Jr.; against *Newsweek*, the Pulitzer Publishing Co. (*St. Louis Post–Dispatch*), and against the *Delta* (Miss.) *Democrat-Times* and its editor, Hodding Carter.[38]

Walker's case reached the Supreme Court of the United States through a suit against the Associated Press which he filed in Texas. He had been awarded $500,000 by the trial court. The Texas Court of Civil Appeals upheld the judgment, and stated without elaboration that the Times v. Sullivan rule was not applicable. The Supreme Court of Texas denied a writ of error,[39] and the United States Supreme Court granted certiorari.

The U.S. Supreme Court decided Associated Press v. Walker and Curtis Publishing Co. v. Butts in the same opinion.[40] Wallace Butts was former athletic director of the University of Georgia, and had brought suit against Curtis for a story in the *Saturday Evening Post* that had accused him of conspiring to "fix" a football game between Georgia and the University of Alabama. Neither Walker nor Butts was a "public official" and the late Justice John M. Harlan's opinion said explicitly that the Court took up the two cases to consider the impact of the Times v. Sullivan rule "on libel

---

[37] Pauling v. National Review, Inc., 49 Misc.2d 975, 269 N.Y.S.2d 11 (1966).

[38] Editor & Publisher, Oct. 5, 1963, p. 10.

[39] Associated Press v. Walker, 393 S.W.2d 671 (Tex.Civ. App.1965).

[40] Curtis Pub. Co. v. Butts, 388 U.S. 130, 87 S.Ct. 1975 (1967).

actions instituted by persons who are not public officials, but who are "public figures' and involved in issues in which the public has a justified and important interest."[41]

Four opinions were delivered by the Court. All agreed that a publication about a "public figure" deserves First Amendment protection. All agreed that both men were public figures. All agreed that Walker should not recover damages against the AP, and most agreed that Butts should recover.

Walker was a "public figure," said Justice John Harlan in writing for four members of the Court, "by his purposeful activity amounting to a thrusting of his personality into the 'vortex' of an important public controversy." Agreeing, in writing for three members, Chief Justice Earl Warren said that "Under any reasoning, General Walker was a public man" in whose conduct society had a substantial interest. Warren said that giving a public figure, such as Walker, an easier burden to meet than a public official in recovering damages for libel[42]

> * * * has no basis in law, logic or First Amendment policy. Increasingly in this country, the distinction between governmental and private sectors are blurred * * *.
>
> Under any reasoning, General Walker was a public man in whose public conduct society and the press had a legitimate and substantial interest.

Harlan argued that the public figure should not have to meet as difficult a standard of proof as the public official. He articulated a lower barrier for the former:[43]

> We consider and would hold that a "public figure" who is not a public official may * * * recover damages for a defamatory falsehood whose substance makes substantial danger to reputation apparent, on a showing of highly unreasonable conduct constituting an extreme departure from the standards of investigation and reporting ordinarily adhered to by responsible publishers.

Then he examined AP's reporting in the Walker case and found no such departure from responsible reporting standards: The AP story was news which required immediate dissemination, the correspondent was competent and his dispatches were internally consistent with a single exception.[44]

So public figure Walker lost his case because Harlan found no "extreme departure from responsible reporting" by the Post and

[41] Ibid., at 134, 87 S.Ct. at 1980.

[42] Ibid., at 163–165, 87 S.Ct. at 1995–1997.

[43] Ibid., at 155, 87 S.Ct. at 1991.

[44] Ibid., at 158–159, 87 S.Ct. at 1993–1994.

Warren found no "actual malice." But public figure Butts, according to both opinions, should win his case against the *Saturday Evening Post,* and keep the $460,000 that he had been awarded at trial. The Post had stated that Butts had revealed his school's football secrets to Alabama coach Paul Bryant just before a game between the schools. The article said that one George Burnett had accidentally been connected, in using the telephone, to the conversation between the two in which Butts told Bryant the secrets. According to the article, Burnett made notes of the conversation as he listened, and the Post obtained his story. Justice Harlan's analysis of the Post's methods of investigation—analysis that was noted with approval in the separate opinion of chief Justice Warren—found the Post wanting. He said, in part: [45]

> The evidence showed that the Butts story was in no sense "hot news" and the editors of the magazine recognized the need for a thorough investigation of the serious charges. Elementary precautions were, nevertheless, ignored. The Saturday Evening Post knew that Burnett had been placed on probation in connection with bad check charges, but proceeded to publish the story on the basis of his affidavit without substantial independent support. Burnett's notes were not even viewed by any of the magazine personnel prior to publication. John Carmichael who was supposed to have been with Burnett when the phone call was overheard was not interviewed. No attempt was made to screen the films of the game to see if Burnett's information was accurate, and no attempt was made to find out whether Alabama had adjusted its plans after the alleged divulgence of information.

Again, there was the application of different standards by Harlan and Warren. Harlan found this kind of reporting to be "highly unreasonable conduct constituting an extreme departure from the standards of investigation and reporting ordinarily adhered to by responsible publishers." And in Chief Justice Warren's opinion, it was evidence of "reckless disregard" of whether the statement were false or not.

Justices Black and Douglas joined the three who endorsed Warren's opinion on a single matter—applying the same actual malice requirement to public figures as to public officials. Thus five justices provided a majority for this standard to prevail over Harlan's "extreme departure" standard. Further, Warren had said he could not believe that "a standard which is based on such an unusual and uncertain formulation" as Harlan's could either guide a jury or afford "the protection for speech and debate that is

---

[45] Ibid., at 157, 87 S.Ct. at 1992.

fundamental to our society and guaranteed by the First Amendment." [46] While Justice Harlan's attempt to place an easier burden upon public figures than public officials through his "extreme departure" standard was persuasive for a few lower courts,[47] his formulation came ultimately to be flatly rejected as a rule for public persons' libel suits.[48]

Then in the famous case of Rosenbloom v. Metromedia, Inc.,[49] in 1971, a plurality of three justices of the U.S. Supreme Court approved extending the actual malice requirement in libel whenever the news was a "matter of public interest." It denied recovery for libel to George Rosenbloom, distributor of nudist magazines in Philadelphia, a private citizen involved in a matter of public interest. Metromedia radio station WIP had said Rosenbloom had been arrested on charges of possessing obscene literature, and linked him to the "smut literature rackets." Later acquitted of obscenity charges, Rosenbloom sued for libel in the WIP broadcasts, and won $275,000 in trial court before losing upon the station's appeal. In the U.S. Supreme Court, five justices agreed that Rosenbloom should not recover. Three of them endorsed the "matter of public interest" rationale, laid out in Justice William J. Brennan's plurality (not a majority) opinion: [50]

> If a matter is a subject of public or general interest, it cannot suddenly become less so merely because a private individual is involved, or because in some sense the individual did not "voluntarily" choose to become involved. The public's primary interest is in the event * * *. We honor the commitment to robust debate on public issues, which is embodied in the First Amendment, by extending constitutional protection to all discussion and communication involving matters of public or general concern, without regard to whether the persons involved are famous or anonymous.

Lower courts accepted the plurality opinion as ruling. The sweep of "matter of public or general interest" was so powerful

[46] Ibid., at 163, 87 S.Ct. at 1995.

[47] Cerrito v. Time, Inc., 302 F.Supp. 1071 (N.D.Cal.1969); Fotochrome, Inc. v. New York Herald Tribune, Inc., 61 Misc.2d 226, 305 N.Y.S.2d 168 (1969); Holmes v. Curtis Pub. Co., 303 F.Supp. 522, 525 (D.S.C.1969); Buckley v. Vidal, 50 F.R.D. 271 (S.D.N.Y.1970); Cervantes v. Time, Inc., 330 F.Supp. 936 (E.D.Mo.1971). See esp. Chapadeau v. Utica Observer–Dispatch, Inc., 38 N.Y.2d 196, 379 N.Y.S.2d 61, 341 N.E.2d 569 (1975) for the New York courts' development of a "fault" standard in libel cases brought by private persons under Gertz v. Robert Welch, Inc., 418 U.S. 323, 94 S.Ct. 2997 (1974).

[48] Hunt v. Liberty Lobby, 720 F.2d 631 (11th Cir.1983), 10 Med.L.Rptr. 1097, 1109.

[49] 403 U.S. 29, 91 S.Ct. 1811 (1971).

[50] Ibid., at 52, 91 S.Ct. at 1824.

that few libel suits, whether by public or private persons were won. Commentators on press law predicted the disappearance of libel suits. But in mid–1974, hardly three years after *Rosenbloom,* the support of a three-justice plurality in that decision for the "matter of public interest" interpretation revealed itself as a shaky foundation. A five-man majority of the U.S. Supreme Court rejected it as a rule in Gertz v. Robert Welch, Inc.[51]

SEC. 28.   DEFINING "PUBLIC FIGURE"

Distinguishing a public from a private person under *Gertz* rests on either of two bases—fame, notoriety, power or influence that render one a public figure for all purposes, or the status that makes one a public figure only for a limited range of issues. In either case, the person assumes special prominence in the resolution of public controversy.

Elmer Gertz, a Chicago lawyer, was retained by a family to bring a civil action against Policeman Nuccio who had shot and killed their son and had been convicted of second degree murder. *American Opinion,* a monthly publication given to the views of the John Birch Society, carried an article saying that Gertz was an architect of a "frame-up" of Nuccio, that he was part of a communist conspiracy to discredit local police, and that he was a Leninist and a "Communist-fronter." Gertz, who was none of these things, brought a libel suit and for six years battled the shifting uncertainties of the courts' attitudes toward "public official," "public figure," and "matter of public interest" for the purposes of libel. A jury found libel *per se* and awarded Gertz $50,000 in damages, disallowed by the trial judge and also by the Seventh Circuit Court of Appeals:[52] Because the *American Opinion* story concerned a matter of public interest, Gertz would have to show actual malice on its part, even though he might be a private citizen. Objecting, Gertz appealed to the U.S. Supreme Court.

Private Individuals Exempted From Actual Malice Rule

With four other justices agreeing, Justice Powell wrote for the majority.[53] The plurality opinion in Rosenbloom v. Metromedia, relied on by the Circuit Court, should not stand. Justice Powell

---

[51] 418 U.S. 323, 94 S.Ct. 2997 (1974). For the position that the "public interest" criterion should be the rule, see Anthony Lewis, New York Times v. Sullivan Reconsidered * * *, 83 Columbia L.Rev. 603 (1983).

[52] Gertz v. Robert Welch, Inc., 471 F.2d 801 (7th Cir.1972). A dozen years after Gertz brought his first action, a federal jury awarded him $400,000 upon re-trial, and the Seventh Circuit Court of Appeals upheld the award: Gertz v. Welch, Inc., 680 F.2d 527 (7th Cir.1982), 8 Med.L.Rptr. 1769.

[53] Gertz v. Robert Welch, Inc., 418 U.S. 323, 94 S.Ct. 2997 (1974).

had no quarrel with requiring public officials and public figures to
prove actual malice in their libel suits.   But he reasoned that the
legitimate state interest in compensating injury to the reputation of
private individuals—of whom, it was found, Gertz was one—requires that such persons be held to less demanding proof of fault by
the offending news medium—only "negligence," rather than the
stern actual malice standard.   They are at a disadvantage, compared with public officials and public figures, where they are
defamed: [54]

> Public officials and public figures usually enjoy signifi-
> cantly greater access to the channels of effective communi-
> cation and hence have a more realistic opportunity to
> counteract false statements than private individuals nor-
> mally enjoy.   Private individuals are therefore more vul-
> nerable to injury, and the state interest in protecting them
> is correspondingly greater.   * * *

> An individual who decides to seek governmental office
> must accept certain necessary consequences of that in-
> volvement in public affairs.   He runs the risk of closer
> public scrutiny than might otherwise be the case.   * * *

> Those classed as public figures stand in a similar
> position.   Hypothetically, it may be possible for someone to
> become a public figure through no purposeful action of his
> own, but the instances of truly involuntary public figures
> must be exceedingly rare.   For the most part those who
> attain this status have assumed roles of special prominence
> in the affairs of society.

> * * * the communications media are entitled to act on
> the assumption that public officials and public figures have
> voluntarily exposed themselves to increased risk of injury
> from defamatory falsehoods concerning them.   No such
> assumption is justified with respect to a private individual.
> He has not accepted public office nor assumed an "influen-
> tial role in ordering society."   * * *

Dissenting Justices Douglas and Brennan wanted to affirm the
Court of Appeals finding that anyone—including Gertz—would
have to prove actual malice in offending words from a story of
general or public interest.   Brennan argued that the *Gertz* decision
damaged the protection which mass media ought to have under the
First Amendment.   Douglas repeated his view that the First
Amendment would bar Congress from passing any libel law; and
like Congress, "States are without power 'to use a civil libel law or

[54] Ibid., at 344–346, 94 S.Ct. at 3009–3010.

any other law to impose damages for merely discussing public affairs'." [55]

Brennan, who had written the plurality opinion in *Rosenbloom,* reiterated his point there: "Matters of public or general interest do not 'suddenly become less so merely because a private individual is involved, or because in some sense the individual did not "voluntarily" choose to become involved.' " [56] He said it is unproved and highly improbable that the public figure will have better access to the media. The ability of all to get access will depend on the "same complex factor * * * : the unpredictable event of the media's continuing interest in the story." As to the assumption that private people deserve special treatment because they do not assume the risk of defamation by freely entering the public arena, Brennan stated that " * * * voluntarily or not, we are all 'public' men to some degree." [57]

Gertz Is Not a "Public" Person

In Gertz v. Welch, the Supreme Court first brushed off the notion that he might be a public **official**.

He'd never had a paid government position and his only "office" had been as a member of mayor's housing committees years before. As for the suggestion that he was a "de facto public official" because he had appeared at the coroner's inquest into the murder (incidental to his representing the family in civil litigation). If that made him a "public official," the court said, all lawyers would become public officials in their status as "officers of the court," which would make little sense.

But the troublesome possibility that Gertz was a public *figure* remained. Because lower courts have so frequently relied on the Supreme Court's treatment of the matter in *Gertz,* detail is called for here.

To begin, the court said, persons in either of two cases "assume special prominence in the resolution of public questions." [58] Also, "they invite attention and comment."

> [A public figure] designation may rest on either of two
> alternative bases. In some instances an individual may
> achieve such pervasive fame or notoriety that he becomes a
> public figure for all purposes and contexts. More common-
> ly, an individual voluntarily injects himself or is drawn
> into a particular public controversy and thereby becomes a

---

[55] Ibid., at 356, 94 S.Ct. at 3015.

[56] Ibid., at 362, 94 S.Ct. at 3018.

[57] Ibid., at 364, 94 S.Ct. at 3019.

[58] Ibid., at 352, 94 S.Ct. at 3013. Succeeding definitions and procedures in determining "public figure" are taken from *Gertz,* pp. 3009 and 3013.

public figure for a limited range of issues. In either case such persons assume special prominence in the resolution of public questions.

1. The first of the two—deemed a public figure for all purposes and in all contexts: One should not be deemed a public personality for all aspects of his life, "absent clear evidence of general fame or notoriety in the community and pervasive involvement in the affairs of society."

Gertz was not a public figure under this first category. He had, indeed, been active in community and professional affairs, serving as an officer of local civil groups and various legal agencies. He had published several works on law. Thus he was well-known in some circles. But he had "achieved no general fame or notoriety in the community." No member of the jury panel, for example, had ever heard of him.

2. The second of the two—where "an individual voluntarily injects himself * * * into a particular public controversy and thereby becomes a public figure for a limited range of issues." Alternative wording used by the court was that "commonly, those classed as public figures have thrust themselves 'into the vortex' of particular public controversies in order to influence the resolution of the issues involved." [59]

In determining the status of this person who has no general fame or notoriety in the community, the court said the procedure should be one of "looking to the nature and extent of an individual's participation in the particular controversy giving rise to the defamation." In this statement, the Court was rejecting the trend under *Rosenbloom* to examine the *topic* of the news to determine whether the public principle held, and instead to examine the *individual* and his role in public life. Doing this for Attorney Gertz, the court found again that he was not a public figure: He had played only a minimal role at the coroner's inquest, and only as the representative of a private client; he had no part in the criminal prosecution of Officer Nuccio; he had never discussed the case with the press; and he "did not thrust himself into the vortex of this public issue * * * " nor "engage the public's attention in an attempt to influence its outcome." Gertz was not, by this second basis, a public figure, and he would not, consequently, have to prove that *American Opinion* libeled him with actual malice. The Supreme Court ordered a new trial.

[59] As a variant of the "limited range of issues" public figure, the Court identified the person who has not *voluntarily* entered a public controversy, but is *drawn* into it. Subsequent decisions have heavily vitiated this concept. See M.L. Rosen, "Media Lament: the Rise and Fall of Involuntary Public Figures," 54 St. John's L.Rev. 487, Spring 1980.

The modification of *Sullivan* and *Rosenbloom* by *Gertz* was a damaging retreat in protection, in the eyes of media commentators. Now, journalists suspected that although there were gains for the media under *Gertz*—in requiring plaintiffs to show fault and in limiting the reach of punitive damages—it was on the whole a great door-opener for libel suits by private plaintiffs who no longer had to prove actual malice.

David A. Anderson, legal scholar and former journalist, argued that even under the protection of the *Rosenbloom* interpretation, the self-censorship by the press which *Sullivan* had sought to minimize in establishing the malice rule and other safeguards, was real.[60] He wrote that the unconventional, non-established media, sometimes known as the "alternative" press, and the world of magazines, are forced to self-censorship under *Gertz*. The people about whom the alternative press writes are frequently from spheres of life not much handled by the established newspaper media, and thus not established as "public figures." Often financially marginal, the unconventional media face a further problem in the high cost of legal defense. Anderson's worry over self-censorship, whether under *Gertz* or under Draconian jury awards even where the greater protection of *Sullivan* applies, runs strongly through the world of the media.[61]

Courts Determine the "Public" and the "Private" under *Gertz*

Whatever the level of press self-censorship under *Gertz* may be, subsequent cases show that media need to be discriminating. Sometimes, distinguishing the "public" from the "private" is not easy, even for the judge, who makes the decision before the case goes to the jury. One judge has said that the two concepts are "nebulous:" "Defining public figures is much like trying to nail a jellyfish to the wall." [62]

Recall that the Gertz decision set up two categories of public figures:

1) Persons (including organizations) who are "all purpose" or "pervasive" public figures because they have pervasive fame or influence, in their own communities if not regionally or nationally.

2) "Limited purpose" (sometimes called "vortex") public figures (including organizations), who voluntarily have injected them-

---

[60] David A. Anderson, "Libel and Press Self–Censorship," 53 Tex.L.Rev. 422 (1975); for an historic pattern supporting Anderson, see Norman L. Rosenberg, *Protecting the Best Men* (Chapel Hill: University of North Carolina Press, 1986).

[61] 10 Med.L.Rptr. # 13, 3/27/84, News Notes; 10 Med.L.Rptr. # 34, 8/21/84, News Notes.

[62] Rosanova v. Playboy Enterprises, Inc., 411 F.Supp. 440, 443 (S.D.Ga.1976).

selves into a matter of public controversy, to help resolve that controversy.

"All-purpose" Public Figures

Sometimes it is easy to see that a person is an "all purpose" or "pervasive" public figure: entertainers Carol Burnett [63] and Johnny Carson,[64] famed evangelist Jerry Falwell, who comments constantly on politics and who has talked of running for President,[65] or a candidate for elective city office.[66]

In seeming contradiction, however, a famous jet-setter with the household-word name of Firestone was held to be a private person.[67] This famous case is discussed later in this chapter.

For an example of a case with local or community involvement, consider the libel suit of attorney Myron Steere, who was labeled an all-purpose public figure. Steere had represented Nellie Schoonover in her homicide trial; she was convicted of first-degree murder. Later, an Associated Press story said the Kansas State Board of Law Examiners had recommended that the Kansas Supreme Court publicly censure Steere for his conduct of her defense. The examiners found that Steere had entered into a "contingency agreement" with Mrs. Schoonover to get all but $10,000 of her late husband's estate if she were acquitted.

Steere sued broadcasters and newspapers that had carried the AP account for defamation, claiming inaccuracies.[68] The trial court held that he would have to prove actual malice because the Kansas Supreme Court said-"appellant was a public figure for all purposes by virtue of his general fame and notoriety in the community." Then it described the reach and breadth of Steere's involvement in the life of the community: He had practiced law in the county for 32 years and had been the county attorney for 8 of those years.[69]

> * * * He has achieved a position of some influence in local affairs capped by his representation of Nellie Schoonover in her well publicized, famous murder trial. We find the totality of his experience in Franklin County gave

[63] Burnett v. National Enquirer, 7 Med.L.Rptr. 1321 (Cal.1981).

[64] Carson v. Allied News Co., 529 F.2d 206 (7th Cir.1976).

[65] Hustler v. Falwell, 485 U.S. 46, 108 S.Ct. 876 (1988).

[66] Redmond v. Sun Publishing Co., 239 Kan. 30, 716 P.2d 168 (1986).

[67] Time, Inc. v. Firestone, 424 U.S. 448, 96 S.Ct. 958 (1976).

[68] Steere v. Cupp, 226 Kan. 566, 602 P.2d 1267 (1979), 5 Med.L.Rptr. 2046. And see Sprouse v. Clay Communication, 158 W.Va. 427, 211 S.E.2d 674 (1975), 1 Med.L.Rptr. 1695, 1704.

[69] Ibid., 573–74, 1273–74, 2050–51. Note, General Public Figures Since Gertz v. Welch, 58 St. John's L.Rev. 355 (Winter 1984).

Myron Steere the requisite fame and notoriety in his community to be declared a public figure for all purposes.

Not only a *person* may be a "public figure." In Ithaca College v. Yale Daily News Pub. Co., Inc., the facts started with the publication of "The Insider's Guide to the Colleges 1978–79," 404 pages of material compiled and edited by the *Yale Daily News*. Through stringers, the editors obtained information on many colleges, and published of Ithaca College such statements as "Sex, drugs, and booze are the staples of life." Ithaca College sued for libel, charging falsity and damage to its business and academic reputation. While Ithaca terms itself a "private" college, the New York Supreme Court said it could not be such in a libel suit.[70] The college assumes a role as a qualified educator of many students, serves the public good, is responsible for fair dealing with its students, the court ruled. It is recognized to be of "general fame or notoriety in the community [with] pervasive involvement in the affairs of society." The court decided that the college was a "public figure for all purposes." Similarly, corporations also may be classified as "public figures." [71]

Efforts to define public figures become especially troublesome where corporations are concerned.[72] For example, an insurance company, because of its power and influence, was held to be a public figure inviting attention and comment from the media.[73] On the other hand, the Supreme Court of the United States refused to hear an Oregon case holding that corporations—specifically banks—are **not** automatically public figures.[74] Note that this case was decided in 1985, several years before the savings and loan/banking crisis became big news, complete with U.S. senators' involvement in keeping regulators at bay in apparent exchange for campaign donations.

"Limited Purpose" Public Figures

Far more common than the person of general fame or notoriety who is a public figure for all purposes is the individual who is such for a "limited range of issues." Thus Dr. Frederick Exner for two decades and more had been "injecting" and "thrusting" himself into the fluoridation-of-water controversy through speeches, litiga-

[70] 105 Misc.2d 793, 433 N.Y.S.2d 530 (1980), 6 Med.L.Rptr. 2180.

[71] See WTSP–TV, Inc. v. Vick (Fla.Cir.Ct.1985), 11 Med.L.Rptr. 1543. But see Blue Ridge Bank v. Veribanc, Inc., 866 F.2d 681 (4th Cir.1989).

[72] Robert Drechsel and Deborah Moon, "Corporate Libel Plaintiffs and the News Media," 21 Am. Bus. L. Journ. 127 (Summer, 1983).

[73] American Benefit Life Ins. Co. v. McIntyre, 375 So.2d 239 (Ala.1979), 5 Med.L.Rptr. 1124.

[74] Bank of Oregon v. Independent News, Inc., 298 Or. 434, 693 P.2d 35 (1985), cert. denied 474 U.S. 826, 106 S.Ct. 84 (1985).

tion, books, and articles. When he brought a libel suit for a
magazine's criticism of his position, he was adjudged a public figure
for "the limited issue of fluoridation" by having assumed leadership and by having attempted to influence the outcome of the issue.
He had taken the role of "attempting to order society" in its
concern with fluoridation.[75]

Harry Buchanan and his firm were retained to perform accounting services for the Finance Committee to Re-elect the President (CREEP) in 1971. Common Cause brought suit in 1972 to
force the Committee to report transactions, and Buchanan's deposition was taken in the matter. In reporting the suit, Associated
Press compared matters involving Buchanan with the handling of
money by convicted Watergate conspirator Bernard L. Barker.
Buchanan sued AP for libel. Was he a public figure? The court
said "yes." There was intense interest in campaign finances at the
time Buchanan was working for CREEP. The system he helped set
up for the committee and the cash transactions in which he took
part were legitimate matters of public scrutiny and concern. Buchanan was a key person for attempts to investigate. He was an
agent of the committee who voluntarily accepted his role, and as
such a public figure.[76]

Other Examples of Limited Purpose Public Figures: The
businessman-president of a state bail-bond underwriters' association attacked a Pennsylvania state commission's report on bail-
bond abuses and attempted to have the commission dissolved; he
had injected himself into controversy and was a public figure.[77]
The United States Labor Party is a public political organization
actively engaged in publishing articles, magazines, and books, and
is a public figure "at least in regard to those areas of public
controversy * * *in which [it has] participated." [78] The Church of
Scientology seeks to play an influential role in ordering society, has
thrust itself onto the public scene, and is a public figure.[79] So is a
Roman Catholic priest who has actively involved himself in the
debate over the independence of Northern Ireland, through radio,
television, and speeches.[80]

If the above-listed persons and organizations strike you as
plainly appropriate public figures in the contexts described, where

[75] Exner v. American Medical Ass'n, 12 Wash.App. 215, 529 P.2d 863 (1974).

[76] Buchanan v. Associated Press, 398 F.Supp. 1196 (D.D.C.1975).

[77] Childs v. Sharon Herald (Pa.Ct.Com.Pls.1979), 5 Med.L.Rptr. 1679.

[78] United States Labor Party v. Anti–Defamation League (N.Y.Sup.Ct.1980), 6
Med.L.Rptr. 2209.

[79] Church of Scientology of California v. Siegelman, 475 F.Supp. 950 (S.D.N.Y.
1979), 5 Med.L.Rptr. 2021.

[80] McManus v. Doubleday & Co., Inc., 513 F.Supp. 1383 (S.D.N.Y.1981), 7 Med.
L.Rptr. 1475.

does the problem arise?   The fact is that there are hard cases disturbing to media people who are dismayed by courts' finding certain individuals to be private even though in the public eye. Consider that to be a problem caused by Gertz v. Welch (1974). Before that decision of the U.S. Supreme Court, the presumption was that government proceedings are public and almost inevitably made public figures out of participants.   Thanks to the Gertz decision, such public figure presumptions need to be used with great caution. Take a notorious case attempting to draw a line between public figures and private persons, Time, Inc. v. Firestone (1974).

Time, Inc. v. Firestone (1976)

Mary Alice Firestone—wife of a prominent member of the wealthy industrial family and member of the "society" elite of Palm Beach, Fla. (the "sporting set," as U.S. Supreme Court Justice Marshall called it)—went to court to seek separate maintenance from her husband, Russell.   He counterclaimed for divorce on grounds of adultery and extreme cruelty.   The trial covered 17 months, both parties charging extramarital escapades ("that would curl Dr. Freud's hair," the trial judge said).   Several times during the 17 months, Mrs. Firestone held press conferences.   She subscribed to a clipping service.   *Time* magazine reported the trial's outcome: Russell Firestone was granted a divorce on grounds of extreme cruelty and adultery, *Time* said.   But the trial judge had not, technically, found adultery, and Mrs. Firestone sued *Time* for libel.[81]   A jury awarded her $100,000 and *Time* appealed, arguing that Mrs. Firestone was a public figure and as such would have to prove actual malice in *Time's* story.

Justice Rehnquist, writing for the majority of five of the U.S. Supreme Court, said "no" to *Time's* appeal.   He quoted various passages from the *Gertz* definition of "public figure" which he said did not fit Mrs. Firestone: "special prominence in the resolution of public questions," "pervasive power and influence," "thrust themselves to the forefront of particular public controversies in order to influence the resolution of the issues involved."   The crux of the matter was that, for all the publicity involved: [82]

> Dissolution of marriage through judicial proceedings is not the sort of "public controversy" referred to in *Gertz,* even though the marital difficulties of extremely wealthy individuals may be of interest to some portion of the reading public.

[81] Time, Inc. v. Firestone, 424 U.S. 448, 96 S.Ct. 958 (1976).
[82] Ibid., at 454, 96 S.Ct. at 965.

In spite of her position in the "Palm Beach 400," her press conferences, and her clipping service, Mrs. Firestone was a "private" individual, and her "private" marital affairs did not "become public for the purposes of libel law solely because they are aired in a public forum."

Predictably, news media were outraged at the designation of Mrs. Firestone as "private." Accustomed to thinking of official proceedings including divorce trials as public matters which could be reported without fear of injuring the privacy of the participants, journalists had to make a conscious effort to think of Mrs. Firestone as in some sense private. Their effort was made more difficult in that her position in society had for years before the divorce placed her among the "newsworthy" and in the public eye. And with her use of clipping services and press conferences during the drawn-out divorce trial, her "public" character had seemed confirmed. What might the decision mean for future cases?

Wolston v. Reader's Digest (1979)

Three years after *Firestone,* the Supreme Court took up another case whose background was also a public court proceeding. And again, the fact that a libel plaintiff's suit arose from his involvement in an official public matter did not destroy private status for his libel suit. Ilya Wolston had been summoned in 1958 to appear before a grand jury that was investigating espionage, but failed to appear. Later, he pleaded guilty to a charge of criminal contempt for failing to respond to the summons and accepted conviction. Sixteen years later, *Reader's Digest* published a book by John Barron on Soviet espionage in the U.S. The book said erroneously that the FBI had identified Wolston as a Soviet intelligence agent. Wolston sued for libel. He asserted that he had been out of the limelight for many years, and that if he had been a public figure during the investigations, he now deserved to be considered private. The lower courts disagreed, saying the long lapse of time was immaterial, that Soviet espionage of 1958 continued to be a subject of importance, and that Wolston thus remained a public figure.

He appealed to the Supreme Court, which by a vote of 8–1 reversed the lower courts and determined that Wolston was a private person who would not have to prove actual malice in his libel suit against the *Reader's Digest.* Justice Rehnquist wrote: [83]

> We do not agree with respondents and the lower courts that petitioner can be classed as such a limited-purpose public figure. First, the undisputed facts do not justify the conclusion of the District Court and the Court of Appeals that petitioner "voluntarily thrust" or "inject-

[83] Wolston v. Reader's Digest Ass'n, Inc., 443 U.S. 157, 99 S.Ct. 2701 (1979).

ed" himself into the forefront of the public controversy surrounding the investigation of Soviet espionage. * * * It would be more accurate to say that petitioner was dragged unwillingly into the controversy. The government pursued him in its investigation.

Hutchinson v. Proxmire (1979)

On the date of the *Wolston* decision, another Supreme Court ruling on the definition of public figure was handed down, and again the decision cast the public figure into a narrower light than many journalists felt warranted. This time, the Court said that researcher Ronald Hutchinson, who had received some $500,000 in federal government grants for his experiments, including some on monkeys' response to aggravating stimuli, was a private figure.[84] He would not have to prove actual malice in his libel suit against Sen. William Proxmire of Wisconsin, who had labeled Hutchinson's work "monkey business" and had given a "Golden Fleece of the Month Award" to government funding agencies which he ridiculed for wasting public money on grants to Hutchinson. A Proxmire press release, a newsletter, and a television appearance were involved, all following Proxmire's announcement of the Award on the senate floor.

Concerned about the narrowing of the definition of "public figure," media attorney James C. Goodale had reasoned in advance of the decision that the lower courts' holding that Hutchinson was, indeed, a public figure deserved to be upheld in the Supreme Court. "Clearly information about how our government grants money and who gets it," he said, "should be the subject of unlimited comment by anyone—especially by a U.S. Senator." [85]

The Supreme Court, however, did not see it that way. It reversed the lower courts, saying that their conclusion that Hutchinson was a public figure was erroneously based upon two factors: one, his success in getting federal grants and newspaper reports about the grants, and two, his access to media as represented by news stories that reported his response to the Golden Fleece Award. But: [86]

> Hutchinson did not thrust himself or his views into public controversy to influence others. Respondents have

[84] Hutchinson v. Proxmire, 443 U.S. 111, 99 S.Ct. 2675 (1979).

[85] "Court Again to Consider Who Is A Public Figure," National Law Journal, Feb. 8, 1979, 23.

[86] Hutchinson v. Proxmire, 443 U.S. 111, 134–135; 99 S.Ct. 2675, 2688 (1979). Proxmire was reported to have settled the suit out of court for $10,000, and the Senate was reported to have assumed his trial costs of more than $100,000. D.S. Greenberg, "Press Was a Co–Villain in Proxmire's Golden Gimmick," Chicago Tribune, April 17, 1980.

not identified such a particular controversy; at most, they point to concern about general public expenditures. But that concern is shared by most and relates to most public expenditures; it is not sufficient to make Hutchinson a public figure. If it were, everyone who received or benefited from the myriad public grants for research could be classified as a public figure.

"Subject-matter classifications"—such as general public expenditures—had been rejected in *Gertz* as the touchstone for deciding who would have to prove actual malice, the Court said: instead, the person and his activities must be the basis. And, finally, the Court said it could not agree that Hutchinson had such access to the media that he should be classified as a public figure; his access was limited to responding to the announcement of the Golden Fleece Award.

"Vortex" Public Figures Not Clearly Defined

Other circumstances complicate the defining of public figures. Justice Powell's definition in *Gertz* and various courts' since (as in *Firestone, Wolston,* and *Hutchinson*), make it crucial to decide whether the person has voluntarily injected himself into a matter of public controversy to help resolve that controversy. American courts, unfortunately, have not drawn clear or predictable lines to separate "public figures" from "private persons." Even so, it may be said that there are many public figures besides those who voluntarily "get involved" and try to influence the outcome of public issues. (Please note, as discussed later in Section 35, older tort law, dating back long before New York Times v. Sullivan, has traditionally provided the defense of "fair comment for media that are sued for their critiques of authors'" works, restaurants, plays, celebrities and public entertainers.) [87]

If persons truly were not public figures before getting media coverage, the mere fact of that coverage will not make them public figures. At times however—although rarely—unwilling persons, through no fault of their own, can become "involuntary public figures." [88] For the most part, however, there are mainly two kinds of "public figures:" The person who, nationally or locally, has pervasive or all-purpose fame, and the "vortex" public figures who thrust themselves into public issues, particularly in an effort to influence the course of events in some significant way.

[87] Prosser, 813–813.

[88] See, e.g., Wolston v. Reader's Digest Ass'n, Inc., 443 U.S. 157, 167, 99 S.Ct. 2701, 2707 (1979), and Waldbaum v. Fairchild Publications, Inc., 627 F.2d 1287, 1295 (D.C.Cir.1980), citing Gertz v. Welch, 418 U.S. 323, 94 S.Ct. 2997 (1974), recognizing that—at least in theory—an involuntary public figure could exist.

The safest generalization for journalists is not to generalize: Get legal advice on close calls whether a person is a "public figure" or a "private figure." At times, courts have ruled that some persons holding elective office—such as an elected but unsalaried county surveyor [89] or a justice of the peace [90]—are private persons.

SEC. 29.   ACTUAL MALICE

Courts examine reporting procedures in testing for actual malice, and find reckless disregard for falsity much more often than knowledge of falsity.

If a libel plaintiff is found by the judge to be a public official or public figure, the plaintiff's next move is to try to show that the offending words were published with actual malice. This term, as we have seen, is defined by the Supreme Court as reckless disregard for falsity in the words, or as knowledge that the publication is false. The burden is on the plaintiff to prove falsity, although the defendant may well undertake to demonstrate truth—a complete defense.

It is worth remembering that, as was said earlier, the actual malice of *Sullivan* is quite different from the concept "malice" as it is usually understood. The word ordinarily has to do with hostility, ill will, spite, intent to harm—as, indeed, it was defined in libel law for generations before *Sullivan,* and as it continues to be defined in its tort-related sense in state libel law where the constitutional standard does not apply.

The Supreme Court has said that "actual malice" is a "term of art, created to provide a convenient shorthand expression for the standard of liability that must be established" [91] where public persons bring libel suits. The court that is trying the libel issue must direct itself to the factual issue as to the defendant's subjective knowledge of actual falsity or his high degree of awareness of probable falsity before publishing.[92]

Very soon after *Sullivan* had established the new definition of actual malice, the Supreme Court began the process of defining "reckless disregard." In Garrison v. Louisiana,[93] a criminal libel

[89] Foster v. Laredo Newspapers, Inc., 19 TX S.Ct.Jrnl. 390, 541 S.W.2d 809 (Tex.1976), cert. denied 429 U.S. 1123, 97 S.Ct. 1160 (1977).

[90] Guinn v. Texas Newspapers, Inc., 738 S.W.2d 303 (Tex.App.1987), 16 Med. L.Rptr. 1024, cert. denied 488 U.S. 1041, 109 S.Ct. 864 (1989). An error-filled article referred to "Guinn," not to Judge Guinn, asserting that Guinn had been convicted of a felony. (In point of fact, Guinn had been the attorney for the convicted thief.)

[91] Cantrell v. Forest City Pub. Co., 419 U.S. 245, 95 S.Ct. 465 (1974).

[92] Orr v. Argus–Press Co., 586 F.2d 1108 (6th Cir.1978).

[93] 379 U.S. 64, 74, 85 S.Ct. 209, 216 (1964).

action, it said that reckless disregard means a "high degree of awareness of probable falsity" of the publication. In a non-media civil libel case where one candidate for public office sued his opponent (St. Amant v. Thompson), the Supreme Court said that for reckless disregard to be found, "There must be sufficient evidence to permit the conclusion that the defendant in fact entertained serious doubts as to the truth of his publication." [94]

Garrison was convicted of criminal libel, and the Supreme Court of the United States reversed the conviction. It said that the fact that the case was a criminal case made no difference to the principles of the Times v. Sullivan rule, and that malice would have to be shown. And the "reckless disregard" of truth or falsity in malice, it said, lies in a "high degree of awareness of probable falsity" on the part of the publisher. Nothing indicated that Garrison had this awareness of falsity when he castigated the Louisiana judges.[95]

Since the first case providing the constitutional protection in libel, the courts have been at pains to distinguish between "reckless disregard of truth" and "negligence." [96] Negligence is not enough to sustain a finding of actual malice. In the leading case, the Court went to this point. Errors in the famous advertisement, "Heed Their Rising Voices," could have been discovered by the *New York Times* advertising staff had it taken an elevator up a floor to the morgue and checked earlier stories on file. Failure to make this check, the Supreme Court said, did not constitute "reckless disregard;" at the worst it was negligence, and negligence is not enough to indicate actual malice.[97]

In Washington Post v. Keogh, a Congressman sued the newspaper for a story by columnist Drew Pearson which the Post carried. The story accused the congressman of bribe-splitting. The Post did not check the accuracy of the columnist's charges. The Federal Court of Appeals held that the Post showed no reckless disregard in not verifying Pearson's charge, regardless of Pearson's shaky reputation for accuracy. The court held that to require such checking by the Post would be to burden it with greater responsibilities of verification than the Supreme Court required of the *New York Times* in the landmark case. It said: [98]

[94] St. Amant v. Thompson, 390 U.S. 727, 731, 88 S.Ct. 1323, 1325 (1968).

[95] 379 U.S. 64, 85 S.Ct. 209 (1964).

[96] Priestley v. Hastings & Sons Pub. Co. of Lynn, 360 Mass. 118, 271 N.E.2d 628 (1971); A.S. Abell Co. v. Barnes, 258 Md. 56, 265 A.2d 207 (1970).

[97] New York Times Co. v. Sullivan, 376 U.S. 254, 288, 84 S.Ct. 710, 730 (1964).

[98] Washington Post Co. v. Keogh, 125 U.S.App.D.C. 32, 365 F.2d 965, 972–973 (1966).

Verification is * * * a costly process, and the newspaper business is one in which survival has become a major problem. * * * We should be hesitant to impose responsibilities upon newspapers which can be met only through costly procedures or through self-censorship designed to avoid risks of publishing controversial material.

In the foregoing decisions in *Garrison, St. Amant,* and *Keogh,* courts defined reckless disregard by saying what it is *not.*

Other decisions have held that "internal inconsistencies" in a reporter's story do not make reckless disregard; [99] nor does the possibility that the reporter harbored "animosity", or a "grudge" or "ill will" toward the plaintiff; [1] nor does a combination of a reporter's failure to investigate, his possession (but omission from the story) of material contradictory to the hard words, plus the fact that the material was not "hot news" and so could have been further checked.[2] And to repeat, reckless disregard is not carelessness or negligence, which are flaws found often enough in news stories but which must be accepted in news of public persons if freedom is to have the "breathing space" it requires to survive. The jury recognized this in the famous case of Ariel Sharon v. Time, Inc.: While it found *Time* magazine's story about public official Sharon to be false and defamatory, it said specifically that *Time* was negligent and careless, but not possessed of reckless disregard. *Time* had erred but not lied, and was not liable for any of the $50 million that Sharon sought.[3]

The cases of public-person plaintiffs who must accept without compensation the negligent, the careless—indeed the "irresponsible" and the "unreasonable" [4]—sometimes warrant the journalist's reflection: Floyd Rood, a tireless worker and publicist in youth assistance efforts including drug rehabilitation, was said in a news story to have begun a money-raising project "to help solve his drug addiction problem." The word "his" was wrong; it had accidentally been changed from "the" in wire transmission. He lost his suit.[5] Alderwoman Glover, said erroneously by a newspaper to have had abortions, could not recover for libel, for the newspaper had been

[99] Foster v. Upchurch, 624 S.W.2d 564 (Tex.1981), 7 Med.L.Rptr. 2533.

[1] Lancaster v. Daily Banner–News Pub. Co., Inc., 274 Ark. 145, 622 S.W.2d 671 (1981), 8 Med.L.Rptr. 1093; Curtis v. Southwestern Newspapers, 677 F.2d 115 (5th Cir.1982), 8 Med.L.Rptr. 1651.

[2] McNabb v. Oregonian Pub. Co., 69 Or.App. 136, 685 P.2d 458 (1984), 10 Med.L.Rptr. 2181.

[3] Time, Feb. 4, 1985, 64; 599 F.Supp. 538 (S.D.N.Y.1984).

[4] Lawrence v. Bauer Pub. & Printing Ltd., 89 N.J. 451, 446 A.2d 469 (1982), 8 Med.L.Rptr. 1536, 1543.

[5] Rood v. Finney, 418 So.2d 1 (La.App.1982), 8 Med.L.Rptr. 2047.

no more than negligent in its mistake.[6]

Turning now to some cases where reckless disregard *was* found in news: The earliest was the 1967 case, Curtis Publishing Co. v. Butts, discussed at pages 159 to 161, in which the former athletic director of the University of Georgia sued for a *Saturday Evening Post* story accusing him of conspiring to "fix" a football game between Georgia and Alabama. The Post had relied on the story of Burnett, a man serving on probation in connection with bad check charges, had not seen Burnett's notes about the alleged telephone conversation he said he had overheard, had not interviewed a man supposedly in the company of Burnett at the time of the phone conversation. Furthermore, the story was not "hot news" that demanded immediate publication. In the words of Chief Justice Earl Warren, this was reckless disregard of whether the statements were true or false.[7]

Investigative Reporting and the Tavoulareas Case (1985)

To journalists, investigative reporting is a high calling, a valued enterprise. They don't mind when they are called "muckrakers" when they try to find and to expose societal ills or corporate or governmental wrongdoing. It came as a shock, therefore when for a time the Washington Post was on the losing end of a $2 million libel award, with its investigative aggressiveness being used against the paper as evidence of its "actual malice."

The feisty and aggressive Mobil Oil Co. president, William Tavoulareas, sued the Post for a story saying he had "set up" his son to head an international tanker fleet carrying petroleum, implying misuse of his corporate position. Tavoulareas, a public figure, sued the Post for $100 million, claiming actual malice (knowing falsity or reckless disregard for the truth) by the newspaper.[8] The jury agreed and awarded him $250,000 compensatory and $1.8 million punitive damages. But after reviewing the facts at length, the judge threw out the jury award (rendered a "judgment n.o.v."). He said that while the story in question was far short of being a model of fair, unbiased investigative journalism, there was "no evidence in the record * * * to show that it contained knowing lies or statements made in reckless disregard of the truth," and no evidence to support the jury's verdict.[9]

The U.S. Court of Appeals, District of Columbia Circuit, reversed the trial judge on a 2–1 vote, and reinstated the jury verdict

[6] Glover v. Herald Co., 549 S.W.2d 858 (Mo.1977), 2 Med.L.Rptr. 1846.

[7] Curtis Pub. Co. v. Butts, 388 U.S. 130, 155, 87 S.Ct. 1975 (1967).

[8] Tavoulareas v. Washington Post Co., 567 F.Supp. 651 (D.D.C.1983), 9 Med. L.Rptr. 1553.

[9] Ibid., 1555, 1561.

of $2.05 million.[10]   The majority found clear and convincing evidence of reckless disregard under the rules of *Butts, St. Amant,* and *Garrison* and added these other indicators of fault in the story: (1) The story carried on its face the warning to the newspaper that it had high potential for harm to Tavoulareas' reputation; (2) the journalists "were motivated by a plan to 'get' the plaintiffs, and deliberately slanted, rejected and ignored evidence contrary to the false premise of the story:" (3) the reporter's interview notes "reflect exactly the opposite of what he was told by the interviewees;" (4) the newspaper refused to retract the story or to print Tavoulareas' letter to the paper.[11]

In elaborating, Judge George MacKinnon (joined by Judge, and later, Supreme Court Justice Antonin Scalia) raised alarm among journalists. The Post's policy of exposing wrongdoing in public life might be characterized as "hard hitting investigative journalism" or as "sophisticated muckraking," the Court said, and either "certainly is relevant to the inquiry of whether a newspaper employee acted in reckless disregard of whether a statement is false or not." The suggestion that a newspaper's devotion to these two honored traditions in journalism might be evidence of reckless disregard of falsity shocked the field.

Judge J. Skelly Wright, at almost total odds with the court majority, spoke for countless journalists in his long, ranging dissent that rejected MacKinnon's analysis. Holding that a newspaper policy of investigative journalism and muckraking could be evidence of reporters' acting in reckless disregard of falsity endangered the First Amendment, Wright declared: [12]

> It is a conclusion fraught with the potential to shrink the First Amendment's "majestic protection" * * *.
>
> Muckraking—a term developed when writers like Lincoln Steffens, Ida Tarbell, and Upton Sinclair relentlessly exposed pervasive corruption—may be seen to serve that high purpose even if it offends and startles * * *.

Wright found in the majority opinion "deep hostility to an aggressive press" that "is directly contrary to the mandates of the Supreme Court and the spirit of a free press," and concluded that

---

[10] Tavoulareas v. Washington Post, 759 F.2d 90 (D.C.Cir.1985), 11 Med.L.Rptr. 1777. The same judges denied a petition of the Post to re-hear the case on another 2–1 vote, 763 F.2d 1472 (D.C.Cir.1985); but the 3–member panel's decision was vacated by the full Circuit Court (10 judges), which voted to hear the case *en banc*: Ibid., 1481.

[11] Ibid., 1809–1810.

[12] Ibid., 1798, 1821–1822. For coverage of similar reactions from journalists, see Peter Prichard, "Tavoulareas Case Returns—with Bite," Quill, May 1985, 25; "Anthony Lewis, Getting Even," New York Times, 4/11/85, A27; Anon., "Press Must Be Tough, but Fair," Milwaukee Journal, 4/12/85, 14.

"neither a newspaper's muckraking policy nor its hard- hitting investigative journalism should *ever* be considered probative of actual malice."

Ultimately, the Washington Post was rescued by a rehearing of the case by the full panel of the U.S. Court of Appeals for the District of Columbia. That court (with Supreme Court Justice–Designate Antonin Scalia not participating) voted 7–1 to throw out the jury's $2.05 million verdict. The court decided that actual malice had not been proven against the Washington Post. Further, a reputation for "sensational" or investigative reporting was *not* to be taken as evidence of actual malice.[13]

Court-determined indicators of "reckless disregard" (which amount to court-determined standards of news reporting) do not end with those at issue in *Tavoulareas*. They include: where a reporter did not make personal contact with anyone involved in the event before writing;[14] where a publication relied on an obviously biased source, was advised of the falsity of information, and published with no further investigation of the story;[15] where the publication printed although the story was inherently improbable.[16] Ill will of the reporter toward the subject of the story may in some cases contribute to a finding of reckless disregard.[17]

Defining Reckless Disregard: Harte–Hanks v. Connaughton (1989)

The *Connaughton* decision of 1989 marked the first time in two decades that the U.S. Supreme Court held against the media in a public figure libel case.[18] (Keep in mind, however that the media have lost some public figure libel cases over the years. See, for example, the $3.05 million libel loss incurred in Brown & Williamson v. Jacobson in 1987.)[19]

Harte–Hanks Communications, Inc. v. Connaughton says that the media may be held responsible for defamation in reporting on a candidate for public office if a jury could reasonably find "actual

[13] Tavoulareas v. Washington Post Co., 817 F.2d 762 (D.C.Cir.1987), cert. denied by the Supreme Court of the United States, 484 U.S. 870, 108 S.Ct. 200 (1987).

[14] Akins v. Altus Newspapers, Inc., 609 P.2d 1263 (Okl.1977).

[15] Stevens v. Sun Pub. Co., 270 S.C. 65, 240 S.E.2d 812 (1978).

[16] Hunt v. Liberty Lobby, 720 F.2d 631 (11th Cir.1983), 10 Med.L.Rptr. 1097, 1107.

[17] Cochran v. Indianapolis Newspapers, Inc., 175 Ind.App. 548, 372 N.E.2d 1211 (1978), 3 Med.L.Rptr. 2131; Tavoulareas v. Washington Post, 759 F.2d 90, 114 (D.C.Cir.1985), 11 Med.L.Rptr. 1777, 1820, vacated 763 F.2d 1472 (1985), affirmed 817 F.2d 762 (D.C.Cir.1987).

[18] Harte–Hanks Communications, Inc. v. Connaughton, 491 U.S. 657, 109 S.Ct. 2678 (1989), 16 Med.L.Rptr. 1881; News Media & the Law, Summer, 1989, p. 16.

[19] Brown & Williamson Tobacco Corp. v. Jacobson, 827 F.2d 1119 (7th Cir.1987), 14 Med.L.Rptr. 1497, cert. denied 485 U.S. 993, 108 S.Ct. 1302 (1988).

malice" misconduct by news organizations. The key here turned on how "reckless disregard for the truth" was defined.

The case arose in 1983 because of judicial election reporting by the Hamilton, Ohio, Journal–News, owned by Harte–Hanks until 1986. The newspaper published a story about municipal judge candidate Daniel Connaughton. The newspaper, which had endorsed Connaughton's opponent, published assertions that Connaughton had promised a grand jury witness and her sister jobs and trips if they would provide testimony embarrassing to his opponent for the judgeship.[20] (It did not help appearances that the Journal–News was in a circulation battle with the Cincinnati Enquirer, a newspaper which endorsed Connaughton.)

Connaughton lost the election, and sued the Hamilton Journal–News for defamation. The newspaper tried to defend itself by asserting a "neutral reportage" (see discussion near end of this chapter) privilege to present accurate and unbiased accounts of charges against a public figure/political candidate. The newspaper asked unsuccessfully for a summary judgment.[21]

Hindsight suggests that the Journal–News exposed itself to liability by failing to investigate thoroughly. When questioned by a reporter, Connaughton reportedly denied offering grand jury witnesses jobs or trips. Perhaps most damaging to the newspaper: It published its attack on Connaughton without interviewing key sources—who had been identified to the newspaper as such—whose denials could have put an end to the derogatory stories about Connaughton. Also, the newspaper decided not to listen to tape recordings available to it which could have provided additional information. As Justice John Paul Stevens wrote for the Court: [22]

> ... [D]iscrepancies in the testimony of Journal-News witnesses may have given the jury the impression that the failure to conduct a complete investigation involved a deliberate effort to avoid the truth.

And that adds up to actual malice. The key lesson for journalists is that they must not cut corners. They should always assume that non-journalists—such as members of a jury—may eventually be looking over their shoulders. The practical reporter's internal voice must keep asking: "If we publish this, will I be able to explain what I did to a jury?"

The jury in the Connaughton case did not believe the newspaper's explanations, and assessed damages totaling $200,000: $5,000

[20] 491 U.S. 657, 660, 109 S.Ct. 2678, 2682 (1989), 16 Med.L.Rptr. at 1883.
[21] Ibid.

[22] Harte–Hanks Communications, Inc. v. Connaughton, 491 U.S. 657, 684, 109 S.Ct. 2678, 2694 (1989), 16 Med.L.Rptr. at 1881, 1893.

compensatory, and \$195,000 punitive.[23]   Upholding that outcome, Justice Stevens wrote: [24]

> ... [I]t is clear that the conclusion concerning the newspaper's departure from accepted standards and the evidence of motive were merely supportive of the court's ultimate conclusion that the record "demonstrated a reckless disregard as to the truth or falsity ... [of the largely unsupported allegations against Connaughton] ... and thus provided clear and convincing proof of 'actual malice' as found by the jury." 842 F.2d at 847.   Although courts must be careful not to place too much reliance on such factors, a plaintiff is entitled to prove the defendant's state of mind through circumstantial evidence, see Herbert v. Lando, 441 U.S. 153, 150 (1979).

Knowing Falsity

The "reckless disregard" aspect of actual malice, is shown rather often in libel suits.   But the second aspect—knowing falsehood—is far less frequently found.   One case involved a suit by State Sen. Richard Schermerhorn of New York.   He was interviewed by reporter Ron Rosenberg of the Middletown *Times Herald Record* about the senator's proposal for the redevelopment plan (the NDDC) in Newburgh.   They discussed a community controversy about whether minorities' chances for benefiting from NDDC were sufficient.   Rosenberg wrote a story which was published under the headline SCHERMERHORN SAYS NDDC CAN DO WITHOUT BLACKS.   There was no reference to this in the story. A storm of protest against the senator arose, and Senators Beatty and von Luther proposed a resolution of censure in the Senate against Schermerhorn.   In a later story, Beatty was quoted as saying that he had access to tapes in which Schermerhorn made subtle anti-black and anti-Semitic statements.

Schermerhorn denied making the headline statement and told his Senate colleagues that if there were tapes showing he had made such statements, he would be unfit to serve in the Senate and would resign.   He brought a libel suit, and charged knowing falsehood.[25]   At trial, Rosenberg agreed that Schermerhorn had not told him what the headline reported, and that a copy editor—who

[23] Damages are discussed in Sec. 24.

[24] Harte–Hanks Communications, Inc. v. Connaughton, 491 U.S. 657, 667, 109 S.Ct. 2678, 2686 (1989), 16 Med.L.Rptr. at 1886.   Justice Stevens also emphasized judges' constitutional duty to " 'exercise independent judgment and determine whether the record establishes actual malice with convincing clarity,' " quoting Bose v. Consumer's Union, 466 U.S. 485, 514, 104 S.Ct. 1949, 1967 (1984): See 10 Med.L.Rptr. 1625, 1882.

[25] Schermerhorn v. Rosenberg, 73 A.D.2d 276, 426 N.Y.S.2d 274 (1980), 6 Med. L.Rptr. 1376.

was never produced at the trial—had written it. But both von Luther and Beatty testified, that, in telephone calls to them, Rosenberg had assured them that Schermerhorn had said that the NDDC could do without blacks, and von Luther added that Rosenberg volunteered that he had a tape in which Schermerhorn made racial and ethnic slurs. The tape was never produced, although both senators testified that they made repeated requests for it.

The jury was unconvinced that a copy editor who never showed up for Rosenberg's trial had written the headline, and in addition, the jury had von Luther's and Beatty's testimony that Rosenberg assured them the headline was accurate. The jury brought in a verdict of $36,000 in damages for Schermerhorn. The New York Supreme Court, Appellate Division, upheld the verdict on three of four counts saying "In our view, then, the evidence was sufficient to sustain the jury's determination that Rosenberg * * * had composed a defamatory headline with actual knowledge that the matter asserted therein was false." [26]

Altered Quotes: Masson v. The New Yorker, Alfred A. Knopf, and Janet Malcolm (1991)

If a writer alters an interview subject's quotations materially, is that "knowing falsity?" That was a key issue in a decade-long defamation suit which resulted in a Supreme Court decision [27] and which finally seemed to have been resolved by a November, 1994, jury verdict. The case, described as a soap-opera for the highly literate, involved a defamation suit by a flamboyant psychiatrist against a gifted writer of biographical profiles whose work frequently appears in The New Yorker. Once the case reached Supreme Court, its ruling meant that the psychiatrist had overcome a lower court's summary judgment ruling against him and could force the author to trial on his libel suit. [28] So in the fall of 1994, the dispute was back where it had started in 1983, in a U.S. district court in San Francisco.[29]

In 1983, psychiatrist Jeffrey M. Masson sued for defamation based on a two-part article by Janet Malcolm, first appearing in The New Yorker, and later published in book form by Knopf. The article/book stemmed from Ms. Malcolm's extensive tape-recorded

[26] Ibid., 1381. See also Morgan v. Dun & Bradstreet, Inc., 421 F.2d 1241 (5th Cir.1970); Sprouse v. Clay Communication, Inc., 158 W.Va. 427, 211 S.E.2d 674 (1975).

[27] Masson v. New Yorker Magazine, Inc., 501 U.S. 496, 111 S.Ct. 2419 (1991), 18 Med.L.Rptr. 2241.

[28] Masson v. New Yorker Magazine, Inc., 881 F.2d 1452 (9th Cir.1989), 16 Med.L.Rptr. 2089.

[29] Seth Mydans, "New Libel Trial Opens With Blocks," The New York Times, Oct. 4, 1994, p. A13.

interviews with Dr. Masson and dealt with his dismissal from his post as projects director of the Sigmund Freud Archives.

In his lawsuit, Dr. Masson argued that Ms. Malcolm had " ... fabricated words attributed to him with quotation marks, and misleadingly edited his statements to make him appear 'unscholarly, irresponsible, vain and lacking in personal honesty or moral integrity.' " [30] Masson contended that the magazine and Knopf knew of author Malcolm's misconduct before the book and the article were published.

All three defendants were granted summary judgments by a federal district court on the grounds that Dr. Masson had not established actual malice: " 'No clear and convincing evidence exists that would justify a holding that ... [the defendants] entertained serious doubts about the truth of the disputed passages.' " [31]

As a public figure, Dr. Masson was required by the Constitution to prove actual malice, and he had argued that a jury could find that standard of fault based on evidence of deliberately fabricated quotes that had been attributed to him. Dr. Masson presented evidence that several quotes ascribed to him did not appear on Ms. Malcolm's tape recordings, and contended that the writer herself had altered other quotes.

After the 1991 Supreme Court decision remanded the Masson case to the Ninth Circuit Court of Appeals, that court held the jury issue was whether Ms. Malcolm and the magazine abused the public trust by knowingly or recklessly published falsehoods. [32]

One of the disputed passages as published in Ms. Malcolm's writings involved her use of quotation marks around Dr. Masson's description of his plans to occupy Maresfield Gardens (home of the Freud Archives) after the elderly Anna Freud's death. Consider Justice Kennedy's repetition of that passage, and his comment upon it: [33]

> " 'It was a beautiful house, but it was dark and sombre and dead. * * * I would have renovated it, opened it up, brought it to life. Maresfield Gardens would have been a place of scholarship but also of sex, women, fun. It would have been like the change in The Wizard of Oz, from black-and-white into color.' " In the Freud Archives 33.

[30] 881 F.2d at 1453, 16 Med.L.Rptr. at 2089–2090.

[31] 881 F.2d at 1454, 16 Med.L.Rptr. at 2090.

[32] Masson v. The New Yorker, Alfred A. Knopf, and Janet Malcolm, 960 F.2d 896, 902–903 (9th Cir.1992), 20 Med.L.Rptr. 1009, 1014–1015.

[33] Masson v. New Yorker Magazine, Inc., 501 U.S. at 503, 111 S.Ct. at 2426 (1991), 18 Med.L.Rptr. at 2245.

[Justice Kennedy then commented:] The tape recordings contain a similar statement, but in place of the reference to "sex, women and fun," and the Wizard of Oz, petitioner [Masson] commented [in the tape recorded interview]:

"[I]t is an incredible storehouse. I mean, the library, Freud's library alone is priceless in terms of what it contains; all his books with his annotations in them; the Schreber case annotated, that kind of thing. It's fascinating."

Even though the Supreme Court's 7–2 decision meant that Ms. Malcolm could not escape a libel trial via summary judgment,[34] the majority opinion was a great relief to lawyers for the news media.[35] Justice Anthony M. Kennedy wrote that deliberate misquotation of a public figure cannot be libelous unless the wording changes the meaning of what really was said.[36]

Some excerpts from Justice Kennedy's opinion follow: [37]

In general, quotation marks around a passage indicate to the reader that the passage reproduces the speaker's words verbatim. They inform the reader that he or she is reading the statement of the speaker, not a paraphrase or other indirect interpretation by an author. By providing this information, quotations add authority to the statement and credibility to the author's work.

* * *

Second, regardless of the truth or falsity of the factual matters asserted within the quoted statement, the attribution may result in injury to reputation because the manner of expression or even the fact that the statement was made indicates a negative personal trait or an attitude the speaker does not hold.

* * *

Justice Kennedy noted that in some circumstances, as in a printed hypothetical conversation or in a work of fiction, a writer's use of quotation marks will not be understood be readers to mean

[34] "Summary judgment" procedures terminate a lawsuit unless the plaintiff can make a good showing of having a strong case.

[35] Linda Greenhouse, "Justices Refuse to Open a Gate for Libel Cases," The New York Times, June 21, 1991, p. A1.

[36] Masson v. New Yorker Magazine, Inc., 501 U.S. at 516, 111 S.Ct. at 2432 (1991), 18 Med.L.Rptr. at 2250–2251.

[37] Masson v. New Yorker Magazine, Inc., 501 U.S. at 511, 111 S.Ct. at 2430–2431 (1991), 18 Med.L.Rptr. at 2248.

the reproduction of actual conversations.[38]

* * *

In some sense, any alteration of a verbatim quotation is false. But writers and reporters by necessity alter what people say, at the very least to eliminate grammatical and syntactical infelicities.

(Among journalists, editing to "fix" an interviewee's syntax is by no means an agreed-upon procedure. For one thing, if a print journalist is reporting on words captured "live" in all their ungrammatical splendor, editorial splicing to make a flaming illiterate's words read as if they were spoken by George Will or Sam Donaldson will make the print media appear foolish. Also, what if the grammatical atrocities are spoken by, say, a State Higher Education Commissioner or a U.S. Department of Education official? Can they be edited into proper English without truly deceiving the public?)

Justice Kennedy's decision spoke cautiously to the issues at hand, declaring: [39]

If every alteration constituted the falsity required to prove actual malice, the practice of journalism, which the First Amendment standard is designed to protect, would require a radical change, one inconsistent with our precedents and First Amendment principles.

* * *

We conclude that a deliberate alteration of the words uttered by a plaintiff does not equate with knowledge of falsity for purposes of *New York Times v. Sullivan* ... and *Gertz v. Robert Welch* ... unless the alteration results in a material change in the meaning conveyed by the statement. The use of quotations to attribute words not in fact spoken bears in a most important way on that inquiry, but it is not dispositive in every case.

Deliberate or reckless falsification that comprises actual malice turns upon words and punctuation only because words and punctuation express meaning. Meaning is the life of language. And for the reasons we have given, quotations may be a devastating instrument for conveying false meaning. * * * [R]eaders of In the Freud Archives may have found Malcolm's portrait of petitioner especially

[38] Masson v. New Yorker Magazine, Inc., 501 U.S. at 514, 111 S.Ct. at 2431 (1991), 18 Med.L.Rptr. at 2248.

[39] Masson v. New Yorker Magazine, Inc., 501 U.S. at 514, 517–518, 111 S.Ct. at 2431, 2433 (1991), 18 Med.L.Rptr. 2241, 2249, 2251.

damning because so much of it appeared to be a self-portrait, told by petitioner in his own words. And if the alterations of petitioner's words gave a different meaning to the statements ... then the device of quotations might well be critical in finding the words actionable.

The Supreme Court's majority thus overturned the summary judgment, ruling that defendants Janet Malcolm and the New Yorker magazine could be taken to trial on the issue of libel. (Later, the magazine was removed from the case, in part because of its reputation for accuracy in editing and in part because Ms. Malcolm was regarded as an independent contractor, not a New Yorker employee.) In a minority opinion, Justices White and Scalia argued that under New York Times v. Sullivan, reporting a known falsehood is sufficient proof of actual malice.[40]

Journalists and legal commentators differed on the potential impact of Masson v. New Yorker. Jane Kirtley, director of the Reporters Committee for Freedom of the Press, said " '[a] lot more reporters are going to start using tape recorders in addition to notebooks—a kind of belt and suspenders protection.' "[41] The New York Times, however, said editorially that the Supreme Court had produced a measured decision meaning that[42]

... fallible journalists won't be held to stenographic exactitude for everything they put between quotation marks. Yet if a deliberately altered quote makes the speaker look like a self-confessed fool or rascal, the journalists had better be prepared to defend themselves in court.

Masson v. Malcolm: The Jury Returns (1994)

On November 2, 1994 a federal district court jury ruled in favor of Janet Malcolm. Its verdict said that her 1983 profile of Dr. Jeffrey Masson—although libelous in one passage—was not a product of the actual malice required for the psychiatrist to collect damages for defamation.[43]

This evidently meant the end of a 10-year-old battle in which Dr. Masson sought $7 million in damages. Ms. Malcolm continued to assert that her article was accurate, although she conceded that she had engaged in "compression," taking separate statements and molding them into a unified statement. In fact, the one quote the

[40] Masson v. New Yorker Magazine, Inc., 501 U.S. at 526, 111 S.Ct. at 2437–2438 (1991), 18 Med.L.Rptr. at 2255.

[41] Tony Mauro, "Journalists may need taped evidence of quotes," USA Today, June 21, 1991, p. 8A.

[42] "Misquotations, Measured," The New York Times, June 21, 1991, p. A12.

[43] The Associated Press, "Jury clears writer, says falsehoods not deliberate, reckless," The Knoxville News–Sentinel, Nov. 3, 1994, p. A8.

jury held to be libelous (even if not actionable defamation because of the absence of knowing falsity) was the product of compressing quotations.[44]

As published in Ms. Malcolm's article, these sentences were juxtaposed:

> " 'Because it is the honorable thing to do.' Well, he had the wrong man." [45]

However, the tapes of Malcolm's interviews with Dr. Masson revealed that there were 35 intervening words between the two sentences quoted above. In those words—present in the tapes but excluded from the article—Freud Archives director Kurt Eissler, who had dismissed Dr. Masson from his post as projects director—was urging Masson to accept his firing quietly, to remain silent and then there might be the possibility of someday getting his job back. This silence was sought, evidently, in the context of Eissler urging Masson not to "poison" or upset the aged Anna Freud's last days. The second sentence quoted above—"Well, he had the wrong man"—this was Dr. Masson's saying he would not remain quiet, **not**—as the compressed quote may be read—that Dr. Masson was saying that he refused to do the honorable thing.[46]

First Amendment lawyer James C. Goodale told The Wall Street Journal that the verdict should " 'give reporters more confidence in reporting substantially what their sources say,' rather than being tied to someone's exact words." [47] It should also send the message that quotes are "massaged" or "compressed" at a writer's ethical if not legal peril.

NBC's "Dateline" and the Pickup Fire Debacle

As media properties such as newspapers and television networks scrambled to hang onto their revenue shares, big stories about ethical lapses by the "news media" are more undesirable than ever. Adding to general public dissatisfaction with "the media" was the revelation in 1993 that a November 17, 1992 "Dateline NBC" television program had rigged "sparking devices" to make sure that a General Motors pickup truck would burst into flames during a staged collision. GM full-size pickup trucks made with side-mounted gasoline tanks from 1973 to 1987 were blamed for a number of truck fires.

---

[44] Edward Felsenthal, "New Yorker's Malcolm Is Cleared of Libel," The Wall Street Journal, Nov. 3, 1994, P. B12.

[45] David Margolick, "Psychoanalyst Loses Libel Suit Against a New Yorker Reporter," Nov. 3, 1994, pp. A1, A14.

[46] Ibid., and Felsenthal, op. cit.

[47] Felsenthal, op. cit.

After the NBC broadcast showing the staged crashes, General Motors officials told NBC News the "Dateline NBC" segment was unfair, and asked to inspect the vehicles used in the crashes. The network responded that "the vehicles had been junked and were not available." [48]

In January, 1993, GM evidently was tipped off that the staged fiery crash was not all it seemed. On January 18, GM got an injunction against the Indianapolis-based Institute for Safety Analysis, which had conducted the crash tests for NBC, order the Institute from destroying the vehicles used in the crash tests. The vehicles later were retrieved from a junkyard by GM.[49]

In February, 1993, after asking NBC for a retraction, GM filed a libel suit against the network, claiming the rigged tests were blatantly deceptive and caused irreparable harm, GM charged that the "crash test" fires had been touched off by radio transmitters which caused model rocket engines affixed to gasoline tanks to ignite.

Michael Gartner, then NBC News president, at first defended the Dateline NBC segment, comparing the sparking devices used in the crash tests to a heated headlight lamp filament, and declared the broadcast to be "fair and accurate." [50] Later, at Gartner's direction, NBC anchors Stone Phillips and Jane Pauley apologized on "Dateline NBC" for the rigged pickup crash tests. General Motors quickly dropped its lawsuit against NBC, and, on March 2, Gartner resigned from the presidency of NBC News, although no one had accused him of having personal knowledge of the deception.[51]

Although the lawsuit was dropped, the reputation of NBC News was not enhanced by the rigged pickup truck crash misadventure. Although this kind of credibility shortfall may lead to more jurors hostile to media in lawsuits, NBC's crash tests can be seen as disserving the public in another way. General Motors pickup trucks with side-mounted gas tanks were the subject of a National Highway Safety Administration (NHSA) study of whether the trucks should be recalled. Refitting nearly five million vehicles with new tanks would be a huge expense for GM. Late in 1994, GM reached agreement with the U.S. Department of Transportation to give $51 million to safety programs in exchange for not

[48] Doron P. Levin, "In Suit, GM Accuses NBC of Rigging Crash Tests," The New York Times, Feb. 2, 1993, p. A11.

[49] Ibid.

[50] Adler, op. cit.

[51] Ken Auletta, "Changing Channels," The New Yorker, March 15, 1993, p. 38.

recalling the pickups.[52]

Slipshod journalism has its price. As pointed out by Paul McMasters, executive director of the Freedom Forum First Amendment Center at Vanderbilt University, this crash test flap enabled GM to divert attention from the real issue: Are those pickup trucks as safe as they should be? [53]

SEC. 30. SPECIAL ISSUES: JURIES, SUMMARY JUDGMENT, NEUTRAL REPORTAGE, DISCOVERY

Juries

If "actual malice" leaves journalists uncertain about the fine distinctions and contradictions among courts, it presents a broader problem for juries called upon to analyze and employ it in deciding libel suits.[54] Jurors' minds must be cleared of predispositions to consider that the ill will or spite associated in plain English with "malice" is not really at issue, but rather, knowing or reckless falsehood by the publisher. This may involve a difficult "turnaround" in jurors' thought processes, and possibly resentment at the idea that a writer/publisher who harbors spite, hatred, or ill will against the plaintiff nevertheless may be legally immune from a libel judgment. Justice Potter Stewart said, after 15 years' experience with the Times v. Sullivan actual malice, that he "came greatly to regret" the Court's employment of that term: [55]

> For the fact of the matter is that "malice" as used in the New York Times opinion simply does not mean malice as the word is commonly understood. In common understanding, malice means ill will or hostility * * *. As part of the * * * standard enunciated in the New York Times case, however, "actual malice" has nothing to do with hostility or ill will * * *.

And if a judge and attorneys in the case succeed in making the legal definition clear, there remains another problem for jurors enmeshed in libel law. Justice Goldberg of the United States Supreme Court warned of problems for juries in New York Times

[52] James Bennett, "U.S. and G.M. End Truck Case Without Recall," The New York Times, Dec. 3, 1994, p. A1.

[53] Remarks at Region 3 Society of Professional Journalists conference, Knoxville, TN, March 6, 1993.

[54] Marc Franklin, "Good Government and Bad Law * * *," 18 Univ. S.F.L.Rev. 1, 8 (1983); 10 Med.L.Rptr. #12, 3/20/84, News Notes; 8 Ibid. #39, 11/30/82, News Notes; Randall P. Bezanson, Gilbert Cranberg, and John Soloski, Libel Law and the Press: Myth and Reality (New York: The Free Press, 1987), p. 237 and passim.

[55] Herbert v. Lando, 441 U.S. 153, 199, 99 S.Ct. 1635, 1661 (1979).

Co. v. Sullivan: [56] "The requirement of proving actual malice * * * may, in the mind of the jury, add little to the requirement of proving falsity, a requirement which the Court recognizes not to be an adequate standard."

After trial Judge Oliver Gasch in *Tavoulareas* found the jury's verdict of some $2 million insupportable and disallowed it, Attorney Steven Brill interviewed five of the six jurors.[57] Brill found that they did not understand that falsity must be knowing or reckless to justify an award. They further believed that the *Post* was required to show the truth of its charges, whereas, of course, the rule actually was that Tavoulareas was required to show falsity.[58]

Brill asserted that the *Post* attorneys did not drum these points into the jury's minds, and talked to the jury of ordinary citizens in language appropriate to lawyers not laymen. As for Judge Gasch, his instructions to the jury consisted of almost two hours of review of legal points involved, bound to be difficult for jurors.[59]

A procedure widely praised as a clarification of the task for a jury was initiated in 1985 by Federal Judge Abraham Sofaer. Ariel Sharon, former defense minister of Israel, brought a libel suit for $50 million against *Time* magazine for its report that Sharon had discussed with Christian Phalangists of Lebanon the need for them to take revenge against assassins, just before the massacre of hundreds of Palestinians by Phalangists. In his instructions, Judge Sofaer had the jury take up three questions, one at a time, and report its finding on each before proceeding. First, he asked the jury, was the story defamatory? ("Yes," the jury found.) Next, was it false? ("Yes," the jury found.) Finally, was it done with actual malice? ("No," the jury found, and thus, *Time* was not liable for damages.) [60]

In the libel case brought by Gen. William C. Westmoreland against CBS in 1985—perhaps unequalled in the publicity attending it and costliness to the participants— [61] Judge Pierre Laval used another device to aid the jury: He simply barred the use of the confusing term "actual malice" during the trial, substituting the

[56] 376 U.S. 254, 299, 84 S.Ct. 710, 736 (1964).

[57] Steven Brill, "Inside the Jury Room at the Washington Post Libel Trial," American Lawyer, Nov. 1982, 1, 93, 94.

[58] Ibid., 1, 90.

[59] Ibid., 92. The Libel Defense Resource Center prepared a manual of jury instructions on libel: LDRC Bulletin # 10, Spring 1984, 1–2. Proof of Actual Malice in Defamation Actions: an Unsolved Dilemma, 7 Hofstra L.Rev. 655, 701.

[60] Time, Feb. 4, 1985, 64, 66.

[61] The 18–week trial may have cost the parties well over $10 million in expenses, New York Times, Feb. 19, 1985, 10, 26; and see Ibid., from mid-October 8, 1984, to Feb. 19, 1985, for the extent of coverage.

"state of mind" of the journalists as a clearer criterion.[62] West-moreland, who sued for "CBS Reports'" accusation that he engaged in a "conspiracy" to understate enemy troop strength when he was Commander of United States forces during the Vietnam War, withdrew his suit after 18 weeks of testimony. The jury was never put to the test of grappling with "actual malice" and "state of mind."

The troubling problem of legal technicalities confronting juries by no means ends the question of how media faced with libel suits need to cope with prejudice.[63] For example, widespread anti-media attitudes of recent decades are likely to be represented within the cross-section of people that often comprises a jury. A juror's support for media's rights to publish may be wiped out by resentment of and lack of trust in powerful institutions. Jurors react badly to perceived arrogance, inaccuracy, and invasion of privacy by newspapers, magazines, and broadcasters.

The many awards by juries of enormous judgments for libel—particularly punitive damages—suggest powerfully that jurors often are disposed to punish media. Jurors often, also, tend to sympathize with the individual whose reputation, feelings, and status among his friends seem tarnished by the rich media corporation, seen by the jury as callous and careless. Where unfairness in media stories is at issue in libel trials, such juror hostility may put a high price on freedom of expression.

Summary Judgment

If a judge at the threshold of a libel trial finds that a plaintiff is a public figure or public official, the case moves at once to a second pretrial consideration, of great importance to the defending news medium and the plaintiff. The plaintiff alleges actual malice, and the defendant ordinarily denies it and moves that the judge dismiss the case in a "summary judgment" for the defendant. Winning such a motion avoids a trial. Avoiding libel trials is desirable for a number of reasons. First, to defend the average libel suit through a trial will cost an average of $175,000, according to a 1991 study by John Soloski.[64] Second, the extended distraction and emotional drain of a libel suit add up to a real threat to vigorous reporting.

[62] Washington Post National Weekly Edition, March 11, 1985, 28.

[63] See James J. Brosnahan, First Amendment Jury Trials, 6 Litigation 4, 28 (Summer 1980); see Bezanson, et al., op. cit.

[64] John Soloski, draft proposal for The Libel Law Reform Movement (with Randall Bezanson), published in 1992 by the Guilford Press of New York; "Libel Law and Journalistic Malpractice: A Preliminary Analysis of Fault in Libel Litigation," paper presented to the Law Division at the August, 1991, convention of the Association for Education in Journalism and Mass Communication.

The importance of summary judgment to the media's defense and to the public need for robust, uninhibited, wide-open reporting was laid out in the decision in Washington Post Co. v. Keogh,[65] an early case that interpreted Times v. Sullivan:

> In the First Amendment area, summary procedures are * * * essential. For the stake here, if harassment succeeds, is free debate. One of the purposes of the *Times* principle, in addition to protecting persons from being cast in damages in libel suits filed by public officials, is to prevent persons from being discouraged in the full and free exercise of their First Amendment rights with respect to the conduct of their government.

In ruling on the motion for summary judgment by the defendant, the judge must make a decision: Is there a "genuine issue of material fact"—a substantial claim by the plaintiff supported by evidence—that there was knowing or reckless falsity in the publication?[66]

Chief Justice Warren Burger of the United States Supreme Court in 1979 wrote a famous footnote—number 9 in Hutchinson v. Proxmire—casting doubt on the appropriateness of summary judgment in libel cases. Lower courts take his admonition into account and sometimes have found it a basis for denial of summary judgment, but summary judgments seem to be granted defendants far more often in libel suits brought by public people than they are denied.[67] Despite the famed footnote, many defamation actions— perhaps as many as 75 per cent of those brought by public figures or officials in the last decade—have been ended by grants of summary judgments to media defendants.

In a decision helpful to the media, the Supreme Court ruled in Jack Anderson v. Liberty Lobby, Inc.(1986) that public official or public figure suits must be ended before trial by summary judgment unless libel can be shown with "convincing clarity." Anderson was sued after articles said to portray Willis Carto and Liberty Lobby as Neo–Nazi, racist, and fascist.

Plaintiffs Carto and Liberty Lobby argued against the summary judgment, saying that the researcher for the Jack Anderson

---

[65] 125 U.S.App.D.C. 32, 365 F.2d 965, 968 (1966).

[66] Restatement, Second, Torts, Vol. 3, p. 220. Cerrito v. Time, Inc., 449 F.2d 306 (9th Cir.1971); Hayes v. Booth Newspapers, Inc., 97 Mich.App. 758, 295 N.W.2d 858 (1980), 6 Med.L.Rptr. 2319.

[67] Hutchinson v. Proxmire, 443 U.S. 111, 99 S.Ct. 2675 (1979). Yiamouyiannis v. Consumers Union of U.S., Inc., 619 F.2d 932 (2d Cir.1980), 6 Med.L.Rptr. 1065. Defendants' motions for summary judgment in the 1980s have been successful about 75% of the time, and Burger's "footnote 9" has been used rarely: Libel Defense Resource Center Bulletin # 13, Spring 1985, 10.

column's articles had relied on several unreliable sources and because there were inaccuracies in the articles. Writing for the Supreme Court, Justice White wrote that trial judges must decide, based on pre-trial affidavits, whether a public plaintiff can meet the actual malice standard by "clear convincing evidence." If not, summary judgment should be granted.[68]

Police Chief Prease alleged in a suit that stories in the Akron, (O.) *Beacon Journal* libeled him. Assistant Managing Editor Timothy Smith said that all statements in the stories were made in good faith with no serious doubts about their accuracy, and the Chief did not refute Smith. Thus the judge found that there was no issue between them about actual malice—no "genuine issue of material fact" that would have to be argued before a jury for decision. He granted summary judgment for the newspaper.[69]

But the United States Court of Appeals, Fourth District, found such an issue in Fitzgerald v. Penthouse Intern., Ltd.,[70] and reversed a trial court's grant of summary judgment to *Penthouse*. Fitzgerald, a specialist in the use of dolphins as military weapons, sued *Penthouse* for an article about his work that might have been construed as an allegation of espionage—selling dolphins trained as "torpedoes" to other nations, for "fast bucks." The Court found that *Penthouse* relied almost exclusively for its story upon a questionable source, and detailed his "many bold assertions about the United States intelligence community" which in some cases "invite skepticism." It quoted St. Amant v. Thompson: [71] Recklessness may be found "where there are obvious reasons to doubt the veracity of the informant or the accuracy of his reports." Fitzgerald had presented a factual question about whether *Penthouse* had "obvious reasons to doubt" its source; *Penthouse* would have to go to trial on the matter of actual malice.

Neutral Reportage

A sometimes useful—but not-to-be-trusted—defense against libel lawsuits goes under the name of "neutral reportage." The neutral reportage argument is one which lawyers sometimes use on behalf of media clients, but as of 1992, that defense had not attained the status of a reliable constitutional defense.

Back in 1977, Judge Irving Kaufman of the U.S. Court of Appeals, Second Circuit, pioneered the neutral reportage concept in

[68] 477 U.S. 242, 106 S.Ct. 2505 (1986), 12 Med.L.Rptr. 2297.
[69] Prease v. Poorman (Ohio Com.Pls.1981), 7 Med.L.Rptr. 2378.
[70] 691 F.2d 666 (4th Cir.1982), 8 Med.L.Rptr. 2340.
[71] 390 U.S. 727, 732, 88 S.Ct. 1323, 1326 (1968).

Edwards v. National Audubon Society, Inc.[72]　Judge Kaufman wrote for the court that the Constitution protects accurate, unbiased news reporting of accusations made against public figures regardless of the reporter's view of their truth.　This concept is related to the long-standing common-law and statutory doctrine of qualified privilege immunity from successful libel suit for fair and accurate reports of official proceedings. (See Sec. 33.)

The case arose when The New York Times carried a story reporting accurately a National Audubon Society's written statement that some scientists were paid to lie about the effects of the pesticide DDT upon birds.　This outraged scientists who were implicated, and they brought a libel suit against the Society and the Times.　Overturning a jury verdict for the scientists, Judge Kaufman wrote for the Court of Appeals that "a libel judgment against the *Times,* in face of this finding of fact, is constitutionally impermissible."　He reasoned: [73]

> At stake in this case is a fundamental principle.　Succinctly stated, when a responsible, prominent organization like the National Audubon Society makes serious charges against a public figure, the First Amendment protects the accurate and disinterested reporting of those charges, regardless of the reporter's private views of their validity. * * * What is newsworthy about such accusations is that they were made.　We do not believe that the press may be required under the First Amendment to suppress newsworthy statements merely because it has serious doubts regarding their truth.

Judge Kaufman applied this doctrine only to situations where the press was not taking sides or was deliberately distorting statements in order to launch a personal attack.　But in this case, the judge said, reporter John Devlin of The Times wrote an accurate account, did not take the Audubon Society's side in his article.　Further, Devlin's article included the scientists' indignant responses to the Audubon Society's charges.　Judge Kaufman's opinion termed Devlin's work "an exemplar of fair and dispassionate reporting.... Accordingly, we hold that it was privileged under the First Amendment." [74]

Welcome as the "neutral reportage" concept was to the news media, it quickly was met by an opposing view from another U.S. Court of Appeals.　Writing in Dickey v. CBS (1978), Judge Hunder

---

[72] 556 F.2d 113 (2d Cir.1977).　See Kathryn D. Sowle, "Defamation and the First Amendment: The Case for a Constitutional Privilege of Fair Report," 54 NYU Law Review 469 (June, 1969).

[73] Edwards v. National Audubon Society, Inc., 556 F.2d 113, 120 (2d Cir.1977).

[74] Ibid.

ruled for his court that "no constitutional privilege of neutral reportage exists." [75] That case involved a libel action resulting from a television broadcast of a pretaped talk show in which a Pennsylvania Congressman accused a public figure of accepting payoffs. Although CBS won the case, it was not on "neutral reportage" grounds, which Judge Hunder said flew in the face of the much-cited decision in St. Amant v. Thompson (1964) [76] (mentioned earlier at page 172.) Judge Hunder criticized the Audubon decision: [77]

> While the Second Circuit [in Edwards v. Audubon Society] found that there can be no liability despite the publisher's "serious doubts" as to truthfulness, *St. Amant* holds that for libel against a public figure to be proved, "[t]here must be sufficient evidence to permit the conclusion that the defendant in fact entertained *serious doubts* as to the truth of his publication. Publishing with such doubts shows reckless disregard for truth or falsity and demonstrates actual malice."

* * *

> We therefore conclude that a constitutional privilege of neutral reportage is not created * * * merely because an individual newspaper or television or radio station decides that a particular statement is newsworthy.

Since the Dickey case of 1978, the concept of neutral reportage has had an uneven and generally unpredictable history of acceptance and rejection, but it may be said that at times it has proven to be a useful defense for the media. A number of states have accepted the neutral reportage doctrine, including Florida and Ohio; [78] others have rejected it. [79] In Illinois in the 1980s, one Appellate Court adopted the neutral report privilege, another rejected it, and the state's Supreme Court refused to consider the

[75] Dickey v. CBS Inc., 583 F.2d 1221 (3d Cir.1978).

[76] 390 U.S. 727, 731, 88 S.Ct. 1323, 1325 (1968).

[77] Dickey v. CBS, Inc., 583 F.2d 1221, 1225–1226 (3d Cir.1978).

[78] El Amin v. Miami Herald Pub. Co. (Fla.1983), 9 Med.L.Rptr. 1079; Horvath v. Telegraph (Ohio App.1982), 8 Med.L.Rptr. 1657. See especially John B. McCrory et al., "Constitutional Privilege in Libel Law," 1993 Revision by Robert D. Sack et.al., in James C. Goodale, Communications Law 1993, Vol. II (New York: Practising Law Institute, 1993), pp. 355–363.

[79] New York: Hogan v. Herald Co., 84 A.D.2d 470, 446 N.Y.S.2d 836 (1982), 8 Med.L.Rptr. 1137, affirmed 58 N.Y.2d 630, 458 N.Y.S.2d 538, 444 N.E.2d 1002 (1982), 8 Med.L.Rptr. 2567; Kentucky: McCall v. Courier–Journal and Louisville Times Co., 623 S.W.2d 882 (Ky.1981), 7 Med.L.Rptr. 2118; Michigan: Postill v. Booth Newspapers, Inc., 118 Mich.App. 608, 325 N.W.2d 511 (1982), 8 Med.L.Rptr. 2222.

issue.[80]

Efforts to use—and get wider recognition for—the defense of neutral reportage continued into the 1990s. When the defense has succeeded, it has been in situations where the plaintiff was a public figure and where the report involved was fair and accurate without the espousal of a point of view by the news medium.[81] For example, the defense failed in Cianci v. New Times Publishing Co. There, *New Times* was found by the Second Circuit (enunciator of the *Edwards* doctrine) to have violated many of the qualifications limiting the privilege. The publication was flatly denied the neutral reportage privilege for its story suggesting falsely that a mayor had been a rapist.[82]

In 1989, in a case setting (at least temporarily) a record for punitive damages against a newspaper in a case surviving the appeals process, the neutral reportage case was rejected as inapplicable. The Pittsburgh Post–Gazette paid (including $561,000 in interest) damages totaling $2.8 million. (Of that amount, a total of $2 million was in punitive damages.) In that case, DiSalle v. P–G Publishing Co.[83], a Pennsylvania court held:

> . . . [I]f neutral reportage is to be recognized as a constitutional privilege, it can offer protection irrespective of the publisher's belief in the truth or falsity of the charges only when a public official or public figure levels a false charge against a public official or figure.

On the other hand, as attorney Robert McGough said after representing the Pittsburgh–Post Gazette in this case, newspapers commonly report on accusations by private parties against public officials " 'without knowing or caring whether the accusation is true . . . In Pennsylvania, it is now not enough to report the accusation accurately.' "[84]

Neutral reportage, then, is an unreliable defense. The policy decision to publish or broadcast a story involving defamatory charges in an unprivileged situation—even against a person or entity appearing to be a "public official" or a "public figure"— should be checked out not only by journalists but by their legal advisers before publication.

[80] Fogus v. Capital Cities Media, Inc., 111 Ill.App.3d 1060, 67 Ill.Dec. 616, 444 N.E.2d 1100 (1982), 9 Med.L.Rptr. 1141, 1143.

[81] Goodale, loc. cit.

[82] Cianci v. New Times Publishing Co., 639 F.2d 54 (2d Cir.1980), 6 Med.L.Rptr. 1625.

[83] Albert Scardino, "Pittsburgh Paper Pays $2.8 million Libel Award," The New York Times, July 12, 1989, p. 9; DiSalle v. P.G. Publishing Co., 375 Pa.Super. 510, 544 A.2d 1345, 1363 (1988), 15 Med.L.Rptr. 1873.

[84] Scardino, loc. cit.

Discovery

The libel plaintiff knows that he will be faced at the outset of his action with a motion for summary judgment by the defendant, and seeks evidence in advance of the trial to counter the motion he knows will come. Often using "discovery proceedings," his attorney confronts the defendant with questions aimed at helping prepare the case. Meanwhile, the defendant news medium is interrogating the plaintiff in similar discovery. Plaintiffs commonly seek evidence, during discovery, of actual malice on the part of the journalist, for their "threshold" showing of this essential ingredient at the outset of the trial. Another element often sought is the identity of confidential sources of the reporter's information—persons quoted in a story, but not named. Refusal by the journalist to testify in discovery proceedings can result in citation for contempt of court.

In one of the most celebrated media cases of the 1970s, Barry Lando and Mike Wallace of CBS' "60 Minutes" refused to answer questions in discovery proceedings that sought to probe their "state of mind" in preparing a segment on one Col. Anthony Herbert. Herbert, a public figure, was suing for words in the broadcast which, he said, portrayed him as a liar in his accusations that his superiors covered up reports of Vietnam War crimes. He was seeking evidence of actual malice on the part of Lando and Wallace. Confronted in discovery proceedings that lasted a year and produced almost 3,000 pages of Lando's testimony alone, Lando refused to respond when it came to inquiries into his state of mind in editing and producing the program, and into the editorial process in general. He said this was a realm of journalistic work that must not be intruded upon for fear of its chilling effect on expression protected by the First Amendment.

While the Court of Appeals, Second District, held on a 2–1 vote that First Amendment interests warranted an absolute evidentiary privilege for Lando, the U.S. Supreme Court reversed, saying that the First Amendment does not prohibit plaintiffs from directly inquiring into the editorial processes of those whom they accuse of defamation.[85] Journalists in libel cases had been testifying as to their motives, discussions, and thoughts relating to their copy, for a century and more before Times v. Sullivan without objecting to the process, said Justice White in writing the majority opinion; and Times v. Sullivan "made it essential to proving liability that plaintiffs focus on the conduct and state of mind of the defendant." He elaborated: [86]

[85] Herbert v. Lando, 441 U.S. 153, 99 S.Ct. 1635 (1979), 4 Med.L.Rptr. 2575.
[86] Ibid., at 160, 99 S.Ct. at 1641, 4 Med.L.Rptr. at 2578.

To be liable, the alleged defamer of public officials or of public figures must know or have reason to suspect that his publication is false. In other cases proof of some kind of fault, negligence perhaps, is essential to recovery. Inevitably, unless liability is to be completely foreclosed, the thoughts and editorial processes of the alleged defamer would be open to examination.

A few newspaper editorials and media voices recognized that the *Herbert* decision had broken no new ground and presented no fresh menace to the First Amendment, but attacking of the Supreme Court was far more common as media took the view that the justices had violated the integrity of the "editorial process" and the First Amendment.[87] Alarmed reactions of shock over presumed new damage by the Court to the First Amendment were often without understanding that what the Court was finding was in line with what lower courts had found for decades or for a century. In general, press reactions spoke eloquently to journalists' superficial education in the history of press freedom, and to their necessary occupational fix upon the world's current "hot scoop," unalloyed by knowledge of the history in which their own First Amendment roots were embedded.

Discovery in libel had arrived to stay, the *Herbert* case confirming its applicability. Said one media attorney at the time:[88] "While there was an outcry from some representatives of the press at the time, it now seems unlikely that the opinion will have any dramatic effect. Before *Herbert* journalists had routinely testified about the editorial process in establishing their freedom from 'actual malice' or 'fault.' As a result of *Herbert,* they will continue to do so."

Because the discovery process can be so intrusive, sensible journalists (or public relations or advertising people who get involved in litigation) should always conduct themselves carefully. Self-protective reporters have long understood that their story notes (or tape recordings, or video out-takes) may be subpoenaed as part of the discovery process in litigation. If you and your newspaper are being sued for libel by a mayor, do you want to explain the doodles you've sketched on your note pad to a jury? What if you've drawn a passable likeness of the mayor but added fangs? But—as pointed out in Chapter 4—even if you have embarrassing materials in your notes or in video outtakes, do *not* destroy any materials relating to litigation once "the papers have been filed" to start a legal action. Don't destroy such materials while there is still any

[87] Editorials on File, April 16–30, 1979, pp. 437–446.

[88] Robert D. Sack, "Special Discovery Problems in Media Cases," Communications Law 1980, I, 235, 242 (Practising Law Institute 1980).

possibility of an appeal or further proceedings. If you do, the court may assume that destruction of materials subject to discovery is evidence of actual malice,[89] or may be punishable as contempt of court.

[89] See Brown & Williamson Tobacco Corp. v. Jacobson, 827 F.2d 1119 (7th Cir.1987), discussed at pp. 123–125.

Chapter 6

DEFENDING AGAINST LIBEL SUITS
UNDER STATE LAW

Sec.
31. Determining Who Is "Private."
32. Ending Strict Liability in Libel.
33. Qualified Privilege as a Defense.
34. Truth as a Defense.
35. Opinion and Fair Comment as Defenses.
36. Retraction.

SEC. 31. DETERMINING WHO IS "PRIVATE"

Since the 1974 decision in Gertz v. Robert Welch, Inc. provided that private persons' libel suits have a lower barrier to clear than public persons', determining who is "private" has been of first importance in defamation actions.

If a person brings a libel suit against a news medium, one of the defense attorney's fondest hopes is that the judge will rule that the plaintiff is a public person: a "public official" or a "public figure." As discussed in the preceding chapter, the public person has to prove "actual malice" in order to win a libel suit.[1]

This chapter concentrates on what happens when private persons bring libel suits. When that happens, news media often make use of state statutes and state constitutions as their defenses,[2] thanks to the important decision in Gertz v. Robert Welch.[3] In *Gertz,* the U.S. Supreme Court said that society's stake in getting news about private persons is not as great as where public persons are involved. To put it another way, society places a high value in protecting private persons against libel. Thus, private persons may meet a less demanding test—proving negligence—than having to meet the constitutional barrier of proving actual malice.

---

[1] See Sec. 25, above. Public persons have to prove "actual malice"—publication of a defamatory falsehood with knowledge of falsity or reckless disregard for the truth.

[2] See Robert D. Sack, "Common Law Libel and the Press: A Primer," in James C. Goodale, chairman, Communications Law 1993, Vol. 2 (New York: Practising Law Institute, 1991), pp. 35–142; Comment, "The Impending Federalization of Missouri Defamation Law," 43 Mo.L.Rev. 270 (1978), discussing relationships of traditional and constitutional principles in the law of defamation.

[3] 418 U.S. 323, 94 S.Ct. 2997 (1974).

The reasons for this were detailed in an earlier discussion of *Gertz* (above, Sec. 28). Briefly, the Court said that private people have not accepted the risk of exposing themselves to the rough-and-tumble give-and-take of public scrutiny and controversy associated with public life. Further, it said, private people do not have the access to media that public people do, to refute false and disparaging news. Another reason that is sometimes given is that private people do not have the immunity from successful libel suits that public officials have in making statements from the platform of libel-proof official proceedings.[4]

Then who is a private person? A central test is that persons are private unless they voluntarily thrust themselves into the "vortex" of public controversy in order to influence the outcome of that controversy. It is worth repeating earlier points: One, of course, is that a person's presence in an official proceeding which is open to the public does not automatically destroy his private status (as with Ilya Wolston, Attorney Gertz, Mrs. Firestone, above).

Another is that the media cannot make a private person public merely by bringing the person into the news. That is illustrated by Hutchinson, of course, and also by Mrs. Mary Troman.[5] Mrs. Troman was drawn into a public controversy by a newspaper which, she said, implied that her home was a gang headquarters when it was no such thing. The court ruled that she was private. She had not in any way "injected" herself into a public controversy, nor had she invited public attention or comment.[6]

At the start of Chapter 5 we saw an attorney declared a public figure for all purposes: Myron Steere had been county attorney for eight years, with substantial publicity. He also had been special counsel for the board of county commissioners in a controversy over a new courthouse and was an officer and representative for many professional, fraternal and social activities. He had achieved influence in local affairs in his 32–year career in law practice in the county was now capped by representing a woman in her well-publicized, famous murder trial.

Yet attorney Paul Littlefield was not a public figure even though involved in a topic of public interest: his own disciplinary proceedings by the Iowa State Bar Association and the Iowa Supreme Court for practicing law while he was on probation. He brought a libel suit for an erroneous news story about the proceedings, and was declared a public figure by the trial court, which said he was drawn into a public forum and debate as a result of his "purposeful act of practicing law in Iowa in direct contravention of

---

[4] Ibid., at 344–45, 94 S.Ct. at 3009–3010.

[5] Troman v. Wood, 62 Ill.2d 184, 340 N.E.2d 292 (1975).

[6] Ibid.

his probation." But the U.S. Court of Appeals for the 8th district did not agree. It was Littlefield's status as a person, not the high public interest in his story, that was crucial: [7]

> We fail to see anything in Littlefield's status indicating that he has ready access to effective means of self-help or that he has voluntarily assumed the risks of public exposure by thrusting himself into a public controversy with a view toward influencing its resolution.

Shifting from professional people to the realm of business and commerce, corporations and business firms are intensely "public" in their reliance on the public's patronage. That may or may not be enough to make them public figures in libel actions. A San Francisco department store, City of Paris, advertised a close-out sale, and media reported widely its going-out-of-business. The store's agent in the sale, Vegod Corp., was said by KGO–TV to have brought inferior goods in during the sale, the story relying on the Better Business Bureau as its source for charges which included the "deceiving" of the public. Vegod sued, and claimed to be "private." The California Supreme Court agreed in a decision that said of the "public controversy test": [8]

> Criticism of commercial conduct does not deserve the special protection of the actual malice test. Balancing one individual's limited First Amendment interest against another's reputation interest * * *, we conclude that a person in the business world advertising his wares does not necessarily become part of an existing public controversy.

In 1985, the United States Supreme Court ruled in a case where it found a plaintiff to be a private person involved in a matter of *private* concern. Greenmoss Builders sought punitive damages from Dun & Bradstreet's false, confidential report, sent to five subscribers to its credit-reporting service, that Greenmoss had declared bankruptcy. Presumed and punitive damages had been barred to private plaintiffs in Gertz v. Robert Welch unless they could show actual malice. But Justice Lewis Powell wrote in a 5–4 decision that the *Gertz* rule applied only where the subject was a matter of public concern, and that this credit report was "solely in the individual interest of the speaker and its specific business

[7] Littlefield v. Fort Dodge Messenger, 614 F.2d 581, 584 (8th Cir.1980), 5 Med. L.Rptr. 2325, certiorari denied 445 U.S. 945, 100 S.Ct. 1342. See also Dodrill v. Arkansas Democrat Co., 265 Ark. 628, 590 S.W.2d 840 (1979), certiorari denied 444 U.S. 1076, 100 S.Ct. 1024 (1980), a "private" attorney. Gertz himself, of course, was a "private" attorney.

[8] Vegod Corp. v. ABC, 25 Cal.3d 763, 160 Cal.Rptr. 97, 603 P.2d 14 (1979), 5 Med.L.Rptr. 2043, 2045. And see Robert E. Drechsel and Moon, D., Corporate Libel Plaintiffs and the News Media * * *, 21 Am. Business L.Journ. 127, Summer 1983.

audience." [9]   The special protection given to speech by the *Gertz* rule and by *Sullivan*—to further robust debate on public issues— was not applicable here.   The Court upheld a jury award to Greenmoss of $50,000 compensatory damages and $300,000 punitive damages.

SEC. 32.   ENDING STRICT LIABILITY IN LIBEL

The law may no longer presume injury to persons as a result of false defamation even though it is libelous on its face.

Gertz v. Robert Welch, Inc. told private people they would not have to meet the constitutional demand of proving actual malice against publishers in bringing libel suits.   What, then, would be required of them?   Justice Powell wrote for the majority that the states might set their own standards of liability for private people to prove, except that the Constitution would not permit states to impose "liability without fault."   Powell was saying that state standards could not include an ancient rule in libel *per se*—that for those words which are damaging on their face, the law presumes injury to reputation and liability for libel by the publisher; the only question is the amount of damages that may be recovered.[10]   This was the long-standing rule of "strict liability" in libel, and the Court was saying that the media must be shielded from strict liability.   The standard of fault for private people to prove, Powell said, need be no more than "negligence," instead of the "actual malice" of *Sullivan*.   The Powell opinion significantly returned to the states much of the jurisdiction in libel cases that had been lost to them through the sweep of *Sullivan,* even as it made it plain that there must not be a return to "automatic" liability for defamation.

The *Gertz* majority then turned its attention to damage awards, outlining further restrictions on the states.   The states have a "strong and legitimate * * * interest in compensating private individuals for injury to reputation," but compensation may not be limitless.   A private plaintiff proving negligence can collect only "compensation for actual injury," otherwise known as "compensatory" or "general" damages.[11]   To collect punitive damages, private persons (like public officials or public figures) have to prove "actual malice" rather than mere negligence.   It found that awarding presumed damages ("compensatory" or "general" damages) or punitive damages where there is no demonstrated loss, "unneces-

[9] Dun & Bradstreet, Inc. v. Greenmoss Builders, Inc., 472 U.S. 749, 105 S.Ct. 2939, 2947 (1985).

[10] Gertz v. Robert Welch, Inc., 418 U.S. 323, 346, 94 S.Ct. 2997, 3010 (1974); Prosser, 780–781.

[11] Gertz v. Robert Welch, Inc., 418 U.S. 323, 348, 94 S.Ct. 2997, 3011 (1974).

sarily compounds the potential of any system of liability for defamatory falsehood to inhibit the vigorous exercise of First Amendment freedoms." [12]

Precisely what the Court meant by the permitted "compensation for actual injury" was not spelled out, but Justice Powell made it plain that he was not speaking strictly of compensation for proved dollar losses flowing from false defamation: [13]

> We need not define "actual injury," as trial courts have wide experience in framing appropriate jury instructions in tort action. Suffice it to say that actual injury is not limited to out-of-pocket loss. Indeed, the more customary types of actual harm inflicted by defamatory falsehood include impairment of reputation and standing in the community, personal humiliation, and mental anguish and suffering. * * * all awards must be supported by competent evidence concerning the injury, although there need be no evidence which assigns an actual dollar value to the injury.

The Negligence "Standard"

The Court's reliance on the ambiguous label of "negligence" has caused substantial problems for media defendants ever since the 1974 decision in Gertz v. Welch. As Justice Brennan predicted in his dissent, the majority opinion in *Gertz* requires media to observe a "reasonable care standard" (i.e. the "negligence standard"). Such a fluid concept, he suggested, could give state court juries intent on punishing unpopular views "a formidable weapon for doing so." He argued that the negligence concept in libel cases would lead to self-censorship because publishers would feel compelled to weigh carefully "a myriad of uncertain factors before publication." Even if recovery were limited under rules requiring proof of "actual injury" to reputation, that would not stop self-censorship arising from fear of having to defend a publication or broadcast against libel suit.[14]

Brennan feared that the decision would damage the media's protection, and Chief Justice Burger thought it could inhibit some editors.[15] Justice Byron White, on the other hand, declared the decision endangered the ordinary citizen who might be defamed. White's opinion, the longest in the case, placed his central objections to the majority in its "scuttling the libel laws of the States in

[12] Gertz v. Robert Welch, Inc., 418 U.S. 323, 348–351, 94 S.Ct. 2997, 3011–3012 (1974).

[13] Ibid.

[14] Ibid., at 366, 94 S.Ct. at 3020.

[15] Ibid., at 354, 94 S.Ct. at 3014.

* * * wholesale fashion." [16]   No longer would private plaintiffs have to prove only libel *per se*.   They also would have to prove "fault" on the part of the publisher, variously referred to in the Gertz opinions as "negligence" or lack of "reasonable care."   Also, private plaintiffs no longer could receive damages based on the publication of damaging words as under the libel *per se* rule; they would have to prove actual damage to their reputations.[17]

Standards of Fault in the States

In *Gertz,* the Supreme Court's majority put the burden of defining the standard of fault to be used onto the state courts: "We hold that, so long as they do not impose liability without fault, the States may define for themselves the appropriate standard of liability for a publisher or broadcaster of defamatory falsehood injurious to a private individual." [18]   The result, unsurprisingly, has been to encourage lack of uniformity in libel law among the states.   Note, also, that the majority in Gertz v. Welch—by not spelling out a lesser standard of fault—by indirection invited the states to fall back to the familiar (if squishy) concept of negligence.   The dissent by Justice William O. Douglas made that point: [19]

The standard announced today leaves the States free to "define for themselves the appropriate standard of liability for a publisher or broacaster" in the circumstances of this case.   This of course leaves the simple negligence standard as an option with the jury free to impose damages upon a finding that the publisher failed to act as "a reasonable man."   With such continued erosion of First Amendment protection, I fear that it may well be the reasonable man who refrains from speaking.

Robert D. Sack and Sandra S. Baron have found that at least two-thirds of the states–34 in 1994–have adopted the negligence standard in private figure defamation lawsuits.[20]

But states were not restricted to the "negligence" which Justice Powell implied in *Gertz*.   Some states have chosen other standards which are more difficult for plaintiffs to prove against media defendants.   Consider New York, important because of the amount of libel litigation in that state.   New York has fashioned a standard known by the shorthand label of "gross irresponsibility by

[16] Ibid., at 370, 94 S.Ct. at 3022.

[17] Ibid. at 374–377, 94 S.Ct. at 3024–3025.

[18] Ibid., at 346, 94 S.Ct. at 3010.

[19] Douglas dissent, 418 U.S. 323, 360, 94 S.Ct. 2997, 3017 (1974).

[20] Robert D. Sack and Sandra S. Baron, Libel, Slander and Related Problems, 2d ed.   (New York: Practising Law Institute, 1994), p. 340.

the news medium," to be applied when a private figure lawsuit falls "arguably within the sphere of legitimate public concern." [21]

John B. McCrory and colleagues have listed four states—Alaska, Colorado, Indiana, and New Jersey—as using an "actual malice" standard, at least as applied to private individuals involved in a matter of public interest.[22] In addition, four states—Connecticut, Louisiana, and Montana, and New Hampshire—were "undecided" on a standard of fault in private figure defamation cases as.[23]

Which Guideline? "Reasonable Journalist" or "Reasonable Person?"

As John B. McCrory, Robert D. Sack, and others have noted, the question arises whether the standard of conduct is going to be the traditional "reasonable man" or "reasonable person" standard of general negligence law, or whether a standard of conduct set by the media industry will be the guidepost.[24]

Both kinds of standards pose problems for media defendants. With the reasonable person standard, the non-journalists sitting on juries seem to have an inborn belief that by definition, journalists are not reasonable persons: journalists are intrusive and tell things that shouldn't be told. And if an industry standard is used—such as Justice Harlan's formulation, "standards of investigation and reporting ordinarily adhered to by responsible publishers," [25] then expert witnesses for a lawsuits two sides will no doubt disagree over what those standards properly should be. And once again, non-journalists—jurors and judges—will sit in a position to second-guess reporters, editors, and broadcasters.

Courts and Setting of Journalistic Standards

In no part of journalism law have the courts more clearly and consistently entered the realm of setting journalistic standards than where they judge the level of "fault"—whether the fault of

[21] Chapadeau v. Utica Observer–Dispatch, Inc., 38 N.Y.2d 196, 379 N.Y.S.2d 61, 341 N.E.2d 569 (1975). The similarity to Justice John Marshall Harlan's standard for public figures to meet in Curtis Pub. Co. v. Butts, 388 U.S. 130, 157, 87 S.Ct. 1975, 1992 (1967) has been commented upon by several observers, including Sack and Baron, op. cit., at p. 350.

[22] McCrory, et al., in Goodale, chairman, Communications Law, 1993 (Vol. 1) at pp. 320–321. The authors note that Alaska has conflicting U.S. district court decisions, so the fault standard for Alaska may be a question for the state's supreme court to resolve.

[23] Ibid., pp. 321–322.

[24] John B. McCrory, Robert C. Bernius, Robert D. Sack, et al., "Constitutional Privilege in Libel Law" in James C. Goodale, chairman, Communications Law 1993, Vol. 2, pp. 322–327; Sack and Baron, op. cit., p. 344.

[25] Curtis Pub. Co. v. Butts, 388 U.S. 130, 87 S.Ct. 1975 (1967).

actual malice or the fault of negligence or gross irresponsibility. Courts examine carefully the reporting and writing process at least as much when a plaintiff is private as when he is public.

In Tennessee, the state Supreme Court decided that it was up to the jury to say whether there had been negligence in a reporter's reliance on a single police record to suggest mistakenly that a woman was an adulterer. Using the "arrest report" of the Memphis police, a Press–Scimitar reporter wrote a story saying that Mrs. Nichols had been shot. The suspect, said the story, was a woman who went to the Nichols home and found her own husband there with Mrs. Nichols. The story used "police said" and "police reported" in attribution, the reporter testifying that these were common terms used to indicate that a source was either a written police record or a policeman's spoken words.

Had the reporter gone to the police record called the "offense report," he would have learned that not only was Mrs. Nichols with the suspect's husband (named Newton), but also Mr. Nichols and two neighbors. There would thus have been no suggestion that Mrs. Nichols was having an adulterous affair and had been "caught" by Mrs. Newton. Almost a month later, the newspaper printed a story correcting the implication of the first story. But Mrs. Nichols sued for libel, and testified at trial that the article had torn up her home, children, and reputation, that the family had had to move, that she had had telephone calls asking how much it cost to get the newspaper to run the correcting account. A friend testified that after the initial story, people gossipped about Mrs. Nichols and "said that she was a whore." Before the case went to the jury for decision, the trial court granted the newspaper a directed verdict: While "no fault had been shown" on the part of the reporter, the trial court said, it did note its uncertainty as to what standard of fault was required on the basis of *Gertz*. The Tennessee Court of Appeals, which reversed the trial court decision on several grounds, said that the standard of liability was "ordinary care." The case then went to the Tennessee Supreme Court, which in upholding the Court of Appeals and sending the case back for trial, laid down Tennessee's requirement upon private libel plaintiffs: negligence.[26]

> In determining the issue of liability the conduct of defendant is to be measured against what a reasonably prudent person would, or would not, have done under the same or similar circumstances. This is the ordinary negligence test that we adopt, not a "journalistic malpractice" test whereby liability is based upon a departure from

[26] Memphis Pub. Co. v. Nichols, 569 S.W.2d 412, 418 (Tenn.1978), 4 Med.L.Rptr. 1573.

supposed standards of care set by publishers themselves
* * *.

In General Products v. Meredith, an article on wood stoves in
Better Homes and Gardens Home Plan Ideas Magazine warned
against fire danger with the use of triple-walled chimneys in certain
stoves. The manufacturer (found to be "private") of one type, not
subject to the hazards of creosote buildup, brought suit. The
federal District Court denied part of the magazine's motion for
summary judgment, saying that there was evidence of possible
negligence by the reporter in his fact gathering: [27]

> * * * he relied on an earlier book and article and did
> not examine them directly, but drew on his general recall
> of their content. He did not contact the author of either
> source for an update, was not aware that the information
> in the magazine article had been repudiated by a subse-
> quent article in another publication, and did not contact
> anyone in the industry on testing relevant to his subject.

A KARK–TV reporter who happened to be near the scene of
police activity in a shopping center store was alerted to the fact,
and a camera crew from the station was sent. The crew filmed the
scene of police handcuffing two men and placing them in a squad
car. Reporter Long questioned the police but got no comment, and
interviewed a store clerk from whom she received vague responses.
Her story accompanying the broadcast film called the event a
"robbery attempt," and said that the two men "allegedly held a
store clerk hostage." But the handcuffed men were never arrested,
merely detained until police determined that the "tip" on which
they acted was false and there had been no robbery attempt. On
libel trial, each plaintiff was awarded $12,500.[28]

The Arkansas Supreme Court said there was enough evidence
of reporting negligence for the trial court to send that issue to the
jury: a news report relying completely on information from a police
scanner, without any checking, an on an eye-witness account from
a reporter who didn't know the context for what she observed, was
not "found to be due care as a matter of law." [29]

If reports from a police "scanner" were suspect in that case, a
news story about a gunshot death, based on a written report to
media from a police "hot line" was not negligent. The line was
started to lessen the need for interviews with police. The reporter,

[27] General Products Co., Inc. v. Meredith Corp., 526 F.Supp. 546 (E.D.Va.1981), 7
Med.L.Rptr. 2257, 2261.

[28] KARK–TV v. Simon, 280 Ark. 228, 656 S.W.2d 702 (1983), 10 Med.L.Rptr. 1049.
The Arkansas Supreme Court reversed and remanded the case because of the trial
court's error in permitting the jury to consider punitive damages, even though it
granted none.

[29] Ibid., at 704, 10 Med.L.Rptr. at 1051.

who had often used the "hot line" and found it reliable, accurately quoted the report's statement that the shooting occurred during a domestic argument. Later, the shooting was ruled accidental. The husband sued the newspaper for implying that he intentionally shot his wife, saying the reporter should have waited for a more "official" report. The Court found no negligence.[30] Nor, in another case, was there negligence in a reporter's failure to interview all eight persons arrested on drug charges, before publishing a story in which a father and son of the same name were confused. The court said that the reporter "undoubtedly could have taken additional steps to insure the accuracy of his facts." But he had talked with several officials, with an attorney, and with neighbors of the raided house, and had listened to a tape of a news conference about the event. His "procedures were well within the bounds of professionalism in the news gathering business." The court found no negligence.[31]

Illinois' Supreme Court adopted negligence as its standard, saying recovery might be had on proof that the defendant knew the statement to be false, or "believing it to be true, lacked reasonable grounds for that belief." It added that a journalist's "failure to make a reasonable investigation into the truth of the statement is obviously a relevant factor." [32] And it quoted the Kansas Supreme Court with approval as further elaboration of what "negligence" means: " * * * the lack of ordinary care either in the doing of an act or in the failure to do something. * * * The norm usually is the conduct of the reasonably careful person under the circumstances." [33]

If it's any help to the reporter, it may be noted that the word "care" is used in various courts' discussions of negligence. It is simply the "care" of the reasonably prudent person in the Arizona and Tennessee cases discussed above. And in the Illinois and Kansas cases just mentioned, the guideline is "ordinary care," while it is "reasonable care" (Washington),[34] and "due care" (Ohio).[35]

One analyst found that the first decade's use of the negligence standard demonstrated high uncertainty and severe contradictions in results, plus a likelihood that it produces self-censorship by

[30] Phillips v. Washington Post (D.C.Sup.Ct.1982), 8 Med.L.Rptr. 1835.

[31] Horvath v. Ashtabula Telegraph (Ohio App.1982), 8 Med.L.Rptr. 1657, 1662.

[32] Troman v. Wood, 62 Ill.2d 184, 340 N.E.2d 292, 298–299 (1975).

[33] Ibid., 299; Gobin v. Globe Pub. Co., 216 Kan. 223, 531 P.2d 76 (1975).

[34] Taskett v. KING Broadcasting Co., 86 Wash.2d 439, 445, 546 P.2d 81, 85 (1976).

[35] Thomas H. Maloney and Sons, Inc. v. E.W. Scripps Co., 43 Ohio App.2d 105, 334 N.E.2d 494 (1974).

media. He wrote in 1984 that the *Gertz* approach has failed,[36] and the view from 1994 indicates that the term "negligence" continues to be excruciatingly vague.

"Gross Irresponsibility"

In New York, the fault of negligence is not serious enough for a private individual to maintain a libel suit. The New York Court of Appeals has specified that, where the subject matter is of public concern, recovery for the private individual depends on his establishing "that the publisher acted in a grossly irresponsible manner without due consideration for the standards of information gathering and dissemination ordinarily followed by responsible parties." [37] The Utica *Observer-Dispatch* had reported two different episodes involving drug-charge arrests in a single story. At one point, it incorrectly brought together school teacher Chapadeau and two other men at a drug-and-beer party, referring to "the trio." Chapadeau was not there, and he brought a libel action. The Court of Appeals noted the error but also pointed out that the story was written only after two authoritative agencies had been consulted, and that the story was checked by two desk hands at the newspaper. "This is hardly indicative of gross irresponsibility," said the court. "Rather it appears that the publisher exercised reasonable methods to insure accuracy." [38] Summary judgment for the newspaper was upheld. It was denied, however, where a television reporter who had broadcast an account of fraudulent practices concerning burial expenses could recall little or nothing about his sources and how he obtained the information, and made little or no effort to authenticate his report. A jury, said the appeals court, would have to decide whether that was gross irresponsibility.[39]

Actual Malice

Private-person plaintiffs face a tougher test in some states, including Indiana, Colorado, and Wisconsin. Indiana is one of a minority of states continuing to adhere to the *Rosenbloom* plurality view that private persons involved in a matter of public interest need to prove actual malice to collect libel damages. Indiana's

---

[36] Marc Franklin, What Does Negligence Mean in Defamation Cases?, 6 Comm/Ent 259, 276–281 (Winter, 1984), and see pp. 266–271 for an excellent analysis of journalistic practices as examined by courts under the negligence standard.

[37] Chapadeau v. Utica Observer–Dispatch, Inc., 38 N.Y.2d 196, 379 N.Y.S.2d 61, 64, 341 N.E.2d 569, 571 (1975). The similarity to U.S. Supreme Court Justice Harlan's recommended standard for public figures to meet, in Curtis Pub. Co. v. Butts, 388 U.S. 130, 87 S.Ct. 1975 (1967), above, p. 117, is too striking to avoid a connection.

[38] Ibid., at 65, 341 N.E.2d at 572. See also Goldman v. New York Post Corp., 58 A.D.2d 769, 396 N.Y.S.2d 399 (1977).

[39] Meadows v. Taft Broadcasting Co., Inc., 98 A.D.2d 959, 470 N.Y.S.2d 205 (1983), 10 Med.L.Rptr. 1363.

Court Appeals, ruling in 1974 only six months after Gertz v. Welch was decided by the U.S. Supreme Court, said that Indiana's own constitution called for this rigorous barrier to recovery for libel, rather than for a negligence standard. The court said that differentiating requirements between public and private persons' libel suits "makes no sense in terms of our constitutional guarantees of free speech and press." [40]

In Colorado, similarly, the state supreme court has denied plaintiffs use of the *Gertz* negligence rule. A defamation defendant should be held liable in Colorado "if, and only if, [the publisher] knew the statement to be false and made the statement with reckless disregard for whether it was false or not."

The Colorado Supreme Court evidently believed that freedom of expression would be damaged with a weaker standard of fault than Times v. Sullivan actual malice in private figure cases.[41] New Jersey and Wisconsin's private person standards are harder to characterize. In New Jersey, private persons have to prove actual malice if they had the experience and awareness to realize that their private activities could bring about public interest and publicity. This seems to blur any distinction between public persons and private persons almost beyond recognition.[42] Wisconsin's Supreme Court has hinted that private plaintiffs would have to prove actual malice if the stories they sued over involved items of public interest,[43] yet the safest approach here is to treat the Badger state as relying on the negligence approach from Gertz v. Welch.[44]

It should be obvious from these examples that there is great variation in libel law from state to state, and that the late William L. Prosser was correct when he wrote animatedly about the haphazard, unplanned growth of this area of law.[45]

[40] Aafco Heating and Air Conditioning Co. v. Northwest Publications, 162 Ind. App. 671, 321 N.E.2d 580 (1974); see also Chang v. Michiana Telecasting (N.D.Ind. 1987), 14 Med.L.Rptr. 1889, 1900, and Bandido's, Inc. v. Journal Gazette Co., 575 N.E.2d 324 (Ind. Ct.App.1991), 19 Med.L.Rptr. 1178, 1181–1182 ("actual malice" is the standard to be used at trial, not in defendant's motion for summary judgment).

[41] Walker v. Colorado Springs Sun, Inc., 188 Colo. 86, 538 P.2d 450 (1975), cert. denied 423 U.S. 1025, 96 S.Ct. 469 (1975).

[42] Sisler v. Gannett Co., 104 N.J. 256, 516 A.2d 1083, 1093 (1986), 13 Med.L.Rptr. 1577.

[43] See, e.g., Denny v. Mertz, 106 Wis.2d 636, 318 N.W.2d 141 (1982); for state-by-state (and federal circuit-by-circuit) coverage updated each year, see, e.g. Henry R. Kaufmann, ed., LDRC 50–State Libel Survey 1994–1995 (New York: Libel Defense Resource Center, 1994).

[44] John Dawson and Lisa M. Arent, "Survey of Wisconsin Libel and Privacy Law," in Kaufman, op. cit., p. 811. In addition to Denny v. Mertz (see preceding footnote), the authors cited Van Straten v. Milwaukee Journal, 151 Wis.2d 905, 447 N.W.2d 105 (App.1989), where a story about inmates exposed to AIDS virus was held to be of public concern.

[45] Prosser, Law of Torts, 4th ed. (1976), pp. 737–738.

Proving "Actual Injury"

Having proved fault at some level—actual malice, negligence, gross irresponsibility—the plaintiff next, as we saw in Justice Powell's majority opinion in the landmark *Gertz* case, must go on to prove actual injury. No longer, as under old tort rules, will injury be presumed in libel cases except where the plaintiff shows *Sullivan* malice. Powell said that this could include various injuries— "impairment of reputation and standing in the community, personal humiliation, and mental anguish and suffering," as well as actual out-of-pocket loss.

Attorney Paul Littlefield, in a case discussed above,[46] was not successful in showing injury. Littlefield had been prohibited from the practice of law for three years, after he had been convicted of attempting to commit a felony. Further, he was found to have resumed practicing in violation of his probation. He brought a libel suit against the Fort Dodge Messenger for an erroneous report (it said he had pleaded guilty to a felony, a more serious offense than "attempting to commit a felony"). His injury, he testified, was that he was dismissed from his employment with the federal government after his supervisor made a trip to Fort Dodge, Ia., where he learned of Littlefield's disbarment. The court denied that there was injury: [47]

> Littlefield failed to prove either (1) that his supervisor ever believed him to be a felon, or (2) that such belief, rather than knowledge of his disbarment, was the motivating factor in his termination. Moreover, Littlefield failed to prove any link between the article of which he complains, published in 1974, and his superviser's 1976 discovery of his disbarment. Thus, Littlefield failed to prove any actual damage resulting from the article.

SEC. 33.   QUALIFIED PRIVILEGE AS A DEFENSE

News media may publish defamation from legislative, judicial or other public and official proceedings without fear of successful libel or slander action; fair and accurate reports of these statements are privileged.

Since long before the landmark year 1964 and the constitutional defense developed in and after New York Times Co. v. Sullivan, libel suits have been defended under statutory and common law provisions termed *qualified privilege, fair comment and criticism,* and *truth.* As noted earlier, the theory that free expression contrib-

---

[46] Littlefield v. Fort Dodge Messenger, 614 F.2d 581 (8th Cir.1980), 5 Med.L.Rptr. 2325, certiorari denied 445 U.S. 945, 100 S.Ct. 1342 (1980).

[47] Ibid., at 584, 5 Med.L.Rptr. at 2327.

utes to the public good in a self-governing society underlies the older defenses as well as the constitutional defense.

In some circumstances it is so important to society that people be allowed to speak without fear of a suit for defamation that their words are given immunity from a finding of libel or slander. The immunity is called privilege. For purposes of the mass media, it is applicable especially in connection with government activity.[48] The paramount importance of full freedom for participants in court, legislative or executive proceedings to say whatever bears on the matter, gives all the participants a full immunity from successful libel action. The immunity for the participant in official proceedings is called "absolute" privilege. No words relevant to the business of the proceeding will support a suit for defamation. If a person is defamed in these proceedings, he cannot recover damages.

Public policy also demands, in an open society, that people know to the fullest what goes on in the proceedings. For this reason, anyone who reports proceedings is given a limited or "qualified" immunity from successful suit for defamation. For the public at large, "anyone" ordinarily means the mass media. The protection is ordinarily more limited for the reporter of a proceeding than for the participant in the proceeding. It is thus called "qualified" (or "conditional") privilege.[49]

It may be argued that the mere fact of a person's participation in an official proceeding makes him a "public figure," and so puts him under the rigorous requirements of proving *Sullivan's* actual malice in a libel suit. The response, of course, is that neither Attorney Gertz nor Mrs. Firestone became a public figure through taking part in official court proceedings that resulted in news stories about them. As discussed in Chapter 5, both received damages for libel.

It has been held that any citizen has *absolute* immunity in any criticism he makes of government. The City of Chicago brought a libel suit against the *Chicago Tribune,* claiming damages of $10 million through the *Tribune's* campaign coverage in 1920. The stories had said that the city was broke, that its credit "is shot to pieces," that it "is hurrying on to bankruptcy and is threatened with a receivership for its revenue."

[48] For other circumstances where it applies, see Prosser, pp. 804–805; see also Robert Sack and Sandra Baron, op. cit., Chapter 6, pp. 361–408.

[49] A few states give absolute privilege to press reports of official proceedings, e.g. Thompson's Laws of New York, 1939, Civ.P. § 337, Wis.Stats.1931, § 331.05(1). And as we have seen in Ch. 4, Sec. 22, broadcasters are immune from defamation suits brought for the words of politicians in campaign broadcasts: Farmers Educational & Coop. Union of America v. WDAY, Inc., 360 U.S. 525, 79 S.Ct. 1302 (1959).

The court denied the city's claim. It said that in any libelous publication concerning a municipal corporation, the citizen and the newspaper possess absolute privilege.[50]

> Every citizen has a right to criticize an inefficient government without fear of civil as well as criminal prosecution. This absolute privilege is founded on the principle that it is advantageous for the public interest that the citizen should not be in any way fettered in his statements
> . . . [51]

Qualified privilege in reporting official proceedings is the heart of the concern here. The privilege arose in the law of England, the basic rationale having been developed before the start of the nineteenth century in connection with newspaper reports of court proceedings.[52] While American courts relied on English decisions, America was ahead of England in expanding the protection for press reports. The immunity was broadened to cover the reporting of legislative and other public official proceedings by the New York legislature in 1854, 14 years before privilege for reporting legislative bodies was recognized in England.[53] Other states readily adopted the New York rule.

In America a famous figure in jurisprudence stated the heart of the rationale for qualified privilege in an early case that has been relied upon by American courts countless times since. Judge Oliver Wendell Holmes, Jr., then of the Massachusetts bench and later a justice of the United States Supreme Court, wrote the words in Cowley v. Pulsifer (1884).[54] Publisher Royal Pulsifer's *Boston Herald* had printed the content of a petition seeking Charles Cowley's removal from the bar, and Cowley sued. Judge Holmes wrote that the public must have knowledge of judicial proceedings, not because one citizen's quarrels with another are important to public concern,

> * * * but because it is of the highest moment that those who administer justice should always act under the sense of public responsibility, and that every citizen should be able to satisfy himself with his own eyes as to the mode in which a public duty is performed.

[50] City of Chicago v. Tribune Co., 307 Ill. 595, 139 N.E. 86, 90 (1923).

[51] See also Grafton v. ABC, 70 Ohio App.2d 205, 435 N.E.2d 1131 (1980), 7 Med.L.Rptr. 1134, 1136, quoting Capital District Regional Off–Track Betting Corp. v. Northeastern Harness Horsemen's Ass'n, 92 Misc.2d 232, 399 N.Y.S.2d 597, 598 (1977).

[52] Curry v. Walter, 170 Eng.Rep. 419 (1796); King v. Wright, 101 Eng.Rep. 1396 (1799).

[53] New York Laws, 1854, Chap. 130; Wason v. Walter, L.R. 4 Q.B. 73 (1868).

[54] 137 Mass. 392, 394 (1884).

The advantage to the nation in granting privilege to press reports, he stressed, is "the security which publicity gives for the proper administration of justice." [55]

The privilege is "qualified" in the sense that it must be fair and accurate. (For example, an accurate quote misleadingly published out of context may not be privileged if defamatory.) Also, in some jurisdictions, the privilege will not hold if the report of the proceeding is made with malice (in the sense of ill will). Fundamentally, however, if a news account is a fair and accurate summary of a public official proceeding or record, the citizen or reporter will be protected by the "reporter's privilege." Also, the story must be one of a "public and official proceeding," not a report of related material that emerges before, after, or in some way outside the proceeding.

Fair and Accurate Reports

Errors can destroy qualified privilege. Ponder the perils of careless note-taking, the constant danger of a misspelled name, the arcane and technical jargon and findings of law courts, and all the slip-ups of life that happen under tight deadlines. Further, if the report of an official proceeding is not fair to people involved in it, the reporter can be in trouble. We have seen in the previous chapter how Mrs. Firestone won a libel judgment for $100,000 from Time, Inc., for its error in reporting that her husband's divorce was granted on grounds of adultery.

In the case of Anthony Liquori of Agawam, Mass., a newspaper reporter made an error in an address after extracting other materials from a court record about a "breaking" case in which a man of the same name from Springfield pleaded guilty and was convicted. The reporter took an address from a phone book; the innocent Liquori was wrongly identified and sued the Republican Company, publisher of the Springfield papers which carried separate stories, both erroneous. The Republican defended with a plea of qualified privilege, arguing that the defense should hold "because the newspaper articles were a substantially accurate report of a judicial proceeding." [56] It asserted that since only the address of the accused was inaccurate, it had published an article which was "substantially true and accurate and entirely fair," and that no more was required. But citing several previous cases about fair and accurate press reports of official proceedings, the Massachusetts Appeals Court said: [57] " * * * an article which labels an innocent man as a criminal because it refers erroneously to his

[55] Ibid.

[56] Liquori v. Republican Co., 8 Mass.App.Ct. 671, 396 N.E.2d 726, 728 (1979), 5 Med.L.Rptr. 2180.

[57] Ibid., at 728–29, 5 Med.L.Rptr. at 2181.

street address, which the reporter gained from a source outside the court records, is neither substantially accurate nor fair." It denied qualified privilege for the Republican. A wrong name, taken accurately from official police records, on the other hand, is privileged.[58]

Not every inaccuracy in reporting proceedings is fatal, however. Privilege did not fail in Mitchell v. Peoria Journal–Star, Inc.,[59] merely because the news story of a court action for liquor ordinance violation got the violators' place of arrest wrong. In Josephs v. News Syndicate Co., Inc.,[60] the newspaper did not lose privilege because somehow the reporter incorrectly slipped into his story of a burglary arrest the statement that the accused had been found under a bed at the scene of the burglary.

Opinion and Extraneous Material

One way to destroy immunity for a news story is to add opinion or material extraneous to the proceeding. It is necessary for reporters to stick to the facts of what comes to light under officials' surveillance. Radio station KYW in Philadelphia broadcast a "documentary" on car-towing rackets, and Austin Purcell sued for defamation. The broadcast had used a judicial proceeding as a basis: a magistrate's hearing at which Purcell was convicted of violating the car-tow ordinance. (Purcell later was exonerated, on appeal.) But the producer of the documentary wove into his script some material he had gathered from other sources—the voices of a man and a woman claiming that they had been cheated and a conversation with detectives. Anonymous voices on the tape called Purcell a "thug" and a "racketeer." The producer added comment of his own to the effect that "the sentencing of a few racketeers is not enough." That was defamation, the court said, and it was not protected by qualified privilege. The documentary lost the protection of qualified privilege because it contained "exaggerated additions." [61]

"Old–Style Malice"

New York Times Co. v. Sullivan (1964) gave the term "actual malice" a restricted meaning where public officials and figures are

---

[58] Biermann v. Pulitzer Pub. Co., 627 S.W.2d 87 (Mo.App.1981), 7 Med.L.Rptr. 2601. See also Murray v. Bailey, 613 F.Supp. 1276 (N.D.Cal.1985), 11 Med.L.Rptr. 1369. Report saying plaintiff arrested for drunk driving and assault and battery privileged as fair report when in fact plaintiff had been arrested for public intoxication and resisting arrest. Book author's later erroneous statement "convicted of drunken driving" held not privileged.

[59] 76 Ill.App.2d 154, 221 N.E.2d 516 (1966).

[60] 5 Misc.2d 184, 159 N.Y.S.2d 537 (1957).

[61] Purcell v. Westinghouse Broadcasting Co., 411 Pa. 167, 191 A.2d 662, 666 (1963). Ibid., 668. See also Jones v. Pulitzer Pub. Co., 240 Mo. 200, 144 S.W. 441 (1912); Robinson v. Johnson, 152 C.C.A. 505, 239 Fed. 671 (1917); Embers Supper Club, Inc. v. Scripps–Howard Broadcasting Co., 9 Ohio St.3d 22, 457 N.E.2d 1164 (1984), 10 Med.L.Rptr. 1729.

concerned. Actual malice means that the publisher knew the words were false, or had reckless disregard for whether they were false or not. Malice before that decision was defined in many ways, including ill will toward another, hatred, intent to harm, bad motive, or lack of good faith. It used to be that people who claimed that news stories of government proceedings libeled them, often charged "malice" in the stories, in terms such as these. Such definitions of "old-style malice" are still alive for libel that does not proceed under the constitutional protection provided by New York Times v. Sullivan.

Consider a case in which the St. Paul Dispatch was accused of a malicious report based on a complaint filed in district court. The newspaper's story said that William and Frank Hurley had been accused of depleting almost all of the estate of an aged woman before her death. Some $200,000 was involved. The Hurleys sued for libel, saying that the report was malicious and therefore not privileged.

The court did not agree, and in effect said the paper had showed neither "old style malice" (an inaccurate report " 'made solely for the purpose of causing harm to the person defamed' ") nor the harder to prove "actual malice" under the New York Times rule. The court ruled the Hurleys could not win their suit because they could produce no evidence of malice at the trial.[62]

Other courts have used old definitions of malice, where qualified privilege is pleaded, alongside knowing or reckless falsehood. Thus one says there is no malice in that which "the publisher reasonably believed to be true;" another speaks of malice as "intent to injure," and another of malice as "ill will." [63]

Official Proceedings

Reports of official activity outside the proceeding—the trial, the hearing, the legislative debate or committee—may not be protected. Some official activity has the color of official proceeding but not the reality.

To start with the courts: Any trial including that of a lesser court "not of record" such as a police magistrate's furnishes the basis for privilege.[64] The ex parte proceeding in which only one party to a legal controversy is represented affords privilege to

[62] Hurley v. Northwest Publications, Inc., 273 F.Supp. 967, 972, 974 (D.Minn. 1967).

[63] Bannach v. Field Enterprises, Inc., 5 Ill.App.3d 692, 284 N.E.2d 31, 32 (1972); and Brunn v. Weiss, 32 Mich.App. 428, 188 N.W.2d 904, 905 (1971). See, also, Orrison v. Vance, 262 Md. 285, 277 A.2d 573, 578 (1971), 3 Med.L.Rptr. 1170.

[64] McBee v. Fulton, 47 Md. 403 (1878); Flues v. New Nonpareil Co., 155 Iowa 290, 135 N.W. 1083 (1912); See also Sack, *loc. cit.*

reporting.[65] So does the grand jury report published in open court.[66]

In many states, the attorneys' "pleadings" filed with the clerk of court as the basic documents starting a lawsuit are *not* proceedings that furnish protection. In those states the judge must be involved; an early decision stated the rule that for the immunity to attach, the pleadings must have been submitted "to the judicial mind with a view to judicial action," [67] even if only in pretrial hearings on motions.

A 1927 New York decision, as so often in defamation, led the way for several states' rejecting this position and granting protection to reports of pleadings. Newspapers had carried a story based on a complaint filed by Mrs. Elizabeth Nichols against Mrs. Anne Campbell, claiming the latter had defrauded her of $16,000. After the news stories had appeared, Mrs. Nichols withdrew her suit. Mrs. Campbell filed libel suit. Acknowledging that nearly all courts had refused qualified privilege to stories based on pleadings not seen by a judge, the New York Court of Appeals said it would no longer follow this rule.

The New York high court conceded that it is easy for a malicious persons to file pleadings in order to vent hostility against others in news stories, and then withdraw the lawsuits. But it said that this can happen also after judges are in the proceeding; suits have been dropped before verdicts have been reached. It added that newspapers had so often printed stories about actions started before they reached a judge that "the public has learned that accusation is not proof and that such actions are at times brought in malice to result in failure." [68] The newspapers won.

That set up what is sometimes called the "Campbell Rule," which says that pleadings may be reported on, fairly and accurately, as soon as they are filed with a court and before a judge has acted upon them. Perhaps 20 states follow this rule today. That is, the filing of a pleading is a reportable public and official act appears to be a public and official act in the course of judicial proceedings in the District of Columbia and in a number of states, including Alabama, California, Georgia, Kentucky, Nevada, New York, Ohio, Pennsylvania, South Carolina, Tennessee, Texas, Washington and Wyoming.

[65] Metcalf v. Times Pub. Co., 20 R.I. 674, 40 A. 864 (1898).

[66] Sweet v. Post Pub. Co., 215 Mass. 450, 102 N.E. 660 (1913).

[67] Barber v. St. Louis Post Dispatch Co., 3 Mo.App. 377 (1877); Finnegan v. Eagle Printing Co., 173 Wis. 5, 179 N.W. 788 (1920).

[68] Campbell v. New York Evening Post, 245 N.Y. 320, 327, 157 N.E. 153, 155 (1927).

The Campbell Rule, increasingly, seems to be "the modern rule," with more and more courts' language tending toward making the contents of pleadings starting a lawsuit a public record to be reported upon.[69] That is fortunate for reporters, editors and broadcast news directors, many who long have assumed that once a pleading is filed with a court clerk, it is fair game.

But other states have not chosen to follow this rule. Massachusetts specifically rejected it in 1945. *The Boston Herald–Traveler* had published a story based on pleadings filed in an alienation of affections case, had been sued for libel, and had lost. The state Supreme Court said: [70]

> * * * the publication of accusations made by one party against another is neither a legal nor a moral duty of newspapers. Enterprise in that matter ought to be at the risk of paying damages if the accusations prove false. To be safe, a newspaper has only to send its reporters to listen to hearings rather than to search the files of cases not yet brought before the court.

Even in those jurisdictions where "pleadings" are privileged, careful adherence to basic rules of reporting is a must. That is, it should be made clear where the information is from: Attribution to the privileged document is good self-protection. The best rule, of course, is to play fair. Ethical reporters and editors will want to make sure that stories explicitly say that a pleading beginning a lawsuit tells only the plaintiff's side of the story. Reporters may wish to go further, phoning lawsuit defendants or the defendants' attorneys to give them an opportunity to comment. (It is likely that defendants may be unwilling to comment in the face of pending litigation, but it never hurts to ask and it will indicate reportorial fairness.)

Stories based on the following situations were outside "official proceedings" of courts and did not furnish news media the protection of qualified privilege: A newsman's interview of ("conversation with") a United States commissioner, concerning an earlier arraignment before the commissioner; [71] the words of a judge [72] and of an attorney [73] in courtrooms, just before trials were convened formally, and the taking by a judge of a deposition in his courtroom, where he was acting in a "ministerial capacity" only, not as a

[69] Henry R. Kaufman, ed., Libel Defense Resource Center (LDRC) 50–State Survey, 1991 (New York: LDRC, 1991).

[70] Sanford v. Boston Herald–Traveler Corp., 318 Mass. 156, 61 N.E.2d 5 (1945): But see Sibley v. Holyoke Transcript–Telegram Pub. Co., Inc., 391 Mass. 468, 461 N.E.2d 823 (1984), 10 Med.L.Rptr. 1557.

[71] Wood v. Constitution Pub. Co., 57 Ga.App. 123, 194 S.E. 760 (1937).

[72] Douglas v. Collins, 243 App.Div. 546, 276 N.Y.S. 87 (1934).

[73] Rogers v. Courier Post Co., 2 N.J. 393, 66 A.2d 869 (1949).

judge.[74] In Bufalino v. Associated Press,[75] the wire service did not actually demonstrate that it relied on FBI records, nor did it identify "officials" who were unnamed sources. So, the AP did not show that it was within the scope of privilege. In a Louisiana case,[76] a newspaper reporter was held to be outside the privilege because he relied on another newspaper's story, even though the latter was based on a sheriff's press release.

Executive Officers and Privilege

Shift now to news stories about the executive and administrative branch of government. When government officials hold a hearing or issue a report or even a press release, absolute privilege usually protects them. And where absolute privilege leads, qualified privilege for press reports ordinarily follows. Yet while major and minor federal officials enjoy the privilege under federal decisions, state courts have not been unanimous in granting it.[77]

The formal hearings of many administrative bodies have a quasi-judicial character, in which testimony is taken, interrogation is performed, deliberation is engaged in, and findings are reported in writing. The reporter can have confidence that such proceedings are "safe" to report. The minutes of a meeting and audits of a city water commission were the basis for a successful plea of privilege by a newspaper whose story reflected badly on an engineer.[78] The Federal Trade Commission investigated a firm and an account based on the investigation said that the firm had engaged in false branding and labeling; the account was privileged.[79] A news story reporting that an attorney had charged another with perjury was taken from a governor's extradition hearing, a quasi-judicial proceeding, and was privileged.[80]

Also, informal hearings or investigations carried out by executive-administrative officers, even those outside of hearing-chambers and without the banging of a gavel, usually furnish privilege. For example, a state tax commissioner audited a city's books and reported irregularities in the city council's handling of funds. A story based on the report caused a suit for libel, and the court held that the story was protected by privilege.[81]

[74] Mannix v. Portland Telegram, 144 Or. 172, 23 P.2d 138 (1933).

[75] 692 F.2d 266 (2d Cir.1982), 8 Med.L.Rptr. 2384.

[76] Melon v. Capital City Press, 407 So.2d 85 (La.App.1981), 8 Med.L.Rptr. 1165.

[77] Barr v. Matteo, 360 U.S. 564, 79 S.Ct. 1335 (1959); Prosser, pp. 802–803; Kaufman, LDRC 50–State Survey.

[78] Holway v. World Pub. Co., 171 Okl. 306, 44 P.2d 881 (1935).

[79] Mack, Miller Candle Co. v. Macmillan Co., 239 App.Div. 738, 269 N.Y.S. 33 (1934).

[80] Brown v. Globe Printing Co., 213 Mo. 611, 112 S.W. 462 (1908).

[81] Swearingen v. Parkersburg Sentinel Co., 125 W.Va. 731, 26 S.E.2d 209 (1943).

Yet not every investigation provides a basis for the defense of qualified privilege; reporters and city editors especially need to know what the judicial precedent of their state is. In a Texas case, a district attorney investigated a plot to rob a bank and obtained confessions. He made the confessions available to the press. A successful libel suit brought was brought on the basis of the resulting news story. The confessions were held insufficient executive proceedings to provide the protection.[82]

Police reporters need to be especially alert to libel dangers. "Blotters" listing the records of arrests and charges made are sources for many news stories. Their status as a basis for a plea of privilege varies from state to state.[83] Police stations generally have a written record—now often kept on computer—which keeps track of incidents and activities around the clock. These reports vary in form and completeness; blotters usually are starting points in the reporting process, with additional checking—including interviewing of officials—needed to get reasonably complete information. As suggested earlier, larger departments often establish some form of police "hot line," which—for safety's sake—probably ought to be regarded as unprivileged.[84]

Oral reports of preliminary investigations by policemen do not support a plea of privilege in some states. The *Rutland Herald* published a story about two brothers arrested on charges of robbery, and included this paragraph:

> Arthur was arrested on information given to police by the younger brother, it is said. According to authorities, Floyd in his alleged confession stated that Arthur waited outside the window in the rear of the clothing store while Floyd climbed through a broken window the second time to destroy possible clues left behind.

[82] Caller Times Pub.Co. v. Chandler, 134 Tex. 1, 130 S.W.2d 853 (1939). But see Woolbright v. Sun Communications, Inc., 480 S.W.2d 864 (Mo.1972).

[83] Sherwood v. Evening News Ass'n, 256 Mich. 318, 239 N.W. 305 (1931); M.J. Petrick, "The Press, the Police Blotter and Public Policy," 46 Journalism Quarterly 475, 1969.

[84] See note 30, above; see also Phillips v. Evening Star Newspaper Co., 424 A.2d 78 (D.C.App.1980), 6 Med.L.Rptr. 2191.

A suit for libel was brought, and the court denied qualified privilege to the story. It reviewed other states' decisions on whether statements attributed to police were a basis for privilege in news, and held that "a preliminary police investigation" is not a proper basis.[85]

The State of New Jersey has provided by statute that "official statements issued by police department heads" protect news stories, and Georgia has a similar law.[86] In other states, courts have provided the protection through decisions in libel suits. In Kilgore v. Koen,[87] an Oregon case, privilege was granted to a story in which deputy sheriffs' statements about the evidence and arrest in a case involving a school principal were the newspaper's source.

Legislative Branch Reporting

As for the legislative branch, the third general sphere of government, state statutes have long declared that the immunity holds in stories from legislative settings. A New York law led the way in this declaration even before the privilege was recognized in England.[88] For debates on the floor of Congress or of a state legislature, there has been no question that protection would apply to news stories. A few early cases indicated that stories of petty legislative bodies such as a town council [89] would not be privileged; but today's reporter need have little fear on this count.

In news stories about a New Jersey municipal council meeting, the city manager was quoted as saying that he was planning to bypass two policemen for promotion because they were insubordinate and "I should have fired them." There was some question as to whether the meeting was the regular one, or a session held in a conference room later. The New Jersey Supreme Court said that that didn't matter. It was not only an official but also a public meeting, at which motions were made by councilmen, heated discussion ensued, and the city manager was questioned by councilmen. Privilege held for the newspaper.[90]

One question about reporting legislatures was settled in a series of "chain" libel suits in the 1920s against several major newspapers. The "qualified privilege" immunity holds for news

[85] Lancour v. Herald & Globe Ass'n, 111 Vt. 371, 17 A.2d 253 (1941); Burrows v. Pulitzer Pub. Co., 255 S.W. 925 (Mo.App.1923); Pittsburgh Courier Pub. Co. v. Lubore, 91 U.S.App.D.C. 311, 200 F.2d 355 (1952).

[86] Henry R. Kaufman, LDRC 50–State Survey 1990–91, pp. 249 and 263, citing O.G.C.A. § 51–5–7 and N.J.S.A. 2A:43–1.

[87] 133 Or. 1, 288 P. 192 (1930).

[88] New York Laws, 1854, Chap. 130; Wason v. Walter, L.R. 4 Q.B. 73 (1868).

[89] Buckstaff v. Hicks, 94 Wis. 34, 68 N.W. 403 (1896).

[90] Swede v. Passaic Daily News, 30 N.J. 320, 153 A.2d 36 (1959).

reports of committees of legislative bodies.[91] (Chain libel suits exist where one plaintiff sues a publisher in several states or jurisdictions on the basis of one allegedly defamatory report.)

Legislative committees have a long history of operating under loose procedural rules.[92] Irregular procedures raise the question whether committee activity always meets the requirements of a "legislative proceeding" which is the basis for immunity in news reports.[93] In reporting committee activity, the reporter may sense danger signals if the committee:

Holds hearings without a quorum;

Publishes material that its clerks have collected, without itself first investigating charges in the material;

Has not authorized the work of its subcommittees;

Has a chairman given to issuing "reports" or holding press conferences on matters that the committee itself has not investigated.

When state and congressional investigating committees relentlessly hunted "subversion" in the 1940s and 1950s, thousands of persons were tainted with the charge of "communist" during the committee proceedings. High procedural irregularity was common. Yet only one libel case growing out of these irregular proceedings reached the highest court of a state, and the newspaper successfully defended with a plea of privilege.[94]

Again, there is much variation concerning privilege from jurisdiction to jurisdiction. It may be generalized that accurate and fair accounts of meetings which are both open to the public and deal with matters of public concern are privileged.[95] Matters get trickier when there is a newsworthy story which becomes available through confidential or secret reports dealing with charges of official misconduct.

The American Broadcasting Co. was sued after it telecast correspondent Bettina Gregory's five part series about scandals in the General Services Administration (GSA). From a confidential

[91] Cresson v. Louisville Courier–Journal, 299 Fed. 487 (6th Cir.1924).

[92] Walter Gellhorn (ed.), The States and Subversion (Ithaca: Cornell Univ.Press, 1952); Ernst J. Eberling, Congressional Investigations (New York: Columbia Univ. Press, 1928); more recently, lax legislative evidence rules have resulted in dropping prosecutions against "Iran-contra" scandal defendants. (Because of such loose procedures, it was determined those defendants who testified before Congress on TV later could not get a fair trial.) See, e.g., David Johnston, "Judge in Iran–Contra Trial Drops Case Against North After Prosecutor Gives Up," The New York Times, Sept. 17, 1991, p. A1.

[93] H.L. Nelson, Libel in News of Congressional Investigating Committees (Minneapolis: Univ. of Minn.Press, 1961), Chs. 1, 2.

[94] Coleman v. Newark Morning Ledger Co., 29 N.J. 357, 149 A.2d 193 (1959).

[95] Sack, in Goodale, ed., Communications Law 1991, Vol. I, p. 62.

source, ABC received—and used as source material—some leaked GSA internal reports. Those reports led to broadcasting assertions that Excelon Security Co., which had been under GSA contract to provide security services, had provided guards who did not have security clearances.

The ABC broadcast added that unnamed top federal, county, and city officials said "the President of Excelon is alleged to have connection with organized crime."

Excelon president Salvatore J. Ingenere sued, arguing that the documents were erroneous and were not privileged because the GSA documents were internal memos not intended for publication. Ingenere lost his suit when the U.S. district court ruled that " ... the Massachusetts common law fair use report privilege extends to the fair and accurate reporting of confidential government reports that reveal possible government misconduct." [96]

Public Proceedings

The Restatement (Second) of Torts, that oft-quoted and influential summary of how law *ought* to be, says: [97]

> The publication of defamatory matter * * * in a report of an official action or proceeding or of a meeting open to the public that deals with a matter of public concern is privileged if the report is accurate and complete and a fair abridgement of the occurrence is reported.

Way back in 1854, the New York legislature enacted a statute saying something quite similar to the passage from the Restatement, dealing with a "fair and true report * * * of any judicial, legislative or public official proceeding." [98] Some 102 years later, in 1956, the New York legislature removed the word "public" from that statute. The change was made after editorial campaigning by New York City newspapers. The deletion of the word "public" made it possible to have immunity in publishing news of an official proceeding even though the proceeding was not public.[99]

In some cases, efforts to use the fair report privilege as a defense to libel suits growing out of coverage of secret government proceedings do not succeed. Despite the elimination of the word "public" from from the New York statute, the state Court of Appeals ruled in 1970 that news stories of matrimonial proceed-

[96] Ingenere v. ABC (D.Mass.1984), 11 Med.L.Rptr. 1227.

[97] Restatement (Second) of Torts, S 611 (1977).

[98] New York Laws, 1854, Chap. 130; Danziger v. Hearst Corp., 304 N.Y. 244, 107 N.E.2d 62 (1952).

[99] Editor & Publisher, May 5, 1956, p. 52; See New York State Legislative Annual, 1956, pp. 494–495. Shiles v. News Syndicate Co., 27 N.Y.2d 9, 313 N.Y.S.2d 104, 107, 261 N.E.2d 251 (1970).

ings—secret under New York law—are protected by qualified privilege.

That New York situation carries a message to all mass communicators: *Know the law of the state in which you work.* Outside of New York, journalists sometimes have lost immunity when they reported libelous stories after gaining access to secret governmental or quasi-governmental proceedings. In an old case, McCurdy v. Hughes, a newspaper reported on a secret meeting of a disciplinary board of a state bar association in which a complaint against an attorney was considered. The attorney brought a libel suit for derogatory statements in the story and won.[1]

Reporting gets tricky for the news media in those times where a meeting or record is not both *public* and *official*. Obviously, some government records do not have public status. If news media publish such non-public or secret materials containing defamatory information, the public interest in those materials needs to be compelling to afford the media protection from liability.

Take, for example, Time magazine's 1978 publication of an article about suspected criminal activities of a Congressman from Pennsylvania named Daniel J. Flood. The Medico v. Time, Inc. defamation suit resulted, beginning when the magazine—in an article tying the Congressman to the Mafia—published these words: "The suspected link, the Wilkes–Barre firm of Philip Medico and his brothers. The FBI discovered more than a decade ago that [Congressman Daniel] Flood steered Government business to the Medicos and often traveled in their company jet." Time's article was based on secret FBI files.[2]

In addition, the magazine story called Medico a member of an organized crime "family" and referred to him as a Mafia "capo" or chief. Time magazine, however, argued that the gist of its article was that the Federal Bureau of Investigation had recorded "Pennsylvania Rackets Boss" Russell Bufalino's description of Philip Medico.

The trial court refused to find that Time's article could be defended as true, but ultimately held that the article was protected under Pennsylvania's common law privilege to report official proceedings. The court recognized that Time had summarized secret FBI reports which had been given the magazine without authorization. But because Time's article was a fair and accurate report of the FBI documents, the trial judge ruled that publication was privileged. Recognizing the great public concern over allegations of wrongdoing by a member of Congress, it was held that secret FBI

[1] McCurdy v. Hughes, 63 N.D. 435, 248 N.W. 512 (1933).

[2] Medico v. Time, Inc., 643 F.2d 134, 141 (3d Cir.1981), 6 Med.L.Rptr. 2529, 2535, cert. denied 454 U.S. 836, 102 S.Ct. 139 (1981).

documents concerning Philip Medico were " 'a report of an official proceeding or meeting.' " [3]

Upholding the trial court, a U.S. Court of Appeals found that important "policies underlie the fair report privilege." First is an "agency theory," where one who reports on a public, official proceeding represents people who could not attend. But, said the appeals court, the agency rationale would not work for proceedings or reports not open to the public. A second policy—and the one the appeals court embraced—is a "theory of public supervision." [4]

> As public inspection of courtroom proceedings may further the just administration of the laws, public scrutiny of the records of criminal investigatory agencies may often have the equally salutary effect of fostering among those who enforce the laws "the sense of public responsibility." For example, exposing the content of agency records may, in some cases, help ensure impartial enforcement of the laws.

A final note about the word "public" in connection with qualified privilege: The immunity to lawsuit for reporting is clearest when the meeting or record is both *public* and *official*. Perhaps there is an emerging standard suggesting that even if a meeting or record is not both public and official, it is important for the community to know what is happening where matters of public welfare and concern are involved.[5] As for private gatherings of stockholders, directors, or members of an association or organization, they are no basis for privilege in news reports.

SEC. 34. TRUTH AS A DEFENSE

Most state laws provide that truth is a complete defense in libel cases, but some require that the publisher show "good motives and justifiable ends." The United States Supreme Court has not ruled on whether truth may ever be subjected to civil or criminal liability.

The defense of truth (often called "justification") in civil libel has ancient roots developed in the common law of England. It was taken up by American courts as they employed the common law in the colonial and early national periods, and was transferred from the common law to many state statutes. Its basis appeals to

[3] Ibid., pp. 137–139.

[4] Ibid., pp. 139, 140, quoting Judge (later Mr. Justice Holmes) from Cowley v. Pulsifer, 137 Mass. 392, 394 (1884).

[5] See Robert D. Sack, op. cit., pp. 105–108, citing Kilgore v. Younger, 30 Cal.3d 770, 796, 180 Cal.Rtpr. 657, 673, 640 P.2d 793, 797 (1982), and Crane v. Arizona Republic, 729 F.Supp. 698 (D.C.Cal.1989).

common sense and ordinary ideas of justice: Why, indeed, should an individual be awarded damages for harm to his reputation when the truth of the matter is that his record does not merit a good reputation? To print or broadcast the truth about persons is no more than they should expect. In addition the social good may be served by bringing to light the truth about people whose work involves them in the public interest.

It is held by some courts that truth alone is a complete defense, regardless of the motives behind its publication, and this squares with the libel statutes in most states. Some state laws continue to qualify, and provide that truth is a defense if it is published "with good motives and justifiable ends." [6] The qualifying term goes back to 1804, when Alexander Hamilton used it in his defense of newspaperman Harry Croswell in a celebrated New York criminal libel case.[7] So far as the comatose *criminal* libel offense is concerned, however, the United States Supreme Court has ruled that the Hamiltonian qualification is unconstitutional, and may not be required of a defendant.[8]

The Supreme Court has shied away from ruling that truth is always a defense. Justice White wrote in Cox Broadcasting Co. v. Cohn that the Court had not decided the question "whether truthful publications may ever be subjected to civil or criminal liability." Earlier cases, he said, had "carefully left open the question" whether the First Amendment requires "that truth be recognized as a defense in a defamation action brought by a private person * * *." [9]

The Burden of Proving Truth

Since the Supreme Court rules of *Sullivan* and *Gertz* have made it plain that some level of fault on the part of the media must be shown—from knowing falsity to negligence—the burden of pleading and showing falsity has largely been on the plaintiff where he is a public person. Yet the *Restatement of Torts (Second)* takes the position that it cannot yet be said that the burden is inescapably on the plaintiff: [10]

[6] State statutes and constitutional provisions are collected in Angoff, op. cit. See also Note, 56 N.W.Univ.L.Rev. 547 (1961); Garrison v. Louisiana, 379 U.S. 64, 85 S.Ct. 209 (1964), footnote 7.

[7] 3 Johns.Cas. 337 (N.Y.1818).

[8] Garrison v. Louisiana, 379 U.S. 64, 85 S.Ct. 209 (1964).

[9] Cox Broadcasting v. Cohn, 420 U.S. 469, 490, 95 S.Ct. 1029, 1043–1044 (1975), a privacy decision. But see Restatement, Second, Torts, § 581A, p. 235, which says "There can be no recovery in defamation for a statement of fact that is true * * *."

[10] Ibid., § 613, p. 310.

Placing the burden on the party asserting the negative necessarily creates difficulties, and the problem is accentuated when the defamatory charge is not specific in its terms but quite general in nature. Suppose, for example, that a newspaper published a charge that a storekeeper short-changes his customers when he gets a chance. How is he expected to prove that he has not short-changed customers when no specific occasions are pointed to by the defendant?

Some courts have said that the burden of proof rests on the plaintiff to show defamation and to prove damages. It is clear that defendants in libel suits frequently have been at pains to prove that an alleged libel is true.[11] In 1986, however, in Philadelphia Newspapers v. Hepps, the U.S. Supreme Court held 5–4 that it is unconstitutional to put the burden of proving truth on a media defendant where the story involved deals with a matter of public concern.

The *Hepps* case was a close call, a 5–4 decision, but it nevertheless tilted the scales in favor of the media for expression "of a public concern." Justice Sandra Day O'Connor wrote for the majority that the old " * * * common-law presumption that defamatory speech is false cannot stand when a plaintiff seeks damages against a media defendant for speech of public concern." [12]

The news media, in other words, should not be punished for statements that *may* be true. This decision invalidated similar rules in eight other states, including New Jersey. Before the Hepps decision, a dozen or more other states—including New York and Connecticut—had already shifted the burden of proof concerning falsity to the plaintiffs.[13]

Not every detail of an allegedly libelous story must be proved accurate in order to rebut a charge of "falsity," but rather, that the story is "substantially" true.[14] But no formula can measure just what inaccuracy will be tolerated by a particular court.

In an old but illustrative case, the *New York World–Telegram and Sun* tried to establish truth of the following statement from its pages, but failed:

---

[11] See Memphis Pub. Co. v. Nichols, 569 S.W.2d 412 (Tenn.1978), 4 Med.L.Rptr. 1573.

[12] Philadelphia Newspapers, Inc. v. Hepps, 475 U.S. 767, 106 S.Ct. 1558, 1561 (1986), 12 Med.L.Rptr. 1977, 1981.

[13] Stuart Taylor, Jr., Supreme Court Adds Protection for News Media in Libel Actions, The New York Times, April 22, 1986.

[14] Hein v. Lacy, 228 Kan. 249, 616 P.2d 277 (1980), 6 Med.L.Rptr. 1662, 1666; Prosser, 825.

John Crane, former president of the UFA now under
indictment, isn't waiting for his own legal developments.
Meanwhile, his lawyers are launching a $$$$$ defamation
suit.

Focusing on the word "indictment," Crane brought a libel suit
against the newspaper and the columnist who wrote the item. He
said that the defendant knew or could have learned the falsity of
the charge by using reasonable care.

The defendants tried to dodge the libel action, arguing that the
facts about John Crane already had been widely punished and
commented up by the press of the city. The lame argument that
the phrase "under indictment" was used in a figurative, non-legal
sense failed, and Crane won his suit against the newspaper. The
court held that "under indictment" means a legal action by a grand
jury to begin criminal charges, and that the use of the term to
mean accusation by private persons is rare.[15] In any case, you
cannot prove the truth of one charge against a person by showing
he or she was suspected or guilty of another.[16]

The same term—"indictment"—was used by another newspaper in an incorrect way, but was held *not* to be libelous. The word
appeared in connection with conflict-of-interest findings discussed
in an editorial. A councilman was never truly indicted, but rather
was charged by delivery of a summons, and convicted. The court
held that "indictment" was substantially accurate, and although
technically incorrect, did not constitute defamation.[17]

Thus loose usage of certain technical terms does not always
destroy a plea of truth. This is what a court ruled when a
Massachusetts newspaper said that a man named Joyce had been
"committed" to a mental hospital when actually he had been
"admitted" to the hospital at the request of a physician as the state
law provided. The newspaper's words that caused the man to
bring a libel suit were that the man "charges * * * that his
constitutional rights were violated when he was committed to the
hospital last November." In ruling for the newspaper which pleaded truth, the court said: [18]

> Strictly * * * "commitment" means a placing in the
> hospital by judicial order * * *. But the words [of the
> news story] are to be used in their "natural sense with the

[15] Crane v. New York World Telegram Corp., 308 N.Y. 470, 126 N.E.2d 753 (1955); Friday v. Official Detective Stories, Inc., 233 F.Supp. 1021 (E.D.Pa.1964).

[16] Sun Printing and Pub. Ass'n v. Schenck, 40 C.C.A. 163, 98 Fed. 925 (1900); Kilian v. Doubleday & Co., 367 Pa. 117, 79 A.2d 657 (1951); Yarmove v. Retail Credit Co., 18 A.D.2d 790, 236 N.Y.S.2d 836 (1963).

[17] Schaefer v. Hearst Corp. (Md.Super.1979), 5 Med.L.Rptr. 1734.

[18] Joyce v. George W. Prescott Pub. Co., 348 Mass. 790, 205 N.E.2d 207 (1965).

meaning which they could convey to mankind in general."
This meaning of the word "commitment" was placing in
the hospital pursuant to proceedings provided by law.   In
so stating as to the plaintiff * * * the defendant reported
correctly.

Of course, writers or broadcasters who are highly attuned to
nuances in word meanings may save their employers the expense
and trouble of even successful libel defenses by avoiding gaffes such
as confusing "commit" with "admit."   While news media continue
to be staffed in part by writers insensitive to shades of meaning,
however, they may take some comfort in the law's willingness—
however unpredictably—to bend on occasion.

Courts frequently hold that truth will not be destroyed by a
story's minor inaccuracies.   Thus truth succeeded although a newspaper had printed that the plaintiff was in police custody on August
16, whereas he had been released on August 15; [19] and it was not
fatal to truth to report in a news story that an arrest, which in fact
took place at the Shelly Tap tavern, occurred at the Men's Social
Club.[20]

In accord with the maxim that "tale bearers are as bad as tale
tellers," it is no defense for a news medium to argue that it
reported accurately and truthfully someone else's false and defamatory statements.   The broadcaster or newspaper reporter writes at
the employer's peril and at his or her own peril, too.   The words "it
is reported by police" or "according to a reliable source" do not
remove from the news medium faced with a libel suit the job of
proving that the allegation or rumor itself is true.[21]   Liability under
the "republication" rule persists.[22]

Even though every fact in a story is truthful, an error of
omission can result in libel.   Recall, now, from Sec. 32, the *Memphis Press–Scimitar's* accurate facts about the shooting of Mrs.
Nichols.   A woman had gone to the home of Mrs. Nichols, and
there, the newspaper said on the basis of a police arrest report,
found her own husband (Newton) with Mrs. Nichols.   The implication of an adulterous affair between the two was plain in the story,
all of whose facts were accurate.   Mrs. Nichols brought libel suits.
The Press–Scimitar had omitted much from the story, as shown by
a separate police document (the "offense report"): Not only were
Mrs. Nichols and Mr. Newton at the home, but also Mr. Nichols

[19] Piracci v. Hearst Corp., 263 F.Supp. 511 (D.Md.1966), affirmed 371 F.2d 1016
(4th Cir.1967).

[20] Mitchell v. Peoria Journal–Star, Inc., 76 Ill.App.2d 154, 221 N.E.2d 516 (1966).

[21] Miller, Smith & Champagne v. Capital City Press, 142 So.2d 462 (La.App.1962);
Dun & Bradstreet, Inc. v. Robinson, 233 Ark. 168, 345 S.W.2d 34 (1961).

[22] Cianci v. New Times Pub. Co., 639 F.2d 54 (2d Cir.1980), 6 Med.L.Rptr. 1625,
1629–1630.

and two other people. Had these facts been in the news story, there would have been no suggestion of an affair. The Press–Scimitar pleaded truth of its words, but the Tennessee Supreme Court said: [23]

> In our opinion, the defendant's reliance on the truth of the facts stated in the article in question is misplaced. The proper question is whether the *meaning* reasonably conveyed by the published words is defamatory * * *. The publication of the complete facts could not conceivably have led the reader to conclude that Mrs. Nichols and Mr. Newton had an adulterous relationship. The published statement, therefore, so distorted the truth as to make the entire article false and defamatory. It is no defense whatever that individual statements within the article were literally true.

Even ill will and an intent to harm will not affect truth where it is said of a public person; knowing or reckless falsehood must be shown.[24] As we have seen, however, against a *private* person's suit, some states provide that truth is a good defense only if made with good motives and for justifiable ends—that ill will (the "malice" of old tort law) may defeat the defense.[25] Belief in the truth of the charge may be useful in holding down damages, if it can be established to the satisfaction of the court. Showing honest belief indicates good faith and absence of malice, important to the mitigation of general damages and the denial or lessening of punitive damages to the successful suit-bringer in a libel case.

An article about a public official's criminal conviction failed to state that, upon retrial, the official was acquitted, and the defense of truth was denied the magazine.[26] Also, courts have refused to accept the plea of truth where news media would not identify anonymous sources upon whom defamatory stories were based.[27]

"Substantial Accuracy"

Mass communicators should keep in mind that "accuracy" and "truth" are not identical in law. Suppose that your source, a member of Congress, stops you on the street and says: "Your hometown banker, J.Q. Milquetoast, has embezzled thousands of dollars from three different banks."

---

[23] Memphis Pub. Co. v. Nichols, 569 S.W.2d 412, 420 (Tenn.1978), 4 Med.L.Rptr. 1573, 1579. See also for true facts but false implication, Dunlap v. Philadelphia Newspapers, Inc., 301 Pa.Super. 475, 448 A.2d 6 (1982), 8 Med.L.Rptr. 1974.

[24] Schaefer v. Lynch, 406 So.2d 185 (La.1981), 7 Med.L.Rptr. 2302.

[25] Sack, 130–131.

[26] Torres v. Playboy Enterprises (D.S.Tex.1980), 7 Med.L.Rptr. 1182.

[27] Dowd v. Calabrese, 577 F.Supp. 238 (D.D.C.1983), 10 Med.L.Rptr. 1208, 1213.

If you quote your source exactly, that will be **accurate**.

To prove **truth**, however you will have to prove that your source's statement about the banker is accurate too, and that Milquetoast indeed had embezzled thousands of dollars from banks.[28]

SEC. 35.   OPINION AND FAIR COMMENT AS DEFENSES

State statutes and the common law provide the doctrine of fair comment and criticism as a defense against libel suits brought by people and institutions who offer their work to the public for its approval or disapproval, or where matters of public interest are concerned. Despite assertions that the old fair comment defense was superseded by constitutional protections for opinion, its principles still are in use by media and courts. Furthermore, the effect of *Milkovich v. Lorain Journal* (1990) on the "opinion defense" stemming from expansive readings of *Gertz v. Welch* (1974) must be considered.

Fair Comment Under Common Law and State Statutes

Opinion embraces comment and criticism. The defense of fair comment was shaped to protect the public stake in the scrutinizing of important public matters. Comment and criticism have permeated news and editorial pages and broadcasts, explaining, drawing inferences, reacting, evaluating. The law protects even scathing criticism of the public work of persons and institutions who offer their work for public judgment: public officials and figures; those whose performance affects public taste in such realms as music, art, literature, theater, and sports; and institutions whose activities affect the public interest such as hospitals, schools, processors of food, public utilities, drug manufacturers. Under fair comment legal immunity against a defamation action is given for the honest expression of opinion on public persons and/or matters of public concern.[29]

Even the most public persons have some small sphere of private life. Although one's private character of course can deeply affect one's public acts, there are circumstances in which comment on private acts and personal character is not embraced by the

---

[28] See, e.g., Rouch v. Enquirer & News, 440 Mich. 238, 487 N.W.2d 205 (1992), 20 Med.L.Rptr. 2265.

[29] Prosser, 812–816; Harper and James, Law of Torts (Boston, 1956). See also New York Times Co. v. Sullivan, 376 U.S. 254, 271, 84 S.Ct. 710, 721 (1964) quoting Cantwell v. Connecticut, 310 U.S. 296, 310, 60 S.Ct. 900, 906 (1940).

protection of fair comment.[30]   The wide sweep of *Sullivan,* it will be remembered, protects only statements about public persons' *public* acts; and courts continue to hold that public persons retain a private sphere.[31]

True and False Statements of "Fact"

States have varied in their fair comment rules. Most have said that the protection for comment does not extend to that which is falsely given out as "fact."   This presents at the outset the often difficult problem of separating facts—which are susceptible of proof—from opinion—which cannot be proved true or false. As you will see, courts efforts to distinguish between statements of fact and of opinion have created one of the slipperiest slopes in all of American law.   Beyond the problem of making that often cloudy distinction is the diversity of rules from state to state.   The majority of states have insisted on the rule of "no protection for misstatement of fact."   Oregon's Supreme Court, for example, held "it is one thing to comment upon or criticize * * * the acknowledged or proved act of a public man, and quite another to assert that he has been guilty of particular acts of misconduct." [32]   Under this interpretation, "charges of specific criminal misconduct are not protected as 'opinions.' " [33]

But under common law, a minority of states provided protection for false statements of fact.   One variation was illustrated by Snively v. Record Publishing Co., an old California decision.[34]   The Los Angeles police chief brought suit against a newspaper for a cartoon which suggested he was receiving money secretly for illegal purposes.   The California Supreme Court held that even if the charge of criminality were false, the cartoon was protected by fair comment.   Political cartoons, indeed, do receive added "running room" from the courts.   They are regarded as exaggerated statements which by their nature stretch facts to make a point.[35]

Substantial variation developed from state to state on the question of how directly and completely opinion had to be sup-

[30] Post Pub. Co. v. Moloney, 50 Ohio St. 71, 89, 33 N.E. 921 (1893); Harper and James, 461.

[31] Zeck v. Spiro, 52 Misc.2d 629, 276 N.Y.S.2d 395 (1966); Stearn v. MacLean–Hunter Ltd., 46 F.R.D. 76 (S.D.N.Y.1969); Standke v. B.E. Darby & Sons, Inc., 291 Minn. 468, 193 N.W.2d 139, 144 (1971).   Note, Fact and Opinion after Gertz v. Robert Welch, Inc., 34 Rutgers L.Rev. 81, 88–89 (Fall 1981).

[32] Marr v. Putnam, 196 Or. 1, 246 P.2d 509, 524 (1952); Otero v. Ewing, 162 La. 453, 110 So. 648 (1926).

[33] Cianci v. New Times Pub. Co., 639 F.2d 54, 63 (2d Cir.1980), 6 Med.L.Rptr. 1625, 1635; Restatement (Second) of Torts, # 571.

[34] Snively v. Record Pub. Co., 185 Cal. 565, 198 P.1 (1921).

[35] See Keller v. Miami Herald Pub. Co., 778 F.2d 711 (11th Cir.1985), and Hustler Magazine v. Falwell, 485 U.S. 46, 108 S.Ct. 876 (1988), 14 Med.L.Rptr. 2281.

ported by accompanying implications or assertions of fact. In point is the case of private citizen Rollenhagen of Orange, Calif., an auto mechanic about whom CBS aired a television story. After one of his customers had complained to police about his charges for repairs, they arrested him for failure to give a written estimate in advance of auto repairs as required under California law, hand-cuffed him, and led him past a CBS camera crew. CBS interviewed auto mechanic Rollenhagen and the police, who said the customer had been victimized—and then ran the story. Rollenhagen sued for defamation, claiming the story was false, but a California Court of Appeal ruled that the story was protected by the state law of fair comment on matters of public interest. The court said that while Gertz v. Welch (1974) had recently permitted states to let private persons recover where there was negligence in a matter of public concern, California had not adopted that rule, but stayed with its half-century-old fair comment statute.[36]

A question of "fact" faces the writer under some states' rules of fair comment: the comment must be based on facts—facts stated with the comment, or facts that are known or readily available to the reader. The Fisher Galleries asked art critic Leslie Ahlander of the *Washington Post* to review an exhibition of paintings by artist Irving Amen. Later, Mrs. Ahlander's column carried this comment:

> [The Amen prints and paintings] are so badly hung among many commercial paintings that what quality they might have is completely destroyed. The Fisher Galleries should decide whether they are a fine arts gallery or a commercial outlet for genuine "hand-painted" pictures. The two do not mix.

Fisher sued for libel, and the *Post* defended on the grounds of fair comment and criticism. Fisher argued that in order for opinion to be protected by the fair comment doctrine, the facts upon which it is based must be stated or referred to so that the reader may draw his own conclusions. The court acknowledged that this is the rule in some jurisdictions.[37] But it instead took that view that the facts do not necessarily have to be stated in the article, but may be facts "known or readily available to the persons to whom the comment or criticism is addressed * * *."[38]

Besides the problem of "fact," the ancient question of what constituted "malice" entered the picture and had much to do with

[36] Rollenhagen v. Orange, 116 Cal.App.3d 414, 172 Cal.Rptr.49 (1981), 6 Med. L.Rptr. 2651, 2564. See Calif. Civil Code Sec. 47, sub.3, granting qualified privilege to all publications concerning a matter of legitimate public interest.

[37] A.S. Abell Co. v. Kirby, 227 Md. 267, 176 A.2d 340 (1961); Cohalan v. New York Tribune, 172 Misc. 20, 15 N.Y.S.2d 58 (1939).

[38] Fisher v. Washington Post Co., 212 A.2d 335, 338 (D.C.App.1965).

what was "fair." Malice would destroy the protection of fair comment; and malice for centuries before New York Times Co. v. Sullivan had been defined in various ways. Furthermore, various characteristics of "unfair" expression were sometimes treated as suggesting malice. Thus from state to state and jurisdiction to jurisdiction, malice could be pretty much what the court felt it ought to be: ill-will, enmity, spite, hatred, intent to harm; "excessive publication," [39] vehemence,[40] words that were not the honest opinion of the writer,[41] words which there was no "probable cause to believe true," [42] words showing reckless disregard for the rights of others, words which a reasonable man would not consider fair.[43] Malice still can be "adduced" [44] from such qualities of expression in some jurisdictions where qualified privilege or fair comment is at issue.

Thus the West Virginia Supreme Court held in denying fair comment's protection against the *Charleston Gazette* which had tongue-lashed several legislators who sued it for saying, among other things, that they had sold their votes. The court said that " ...if such comment is unfair or unreasonably violent or vehement, immunity from liability is denied." [45]

But in another state—Iowa—there was no suggestion in a Supreme Court decision that "matters of public interest must be discussed temperately." Journalists everywhere know the case of the Cherry sisters, one of the most famous in the annals of libel in America. The *Des Moines Leader* successfully defended itself in their libel suit, using the defense of fair comment. It started when the Leader printed this:

> Billy Hamilton, of the *Odebolt Chronicle* gives the Cherry Sisters the following graphic write-up on their late appearance in his town: "Effie is an old jade of 50 summers, Jessie a frisky-filly of 40, and Addie, the flower of the family, a capering monstrosity of 35. Their long skinny arms, equipped with talons at the extremities, swung mechanically, and anon waved frantically at the suffering audience. The mouths of their rancid features opened like caverns, and sounds like the wailing of damned souls issued therefrom. They pranced around the stage with a motion that suggested a cross between the *danse du*

[39] Pulliam v. Bond, 406 S.W.2d 635, 643 (Mo.1966).
[40] England v. Daily Gazette Co., 143 W.Va. 700, 104 S.E.2d 306 (1958).
[41] Russell v. Geis, 251 Cal.App.2d 560, 59 Cal.Rptr. 569 (1967).
[42] Taylor v. Lewis, 132 Cal.App. 381, 22 P.2d 569 (1933).
[43] James v. Haymes, 160 Va. 253, 168 S.E. 333 (1933).
[44] Goldwater v. Ginzburg, 414 F.2d 324, 342 (2d Cir.1969).
[45] England v. Daily Gazette Co., 143 W.Va. 700, 104 S.E.2d 306, 316 (1958).

ventre and fox trot,—strange creatures with painted faces and hideous mien. Effie is spavined, Addie is stringhalt, and Jessie, the only one who showed her stockings, has legs and calves as classic in their outlines as the curves of a broom handle."

There was nothing moderate about Billy Hamilton's criticism of these Three Graces, but the Iowa Supreme Court said that that did not matter. What Hamilton wrote about the three sisters, and the Leader reprinted, was fair comment and criticism: [46]

> One who goes upon the stage to exhibit himself to the public, or who gives any kind of a performance to which the public is invited, may be freely criticized. He may be held up to ridicule, and entire freedom of expression is guaranteed to dramatic critics, provided they are not actuated by malice or evil purpose in what they write. * * * Ridicule is often the strongest weapon in the hands of a public writer; and, if fairly used, the presumption of malice which would otherwise arise is rebutted * * *.

Opinion Under the Constitution

Opinion defenses against defamation, although remarkably useful, sometimes promise more than they deliver. True, as noted in Chapter 4 (Sec. 19), the First Amendment has been held to protect exaggerated, extravagant give-and-take in labor and political disputes. In such settings, deep feelings give rise to name-calling, to "rhetorical hyperbole" that is not to be construed literally.

Examples of epithets protected in labor or political disputes include:

— "Scabs" and "traitors" as used in a union publication against non-union workers.[47]

— "Blackmail" and "unethical trade" in a land-use dispute.[48]

— "Fellow traveler of the fascists" in a denunciation of a leader of a political fringe group.[49]

Such opinion was protected by courts, defined as immunized by *the context in which it occurred,* in labor or political disputes.[50]

[46] Cherry v. Des Moines Leader, 114 Iowa 298, 86 N.W. 323 (1901).

[47] Old Dominion Branch No. 496, Nat. Ass'n of Letter Carriers, AFL–CIO v. Austin, 418 U.S. 264, 94 S.Ct. 2770 (1974).

[48] Greenbelt Cooperative Pub. Ass'n v. Bresler, 398 U.S. 6, 90 S.Ct. 1537 (1970).

[49] Cianci v. New Times Pub. Co., 639 F.2d 54, 62 (2d Cir.1980), 6 Med.L.Rptr. 1625, 1631, quoting Buckley v. Littell, 539 F.2d 882 (2d Cir.1976).

[50] Sack, 157–58, 160–61.

With less than perfect consistency, courts distinguish hyperbole from specific charges of crime and wrongdoing. For example, charging one with a "SS [Nazi] background" and being associated with the Gestapo are not opinion or hyperbole, nor is "outright extortion" spoken of a councilman.[51]

In addition to such protection for rhetorical hyperbole, additional constitutional immunity was deduced by many courts from a dictum—a kind of judicial aside—written by U.S. Supreme Court Justice Lewis Powell in the majority opinion in Gertz v. Robert Welch, Inc.[52]

> Under the First Amendment there is no such thing as a false idea. However pernicious an idea may seem, we depend for its correction not on the conscience of judges and juries but on the competition of other ideas. But there is no constitutional value in false statements of fact.

Under this statement apparently giving an absolute protection for opinion, the Second Restatement of Torts (1977) said—prematurely, it has turned out—that common-law fair comment had been obliterated. It declared that only where a statement in the form of opinion implies the allegation of undisclosed defamatory facts as the basis is the statement actionable.[53]

Such a statement is "mixed" opinion, and not protected as "pure" opinion is. ("Mixed" opinion refers to an opinion expressed in such a way to appear to be based on facts, and where the opinion is expressed so as to imply there are undisclosed facts justifying the defamatory statement. "Pure" opinion, on the other hand, is based on provable facts which are explicitly stated as support for the opinion. [Restatement (Second) of Torts (1977), § 566, Comment b.])

After *Gertz,* many courts enthusiastically supported—and added to—the Supreme Court's statement that "there is no thing as a false idea." Under that slogan, constitutional support flourished, protecting expressions of opinion against defamation lawsuits. For example, the Massachusetts Supreme Judicial Court, using approaches from *Gertz,* from the Restatement of Torts, and from elements of rhetorical hyperbole. In doing so, it illustrated the horrendous difficulty in distinguishing between fact and opinion.

[51] Good Government Group of Seal Beach, Inc. v. Superior Court, 22 Cal.2d 672, 150 Cal.Rptr. 258, 586 P.2d 572 (1978).

[52] 418 U.S. 323, 339–340, 94 S.Ct. 2997, 3007 (1974). For a case boldly using *Gertz* to create an "opinion defense," see Miskovsky v. Oklahoma Publishing Co., 654 P.2d 587 (Okl.1982), cert. denied 459 U.S. 923, 103 S.Ct. 235 (1982), 8 Med.L.Rptr. 2302; see also discussion in Goodale, ch., Communications Law 1993, Vol. II, at p.153, including In re Yagman, 796 F.2d 1165, 1186 (9th Cir.1986): " ' "an opinion is simply not actionable defamation." ' "

[53] Restatement (Second) Torts (1977), S566, Comment b.

In that case, reporter Cole was fired from WBZ–TV for "reasons of misconduct and insubordination," an official statement from the general manager said. Newspapers reported the firing and the reasons, and added that station spokesman Konowitz elaborated by telephone to them that "unofficially" the firing also was based on "sloppy and irresponsible techniques". Cole sued for libel, seeking damages for those "unofficial words." In upholding the station's position, the court ruled that Konowitz's words could be viewed only as expressions of opinion regarding Cole's reporting abilities. It said: [54]

> Whether a reporter is sloppy and irresponsible with bad techniques is a matter of opinion. The meaning of these statements is imprecise and open to speculation. They cannot be characterized as assertions of fact. They cannot be proved false. "An assertion that cannot be proved false cannot be held libelous." Hotchner v. Castillo–Puche, 55 F.2d 910, 913 * * *.

It may puzzle journalists that one cannot prove such charges false. After all, the United States Supreme Court and other courts often have canvassed reporters' techniques, finding them acceptable at times despite angry charges by plaintiffs, flawed and faulty at other times, and on the basis of the latter sometimes have granted libel judgments.[55]

But the Massachusetts Court found precedent for its judgment: One writer, for example, had called a judge one of the ten worst judges in New York, said he had made a sufficient pattern of incompetent decisions and should be removed from office. The New York court denied recovery for these "opinions," saying that the defendants had simply expressed "their opinion of his judicial performance," and the judge could not recover "no matter how unreasonable, extreme or erroneous these opinions might be." [56] (The statement that the judge was "probably corrupt," on the other hand, was an accusation of crime that could be proved true or false.) In another case, "liar" merely expressed an opinion and could not be libelous however mistaken the opinion might be.[57] In

[54] Cole v. Westinghouse Broadcasting Co., Inc., 386 Mass. 303, 435 N.E.2d 1021 (1982), 8 Med.L.Rptr. 1828, 1832–1833. See also Marc A. Franklin, "The Plaintiff's Burden in Defamation * * *," 25 William and Mary L.Rev. 825, 868 (1983–1984), arguing that "goodness" and "badness" are evaluative statements, "simply not concepts that can be judicially characterized as being either true or false."

[55] Curtis Pub. Co. v. Butts, 388 U.S. 130, 87 S.Ct. 1975 (1967), finding the Associated Press reporter's techniques blameless and the Saturday Evening Post's constituting "reckless disregard." Where reckless disregard is found, it is commonly for bad reporting techniques.

[56] Citing Rinaldi v. Holt, Rinehart & Winston, Inc., 42 N.Y.2d 369, 376, 380–382, 397 N.Y.S.2d 943, 950–951, 366 N.E.2d 1299 (1977).

[57] Citing Edwards v. National Audubon Soc., Inc., 556 F.2d 113, 131 (2d Cir.1977).

another, "fascist" and fellow traveler of fascism were matters of opinion and protected ideas—but in this case,[58] the claim that the plaintiff had lied about people in his work as a journalist was ruled to be an assertion of fact.

The unsettled nature of the law as to opinion and comment under the Constitution was strikingly illustrated in Evans v. Ollman, a 1984 decision of the Court of Appeals, District of Columbia Circuit. Eleven judges sitting *en banc* delivered seven opinions. The majority found for two defendant newspaper columnists, and the U.S. Supreme Court refused to accept the plaintiff's appeal, in effect upholding the decision.[59] Bertell Ollman, a Marxist professor of political science at New York University under appointment procedures to head the department of government at the University of Maryland, sued syndicated newspaper columnists Evans and Novak. Their column stated that Ollman "is widely viewed in his profession as a political activist," whose "candid writings avow his desire to use the classroom as an instrument for preparing what he calls 'the revolution'." It also reported that an unnamed political scientist said that Ollman "has no status within the profession, but is a pure and simple activist."

Writing for himself and three others, Judge Kenneth W. Starr found this to be opinion protected under the First Amendment and the *Gertz* dictum. Judge Robert Bork, joined by three others, considered the statements in the column to be rhetorical hyperbole, and as such a category of words different from either "fact" or "opinion," but protected by the First Amendment. Judge (now Justice) Antonin Scalia, writing as one of five who dissented in part from the judgment, called the statement as to Ollman's status in the profession "a classic and cooly crafted libel," and treated it as an unprotected statement of fact.[60]

Judge Starr noted the difficulty and the "dilemma" that courts often face in distinguishing between fact and opinion. For doing

[58] Buckley v. Littell, 539 F.2d 882, 884–885 (2d Cir.1976). Decisions that have found indications of "undisclosed defamatory facts" and denied protection include: Braig v. Field Communications, 310 Pa.Super. 569, 456 A.2d 1366 (1983), 9 Med. L.Rptr. 1057, allegation that "Judge Braig is no friend of the Police Brutality Unit"; Nevada Independent Broadcasting Corp. v. Allen, 99 Nev. 404, 664 P.2d 337 (1983), 9 Med.L.Rptr. 1770, in a statement questioning whether a political candidate was "honorable"; Grass v. News Group Publications, Inc., 570 F.Supp. 178 (S.D.N.Y. 1983), 9 Med.L.Rptr. 2129, saying that Lew made the business a great success, while "Alex minded the store back home" and "was always in the shade when Lew was around."

[59] Ollman v. Evans, 750 F.2d 970 (D.C.Cir.1984), 11 Med.L.Rptr. 1433; appeal refused by Supreme Court, L. Greenhouse, "Supreme Court Roundup," New York Times, 5/29/85, 8.

[60] Ibid., at 1038, 11 Med.L.Rptr. at 1491.

so, he shaped a four-part test which periodically is used in in decisions grappling with this perplexing realm of libel law: [61]

1. The inquiry must analyze the common usage or meaning of the words. Do they have a precise meaning such as a direct charge of crime, or are they only loosely definable?

2. Is the statement verifiable—"objectively capable of proof or disproof?"

3. What is the "linguistic" context in which the statement occurs? Here the article or column needs to be taken "as a whole": "The language of the entire column may signal that a specific statement which, standing alone, would appear to be factual, is in actuality a statement of opinion."

4. What is the "broader social context into which the statement fits?" Here there are signals to readers or listeners that what is being read or heard is likely to be opinion, not fact. An example would be the labor dispute of *Old Dominion* (above, Sec. 19), with its exaggerated rhetoric common in such circumstances. Another signal would be whether the article appeared on an editorial page—where opinion is expected—or in a front-page news story.

Despite the assertion in the Restatement (Second) of Torts in 1977, Gertz v. Robert Welch, Inc., did not obliterate the old libel defense of fair comment. Years later, some courts were still using common-law fair comment. [62]

For example, the Illinois Appellate Court, Fifth District, in 1982 held that repeated charges of "liar" against a county official in a newspaper editorial, and warning of two more years of his "lying leadership," were not protected opinion. For while a single charge of "liar" about a single event had been held not actionable in Illinois, the cumulative force of several such charges was "an actionable assault on the plaintiff's character in general, not mere criticism of his conduct in a particular instance." [63] The Court found that these were factual assertions, not expressions of opinion and not rhetorical hyperbole as argued by the defendant. Once more, the charge of "liar" had been found to be unprotected. It is unsafe, like accusations of criminal activity even in the form of "In

[61] Ibid., at 979–983, 11 Med.L.Rptr. at 1440–1444.

[62] Sack, 178–82; Note, Fact and Opinion after Gertz v. Robert Welch, Inc., 34 Rutgers L.Rev. 81, 126 (Fall 1981); Jerry Chaney, Opinion Dicta New Law of Libel? 10 Med.Law Notes # 2, 5 (Feb., 1983); 10 Med.L.Rptr. # 15, 4/10/84, News Notes; Prosser & Keetan, Law of Torts, 5th ed. (1984), 831; Cianci v. New Times, 639 F.2d 54 (2d Cir.1980), 6 Med.L.Rptr. 1625, 1634. Goodrich v. Waterbury Republican–American, Inc., 188 Conn. 107, 448 A.2d 1317 (1982), 8 Med.L.Rptr. 2329; Orr v. Argus–Press Co., 586 F.2d 1108 (6th Cir.1978); Tawfik v. Loyd (N.D.Tex.1979), 5 Med.L.Rptr. 2067.

[63] Costello v. Capital Cities Media, Inc., 111 Ill.App.3d 1009, 67 Ill.Dec. 721, 445 N.E.2d 13 (1982), 9 Med.L.Rptr. 1434.

my *opinion,* he is a rapist"[64] ... a dangerous form of comment taken up in the 1990 U.S. Supreme Court decision discussed below.

Milkovich v. Lorain Journal Co. (1990)

As is evident from the preceding pages, Gertz v. Welch, Inc. (1974) generated numerous court decisions referred to under the general label of a "constitutional opinion defense." This defense was warmly welcomed by many commentators, adopted by many appellate courts, and rejected by some others.[65] When this defense was accepted, it meant that statements of opinion—variously defined—were held not to be actionable defamation. That opinion defense has been diluted, in substantial measure, by the U.S. Supreme Court decision in 1990 in a 15–year–old libel case, Milkovich v. Lorain Journal.[66]

Michael Milkovich, Jr., a retired high school wrestling coach whose teams won numerous state championships, taught the news media a practical lesson. Packaging attacks on individuals' reputations as "opinion" appears more risky after the Supreme Court's decision.

In 1974, Milkovich was coaching the Maple Heights (Ohio) High School wrestling team against Mentor High School when a fight broke out. Several persons were hurt. Later, Coach Milkovich was among those testifying in an investigation by the Ohio State High School Athletic Association (OSHAA). His Maple Heights team was put on probation and ruled ineligible for the 1975 state tournament, and Coach Milkovich was censured for his role in the fight. After OSHAA was sued by some Maple Heights parents and wrestlers, an Ohio Court of Common Pleas overturned the probation and ineligibility orders.[67]

The following day, a column by sportswriter J. Theodore Diadiun appeared in the News–Herald, a newspaper published by the Lorain Journal Co. The column's headline said: "Maple beat the law with the 'big lie.' " A headline on the jump page read, " * * * Diadiun says Maple told a lie." The column said, in part:[68]

" ' * * * a lesson was learned (or relearned) yesterday by the student body of Maple Heights High School, and by

[64] Cianci v. New Times Pub. Co., 639 F.2d 54, 63 (2d Cir.1980), 6 Med.L.Rptr. 1625, 1631; Ollman v. Evans, 750 F.2d 970 (D.C.Cir.1984), 11 Med.L.Rptr. 1433, 1443.

[65] See discussion in David A. Anderson, "Is Libel Law Worth Reforming?", 140 *Pa.L.Rev.* (Dec.1991) pp. 505–510.

[66] Milkovich v. Lorain Journal Co., 497 U.S. 1, 110 S.Ct. 2695 (1990), 17 Med. L.Rptr. 2009.

[67] 497 U.S. at 4, 110 S.Ct. at 2698 (1990), 17 Med.L.Rptr. at 2010.

[68] 497 U.S. at 6, 110 S.Ct. at 2698 (1990), 17 Med.L.Rptr. at 2011.

anyone who attended the Maple–Mentor wrestling meet of last Feb. 8.

* * *

" 'It is simply this: If you get in a jam, lie your way out.

* * *

" 'The teachers responsible were mainly Maple wrestling coach, Mike Milkovich, and former superintendent of schools, II. Donald Scott.

* * *

" 'Anyone who attended the meet, whether he be from Maple Heights or Mentor, or impartial observer, knows in his heart that Milkovich and Scott lied at the hearing after each having given his solemn oath to tell the truth.

" 'But they got away with it.

" 'Is this the kind of lesson we want our young people learning from their high school administrators and coaches?

" 'I think not.' "

Milkovich sued for defamation, and 15 years later—in 1990–the U.S. Supreme Court granted certiorari "to consider the important questions raised by the Ohio courts' recognition of a constitutionally required 'opinion' exception to the application of its defamation laws." [69]

Writing for the Court, Chief Justice William H. Rehnquist summarized cases constitutionally limiting the application of state defamation laws, from New York Times v. Sullivan (1964) through *Gertz* and Philadelphia Newspapers v. Hepps. (See discussions of these cases at text Secs. 28 and 34.) In addition, the Chief Justice cited Harte–Hanks v. Connaughton (1989) (discussed in Sec. 29): " 'The question whether the evidence in the record in a defamation case is sufficient to support a finding of actual malice is a question of law.' " [70]

The Chief Justice wrote: [71]

Respondents would have us recognize ... still another First Amendment-based protection for defamatory statements which are categorized as "opinion" as opposed to

[60] 497 U.S. at 10, 110 S.Ct. at 2701 (1990), 17 Med.L.Rptr. at 2013.
[70] 497 U.S. at 17, 110 S.Ct. at 2705 (1990), 17 Med.L.Rptr. at 2016.
[71] 497 U.S. 17, 110 S.Ct. at 2705–2706, 17 Med.L.Rptr. at 2017.

"fact." For this proposition they rely on the following dictum from our opinion in *Gertz:*

> "Under the First Amendment there is no such thing as a false idea. However pernicious an opinion may seem, we depend for its correction not on the conscience of judges and juries but on the competition of ideas. But there is no constitutional value in false statements of fact."

Judge Friendly appropriately observed that this passage "has become the opening salvo in all arguments for protection from defamation actions on ground of opinion, even though the case did not remotely concern the question." Cianci v. New Times Publishing Co., 639 F.2d 54, 62 (C.A.2 1980). Read in context, though, the fair meaning of the passage was merely a reiteration of Justice Holmes' classic "marketplace of ideas" concept * * * [See Chapter 1, Sec. 2.]

> Thus we do not think this passage from *Gertz* was intended to create a wholesale defamation exemption for anything that might be labeled "opinion." * * * Not only would such an interpretation be contrary to the tenor and context of the passage, but it would also ignore the fact that expressions of "opinion" may often imply an assertion of objective fact.

> If a speaker says, "In my opinion John Jones is a liar," he implies a knowledge of facts which led to the conclusion that Jones told an untruth. Even if the speaker states the facts upon which he bases his opinion, if those facts are either incorrect or incomplete, or if his assessment of them is erroneous, the statement may still imply a false assertion of fact. Simply couching such statements in terms of opinion does not dispel these implications; and the statement, "In my opinion Jones is a liar," can cause as much damage to reputation as the statement "Jones is a liar."

Chief Justice Rehnquist wrote: "It is worthy of note that at common law, even the privilege of fair comment did not extend to 'a false statement of fact, whether it was expressly stated or implied from an expression of opinion.' *Restatement (Second) of Torts* * * * Sec. 566 Comment *a.*" [72]

The Chief Justice expressed a desire to avoid drawing lines between opinion and fact. " * * * [W]e think the 'breathing space' which 'freedoms of expression require' to survive *Hepps,* 475 U.S.

---

[72] 497 U.S. at 19, 110 S.Ct. at 2706 (1990), 17 Med.L.Rptr. at 2017.

at 772, 106 S.Ct. at 1561 (quoting *New York Times,* 376 U.S. at 272, 84 S.Ct. at 721), is adequately secured by existing constitutional doctrine without the creation of an artificial dichotomy between 'opinion' and 'fact.' " [73]

Thus, unlike the statement, "In my opinion Mayor Jones is a liar," the statement "In my opinion, Mayor Jones shows his abysmal ignorance by accepting the teachings of Marx and Lenin" would not be actionable. *Hepps* ensures that a statement of opinion relating to matters of public concern which does not contain a provably false factual connotation will receive full constitutional protection.

It is to be doubted that the preceding paragraphs are going to settle legal squabbles over what is "fact," "opinion," or, as the Chief Justice stated earlier, an expression of opinion implying an "objective fact." [74]

Chief Justice Rehnquist listed several decisions limiting the severity of libel laws against defendants: [75]

— The *Bresler–Letter Carriers–Falwell* line of cases, protecting name-calling statements that cannot reasonably be interpreted as representing "actual facts" about a person.

— "The *New York Times, Butts,* and *Gertz* culpability requirements further ensure that debate over public issues remains 'uninhibited, robust and wide-open.' New York Times, 376 U.S., at 270 [1964]."

— Finally, the enhanced independent appellate review required by *Bose Corp.* provides assurance that determinations about libel will be made so as not to "constitute a forbidden intrusion into the field of free expression. *Bose,* 466 U.S. at 490 * * *"

Chief Justice Rehnquist concluded that the language the newspaper columnist used against Coach Milkovich was "loose, figurative or hyperbolic," and that the column's connotation that the coach had committed perjury was susceptible of being proved true or false.[76]

Dissenting, Justice Brennan—joined by Justice Marshall—seemingly agreed with the majority's rendition of the facts in the Milkovich case. Unlike the majority, however, Brennan characterized the columnist's words about the coach as "patently conjecture." Therefore, he disagreed with the finding that columnist

[73] 497 U.S. at 20, 110 S.Ct. at 2706 (1990), 17 Med.L.Rptr. at 2017.

[74] 497 U.S. at 19, 110 S.Ct. at 2706 (1990), 17 Med.L.Rptr. at 2018.

[75] 497 U.S. at 20–22, 110 S.Ct. at 2706–2707 (1990), 17 Med.L.Rptr. at 2018.

[76] Ibid.

Diadiun's statements were actionable because they implied an assertion of fact that the coach had perjured himself. Brennan countered: [77]

> Diadiun not only reveals the facts upon which he is relying but makes it clear at which point he runs out of facts and is simply guessing. Read in context, such statements simply cannot reasonably be interpreted as implying such an assertion of fact.

Brennan, in line with his years of supporting press freedom, suggested ways in which conjecture and opinion not grounded in verifiable fact could serve a very real public interest. Justice Brennan asked: [78]

> Did NASA officials ignore sound warnings that the Challenger Space Shuttle would explode? Did Cuban–American leaders arrange for John Fitzgerald Kennedy's assassination? Was Kurt Waldheim a Nazi officer? Such questions are matters of public concern long before all the facts are unearthed, if they ever are.

The *Milkovich* decision means that news organizations are well advised to look to their ethics. Reporters and their bosses had best repress the desire to clobber reputations—especially *private* reputations—with opinion statements if the underlying facts are squishy. The noted media attorney Bruce Sanford put it another way: He predicted that " 'our public debate will be more flannel-mouthed and more cautious' " because of self-censorship to avoid possible libel suits.[79] Caution may be indicated. The Lorain Journal Co. reportedly spent more than $500,000 in defending and losing the Milkovich libel suit.[80] And, the Milkovich decision does have its strange aspects. As Sanford noted, it is ironic that the more far-fetched " * * * or obviously absurd the commentary, the more constitutional protection it will have." Unsurprisingly, Sanford—along with a number of other lawyers who defend media clients—initially looked at this decision and predicted tough times ahead for the news media where defamation is concerned.[81]

Are Statements "Opinion" or Provable Fact?

Milkovich v. Lorain Journal (1990) proved perplexing for commentators, some who believed that the opinion defense based on a

[77] 497 U.S. at 28, 110 S.Ct. at 2711 (1990), 17 Med.L.Rptr. at 2019.

[78] 497 U.S. at 34–35, 110 S.Ct. at 2714 (1990), 17 Med.L.Rptr. at 2021.

[79] Bruce Sanford, "Libel Defeat Is Troublesome For Broadcast News," *RadioWeek* July 16, 1990, p. 4.

[80] David Margolick, "How a '74 Fracas Led to a High Court Libel Case," The New York Times, April 20, 1990.

[81] Sanford, loc. cit.

selective reading of Gertz v. Welch (1974) was all but defunct. Perhaps not. For, as Robert Sack and Sandra Baron have suggested, " ... most courts considering opinion since Milkovich have reached the results they likely would have reached before." [82]

Opinions, by their nature, are not objectively provable. Consider Unelko Corp. v. Rooney, a useful case making an effort find a fact/opinion distinction involving CBS curmudgeon Andy Rooney. "It didn't work," Rooney said during a broadcast about Rain–X, a windshield rain-repellent manufactured by Unelko. The Ninth Circuit Court of Appeals held this was an objectively supportable comment, a statement of fact not protected under *Milkovich*. The court expressed three tests for trying to draw a line between fact and opinion: [83]

1) Is figurative or hyperbolic language used of the kind not to be understood literally?

2) Was the general tenor of Rooney's broadcast commentary perceived as satirical or humorous?

3) Could the statement "It didn't work" be proved true or false?

Rooney and CBS actually defended successfully against this suit brought under California defamation law. Even though their case was undermined by the court's reading of Milkovich v. Lorain Journal (1990), the defendants won because Unelko did not show that Rooney's statement was false and because of public interest in whether products actually work as represented.

Moldea v. New York Times Co. (1994)

Litigation brought by an author against The New York Times Book Review may provide additional clues for what the Milkovich decision of 1990 (see above) means to protection of statements of opinion from libel suits. Dan Moldea wrote a book titled Interference: How Organized Crime Influences Professional Football. He asserted that an unfavorable review by Times sportswriter Gerald Eskenazi damaged the book's reception and injured Moldea's reputation and earning ability. The review said Moldea's book contained " 'too much sloppy journalism to trust the bulk of this book's 512 pages including its whopping 64 pages of footnotes' " and then listed some examples of what the reviewer saw as short-

---

[82] Robert D. Sack and Sandra S. Baron, Libel, Slander and Related Problems, 2nd ed. (New York: Practising Law Institute, 1994), p. 214. Bryan Denham, a graduate student at Tennessee, reached a similar conclusion in his 1994 unpublished paper, "Legal Analyses of Milkovich: Consistencies and Contradictions."

[83] 912 F.2d 1049, 1051 (9th Cir.1990), 17 Med.L.Rptr. 2317, 2320–2321.

comings.[84]

Moldea's defamation and false light invasion of privacy suit against The Times was at first unsuccessful, with a U.S. district court granting the newspaper summary judgment. That court ruled that the reviewer's statements could not be legally actionable as defamation because they were merely statements of opinion and thus unverifiable; no reasonable juror, this court said could find them to be true or false.[85]

In a 2–1 decision, however, a panel of the Court of Appeals, D.C. Circuit, at first found in favor of Moldea, ruling that some of the characterizations in Moldea's book were potentially actionable because they were verifiable, and could not be held to be true as a matter of law.[86]

But on rehearing, the Court of Appeals held that Gerald Eskenazi's review of Moldea's book was not defamatory. First, the genre of the writing and the context in which it appears must be taken into effect: [87]

> In contrast to the situation in *Milkovich*, the instant case involves a context, a book review, in which the allegedly libelous statements were evaluations quintessentially of a type readers expect to find in that genre. The challenged statements in the Times review consist solely of the reviewer's comments on a literary work and therefore must be judged with an eye toward readers' expectations and understandings of book reviews. * * *

> There is a long and rich history in our cultural and legal traditions of affording reviewers latitude to comment on literary and other works. The statements at issue in the instant case are assessments of a book, rather than direct assaults on Moldea's character, reputation, or competence as a journalist. * * * [W]hile a critic's latitude is not unlimited, he or she must be given the constitutional "breathing space" appropriate to the genre. New York Times v. Sullivan, 376 U.S. 254, 272 (1964).

The Times's petition for rehearing had real impact, for the court said in "Moldea (II):" "We believe that the Times has suggested the appropriate standard for evaluating critical reviews: 'The proper analysis would make commentary actionable only when

[84] Moldea v. New York Times Co., 22 F.3d 310 (D.C.Cir.1994), 22 Med.L.Rptr. 1673, 1674.

[85] Ibid., citing Moldea v. New York Times Co., 793 F.Supp. 335 (D.D.C.1992), 19 Med.L.Rptr. 1931.

[86] Ibid., p. 1673, citing "Moldea (I), 15 F.3d at 1146–1148.

[87] Ibid., pp. 1676–1677.

the interpretations are unsupportable by reference to the written work.' " [88] The court declared that [89]

> this "supportable interpretation" standard provides that a critic's interpretation must be rationally supportable by reference to the actual text he or she is evaluating, and thus would not immunize situations analogous to Milkovich in which a writer launches a personal attack, rather than interpreting a book.

The Court of Appeals decision in "Moldea (II)" meant that the district court's original grant of summary judgment to The Times was upheld, and thus halted Moldea's claims for both defamation and false light privacy.

SEC. 36. RETRACTION

A full and prompt apology following the publication of a libel will serve to mitigate damages awarded to the injured.

The news medium that has libeled a person may retract its statement, and in doing so, hope to lessen the chances that huge damages will be awarded to the injured party. The retraction must be full and without reservation, it should be no attempt to justify the libel, and it must be given the prominence in space or time that the original charge received. But while a full and timely apology may go to mitigate damages, it is in no sense a complete defense. Into the mid–1990s, the law reasons that many persons who saw the original story may not see the retraction.

In spite of a thorough retraction in one case, it was estimated that the broadcaster involved agreed to an out-of-court settlement in the range of one-fourth to one-half of a million dollars.[90] Under state statutes, a full and prompt retraction serves to negate punitive damages, for it is considered evidence that the libel was not published with common-law malice (ill will). Under the constitutional (*Sullivan*) doctrine, however, retraction was placed in a somewhat ambiguous condition, jurisdictions varying in whether it negates actual malice (knowing or reckless falsehood) or not.[91]

[88] Ibid., p. 1677, quoting the Times's Petition for Rehearing (emphasis deleted).

[89] Ibid., p. 1677. The Court of Appeals found similar approaches to the "supportable interpretation" standard in Bose Corp. v. Consumers' Union, 466 U.S. 485, 104 S.Ct. 1949 (1984), and in Masson v. Malcolm, 111 S.Ct. at 2434, quoting Bose, 466 U.S. at 512, 513, concerning statements not so obviously false as to sustain a finding of "actual malice."

[90] Green v. WCAU–TV, 8 Med.L.Rptr. #35, 11/2/82, News Notes.

[91] Donna L. Dickerson, Retraction's Role Under the Actual Malice Rule, 6 Communications and the Law #4, 39 (Aug. 1984).

Many states—33 in 1994—have retraction statutes,[92] some providing that punitive damages may not be awarded if retraction is made properly and the publisher shows that he did not publish with malice. Others have gone further, providing that only "special" (actual monetary) damages may be awarded following a retraction and demonstration of good faith on the part of the publisher. California may have the statute most favorable to publishers. It provides that a proper retraction limits recovery to special damages, no matter what the motives of the publisher.[93]

Some retraction statutes have been attacked as unconstitutional, one reason being that they sometimes are applicable only to newspapers and as such are discriminatory. Many persons may publish libel in non-newspaper form, but not have the advantage of retraction statutes in these states. In Park v. Detroit Free Press Co., a Michigan retraction statute was held unconstitutional, the Court holding that "It is not competent for the legislature to give one class of citizens legal exemptions from liability for wrongs not granted to others." [94] The Supreme Court of Kansas held that state's retraction provision unconstitutional. The decision went to the law's preventing recovery of general damages, and said: [95]

> The injuries for which this class of damages is allowed are something more than merely speculative * * *. In short, they are such injuries to the reputation as were contemplated in the bill of rights * * *.

Where punitive damages only are barred to the defamed, however, the constitutionality of the statute ordinarily has been upheld.[96]

"SLAPP" Lawsuits

In the late 1980s, the phrase "getting SLAPPED" took on First Amendment meaning. "SLAPP" became well known as the acronym for "Strategic Lawsuits Against Public Participation."

For example, suppose a number of citizens of Clearwater City starts a petition to pressure the Blanking Paper Company upstream

---

[92] Henry R. Kaufman, "Special Report: The Potential Reform of State Retraction Statutes Under the Uniform Correction or Clarification of Defamation Act," in LDRC [Libel Defense Resource Center] 50–State Survey, 1993–1994, at p. xvii (New York: LDRC, 1993); for a list of state retraction laws, see Sack and Baron, op. cit., pp.837–865.

[93] T.M. Newell and Albert Pickerell, "California's Retraction Statute: License to Libel?," 28 Journ.Quar. 474, 1951. For State retraction statutes, see Sack, App. IV, 589.

[94] 72 Mich. 560, 40 N.W. 731 (1888). See also Madison v. Yunker, 180 Mont. 54, 589 P.2d 126 (1978).

[95] Hanson v. Krehbiel, 68 Kan. 670, 75 P. 1041 (1904).

[96] Comer v. Age–Herald Pub. Co., 151 Ala. 613, 44 So. 673 (1907); Meyerle v. Pioneer Pub. Co., 45 N.D. 568, 178 N.W. 792 (1920).

to stop polluting the Clearwater River. If pollution controls are too expensive for the paper company at the moment, one alternative—which came into increasing use in the late 1980s—is to sue the petitioners for defamation (or some other legal claim). If, as is likely, the citizens' group does not have pockets as deep as Blanking Paper Company, the citizens may be intimidated into shutting up. If they do, they will have been SLAPPED.

The term SLAPP was coined by Professors Penelope Canan and George W. Pring of the University of Denver. They charted the phenomenon of ordinary-looking civil damage suits which in reality were "clearly reactions against past or anticipated opposition on political issues." [97]

In 1988, Canan and Pring surveyed 100 SLAPP suits. The most frequent legal claims used to try to squelch complaining citizens were defamation, business torts and abuse of process, while other filers opted for claims including conspiracy, violation of civil rights, and nuisance lawsuits. [98]

Although courts ultimately dismiss 80 percent of the SLAPP suits, that may still mean that protesting parties have been silenced because of lengthy, costly litigation. Some states, however, have reacted by considering legislation to slow down SLAPP suits. In 1989, for example, Washington passed a statute giving immunity from civil liability for any person who is sued for giving information to a governmental body. [99]

In addition, some people fight back. Early in 1990, reporter Lee McEachern of KQED–TV, San Francisco, told of three Bakersfield, California, farmers who were sued for placing a newspaper ad critical of J.G. Boswell, "the world's largest farming company."

The farmers counter-sued, and a jury held that the SLAPP lawsuit against them had deprived them of their constitutional rights of speech, press, and petition. The three farmers were awarded damages totaling $13.5 million, McEachern told the Mac-Neil–Lehrer News Hour. [1]

The Biggest "SLAPP" Suit Yet?

To underline its contention that cigarette manufacturers don't add nicotine to keep smokers hooked, Philip Morris Companies filed a **$10 Billion** defamation suit against the ABC network in March

[97] Penelope Canan and George W. Pring, "Studying Strategic Lawsuits Against Public Participation * * *," 22 Law and Society Review No. 2 (1988), pp. 385–395.

[98] Ibid.

[99] Amy Dockser Marcus, "Law: Intimidation Lawsuits Creep Up on Critics," Wall Street Journal, Feb. 4, 1990, p. 81.

[1] Lee McEachern, "Focus—Getting Slapped," MacNeil–Lehrer News Hour, Feb. 19, 1990.

of 1994. The lawsuit, filed in circuit court in Richmond, Virginia, argued that the company was greatly harmed by statements broadcast on ABC's magazine program, "Day One," and on other ABC News programs broadcast in February and March of 1994.

Statements complained of asserted-in the words of a New York Times story-"that cigarette companies laced cigarettes with extra nicotine." Philip Morris' Murray Bring, vice president and general counsel, said " 'These allegations are not true, and ABC knows they are not true.' " [2]

About that same time, Dr. David Kessler, commissioner of the Food and Drug Administration (FDA), had stated that the FDA had accumulated enough evidence to suggest cigarette manufacturers " 'commonly add nicotine to cigarettes to deliver specific amounts,' " adding that Congress should consider regulating nicotine as a drug.[3]

Although The New York Times did not refer to the $10 billion lawsuit against the media as a SLAPP suit, an editorial nevertheless depicted the litigation as a bullying tactic to intimidate the network. The editorial referred to accusations of the cigarette industry's "ability to control the dose of addictive nicotine delivered to smokers" as the industry's "vulnerable underbelly." [4]

Other Costs of Defamation

The damages paid out in defamation cases are only part of the cost to the media, only part of the "chilling effect." Court and lawyer costs can be massive: as high as $10 million for CBS to defend the libel suit brought by General William Westmoreland and more than $3 million for Time magazine to defend against a suit brought by General Ariel Sharon.[5] Beyond court-related costs, there are costs of journalists' and editors/news directors' time spent in giving depositions.

Although there is an elegance and a nobility about New York Times v. Sullivan (1964) and many of the cases following it, the romance of the "constitutional defense" to libel has begun to pall on a number of observers. Eugene Roberts, then editor of The Philadelphia Inquirer, reported late in 1987 that his newspaper was

[2] Michael Janofsky, "Philip Morris Accuses ABC of Libel," The New York Times, March 25, 1994, p. A7. See also the Roger Rosenblatt essay, "How Do They Live With Themselves?", The New York Times Magazine, March 20, 1994, p. 40ff.

[3] Ibid., quoting Kessler letter to the Coalition on Smoking OR Health.

[4] "Philip Morris Lashes Back," editorial in The New York Times, April 3, 1994, Sec. 4, p. 10.

[5] For extended discussions of these cases, see Renata Adler, Reckless Disregard (New York: Knopf, 1986) and Rodney A. Smolla, Suing the Press (New York: Oxford, 1986).

being sued by two state supreme court justices after articles investigating the need for court reform in Pennsylvania.

Roberts said: "The Westmoreland and Sharon cases are the best known, but they are the merest tip of the iceberg." He referred to a $250 million libel suit against California's McClatchy Newspapers, withdrawn after three years of attorneys' fees. And in Arizona, the Sheriff Dick Godbehere of Maricopa County had brought a $64 million libel suit against the Arizona Republic and the Phoenix Gazette.

Roberts suggested that the "actual malice loophole," instead of protecting press freedom as the Supreme Court intended had provided tools of harassment for public officials to use with the help of friendly, anti-media juries.[6]

Katherine P. Darrow, General Counsel of The New York Times had a similarly chilling message late in 1987. She said that the average affirmed award for a person who prevails in a libel suit is $145,000. But that amount—obviously substantially large—did not concern her a great deal. After all, she said, only about 10 per cent of all the libel cases started ever get to trial.

What did worry her was the cost of defense. To handle a hypothetical average suit—including pre-trial matters such as discovery, motions, plus the trial itself and an appeal. Figuring the hours billed at typical rates for the U.S. outside of New York City, she estimated a cost through trial of nearly $150,000.

She said this meant that newspapers will be in for a period of high legal defense expenses. Large newspapers may well be able to survive, and even thrive, but small publications could be chilled into silence by the threat of libel, if not actually sued into oblivion.[7]

And if defamation law is seen as a threat for the media, it is not working for most plaintiffs, either. The famed "Iowa Study" of libel showed in the late 1980s that plaintiffs chances of winning a libel suit are about one in five. Plaintiffs' attorneys tend to be more optimistic than libel suit success rates justify, but most plaintiffs should understand that the odds against winning are long.[8]

The Iowa study indicated, quite simply, that the law of defamation does not and can not work because it is built upon an untenable assumption that libel plaintiffs somehow can be mended

[6] Eugene L. Roberts, "When Freedom of Expression Becomes a Financial Burden," remarks on receiving the John Peter Zenger award, University of Arizona, Tucson, Nov. 13, 1987.

[7] Katherine P. Darrow, "Libel and Newspapers: Is this the Big Chill?", speech at University of Missouri, Oct. 28, 1987.

[8] Randall P. Bezanson, Gilbert Cranberg, and John Soloski, Libel Law and the Press: Myth and Reality (New York: Free Press, 1987) pp. 72–76.

by monetary damage awards. But plaintiffs themselves, on the other hand, want to set the record straight, to correct falsehoods published about them.[9]

Media attorney Floyd Abrams declared in 1988 that libel law " ' ... doesn't really protect individual reputations, and, on the other hand, it does chill freedom of expression.' " [10] Abrams had company in holding that view. The Libel Dispute Resolution Program of the Iowa Libel Research Project and the American Arbitration Association is proposed an alternative. One alternative—a proposed "Uniform Defamation Act"—offered suggested statutory language. Such language, if adopted by state legislatures, would have had disputants who might otherwise wind up as plaintiff and defendant in a defamation lawsuit to agree to submit to an arbitration hearing before a neutral arbitrator.

Such a proceeding would reach a decision on whether reputational harm has been done and whether the challenged statements are true or false. A brochure describing this project said, "Fault-related questions such as malice, negligence, and the reasonableness of editorial procedures, and discovery * * * will be prohibited." Money damages would not be awarded by the arbitrator, and the remedy was likely to be publication or broadcast of the arbitrator's brief statement of the findings.[11]

Late 1988 saw the proposal of the Northwestern Libel Reform Project. This effort by the Annenberg Washington Program of Northwestern University was directed by Newton N. Minow, formerly chairman of the Federal Communications Commission under President Kennedy.

One rationale for libel reform efforts may be found in a number of inconclusive defamation cases—cases such as those involving General William Westmoreland against CBS and William Tavoulareas against the Washington Post. After millions of dollars had been expended by both sides in the Westmoreland case, the General withdrew from the suit, with both sides claiming vindication. Tavoulareas had been awarded $2 million in his lawsuit against the Washington Post. That amount, the Libel Reform Project noted, would have paid the lawyers' fees for Tavoulareas, but the award was overturned on appeal.[12]

[9] Ibid., p. 4.

[10] Roselle L. Wissler, et al., "Why Current Libel Law Doesn't Work", The Judges' Journal (Spring 1988) p. 29.

[11] Resolving Libel Disputes, booklet available from Iowa Libel Research Project, College of Law, University of Iowa, Iowa City, Iowa 52242.

[12] Proposal for the Reform of Libel Law, Annenberg Washington Program in Communications Policy Studies, October 17, 1988, pp. 9–10.

The Libel Reform Project's proposed model statute would require that all plaintiffs *must* seek a retraction or opportunity to reply before filing suit. The plaintiff who did not get a retraction or an opportunity to reply would be entitled to file suit. But the Libel Reform Project's proposed law would hold out an option to avoid the lengthy and expensive process of current libel law. How? By agreeing to a declaratory judgment lawsuit. The only issue in such a suit would be truth or falsity of the defamatory statement. The losing party would pay the winner's attorney's fees. But on the other hand, plaintiffs' lawyers—and the plaintiffs themselves—may not wish to give up the possibility of the occasional big libel award.

This proposed statute accepted the idea of neutral reportage: there could be no liability for accurately reporting the words of others. It would also grant no more than "reasonable compensation based upon proof of actual injury," and would abolish presumed and punitive damages.[13]

There was little initial enthusiasm and there was overt opposition for the Libel Reform Project's suggestions from many media leaders and lawyers. Criticisms of its proposals surfaced quickly. Attorney Jane Kirtley, executive director of the Reporter's Committee for Freedom of the Press, argued that the Libel Reform Project was in effect urging the jettisoning of the principles of New York Times v. Sullivan, abandoning the doctrine that news media cannot be held responsible for "false statements published without fault."

Kirtley conceded that a declaratory judgment lawsuit would be cheaper to litigate. However, she said: "[T]he cost in human terms—the public pillorying of both complainant and publisher—will not be significantly reduced for the simple reason that the ultimate question of truth is just not that easy to answer."[14]

The Uniform Correction Act Proposal

In 1993, the National Conference of Commissioners on Uniform State Laws adopted a proposal by a vote of 40–8 to approve a Uniform Correction Act. This proposal was approved in February, 1994, by the American Bar Association House of Delegates. The model Uniform Correction Act, if passed by legislatures of individual states, could provide nationwide consistency in retraction statutes.[15]

[13] Ibid., pp. 15–17, 19–24.

[14] Jane Kirtley, "Proposal to reform libel law has troubling aspects," Editor & Publisher, Nov. 5, 1988, p. 52ff.

[15] Kaufman, 1993–1994, loc. cit.; telephone interview with Dr. John Soloski, University of Iowa, Nov. 11, 1994.

In a state where the Uniform Correction Act is adopted, any person wishing to sue for defamation (or false light privacy) would be required to request a retraction before filing suit. The would-be plaintiff also would be required to provide evidence of the error/defamation to the publisher. If a sufficient, good faith clarification or correction is made (or if one is not sought 90 days after the aggrieved individual learns of the publication), all that a plaintiff could win is damages amounting to actual monetary loss provably resulting from the publication.[16]

Efforts were to be made in 1995 to introduce the Uniform Correction Act into the legislatures of several states. Chances for widespread passage of the Uniform Correction Act will be affected by the concern of libel plaintiffs' lawyers, who may hate to see stronger retraction procedures cut into potential big-dollar libel victories. Also, would limiting libel plaintiffs' ability to collect lawsuit damages to their reputations infringe on any constitutional rights of individuals? Stay tuned.

[16] Ibid., for text draft of Uniform Correction Act, pp.xxxi-xlviii. (Long title: "Uniform Correction or Clarification of Defamation Act.")

Chapter 7

THE LAW OF PRIVACY AND THE MEDIA

SEC. 37. DEVELOPMENT OF PRIVACY LAW

Privacy—"the right to be let alone"—is protected by an evolving area of tort law and has been recognized as a constitutional right by the Supreme Court of the United States.

Privacy—roughly defined as "the right to be let alone" [1]—is one of the nation's hottest issues in the 1990s. It is often said that the United States has become "The Information Society." Increasingly, it is difficult for individuals to keep information about themselves from indiscriminate use by government agencies or business interests. The worry of the 1970s—when privacy was seen to be in peril by politicians, legal scholars, anthropologists, and citizen activists—was the nightmare of the 1980s [2] and may be the reality of the 1990s.

It can't happen here? Don't bet your life on it. Remember that government's stake in information about individuals has implications for *control*. Knowledge is power.

Think about cable television. We are moving steadily toward a nation interconnected, by satellite transmission if not by wire, to

---

[1] Thomas M. Cooley, A Treatise on the Law of Torts, 2d ed. (Chicago: Callaghan and Co., 1888) p. 29.

[2] See, e.g., Arthur R. Miller, The Assault on Privacy (Ann Arbor: University of Michigan Press, 1971); Don R. Pember, Privacy and the Press (Seattle: University of Washington Press, 1972); Alan Westin, Privacy and Freedom (New York: Atheneum, 1967); Subcommittee on Constitutional Rights of the Committee on the Judiciary, United States Senate, Ninety Second Congress, First Session ("The Ervin Subcommittee"), February 23–25, March 2–4, 9–11, 15 and 17, Parts 1 and 2, pp. 1–2164, *passim;* Final Recommendations of the Privacy Study Commission, and Warren Freedman, The Right to Privacy in the Computer Age (New York: Quorum Books, 1987), and George Orwell, 1984.

interactive (two-way) in-the-home cable television systems. The cornucopia of services offered by cable television and/or the Information Highway is dazzling. The technology is now here for use of cable TV for shopping, mail delivery, consulting with physicians, communicating with one's elected representatives, answering polls, and on and on. Think also about the price in lost privacy being paid for such a collection of services, when commercial interests are thirsting to know even more about your buying habits and when it's likely that your E–Mail is not secure from prying eyes.

Clipping Privacy With Clipper Chips

George Orwell's nightmarish vision of a privacy-free society was spelled out in his novel, **1984**. What Orwell feared could be seen in 1994's disputes over Clipper Chips.

A clipper chip—more technically called the " 'key escrow data encryption system' "—was designed to protect telephones and computers from intrusion by "outsiders," outsiders, that is, except the U.S. government.[3] These devices are sealed computer chips that can't be opened for inspection without being destroyed. The problem? Only the U.S. government would have the "keys" needed to read coded messages.[4]

Some background. By the early 1990s, the Federal Bureau of Investigation was complaining publicly that new telephone equipment made it difficult to wiretap phone calls by suspected criminals. New high-volume phone lines carrying digital signals move so much data that the Department of Justice proposed a bill to require a change " 'if those phone systems impede the Government's ability to conduct lawful electronic surveillance.' "[5]

In 1994 the Clinton Administration adopted—and apparently later rejected—the technology developed by the National Security Agency, to require use of clipper chips "to enable law enforcement agencies to intercept coded telephone and computer communications." Despite furious protests from civil liberties groups, the Commerce and Justice departments urged federal agencies to specify that corporations to make use of clipper chips in manufacturing computer and telephone equipment.[6]

U.S. manufacturers including I.B.M., Apple and Microsoft declared that Americans won't trust equipment containing govern-

[3] Peter H. Lewis, "Collisions in Cyberspace on Data Encryption Plan," The New York Times, March 26, 1994, p. 17.

[4] Ibid.; John Markoff, "U.S. as Big Brother of Computer Age," The New York Times, May 6, 1983, p. C1.

[5] Anthony Ramirez, "As Technology Makes Wiretaps More Difficult, FBI Seeks Help," The New York Times, March 8, 1992, Sec. 1, p. 12.

[6] Lewis, op. cit.; Edmund L. Andrews, "U.S. Plans to Push Computer Coding Police Can Read," The New York Times, March 8, 1992, Sec. 1, p.12.

ment-built coding devices with secret technology, and that this also could prove devastating to U.S. exports of computers and telephone equipment. As a result, the clipper chip proposal, which could have undermined individual and corporate efforts to encrypt their databases to keep them from prying eyes, was shelved, at least for the time being. But as Jane Kirtley of the Reporters Committee on Freedom of the Press has written, FBI Director Louis Freeh lobbied Congress into passing his "digital telephony" bill late in 1994. That bill, which will cost taxpayers $500 million, forces telephone companies to make their communications networks accessible to wiretaps by law enforcement agencies. So now the paranoid world of international espionage intrudes into American business and society. Even more than lone-wolf hackers, the NSA's clipper chip could remove expectations of privacy. Some computer experts argue that there is no way to be sure "that the National Security Agency has not built a 'trap door' that could allow unauthorized Government eavesdropping." [7]

So it is that the technology which serves us may also ensnare us. Infrared telephoto lenses "see in the dark." Super-sensitive directional microphones can hear across sizable distances. Dossiers are compiled by credit bureaus, and by myriad government agencies. All of these things were continuing phenomena, parts of what Vance Packard called "The Naked Society" back in 1964.[8] Arthur Miller of the Harvard School of Law produced an all-too prophetic study, The Assault on Privacy, investigating credit bureau abuses and use of systems for data collection and information storage and retrieval. Acknowledging the helpful uses of such technology, Professor Miller then warned: "we must be concerned about the axiom ... that man must shape his tools lest they shape him." [9]

Privacy is worth fighting for, against governmental stupidity or arrogance, or against the prying of businesses or private individuals. Louis D. Brandeis, one of the Supreme Court's greatest justices, once wrote that the makers of the American Constitution "sought to protect Americans in their beliefs, their thoughts, their emotions and their sensations. They [the Constitution's framers] conferred, as against the Government, the right to be let alone—the most comprehensive of rights and the right most valued by civilized man." [10]

Privacy is a problem for each citizen, a desired right to be fought for and zealously guarded. Privacy is also a communica-

[7] Markoff, loc. cit.; Jane Kirtley, "Examine Privacy Arguments Carefully," Virginia's Press, Oct. 31, 1994, p. 5.

[8] Vance Packard, The Naked Society (New York: David McKay and Co., 1964).

[9] Miller, op. cit., pp. 7–8.

[10] Olmstead v. United States, 277 U.S. 438, 48 S.Ct. 564 (1928).

tions media problem, one to be reported upon. And finally, privacy is a media problem in another sense because missteps by newspapers, magazines and radio and television stations have resulted in hundreds of privacy lawsuits.

Privacy is nowhere mentioned in the Constitution, and its absence is understandable. In America during the Revolutionary generation, most people lived on farms. Urban residents made up not much more than 10 per cent of the new nation's population. When the Constitution was ratified, Philadelphia, then the nation's largest city, had little more than 40,000 residents. When people were out-of-doors, there was little real need for any specific Constitutional statement of a right to privacy. Indoors, privacy was another matter. In 18th Century America, homes often had living, eating and sleeping accommodations for an entire family in the same room. In public inns, travelers often had to share rooms— and sometimes beds—with other wayfarers.[11]

Although privacy was not mentioned in the Constitution by name, its first eight amendments, plus the Fourteenth Amendment, include the right to be secure against unreasonable search and seizure and the principle of due process of law. Taken together with the Declaration of Independence's demands for the right to "life, liberty and the pursuit of happiness," it can be seen that concerns were expressed, early in this nation's life, for something akin to a "right to be let alone."

Since 1960, the Supreme Court of the United States has recognized privacy as a constitutional right, a right which to some extent protects citizens from intrusions by government or police agencies.[12]

Here, a useful distinction may be made between the *right* of privacy and the *law* of privacy. As Professor James Willard Hurst of the University of Wisconsin Law School has written, American legal history is full of concern for a broad *right* to privacy, represented by interests protected in the Constitution's Bill of Rights. (The Constitution, of course, protects citizens only against *government* actions.) The narrower tort *law* of privacy as enunciated by judges and legislatures deals with invasions of personal privacy by individuals or businesses, providing an avenue for monetary damages.[13]

The tort *law* of privacy is also quite new. It has been traced to an 1890 *Harvard Law Review* article written by two young Boston

[11] Pember, Privacy and the Press, p. 5.

[12] See Mapp v. Ohio, 367 U.S. 643, 81 S.Ct. 1684 (1961): Griswold v. Connecticut, 381 U.S. 479, 85 S.Ct. 1678 (1965).

[13] James Willard Hurst, Law and Conditions of Freedom (Madison, Wis.: University of Wisconsin Press, 1956) p. 8.

law partners, Samuel D. Warren and future Supreme Court Justice Louis D. Brandeis. The article, often named as the best example of the influence of law journals on the development of the law, was titled (or perhaps, mis-titled) "The Right to Privacy."

If this law journal article was the start of a law of privacy in America, it should also be noted that the newspaper press may have been involved too. Standard accounts of the origins of the Warren–Brandeis article have it that Warren and his wife had been greatly annoyed by newspaper stories about parties which they gave. This irritation, so the story goes, led to the drafting of the article, now thought to have been written primarily by Brandeis. The co-authors asserted that an independent action for privacy could be found within then- established areas of the law such as defamation and trespass to property. Warren and Brandeis wrote: [14]

> The press is overstepping in every direction the obvious bounds of propriety and of decency. Gossip is no longer the resource of the idle and of the vicious, but has become a trade which is pursued with industry as well as effrontery. To satisfy a prurient taste the details of sexual relations are spread broadcast in the columns of the daily papers. To occupy the indolent, column upon column is filled with idle gossip, which can only be procured by intrusion upon the domestic circle. The intensity and complexity of life, attendant upon advancing civilization, have rendered necessary some retreat from the world, and man, under the refining influence of culture, has become more sensitive to publicity, so that solitude and privacy have become more essential to the individual; but modern enterprise and invention have, through invasions upon his privacy, subjected him to mental pain and distress, far greater than could be inflicted by mere bodily injury.

But as a judge in a Missouri appeals court noted in 1911, the concept of a right of privacy was not new at all. Privacy, the judge wrote, "is spoken of as a new right, when in fact it is an old right with a new name. Life, liberty, and the pursuit of happiness are rights of all men." [15]

From such beginnings an expanding law of privacy has emerged. In 1901, a package of flour led to an early—and famous—privacy case in New York: Roberson v. Rochester Folding Box Co. The judges of two New York courts were evidently readers of the Harvard Law Review, because they would have allowed recovery in a privacy lawsuit brought by Miss Abigail M. Roberson.

[14] Samuel Warren and Louis D. Brandeis, "The Right to Privacy," 4 Harvard Law Review (1890) p. 196.

[15] Munden v. Harris, 153 Mo.App. 652, 659–660, 134 S.W. 1076, 1078 (1911).

She had sued for $15,000 because her likeness was used to decorate posters advertising Franklin Mills flour without her consent. But New York's highest court—the Court of Appeals—ruled that she could not collect because there was no precedent which established a "right of privacy." Despite Miss Roberson's unwilling inclusion in an advertising campaign featuring the slogan of "The Flour of the Family," the Court of Appeals held that if her claim were allowed, a flood of litigation would result, and that it was too difficult to distinguish between public and private persons.[16]

The *Roberson* decision, however, hinted broadly that if the New York legislature wished to enact a law of privacy, it could do so. Considerable public outcry and a number of outraged newspaper editorials greeted the outcome of the *Roberson* case. The next year, in 1903, the New York legislature passed a statute which made it both a misdemeanor and a tort to use the name, portrait, or picture of any person for advertising or "trade purposes" without that person's consent. Note that this was narrowly drawn legislation, limited to the kind of fact situation which had arisen in *Roberson*.[17]

In 1905, two years after the New York privacy statute was passed, the Georgia Supreme Court provided the first major judicial recognition of a law of privacy. An unauthorized photograph of Paolo Pavesich and a bogus testimonial attributed to him appeared in a newspaper advertisement for a life insurance company. The Georgia court ruled that there is a law of privacy which prevents unauthorized use of pictures and testimonials for advertising purposes.[18]

Since the 1905 *Pavesich* decision, the tort of privacy has grown mightily. The late William L. Prosser, for many years America's foremost torts scholar, outlined four kinds of torts included under the broad label of "invasion of privacy." [19]

1. Intrusion on the plaintiff's physical solitude.

2. Publication of private matters violating the ordinary decencies.

[16] 171 N.Y. 538, 64 N.E. 442, 447 (1902).

[17] New York Session Laws 1903, Ch. 132, §§ 1–2, now known as §§ 50–51, New York Civil Rights Law.

[18] Pavesich v. New England Life Ins. Co., 122 Ga. 190, 50 S.E. 68, 79 (1905).

[19] Barbieri v. News–Journal Co., 56 Del. 67, 189 A.2d 773, 774 (1963). The Delaware Supreme Court summarized Dean Prosser's analysis of the kinds of actions to be included by the law of privacy. For fuller treatment, see Prosser's much-quoted "Privacy," 48 California Law Review (1960), pp. 383–423, and his Handbook of the Law of Torts, 4th Ed. (St. Paul, Minn., West Publishing Co., 1971, pp. 802–818).

3. Putting plaintiff in a false position in the public eye, as by signing that person's name to a letter or petition, attributing views not held by that person.

4. Appropriation of some element of plaintiff's personality— his or her name or likeness—for commercial use.

It should be noted that these are not mutually exclusive categories; more than one of these four kinds of privacy actions may be present in the same case.

The law of privacy—or one of its four sub-tort areas as listed above—has now been recognized by federal courts, in the District of Columbia, and at least 49 states.[20] Court ("common law") recognition came in most states, and statutes recognizing the law of privacy were passed in other states, including: California, Nebraska, New York, Oklahoma, Utah, Virginia, and Wisconsin. Even in those states which were slow to recognize the law of privacy, privacy interests were apt to be protected under other legal actions such as libel or trespass.[21]

Professor Prosser noted that an action for invasion of privacy is much like the old concept *"libel per se:"* a plaintiff does not have to plead or prove actual monetary loss ("special damages") in order to have a cause of action. In addition, a court may award punitive damages. But while actions for defamation and for invasion of privacy have points of similarity, some see major differences. As a Massachusetts court said, "The fundamental difference between a right to privacy and a right to freedom from defamation is that the former directly concerns one's own peace of mind, while the latter concerns primarily one's reputation." [22]

[20] Victor A. Kovner, Harriette K. Dorsen, Suzanne Telsey, "Recent Developments In Intrusion, Private Facts, False Light, and Commercialization Claims," in James C. Goodale, chairman, Communications Law 1993 Vol. I (New York: Practising Law Institute, 1993); see especially his sampling of recent authorities for the four sub-torts which make up the law of privacy, "State Recognition of the Four Torts," pp. 883ff. Minnesota appeared to be the last holdout in 1993, and even there, some recognition has occurred in the area of appropriation- commercialization.

[21] State privacy statutes include California Civil Code, Section 3344, which is similar to the New York privacy statute, New York Civil Rights Law §§ 50–51. Wisconsin Statute § 895.50 recognized all four torts, thus overruling the notorious intrusion case, Yoeckel v. Samonig, 272 Wis. 430, 75 N.W.2d 925 (1956). A woman brought suit, alleging that her picture had been taken in the restroom of Sad Sam's Tavern. The Wisconsin Supreme Court decided that in the absence of statutory enactment, there was no right to privacy in Wisconsin. For a similar statute, see Nebraska Civil Rights Rev.Stat. § 2–201–211. Utah Code Annotated §§ 76–9–401– 403, 406 deals with intrusion, and U.C.A. § 76–9–401, 406 covers misappropriation (right of publicity). Virginia Code § 8.01–40 covers right of publicity; Kovner, op. cit.

[22] Themo v. New England Newspaper Pub. Co., 306 Mass. 54, 27 N.E.2d 753, 755 (1940). Note that Professor Prosser could not have forecast the U.S. Supreme Court decision in the libel case of Gertz v. Welch, Inc., 418 U.S. 323, 94 S.Ct. 2997 (1974), which demolished the old *libel per se* standard in rejecting the concept of liability without fault.

While such a distinction may exist in theory, in practice the distinction between defamation and invasion of privacy is blurred. Privacy, it would seem, may often be regarded as a close cousin of defamation. Some publications, indeed, may be both defamatory and an invasion of privacy, and shrewd attorneys often sued for both libel and invasion of privacy on the basis of a single publication.[23]

Privacy actions also resemble defamation lawsuits in that the right to sue belongs only to the affronted individual. As a rule, relatives or friends cannot sue because the privacy of someone close to them was invaded, unless their own privacy was also invaded. In general, as with defamation, the right to sue for invasion of privacy dies with the individual.[24]

When considering privacy law, two things should be kept in mind:

First, the law of privacy is not uniform. In fact, one judge once compared the state of the law to a haystack in a hurricane. There is great conflict of laws from state to state and from jurisdiction to jurisdiction.

Second, when courts or legislatures become involved with the law of privacy, they are attempting to balance interests. On one side of the scale, you have the public interest in freedom of the press and the right to publish. On the other side, you have the individual's right to privacy.

SEC. 38. "INTRUSION" AS INVASION OF PRIVACY

Invading a person's solitude, including the use of microphones or cameras, has been held to be actionable.

Journalists are often seen as invaders of privacy *par excellence,* but they are rank amateurs compared to governmental units, including police and intelligence-gathering agencies. In times such as these, journalists are in an anomalous position where privacy is concerned. The federal Privacy and Freedom of Information Acts are somewhat at cross purposes.[25] Obviously, individuals using

[23] In general, although invasion of privacy and defamation are often included as elements of the same lawsuit, usually courts have not allowed a plaintiff to collect for both actions in one suit. "Duplication of Damages: Invasion of Privacy and Defamation," 41 Washington Law Review (1966), pp. 370–377; see, also, Brink v. Griffith, 65 Wash.2d 253, 396 P.2d 793 (1964), and Donald Elliott Brown, "The Invasion of Defamation by Privacy," Stanford Law Review 23 (Feb., 1971), pp. 547–568.

[24] Bremmer v. Journal–Tribune Pub. Co., 247 Iowa 817, 76 N.W.2d 762 (1956); Wyatt v. Hall's Portrait Studio, 71 Misc. 199, 128 N.Y.S. 247 (1911). In at least one state, heirs can sue for invasion of privacy. For example, see the Utah intrusion statute, U.C.A. §§ 76–9–401–403, 406.

[25] See Chap. 14, Sec. 82.

federal and state Freedom of Information legislation to pry information out of government are at times going to dig up facts which persons involved will feel to be an invasion of their privacy.

In the area called "intrusion on the plaintiff's physical solitude," the media must beware of the modern technology which they call upon to gather and to broadcast news. Microphones—some of which can pick up quiet conversations hundreds of feet away—and telephoto lenses on cameras should be used with care.

More than 200 years ago, Sir William Blackstone's *Commentaries* (1765) considered a form of intrusion, calling eavesdropping one of a list of nuisances which law could punish. Eavesdroppers were termed "people who listen under windows, or the eaves of a house, to conversation, from which they frame slanderous and mischievous tales." [26] Now, the tort subdivision of intrusion includes matters from illegal entry into a house to surreptitious tape recording (in some instances) to window- peeping.

Trouble sometimes has found photographers. Courts have held that it is not an invasion of privacy to take someone's photograph in a public place. Here, photographers are protected on the theory that they "stand in" for the public, taking pictures of what any persons could see if they were there. It follows, of course, that photographers should beware of taking photos in private places. When journalists or photographers invade private territory, they and their employer could be in trouble.

Barber v. Time provides a classic example. In 1939, Mrs. Dorothy Barber was a patient in a Kansas City hospital, being treated for a disease which caused her to eat constantly but still lose weight. A wire service (International News Service) photographer invaded her hospital room and took her picture despite her protests. This resulted in stories about Mrs. Barber's illness appearing in Kansas City-area newspapers for several days. Time Magazine then purchased the picture from the wire service, and published it along with a 150–word story taken largely from an original wire-service story. Time's headline said "Starving Glutton;" a cutline under the picture said "Insatiable–Eater Barber; She Eats for Ten." Mrs. Barber won $3,000 in damages from Time, Inc.[27]

In the late 1970s, a television film crew's intrusion onto private property caused a CBS-owned station huge legal costs, although it wound up paying a minor damage award of only $1,200. Minor

[26] Sir William Blackstone's Commentaries on the Law, ed. by Bernard C. Gavit (Washington, D.C., Washington Book Co., 1892) p. 823.

[27] Barber v. Time, Inc., 348 Mo.1199, 159 S.W.2d 291, 295 (1942). Time purchased the picture from "International," a syndicate dealing in news pictures, and mainly followed the wording of an account furnished by United Press.

award or not, the case of LeMistral v. Columbia Broadcasting System underlines the principle that journalists must ask themselves whether they are attempting to report from a private place. In the LeMistral case, WCBS–TV reporter Lucille Rich and a camera crew charged unannounced into the famous and fashionable LeMistral Restaurant in New York City. The reporter-camera team was doing a series on restaurants cited for health-code irregularities. The arrival of the camera crew—with lights on and cameras rolling—caused a scene of confusion which a slapstick comedian would relish. (Persons lunching with persons other than their spouses were reported to have slid hastily under tables to try to avoid the camera.) The restaurant's suit for invasion of privacy and trespass resulted in a jury award against CBS of $1,200 in compensatory damages and $250,000 in punitive damages. On appeal, the case was sent back to the trial judge for reconsideration and, ultimately, cancellation of the punitive damage award.[28]

If you can see something in a public place, you can photograph it. However, photographers can go too far even in public places if their behavior becomes annoyingly intrusive. Ron Galella, a self-styled "paparazzo," was making a career out of taking pictures of Jacqueline Kennedy Onassis and her children. Paparazzi, in the words of U.S. Circuit Judge J. Joseph Smith, "make themselves as visible to the public and obnoxious to their photographic subjects as possible to aid in the advertisement and wide sale of their works."

Galella's fixation on taking pictures of Mrs. Onassis and children ultimately led to issuance of an injunction against the photographer. He was forbidden to approach within 25 feet of Mrs. Onassis or within 30 feet of her children.[29] Temptation proved too strong for Galella, however. In 1981, on four different occasions, Galella was again too close and too obnoxious in his photographic shadowing of Mrs. Onassis and her children. U.S. District Judge Cooper found Galella to be in contempt of the court's 1975 order, subjecting the persistent photographer to liability for a heavy fine and/or imprisonment.[30]

If photographers can see their quarry from a public spot, without going through strange gyrations or trespassing onto private property, no liability should result. The *Crowley* (La.) *Post-Signal* was sued for invasion of privacy by Mr. and Mrs. James Jaubert. The Jauberts returned from a trip to discover that a photograph of their home had been published on the *Post-Signal's* front page,

[28] Le Mistral, Inc. v. Columbia Broadcasting System, 61 A.D.2d 491, 402 N.Y.S.2d 815 (1st Dept.1978); TV Guide, May 3, 1980, p. 6.

[29] Galella v. Onassis, 487 F.2d 986 (2d Cir.1973).

[30] 533 F.Supp. 1076, 1108 (S.D.N.Y.1982), 8 Med.L.Rptr. 1321–1325.

with this caption: "One of Crowley's stately homes, a bit weather-worn and unkempt, stands in the shadow of a spreading oak."

The Jauberts sought $15,000 for invasion of privacy, including mental suffering and humiliation; they were awarded a total of $1,000 by the trial court. The Louisiana Supreme Court ruled that because the photograph was taken from the middle of the street in front of the Jaubert house, and because passers-by were presented with an identical view, there was no invasion of privacy.[31]

Ethical as well as legal considerations get involved in most privacy cases. In the case known as Cape Publications v. Bridges, Hilda Bridges Pate sued for invasion of privacy for a photograph published by the Florida newspaper, Cocoa Today. During the summer of 1977, Hilda Bridges Pate was abducted by her estranged husband. He went to her place of employment and—at gunpoint—forced her to go with him to their former apartment.[32]

Police were summoned and were surrounding the apartment. The husband forced her to undress in an effort to prevent her from trying to escape. The husband shot himself to death. Police heard the gunshot, stormed the apartment, and rushed the partially clad Ms. Pate to safety across a public parking lot as she clutched a dishtowel to her body. At the trial, a Florida jury awarded Ms. Pate $1 million in compensatory damages and $9 million in punitive damages.

In erasing the damage awards, the Florida Court of Appeal, Fifth District said, "The published photograph is more a depiction of grief, fright, emotional tension and flight than it is an appeal to other sensual appetites." In short, it was a newsworthy story. Judge Dauksch said, "The photograph revealed little more than could be seen had * * * (Ms. Pate) been wearing a bikini, and somewhat less than some bathing suits seen on the beaches." Judge Dauksch added that courts should be slow to interfere with newspapers' publishing of news in the public interest.[33]

Dietemann v. Time, Inc.

Over the years, there have been relatively few cases of "intrusion" privacy lawsuits against the news media. Life Magazine—a

[31] Jaubert v. Crowley Post–Signal, Inc., 375 So.2d 1386 (La.1979), 5 Med.L.Rptr. 2084.

[32] Cape Publications, Inc. v. Bridges, 423 So.2d 426 (Fla.App. 5th Dist.1982), 8 Med.L.Rptr. 2535. See discussion in The News Media & The Law, Jan./Feb. 1984, at p. 41, noting that the Florida Supreme Court and the Supreme Court of the United States refused to review this decision in fall, 1983.

[33] 423 So.2d 426, 427 (Fla.App. 5th Dist.1982), 8 Med.L.Rptr. 2535, 2536. In footnote 2, Judge Dauksch quoted the Restatement (Second) of Torts, Sec. 652 D, Comment G, on the definition of news: " 'Authorized publicity, customarily referred to as "news," includes publications concerning crimes, arrests, police raids, suicides, marriages, divorces, accidents, fires, catastrophes of nature, narcotics-related deaths, rare diseases, etc., and many other matters of genuine popular appeal.' "

Time, Inc., publication—bit the privacy bullet, however, in the 1971 decision in Dietemann v. Time, Inc.   In that case, reporters from Life, cooperating with the Los Angeles, California district attorney and the State Board of Health, did some role-playing to entrap a medical quack.   Reporter Jackie Metcalf and photographer William Ray went to the home of journeyman plumber A.A. Dietemann, a man who was suspected of performing medical services without a diploma or state license.   Mrs. Metcalf and Mr. Ray gained admittance to Dietemann's house by claiming that they had been sent by (if you'll pardon the expression) the plumber's friends.

Mrs. Metcalf complained that she had a lump in her breast, and while Dietemann conducted his "examination," Ray was secretly taking pictures.   Life later published pictures from Dietemann's home, and also reported on his "diagnosis."   He said Mrs. Metcalf's difficulty was caused by eating some rancid butter 11 years, 9 months and 7 days prior to her visit to his home.[34]

Mrs. Metcalf, meanwhile, had a transmitter in her purse, and was relaying her conversations with Dietemann to a receiver/tape recorder in an auto parked nearby.   That auto contained the following eavesdroppers: another Life reporter, a representative of the DA's office, and an investigator from the California State Department of Public Health.   This detective work resulted in a conviction of Dietemann for practicing medicine without a license.   The plumber sued for damages totaling $300,000 for invasion of his privacy.   A jury, recognizing that Dietemann was not suing from a position of great strength as a convicted medical man-sans-license, nevertheless awarded Dietemann $1,000 for invasion of privacy.

In an opinion by Judge Shirley Hufstedler, a United States Court of Appeals upheld the damage award, disagreeing with Life magazine attorneys' arguments that concealed electronic instruments were "indispensable tools of investigative reporting."   Judge Hufstedler wrote: [35]

> Investigative reporting is an ancient art;   its successful practice long antecedes the invention of miniature cameras and electronic devices.   The First Amendment has never been construed to accord newsmen immunity from torts or crimes committed during the course of newsgathering.

McCall v. Courier–Journal and Louisville Times Co.

This case is discussed under the general heading of "Intrusion," and that certainly is an element here.   Like a number of other privacy cases, however, it involves a number of issues.   In this case, there was a libel suit, plus privacy law claims which are

[34] Dietemann v. Time, Inc., 449 F.2d 245, 246 (9th Cir.1971).

[35] Ibid., at p. 249.

labeled "false light;" the false light tort area is discussed later in this chapter. McCall v. Courier- Journal and Times arose when Louisville Times reporters outfitted drug suspect Kristie Frazier's purse with a tape recorder. She had told them that attorney Tim McCall had said that if she would pay him $10,000, he could keep her out of jail. Ms. Frazier then returned to McCall's law office with tape recorder running and had another conversation with him. As the fact situation was summarized by The Reporters Committee for Freedom of the Press: [36]

> The transcript of the conversation revealed that McCall said that the case could not be "fixed" and warned Frazier not to speak in such terms. But he did say that he was going fishing with one of the judges involved, and that once the prosecutor knew McCall had elicited a substantial fee, he would be more sympathetic to her cause.

While Ms. Frazier was in McCall's office taping their conversation, he asked her several times whether she was using a recording device. She denied doing so. Once Ms. Frazier handed the tape over to Louisville Times reporters it was used as the basis for an article. The article said, in part, "The Times requested that Miss Frazier tape-record the conversation because the newspaper was attempting to investigate her allegations that McCall offered to 'fix' her case for $10,000. However, the Times found no indication of any 'fix.' " The Times, even so, repeated Frazier's allegations.[37]

Attorney McCall sued for invasion of privacy and libel. He declared that the secret taping was a wrongful act, and that he had been libeled because the article implied that he had offered to fix the case and was published in reckless disregard of his rights. McCall asked $6 million in damages. The Louisville Times published a story about McCall's lawsuit, summarizing its first article. McCall then amended his complaint, adding the contention that the Times' second article was libelous, too.

Subsequently, the Kentucky Supreme Court ruled that a summary judgment should not have been granted to the newspaper; the matter should be allowed to go to trial on the libel and false light claims. The Kentucky Supreme Court, however, was not impressed with the intrusion aspect of Attorney McCall's suit, instead concentrating on false light privacy and libel.

The Kentucky Supreme Court sent the case back to the trial court for reconsideration.[38] Before that trial could begin again, the newspaper company agreed to pay Attorney McCall $75,000 to

[36] News Media & the Law, Oct.-Nov. 1980, p. 31.

[37] News Media & the Law, Oct.-Nov. 1980, p. 31.

[38] McCall v. Courier–Journal and Louisville Times Co., 623 S.W.2d 882, 887 (Ky.1981), 7 Med.L.Rptr. 2118, 2125.

settle the $6 million libel and invasion of privacy lawsuit. Paul Janensch, then executive editor of the Louisville newspapers, said the settlement was reached to avoid another costly and time-consuming trial. On the other hand, McCall's attorney told the Associated Press that the newspaper " 'did not want to face a jury in this community which would call it to account for both the wrongful invasion of McCall's privacy and improper reporting.' " [39]

Cassidy v. ABC

Although people generally may dislike hidden tape recorders, they may be even more hostile to hidden television cameras. Sometimes, as Chicago policeman Arlyn Cassidy learned, you can be on TV at an inopportune moment. Cassidy was working as an undercover vice squad agent assigned to investigate a massage parlor.

Policeman Cassidy testified that he had paid a $30 admission fee to see "de-luxe" lingerie modeling. He was then taken to a small cubicle by one of the models, and noticed "camera lights" on each side of the bed. He told the model the lights made the room warm, and then reclined on the bed and watched the model change her lingerie several times. As an Illinois judge described the scene, Cassidy made several suggestive remarks to the model and then arrested her for solicitation after she "established 'sufficient' physical contact." Three other vice squad officers then joined Officer Cassidy, asking if anyone was in the adjoining room. [40]

At that moment, someone rushed out of Room No. 2, yelling "Channel 7 News." That's right, a camera crew from Chicago's American Broadcasting Company television outlet had been in the adjoining room, filming Officer Cassidy and the model through a two-way mirror. The television station personnel testified that they had received complaints from the massage parlor's manager that his establishment was the subject of police harassment.

The whole television situation rubbed Officer Cassidy the wrong way. He complained that the camera crew's activities violated Illinois' anti-eavesdropping statute [41] and that his common law right to privacy was violated. [42] The Illinois Appellate Court had difficulty in terming a television camera "an eavesdropping device," the more so because the noise of the camera's operation drowned out sounds from the other room. Furthermore, Cassidy had noticed the lights and asked the model whether they were "on TV." She replied, "Sure, we're making movies." Under such

[39] The Associated Press, "Louisville Times, attorney settle suit," story published in The Kentucky Kernel, newspaper of the University of Kentucky, Nov. 24, 1982, p. 5.

[40] Cassidy v. ABC, 60 Ill.App.3d 831, 17 Ill.Dec. 936, 377 N.E.2d 126 (1978).

[41] Ibid., at 937, 377 N.E.2d at 127; see § 14–2, Oh. 38, Ill.Rev. Stat. (1975).

[42] Ibid., at 937, 377 N.E.2d at 127.

circumstances, Officer Cassidy was believed by the court not to have much of an expectation of privacy.

In addition, Cassidy's effort to assert a cause of action under the "intrusion" theory of privacy failed, on grounds that Cassidy was a public official on duty at the time he heard those stirring words, "Channel 7 News." [43]

Use of Tape Recorders

The Dietemann and Cassidy cases should inspire journalists to think carefully about their use of cameras, tape recorders, and electronic listening and transmitting gear. Professor Kent R. Middleton, in an important article on the **legality** of journalists' use of tape recorders, concluded: "Reporters may record or transmit conversations they overhear, they participate in, or they record with permission of one party." Recording with the permission of one party—that's called "consensual monitoring" in legal jargon—is what is involved here for the press.[44]

Does one-party consent sound confusing, or merely ludicrous? What would one-party consent do to the law of embezzlement or robbery? What "consensual monitoring" actually does as a legal concept is forbid an unauthorized third party from intercepting a conversation, as in the case of an illegal (not authorized by a court) tap on a telephone line, listening in on two other parties.

Please note that this section is discussing what is legal, and not necessarily what is ethical. The authors of this text know that many reporters often record conversations—particularly telephone conversations—without giving notice that a tape recorder is running.

It is legal in most states for a reporter to conceal a tape recorder in pocket or purse while talking to news sources. Note, however, that roughly one-quarter of the states have statutes outlawing such use of recorders. Victor Kovner and co-authors reported in 1993 reported that such "participant monitoring" was forbidden by statute in 10 states: California, Florida, Maryland, Massachusetts, Maryland, Montana, New Hampshire, Oregon, Pennsylvania, and Washington.[45] Furthermore, in Shevin v. Sunbeam Television Corporation, the Florida Supreme Court ruled that the Florida statute forbidding interception of telephone messages

[43] Ibid., at 938, 942, 377 N.E.2d at 128, 132.

[44] Kent R. Middleton, "Journalists and Tape Recorders: Does Participant Monitoring Invade Privacy?", 2 COMM/ENT Law Journal (1980) at pp. 299–300.

[45] Victor A. Kovner, Harriette K. Dorsen, and Suzanne L. Telsey, "Recent Developments in Intrusion, Private Facts, False Light, and Commercialization Claims," in James C. Goodale, chairman, Communications Law 1993, Vol. I (New York: Practising Law Institute, 1993), p. 636.

without consent of all parties involved did not violate a reporter's First Amendment rights.[46]

Many reporters routinely record telephone conversations without telling the party on the other end of the line, or without a warning "beep" signal as required by the Federal Communications Commission.[47] This kind of surreptitious recording may not violate specific state law, but it is forbidden by telephone company tariffs, as Middleton has written. If a person is somehow caught while secretly recording phone conversations, the telephone company could cut off phone service. That, however, seems to be only a remote possibility.[48] Furthermore, as privacy expert Victor A. Kovner has noted, the FCC in 1983 advanced a "Notice of Proposed Rule–Making" to get rid of the "beep-tone" rule but nothing has come of it. The FCC argued that technology of recent years made the rule in unenforceable.[49]

Boddie v. ABC (1984)

In addition to state provisions and telephone company "tariffs" [rules] overseen by the Federal Communications Commission (FCC), there is also the Electronic Communications Privacy Act of 1986.[50] Despite its name, it turns out to be less protective of privacy than the statute it amended where the sneaky interception of voices and other messages by electronic means is concerned.[51]

The 1968 "Federal Wiretap Statute" allowed taping or intercepting communications when one of the parties in the conversation doing the taping. This applied unless the taping was done for the purpose of committing a tort or a crime "or for the purpose of committing any other injurious act." [52]

While the 1968 statute was still in force, Sandra Boddie sued the American Broadcasting Companies for a report on its "20⁄20" program. She sought damages for defamation, false light invasion of privacy, and violation of the Federal Wiretap Statute. The ABC report causing Ms. Boddie's suit discussed allegations that Judge

[46] Shevin v. Sunbeam Television Corp., 351 So.2d 723 (Fla.1977), rehearing denied 435 U.S. 1018, 98 S.Ct. 1892 (1978). See also Victor A. Kovner, "Recent Developments in Intrusion, Private Facts, False Light, and Commercialization Claims," in James C. Goodale, chairman, Communications Law 1991, Vol. II, pp. 15–26.

[47] Middleton, pp. 304–309.

[48] Ibid., pp. 319–320; Kovner, op. cit., pp. 24–25, citing 47 CFR 64.501; Section 73.1206. FCC Rules.

[49] Kovner, ibid., citing FCC Docket No. 20840, 1983.

[50] Electronic Communications Privacy Act of 1986, Pub.L. No. 99–508, 18 U.S.C.A. § 2510.

[51] See 18 U.S.C.A. § 2511, as discussed in Boddie v. ABC, 694 F.Supp. 1304, 1305–1306 (N.D.Ohio 1988), 16 Med.L.Rptr. 1100, 1101, 1103.

[52] See Marc Franklin and David A. Anderson, *Cases and Materials on Mass Media Law,* 4th ed. (Westbury, N.Y.: Foundation Press, 1989), p. 492.

James Barbuto of Akron, Ohio, granted leniency to criminal defendants in exchange for sex.

During $^{20}\!/_{20}$'s investigations of Judge Barbuto, ABC television personality Geraldo Rivera interviewed Ms. Boddie. She agreed to be interviewed but refused to appear on camera. Unknown to Ms. Boddie, Rivera and an ABC producer/reporter, Charles C. Thompson, recorded her interview by using hidden microphones and a hidden videotape camera. A part of the surreptitiously taped interview was televised by ABC in a broadcast report titled "Injustice for All." [53]

Ms. Boddie's lawsuit against ABC went through several incarnations [54] but ultimately was unsuccessful. She had sued—and her right to a cause of action had been upheld—under the 1968 Federal Wiretap Statute. [55] But in 1986, after the U.S. Court of Appeals (6th Cir.) had ruled that Ms. Boddie had a cause of action under the 1968 Federal Wiretap Statute,[56] Congress amended the statute, removing the vague phrase "any other injurious act."

In 1988, however, the U.S. District Court (N.D.Ohio) concluded that the Federal Wiretap Statute, as amending the 1986 Privacy Act, had to be applied in Ms. Boddie's lawsuit, saying that the later Act merely clarified Congressional intent in the 1968 Federal Wiretap Statute.[57]

> * * * Congress never intended, at least in cases involving media defendants and giving rise to First Amendment considerations, to provide a cause of action for gathering and disseminating news that does not raise to the level of a crime or a tort * * *.

So Ms. Boddie came up empty in her lawsuit against Geraldo Rivera and ABC.

Pearson v. Dodd

In a case which raises the question of the extent of reportorial involvement in removing documents from the office of a public official, Senator Thomas Dodd of Connecticut failed to collect in an

---

[53] Boddie v. American Broadcasting Companies, Inc., 731 F.2d 333, 335 (6th Cir.1984), 15 Med.L.Rptr. 1923, 1924–1925.

[54] Ibid.

[55] Boddie v. American Broadcasting Companies, Inc., 694 F.Supp. 1304 (N.D.Ohio 1988), 16 Med.L.Rptr. 1100, quoting 1968 Federal Wiretap Statute, 18 U.S.C.A. § 2511(2)(d) at p. 1101.

[56] Boddie v. American Broadcasting Companies, Inc., 694 F.Supp. 1304, 1305 (N.D.Ohio 1988), 16 Med.L.Rptr. 1100, 1101.

[57] Ibid., at 1309, 16 Med.L.Rptr. at 1104. For another case involving Geraldo Rivera where ABC also dodged the privacy bullet—this time involving taping a conversation on a public street—see Brooks v. ABC, Inc., 999 F.2d 167 (6th Cir.1993), 21 Med.L.Rptr. 1756.

intrusion-invasion of privacy lawsuit against sensational columnists Drew Pearson and Jack Anderson. Pearson and Anderson had done great harm to Dodd's reputation and career. They had published papers taken from Dodd's office files which showed an appropriation of campaign funds for personal purposes.

The exposé of Dodd began during the summer of 1965 when two employees and two former employees of Senator Dodd removed documents from his files, photocopied them, and then replaced the originals in their filing cabinets. The copies were turned over to Anderson, who knew how they had been obtained. The Pearson–Anderson "Washington Merry–Go–Round" column then ran six stories about the Senator, dealing—among other matters—with his relationship with lobbyists for foreign interests.

Dodd argued that the manner in which the information for the columns was obtained was an invasion of his privacy. After hearing Pearson and Anderson's appeal from a lower court judgment,[58] Court of Appeals Judge J. Skelly Wright said that Dodd's employees and former employees had committed improper intrusion when they removed confidential files to show them to outsiders. And what of the journalists? [59]

> If we were to hold appellants [Pearson and Anderson] liable for invasion of privacy on these facts, we would establish the proposition that one who receives information from an intruder, knowing it has been obtained by improper intrusion, is guilty of a tort. In an untried and developing area of tort law, we are not prepared to go so far.

Florida Publishing Co. v. Fletcher

In 1972, 17-year-old Cindy Fletcher was alone one afternoon at her Jacksonville, Fla., home when a fire of undetermined origin did severe damage to the house. She died in the blaze. When the Fire Marshal and a police sergeant arrived at the house to make their investigation, they invited news media representatives to join them as was their standard practice.

The Fire Marshal desired a clear picture of the "silhouette" left on the floor after the removal of Cindy Fletcher's body to show

[58] Dodd v. Pearson, 279 F.Supp. 101 (D.D.C.1968).

[59] 133 U.S.App.D.C. 279, 410 F.2d 701, 704–705 (D.C.Cir.1969). See also Bilney v. Evening Star Newspaper Co., 43 Md.App. 560, 406 A.2d 652 (1979), 5 Med.L.Rptr. 1931, in which a newspaper was sued for intrusion because it had published confidential academic records of members of the University of Maryland basketball team. The records involved were held to be newsworthy, and the lawsuit against the paper was dismissed because it was not demonstrated that reporters had solicited or encouraged reading of confidential records. The material involved came unasked for, from an unnamed source.

that the body was already on the floor before the fire's heat damaged the room. The marshal took one Polaroid photograph of the outline, but that picture was unclear and he had no more film. A photographer for the Florida *Times-Union* was then asked to take the silhouette picture, which was made part of the official investigation files of both the fire and police departments.

This picture was not only part of the investigative record, it was also published—along with other pictures from the fire scene—in a Times–Union story on September 16, 1972. Cindy's mother, Mrs. Klenna Ann Fletcher, first learned of the facts surrounding the death of her daughter by reading the newspaper story and by seeing the published photographs.

Mrs. Fletcher sued the newspaper ["Florida Publishing Company"] and alleged three things: "(1) trespass and invasion of privacy, (2) invasion of privacy, and (3) wrongful intentional infliction of emotional distress—seeking punitive damages."[60] The trial court dismissed Count 2 and granted summary judgments in favor of the newspaper on counts 1 and 3. Speaking to the question of trespass, the trial judge said: [61]

> "The question raised is whether the trespass alleged in Count I of the complaint was consented to by the doctrine of common custom and usage.

> "The law is well settled in Florida that there is no unlawful trespass when peaceable entry is made, without objection, under common custom and usage."

Numerous affidavits had been filed by the news media saying that "common custom and usage" permitted the news media to enter the scene of a disaster.[62]

Mrs. Fletcher appealed from the trial court to Florida District Court of Appeal, First District, which held that she should have been able to go to trial on the issue of trespass.[63] The Florida Supreme Court, however, ruled that no actionable trespass or invasion of privacy had occurred. The Florida Supreme Court quoted approvingly from a dissenting opinion by Florida District Court of Appeal Judge McCord: [64]

---

[60] Florida Pub. Co. v. Fletcher, 340 So.2d 914, 915–916 (Fla.1976).

[61] Quoted at Ibid., p. 916.

[62] Ibid. Affidavits came from such sources as the Chicago Tribune; ABC–TV News, New York; the Associated Press; the Miami Herald; United Press International; the Milwaukee Journal, and the Washington Post.

[63] Ibid., pp. 917–918.

[64] Ibid., pp. 918–919. See also Higbee v. Times–Advocate, Inc., (S.D.Cal.1980), 5 Med.L.Rptr. 2372, dismissing a federal violation of civil rights claim but ruling that a photo taken inside plaintiffs' home was a matter of state tort law. Escondido, Calif., law enforcement officers had invited the press to be present during the execution of

"*It is my view that the entry in this case was by implied consent.*

* * *

"Implied consent would, of course, vanish if one were informed not to enter at that time by the owner or possessor or by their direction. But here there was not only no objection to the entry, but *there was an invitation to enter by the officers investigating the fire.*"

When a reporter does not have any kind of permission to be on private property, however, the result could be troublesome. That's one message of a 1980 case, Oklahoma v. Bernstein, as decided by an Oklahoma District Court (Rogers County). Benjamin Bernstein and a number of other reporters had been arrested for trespassing onto private property. In hot pursuit of a newsworthy event, they followed protesting demonstrators onto the construction site of a Public Service Company of Oklahoma (PSO) nuclear power plant, Black Fox Station.

Despite showings of extensive governmental support (e.g. use of eminent domain to acquire part of the site for PSO, government-guaranteed loans, and close continuing supervision from the Nuclear Regulatory Commission), the Black Fox site was held to be private property. Although the Oklahoma court held that protests at the construction site were newsworthy, and although PSO was trying to minimize news coverage of an important public controversy, the reporters were found guilty of trespass.[65]

Also, consider the decision in Anderson v. WROC–TV (1981). Two Rochester, New York, television stations accepted the invitation of Humane Society investigator Ronald Storm to accompany him as he served a search warrant. The warrant authorized Storm to enter the house occupied by Barbara P. Anderson and Joy E. Brenon, to seize animals which might be found confined in an overcrowded, unhealthy situation or not properly cared for.

When investigator Storm served the search warrant, television photographers and reporters accompanied him into the home of Ms. Anderson and Ms. Brenon, and filmed the interior. Ms. Brenon asked the television people to stay outside her home, but they entered anyway. Stories about the search were broadcast that evening on news shows of WROC–TV and WOKR–TV.[66]

a search warrant. For a contrary view, see Kent R. Middleton, "Journalists, Trespass and Officials: Closing the Door of Florida Publishing Co. v. Fletcher," 16 Pepperdine Law Rev. 259 (1989).

[65] Oklahoma v. Bernstein (Okl.D.C., Rogers County 1980), 5 Med.L.Rptr. 2313, 2323–2324.

[66] Anderson v. WROC–TV, 109 Misc.2d 904, 441 N.Y.S. 220 (1981), 7 Med.L.Rptr. 1987, 1988.

Citing Dietemann v. Time, Inc.,[67] the New York Supreme Court, Monroe County, held that the First Amendment right to gather news does not allow members of the press to get away with committing crimes or torts in the course of newsgathering. Reporters are not above the law. In this case, a resident of the house told television station employees to stay out of her house, and they did not do so. In addition, the New York Court distinguished this case from Florida Publishing Company v. Fletcher,[68] noting that the entry of a Humane Society editor had less news value than a fire which had caused a death: [69]

> As the plaintiffs correctly argue, one may not create an implied consent by asserting that it exists and without evidence to support it. In passing, and as previously noted, it also appears * * * that the entry was made in disregard of plaintiff Joy Brenon's express instructions to stay out.

Baugh v. CBS (1993)

A 1993 case hung up another caution flag for broadcasters. Baugh v. CBS arose when the network's "Street Stories" public affairs magazine program broadcast an episode titled "Stand By Me." The broadcast covered the Alameda County, California "Mobile Crisis Intervention Team," which aids crime victims. The broadcast focused on the work of Elaine Lopes, helping victims through crises, giving emotional support and information on how to deal with the legal system.

CBS correspondent Bob McKeown's broadcast included videotape of Mrs. Yolanda Baugh talking with Ms. Lopes, describing how her husband started "beating on me and kicking on me and hitting me in the face." [70] After CBS aired the broadcast, Ms. Baugh and her daughter sued for invasion of privacy (private facts, appropriation and intrusion) and intentional infliction of emotional distress.

Mrs. Baugh's lawsuit asserted that while talking with police, she heard people coming into her house, but she ushered them out of the house, saying " 'Get the hell out of here.' " But, she said, a police officer told her something like this: " 'It's okay. They [the CBS camera crew] are from the DA's office. They are here to help you.' " [71]

---

[67] 109 Misc.2d 904, 441 N.Y.S. 220, 227 (1981), 7 Med.L.Rptr. 1997, 1990, discussing Dietemann v. Time, Inc., 449 F.2d 245 (9th Cir.1971).

[68] 340 So.2d 914 (Fla.1976).

[69] 109 Misc.2d 904, 441 N.Y.S.2d 220, 227 (1981), 7 Med.L.Rptr. 1987, 1992.

[70] Baugh v. CBS, Inc., 828 F.Supp. 745 (N.D.Cal.1993), 21 Med.L.Rptr. 2065, 2067.

[71] Ibid.

About two months later, Mrs. Baugh said, she learned from social worker Elaine Lopes that her story would be broadcast. When Ms. Baugh objected that she did not want to be on television. On March 23, 1992—more than two weeks before CBS aired the episode of "Street Stories" containing footage of Mrs. Baugh—she talked to a producer at CBS, who—she said—told him he might be able to obscure her face on the screen. Mrs. Baugh told him that was not sufficient. She added,[72]

" ...about a week later, I was contacted on the phone by a man who identified himself as a CBS lawyer in New York. In a rude, uncaring and arrogant manner, he told me that I had no case against CBS and there is nothing I could do."

Mrs. Baugh failed in her claim of trespass or intrusion, because in this context, "no trespass can be found if actual consent to entry was given," even if the consent was given by police who should not have given it.[73] On the other hand, the court refused to dismiss Mrs. Baugh's claim for intentional infliction of mental distress.[74]

Ayeni v. CBS (1994)

In conflict with the "no trespass" finding of Baugh v. CBS, a 1994 U.S. district court decision in Ayeni v. CBS held that federal agents' permission for TV journalists to search a home was insufficient permission to avoid liability. Tawa Ayeni, wife of a man suspected of involvement in a credit card fraud operation, was home with her son Kayode, a minor, when a U.S. Treasury Department agent carried out a search warrant. Six federal agents—four or five Secret Service agents and one or two postal inspectors—went to the Ayeni's residence. Mrs. Ayeni, clad in her dressing gown, opened the door slightly but the agents pushed their way into her home at about 6 p.m.

About 8:15 pm., Treasury Agent James Mottola entered the Ayenis' apartment with a CBS news crew from "Street Stories." Mrs. Ayeni complained that the crew was not identified as CBS employees, saying that she thought the CBS camera crew members and "Street Stories" producer Meade Jorgensen were " 'part of the team executing the warrant.' "[75]

CBS and "Street Stories" producer Jorgensen both claimed they enjoyed a qualified immunity because "they were acting with the permission of government agents ... [and] should be entitled to the qualified immunity enjoyed by government officials."[76] This

[72] Ibid., 2068.

[73] Ibid., 2072, quoting Miller v. NBC, 187 Cal.App.3d 1463, 1480–1481.

[74] Ibid., p. 2073.

[75] Ayeni v. CBS Inc., 848 F.Supp. 362 (E.D.N.Y.1994), 22 Med.L.Rptr. 1466, 1467.

[76] Ibid., 1469.

audacious claim was slapped down by District Judge Weinstein, who held that the presence of CBS crew members invited in by a U.S. agent "so that they could titillate and entertain others was beyond the scope of what was lawfully authorized by the warrant." Concluding that the Ayeni lawsuit against CBS should not be dismissed, the judge declared: [77]

> CBS had no greater right than that of a thief to be in the home, to take pictures, and to remove the photographic record. * * *

> The images, though created by the camera, are a part of the household; they cannot be removed without permission or official right.   The television tape was seizure of information for non-governmental purposes.

In addition, a U.S. Court of Appeals ruled that Treasury Agent Mottola violated the Fourth Amendment proscriptions against unreasonable search and seizure by allowing the CBS crew into the Ayenis' home.   Furthermore, he was held to be personally liable for damages for permitting the videotaping intrusion, which went beyond the scope of the search warrant.[78]

SEC. 39.   PUBLICATION OF PRIVATE MATTERS

With the law of privacy, "truth can hurt."   Unlike the law of defamation, truth is not necessarily a defense to a lawsuit for invasion of privacy.

The case of Dorothy Barber discussed in the last section was not only an incident of "intrusion," but also involved a second sub-area of privacy law: "publication of private matters violating the ordinary decencies."   In this area of law, missteps by the mass media have led to a substantial number of lawsuits.   In publishing details of private matters, the media may make accurate reports and yet—at least on some occasions—be found liable for damages. A suit for defamation would not stand where the press has accurately reported the truth, but the press could nevertheless lose an action for invasion of privacy based on the same fact situation. Here, the truth sometimes hurts.

In most cases, the existence of a public record usually has precluded recovery for invasion of privacy.   Even if persons are embarrassed by publication of dates of a marriage or birth,[79] or information which is a matter of public record,[80] publication accurately based on such records have escaped successful lawsuits.

---

[77] Ibid., p. 1470.

[78] Ayeni v. Mottola, 35 F.3d 680 (2d Cir.1994), 22 Med.L.Rptr. 2225.

[79] Meetze v. Associated Press, 230 S.C. 330, 95 S.E.2d 606 (1956).

[80] Stryker v. Republic Pictures Corp., 108 Cal.App.2d 191, 238 P.2d 670 (1951).

Where there is a legitimate public record—and where the media's use of that record is not forbidden by law—the material generally may be used for publication. In 1960, the Albuquerque (N.M.) *Journal* published a story which said that a 16–year-old boy had sexually assaulted his younger sister: [81]

The younger sister, Delores Hubbard, sued for invasion of privacy, asserting that she had suffered extreme humiliation and distress and that the story "caused her to be regarded as unchaste, and that her prospects of marriage have been adversely affected thereby." Attorneys for the newspaper, however, brought proof that the *Albuquerque Journal's* story was an exact copy of an official court record. In upholding a lower court's judgment for the newspaper, the New Mexico Supreme Court ruled that because this was a public record, the newspaper enjoyed privilege.[82]

Sipple v. Chronicle Publishing Co. (1984)

It should be apparent that much in the law of privacy is unpredictable, and the "private facts" area is no exception. Consider the lawsuits brought by Oliver Sipple, the ex-Marine who saved President Gerald Ford's life in 1975 by deflecting the aim of a would-be assassin, Sarah Jane Moore. Two days after the incident, the San Francisco Chronicle's famed columnist Herb Caen wrote that San Francisco's gay community was proud of Sipple's action, and that it might dispel stereotypes about homosexuals.[83]

Sipple objected that his sexual orientation had nothing to do with saving the President's life, and filed suit against The San Francisco Chronicle, Herb Caen, The Los Angeles Times, and several other newspapers, seeking $15 million in damages. Sipple argued that printing facts about his private life without his consent exposed him to ridicule. The Los Angeles Times countered that Sipple, as a person thrust into the "vortex of publicity" of an event of worldwide importance had become a newsworthy figure. "[M]any aspects of his life became matters of legitimate public interest." Individuals who become public persons give up part of their right of privacy, the *Times* contended. Finally, in April, 1980, a California trial court—without giving any reasons—dismissed the invasion of privacy suit against the San Francisco Chronicle and other newspapers.[84]

Sipple appealed against the dismissal, asking the California Court of Appeal, First District, to reinstate his privacy lawsuit.

---

[81] Hubbard v. Journal Pub. Co., 69 N.M. 473, 474, 368 P.2d 147, 148 (1962).

[82] 69 N.M. 473, 474–475, 368 P.2d 147, 148–149 (1962).

[83] The News Media & The Law, Oct./Nov. 1980, p. 27.

[84] Sipple v. Chronicle Publishing Company, 154 Cal.App.3d 1040, 201 Cal.Rptr. 665 (1st Dist.1984), 10 Med.L.Rptr. 1690, 1693–1694.

The appellate court held, however, that Sipple's case was correctly terminated by the lower court. The Court of Appeal said that the facts about Sipple as a member of San Francisco's gay community were already quite widely known: "in the public domain." In addition, the Court of Appeal held that Sipple was indeed newsworthy after saving President Ford's life.

Sipple, of course, was involved in an event of international importance. When the newsworthiness is less, the privacy protection for individuals can be correspondingly greater. Toni Ann Diaz, for example, had achieved a limited newsworthiness as the first woman student body president at a northern California school, the College of Alameda.

Diaz v. Oakland Tribune

In 1978, Oakland Tribune columnist Sidney Jones published truthful—yet highly private—information about Ms. Diaz.[85]

> "More Education Stuff: The students at the College of Alameda will be surprised to learn their student body president Toni Diaz is no lady, but is in fact a man whose real name is Antonio.

> "Now I realize, that in these times, such a matter is no big deal, but I suspect his female classmates in P.E. 97 may wish to make other showering arrangements."

The trial court jury awarded Ms. Diaz a total of $775,000, finding that the information about the sex change was not newsworthy and would be offensive to ordinary readers.[86]

Late, although obviously in sympathy with Ms. Diaz, the California Court of Appeal, First District, sent the matter back to the lower court for a new trial. The appellate court held that the trial judge had committed reversible error in not emphasizing to the jury that a newspaper has a right to publish newsworthy information. Also, it was held that jury instructions should have made it clear that plaintiff Diaz had to carry the burden of proof in trying to show that the article she complained of was not newsworthy.[87]

The court held that there was little evidence that the gender-corrective surgery was part of the public record. It did not consider Diaz's Puerto Rican birth certificate to be a public record in this instance. Given Diaz's efforts to conceal the operation, and considering Diaz's needs for privacy and the notoriety received as the first woman student body president at that college, the question of the

---

[85] Diaz v. Oakland Tribune, Inc., 139 Cal.App.3d 118, 188 Cal.Rptr. 762, 766 (1983), 9 Med.L.Rptr. 1121, 1122.

[86] The News Media and the Law, Oct./Nov. 1980, p. 28.

[87] 139 Cal.App.3d 118, 188 Cal.Rptr. 762 (1983), 9 Med.L.Rptr. 1121.

story's newsworthiness—the judge said—should have been left to a jury.[88] The court added that there was no merit in the Oakland Tribune's claim that the story was made newsworthy by the changing roles of women in society.

The appellate court then sent the case back to the trial level, but a second jury never heard the Diaz case. After the decision by the California Court of Appeal, First District, the case was reportedly settled out of court for between $200,000 and $300,000.

Howard v. Des Moines Register (1979)

The case of Howard v. Des Moines Register and Tribune Co. also raised both legal and ethical concerns. *Register* reporter Margaret Engel did an investigative story on a county home, and published the name of a young woman who had undergone forced sterilization. The article included this passage: "He [Dr. Roy C. Sloan, the home's psychiatrist] said the decision to sterilize the resident Robin Woody was made by her parents and himself." The article, based on public records, also noted that the woman was 18 years old in 1970 at the time of her sterilization, and was not mentally retarded or disabled, but an " 'impulsive, hair-triggered, young girl' in the words of Dr. * * * Sloan." [89]

The *Register* defended itself successfully against a private facts lawsuit, with the court concluding that in this context, use of the defendant's name was justified. In granting the *Register* a summary judgment, an Iowa District Court said that the relationship between the disclosure and a story's newsworthiness should be considered. In this case, use of Robin Woody's name was said to lend personal detail, specificity and credibility to a story on a newsworthy topic, care of residents in a county home.[90]

In at least six states, statutes prohibit publishing the *identity* of a rape victim. Those states are Alaska, Florida, Georgia, South Carolina, and New York.[91] A case based upon the South Carolina statute resulted in a 1963 Federal District Court ruling indicating that such statutes were valid. However, a 1975 Supreme Court of the United States decision held otherwise when publication of a rape victim's name was based on a public record.[92]

[88] 139 Cal.App.3d 118, 188 Cal.Rptr. 762, 763 (1983), 9 Med.L.Rptr. 1121, 1127.

[89] Howard v. Des Moines Register and Tribune Co., 283 N.W.2d 289, 302 (Iowa 1979).

[90] Ibid., p. 303.

[91] Alaska Stat. 12.61.140 (1991); West's Fla.Ann. 794.03; Ga.Stat. 26–9901; New York L. 1991 c. 251; S.C.Ann. Code 16–81; see Kovner, et.al., in Goodale, op. cit. Vol. I, pp. 663–665.

[92] Cox Broadcasting Corp. v. Cohn, 420 U.S. 469, 95 S.Ct. 1029 (1975); Nappier v. Jefferson Standard Life Ins. Co., 213 F.Supp. 174 (D.S.C.1963).

But what if there is a state statute against publication of names of victims of sexual assault? Consider Cox Broadcasting v. Cohn and later cases dealing with news reports identifying rape victims. Although key cases say the First Amendment protects publication of material taken accurately from public records, a backlash against publication of names of rape victims may be underway.

Cox Broadcasting Corp. v. Cohn (1975)

Cox Broadcasting v. Cohn grew out of tragic circumstances. In August, 1971, 17-year-old Cynthia Cohn was gang-raped and died, and six youths were soon indicted for the crimes against her. There was considerable coverage of the event, but the identity of the victim was not disclosed until one defendant's trial began. In April of 1972, five of the six youths entered pleas of guilty to rape or attempted rape, the charge of murder having been dropped. Those guilty pleas were accepted, and the trial of the defendant who pleaded not guilty was set for a later date.[93]

A Georgia statute forbids publication of the identity of a rape victim. Despite this, a television reporter employed by WSB–TV—a Cox Broadcasting Corporation station—learned Cynthia Cohn's name from indictments which were open to public inspection. Later that day, the reporter broadcast her identity as part of his story on the court proceedings, and the report was repeated the next day.[94]

Martin Cohn sued Cox Broadcasting, claiming that the broadcasts which had identified his daughter invaded his own privacy by reason of the publication of his daughter's name. After hearing the Cohn case twice, the Georgia Supreme Court ruled that the statute forbidding publication of the name of a rape victim was constitutional * * * " 'a legitimate limitation on the right of freedom of expression contained in the First Amendment.' " [95]

The Supreme Court of the United States disagreed by a vote of 8–1. Writing for the Court, Mr. Justice White said: [96]

> The version of the privacy tort now before us—termed in Georgia the "tort of public disclosure" * * * is that in which the plaintiff claims the right to be free from unwanted publicity about his private affairs, which, although

[93] Cox Broadcasting Corp. v. Cohn, 420 U.S. 469, 471, 95 S.Ct. 1029, 1034–1035 (1975).

[94] 420 U.S. 469, 471, 95 S.Ct. 1029, 1034–1035 (1975).

[95] 420 U.S. 469, 475, 95 S.Ct. 1029, 1036 (1975). Justices Powell and Douglas filed concurring opinions, and Justice Rehnquist dissented, stating that the Supreme Court did not have jurisdiction in this case for want of a final decree or judgment from a lower court.

[96] 420 U.S. 469, 489, 95 S.Ct. 1029, 1043 (1975).

wholly true, would be offensive to a person of ordinary sensibilities. Because the gravamen [gist] of the claimed injury is the publication of information, whether true or not, the dissemination of which is embarrassing or otherwise painful to an individual, it is here that claims of privacy most directly confront the constitutional freedoms of speech and press.

Justice White wrote that truth may not always be a defense in either defamation or privacy actions. First, concerning defamation: "The Court has * * * carefully left open the question whether the First and Fourteenth Amendments require that truth be recognized as a defense in a defamation action brought by a private person as distinguished from a public official or a public figure." Writing about privacy, he continued, "In similar fashion, Time v. Hill, supra, [385 U.S. 374 at 383 n. 7, 87 S.Ct. 534 at 539 (1967)] expressly saved [reserved] the question whether truthful publication of very private matters unrelated to public affairs could be constitutionally proscribed." [97] Thus the Supreme Court recognized—but backed away—from a troubling constitutional question: May a state ever define and protect an area of privacy free from unwanted *truthful* publicity in the press?

Having recognized this problem, Justice White then turned his majority opinion to narrower and safer ground. In *Cox Broadcasting,* the key question was whether Georgia might impose sanctions against the accurate publication of the name of a rape victim, when that name had been obtained from records of a prosecution which are open to public inspection. Justice White concluded that the news media could not be punished from quoting accurately from a public record.[98]

He wrote that the news media have a great responsibility to report fully and accurately the proceedings of government, "and official records and documents open to the public are the basic data of governmental operations." [99]

Smith v. Daily Mail (1979)

In 1979, the Supreme Court of the United States followed its reasoning from *Cox Broadcasting* in deciding Smith v. Daily Mail Publishing Co. *Smith* was a case which cut across areas of constitutional limitations on prior restraint, privacy, and free press-fair trial considerations. It arose in February, 1978, when a 14–year-old junior high school student in St. Albans, W.Va., shot and killed

[97] 420 U.S. 469, 490, 95 S.Ct. 1029, 1044 (1975).

[98] 420 U.S. 469, 491, 95 S.Ct. 1029, 1044 (1975).

[99] 420 U.S. 469, 492, 95 S.Ct. 1029, 1044–1045 (1975), citing Sheppard v. Maxwell, 384 U.S. 333, 350, 86 S.Ct. 1507, 1515 (1966).

a 15–year-old fellow student. Reporters for nearby Charleston newspapers learned the identity of the youth accused of the shooting by their routine monitoring of the police radio. The Charleston *Daily Gazette*—and later, the *Daily Mail*—used the youth's name in their stories, in violation of a West Virginia statute forbidding newspapers' use of names of juveniles accused of crimes without a written court order.[1]

The state of West Virginia contended that even though this statute amounted to a prior restraint on speech, the state's interest in protecting the identity of juveniles caught up in the legal process overcame the presumption against the constitutional validity of prior restraints. In declaring the West Virginia statute unconstitutional by a vote of 8–0, Chief Justice Burger wrote: "At issue is simply the power of a state to punish the truthful publication of an alleged juvenile delinquent's name lawfully obtained by a newspaper. The asserted state interest cannot justify the statute's imposition of criminal sanctions on this type of publication."[2]

The Florida Star v. B.J.F. (1989)

The general rule for journalists is that if material is part of a public record (such as a record of a judicial proceeding) it can be reported truthfully and accurately without legal penalty. In 1989, the U.S. Supreme Court cautiously upheld this generalization in The Florida Star rape reporting case.[3]

This case arose when a Jacksonville weekly newspaper published an item reporting a woman's complaint to the Sheriff's Department that she had been robbed and sexually assaulted. The department prepared a report using B.J.F.'s full name, and put it in the department's press room. Access to the reports in this room was unrestricted.

A reporter-trainee for The Florida Star copied the report verbatim, and a reporter then wrote an accurate one-paragraph "Police Reports" item, which was published. This violated the newspaper's own policy by identifying a rape victim; the newspaper had not done so previously. This mistake by the newspaper came under a Florida statute making it unlawful to " 'print, publish, or

---

[1] West Virginia Statute § 49–7–3; Smith v. Daily Mail Pub. Co., 443 U.S. 97, 99 S.Ct. 2667 (1979).

[2] 443 U.S. 97, 105, 99 S.Ct. 2667, 2672 (1979). See also the key prior restraint cases as discussed in Chapter 1: Near v. Minnesota ex rel. Olson, 283 U.S. 697, 51 S.Ct. 625 (1931); Organization for a Better Austin v. Keefe, 402 U.S. 415, 91 S.Ct. 1575 (1971); New York Times Co. v. United States, 403 U.S. 713, 91 S.Ct. 2140 (1971), and Nebraska Press Ass'n v. Stuart, 427 U.S. 539, 96 S.Ct. 2791 (1976).

[3] 491 U.S. 524, 109 S.Ct. 2603 (1989), 16 Med.L.Rptr. 1801.

broadcast . . . in any instrument of mass communication' the name of a victim of a sexual offense." [4]

"B.J.F." sued for invasion of privacy, claiming that the Jacksonville weekly negligently had violated the Florida statute. She contended that because of the publication of her name, she had suffered emotional distress, and that her mother had received a threatening phone call from a man who said he would rape B.J.F. again. The plaintiff testified that she had been forced to change her phone number and residence and to get mental health counseling.

Despite the newspaper's plea that it had learned the name from the incident report issued by the Sheriff's Department, and that printing the rape victim's name was an inadvertent violation of the newspaper's own policy, the trial court denied the newspaper's motion to dismiss. The court then accepted plaintiff's motion for a directed verdict, awarding $75,000 in compensatory damages and $25,000 in punitive damages.[5] The directed verdict was upheld by Florida's First District Court of Appeal, and the U.S. Supreme Court noted probable jurisdiction.[6]

By a 6–3 majority, the Supreme Court held for the newspaper. Justice Thurgood Marshall's opinion announced the judgment of the Court: It was carefully confined to the specific fact situation. The Court again avoided deciding the important constitutional issue of whether the press can ever have criminal responsibility or civil liability for publishing a truthful but privacy-invading story.[7] Note also that this decision did not declare unconstitutional the Florida statute which makes it a crime to publish a rape victim's name.[8]

Justice Marshall turned to Smith v. Daily Mail (1979), discussed above, for his rationale in The Florida Star case, invoking the application of "limited principles that sweep no more broadly than the appropriate context of the instant case." The Smith v. Daily Mail formulation, Justice Marshall wrote, protects only publication of information which a news medium has "lawfully obtained,"

> Applied to the instant case, the *Daily Mail* principle clearly commands reversal. The first inquiry is whether the newspaper "lawfully obtained truthful information about a matter of public significance." 443 U.S. at 103.

[4] Florida Stat. § 794.03, quoted in Ibid.

[5] 491 U.S. at 529, 109 S.Ct. at 2607 (1989), 16 Med.L.Rptr. at 1803.

[6] Ibid.

[7] 491 U.S. at 529, 109 S.Ct. at 2607 (1989), 16 Med.L.Rptr. at 1804.

[8] 491 U.S. at 533–536, 109 S.Ct. at 2609–2610 (1989), 16 Med.L.Rptr. at 1805–1806.

It is indisputed that the news article describing the assault on B.J.F. was accurate. In addition, appellant [the newspaper] lawfully obtained B.J.F.'s name. * * *

Some of Justice Marshall's words suggested that the Court *might* be willing to look favorably upon punishment for publishing truthful information if the statute were narrowly drawn. But where government "has failed to police itself in disseminating information," imposition of damages against the media cannot stand.[9]

In dissent, Justice White complained bitterly that for B.J.F. " * * * the violation she suffered at a rapist's knife point marked only the beginning of her ordeal."

Macon Telegraph v. Tatum (1993)

A 1993 Georgia case, however, resulted in a $100,000 jury award against a newspaper—upheld by the Georgia Court of Appeals—under that state's statute forbidding identification of rape victims. Macon Telegraph v. Tatum resulted from newspaper stories about a woman who shot and killed an intruder in her bedroom about 4 a.m. on a Saturday morning. Police ultimately cleared this incident as justifiable homicide.[10]

Although a Georgia statute [11] forbids publication of names of sexual assault victims, the Macon Telegraph published two articles about the incident, identifying Ms. Tatum, mentioning the street on which she lived, but without mentioning that a rape or an assault with intent to commit rape had occurred. The newspaper's first article, however, was headlined "Woman Kills Attacker in Bedroom," and included the information that the intruder had his pants unzipped.

The factual record in this case was in dispute, with the newspaper claiming that the woman's name and address were already available. The newspaper also argued that there was a question whether Ms. Tatum had been the victim of a sexual assault, and if so, the newspaper was not aware of it. Police, on the other hand, testified that Ms. Tatum's name had been released to the press only on condition that it not be published, and that it had been made clear that police were treating the incident as a sexual assault. Further, police declared it was understood that Ms. Tatum's name be published only with her permission, and that publication of her

---

[9] 491 U.S. at 536, 109 S.Ct. at 2611 (1989), 16 Med.L.Rptr. at 1806.

[10] Macon Telegraph v. Tatum, 208 Ga.App. 111, 430 S.E.2d 18 (1993), 21 Med. L.Rptr.1116, 1117.

[11] OCGA Sec. 16–6–23.

name without permission would violate the Georgia Rape Shield Statute.[12]

Late in 1993, however, the Georgia Supreme Court reversed, finding in favor of the newspaper: [13]

> * * *[W]e hold that Tatum, who committed a homicide, however justified, lost her right to keep her name private. When she shot Hill, Tatum became the object of a legitimate public interest and the newspaper had the right under the Federal and State constitution to accurately report the facts regarding the incident, including her name.

Patti Bowman, Rape Charges, and Privacy Law

Salacious details in allegations of sexual misconduct and victimization were much in the news in the fall of 1991. One case involved the televised trial of rape charges against William Kennedy Smith, nephew of Massachusetts Senator Edward Kennedy. The 30–year–old woman who brought the rape charges was identified in a grocery-store tabloid paper. Then, in a lowest-common-denominator approach to journalistic value, some establishment news media including NBC News and The New York Times also identified the complainant as Patti Bowman. Yet at her trial in a Florida court, when she testified, her face was obscured by an electronically generated blue blur. William Kennedy Smith was acquitted quickly by a six-person jury, but the trial generated nation-wide distaste, and raised the question whether women will now be more reluctant to face the legal process to pursue rape charges.[14]

Lurid media coverage of the William Kennedy Smith rape trial and acquittal resulted in charges against a newspaper of violating Florida Statute 794.03. That statute specifies criminal sanctions against anyone revealing the identity of the victim of a sexual offense "in any instrument of mass communication."

William Kennedy Smith was not convicted of rape. Patti Bowman, however, brought charges against The Globe under the Florida statute mentioned above. Eventually, both a Florida trial court and a Florida District Court of Appeal held that the Florida statute demanding criminal penalties for identifying victims of sexual offenses "violates free speech and free press provisions of

---

[12] Ibid., p. 1117.

[13] Macon Telegraph Publishing Co. v. Tatum, 263 Ga. 678, 436 S.E.2d 655 (1993), 22 Med.L.Rptr. 1126, 1127.

[14] See, e.g., "The Trial You Won't See," Newsweek, Dec. 16, 1991, p. 21; David Margolick, "Smith Acquitted of Rape Charge After Brief Deliberation by Jury," The New York Times, Dec. 12, 1991.

the Constitutions of Florida and the United States ...," is over-broad and an unconstitutional prior restraint.[15]

The "Social Value" Test: A California Aberration?

In decisions separated by 40 years, California courts added an element to privacy law: the existence of a public record did not necessarily serve as a defense to a lawsuit for invasion of privacy. One of the most famous—and wrong-headed—cases involving the disclosure of embarrassing private facts came in the 1931 case of Melvin v. Reid, which for many years was regarded as a leading decision in the law of privacy. Gabrielle Darley Melvin sued when a motion picture—"The Red Kimono"—was made about her life as a prostitute and her trial for murder in 1918. But Gabrielle Darley had been acquitted of the murder charge, and thereafter led a changed life: she got married, found many friends who were not aware of her tawdry past, and became an accepted member of society.[16]

Although the court found that a movie could be made about Mrs. Melvin's life without penalty—because the facts were part of a public record—it was found that damages could be recovered for the use of her name, both in the motion picture and in advertisements for it. Strangely, the California Supreme Court said that privacy as a tort action did not then (in 1931) exist in California. However, Justice Marks found provisions in the California state constitution, such as Section 1, Article I: "men are by nature free * * * and have certain inalienable rights, among which are pursuing and obtaining safety and happiness." [17]

So it was that Mrs. Melvin won her lawsuit, even though Justice Marks denied the existence of the tort of invasion of privacy in California. One especially curious thing about Melvin v. Reid is that the California Supreme Court gave little heed to the qualified privilege attached to reports made from public records. But then, in 1931, a movie such as "The Red Kimono" was not believed to be a defensible part of "the press" which is protected by the First Amendment.[18] The court suggested strongly that if the motion

---

[15] Florida v. Globe Communications Corp., 622 So.2d 1066, 1067 (Fla. Ct. of App., 4th Dist., 1993), 21 Med.L.Rptr. 2129.

[16] Melvin v. Reid, 112 Cal.App. 285, 297 P. 91 (1931).

[17] This was indeed a curious reading of the state's constitution. Usually, constitutions or bills of rights are seen as protecting individuals from the actions and powers of governments, rather than establishing protection against the actions of other individuals. See Pember, Privacy and the Press, p. 98.

[18] For years, courts were reluctant to accord First Amendment protection to motion pictures. See, e.g., Mutual Film Corp. v. Industrial Commission of Ohio, 236 U.S. 230, 35 S.Ct. 387 (1915); Joseph Burstyn, Inc. v. Wilson, 343 U.S. 495, 72 S.Ct. 777 (1952) was the case which first termed movies a significant medium for the expression of ideas.

picture company had used only those aspects of Gabrielle Darley's life which were in the trial record or public record of her case, then the film would have been privileged. Even so, Gabrielle Darley's name surely was part of the public record and it would seem that using it should have been "privileged."

In 1968, *Readers Digest* magazine published an article titled "The Big Business of Hijacking," describing various truck thefts and the efforts being made to stop such thefts. Dates ranging from 1965 to the time of publication were mentioned throughout the article, but none of the hijackings mentioned had a date attached to it in the text.[19]

One sentence in the article said: "Typical of many beginners, Marvin Briscoe and [another man] stole a 'valuable-looking' truck in Danville, Ky. and then fought a gun battle with the local police, only to learn that they had hijacked four bowling-pin spotters."

There was nothing in the article to indicate that the hijacking had occurred in 1956, some 11 years before the publication of the *Reader's Digest* article. In the words of the California Supreme Court, "As a result of defendant's [Reader's Digest's] publication, plaintiff's 11–year-old daughter, as well as his friends, for the first time learned of the incident. They thereafter scorned and abandoned him." [20] Briscoe argued that he had since "gone straight" and that he had become entirely rehabilitated, and led an exemplary and honorable life, making many friends in respectable society who were not aware of the hijacking incident in his earlier life.

Briscoe conceded the truth of the facts published in the *Reader's Digest* article, but claimed that the public disclosure of such private facts humiliated him and exposed him to contempt and ridicule. He conceded that the *subject* of the article might have been "newsworthy," but contended that the use of his *name* was not, and that *Reader's Digest* had therefore invaded his privacy.

Writing for a unanimous California Supreme Court, Justice Raymond E. Peters agreed with Briscoe's arguments, saying: [21]

> Plaintiff is a man whose last offense took place 11 years before, who has paid his debt to society, who has friends and an 11–year-old daughter who were unaware of his early life—a man who has assumed a position in "respectable society." Ideally, his neighbors should recognize his present worth and forget his past life of shame. But men are not so divine as to forgive the past trespasses

[19] Briscoe v. Reader's Digest Ass'n, 4 Cal.3d 529, 93 Cal.Rptr. 866, 868, 483 P.2d 34, 36 (1971).

[20] Ibid.

[21] 4 Cal.3d 529, 93 Cal.Rptr. 866, 873–75, 483 P.2d 34, 41–42 (1971).

of others, and plaintiff therefore endeavored to reveal as little as possible of his past life. Yet, as if in some bizarre canyon of echoes, petitioner's past life pursues him through the pages of Reader's Digest, now published in 13 languages and distributed in 100 nations, with a circulation in California alone of almost 2,000,000 copies.

In a nation built upon the free dissemination of ideas, it is always difficult to declare that something may not be published. * * * But the rights guaranteed by the First Amendment do not require total abrogation of the right to privacy. The goals sought by each may be achieved with a minimum of intrusion on the other.

Although the California Supreme Court was not in a position to award damages to Mr. Briscoe, it did send his case back to a lower court for trial. Justice Peters declared that although there was good reason to discuss the crime of truck hijacking in the media, there was no reason to use Briscoe's name. A jury, in the view of the California Supreme Court, could certainly find that Mr. Briscoe had once again become an anonymous member of the community.[22]

Despite such sweeping language, Briscoe did not win his lawsuit. The case was removed to the U.S. District Court, Central District of California, where Judge Lawrence T. Lydick granted a summary judgment to the *Reader's Digest.* Judge Lydick concluded that the article complained of by Briscoe was newsworthy and published without [actual] malice or recklessness. Further, the judge concluded that the article disclosed no private facts about Marvin Briscoe and that it did not invade his privacy.[23]

The language of the California Supreme Court in Briscoe lingered on. Take the case of Milo Conklin, who brought suit for invasion of privacy because the *Modoc County Record* published this item under the caption, "Twenty Years Ago Today in Modoc County: MILO CONKLIN has been charged with the murder of his brother-in-law, Louis Blodgett, in Cedarville Sunday."

The statement was true. Conklin had been tried for, and convicted of, Blodgett's murder. He served a prison sentence, completed parole, remarried, fathered two children, and rehabilitated himself. Conklin, at all material times, was a resident of

[22] 4 Cal.3d 529, 93 Cal.Rptr. 866, 875, 483 P.2d 34, 43 (1971).

[23] Briscoe v. Reader's Digest Ass'n (C.D.Cal.1972), 1 Med.L.Rptr. 1852, 1854. This decision in favor of the magazine which was not reported in Federal Supplement, was a kind of "best kept secret;" the finding here (evidently unknown other than in the media law reporting service, Media Law Reporter) was either unnoticed or ignored by courts in deciding Forsher v. Bugliosi, 26 Cal.3d 792, 163 Cal.Rptr. 628, 608 P.2d 716 (1980) and Conklin v. Sloss, 86 Cal.App.3d 241, 150 Cal.Rptr. 121 (3d Dist.1978), 4 Med.L.Rptr. 1998.

Cedarville, California, a hamlet of 800 in the northeast corner of California. It is hard to believe that a town of 800 could forget that it had a convicted murderer in its midst. The California Court of Appeal, Third District, nevertheless accepted Conklin's argument that some of his friends and acquaintances for the first time had learned of his unsavory past and abandoned him.[24]

The defendant newspaper replied that the statement was privileged under a California statute which says that a privileged publication is made by [25]

> * * * a fair and true report in a public journal, of (1) a judicial, (2) legislative, or (3) other public official proceeding, or (4) of anything said in the course thereof....

Although this statutory language evidently conferred a privilege to protect the *Modoc County Record* from successful suit, the *Briscoe* case surfaced again to haunt the press. A California Court of Appeal held that Conklin's case should be taken to trial on the issue of whether publication of items of public record from 20 years earlier were "newsworthy," [26] leaving the potential for a jury to tell a newspaper its business.

Some of the sting of *Briscoe* may have been lessened, however, by the California Supreme Court's 1980 decision in Forsher v. Bugliosi. Bugliosi, at one time a prosecuting attorney in the trial of Charles Manson and his "Family" for the "Tate–Labianca killings." Bugliosi was co-author of Helter–Skelter, a book purporting to be an inside view of the killings, the trial, and the Manson Family. James Forsher, who was mentioned in the book as having been on the periphery of the Manson Family's activities in a minor and non-criminal way, sued for invasion of privacy and libel. In his privacy claim, Forsher contended that there was no informational or social value in using his name in connection with retelling of past events. Justice Manual's opinion in *Forsher* limited the impact of the *Briscoe* decision to cases involving rehabilitated criminals who were harmed by publication of their criminal records.[27]

> California courts have refrained from extending the Briscoe rule to other fact situations. * * * *Briscoe* * * *
> [held] that "where the plaintiff is a past criminal and his

[24] Conklin v. Sloss, 86 Cal.App.3d 241, 150 Cal.Rptr. 121 (3d Dist.1978), 4 Med.L.Rptr. 1998, 1999.

[25] West's Ann.Cal.Civil Code § 47, subs. 4.

[26] 86 Cal.App.3d 241, 150 Cal.Rptr. 121, 125 (3d Dist.1978), 4 Med.L.Rptr. 1998, 2001. See also Restatement of Torts, § 857, comment c, quoted with approval by the court at 150 Cal.Rptr. 125.

[27] Forsher v. Bugliosi, 26 Cal.3d 792, 163 Cal.Rptr. 628, 636–637, 608 P.2d 716, 724, 726 (1980).

name is used in a publication, the mere lapse of time may provide a basis for an invasion of privacy suit."

* * *

Time Lapse

One of the problems referred to in Briscoe v. Reader's Digest Ass'n involved the so-called time lapse question.[28] How much time must pass before a person recovers from unwanted publicity, loses his or her newsworthiness, and again can be said to have regained anonymity? Take the case of William James Sidis, a person who did not seek publicity but who was found by it. In 1910, Sidis was an 11-year-old mathematical prodigy who lectured to famed mathematicians. He was graduated from Harvard at 16, and received a great deal of publicity. More than 20 years after his graduation, the New Yorker Magazine—in its August 14, 1937 issue—ran a feature story about Sidis plus a cartoon, with the captions "Where Are They Now?" and "April Fool." The article told how Sidis lived in a "hall bedroom of Boston's shabby south end," working at a routine clerical job, collecting streetcar transfers and studying the history of American Indians. Sidis sued for invasion of privacy, but a United States Court of Appeals ultimately held that he could not collect damages.

The court conceded that the New Yorker had perpetrated "a ruthless exposure of a once public character, who has since sought and has now been deprived of the seclusion of private life." Even so, the lawsuit did not succeed.[29]

> * * * [W]e are not yet disposed to afford to all of the intimate details of private life an absolute immunity from the prying of the press. Everyone will agree that at some point the individual interest in obtaining information becomes dominant over the individual's desire for privacy. * * * At least we would permit limited scrutiny of the "private" life of any person who has achieved, or has had thrust upon him, the questionable and indefinable status of a "public figure." * * *

* * *

The article in the *New Yorker* sketched the life of an unusual personality, and it possessed considerable popular news interest.

We express no comment on whether or not the newsworthiness of the matter printed will always constitute a

---

[28] See Chief Justice Raymond E. Peters opinion, 4 Cal.3d 529, 93 Cal.Rptr. 866, 873–75, 483 P.2d 34, 41–42 (1971).

[29] Sidis v. F–R Pub. Corp., 113 F.2d 806 (2d Cir.1940).

complete defense. Revelations may be so intimate and so unwarranted in view of the victim's position as to outrage the community's notions of decency. But when focused upon public characters, truthful comments upon dress, speech, habits, and the ordinary aspects of personality will usually not transgress this line.

The court implied that the invasion of privacy must be so severe that it would cause more than minor annoyance to an hypothetical "average" or "reasonable" man of "ordinary sensibilities." William James Sidis was an unusually sensitive man, and it has been speculated that the *New Yorker* article was in large measure responsible for his early death.[30]

The outcome of the Sidis case represents a general pattern. American courts usually have ruled against "time lapse" privacy lawsuits. Two post–1980 cases support that view: Underwood v. First National Bank [31] and Roshto v. Hebert.[32] In the Underwood case, Thomas G. Underwood sued the First National Bank of Blooming Prairie, Minn. In 1980, the bank published a history of its community. That history included a short summary of the first degree murder trial—and conviction—of Underwood for shooting a policeman to death. Underwood claimed that the version in the book was defamatory (that he had killed the policeman in a running gunfight, not—as said in the book—shooting him when he was down on the ground). Additionally, he argued that the "Hot News" that made him a public figure in 1952 was now "Old News," and that appropriating Underwood's name for such an old story invaded his privacy.[33] The Minnesota District Court, assuming for the sake of argument that the law of privacy has been adopted in Minnesota, nevertheless granted the bank's motion for summary judgment, halting Underwood's libel and privacy suit.[34]

In Roshto v. Hebert, the Heberts' newspaper—The Iberville South—found itself sued for invasion of privacy because of its regular "Page from our Past" feature. In 1973, this weekly newspaper reproduced the entire front page from its April 4, 1952, edition, which included an article about the cattle theft trial of three brothers, Carlysle, Alfred, and E.R. Roshto. Four years later, in 1977, the newspaper reproduced the front page of the November 14, 1952, edition, containing another article about the Roshto

---

[30] Prosser, "Privacy," California Law Review, Vol. 48 (1960) at p. 397.

[31] Underwood v. First National Bank (Minn.Dist.Ct.1982), 8 Med.L.Rptr. 1278.

[32] Roshto v. Hebert, 439 So.2d 428 (La.1983), 9 Med.L.Rptr. 2417.

[33] 8 Med.L.Rptr. 1278, 1279, 1280.

[34] Ibid., 1281. The judge noted that historically, the Minnesota Supreme Court has been reluctant to recognize the tort of invasion of privacy; it is the last holdout among the 50 states.

brothers—this time discussing their sentencing to prison after their sentences were affirmed on appeal.[35]

The Louisiana Supreme Court ruled in favor of the defendant newspapers, although giving some indications of reluctance: [36]

> Defendants were arguably insensitive or careless in reproducing a former front page for publication without checking for information that might be currently offensive to some members of the community. However, more than insensitivity or simple carelessness is required for the imposition of liability for damages when the publication is truthful, accurate and non-malicious.

Finally, consider the 1983 case of Doe v. Sarasota–Bradenton Television. "Jane Doe" was raped, and agreed to testify against her assailant at his upcoming trial. It was important to her that her name and photograph would not be displayed or photographed in connection with this trial.

In March, 1982, "Jane Doe" testified at the rape trial. A news team from the Sarasota–Bradenton Florida Television Company was present in the courtroom. (As noted in Chapter 15, Section 88, below, under Florida law, news cameras are allowed in that state's courtrooms.) That night, the TV station ran a video tape of the trial featuring "Jane Doe's" testimony. As the video tape ran, a newscaster identified "Jane Doe" by name to the viewing audience.[37]

"Jane Doe" sued the TV station, seeking damages under a Florida statute [38] and for common-law invasion of privacy and for intentional infliction of emotional distress. The trial court found in favor of the television station, dismissing the woman's complaint.[39]

A Florida Court of Appeal agreed that this lawsuit must be dismissed, as under Cox Broadcasting Corp. v. Cohn, a case discussed at a few pages earlier.[40] The District Court of Appeal noted that in both the Cox Broadcasting and the "Jane Doe" cases, the broadcasts complained of contained completely accurate but pain-inflicting information. The Florida court had harsh words for the TV station: [41]

[35] Roshto v. Hebert, 439 So.2d 428, 429 (La.1983), 9 Med.L.Rptr. 2417, 2418.

[36] 439 So.2d 428, 432 (La.1983), 9 Med.L.Rptr. 2417, 2420.

[37] Doe v. Sarasota–Bradenton Florida Television Co., Inc., 436 So.2d 328 (Fla. App.2d Dist.1983), 9 Med.L.Rptr. 2074.

[38] Ibid., quoting Florida Statute section 794.03.

[39] Ibid., at 329, 9 Med.L.Rptr. at 2075.

[40] 420 U.S. 469, 95 S.Ct. 1029 (1975).

[41] Ibid., at 329, 9 Med.L.Rptr. at 2075–2076.

We deplore the lack of sensitivity to the rights of others that is sometimes displayed by such an unfettered exercise of first amendment rights.

* * *

The publication added little or nothing to the sordid and unhappy story; yet, that brief little- or-nothing addition may well affect appellant's [Jane Doe's] well-being for years to come.

The court chastised the prosecution—representatives of the State of Florida—"for not having sought a protective order regarding cameras in the courtroom or other proper steps to support its alleged assurance" to Jane Doe that she could testify in the rape trial without her name and picture being used. Further, the court said that it recognized the frequent conflict between freedom of the press and the right of privacy. It then urged "compassionate discretion" by the media in such situations.[42]

Virgil v. Time, Inc. (1975)

Another case encouraging recovery in a privacy lawsuit *even when a truthful report is made by the news media* is Virgil v. Time, Inc. Sports Illustrated, a Time, Inc. publication, published an article on body surfing in February, 1971. The article devoted much attention to Mike Virgil, a surfer who was well known at "The Wedge," a dangerous beach near Newport Beach, California. Sports Illustrated staff writer Curry Kirkpatrick had interviewed Virgil at length—which obviously required a kind of consent from Virgil—and Virgil had also consented to the taking of pictures by a free-lance photographer working with Kirkpatrick.

Before the article was published, another Sports Illustrated employee called Virgil's home and verified some of the information with his wife. At this point, Virgil "revoked all consent" for publication of the article and photographs and indicated that he did not want his name used in the story. Circuit Judge Merrill summarized Virgil's attempt to revoke his consent:[43]

While not disputing the truth of the article or the accuracy of the statements about him which it contained, and while admitting that he had known that his picture was being taken, the plaintiff indicated that he thought the article was going to be limited to his prominence as a surfer at The Wedge, and that he did not know that it would contain references to some rather bizarre incidents in his life that were not directly related to surfing.

[42] Ibid., at 330, 9 Med.L.Rptr. at 2076, 2077.
[43] Virgil v. Time, Inc., 527 F.2d 1122, 1124 (9th Cir.1975).

It can be objected that Judge Merrill was placing himself in the editor's chair: is it for a *judge* to say whether some of the "bizarre incidents" in Virgil's life are "not directly related to surfing?" If a person persists in body-surfing at a place known as one of earth's most dangerous beaches, might not some of his other actions—such as extinguishing a cigarette in his mouth, or diving down a flight of stairs because "there were all these chicks around"—illustrate an unusually reckless (and therefore newsworthy?) approach to life? [44]

It was argued for the magazine—which had proceeded, on advice of counsel, to publish the article even after Virgil "revoked" his consent—that Virgil had voluntarily made public the facts he complained about. Judge Merrill disagreed, in words which frightened reporters and editors: [45]

> Talking freely to a member of the press, knowing the listener to be a member of the press, is not then in itself making public. Such communication can be said to anticipate that what is said will be made public since making public is the function of the press, and accordingly such communication can be construed as a consent to publicize. Thus if publicity results it can be said to have been consented to. However, if consent is withdrawn prior to the act of publicization, the consequent publicity is without consent.

Judge Merrill paid particular attention to the Restatement, Second, Torts § 652D (Tentative Draft No. 21, 1975), saying that unless a subject is newsworthy, the publicizing of private facts is not protected by the First Amendment.[46] He then quoted a comment from the Restatement of Torts, Second: [47]

> "In determining what is a matter of legitimate public interest, account must be taken of the customs and conventions of the community; and in the last analysis what is proper becomes a matter of the community mores. The line is to be drawn when the publicity ceases to be the giving of information to which the public is entitled, and becomes a morbid and sensational prying into public lives for its own sake. ..."

The Restatement, Second, described the elements of a lawsuit for publication of embarrassing private facts in a way which has encouraged judges to "play editor." [48]

[44] Ibid., p. 1125n, quoting the Sports Illustrated article.

[45] Ibid., p. 1127.

[46] Ibid., p. 1128.

[47] Restatement quoted in Ibid., pp. 1129, 1129n.

[48] Restatement, Second, Torts, § 652D.

One who gives publicity to a matter concerning the private life of another is subject to liability to the other for invasion of privacy, if the matter publicized is of a kind that

(a) would be highly offensive to a reasonable person and

(b) is not of legitimate concern to the public.

In an action which startled constitutional lawyers, the Supreme Court refused to review the Court of Appeals decision in *Virgil*.[49] This meant that the *Virgil* case went back to the District [trial] Court, which decided—fortunately for Sports Illustrated— that the article about Virgil was "newsworthy."[50] But was this a victory for the magazine? Constitutional law specialists Alan U. Schwartz and Floyd Abrams said otherwise. Schwartz complained, "Under this formula truth becomes immaterial. The test is whether community mores (and *what* community? one may ask) have been offended. The peril to the journalist is extreme."[51] Abrams declared, "the test set forth by the Court in the Virgil case contains language so broad ('morbid and sensational prying'), so open-ended ('a reasonable member of the public') and so subjective ('decent standards') that it makes it all but impossible to determine in advance what may be published and what not."[52]

Campbell v. Seabury Press (1980)

Private facts—sometimes termed the "truthful tort" area— were also at issue in Campbell v. Seabury Press. Civil rights leader Will D. Campbell wrote his autobiography, Brother to a Dragonfly, which included an account of his deceased brother, Joe. Campbell wrote about his brother's addiction to drugs and the effects of that addiction on his personality, his family life, and on Will Campbell himself. Carlyne Campbell, Joe's first wife, sued for defamation and invasion of privacy, complaining about the book's portrayal of her marital relationship with Joe Campbell. Seabury Press was granted a summary judgment by the U.S. District Court on grounds that a public interest privilege under the first Amendment protected such disclosures.[53]

[49] Virgil v. Time, Inc., 527 F.2d 1122, 1130–1132 (9th Cir.1975), certiorari denied 425 U.S. 998, 96 S.Ct. 2215 (1976). Justices Brennan and Stewart said they would have granted certiorari.

[50] Floyd Abrams, "The Press, Privacy and the Constitution," New York Times Magazine, August 21, 1977, pp. 11ff, at p. 13; Virgil v. Sports Illustrated, 424 F.Supp. 1286 (S.D.Cal.1976).

[51] Schwartz, op.cit., p. 32.

[52] Abrams, op.cit., pp. 13, 65.

[53] Campbell v. Seabury Press, 614 F.2d 395 (5th Cir.1980), 5 Med.L.Rptr. 2612.

Carlyne Campbell appealed, arguing that her lawsuit should not be dismissed because there was no logical connection between the matters of legitimate public interest and her home life with Joe Campbell. The Court of Appeals for the Fifth Circuit upheld the dismissal of her case, and articulated a constitutional rationale favorable to the news media. In a per curiam opinion, Circuit Judges Charles Clark, Robert S. Vance, and Sam D. Johnson wrote: [54]

> The first amendment mandates a constitutional privilege applicable to those torts of invasion of privacy that involve publicity. See Cox Broadcasting Corp. v. Cohn, * * * This broad constitutional privilege recognizes two closely related yet analytically distinct privileges. First is the privilege to publish or broadcast facts, events, and information relating to public figures. Second is the privilege to publish or broadcast news or other matters of public interest. See Smith v. Doss, 251 Ala. 250, 253, 37 So.2d 118, 120 (1948). * * * [This news privilege] is not merely limited to the dissemination of news either in the sense of current events or commentary upon public affairs. Rather, the privilege extends to information concerning interesting phases of human activity and embraces all issues about which information is needed or appropriate so that individuals may cope with the exigencies of their period.

As privacy and media law expert Harvey Zuckman has noted, because of the Fifth Circuit's "liberal outlook on the newsworthiness or public interest privilege, counsel for your newspapers may wish to consider attempting removal of private fact and even 'false light' cases from state courts where they are usually filed to the local United States District Court. If that court is located in Florida, Georgia, Alabama, Mississippi, Louisiana or Texas, it will be governed by the law of the *Campbell* case." [55]

SEC. 40. FALSE PUBLICATIONS WHICH INVADE PRIVACY

Putting a person in a false position before the public has proven costly for many publications.

A third sub-area of privacy law, "putting plaintiff in a false position in the public eye," is one which holds great dangers of lawsuits for the mass media. The first invasion of privacy case

---

[54] 614 F.2d 395, 396 (5th Cir.1980), 5 Med.L.Rptr. 2612.

[55] Harvey Zuckman, "The Right of Privacy and the Press," talk at Southern Newspaper Publishers Association seminar, The University of Texas–Austin, Oct. 13, 1980.

dealing with the mass media to be decided by the Supreme Court of the United States involved a "false position in the public eye." [56]

This branch of privacy law has roots which go back to an outraged English poet, Lord Byron, who successfully sued to prevent the publication of inferior poems under Lord Byron's name.[57] In more recent years, the media—or people who use the media—have misrepresented the views of other people at their peril.

Cain v. Hearst (1994)

False-light privacy has been accepted by courts of most states, although growing resistance to this rather shapeless, defamation-like tort has become evident since 1980. In Cain v. Hearst (1994), the Texas Supreme Court refused to adopt the false light tort. Clyde Cain, a Texas prison inmate, had sued the Houston Chronicle for putting him in a false light by calling him a burglar, thief, pimp, and killer. Cain's false light suit objected to the newspaper's writing that he was "believed to have killed as many as eight people," complaining that the published statement put him in a false light; he evidently had killed only three.

Rejecting false light privacy by a vote of 5–4, the Texas Supreme Court said that the false light action "duplicates the tort of defamation while lacking many of its procedural limitations." That court then listed a total of eight other jurisdictions not accepting false light privacy: Mississippi, Missouri, New York, North Carolina, Ohio, Virginia, Washington, and Wisconsin.[58]

[56] Time, Inc. v. Hill, 385 U.S. 374, 87 S.Ct. 534 (1967). It should be noted that this third area of privacy overlaps a fourth area discussed later in this chapter, "appropriation of some element of plaintiff's personality for commercial use." This overlapping is especially apparent in cases involving spurious testimonials in advertisements. See, e.g., Flake v. Greensboro News Co., 212 N.C. 780, 195 S.E. 55 (1938) where a woman's picture was placed, by mistake, in an advertisement; Fairfield v. American Photocopy Equipment Co., 138 Cal.App.2d 82, 291 P.2d 194 (1955).

[57] Lord Byron v. Johnston, 2 Mer. 29, 35 Eng.Rep. 851 (Chancery 1816).

[58] Cain v. Hearst Corporation, 37 TX S.Ct.Jrnl. 1151, 878 S.W.2d 577 (Tex.1994), p. 1151, and listing jurisdictions outside of Texas which had not adopted false light privacy. The Texas court listed: Mitchell v. Random House, 865 F.2d 664, 672 (5th Cir.1989) (Mississippi); Sullivan v. Pulitzer B'cstg., 709 S.W.2d 475, 480 (Mo.1986); Arrington v. New York Times Co., 55 N.Y.2d 433, 449 N.Y.S.2d 941, 434 N.E.2d 1319, 1323 (1982); Renwick v. News & Observer Pub. Co., 310 N.C. 312, 312 S.E.2d 405, 410 (1984); Yeager v. Local 20, Teamsters, 60 Ohio St.3d 369, 453 N.E.2d 666, 669–670 (1983); Falwell v. Penthouse Int'l., 521 F.Supp. 1204, 1206 (W.D.Va.1981) (Virginia); Hoppe v. Hearst Corp., 53 Wash.App. 668, 770 P.2d 203, 208, n.5 (Wash.Ct.App.1989). Add to these Zinda v. Louisiana Pacific Corp., 149 Wis.2d 913, 440 N.W.2d 548, 555 (1989), holding that Wisconsin's privacy statute does not provide a cause of action for putting a person in a false light in the public eye. The Texas Supreme Court also cited Diane Lenheer Zimmerman, "False Light Invasion of Privacy: The Light that Failed," 64 N.Y.U. Law Rev. 364, 452 (1989).

Can Photographs Lie?

The old saying that "photographs don't lie" is perhaps true most of the time, but photos—and especially their captions—must be carefully watched by editors. Pictures which would give, or are used in such a way that they give, a misleading impression of a person's character are especially dangerous. The *Saturday Evening Post* was stung by a privacy lawsuit in Peay v. Curtis Publishing Co. The magazine published an article about Washington, D.C., taxicab drivers titled "Never Give a Passenger an Even Break." The court noted that this article painted the city's drivers as "ill mannered, brazen, and contemptuous of their patrons * * * dishonest and cheating when opportunity arises." [59] The *Saturday Evening Post's* article was worth money to cab-driver Muriel Peay, whose picture had been used, without her permission, to illustrate the article.

The Curtis Publishing Company lost another invasion of privacy lawsuit only three years later, and the cause was again careless use of a picture. Back in 1947, ten-year-old Eleanor Sue Leverton was knocked down by a careless motorist. A news photographer snapped a picture of a woman helping the little girl to her feet. This photo was published in a Birmingham, Ala., newspaper. To this point, there was no action for invasion of privacy possible for young Miss Leverton.

But 20 months after the little girl was hit by the car, the *Saturday Evening Post* used her picture to illustrate an article headlined "They Ask to Be Killed." The little girl's picture was captioned, "Safety education in schools has reduced child accidents measurably, but unpredictable darting through traffic still takes its sobering toll." In a box next to the headline, these words appeared: "Do you invite massacre by your own carelessness? Here's how to keep them alive." A Federal Court of Appeals said:[60]

> The sum total of all this is that this particular plaintiff, the legitimate subject for publicity for one particular accident, now becomes a pictorial, frightful example of pedestrian carelessness. This, we think, exceeds the bounds of privilege.

The lesson for photo-editors should be plain: if a picture is not taken in a public place or if that picture—or its caption—places someone in a false light, don't use it. The exception, of course, would be when you have received permission, in the form of a signed release, from the persons pictured. Two invasion of privacy

[59] Peay v. Curtis Pub. Co., 78 F.Supp. 305 (D.D.C.1948); Fowler v. Curtis Pub. Co., 78 F.Supp. 303, 304 (D.D.C.1948).

[60] Leverton v. Curtis Pub. Co., 192 F.2d 974 (3d Cir.1951).

lawsuits by Mr. and Mrs. John W. Gill, one successful and one not, illustrate the point rather neatly.

Mr. and Mrs. Gill were seated on stools at a confectionery stand which they operated at the Farmer's Market in Los Angeles. Famed photographer Henri Cartier–Bresson took a picture of the Gills, as Mr. Gill sat with his arm around his wife. The photograph was used in *Harper's Bazaar* to illustrate an article titled "And So the World Goes Around," a brief commentary having to do with the poetic notion that love makes the world go 'round. Although the Gills sued, they failed to collect from the Hearst Corporation, publisher of the magazine. The court held that the Gills had no right to collect since they took that voluntary pose in public and because there was nothing uncomplimentary about the photograph itself.[61]

Although they couldn't collect from the Hearst Corporation for invasion of privacy, Mr. and Mrs. Gill already had won damages from the Curtis Publishing Company. The *Ladies Home Journal,* a Curtis publication, had printed the very same photograph taken at the Farmer's Market but had made that photo an invasion of privacy by using faulty captions. The *Journal* used the Gills' picture to illustrate an article titled "Love." Underneath the picture was this caption "Publicized as glamourous, desirable, 'love at first sight' is a bad risk." The story termed such love "100% sex attraction" and the "wrong" kind. The court held that the article implied that this husband and wife were "persons whose only interest in each other is sex, a characterization that may be said to impinge seriously upon their sensibilities." [62]

Context Providing a "False Light"

A 1984 Texas case suggests that the context in which something is published can cause lawsuits for defamation or for invasion of privacy. Jeannie Braun, trainer of "Ralph the Diving Pig" at Aquarena Springs Resort, San Marcos, Texas, took violent exception to having her picture displayed in Chic, a Larry Flynt-published magazine specializing in female nudity and photos and cartoons of an overtly sexual nature.

Part of Mrs. Braun's job at Aquarena Springs was to tread water while holding out a baby bottle of milk. Ralph the pig would then dive into the pool and feed from the bottle. Pictures and postcards were made of Ralph diving toward Mrs. Braun. Mrs. Braun had signed a release saying the picture could be used for advertising and publicity as long as the photo was used in good taste, without embarrassment to her and her family.

---

[61] Gill v. Hearst Pub. Co., 40 Cal.2d 224, 253 P.2d 441 (1953).

[62] Gill v. Curtis Pub. Co., 38 Cal.2d 273, 239 P.2d 630 (1952).

Once the picture appeared in Chic—surrounded by pictures and cartoons full of sexual content (captions on other items included "Lust Rock Rules" and "Chinese Organ Grinder")—Mrs. Braun sued for a total of $1.1 million for defamation and invasion of privacy. After ruling that Mrs. Braun was a private individual, the Court of Appeals for the Fifth Circuit took issue with the trial court's damage awards totaling $95,000. That figure represented defamation damages ($5,000 actual and $25,000 punitive) and false light privacy damages ($15,000 actual and $50,000 punitive). The appeals court said that as a matter of public policy, punitive damages should not be awarded in one case for both defamation and false-light privacy invasion. Therefore, the appeals court said that only the damages assessed for invasion of privacy—$65,000— should be awarded.[63]

Duncan v. WJLA–TV

The "false light" area of law is so close to libel that—with evidently increasing frequency—people sue for both invasion of privacy and defamation. Take the case of Duncan v. WJLA–TV (1984), which illustrated, once again, that incautious picture captioning (or the television equivalent, "voice-overs") has its perils. A young woman named Linda K. Duncan was standing on a street corner in Washington, D.C. Meanwhile, WJLA–TV was shooting a "journalist-in-the-street" format story featuring reporter Betsy Ashton.

WJLA–TV broadcast two versions of a news story based on this videotaping of Ms. Ashton. For the 6 p.m. newscast, the camera was aimed down K street and focused on pedestrians on the corner behind reporter Ashton. The camera zeroed in on Linda Duncan, as she faced toward the camera and could be seen clearly. Then, the camera shifted back to reporter Ashton, who talked about her story, a new treatment for genital herpes.[64]

For the 11 p.m. newscast, a substantial amount of editing was done. Instead of the street scene including reporter Betsy Ashton in the foreground, reliance was placed on a "voice-over" as spoken by news anchor David Schoumacher. For the 11 p.m. version, Ms. Duncan was seen turning into the camera, and then pausing. As she did so, Schoumacher intoned: "For the twenty million Americans who have herpes, it's not a cure." The 11 p.m. version of the story concluded with Ms. Duncan turning away and walking off down the street.[65]

[63] Braun v. Flynt, 726 F.2d 245, 258 (5th Cir.1984), 10 Med.L.Rptr. 1497, 1498, 1499, 1507–1508.

[64] Duncan v. WJLA–TV, Inc. (D.D.C.1984) 10 Med.L.Rptr. 1395, 1398.

[65] Ibid.

A United States District Court ruled that the 6 p.m. broadcast was neither defamatory nor a false light invasion of privacy—as far as the 6 p.m. broadcast was concerned. The earlier broadcast was said to provide sufficient context for viewers not to associate the subject matter of the news story with Ms. Duncan. The court said, however, that the 11 p.m. newscast presented different questions and should be submitted to a jury for consideration.[66] Ms. Duncan won a small damage award from WJLA–TV.

Fictionalization

The misuse of pictures or photographs is one way to get involved in a privacy lawsuit. So is *fictionalization*. Fictionalization, as used by the courts, involves more than mere incidental falsity. Fictionalization appears to mean the deliberate or reckless addition of untrue material, perhaps for entertainment purposes or to make a good story better. Although the courts' rules for determining fictionalization are by no means clear, journalists should be warned to look to their ethics and accuracy. "Hyping" or "sensationalizing" a story by adding untrue materials so that a false impression is created concerning the subject of the story may be actionable.

Triangle Publications, which produced magazines such as *Timely Detective Cases* and *Uncensored Detective,* lost a privacy suit because of fictionalization. Robert H. Garner and Grace M. Smith had become legitimate objects of news interest because they were on trial for the murder of her husband. Mr. Garner and Mrs. Smith were convicted of the murder. Meanwhile, magazines published by Triangle carried numerous articles about the crime, adding some untrue elements to their stories. The magazines claimed that Mr. Garner and Mrs. Smith had had "improper relations with each other." However, after the detective magazines had published their stories, the convictions of Mr. Garner and Mrs. Smith were reversed.

A Federal District Court held that there could be no liability for presenting news about a matter of public interest such as a murder trial. However, Triangle Publications could be liable for a privacy lawsuit because when the magazines [67]

> enlarged upon the facts so as to go beyond the bounds of propriety and decency, they should not be cloaked with and shielded by the public interest in dissemination of "information." * * *

[66] Ibid.

[67] Garner v. Triangle Publications, Inc., 97 F.Supp. 546, 550 (S.D.N.Y.1951). For similar holdings, see Hazlitt v. Fawcett Publications, Inc., 116 F.Supp. 538 (D.Conn. 1953); Reed v. Real Detective Pub. Co., 63 Ariz. 294, 162 P.2d 133 (1945).

It appears, however, that minor errors in fact will not be sufficient to defeat the defense of newsworthiness, which will be discussed later. In the first media-related privacy case to reach the Supreme Court of the United States, it was held that Constitutional protections for speech and press forbid recovery for false reports "in the absence of proof that the defendant published the report with knowledge of its falsity or in reckless disregard of the truth." [68]

Another lawsuit for fictionalization involved the famed Warren Spahn, the left-handed pitcher who won more than 300 games during a long career with the Boston—and later the Milwaukee—Braves. Spahn was a hero to many baseball card collectors in the 1950s and early 1960s, and some people wanted to cash in on "Spahnie's" success. Writer Milton J. Shapiro and publisher Julian Messner, Inc., brought out a book titled *The Warren Spahn Story,* aimed at a juvenile audience. Throughout this book, Spahn's feats were exaggerated. For one thing, Spahn was portrayed as a war hero, which he was not. An elbow injury finally brought an end to Spahn's career; author Shapiro consistently wrote about Spahn's "shoulder injury." Such inaccuracies were topped off by page after page of fictional dialogue—words attributed to Spahn and his associates but which had been invented by author Shapiro.[69]

Shapiro and Julian Messner, Inc. argued strenuously that Spahn was a public figure who enjoyed no right to privacy.[70] Justice Charles Breitel of the Appellate Division, New York Supreme Court disagreed with contentions that Spahn no longer possessed a right of privacy, and said the fact that the fictionalization was laudatory was immaterial.[71]

If, indeed, writers cannot suppress the impulse to fictionalize, they would be more likely to avoid a lawsuit if they do not use the names of actual people involved in an event upon which they base their fictionalization. Where there is no identification, courts will not be able to find for the plaintiffs.[72] But where there is both

[68] Time, Inc. v. Hill, 385 U.S. 374, 388, 87 S.Ct. 534, 542 (1967). See also Binns v. Vitagraph Corp. of America, 210 N.Y. 51, 103 N.E. 1108 (1913); Stryker v. Republic Pictures Corp., 108 Cal.App.2d 191, 238 P.2d 670 (1951).

[69] Spahn v. Julian Messner, Inc., 43 Misc.2d 219, 230–232, 250 N.Y.S.2d 529, 540–542 (1964).

[70] See Time, Inc. v. Hill, 385 U.S. 374, 87 S.Ct. 534 (1967).

[71] 23 A.D.2d 216, 221, 260 N.Y.S.2d 451, 456 (1965).

[72] Bernstein v. NBC, 129 F.Supp. 817 (D.D.C.), affirmed 98 U.S.App.D.C. 112, 232 F.2d 369 (1956); Smith v. NBC, 138 Cal.App.2d 807, 292 P.2d 600 (1956).

identification and fictionalization, the publisher is in danger of losing a suit.[73]

Cantrell v. Forest City Publishing Co. (1974)

Major fact errors—or large swatches of fictionalizing—in something purporting to be a news story—can mean serious difficulty for the news media. Consider the case known as Cantrell v. Forest City Publishing Company. Mrs. Margaret Mae Cantrell and her son sued the company for an article which appeared in the Cleveland Plain Dealer in August of 1968, claiming that the article placed her and her family in a false light.

The facts underlying the lawsuit were these: In December, 1967, Mrs. Cantrell's husband was killed—along with 43 other persons—when the Silver Bridge across the Ohio River at Point Pleasant, W.Va., collapsed. Cleveland *Plain Dealer* reporter Joseph Eszterhas had covered the disaster and he wrote a news feature on Mr. Cantrell's funeral. Five months later, Eszterhas and photographer Richard Conway returned to Point Pleasant and went to the Cantrell residence. Mrs. Cantrell was not there, so Eszterhas talked to the Cantrell children and photographer Conway took 50 pictures. Eszterhas' story appeared as the lead article in the August 4, 1968, edition of the *Plain Dealer's* Sunday magazine.

The article emphasized the children's old, ill-fitting clothes and the poor condition of the Cantrell home. The Cantrell family was used in the story to sum up the impact of the bridge collapse on the lives of people in the Point Pleasant area. Even though Mrs. Cantrell had not been present during Eszterhas' visit to her home, he wrote: [74]

> "Margaret Cantrell will talk neither about what happened nor about how they are doing. She wears the same mask of non-expression she wore at the funeral. She is a proud woman. She says that after it happened, the people in town offered to help them out with money and they refused to take it."

In a ruling that Mrs. Cantrell should be allowed to collect the $60,000 awarded by a U.S. District Court jury, the Supreme Court said: [75]

> * * * the District Judge was clearly correct in believing that the evidence introduced at trial was sufficient to

[73] Mau v. Rio Grande Oil Co., 28 F.Supp. 845 (N.D.Cal.1939); Garner v. Triangle Publications, Inc., 97 F.Supp. 546 (S.D.N.Y.1951). But see Leopold v. Levin, 45 Ill.2d 434, 259 N.E.2d 250 (1970), where a fictional treatment of Nathan Leopold's participation in the famed 1924 murder of Bobby Franks was declared to be protected by the First Amendment despite the addition of fictional embellishments.

[74] 419 U.S. 245 at 248, 95 S.Ct. 465 at 468 (1974), quoting Eszterhas, "Legacy of the Silver Bridge," The Plain Dealer Sunday Magazine, Aug. 4, 1968, p. 32, col. 1.

[75] 419 U.S. 245, 253, 95 S.Ct. 465, 470–471 (1974).

support a jury finding that the respondents Joseph Eszterhas and Forest City Publishing Company had published knowing or reckless falsehoods about the Cantrells.   There was no dispute during the trial that Eszterhas, who did not testify, must have known that a number of the statements in the feature story were untrue.   In particular, his article plainly implied that Mrs. Cantrell had been present during his visit to her home and that Eszterhas had observed her "wear[ing] the same mask of non-expression she wore [at her husband's] funeral."   These were "calculated falsehoods," and the jury was plainly justified in finding that Eszterhas had portrayed the Cantrells in a false light through knowing or reckless untruth.

Bindrim v. Mitchell

The flip side of a journalist lapsing into fiction is a person who purports to write a novel with a story line which parallels too closely to actual persons and events.   In point here is the case of Bindrim v. Mitchell.   Although it was a libel action, the plaintiff— Paul Bindrim, Ph.D., a licensed clinical psychologist—could just as well have sued for invasion of privacy under the false light theory.   Dr. Bindrim used the so-called "Nude Marathon" in group therapy in order to help people shed their psychological inhibitions along with the removal of their clothes.   And then a novelist showed up and wanted to join his nude encounter group.[76]

Gwen Davis Mitchell had written a best-selling novel in 1969, and then set about writing a novel about women of the leisure class.   When she asked to register in Dr. Bindrim's therapy group, he told her she could not come into the group if she planned to write about it in a novel.   Bare-facedly, she said she would attend the sessions for therapeutic reasons and had no intention of writing about the group.   Dr. Bindrim then brought to her attention a written contract, which included this language: [77]

> "The participant agrees that he will not take photographs, write articles, or in any manner disclose who has attended the workshop or what has transpired.   If he fails to do so he releases all parties from this contract, but remains legally liable for damages sustained by the leaders and participants."

Ms. Mitchell reassured Dr. Bindrim that she would not write about the session, paid her money, signed the contract, and attended the nude marathon.   Two months later, she entered into a

[76] Bindrim v. Mitchell, 92 Cal.App.3d 61, 69, 155 Cal.Rptr. 29, 33 (1979), 5 Med.L.Rptr. 1113, certiorari denied 444 U.S. 984, 100 S.Ct. 490 (1979).

[77] 92 Cal.App.3d 61, 69, 155 Cal.Rptr. 29, 33 (1979).

contract with Doubleday publishers and was to receive $150,000 in advance royalties for her novel, which was subsequently published under the name "Touching." It depicted a nude encounter session in Southern California led by "Dr. Simon Herford." The fictional Dr. Herford was described in the novel as a *psychiatrist,* " 'a fat Santa Claus type with long white hair, white sideburns, a cherubic rosy face and rosy forearms.' "

Dr. Bindrim, on the other hand, a psychologist, was clean shaven and had short hair. He alleged that he had been libeled, because dialogue in the novel set in encounter groups included some sexually explicit language which tapes of actual sessions run by Dr. Bindrim did not contain. As a therapist, the psychologist did not use such insulting and vulgar language.[78]

Despite these differences—and perhaps in part because author Mitchell had actually attended Dr. Bindrim's therapy group—it was held that there were sufficient similarities between the fictional Dr. Herford and the real Dr. Bindrim for identification to have taken place. Also, the situation was not improved for the author because she had signed the contract not to write about the sessions. Doubleday and Ms. Mitchell were ordered to pay damages totaling $75,000. This case thus hangs out a warning against slipshod disguising of fictional characters who are based on real, live persons.[79]

SEC. 41. APPROPRIATION OF PLAINTIFF'S NAME OR LIKENESS

The appropriation or "taking" of some element of a person's personality for commercial or other advantage has been a source of many privacy lawsuits.

Often, careless use of a person's name or likeness will be the misstep which results in a privacy action. The first widely known privacy cases, Roberson v. Rochester Folding Box Co.[80] and Pavesich v. New England Life Ins. Co.,[81] both discussed earlier in this chapter, turned on taking a person's name or picture for advertising purposes.

The use of a name, by itself, is not enough to bring about a successful lawsuit. For example, a company could publish an advertisement for its breakfast cereal and say that the cereal "gave Fred Brown his tennis-playing energy." There are, of course, many Fred Browns in the nation. However, should the cereal

[78] 92 Cal.App.3d 61, 70, 75, 155 Cal.Rptr. 29, 34, 37 (1979).

[79] 92 Cal.App.3d 61, 82–83, 155 Cal.Rptr. 29, 41 (1979).

[80] 171 N.Y. 538, 64 N.E. 442 (1902).

[81] 122 Ga. 190, 50 S.E. 68 (1905).

company, without explicit permission, identify a *particular* individual—such as "Olympic High Hurdle Champion Fred Brown"—then Mr. Brown, the hurdler, would have an action for invasion of privacy. Thus a *name* can be used, as long as a person's *identity* is not somehow appropriated.

A good example of this point is a suit which was brought by a Joseph Angelo Maggio, who claimed that the use of a name— "Angelo Maggio"—in James Jones' best-selling novel, *From Here to Eternity,* invaded his privacy. The court ruled, however, that although the name was the same as that of the plaintiff, the plaintiff's *identity* had not been taken. The fictional "Angelo Maggio" was held not to be the same individual as Joseph Angelo Maggio.[82]

Persons who use the media should develop a kind of self-protective pessimism: it should always be assumed that if something could go wrong and result in a lawsuit, it might indeed go wrong. This is, of course, an almost paranoid approach, but it can help to avoid much grief. Take, for example, the case of Kerby v. Hal Roach Studios, Inc., where a simple failure to check as obvious a reference as a telephone directory led to a lost lawsuit. A publicity gimmick boosting one of the *Topper* movies involved the studio's sending out 100 perfumed letters to men in the Los Angeles area. These gushy letters were signed: [83]

> Fondly,
>
> Your ectoplasmic playmate,
>
> Marion Kerby.

Marion Kerby was the name of one of the characters—a female ghost—portrayed in the movie. Unfortunately for the Hal Roach Studios, there was a real-life Marion Kerby in Los Angeles, an actress and public speaker. She was the only one listed in the Los Angeles telephone directory. Miss Kerby, after being annoyed by numerous phone calls and a personal visit, sued for invasion of privacy, and ultimately collected.[84]

Sometimes the out-and-out use of a person's name or likeness *is* permissible in an advertisement—*if* a court decides that the use of the name or likeness is "incidental." Take Academy Award and Emmy Award-winning actress Shirley Booth, who was vacationing in Jamaica some years ago. A *Holiday* magazine photographer

---

[82] People on Complaint of Maggio v. Charles Scribner's Sons, 205 Misc. 818, 130 N.Y.S.2d 514 (1954). See also, Uproar Co. v. National Broadcasting Co., 8 F.Supp. 358 (D.C.Mass.1934), affirmed 81 F.2d 373 (1st Cir.1936); Nebb v. Bell Syndicate, 41 F.Supp. 929 (S.D.N.Y.1941).

[83] Kerby v. Hal Roach Studios, Inc., 53 Cal.App.2d 207, 127 P.2d 577, 578 (1942).

[84] Ibid., at 578. It should be noted that this case is also a good example of the privacy tort category called "false position in the public eye."

asked, and received, permission to take her picture, and that picture was later used in a *Holiday* feature story about Jamaica's Round Hill resort. Several months later, however, the same picture appeared in full-page promotional advertisements for *Holiday* in *Advertising Age* and *New Yorker* magazines. Beneath the picture of the actress were the words "Shirley Booth and Chapeau, from a recent issue of *Holiday*." [85]

Miss Booth sued *Holiday's* publisher, the Curtis Publishing Co., in New York, claiming invasion of privacy on the ground that *Holiday's* advertising use of that picture was impermissible. New York's privacy statute, after all, prohibits use of a person's name or likeness "for purposes of trade" unless the person involved has given consent.[86] Curtis Publishing responded that this sort of promotional advertising was needed to help magazine sales, thus supporting the public's interest in news.[87]

Miss Booth won $17,500 at the trial level, but that finding was reversed on appeal. Finding for the Curtis Publishing Co., Justice Charles D. Breitel termed *Holiday's* advertising use of the picture "incidental," and therefore not prohibited by New York's privacy statute.[88]

As Victor A. Kovner has pointed out, there has been a growing number of misappropriation claims founded on unauthorized use of a person's photograph or likeness, in articles and on covers of magazines and books. "[T]he general rule," Kovner said, "is that a picture reasonably related to an article or book on a matter of public interest will not be actionable." [89]

A case in point is Arrington v. New York Times, where the newspaper—without permission—ran a photograph of a young black man on the cover of its Sunday magazine section. The man's likeness was recognizable, but his name was not used. The newspaper argued that it had taken his picture to illustrate an article titled "The Black Middle Class: Making It," using his picture to illustrate upward mobility of blacks.

Use of Arrington's photo in those circumstances was held not to violate New York's Civil Rights Act, §§ 50–51, dealing with

[85] Booth v. Curtis Pub. Co., 15 A.D.2d 343, 223 N.Y.S.2d 737 (1962).

[86] Sections 50–51, New York Civil Rights Law, McKinney's Consolidated Laws, Ch. 6. See 15 A.D.2d 343, 223 N.Y.S.2d 737, at 739 (1962).

[87] Booth v. Curtis Pub. Co., 15 A.D.2d 343, 349, 223 N.Y.S.2d 737, 743–744 (1962).

[88] 11 N.Y.2d 907, 228 N.Y.S.2d 468, 182 N.E.2d 812 (1962). See also, University of Notre Dame du Lac v. Twentieth Century–Fox Film Corp., 22 A.D.2d 452, 256 N.Y.S.2d 301 (1965).

[89] Victor A. Kovner, "Privacy," in James C. Goodale, chairman, Communications Law 1987 Vol. I, p. 282; see also Vol. II (1993), pp. 832–865.

appropriation of a person's name or likeness for commercial purposes.[90]

On the other hand, unauthorized use of a black student's photograph on the cover of a book aimed at students hoping to go to college was ruled to be a violation of the New York Civil Rights Statute. Valerie Spellman was initially awarded $120,000 in compensatory damages and $250,000 in punitive damages, but an appellate court threw out all but $1,500 in compensatory damages. Note that she had given verbal consent to having her picture taken, but never gave the written consent required by the statute.[91]

The Arrington and Spellman cases are "mild" fact situations. Sexy photos or pictures which are published without permission are apt to lead to being sued and, perhaps, to being sued successfully.

The gasp-and-giggle genre of magazines continues to make problems for itself. Take, for example, the fact situations in Ali v. Playgirl. A frontally nude black boxer, his hands taped, was pictured—in something "between representational art and a cartoon"—sitting in the corner of a boxing ring. The features on the black male resembled former heavyweight boxing champion Muhammad Ali. Ali's name was not used, but the drawing was accompanied by some doggerel referring to the figure as "the Greatest." Ali, of course, made a career out of calling himself "the Greatest" and came to be so identified in the public mind. Ali was granted a preliminary injunction to halt further circulation of the February, 1978 issue of Playgirl which contained the offensive picture.[92]

Author-playwright A.E. Hotchner's attempt to write an intimate biography of American literary giant Ernest Hemingway led to a privacy suit under the New York statute. Hemingway had died in 1961, and his widow, Mary Hemingway, sued to enjoin Random House from publishing Hotchner's manuscript. Hotchner's biography covered the Nobel laureate's life from 1948, when Hemingway and Hotchner first met in a bar in Havana, Cuba, up to the time of Hemingway's death. New York Supreme Court Judge Harry B. Frank wrote of Hotchner's book: [93]

> The format and narrative style of the work make immediately apparent that it is intended as a subjective presentation from the vantage of the friendship, camaraderie, and personal experiences that the younger author shared with the literary giant. Their adventures, their

[90] (New York Supreme Court 1980), 5 Med.L.Rptr. 2581, 2584.

[91] (New York County Civil Court 1978), 3 Med.L.Rptr. 2407, 2408.

[92] Ali v. Playgirl, Inc., 447 F.Supp. 723 (S.D.N.Y.1978), 3 Med.L.Rptr. 2540, 2546.

[93] Estate of Hemingway v. Random House, Inc., 49 Misc.2d 726, 268 N.Y.S.2d 531, 534 (1966).

travels, their meetings are all set forth in detail and the portrait of Hemingway that emerges is shaded in terms of the unique self that he manifested and revealed in the course of his particular relationship with Hotchner.

Mary Hemingway's suit for an injunction complained, among other things, that the Hotchner manuscript violated her statutory right of privacy under Section 51 of the New York Civil Rights Law. Mrs. Hemingway was mentioned in various places throughout the book, and she charged that those references to her amounted to an invasion of her privacy. Judge Frank rejected Mrs. Hemingway's privacy contentions and allowed Random House to publish the book, saying that given the public's need to be informed, a biography of this sort outweighed privacy considerations.[94]

In other lawsuits dealing with "appropriation," it has been held that the taking or appropriation need not be for a financial gain in those jurisdictions where the common-law right of privacy is recognized. Just as long as someone's identity or likeness is used for some advantage, an action for invasion of privacy may succeed. An example of this occurred when a political party used a man's name as a candidate when he had not given his consent.[95] However, a number of states—including New York, Oklahoma, Virginia, Utah and California—have privacy statutes requiring proof of monetary advantage gained by the publication.[96] It has often been urged that everything published by the mass media is done "for purposes of trade." In defense of press freedom, however, courts have repeatedly held that just because a newspaper, magazine, or broadcasting station makes a profit does not mean that everything published is "for purposes of trade."[97]

Actress Ann–Margret brought an invasion of privacy action under Section 51 of the New York Civil Rights Law, asking damages from *High Society* magazine. She contended that including her photograph, nude to the waist, in a publication known as *High Society Celebrity Skin* amounted to use of her likeness, without her consent, for purposes of trade, and also invaded her right of publicity. Although he dismissed her suit, a sympathetic federal judge wrote:[98]

> The defendants * * * publish a magazine * * * which specializes in printing photographs of well-known women

[94] 49 Misc.2d 726, 268 N.Y.S.2d 531, 534 (1966).

[95] State ex rel. La Follette v. Hinkle, 131 Wash. 86, 229 P. 317 (1924).

[96] McKinney's N.Y. Civil Rights Law §§ 50–51; Virginia Code 1950, § 8–650; 15 Oklahoma Statutes Anno. § 839.1; Utah Code Ann. 1953, 76–4–8, and § 3344, California Civil Code.

[97] See, e.g., Time, Inc. v. Hill, 385 U.S. 374, 395, 87 S.Ct. 534, 546 (1967).

[98] Ann–Margret v. High Society Magazine, Inc., 498 F.Supp. 401, 403–404 (S.D.N.Y.1980), 6 Med.L.Rptr. 1774, 1775.

caught in the most revealing situations and positions that the defendants are able to obtain. In view of such content, the plaintiff has attempted to characterize Celebrity Skin as hard-core pornography. That description, however, by contemporary standards, appears inappropriate. A more apt description would be simply "tacky."

Judge Goettel's sympathies might have been with Ann–Margret, but he ruled that she could not collect for invasion of privacy. The actress, "who has occupied the fantasies of many moviegoers over the years," chose to perform unclad in one of her films; that is a matter of public interest.

The judge then expressed a non-authoritarian view of what constitutes newsworthiness, a view which seems to have lost favor in some other courts.[99] Judge Goettel wrote: [1]

> And while such an event may not appear overly important, the scope of what constitutes a newsworthy event has been afforded a broad definition and held to include even matters of "entertainment and amusement, concerning interesting phases of human activity in general." Paulsen v. Personality Posters, Inc., * * * 113 F.2d 806 at 809. As has been noted, it is not for the courts to decide what matters are of interest to the general public. See Goelet v. Confidential, Inc. * * * 5 A.D.2d 226 at 229–30, 171 N.Y.S.2d 223 at 226.

The Right of Publicity

As a general rule, the right of privacy dies with the individual. As tort scholar William L. Prosser noted, "there is no common law right of action for a publication concerning one who is already dead." However, as with most general rules, there are exceptions. A workable lawsuit for invasion of privacy may exist after a person's death, "according to the survival rules of the particular state." [2]

Similarly, there is a general rule that relatives have no right of action for an invasion of the privacy of a deceased person. A satirical national television show, "That Was the Week that Was," included this statement in a broadcast over the National Broadcasting Company network: "Mrs. Katherine Young of Syracuse, New York, who died at 99 leaving five sons, five daughters, 67 grandchil-

---

[99] See, e.g., Briscoe v. Reader's Digest Ass'n, 4 Cal.3d 529, 93 Cal.Rptr. 866, 483 P.2d 34 (1971); Virgil v. Time, Inc., 527 F.2d 1122 (9th Cir.1975).

[1] Ann–Margret v. High Society, 498 F.Supp. 401, 405 (S.D.N.Y.1980), 6 Med. L.Rptr. 1774, 1776.

[2] William L. Prosser, Handbook of the Law of Torts, 4th ed., St. Paul, Minn.: West Publishing Co., 1971, at p. 815, citing the highly confusing decision in Reed v. Real Detective Pub. Co., 63 Ariz. 294, 162 P.2d 133 (1945).

dren, 72 great grandchildren, and 73 great-great grandchildren—
gets our First Annual Booby Prize in the Birth Control Sweep-
stakes." Two of Mrs. Young's sons sued for invasion of privacy,
but failed because there is no relative's right to sue for invasion of
the privacy of a deceased person.[3]

But what about famous people? What about performers, even
those as wildly different as Bela Lugosi or Elvis Presley? Their
likenesses, their personas, are still valuable commercial properties
long after their deaths. For example, the legal ghost of the late
horror-film star Bela Lugosi came back in the courtrooms to haunt
Universal Pictures Company, although Universal eventually won its
case after a series of lengthy court battles. Lugosi, famed for his
portrayal of Count Dracula, died in 1956. In 1960, however,
Universal began to capitalize on his fame, entering into licensing
agreements to allow manufacturing of a number of items, including
shirts, cards, games, kites, bar accessories and masks—all with the
likeness of Count Dracula as played by Bela Lugosi.[4]

Lugosi's son and widow sued to recover profits made by Universal Pictures in its licensing arrangements, claiming a "right of
property or right of contract which, upon Bela Lugosi's death,
descended to his heirs." [5] Although the Lugosis won their suit at
the trial court level, the California Supreme Court ultimately voted
4–3 that the exclusive right to profit from his name and likeness
did not survive the actor's death. The California Supreme Court
said, in adopting California Court of Appeal Presiding Justice
Roth's opinion as its own:

> "Such ' * * * a right of value' to create a business,
> product or service of value is embraced in the law of
> privacy and is protectable during one's lifetime but it does
> not survive the death of Lugosi."

More has been heard, however, in the area of law involving
profiting from celebrities' names or likenesses after their deaths.
Courts in different regions of the nation give contradictory signals.
Cases involving the legendary Elvis Presley are illustrative:

> (1) In Factors, Etc. v. Pro Arts, Inc., the Court of Appeals for
> the Second Circuit held in 1978 that there *was* a property
> right in Presley's name and likeness which continued on
> for his heirs after Presley's death.[6]

[3] Young v. That Was the Week that Was, 423 F.2d 265 (6th Cir.1970); accord: see
Maritote v. Desilu Productions, Inc., 345 F.2d 418 (7th Cir.1965); Ravellette v.
Smith, 300 F.2d 854 (7th Cir.1962).

[4] Bela George Lugosi v. Universal Pictures, No. 877975, Memorandum Opinion,
Superior Court of California for the County of Los Angeles, published in full in
Performing Arts Review, Vol.3, No.1 (1972), pp. 19–62.

[5] Ibid., pp. 21, 27–28.

[6] Factors Etc., Inc. v. Pro Arts, Inc., 579 F.2d 215 (2d Cir.1978).

(2) On the other hand, the Court of Appeals for the Sixth Circuit concluded in Memphis Development Foundation v. Factors, Etc. that Presley's heirs could *not* assign exclusive rights to use Presley's name and likeness. Thus, a Memphis firm which was selling—without authorization—statuettes of Elvis was allowed to go right on doing just that.[7]

As Victor Kovner has written, there is great disagreement among a number of courts[8] on "survivability" of name and likeness. Any persons, however, can assign rights to commercially develop their names or images.

Beyond that, actors imitating the famed late comedians, Stan Laurel and Oliver Hardy lost a suit to heirs of Laurel and Hardy.[9] Similarly, the right of publicity was recognized in a case involving the late mystery author, Agatha Christie. In this case, heirs of Miss Christie failed to collect, however, because the account was so obviously a fiction.[10]

Other cases have held that there is a kind of a property right in a person's picture or likeness. Bubble-gum "trading cards" offer cases in point. Beginning with Judge Jerome D. Frank's 1953 decision in Haelan Laboratories, Inc., v. Topps Chewing Gum, several cases involved players' photographs. Judge Frank wrote of a "right of publicity" apart from a right of privacy which compensates a person for mental suffering because that person has received unwanted publicity. Judge Frank said: "We think that in addition to an independent right of privacy * * * a man has a right in the publicity value of his photograph, i.e., the right to grant the exclusive privilege of publishing his picture * * *. This right might be called a 'right of publicity.' "[11]

Consider "right of publicity" cases involving outfielder Ted Uhlaender and slugging first baseman Orlando Cepeda. Both sued for compensation for the unauthorized use of their names for

[7] Memphis Development Foundation v. Factors Etc., Inc., 616 F.2d 956 (6th Cir.1980).

[8] Kovner et al., 1993, Vol. I at p. 870, citing eight states with commercialization statutes providing for a property right to publicity surviving death: California, Florida, Georgia, Nebraska, Oklahoma, Utah, Virginia, and Tennessee. Tennessee adopted the "Personal Rights Protection Act of 1984"—protecting a property right in name, etc.—10 years after death, on June 5, 1984.

See also the remarkably useful LDRC [Libel Defense Resource Center] 50–State Survey 1984: Current Developments in Media Libel and Invasion of Privacy Law, ed. by Henry R. Kaufman. See state-by-state listings on court decisions and relevant statutes.

[9] Price v. Worldvision Enterprises, Inc., 455 F.Supp. 252 (S.D.N.Y.1978), affirmed 603 F.2d 214 (2d Cir.1979).

[10] Hicks v. Casablanca Records, 464 F.Supp. 426 (S.D.N.Y.1978).

[11] Haelan Laboratories, Inc. v. Topps Chewing Gum, Inc., 202 F.2d 866 (2d Cir.1953).

advertising or promotional purposes. In the *Uhlaender* case, a court decided that a public figure such as a baseball player has a property or proprietary interest in his public personality. This included his identity, as embodied in his name, likeness, or other personal characteristics. This property interest—in effect the "right of publicity" of which Judge Frank wrote in 1953 in the *Haelan Laboratories* case—was held in *Uhlaender* to be sufficient to support an injunction against unauthorized appropriation.[12]

As if celebrities such as Bela Lugosi, Elvis Presley, and baseball players didn't add enough flair to the law of privacy, what about Hugo "Human Cannonball" Zacchini? Zacchini was doing his thing at the Geauga County Fair in Burton, Ohio—being shot out of a cannon into a net 200 feet away. This high-calibre entertainer, however, took exception to being filmed by a free-lancer working for Scripps–Howard Broadcasting. Zacchini noted the free-lancer and asked him not to film the performance, which took place in a fenced area, surrounded by grandstands.

The television station broadcast the film of the 15–second flight by Zacchini, with the newscaster saying this:[13]

> "This * * * now * * * is the story of a *true spectator* sport * * * the sport of human cannonballing * * * in fact, the great *Zacchini* is about the only human cannonball around these days * * * just happens that, *where* he is, is the Great Geauga County Fair, in Burton * * * and believe me, although it's not a *long* act, it's a thriller * * * and you really need to see it *in person* to appreciate it. * * * "

Zacchini sued for infringement of his "right of publicity," claiming that he was engaged in the entertainment business, following after his father, who had invented this act. He claimed that the television station had "showed and commercialized the film of his act without his consent," and that this was "an unlawful appropriation of plaintiff's professional property."

The Ohio Supreme Court rejected Zacchini's claims, saying that a TV station has a privilege to report in its newscasts "matters of legitimate public interest which would otherwise be protected by an individual's right of publicity." The TV station could be held liable, but only when the actual intent of the station was to appropriate the benefit of the publicity for some non-privileged

[12] Uhlaender v. Henricksen, 316 F.Supp. 1277 (D.Minn.1970); Cepeda v. Swift & Co., 415 F.2d 1205 (8th Cir.1969).

[13] Zacchini v. Scripps–Howard Broadcasting Co., 433 U.S. 562, 97 S.Ct. 2849 (1977).

private use, or unless the actual intent was to injure the individual involved.[14]

The Supreme Court of the United States disagreed, saying that Zacchini was not contending that his act could not be reported as a newsworthy item.[15]

It is evident, and there is no claim here to the contrary, that petitioner's state-law right of publicity would not serve to prevent respondent from reporting the newsworthy facts about petitioner's act. Wherever the line in particular situations is to be drawn between media reports that are protected and those that are not, we are quite sure that the First and Fourteenth Amendments do not immunize the media when they broadcast a performer's entire act without his consent.

* * *

The broadcast of a film of petitioner's entire act poses a substantial threat to the economic value of that performance.

* * *

We conclude that although the State of Ohio may as a matter of its own law privilege the press in the circumstances of this case, the First and Fourteenth Amendments do not require it to do so.

A five-member majority of the Supreme Court then sent the Zacchini case back to the Ohio courts for a decision on whether the Human Cannonball should recover damages. In dissent, Justice Powell—who was joined by Justices Brennan and Marshall—wondered just what constituted "an entire act." [16] As attorney Floyd Abrams has asked—following Justice Powell's question—does the "entire act" include the fanfare and getting into the cannon, possibly lasting for several minutes? [17]

SEC. 42. DEFENSES: NEWSWORTHINESS, THE CONSTITUTION, AND CONSENT

Traditionally, the media's most useful defense against an invasion of privacy lawsuit has been the concept of "newsworthiness," although the "actual malice" rule may supersede it.

[14] Ibid., at 565–566, 97 S.Ct. at 2852.

[15] Ibid., at 574–579, 97 S.Ct. at 2857–2859.

[16] Ibid., at 58, 97 S.Ct. at 2860.

[17] Floyd Abrams, "The Press, Privacy, and the Constitution," New York Times Magazine, August 21, 1977, at pp. 11ff.

Newsworthiness, for many years, was a splendid defense in "private facts" invasion of privacy lawsuits. It is still a major factor, and in some cases may be *the* prime factor in a successful defense against an invasion of privacy lawsuit. However, a number of cases and the oft-quoted discussion of privacy in the Restatement of Torts, Second, suggest that this defense is undergoing erosion.[18]

Somewhat as Pontius Pilate asked "What is truth?," one may ask, "What is news?" No two journalists ever seem to be able to agree on a clear-cut definition of the term, but presumably, they know it when they see it. Courts, in numerous privacy cases, have tried with indifferent success to define news and newsworthiness. One court has even called news "that indefinable quality of information which arouses public attention."

Editors and reporters assert that "news is what we say it is" or that news is "whatever interests people." For years, many judges confronted with privacy cases tended to accept journalists' definitions.[19] Two cases discussed at some length in Section 39 of this chapter—Virgil v. Time, Inc. (1975)[20] and Campbell v. Seabury Press (1980)[21]—illustrate the tension between two ways of defining news. In *Virgil,* the Circuit Court judge evidently believed that courts (and juries) should set standards of newsworthiness. Using the Restatement's formulation, judges and juries are to work out a kind of "community standard" in a privacy case, determining whether the matter publicized would be "highly offensive to a reasonable person" and whether it is "of legitimate concern to the public."[22]

In *Campbell,* however, the judge viewed newsworthiness in a way far more favorable to the press. The court there said that the First Amendment commands a newsworthiness privilege. As Harvey Zuckman has pointed out, *Campbell* held that the information publicized need not be limited to news dissemination or commentary on public affairs. The privilege "extends to 'information concerning interesting phases of human activity and embraces all issues about which information is needed or appropriate for coping with the exigencies of their period.'"[23] And that can include

[18] Restatement, Second, Torts, § 652D.

[19] Sweenek v. Pathe News Inc., 16 F.Supp. 746, 747 (E.D.N.Y.1936); Sidis v. F–R Pub. Co., 113 F.2d 806, 809 (2d Cir.1940); Associated Press v. International News Service, 245 Fed. 244, 248 (2d Cir.1917), affirmed 248 U.S. 215, 39 S.Ct. 68 (1918); Jenkins v. Dell Pub. Co., 251 F.2d 447, 451 (3d Cir.1958).

[20] Virgil v. Time, Inc., 527 F.2d 1122 (9th Cir.1975).

[21] Campbell v. Seabury Press, 614 F.2d 395 (5th Cir.1980).

[22] Restatement, Second, Torts, § 652D.

[23] Zuckman, "The Right of Privacy and the Press," presentation at Southern Newspaper Publishers Association law symposium, Austin, Texas, October 13, 1980.

information about persons who have not sought out—or who have actively tried to avoid—publicity.

Often, of course, people are caught up in the news when they would much rather retain the anonymity of private persons. But when an event is classified as news, the courts have uniformly forbidden recovery for substantially accurate accounts of an event which is of public interest. A rather extreme case in point here involved the unfortunate John Jacova, who had bought a newspaper at a Miami Beach hotel's cigar counter. As Jacova innocently stood at the counter, police rushed into the hotel in a raid and mistook Jacova for a gambler. Jacova was taken into custody, but was released after he showed identification. Mr. Jacova was understandably annoyed later in the day to see himself on television being questioned by policemen. He sued the television stations for invasion of privacy. He was not allowed to collect, however, because the court ruled that Jacova had become an "unwilling actor" in a news event.[24]

Mrs. Lillian Jones—much against her will—originated the "unwilling public figure" rule in a famous privacy case decided in 1929. Her husband was stabbed to death on a Louisville street in her presence. The Louisville *Herald-Post* published a picture of Mrs. Jones, and quoted her as saying of her husband's attackers: "I would have killed them." The court expressed sympathy and acknowledged the existence of a right to privacy, but added:[25]

> There are times, however, when one, whether willing or not, becomes an actor in an occurrence of public or general interest. When this takes place, he emerges from his seclusion and it is not an invasion of his right to privacy to publish his photograph with an account of such occurrence.

Even in the early 1980s there appeared to be an "involuntary public figure" category in privacy law. But that appears to fly in the face of developments in the law of libel. As discussed in Chapter 5, Section 28, the "involuntary public figure" category has been virtually killed off in libel law by the Supreme Court of the United States.[26] Will the Supreme Court shove the libel rule into the law of privacy, further weakening newsworthiness as a defense? Developments in this area need to be watched carefully by journalists and by their attorneys.

[24] Jacova v. Southern Radio and Television Co., 83 So.2d 34 (Fla.1955); see, also, Hubbard v. Journal Pub. Co., 69 N.M. 473, 368 P.2d 147 (1962); Elmhurst v. Pearson, 80 U.S.App.D.C. 372, 153 F.2d 467 (1946).

[25] Jones v. Herald Post Co., 230 Ky. 227, 18 S.W.2d 972 (1929).

[26] See also Time, Inc. v. Firestone, 424 U.S. 448, 96 S.Ct. 958 (1976), and Wolston v. Reader's Digest Ass'n, Inc., 443 U.S. 157, 99 S.Ct. 2701 (1979).

What of people who seek fame, public office, or otherwise *willingly* bring themselves to public notice? Public figures have been held to have given up, to some extent, their right to be "let alone." Persons who have sought publicity—actors, explorers, or politicians to give a few examples—have made themselves "news" and have parted with some of their privacy. In one case, a suit by a former husband of movie star Janet Leigh was unsuccessful despite his protestations that he had done everything he could to avoid publicity. Her fame rubbed off on him.[27]

Even so, when the media go "too far," celebrities can bring successful privacy lawsuits. The taking of a name of a public figure, for example, to advertise a commercial product without his consent would be actionable. Also, even newsworthy public figures can collect damages when fictionalized statements are published about them. Some areas of life are sufficiently personal and private that the media may intrude only at their peril. Private sexual relationships, homes, bank accounts, and private letters of an individual would all seem to be in a danger zone for the media.[28]

Unwilling subjects of photographs or motion pictures have caused considerable activity in the law of privacy. Consider the case of Frank Man, a professional musician who made the scene at the Woodstock Festival in Bethel, N.Y., in August of 1969. At someone's request, Man clambered onto the stage and played "Mess Call" on his flugelhorn to an audience of movie cameras and 400,000 people. Subsequently, Warner Bros., Inc. produced and exhibited a movie under the title of "Woodstock." Man claimed that the producers and distributors of the film included his performance without his consent, and brought suit in New York against Warner Bros.

A United States District Court said:[29]

The film depicts, without the addition of any fictional material, actual events which happened at the festival. Nothing is staged and nothing is false. * * *

There can be no question that the Woodstock festival was and is a matter of valid public interest.

Man argued that a movie depicting Woodstock could no longer be treated as news because of the lapse of time. The court replied that "the bizarre happenings of the festival were not mere fleeting news but sensational events of deep and lasting public interest."

[27] Carlisle v. Fawcett Publications, Inc., 201 Cal.App.2d 733, 20 Cal.Rptr. 405 (1962).

[28] See Garner v. Triangle Publications, 97 F.Supp. 546 (S.D.N.Y.1951); Bazemore v. Savannah Hospital, 171 Ga. 257, 155 S.E. 194 (1930); Baker v. Libbie, 210 Mass. 599, 97 N.E. 109 (1912).

[29] Man v. Warner Bros. Inc., 317 F.Supp. 50, 53 (S.D.N.Y.1970).

The court concluded that Frank Man, by his own volition had placed himself in the spotlight at a sensational event. He had made himself newsworthy, and thus deprived himself of any right to collect for invasion of privacy.[30]

It should not, however, be inferred that all factual reports of current events have been—or will be—held absolutely privileged. Film Producer Wiseman produced a film—"The Titicut Follies"—which showed conditions in a mental hospital, with individuals identifiable. The film showed naked inmates, forced feeding, masturbation and sadism, and the court concluded that Wiseman's film had—by identifying individuals—gone beyond the consent which mental hospital authorities had given him to make the film. The film was taken out of commercial distribution, but was not destroyed. The court ruled that the film was of educational value, and that it could be shown to special audiences such as groups of social workers, or others who might be moved to work toward improving conditions in mental hospitals.[31]

The protection of newsworthiness may vanish suddenly if a careless or misleading caption is placed on a picture. Consider the case of Holmes v. Curtis Publishing Company.

"MAFIA: SHADOW OF EVIL ON AN ISLAND IN THE SUN" screamed the headline on a feature story in the February 25, 1967 issue of the *Saturday Evening Post*. Published along with the article was a picture of James Holmes and four other persons at a gambling table, evidently playing blackjack. This picture was captioned, "High–Rollers at Monte Carlo have dropped as much as $20,000 in a single night. The U.S. Department of Justice estimates that the Casino grosses $20 million a year, and that one-third is skimmed off for American Mafia 'families.'"

Holmes objected to publication of this article, and sued for libel and invasion of privacy, arguing that the picture and caption had placed him in a false light. Holmes was not mentioned by name in the article, but he was, however, the focal point of the photograph. A United States district court in South Carolina noted that the article dealt with subjects of great public interest—organized crime, the growth of tourism in the Bahama Islands, and legalized gambling.

The court refused to grant the Curtis Publishing Company's motions that the libel and privacy lawsuits by Holmes could not stand because of precedents such as New York Times Co. v.

---

[30] Ibid.

[31] Commonwealth v. Wiseman, 356 Mass. 251, 249 N.E.2d 610 (1969). In 1991, more general showings were allowed. See, also Daily Times Democrat v. Graham, 276 Ala. 380, 162 So.2d 474 (1964), where a woman collected for invasion of privacy after a newspaper used her identifiable picture as she emerged from a "fun house" where a jet of air blew her dress above her waist.

Sullivan [32] and Time, Inc. v. Hill.[33] Instead, the court declared that the libel and privacy issues would have to go to trial: [34]

> Certainly defendant's caption is reasonably capable of amounting to a defamation, for one identified as a high-stakes gambler of having a connection with the Mafia would certainly be injured in his business, occupation, and/or reputation.

> As to plaintiff's action for privacy, there appears no question that if it were not for defendant's caption beneath plaintiff's photograph, this court would be justified in dismissing plaintiff's invasion of privacy cause of action. But such is not the case. Conflicting inferences also arise from the record as it stands today which preclude disposition of this cause of action summarily.

Time, Inc. v. Hill and "Actual Malice"

The law of privacy is much like a jigsaw puzzle with some pieces missing: it is sometimes hard to discern a meaningful pattern. Just as the defense of newsworthiness—discussed in the preceding section—is in flux, the Constitution-based defense growing out of the 1967 Supreme Court decision in Time, Inc. v. Hill also is undergoing change.

When the Supreme Court weighed the right to privacy against the First Amendment freedom to publish, the freedom to publish was given preference. Time, Inc. v. Hill was noteworthy in one respect because the losing attorney was Richard Milhous Nixon, more recently known as sometime President of the United States. This decision is important because it represents the first time that the Supreme Court decided a privacy case dealing with the mass media.

In 1952, the James J. Hill family was minding its own business, living in the suburban Philadelphia town of Whitemarsh. On September 11, 1952, however, the Hills' anonymity was taken away from them by three escaped prisoners. The convicts held Mr. and Mrs. Hill and their five children hostage in their own home for 19 hours. The family was not harmed, but the Hills—much against their wishes—were in the news.[35] Their story became even more sensational when two of the three convicts who had held them hostage were killed in a shoot-out with police.[36]

[32] 376 U.S. 254, 84 S.Ct. 710 (1964).

[33] 385 U.S. 374, 87 S.Ct. 534 (1967).

[34] Holmes v. Curtis Pub. Co., 303 F.Supp. 522, 527 (D.S.C.1969).

[35] 385 U.S. 374, 377, 87 S.Ct. 534, 536 (1967).

[36] Pember, Privacy and the Press, p. 210.

In 1953, Random House published Joseph Hayes' novel, The Desperate Hours, a story about a family which was taken hostage by escaped convicts. The novel was later made into a successful play and, subsequently, a motion picture.

The publicity which led the Hills to sue for invasion of their privacy was an article published in 1955 by *Life* magazine. The article, titled "True Crime Inspires Tense Play," described the "true crime" suffered by the James Hill family of Whitemarsh, Pennsylvania.[37]

Life's pages of photographs included actors' depiction of the son being "roughed up" by one of the escaped convicts. This picture was captioned "brutish convict." Also, a picture titled "daring daughter" showed the daughter biting the hand of a convict, trying to make him drop the gun.[38]

The Joseph Hayes novel and play, however, did not altogether match up with *Life's* assertion that Hayes' writings were based on the ordeal of the Hill family. For one thing, Hayes' family was named "Hilliard," not Hill. Also, the Hills had not been harmed by the convicts in any way, while in the Hayes novel and play the father and son were beaten and the daughter was "subjected to a verbal sexual insult."

Hill sued for invasion of privacy under the privacy sections of New York's Civil Rights Law, which provides that a person whose name or picture was so used "for purposes of trade" without his consent could "sue and recover damages" for any injuries sustained by reason of such use.[39]

The Hills sought damages on grounds that the *Life* article "was intended to, and did, give the impression that the play mirrored the Hill family's experience, which, to the knowledge of defendant * * * was false and untrue." In its defense, Time, Inc., argued that "the subject of the article was 'a subject of legitimate news interest,' 'a subject of general interest and of value and concern to the public' at the time of publication, and that it was 'published in good faith without any malice whatsoever * * *.' "[40]

The trial court jury awarded the Hills $50,000 compensatory and $25,000 punitive damages. On appeal, the Appellate Division of the Supreme Court of New York ordered a new trial on the question of damages, but upheld the jury's finding that *Life* maga-

---

[37] Life, Feb. 28, 1955.

[38] 385 U.S. 374, 377, 87 S.Ct. 534, 536–537 (1967).

[39] Sections 50–51, New York Civil Rights Law, McKinney's Consolidated Laws, Ch. 6.

[40] 385 U.S. 374, 378, 87 S.Ct. 534, 537 (1967).

zine had invaded the Hill's privacy. The Appellate Division bore down hard on the issue of fictionalization.[41]

At the new trial on the issue of damages, a jury was waived and the court awarded $30,000 compensatory damages with no punitive damages.

When the *Hill* case reached the Supreme Court, issues of freedom of speech and press raised in the appeal by Time, Inc. were considered. Justice Brennan's majority opinion first dealt with the issue of whether truth could be a defense to a charge of invasion of privacy. Quoting a recent New York Court of Appeals decision, Brennan asserted it was "crystal clear" in construing the New York Civil Rights Statute, "that truth is a complete defense in actions under the statute based upon reports of newsworthy people or event." [42] Brennan added, "Constitutional questions which might arise if truth were not a defense are therefore no concern." [43]

Justice Brennan then wrestled with the issue of fictionalization. He noted that James Hill was a newsworthy person " 'substantially without a right to privacy' insofar as his hostage experience was involved." Hill, however, was entitled to sue to the extent that *Life* magazine "fictionalized" and "exploited for the defendant's commercial benefit." Brennan then turned to a libel case, New York Times v. Sullivan, for guidance.[44]

> Material and substantial falsification is the test. However, it is not clear whether proof of knowledge of the falsity or that the article was prepared with reckless disregard for the truth is also required. In New York Times Co. v. Sullivan * * * we held that the Constitution delimits a State's power to award damages for libel in actions brought by public officials against critics of their official conduct. Factual error, content defamatory of official reputation, or both, are insufficient to an award of damages for false statements unless actual malice—knowledge that the statements are false or in reckless disregard of the truth—is alleged and proved. * * *

> * * *

> We hold that the Constitutional protections for speech and press precluded the application of the New York statute to redress false reports of matters of public interest

[41] 385 U.S. 374, 379, 87 S.Ct. 534, 537 (1967), quoting Hill v. Hayes, 18 A.D.2d 485, 489, 240 N.Y.S.2d 286, 290 (1963).

[42] At the outset of his opinion, Justice Brennan relied heavily upon Spahn v. Julian Messner, Inc., 18 N.Y.2d 324, 274 N.Y.S.2d 877, 221 N.E.2d 543 (1966).

[43] 385 U.S. 374, 383–384, 87 S.Ct. 534, 539–540 (1967).

[44] New York Times Co. v. Sullivan, 376 U.S. 254, 84 S.Ct. 710 (1964), used in Time, Inc. v. Hill, 385 U.S. 374, 386–388, 87 S.Ct. 534, 541–542 (1967).

in the absence of proof that the defendant published the report with knowledge of its falsity or in reckless disregard of the truth.

It should be emphasized that Justice Brennan's opinion in Time v. Hill has not made truth an entirely dependable defense against a lawsuit for invasion of privacy. For one thing, the Supreme Court's adoption of the malice rule from New York Times v. Sullivan applies only to those privacy cases involving falsity. Furthermore, the Supreme Court was badly split in Time v. Hill; a five-Justice majority did vote in favor of *Life* magazine, but only two justices—Potter Stewart and Byron White—agreed with Brennan's use of the "Sullivan rule."

Brennan appeared to prize press freedom's benefits to society more than the individual's right to privacy.[45] If incidental, nonmalicious error crept into a story, that was part of the risk of freedom, for which a publication should not be held responsible. Justice Brennan wrote: [46]

* * *

Erroneous statement is no less inevitable in * * * [a case such as discussion of a new play] than in the case of comment upon public affairs, and in both, if innocent or merely negligent, * * * it must be protected if the freedoms of expression are to have the "breathing space" that they "need * * * to survive."

The "breathing space" mentioned by Justice Brennan—a phrase borrowed from New York Times v. Sullivan—indicated that the Court was giving the press a healthy "benefit of the doubt." Press freedom, Brennan declared, is essential to "the maintenance of our political system and an open society." Yet this freedom, he argued, could be dangerously invaded by lawsuits for libel or invasion of privacy.[47]

"We have no doubt," Brennan wrote, "that the subject of the *Life* article, the opening of a new play linked to an actual incident, is a matter of public interest. 'The line between the informing and the entertaining is too elusive for the protection of * * * [freedom of the press].' " [48]

[45] See the dissent by Mr. Justice Abe Fortas, which was joined by Chief Justice Earl Warren and by Justice Tom C. Clark, 385 U.S. 374, 411, 416, 87 S.Ct. 534, 554, 556 (1967).

[46] 385 U.S. 374, 388–389, 87 S.Ct. 534, 542–543 (1967).

[47] 385 U.S. 374, 389, 87 S.Ct. 534, 543 (1967).

[48] 385 U.S. 374, 388, 87 S.Ct. 534, 542 (1967), quoting Winters v. New York, 333 U.S. 507, 510, 68 S.Ct. 665, 667 (1948).

Time, Inc. v. Hill thus erected an important constitutional shield in false-light privacy cases. If persons caught up in the news as "involuntary public figures" are to recover damages for falsity, they must prove "actual malice" as borrowed from the lore of libel: publication of knowing falsehoods or with reckless disregard for whether a statement was false or not. As noted earlier, the developments in the law of libel have virtually annihilated the "involuntary public person" category, and the question remains whether the "public interest" consideration in privacy law will continue to be a worthwhile defense.[49]

Cantrell v. Forest City Pub. Co., discussed in Section 40 of this chapter, allowed the widow of the victim of the famed collapse of the Point Pleasant Bridge to collect $60,000. The jury found fictionalization amounting to "actual malice" in the sense of a knowing falsehood. However, as noted by Sallie Martin Sharp in a 1981 study, the *Cantrell* majority " * * * invited challenges to the [Time v.] *Hill* opinion when it said:"[50]

> "[T]his case presents no occasion to consider whether a State may constitutionally apply a more relaxed standard of liability for a publisher or broadcaster for false statements injurious to a private person under a false-light theory of invasion of privacy or whether the constitutional standard announced in Time, Inc. v. Hill applies to all false-light cases."

Dr. Sharp found that the Constitution-based defenses growing out of Time, Inc. v. Hill have become increasingly important. Since *Hill* was decided in 1967, she wrote, lower federal and state courts began considering private facts in terms of First Amendment limits * * * "even though the *Hill* case involved false light invasion of privacy."[51]

Beyond that, Victor A. Kovner has asked whether the important libel case of Gertz v. Robert Welch, Inc.[52]—discussed at length in Section 28 of Chapter 5—whether "actual malice's" application in false light privacy cases is limited to public officials and "public figures." Courts of eight states take this position.[53]

---

[49] See also Time, Inc. v. Firestone, 424 U.S. 448, 96 S.Ct. 958 (1976), and Wolston v. Reader's Digest Ass'n, Inc., 443 U.S. 157, 99 S.Ct. 2701 (1979).

[50] Sallie Martin Sharp, "The Evolution of the Invasion of Privacy Tort and Its Newsworthiness Limitations," Ph.D. dissertation, The University of Texas at Austin, 1981. See also Don R. Pember and Dwight L. Teeter, Jr., "Privacy and the Press Since Time, Inc. v. Hill, 50 Washington Law Review (1974) at p. 77.

[51] Sharp, Ibid.

[52] 418 U.S. 323, 94 S.Ct. 2997 (1974).

[53] Kovner, et al. "Recent Developments in Intrusion, Private Facts, False Light, and Commercialization Claims," in Goodale (1993), op. cit., Vol. I at p. 870.

In Wood v. Hustler, one of the frequent lawsuits against that magazine, the Fifth Circuit Court of Appeals took what may be the predominating approach to applying a constitutional standard in a false-light privacy suit by a private person.   (Wood v. Hustler involved Hustler Magazine's publishing a stolen nude photo of a woman after carelessly accepting a faked consent form.)   Circuit Judge Jolly wrote for the court: [54]

> On the particular issue of standard of care under false light [privacy law], the Restatement (Second) of Torts § 652E Caveat & Comments d (1976) leaves open the possibility that liability may be based on a showing of negligence as to truth or falsity.   "If Time v. Hill is modified along the lines of Gertz v. Robert Welch, then the reckless-disregard rule would apparently apply if the plaintiff is a public official or public figure and the negligence rule will apply to other plaintiffs."   Restatement (Second) of Torts § 652E comment d at 399.

Defenses: Consent

In addition to *newsworthiness,* another important defense to a lawsuit for invasion of privacy is *consent.* Logically enough, if a person has consented to have his privacy invaded, he should not be allowed to sue for the invasion. As Warren and Brandeis wrote in their 1890 *Harvard Law Review* article, "The right to privacy ceases upon the publication of the facts by the individual or with his consent." [55]

The defense of consent, however, poses some difficulties.   To make this defense stand up, it must be *pleaded* and *proved* by the defendant.   An important rule here is that the *consent* must be as broad as the invasion.

A young man had consented to have his picture taken in the doorway of a shop, supposedly discussing the World Series.   But the youth was understandably chagrined when *Front Page Detective* used this photograph to illustrate a story titled "Gang Boy."   The Supreme Court of New York allowed the young man to recover damages, holding that consent to one thing is not consent to another.   In other words, when a photograph is used for a purpose not intended by the person who consented, that person may be able to collect damages for invasion of privacy.[56]

In the case of Russell v. Marboro Books, a professional model was held to have a suit for invasion of privacy despite the fact that

[54] Wood v. Hustler Magazine, Inc., 736 F.2d 1084 at 1091 (5th Cir.1984), 10 Med.L.Rptr. 2113 at 2117–2118. This case is discussed, below, at pp. 314–315.

[55] Warren and Brandeis, op. cit., p. 218.

[56] Metzger v. Dell Pub. Co., 207 Misc. 182, 136 N.Y.S.2d 888 (1955).

she had signed a release. (In the states which have privacy statutes—California, New York, Oklahoma, Utah, Wisconsin and Virginia—prior consent in writing is required before a person's name or picture can be used in advertising or "for purposes of trade.") Miss Russell, at a picture-taking session had signed a printed release form: [57]

Model Release

The undersigned hereby irrevocably consents to the unrestricted use by * * * [photographer's name], advertisers, customers, successors and assigns of my name, portrait, or picture, for advertising purposes or purposes of trade, and I waive the right to inspect or approve such completed portraits, pictures or advertising matter used in connection therewith * * *.

Miss Russell maintained that her job as a model involved portraying an "intelligent, refined, well-bred, pulchritudinous, ideal young wife and mother in artistic settings and socially approved situations." Her understanding was that the picture was to depict a wife in bed with her "husband"—also a model—in bed beside her, reading. Marboro books did use the pictures in an advertisement, with the caption "For People Who Take Their Reading Seriously." Thus far, there was no invasion of privacy to which Miss Russell had not consented.

Marboro Books, however, sold the photograph to Springs Mills, Inc., a manufacturer of bed sheets which enjoyed a reputation for publishing spicy ads. The photo was retouched so that the title of the book Miss Russell was reading appeared to be *Clothes Make the Man,* a book which had been banned as pornographic. The advertisement suggested that the book should be consulted for suitable captions, and also suggested captions such as "Lost Weekend" and "Lost Between the Covers." The court held that Miss Russell had an action for invasion of privacy despite the unlimited release that she had signed. Such a release, the court reasoned, would not stand up "if the picture were altered sufficiently in situation, emphasis, background, or context * * * liability would accrue where the content of the picture had been so changed that it is substantially unlike the original." [58]

Even if a signed release is in one's possession, it would be well to make sure that the release is still valid. In a Louisiana case, a man had taken a body-building course in a health studio. This man had agreed to have "before" and "after" photos taken of his physique, showing the plaintiff's body in trunks. Ten years later,

[57] Russell v. Marboro Books, 18 Misc.2d 166, 183 N.Y.S.2d 8 (1959).
[58] Ibid.

the health studio used the pictures in an ad.   The court held that privacy had been invaded.[59]

If the topic of consent in media law does not make for wary publishers, it should.   Hustler magazine was hoaxed by a snapshot and an un-neighborly neighbor, and lost a $150,000 invasion-of-privacy case as a result.   Billy and LaJuan Wood, husband and wife, went for a skinny-dip swim at a secluded spot at a wilderness area in a state park.   After swimming, they playfully took several photos of each other in the nude.   Billy had the film developed by a business using a mechanical developing process, and they treated the snapshots as private, not showing them to others and keeping them out of sight in a drawer in their bedroom.

One Steve Simpson, a neighbor living in the other side of the Woods' duplex, broke into the Woods' home and stole some of the photos.   Simpson and Kelly Rhoades, who was then his wife, submitted the nude photo of LaJuan to Hustler magazine for publication in its "Beaver Hunt" section.

Simpson and Rhoades filled out a consent form that requested personal information.   They gave some true information about LaJuan Wood (her identity, and her hobby of collecting arrowheads), but also gave some false information such as LaJuan's age and a lurid sex fantasy attributed to her.   Kelley Rhoades forged LaJuan's signature and the photograph and consent form were mailed to Hustler in California.   The faked consent form did not list a phone number but gave Kelley Rhoades' address as the place where Hustler was to send the $50 it was to pay for each photo used in the "Beaver Hunt" section.[60]

After Hustler selected LaJuan's photo, Kelley Rhoades received and answered a mailgram addressed to LaJuan and phoned Hustler.   A Hustler staff member then had about a two-minute conversation with Rhoades; that was the extent of the magazine's checking for consent.[61]

Hustler magazine urged that the action should fail under the one-year statute of limitations applying to defamation in Texas. The Court of Appeals, however, chose to keep the privacy action alive under a two-year statute of limitations.[62]   Hustler further

[59] McAndrews v. Roy, 131 So.2d 256 (La.App.1961).

[60] Wood v. Hustler Magazine, Inc., 736 F.2d 1084, 1085–1086 (5th Cir.1984), 10 Med.L.Rptr. 2113–2114.

[61] 736 F.2d 1084, 1086 (5th Cir.1984), 10 Med.L.Rptr. 2113, 2114.

[62] 736 F.2d 1084, 1085 (5th Cir.1984), 10 Med.L.Rptr. 2113, 2114. The Woods had sued for both libel and invasion of privacy; the libel action was ruled out because of the one-year statute of limitations on defamation, Tex.Civ.Stat.Ann.Art. 5524; however, the two-year limitations period of Art. 5526 was held to apply to false-light privacy cases. Billy Woods' invasion of privacy action was disallowed because the publication of the photo did not invade his privacy.

argued that it should not be held liable for placing LaJuan Wood in
a false light because it did not publish in reckless disregard of the
truth, having no serious doubts about the falsity of the consent
form.[63] However, the U.S. Court of Appeals for the Fifth Circuit
held that since LaJuan Wood was a private figure [64] who need prove
only negligent behavior in order to collect damages. In upholding
the trial court damage award to her of $150,000, the Court of
Appeals said: [65]

> Hustler carelessly administered a slipshod procedure
> that allowed LaJuan be placed in a false light in the pages
> of Hustler Magazine. The nature of material published in
> the Beaver Hunt section would obviously warn a reason-
> ably prudent editor or publisher of the potential for defa-
> mation or privacy invasion if a consent form was forged.
> The wanton and debauched sexual fantasies and the inti-
> mate photos of nude models were of such a nature that
> great care was required in verifying the model's consent.

Cher v. Forum International

Consider the famed entertainer "Cher." Evidently she is
determined to control as much of her performer's image as possible.
She willingly consented to and taped an interview with radio talk
show host Fred Robbins, a writer who sells celebrity interviews to
magazines. Cher said she had consented to the interview believing
she had an agreement that the resulting article was to appear in
US magazine. *US* did not run the interview, but instead returned
it to Robbins with a "kill" fee. Robbins then sold the interview to
the sensational tabloid *Star* and to a pocket-sized magazine called
Forum. That publication was owned by Forum International, of
which Penthouse International owned 80% of the stock.[66]

Cher sued, bringing a legal action which had—among other
things—aspects of the "false light" branch of privacy law. She did
not claim that the interview was defamatory, nor did she complain
that private facts had been published without her consent. Instead, her complaint charged breach of contract, unfair competition,
and *misappropriation* of her name and likeness and of her *right to
publicity*. Beyond the legal labels, Cher was complaining about the
appearance she consented to for a much "tamer" kind of magazine,

---

[63] 736 F.2d 1084, 1089 (5th Cir.1984), 10 Med.L.Rptr. 2113, 2116.

[64] See discussion of public figures in defamation law, Chapter 5, Sections 27 and
28.

[65] 736 F.2d 1084, 1092 (5th Cir.1984), 10 Med.L.Rptr. 2113, 2119.

[66] Cher v. Forum International, Ltd., et al., 692 F.2d 634, 638 (9th Cir.1982), 8
Med.L.Rptr. 2484, 2485.

US, only to have it appear in the juicy tabloid *Star* and the generally salacious *Forum,* creating misleading impressions.[67]

Cher accused *The Star* of having falsely represented that she had given that publication an exclusive interview, which would be degrading to her as a celebrity, given the nature of that tabloid. The Court of Appeals held, however, that *The Star's* promotional claim of an "Exclusive Interview" did not constitute knowing or reckless falsity under the doctrine of Time, Inc. v. Hill.[68] Therefore, the judgment against *The Star* was reversed.[69]

Forum magazine, however, after identifying Fred Robbins as the interviewer, made it appear that *Forum* itself was the poser of the questions put to Cher. Cher complained through her attorneys that this created the false impression that she had given an interview directly to *Forum.* She argued that this exploited her celebrity value by implying that she endorsed *Forum.* Her name and likeness were used in promotional subscription "tear out" ads: "There are certain things that Cher won't tell *People* and would never tell *US.* She tells *Forum.*"[70]

The Court of Appeals ruled that publishers can use promotional ads or literature so long as there is no false claim that a celebrity endorsed the publication involved. Court of Appeals Judge Goodwin wrote, " * * * [T]he advertising staff [of Forum] engaged in the kind of knowing falsity that strips away the protection of the First Amendment."[71] The Court of Appeals cut the original damage award to Cher from the trial court's figure of more than $600,000 to roughly $200,000.[72]

When a defendant does not have consent and does invade someone's privacy, good intentions are not a defense. It may be pleaded that the defendant honestly believed that he had consent, but this can do no more than to mitigate punitive damages. Some of the consequences of a publication's not getting a clear and specific consent from persons whose pictures were used in a magazine article may be seen in the case of Raible v. Newsweek. According to Eugene L. Raible, a Newsweek photographer visited his home in 1969, and asked to take a picture of Mr. Raible and his children in their yard for use in "a patriotic article." Then, the October 6, 1969, issue of that magazine featured an article which

---

[67] 692 F.2d 634, 638 (9th Cir.1982), 8 Med.L.Rptr. 2484, 2485.

[68] 385 U.S. 374, 87 S.Ct. 534 (1967).

[69] 692 F.2d 634, 638 (9th Cir.1982), 8 Med.L.Rptr. 2484, 2486.

[70] Ibid. The U.S. Court of Appeals, 9th Circuit, found that Robbins did not participate in the publishing, advertising, or marketing of the articles, and the trial court judgment against him was vacated. Also, it was stipulated at the trial court level that there was no contract between Cher and Robbins.

[71] 692 F.2d 634, 640 (9th Cir.1982), 8 Med.L.Rptr. 2484, 2487.

[72] Ibid.; see also News Media & The Law, Sept./Oct. 1983, pp.17–18.

was headlined on the cover, "The Troubled American—A Special Report on the White Majority." [73] Newsweek did use Mr. Raible's picture (with his children cropped out of it); he was wearing an open sport shirt and standing next to a large American flag mounted on a pole on his lawn. The article ran for many pages thereafter, with such marginal headlines as "You'd better watch out, the common man is standing up," and "Many think the blacks live by their own set of rules." [74] Mr. Raible sued for libel and for invasion of privacy.

Although Raible's name was not used in the story, the court said it was readily understandable that his friends and neighbors in Wilkinsburg, Pa., might consider him to be typical of the "square Americans" discussed in the article. Raible argued that his association with the article meant that he was being portrayed as a " * * * typical 'Troubled American,' a person considered 'angry, uncultured, crude, violence prone, hostile to both rich and poor, and racially prejudiced.' " [75]

District Judge William W. Knox granted *Newsweek* a summary judgment, thus dismissing Mr. Raible's libel claims. Judge Knox declared that since the article indicated that the views expressed are those of the white majority of the United States—of whom Mr. Raible was one—"then we would have to conclude that the article, if libelous, libels more than half of the people in the United States and not plaintiff in particular." [76]

Judge Knox declared, however, that Mr. Raible's invasion of privacy lawsuit appeared to stand on firmer ground. Directing that Raible's privacy lawsuit go to trial, Judge Knox wrote: [77]

> It is true that if plaintiff [Raible] consented to the use of his photograph in connection with *this article,* he would have waived his right of action for invasion of privacy. However, it would appear to the court that the burden of proof is upon the defendant to show just what plaintiff consented to and the varying inferences from this testimony will have to be resolved by the trier of facts.

SEC. 43. DEFENSES: LIMITATIONS AND PROBLEMS

Privacy is a relatively new region of law which has had much unplanned growth. Complexities and confusions affect defenses to privacy lawsuits.

[73] Raible v. Newsweek, Inc., 341 F.Supp. 804, 806, 809 (W.D.Pa.1972).

[74] Ibid., p. 805.

[75] Ibid., p. 806. See also DeSalvo v. Twentieth Century–Fox Film Corp., 300 F.Supp. 742 (D.Mass.1969).

[76] Ibid., p. 807.

[77] Ibid., p. 809.

Journalists should not take much comfort in the defenses available for use against suits for invasion of privacy. As noted in this chapter, the concept of "newsworthiness" can prove to be so elastic that it is dangerously subject to the whims of a judge or jury. Also, some courts now seem to be becoming more restrictive in their definitions of "news" and "public interest." Beyond that, being able to defend successfully against a privacy-invasion suit is only part of the equation: even for winners, the costs in dollars and time expended can be enormous.

As may be seen from reading this chapter, the "privacy" concept is many things: a generalized feeling about a "right to be let alone;" it is a constitutional right against some kinds of *governmental* interference in our lives, and it is a growing and increasingly complex body of tort law. As Victor A. Kovner has suggested, perhaps the privacy area must now receive some drastic rethinking and reworking.[78]

> The torts might simply be referred to as intrusion claims, embarrassing facts or "intimacy" claims, false light claims, misappropriation claims, and right of publicity claims. Privacy has little to do with many of these claims. * * * [O]veruse of the term "invasion of privacy" may only contribute to further misunderstanding of the field and further infringement of First Amendment rights.

Privacy is a new area of law, and has not had the centuries of trial-and-error development that attended the law of defamation. This relative newness is a great source of privacy law's danger for the media. Over time, defenses to defamation were built up: for one thing, truth was made a defense. And where slander is concerned, "special damages"—actual monetary loss—must generally be proved before a plaintiff can collect. Where retraction statutes are in force, a plaintiff must prove special damages once a fair and full apology for the defamation has been published.[79] But with the law of privacy, the media do not have such shields. In only one of the privacy tort sub-groups discussed above—"putting plaintiff in a false position in the public eye"—is truth be a defense to a privacy action. Also, a publication need not be defamatory to invade someone's privacy.

Small wonder, then, that some eminent scholars have viewed the law of privacy as a threat to freedom of the press. Professor William L. Prosser has suggested that the law of privacy, in many respects, comes "into head-on collision with the constitutional

[78] Kovner, in Goodale, Communications Law 1984, Vol. 2, at p. 251.

[79] When the fact situation giving rise to a privacy action also involves defamation, retraction statutes have been held to apply. Werner v. Times–Mirror Co., 193 Cal.App.2d 111, 14 Cal.Rptr. 208 (1961).

guaranty of freedom of the press." He said privacy law may be "capable of swallowing up and engulfing the whole law of public defamation." [80]

If, for example, a newspaper were to be sued for *both* libel and invasion of privacy for the same article, difficulties in making a defense hold up might well arise. If the publication were defamatory, the newspaper might be able to plead and prove truth as a defense. But proving truth would not halt the privacy suit unless the article had to do with "putting plaintiff in a false position in the public eye." It could be possible, if a plaintiff *alleged* that a newspaper printed "embarrassing private facts," that proving the truth of an article might encourage a sympathetic jury to find against the newspaper for invasion of privacy.

This means that an article containing no defamation, based on real facts, and published with the best of intentions or through an innocent mistake could be the basis for a successful invasion of privacy lawsuit. If, indeed, it becomes easier to collect for an invasion of privacy suit than for a defamation action, it has been suggested that privacy suits may supplant libel actions.[81]

The foregoing discussion has concentrated on invasion of privacy as a tort. Privacy, however, is protected not only by tort law—in which individuals may sue for damages if their privacy is invaded. Since 1960, privacy has become a constitutional right, a right which to some extent protects citizens from intrusions by government or police agencies.[82]

Precisely because privacy is a hot political issue, it needs to be watched carefully lest it do great damage to First Amendment concerns. The Freedom of Information Act of the federal government was passed in 1966, and was amended in 1975. And while that was dedicated to disclosure of information, it was accompanied by a measure dedicated to non-disclosure of information (at least where the press is concerned). The Privacy Act of 1974 was passed in an effort to give citizens some control over the government's enormous system of dosiers, and to let individuals see and correct files about themselves. The Privacy Act also limited disclosure of individually identifiable information by federal agencies.

Some observers have contended that the federal Privacy Act is not in conflict with the Freedom of Information Act. Others, including Supreme Court reporter Lyle Denniston, disagree, argu-

[80] Prosser, Handbook of the Law of Torts, 3rd ed., p. 844; 4th ed. (1971), pp. 815–816; "Privacy," 48 California Law Review 383, 401 (1960).

[81] Zuckman, op. cit., citing I Prentice–Hall Government Disclosure Service, p. 30,001 (1980), and Biweekly Comparison of Key Statutes, National Law Journal, February 11, 1980, pp. 12–14.

[82] John W. Wade, "Defamation and the Right of Privacy," 15 Vanderbilt Law Review 1093, 1121 (1962); Prosser, "Privacy" loc. cit.

ing that the emphasis on privacy is likely to damage newsgathering through the loss of "inside" sources of information often vital to covering sensitive stories about government.   His point is that when bureaucrats are torn between disclosure of information and retention of information, the safest course will seem to be against disclosure.

As Professor Harvey Zuckman has suggested, the impact of the federal Privacy Act (1974) on the states has been substantial.   Just six years after the Privacy Act's adoption, one third of the states had passed some sort of privacy act and a like number had legislated to allow expungement [erasure] of non-conviction arrest records.[83]

But why shouldn't arrest records be sealed?   After all, not all persons arrested—and thereby shown to be suspected of committing a crime—*have* committed a crime.   Even when an innocent person is arrested, a so-called "criminal record" is created.   Why shouldn't such records be sealed—hidden away for all time—or expunged, wiped off the record?   Alan Westin has written that there are many instances of suicides and nervous breakdowns resulting from exposures by government investigations, press stories about such situations, and even published research.   Westin said this should " 'constantly remind a free society that only grave social need can ever justify destruction of the privacy which guards the individual's ultimate autonomy [over dissemination of information about oneself].' " [84]

On the other hand, in Minnesota, a teen-aged girl was placed in a foster home with a convicted sex offender.   The Welfare Department that placed her there did not know about the sex offender because the agency was not allowed access to criminal records.   Also, it is—or should be—a truism among journalists that the police and the jails and the courts need the closest scrutiny possible if this society is to retain its key freedoms.   In order to preserve due process of law, information about police and judicial activities must be kept public and published in the press.   As W.H. Hornby, former editor of *The Denver Post,* once declared: [85]

We still need to know who is in jail and what the charges are against him.   We still need to know who has been indicted.   If we don't insist on this knowledge, we are in the same position as the Germans who, in their privacy,

[83] Zuckman, op. cit.

[84] Alan F. Westin, Privacy and Freedom (New York: Atheneum, 1970), pp. 33–34, quoted in Wright, op. cit.

[85] W.H. Hornby, "Secrecy, Privacy and Publicity," Columbia Journalism Review, March–April, 1975, p. 11, quoted in Clancy, op. cit.

wondered about the sighing cargoes of those long freight trains that passed in the night.

"Incitement" and Soldier of Fortune

A quite new and potentially expansive area of media liability is termed "incitement." Where the media are concerned, that means bringing a lawsuit against the makers of a publication or movie or audio tape or disc, blaming the media product for some harmful outcome.

One of the flashier examples of this emergent area of law could be found in Eimann v. Soldier of Fortune Magazine, Inc., where a 1988 jury award of $9.4 million ($7.2 million in punitive damages) was made against Soldier of Fortune magazine. A jury ordered the civil damage award, evidently believing that Soldier of Fortune had published an ad offering the services of a hired killer. The classified ad by John Wayne Hearn offered his services as a Vietnam veteran, a weapons specialist who knew jungle warfare, to undertake "high risk assignments." Hearn, indeed, was serving several life terms for shooting Sandra Black to death in her home in Bryan, Texas. Her husband, Robert Black, was sentenced to death for hiring her killer for $10,000.[86]

Predictably, the huge jury verdict caused Editor & Publisher, a trade journal for the newspaper industry, to call for a reversal. "The Texas decision," said Editor & Publisher, "would mean that a reader with a grudge against a publication could bring suit claiming damages for ads believed to be untruthful or misleading unless the publisher investigated every advertising claim." [87]

Soldier of Fortune escaped liability in this case, however, because the U.S. Court of Appeals (5th Cir.) held that this advertisement was innocuously worded and that the magazine, therefore, had no duty to refuse to publish such a classified ad.[88]

In a 1991 decision, however, an Alabama federal court found Soldier of Fortune liable in the amount of $2 million for wrongful death. The jury also awarded Michael Braun $375,000 in compensatory damages and $2 million (reduced from the jury's award of $10 million) in punitive damages. In Braun v. Soldier of Fortune, brothers Michael and Ian Braun sued the magazine for wrongful death and personal injury, claiming that their father had been

[86] Lisa Belkin, "Magazine is Ordered to Pay $9.4 Million for Killer's Ad," The New York Times, March 4, 1988, p. 9.

[87] Editor & Publisher, "Responsibility for ad content," March 12, 1988.

[88] Eimann v. Soldier of Fortune Magazine, Inc., 880 F.2d 830 (5th Cir.1989), 16 Med.L.Rptr. 2148, 2152.

killed by the person who placed the following classified ad: [89]

> GUN FOR HIRE: 37–year-old professional mercenary desires jobs. Vietnam Veteran. Discreet and very private. Body guard, courier, and other special skills. All jobs considered. Phone (615) * * * or write * * * Gatlinburg, TN 37738.

That advertisement had been placed by Richard Savage. A business associate of Mr. Braun saw the ad and negotiated with Savage. Savage employed Sean Trevor Doutre as a contract killer, with these results: On an August day in 1985, as Richard Braun and his 16–year-old son Michael drove out of their suburban Atlanta home, Doutre stepped in front of the car and fired several shots with an MAC–11 automatic pistol. Father and son rolled out of the car on opposite sides; Doutre fired two shots into the father's head. Doutre then pointed the pistol at 16–year-old Michael Braun, but did not fire. "Instead, Doutre put his finger over his lips signaling Michael to be quiet and ran into the woods." [90]

The Braun court distinguished Savage's Soldier of Fortune ad from the classified ad involved in the Eimann case discussed above. The Braun court refused to grant the magazine summary judgment, holding that the ad carrying phrases such as "Gun for Hire" and "Discreet and Very Private" and "All jobs considered" was far more explicit than the "facially innocuous" language in the ad in the Eimann case. The court held that Soldier of Fortune's ad had harmed the Braun family: [91]

The U.S. Court of Appeals, Eleventh Circuit, allowed the jury verdict to stand, voting 2–1 that a standard of legal duty may be set for publishers. Advertisements should not be published that expose the public to substantial danger of harm.[92]

> We agree with the district court that "the language of this advertisement is such that, even though couched in terms not explicitly offering criminal services, the publisher could recognize the offer of criminal activity as readily as its readers obviously did." * * *

[89] Braun v. Soldier of Fortune Magazine, Inc., 757 F.Supp. 1325 (M.D.Ala.1991), 18 Med.L.Rptr. 1732, 1733.

[90] Ibid.

[91] Ibid., at 1729.

[92] Braun v. Soldier of Fortune Magazine, 968 F.2d 1110, 1121 (11th Cir.1992), 20 Med.L.Rptr. 1777, 1786. The Supreme Court denied certiorari, allowing the $4.375 million jury verdict to stand. Both the National Newspaper Association and the Magazine Publishers Association had filed amicus briefs in behalf of Hustler, arguing that this outcome would make advertising more costly because of the necessity of studying all classified ads before publication. See "High Court Shuns Two Free Speech Cases," The New York Times, Jan. 12, 1993, p. A9.

Early in 1993, the U.S. Supreme Court refused to hear the Braun v. Soldier of Fortune case, thus letting stand the jury's awards against the magazine totaling $4.375 million.[93]

For the most part, however, outcomes of incitement cases against the media have favored defendants. One case which received substantial publicity was Herceg v. Hustler, in which a teenage boy died experimenting with "autoerotic asphyxiation" after he read about it in Hustler magazine. The U.S. Court of Appeals, 5th Circuit, in 1987 reversed a damage award of nearly $200,000 against Hustler.[94] Also, rock stars Ozzy Osbourne and Judas Priest were sued by surviving family members of adolescent family members who committed suicide. Osbourne's lyrics in "Suicide Solution" were held to be entertainment, and that Osbourne's music was not proven to have been intended to cause suicide. In that case, the grieving relatives did not collect damages.[95]

In an even stranger case, a Nevada judge ruled in Vance v. Judas Priest (1989) that subliminal messages do not have First Amendment protection. This case involved a lawsuit by anguished survivors of Raymond Belknap, 18, who committed suicide with a 12–gauge shotgun aimed under his chin, and James Vance, 20, injured in a suicide attempt with the same shotgun, survived for several years thereafter. Vance, horribly disfigured, died three years later in the psychiatric unit of a hospital.

The self-inflicted shootings occurred after Belknap and Vance had spent the afternoon drinking beer, smoking marijuana, and listening to Judas Priest albums. Arguments for the plaintiffs included assertions that subliminal messages urging self-destruction were present in the records along with the overt heavy-metal themes of death, destruction, violent sex and suicide.

A Nevada court held that subliminal messages, which are outside free speech theories, were not protected by the First Amendment.[96] Finding that testimony linking the deaths to the music of Judas Priest was not "inherently incredible," the Nevada district court (2nd District) ordered the case to go to trial. At trial, however, it was held that there was insufficient proof that the defendants put subliminal messages in the songs or that the lyrics caused the suicides.[97]

[93] "High Court Shuns Two Free Speech Cases," The New York Times, January 12, 1993, p. A9.

[94] Herceg v. Hustler Magazine, Inc., 814 F.2d 1017 (5th Cir.1987), 13 Med.L.Rptr. 2345.

[95] McCollum v. CBS, Inc., 202 Cal.App.3d 989, 249 Cal.Rptr. 187 (1988), 15 Med.L.Rptr. 2001.

[96] Vance v. Judas Priest, 16 Med.L.Rptr. 2241, 2257 (Nev.1989).

[97] Outcome cited in Victor A. Kovner, Harriette K. Dorsen, and Suzanne Telsey, "Recent Developments . . .," in James C. Goodale, chairman, Communications Law

1991 (Vol. II), at p. 105, discussing a New York Times story dealing with Priest v. Belknap Records, Aug. 25, 1990, p. 11.

Chapter 8

OBSCENITY

SEC. 44. OBSCENITY AND AMERICAN LAW

Obscene expression has never been considered worthy of constitutional protection, but the growth of the hard-core pornography industry during the 1950s prompted the Supreme Court to create standards to establish what could legally be classified as obscene.

Obscenity was never considered a significant legal issue during the first 170 years of this nation's history. In fact the Supreme Court did not decide to review the constitutionality of existing obscenity laws until 115 years after the first federal anti-obscenity law had been enacted.[1]

The main reason for this long era of judicial neglect was the limited scope of pornographic business in the United States prior to the 1950s. Before this time those who engaged in the sale of sexually explicit materials tended to be small-time operators, specializing in procuring a few erotic books or batches of grainy French postcards for a very select and secretive clientele.[2]

During the 1950s, however, as organized crime began to move into the field, its operation became much more efficient and profit-

---

[1] The first federal anti-obscenity law was contained in the Tariff Act of 1842, U.S. Public Statutes at Large, Vol. 5, Ch 270, forbidding the, "importation of all indecent and obscene paintings, lithographs, engravings and transparencies." In 1957, the United States Supreme Court reviewed the constitutionality of such anti-obscenity laws for the first time in Roth v. United States, 354 U.S. 476, 77 S.Ct. 1304 (1957). In this regard it is informative to note that the word "pornography" itself did not exist in the English language until sometime during the early 1850s, and that it originally referred only to the scientific (or pseudo-scientific) study of prostitutes. See Walter Kendrick, The Secret Museum. New York, Viking Press, 1987.

[2] See the Gathings Committee: Us Congress, House, Select Committee on Current Pornographic Materials, Hearings Before Select Committee, and Report of Select Committee to the House, 83rd Cong. 2d Sess. 1952.H. Rept. 2510 and the Kefauver Committee: U.S. Congress, Senate, Committee on the Judiciary, Obscene and Pornographic Materials, 84th Cong,. 2d Sess. 1956, H. Rept. 2381.

able, employing mass mailings for the first time to promote the sale of slickly produced erotic magazines to a much broader segment of the population.[3] By 1960, annual revenues from the sale of sexually explicit materials were estimated to be in excess of 500 million dollars, earnings that at the time rivaled those of both the American television and motion picture industries.[4]

Prior to this time obscenity had always been assumed to be an illegal form of expression, denied any First Amendment protection. As Justice Holmes had declared in Frohwerk v. United States[5]

> The First Amendment ... cannot have been, and obviously was not, intended to give immunity for every possible use of language.

But in 1957, just as hard-core pornography was emerging as a major industry throughout the nation, the Supreme Court decided to intervene in this field of law for the first time. Concerned that overly broad anti-obscenity statutes might be improperly infringing on protected free speech, the Court acted to impose its own federal guidelines on these laws, requiring them to conform to one uniform standard in determining what could legally be classified as "obscene."[6] Unfortunately, this decision of the Court to assume ultimate authority over obscenity law in the United States was made on the eve of the "sexual revolution," a frenzied era that would soon cast its nine Justices adrift in a flood of obscenity appeals, foundering aimlessly for a time upon its surging waves of controversy.

[3] Federal Bureau of Investigation: Report Regarding the Extent of Organized Crimes Involvement in Pornography (1978). Also see, Attorney General's Commission on Pornography: Final Report (1986), pp. 291–301. Although an earlier government study, the Report of the President's Commission on Obscenity and Pornography (1970), found insufficient evidence to document the extent of mob involvement in this field, (pp. 142–143), its efforts to establish such a connection were admittedly quite limited.

[4] The Granahan Committee: U.S. Congress, House, Committee on the Post Office and Civil Service, Subcommittee on Post Operations, Hearings before Subcommittee and Report of Subcommittee to Committee, 86th Congress, 2d sess. 1960. Although both the Kefauver and the Granahan Committee reports acknowledged the difficulty of accurately estimating the revenues generated by an illegal industry whose major operators were not likely to disclose this information on their tax forms, the figures were considered to be rather conservative projections of actual earnings. For comparative purposes, the total revenues earned by all TV stations in the United States in 1960 was $962 million, while the total domestic box office receipts for all films shown in the U.S. that year was $710 million. Christopher H. Sterling and Timothy R. Haight, The Mass Media: Aspen Institute Guide to Communication Industry Trends. New York, Praeger Publishers, 1976. Table 380–A, p. 207 and Table 340–B, p. 182.

[5] 249 U.S. 204, 39 S.Ct. 249 (1919).

[6] Roth v. United States, 354 U.S. 476, 77 S.Ct. 1304 (1957).

SEC. 45.   THE COMMON LAW ORIGINS

British common law principles drawn from an era of soap-box orators and humble printers could offer only limited guidance to American courts facing the need to develop a legal definition of obscenity for a modern society.

Although nineteenth century America was never a hot-bed of erotic literature, the moral and religious fervor that swept the nation during the 1870s launched crusades to seek out every kind of depravity or vice, wherever it might be found. In 1873, Anthony Comstock, one of these religious crusaders, was able to convince Congress to adopt federal legislation making it a crime to use the mail to distribute obscene materials. During the next few years several State legislatures also responded to the demands of Comstock and his followers by passing their own anti-obscenity laws.

After these laws had been enacted, it was then up to each State court to decide how the term "obscene" should be defined. In the absence of any precedents from earlier American case law, these courts were forced to seek guidance from English common law where a number of judges eventually discovered and applied the standard an English court had established in 1868 in the case of Regina v. Hicklin.

The Hicklin Rule

In *Hicklin,* Lord Chief Justice Cockburn ruled that an anti-Catholic pamphlet, The Confessional Unmasked, was obscene. Lord Cockburn set down this test for obscenity: [7]

> Whether the tendency of the matter charged as obscene is to deprave and corrupt those whose minds are open to such immoral influences and into whose hands a publication of this sort might fall.

In States that followed the "Hicklin rule" it was not necessary to prove that any publication under review was likely to harm or offend a normal adult.[8] All the rule required was proof that the work in question could have a damaging effect on children or abnormal adults—"those whose minds are open to such immoral influences"—in order to satisfy its standard. In time some State courts added the so-called "partly obscene" test to the *Hicklin* rule. If a publication contained one or more obscene passages, the entire work could be classified as obscene.[9]

---

[7] L.R. 3 Q.B. 360, 370 (1868).

[8] See United States v. Bennett, 24 Fed.Cas. 1093, 1103–1104, No. 14,571 (S.D.N.Y. 1879); Commonwealth v. Friede, 271 Mass. 318, 320, 171 N.E. 472, 473 (1930).

[9] Lockhart & McClure, op. cit., p. 343.

Perhaps the most troublesome portion of the *Hicklin* rule, though, was the concept that a book could be classified as obscene if it suggested "thoughts of a most impure and libidinous character." [10] In the law of obscenity, no harm or even likelihood of harm to readers need be shown in order to suppress a book as obscene.[11]

In 1913, Judge Learned Hand wrote an often quoted protest against the *Hicklin* rule, which he termed "mid-Victorian precedent." Although Judge Hand felt compelled to uphold the condemnation as obscene of Daniel Goodman's novel *Hagar Revelley*, the judge wrote: [12]

> I question whether in the end men will regard that as obscene which is honestly relevant to the adequate expression of innocent ideas, and whether they will not believe that truth and beauty are too precious to be mutilated in the interests of those most likely to pervert them to base uses. * * *

Despite his protest, the *Hicklin* rule remained the leading test of obscenity in America until the 1930s.[13]

The Ulysses Decision

About this time, however, other American courts began to relax enforcement of the *Hicklin* rule to some extent. A mother who wrote a book to help her children learn about sex—and who later published the book at the suggestion of friends—successfully defended herself against charges that the book *(Sex Side of Life)* was obscene.[14] And in 1933, James Joyce's famed stream-of-consciousness novel *Ulysses,* now an acknowledged classic, was the target of an obscenity prosecution under the Tariff Act of 1930.[15]

Customs officers had prevented an actress from bringing *Ulysses* into this country. When *Ulysses* reached trial, Judge John Woolsey decided that a literary work deserved be judged in its entirety, rather then by the contents of a few selected passages. On this basis he attacked the *Hicklin* test head-on and ruled that *Ulysses* was art, not obscenity.

[10] Ibid.

[11] See Roth v. United States, 354 U.S. 476, 490, 77 S.Ct. 1304, 1312 (1957); see also dictum by Mr. Justice Frankfurter, Beauharnais v. Illinois, 343 U.S. 250, 266, 72 S.Ct. 725, 735 (1952).

[12] United States v. Kennerley, 209 Fed. 119 (S.D.N.Y.1913).

[13] See, e.g., Commonwealth v. Friede, 271 Mass. 318, 320, 171 N.E. 472, 473 (1930).

[14] United States v. Dennett, 39 F.2d 564, 76 A.L.R. 1092 (2d Cir.1930).

[15] United States v. One Book Called "Ulysses," 5 F.Supp. 182 (S.D.N.Y.1933); Paul and Schwartz, op. cit., p. 66.

His decision has become one of the most noted in the law of
criminal words, even though it by no means brought the end of the
Hicklin rule, which continued to applied in the decisions of other
courts.[16]   Overrated or not, the *Ulysses* decision represents an
often-cited step toward nullifying some of the most restrictive
aspects of the old *Hicklin* standard.

The *Ulysses* decision provided a new definition of obscenity for
other courts to consider: that a book is obscene if it [17]

> tends to stir the sex impulses or to lead to sexually impure
> and lustful thoughts.   Whether a particular book would
> tend to excite such impulses must be the test by the
> court's opinion as to its effect (when judged as a whole) on
> a person with average sex instincts.

Only one portion of the old *Hicklin* rule appeared in Judge
Woolsey's *Ulysses* opinion: the emphasis on thoughts produced by a
book as an indicator of a book's obscene effect on a reader.   This
judicial preoccupation with thoughts—and the tests outlined by
Judge Woolsey in 1933—are markedly similar to rules for judging
obscenity laid down in the Supreme Court's landmark decision in
the 1957 case of Roth v. United States.[18]

SEC. 46.   THE ROTH LANDMARK

**In Roth v. United States, the Supreme Court held that
obscenity is not constitutionally protected expression
and set down its most influential standard for judging
what is—or is not—obscene.**

In 1957 the Supreme Court acted to establish one uniform set
of national standards to define what could properly be categorized
by American law as obscene. In the case of Roth v. United States,
the Court while accepting the premise that obscene speech enjoyed
no constitutional protection, insisted that all anti-obscenity laws
contain specific safeguards to limit their application solely to those
forms of expression that could properly be classified as obscene. [19]

Although this decision is usually referred to as the *Roth* case, it
actually involved two different appeals.   The Court simultaneously
decided a case under the federal obscenity statute [20] (*Roth*) and

[16] See e.g., United States v. Two Obscene Books, 99 F.Supp. 760 (N.D.Cal.1951),
affirmed as Besig v. United States, 208 F.2d 142 (9th Cir.1953).

[17] United States v. One Book Called "Ulysses," 5 F.Supp. 182, 184 (S.D.N.Y.1933).

[18] 354 U.S. 476, 77 S.Ct. 1304 (1957).

[19] Ibid.

[20] United States v. Roth, 237 F.2d 796 (2d Cir.1956).

under a state statute[21] (*People v. Alberts*). Taken together, the *Roth* and *Alberts* cases thus raised the question of the constitutionality of both federal and state anti-obscenity laws.

In the federal prosecution, Roth was convicted of violating the statute by mailing various pamphlets plus a book, *American Aphrodite.* He was sentenced to what was then the maximum sentence: a $5,000 fine plus a five-year penitentiary term. His conviction was affirmed by the United States Court of Appeals, Second Circuit, although the noted jurist Judge Jerome M. Frank questioned the constitutionality of obscenity laws in a powerful concurring opinion.

In words which have been called the beginning of the modern law of obscenity, Judge Frank declared that obscenity laws are unconstitutionally vague.[22]

* * *

The troublesome aspect of the federal obscenity statute * * * is that (a) no one can now show that with any reasonable probability obscene publications tend to have any effects on the behavior of normal, average adults, and (b) that under the [federal] statute * * * punishment is apparently inflicted for provoking, in such adults, undesirable sexual thoughts, feelings or desire—not overt dangerous or anti-social conduct, either actual or probable.

Despite Judge Frank's denunciation of the "exquisite vagueness" of obscenity laws, Roth's conviction was upheld. The Supreme Court then granted certiorari in order to review the case.[23]

Alberts v. California

The State of California prosecution against David S. Alberts was directed at his mail-order business in Los Angeles. In 1955, he was served with a warrant and his business office, warehouse and residence were searched. Hundreds—maybe thousands—of books and pictures were seized.[24] Such books as "Witch on Wheels," "She Made It Pay," and "Sword of Desire"—plus some mail circulars—were found to be obscene. Alberts' conviction was upheld by an appellate court. That court concluded that the words "obscene" and "indecent" were not unconstitutionally vague. The Supreme Court then noted probable jurisdiction.[25]

21 West's Ann.Cal.Pen.Code § 311; People v. Alberts, 138 Cal.App.2d Supp. 909, 292 P.2d 90 (1955).

22 237 F.2d 796, 825 826–827 (2d Cir.1956). See Stanley Fleishman, "Witchcraft and Obscenity: Twin Superstitions," Wilson Library Bulletin, April, 1965, p. 4.

23 352 U.S. 964, 77 S.Ct. 361 (1957).

24 Fleishman, op. cit., p. 10.

25 Alberts v. California, 352 U.S. 962, 77 S.Ct. 349 (1957).

In jointly considering the *Roth* and *Alberts* cases, the Court did not rule on whether the books sold by the two men were in fact obscene. The only issue reviewed in each case was the validity of an obscenity law on its face.[26]

Alberts argued that this mail-order business could not be punished under California law because a state cannot regulate an area pre-empted by the federal obscenity laws. The majority opinion replied that the federal statute deals only with actual mailing and does not prevent a state from punishing the advertising or keeping for sale of obscene literature.[27]

Roth contended, on the other hand, that the power to punish speech and press offensive to morality belongs to the states alone under the powers of the First, Ninth, and Tenth Amendments to the Constitution. The majority opinion discarded this argument, saying that obscenity is not speech or expression protected by the First Amendment.[28] Justice Brennan added, in language which was to greatly affect later decisions in the law of obscenity: [29]

> All ideas having even the slightest redeeming social importance—unorthodox ideas, controversial ideas, even ideas hateful to the prevailing climate of opinion—have the full protection of the guaranties [of free speech and press], unless excludable because they encroach upon the limited area of more important interests. But implicit in the history of the First Amendment is the rejection of obscenity as utterly without redeeming social importance.

Justice Brennan's majority opinion set the stage for obscenity law developments in two ways. First, he affirmed the prevailing common law view that obscenity laws might be used to punish *thoughts;* overt sexual actions are not needed to bring a conviction.[30] Second—and more significantly—he affirmed the common law position that obscenity is *not* legally protected expression.[31]

Those are the two main strands in the law of obscenity. Other strands woven in by concurring and dissenting Justices in Roth v. United States foreshadowed those major and minor themes which would crescendo and diminish during next the 40 years in this complex orchestration of obscenity law.[32]

[26] 354 U.S. 476, 77 S.Ct. 1304, 1307 (1957).

[27] 354 U.S. 476, 493–494, 77 S.Ct. 1304, 1314 (1957).

[28] 354 U.S. 476, 492, 77 S.Ct. 1304, 1313 (1957).

[29] 354 U.S. 476, 484, 77 S.Ct. 1304, 1309 (1957).

[30] 354 U.S. 476, 486–487, 77 S.Ct. 1304, 1309–1310 (1957).

[31] 354 U.S. 476, 482, 77 S.Ct. 1304, 1307 (1957).

[32] For example, Chief Justice Earl Warren's concurrence in Roth argued that the conduct of a defendant was the key point in an obscenity prosecution. For a case

The Roth Test

Writing for the Court, Justice Brennan offered this definition of obscenity: "Obscene material is material which deals with sex in a manner appealing to prurient interest." [33] "Prurient interest," of course, refers to sexually oriented thoughts. Brennan then articulated "the Roth test" for judging whether or not material is obscene: [34]

> * * * whether to the average person, applying contemporary community standards, the dominant theme of the material taken as a whole appeals to prurient interest.

Subsequent decisions have returned for guidance to these words again and again. This "*Roth* test" repudiated some features of the American rendition of the *Hicklin* rule. The practice of judging books by the presumed effect of isolated passages upon the most susceptible persons was rejected because it "might well encompass material legitimately dealing with sex." [35]

However, Justice Brennan's words were obviously not wholly libertarian. Under *Roth,* a book could be declared obscene if it could be assumed that it might induce obscene thoughts in an hypothetical average person.[36] There was no need for the prosecution to prove that there is a "clear and present danger" [37] or even a "clear and possible danger" [38] that the reading of the book in question would lead to antisocial conduct.

Roth: Concurrences and Dissents

Chief Justice Earl Warren was evidently puzzled by the idea that *books* rather than persons were defendants in obscenity prosecutions. His brief concurring opinion in *Roth* has proven to be remarkably predictive since 1957. Chief Justice Warren stated that in an obscenity trial, the conduct of the defendant rather than the obscenity of a book should be the central issue: [39]

which turned on the defendant's conduct, see Ginzburg v. United States, 383 U.S. 463, 86 S.Ct. 942 (1966).

[33] 354 U.S. 476, 487, 77 S.Ct. 1304, 1310 (1957). The terms used in the three "tests" approved in Roth—"lustful desire," "lustful thoughts," and "appeal to prurient interest"—all imply that if a book can be assumed to cause or induce "improper" sexual thoughts, that book can be "banned." The "appeal to prurient interest" test was drawn from the American Law Institute's Model Penal Code, Tentative Draft No. 6 (Philadelphia, American Law Institute, May 6, 1957).

[34] 354 U.S. 476, 489, 77 S.Ct. 1304, 1311 (1957).

[35] 354 U.S. 476, 489, 77 S.Ct. 1304, 1311 (1957).

[36] 354 U.S. 476, 486, 77 S.Ct. 1304, 1310 (1957).

[37] 354 U.S. 476, 489, 77 S.Ct. 1304, 1310 (1957).

[38] U.S. 476, 489, 77 S.Ct. 1304, 1310 (1957), citing Dennis v. United States, 341 U.S. 494, 71 S.Ct. 857 (1951).

[39] 354 U.S. 476, 495, 77 S.Ct. 1304, 1315 (1957).

He concluded that both Roth and Alberts had engaged in "the commercial exploitation of the morbid and shameful craving for materials with prurient effect" and said that the state and federal governments could constitutionally punish such conduct.[40]

Justice Brennan's majority opinion in *Roth* has influenced the course of the law of obscenity. So, in recent years, has Chief Justice Warren's concurring opinion, which insisted that the behavior of the defendant, rather than the nature of the book itself, was the "central issue" in an obscenity case.[41]

Justice Harlan also disagreed with the majority opinion's conclusion that obscenity laws are constitutional because an earlier Supreme Court had found that obscenity is "utterly without redeeming social importance": [42]

> On this basis, the *constitutional* question before us becomes, as the Court says, whether "obscenity," as an abstraction, is protected by the First and Fourteenth Amendments, and the question whether a *particular* book may be suppressed becomes a mere matter of classification, of "fact" to be entrusted to a fact-finder and insulated from independent judgment.

Justice Harlan thus told his fellow justices that the vital question was "what is obscenity?", rather than "is obscenity good or bad?"

While Harlan asked this challenging question of his brethren on the Court, Justice William O. Douglas was joined by Justice Hugo L. Black in a scathing attack on obscenity laws and obscenity prosecutions. This dissent foreshadowed arguments these Justices would advance in obscenity cases which subsequently followed *Roth* to the Supreme Court. Douglas wrote that Roth and Alberts were punished "for thoughts provoked, not for overt acts nor antisocial conduct." He was unimpressed by the possibility that the books involved might produce sexual thoughts: "The arousing of sexual thoughts and desires happens every day in normal life in dozens of ways." [43]

Problems involving freedom of speech and press, it was argued, must not be solved by "weighing against the values of free expression, the judgment of a court that a particular form of expression has 'no redeeming social importance.'" Justice Douglas declared: [44]

[40] 354 U.S. 476, 496, 77 S.Ct. 1304, 1315 (1957).
[41] 354 U.S. 476, 495, 77 S.Ct. 1304, 1314–1315 (1957).
[42] 354 U.S. 476, 497, 77 S.Ct. 1304, 1315 (1957).
[43] 354 U.S. 476, 509, 77 S.Ct. 1304, 1322 (1957).
[44] 354 U.S. 476, 514, 77 S.Ct. 1304, 1324 (1957).

[T]he test that suppresses a cheap tract today can suppress a literary gem tomorrow. All it need do is incite a lascivious thought or arouse a lustful desire. The list of books that judges or juries can place in that category is endless.

SEC. 47. MONITORING COMPLIANCE: THE FEDERAL REVIEW ERA

Once the federal court system had asserted its right to review the constitutionality of all State obscenity laws, it found itself overwhelmed not only by the case-load it assumed, but also by the difficulty of defining obscenity in any uniform or clearly consistent way.

Although *Roth* remains the leading decision on obscenity and said much, later court decisions showed that it actually settled very little. Five years after *Roth* the Supreme Court attempted to refine its definition of obscenity in Manual Enterprises, Inc. v. Day, Postmaster General of the United States. In writing for the Court, Justice Harlan termed *MANual* [sic], *Trim,* and *Grecian Pictorial* "dismally unpleasant, uncouth and tawdry" magazines which were published "primarily, if not exclusively, for homosexuals." [45]

Despite this, a majority of the Supreme Court held that these magazines which presented pictures of nude males were not obscene and unmailable because they were not "patently offensive." Harlan wrote: [46]

Obscenity under the federal statute * * * requires proof of two distinct elements: (1) patent offensiveness; and (2) "prurient interest" appeal.

In 1966, the Supreme Court again tackled the tough problem of defining obscenity as decisions were announced in three cases, the "Fanny Hill" case,[47] Mishkin v. New York,[48] and Ginzburg v. United States.[49]

First announced was the decision in the *Fanny Hill* case. *Fanny Hill,* or more accurately, *Memoirs of a Woman of Pleasure,* was written in England about 1749 by John Cleland. The book was well known in the American colonies and was first published in the United States around 1800. *Fanny Hill,* was also one of the first books in America to be the subject of an obscenity trial; in Massachusetts in the year 1821.[50] More than 140 years later,

[45] 370 U.S. 478, 481, 82 S.Ct. 1432, 1434 (1962).

[46] 370 U.S. 478, 482–486, 82 S.Ct. 1432, 1434–1436 (1962).

[47] 383 U.S. 413, 86 S.Ct. 975 (1966).

[48] 383 U.S. 502, 86 S.Ct. 958 (1966).

[49] 383 U.S. 463, 86 S.Ct. 942 (1966).

[50] Commonwealth v. Peter Holmes, 17 Mass. 336 (1821).

Fanny Hill was back in the courts of Massachusetts, as well as in New York, New Jersey and Illinois.

In Fanny Hill, there is not one of the "four letter words" which have so often brought modern literature before the courts. But although the language was quite sanitary, author Cleland's descriptions of Fanny's sexual gyrations left little to the imagination. Even so, some experts—including poet and critic Louis Untermeyer—testified that Fanny Hill was a work of art and was not pornographic. The experts, however, were asked by a cross-examining prosecuting attorney if they realized that the book contained "20 acts of sexual intercourse, four of them in the presence of others; four acts of lesbianism, two acts of male homosexuality, two acts of flagellation and one of female masturbation." [51]

Fanny Hill, then, is a frankly erotic novel. Justice Brennan summed up the tests for obscenity which the highest court had approved: [52]

> We defined obscenity in *Roth* in the following terms: "[W]hether to the average person, applying contemporary community standards, the dominant theme of the material taken as a whole appeals to prurient interest." 354 U.S. at 489, 77 S.Ct. at 1311. Under this definition, as elaborated in subsequent cases, three elements must coalesce: it must be established that (a) the dominant theme of the materials taken as a whole appeals to a prurient interest in sex; (b) the material is patently offensive because it affronts contemporary community standards relating to the description or representation of sexual matters; and (c) the material is utterly without redeeming social value.

The Supreme Court ruled that the Massachusetts courts had erred in believing that a book could be deemed obscene even though not "unqualifiedly worthless." Justice Brennan, writing for the Court, stated that a book "can not be proscribed unless it is found to be *utterly* without redeeming social value." [53]

Justice Brennan then announced the Court's decision in the *Mishkin* case. Edward Mishkin, who operated a bookstore near New York City's Times Square, was appealing a sentence of three years and $12,500 in fines. Mishkin's publishing specialty was sadism and masochism, and he had been found guilty by New York courts of producing and selling more than 50 different paperbacks.

[51] Cf. the outraged dissent by Justice Tom C. Clark, 383 U.S. 413, 445–446, 86 S.Ct. 975, 990–991 (1966).

[52] 383 U.S. 413, 418, 86 S.Ct. 975, 977 (1966).

[53] 383 U.S. 413, 419, 86 S.Ct. 975, 978 (1966).

Titles involved included *Dance With the Dominant Whip, and Mrs. Tyrant's Finishing School.*[54]

Mishkin's defense, was based on the notion that the books he published and sold did not appeal to the prurient interest of an average person. The average person, it was argued, would be disgusted and sickened by such books.[55] Justice Brennan's majority opinion, however, dismissed Mishkin's argument.[56]

> Where the material is designed primarily for and primarily disseminated to a clearly defined deviant sexual group, rather than the public at large, the prurient-appeal requirement of the *Roth* test is satisfied if the dominant theme of the material taken as a whole appeals to the prurient interest of the members of that group.

After upholding Mishkin's conviction, Mr. Justice Brennan then turned to the *Ginzburg* case. With this opinion, the Supreme Court brought another element to the adjudication of obscenity disputes: the manner in which the matter charged with obscenity was sold.[57]

The *Ginzburg* case involved three publications: "EROS, a hardcover magazine of expensive format; Liaison, a bi-weekly newsletter; and The Housewife's Handbook on Selective Promiscuity, * * * a short book." Justice Brennan took notice of abundant evidence from Ralph Ginzburg's federal district court trial "that each of the accused publications was originated or sold as stock in trade of the sordid business of pandering—the business of purveying textual or graphic matter openly advertised to appeal to the erotic interest of their customers." [58]

Included as evidence of this "pandering" were EROS magazine's attempts to get mailing privileges from the whimsically named hamlets of Intercourse and Blue Ball, Pa. Mailing privileges were finally obtained in Middlesex, N.J.[59] Also, Justice Brennan found "the leer of the sensualist" permeating the advertising for the three publications. *Liaison,* for example, was extolled as "Cupid's Chronicle," and the advertising circulars asked, "Are you a member of the sexual elite?" [60]

The Court was severely split of the *Ginzburg* case, however, with Justices Black, Douglas, Harlan and Stewart all registering

54 383 U.S. 502, 514–515, 86 S.Ct. 958, 966–968 (1966).

55 383 U.S. 502, 508, 86 S.Ct. 958, 963 (1966).

56 383 U.S. 502, 508–509, 86 S.Ct. 958, 963–964 (1966).

57 383 U.S. 463, 465–466, 86 S.Ct. 942, 944–945 (1966).

58 383 U.S. 463, 467, 86 S.Ct. 942, 945 (1966).

59 383 U.S. 463, 467, 86 S.Ct. 942, 945 (1966).

60 383 U.S. 463, 469n, 86 S.Ct. 942, 946 (1966).

bitter dissents. Justice Black set the tone for his dissenting brethren, declaring: [61]

> * * * Ginzburg, * * * is now finally and authoritatively condemned to serve five years in prison for distributing printed matter about sex which neither Ginzburg nor anyone else could possibly have known to be criminal.

Justice Harlan accused the court's majority of rewriting the federal obscenity statute in order to convict Ginzburg, and called the new "pandering" test unconstitutionally vague.[62] And Justice Stewart asserted in his dissent that Ginzburg was not charged with "commercial exploitation," with "pandering," or with "titillation," and to allow him to be convicted on such grounds was to deny him due process of law.[63]

Justice Douglas added his denunciation of the condemnation of materials as obscene not because of their content, but because of the way they were advertised.[64]

Protecting the Young: The Ginsberg Case and the "Variable Obscenity" Concept

As if to confound careless spellers, it happens that one of the most important cases after the Ralph *Ginzburg* case involved a man named *Ginsberg:* Sam Ginsberg. In the 1968 *Ginsberg* case, the Supreme Court held by a 6–3 vote that a New York statute which defined obscenity on the basis of its appeal to minors under 17 was not unconstitutionally vague.

Sam Ginsberg and his wife operated "Sam's Stationery and Luncheonette" in Bellmore, Long Island. In 1965, a mother sent her 16–year-old son to the luncheonette to by some "girlie" magazines. The boy purchased two magazines—apparently *Sir* and *Gent* or similar publications—and walked out of the luncheonette.

On the basis of this sale, Sam Ginsberg was convicted of violation of a New York law making it a misdemeanor "knowingly to sell * * * to a minor under 17 any picture * * * which depicts nudity * * * and which is harmful to minors" and "any * * * magazine * * * which contains * * * [such pictures] and which, taken as a whole, is harmful to minors." [65]

It should be noted that magazines such as the 16–year-old boy purchased from Sam Ginsberg's luncheonette in 1965 had been

---

[61] 383 U.S. 463, 476, 86 S.Ct. 942, 954 (1966).

[62] 383 U.S. 463, 476, 86 S.Ct. 942, 954 (1966).

[63] 383 U.S. 463, 494, 86 S.Ct. 942, 954 (1966).

[64] 383 U.S. 463, 494, 497, 86 S.Ct. 942, 954, 956 (1966).

[65] Ginsberg v. New York, 390 U.S. 629, 634, 88 S.Ct. 1274, 1277 (1968). The statute is Article 484–H of the New York Penal Law, McKinney's Consol. Laws c. 40.

held *not* obscene for adults by the Supreme Court.[66] However the judge at Sam Ginsberg's obscenity trial found pictures in the two magazines which depicted nudity in a manner that was in violation of the New York statute.

The trial judge found that the pictures were "harmful to minors" under the terms of the New York law.

In affirming Ginsberg's conviction, Justice Brennan approved the concept of "variable obscenity." [67] Brennan acknowledged that the magazines involved in the *Ginsberg* case were not obscene for sale to adults, However, he upheld the right of a State to accord to minors under the age of 17 a more restricted right of access than assured to adults to judge and determine for themselves what sex material they may read or see.[68]

In the case that resulted in the fining and jailing of *Eros* publisher Ralph Ginzburg, the Supreme Court served notice that not only *what* was sold but *how* it was sold would be taken into account.[69] The *how* of selling or distributing literature can include a legitimate public concern over the materials which minor children see. In essence, this case established the concept of "variable obscenity", holding that materials not obscene for adults can be found to be obscene if children are allowed access to them.[70]

Indecisiveness: *Redrup* and *Stanley*

In the spring of 1967, the Supreme Court of the United States openly admitted its confusion over obscenity law in a case known as Redrup v. New York.[71] This decision did not *look* important: it took up only six pages in United States Reports and only about four pages were devoted to its unsigned *per curiam* ["by the court"] majority opinion. The other two pages were given over to a dissent by Justice John Marshall Harlan, with whom Justice Tom C. Clark joined.

Redrup was a significant case simply because the Court said that a majority of its members could not agree on a standard which could declare so-called "girlie magazines" and similar publications to be obscene. *Redrup* seemed for a time to be the most important obscenity case since Roth v. United States because it was used by

[66] Redrup v. New York, 386 U.S. 767, 87 S.Ct. 1414 (1967).

[67] Ginsberg v. New York, 390 U.S. 629, 635 n., 88 S.Ct. 1274, 1278 n. (1968), quoting Lockhart and McClure, "Censorship of Obscenity: The Developing Constitutional Standards," 45 Minnesota Law Review 5, 85 (1960).

[68] Ginsberg v. New York, 390 U.S. 629, 635, 88 S.Ct. 1274, 1277–1278 (1968); see Butler v. Michigan, 352 U.S. 380, 77 S.Ct. 524 (1957); Roth v. United States, 354 U.S. 476, 77 S.Ct. 1304, 1309 (1957).

[69] Ginzburg v. United States, 383 U.S. 463, 86 S.Ct. 942 (1966).

[70] Ginsberg v. New York, 390 U.S. 629, 88 S.Ct. 1274 (1968).

[71] 386 U.S. 767, 87 S.Ct. 1414 (1967).

both state and federal courts for several years to avoid many of the complexities of judging whether works of art or literature are obscene.

On June 12, 1967, the date the Court's term ended that year and less than two months after *Redrup* was decided, the Court reversed 11 obscenity convictions by merely referring to Redrup v. New York.[72] Another dozen state or federal obscenity convictions were reversed during the next year, with *Redrup* being listed as an important factor in each reversal.[73]

The majority opinion in *Redrup* placed significant reliance upon the Court's 1966 decision in Ginzburg v. United States. In *Ginzburg,* discussed earlier in this chapter, it will be recalled that the Court took special notice of the *manner* in which magazines or books were sold.[74] *Redrup* echoed this concern, but also took into account the *recipients* of materials charged with obscenity. The Court suggested that convictions for selling or mailing obscenity should be upheld in three kinds of situations:

(1) Where there is evidence of "pandering" sales as in Ginzburg v. United States.

(2) Where there is a statute reflecting "a specific and limited state concern for juveniles." [75]

(3) Where there is "an assault upon individual privacy by publication in a manner so obtrusive as to make it impossible for the unwilling individual to avoid exposure to it." [76]

Beyond these kinds of forbidden conduct *Redrup* gave little guidance. Perhaps, however, it could be assumed that *Redrup* meant this: If the *conduct* of the seller did not fit the three kinds of prohibited actions listed above, and if the *contents* were not so wretched that they would be held to be "hardcore pornography," [77]

[72] Dwight L. Teeter, Jr., and Don R. Pember, "The Retreat from Obscenity: Redrup v. New York," Hastings Law Journal Vol. 21 (Nov., 1969) pp. 175–189.

[73] 386 U.S. 767, 771–772, 87 S.Ct. 1414, 1416–1417 (1967).

[74] 383 U.S. 463, 86 S.Ct. 942 (1966).

[75] Redrup v. New York, 386 U.S. 767, 769, 87 S.Ct. 1414, 1415 (1967). Note that (2) above, announced in Redrup on May 8, 1967, forecast with considerable precision the Court's decision in Ginsberg v. New York, 390 U.S. 629, 88 S.Ct. 1274 (1968).

[76] Ibid., citing Breard v. Alexandria, La., 341 U.S. 622, 71 S.Ct. 920 (1951), and Public Utilities Commission of Dist. of Columbia v. Pollak, 343 U.S. 451, 72 S.Ct. 813 (1952).

[77] 386 U.S. 767, 771n, 87 S.Ct. 1414, 1416n, referring to Justice Potter Stewart's quotation, in his dissent in Ginzburg v. United States, of this definition of hardcore pornography, including writings and "photographs, both still and motion picture, with no pretense of artistic value, graphically depicting acts of sexual intercourse, including various acts of sodomy and sadism, and sometimes involving several participants in scenes of orgy-like character. * * * verbally describing such activities in a bizarre manner with no attempt whatsoever to afford portrayals of

then the materials involved were constitutionally protected.[78]

Stanley v. Georgia (1969)

In 1969, there was hope that the Supreme Court—clearly frustrated by its growing caseload of obscenity appeals-would find some way to bring order to this complex and troublesome area of law. The Court's resolution of Stanley v. Georgia added to this hope.[79]

The *Stanley* case arose when a Georgia state investigator and three federal agents, operating under a federal search warrant, searched the home of Robert E. Stanley, looking for bookmaking records. Evidence of bookmaking was not found, but the searchers found three reels of 8 millimeter film and a projector. They treated themselves to a showing and decided—as did the court- that the films were obscene. When Stanley's appeal reached the Supreme Court, Mr. Justice Thurgood Marshall—writing for a unanimous Court—overturned the conviction, naming two constitutional rights.[80]

(1) A right growing out of the First Amendment, a "right to receive information and ideas, regardless of their social worth." [81]

(2) A constitutional right to privacy tied to the right to receive information and ideas: [82]

> * * * [F]undamental is the right to be free, except in very limited circumstances, from unwanted governmental intrusions into one's privacy. * * * These are the rights that appellant [Stanley] is asserting. * * * the right to satisfy his intellectual and emotional needs in the privacy of his own home.

Because Stanley v. Georgia involved no dangers of either injuring minors or invading the privacy of the general public, the Supreme Court concluded: [83]

> We hold that the First and Fourteenth Amendments prohibit making mere private possession of obscene material a crime. Roth and the cases following that decision

character or situation and with no pretense to literary value." See Ginzburg v. United States, 383 U.S. 463, 499n, 86 S.Ct. 942, 956n (1966).

[78] 386 U.S. 767, 87 S.Ct. 1414, 1416 (1967).

[79] Stanley v. Georgia, 394 U.S. 557, 89 S.Ct. 1243 (1969).

[80] Black, J., concurred in the decision.

[81] 394 U.S. 557, 89 S.Ct. 1243 (1969), citing Winters v. New York, 333 U.S. 507, 510, 68 S.Ct. 665 (1948).

[82] 394 U.S. 557, 564–564, 89 S.Ct. 1243, 1247–1248 (1969).

[83] 394 U.S. 557, 568–569, 89 S.Ct. 1243, 1249–1250 (1969).

are not impaired by today's holding. As we have said, the States retain broad power to regulate obscenity; that power simply does not extend to mere possession by the individual in the privacy of his own home.

Taken together, *Redrup* and *Stanley* suggested to some judges that the strictures of obscenity law had been loosened by the Supreme Court. *Redrup* seemed to indicate that the Court wouldn't define anything but hard-core pornography as obscene. And *Stanley* seemed to hold that anyone had a right to possess sexually explicit literature and films at home. This meant to some judges that if you were able to possess such material privately, someone must have at least a limited right to sell it to you.[84]

Or, suppose an individual had an urge, as Justice Marshall once phrased it, to receive "information and ideas" by viewing "Raunchy Randy and the Virgins of Venus" at a local X-rated movie parlor. Couldn't that person be somehow "publicly private"—when secretly gathering information and ideas in anonymous darkness of that theater? And wouldn't that person be a consenting adult whose privacy or other sensibilities were not being intruded upon? [85] Couldn't it be claimed that individuals have a right to satisfy their own "intellectual and emotional needs" in this way? [86]

Whatever the Supreme Court may have appeared to suggest in its previous decisions, it responded by answering "no" to each of these questions in its 1971 decision, Byrne v. Karalexis. [87] The case involved state prosecutions against theater owners for showing what was then considered to be a shocking Swedish sex film, "I Am Curious (Yellow)".

A federal court attempted to bar these prosecutions by extending the Stanley v. Georgia language that already permitted individuals to receive and possess obscene material to also allow them to view such material in a theater or library. The court contended that "If a rich Stanley can view a film, or read a book, a poorer Stanley should be free to visit a protected theater or library. We see no reason for saying he must go alone." [88]

But in an unsigned *per curiam* decision, the Supreme Court vacated the lower court's order, permitting Massachusetts to prose-

---

[84] See, e.g., Dyson v. Stein, 401 U.S. 200, 91 S.Ct. 769 (1971).

[85] See, e.g., United States v. Articles of "Obscene" Merchandise, 315 F.Supp. 191 (S.D.N.Y.1970), and Paris Adult Theatre I v. Slaton, 413 U.S. 49, 93 S.Ct. 2628 (1973).

[86] Stanley v. Georgia, 394 U.S. 557, 89 S.Ct. 1243 (1969).

[87] 401 U.S. 216, 91 S.Ct. 777 (1971).

[88] 306 F.Supp. 1363 at 1366–1367 (D.Mass.1969).

cute any theater owner who exhibited this film.[89]

SEC. 48.   CREATING A NEW CONSENSUS: THE MILLER STANDARD

In 1973, Chief Justice Burger succeeded in developing a new set of obscenity standards that a majority of the Court could accept.

Miller v. California

The most important of the five obscenity cases decided by the Supreme Court on June 21, 1973—and indeed the most important such case since Roth v. United States (1957)—was Miller v. California. In that case, as in the four others of that date, the Court split 5–4, revealing a new coalition among the Justices where obscenity and pornography were concerned.[90]

This coalition included Justice Byron R. White (appointed by President John F. Kennedy) and four justices appointed by President Richard M. Nixon (Chief Justice Warren Burger, plus justices Harry Blackmun, William Rehnquist, and Lewis Powell). Dissenting in all five of those obscenity cases were Justices Thurgood Marshall, Potter Stewart, William O. Douglas, and the author of the *Roth* test of 1957 and of many of the obscenity decisions thereafter, Justice William J. Brennan, Jr.

Miller v. California arose when Marvin Miller mailed five unsolicited—and graphic—brochures to a restaurant in Newport Beach. The envelope was opened by the restaurant's manager, with his mother looking on, and they complained to police. The brochures advertised four books, Intercourse, Man–Woman, Sex Orgies Illustrated, and An Illustrated History of Pornography, plus a film titled Marital Intercourse. After a jury trial, Miller was convicted of a misdemeanor under the California Penal Code.[91]

Writing for the majority in *Miller,* Chief Justice Burger ruled that California could punish such conduct. He noted that the case involved "a situation in which sexually explicit materials have been thrust by aggressive sales action upon unwilling recipients or juveniles.

[89] 401 U.S. 216, 91 S.Ct. 777 (1971).

[90] Paris Adult Theatre I v. Slaton, 413 U.S. 49, 93 S.Ct. 2628 (1973); United States v. Orito, 413 U.S. 139, 93 S.Ct. 2674 (1973); Kaplan v. California, 413 U.S. 115, 93 S.Ct. 2680 (1973), and U.S. v. Twelve 200–ft. Reels of Super 8 mm Film, 413 U.S. 123, 93 S.Ct. 2665 (1973).

[91] West's Ann. California Pen. Code § 312.2(a) makes it a misdemeanor to knowingly distribute obscene matter. After the jury trial, the Appellate Department, Superior Court of California, Orange County, summarily affirmed the conviction without offering an opinion.

Endeavoring to formulate a new standard, Chief Justice Burger first returned to *Roth's* declaration that obscene materials were not protected by the First Amendment.[92] Then, he denounced the test of obscenity outlined in the Fanny Hill (*Memoirs of a Woman of Pleasure*) case in 1960, nine years after *Roth.* In that case, three justices, in a plurality opinion, held that material could not be judged obscene unless it were proven to be "utterly without redeeming social importance." Burger added: [93]

> While *Roth* presumed "obscenity" to be "utterly without redeeming social value," *Memoirs* required that to prove obscenity it must be affirmatively established that the material is *"utterly* without redeeming social value." Thus, even as they repeated the words of *Roth,* the *Memoirs* plurality produced a drastically altered test that called on the prosecution to prove a negative, i.e., that the material was *"utterly* without redeeming social value"—a burden virtually impossible to discharge under our criminal standards of proof.

The Chief Justice admitted that since the 1957 decision in *Roth,* the Court had not been able to muster a majority to agree to a standard of what constitutes "obscene, pornographic material subject to regulation under the States' police power." [94] In 1973, however, Burger found himself in substantial agreement with four other Justices. He made the most of it, setting out general rules on what States could regulate ("hard-core pornography") and rewording the *Roth* and *Memoirs* tests into a standard reducing the burden of proof necessary to convict persons for distribution or possession of sexually explicit materials.[95]

> * * * [W]e now confine the permissible scope of such regulation to works which depict or describe sexual conduct. That conduct must be specifically defined by the

[92] 413 U.S. 15, 20, 93 S.Ct. 2607, 2613 (1973), citing Roth v. United States, 354 U.S. 476, 77 S.Ct. 1304 (1957).

[93] 413 U.S. 15, 22, 93 S.Ct. 2607, 2613–2614 (1973), citing Memoirs of a Woman of Pleasure v. Massachusetts, 383 U.S. 413, 86 S.Ct. 975 (1966). Emphasis the Court's.

[94] 413 U.S. 15, 22, 93 S.Ct. 2607, 2614 (1973).

[95] 413 U.S. 15, 23–24, 93 S.Ct. 2607, 2614, 2615 (1973). Emphasis the Court's. Chief Justice Burger wrote that a State could, through statute, forbid:

"(a) Patently offensive representations or descriptions of ultimate sexual acts, normal or perverted, actual or simulated.

(b) Patently offensive representations or descriptions of masturbation, excretory functions, and lewd exhibition of the genitals."

Burger also stated that, "Sex and nudity may not be exploited without limit by films or pictures exhibited or sold in places of public accommodation any more than live sex and nudity can be exhibited or sold without limit in such public places. At a minimum, prurient, patently offensive depiction or description of sexual conduct must have serious literary, artistic, political or scientific value to merit First Amendment protection."

applicable state law, as written or authoritatively construed. A state offense must also be limited to works which, taken as whole, appeal to the prurient interest in sex, which portray sexual conduct in a patently offensive way, and which, taken as a whole, do not have serious literary, artistic, political, or scientific value.

The basic guidelines for the trier of fact must be: (a) whether "the average person, applying contemporary community standards" would find that the work, taken as a whole, appeals to the prurient interest * * * (b) whether the work depicts or describes, in a patently offensive way, sexual conduct specifically defined by the applicable state law, and (c) whether the work, taken as a whole, lacks serious literary, artistic, political or scientific value. We do not adopt as a constitutional standard the *"utterly* without redeeming social value" test of Memoirs v. Massachusetts * * *: that concept has never commanded the adherence of more than three Justices at one time.

The majority opinion also declared that it would be unwise to attempt to formulate a uniform national standard to determine what appeals to "prurient interest" or what is "patently offensive." "[O]ur nation is simply too big and diverse for this Court to reasonably expect that such standards could be articulated for all 50 States in a single formulation * * *"[96] The First Amendment, Burger said, did not force citizens in Maine or Mississippi to accept all depictions of sexual conduct that might be tolerated in Las Vegas or New York City.

This new recognition "community standards" in the area of obscenity law also appeared to furnish the Court the justification it had been seeking to reduce its obscenity appeal workload.

The Roth decision in 1957 had forced the Supreme Court to assume the role of final arbiter in deciding what could legally be classified as obscene. As long as only one uniform national standard existed, the Court's nine Justices were its ultimate interpreters, required to review the contents of each salacious film or book that had been banned in order to decide whether or not it was actually obscene under federal law.[97]

Through this recognition of at least some degree of legitimate divergence in local and regional attitudes towards explicit sexual material, it was hoped that the Supreme Court would now be able to avoid a significant number of those obscenity appeals it had

[96] 413 U.S. 15, 30, 93 S.Ct. 2607, 2618 (1973).

[97] Although the Roth opinion itself did not specifically require that a single uniform federal standard be applied in all obscenity cases, Justice Brennan interpreted it as doing so in Jacobellis v. Ohio, 378 U.S. 184, 84 S.Ct. 1676 (1964).

previously been compelled to accept. Since *Miller* permitted "community standards" to be a factor evaluated in determining what was obscene, the Supreme Court could now defer in those matters to the lower courts, pointing out that local judges and juries were much better situated than Supreme Court Justices to interpret and apply local sexual standards. Unfortunately, once again, those who hoped for this result had underestimated the inherent capacity of obscenity law to confound and convolute the judicial system.

Justice Brennan's opposition to these decisions seemed based in large measure on his growing belief that no matter what set of standards were used, obscenity statutes would always be unconstitutionally vague. That is, there are *"scienter"* problems: obscenity laws are by their nature so formless that defendants can not have fair notice as to whether publications or films they distribute or exhibit are obscene. Without fair notice, there may occur a "chilling effect" upon protected speech.

Brennan wrote: [98]

> I am convinced that the approach initiated 15 years ago in Roth v. United States * * * culminating in the Court's decision today, cannot bring stability to this area of the law without jeopardizing First Amendment values, and I have concluded that the time has come to make a significant departure from that approach.

> * * *

> Our experience with the *Roth* approach has certainly taught us that the outright suppression of obscenity cannot be reconciled with the fundamental principles of the First and Fourteenth Amendments. For we have failed to formulate a standard that sharply distinguishes protected from unprotected speech, and out of necessity we have resorted to the *Redrup* approach, which resolves cases as between parties, but offers only the most obscure guidance to legislation, adjudication by other courts, and primary conduct.

> * * *

> I would hold, therefore, that at least in the absence of distribution to juveniles or obtrusive exposure to unconsenting adults, the First and Fourteenth Amendments prohibit the state and federal governments from attempting wholly to suppress sexually oriented materials on the basis of their allegedly "obscene" contents. Nothing in

[98] Brennan dissent in Paris Adult Theatre I v. Slaton, 413 U.S. 49, 90, 93 S.Ct. 2628, 2651 (1973).

this approach precludes those governments from taking action to serve what may be strong and legitimate interests through regulation of the manner of distribution of sexually oriented material.

From the *Miller* decision of 1973 well into the 1980s, the Court split 5–4 in many of the obscenity cases it has decided. The majority followed *Miller,* and favored stringent regulation of sexually explicit material. Time and time again, including many *per curiam* decisions in which the Court upheld obscenity prosecutions without an explanatory opinion, Brennan dissented, constantly contending that obscenity can not be described with sufficient clarity to give defendants fair notice.[99]

The Meanings of *Miller*: Defining "Community Standards"

If the Supreme Court Justices had expected that the new "contemporary community standards" test introduced by the *Miller* case would significantly reduce their obscenity caseload, they were soon to be disappointed.

Jenkins v. Georgia

Mike Nichols' serious film, *Carnal Knowledge,* became the target of an obscenity prosecution in Albany, Georgia. The prosecution took place even though the film contained no frontal nudity or explicit depictions of sexual acts. The manager of a theater, Billy Jenkins, was convicted under a Georgia statute [1] forbidding distribution of obscene material and was fined $750 and sentenced to 12 months in jail. His conviction was affirmed by the Georgia Supreme Court.

Although agreeing with the Georgia Supreme Court that the U.S. Constitution does not require juries in obscenity cases to be instructed according to a hypothetical statewide standard, the Supreme Court of the United States unanimously reversed Jenkins' conviction. Writing for the Court, Justice William H. Rehnquist ruled that *Carnal Knowledge* was not patently offensive. He referred to Miller v. California, which said that a state statute could forbid patently offensive materials, including

"representations or descriptions of ultimate sexual acts, normal or perverted, actual or simulated," and "represen-

[99] See, e.g., Trinkler v. Alabama, 414 U.S. 955, 94 S.Ct. 265 (1973); Raymond Roth v. New Jersey, 414 U.S. 962, 94 S.Ct. 271 (1973); Sharp v. Texas, 414 U.S. 1118, 94 S.Ct. 854 (1974); J–R Distributors, Inc. v. Washington, 418 U.S. 949, 94 S.Ct. 3217 (1974). See also Hamling v. United States, 418 U.S. 87, 140–152, 94 S.Ct. 2887, 2919–2924 (1974).

[1] Jenkins v. Georgia, 418 U.S. 153, 156, 94 S.Ct. 2750, 2753 (1974) citing Ga.Code §§ 26–2011, 26–2105.

tations or descriptions of masturbation, excretory functions, and lewd exhibition of the genitals."

Because *Carnal Knowledge* did not contain any of those specific actions characterized as being obscene in *Miller,* the conviction of Jenkins could not stand.[2]

In essence, the Court was saying that although it was now willing to accept the fact that "contemporary community standards" regarding sexual matters might vary to some extent from region to region, there could be no finding of obscenity anywhere in the United States unless the material in question could reasonably be considered to be obscene.

Hamling v. United States

William Hamling and several co-defendants were convicted on 12 counts of using the mails to deliver obscene advertisements in 1971, two years *before* the *Miller* decision recognized the relevance of local community standards in determining whether the average person could reasonably find that a work appealed to prurient interest.

Hamling and his confederates were attempting to sell an illustrated version of the government's own *Presidential Report of the Commission on Obscenity and Pornography*, offering in their promotional mailer a wide assortment of graphic photographs illustrating those lurid and obscene sexual activities the government report had simply described.

During the trial, conducted in San Diego, California, the judge had refused to allow the defense to introduce the results of a survey of 718 San Diego residents suggesting that a majority of those surveyed felt this brochure should be made available to the public.

When the Supreme Court reviewed the case in 1974, Justice Rehnquist, writing for the majority, concluded that the refusal of the trial judge to admit evidence of community standards did not prejudice the rights of the defendants because the advertisements themselves were clearly obscene.[3]

Justice Brennan, joined by Justices Stewart and Marshall, dissented vigorously. He asserted that material should not be suppressed unless there is distribution to juveniles or obtrusive exposure to non-consenting adults.[4] He also criticized the concept of "community standards" itself, pointing out that national distributors, facing "variegated standards * * * impossible to discern,"

---

[2] 418 U.S. 153, 160, 94 S.Ct. 2750, 2755 (1974).

[3] Hamling v. United States, 418 U.S. 153, 94 S.Ct. 2750 (1974).

[4] 418 U.S. 87, 94 S.Ct. 2887, 2903 (1974).

will be forced to abide by the most repressive standard when distributing sexually oriented materials.[5]

Pope v. Illinois

One recent example of the difficulties lower courts have had in knowing exactly how the "community standards" test should be applied is illustrated by **Pope v. Illinois**.[6] Here the question was whether the artistic value of a work was to be determined by the typical citizen in the community where the case was being tried.

It should be recalled that Miller v. California set out a three-part test:[7]

> (1) Does the material, when viewed by an average person applying contemporary community standards, appeal to prurient interest?

> (2) If so, then is the appeal "patently offensive"?

> (3) Then, even though the material does appeal to prurient interest in a patently offensive manner; does it deserve free speech protection despite such qualities because of having serious literary, artistic, political or scientific value?

In this case—involving sales of magazines to undercover agents in a Rockford, Illinois adult bookstore—the constitutionality of judge's instructions to the jury were challenged. At their trials, the defendants argued that the literary or artistic value of a work should be based on a uniform national standard.[8] The judge rejected this argument, instructing the jury instead to consider its value in terms of, "how it would be viewed by ordinary adults in the whole state of Illinois."

Writing for the majority, Justice White asserted:

> There is no suggestion in our cases that the opinion of the value of an allegedly obscene work is to be determined by reference to community standards. Indeed, Smith v. United States, 431 U.S. 291 (1977) held that, in a federal prosecution for mailing obscene materials, the first and second prongs of the *Miller* test—appeal to prurient inter-

[5] 418 U.S. 87, 94 S.Ct. 2887, 2921 (1974).

[6] Pope v. Illinois, 481 U.S. 497, 107 S.Ct. 1918 (1987). For other examples of the type of problems lower courts have encountered in attempting to apply this standard see Pinkus v. United States, 436 U.S. 293, 98 S.Ct. 1808 (1978)-children not to be included in considering community standards- and Smith v. United States, 431 U.S. 291, 97 S.Ct. 1756 (1977)-jury can find material obscene under federal law even if State in which offense occurs has no anti-obscenity law.

[7] 413 U.S. 15, 23–24, 93 S.Ct. 2607, 2614–1615 (1973).

[8] This has come to be known as the "SLAPS" test; does the material have *Serious* *Literary*, *Artistic*, *Political* or *Scientific* value that protects it from being classified as obscene.

est and patent offensiveness—are issues of fact for the jury
to determine applying contemporary community standards.   The Court then observed that unlike prurient
appeal or patent offensiveness, "[L]iterary, artistic, political, or scientific value ... is not discussed in *Miller* in
terms of contemporary community standards."

White maintained that "artistic value" was not a relative term
that each community could be permitted to establish for itself.

> Just as the ideas a work represents need not obtain
> majority approval to merit protection, neither, insofar as
> the First Amendment is concerned, does the value of a
> work vary from community to community based on the
> degree of local acceptance it has won.   The proper inquiry
> is ... whether a reasonable person would find such value
> in the material, taken as a whole.

Justice John Paul Stevens disagreed.   He pointed out that
reasonable people would often disagree when assessing the literary
or artistic quality of a particular work and to insist that only one
judgement of a work's merit was "reasonable" would impose an
"intolerable orthodoxy" on efforts to control obscenity.   Despite his
objections the jury's verdict was set aside because of what a
majority of the Justices believed to be the trial court's erroneous
instructions describing the standard the jury was to use in evaluating artistic value.

Other Recent Obscenity Issues

Although recent Supreme Court decisions have reduced the
ambiguity of the phrase "contemporary community standards," a
number of other modern obscenity law concepts remain far less
clearly defined.

To what extent, for example, can federal enforcement officials
involve themselves in the process of distributing obscene materials
without being found to have improperly enticed a defendant into
committing a crime?

In United States v. Kuennen,[9] the Supreme Court refused to
review the conviction of an individual whose shipment of obscene
materials from Denmark was first intercepted by U.S. Customs
officials and then re-mailed to him by that agency.   Kuennen
claimed that he had not violated federal postal laws because the law
simply prohibited "causing" obscene materials to be sent through
the mail and in this case it was the federal agency that "caused"
these materials to be mailed to him.   The federal court was
unmoved by his argument, finding although a Customs official may

[9] 901 F.2d 103 (8th Cir.1990), cert. denied 498 U.S. 958, 111 S.Ct. 385 (1990).

have mailed the package to Kuennen, it was the defendant himself who "caused" the mailing of these materials when he ordered them from his foreign supplier.

However, in Jacobson v. United States[10], in a 5–4 decision, the Supreme Court held that a government enforcement agency could not actively solicit customers for obscene materials and then charge them criminally for having responded to the solicitation. In this case an organization secretly sponsored by the government was sending promotional materials offering a wide assortment of explicit child pornography books and magazines to individuals it suspected were already purchasing these materials from other sources.

Keith Jacobson, an elderly Nebraska farmer, received such advertisements for more than two years before he finally ordered a pornographic magazine, *Boys Who Love Boys*, from the organization. On the basis of his order, Jacobson was convicted of violating a federal mail statute by knowingly receiving materials showing minors engaged in sexually explicit activities.

Justice White, writing for the majority, held that while government agents might be permitted to offer citizens an opportunity to commit crimes they are already predisposed to commit, it was illegal entrapment for them to engage in such an elaborate subterfuge to induce an innocent person to commit a crime.

Computer Sex

Efforts by enforcement agencies to prevent the sale of sexually explicit and child pornography films has been made even more difficult by recent technological advances that simplify the process of shipping high-quality video images to home computers.[11] In Oklahoma and Texas individuals have been already been charged with offering to sell obscene CD–ROM images to computer bulletin board members while a New Jersey man has been arrested for possessing digitized pictures depicting sexually explicit images of minor-aged girls.

Are such computer networks personal channels of communication, protected by privacy law from government intrusion? And even if this defense should fail, do current federal and State anti-obscenity laws extend to the sale of sexually explicit digitized CD–ROM images? The only thing that seems certain at this point is that this complex area of law is not likely to become any less complicated in the immediate future.

Yet, while it is too soon to predict how technological advances may affect the field of obscenity law in the future, two recent cases

[10] 112 S.Ct. 1535 (1992).

[11] See, for example, Andrea Gerlin, "Electronic Smut vs. Drawing Fire of Prosecutors, Raising Questions" New York Times, June 27, 1994, p. B3.

suggest that at least for the moment freedom of expression is not being unduly hampered by the existence of such laws.

The Mapplethorpe Exhibit Case

Concern that mid-American juries lacked the sophistication to distinguish between "art" and "smut" lessened to some extent in October 1990 after a Cincinnati, Ohio jury acquitted a local museum director charged with displaying obscene works.[12] Dennis Barrie, director of Cincinnati's Contemporary Arts Center, had scheduled an exhibition of pictures by Robert Mapplethorpe, a nationally recognized photographer who died of AIDS in 1989.

The exhibition included five photos of nude men in sadomasochistic poses and two of children with their genitals exposed. The exhibit had attracted little attention in its previous showings in Philadelphia and Chicago, but at its opening in Cincinnati, Barrie and the Museum were charged with pandering obscenity, and unlawfully displaying pictures of nude children, both misdemeanor offenses carrying maximum sentences of one year in jail, and a fine of $5,000.

To simplify the issue, the State called just one witness to testify as to the artistic merit of the exhibit, a self-styled communications "specialist" whose only claimed expertise as an art critic involved writing songs for the "Captain Kangaroo" television show. In contrast, the defense called more than a dozen expert witnesses, including directors from some of the nation's leading art museums who were unanimous in their assessment of Mapplethorpe as a serious and important artist.

If the prosecution believed the photos themselves would be enough to shock the mostly working class, church-going jury of four men and four women into returning a guilty verdict, they clearly underestimated the intelligence of the panel. After the trial had ended, several jurors admitted being personally offended by these pictures they felt were "lewd", "grotesque" and "disgusting".[13] But even though they felt that these photos did appeal to prurient interests and were patently offensive, they accepted the judgment of art experts who believed these works also had artistic merit, and therefore could not be classified as being obscene.

Reacting in part to public criticism of the federal funding Mapplethorpe had received, Congress amended the statute governing awards made by National Endowment for the Arts, requiring

[12] Contemporary Arts Center v. Ney, 735 F.Supp. 743 (S.D.Ohio 1990). Also see "Jury Finds Merit in Mapplethorpe Exhibit with Verdict of Not Guilty" Milwaukee Journal, October 7, 1990, p. A1.

[13] Isabel Wilkerson, "Obscenity Jurors Were Pulled 2 Ways But Deferred to Art" New York Times October 10, 1990, p. B1. Five of the eight jurors had never visited an art museum.

the NEA to consider "general standards of decency" in deciding who might qualify for funding from the organization. Applying this new standard, NEA denied requests for government funds from several artists who applied for grants, including one who planned theatrical performances of simulated masturbation and another who intended to smear her body with excrement to portray the debasement of women. When these individuals were unable to obtain taxpayer funding they sought, they challenged the new "decency" standard in court.

A California federal district court upheld their challenge, finding the term "decency" to be unconstitutionally vague and overbroad because it prevented applicants from fully understanding what was required of them in order to qualify for federal financial support. [14]

2 Live Crew Case

In June 1990, a U.S. District Court in Fort Lauderdale, Florida had entered a decree forbidding the sale or distribution of a music video "Nasty As They Wanna Be" by rap group *2 Live Crew* anywhere within the jurisdiction of the Court. District Judge Jose A. Gonzales conducted extensive hearings before deciding that the music video was in fact obscene, and therefore could be prevented from being sold.[15]

A local music store owner, Charles Freeman, sold a copy of the music video to an undercover police officer a few days after the decree had been entered and was convicted of violating this ban. Shortly after Freeman's arrest, *2 Live Crew* performed selections from the music video during an all-adult concert in Fort Lauderdale. The three members of the group were each charged with one misdemeanor count of disseminating obscene material, and were tried in October 1991, soon after Freeman's conviction.

The defense maintained that white jurors on the 6 member jury panel would be incapable of understanding this unique form of black artistic expression, but the jury voted unanimously for acquit-

[14] Finley v. National Endowment for the Arts, 795 F.Supp. 1457 (C.D.Cal.1992)

[15] Skyywalker Records, Inc. v. Navarro, 739 F.Supp. 578 (S.D.Fla.1990), 17 Med. L.Rptr. 2073. According to testimony presented at the hearings, this single music video contained more than a dozen references urging violent sex, some 200 descriptions of women as either "bitches" or "ho" (whores), 115 explicit terms for male or female genitalia, 87 descriptions of oral sex, 9 descriptions of male ejaculation, 4 extensive descriptions of group sex, all within a general theme glorifying the debasement and humiliation of women. The declaratory judgement of obscenity entered by the District Judge was later vacated on appeal. The reviewing court pointed out that the judge who had tried the case had not demonstrated that he possessed either the artistic or literary background necessary to find that the work lacked "serious artistic, scientific, literary or political value." Luke Records v. Navarro, 960 F.2d 134 (11th Cir.1992).

tal, finding that the performance was not obscene.[16] Once again, the verdict turned on the "artistic merit" issue, for the jury accepted the judgment of a black English professor that "rapping" represented a serious black cultural art form, whose words were not to be taken at their face value but to be understood in the historical context of black culture.[17]

In both of these recent cases, those who had been predicting that a new wave of artistic censorship would sweep across the nation could take some comfort in the verdicts of two predominately white, working-class juries who respected their obligations as jurors to decide these emotion-packed obscenity issues impartially and objectively. Perhaps, then, there is reason to believe that the time-honored American trial by jury system deserves more respect than its erudite critics have sometimes been willing to accord it.

SEC. 49 BALANCING CONFLICTING SOCIETAL INTERESTS

As private industry content standards continue to become more permissive, pressure is mounting for laws to protect society from mass culture messages that demean certain groups, or erode fundamental tenets of decency.

Motion Picture Industry Standards

Until the late 1940s, five major film companies dominated the motion picture business in the United States. Paramount, MGM, Warner Brothers, Twentieth Century Fox and RKO owned more than 3000 of the nation's first-run motion picture theaters and controlled film industry production, distribution and exhibition by following a policy of trade-offs and cross-preferences with other studio-owned theaters to deny some 15,000 independently owned theaters access to these feature films until their box office appeal had diminished.

This concentration of control within the film industry also allowed the major studios to cooperate in adopting and enforcing a code of industry standards to ensure that no feature film would contain themes or scenes that might be offensive to certain segments of the film audience.[18] Independent film producers had no

[16] "Rap Members Found Not Guilty in Obscenity Trial," New York Times, October 21, 1990, p. 1.

[17] Another factor that may have aided the defense is that the vocals the prosecution recorded at the concert were virtually unintelligible to the jury, providing very little basis for the jury to find the lyrics to be obscene.

[18] The Motion Picture Producers and Distributors of American (MPPDFA) established a film review office in 1922, largely as a public relations gesture to reduce the bad image resulting from a rash of personal scandals in Hollywood. Known as the "Hay's Office", because of its first director, Will Hays, its role in reviewing film

choice but to conform to these standards of decency, because without the industry's "Production Code Seal of Authority" they would be denied access to those essential first-run theaters owned by the major studios.[19]

Then, in 1948, the Justice Department was able to force the major film studios to enter into a Consent Decree in which they agreed to rid themselves of their motion picture theaters.[20]

Losing control of these major first-run theaters also meant that these studios lost the capacity to impose industry standards on feature film content. As television viewing increased during the 1950s, film attendance plunged downward from 90 million a week in 1948 to less than 40 million a week only a decade later.[21] To lure audiences back to the film theaters, their new owners needed motion pictures promising special attractions television couldn't provide. One technique was to use technology to expand the screen, surround the viewer with sound, and portray action on a massive scale.

Another was to show sexier or more provocative dramas than television offered the public. Freed of the constraints of the Hollywood Production Code, theater chains began turning to European producers for daring, far more explicit motion pictures than American audiences had ever seen in the past.

At this point a number of local film boards originally formed in the early 1900s, but then dormant for decades as Hollywood closely supervised motion picture content, suddenly came to life as these new independent films began appearing in their communities. Now as such boards, operating under State authority, began trying to fill that void left by the collapse of industry controls, the issue soon arose about their legal right as government agencies to impose conditions on the local exhibition of feature films.

content did not become significant until the major studios adopted a much more stringent set of standards, known as the Production Code, in the mid 1930s.

[19] In many ways this private content supervisory system closely resembled that employed by National Association of Broadcasters. In both cases, a small group of studios or networks were able to avoid offending audiences by exerting their control over the main channels of distribution, and this power that gave them to deny distribution to material they believed was in bad taste. In television as in film, the later fragmentation of that power diminished their ability to continue to perform that function.

[20] United States v. Paramount Pictures, 334 U.S. 131, 68 S.Ct. 915 (1948). The studios were actually given the option of divesting themselves of either their role as film distributors or film exhibitors, but sensing the threat that television would soon pose for film theaters, they chose to retain their more profitable distribution role.

[21] Christopher Sterling and Timothy Haight, eds. The Mass Media: Aspen Institute Guide to Communication Industry Trends (New York: Praeger, 1978) pp. 34–35.

The first of these cases to challenge the authority of a State to control film content was Burstyn v. Wilson, a 1952 Supreme Court decision involving Roberto Rossellini's film, *"The Miracle."* [22]

This was a story about a simple-minded goatherd who had been raped by a bearded stranger whom she believed to be St. Joseph. The film was accused not of obscenity but of "sacrilege." The New York Education Department had issued a license to allow showing of "The Miracle," but the Education Department's governing body, the New York Regents, ordered the license withdrawn after the regents had received protests that the film was "sacrilegious." Burstyn appealed the license's withdrawal to the New York Courts, claiming that the state's licensing statute was unconstitutional. New York's courts, however, rejected that argument.

The Supreme Court of the United States ultimately ruled unanimously that the New York statute and the term "sacrilegious" were both so vague that they abridged freedom of expression. Although the Court said in *dicta* that a clearly drawn obscenity statute to regulate motion pictures might be upheld, the main thrust of the *Burstyn* decision was toward greater freedom. Not only were films given protection under the First and Fourteenth Amendments, movies which offended a particular religious group need not, for that reason alone, be banned. Thus "sacrilege" can no longer be a ground for censoring movies.

Seven years after the *Burstyn* decision, the Supreme Court—in Kingsley International Pictures Corp. v. New York—again upheld the concept that films are within the protection of the First Amendment. In *Kingsley*, however, the Court specifically refused to decide whether "the controls which a State may impose upon this medium of expression are precisely co-extensive with those allowable for newspapers, books, or individual speech." [23]

In 1961 Times Film Corporation paid the City of Chicago the customary license fee to exhibit the film *"Don Juan"* but then refused to submit the film as required by local ordinance to Chicago's Film Review Board for pre-screening and a license. Instead, in Times Film Company v. City of Chicago, it challenged the city's authority to impose these conditions on the exhibition of a motion

[22] Joseph Burstyn, Inc. v. Wilson, 343 U.S. 495, 72 S.Ct. 777 (1952). Some film historians claim that Mutual Film Corp. v. Industrial Commission of Ohio, 236 U.S. 230, 35 S.Ct. 387 (1915) was the first test of film's free speech rights, a test in which a federal court held that a State law could restrict film distribution because film was not a form of protected expression, but rather only a business. What these historians overlook is that it was not until 1927 that the Supreme Court finally recognized the power of federal courts to overturn State laws restricting free speech, so that in this case, determining whether or not film was a protected form of free speech was really irrelevant to the actual decision, and therefore not a precedent controlling future federal court decisions in this field.

[23] 360 U.S. 684, 689–690, 79 S.Ct. 1362, 1366 (1959).

picture, contending that the ordinance constituted an unconstitutional prior restraint on free speech.

The Supreme Court upheld the city's right to impose these conditions on its local film exhibitors by a 5–4 vote. The majority denied that there was complete freedom to exhibit any motion picture and added, "Nor has it been suggested that all prior restraints are invalid." [24]

Four years later, in Freedman v. Maryland (1965), the Supreme Court invalidated a state prior restraint system. This time, unlike the *Times Film* case, *all* prior restraint was not challenged as unconstitutional. Instead, the Maryland Film Review Board was challenged because it could arbitrarily halt the showing of a film until the exhibitor was able to complete a time-consuming appeal procedure through the State court system. The Maryland review process was held invalid because of insufficient procedural safeguards for the protection of the film exhibitor. But even Justice Brennan—the legendary First Amendment supporter—suggested that an orderly, speedy procedure for prescreening films could be constitutional. [25]

In fact, a later Maryland-based film review system was upheld by an affirming vote of the Supreme Court—in Star v. Preller (1974)—demonstrating that a reasonably structured process was constitutional. The provisions of the new statute, cited with approval by the Court [26]

— Granted the Review Board only five days in which to review and license a film.

— Required, if a license is denied, that the Review Board begin review proceedings within 3 days before the Baltimore City Circuit Court.

— Required that a court make a prompt determination of obscenity (or lack of it) in an adversary hearing before the Review Board can make final denial of the license.

— Required the Board to bear the burden of proof at all stages of the proceeding.

At this time, then, prior restraint of film is still constitutional, but only when strict procedural safeguards are followed. These film industry decisions reflect the difficult role the Supreme Court has had to play when attempting to balance the free speech rights

[24] Times Film Corp. v. Chicago, 365 U.S. 43, 47, 81 S.Ct. 391, 393 (1961), citing Near v. State of Minnesota ex rel. Olson, 283 U.S. 697, 51 S.Ct. 625 (1931).

[25] Freedman v. Maryland, 380 U.S. 51, 85 S.Ct. 734 (1965). For a similar result, see Interstate Circuit, Inc. v. Dallas, 390 U.S. 676, 88 S.Ct. 1298 (1968).

[26] A1 Star v. Preller, 419 U.S. 956, 95 S.Ct. 217 (1974), affirming 375 F.Supp. 1093 (D.Md.1974).

of a film distributor against the inherent right of each State to protect the welfare of its citizens.

In 1968 the major film studios began a new effort to enhance the image of the industry. Unable any longer to enforce standards of good taste, the studios instead established a rating system designed to inform audiences in advance what type of content each film contained. In the original rating system, a "G" designated films suitable for all audiences; "PG" meant parents were cautioned that some material might not be suitable for children; "R" indicated that children under 17 would not be admitted unless accompanied by a parent or guardian; and "X" meant no one under 17 would be admitted.

The rating system had at least two unintended effects. One was to destroy the appeal of the "G" rated film, as children began refusing to attend those films that adults thought were good for them. In 1968, 32 percent of the films released by major studios had a "G" rating, but by 1990, only 4 percent were rated "G".[27]

In contrast, "R" rated films rose from 22 percent of all major releases in 1968 to 48 percent in 1990, as average age of the film audience dropped from 22 to 16, and "R" became virtually synonymous with this age group's favorite film genre; violent, action packed adventures laced with suitable amounts of mayhem and gore.

The other was to make it virtually impossible to successfully market an "X" rated film. Soon after the code was adopted, a number of major newspaper chains established the policy of refusing to accept display ads for "X" rated films, and several television groups began following the same policy a few years later. In addition, most major video rental organizations refused to handle "X" rated films. In view of these severe constraints an "X" rating imposed on the earnings potential of a picture, Hollywood producers generally insisted on contractual agreements that allowed them to re-edit any feature film rated as "X" to delete any scenes that prevented it from receiving a "R" rating.[28]

In time, however, because of the bitter controversies these agreements created between producers-investors and directors attempting to make serious but extremely graphic films such as "Henry and June" or "Tie Me Up! Tie Me Down," the film code was revised in 1990 to distinguish between this type of artistic film

[27] "MPAA Film Ratings 1968–90" Variety November 8, 1991, p. 26. One example of this film industry fear of the dreaded "G" rating was the John Wayne, Katharine Hepburn film, "Rooster Cogburn" where the producers insisted that one violent scene be inserted to guarantee a "PG" rather than "G" rating.

[28] "Taking the Hex Out of X" Time, October 8, 1990, p. 79. No film distributor can escape an "X" rating by refusing to submit the film to the rating board, because all unreviewed films are automatically given an "X" rating.

effort, reclassified as "NC–17" and the typical "X" rated hard core pornographic film.

Unfortunately for the film industry, several States, as well as most newspapers, television stations and video rental organizations, were unimpressed by this distinction drawn by the rating group, continuing to treat the "NC–17" rating as nothing more than an artsy "X." [29]

Although the film industry's rating system is far from perfect, it has at least been designed to perform a public service by notifying audiences in advance what type of content they can expect from each film the industry releases.

Recent efforts to persuade the music industry to adopt a similar code system have been far less successful to date. After agreeing in principle in 1985 to label all violently pornographic or sexually explicit record and music video releases, several years passed before six major music distributors finally declared their willingness in 1990 to begin on a voluntary basis to establish standards for applying notification stickers on all musical cassettes and albums containing obscene or otherwise patently offensive material.

Unfortunately, as soon as this agreement was reached, several States began consideration of legislation that would prevent anyone under the age of 18 from purchasing any record or cassette bearing such a label. The music industry immediately went on the offensive, declaring that they would abandon this labelling effort if any State passed such a law abridging their right of free speech.[30]

While this concern for freedom of expression is certainly praiseworthy, another factor that might have some effect on the attitude of these music distributors is that purchasers under the age of 18 not only accounted for 32 percent of all revenues earned by the music industry in 1988, but also represented the largest age segment of buyers for "heavy metal" and "black/urban" music, the two types of music most likely to be affected by any labeling law.[31]

Rights of Women and Children

To this point we have been focusing primarily on the legal rights of those who create, finance and distribute sexually oriented magazines, books, films or music. We have seen that the marketing of these items cannot be restricted unless a State decides to enact a statute prohibiting their dissemination, and that statute

[29] "NC–17 X'd Out at Blockbuster; Wildmon, AFA Boycott" Variety January 21, 1991, p. 27.

[30] Kevin Zimmerman, "Music Biz Rising to Free–Speech Challenge" Variety, July 25, 1990, p. 53.

[31] Charles Fleming, "Stickers for Minors a Major Headache" Variety, July 25, 1990, p. 1.

conforms in all respects to those protections accorded these corporate entities or individuals by the Constitution.[32]

But what about those in our society who are *victimized* by these materials? Does media free speech carry with it the privilege to ridicule or insult any group with impunity, secure in the knowledge that they have neither the legal right nor the media connections needed to respond to such attacks? In this era of "PC", there is a heightened awareness of the sensitivity of various racial and ethnic groups to comments or depictions that would have been considered perfectly appropriate only a decade ago, but one group in our society still does not appear to have benefitted from this change of attitude.

Today as in the past, certain "sexually oriented" magazines, films and music continue to stereotype women either as mindless sex objects constantly seeking gratification, or as subhuman victims to be subjugated and used. Unfortunately, efforts by militant feminists to ban beauty pageants or bar the viewing of even the most innocent of pin-up pictures have tended to obscure differences between images which glamorize or revere and those that degrade. Clearly, it is one thing for an artist to strive to convey the beauty of the female form to an admiring public and quite another for a hard-core pornographer to display the body of a nude woman in a sordid depiction of sexual debasement merely to gratify the urges of those eager to savor such abuse .[33]

During the 1980s, women's groups in the United States mounted two different types of legal attacks on pornographic materials that dehumanize women. One involved sponsoring a local ordinance that would allow a woman to sue a pornographic dealer for damages sustained as a result of the sale of such materials. The other sought a local law to suppress pornographic material in order to protect the civil rights of women.

The Minneapolis Approach

In Minneapolis, a group of women opposing pornography thought it unwise to involve government in their efforts to prevent

[32] These protections, as defined in California v. Miller, require that there be reasonable findings, based on acceptable evidence, that the material in question does appeal to prurient interests in a patently offensive way, and does not have any serious literary, artistic, political or scientific value.

[33] The Supreme Court also seems to have had its own difficulties through the years in distinguishing art from exploitation. In 1972, in California v. LaRue, 409 U.S. 109, 93 S.Ct. 390, the Court held that nude female dancers performing in a bar were engaged in a form of constitutionally protected expression. However, more recently in Barnes v. Glen Theatre, Inc., 501 U.S. 560, 111 S.Ct. 2456 (1991) a divided Court upheld by a 5–4 vote an Indiana statute requiring female dancers in a barroom setting to be covered by pasties and a G-string, declaring that although a nude dancer in a bar might be conveying a message, the State's interests in safeguarding societal order and public morality would outweigh such free speech considerations.

the dissemination of such material. As Wendy Kaminer, one of the group's leaders, wrote, "Feminists need not and should not advocate censorship, but we have every right to organize politically and to protest material that is degrading and dangerous to women." [34]

Her solution, as that of Andrea Dworkin and Catharine McKinnon—driving forces behind the Minneapolis ordinance—was to sue for violation of their personal rights as women. Since they believed that pornography was sex-based discrimination—"the sexually explicit subordination of women, graphically depicted"—then persons offended by such materials should have the right to sue for damages.[35] However, this approach was eventually abandoned when its supporters failed on two separate occasions to override the veto of Minneapolis Mayor Fraser.

The Indianapolis Ordinance: Prior Restraint

In the spring of 1984, the Indianapolis–Marion County City–County Council passed and then amended an ordinance to define, prevent, and prohibit "all discriminatory practices of sexual subordination or inequality through pornography." Mayor Richard Hudnut signed them into law.[36] The ordinance said, in part: [37]

> 16. "Pornography" is defined in the Ordinance as follows:
>
> "(q) Pornography shall mean the graphic sex—sexually explicit subordination of women, whether in pictures or in words, that also includes one or more of the following:
>
> (1) Women who are presented as sexual objects or who enjoy pain or humiliation; or
>
> (2) Women are presented as sexual objects who experience sexual pleasure in being raped; or
>
> (3) Women are presented as sexual objects tied up or cut or mutilated or bruised or physically hurt, or as dismembered or truncated or fragmented or severed into body parts; or

[34] Wendy Kaminer, "Pornography and the First Amendment: Prior Restraint and Private Action" in Take Back the Night, p. 241.

[35] See Attorney General's Commission on Pornography Final Report (1986). Although the report has been criticized for overstating the causal connection between depictions of sexual violence and violent treatment of women, virtually all social scientists who testified before the Commission agreed that constant exposure to such content would be likely to stimulate a more aggressive attitude towards women by men already tending towards such behavior.

[36] American Booksellers Association, Inc. v. Hudnut, 598 F.Supp. 1316 (S.D.Ind. 1984).

[37] 598 F.Supp. at 1320 (S.D.Ind.1984), 11 Med.L.Rptr. at 1106, quoting Indianapolis ordinance.

(4) Women are presented being penetrated by objects or animals; or

(5) Women are presented in scenarios of degradation, injury, abasement, torture, shown as filthy or inferior, bleeding, bruised, or hurt in a context that makes these conditions sexual, and

(6) Women are presented as sexual objects for domination, conquest, violation, exploitation, possession, or use, or through postures or positions of servility or submission or display.

The use of men, children, or transsexuals in the place of women in paragraphs (1) through (6) above shall also constitute pornography under this section."

Another section of the ordinance made "trafficking in pornography"; the production, sale, exhibition, or distribution of pornographic material unlawful. In addition, the ordinance authorized any woman in the community to file a complaint on behalf of all local women protesting the subordination of women.

In response, the American Booksellers Association—plus other groups and individuals including the Association of American Publishers and the Freedom to Read Foundation of the American Library Association—challenged the constitutionality of the ordinance. It was contended that the ordinance "severely restricts the availability, display and distribution of constitutionally protected, non-obscene materials in violation of the First and Fourteenth Amendments." More specifically, plaintiffs complained that the sweep of the ordinance took in more than materials which are constitutionally unprotected speech (such as obscenity).

Further, these plaintiffs said the ordinance was unconstitutionally vague in not giving adequate notice of what might be a crime under its provisions.

District Judge Barker's lengthy opinion found three major defects in the Indianapolis ordinance; it sought to control speech without reference to applicable constitutional requirements, the expression it sought to control might not meet the obscenity test specified in Miller v. California and the language of the ordinance was, in Judge Barker's view, "impermissibly vague."

In sum, although government has a recognized interest in prohibiting sex discrimination, the judge found that, "that interest does not outweigh the constitutionally protected interest in free speech."

On appeal, a three-judge panel of the U.S. Court of Appeals, Seventh Circuit, affirmed the district court's judgment that the Indianapolis anti-pornography ordinance was unconstitutional.

Circuit Judge Easterbrook said the ordinance did not refer, as in Miller v. California, to prurient interest, offensiveness, or community standards. Further, it concentrated on particular depictions, not judging a work as a whole, and made it irrelevant whether a work had literary, artistic, political, or scientific value.

The ordinance contains four prohibitions. People may not "traffic" in pornography, "coerce" others into performing in pornographic works, or "force" pornography on anyone. Anyone injured by someone who has seen or read pornography has a right of action against the maker or seller.

Even though the appeals court was willing to admit that the subordinate status of women had led to "lower pay at work, insult and injury at home, and battery and rape," it concluded that the definition of illegal pornography contained in this ordinance improperly infringed upon constitutionally protected free speech.[38]

Child Pornography

Although American law has been unsympathetic to the pleas of women to stop the flood of pornographic materials in the United States, child pornography has been treated in an entirely different fashion. Legislation has been created to outlaw using minors to perform or act in the creation of films, books, or magazine articles or other items depicting the sexual exploitation of children.[39]

The measure was designed to put a stop to magazines which could be purchased in 1977 such as "Chicken Delight," "Lust for Children," "Lollitots," and "Child Discipline" that were then being sold. Dr. Judianne Densen–Gerber, president of the Odyssey Institute, made this outraged statement to the Subcommittee on Crime of Congress' Committee on the Judiciary: [40]

> There comes a point where we can no longer defend by intellectualization or forensic debate. We must simply say "I know the difference between right and wrong and I am not afraid to say 'no' or demand that limits be imposed."
>
> Common sense and maternal instinct tell me that this [child pornography that she found in New York, Philadelphia, Boston, Washington, New Orleans, Chicago, San

[38] American Booksellers Association, Inc. v. Hudnut, 771 F.2d 323 (7th Cir.1985); see also, Tamar Lewin, "Canada Court Says Pornography Harms Women and Can Be Banned," The New York Times, Feb. 28, 1992, p. 41.

[39] Senate Bill 1585, 95th Congress, 1st Session, No. 95–438, "Protection of Children Against Sexual Exploitation Act of 1977; Report of the Committee on the Judiciary, United States Senate, on S. 1585.

[40] Prepared Statement of Judianne Densen–Gerber, J.D., M.D., F.C.L.M., President, Odyssey Institute, for submission to The U.S. House of Representatives, Committee on the Judiciary, Subcommittee on Crime, May 23, 1977.

Francisco, and Los Angeles] goes way beyond free speech. Such conduct mutilates children's spirits; they aren't consenting adults, they're victims. The First Amendment isn't absolute.

This legislation, signed into law in 1978 by President Carter, was formally called the "Protection of Children Against Sexual Exploitation Act of 1977." This legislation, in the words of U.S. Senators John C. Culver of Iowa and Charles McC. Mathias of Maryland, was intended to do the following: [41]

— Make it a Federal crime to use children in the production of pornographic materials.

— Prohibit the interstate transportation of children for the purpose of engaging in prostitution, and

— Increase the penalty provisions of the current Federal obscenity laws if the materials adjudged obscene involve the use of children engaging in sexually explicit conduct.

This measure tried to correct loopholes in federal obscenity statutes. Before this law was passed, there was no federal statute prohibiting use of children in production of materials that depict explicit sexual conduct. This statute defined "minor" as any person under the age of 16 years. Penalties for violation of this statutory provision are two–ten years imprisonment and/or a fine of up to $10,000 on first offense, or five–fifteen years imprisonment and/or a fine of up to $15,000 for subsequent offenses.[42]

Committees of the U.S. Senate and House of Representatives found a close connection between child pornography and the use of young children as prostitutes. For example, a 17–year-old Chicago youth who had sold himself on the streets for two years, could often earn close to $500 a week by selling himself two or three times a night to perform various sex acts with "chicken hawks" or pose for pornographic pictures or both.[43]

Kidporn and New York v. Ferber (1982)

In 1982, the Supreme Court of the United States made one thing clear about the murky law of obscenity: it will uphold state

[41] Form letter sent to the author by Senators Culver and Mathias, circa September 1977; letter to the author of October 19, 1977, by Rep. John Conyers, Jr. of Michigan's First District. See Public Law 95–225.

[42] 18 U.S.C.A. § 2251, Chapter 110—Sexual Exploitation of Children. The Mann Act, 18 U.S.C.A. § 2423, prohibits the interstate transportation of minor females for purposes of prostitution and did not include young males until amended in 1977.

[43] Report of the Committee on the Judiciary, United States Senate on S.1585, Protection of Children Against Sexual Exploitation Act of 1977 (Washington, D.C., 1977), p. 7. See also Robin Lloyd, For Money or Love: Boy Prostitution in America (New York: Vanguard Press, 1976).

efforts to punish individuals for the production or sale of "kid-porn."

In New York v. Ferber, the Court declared valid a New York criminal statute prohibiting persons from knowingly authorizing or inducing a child less than 16 years old to engage in a sexual performance.[44] "Sexual performance" was defined by the New York statute as, "any performance or part thereof which includes sexual performance or part thereof which includes sexual conduct by a child less than sixteen years of age." The specific statutory provision tested said: [45]

> A person is guilty [of a class D felony, which carries punishment of up to seven years imprisonment for persons and a fine of up to $10,000 for corporations] of promoting a sexual performance by a child when, knowing the character and content thereof, he produces, directs, or promotes any performance which includes sexual conduct by a child less than sixteen years of age.

The case began when Paul Ira Ferber, proprietor of a Manhattan bookstore specializing in sexually oriented materials, sold two films to undercover police officers. The two films dealt almost exclusively with depictions of boys masturbating. A jury trial convicted Ferber of two counts of promoting a sexual performance and Ferber was sentenced to 45 days in prison.

Ferber's convictions were upheld on first appeal, but the New York Court of Appeals said that the statute section under which Ferber was convicted was too sweeping. The New York Court of Appeals held that Section 263.15 might be used to punish sale or promotion of material protected by the First Amendment. Protected material which seemed to come under the New York statute, the appeals court said, included "medical books and educational sources, which deal with adolescent sex in a realistic but nonobscene manner." [46]

The Supreme Court of the United States granted certiorari. In deciding the case, the Court said that it presented just one question:

> To prevent the abuse of children who are made to engage in sexual conduct for commercial purposes, could

---

[44] 458 U.S. 747, 102 S.Ct. 3348 (1982), 8 Med.L.Rptr. 1809.

[45] McKinney's, New York Penal Law, § 263.1. In addition, as noted by the Court, the New York statute defines a performance as " 'any play, motion picture, photograph or dance' or 'any other visual presentation exhibited before an audience.' " See McKinney's, N.Y.Penal Law § 263.4. "Sexual conduct" is defined as " 'actual or simulated sexual intercourse, deviate; sexual intercourse, sexual bestiality, masturbation, sado-masochistic abuse, or lewd exhibition of the genitals.' " McKinney's, N.Y.Penal Law § 263.3.

[46] 458 U.S. 747, 102 S.Ct. 3348, 3352 (1982).

the New York State Legislature, consistent with the First Amendment, prohibit the dissemination of material which shows children engaged in sexual conduct, regardless of whether such material is obscene?

Writing for the Court, Justice Byron White said:

> Like obscenity statutes, laws directed at the dissemination of child pornography run the risk of suppressing protected expression by allowing the hand of the censor to become unduly heavy. For the following reasons, however, we are persuaded that the States are entitled to greater leeway in the regulation of pornographic depictions of children.

> *First.* It is evident beyond the need for elaboration that a state's interest in "safeguarding the physical and psychological well being of a minor" is "compelling." Globe Newspapers v. Superior Court, 457 U.S. 596, 607, 102 S.Ct. 2613, 2620 (1982), 8 Med.L.Rptr. 1689.

* * *

> *Second.* The distribution of photographs and films depicting sexual activity by juveniles is intrinsically related to the sexual abuse of children in at least two ways. First, the materials produced are a permanent record of the children's participation and the harm to the child is exacerbated by their circulation. Second, the distribution network for child pornography must be closed if the production of material which requires the sexual exploitation of children is to be effectively controlled.

Justice White noted the economic motive involved in the production of such materials. "It rarely has been suggested that the constitutional freedom for speech and press extends immunity to speech or writing used as an integral part of conduct in violation of a valid criminal statute." [47] Further, classifying child pornography as a category outside protection of the First Amendment is compatible with the Supreme Court's earlier rulings.

The Price of "Free" Speech

Today, obscene expression remains the only major form of communication unprotected by law, but the term "obscene" is now narrowly defined by most courts to include only the most revolting forms of sexually explicit depictions or descriptions. If further efforts are made to extend this legal categorization to include violent or hard-core pornography, the Supreme Court may eventually decide to move in one of two opposing directions.

---

[47] Quoting Giboney v. Empire Storage & Ice Co., 336 U.S. 490, 69 S.Ct. 684 (1949).

On one hand, the Court could ultimately rule that no valid social purpose is served by continuing its tightly constrained "obscenity exception," and abolish this category of unprotected expression. In this way State or local governments would be denied legal authority to restrict local sale or distribution of any form of magazine, film or video content, and the Court could escape further involvement in this difficult and divisive area of law.

On the other, the Court could decide, in response to a growing awareness of how much media actually shape our perceptions of each other and the world around us, to expand the "obscenity exception" in order to grant recognition to the inherent legal interests of those in our society victimized by violent pornography or other forms of hate literature.

Those who fear any greater government control over the sale or distribution of pornographic material argue that social scientists have not yet been able to establish a clear causal connection between the viewing of violent pornography and acts of sexual violence.[48] In reality, however, this is about as sensible as assuming that the Earth must be flat because medieval scientists lacked the research skills to prove it was round.

The truth is that because of the awesome complexity of the human mind, and numerous legal and ethical constraints imposed upon behavioral research methodologies, social science remains light years away from being capable of predicting even the most elemental forms of stimulus-response relationships of human behavior. Because of this, it would seem wiser not to rely too heavily on social science at this point for answers to serious questions of public policy. Instead it would appear far more reasonable to follow the tradition of Scottish juries who in addition to being able to find a defendant guilty or not guilty, were allowed to enter a verdict of "not proven" when common sense indicated conclusively that the defendant had committed the crime, but insufficient evidence existed to support the conviction.

Another argument advanced against government restrictions on the free flow of such material is that if certain groups are offended by the content of some particular magazine, film or video, they can simply refuse to buy it. In reality, however, widespread dissemination of these mass media messages of lust, hate or ridicule provides those who are eager to read or view this material reenforcement of those very distorted stereotypes its victims seek to combat. Just as non-smokers in a smoke-filled room, we cannot

[48] The **Final Report of the Attorney General's Commission on Pornography.** U.S. Government Printing Office, 1986, concluded that a significant body of research evidence clearly established such a connection. Predictably, this contention was immediately challenged by several social scientists who asserted that the Report's findings were far broader than warranted by the facts.

escape a polluted cultural environment simply by pretending that it does not exist.

To trust in the power of individual consumer choice to alter the nature of this environment seems about as naive as believing all our ecological problems can be solved through boycotting the products of a few polluters. Recognizing the futility of attempting to save our natural resources through the marketplace alone, the federal government ultimately adopted standards to protect the interests of each citizen in a clean and healthful environment.[49] Similarly, unless American law at some point either assumes responsibility for protecting the interests of those who are unfairly portrayed by the media, or recognizes their right to protect these interests on their own, that media atmosphere in which they must exist seems unlikely to improve.

Still another argument against recognizing any legal right of those aggrieved by their media treatment is that law is incapable of making informed judgments about the quality of media content, and may turn from suppressing smut today to suppressing Shakespeare tomorrow. What this argument overlooks is that our system of law has progressed significantly since the days of the Star Chamber and trial by ordeal.

If a legislature can define and a court or jury can decide at what point similarity in story or melody line constitutes plagiarism; at what moment the aborting of a fetus becomes the murder of a human being; or at what level of mental capacity an individual can be held accountable for the attempted assassination of a president, it would seem that this same legal system has sufficient sophistication to determine when media content is designed to exploit rather than to entertain.

Yet, despite any arguments to the contrary, the traditional mass communication law text would almost certainly praise any Supreme Court decision that abolished the legal category of obscenity, and criticize any effort to extend its scope to include hard-core pornographic or other similar material. This is because the time-honored approach in this field has been to view every law and each judicial decision solely in terms of whether the industry "won" or

[49] The National Environmental Policy Act of 1970, 42 U.S.C.A. § 4321 and the creation of the Environmental Protection Agency in 1970, marked the first major federal recognition of the need to preserve the physical environment. Prior to that time, courts tended to be unsympathetic with environmental concerns that limited industrial development. Typical is the comment the court in Gardner v. International Shoe Co., 319 Ill.App. 416, 49 N.E.2d 328 (1943), that "the restraining of normal business activity is contrary to public policy." Even as late as 1970, in Boomer v. Atlantic Cement Co., 26 N.Y.2d 219, 309 N.Y.S.2d 312, 257 N.E.2d 870 (1970), a court refused to enjoin industrial pollution because damage caused by the pollution was found to be less than the costs of reducing the pollution.

"lost"; that is, whether its free speech rights were ultimately extended or diminished.

From this perspective, however, it is easy to overlook the fact that in most of these legal battles there are other individuals, groups and societal issues caught in the crossfire. A "victory" for the industry in the field of libel, for example, actually represents a defeat for all those who may have been unfairly maligned by media. Similarly, upholding the right of the press to describe details of a criminal investigation may result in prejudicing a jury against the accused, or allow someone who has actually committed a crime to escape justice because of improper pretrial publicity. Releasing broadcasters from their obligations to provide childrens' programming may enhance their freedom of expression, but at a cost of reducing the number of shows designed to fulfill the educational and entertainment needs of the young.

What this suggests is that the study of mass communication law should involve more than simply tallying wins and loses on a scorecard. Any legal victory for the media must be viewed in a broader context; one that looks beyond gauging how much additional freedom media has won to consider at what societal costs this victory has been achieved, and to what benefit for the public.

From this standpoint, then, it may be difficult to rejoice too heartily the victory by the publisher of some violently pornographic magazine over State law, because the extension of the right to disseminate this material certainly exacts its toll from each woman threatened by its message, at no perceptible benefit to our society except for those who avidly study every page.

In the last analysis, though, the only thing that might prove to be more damaging to the interests of the mass communication industry than a series of legal defeats severely curtailing their freedom of expression might be a series of victories granting them virtually absolute freedom from any legal responsibility for their actions. In that case, individuals deprived of any legal means of influencing the conduct of the media are almost certain to resort to vigilante tactics to protect societal interests they believe are too precious to abandon, and to seek through political pressure controls far more repressive than those the media have succeeded in escaping. Ironically, then, what seems most likely to guarantee the broadest possible range of free expression for media in the United States may actually be the continued presence of sufficient legal controls to guarantee that these media will remain responsive to the concerns of each citizen they serve.

Electronic Media Standards

For broadcasters, transmission of obscene programming is a federal criminal offense, and also grounds for FCC revocation of a

broadcast license.[50]   In addition, however, the Commission has
been attempting to establish more rigorous standards for sexually
oriented broadcast programs, prohibiting "indecent" content,
which the agency has defined in general terms as being patently
offensive descriptions of sexual or excretory activities.[51]

The public appears to expect a far higher standard of good
taste from broadcasters, and particularly from television networks,
than from other media simply because even in an era when these
networks attract only 60 percent of the nation's primetime viewers,
they still remain the most powerful and pervasive force in American mass culture.   On a typical evening, any modestly popular
situation comedy scheduled by one of the major television networks
will be viewed by more Americans than will read any best selling
novel or attend any single feature film that entire year.   In other
words, virtually every network television series producer has a
greater opportunity to influence public sentiments, beliefs and
values than even the most popular of novelists or film makers.

Until the early 1980s, all broadcast programming was regulated by the federal government.   Although the amount of supervisory
control the FCC actually exerted over television network program
policies was minimal, the fact that a federal agency was authorized
by law to make television responsive to the concerns of the public
was in itself sufficient to satisfy most citizens.

The deregulation of broadcasting closed this one channel of
legal influence that had been open to the average citizen, at a time
when the industry was dismantling its own private system of
program content standards and looking for ways to attract a
younger, more affluent and less traditional group of listeners and
viewers.[52]

Competition from the Fox Network and a wide array of cable
services forced the three major television networks to become
slightly more venturesome during the 1980s, as both series and
made-for-TV movies began treating topics that would have been
summarily rejected only a decade before.   Although very little that
was broadcast during this era could have been classified as "inde-

[50] For radio and television, this prohibition against the transmission of obscene
content is contained in the criminal provisions of 18 U.S.C.A. § 1464.   A similar
prohibition against the carriage of obscene cable TV programming is contained in
the Cable Policy Act, 47 U.S.C.A. § 559.

[51] The FCC's indecency activities are discussed in the following chapter.

[52] Although the FCC's current crusade against "indecent" programs as described
in Chapter 7 may deserve criticism for attempting to repress constitutionally
protected expression, it is at least an effort by the FCC to demonstrate to the more
than 6,000 individuals who write to the agency each year to complain about such
programs that the federal government is still trying to be responsive to public
concerns about the quality of broadcast service.   See, for example, "Defining the
Line Between Regulation and Censorship" Broadcasting April 15, 1991, p. 74.

cent," much less obscene, American audiences were not accustomed to even mildly risque programs from a medium readily accessible to children in the home.

Yet, because of wide-spread concern caused by broadcasting being released from virtually all of its "public interest" obligations, one of the major results of broadcast deregulation has been to popularize the forming of countless local and national private pressure groups, ranging from religious right to radical left, from *Gay and Lesbian League* to the *AFL-CIO*, to fight for each group's own perceived interests in broadcast programming. Using a broad range of economic, legal and political threats, these groups have already forced a number of stations to modify their programming policies in response to their demands. In a very real sense, then, it can be argued that one of the disadvantages of media having largely unfettered legal freedom is already clearly reflected in these recent experiences of the broadcasting industry.

Part III

MASS COMMUNICATIONS AND GOVERNMENT

Chapter 9

REGULATING BROADCASTING

SEC. 50. LICENSING BROADCASTERS

The licensing process has provided both the legal authority and the procedures essential for the regulation of broadcast service in the United States.

The Radio Act of 1927 marked both the beginning of broadcast regulation in the United States and the end of that era when use of the airwaves was an inherent right of every citizen, limited only by the availability of spectrum space.[1] Section 11 of the Radio Act diminished this *right* to the status of a *privilege*, to be granted by the Federal Radio Commission (FRC) only in circumstances where the agency found that issuing or renewing a broadcast license would serve the "public interest".[2] This same regulatory approach was followed by the Communications Act of 1934 that created the Federal Communications Commission (FCC) to replace the FRC.[3]

Because these governmental bodies were viewed as bestowing a *privilege* upon those they permitted to broadcast, the United States

---

[1] Section 2 of the Radio Act of 1912 required the Secretary of Commerce to issue licenses upon request, allowing conditions to be imposed upon a license only in instances where its operation might interfere with those of other licensed stations.

[2] Section 11, Radio Act of 1927, "If upon examination of any application for a station license or for the renewal or modification of a station license the licensing authority shall determine that public interest, convenience or necessity would be served by the granting thereof, it shall authorize the issuance, renewal or modification thereof in accordance with such finding."

[3] Communications Act of 1934, Public Law 416, 73d Congress, Secs. 307–309.

Supreme Court upheld their authority as regulatory agencies to impose conditions on the private use of this public resource of broadcast spectrum space, including a requirement that broadcast programming serve the interests of the public.[4] As a later Supreme Court decision would declare in even stronger terms, such government program standards were viewed as enhancing, rather than repressing broadcast freedom of expression because,

> When there are substantially more individuals who want to broadcast than there are frequencies to allocate, it is idle to posit an unabridgeable First Amendment right to broadcast comparable to the right of individuals to speak, write or publish ... the people as a whole retain their interest in free speech and their collective right to have the medium function consistently with the ends and purposes of the First Amendment.[5]

It is this broadcast licensing power, then, that has furnished the federal government with both the legal authority essential to regulate American broadcast service and that administrative process necessary to enforce its regulatory policies during the past seven decades.

The licensing process itself has always been more a matter of form than of substance. Applications for a construction permit, a broadcast license or renewal of a license each require the completion of countless forms, all filed in multiple copies with the Commission in Washington. There a small desk-bound staff of less than two dozen civil servants processes this paperwork to determine whether each application should be approved.[6]

The forms themselves are generally prepared for the broadcaster by one of the major communication law firms in Washington that specializes in dealings with the FCC. These attorneys, often former FCC employees, are in daily contact with the Commission staff to resolve any problems that might arise from their clients' broadcast filings. In nearly all cases, the end result of the process is that the application for the permit, license or license renewal is eventually granted.[7]

[4] National Broadcasting Company, et al. v. United States, et al., 319 U.S. 190, 63 S.Ct. 997 (1943). See also, chapter 3, Sec. 14 of this text for a more extensive discussion of this decision.

[5] Red Lion Broadcasting Co. v. FCC, 395 U.S. 367, 89 S.Ct. 1794 (1969).

[6] For an excellent description of this administrative process, see Barry Cole and Mal Oettinger, Reluctant Regulators: The FCC and the Broadcast Audience (Reading, MA: Addison–Wesley, 1978).

[7] In 1976, for example, the FCC processed 2995 applications for renewal of broadcast licenses of which just 23 were designated for hearing, and only 8 ultimately denied. In other words, 99.2% of all renewal applicants were approved without hearing and only 3/10 of 1% were eventually denied. Cole, Oettinger, op. cit., p. 147.

However, in that very small percentage of cases where a broadcast license application cannot be approved because, "a substantial and material question of fact is presented, or the Commission for any reason is unable to make the finding specified," the applicant is notified of the Commission's intention to hold a hearing before deciding what action should be taken.[8]

In most instances, a broadcaster unsuccessful at the informal hearing level still has the right to have this administrative finding reviewed both within the FCC itself and then by the Court of Appeals for the District of Columbia before being forced to accept an adverse Commission decision.[9]

The FCC does not monitor broadcast transmissions and so at time of renewal, it has always had to rely upon the records or "logs" of programming maintained by each station in determining whether the broadcaster has complied with the program proposals the station filed with the Commission when the license was last renewed.[10]   During the 1980s the agency reduced this level of supervision even further, releasing broadcasters from the obligation to submit program logs to the Commission at the time of a station's license renewal.[11]

In 1991, however, the Commission decided to begin enforcing certain basic broadcast rules more aggressively, using its forfeiture power to impose monetary fines on licensees violating these rules. This tactic allowed the FCC to react to these violations much more quickly and efficiently than if it threatened a broadcaster's license, because many of the procedural safeguards of the licensing process did not apply in cases where the Commission sought only a monetary penalty.

[8] U.S.C.A. Title 47, § 309(e). Recently, one of the few comparative standards the FCC had been using in deciding among competing candidates for a broadcast license was overturned by the court in Bechtel v. FCC, 957 F 2d 873 (D.C.Cir.1992). The court questioned the validity of the "integrated ownership" standard the Commission claimed to have been following since 1965, asking the FCC to produce one case during those years in which an applicant who received a license after pledging to personally manage a station had actually done so. Rather than respond to this challenge, the agency decided in April 1992 to review its entire comparative licensing process. See Reexamination of the Policy Statement on Comparative Broadcast Hearings, 7 FCC Rcd 2664 (1992); see also, Anchor Broadcasting, 72 R.R. 2d 98 (1993).

[9] U.S.C.A. Title 47, § 402(b). Although a broadcaster may also seek U.S. Supreme Court review of an adverse Court of Appeals decision, the Supreme Court agrees to review, or accept certiorari only in a very limited number of appeal situations each year.

[10] For a more detailed description of this license renewal process and its flaws, see Don R. Le Duc, Beyond Broadcasting: Patterns in Policy and Law (White Plains, NY: Longman, 1987) pp. 43–56.

[11] Revision of Applications of Renewals of License of Commercial and Non–Commercial AM, and Television Licensees, 50 R.R. 2d 704 (1981).

After adopting a comprehensive *Table of Forfeitures* which for the first time specified the specific monetary amount that would be levied for each type of rule violation, the agency started almost immediately to invoke its new sanctions. [12] During 1993 alone the Commission imposed fines totally more than one million dollars on some 140 different broadcasters for violations ranging from technical offenses such as inadequate tower lighting or failure to maintain public files to more serious charges of inadequate compliance with EEO requirements, improper political advertising practices or violation of the Commission's indecency standards. [13]

For the most part, though, broadcasters have tended to conform to Commission regulatory policies not because of any fear of forfeiture, or concern about what the licensing process might reveal about their programming practices, but rather because even the slightest threat to a station's license is a risk worth avoiding at virtually any cost.

This type of indirect rule worked particularly well during an era when the Commission could decide for itself when its under-staffed Broadcast Bureau was capable of using the license renewal process to enforce certain specific FCC regulatory standards. Until the mid 1960s, only a competing broadcaster could compel the FCC to conduct a comparative hearing before awarding or renewing a broadcast license of another station in that market, and then only if the evidence clearly indicated that the award could cause intolerable transmission interference or severe economic injury to the complaining broadcaster.[14]

In all other situations, the Commission had sole authority to decide whether the public interest demanded that it conduct an elaborate and time consuming hearing before renewing a broadcast license. Not surprisingly, it rarely did.

In 1966, however, a federal court found that the FCC had been wrong in assuming that because the Commission was created to protect the interests of the public, members of the public themselves had no right to become involved in a broadcast licensing

---

[12] In re Standards for Assessing Forfeitures, 69 R.R. 2d 823 (1991), affirmed on reconsideration 70 R.R. 2d 11206 (1992). In July 1994, the U.S. Court of Appeals for the D.C. District upheld a U.S. Telephone Association challenge of this new uniform forfeiture schedule, holding that the FCC had failed to give those broadcasters, cable operators and telephone company licensees it affected adequate opportunity to comment on the new schedule before it was adopted. The Court did not find the concept of uniform fines to be unacceptable in itself but did question the equity of this particular schedule of fines that seemed to be overly severe in punishing telephone company regulatory violations.

[13] "Informal Listing of FCC Forfeiture Proceedings 1993", Mass Media Bureau, 1994. (mimeo). However, in U.S. Telephone Assn. v. FCC, 28 F.3d 1232 (D.C.Cir. 1994) a federal court overturned the Commission's uniform schedule, holding that the penalties it had established for telephone carrier violations were excessively high.

[14] Title 47, U.S.C.A. § 316(b).

proceeding.[15] This decision, authorizing members of a community to to challenge in federal court any license renewal granted by the Commission without adequate evidence of the local station's effective past performance, set off such a massive barrage of "citizen group" license challenges that the entire structure of American broadcast regulation seemed imperiled for a time.

RENEWING THE BROADCAST LICENSE

Recognizing the right of citizen groups to challenge the renewal of a broadcast license created new constraints upon broadcast freedom of expression.

During the period from 1970 to 1977, the FCC received a total of 447 citizen petitions or objections involving the licenses of 936 broadcast stations; almost 10 percent of all the commercial broadcasters then being licensed by the Commission.[16] Many in the broadcast industry felt that they had been betrayed by the courts, and abandoned by a Commission no longer capable of protecting them from private pressures. After complying with FCC rules for almost a half century with the understanding that the agency posed the only threat to their licenses, they were now suddenly being forced to defend themselves from citizen challenges as well, attacks upon an unprotected flank that left them vulnerable to interest group demands.

The FCC tried to end this siege of license renewal challenges in 1970 by proposing rules that made it virtually impossible to deny license renewal to an existing broadcast station, but a federal court refused to allow these rules to be adopted.[17] As the 1970s drew to a close, this "citizen group" movement lost its momentum, frustrated by the Commission's skilled use of procedural delay to deny them the hearings they sought. But this chaotic era of widespread license challenge had convinced the broadcast industry that it could no longer rely upon the FCC or the Communications Act of 1934 to protect their broadcast licenses from challenge.

Instead, the primary political objective for broadcasters during the 1980s became convincing Congress to adopt new legislation capable of sheltering existing broadcast station licenses from citizen group attack much more effectively at time of renewal. In 1981,

[15] Office of Communication of the United Church of Christ v. FCC, 359 F.2d 994 (D.C.Cir.1966).

[16] Comptroller General, Report to the Congress, "Selected FCC Regulatory Policies and Consequences for Commercial Radio and Television," CED 79–62, 4 June 1979, p. 17.

[17] The FCC rules were proposed in "Policy Statement Concerning Comparative Hearings Involving Regular Renewal Applicants," 22 FCC2d 424 (1970). The rules were rescinded when challenged by a public service law firm in Citizens Communication Center v. FCC, 447 F.2d 1201 (D.C.Cir.1971).

Congress did act to reduce the dimensions of the license renewal problem to some extent by increasing the length of each television station license from three years to five, and lengthening each radio license period from three years to seven.[18] However, Congress has refused thus far to grant the industry the broad license renewal protection it has been seeking, forcing the FCC to try to provide these safeguards under the more restrictive language of the Communications Act of 1934.[19]

The Commission's decision to attempt to protect broadcasters from citizen organized license challenges is based upon the belief that such private pressure can pose a greater, if more subtle threat to broadcast freedom of expression that any federal regulatory policy may have posed in the past. Although the First Amendment shields broadcasting from government censorship, it provides no legal protection against private pressure. In addition, while government regulation is a public process, open for all to observe, interest group negotiations typically are conducted in secret, with concessions being granted without public knowledge or consent.

Ironically, then, the same FCC that was once viewed by the industry as the enemy of broadcast free speech is now the industry's only ally in the struggle to safeguard those free speech rights from the influence of self-styled "citizen groups."

But why should broadcast industry be so susceptible to such private pressure, particularly since any "citizen group" license challenge will ultimately be brought to the FCC for resolution? Those who champion the First Amendment rights of broadcasting are often critical of stations or networks willing to negotiate their programming practices with these interest groups, arguing that such broadcast organizations have the financial resources to protect, rather than bargain away their precious freedom of expression.

What these critics fail to realize is that while a media organization may have such resources, the decision to fight rather than negotiate a license challenge must be made by some highly paid executive within this organization, generally the station manager, whose dependence upon that generous salary to meet monthly mortgage payments and other financial obligations makes this employee far more vulnerable to such private pressure than any abstract concept of broadcast free speech would suggest.

Continuing controversy over station programming practices tends to disrupt normal business operations, is likely to damage a

18 Omnibus Reconciliation Act of 1981, 95 Stat. 736–37, as amended by Public Law 97–259.

19 See, for example, "FCC: Time to Modernize Comparative Renewal," Broadcasting, June 27, 1988, p. 35.

station's public image in the area it serves, and is almost certain to be viewed with alarm and displeasure at the corporate headquarters of the station's group owner. In addition, even a successful defense of a station's license may result in uncompensated legal expenses ranging from 100,000 to 500,000 dollars.[20] With these facts in mind, then, it may be easier to understand why a number of broadcast stations have yielded to the programming demands of well organized, politically sophisticated pressure groups, and why both the industry and the FCC view such privately negotiated programming concessions with such concern.

The FCC was finally able to adopt a revised set of license renewal rules in 1989, designed to discourage the challenging of a broadcast license merely to profit from a subsequent payment by the licensee to withdraw the challenge.[21] The new rules require that the Commission approve in advance all negotiated settlements between the license holder and a challenger or competing applicant. No settlement will be approved if payments to the challenger exceed what the FCC finds to be the "legitimate and prudent" expenses actually incurred by the challenger during the proceeding.

In addition, other forms of indirect compensation are now also presumed to violate the agency's settlement standards, such as an agreement by the station to hire or retain any member of the challenging organization, or to schedule specific programming produced or provided by that organization.

A survey of renewal proceedings conducted soon after the new rules were adopted disclosed a significant decrease in the number of challenges being filed, suggesting that these new procedural safeguards were achieving their desired policy objectives. Encouraged by these results, the FCC decided in May 1990 to impose similar settlement payment restrictions on all future comparative hearings involving new broadcast license applications as well.

After two decades of rulemaking and litigation, the Commission finally appears to have developed renewal standards capable of discouraging the filing of improperly motivated license challenges, while at the same time continuing to permit legitimate challenges to be evaluated fairly and impartially. Although the broadcast industry might have hoped for an even more elaborate set of regulatory safeguards to shelter licensees from the threat of other

[20] For example, WBBM–TV Chicago viewed it as a "victory" when they were able to settle a license challenge brought by Center City for *only* $187,000; reimbursement of Center City's legal expenses in filing the challenge. See "Settlement Reached in WBBM–TV Chicago Challenge", Broadcasting, July 18, 1988, p. 33.

[21] Broadcast Renewal Process, 66 RR2d 708 (1989); petition for reconsideration denied, 67 RR2d 1515 (1990) also see 67 RR2d 1526 (1990) for the adoption of similar standards for citizen petitions to deny applications for new stations, license modifications and transfer applications.

types of unjustified challenges, this appears to be the most extensive protection of a broadcaster licensee's renewal rights that the FCC, as an agency of Congress, has the legal authority to provide.

SEC. 51. BROADCAST PROGRAM STANDARDS

Broadcast program requirements have always been stated in general terms to avoid encroaching unnecessarily upon the free speech rights of the broadcast licensee.

In 1929, only two years after it began regulating broadcast service in the United States, the FRC issued its first comprehensive description of federal broadcast program policy. Beginning a regulatory tradition that would endure until the 1980s, the agency pointed out in this earliest public programming statement that it would not establish any list of *preferred* program categories. Instead, the FRC simply directed each station to offer its audience a balanced schedule of different types of programs capable of serving the needs of every segment of the station's audience. The Commission described its program policy objectives in this way:

> The tastes, needs and desires of all substantial groups among the public should be met, in fair proportion, by a well-rounded program schedule, in which entertainment, religion, education and instruction, important public events, discussions of public questions, weather, market reports, news and matters of interest to all members of the family find a place.[22]

Network Program Control

The FRC soon discovered, however, that it was difficult to achieve even these rather basic and generalized programming goals because stations had begun to rely upon national broadcast networks to provide a substantial portion of their daily program schedule. Network broadcasting had existed since 1924, but it was not until 1929 that NBC and the newly formed CBS became the dominant national programming and advertising forces in American radio.[23]

Stations were eager to affiliate with one of the major broadcast networks because they offered the type of popular, professionally produced entertainment shows no local station could hope to duplicate. To become a network affiliate, however, a station had to agree to carry a substantial number of network programs each

[22] In the matter of the application of Great Lakes Broadcasting, 3 FRC Annual Reports 32 (1929).

[23] NBC actually operated two separate radio networks until 1941, the "Red" network which it retained, and the "Blue" network sold in 1941 and renamed the American Broadcasting Company in 1945.

week, and to reserve other portions of its broadcast schedule to be used for whatever programs the network chose to provide.

Both the FRC and the FCC saw the networks as distorting that balance in the various forms of programming these regulatory bodies had sought to encourage; furnishing affiliate stations with a vast array of light entertainment shows while offering virtually no public affairs, educational or childrens' programming.

Yet neither agency had authority to regulate the networks *directly*, because networks did not use the broadcast spectrum to distribute their programs, delivering them instead to their affiliated stations through privately leased telephone lines. Since the networks required no broadcast license to operate these non-spectrum programming services, there was no legal basis for imposing any public interest standards upon the shows they provided their affiliate stations.[24]

Unable to regulate network program practices directly, the FCC began during the late 1930s to use its licensing authority instead to force the network affiliate stations themselves to reclaim from their national network the right to program a larger proportion of their own daily broadcast schedule. In 1940, the Commission adopted rules that established severe restrictions on the amount of broadcast time any station could devote to network programming, including an enforcement provision that allowed the Commission to revoke the broadcast license of any station exceeding these network time limitations.[25]

In 1970, the Commission tried a somewhat similar tactic in television, restricting network affiliate television stations in major markets to only three hours of network supplied prime-time programming each evening.[26] This "Prime Time Access Rule", modified and amended several times to make it more effective, was designed to stimulate local station production during the most popular viewing period of the day, or at the very least to provide non-network program suppliers with access to major market television audiences.

Neither of these efforts was particularly successful. The Commission's vision of a locally oriented broadcast service, offering a broad and balanced assortment of public affairs, educational and other programs overlooked those powerful economic incentives that

[24] Each network did own and operate broadcast stations itself, (O & O stations) but the tactic of trying to influence national network program practices through regulations imposed upon these network owned stations never worked successfully.

[25] FCC rules CFR § 47. 3.101–3.108. The NBC v. US Supreme Court opinion that approved these rules is discussed in chapter 3, Sec. 14.

[26] 23 FCC2d 282 (1970); modified by 44 FCC2d 1081, and further modified by 46 FCC2d 829.

propelled the broadcast industry towards nationwide delivery of popular entertainment financed by national advertising.

Through the years, however, the FCC and the broadcast networks managed to develop a rather close working relationship on most regulatory issues. The FCC was useful to the networks, because by regulating broadcasting, it shielded the industry from other, more powerful political pressures, and furnished broadcasting with a stable and predictable legal environment in which the networks could prosper. On the other hand, the FCC had to rely upon the networks to carry out programming reforms the Commission did not have the legal authority to achieve on its own.[27]

Abolishing Format Requirements

Although the Commission was constantly involved in efforts to improve the quality of network broadcast service, it was generally reluctant to interfere in any way with the programming practices of individual broadcast stations. As long as stations were not violating any specific FCC programming rule, the agency was willing to allow broadcasters the widest possible discretion in selecting their own format or schedule.

Thus, in 1970, when a classical music station was being sold to investors who intended to change its musical format, the Commission routinely approved the sale, even though a citizens' group had petitioned the FCC to deny the license transfer. Upon appeal, the court reversed the Commission decision, ordering the FCC to conduct a hearing to determine whether the sale would result in depriving the audience in that broadcast market of its only source of this type of programming.[28] In response to the FCC's argument that it was not authorized to act as a "national arbiter of taste," the court declared,

> The Commission is not dictating tastes when it seeks to discover what they presently are, and to consider what assignment of channels is feasible and fair in terms of their gratification.[29]

Four years later the Commission was faced with another sale of a classical music station to a group eager to convert it into a "top 40" outlet, and once again the agency approved the sale without permitting the local citizens' group the hearing they had requested to oppose the license transfer and change of format. The court

[27] For one example of such close FCC–network cooperation, see the "Family Viewing" opinion in Writers Guild of America West, Inc. v. FCC, 423 F.Supp. 1064 (C.D.Cal.1976).

[28] Citizens Committee to Preserve the Voice of Arts in Atlanta v. FCC, 436 F.2d 263 (D.C.Cir.1970).

[29] Ibid., 272 n. 7.

again reversed the FCC decision, this time with the observation that,

> We think it axiomatic that preservation of a format that would otherwise disappear; although economically and technologically viable and preferred by a significant number of listeners, is generally in the public interest.[30]

At this point the Commission decided to conduct a public policy hearing to determine what its future role in such program format controversies should be. At the conclusion of these deliberations, the FCC adopted the rather daring stance that despite any instructions it had received from the federal court of appeals, it would no longer allow itself to be involved in any regulation of broadcast station formats because, as the Commission explained it,

> Our reflection ... has fortified our conviction that our regulation of entertainment formats as an aspect of the public interest would produce an unnecessary and menacing entanglement in matters that Congress meant to leave to private discretion.[31]

A citizens' group immediately appealed this FCC policy decision, but after it had been reversed at the Court of Appeals level, the Supreme Court decided to consider this format regulation issue itself for the first time. In Federal Communications Commission v. WNCN Listeners Guild [32] the Commission's position was upheld by the court, on the basis that the FCC's format policy reflected a reasonable balance between, "promoting diversity in programming and ... avoiding unnecessary restrictions upon licensee discretion."

Indecent Programming

Yet, even though the Commission has been reluctant to become involved in most phases of local station programming, one specific type of programming has been singled out recently by the FCC for close supervision. Both the Radio Act of 1927 and the Communications Act of 1934 contained regulatory provisions authorizing the imposition of fines and possible revocation of the license of any station broadcasting obscene, indecent or profane language.[33]

[30] Citizens Committee to Save WEFM v. FCC, 506 F.2d 246 (D.C.Cir.1973).

[31] "Changes in the Entertainment Formats of Broadcast Stations," 37 RR2d 1679, 1976.

[32] 450 U.S. 582, 101 S.Ct. 1266 (1981).

[33] In 1948, Congress transferred these statutory provisions to the U.S. Criminal Code, Title 18, U.S.C.A. § 1464, because they also contained criminal penalties (imprisonment of up to 5 years) that could be enforced more effectively by the U.S. Justice Department. However, the FCC was granted continuing authority to penalize broadcasters under the new code section.

As discussed in Chapter 8 of this text, punishing "obscene" broadcast language presented no constitutional problem for either federal regulatory agency, because speech or conduct found to be obscene is not recognized by American law as meriting First Amendment protection.[34] "Indecent" or "profane" speech, on the other hand, is constitutionally protected, and so regulatory efforts to discourage such utterances or to penalize stations for scheduling an "indecent" or "profane" program impose greater constraints upon the broadcast medium than upon any other form of American mass communication.

In reality, though, the broadcast networks and their industry association, the National Association of Broadcasters (NAB), were able to shield the FRC and FCC from the problem of tasteless broadcast content until the early 1970s. Each of the networks demanded that their affiliated stations follow NAB program standards far more restrictive in areas of public taste than any regulatory agency could have required, and while independent stations were not bound by these agreements, they hesitated to isolate themselves in this way from the protection of the NAB.

As the 1970s began, however, a number of smaller, typically urban market FM stations saw an opportunity to attract a larger audience with a new format called "topless radio," featuring sexually oriented talk shows to capitalize upon the so-called new morality of that era. By 1973, stations adopting the "topless" format had become top-rated during their sex talk segments in several major markets, as letters of complaint from outraged listeners began flooding the FCC.[35]

In that same year the FCC imposed a $2,000 fine upon a station that had presented a particularly explicit discussion of oral sex techniques, pointing out,

> We are emphatically not saying that sex per se is a forbidden subject on the broadcast medium ... sex and obscenity are not the same things.[36]

but holding that because the program had been broadcast at a time when a substantial number of children could be presumed to be listening, the station had disregarded its public interest responsibilities towards that special segment of its audience.

---

[34] See chapter 8.

[35] The FCC received more than 2,000 letters from listeners complaining about these programs in 1972; in 1974, they received more than 20,000 letters of complaint. "Programming of Violent, Indecent or Obscene Material", Broadcast Management/Engineering, June 1975, pp. 22–24.

[36] Sonderling Broadcasting, 27 RR2d 285 (1973).

A citizens' group petitioned for a hearing to challenge the Commission's decision, but a federal appeals court upheld both the FCC action and its right to reject such a petition.[37]

In that same year, another station, in a mid-afternoon program, featured an excerpt from a comedy album of George Carlin, his "Filthy Words" routine, discussing in detail the nuances of several of the seven four-letter words he said couldn't be mentioned on radio or television. The FCC issued a declaratory ruling against the station, this time defining its position on indecency with even greater clarity. According to the Commission, "indecent" programming was that which,

> . . . describes, in terms patently offensive as measured by contemporary community standards for the broadcast medium, sexual or excretory activities and organs, at times of the day where there is reasonable risk that children may be in the audience.[38]

The FCC's newly established indecency standard was overturned almost immediately by a federal appeals court, but at that point the Supreme Court intervened to consider whether more stringent restrictions could legally be imposed upon broadcast free speech than other forms of media expression.

A majority of the Justices affirmed the Commission's position, basing their affirmation of the FCC's right to hold broadcasting to a higher standard of care in this area of speech on two special characteristics of the medium, its pervasiveness and its unique accessibility to children.[39] In addition, the crucial factor in the view of the court was that the FCC was not attempting to ban the broadcasting of indecent programs, but only to require that such programs be scheduled at times when they were not likely to reach a large youthful audience.

Although a divided Court had affirmed the right of the Commission to treat indecent programming as a nuisance, "channeling" it away from younger viewers or listeners, the new "marketplace" oriented FCC of the 1980s seemed reluctant to exercise this power. Despite complaints from various citizen groups about the explicit nature of certain new "shock" radio formats, the agency decided initially to restrict its definition of "indecent" only to broadcasts containing one or more of those famous seven words George Carlin

[37] Illinois Citizens Committee for Broadcasting v. FCC, 515 F.2d 397 (D.C.Cir. 1974).

[38] Pacifica Foundation, 56 FCC2d 946 (1975).

[39] FCC v. Pacifica Foundation, 438 U.S. 726, 98 S.Ct. 3026 (1978). It's important to note, however, that the FCC's indecency definition was upheld by a narrow 5–4 vote, suggesting quite clearly that its authority to enforce this type of content control would be narrowly construed.

had uttered in the monologue that led to the *Pacifica* action.[40]

In 1987, however, the Commission, under pressure from Congress, began to assert that authority the Supreme Court had authorized almost a decade earlier. The FCC sent public notices to two broadcast stations the agency found to be in violation of the rule, and declared its intention to adopt rules reestablishing the broader definition of indecency it had followed during the 1970s.

Channeling Indecency to a Safe Harbor

Following the "channeling" approach the Supreme Court had approved in *Pacifica,* the FCC declared that indecent programming would be punished only if were scheduled at a time when there was "reasonable risk that children might be in the audience."[41] Originally the Commission had stated that programs scheduled after 10 p.m. could be aired without concern for their accessibility to children. However, when audience research revealed that a substantial number of children were still listening or viewing at 10 p.m. each evening, the FCC narrowed its "safe harbor;" making the period from midnight to 6 a.m. the only appropriate time for such "adult" programming.

This new campaign by the Commission to shield young viewers and listeners from indecent broadcast programming was immediately attacked by a coalition of public interest and trade organizations.[42] Upon review, the D.C. Court of Appeals affirmed the fundamental right of the FCC to restrict indecent programming to those hours of the day when children were least likely to be present in the broadcast audience. In this instance, however, the Court held that the Commission had not adequately documented its claim that the midnight to 6 AM period it selected as a "safe harbor" for such programming was actually the most narrowly drawn one capable of realizing this policy objective.

[40] The "shock" radio format goes one step beyond "topless," trying to offend the sensibilities of as many different groups in our society as possible by using racial jokes, ethnic slurs and other forms of base humor to attract an audience.

[41] New Indecency Enforcement Standards, 62 RR2d 1218 (1987).

[42] Action for Children's Television v. FCC, 852 F.2d 1332 (D.C.Cir.1988). It is interesting to note that this legal challenge was spearheaded by the nation's largest and most influential advocacy group for the broadcast programming rights of young viewers and listeners. Through the years ACT has constantly campaigned for more extensive government restrictions on broadcast commercials to protect American youth from the damaging effects of advertising, but its leaders apparently saw no similar need to protect young viewers from the damaging effects of indecent programming, defined by the FCC as "describing or depicting sexual or excretory activities in a patently offensive manner." ACT has explained that it opposes any governmental restrictions on "indecent" broadcasts because indecency is expression protected by the First Amendment. The only problem with that explanation is that commercial speech is also expression protected by the First Amendment.

As the FCC was preparing to justify its six hour indecency "harbor" as being the least extensive time period required to achieve its goal, Congress acted to make the agency's already difficult legal position virtually impossible to defend. In October 1988 Congress passed legislation that compelled the Commission to enforce an absolute *ban* on indecent broadcast programming on a *24 hour a day basis.*[43] The FCC had no choice but to comply with this Congressional directive, even though it meant that the agency would now be required to *prohibit* a constitutionally protected form of expression it had sought only to channel within a "safe harbor" of time.

When the Commission announced its intention to begin enforcing a total ban on indecent programming in January 1989, the same coalition of media and public interest groups was able to obtain an order from the D.C. Court of Appeals preventing the Commission from implementing this new rule until its validity could be determined by the Court. In doing so, however, the Court granted the FCC permission to continue the enforcement of its indecency standards on a provisional basis in order to gather further documentation relating to the nature of this indecent programming it could submit when the case was ultimately heard by the Court.

After completing its review in July 1990, the Commission voted unanimously to adopt a report supporting a 24 hour a day ban of both indecent radio and television program content, arguing that because at least some portion of the broadcast audience was likely to be composed of children at all times of the day and night, anything less than a total ban of such programming would not achieve the objectives of the regulation.[44]

In April 1991 the U.S. Court of Appeals struck down the 24 hour a day ban of indecent broadcast programming, but directed the FCC to consider once again the possibility of establishing a reasonable defined "safe harbor" for indecent content capable of

[43] Public Law 100–459, § 608 (1988). Two months later the FCC adopted an order enforcing this ban. See 67 RR2d 1714.

[44] 67 RR2d 1714 (1990). To understand more clearly the type of content that triggered the FCC action, and that had motivated the more than 6,000 indecency complaints the FCC had been receiving annually since the mid 1980s, here are a few excerpts from some of those programs broadcast during a time of day when a substantial number of children could be expected to be in the broadcast audience: WLUP Chicago, " * * * went down on that other woman and oh God, you had your tongue in her vagina. It was fabulous * * * "; KSJO, San Jose, "I'd love to lick the matzo balls right off your butt * * * I'd like to have a smorgasbord in your butt. I'd like to have matzos in there with borscht, everything. I'd just have a buffet * * * "; WLLZ Detroit, "He puts Penthouse on his desk/he's got big muscles in his wrist/he holds his organ in his fist/He gives his pink dolphin a mighty twist * * * All the girls in the office they say, 'Hard-on, hard-on, beg my pardon.' Walk with an erection"; WMCA New York, "When you can't call welfare people 'sluts' and 'whores,' 'cocksuckers' or 'freeloaders,' then our English language serves no purpose."

channeling such programs away from children without unduly restricting adult access to them.[45]

Freed by the Court of its Congressionally imposed burden to *ban* indecent broadcasting from the airwaves, the FCC tried initially to enlarge its "safe harbor" from six to ten hours a day, permitting such programs to be aired at any time between 8 P.M. and 6 A.M. But when Congress attached a 12 P.M. to 6 A.M. "safe harbor" provision to the Public Broadcasting funding bill of 1992, the FCC was forced to revert to a uniform midnight to 6 A.M. "harbor" for all its licensees, aware that it could not justify punishing one group of broadcasters for scheduling indecent program material during a time period when another group was free to schedule such programming without penalty.[46]

The FCC also attempted during this era to strengthen its case for a "safe harbor" through research designed to respond to judicial criticisms of its earlier findings.[47] In November 1993 a 3–judge D.C. Court of Appeals panel found the Commission's new arguments to be no more convincing than their old ones, but in January 1994 this panel was set aside by a majority of the D.C. Appeals Court judges, with a new hearing then scheduled to review the entire broadcast indecency issue.[48]

Yet, whatever the outcome of this litigation, the best solution to this problem seems to already have been proposed by the National Association of Broadcasters. Rather than urging broadcast owners to test the limits of public permissiveness, the NAB instead pleaded with them to monitor their station's programming more carefully in order to prevent the transmission of explicit sexual or scatological references intended primarily to shock or offend. Unfortunately, this plea is likely to continue to be ignored by that small group of broadcasters who have already demonstrated their willingness to do anything, no matter how degrading or tasteless, to attract an audience. That, in turn, will exert public pressure on the FCC to intrude once more into this sensitive area of broadcast program content, for as Justice Stewart once observed,

> Patently offensive, indecent material presented over
> the airwaves confronts the citizen not only in public, but
> also in the privacy of the home, where the individual's

[45] ACT v. FCC, 932 F.2d 1504 (D.C.Cir.1991) cert. den. 112 S.Ct. 1281 (1992).

[46] Public Telecommunications Act of 1992, Pub. Law 102–356. § 16(a), 106 Stat. 949, 954.

[47] Broadcast Indecency, 71 R.R. 2d 1116 (1992). In this proceeding the FCC specified for the first time the age range of those it sought to protect (those 17 or younger) and gathered more detailed broadcasting rating information to demonstrate more clearly how the new rules would protect the largest number of children while imposing the least severe degree of programming constraint on broadcasters.

[48] ACT v. FCC, 74 R.R. 2d 229 (1993).

right to be left alone clearly outweighs the First Amendment rights of the intruder.[49]

Broadcast Hoaxes

From 1938 onward, when Orson Welles's *Mercury Theater* adaptation of H.G. Well's *War of the Worlds* caused panic among thousands of Americans who were convinced by the broadcast program that Mars had attacked the United States, the FCC has never been amused by any effort, however clever or humorous, to tease or frighten a broadcast audience.[50]

In 1992 the Commission reacted to complaints about a series of broadcast hoaxes that had aired during the previous two years by adopting new rules authorizing it to fine stations a maximum of $25,000 for knowingly broadcasting

> ... information or other material it knows to be false if it is foreseeable that broadcast of the information could cause substantial public harm, and if the broadcast of the information does in fact directly cause substantial public harm.[51]

Recent hoax broadcasts have included a news report asserting that the United States was under nuclear attack, another claiming that a popular radio personality had just been shot and a third involving a talk show host who had arranged for a caller to confess falsely on air to having just committed a murder.[52]

The agency will consider such harm to be "foreseeable" if the broadcaster could reasonably expect that public harm will occur. In this context, the FCC pointed out that an April Fools Day newscast claiming that a local football team had just traded one of its stars would not come under this rule, because while it might distress some fans, it would not create that degree of harm or damage contemplated by the rule.

SEC. 52. POLITICAL ACCESS RULES

Despite deregulation, Congress still requires the FCC to enforce all equal access broadcast requirements.

[49] FCC v. Pacifica Foundation, 438 U.S. 726, 98 S.Ct. 3026 (1978). The court also pointed out in a footnote (28) that those who seek indecent materials are not limited in access to them by this ruling, since they are so readily available from so many other sources in American society.

[50] For a vivid description of some of the public hysteria caused by this broadcast, see "Radio Listens in Panic, Taking War Drama As Fact", New York Times, October 31, 1938, p. 1.

[51] Amendment of Part 73 Regarding Broadcast Hoaxes.

[52] Nuclear attack; Emmis Broadcasting, KSHE–FM, 69 R.R. 2d 195 (1991); false report of a shooting, Letter to Frank Battaglia, President, North American Broadcasting Co. 70 R.R. 2d 1329 (1992); false report of a murder; General Manager, Radio Station KROQ–FM, 6 F.C.C. R. 7262 (1991).

The "equal time", or more accurately the "equal opportunities" requirement for political candidates has been an obligation imposed upon broadcasting since the Radio Act of 1927 was adopted.   Section 18 of the Radio Act became the well known Section 315 of the Communications Act of 1934, stating,

> If any licensee shall permit any person who is a legally qualified candidate for any political office to use a broadcasting station, he shall afford equal opportunities to all other such candidates for that office in the use of such broadcasting station . . .

This section also denied the broadcaster any authority to censor political candidates exercising their rights of access under the terms of Section 315.

In 1959, a political candidate used this access to make defamatory remarks about his opponent.   The opponent sued the broadcast station for airing these defamatory statements, but in Farmers Educational & Cooperative Union of America v. WDAY, Inc.,[53] the Supreme Court held that in establishing the terms and conditions for such political broadcast access, Congress had preempted state defamation law and created an absolute privilege that shielded the broadcast station from legal liability for statements made by such candidates.

During this same era, television news coverage of public events began raising a question Congress had no reason to consider when Section 315 was adopted.   If a political candidate could be seen by viewers in film clips of a news event broadcast by a television station, was such an appearance a "use" of broadcast facilities requiring the station to offer all opponents of that candidate equal access to television time?

The Commission decided in 1959 that such an appearance did constitute a "use" under the Act, even though broadcast journalists had pointed out that if each televised glimpse of a candidate triggered an obligation by a station to make free time available to all opponents, it would be virtually impossible for a television station to provide its viewers with adequate local news coverage during an election campaign.[54]

Congress reacted promptly by amending Section 315 to exempt from its equal opportunities requirement any appearance by a legally qualified candidate on a

(1) bona fide newscast

(2) bona fide news interview

---

[53] 360 U.S. 525, 79 S.Ct. 1302 (1959).

[54] Columbia Broadcasting System, 26 FCC2d 715 (1959).

(3) bona fide documentary (if the appearance of the candidate is incidental to the presentation of the subject or subjects covered by the news documentary), or

(4) on-the-spot coverage of bona fide news events (including but not limited to political conventions and activities incidental thereto) . . .

This amendment offered broadcast journalists the protection from equal access obligations necessary to cover most news events, but in special situations not fitting neatly into one of these four exempted categories of coverage, the FCC has been reluctant to extend the scope of such exemptions. In 1960, for example, Congress was forced to suspend the application of Section 315 to presidential candidates to permit the three television networks to broadcast the famous Kennedy–Nixon debates without being required to provide an equal amount of free network broadcast time to all minor party presidential candidates.

In 1975, however, the Commission reversed its earlier position that neither broadcast coverage of political candidate debates nor candidate press conferences came within the exemption Congress had granted for on-the-spot coverage of bona fide news events.[55] It now held that debates were exempt from Section 315 requirements if they were controlled by someone other than the candidates or the broadcaster, and also exempted coverage of press conferences if they were "newsworthy and subject to on-the-spot coverage."[56]

The League of Women Voters acted as the independent host of these presidential debates for the television networks in 1976 and 1980. Since 1984, however, the Commission no longer has required the presence of an outside sponsoring organization in order to exempt political debates from 315 requirements, finding no basis for its previous belief that such an independent group was needed to insure impartial coverage of such debates.[57]

In 1991 the Commission relaxed its equal access requirements still further, expanding the "spot news" exemption of Section 315 to permit the broadcasting of candidate-prepared campaign state-

[55] Petition of Aspen Institute and CBS, 35 RR2d 49 (1975). In Petition of Henry Geller, et al., 54 RR2d 1246 (1983) the FCC relaxed its political candidates' debates rules still further, allowing broadcasters themselves to sponsor debates between political candidates without being required by Section 315 to extend this right of debate to all candidates for the office in question.

[56] This change in FCC policy was sustained by the court of appeals in Chisholm v. FCC, 538 F.2d 349 (D.C.Cir.1976), cert. denied 429 U.S. 890, 97 S.Ct. 247 (1976). Senator Kennedy challenged the new press conference exemption, claiming that President Carter had used such a conference to attack Kennedy, then a competing presidential candidate. The FCC's position was upheld in Kennedy for President Committee v. FCC, 636 F.2d 432 (D.C.Cir.1980).

[57] The FCC's position was affirmed in League of Women Voters Educ. Fund v. FCC, 731 F.2d 995 (D.C.Cir.1984).

ments and interviews limited to the two major presidential candidates without obligating a station to offer lesser candidates equal access.[58]

Through the years the FCC has also extended its category of broadcast programs exempted from political access requirements to include entertainment shows that provide news or current event coverage as regularly scheduled segments of the program. In this way, not only "Today", "Good Morning America" and "This Morning" but even "Donahue", "Entertainment Tonight" and "Entertainment This Week" have been able to invite political candidates to discuss public issues without exposing the network or station carrying them to "equal time" demands by rival candidates.[59]

On the other hand, the Commission has held rigidly to its position that any "use" of station time by a political candidate not expressly exempted by Section 315 creates an obligation for equal access. For example, the FCC declared that any station broadcasting a Ronald Reagan film during any campaign period in which he was a political candidate would obligate that station to offer all his legally qualified opponents the same degree of access to its audience.[60]

In 1991 the agency did modify this policy significantly, declaring that an appearance by a political candidate would be considered a "use" only when the candidate's voice or picture was authorized or sponsored by the candidate or the candidate's campaign committee. [61] Recognizing the increasingly common practice in negative campaign commercials to include audio clips or video footage of a candidate's opponent, the FCC wanted to clarify its position that

[58] Request of King Broadcasting Company Licensee of KING–TV, Seattle, Washington for a Declaratory Ruling. 69 R.R. 2d 1017 (1991). However, in reversing earlier decisions denying these exemptions in Request for Declaratory Ruling by WEBE, 108 Radio Co. 63 R.R. 2d 1748 (1987) rev'd and remanded sub nom., King Broadcasting Co. v. FCC, 860 F.2d 465 (1988), the Commission did caution broadcasters that failure to include a major third-party presidential candidate in their news coverage might risk the loss of the spot news exemption the agency had authorized.

[59] Although the Donahue exemption was originally denied by the FCC, it was subsequently granted in 1984 despite the show's rather sporadic commitment to coverage of significant political events or issues. See Multimedia Entertainment 56 RR2d 143 (1984). In justifying its exemption for show business promotional programs such as "Entertainment Tonight," the FCC observed that the news exemption to Section 315 is not based on "the subject matter reported" but only on whether a program "reports news of some area of current events". In addition, the agency pointed out that if it began deciding in each case whether the information provided by a particular program was sufficiently important or significant to justify an exemption, it could be involving itself more deeply in the evaluation of broadcast program content than the First Amendment would permit. Request for Declaratory Ruling by Paramount Pictures Corp. (1988).

[60] In re Adrian Weiss, 36 RR2d 292 (1976). See also In re Pat Paulsen, 23 RR2d 861 (1972), affirmed 491 F.2d 887 (9th Cir.1974).

[61] Codification of the Commission's Political Programming Policies, 70 R.R. 2d 239 (1991).

unauthorized use of a political opponent's voice or image would not then entitle the candidate who produced such ads to claim air time on the basis of this "appearance" by the opponent.

Under this new standard, then, the broadcast of an old feature film of a candidate such as Ronald Reagan would no longer provide his political opponents with a right of equal access unless Reagan or his campaign committee had actually approved or authorized the scheduling of the film.

At the same time, though, the Commission refused to alter its policy regarding typical broadcast employees, a policy that still effectively denies any broadcast performer the right to run for political office. The FCC has defined "use" of broadcast facilities to include virtually any type of on-air performance, including working under an assumed name as the radio host of a weekly dance show.[62] Under this strict interpretation of the rules, as soon as a broadcast performer becomes a political candidate, each subsequent on-air performance obligates the station to provide a similar amount of free air time to each of the employee's political opponents.

In one recent case, station management estimated that it would be required to provide more than 33 hours of free broadcast response time if a television reporter went ahead with his plans to become a candidate for a town council position.[63] Not surprisingly, the reporter was ordered by the station to make an immediate choice between a career in politics and one in broadcasting.

Yet, it would be unfair to blame the FCC too severely for this unfortunate result, because Congress has allowed the Commission virtually no discretion in the enforcement of this broadcast "use" standard. Despite the fact that both the NAB and the Radio Television News Directors Association (RTNDA) have on several occasions urged that Congress amend Section 315 to allow broadcast employees to exercise this basic right of citizenship, Congressional leaders have seemed content to continue treating broadcasting as a less legally privileged medium.

Nowhere is that attitude of Congress more clearly reflected than in legislation it enacted in 1971 to take advantage of broadcasting's status as a federally regulated medium. In that year the Communications Act was amended by Congress to compel each broadcast station to provide candidates for federal office a reasonable amount of broadcast time, and to furnish time for purchase by federal candidates at the lowest rate charged regular advertisers for

[62] See Letter to WUGN, 40 FCC 2d 293 (1958).
[63] Branch v. FCC, 824 F.2d 37 (D.C.Cir.1987), 14 Med.L.Rptr. 1465.

that same time period.[64]   In essence, members of Congress had decided to combat the rising costs of federal election campaigns by imposing upon broadcasting, the only medium controlled by government, requirements designed to reduce their own campaign costs at the broadcast industry's expense.

The first major test of this new legislation occurred in 1980, when the Carter–Mondale Committee sought to purchase a half hour of prime time from each network to present a documentary portraying President Carter's first term accomplishments just after Carter's formal announcement of his intention to seek a second term.   When none of the networks were willing to provide the full 30 minutes of time the Committee demanded, the group filed a complaint with the FCC.[65]   The Commission found the networks in violation of the "reasonable access" rule, and on appeal, the Supreme Court, in a five to four decision, narrowly affirmed this finding.[66]

In 1990, an extensive FCC audit revealed that more than two-thirds of the 30 radio and televisions stations the agency had investigated were not charging political candidates the lowest advertising rates required by federal law.[67]   The Commission also discovered that a substantial number of these stations had not fully informed candidates of the availability of lower priced packages of advertising for which they qualified.   As a result of this audit the FCC adopted new rules requiring stations to make full disclosure to political candidates of all advertising unit rates offered to any of the station's regular commercial accounts. [68]

However, when several politicians who had been candidates during the 1990 election campaign sued broadcast stations to recover what they claimed were excessive charges for political commercials, the FCC quickly intervened to shield broadcasters from such litigation, asserting that the Commission had sole authority to decide when a station was in violation of federal political broadcast advertising laws. [69]   Instead of permitting such contro-

---

[64] The "reasonable access" amendment created section 312(a)(7) of the Communications Act, and the "lowest rate" provision became section 315(b).

[65] Networks were reluctant to sell a large block of prime time for a political program during a non-election year, aware that inserting such a political documentary into a regular evening lineup of shows would substantially reduce the audience for all programs following the political program the evening it was scheduled.   CBS offered a 5 minute prime time segment, and ABC a full 30 minute prime time slot during a non-rating period in January, but the Committee refused these offers.

[66] CBS, Inc. v. FCC, 453 U.S. 367, 101 S.Ct. 2813 (1981).

[67] Political Program Audit, 68 R.R. 2d 113 (1990).

[68] Codification of the Commission's Political Programming Policies, 70 R.R. 2d 219 (1991).

[69] Exclusive Jurisdiction with Respect to Potential Violations of the Lowest Unit Charge Requirements of Section 315 (b), Communications Act, 70 R.R. 2d 1 (1991).

versies to be decided by the courts, the agency offered candidates two options for resolving future broadcast advertising rate disputes; either to submit them to a neutral arbitrator for a binding decision, or to ask the Commission to determine the proper charges through the agency's complaint process.

Considering the advantages that politicians currently obtain from the "equal opportunities," "lowest advertising rate" and "reasonable access" provisions of the Communications Act of 1934, it seems highly unlikely that Congress will ever be eager to release broadcasting from the constraints of regulation so long as these benefits continue to result from such control. [70]

SEC. 53.   FAIRNESS DOCTRINE OBLIGATIONS

Although the FCC has repealed the Fairness Doctrine, it has never been declared unconstitutional by the courts, and easily could be reinstituted at any time by Congress or the Commission.

In contrast, the "fairness doctrine", the other major public issue oriented principle of broadcast regulation, has never been as directly related to Congressional self-interest.   In fact, Congress never bothered to formally codify the doctrine, simply declaring when amending the "equal opportunities" provision of Section 315 in 1959 that it had no intention of relieving broadcasters,

> ... from the obligations imposed upon them under this Act to operate in the public interest and to afford reasonable opportunity for the discussion of conflicting views on issues of public importance.[71]

The concept of broadcast "fairness" emerged instead from years of specific decisions made by the FRC and FCC in determining the exact extent of a licensee's obligation to provide the public with balanced coverage of controversial matters of public importance.   In 1949, the FCC issued the first formal description of this doctrine, declaring,

> One of the most vital questions of mass communications in a democracy is the development of an informed public opinion through the public dissemination of news and ideas concerning the vital public issues of the day.[72]

[70] Congress has always favored the "equal opportunities" provision of Section 315, because while virtually every incumbent can gain constant broadcast access to constituents between elections through news items most local stations are eager to carry, any challenger is restricted by § 315 during the campaign period to access under the same terms and conditions as the incumbent, thus protecting the incumbent's pre-election advantage.

[71] Public Law No. 274, 86th Congress 1959.

[72] Editorializing by Broadcast Licensees, 13 FCC 1246 (1949).

Elaborating on this concept, the Commission established a twofold obligation for every broadcaster; to devote a reasonable amount of time to the coverage of important public issues, and to provide this coverage in a fair and balanced manner.

In 1969, the Supreme Court had its first opportunity to consider the First Amendment issues raised by the fairness doctrine. Although only one narrow portion of the doctrine, its personal attack rule, was truly at issue, the consolidation of this case with an action brought by a group of broadcast news directors allowed the court to consider the broader constitutional implications of this Commission policy.

Justice White, speaking for a unanimous court, declared in affirming the doctrine that the federal government did have the constitutional authority to require broadcasters to furnish their audiences with balanced coverage of controversial issues of public importance because,

> It is the purpose of the First Amendment to preserve an uninhibited marketplace of ideas in which truth will ultimately prevail, rather than to countenance monopolization of that market, whether it be by the Government itself or a private licensee.... It is the right of the viewers and listeners, not the right of the broadcasters, which is paramount.[73]

In 1967 the Commission had taken the position that in accepting cigarette advertising, a station obligated itself under the fairness doctrine to present programming or public service announcements balancing the advocacy of smoking with information describing the threat that cigarette smoking posed to health.[74] By establishing this precedent, the FCC soon found itself under pressure from a wide range of interest groups demanding that this "counteradvertising" broadcast obligation be extended to require informational messages criticizing virtually every product advertised on television or radio.

Expanding the scope of the fairness doctrine in this way would have made it extremely difficult for broadcasters to continue to compete with newspapers or magazines for advertising revenues, since few advertisers would be likely to use a medium that was obligated by law to provide free air time to those who wished to criticize the products they had paid to promote. As a result, when the Federal Trade Commission (FTC) filed a brief with the FCC in 1972 that urged the Commission adopt broadcast counteradvertising rules as a "suitable approach to some of the present failings of advertising which are beyond the FTC's capacity," the FCC realized

---

[73] Red Lion Broadcasting Co. v. FCC, 395 U.S. 367, 89 S.Ct. 1794 (1969).

[74] Banzhaf v. FCC, 405 F.2d 1082 (D.C.Cir.1968).

that it was being maneuvered into a regulatory position that would undercut the financial base of the entire broadcast industry.[75]

In 1974 the Commission rejected this FTC proposal and issued a policy statement effectively removing all product advertising from the requirements of the fairness doctrine, except in situations where the advertising itself expressly raised a controversial issue of public importance.[76] In this same policy statement the FCC also tried to clarify basic broadcast obligations under the doctrine, concluding that broadcasters needed only to devote a reasonable amount of time to the coverage of public issues, and through this coverage, to provide opportunities for the presentation of contrasting points of view relating to these issues.

Citizen groups viewed this effort at clarification as an attempt to retreat from regulatory guidelines that in the past had been construed by the agency itself as requiring broadcasters actively to seek out controversial issues of public importance and to assume primary responsibility for providing balanced coverage of these issues. Eventually, however, the FCC's new, more limited definition of broadcast fairness doctrine obligations was sustained by the courts.[77]

As the 1980s began, even this more narrowly defined set of fairness obligations soon appeared too repressive of free speech for an FCC now fully committed to a policy of deregulation. In 1981, the Commission asked Congress to repeal the fairness doctrine, pointing to what it felt was an ever increasing inequity between the programming requirements broadcasters had to accept, and the much less extensive programming obligations the agency could legally impose upon all other forms of competing electronic media service.[78]

When Congress failed to respond to the FCC's request, the agency launched its own extensive investigation of the doctrine's effects on broadcast free speech. In 1985, the Commission released its report based on this investigation, concluding the fairness doctrine no longer served the public interest.[79] This was true, according to the report, because a rapid expansion in the number of information services available to American audiences made them far less dependent upon broadcasting to be informed than they had been when the doctrine was adopted. In the absence of such

[75] FTC Docket 19.260.

[76] In the Matter of Handling of Public Issues under the Fairness Doctrine, 48 FCC 2d 1 (1974).

[77] National Citizens Committee for Broadcasting v. FCC, 567 F.2d 1095 (D.C.Cir. 1977), cert. denied 436 U.S. 926, 98 S.Ct. 2820 (1978).

[78] FCC Report No. 5068, Setting Forth Proposals for Amending the Communications Act (Sept. 17, 1981).

[79] Fairness Report, 102 FCC 2d 143 (1985).

continuing dependence, further intrusion by government in this area of broadcast free speech was not only unwarranted, in the Commission's view, but also dangerous, because it provided too many opportunities for political pressure to affect broadcast coverage of public issues.

Congress reacted to this FCC report by ordering the agency *not* to alter any of its existing fairness doctrine enforcement policies for a two year period ending in August 1987. Instead, the Commission was directed to complete, within this two year period, a detailed assessment of various alternative methods the agency might recommend for continuing to protect the public's interest in balanced treatment of controversial issues without unnecessarily infringing upon a broadcaster's editorial discretion.

During the preparation of its 1985 Fairness Doctrine report, the FCC had actually enforced its provisions for the first time in nearly a decade. In 1984 the Commission found that *Meredith Broadcasting*, owner of a television station in Syracuse, New York violated the doctrine's provisions by refusing to balance editorial advertisements supporting the building of a nuclear power plant with anti-nuclear energy public service announcements pointing out the drawbacks of this source of energy.[80]

Perhaps it was only coincidental that the Commission had decided to begin enforcing the doctrine again at this particular time, but there certainly was a clear tactical advantage in doing so. As long as Congress remained unwilling to relieve the FCC of its statutory obligation to enforce the fairness doctrine, the only avenue open for the Commission to escape this responsibility was to give the D.C. Court of Appeals the opportunity to declare its efforts to punish an alleged fairness doctrine violator to be unconstitutional and therefore unenforceable; exactly the situation that the *Meredith* case just happened to present.

But whatever the FCC's intentions, the Court of Appeals acted instead in Telecommunications Research and Action Center (TRAC) v. FCC to free the Commission from its legal obligation to enforce the fairness doctrine without considering the constitutionality of the doctrine itself.[81] In this relatively obscure case decided just prior to *Meredith*, the Court held that the FCC was not obligated to make broadcast teletext services conform to fairness doctrine standards because, contrary to the prevailing view, the attempt of Congress in 1959 to incorporate the doctrine into the Communication Act had not been clear or specific enough to actually *codify* it into law.

[80] In re Syracuse Peace Council, 57 RR2d 519 (1984).

[81] 801 F.2d 501 (D.C.Cir.1986).

As a result, when the Court returned the *Meredith* case to the Commission, it instructed the FCC to resolve the controversy simply on the basis of whether the agency *itself* believed the fairness doctrine served the public interest, because in its *TRAC* decision the Court had already released the Commission from any Congressional imposed obligation to enforce the doctrine.[82]

As the year 1987 began, members of Congress who wanted to preserve the doctrine realized that they would soon have to add a new, more clearly stated "fairness" clause to the Communications Act in order to prevent the FCC from exercising the freedom the Appeals Court had just given it to rescind the doctrine on its own. Congressional leaders succeeded in marshalling new "fairness" legislation through both houses of Congress during the spring of 1987 and a bill codifying the doctrine was presented to President Reagan by mid-June.[83]

During this period of feverish legislative activity, the NAB decided not to oppose this attempt to codify the fairness doctrine, fearing that such opposition might antagonize members of Congress whose support was needed for more important comparative renewal legislation.[84] Yet, even though the broadcast industry had been unwilling to campaign publicly to extend its right of freedom of expression under these circumstances, President Reagan decided on his own to veto the bill, a veto Congress lacked the votes to override.

After this veto, the FCC stood alone in the political spotlight. The Court of Appeals had found no language in the Communications Act compelling the Commission to continue to enforce the doctrine, and Congress had failed in its efforts to insert a new fairness doctrine provision in the Act.

At the time the agency was still bound by instructions from Congress not to abandon its enforcement of the doctrine prior to August 1987, when it was to provide Congress with a list of alternative methods for achieving the same objectives of balance in the broadcast coverage of controversial issues. On August 4, 1987, it issued this study Congress had requested.[85] At the same time, however, the agency released its decision in the *Meredith* case,

[82] Meredith Corp. v. FCC, 809 F.2d 863 (D.C.Cir.1987). Because the Supreme Court had found that the fairness doctrine did not infringe upon broadcaster First Amendment rights in the *Red Lion* case, the lower court obviously preferred to avoid basing its decision on constitutional grounds.

[83] S. 742 was passed by the Senate on April 21 and H.R. 1934 was passed by the House in May. The reconciled bill was vetoed by President Reagan on June 19, 1987, and unable to override the veto, the legislation was returned to committee without action.

[84] "CBS's Bob McConnell and the Story Behind the Veto", Broadcasting, July 6, 1987, p. 33.

[85] Fairness Alternatives, 63 RR2d 488 (1987).

rescinding all broadcast fairness doctrine requirements, except those rules relating to "personal attack" and "political editorializing".[86]

Supporters of the doctrine in Congress reacted angrily to the Commission's action, drafting new fairness legislation while seeking some approach that could shelter it from presidential veto. But despite their best efforts, this second attempt to make the fairness doctrine part of the Communications Act also failed to survive President Reagan's veto in December 1987.

On review, the FCC's decision to rescind the Fairness Doctrine was upheld by a divided three-judge panel.[87] The Court found that the Commission had not acted in an arbitrary or capricious manner in abolishing both of the Doctrine's requirements; to seek out controversial issues of public importance and to cover them in a balanced, impartial fashion. In essence, the majority decision accepted the FCC's conclusions that the Fairness Doctrine tended to discourage broadcast coverage of controversial public issues and also tended to encourage too great a degree of governmental interference in areas of broadcast freedom of expression.

Each judge wrote a separate opinion. Judge Starr, while concurring in the result, argued that the constitutionality of the Doctrine itself was so closely interwoven into the Commission's action that its validity under the First Amendment needed to be considered independently by the court before reaching its decision. On the other hand, Judge Wald in his dissent contended that although no independent consideration of First Amendment issues was necessary, the FCC had not adequately demonstrated the need to repeal the "first prong" of the Doctrine, the requirement "to seek out controversial issues" when finding that the second or "balance" prong no longer serves the public interest.

At this point, then, the Commission's decision to repeal the basic requirements of the Fairness Doctrine has been sustained by the D.C. Court of Appeals, but because of the Court's refusal to base its decision on constitutional grounds, Congress has not been precluded from adopting legislation in the future that would once again require the FCC to enforce its requirements.

In the meantime the FCC continues to reduce the range of its fairness doctrine obligations, deciding by a 3–2 vote in 1992 that it will no longer enforce one of the doctrine's corollaries, the require-

[86] In re Complaint of Syracuse Peace Council Against WVTH, Memorandum Opinion and Order, 63 RR2d 542 (1987). See also "The Decline and Fall of the Fairness Doctrine: Fairness Held Unfair," Broadcasting, Aug. 19, 1987, p. 27.

[87] Syracuse Peace Council v. FCC, 867 F.2d 654 (D.C.Cir.1989). See also the FCC reconsideration of its Meredith Broadcasting decision that formed the basis for this appeal in Syracuse Peace Council, 64 RR2d 1073 (1988).

ment of fairness in broadcast coverage of elections or ballot issues.[88] In a 7–5 vote affirming the Commission's decision, a federal appeals court agreed that the agency was not obligated to enforce any element of the doctrine unless Congress enacted legislation that required it to do so.[89]

SEC. 54. PERSONAL ATTACKS AND POLITICAL EDITORIALS

When a broadcast attacks the integrity or character of a person or group, or an editorial supports or opposes a political candidate, the station must promptly notify the person attacked or opposed, furnishing that person with the content of the attack, and offering air time to respond.

An attack upon the character, honesty, or integrity of a person or group during a broadcast of a controversial issue of public importance is one situation still governed by the rules of the fairness doctrine. The other occurs when a station broadcasts an editorial supporting or opposing a political candidate.

The Commission has justified its reluctance to rescind either of these rather specialized fairness rules until it has considered them more carefully by explaining that neither of these corollaries appears to infringe significantly upon the editorial judgment of broadcasters.[90]

These Commission rules require that the broadcaster must notify the target of the attack promptly, and furnish this person with a transcript, tape or summary of the attack. Also, an offer of time to reply must be given. Where the licensee has broadcast an editorial endorsing or opposing a political candidate, the opposing candidates are to be notified within 24 hours after the endorsement or attack, and furnished with the transcript and an offer of time.[91]

Personal attacks occurring during bona fide newscasts, news interviews and commentaries are *exempted* from these fairness requirements.[92] This leaves station editorials and documentaries among the types of programs that do impose these special responsibilities upon broadcasters.

[88] Arkansas AFL–CIO v. KARK–TV, 70 R.R. 2d 369 (1992).

[89] Arkansas AFL–CIO v. FCC, 980 F.2d 1190 (8th Cir.1992).

[90] Another reason for being somewhat reluctant to repeal the "personal attack" rule could be that it was this specific rule the Supreme Court found to be constitutional in the *Red Lion* decision. See Syracuse Peace Council, 64 RR 2d 1873 (1988).

[91] 32 Fed.Reg. 10303–ff (1967).

[92] 32 Fed.Reg. 11531 (1967).

While the FCC contends that notification requirements such as those imposed by personal attack and political editorial rules do not exert the same degree of "chilling effect" on broadcast freedom of expression as regulations directly affecting program content, there are those who disagree with this assessment. It has been argued, for example, that personal attack rules do not serve the claimed FCC objective of airing crucial public issues.

Instead, according to these critics, it is only when issues retreat and name-calling comes to the fore that the personal attack rules require reply opportunity. "To a large extent, the personal attack rules generate name calling exercises, allowing those parties whose personalities are criticized to rebut the charges without requiring rebuttal opportunities on the more substantive issues." [93]

There is no way of being able to determine at this point whether the personal attack and political editorializing rules have been preserved to achieve some long term policy objective of the Commission, or have only been spared until the agency can find a valid justification for their recision. In either case, they now represent the last remaining regulatory vestiges of that once broad and powerful doctrine that shaped the programming policies of broadcast stations and networks throughout the United States.

SEC. 55.   PUBLIC BROADCASTING

Created to offer an alternative to commercial radio and television, public broadcasting has been sheltered from direct FCC control by a separate set of regulations.

Unlike most other Western industrial nations, no special provisions were made for non-commercial broadcasting when broadcast regulation began in the United States. Those college and university radio stations that had already received a broadcast license from the Commerce Department during the early 1920s were permitted to remain on the air, but no spectrum space was specifically set aside by either the Radio Act of 1927 or the Communications Act of 1934 to encourage the development of a nationwide educational or cultural broadcasting service.[94]

[93] Steven J. Simmons, "The FCC Personal Attack and Political Editorializing Rules Reconsidered," Pennsylvania Law Review (Fall 1977) p. 990.

[94] Many of the earliest radio stations had been experimental projects of some college physics or engineering department. Yet as late as 1927, when the FRC began issuing broadcast licenses, most of the more than 200 noncommercial stations it licensed were still operated by educational institutions. Within the decade however, their number had dwindled to less than 30, victims of both a Depression era economy and the absence of any clearly defined educational broadcasting objectives. Most were purchased by commercial broadcasters, eager to obtain their valuable frequency assignments. Section 307(c) of the Act of 1934 did require the FCC to report to Congress on the advisability of allocated fixed percentages of radio

In 1945, as part of its revised approach to broadcast frequency assignments, the FCC allotted some 10 percent of the new FM service spectrum space to non-commercial applicants and in 1952, following the same approach, it allotted a similar percentage of the television spectrum for non-commercial stations.[95]   However, this belated recognition of non-commercial broadcast service did little to stimulate the growth of educational broadcasting in the United States.   By 1960, for example, there were only 162 educational FM stations in operation throughout the nation, and only 44 educational television stations.

What these educational television stations lacked in particular was any major source of funding capable of underwriting the massive production costs demanded by even a relatively modest television program schedule.   In 1962 the federal government passed the first significant piece of legislation offering financial support for educational television, the Educational Television Facilities Act.

Five years later an extremely influential report issued by the Carnegie Commission on Educational Television resulted in Congress enacting the Public Broadcasting Act of 1967.   This Act created the Corporation for Public Broadcasting (CPB), a non-profit, non-governmental organization charged with funding all forms of educational broadcasting in the United States.[96]

To protect this new non-commercial service from being dominated by a centralized bureaucracy in Washington, CPB was denied the right to provide any type of broadcast service of its own to the general public.   Instead, it was directed to work with existing public broadcast stations to develop new forms of culturally or educationally oriented radio and television programming.

In 1970 CPB and a coalition of public broadcast stations formed the Public Broadcast Service (PBS) and National Public

broadcasting facilities to various types of non-commercial broadcasters but the Commission reported back to Congress in 1935 that existing commercial stations were providing sufficient cultural and education programming to make any special non-commercial allocations unnecessary.

[95] The first FCC attempt to reserve space for non-commercial FM broadcasting actually occurred in 1940, but World War II suspended efforts to implement this allocation plan and it was substantially modified when reintroduced in 1945.   Radio broadcast licenses have always been issued nationwide on a first-come, first-serve basis, only conditioned on an applicant being able to establish that transmission on the frequencies assigned will not interfere with other existing radio broadcast signals.   In contrast, the FCC's FM and TV license allocation programs have assigned each specific authorized FM or TV channel to a particular locality in the United States, and designed a specified segment of the FM band and a specific proportion of all TV channels for non-commercial use.

[96] The Carnegie Commission had recommended the term "public" rather than "educational" to describe the new non-commercial broadcast services it proposed, contended that to label them as "educational" would unduly restrict their role as alternatives to commercial broadcasting.

Radio (NPR), organizations established to distribute public radio and television programs to member stations. Four years later CPB and its member television stations created the Station Program Cooperative (SPC) plan, further decentralizing public television operation by making local stations primarily responsible for deciding which specific proposed television series productions will be funded.

When Congress established the Corporation for Public Broadcasting in 1967, it inserted new regulatory language in the Communications Act of 1934 specially designed to govern its functions.[97] The question soon arose whether by creating a separate set of regulatory requirements for public broadcasting, Congress had thereby exempted these stations from all other obligations imposed on broadcasters by the Communications Act.

In Accuracy in Media, Inc. v. FCC a federal court found that because Congress had included specific language in the Act of 1967 requiring public broadcasters to provide balanced and objective programming, it was Congress rather than the FCC that should be primarily responsible for supervising compliance with its directive.[98]

This special regulatory language governing non-commercial broadcasting had also denied those stations receiving funding from CPB the right to editorialize. In a 5–4 decision, the U.S. Supreme Court struck down this ban as an unconstitutional abridgement of broadcast free speech.[99]

In Muir v. Alabama Educational Television Commission, a majority of the huge en banc panel of 22 federal judges held that public broadcast stations had the same degree of editorial freedom in selecting and scheduling their programming as all other broadcasters.[1] Viewers challenging the refusal of two public broadcast stations to carry a controversial PBS documentary had argued that their tax supported status transformed them into "public forums" with less discretion to ignore the demands of the citizens who

---

[97] Statutory provisions of the Communications Act of 1934 that relate to CPB and public broadcasting are found in Section 390–399 of the Act of 1934.

[98] 521 F.2d 288 (D.C.Cir.1975), cert. denied 425 U.S. 934, 96 S.Ct. 1664 (1976). The court was particularly impressed by the argument that Congress had sought to shelter public broadcasting as much as possible from federal interference, and FCC regulation in the area of program content would operate to undercut that objective.

[99] FCC v. League of Women Voters of California, 468 U.S. 364, 104 S.Ct. 3106 (1984). In this instance, the station editorializing was not a public broadcaster but rather a non-commercial station that had accepted funding from CPB and therefore came under the federal statute.

[1] 688 F.2d 1033 (5th Cir.1982). The large panel of judges resulted from the consolidation of appeals from two conflicting lower court actions resulting from the refusal of two public broadcast stations to carry the controversial documentary "Death of a Princess" that portrayed Saudi Arabian society as being primitive and barbaric.

provided their funding, but the majority opinion rejected this distinction between commercial and non-commercial public interest standards.

Although most non-commercial licenses in the United States are held by public broadcast stations operated by state or local governments, universities, or school districts, other non-profit organizations are also licensed to broadcast by the FCC. Religious groups or institutions do not qualify for a reserved educational broadcast channel unless the primary emphasis of their programming is on education, but they as well as other community supported broadcasters such as "Pacifica" are authorized to receive a non-commercial broadcast license.

Periodic campaigns have been waged to deny religious broadcasters spectrum space because their opponents contend they are too narrowly oriented to serve the interests of the general public.[2] The FCC has never accepted this argument, however, maintaining that religious and other non-commercial broadcasters perform a useful service by enhancing that degree of diversity available to American broadcast audiences.

[2] See Multiple and Religious Ownership of Educational Stations, 34 RR2d 1217 (1975). The Commission rejected this argument, but does employ the "fair break" principle first described in Noe v. FCC, 260 F.2d 739 (D.C.Cir.1958), requiring a broadcast licensee to give all listeners reasonable access to views opposing those held by the broadcaster.

Chapter 10

DEREGULATION AND THE NEW MEDIA

Since 1927, the entire regulatory structure of American broadcasting has rested upon a single base of authority, the privilege of spectrum access, furnishing both the legal justification and those administrative procedures needed for federal control of broadcast service in the United States.

Through licensing standards derived from this authority, the FRC and FCC labored diligently to establish and maintain a nationwide system of locally oriented radio and television stations, with each licensee granted an exclusive territorial right to disseminate programming on one specially reserved segment of spectrum frequencies.

Cable television posed the first serious threat to this traditional regulatory structure. Its wired systems did not require any spectrum space, and their coaxial lines had the capacity to flood previously sheltered broadcast markets with new channels of programming. As a result, cable TV, operating outside licensing authority of the FCC, was free to fragment local television audiences and diminish station advertising revenues.

Cable TV emerged as unexpectedly as radio broadcasting had developed during the 1920s. Once again, the federal government would be forced to react to a crisis it had not foreseen, and to adopt laws to resolve the immediate problem without time to consider the long range policy implications of those laws.

SEC. 56. REGULATING CABLE TV

Cable TV has been regulated by the FCC as a by-product of broadcast service, its presence tolerated only to the extent that it did not impair the quality of that service.

No one actually "invented" cable television. During the 1930s, Bell Labs had perfected coaxial cable, a specially constructed high-capacity conduit capable of delivering a vast number of different communication services within a single wire.   Even in the late 1940s, however, when AT&T began using this cable to distribute network programs to affiliated television stations, there was no thought of connecting individual households to such a coaxial delivery system.

In truth, the emergence of cable TV was simply an historical accident, caused by a noble but flawed policy effort of the FCC to design a system of "community oriented" local television in the United States.   The FCC television allocation plan of 1952 provided for more than 2000 television stations to serve some 1300 different communities throughout the nation.[1]   The engineering staff of the Commission had based its television service projections on just such a fully operational system.   Unfortunately, only 530 of these 2000 stations were actually in operation at the end of that decade, even though nearly 85 percent of all American homes already were television households.[2]

What the FCC planners had failed to foresee was that no one would apply for a television license in any of those communities too small to generate enough advertising revenues to interest a television network in providing the station with programming.   As a result, instead of establishing a nationwide system of local television stations, the Commission succeeded only in creating conditions that would allow a new, more effective system of television program distribution to develop.

The Community Antenna Era

Originally "community antennas," as cable systems were then called, were exactly that; shared master antenna hookups that allowed a cluster of homes located just beyond the coverage area of the nearest television station to receive a marginally acceptable picture.[3]   During the early 1950s these primitive aerials were viewed as being nothing more than a temporary solution to an immediate problem, destined to disappear in time as newly licensed stations began filling in each of the many gaps remaining in national network television coverage.

Within a few years, however, it became clear the Commission would not abandon its original television station allocation policy despite the plan's obvious limitations.   As late as 1958, some 34

[1] 6th Report and Order, 17 Reg. 3905–4100 (May 2, 1952) allocated 2,053 television stations to 1,291 different communities in the United States, many with populations of less than 50,000.

[2] U.S. Congress, Senate, Committee on Interstate and Foreign Commerce, Television Inquiry: Television Allocations 86th Cong. 2nd sess. 1960, p. 4587.

[3] As in the early days of radio, many of these first community antenna operators were actually appliance stores, trying to stimulate demand for the TV receivers they wanted to sell by providing television reception to households that otherwise would have been unable to receive a broadcast television signal.

percent of America's television households still could receive only one television channel.[4] Located in less populous markets without an audience base large enough to support additional affiliate television stations, these viewers had access to only one of those three sources of network fare they were eager to watch each evening.

During this era an enterprising community antenna operator asked the the FCC's Common Carrier Bureau for permission to use a microwave system to deliver to his system the network programming not available in his area from nearby network affiliate stations.[5] Because communication common carrier regulation at that time involved nothing more than a review of the reasonableness of the charges for service, his request was routinely granted.[6]

The CATV Era

Microwave relays opened an entirely new domain for CATV operators, allowing them for the first time to enter larger communities where some television service was already available. Until this time, a cable system could only improve the quality of existing over-the-air television service.

Now, however, cable TV could attract far more subscribers by offering them channels of network programs they were unable to receive over-the-air. Although those affiliate stations whose network programs were being exported by CATV systems without payment or permission were the first to complain about this usage, they really sustained no economic injury through this unauthorized carriage of their signals.[7] Few of the programs being exported by CATV were actually owned by these stations, and the wider circulation each station's advertising messages gained through cable dissemination actually increased rather than diminished their potential to earn revenues.

Instead, the damage was being inflicted upon small market television stations located in those communities where the CATV systems were operating. Until this time, station managers had

---

[4] U.S. Congress, Senate, Committee on Interstate and Foreign Commerce, "VHF Boosters and Community Antenna Legislation"; Hearings on S. 1739 ... 86th Congress, 1st sess. 1959, p. 455.

[5] FCC 54–58; In the Matter of J.E. Belnap. For a discussion of the impact this decision had upon cable TV development and regulation in the 1950s and 1960s, see Don R. Le Duc, Cable Television and the FCC (Philadelphia) Temple University Press, 1973) pp. 74–77.

[6] In a 1961 case, Federal Power Com'n v. Transcontinental Gas P.L. Corp., 365 U.S. 1, 81 S.Ct. 435, the Supreme Court approved the common carrier regulatory approach of looking beyond simple authorization of a service to determine whether the ultimate result of its use would be in the public interest. It was this decision that gave the FCC authority to begin denying cable TV its microwave relay requests in Carter Mountain Transmission Corp. v. FCC, 321 F.2d 359 (D.C.Cir.1963).

[7] Intermountain Broadcasting & Television Corp. v. Idaho Microwave, Inc., 196 F.Supp. 315 (D.Idaho 1961).

generally been pleased with the community antenna systems that sprang up along the edges of their coverage contours, for they extended a station's effective transmission range at no cost to the broadcaster.

Now, however, these CATV systems were providing competing television channels to subscribers in the broadcaster's own market, substantially reducing the number of viewers watching the local station's programs. What had been a symbiotic relationship between the station and community antenna had been transformed into a parasitic one, for CATV was preying on small one station markets in the weakest financial condition. Yet, ironically, it was the marginal nature of these markets that sheltered CATV from immediate federal regulatory reaction.

Because the networks and the major stations instrumental in shaping industry policies saw little need to protect the economic welfare of stations in markets that cumulatively represented less than one percent of the total television audience, they made no effort to convince the FCC to intervene to prevent this damaging competition.[8]

In 1960, at the urging of several members of Congress whose small market television broadcasters faced such CATV competition, a Congressional committee considered legislation that would place the cable industry under FCC's regulatory jurisdiction. The FCC vigorously opposed the legislation, declaring that it did not believe the cable threat to be severe enough to justify the heavy administrative burden its supervision would impose upon the agency.[9] Ultimately the bill died in committee and because Congress would not adopt any cable TV legislation during the next 20 years, the FCC was compelled to operate continually at the very edge of its legal authority when dealing with cable, uncertain when the federal courts might find the agency had exceeded the boundaries of its Congressionally delegated power over cable TV.

Local Cable TV Controls

Because the federal government had not claimed exclusive control over cable TV, local governments began to exert their own legal authority to impose program service obligations upon cable operators who wanted to construct cable systems in their communities. They were able to do this without unconstitutionally abridg-

[8] For a more complete discussion of this era of cable TV growth, see Le Duc, Op.Cit. pp. 82–113.

[9] "In the Matter of Inquiring into the Impact of CATV ... upon the Orderly Development of Television Broadcasting." Docket 12443, 18 RR2d 1573 (1959). The FCC realized that without constitutional authority to license each cable system, the agency would have no power to prevent the damaging impact CATV competition had upon broadcast stations, and yet would be held responsible for such damage because of being given this responsibility for cable supervision.

ing the free speech rights of the cable operator because of one special characteristic of cable TV operation.

It was virtually impossible to construct a cable system without first obtaining a public *easement*, the property right a cable operator needed from local government to permit the system's cable to be strung across the municipality's streets and other public rights-of-way. Within a short time, however, local governments began to realize if a cable operator expected to benefit from this use of public property, the citizens of the community to be served also had a right to benefit from this use of their land.

The contract that local governments offered an operator interested in providing cable TV service became known as the *franchise agreement*, offering the operator the privilege of a "public easement" to construct the cable system in return for an annual lease payment, called the *franchise fee,* and other regulatory requirements imposed on the system for the benefit of the citizens of that community who were the rightful owners of this municipal property.

As large corporations began buying groups of small CATV systems in the early 1960s, they started to exert strong influence upon the industry's trade group, the National Cable Television Association (NCTA), to *support*, rather than oppose federal regulation of cable TV. These new corporate cable owners found it extremely inconvenient to manage cable systems operating under vastly different local franchise agreements, and so they favored the broadest possible federal preemption of cable control to reduce the degree of diversity among these local cable laws.

The NAB and NCTA tried to draft a jointly sponsored cable TV bill to submit to Congress that would grant the FCC at least some type of regulatory authority over cable TV. However, by 1964, bitter factional clashes between the new pro-regulatory and the old anti-regulatory groups within NCTA had become too intense to allow for any hope of future agreement on the "industry consensus" legislation Congress had requested.

As these industry negotiations were ending in failure, several of the larger, corporate owned CATV systems were preparing to enter a number of the "top 100," or largest 100 American broadcast markets, where 90 percent of the nation's television homes were located. Suddenly cable's competitive threat was no longer viewed as a minor one by broadcast industry leaders, and the FCC now shared this viewpoint.

Federal Cable Microwave Constraints

Although the FCC had no legal authority to regulate cable, it did have such authority over the microwave relay services essential to deliver the additional television signals cable TV needed to attract subscribers in major markets.[10] In 1963, the Commission had actually begun, on a case-by-case basis, to decide whether approving an application for a particular cable microwave relay would lessen the financial capacity of local television stations in the cable system's area to provide effective broadcast service.

When the FCC began to deny microwave applications on this basis, a federal court upheld the agency's right to use this power to protect the public's interest in maintaining the quality of broadcast television.[11] Then in 1965 the FCC declared that it would no longer authorize *any* applications to microwave television programs into a "top 100" broadcast market until the agency was able to adopt permanent cable microwave rules.[12] In the end, this "temporary" freeze on microwave applications would actually remain in force for more than seven years, effectively denying the cable TV industry any growth opportunities in the nation's most profitable broadcast markets from 1965 to 1972.

Although the Commission has been widely criticized for suppressing cable industry expansion during this extended period of time, it is only fair to point out that Congress was at least equally to blame for the agency's conduct. The FCC was convinced that it would not be in the public interest to allow the cable industry to undermine the economic stability of television stations, while at the same time offering the public virtually no programming of its own and contributing nothing to the production costs of those television programs it carried.

Cable TV was free to take and distribute whatever broadcast programming it wanted without permission or payment simply because the only legally recognized property rights in these programs were defined by the Copyright Act of 1909, a law adopted before the birth of radio broadcasting. Because it had been written in the era of vaudeville and the musical hall, the Act of 1909 protected copyrighted material from infringement only if it was being "performed" without permission. In 1968, the Supreme

[10] To attract paying subscribers in major markets, cable TV had to offer viewers more service than those three network channels virtually all households in urban area could already receive with a simple antenna. This meant that programming from non-network stations in distant markets had to be imported as well, offering different film packages, syndicated programs and sports than local stations provided. Until 1975, when the first communication satellites began operation, there was no other means for delivering television signals from one market to another except by microwave network.

[11] Carter Mountain Transmission Corp. v. FCC, 321 F.2d 359 (D.C.Cir.1963), cert. denied 375 U.S. 951, 84 S.Ct. 442 (1963).

[12] "Proposed Rulemaking in Docket 15971", 1 FCC2d 463 (1965). By making this an interim or temporary rule, the FCC protected it from being challenged in federal court, because the court, except in an exceptional case, will not hear an appeal from an order until the action is final.

Court affirmed earlier decisions by several lower federal courts that mere delivery of a television program by a cable TV system was not a "performance" of that program, and therefore that television programming was not protected by the Copyright Act of 1909 from unauthorized cable TV usage.[13]

Congress had begun efforts to revise the copyright law to include cable TV carriage of broadcast programming in 1965, but it took more than a decade to accomplish this task and cable TV would not actually come under the provisions of the new Copyright Act of 1976 until January 1, 1978.[14] During this entire era, the FCC stood as the broadcast industry's only legal defense again cable TV's unauthorized use of television programming.

In 1968 the Supreme Court affirmed for the first time the Commission's use of its microwave relay authority to discourage cable TV from entering major broadcast markets.[15] At that point the FCC announced its intention to launch a series of full scale hearings to develop rules and long range policy for the development of cable TV service in the United States. Four years later the agency completed these deliberations, and in March 1972, it issued these new rules, declaring that the era of modern cable TV service in the United States had finally begun.[16]

In reality, the FCC would continue to make it virtually impossible for cable TV systems to serve the 50 largest broadcast markets, where 75 percent of the television audience was located, until the Copyright Act of 1976 came into force. However, from 1972 onward, the cable TV industry would at least be regulated by rules designed for its systems, rather than solely for the protection of its broadcast industry competitor.

Cable TV had sprung up like a weed in a carefully cultivated garden. In attempting to create favorable conditions for the growth of locally oriented television service, the FCC had succeeded only in providing fertile opportunities for a rival distribution system to take root.

In this environment cable TV was the intruder, the electronic medium to be restrained in order to encourage more useful growth. Viewed from this perspective, it is easier to understand why the

[13] Fortnightly Corp. v. United Artists Television, Inc., 392 U.S. 390, 88 S.Ct. 2084 (1968).

[14] Title 17, United States Code, "Copyright Act of 1909" was rescinded and replaced by the new Title 17, as enacted by Public Law No. 94–553, 94th Stat. 2541 (1976).

[15] United States v. Southwestern Cable Co., 392 U.S. 157, 88 S.Ct. 1994 (1968), in which the high court affirmed the FCC's authority to regulate cable TV's use of television signals as being a reasonable ancillary of its power to regulate broadcasting in the public interest.

[16] "Third Report and Order on Docket 18397", 24 RR2d 1501 (1972).

FCC simply suppressed cable TV, rather than trying to incorporate its systems within plans to provide more effective distribution of the nation's television services. Unfortunately, the damage caused by this repression would become all too apparent in the near future, when the cable industry did not have the financial capacity necessary to fulfill the promises it made to citizens in a number of American cities.

SEC. 57. FEDERAL CABLE TV REGULATION

Cable TV was the first of the "new media," its multi-channel distribution system providing an entirely different form of communication service than the single channel broadcast station.

The 1972 FCC cable rules required every new system being constructed in one of the largest 100 broadcast markets to provide its subscribers with a minimum of 20 channels, and to set aside specific channels for educational, governmental, leased and public access programming. While the FCC denied local governments any regulatory authority over cable TV's television signal carriage or program origination practices, it permitted municipal or state cable regulators to continue to establish franchise boundaries, select cable operators, determine terms of service and decide upon the amount to be collected as a franchise fee, although each of these powers now had to be exercised within standards set by the federal government.

It was difficult for the Commission to regulate cable TV effectively, because the agency had no constitutional authority to deny these non-spectrum communication systems permission to operate. Instead, the agency could only deny those cable systems in violation of its rules the right to carry broadcast signals, and if necessary, to enforce this denial through a federal court order. However, since the effect of this order would be to prevent the system's subscribers from receiving those services for which they were willing to pay, it was an action the Commission was obviously reluctant to take.

Initially, the FCC imposed an extremely elaborate system of restrictions upon the importation of television signals to major market cable systems, but after the Copyright Act of 1976 established a system compensating broadcasters and program suppliers for cable TV carriage, the Commission rescinded most of these restraints. By 1983, the only major FCC rule remaining in this field was "must carry", requiring cable TV systems to provide channel space for all local television stations their subscribers could receive over-the-air.

Even though the new copyright law did require cable TV systems to begin paying for the television programming they were importing, the terms and conditions of payment reflected a clear legislative victory for the cable industry. Cable was granted a *compulsory license* by the Copyright Act, compelling television stations and program suppliers to allow cable TV to carry their programs in return for a program use fee to be determined by a government body, the Copyright Royalty Tribunal. The Tribunal was empowered by the Act to collect from each cable system a percentage of that system's gross subscriber revenues to be used to compensate these television program suppliers.[17]

In gaining the "compulsory license," the cable industry was able to avoid having to pay the marketplace value for the programs it used. When the first distribution was made from this cable copyright pool, program suppliers complained bitterly that payments they received from the Tribunal were not only far less than the actual value of these programs, but even less than the financial damage they sustained because of this cable TV usage.[18]

In 1982 the Tribunal instituted new proceedings to adjust the amount of subscriber revenues each system would be required to pay into the copyright revenue pool. Until that time, cable systems paid only 0.625 percent of their annual revenues to import one distant television signal, and another 0.425 percent for each additional distant signal imported. Program suppliers urged the Tribunal to increase this fee substantially, because by bringing major feature films packages and popular series programming into areas where they had not yet been sold to local stations, cable TV was significantly diminishing the value, and thus the price of these features as "first run" attractions for television stations in that market where the cable system was located.[19]

After lengthy deliberations the Tribunal finally decided upon new rates for cable systems to pay for each distant television signal imported, almost 10 times higher than the base percentages established only four years before.[20] Although the cable industry com-

[17] This "secondary transmission" cable copyright payment procedure is described in Title 17, U.S.C.A. §§ 801–810.

[18] The Tribunal collected $15 million from cable systems during 1978, the first year this system was in operation. The distribution formula granted 75% of this money to program and movie syndicators, 12% to sports organizations and only 3.5% to television stations. This allocation was approved by the courts in National Ass'n of Broadcasters v. Copyright Royalty Tribunal, 675 F.2d 367 (D.C.Cir.1982).

[19] This problem became more severe in 1980 when the FCC rescinded its "syndicated exclusivity" rules, that until this time had forced cable TV to "black out" programs on those channels it imported that local stations held exclusive rights to broadcast in that market.

[20] CRT 1982 "Distribution Proceeding and Partial Distribution of Fees" 48 Fed.Reg. 46412 (Oct. 12, 1983). This determination was sustained by the courts in

plained bitterly about this massive increase in its copyright fee payments, the actual economic impact of these higher copyright rates upon cable systems was not very severe, simply because cable operators were by this time far less dependent upon broadcast stations for cable system programming.[21]

Cable Satellite Networks

Between 1975 and 1980, satellite delivered pay-TV services, superstations, and advertising supported cable networks not only reduced cable TV's dependence on the broadcast industry for programming, but also furnished cable systems with new sources of revenue. Home Box Office (HBO) launched the first cable pay-TV service in 1975, offering system owners the opportunity to earn profits from a vacant channel by devoting it to the delivery of the HBO service.

In 1977, USA, the first advertising supported cable TV network, began operation. It sought, at least initially, to cover its costs and generate profits solely on the basis of the commercials it could place in its programming. Although cable operators receive no payment from these advertising supported channels, and in most cases are now charged a monthly per subscriber fee for the privilege of carriage, systems can earn money from placing local advertising in network time slots provided, and are likely to attract a greater number of subscribers because of offering these additional channels of programming.

So-called "superstation" cable service began in 1976, when Ted Turner, owner of a small UHF station in Atlanta, started delivering his station's programming by satellite to cable systems throughout the nation. Turner, whose ownership of the Atlanta Braves and part-ownership of the Atlanta Hawks allowed him to offer professional sports as well as the usual assortment of older syndicated series programs, generated his revenues through the higher advertising rates he could charge sponsors for his vastly expanded national cable viewing audience. By the mid–1980s, his service was already reaching more than 12.5 million American homes, or roughly one-sixth of all television households in the United States.

By 1980, cable TV system operators could choose among five competing pay-TV services, six "superstations" and more than 40 advertising supported cable networks, such as Entertainment and

National Cable Television Ass'n v. Copyright Royalty Tribunal, 689 F.2d 1077 (D.C.Cir.1982).

[21] In December 1993, Congress abolished the Copyright Royalty Tribunal, replacing this tax-supported agency with ad hoc arbitration panels chosen by the Librarian of Congress and working in consultation with the Register of Copyrights. Copyright owners will now be required to provide the funding for these panels that will decide how to allocate the compulsory license payments that cable systems and juke box owners make annually to those who own the programs and music they use.

Sports Network (ESPN), Cable Satellite Public Affairs Network (C–SPAN), Cable News Network (CNN) and a host of other general and specialized program services to fill their systems' channels.

Ironically, this explosive growth in new satellite delivered services that transformed cable TV from a passive relay system for broadcast services into a truly unique and independent electronic medium was also the unanticipated by-product of an FCC major policy decision involving a different form of communication.

When the FCC authorized domestic communication satellite service in 1972, no one could foresee how its competitive "open skies" satellite policy would affect future cable TV service in the United States.[22] Until this time AT&T had held a virtual monopoly over the national distribution of television programming. Broadcast networks were charged a relatively low rate to deliver their programs to affiliate stations, because they were willing to pay for 24 hour a day usage of special AT&T television circuits set aside specifically for this purpose. When other television distributors tried to lease similar circuits from AT&T on an occasional use basis, however, the charge for this service was prohibitively high, because AT&T was forced to reroute thousands of telephone circuits to find the space necessary to deliver a full-sized television channel.

The Commission's policy decision to encourage competition by opening the communication satellite field to any organization meeting basic qualifications standards was not designed with the intention of ending this AT&T monopoly over national television delivery, but rather in the hope of reducing AT&T's domination over nationwide distribution of telephonic, telegraphic and other personal and business messages.[23] However, when Western Union's Westar I and RCA's Americom were finally launched in the mid–1970s, these new satellite system owners were eager to lease their unused delivery channels to video program organizations at rates far lower than AT&T had been charging.

The other factor that had inhibited the growth of new nationwide television services had been the absence of local outlets to distribute these programs. Most broadcast markets had only three television stations, each already affiliated with a major network. As cable TV began to expand during the mid–1970s, however, with the 20 channel system capacity required by the FCC rules, virtually all operators had vacant channels available to serve as those local outlets that national satellite delivered program services required.

[22] "Domestic Communication Satellite Facilities," 35 FCC2d 844 (1972).

[23] The FCC Common Carrier Bureau had begun this policy effort to reduce the AT&T–Bell domination of American personal and business communication services in 1959 by allowing carriers other than AT&T to operate microwave relay networks.

Thus, through another fortunate historical accident, the emergence of privately owned, competitively priced national domestic satellite system service happened to coincide with the growing demand of urban multi-channeled cable systems for additional programming to result in the establishment of a much more independent and prosperous cable industry.

The Urban Cable System Era

Unfortunately, though, extensive campaigns launched by each of the major cable ownership groups to capture as many urban cable franchises as possible once the FCC signal importation restrictions had been lifted, left most of these multiple system owners (MSOs) in a very precarious financial position as the 1980s began. In their eagerness to win franchise agreements from major city governments, each applicant tried to outbid all other competitors by offering an impressive range of communication services without carefully considering the operational costs involved. Adding to their difficulties was the fact that as many of these urban systems were being built in 1978 and 1979, interest rates on the substantial investment needed for cable construction soared to more than 20 percent.[24]

If the cable industry had been allowed by the FCC to expand gradually in urban markets through the years, it seems reasonable to assume that this period of frantic franchise speculation would have been avoided. Instead, the net result of all this destructive bidding was simply a trail of broken cable franchise promises, denying subscribers those benefits that had earned the MSO its franchise.

During the late 1970s, cable growth came to a virtual halt as financially overextended MSOs sought the additional funding essential to complete those systems they were already committed to build. The timing couldn't have been more unfortunate for the cable industry, because, ironically, that very satellite delivered programming that could have made cable TV successful in major television markets was now seen by direct broadcast satellite (DBS), multi-channel, multi-point, distribution system (MMDS) and low power television (LPTV) promoters as being the program services that would allow them to invade these markets and claim that urban audience cable TV was still struggling to reach.[25]

[24] For a detailed summary of many of these urban market problems, see "Cable Franchising Update," Broadcasting July 12, 1982, p. 37.

[25] As late as 1981, more than 60% of all American cable TV systems still had no more than a 12 channel delivery capacity, a capacity reduced even further by franchise and FCC signal carriage rules. Sydney Head and Christopher Sterling, Broadcasting in America 4th ed. (Boston: Houghton Mifflin, 1982) p. 296.

Cable TV had been the first of the "new media." What made cable TV different from broadcasting was its program delivery function. Each radio or television station must depend upon a single channel of communication to entertain and inform its audience and earn its advertising revenues. In contrast, a cable system serves as a broadcast spectrum for its subscribers, allowing them to select from among those various channels of programming it provides.

This difference gave cable TV a tremendous competitive advantage over the individual television station. The cable system did not have to displace a popular, profitable program in order to provide more specialized features for particular segments of the audience. Instead, popular and specialized programs could be distributed simultaneously, attracting as paying subscribers not only those seeking mass appeal features, but also viewers especially interested in sports, politics, religion, culture, news or any of the many other cable delivered services. In fact, cable systems soon began packaging groups of these program channels in various priced "tiers" of subscriber fees, allowing operators to profit to an even greater extent from the diversity of services the system offered.

Yet, although cable TV was able to exploit this multi-channel distribution system advantage when competing with broadcasting, its massively expensive coaxial distribution system made it vulnerable to challenge from newer multi-channeled systems far less expensive to build, and capable of beginning service much more rapidly than cable.

Until this point, the cable industry had been totally committed to the principle of free competition in a marketplace environment to determine which form of electronic media service should prevail. During the 1980s, that commitment became somewhat less than total.

SEC. 58.   NEW MEDIA COMPETITION

The authorization of each new electronic medium made it increasingly difficult for the FCC to maintain the "level regulatory playing field" it had pledged to provide each competitor.

In 1972, the Commission formulated its "open skies" satellite policy without intending to attempt to stimulate the growth of electronic media services in the United States. During the 1980s, the Commission formulated its "new media technology" policies with exactly this purpose in mind. Only time will tell whether or not the FCC's carefully planned regulatory strategy will be as successful as those results it has achieved largely by chance.

Direct Broadcast Satellite Systems

The FCC announced its intention in October 1980 to establish regulatory policies for the development of direct broadcast satellite (DBS) service in the United States. This action was motivated at least in part by the concern that American lagged behind Canada, Western Europe and Japan in the development of DBS technology. "Direct broadcast" satellites are specially designed to transmit a focused, far more powerful signal covering a more limited amount of territory than the ordinary communication satellite. Because of this greater power, DBS signals can be received on a much smaller "dish" or antenna than the regular satellite, reducing the size and cost to a point where individual households could easily afford to purchase this reception equipment.[26]

Satellite Television Corporation, a subsidiary of Comsat, had submitted a proposal to the FCC in 1979 to develop a six channel DBS pay-TV service, to be delivered through a system of several satellites deployed in orbital slots capable of providing nationwide coverage. In October 1981 the Commission accepted this application, and at the same time approved applications from several other organizations interested in providing various forms of DBS service, including CBS, RCA, American Communications, and Western Union Telegraph.[27]

The following year the FCC adopted a simplified set of regulations especially designed for DBS service, exempting these systems from traditional broadcast ownership and political access requirements.[28] The Commission hoped through what it called this "flexible" new approach to avoid imposing unnecessary regulatory burdens upon new media in the earliest stages of their development, before it was clear precisely what type of federal supervision they might require.

The National Association of Broadcasters challenged what it saw as unfair regulatory advantages given an electronic media competitor, and this challenge was sustained on appeal.[29] The court found that the Commission had no right to exempt DBS systems who came within the statutory definition of "broadcasting" from requirements Congress had imposed upon all those providing broadcast service in the United States.

---

[26] The large backyard dish necessary to receive regular satellite transmissions today still costs about $2,000. The tiny DBS dish, only 3 feet in diameter, costs between $400–500, and when mass marketing allows them to be made in quantity, it is estimated that they may retail for only $200–$250.

[27] "Notice of Proposed Policy Statement and Rulemaking in General Docket 80–603," adopted Oct. 22, 1981, 88 FCC2d 100 (1981).

[28] "In the Matter of Inquiry into the Development of Regulatory Policy in Regard to Direct Broadcasting Satellites ...," 51 RR2d 1341 (1981).

[29] National Association of Broadcasters v. FCC, 740 F.2d 1190 (D.C.Cir.1984).

In the end, however, it was not the regulatory but the financial demands of launching and operation that discouraged those who had filed DBS applications with the Commission from actually beginning to provide this service. Subscription Television, the pioneer in this field, abandoned its DBS plans in 1984, and CBS, RCA and others soon followed its example. United States Communications tried a lower powered communication satellite to provide direct-to-home broadcast service to those households with larger dish antennas, but this venture ended in receivership less than two years after it was launched.

From the beginning, DBS promoters had realized that it would take an estimated $150 million to launch even a modest single satellite, three channel service. During the early 1980s, however, it was still assumed that the novel appeal of first run feature films, unedited and uninterrupted by commercials would attract enough DBS subscriber households to recoup these costs in a reasonable period of time. By 1985, as the VCR and the VCR rental stores were becoming national institutions, the appeal of the first run feature film no longer seemed unique enough to justify such a substantial investment.

As the 1990s began, it seemed that "Sky Cable," a true high power DBS proposal uniting General Electric's NBC, Rupert Murdoch's News Corporation, Cablevision and satellite supplier Hughes would soon establish the first DBS service in the United States. But despite the fact that Hughes held the only group of orbital locations capable of providing DBS service to the entire continental United States, the consortium collapsed within a year, leaving the Hughes as the only partner still eager to continue the project.

In 1991 Hubbard Broadcasting (USSB) agreed to finance a portion of the Hughes DBS project and by mid 1994, their joint venture was ready for launch. Hughes, operating as "DirecTv", will offer some 40 program channels and set aside an additional 40 channels for a PPV feature film service, while Hubbard's "USSB," will provide a competing 30 channels of program services from the same satellites.[30]

At the moment "Primestar," a non-DBS, medium power satellite system owned by several cable MSOs and GE American Communication, will be their only significant satellite competitor. But this system that now serves some 700,000 subscriber homes has

[30] Rich Brown, "Dishing Up Full–Power DBS," Broadcasting, March 28, 1994, p. 48. After an initial investment of $600–$700 per household for the 18 inch dish antenna and other reception equipment, subscribers can select from among various program packages, ranging in price from $7.95 for USSB's basic package of MTV, VH1, Nickelodeon, Nick at Nite, All News Channel, Comedy Central and Lifetime to $29,95 per month for DirecTv's "Total Choice" that includes more than 30 program channels.

been hampered by the larger dish antenna its transmissions requires, limiting its growth potential in urban areas.

The cable industry claims to be unconcerned by DBS, pointing to advances in channel compression technology they expect will soon increase by a factor of 10 the number of channels each cable system will have the capacity to deliver. This they believe will provide cable systems with a significant competitive advantage over even the most advanced DBS system of that era, limited as they will be by the spectrum space allocated for their transmissions to no more than 120 digitally compressed channels of service.

In reality, however, digital compression could have exactly the opposite effect. Without even considering how the cable industry will find the funds to obtain or produce sufficient programming and services to fill 100, let alone 500 video channels, the fact is that cable TV channel expansion must take place gradually on a system-by-system basis and is unlikely to extend into those rural cable markets targeted by DBS systems within the foreseeable future. On the other hand, the moment a DBS satellite is launched its entire nationwide system of channels are digitally compressed and capable immediately of offering its entire audience that abundance of services made possible by this new technology.

High Definition TV Service

Perhaps the most important benefit that digital band compression can offer both cable TV and DBS is in furnishing them the channel space required to deliver future high definition television (HDTV) services. Until recently, this advantage seemed relatively unimportant, because foreign dominance in the field of high definition technology had made the U.S. government reluctant to promote the development of this service in the United States. But when American advances in digitally transmitted HDTV finally surpassed the analog based techniques of Japan and Europe in 1990, the FCC moved rapidly to encourage its growth.

In April 1992 the FCC announced its plan to begin assigning UHF frequencies for broadcast HDTV transmission (termed ATV by the agency for "Advanced TV") immediately after it adopted a universal American standard for digitally transmitted ATV. Each existing television station would then be allowed five years (later extended to six) from the date of the adoption of this standard to begin the transmission of high definition (ATV) programming on its newly assigned high definition channels or risk the loss of its channel assignment to a rival applicant.

Those broadcasters satisfying this initial deadline would then have another 10 years to convert to full-time high definition TV operation, at which time the Commission would revoke all existing

VHF (2–13) channel allocations, reassigning every television station to what would then be an all-UHF band HDTV American broadcast service.

Response to this visionary plan was prompt and predictable. The decision to deny non-broadcasters an opportunity to receive an ATV license angered public interest groups, while TV station owners complained that it would cost an estimated $12 million for each station to convert to high definition operation. Public TV stations felt particularly threatened by this massive demand on their limited financial resources, while VHF stations opposed the eventual loss of their more valuable channel assignments.

Yet despite these bitter factional fights, the effort to launch digitally delivered high definition television in the United States continues unabated, an effort that will also have a profound effect on future development of cable TV and other new media.

The HDTV "grand alliance," seven major electronic firms committed to the development of universal technical standards for HDTV in the United States, had settled on four of the five subsystem standards (picture format, audio, compression, data packets) by October 1993.[31] When the fifth subsystem, a Zenith "VSB" transmission standard was selected by the FCC's industry advisory committee in February 1994 for both over-the-air and cable HDTV delivery, it cleared the way for final testing of HDTV in the United States, a process scheduled to be completed by March 1995.

The driving force behind this federal effort to encourage the launching of high definition television has been industrial policy. During the few years rapid advances in American digital technology have thrust the United States into the lead in the race to dominate the world market for HDTV hardware. Rapid deployment of high definition television in the United States will allow the American electronic and computer industries to consolidate their control over the global market for a wide range of digital transmission and reception devices.

But whatever the motivation, the fact remains that although the FCC has focused primarily on broadcast stations in framing its HDTV regulations, both cable TV and DBS seem much better situated than broadcasters to benefit from its introduction. Because of their ability to underwrite the increased production costs of HDTV programs through higher subscriber fees, these media are almost certain to profit in the long run from HDTV development far more than their advertising-dependent broadcast competitors.

[31] These seven electronic firms combined into three development groups: (1) AT&T/Zenith Electronics; (2) General Instrument/MIT; (3) Phillips Consumer Electronics/David Sarnoff Research/Thomson Consumer Electronics.

Satellite Master Antenna Systems

In contrast to DBS or HDTV, satellite master antenna television (SMARTV) systems are not really "new technology" at all, but simply a modern version of the old fashioned community antenna. SMARTV operators erect large satellite receiving dishes on top of high-rise apartment buildings in major cities, and then distribute the satellite delivered programming received through cable to each apartment in the complex.

SMARTV systems charge apartment subscribers for their wired service, just as cable systems do. However, unlike cable TV, these self-contained systems do not cross city property to deliver their service, and so do not require an easement or franchise grant from the municipality in order to operate.[32]

Although these systems serve only those tenants within a single building, and so are not in competition with cable TV on a city-wide basis, they still can have a damaging impact upon cable revenues by depriving a cable system its most profitable potential subscriber revenues. The per subscriber cost of cabling a densely populated high-rise building has been estimated to be five to ten times lower than serving individual households, so each new SMARTV system doesn't simply deprive cable an additional group of subscribers, but also denies it the most valuable type of service opportunity.

Municipal governments have tended to be very sympathetic to cable TV in this situation, because local cable systems typically pay the city from three to five percent of their annual subscriber revenues as a franchise fee. In 1983, a SMARTV operator in New Jersey was prevented from installing a satellite reception system because of failing to comply with the regulatory requirements of the New Jersey Cable Television Act. The operator requested the FCC to intervene and deny state or local governments the right to regulate SMARTV construction or operation.

State officials argued that since the FCC had chosen not to regulate SMARTV systems, state and local authorities retained the right to impose rules upon these systems so as to balance their competitive relationship with locally regulated cable TV. The FCC rejected this argument, denying state or local governments any regulatory authority over SMARTV, despite the competitive threat these unregulated services might pose for cable TV. Another state

---

[32] SMARTV systems are also unlike the 2.5 million "home dish" installations, where individual households receive their programming direct from satellite. SMARTV operators are licensed by satellite programmers to distribute their channels for profit, sharing these profits with the programmers. Home dish owners are not licensed in this manner, but most satellite services now scramble their transmissions so that these individuals must pay to unscramble and view these transmissions.

cable regulatory body immediately challenged the FCC's decision to preemptive SMARTV jurisdiction, but the Commission was affirmed on appeal.[33]

MMDS: "Wireless" Cable Systems

In 1982, the court had also affirmed the FCC's authority to assert preemptive federal control over all microwave relay services.[34] Microwave is a very high frequency radio relay, developed by AT&T in the 1940s to substitute whenever possible for more expensive telephone wire or cable trunk lines. A microwave relay, unlike a regular radio transmission, must be focused like a beam of light, and travels in a narrow path as aimed for some 25 to 30 miles unless obstructed, as light would be obstructed, by a hill or tall building.

Until the late 1970s, microwave networks were used almost exclusively to send information or messages from one place to another. At that point, some multi-point system (MDS) operators in urban areas began to develop new microwave markets by relaying pay-TV programs to hotels and high-rise apartments. The design of a MDS system differs in one significant respect from that of the traditional point to point microwave relay. While the relay service consists of a single beam traveling in a straight line, MDS systems transmit several beams of microwave signals simultaneously that fan out from their transmission hub in different directions like spokes on a wheel. This design not only made it possible for a MDS system to deliver its pay-TV channel to virtually any hotel or apartment building within range of one of its transmissions, but also to deliver the same pay-TV service directly to every individual household in the path of one of these beams as well.

It was at this point that the FCC moved in to prevent the New York cable commission from establishing regulatory standards to control the competitive impact of MDS upon cable TV. MDS itself posed nothing more than a minor competitive threat to cable TV, because each MDS system had been assigned only one television channel of microwave frequencies.

In 1983, however, the FCC revised its rules to create a more powerful new major market competitor for cable, the "multi-channel, multi-point distribution service" (MMDS). The Commission reallocated frequencies from another microwave service to provide each of those new MMDS systems it would license sufficient microwave bandwidth to deliver four separate channels of television

[33] New York State Commission on Cable Television v. FCC, 749 F.2d 804 (D.C.Cir. 1984).

[34] Orth–O–Vision, 44 RR2d 329 (1978), reconsidered 48 RR2d 503 (1980); affirmed in New York State Commission on Cable Television v. FCC, 669 F.2d 58 (2d Cir.1982).

service, with the right to lease additional microwave frequency bands for television delivery from other operators in that market.[35]

After receiving more than 16,500 applications for MMDS licenses during the brief period the agency had set aside to accept such filings, the FCC decided to select successful applicants by means of a lottery, rather than trying to evaluate each license application individually.[36] The Commission held the first of these lotteries in September 1985, but the growth of MMDS, also known as "multi-channel television" (MCTV) and "wireless cable" has been far less spectacular thus far than originally expected.

The most successful of the systems are those that serve major urban markets without any significant cable TV system competition. MMDS systems have already started operation in Philadelphia, San Francisco, Washington D.C., Cleveland and several smaller markets. The Cleveland operation is undoubtedly the most impressive at the moment, offering 12 channels of service, including "Showtime" pay TV.[37]

MMDS operators are claiming that the cable TV industry is conspiring with cable program suppliers to deny "wireless cable" the type of premium pay-TV and satellite network services these systems need to attract subscribers.[38] However, the fact that MMDS has been unable to compete in markets where cable TV is already in operation may simply suggest that no electronic medium restricted by spectrum space limitations to less than a dozen channels can ever hope to attract subscribers away from a wired system offering three to four times that number of program channels.

Low Power TV

The final "new medium" of this era was actually an old fashioned single channel distribution system, which is probably the reason it has failed thus far to have any significant impact upon American electronic media service. The concept of low power television (LPTV) was drastically revised by the Commission in March 1982, to transform it from a one-per-applicant, non-commercial broadcast public access service to a facility that could be group owned, operated as part of a nationwide network and used to distribute scrambled pay-TV services.[39]

[35] ITFS Service, 54 RR2d 107 (1983).

[36] Further Notice of Proposed Rulemaking in General Docket 80–122, adopted Oct. 12, 1983, 48 Fed.Reg. 49309. Congress had granted the FCC the authority to use a lottery to select licensees in the Omnibus Spending Bill of 1981.

[37] "Wireless Cable Ready to Grow," Broadcasting Oct. 5, 1987, p. 46.

[38] "Microband Fights for "Wireless Cable," Variety August 3, 1988, p. 80.

[39] "Report and Order on Docket 78–253," adopted Mar. 4, 1982, 17 Fed.Reg. 21468.

Changing the orientation of these stations attracted a substantial amount of interest, and within a matter of weeks, the FCC was buried under a backlog of 32,000 applications for the 4,000 LPTV licenses available to be issued. The FCC began processing these applications in September 1983, issuing licenses, using a lottery process, at a rate of about 100 a month. In 1988, however, less than 10 percent of those original licenses were actually in use, with some 380 LPTV stations on the air and another 150 in the construction permit stage.[40] Perhaps after the initial enthusiasm had worn off, those who had so eagerly sought the opportunity to operate a LPTV station realized more clearly than the Commission what the future prospects actually were for a small single channel medium in a world of multi-channel media competitors.

Although it may be too soon to evaluate the successes and failures of the Commission's "new media" competition policies of the early 1980s, certain characteristics of this competition now seem clearer than they did only a few years ago.

The one unexpected factor that made competitive conditions for new media far more difficult than anticipated was the impressive resurgence of the cable industry from 1981 through 1985, as national economic conditions improved, and interest rates dropped substantially. The number of cable subscribers more than doubled during these four years, increasing from 7.8 to 20.4 million, as the number of households able to obtain cable TV service rose from 43 to 72 percent of all American homes.[41]

The FCC began these "new media" proceedings in 1980 with the assumption that cable TV growth in major markets had been stunted, leaving gaping holes in national satellite service coverage that could be filled by DBS, MMDS and LPTV. By the time the Commission was able to begin licensing these "new media" applicants in 1984 and 1985, those holes were being filled instead by revitalized urban cable TV systems, making it difficult for these "new media" with their unproven service records and far more limited channel capacity to attract their own subscribers.

The greatest problem for these "new media" is that they have lacked any unique communication services of their own to attract viewers away from established media. DBS operators had seen themselves as "first run pay-TV feature film distributors" until the rapid emergence of the VCR and expansion of the film cassette rental industry made this appeal far less powerful. MMDS, SMARTV and LPTV offered no programming that cable TV couldn't provide, and had less channel capacity to deliver such programming than their cable competitor. As a result, it seems

[40] "By the Numbers", Broadcasting April 4, 1988, p. 14.
[41] Arthur D. Little, "Prospects for Cable TV: Outlook 1985–1990," May 1985.

unlikely that any of these "new media" in their present form can survive direct cable TV competition unless they are able to develop unique entertainment or informational features not available from cable, or can provide service at a cost so much lower than cable TV that they can attract viewers on that basis alone.[42]

While the first years of this "new media" era may not have revealed any challenger as yet capable of displacing cable TV in urban markets, it did reveal for the first time the incredibly difficult task the FCC would have in trying to maintain a "level regulatory playing field" among competing forms of electronic mass media.[43] The Commission has pledged its commitment to the principal of fair and equitable regulatory treatment of all electronic media, but as the agency discovered during this era, its authority to achieve this objective is restricted in several ways.

For one thing, as the FCC learned in the DBS case, it has only limited discretion in designing its rules to reflect the special characteristics of the medium being regulated.[44] Although the agency might believe certain basic broadcast standards to be irrelevant to satellite communication, hindering rather than encouraging its development, it is required by law to enforce all requirements established by Congress for that class of communication service without concern for their effect upon that particular medium.

[42] Industry experts estimate the per-subscriber cost of providing cable TV service to be $2,000 per household while the per-subscriber cost of furnishing each MMDS subscriber with a dish antenna and necessary conversion equipment is less than $500 per household. At this point, however, in part because of much lower sales volume, MMDS subscriptions are still priced somewhat higher than comparable cable rates; e.g. a $25.95 monthly charge in the typical MMDS service area for 12 basic MMDS delivered program channels and one premium service.

[43] The most powerful future cable TV challenger appears to be the local telephone company, already wired to each subscriber home, and moving towards an all fiber optic network system that would have the capacity to deliver far more video channels than the typical cable system. This telephone company competitive threat is discussed in Chapter 17.

[44] In June 1988, the D.C. Court of Appeals affirmed an FCC ruling that neither subscription TV nor direct broadcast satellites are "broadcast" technologies, allowing the agency to exempt these distribution systems from certain regulatory requirements imposed by Congress on broadcasters. National Ass'n for Better Broadcasting v. FCC, 849 F.2d 665 (D.C.Cir.1988). The FCC had argued that "broadcasting," as defined by the Communications Act of 1934, applies only to spectrum transmissions intended for the general public. Because neither STV nor DBS transmissions were intended for general public, but only for those members of the audience willing to pay for the decoding of these transmissions, the Court agreed that the agency need not apply to these services Congressional regulations intended only for traditional broadcasters. During the same year, however, a different 3-judge D.C. Court of Appeals panel denied the FCC authority to award Instructional Television Fixed Service (ITFS) licenses by lottery without complying with Congressional minority preference requirements relating to such lottery awards. Telecommunications Research and Action Center v. FCC, 836 F.2d 1349 (D.C.Cir.1988). These conflicting decisions make it difficult to determine exactly how much discretion the FCC actually has in attempting to modify statutory requirements to encourage new media development.

For another, as the Commission discovered in the SMARTV and MMDS preemption controversies, since it could not free cable TV from lawful local regulation, its only alternatives were to allow similar local restraints to be imposed upon these media, or to grant them a freedom cable TV did not enjoy.   It chose regulatory freedom over a "level playing field" for SMARTV and MMDS, as the court forced it to choose the "level playing field" over regulatory freedom in the DBS case, but in neither instance did the Commission achieve the true equality in regulatory treatment it was seeking.

Unfortunately, this principle is becoming more difficult for the FCC to observe with each passing year, because as each new medium attempts to expand its own special rights and interests, it is virtually impossible for the Commission to maintain that balance among those media regulatory constraints it is required to preserve.

SEC. 59.   DEREGULATION, REREGULATION AND THE MARKETPLACE

As the level of electronic media competition increases, each medium appears to be less concerned with freeing itself from government control than with finding a regulatory solution to its own competitive problems.

The greatest obstacle in the path of FCC efforts to establish a equitable regulatory environment in which all electronic media can compete under the same general legal obligations is the Communications Act of 1934.   As long as Congress is recognized by the courts as having the constitutional authority to impose conditions upon the exercise of broadcast free speech, the Commission has no choice but to enforce those conditions.

Because of this obligation, it is difficult for the FCC to provide broadcasting with a truly level regulatory playing field, for while the agency must require broadcasters to conform to various programming standards, its constitutional authority to impose similar content standards upon competing electronic media is far less extensive.[45]   More significantly, perhaps, because the FCC is powerless to reduce the regulatory burden of the broadcast industry, the only alternative it has for restoring balance to the "playing field" is to increase those legal obligations it imposes upon all other electronic media.

As these circumstances might suggest, the FCC is constantly being pressured by the broadcast industry to extend and expand its

---

[45] Congress itself imposed the equal access for political candidates obligations of Sec. 315 upon cable TV program origination channels when it enacted the Federal Elections Campaign Act of 1971;   Pub.L. No. 92–225, 86 Stat. 3 (1972).

regulatory controls over cable TV and other media competitors. It was the National Association of Broadcasters that challenged the Commission's attempt to limit the regulatory obligations of DBS systems, and that ultimately prevented the FCC from carrying out its proposed policy of "flexible" supervision of new media. Similarly, the broadcast industry opposed the creation of low power television stations because the FCC had established no "local service" requirements for these facilities.[46] Through the years, however, broadcast pressure for more extensive regulation has been most consistently applied to the field of cable television.

"Must Carry" and Syndicated Exclusivity

Every Commission effort to reduce the federal constraints on cable TV system operation has been attacked by a broadcast organization, and on several occasions the NAB has threatened to turn to Congress for relief when the FCC, in its deregulatory fervor, seemed too eager to release cable TV systems from various regulatory requirements of the past.[47] This industry pressure became even more intense in 1985, when a federal court found that the Commission's cable TV "must carry" rules were far too broad in their scope to be legally enforceable.[48]

The FCC had adopted rules in the mid 1960s that made it mandatory for cable systems to carry all locally viewed television stations. The agency's basis for enacting this regulation at that time was that in the absence of such a requirement, a cable operator might be tempted to injure a local station economically by refusing to deliver its signal to cable subscribers in its area of service.

The court did not declare the concept of "must carry" to be unconstitutional on its face, but simply held that the magnitude of this potential problem was not great enough to justify the degree of interference the rule imposed upon the free speech rights of the cable system to select the programming it would deliver to its subscribers. Initially, the FCC decided not to appeal this decision or attempt to re-draft the "must carry" rules in narrower terms that might satisfy the court, but under extreme pressure from the NAB and several members of Congress, the Commission was forced, within a few weeks, to reverse its position.[49]

[46] "Notice of Proposed Rulemaking in BC Docket 78–258, 82 FCC2d 47 (1980).

[47] See, for example, Malrite T.V. of New York v. FCC, 652 F.2d 1140 (2d Cir.1981) cert. denied 454 U.S. 1143, 102 S.Ct. 1002 (1982) opposing FCC recision of the cable distant signal and syndicated exclusivity rules.

[48] Quincy Cable TV, Inc. v. FCC, 768 F.2d 1434 (D.C.Cir.1985).

[49] Compare "FCC Decides Against Must–Carry Appeal," Broadcasting August 15, 1985, p. 28 with "Must Carry: Coming to a Boil at FCC," Broadcasting Sept. 23, 1985, p. 23.

In March 1986 the NAB was successful in wresting significant cable signal carriage concessions from the NCTA. By August of the same year, the FCC had adopted new "must carry" rules closely following the terms of this consensus agreement.[50] However, the court had not been a party to this carefully coordinated consensus, and in December 1987 it struck down this second effort to impose signal carriage requirements upon cable TV as still being unreasonably intrusive upon cable's First Amendment rights.[51]

Prevented by the court from regulating cable TV in this way, the FCC decided to pursue another tactic to limit cable TV's programming choices. When the Commission reopened its "must carry" proceedings in 1985, it indicated that if mandatory carriage should prove to be unenforceable, it might decide instead to reimpose its syndicated exclusivity rule upon cable systems. At the time, this was seen as nothing more than subtle pressure to encourage the cable industry to come to terms on a "must carry" consensus agreement.

When "must carry" requirements were overturned by the court, however, the FCC, at the urging of the broadcast industry, actually carried out its threat, proceeding not only to draft new syndicated exclusivity rules, but also to make a formal recommendation to Congress that cable TV's compulsory copyright license be revoked as well.[52] These new syndicated exclusivity rules, replacing the ones the FCC had repealed in 1980, required cable systems once again to delete from their channels any syndicated programs they imported from a distant stations if a local television station had been granted an exclusive right to broadcast these programs in the market served by the cable system.[53]

In 1980 the FCC had decided these rules that forced a cable system to "black out" various program channels on a regular basis imposed a costly administrative burden on the cable operator, frustrated and inconvenienced the system's viewers, and was no longer necessary to protect the economic interests of local stations.[54] Now, eight years later, the agency seemed convinced that these same rules were both reasonable and necessary.

[50] "Must Carry Rules", 61 RR2d 792 (1986).

[51] Century Communications Corp. v. FCC, 835 F.2d 292 (D.C.Cir.1987).

[52] Compulsory Copyright License for Cable Retransmission, 66 R.R. 2d 1259 (1988).

[53] "Syndicated" programs include any programming that is not currently being distributed by a major television network to its affiliated stations on a regular basis. This would include feature film packages, old network series programming (termed "off-network" syndication) non-network game and talk shows (termed "first-run" syndication) and non-network sporting events.

[54] "In the Matter of Community Antenna Television Syndicated Program Exclusivity Rules," 48 RR2d 171 (1980).

Lacking any logical explanation for this change in regulatory attitude, it can only be assumed that "syndicated exclusivity" illustrates how the FCC's "level playing field" principle can result in increasing the regulatory burdens of broadcast industry media competitors. When judicial recognition of cable TV's freedom of expression denied the Commission the authority needed to maintain the regulatory balance it sought between broadcast and cable program carriage rights, the agency simply imposed other signal carriage restraints upon cable to restore that balance.

Limiting Local Cable Control: The Cable Policy Act of 1984

Although the FCC had not been sympathetic to cable industry's pleas to permit local authorities to impose upon MMDS and SMARTV systems the same type of franchise obligations required of cable systems in order to equalize their regulatory burden, the Commission did attempt to equalize their local media regulatory requirements in another way. Rather than increasing the regulatory burden of these new media competitors, the agency worked instead to reduce the degree of authority local franchise regulators could exercise over cable TV.

To achieve this objective, the FCC began claiming exclusive federal control over a number of cable TV regulatory powers previously exercised by local cable franchising bodies. This tactic was designed to pressure the National League of Cities (NLC), the lobbying group for city governments, into reaching a consensus agreement with the NCTA on federal legislation to regulate cable before the Commission's preemptive actions diminished local cable TV authority to a point where NLC would have no bargaining power left in these negotiations.[55]

The *Cable Communications Policy Act of 1984* that resulted from these negotiations significantly reduced the regulatory authority of local governments.[56] Although the cable franchising process remained under the control of the local cable regulatory body, the powers these local bodies could exercise were significantly reduced by a broad range of new federal restrictions.

[55] During this era, the FCC denied municipalities the right to regulate the rates of any cable service other than the "basic," lowest-price tier of service in Community Cable TV, 54 RR2d 1351 (1983) and opened dockets to consider establishing stricter franchise fee limitations and access requirements. Pressure was increased still further by the Supreme Court decision in Capital Cities Cable, Inc. v. Crisp, 467 U.S. 691, 104 S.Ct. 2694 (1984) that held that states could impose no content restrictions on broadcast signals imported to local cable systems because the FCC had preempted this area of cable regulation.

[56] 47 U.S.C.A. §§ 521–559. The Act also amended the Communications Act of 1934 to grant the FCC *direct* regulatory authority over cable TV, rather than the derivative broadcast-related jurisdiction over cable TV the agency had been forced to depend on for more than a quarter of a century.

The Act denied local governments the right to specify particular programming or information services that applicants for a franchise would be required to provide, denied them the right to impose any content standards whatsoever on constitutionally protected cable programming, and did not allow them to prevent a cable operator from deleting any program service that the operator believed was "commercially impracticable" for the system to carry.[57]

Renewal of a cable franchise was virtually guaranteed, furnishing a cable operator the type of shelter from regulatory pressure any broadcaster would envy.[58] The Act also denied the franchising authority the right to regulate cable TV as a common carrier meaning, among other things, that a cable operator could legally refuse to provide any type of access to system channels other than that offered by its public, educational and government access channels.

Franchise fees were fixed at a maximum of five percent of system gross revenues, and local governments were no longer allowed to regulate the rates the cable system charged local subscribers.[59] Considering the fact that a city does grant a cable system a valuable and essential public property right of easement, and therefore has both the right and the obligation to obtain in return certain benefits for the use of this public property, the Cable Act appeared to extend federal preemptive power over local cable regulation about as far as federal law could logically reach.

Yet, this new recognition of cable TV's First Amendment rights carried with it certain risks many in the cable industry seemed unwilling to face.[60] For example, judicial recognition of cable's First Amendment right to be free of "must carry" requirements

[57] 47 U.S.C.A. §§ 544–545.

[58] A cable franchise can not be denied renewal unless the cable regulator can establish that the operator has substantially violated the terms of the existing franchise agreement, has provided unreasonably inadequate service, lacks the necessary financial, technical or legal ability to fulfill the promises made in the proposal or has filed a renewal proposal that does not adequately meet the future needs of the community. The decision to deny may be appealed, and in federal court, and the franchise authority has the burden of establishing the reasonableness of its action. 47 U.S.C.A. § 546.

[59] Maximum franchise fees are established by 47 U.S.C.A. § 542. Section 543 still allows regulation of basic rates, but only in localities unable to receive three television stations off air. The FCC was granted authority by Congress to determine when "effective TV service" was lacking so as to require continued rate regulation. This standard, challenged in American Civil Liberties Union v. FCC, 823 F.2d 1554 (D.C.Cir.1987) was sustained by the court. The FCC amended these rules to include more specific technical standards in 64 RR2d 1276 (1988).

[60] For a useful discussion of cable TV's First Amendment concerns, see "Cable's Catch–22: Whether to Be or Not to Be a Full First Amendment Player," Broadcasting, Dec. 21, 1987, p. 28.

was not something the NCTA had sought.[61]   The mandatory carriage rules had been challenged by one maverick cable operator, not the industry itself, because the NCTA understood this obligation to be only a small part of a larger reciprocal agreement in effect with the NAB, whereby cable would carry local television signals in return for the broadcast industry's continuing support for compulsory licensing and cable deregulation policies.[62]

Even more significantly, complete First Amendment recognition of cable TV's rights as a communications medium threatened the most precious right each system possessed, it's exclusive franchise agreement.   Unsuccessful cable franchise applicants in several cities attempted to force local regulatory bodies to allow them to build competing cable systems without a franchise in the local cable system's service area, arguing that preventing them from doing so unconstitutionally abridged their right to communicate with the public.[63]

Considering the competitive threat that such a First Amendment position posed for all major cable companies now operating under an exclusive franchise agreement, it is not surprising that the NCTA steadfastly opposed what the cable industry saw as being this "unrealistically absolutist" view of freedom of expression.[64] On the other hand, several cable TV operators safe from competitive challenge did vigorously assert their First Amendment status, not to protect their freedom of expression, but simply to avoid

[61] "FCC Must–Carry Rules Overturned by a Washington Appeals Court," *Variety* Dec. 16, 1987, p. 34.

[62] It's important to realize, when considering the close working relationship between the NAB and NCTA in many policy areas, that the two industries are not really that distinct, since over ⅓ of all cable systems are owned by broadcast interests.

[63] The most famous of these cases is City of Los Angeles v. Preferred Communications, Inc., 476 U.S. 488, 106 S.Ct. 2034 (1986).   The Supreme Court remanded this case to a California District Court for a determination of whether the exclusive cable TV franchise might be justified in this case because of other, more compelling societal needs the agreement served.   The trial court judge held that several of the city's major cable franchise requirements to be more restrictive than necessary to achieve the municipality's proper regulatory objective of providing for safe and efficient use of utility poles and conduits.   It upheld provisions favoring local franchise applicants, but struck down those limiting the length of the franchise agreement, requiring state-of-the-art equipment, and compelling the operator to provide six free public access and two leased channels, finding in each case that these constraints on the free speech rights of the cable applicant were greater than necessary to realize any valid public policy objective of the city.   Preferred Communications Inc. v. City of Los Angeles, 68 RR2d 121 (C.D.Cal.1990).   See also Century Federal, Inc. v. City of Palo Alto, Cal., 648 F.Supp. 1465 (N.D.Cal.1986) where a decision by several California cities to grant an exclusive cable franchise was declared by the court to be a clearly unconstitutional abridgment of free speech. The Cable Act of 1992 has made this issue moot, requiring municipalities to allow all parties who wish to provide the community with cable service to do so unless the local government can demonstrate some compelling reason for not doing so.

[64] Op. cit., footnote 61.

paying franchise fees they claimed imposed a discriminatory burden upon their activities as a communications medium.[65]

The Cable Act of 1992

Ironically, if the cable industry had not won such an over-whelming victory in maneuvering its own legislation through Congress in 1984, it seems highly unlikely that a powerful coalition of broadcasters and consumer activists would have been capable of uniting so successfully a few years later to deny cable the spoils of that victory. From 1986 onward, a cable industry now freed from virtually all regulatory controls began to increase cable subscriber rates each year, delete or shift local broadcasters to less attractive cable channels, deny media competitors access to its programming, and use its new prosperity to wrest from television networks various sports and special events programs that had previously been available to broadcast audiences.

As public opposition to cable TV mounted, this anti-cable coalition was eventually able to cobble together a package of legislative proposals designed to satisfy all special interests except those of the cable industry. The bill, euphemistically titled the *Cable Television Consumer Protection and Competition Act of 1992* became law on Oct. 5, 1992 when both Houses of Congress voted to override President Bush's veto of the bill.[66]

In addition to denying local governments the right to grant exclusive cable franchise awards, this legislation contained five major regulatory elements that the FCC was directed by Congress to implement by October 5, 1993.[67]

1. Retransmission Consent/Must Carry

The bill gave broadcasters the right to negotiate for cable TV payment for the carriage of their signals. At the end of every three year period a commercial TV station now has the option of deciding whether to seek a cash payments or other benefits from the local cable system for carriage of its signal or simply require that its signal be carried by the system.[68] Noncommercial stations receive automatic mandatory carriage rights and are not eligible for retransmission consent payment.

---

[65] Central Telecommunications, Inc. v. TCI Cablevision, Inc., 800 F.2d 711 (8th Cir.1986); Erie Telecommunications, Inc. v. City of Erie, 659 F.Supp. 580 (W.D.Pa. 1987).

[66] Pub. Law 102–385, 106 Stat. 1460.

[67] 47 U.S.C.A. § 541(a)(1) orders a local government not to "unreasonably refuse to award" a cable franchise to a potential competitor of any operator it authorizes to provide local cable TV service.

[68] 47 U.S.C.A. §§ 614, 615.

Cable systems with 12 channels or less must carry at least 3 local television signals, while systems with more than 12 channels must reserve up to one third of their channel capacity for broadcast station transmissions.

When the smoke of battle cleared and the October 1993 deadline for mandatory carriage agreements had arrived, virtually all television stations had agreed to carriage without any monetary compensation from their local cable systems. However, a significant number of stations were able to obtain other benefits in return for the right of signal carriage, including free station promotions, advertising insertions and/or the right to take over and program one of the cable system's channels.[69]

In addition, ABC, NBC, Fox and major group television owners Multimedia and Tribune were all able to use retransmission consent to obtain the channels from cable systems needed to launch their own new cable networks.[70]   Only CBS failed to take advantage of the new rules, holding out for a cash payment until the agreement deadline and then having no choice but to grant cable systems a one-year extension of their right to continue to carry the network's seven stations without charge.[71]

2. Indecency

The bill also authorized the FCC to adopt rules to regulate indecent cable TV program content.[72]   In February 1993 the Commission adopted a new set of regulations giving cable operators the right to restrict any indecent programming to one designated channel and to encode that channel so it would be available only to those subscribers who request it. [73]

In addition, the Commission prohibited obscene or indecent programs on cable public access, educational and government channels and authorized cable operators to require certification from its suppliers that programs provided for carriage were not indecent or obscene.

[69] Joe Flint, "Stations Stay for No Pay," Broadcasting Oct 11, 1993, p. 6.

[70] Steve McClellan, "Retrans Plans: Programming the New Channels," Broadcasting, Oct. 11, 1993, p. 16. ABC launched a second sports channel, ESPN2; NBC, a talk-oriented network, "America's Talking"; Fox, "FX," a general entertainment channel; Multimedia, "Talk Channel" and Tribune, the "Food Channel."   In addition, 22 local TV stations were successful in obtaining the right to program a local cable TV system channel. Sadly, the chief victim of this broadcaster success seems to have been the unique cable public service channel C–SPAN, that has already lost almost 3 million viewers because cable systems have been forced to make channel space available on their systems for the various new local television station and network program services they are now required by law to carry.

[71] Joe Flint, "CBS Blinks, Leaves Table Empty Handed," Broadcasting, Oct. 4, 1993, p. 6.

[72] 47 U.S.C.A. para. 532.

[73] Indecent Programming, 71 R.R. 2d 1177 (1993).

3. Subscriber Rate Regulation

The Commission was directed by the bill to determine which cable systems faced sufficient competition to be exempted from basic rate regulation. All other systems were made subject to local basic tier rate regulation.[74] The FCC also agreed to accept petitions to regulate other tiers of cable service where the rate charged by the cable system exceeded that amount deemed reasonable by the Commission.

In April 1993, the Commission issued its First Report and Order on cable rate regulation.[75] It decided that effective competition existed when a second cable system or other multi-channel video provider reached at least 50% of first system's service area households and served more than 15% of those households. The agency found that cable systems not facing effective competition charged rates on the average 10% higher than systems facing such competition. Based on this finding, the Commission immediately imposed a freeze on cable rate increases and in September 1993 ordered a roll-back on charges for a wide variety of subscriber service charges.

Then, in February 1994, the FCC ordered a further decrease in cable subscriber charges, claiming the overall effect of its decree would be to decrease monthly cable bills by an average of seven percent.[76]

4. Media Competitor Program Access

Reacting to a claim by DBS, MMDS and LPTV operators that major cable organizations were using their economic power to prevent cable program networks from selling their services to these rival distribution services, the FCC was directed to adopt rules to end such anti-competitive practices.

The FCC responded by imposing a 10 year ban on any cable TV system asserting an exclusive right to distribute the programming it purchased from its program suppliers, but at the same time the agency decided to allow any exclusive program contracts already in effect on June 1, 1990 to continue to be enforced.[77]

In 1994, the Commission enforced this program access requirement for the first time, compelling Time Warner to make *Court TV*, a cable network in which it has a major ownership interest,

---

[74] "Basic tier" requires the cable system to provide nothing more than local television broadcast signals and the community public access, educational, leased and governmental channels.

[75] Cable Rate Regulation, 72 R.R. 2d 216 (1993).

[76] Implementation of Cable Act of 1992; Rate Regulation 74 R.R. 2d 1077 (1994).

[77] 47 U.S.C.A. para. 628; 72 R.R. 2d 649 (1993).

available to all non-cable video delivery services.[78]   Time Warner
had refused to allow Liberty TV, a SMARTV operator competing
with Time Warner's New York cable system, to distribute Court TV
to its customers.   Because *Court TV* was not in operation before
the FCC's June 1, 1990 deadline, the Commission refused to permit
Warner to claim an exclusive program contract with this program
network.

5. Ownership Limitations

The Commission was directed by Congress to establish restrictions on the number of subscribers a single cable operator can serve
and on the amount of ownership interest a cable organization could
have in a cable program network or service.[79]   The FCC is considering regulations that would prevent any single cable organization
from serving more than 25% of the nation's cable households,
placing a 40% cap on the number of cable channels that carry
program services owned by the system and restricting cable system
ownership of its local MMDS or SMARTV competitors.

6. Other Directives

The law also required the FCC to conduct an investigation of
the trend of national, regional and local sports programming being
diverted from broadcast to cable, pay TV and PPV services; to
determine whether TV stations carrying 24–hour a day home
shopping programs should be eligible for must-carry; to establish
public interest requirements for DBS operators, including pricing
rules and minimum noncommercial and educational channel carriage; and to expand the cable TV job categories covered by cable
TV EEO rules from nine to 15, including such positions as general
manager and chief technician.

In response to these various directives a Commission study in
June 1993 found no evidence of any significant migration of sporting events from broadcasting to pay TV; found that home shopping
networks were eligible for must-carry protection; began proceedings to more clearly establish the public service obligations of DBS
operators and launched an inquiry to determine the level of EEO
compliance of the nation's cable systems.

Judicial Review of the 1992 Cable Act

Because of Congressional concern that the Act's must-carry
requirements might be overturned by a federal court as the FCC's
earlier must-carry regulations had been, this legislation created a
special review process just for this portion of the Act.   To deter-

[78] In the Matter of Time–Warner Cable 75 R.R.2d 350 (1994).
[79] 11. 47 U.S.C.A. para. 533 (f)(1).

mine the legality of must-carry as quickly as possible, Congress provided for a *direct* appeal to the Supreme Court as a matter of *right* from a decision of a special 3 judge D.C. District Court panel convened solely to review its must-carry provisions. [80]

Turner Broadcasting immediately sought an injunction to prevent the the Act from being enforced until its constitutionality had been determined, but this plea was rejected. [81]

Several cable organizations, including Time–Warner, the Discovery Channel, and Daniels Cablevision, then attempted to challenge the constitutionality of eleven separate provisions of the 1992 Act and two provisions of the Cable Act of 1984. In September 1993, U.S. District Judge Jackson rejected virtually all of the challenges, ruling that the key provisions of the 1992 Act; rate regulation, program access and retransmission consent were all valid exercises of federal regulatory power.[82] Jackson did find three provisions of the Act to be unconstitutional: the banning of unscrambled pay-TV previews of R-rated films; regulatory limitations on the maximum size of cable conglomerates; and educational and non-commercial program channels requirements imposed on DBS operators, but none of these findings gave the cable systems the relief they had sought.

Earlier, Judge Jackson had refused Time Warner's request to review the the constitutionality of the must carry provisions of the 1992 Act as part of this action, indicating that this crucial decision would be made by the 3 judge panel Congress had established for this purpose.[83]

In March 1993, the District Court panel voted 2–1 to uphold the constitutionality of the Act's must-carry provisions.[84] Writing for the majority, District Judge Jackson declared that although the Act's must-carry requirements did infringe to some extent on the first amendment rights of cable operators, the *O'Brien test* had been satisfied because must-carry did not impose a heavier burden on speech than necessary to protect a significant government interest, the preservation of broadcast service in the United

[80] Cable Act of 1992, Section 23, 47 U.S.C.A. § 555 (c) (1). Although the Act provided for this Supreme Court review as a matter of right *only* if one or more of its must-carry provisions was found by this Court to be *unconstitutional*, the Supreme Court accepted the direct appeal even though the lower court upheld the constitutionality of must-carry.

[81] Turner Broadcasting v. FCC, 810 F.Supp. 1308 (D.D.C.1992). On appeal, Chief Justice Rehnquist denied Turner's request for injunctive relief, 113 S.Ct. 1806 (1993).

[82] Time Warner Entertainment v. FCC; Discovery Communication v. United States, 835 F.Supp. 1 (D.D.C.1993).

[83] Time Warner v. FCC, 810 F.Supp. 1302 (D.D.C 1992).

[84] Turner Broadcasting System v. FCC, 819 F.Supp. 32 (D.D.C.1993).

States. [85]   District Judge Sporkin concurred in the result, but did not agree that these provisions of the Act imposed any significant burden on free speech rights of the cable operator.

Circuit Judge Williams dissented, contending that the must-carry requirements were in reality *content based* regulation of speech, requiring a much more compelling demonstration of government interest to justify their imposition than existed in this case.[86]

The Supreme Court promptly granted certiorari, but then found itself unable to come to any clear consensus regarding constitutional issues raised by the Act's must-carry requirements. Eventually, in a decision cluttered with five separate opinions, it voted 5–4 to send the case back to the District Court for further review.   Writing for the majority in *Turner Broadcasting v. United States,* Justice Kennedy declared although these provisions of the new cable act were "justified," the lower court had not adequately demonstrated that broadcasting was in genuine jeopardy and in need of the protections afforded by must-carry.[87]

Chief Justice Rehnquist, Justice Souter and Justice Blackmun joined in Kennedy's opinion.   Justice Stevens concurred in the result, but wrote a separate opinion asserting that he believed the provisions in question to be constitutional, agreeing to remand the case to the lower court for further review only to provide the fifth vote necessary to sustain these sections of the Act.

Justice O'Connor, joined by Justices Scalia, Thomas and Ginsburg, not only found the Act's must carry provisions to be *content based,* but also so broad in their scope as to be unconstitutional even with a content-neutral construction.   Her opinion categorized must-carry as being an impermissible restriction on a cable operator's editorial discretion as well as the cable programmer's freedom of expression, restricting their ability to provide the programming of their choice and forcing them to distribute programming they would prefer not to provide.

The decision was obviously less than a total victory for either side. Broadcasters appeared to have gained more in the short run, because the decision left the Act's must-carry rules in force during this period of judicial review.   Yet, the cable industry could find encouragement in the fact every Justice except Stevens concurred in the belief that cable should receive greater protection under the First Amendment than broadcasting, and perhaps even more en-

[85] 819 F.Supp. at 45–47. The "O'Brien test" cited by the opinion was developed in United States v. O'Brien, 391 U.S. 367, 88 S.Ct. 1673 (1968) and refined recently in Ward v. Rock Against Racism, 491 U.S. 781, 109 S.Ct. 2746 (1989).

[86] 819 F.Supp. pp. 61–62.

[87] Turner Broadcasting v. FCC, 114 S.Ct. 2445 (1994).

couragement from Justice Breyer, a purported deregulationist, replacing Justice Blackmun on the Court when the case was reconsidered.

Now that the Supreme Court has issued its crucial "must carry" decision, it could decide to review those other portions of the 1992 Act that Judge Jackson affirmed in his earlier *Times Warner* decision. That decision may now be appealed, but most experts believe that the First Amendment issues raised in the *Turner Broadcasting* case had offered the cable industry its best opportunity to undermine the Act.

Free Speech and Competition: Media Promise v. Performance

Nothing in this recent history of electronic media deregulation appears to reveal a strong commitment from any segment of the media industry for either a more competitive media marketplace or a broader recognition of electronic media free speech rights.[88]   In fact, *Broadcasting,* the "fifth estate's" own trade journal, began for the first time in the magazine's history to publish editorials critical of both broadcast and cable TV industry leaders for being so eager to trade away free speech rights merely to safeguard their short term economic interests.[89]   Responding to a strongly worded letter from a broadcast lobbying group pointing out that *Broadcasting* magazine had no right to speak for the industry, it commented editorially,

> ... "Committed to the First Amendment and the Fifth Estate" has been represented on this page for almost 57 years without facing challenge from a significant portion of the industry we cover ...   We have never said we were speaking for the industry; on the other hand, until these recent divisions, it appeared that the magazine and the industry leadership were in essential agreement.   Our policy hasn't change; one wonders what has.

* * *

[88] For example, the NAB recently commissioned and published a study *opposing* a "marketplace" approach to broadcast service in the United States.   Titled "Is More Necessarily Better?"   the report criticizes FCC efforts to license additional broadcast facilities that the agency's engineering bureau indicates can operate without creating interference for existing stations.   In this report, this marketplace concept is described as being both *ineffective* and *destructively competitive*.   "NAB Shies Away from Crowded Marketplace," Broadcasting, July 4, 1988, p. 47.

[89] See, for example, "On the Sidelines", Broadcasting, April 27, 1987, p. 122, criticizing the broadcast industry's willingness to deal away the "Fairness Doctrine" in return for comparative license renewal relief; "Cutting and Running", Broadcasting June 27, 1988, p. 90, opposing industry acceptance of permanent federal free speech restrictions to obtain guarantees of continued spectrum usage without charge, and "Fish or Fowl?"   Broadcasting, December 21, 1987, p. 112, urging the cable TV industry not to sell out its free speech rights simply to shield its franchises from competition.

If broadcasters are content to operate more as crown carriers than as First Amendment speakers, then little may be lost by submitting to the fairness doctrine as well. And if the theory is that broadcasters will enjoy more economic benefit from a public interest standard than they will pay to the government in tribute, then you pays your money and you takes your chance. Our own view is that broadcasters stand to lose their freedom and keep their insecurity—the worst of both worlds.[90]

Why should the broadcast industry, finally free of what industry leaders have always described as the "chilling" free speech effects of Fairness Doctrine, have been willing to negotiate with Congress for its return? Or, why should an industry so bitterly opposed to its second class status as a regulated medium accept continued government supervision of program content when the opportunity existed to escape these constraints upon broadcast free speech? The answer is simply that for the typical broadcaster, a guaranteed right of license renewal is far more precious than any abstract concern about freedom of expression. If the price for such renewal legislation is acceptance of the Fairness Doctrine, the industry has shown itself willing to pay it. By the same token, if total programming freedom would come only at the cost of a spectrum use fee or public auction of spectrum space, broadcast free speech does not appear at the moment to be worth that price.[91]

Similarly, while the cable TV industry seeks First Amendment recognition as a medium, it did not desire complete freedom of expression if the cost it paid for that right was the loss of its exclusive franchise privilege. Nor does the cable industry see anything contradictory in advocating a marketplace approach for establishing the price of its cable subscriber fees, and yet opposing such an approach for determining the price it must pay for cable programming. And by the same token, weren't broadcasters embarrassed about invoking the power of the federal government to extort payments from cable systems for their broadcast signals that they were unable to obtain through marketplace negotiations with these same systems?

[90] "Hanging in There for the First Amendment," Broadcasting July 25, 1988, p. 114.

[91] During the past decade, Congress has considered a number of bills that would have transformed broadcasting's "public interest" programming responsibilities into a simple financial obligation for use of a public resource. By paying the reasonable value for the license privilege, a broadcaster would thereby be freed of any responsibilities to the public in terms of program service. Because of this, all federal broadcast content regulation would end when this legislation took effect. The broadcast industry has not supported any of these "reasonable value" bills. One reason for the industry's lack of enthusiasm for this approach might be reflected in the fact that the value of one Chicago network television license was recently estimated to be in excess of $600 million.

In reality, of course, the media industries are no different from other political and economic groups in our society, in that they can distinguish between a general principle and its specific application in deciding when a theoretical commitment must be abandoned to achieve a particular goal.   Thus, to media leaders, "free speech," "deregulation" and "marketplace" are not sacred ends in themselves, but simply concepts invoked to realize certain industry objectives; and therefore useful only to the extent that they aid in attaining those objectives.

In that sense, then, while "freedom of expression" remains a noble aspiration for all electronic media, it is often the first casualty in policy skirmishes among media competitors.   Deregulation has not as yet resulted in freeing electronic media from government content control, in large part because winning such "free speech" rights has not been a primary policy objective of electronic media during this era.   Perhaps at some future date, when the competitive boundaries of each of these media empires have been more clearly established, that time will finally arrive.

Chapter 11

REGULATION OF ADVERTISING

SEC. 60. FROM *CAVEAT EMPTOR* TO CONSUMER PROTECTION

The history of advertising in the United States has seen a gradual change away from the motto of *caveat emptor* ("let the buyer beware").

It is hardly news that advertising is both a necessity and a nuisance in American society. It encourages and advances the nation's economy by providing information to the public about goods and services. Although its economic role in supporting the news media has been criticized, advertising has paid the bills for most of the news and vicarious entertainment which we receive. Historically, we owe advertising another debt. The rise of advertising in the 19th Century did much to free the press from excessive reliance on political parties or government printing contracts—which tended to color news columns with their bias.

Despite advertising's undeniably worthwhile contributions, this chapter unavoidably must emphasize the seamy side of American salesmanship. We will concentrate to a great extent upon issues raised by cheats and rascals. There can be little question that all too much advertising has been—and is—inexact, if not spurious and deceitful. Better units of the communications media now operate their advertising as a business with a definite obligation to the public. The realization evidently has dawned that unless advertising is both truthful and useful, the public may react unfavorably.

456

Advertising in the United States has a colorful if sometimes sordid past. From the first days of the nation throughout the Nineteenth Century, the philosophy motivating advertising was largely *laissez faire*. Too much advertising, in spirit if not to the letter, resembled this 1777 plug for "Dr. RYAN's *incomparable* WORM *destroying* SUGAR PLUMBS, *Necessary to be kept in all* FAMILIES:" [1]

> The plumb is a great diuretic, cleaning the veins of slime; it expels wind, and is a sovereign medicine in the cholic and griping of the guts. It allays and carries off vapours which occasion many disorders of the head. It opens all obstructions in the stomach, lungs, liver, veins, and bladder; causes a good appetite, and helps digestion.

Such exploitation of the *laissez faire* philosophy went unpunished for more than a century of this nation's existence. There was little or no regulation; what would be termed unreliable or even fraudulent advertising was published by some of the most respectable newspapers and periodicals. The general principle seemed to be that advertising columns were an open business forum with space for sale to all who applied.

Before 1900, advertising had little established ethical basis. The liar and the cheat capitalized on glorious claims for dishonest, shoddy merchandise. The faker lured the ill and suffering to build hopes on pills and tonics of questionable composition. Cures were promised by the bottle. Fortunes were painted for those who invested in mining companies of dubious reliability. Foods often were adulterated.

Exposés of frauds and fraud promoters who were using advertising to ensnare new prospects were important early in the Twentieth Century. Mark Sullivan exposed medical fakes and frauds in the *Ladies Home Journal* in 1904. Upton Sinclair's novel, *The Jungle,* revolted readers with its description of filthy conditions in meat-packing plants. Spurred by such exposés, Congress passed the Pure Food and Drug Act in 1906. Despite being a truth-in-labeling measure the 1906 statute did nothing to insure truth in advertising.[2]

Campaigning against advertising chicanery, many magazines and newspapers exposed fraudulent practices.[3] Some newspapers of this period, including the Cleveland Press and other Scripps–McRae League papers, monitored advertisements, refusing those which appeared to be fraudulent or misleading. A Scripps–McRae

[1] Pennsylvania Gazette, March 12, 1777.

[2] Ibid.

[3] H.J. Kenner, The Fight for Truth in Advertising (1936) pp. 13–14; Alfred McClung Lee, The Daily Newspaper in America (1937), p. 328.

official asserted that the newspaper group turned away approximately $500,000 in advertising revenue in one year by rejecting advertisements.

Such self-regulation has grown considerably over the years, and legal restraints have grown, too. People working in advertising come under all the laws which affect other branches of mass communications, including libel, invasion of privacy, copyright infringement, and obscenity. In addition, there are batteries of statutes and regulatory powers aimed at advertising *in addition to* the laws which affect, for example, the editorial side of a newspaper. There's the Food and Drug Administration (FDA), the Securities Exchange Commission (SEC), the Federal Communications Commission (FCC), and quite an alphabet soup of other federal agencies which gets into the advertising regulation act. Beyond that, there is increasing activity at the state level to attempt to control false or deceptive advertising. This chapter, then, can be only a sparse survey of advertising regulatory structures.

SEC. 61. FEDERAL ADMINISTRATIVE CONTROLS: THE FEDERAL TRADE COMMISSION

The most important federal government controls over advertising have been exercised by the Federal Trade Commission, which has experienced considerable controversy in recent years.

The Federal Trade Commission

During the 20th Century, the Federal Trade Commission became more important than other official controls over advertising. The FTC Act was passed in 1914 to supplement sanctions against unfair competition which had been provided by the Sherman Anti-Trust Act of 1890 and by the Clayton Act of 1914.[4] Gradually, the FTC grew in power and assumed an increasingly important place in regulating advertising.

The Federal Trade Commission is an example of administrative rule and law-making authority delegated by Congress. Five Federal Trade Commissioners are appointed by the President and confirmed by the Senate for five-year terms. No more than three of the five commissioners may be from the same political party. The strength of the FTC as a regulatory agency has varied greatly over the years, changing with the level of Congressional support and with the variable political attitudes toward the effectiveness of government efforts to control unfair competition.

---

[4] Sherman Act, 26 Stat. 209 (1890), 15 U.S.C.A. § 1; Clayton Act, 38 Stat. 730 (1914), 15 U.S.C.A. § 12.

The FTC machinery—which is described later at some length—
is set up to enforce Section 5 of the Federal Trade Commission Act,
which says: "Unfair methods of competition in commerce, and
unfair or deceptive practices in commerce, are declared unlawful." [5]

Early FTC cases which came before the courts cast doubt on
the Commission's powers over advertising.[6] However, in 1921,
something as mundane as partly wool underwear masquerading as
real woollies gave the FTC the case it needed to try to establish its
authority. For many years the Winsted Hosiery Company had
been selling its underwear in cartons branded with labels such as
"Natural Merino," "Natural Wool," or "Australian Wool." In fact,
none of this company's underwear was all wool, and, some of its
products had as little as 10 per cent wool.

The FTC complaint against Winsted Hosiery asked the company to show cause why the use of its brands and labels which seemed
deceptive should not be discontinued. After hearings, the FTC
issued a cease and desist order against the company. On appeal,
the FTC lost, with a United States Circuit Court saying: the
agency was powerless to prevent use of misleading labels.[7]

In 1922, however, the Supreme Court of the United States
upheld the FTC in language broad enough to support the Commission's power to control false labeling and advertising as unfair
methods of competition. Speaking for the Court, Justice Brandeis
declared that the Commission was justified in its conclusions that
the hosiery company's practices were unfair methods of competition. He authorized the Commission to halt such practices. Brandeis said, "when misbranded goods attract customers by means of
the fraud which they perpetrate, trade is diverted from the producer of truthfully marked goods." [8]

Despite the efforts of the Federal Trade Commission, the idea
of consumer protection had little support from the Courts during
the early 1930s. In 1931, the *Raladam* case, for example, cut
sharply into the FTC's attempts to defeat the ancient, amoral
doctrine of caveat emptor, "let the buyer beware." The Raladam
Company manufactured an "obesity cure" containing "desiccated
thyroid." This preparation, sold under the name of "Marmola,"
was advertised in newspapers and on printed labels as being the
result of scientific research. It was claimed that "Marmola" was

[5] 15 U.S.C.A. § 45(a)(1).

[6] Federal Trade Commission v. Gratz, 253 U.S. 421, 40 S.Ct. 572 (1920); L.B.
Silver Co. v. Federal Trade Commission of America, 289 Fed. 985 (6th Cir.1923).

[7] Winsted Hosiery Co. v. Federal Trade Commission, 272 Fed. 957, 961 (2d
Cir.1921).

[8] Federal Trade Commission v. Winsted Hosiery Co., 258 U.S. 483, 493–494, 42
S.Ct. 384, 385–386 (1922).

"safe and effective and may be used without discomfort, inconvenience, or danger of harmful results to health."

The FTC complaint focused upon the likelihood of actual physical harm to consumers who used Marmola believing it safe as claimed. The Supreme Court, however, disallowed the FTC's order that the Raladam Corporation cease such advertising. Speaking for the Court, Justice George Sutherland ruled that Section 5 of the FTC Act did not forbid the deception of consumers unless the advertising injured competing business in some way. Accordingly, the FTC was not allowed to work directly for consumer protection.[9]

The FTC's authority over advertising grew slowly. As late as 1936—when the FTC had been in operation for some 22 years—the famed Judge Learned Hand of a U.S. Circuit Court decided a case against the FTC and in favor of an advertising scheme for encyclopedias which involved false representation. The publisher of the encyclopedias tried to lure customers into believing that the company gave them a set of encyclopedias "free," and that the customer's payment of $69.50 was only for a loose leaf supplement to the encyclopedia. The $69.50 was actually the combined regular price for both books and supplements. Despite this, Judge Hand could declare:[10] "Such trivial niceties are too impalpable for practical affairs, they are will-o'-the-wisps, which divert attention from substantial evils."

When this case reached the Supreme Court, Justice Hugo L. Black reacted indignantly, saying the sales method used to peddle the encyclopedia "successfully deceived and deluded its victims."[11] In overturning Judge Hand's "let the buyer beware" ruling in the lower court, Justice Black added:[12]

> The fact that a false statement may be obviously false to those who are trained and experienced does not change its character, nor take away its power to deceive others less experienced. There is no duty resting upon a citizen to suspect the honesty of those with whom he transacts business. Laws are made to protect the trusting as well as the suspicious.

In 1938, the year after the Supreme Court endorsed the concept of consumer protection from advertising excesses, Congress acted to give the FTC greater authority over deceptive advertising.

[9] Federal Trade Commission v. Raladam Co., 283 U.S. 643, 644, 51 S.Ct. 587, 589 (1931).

[10] Federal Trade Commission v. Standard Educ. Society, 302 U.S. 112, 116, 58 S.Ct. 113, 115 (1937), quoting Judge Hand's opinion in the same case in the Circuit Court, 86 F.2d 692, 695 (2d Cir.1936).

[11] 302 U.S. 112, 117, 58 S.Ct. 113, 115 (1937).

[12] 302 U.S. 112, 116, 58 S.Ct. 113, 115 (1937).

The 1938 Wheeler–Lea Amendment changed Section 5 of the Federal Trade Commission Act to read: "Unfair methods of competition *in commerce,* and unfair or deceptive acts or practices in commerce, are hereby declared unlawful."[13]   Note the italicized phrase. These words were added by the Wheeler–Lea Amendment, and this seemingly minor change in phrasing proved to be of great importance.   The italicized words removed the limits on FTC authority imposed by the *Raladam* decision.   No longer would the FTC have to prove that a misleading advertisement harmed a competing business.   Now, if an advertisement deceived consumers, the FTC's enforcement powers could be put into effect.[14]

Aiming at false advertising, the Wheeler–Lea Amendment also inserted Sections 12 and 15(a) into the Federal Trade Commission Act.   Section 12 provides: [15]

It shall be unlawful for any person, partnership, or corporation to disseminate, or cause to be disseminated, any false advertisement—(1) by United States mails, or in [interstate] commerce by any means, for the purpose of inducing, or which is likely to induce, directly or indirectly, the purchase in commerce of food, drugs, devices or cosmetics.

Section 15(a) of the FTC Act says:

The term "false advertising" means an advertisement, other than labeling, which is misleading in a material respect; and in determining whether any advertisement is misleading, there shall be taken into account (among other things) not only representations made or suggested by statement, word, design, device, sound, or any combination thereof, but also the extent to which the advertisement fails to reveal facts material in the light of such representations or material with respect to consequences which may result from the use of the commodity * * *.

Such statutory changes gave the FTC some of the power it sought to protect consumers.   As FTC Commissioners Everette MacIntyre and Paul Rand Dixon wrote in the 1960s, the Wheeler–Lea "amendment put the consumer on a par with the businessman from the standpoint of deceptive practices." [16]

[13] 52 Stat. 111 (1938);   15 U.S.C.A. § 45.   Italics added.

[14] Ibid.;   Earl W. Kintner, "Federal Trade Commission Regulation of Advertising," Michigan Law Review Vol. 64:7 (May, 1966) pp. 1269–1284, at pp. 1275–1276, 1276n.

[15] Section 12, 52 Stat. 114 (1938), 15 U.S.C.A. § 52;   Section 15(a), 52 Stat. 114 (1938), 15 U.S.C.A. § 55(a).

[16] Everette MacIntyre and Paul Rand Dixon, "The Federal Trade Commission After 50 Years," Federal Bar Journal Vol.24:4 (Fall,1964) pp. 377–424, at p. 416.

Even so, this commission was often called "toothless" and other less flattering things. The delays which have attended FTC enforcement procedures—especially those involved in lengthy court battles—became legendary. An often cited example was the famed "Carter's Little Liver Pills" case. In 1943, the FTC decided that the word "liver" was misleading, and a classic and lengthy battle was on. Carter's Little Liver Pills had been a well known laxative product for 75 years. It took the FTC a total of 16 years—from 1943 to 1959—to win its point before the courts and get "liver" deleted.[17]

In addition, the FTC could not hope to regulate all advertising in (or affecting) interstate commerce—it could merely regulate by example, by pursuing a relatively small number of advertisers who appeared to operate in a deceptive fashion, in hopes that this would encourage others to tone down their advertising claims. It has been objected that during most of the FTC's history, it had tended to go after "little guys" or unimportant issues, too often ignoring misdeeds by big and powerful corporations which tied into important issues.

Beyond that, the FTC's enforcement machinery, for the most part, was creaky and slow. If an advertising campaign on television is deemed "deceptive" or "false and misleading" by the FTC, the ad campaign might have run its course (generally several months) before the FTC could have any impact. In lawyer's jargon, such cases had become moot, or meaningless by the time they were finally resolved.

The FTC has several weapons to use against misleading advertising; "getting the FTC's attention" is accomplished in a variety of ways. Letters from consumers or businesses, inquiries from Congress, or articles on consumer issues all may trigger FTC actions: [18]

(1) **"Voluntary Compliance" (Consent Orders):** When the FTC suspects that a violation of law occurred, it will begin an investigation. Typically, such investigations are non-public, the FTC says, "in order to protect both the investigation and the company" being investigated. One mechanism available to the Commission is to try to get what is termed "voluntary compliance" by negotiating a "consent order" with the company. "A company that signs a consent order need not admit that it violated the law, but must

[17] Carter Products, Inc. v. Federal Trade Commission, 268 F.2d 461 (9th Cir. 1959), certiorari denied 361 U.S. 884, 80 S.Ct. 155 (1959).

[18] Federal Trade Commission, "A Guide to the Federal Trade Commission," 1992 pamphlet, p. 19.

agree to stop the disputed practices . . ." as outlined by the FTC in a complaint.

(2) **Administrative Complaints:** If a consent agreement is not reached, the FTC may issue an administrative complaint. As the 1992 "Guide to the Federal Trade Commission" says, "If an administrative complaint is issued, a formal proceeding before an administrative law judge begins that is much like a court trial: evidence is submitted; testimony is heard; and witnesses are examined and cross-examined. If a law violation is found, a cease and desist order . . . may be issued. Initial decisions by administrative law judges [Civil Service employees independent of the FTC] may be appealed to the full Commission." If the finding of a law violation is the FTC may issue a **cease and desist order**. Appeals from a final FTC decision may be made to a U.S. Court of of appeals and, ultimately, to the U.S. Supreme Court. Violation of such an order is punishable by a civil penalty of $10,000 a day for each offense.[19]

(3) **Other FTC Sanctions:** In situations where substantial harm to consumers, as in cases of suspected fraud, "the FTC can go directly to court to obtain an injunction, civil penalties, or consumer redress. . . . By going directly to court, the FTC can stop the fraud" . . . to try to minimize the number of consumers injured.

(4) **Publicity:** The FTC publicizes complaints and cease and desist orders which it promulgates. News releases on such subjects are issued regularly to the media, and publicity has proven to be one of the strongest weapons at the FTC's disposal.[20]

It can be seen from the foregoing list of FTC activities that the Commission is not dependent solely on harsh actions such as cease-and-desist orders or court procedures. The Commission also takes positive steps to attempt to clarify its view of fair advertising practices. The Commission has three major programs which provide guidance to competitors and consumers. These are:

1. INDUSTRY GUIDES. This program involved issuing interpretations of the rules of the Commission to its staff. These guides are made available to the public, and are aimed at certain significant practices of a particular industry, especially those involved in advertising and labeling. The guides can be issued by the Commission as its inter-

---

[19] Ibid.; Rosden & Rosden, op. cit., Vol. II, § 25.06.

[20] Federal Trade Commission, Your FTC: What It Is and What It Does, p. 19.

pretation of the law without a conference or hearings, and, therefore, in a minimum of time.

2. ADVISORY OPINIONS. In 1962, the FTC began giving advisory opinions in response to industry questions about the legality of a proposed industry action. Advisory opinions generally predict the FTC's response, although the Commission reserves the right to reconsider its advice if the public interest so requires.[21]

3. TRADE REGULATION RULES. The FTC publishes a notice before issuing a Trade Regulation Rule on a specific practice. Industry representatives may then comment on the proposed Trade Regulation before the rule is adopted and put into effect.[22]

Voluntary compliance with laws and FTC rules is not always forthcoming. The FTC sometimes is compelled to begin a case against an advertiser. Cases sometimes open after a complaint from an aggrieved citizens or competitors who have suffered losses because of what they believe to be illegal activity. The FTC also screens advertisements, looking for false or misleading statements. When a suspicious advertisement is found, a questionnaire is sent to the advertiser. The FTC may also request samples of the product advertised, if practicable. If the product is a compound, its formula may be requested. Copies of all advertisements published or broadcast during a specified period are requested, together with copies of supplementary information such as booklets, folders, or form letters.

Product samples may be inspected by the FTC or referred to another appropriate government agency for scientific analysis. If false or misleading advertising claims are indicated by such an examination, the advertiser is advised of the scientific opinions of the Commission's experts. Advertisers are allowed to submit evidence in support of their advertisements.

In recent years, the FTC has become much more active in challenging nutritional claims made for various food products in our health-obsessed society. The Commission has developed standards to be used to determine when a processed food can be called "lite" or "light", and is challenging the right of those marketing products with a substantial amount of saturated fat from claiming they are "cholesterol free."

The Federal Trade Commission established guidelines in 1992 requiring documentation of advertising claims that use of a particular product benefits the environment. The FTC standards allow an

---

[21] Rosden and Rosden, Law of Advertising, III, § 32.04.

[22] Ibid., § 32.05.

advertiser to claim that a product is "ozone safe," "biodegradable" or "compostable" only if the manufacturer can produce evidence that the ecological benefits of the product are substantial.

In explaining its guidelines the FTC declared that the term "ozone safe" or "ozone friendly" should not be used unless the product contains no chlorofluorocarbons or other ozone depleting chemicals. By the same token, the use of the word "biodegradable" should be limited to products that break down into elements found in nature within a reasonable period of time.

Strengthening the FTC—The 1970s

Strengthening of the FTC's regulatory powers came in 1973 in a stealthy fashion. While an energy crisis absorbed attention of Congress and of the public in 1973, a rider to the Trans–Alaska Pipeline Authorization Act gave the FTC powers which it had sought for years.[23] Thanks to that rider, the FTC was given the power to go to a federal court and ask for an injunction against an advertisement which is—in the eyes of the Commission—clearly in violation of federal law prohibiting false or misleading advertising. This injunctive sanction is not likely to be much used because it is so drastic. However, an injunction could—in critical instances— put a stop to ads which might otherwise continue to run through their campaign cycle, be it three months or six months or nine months, before the FTC could act.

More help was on the way for the FTC. In January, 1975, the "Consumer Product Warranties and Federal Trade Commission Improvements Act"—hereafter referred to as the Moss–Magnuson Act—was signed into law by President Gerald R. Ford.[24] One part of this measure was designed to provide minimum disclosure standards for written consumer product warranties.

Before the Moss–Magnuson Act, jurisdiction of the FTC was limited to advertising *in* interstate commerce. In 1941, the Supreme Court held that an Illinois company which limited its sales to wholesalers located only in Illinois was not "in [interstate] commerce," [25] and was thus beyond the reach of FTC control. Now, under the Moss–Magnuson statute, the FTC can regulate advertising *affecting* commerce. A small change, on the surface, but not in actuality. This wording change gave the FTC the power, in effect,

[23] 15 U.S.C.A. § 53. See Note, " 'Corrective Advertising' Orders of the Federal Trade Commission," 85 Harvard Law Review (Dec.1971), pp. 485–486. The FTC already has injunctive powers to deal with advertising for products which could pose an immediate health threat to consumers: medical devices, foods, drugs, and cosmetics.

[24] Pub. L. 93–637, 88 Stat. 2183 (1975).

[25] Federal Trade Commission v. Bunte Bros., 312 U.S. 349, 61 S.Ct. 580 (1941).

to say that *all* commerce affects interstate commerce, and therefore is under FTC jurisdiction.[26]

Also, the Moss–Magnuson Act gave the power to the Commission to get beyond "regulation by example"—that is, to do more than let a shave cream manufacturer know with a cease-and-desist order that an advertising campaign was considered misleading by the FTC. The FTC was enabled to issue Trade Regulation Rules which can apply to an entire product type or industry. Trade Regulation Rules—when formally issued by the FTC—have the force of law. Fines for violation of a Trade Regulation Rule through misleading advertising can draw fines of up to $10,000 a day, so the FTC was given the clout to get advertisers to pay attention.[27]

Weakening the FTC—The 1980s

Although the Magnuson–Moss Act strengthened FTC powers, the activist stance of the FTC during the late 1970s brought a counter-attack from the business community plus 1980 legislation to weaken the FTC. Although the Great Sugar Imbroglio—an abortive FTC rulemaking to regulate sugar in cereals heavily advertised to children—was by no means the only source of the FTC's troubles, it may be used as an example of Commission behavior that horrified business and industry. In 1977 and 1978,[28]

> [t]he FTC staff proposed rules that would have resulted in a ban of most children's television advertising. The FTC primarily premised its far-reaching rulemaking proceeding on "unfairness," a standard with few legal precedents, rather than on "deception," a well-established standard with more confining limits.

Issues involved in the regulation of children's advertising—including FTC hearing on whether some sugary foods should be banned—provided a sticky situation for the commission. In 1977 and 1978, FTC Chairman Michael Pertschuk made a variety of statements critical of techniques used in children's advertising.

The FTC soon began a major trade regulation rulemaking procedure on "Children's Advertising," under Section 18 of the Magnuson–Moss Act.[29] The Association of National Advertisers and the Kellogg Company, after asking without success that Pertschuk disqualify himself from hearings on the subject, then went to court for an order to restrain Pertschuk from further involvement. It was contended that the chairman had prejudged fact issues and would not be able to participate fairly in the rulemaking proce-

[26] Moss–Magnuson Act, Pub.L. 93–637, 88 Stat. 2183 (1975).

[27] Ibid.

[28] Foote and Mnookin, op. cit., p. 90.

[29] 15 U.S.C.A. § 57a.

dure.[30]   Pertschuk, in fact, had said: " 'Advertisers seize on the child's trust and exploit it as a weakness for their gain.* * * ' " and " 'Cumulatively, commercials directed at children tend to distort the role of food.* * *   Rarely is their emphasis on good nutrition.' " [31]

A U.S. district court disqualified Pertschuk from the proceeding, saying that administrative hearings must both be fair and look fair, and that Pertschuk did not meet those criteria.   Late in 1979, however, the U.S. Court of Appeals, District of Columbia Circuit, ruled that Pertschuk's dual role of advocate and administrator was permissible; the Association of National Advertisers had not shown that the Chairman's mind was unalterably closed concerning the proceeding on children's advertising.[32]

The FTC Improvements Act of 1980

Although that Court of Appeals supported the FTC's activism, Congress in 1980 passed the whimsically named Federal Trade Commission Improvements Act of 1980.[33]   This legislation removed "unfairness" [34] as a basis for regulation of commercial advertising. Instead of being able to forbid "unfair" ads the FTC had to show out-and-out *deception,* which is harder to prove.   Also, the 1980 act removed FTC powers to make rules on children's advertising and the funeral industry.   In addition, the FTC was given the additional problem of having Congress breathing down its neck.   Under the 1980 "Improvements Act," a 90–day review period was established for any proposed FTC Trade Regulation Rules.   If both Houses of Congress pass a resolution objecting to the rule, the rule is overturned.   This procedure has been called the "two-House legislative veto." [35]

FTC Organization and Advertising Regulation

The Federal Trade Commission looks formidable on a table of organization, until one realizes that its entire budget—to handle

[30] Association of National Advertisers v. FTC, 4 Med.L.Rptr. 1716, 1718 (D.C.D.C. 1978).

[31] The News Media & The Law, Vol. 3: No. 2 (May/June 1979), p. 18.

[32] Association of National Advertisers v. FTC, 627 F.2d 1151 (D.C.Cir.1979), 5 Med.L.Rptr. 2233, 2236, 2245–2247.   Despite this ruling, Pertschuk withdrew from the administrative rulemaking procedure.

[33] Pub.L.No. 96–252, 94 Stat. 374 (1980).

[34] Foote and Mnookin, op. cit., pp. 90–91; see also discussion in text in preceding footnote number 36.

[35] Pub.L.No. 96–252, 94 Stat. 374 (1980), § 21, discussed in Earl W. Kintner, Christopher Smith, and David B. Goldston, "The Effect of the Federal Trade Commission Improvements Act of 1980 on the FTC's Rulemaking and Enforcement Authority," 58 Washington University Law Quarterly No. 4 (Winter, 1980) pp. 847–859, at 853.   This legislative veto provision stays in effect until September 30, 1982, and contains a provision for expedited judicial review should this provision's constitutionality be attacked through a lawsuit.

antitrust matters and to protect consumers, including regulation of advertising—was roughly $80 million in 1994. Even if $40 million of that were used to regulate advertising, keep in mind that the FTC's advertising regulation resources are dwarfed by the enormous size of the U.S. advertising industry: $130 billion or more per annum. The FTC has three bureaus: [36]

- The Bureau of Competition, the FTC's antitrust arm
- The Bureau of Economics, which aids the FTC in predicting the economic consequences of its actions
- The Bureau of Consumer Protection, which has a broad mandate to protect consumers against unfair, fraudulent, or deceptive practices.

The **Bureau of Consumer Protection** has five divisions all having some relationship to advertising regulation. These divisions are: [37]

1) **The Division of Advertising Practices.** This unit will be discussed at some length, below.

2) **The Division of Credit Practices,** which enforces many consumer credit statutes, including the Equal Credit Opportunity Act, the Fair Credit Reporting Act, and the Truth in Lending Act.

3) **The Division of Marketing Practices**, which concentrates its enforcement activities on matters including fraudulent telemarketing schemes, "900" number telephone programs, consumer problems with warranty or contract obligations, and health or safety problems in major consumer products.

4) **The Division of Service Industry Practices**, which includes enforcement activities related to consumer fraud in sale of investment goods and services, art, precious metals, gems, and rare coins. Also within this division's concerns are fraud or deception in advertising and sale of health care services, plus claims relating to cures and remedies and deceptive marketing of health care programs.

5) **The Division of Enforcement** checks on compliance with cease and desist orders issued by the Commission and enforces a number of laws and trade regulation rules, including requirements that companies ship purchases made by mail when promised. This division also enforces The Unordered Merchandise Statute, which allows consumers to keep, as gifts, unordered merchandise delivered to them through the U.S. Mail. Other rules enforced here involve disclosure of energy costs of home appliances, octane ratings of gas, and efficiency ratings of home insulation. Also within

[36] A Guide to the Federal Trade Commission, 1992 ed., pp. 6–18.
[37] Ibid., pp. 6–11.

this division is enforcement of rules requiring proper labeling of wool, furs, and textiles.

The Division of Advertising Practices

FTC literature summarizes the scope of the Division of Advertising Practices' law enforcement activities in this fashion: [38]

- Tobacco and alcohol advertising, including monitoring for unfair practices or deceptive claims, and reporting to Congress on cigarette and smokeless tobacco labeling, advertising, and promotion.

- Advertising claims for food and over-the-counter drugs, particularly those relating to nutritional or health benefits of foods and safety and effectiveness of drugs or medical devices.

- Performance and energy-savings claims made for energy-related household and automotive products.

- Environmental performance claims made for consumer products, including claims that products are environmentally save, ozone-friendly, or biodegradable.

- Infomercials, long-form (30–minute) advertising, to ensure that both the format and content of programs are non-deceptive.

- General advertising at the national and regional level, particularly advertising making objective claims that are difficult for consumers to evaluate.

SEC. 62.   DECEPTIVENESS: THE FTC'S DEFINITION

Even literally true statements may cause an advertiser difficulty if those statements are part of a deceptive advertisement.

Since the mid–1980s, the Federal Trade Commission has defined deceptive advertising as **"a material representation, omission, or practice that is likely to mislead a consumer acting reasonably under the circumstances."** Taking this definition apart, "material representation" may be taken to mean an important or decision-influencing statement in an advertisement. Also, the consumer who is to be protected is not naive or foolish, but a reasonable person who is acting sensibly. This is some distance from the old, avaricious slogan of caveat emptor ("let the buyer beware"), but it will not protect persons who do not protect themselves by "acting reasonably under the circumstances." [39]

---

[38] A Guide to the Federal Trade Commission, 1992 ed., pp. 6–7.

[39] AMREP Corporation v. FTC, 768 F.2d 1171, 1177 (10th Cir.1985).

Note that the definition does not refer to "false advertising." As noted advertising law scholar Ivan L. Preston has noted, many people will say regulators regulate "false advertising." He cautions: [40]

> That's fine for ordinary usage, but technically it's better to use the term **deceptive advertising**. By strict definition, **false** means only claims that are explicitly, literally false. However, ads also make claims [often by omission of key facts] that are explicitly true but produce false meanings.

Consider a photo album sales scheme. Door-to-door salesmen told customers that for $39.95, they could receive a "free" album by purchasing 10 photographic portraits at the "regular price" of the photographs alone. In one sense, that was true, but not to the Federal Trade Commission.

The FTC ordered the company selling the photo albums to stop suggesting that its albums were given away free, when in fact the albums were part of a $39.95 package deal. The company was also ordered to stop claiming that it sold only to "selected persons" and that a special price was involved. The photo album company retorted that its sales pitch was the literal truth, and that the FTC's cease-and-desist order should, therefore, be set aside by the courts.[41] The company argued that its customers actually were "selected;" that the word "few" is a relative term which is very elastic, and that the $39.95 price was in fact "promotional" because it tended to support the sale of the albums.

A U.S. Court of Appeals upheld the FTC's cease-and-desist order. The court announced that there should be a presumption of validity when courts reviewed FTC orders involving advertising. Tendencies of advertisements to mislead or deceive were held to be factual questions which would be determined by the FTC. Finally, the Circuit Court vigorously upheld the idea that even literal truthfulness of statement cannot protect an advertisement if it is misleading. Even though separate words and claims may be truthful by themselves, they may be regulated if used in a combination which adds up to deceptiveness.[42]

Deception by Omission

In some advertisements, what is **not** said may be more important—and deceptive—than what is said. Omitted material, in other words, may make an implied claim which is misleading. The

---

[40] Ivan L. Preston, The Tangled Web They Weave: Truth, Falsity and Advertisers (Madison: University of Wisconsin Press, 1994), p.9.

[41] Kalwajtys v. Federal Trade Commission, 237 F.2d 654, 655–656 (7th Cir.1956).

[42] 237 F.2d 654, 656 (7th Cir.1956).

case of Bristol–Myers v. FTC (1984) involved various Young & Rubicam advertising campaigns for Bufferin, the well known pain reliever. For a time, Bufferin ads claimed that "doctors recommended Bufferin more than any other 'leading brand' of OTC [over-the-counter] internal analgesic." The FTC found it was true that from 1967 through 1971, Bufferin was recommended by doctors more often than Bayer, Excedrin, and Anacin—all, like Bufferin, aspirin-based pain relievers. Upholding an FTC finding of deceptiveness against Bristol–Myers, the Second Circuit stated: [43]

> However the Commission found that the ads conveyed the message that physicians recommend Bufferin more than any other OTC internal analgesic, and not just the three other leading brands of aspirin-based products. Since in fact doctors recommend Tylenol, Ascriptin and generic aspirin more often than Bufferin, the FTC found the message conveyed by the ads false and misleading.

Similarly, an over-reaching claim in an advertisement can cause difficulties for the advertiser. In the 1973 case of Firestone Tire & Rubber Co. v. FTC, the Commission took exception to ads with the slogan, " 'When you buy a Firestone tire—no matter how much or how little you pay—you get a safe tire.' " Note that the advertisement made no overt claim that all Firestone tires are safe, but the FTC ruled that the ad's language contained an implied message that all Firestone tires are absolutely safe. A U.S. Court of Appeals upheld the FTC's cease-and-desist order against Firestone.[44]

Television Ad Mock–Ups

To what extent can "reality" be suspended during the filming of a television commercial without producing an ad that improperly misleads the public? Products such as butter and ice cream that would melt under the hot studio lights of yesteryear had to be adulterated in some fashion in order to be filmed. New cars are parked under powerful floodlights to accentuate the sheen of their finishes, and the complexions of many of those breathtakingly beautiful models shown in cosmetic ads have been artfully retouched in the photo lab. Do such common practices actually deceive consumers and cause them to buy goods they would otherwise refuse to purchase?

The FTC attempted to establish a standard of non-deception in this field of television advertising during the early 1960s that is not likely to be recorded in the annals of history as one of bureaucra-

[43] Bristol–Myers Company v. FTC, 738 F.2d 554, 563 (2d Cir.1984).

[44] Firestone Tire & Rubber Co. v. FTC, 481 F.2d 246, 249 (6th Cir.1973), cert. den. 414 U.S. 1112, 94 S.Ct. 841 (1973).

cy's finest hours. The FTC's great "sandpaper caper" dragged on for five years at substantial expense to the American taxpayer and only minimal benefit to the American consumer.[45]

An aerosol shaving cream client, Rapid Shave, had commissioned the Ted Bates advertising agency to produce a series of television commercials dramatizing the superior qualities of that product. Realizing that all shaving creams were pretty much alike, some creative genius at the agency came up with the idea of demonstrating on camera that Rapid Shave could not only soften tough beards but even soften the roughest type of sandpaper. But when the agency tried to film the commercial, the shaving cream dampened the sandpaper, causing it to rip as it was being shaved. Rather than abandon the idea, the agency decided instead to coat a piece of plastic with sand to make it look like sandpaper, and use this plastic replica in its Rapid Shave campaign.

As the "sandpaper" was shown being shaved in the commercial, an announcer intoned, "To prove RAPID SHAVE'S super-moisturizing power, we put it right from the can onto this tough dry sandpaper. It was applied * * * soak * * * and off in a stroke." [46]

One hopes that few consumers would rush out to buy Rapid Shave simply to shave sandpaper. Colgate–Palmolive, the manufacturer of Rapid Shave, may well have been startled when the FTC issued a complaint contending that this ad constituted a deceptive advertising practice. However, when an FTC hearing examiner discovered that sandpaper actually could be shaved with Rapid Shave after it had soaked to the paper for an hour or so, he dismissed the complaint.[47]

Unwilling to allow the public to be led astray by this sandpaper hoax, the FTC reversed the hearing examiner's finding and issued a cease and desist order declaring that all depictions in advertisements that were not "accurate representations were illegal."

But when a Court of Appeals considered the FTC order, it expressed concern that the flexible Article 5 of the FTC Act was being used in a new area. Article 5 provides:

> Unfair methods of competition in commerce, and un-
> fair or deceptive acts or practices in commerce, are de-

[45] Federal Trade Commission v. Colgate–Palmolive Co., 380 U.S. 374, 85 S.Ct. 1035 (1965). For an amusing account of this case, see Daniel Seligman, "The Great Sandpaper Shave: A Real–Life Story of Truth in Advertising," Fortune (Dec.1964) pp. 131–133ff.

[46] 380 U.S. 374, 376, 85 S.Ct. 1035, 1038 (1965).

[47] 380 U.S. 374, 376–377, 85 S.Ct. 1035, 1038 (1965).

clared unlawful.[48]

The Circuit Court of Appeals concluded that the FTC was going too far in declaring all mock-ups illegal. The court declared, "where the only untruth is that the substance [the viewer] sees on the screen is artificial, and the visual appearance is otherwise a correct and accurate representation of the product itself, he is not injured." [49]

In May, 1963, the Commission issued its final order that Colgate and Bates cease and desist from: [50]

> Unfairly or deceptively advertising any * * * product by presenting a test, experiment or demonstration that (1) is represented to the public as actual proof of a claim made for the product which is material to inducing a sale, and (2) is not in fact a genuine test, experiment or demonstration being conducted as represented and does not in fact constitute actual proof of the claim * * *.

Although Colgate and Bates also challenged the 1963 FTC order, the Supreme Court of the United States made the order stick. Note that the use of *all* mock-ups in televised commercials was not forbidden as deceptive. The Court found that "the undisclosed use of plexiglas" in the Rapid Shave commercials was "a material deceptive practice." But there is a fine line between the forbidden kind of "demonstration" in the Rapid Shave commercial and an acceptable "commercial which extolled the goodness of ice cream while giving viewers a picture of a scoop of mashed potatoes appearing to be ice cream." The Court tried to draw just such a distinction.[51]

Marbles in the Soup

The Campbell Soup Company, however, slipped over the fine line between "demonstration" and "deception," at least in the eyes of the Federal Trade Commission. Campbell Soup consented to stop the practice of putting marbles in bowls of soup to force solid

[48] 380 U.S. 374, 376n, 85 S.Ct. 1035, 1038n, quoting 38 Stat. 719, as amended, 52 Stat. 111, 15 U.S.C.A. § 45(a)(1).

[49] 380 U.S. 374, 381, 85 S.Ct. 1035, 1040 (1968), quoting 310 F.2d 89, 94 (1st Cir.1962).

[50] 380 U.S. 374, 382, 85 S.Ct. 1035, 1041 (1965), quoting Colgate Palmolive Co., No. 7736, FTC May 7, 1963. This clause was added by the FTC for the benefit of Ted Bates & Co., because advertising agencies do not always have all the information about a product that a manufacturer has. The clause said, " 'provided, however, that respondent [Bates] neither knew nor had reason to know that the product, article or substance used in the test, experiment, or demonstration was a mock-up or a prop.' "

[51] 380 U.S. 374, 390, 85 S.Ct. 1035, 1045, 1047 (1965).

chunks of meat and vegetables to the surface, making them visible to viewers of television ads.[52]

SEC. 63.   CORRECTIVE ADVERTISING ORDERS OF THE FTC

The Federal Trade Commission has attempted to enforce truth in advertising by requiring some advertisers to correct past misstatements.

After being roughly handled by critics ranging from Ralph Nader to the American Bar Association during the late 1960s, the Federal Trade Commission of the 1970s became much more active than in previous years. Symptomatic of this increased activity was an FTC complaint against Standard Oil Company of California. The company's advertising had been claiming that its Chevron gasoline, thanks to an additive called F–310, could significantly decrease harmful substances in auto exhaust emissions, thus helping to reduce air pollution. This sort of "we're good for the environment" advertising has been termed "Eco–Porn" (ecological pornography) by cynical critics of advertising.

The FTC issued a cease and desist order to halt allegedly misleading F–310 advertising claims, but the matter did not end there. The FTC also demanded that the Standard Oil Company run "corrective" ads for a year, adding another FTC sanction to use against deceptive advertising in addition to a cease-and-desist order. In the Chevron F–310 case, the Standard Oil Company of California had to disclose that its earlier advertising campaign had included false and deceptive statements. The Commission said that 25 per cent of the advertising for Chevron—either published space or broadcast time—should be devoted to making "affirmative disclosures" about the earlier advertising.[53] An FTC administrative judge dismissed charges against the F–310 ads, but he was then overruled by the Commission. The FTC then re-instituted its cease-and-desist order. The U.S. Court of Appeals for the Ninth Circuit held that the FTC was correct in concluding that the F–310 commercials had a tendency to mislead consumers. However, the FTC was held to have erred in having issued an order against Standard Oil Company asking the company to refrain from making

[52] Campbell Soup Co., 3 Trade Reg.Rep. Para. 19,261 (FTC, 1970); the Campbell Soup Co. consented to stop the practice of putting marbles in soup bowls to force solid chunks of meat and vegetables to the surface of the soup so as to be visible to viewers of television ads.

[53] 3 Trade Reg.Rep.Para. 19,420 (FTC Complaint issued, Dec. 29, 1970). See also William F. Lemke, Jr., "Souped Up Affirmative Disclosure Orders of the Federal Trade Commission," 4 University of Michigan Journal of Law Reform (Winter, 1970) pp. 180–181; Note, " 'Corrective Advertising' Orders of the Federal Trade Commission," 85 Harvard Law Review (December, 1971) pp. 477–478.

certain representations about F–310 "or any other product in commerce" unless every statement is true and completely substantiated. The court said that order was too broad, and had to be narrowed to deal only with gasoline additive F–310.[54]

Other corporate defendants in cases where the FTC has sought to obtain corrective advertising include Coca Cola, for claims made about nutrient and vitamin content of its Hi–C fruit drinks,[55] and ITT Continental Baking Company, for ads implying that eating Profile Bread could help people to lose weight. The FTC charged that Profile was different from other bread only in being more thinly sliced, meaning that there were seven fewer calories per slice. ITT Continental Baking Company consented to a cease and desist order which does two things: first, it prohibits all further claims of weight-reducing attributes for Profile Bread, and second, the company has to devote 25 per cent of its Profile advertising for one year to disclosing that the bread is not effective for weight reduction.[56]

The FTC—as if to confound some of its earlier critics—showed increasing willingness to move against advertising campaigns by big-name firms or products. "Listerine Antiseptic Mouthwash," a product of the Warner–Lambert Company had advertised its product for years as preventing or alleviating the common cold. The FTC ordered in 1972 that Warner–Lambert disclose in future advertisements that: "Contrary to prior advertising, Listerine will not help prevent colds or sore throats or lessen their severity." Hearing the case on appeal, the Court of Appeals for the Fifth Circuit affirmed the order, but dropped the phrase "Contrary to Prior Advertising." [57] Writing for the court in 1977, Circuit Judge J. Skelly Wright found persuasive scientific testimony that gargling Listerine could not help a sore throat because its active ingredients could not penetrate tissue cells to reach viruses.[58] "[T]he Commission found that the ability of Listerine to kill germs by millions on contact is of no medical significance in the treatment of colds or sore throats. Expert testimony showed the bacteria in the oral cavity, the 'germs' which Listerine purports to kill, do not cause colds and play no role in cold symptoms." In this case the Warner–Lambert Company was not playing for small monetary stakes. The FTC required the corrective advertising statement to appear in

[54] Standard Oil Co. of California v. FTC, 577 F.2d 653, 658 (9th Cir.1978).

[55] 3 Trade Reg.Rep. Para. 19,351 (FTC, 1970).

[56] 3 Trade Reg.Rep. Para. 19,780 (FTC, Aug. 17, 1971); Note, " 'Corrective Advertising' Orders of the Federal Trade Commission," 85 Harvard Law Review (December, 1971), p. 478.

[57] Warner–Lambert Co. v. FTC, 562 F.2d 749, 762 (D.C.Cir.1977).

[58] Ibid., p. 754.

Listerine advertising until about $10 million had been spent on touting the mouthwash.

The Warner–Lambert Company also played for high legal stakes by challenging the very authority of the FTC to issue "corrective advertising" orders.   The Commission contended, on the other hand, that the affirmative disclosure that Listerine will not prevent colds or lessen their severity is needed to give effect to a cease and desist order which would remove the misleading claim from the mouthwash's ads.[59]

The Court of Appeals upheld the FTC's order against Listerine, approving the Commission's standard for imposing corrective advertising.   The FTC standard said if a deceptive advertisement played a substantial role in creating or reinforcing "in the public's mind a false and material belief which lives on after the false advertising ceases," then there is clear harm to competitors and to the consuming public.   Since merely ceasing the ad cannot avert injury to the public, the FTC said it could require corrective ads: "affirmative action designed to terminate the otherwise continuing ill effects of the advertisement." [60]

Comparative Advertising

People reading or viewing advertising sometimes see claims made that Product A is "better," "more effective," etc. than Product B.   This is what is known as "comparative advertising" and has been encouraged by the Federal Trade Commission in the belief that this will assist consumers in getting more needed information about products.   This comparative advertising, however, must be susceptible of substantiation; false and misleading comparative statements will draw legal consequences.

For example, consider American Home Products [makers of Anacin] v. Johnson and Johnson [makers of Tylenol].   Anacin ads based on the theme "Your Body Knows" contended that Anacin was superior to Tylenol, that it was more effective in reducing inflammation, and that it worked faster than Tylenol.   Johnson and Johnson [Tylenol] complained to the three television networks that the Anacin advertising was deceptive and misleading.   American Home Products [Anacin] countered by suing Johnson and Johnson, claiming that the makers of Tylenol violated the Lanham Trademark Act by disparaging a competitor's product,[61] seeking an injunction against Tylenol advertising.[62]

[59] Ibid., p. 756.

[60] Ibid., p. 762.

[61] Lanham Trademark Act, 44 Fed.Reg. 4738 § 43(a).

[62] American Home Products Corp. v. Johnson and Johnson, 436 F.Supp. 785 (S.D.N.Y.1977), affirmed 577 F.2d 160 (2d Cir.1978).

This lawsuit backfired, however, because a federal district court dismissed the American Home Products [Anacin] suit and instead slapped a permanent injunction on American Home Products forbidding publishing of a misleading advertisement.[63]

The Lanham Act (Sec. 43a) & Deceptive Advertising

The Lanham Trademark Act is another lever to be used along with the FTC Act to discourage deceptive advertising or promotional activities. Section 43(a) of the Lanham Act, as amended in 1989, makes it possible for persons who believe they are injured by deceptive advertising to sue for damages. P. Cameron DeVore and Robert D. Sack have written that the present Section 43(a) is intended to operate as a commercial defamation act. That portion of the Lanham Act says that individuals who misrepresent "the nature, characteristics, qualities or geographical origins of his or her or another person's goods, services, or commercial activities shall be liable in a civil action [brought] by any person who believes that he or she is likely to be damaged by such act."[64]

And the Lanham Act can be used to protect against unauthorized use of trademarks. The gigantic brewing firm of Anheuser-Busch sued Balducci Publications because its magazine—"Snicker"—had run a fictitious parody ad for "Michelob Oily," using the beer manufacturer's familiar trademarks as part of the effort at humor. The brewer won what it sought: $1 in damages plus an injunction against further use of the trademark by the magazine.[65]

Another part of Section 43(a) of the Lanham Act allows an individual or company to sue for damages for confusion created by an advertisement misrepresenting a product. That is precisely what singer Tom Waits did when a singer imitating Waits was used in a Frito–Lay commercial to tout a new product. Holding that Waits has a recognizable product (his voice), the Court of Appeals for the Second 9th Circuit upheld a $2.375 million judgment for Waits for linking his identity to a commercial product without his permission.[66]

Comparative advertising cases can involve both ad regulation and copyright law. Triangle Publications—when publishers of *TV Guide*—sued Knight-Ridder Newspapers, publishers of *The Miami*

[63] Ibid.

[64] P. Cameron DeVore and Robert D. Sack, "Advertising and Commercial Speech," in James C. Goodale, chairman, Communications Law 1993 (New York: Practising Law Institute, 1993), p. 175, see Lanham Act as amended in 1987, Sec. 43(a), 15 U.S.C.A. Sec. 1125(a) (1988).

[65] Anheuser-Busch v. Balducci Publications, 28 F.3d 769 (8th Cir.1994), 22 Med. L.Rptr. 2001.

[66] Waits v. Frito–Lay, Inc., 978 F.2d 1093, 1101–1105 (9th Cir.1992).

Herald. The newspaper had started a television program guide as a Sunday supplement.

The *TV Guide* complaint stemmed from the newspaper's use of a copyrighted cover in a promotional ad. Ultimately, it was held that *The Herald*'s use of the *TV Guide* cover in the context of a truthful comparative advertisement was indeed a "fair use".[67] (See Copyright, Chap. 12, Sec. 76.)

Advertising Substantiation

Since the early 1970s, the FTC has set down requirements that advertisers make available proof—"substantiation," in FTC terminology—to back up their claims. At the start of its substantiation efforts, the Commission demanded of entire industries—e.g. soap and detergents, air conditioners, deodorant manufacturers—that they come forward to back up their claims. An early case in the substantiation area was the FTC proceeding, In re Pfizer, Inc., decided in 1972. Pfizer, a chemical/drug manufacturing concern, had advertised its "Un–Burn" product with claims that its application would stop the discomfort of sunburn by tuning out nerve endings. The FTC told Pfizer that unless it could prove such a claim, that would be considered an unfair (and therefore illegal) trade practice. That meant an advertiser should have "a reasonable basis [for its claims] before disseminating an ad." [68] As FTC Associate Director for Advertising Practices Wallace S. Snyder wrote in 1984, " * * * ads for objective claims imply that the advertiser has a prior reasonable basis for making the claim. In light of the implied representation of substantiation, therefore, a performance claim that lacks a reasonable basis is deceptive." [69]

State Regulation of Advertising

In the 1980s, a time in which "deregulation" was a major theme of the Reagan Administration, one effect was a continued scaling back of the aggressiveness of the nation's prime governmental regulator of advertising, the Federal Trade Commission. But from the mid–1980s on, occasional comments were heard from leaders in the advertising business to the effect that deregulation had its problems, too. Although "getting government off the back of business and the public" was good for political mileage, when

[67] Triangle Publications, Inc. v. Knight–Ridder Newspapers, Inc., 626 F.2d 1171 (5th Cir.1980), affirming 445 F.Supp. 875 (S.D.Fla.1978), 3 Med.L.Rptr. 2086; see also DeVore and Sack, op. cit., p. 476.

[68] Wallace S. Snyder, "Advertising Substantiation Program," in Christopher Smith and Christian S. White, chairmen, The FTC 1984 (New York: Practising Law Institute, 1984), p. 121; In re Pfizer, Inc., 81 FTC 23 (1972).

[69] Snyder, loc. cit., citing General Dynamics Corp., 82 FTC 488 (1973), and also Firestone Tire & Rubber Co., 81 FTC 398 (1972), affirmed 481 F.2d 246 (6th Cir.1972), certiorari denied 414 U.S. 1112, 94 S.Ct. 841 (1973).

FTC regulation diminished, state regulatory efforts to some extent moved into the void. Perhaps it might be said that regulators, like nature, abhor a vacuum.

Advertising executives had reason to worry as state ad regulation became more insistent. Whatever their feelings about the FTC, state-to-state regulatory differences in the 1980s threatened to assemble a crazy-quilt pattern of regulations.

Part of the rise of more aggressive state regulation of advertising may be found in the National Association of Attorneys' General. In February, 1988, Daniel Oliver, then chairman of the Federal Trade Commission, expressed some doubts about the states' consumer-protection, saying the state attorneys general were exceeding their authority. Oliver added, "Obviously, deregulation gives the opportunity for the most restrictive of attorneys general to bring cases that will have national effect, and that's not what the American consumer needs." [70]

The New York Times reported that attorneys general of New York, Texas, California, Missouri, Kansas, Illinois, Minnesota and Wisconsin created a study group to look into consumer complaints about airline fares. "The group reported last fall that airline advertising was deceptive and that it amounted to a 'bait-and-switch' practice," and later distributed enforcement guidelines on false advertising. One consumer advocate even told The New York Times in 1988 that many activists were working with state attorneys general, getting action to resolve complaints also filed—evidently with little result—with Federal agencies.[71]

In 1992, however, the U.S. Supreme Court held 5–3 that the Airline Deregulation Act of 1978 denies a State the right to enforce any law relating to air carrier rates, routes or services and also denies it the right to regulate advertising pertaining to those matters. Dan Morales, former Attorney general of Texas, had sued Trans World Airlines for failing to follow advertising disclosure requirements relating to "frequent flyer" programs established by the National Association of Attorneys General.

Speaking for the Supreme Court's majority, Justice Antonin Scalia found that the state requirements imposed unnecessarily heavy financial burdens on airlines. He held requiring airlines to create different ads to conform to the laws of various states did not benefit consumers to the extent necessary to justify such a burden.[72]

[70] M.D. Hinds, "States Are Taking Lead on Consumer Protection," The New York Times, Feb. 8, 1988, p. 12.

[71] Ibid.

[72] Morales v. Trans World Airlines, 112 S.Ct. 2031 (1992).

In the late 1980s, under FTC Commission Chair Janet Steiger, the Commission to a considerable extent repaired relations with the National Association of [State] Attorneys General (NAAG). (One wit speculated that NAAG might also stand for National Association of Aspiring Governors.) State Attorneys General, whose concern for consumers seemed on some occasions to be fueled by high-profile cases useful to the politically ambitious, had been free-lancing on national problems. Thus, an advertisement might be acceptable (or at least not challenged) in many states but might be unacceptable "bait and switch" advertising to the Attorney General of, say, the New York. The result was that one state could cause restructuring of a national advertising campaign.

SEC. 64. OTHER FEDERAL ADMINISTRATIVE CONTROLS

In addition to the Federal Trade Commission, many other federal agencies—including the Food and Drug Administration, the Federal Communications Commission, and the United States Postal Service—exert controls over advertising in interstate commerce.

Although of paramount importance as an advertising regulator, the FTC does not stand alone among federal agencies in its fight against suspect advertising. Federal agencies which have powers over advertising include:

(1) The Food and Drug Administration

(2) The United States Postal Service

(3) The Securities and Exchange Commission

(4) The Alcohol and Tobacco Tax Division of the Internal Revenue Service

Such a list by no means exhausts the number of federal agencies which, tangentially at least, can exert some form of control over advertising. Bodies such as the Federal Aeronautics Administration and the Interstate Commerce Commission and the Federal Power Commission have power to curtail advertising abuses connected with matters under each agency's jurisdiction.[73]

1. Food and Drug Administration

The Food and Drug Administration's (FDA) activities in controlling labelling and misbranding overlap the powers of the FTC to a considerable degree. The Pure Food and Drug Act gives the FDA

---

[73] See Note, "The Regulation of Advertising," Columbia Law Review Vol. 56:7 (Nov. 1956) pp. 1019–1111, at p. 1054, citing 24 Stat. 378 (1887), 49 U.S.C.A. § 1 (ICC); 41 Stat. 1063 (1920), 16 U.S.C.A. § 791(a) (FTC); 52 Stat. 1003 (1938), as amended, 49 U.S.C.A. § 491.

jurisdiction over misbranding and mislabeling of foods, drugs, and cosmetics.[74] The FTC, however, was likewise given jurisdiction over foods, drugs, and cosmetics by the Wheeler–Lea Amendment.[75] It used to be said that the FTC and the FDA have agreed upon a division of labor whereby FTC concentrates on false advertising and the FDA focuses attention on false labelling.[76] However, this division of labor is quite inexact. Pamphlets or literature distributed with a product have been held to be "labels" for purposes of FDA enforcement.[77]

Unlike the five-commissioner FTC—with no more than three individuals from one political party—the FDA is headed by one individual. That can add up to more aggressive approaches to high-profile controversies by the FDA than the FTC will take on. The high-energy Dr. David Kessler, a physician and a lawyer, became FDA Commissioner in 1991. In the 1990s, the FDA was handed increased responsibility for blood safety and drugs from aspirin to AIDS medications. As science writer Herbert Burkholz wrote, "25 cents out of every dollar spent by the American consumer goes for products regulated by the FDA."

The FDA also has responsibility for inspection of fish and meat and food products, under the 1938 Federal Food, Drug, and Cosmetic Act. Dr. Kessler faced daunting challenges, but set about streamlining FDA investigations and enforcement, and was much in the headlines in 1994 as he took on tobacco industry claims that nicotine is not addictive. Among Dr. Kessler's suggestions to Congress was the possibility of regulating nicotine as a drug (to be sold by pharmacies?) and restricting cigarette advertising to protect children from intentional or unintentional encouragement to smoke.[78] As the FDA took on the tobacco industry, the FTC decided not to take on the "Joe Camel" billboards and magazine ads criticized on the theory they are aimed at making cigarette smoking attractive to children.

2. The U.S. Postal Service

Postal controls over advertising can be severe. Congress was provided with lawmaking power to operate the postal system under Article I, Section 8 of the Constitution. This power was long

[74] 52 Stat. 1040 (1938), 21 U.S.C.A. § 301.

[75] See "The Wheeler Lea Amendment" to the Federal Trade Commission Act, 52 Stat. 111 (1938), as amended, 15 U.S.C.A. § 45(a)(1).

[76] See, for example, 2 CCH Trade Reg.Rep. (10th ed.), Paragraph 8540, p. 17,081 (1954).

[77] See United States v. Kordel, 164 F.2d 913 (7th Cir.1947); United States v. Article of Device Labeled in Part "110 V Vapozone," 194 F.Supp. 332 (N.D.Cal. 1961).

[78] Philip J. Hilts, "Ban on Cigarettes Could be Avoided, FDA Chief Says," The New York Times, June 29, 1994, pp. A1, A10.

delegated by Congress to a Postmaster General and his Post Office Department. It has long been established that the mails could not be used to carry things which, in the judgment of Congress, were socially harmful.[79] The Postmaster General had the power to exclude articles or substances which Congress has proscribed as non-mailable. With the passage of the Postal Reorganization Act of 1970, the Post Office Department was abolished as a Cabinet-level agency, and was replaced by the United States Postal Service, a subdivision of the Executive branch.[80]

Perhaps the Postal Service's greatest deterrent to false advertising is contained in the power to halt delivery of materials suspected of being designed to defraud mail recipients.[81] The Postal Service can order nondelivery of mail, and can impound suspected mail matter.[82]

The administrative fraud order is not the only kind of mail fraud action available to the Postal Service. Instead of administrative procedure through the Service, a *criminal* mail fraud case may be started. Criminal cases are prosecuted by a U.S. attorney in a United States District Court. Conviction under the federal mail fraud statute can result in a fine of up to $1,000, imprisonment for up to 5 years, or both.[83] Criminal fraud orders are used when the U.S. Postal Service wishes to operate in a punitive fashion. The administrative fraud orders, on the other hand, are more preventive in nature.

3. The Securities and Exchange Commission

Securities markets are attractive to fast-buck artists, so the sale and publicizing of securities are kept under a watchful governmental eye. Most states have "Blue Sky" laws which enable a state agency to halt the circulation of false or misleading information about the sale of stocks, bonds or the like.[84] The work of the Securities and Exchange Commission, however, is far more important in protecting the public.

After the stock market debacle of 1929, strong regulations were instituted at the federal level to prevent deceptive statements about securities. Taken together, the Securities Act of 1933 [85] and the

---

[79] See, for example, early federal tax laws on obscenity discussed in Chapter 11, or see Public Clearing House v. Coyne, 194 U.S. 497, 24 S.Ct. 789 (1904).

[80] 39 U.S.C.A. § 3003.

[81] Ibid., III, § 50.02.

[82] Ibid., Rosden & Rosden II, § 18.02, n. 17.

[83] 18 U.S.C.A. § 1341; Ague, ibid., p. 61.

[84] See Note, "The Regulation of Advertising," Columbia Law Review op. cit. p. 1065.

[85] 48 Stat. 74 (1933), 15 U.S.C.A. § 77.

Securities Exchange Act of 1934 [86] gave the S.E.C. great power over the sale and issuance of securities.

Sale of securities to investors cannot proceed until complete and accurate information has been given, registering the certificates with the S.E.C.[87] A briefer version of the registration statement is used in the "prospectus" circulated among prospective investors before the stock or bond can be offered for sale.[88] If misleading statements have been made about a security "in any material respect" in either registration documents or in the prospectus, the Commission may issue a "stop order" which removes the right to sell the security.[89] Furthermore, unless a security is properly registered and its prospectus accurate, it is a criminal offense to use the mails to sell it or to advertise it for sale.[90]

An unscrupulous seller of securities has more to fear than just the S.E.C. Under a provision of the United States Code, a person who has lost money because he was tricked by a misleading prospectus may sue a number of individuals, including persons who signed the S.E.C. registration statement and every director, officer, or partner in the firm issuing the security.[91]

4. The Alcohol and Tobacco Tax Division, Internal Revenue Service

Ever since this nation's unsuccessful experiment with prohibition, the federal government has kept a close eye on liquor advertising. The responsible agency is the Alcohol and Tobacco Tax Division of the Internal Revenue Service.[92] Liquor advertising may not include false or misleading statements, and may not disparage competing products. False statements may include misrepresenting the age of a liquor, or claiming that its alcoholic content is higher than it is in reality.[93]

The Alcohol and Tobacco Tax Division has harsh sanctions at its disposal. If an advertiser violates a regulation of the Division, he is subject to a fine, and could even be put out of business if his federal liquor license is revoked.[94]

[86] 48 Stat. 881 (1934), as amended, 15 U.S.C.A. §§ 78(a)–78(jj).

[87] 48 Stat. 77 (1933), as amended, 15 U.S.C.A. § 77(f).

[88] 48 Stat. 78 (1933), 15 U.S.C.A. § 77(j).

[89] 48 Stat. 79 (1933), as amended, 15 U.S.C.A. § 77(h)(b) and (d). For an example of litigation charging false statements in the sale of corporate bonds, see Escott v. BarChris Construction, 283 F.Supp. 643 (S.D.N.Y.1968).

[90] 48 Stat. 84 (1933), as amended, 15 U.S.C.A. § 77(e).

[91] 48 Stat. 82 (1933), 15 U.S.C.A. § 77(k).

[92] 27 U.S.C.A. § 205.

[93] Ibid.

[94] Ibid.

The FTC and other federal agencies by no means provide the whole picture of controls over advertising. There are many state regulations affecting political advertising and legal advertising by government bodies, but they cannot be treated here. States also regulate the size and location of billboards, but space does not permit discussion of these statutes. We now turn to consideration of some of the ways in which states have regulated commercial advertising in the mass media.

SEC. 65.   THE PRINTERS' INK STATUTE

Most states have adopted some version of the model statute which makes fraudulent and misleading advertising a misdemeanor.

One of the best known restraints upon advertising exists at the state level in the various forms of the Printers' Ink statute adopted in 48 states. *Printer's Ink* magazine, in 1911, advocated that states adopt a model statute which would make false advertising a misdemeanor. Leaders in the advertising and publishing world realized the difficulty in securing prosecutions for false advertising under the usual state fraud statutes. Considerable initiative in gaining state enactment of Printers' Ink statutes was generated through the Better Business Bureau and through various advertising clubs and associations.

All but two states—Delaware and New Mexico—have some version of the Printers' Ink statute on their books.[95] Although the Printers' Ink statute is famous, its fame is greater than its present-day usefulness as a control over advertising. Relatively few relevant cases exist which indicate that the statute has seen little use in bringing cheating advertisers to court. The Printers' Ink statute may still be useful as a guideline, or in providing a sanction which local Better Business Bureaus may threaten to invoke even if they seldom do so.[96]

The Printers' Ink statute is aimed and enforced primarily against advertisers rather than against units of the mass media which may have no knowledge that an ad is false or misleading.[97] This statute was widely adopted, apparently because the common law simply did not provide adequate remedies against false advertising, especially in an economy which has grown so explosively.

[95] "Basis for State Laws on Truth in Publishing—The Printers' Ink Model Statute," Reprint, Printers' Ink Publishing Corp., 1959. Note, "Developments in the Law—Deceptive Advertising," Harvard Law Review, op. cit., p. 1122.

[96] Note, "The Regulation of Advertising," op. cit. p. 1057.

[97] Ibid., pp. 1059–1060; State v. Beacon Publ. Co., 141 Kan. 734, 42 P.2d 960 (1935).

The model statute is more flexible than common law prosecutions or fraud statutes. It does not make *scienter,* guilty knowledge or intent to publish false advertisements an element of the offense. Many states, however, have variants of the Printers' Ink statute which are not as comprehensive as the model law in that some element of *scienter* must be shown for conviction.[98]

SEC. 66. LOTTERIES

Federal and state prohibitions on advertising or publicizing of lotteries are changing as many states have started lotteries as revenue measures.

The theory of laws forbidding advertising or publicizing lotteries is that the public needs to protected from gambling. And in practice, most people in the areas of advertising, public relations and journalism paid scant attention to the federal and state lottery ad statutes. As a practical matter, church bingo socials or merchants' promotional lottery schemes are rarely prosecuted.

What then, is a lottery? There are three elements:

(1) *Consideration*—This usually means money paid to purchase a lottery ticket or a chance on an auto or some other item which a service organization is offering to raise money. But in some states, consideration need not be money paid. Just the effort required to enter a contest, as going to a store to get an entry blank or having to mail a product label, at times has been termed "consideration." [99]

(2) *Prize*—A prize in a lottery is something of value, and generally of greater worth than the consideration invested.

(3) *Chance*—The element of chance—the gambling element—is what led Victorian–era Congressmen to pass the first federal statutes against lotteries in 1890. There can, however, be an element of certainty accompanying the buying of chances in a lottery. For example, if a woman buys a newspaper subscription she is certain to receive the newspaper which includes a chance in a prize contest, but—many years ago—one court termed that promotion a lottery.[1]

In May 1990, a new federal law, the "Charity Games Act," went into effect, permitting print or broadcast promotion and advertising of lotteries conducted by non-profit organizations and of

---

[98] Note, "Developments in the Law of Deceptive Advertising," Harvard Law Review loc. cit.

[99] Brooklyn Daily Eagle v. Voorhies, 181 Fed. 579 (C.C.N.Y.1910).

[1] Stevens v. Cincinnati Times–Star Co., 72 Ohio St. 112, 73 N.E. 1058 (1905).

all official state lotteries in any state conducting such lotteries.[2] The new law also allows commercial corporations to advertise occasional lotteries as long as such a promotional activity is not related to the corporation's usual course of business.

Congressional lottery legislation has aimed at helping states to control that form of gambling. In general, federal law makes broadcasting of a lottery advertisement a crime. However, an exception was made to allow broadcasters to carry ads for state-run lotteries on those stations licensed in states which themselves have lotteries.[3]

Radio and television broadcasts, however, don't stop at state lines. This was the underlying problem confronting the U.S. Supreme Court involving a North Carolina radio station owned by Edge Broadcasting Co. That broadcaster is located in the non-lottery state of North Carolina. The radio station, however, is only three miles from the Virginia state line, and Virginia does have a state lottery. More than 90% of the radio station's audience lives in Virginia.

The radio station challenged the federal ban on broadcasting lottery ads, and a federal district court and a U.S. Court of Appeals held that the ban was unconstitutional. The Court of Appeals held 2–1 that there was no reasonable fit between the goal of protecting North Carolina listeners and the means chosen to achieve it. The reason? About 10% of the listeners in North Carolina could get the same lottery information from Virginia media.[4]

The U.S. Supreme Court, however, reversed the appellate court by a margin of 7–2. Writing for the Court, Justice Byron White found that despite its minimal impact in this case, the federal statute was sufficiently effective in advancing a state's legitimate governmental aim of restricting dissemination of gambling ads. This upheld the constitutionality of the federal ban on advertising lotteries over stations which are not physically located in states having state lotteries.[5]

SEC. 67.   SELF–REGULATION

Leading communications companies have developed standards to govern their acceptance or rejection of advertising.

Publishers and broadcasters must know the legal status of advertising. If it can be proved that they knew that an advertise-

[2] Public Law 100–667, 132, amending Sec. 43(a) Title 15 USC 1125(a).

[3] 18 U.S.C.A. § 1307.

[4] 956 F.2d 263 (4th Cir.1992).

[5] U.S. v. Edge Broadcasting Co., 113 S.Ct. 2696 (1993), 21 Med.L.Rptr. 1577.

ment is fraudulent, they may be held responsible for that ad along with the person or company who placed it in the publication. Advertising departments on many newspapers, moreover, often serve as a kind of advertising agency. In this capacity, the advertising staff must be able to give knowledgeable counsel and technical advice to advertisers.

In general, publishers are not liable to the individual consumer for advertising which causes financial loss or other damage unless the publisher or his employees knew that such advertising was fraudulent or misleading. The absence of liability for damage, however, does not mean that there is an absence of responsibility to the public generally and to individual readers of a publication.

The newspaper or broadcast station which permits dishonest or fraudulent advertising hurts its standing with both its readers and its advertisers. Publishers and broadcasters, who perceive psychological and economic advantages in refusing dishonest advertising, also appear to be becoming more cognizant that they have a moral duty to protect the public.

Responsible media units go to great lengths to ensure that advertising which they publish or broadcast is honest. Some newspapers' advertising acceptance statements, such as the one used by the Dallas Morning News, are very specific, spelling out advertisements which will not be accepted for publication. For example, the Dallas Morning News says it will not accept "bait and switch" ads: "Advertisements describing goods not available and not intended to be sold on request, but used as 'bait' to lure customers." Other newspapers provide long lists of ads that are not acceptable; some include fortune tellers, palm readers, and faith healers, along with forbidding publication of ads for illegal or harmful activities or substances.[6]

The National Advertising Division/National Advertising Review Board

In Addition to self-regulation by individual media units, a broader voluntary alternative exists in the National Advertising Division of the Council of Better Business Bureau and the National Advertising Review Board (NAD/NARB). These organizations serve as unofficial channels to try to resolve advertising disputes. Established in the 1970s by the Council of Better Business Bureaus and major advertising associations,[7] the NAD receives questions and complaints about **national** advertising, and conducts preliminary discussions with advertisers. Its purview is strictly national

[6] Advertising Standards of Acceptability in the Dallas Morning News, pamphlet dated August, 1983.

[7] The American Advertising Federation, the American Association of Advertising Agencies, and the Association of National Advertisers.

advertising which is suspected of deception. The NAD takes complaints from individuals and companies and also generates some of its own "cases" by monitoring national advertising in print and electronic mass media. During 1991, NAD Case Reports closed 88 cases, with challenges competitors making up 71% of the total; 14% came from NAD's own activities, 6% came from customer complaints, and 2% from local Better Business Bureaus.[8]

If an advertiser and the NAD cannot agree after initial discussions, NAD publishes a report outlining the issues for referral to the NARB[9] Later, the NARB will produce its own report on the specific controversy. For example, the NAD in 1992 investigated Norelco's 950 RX electric razor, in response to an inquiry about how accurately a TV animation depicted "the action of the lift and cut system." After Norelco produced copies of six United States patents plus microphotography showing the lift and cut system actually in operation, the NAD concluded that the animated claim in the TV ad was substantiated. Findings such as these—including some which are adverse to advertisers and then referred to the NARB for further review—are published in NAD Reports. The reports contain the disclaimer that if an advertisement is changed or stopped, that "is not be taken as an admission of impropriety on any advertiser's part."

Nevertheless, some advertisers who face NAD questions do discontinue or modify ads, or provide substantiation before running the ads again. Take the case of a consumer who complained that the U.S. Postal Service had not lived up to its TV ads claiming "Two, Two, Two, Two–Day Priority Mail. Two. That's delivery in just two days of up to two pounds for just $2.90." The ad did have a disclaimer, "Some restrictions Apply." In fact, a consumer who mailed documents from Michigan to Connecticut discovered that his shipment took 10 days, not two. This NAD inquiry resulted in the Postal Service agreeing to add a statement telling customers to consult their local post office for details.[10]

SEC. 68. THE RIGHT TO REFUSE SERVICE

A newspaper or magazine is not a public utility and therefore may choose those with whom it cares to do business.

A newspaper or magazine is a private enterprise and as such may carry on business transactions with whom it pleases. If its managers so desire they may refuse to sell newspapers to individu-

[8] NAD Case Reports, Sample Issue, 1992.

[9] NAD Case Reports, Feb. 17, 1992.

[10] NAD Case Reports, Feb. 17, 1992.

als or news agents, or to publish news stories about any particular event or on any opinion. By weight of legal authority, a newspaper is not a public utility.

There is periodic pressure to create a "right of access" to advertising if not to the news space of the media. Arguments heard touting a right to buy ads run something like this:

> The free marketplace of ideas is not working at all well during the latter third of the 20th Century. Competition among newspapers, magazines, and the electronic media is so diminished that only ideas acceptable to the nation's establishment can gain a hearing. Laissez faire in the media has come to mean, as John P. Roche once said in another context, "Every man for himself—as the elephant said, dancing among the chickens." Government has an affirmative obligation to stop the discriminatory refusal of advertisements and notices in publications.

Such arguments, thus far, have not succeeded. If a change does come which affects the right to refuse advertising, it would seem that advertising with a political or otherwise socially significant message might first be forced upon publishers before the right to refuse ordinary commercial advertising would be affected. An old but important case decided in 1931 declared: [11]

> If a newspaper were required to accept an advertisement, it could be compelled to publish a news item. If some good lady gave a tea, and submitted to the newspaper a proper account of the tea, and the editor of the newspaper ... refused to publish it, she, it seems to us, would have as much right to compel the newspaper to publish the account as would a person engaged in business to compel a newspaper to publish an advertisement. . . .

> Thus, as a newspaper is strictly a private enterprise, the publishers thereof have a right to publish whatever advertisements they desire and to refuse to publish whatever advertisements they do not desire to publish.

Non-private entities, however—such as transit authorities or state-owned publications—can not refuse advertising with impunity. A California case involved a group called Women for Peace. In 1964, Women for Peace sought to place advertising placards in buses owned by the Alameda–Contra Costa Transit District. The placards said:

[11] Shuck v. Carroll Daily Herald, 215 Iowa 1276, 1281, 247 N.W. 813, 815, 87 A.L.R. 975 (1933). See also Friedenberg v. Times Publishing Co., 170 La. 3, 127 So. 345 (1930); In re Louis Wohl, Inc., 50 F.2d 254 (D.Mich.1931). See also Miami Herald Pub. Co. v. Tornillo, 418 U.S. 241, 94 S.Ct. 2831 (1974).

"Mankind must put an end to war or war will put an end to mankind."   President John F. Kennedy.

Write to President Johnson: Negotiate Vietnam. Women for Peace, P.O. Box 944, Berkeley.[12]

The private advertising agency which managed advertising for the transit district rejected the placards.   It was declared that "political advertising and advertising on controversial subjects are not acceptable unless approved by the [transit] district, and that advertising objectionable to the district shall be removed * * *."[13]

After a trial and two appeals, the Women for Peace finally won their case in 1967 before the California Supreme Court. The court said that the ad was protected by the First Amendment and that once a public facility is opened for use of the general public, arbitrary conditions cannot be imposed upon the use of that facility.[14]

The California Supreme Court declared.[15]

We conclude that defendants, having opened a forum for the expression of ideas by providing facilities for advertisements on its buses, cannot for reasons of administrative convenience decline to accept advertising expressing opinions and beliefs within the ambit of First Amendment protection.

In 1969, a college newspaper was told it could not refuse political advertising. A number of non-students wished to place political ads in the *Royal Purple,* the official campus newspaper at Wisconsin State University–Whitewater. Their requests for advertising space were denied on the ground that the newspaper had a policy against accepting "editorial advertisements"—those advertisements expressing political views. Refusal of the advertisements led to suits charging that the plaintiffs' First and Fourteenth Amendment rights had been violated by Wisconsin, acting through the regents of the state colleges, and by the university itself. This refusal, it was claimed, amounted to "state action" because the board of regents—a state agency—had delegated policy-setting powers to the president of the university and to the student publications board.[16]

[12] Wirta v. Alameda–Contra Costa Transit District, 68 Cal.2d 51, 64 Cal.Rptr. 430, 432, 434 P.2d 982, 984 (1967).

[13] Ibid.

[14] 68 Cal.2d 51, 64 Cal.Rptr. 430, 433, 434 P.2d 982, 985 (1967), citing Danskin v. San Diego Unified School District, 28 Cal.2d 536, 171 P.2d 885 (1946).

[15] 68 Cal.2d 51, 64 Cal.Rptr. 430, 432, 434 P.2d 982, 984 (1967).

[16] Lee v. Board of Regents of State Colleges, 306 F.Supp. 1097 (W.D.Wis.1969).

U.S. District Judge James Doyle ruled that the *Royal Purple* should have accepted the advertisements: [17]

> Defendant's acceptance of commercial advertisements and of those public service advertisements that do not "attack an institution, group, person or product" and their rejection of editorial advertisements constitutes an impermissible form of censorship.

> There can be no doubt that defendants' restrictive advertising policy—a policy enforced under color of state law—is a denial of free speech and expression.

Note that the theme of state action runs through all of the above cases in which courts have listened with sympathy to demands that advertisements be accepted. That is, the agency refusing to accept an advertisement was either a transit authority funded by public money [18] or an official campus newspaper on a tax-supported campus which had advertising acceptance rules set up under delegated state authority.[19] In the absence of a strong showing of state action, however, the general rule is that advertisements may be refused by the print media.

One possible exception to that rule—and a rare and hard to prove exception at that—might be if a newspaper, for example, refused ads in some sort of an anticompetitive scheme to injure another business. One example is offered by Home Placement Service v. Providence Journal Company, in 1982. The U.S. Court of Appeal for the First Circuit ruled that a newspaper's refusal to accept classified ads from a rental referral business was held to violate antitrust provisions of the Sherman Act.

This was a special case, however. On the one hand, it is understandable why the Providence Journal didn't want to carry Homefinders' ads. Homefinders would advertise a property with an untraceable location, and then—once someone called the phone number listed in the ad—the person was told that the listed property was " 'no longer available, but if the prospective tenant would merely come to Homefinders' office and pay the fee of $20, other listings would be made available.' " On the other hand, the newspaper's refusal of the ads appeared a bit strange because The Providence Journal, the only metro daily in the area, itself served as a rental referral agency through its advertising columns. The Court of Appeal said that the evidence in the case " * * * indicates

[17] Ibid., 1101, affirmed 441 F.2d 1257 (7th Cir.1971).

[18] Cf. Kissinger v. New York City Transit Authority, 274 F.Supp. 438, 441 (S.D.N.Y.1967); Wirta v. Alameda–Contra Costa Transit District, 68 Cal.2d 51, 64 Cal.Rptr. 430, 432, 434 P.2d 982, 984 (1967); Planned Parenthood v. Chicago Transit Authority, 592 F.Supp. 544 (N.D.Ill.1984).

[19] Lee v. Board of Regents of State Colleges, 441 F.2d 1257 (7th Cir.1971), affirming 306 F.Supp. 1097 (W.D.Wis.1969).

the simplest form of attempted strangulation of a competitor by refusal to deal." The Court said this conduct violated both Sections 1 and 2 of the Sherman Act.[20]

One other situation where an ad refusal might bring legal trouble involves contract law. If a newspaper has entered into a contract to carry advertising, and then refuses to do so, that could be a problem. That's the message from a 1982 Indiana case, Herald–Telephone v. Fatouros, a case involving a political ad which was accepted—as was payment for the ad—and then the message was refused because it might be "inflammatory." The Indiana Court of Appeals, Fourth District, said: [21]

> * * * we agree * * * that a newspaper has a right to publish or reject advertising as its judgment dictates. However, once a newspaper forms a contract to publish an advertisement, it has given up the right to publish or not publish the ad ...

In more usual cases, however, the media are free to refuse ads, as in Person v. New York Post Corp., 1977. The plaintiff asked a court order to prevent the newspaper from refusing to run a "tombstone" ad on a financial matter. Instead, the federal district court declared that it is a newspaper's prerogative to accept or reject ads as it sees fit.[22]

The *Resident Participation* Case

One of the most eloquent pleas for forced access to advertising space can be found in an air pollution dispute in Denver, Colorado. The setting in Denver should be idyllic—a city ringed by the magnificent Rocky Mountains, close to some of the American continent's most spectacular scenery. But not all was well in Denver during the late 1960's: on some days, Denver residents suffered from an eyeburning smog which would seem more at home in Los Angeles, California, roughly 950 miles away.

When word got out that Pepcol, Inc.—a subsidiary of the giant conglomerate Beatrice Foods, Inc.—was going to build a rendering plant within the city limits of Denver, a protest resulted. A citizens group calling itself Resident Participation of Denver, spurred by visions of a malodorous plant processing "dead animals,

[20] Home Placement Service, Inc. v. Providence Journal Co., 682 F.2d 274, 276, 279 (1st Cir.1982), 8 Med.L.Rptr. 1881, 1884, reversed in part at 739 F.2d 671 (1st Cir.1984). Although lawyers' fees ran to over $35,000, the *treble damage* award was a mere $3.

[21] Herald Telephone v. Fatouros, 431 N.E.2d 171 (Ind.App. 4th Dist.1982), 8 Med.L.Rptr. 1230, 1231.

[22] Person v. New York Post Corporation, 427 F.Supp. 1297 (E.D.N.Y.1977), affirmed 573 F.2d 1294 (2d Cir.1977).

guts, and blood" and producing "disgusting" garbage,[23] attempted to place advertisements in Denver's two competing daily newspapers, the *Denver Post* and the *Rocky Mountain News.* The newspapers rejected the ads on the ground that the proposed wording called for a boycott of Beatrice Foods products, and boycott advertising is forbidden by Colorado statute.[24]

Undaunted, the Resident Participation group re-worded its advertising copy to avoid any reference to boycott, but listed each Beatrice Foods products as Meadow Gold milk, cheese, and ice cream, and Zooper Dooper fruit drinks and ice cream. The advertisement, as rewritten, included suggested letters: readers were to be asked to clip out, sign, and mail the letters, thereby protesting the rendering plant project to city and state officials. Both newspapers again refused to print the advertisements.[25]

Resident Participation then sought a court order under the First Amendment to force the newspapers to punish the advertisements. The newspapers countered with arguments that the First Amendment forbids only official abridgments of free speech and press, not merely private ones, and this was an argument the ecology group was unable to overcome. Nevertheless, Resident Participation argued strenuously to have the court consider the newspapers refusals to publish the advertisements as a kind of official or state action. This was claimed because of the newspapers "enjoy monopoly control in a vital area of public concern," and because Colorado statutes require publication of legal notices in newspapers of general circulation.[26]

Resident Participation also contended that the state and city are involved in the newspaper business because of sections of the Colorado Revised Statutes which require that legal notices be published in newspapers of general circulation.[27] Other provisions which were said to make newspapers a public business included a statute which exempts editors and reporters from jury service,[28] and a Denver ordinance which allows newspaper vending machines on public property, including sidewalks.[29]

[23] Plaintiffs Exhibit "A," Resident Participation, Inc. Newsletter quoted in brief in Resident Participation of Denver, Inc. v. Love, 322 F.Supp. 1100 (D.Colo.1971). The authors thank Thomas A. Stacey, graduate student in journalism at the University of Wisconsin–Madison, for his assistance.

[24] Colo.Rev.Stat.Ann. § 80–11–12.

[25] Resident Participation of Denver, Inc. v. Love, 322 F.Supp. 1100, 1101 (D.Colo. 1971).

[26] Ibid., 1102.

[27] Colorado Rev.Stat.Ann. §§ 49–10–3, 49–8–1, 49–22–5, 49–22–11 (1963).

[28] Colo.Rev.Stat.Ann. § 7801–3 (1963).

[29] Denver Municipal Code, §§ 339G, 334.1–2.

A three-judge federal district court rejected these arguments with dispatch, saying it could find nothing "remotely suggesting that these measures are sufficient to justify labeling the newspapers conduct state action." [30]

As the Resident Participation case showed, general circulation newspapers cannot be compelled to accept and publish controversial advertisements. Some newspapers, however, publish controversial political advertisements as a matter of responsibility to the public. In the spring of 1972, for example, The New York Times published two advertisements which drew considerable protest from readers. The first advertisement, signed by a group of citizens calling themselves "The National Committee for Impeachment," demanded the removal from office of President Richard M. Nixon, alleging violations of law and the Constitution in his prosecution of the Vietnam war. A second advertisement, an open letter to President Nixon signed by Norman F. Dacey, inveighed against the President for a Middle East policy termed "blind support" for Israel.[31]

Readers responded to these advertisements with hundreds of letters, and many of those letters criticized *The Times* for publishing such emotionally loaded and politically heated ads, opinions with which neither *The Times*—nor a large part of its readership agreed. That criticism of *The Times* was expressed so frequently and with such obvious sincerity that *The Times* published an editorial, "Freedom to Advertise." The editorial argued that the newspaper felt an obligation to give the public opportunities to express its views, even views violently opposed to the newspaper's, through "various outlets in this newspaper including the advertising columns." [32]

It has long been held by American courts that a newspaper or magazine is a private enterprise, and that it may choose to omit certain news items or to refuse certain advertising. In recent years, and in part because of the thrust given to a "new right of access" by Professor Jerome Barron, the old "right to refuse ads" has undergone considerable challenge. Nevertheless, this generalization may still be made: unless the publication or agency which is to carry an advertisement is clearly some sort of a public entity because of some kind of "state action," an advertisement lawfully may be refused.

Take the case of a film exhibitor who was angered because the *Los Angeles Times* altered advertising copy for a movie, The Killing of Sister George, slightly changing a drawing of a female figure and omitting a reference to "deviate sexual conduct". *The Times*, by

[30] 322 F.Supp. 1100, 1103 (D.C.Colo.1971).

[31] See New York Times, May 31 and June 6, 1972.

[32] New York Times, June 16, 1972. © 1972 by The New York Times Company.

virtue of its enormous advertising revenues, was said by the film distributor to have attained a "substantial monopoly in Southern California." It was further argued that the *Times's* "semi-monopoly and quasi-public position" amounted to state action. The United States Court of Appeals for the 9th Circuit rejected the film distributors arguments, saying: "Unlike broadcasting, the publication of a newspaper is not a government conferred privilege. As we have said, the press and the government have had a history of disassociation." [33]

The right to refuse ads seemed to be holding solidly in the 1990s.

Newspaper Liability for Allegedly Discriminatory Ads?

Sometimes, despite the quest for revenue, newspapers might be better off if they would refuse some advertisements. Ragin v. New York Times [34] and Housing Opportunities Made Equal v. Cincinnati Enquirer [35] both addressed the question of whether a newspaper is liable for publishing advertising that may violate the standards of the Federal Fair Housing Act. Based on conflicting outcomes, the answer seemed to depend on the federal circuit where the newspaper is located.

The New York Times was sued by a group of African Americans who asserted that the newspaper's real estate ad section over two decades rarely displayed pictures of blacks as prospective home owners or renters, an omission constituting a racial preference in violation of federal law. The Second Federal Circuit refused to dismiss the action, holding that a jury might reasonably conclude that such a pattern over a long period of time was not protected commercial speech because it would be an illegal activity.[36]

On the other hand, the Sixth Federal Circuit Court of Appeals dismissed similar allegations brought against the Cincinnati Enquirer, finding that a series of housing ads depicting only whites constituted legally protected commercial free speech. Further, the Sixth Circuit held that the newspaper should not be reburied to serve as an arm of government reviewing all housing advertise-

---

[33] Associates & Aldrich Co. v. Times Mirror Co., 440 F.2d 133, 136 (9th Cir.1971); see also Adult Film Ass'n of America v. Times Mirror Co., 3 Med.L.Rptr. 2292, Civil Action No. C217216 (L.A.Cty.Sup.Ct.1978), upholding a newspaper's right to refuse ads.

[34] Ragin v. New York Times, 923 F.2d 995 (2d Cir.1991).

[35] Housing Opportunities Made Equal v. Cincinnati Enquirer, 943 F.2d 644 (6th Cir.1991).

[36] Ragin v. New York Times, 923 F.2d 995 (2d Cir.1991), cert. den. 112 S.Ct. 81 (1991).

ments it accepted to make sure that they reflected a proper mixture of races.[37]

SEC. 69.   BROADCAST ADVERTISING

Broadcasters also have the right to refuse to accept advertising messages, except for federal political candidate ads during an election period.

In Columbia Broadcasting System Inc. v. Democratic National Committee, the Supreme Court held that radio and television stations are not legally required to broadcast any advertisements they do not want to accept.[38]   By a 7–2 vote, the Court recognized a right for broadcasting similar to the print media's "right to refuse service".

This case dealt with the efforts of a political party and an anti-war group to get airtime for their respective viewpoints.   Business Executives' Move for a Vietnam Peace (BEM) was the anti-war group that filed a complaint with the FCC alleging that a radio station in Washington D.C., WTOP had violated the fairness doctrine by refusing to sell the group time to broadcast a series of one-minute spot announcements against the Vietnam conflict.   WYOP refused, saying it already had presented full and fair coverage of all important viewpoints concerning U.S. policy in Southeast Asia.

A few months later, the Democratic National Committee (DNC) sought a declaratory ruling from the FCC on this statement:

> That under the First Amendment ... and the Communications Act, a broadcaster may not, as a general policy, refuse to sell time to responsible entities ... for comment on public issues.

The Commission rejected the demands of both DNC and BEM, but the Court of Appeals reversed the FCC, declaring that a flat ban on paid public-issue announcements was "in violation of the First Amendment, at least when other types of paid announcements are accepted." [39]

The Supreme Court, however, upheld the FCC's decision by a margin of 7 to 2.   Chief Justice Burger's plurality opinion—he was joined by Justices Rehnquist and Stewart—concluded that broadcast licensees were not common carriers.

He compared a newspaper's right of editorial judgment with that of a broadcast licensee, finding that the broadcaster's degree of

---

[37] Housing Opportunities Made Equal v. Cincinnati Enquirer, 943 F.2d 644 (6th Cir.1991).

[38] CBS, Inc. v. Democratic Nat. Committee, 412 U.S. 94, 93 S.Ct. 2080 (1973).

[39] Business Executives' Move for Vietnam Peace v. FCC; Democratic National Committee v. FCC, 450 F.2d 642 (D.C.Cir.1971) overturning Business Executives, 24 FCC2d 242 (1970) and Democratic National Committee, 25 FCC2d 216 (1970).

freedom was somewhat less extensive than that of the newspaper publisher. Broadcasters are supervised—and periodically licensed—by the FCC which must "oversee without censoring." [40] Even so, the opinion declared, government control over broadcast licensees is not broad enough to transform their stations into "common carriers" or "public utilities", compelled to accept and deliver whatever message any individual might be willing to pay to have transmitted.

Burger wrote,

> For better or worse, editing is what editors are for, and editing is selection and choice of material. That editors—newspaper or broadcast—can and do abuse this power is beyond doubt, but that is not reason to deny the discretion Congress provided. Calculated risks of abuse are taken in order to preserve higher values.

The concurring and dissenting opinions galloped off in several directions. Justice Douglas's concurrence declared that TV and radio stand in the same protected position under the First Amendment as newspapers and magazines. And Douglas, along with Justice Stewart, was highly critical of any claimed "right of access", arguing that if government can *require* publication, then freedom of the press would be lost. Justices Brennan and Marshall dissented from the majority view, contending that if time could not be purchased for the airing of controversial political and social viewpoints, then broadcasting would continue to be filled with nothing but bland, noncontroversial programming.

Based upon this decision, then, a broadcaster has the judicially recognized right to refuse to sell commercial time to anyone except those within that one specific category guaranteed advertising access by Congress; legally qualified candidates for federal elective offices.[41]

Action for Children's Television (ACT), a citizens' group, had been pressuring the FCC since the early 1970s to reduce the amount of commercialism in television programs produced for children. In 1986, the Commission eliminated the commercial guidelines it had established for television broadcast licensees, including limitations on the number of commercial minutes per hour of programs designed for children.[42] ACT challenged this FCC action, and the Court of Appeals, D.C. Circuit, sustained the

---

[40] 412 U.S. 94, 93 S.Ct. 2080 (1973).

[41] Title 47 Section 312(a)(7) provides that station licenses may be revoked for refusing to allow reasonable access or to allow the purchase of reasonable amounts of time by legally qualified candidates for federal elective offices. For a more detailed discussion of this requirement, see chapter 12.

[42] Programming Commercialization Policies, 60 RR2d 526 (1986).

challenge, declaring that the Commission had not presented adequate justification for its assumption that the marketplace would operate to prevent over-commercialization of children's programs.[43]

In October 1988, a consensus children's television advertising bill, reflecting the compromise agreement the NAB had negotiated with various interest groups, was enacted by Congress but vetoed by President Reagan.[44]

Two years later Congress passed new legislation with many of the same provisions contained in the earlier compromise agreement. This time, however, President Bush's failure to veto the "Children's Television Act" allowed it to become law in October 1990.[45] The Act limited advertising contained in weekday television or cable TV programs intended for children to 10½ minutes per hour, while allowing 12 minutes per hour on the weekend.

In addition, the law also requires broadcasters to meet the educational needs of children or face possible license revocation by the FCC, and established a federal endowment to fund the production of educational programs for children. At the insistence of Action for Children's Television, the bill also directed the FCC to determine whether certain "super-hero" cartoon strips based on toy characters merchandised by the advertiser constitute "program-length" commercials, and therefore automatically violate the law by exceeding maximum advertising time standards for such programs.

In January, 1992, the FCC began an audit of broadcast stations to determine the degree of compliance with the rules the Commission adopted to enforce the Children's Television Act of 1990. The audit revealed seven stations and three cable systems in apparent violation of one or more provisions of the Act. Only one of the stations cited by the FCC was able to provide a satisfactory explanation of its programming practices. The others were either fined

[43] Action for Children's Television v. FCC, 821 F.2d 741 (D.C.Cir.1987). For more than a half century, the National Association of Broadcasters had been actively involved in limiting the amount of commercialization in programs designed for children, working with the networks to voluntarily limit the number of commercial minutes per hour. In 1982, however, the Justice Department decided to bring an antitrust action against the NAB, charging that its commercial codes were in constraint of trade. At that point, the NAB was forced to enter into a consent agreement to abandon all efforts to negotiate for further limitations upon broadcast advertising. See United States v. National Association of Broadcasters, 536 F.Supp. 149 (D.D.C.1982). As a result, the FCC's rescission of its commercial time limitations in 1986 left broadcasters free of any regulatory or self regulatory constraints upon commercialization.

[44] "Congress, in Overtime, Passes TVRO, Children's Ad bills," Broadcasting, October 24, 1988, p. 27.

[45] Children's TV Act of 1990, PL 101–437, 47 U.S.C.A. §§ 303a, 303b, 394. Implemented by the FCC, In the Matter of Policies and Rules Concerning Children's Television Programming, 68 RR2d 1615 (1991). See also, "President's Pocket Unveto Allows Children's Bill to Become Law," Broadcasting, October 22, 1990, p. 35.

or admonished.   One TV station, KWHE, Honolulu, was fined
$20,000 for its violations and two other stations, WFTS Tampa and
WTTA St. Petersburg were each fined $10,000.[46]

Continuing its effort to get compliance with the Act, the FCC
decided in February, 1993, to delay renewing the licenses of seven
TV stations in Ohio and Michigan until the stations demonstrated
they were meeting the educational needs of children.[47]

The Commission also issued a notice of inquiry to determine
whether it was proper for broadcasters to log entertainment shows
for children as programs meeting their informational needs, and
whether short "educational" inserts could properly be considered
as fulfilling broadcasters' obligations to children.[48]

Although the National Association of Broadcasters supported
the legislation, its constitutionality has been challenged by the
Radio–Television News Directors Association.   The RTNDA claims
the bill violated the First Amendment rights of broadcasters by
requiring them, "to provide programming and supporting advertising material as the federal government demands." [49]

Yet even if the Act does prove to be constitutional, its value in
protecting children from the hazards of over-commercialization
may turn out to be less significant than hoped.   Recent studies of
children's viewing behavior have revealed a continuing downward
trend in the amount of time spent watching broadcast television
each day.[50]   These studies do not suggest that children are actually
viewing less video entertainment each year, but rather that they
are spending more of their time watching rented cassettes on the
family VCRs where they can expose themselves to program-length
commercials like "The Care Bears Battle the Freeze Machine",
"Transformers: The Ultimate Doom" or "Mutant Ninja Turtles"
to their hearts' content without interference from any well-inten-
tioned adult interest group.

SEC. 70. ADVERTISING AND THE CONSTITUTION

Beginning in 1975, some commercial advertising began to receive protection under the First Amendment.

Commercial speech often is referred to as a stepchild of the
First Amendment.   Over the years, commercial speech—or adver-

[46] Harry Jessell, "Six TV's Hit for Violating Kids TV Rules," Broadcasting, Jan.
18, 1993, p. 95.

[47] "FCC Means Business," Broadcasting, Feb. 1, 1993, p. 36.

[48] Policies and Rules Concerning Children's Television Programming, 58 Fed. Reg.
14367 (1993).

[49] "Media Groups Challenge Kidvid Bill Constitutionality," Variety January 28,
1991, p. 44.

[50] See, for example, Nielsen 1990, Report on Television.

tising, to use an everyday term—was denied freedoms of speech and press granted to unconventional religious minorities,[51] to persons accused of blasphemy,[52] to free-love advocates,[53] and to persons sued for defaming public officials or public figures.[54]   During the 1970s and 1980s, the Supreme Court—however grudgingly and qualifiedly—held that just because a message is disseminated as paid-for advertising does not wipe out all First Amendment protection for that message.[55]   By the early 1990s, however, Supreme Court backing for constitutional support for advertising evidently was backsliding.[56]

Back in 1942, evidently with little reflection or receiving of evidence, the Supreme Court of the United States denied advertising First Amendment protection in Valentine v. Chrestensen.[57]   In 1940, F.J. Chrestensen owned a World War I submarine moored at an East River pier in New York City.   As World War II threatened to engulf the U.S., Chrestensen was trying to make money by charging for tours of a "U–Boat."   New York City officials, however, ordered him not to distribute handbills advertising the submarine.   Chrestensen's handbill listed an admission fee.   New York City Police Commissioner Lewis J. Valentine said that the city's Sanitary Code forbade distributing commercial advertising matter in the streets.[58]

Chrestensen changed his handbill.   One side then consisted of a notice about the submarine, but reference to the admission fee was deleted.   The other side of the redone handbill was used to protest against city policies he disliked.   Police officials then told Chrestensen he could distribute a handbill criticizing the city, but that invitation to visit the submarine was a commercial ad and was not permitted.   In 1942, the Supreme Court held unanimously that although streets may be used to communicate information and

[51] Minersville School Dist. v. Gobitis, 310 U.S. 586, 60 S.Ct. 1010 (1940).

[52] Joseph Burstyn, Inc. v. Wilson, 343 U.S. 495, 72 S.Ct. 777 (1952).

[53] Kingsley Intern. Pictures Corp. v. Regents of N.Y.U., 360 U.S. 684, 688–689, 79 S.Ct. 1362, 1365 (1959).

[54] See New York Times Co. v. Sullivan, 376 U.S. 254, 84 S.Ct. 710 (1964) and later cases, including Rosenblatt v. Baer, 383 U.S. 75, 86 S.Ct. 669 (1966); Curtis Pub. Co. v. Butts, Associated Press v. Walker, 388 U.S. 130, 87 S.Ct. 1975 (1967), and St. Amant v. Thompson, 390 U.S. 727, 88 S.Ct. 1323 (1968).

[55] Bigelow v. Virginia, 421 U.S. 809, 95 S.Ct. 2222 (1975); Virginia State Board of Pharmacy v. Virginia Citizens Consumer Council, 425 U.S. 748, 96 S.Ct. 1817 (1976).

[56] See Posadas de Puerto Rico v. Tourism Co., 478 U.S. 328, 106 S.Ct. 2968 (1986); Board of Trustees of the State University of New York v. Fox, 492 U.S. 469, 109 S.Ct. 3028 (1989), and Austin v. Michigan Chamber of Commerce, 494 U.S. 652, 110 S.Ct. 1391 (1990).

[57] 316 U.S. 52, 62 S.Ct. 920 (1942).

[58] Valentine v. Chrestensen, 316 U.S. 52, 54, 62 S.Ct. 920, 921 (1942).

disseminate opinion, the Constitution does not restrain government from controlling "purely commercial advertising." [59]

The Court's decision in Valentine v. Chrestensen was brief, only five pages in the official *United States Reports*. Mr. Justice Owen J. Roberts' opinion for the Court—which slipped in the virtually unsupported statement that commercial advertising is not entitled to First Amendment protections—ignored a number of relevant cases he might well have cited.[60]

But that's where matters stood; 1942's Valentine v. Chrestensen decision stated the law for some years to come. In 1959, in a now-famous concurring opinion in Cammarano v. United States, Justice William O. Douglas complained that the Chrestensen decision was "casual, almost offhand. And it has not survived reflection." Cammarano, a beer distributor, had tried to deduct, as a business expense, a contribution to a fund used to buy political ads to oppose a ballot measure which would have turned all wine and beer sales over to a state agency. Although he concurred in the decision denying Cammarano the IRS deduction, Justice Douglas wrote: " * * * I find it impossible to say that the owners of the * * * business who were fighting for their lives in opposing these initiative [ballot] measures were not exercising First Amendment rights." [61]

N.Y. Times v. Sullivan (1964) and Advertising

Oddly enough, a "breakthrough" case toward protecting advertising under the Constitution is little thought of as a "commercial speech case." In part, however, that's exactly what the landmark 1964 libel decision of New York Times v. Sullivan was. In that case, the Supreme Court granted First Amendment protection for advertisements which deal with important political or social matters. The *Sullivan* case, discussed fully in libel chapters earlier in this book, carefully distinguished the advertising involved in Valentine v. Chrestensen from the advertising at issue in New York Times v. Sullivan. Libel plaintiff Sullivan's attorneys argued that libelous statements had been published in an advertisement by The New York Times. Therefore, the plaintiff's contention was that "the constitutional guarantees of freedom of speech and of the press are inapplicable * * * at least so far as the Times is con-

[59] Ibid.

[60] See Mr. Justice William O. Douglas's concurring opinion in Cammarano v. United States, 358 U.S. 498, 513–515, 79 S.Ct. 524, 533–535 (1959), listing two cases prior to the Chrestensen case which approved broad control over commercial advertising: Fifth Avenue Coach Co. v. New York, 221 U.S. 467, 31 S.Ct. 709 (1911), and Packer Corp. v. Utah, 285 U.S. 105, 52 S.Ct. 273 (1932). Justice Douglas noted that in the latter case, no First Amendment issue was raised.

[61] 358 U.S. 498, 79 S.Ct. 524 (1959).

cerned, because the allegedly libelous statements were published as part of a paid, 'commercial' advertisement." [62]

The Supreme Court held that such a reliance on the rule Valentine v. Chrestensen was "wholly misplaced." Writing for the *Sullivan* majority, Justice William J. Brennan, Jr. declared: [63]

> The publication here [in Times v. Sullivan] was not a "commercial" advertisement in the sense in which the word was used in *Chrestensen*. It communicated information, expressed opinion, recited grievances, protested claimed abuses, and sought financial support on behalf of a [civil rights] movement whose existence and objectives are matters of the highest public concern. * * * That the Times was paid for publishing the advertisement is as immaterial in this connection as is the fact that newspapers and books are sold. * * * Any other conclusion would discourage newspapers from carrying "editorial advertisements" of this type, and so might shut off an important outlet for the promulgation of information and ideas by persons who do not themselves have access to publishing facilities . . .

What advertising, then, was protected by the First Amendment after New York Times v. Sullivan (1964)? Not all advertising—and especially, not advertising for an illegal activity—the Supreme Court said in Pittsburgh Press Co. v. Pittsburgh Commission on Human Relations (1973). A Pittsburgh ordinance empowered the city's human relations commission to issue cease and desist orders against discriminatory hiring practices. The Pittsburgh Press ran "Help Wanted" ads in columns labeled "Jobs—Male Interest," and "Jobs—Female Interest." The city commission sought a cease and desist order.[64]

Arguing for the Pittsburgh Press, attorneys contended that the order violated the First Amendment because it tampered with the newspaper's editorial judgment in accepting and placing ads. Writing for the Court's five-member majority, Justice Lewis Powell disagreed: Discrimination in employment is illegal commercial activity under the city's ordinance. "We have no doubt that a newspaper constitutionally could be forbidden to publish a want ad proposing a sale of narcotics or soliciting prostitutes." [65]

[62] New York Times Co. v. Sullivan, 376 U.S. 254, 265–266, 84 S.Ct. 710, 718 (1964).

[63] Ibid.

[64] 413 U.S. 376, 377, 93 S.Ct. 2553, 2555 (1973).

[65] Pittsburgh Press Co. v. Pittsburgh Commission on Human Relations, 413 U.S. 376, 387, 93 S.Ct. 2553, 2560 (1973).

Dissenting in *Pittsburgh Press,* Chief Justice Warren Burger declared that the cease and desist order against the newspaper was in fact a prior restraint on publication.[66]

Bigelow v. Virginia (1975)

It should be emphasized that the Court, in New York Times v. Sullivan, drew a distinction between "commercial advertising" which attempted to sell products or services and other kinds of expression. This distinction, however, was too oversimplified. Some products or services—by their very nature—are matters of public debate or controversy, and advertisements for those products or services may have the characteristics and importance of political speech. A 1975 Virginia case involving advertising about the availability and legality of abortions in New York—the case called Bigelow v. Virginia—showed that "commercial speech" can have some degree of constitutional protection.

Early in 1971, an advertisement was published in The Virginia Weekly, a newspaper focusing its coverage on the University of Virginia. Jeffrey C. Bigelow was managing editor and a director of the newspaper when it published this ad: [67]

"UNWANTED PREGNANCY
LET US HELP YOU
Abortions are now legal in New York

There are no residency requirements.
FOR IMMEDIATE PLACEMENT IN
ACCREDITED HOSPITALS AND
CLINICS AT LOW COST
Contact
WOMAN'S PAVILION
515 Madison Avenue
New York, N.Y. 10022
or call any time
(212) 371–6670 or (212) 371–6550
AVAILABLE 7 DAYS A WEEK
STRICTLY CONFIDENTIAL. We will
make all arrangements for you and help
you with information and counseling."

A Virginia court convicted Bigelow of violating a section of the Virginia Code: "If any person, by publication, lecture, advertisement, or by the sale or circulation of any publication, or in any other manner, shall encourage or prompt the procuring of an

[66] Pittsburgh Press Co. v. Pittsburgh Commission on Human Relations, 413 U.S. 376, 394, 93 S.Ct. 2553, 2563 (1973).

[67] Bigelow v. Virginia, 421 U.S. 809, 810, 95 S.Ct. 2222, 2227 (1975).

abortion or miscarriage, he shall be guilty of a misdemeanor." [68] The Virginia Supreme Court affirmed Bigelow's conviction, declaring that because the ad involved was a "commercial advertisement," Bigelow's First Amendment claim was not valid. Such an advertisement, said the Virginia Supreme Court, " 'may be constitutionally prohibited by the state, particularly where, as here, the advertising relates to the medical-health field.' " [69]

The Supreme Court overruled the Virginia Supreme Court. Writing for a 7–2 majority, Justice Harry Blackmun concluded that Virginia courts erred in assuming that advertising is not entitled to First Amendment protection. Justice Blackmun distinguished the Virginia case from *Chrestensen*. He wrote that the handbill ad involved in *Chrestensen* did no more than propose a purely commercial transaction, while The Virginia Weekly's ad about abortions "contained factual material of clear 'public interest.' " [70]

The existence of the Women's Pavilion in New York City was "not unnewsworthy" and also pertained to constitutional privacy interests.[71] A State, Justice Blackmun wrote, "may not * * * bar a citizen of another State from disseminating information about an activity that is legal in another State." Although advertising "may be subject to reasonable regulation that serves a legitimate public interest," some commercial speech is still worthy of constitutional protection. "The relationship of speech to the marketplace of products or services does not make it valueless in the marketplace of ideas," Justice Blackmun declared.[72]

What Justice Blackmun's majority opinion called for, of course, is a balancing of interests. The courts, and most especially the Supreme Court, have final say in deciding what is "merely" commercial speech as compared to ads which are "newsworthy" or politically or socially important enough to be anointed with "the public interest." Such vagueness, of course, lends little predictability to this area of the law.

Virginia State Board of Pharmacy v. Virginia Citizens Consumer Council, Inc. (1976)

What the Supreme Court started in 1975 with the *Bigelow* case continued the next year with the decision in the Virginia State Board of Pharmacy (VSBP) case. In fact, an excellent study of advertising law emphasized—as of 1991—that VSBP represented

[68] Bigelow v. Virginia, 421 U.S. 809, 814, 95 S.Ct. 2222, 2228 (1975).

[69] Bigelow v. Virginia, 421 U.S. 809, 814, 95 S.Ct. 2222, 2229 (1975), quoting Bigelow v. Commonwealth, 213 Va. 191, 193–195, 191 S.E.2d 173, 174–176 (1972).

[70] Bigelow v. Virginia, 421 U.S. 809, 822, 95 S.Ct. 2222, 2233 (1975).

[71] Ibid., citing Roe v. Wade, 410 U.S. 113, 93 S.Ct. 705 (1973), and Doe v. Bolton, 410 U.S. 179, 93 S.Ct. 739 (1973).

[72] Bigelow v. Virginia, 421 U.S. 809, 826, 95 S.Ct. 2222, 2235 (1975).

the decision in which the Supreme Court gave broadest First Amendment protection for commercial advertising.[73]

The Virginia State Board of Pharmacy case was not directly about a political or social issue. Instead, it dealt with a matter of price advertising. It arose because a Virginia statute forbade "the advertising of the price for any prescription drug." This statute was challenged in a lawsuit by two consumer organizations and by a Virginia citizen who had to take prescription drugs on a daily basis. The plaintiffs claimed that the First Amendment entitled users of prescription drugs to receive information from pharmacists—through advertisements or other promotional means—about the price of those drugs.[74]

By a 7–1 vote expressed via Justice Blackmun's majority opinion in *Virginia State Board of Pharmacy,* the Court overturned the state's ban on advertising of prescription drug prices.[75]

> ... [T]he question whether there is a First Amendment exception for "commercial speech" is squarely before us. Our pharmacist does not wish to editorialize on any subject, cultural, philosophical, or political. He does not wish to report any particularly newsworthy fact, or to make generalized observations even about commercial matters. The "idea" he wishes to communicate is simply this: "I will sell you the X prescription drug at Y price."

The Supreme Court declared that the consumer had a great interest in the free flow of commercial information—perhaps a greater interest than in the day's most important political debate. The individuals hardest hit by the suppression of prescription price information, wrote Justice Blackmun, were the poor, the sick and the old. Therefore, despite the State of Virginia's interest in protecting professionalism among pharmacists, the societal interest in making prescription price information available through advertising was protected under the First Amendment. Thus, the Supreme Court declared the Virginia statute invalid.[76]

Subsequent cases indicated that commercial speech could receive constitutional protection in a variety of areas. Later in 1976, for example, the Horner–Rausch Optical Co. case, decided by a

---

[73] For an excellent discussion of the Virginia Board of Pharmacy case and, indeed, of the key cases involving advertising and the First Amendment, see Richard T. Kaplar, Advertising Rights, The Neglected Freedom: Toward a New Doctrine of Commercial Speech (Washington, D.C.: The Media Institute, 1991).

[74] Virginia State Board of Pharmacy v. Virginia Citizens Consumer Council, Inc., 425 U.S. 748, 96 S.Ct. 1817 (1976).

[75] Virginia State Board of Pharmacy v. Virginia Citizens Consumer Council, Inc., 425 U.S. 748, 759–761, 96 S.Ct. 1817, 1824–1825 (1976).

[76] Virginia State Board of Pharmacy v. Virginia Citizens Consumer Council, Inc., 425 U.S. 748, 763, 96 S.Ct. 1817, 1826 (1976).

Tennessee court, declared an administrative regulation against price ads for eyeglasses to be unconstitutional.[77] And in 1977, the U.S. Supreme Court decided the now famous "lawyer ad case," Bates v. State Bar of Arizona.[78]   By a 5–4 margin, the Court held that lawyers have a constitutional right to advertise their prices for their various services.

Justice Blackmun's majority opinion in *Bates* said, "[I]t is entirely possible that advertising will serve to reduce, not to advance, the cost of legal services to the consumer."   In this case, the consumer's need for information about the cost of legal services was held to outweigh the legal profession's interest in having a regulated self-restraint against virtually all kinds of advertising by attorneys.   The majority opinion added that the time, place and manner of advertising may be regulated, and that false or misleading advertising by lawyers may be forbidden.[79]

> In holding that advertising by attorneys may not be subjected to blanket suppression, and that the advertisement in question is protected, we, of course, do not hold that advertising by attorneys may not be regulated in any way.   * * * Advertising that is false, deceptive or misleading of course is subject to restraint.

> * * *

> The constitutional issue in this case is only whether the State may prevent the publication in a newspaper of appellants' truthful advertisement concerning the availability and terms of routine legal services.   We rule simply that the flow of such information may not be restrained, and we therefore hold the present application of the disciplinary rule against appellants to be violative of the First Amendment.

The Bellotti Case (1978): Protecting Corporate Speech

If abortion clinics, pharmacists, and lawyers have some First Amendment protection for their ads, what about corporations right to exercise political speech?   In First National Bank of Boston v.

[77] Horner–Rausch Optical Co. v. Ashley, 547 S.W.2d 577 (Tenn.App.1976).

[78] Bates v. State Bar of Arizona, 433 U.S. 350, 97 S.Ct. 2691 (1977).

[79] Bates v. State Bar of Arizona, 433 U.S. 350, 383, 384, 97 S.Ct. 2691, 2706, 2708, 2709 (1977).   Advertising by attorneys can go too far, however, when it includes a lawyer's visiting the family of a person injured in an auto accident, and even visiting with the driver herself in her hospital room.   Personal solicitation of that nature (bedpan chasing?) is unreasonable. See Ohralik v. Ohio State Bar Ass'n, 436 U.S. 447, 98 S.Ct. 1912 (1978).   If lawyer advertising is fundamentally misleading, it will not be tolerated: See Peel v. Attorney Registration and Disciplinary Com'n of Illinois, 496 U.S. 91, 110 S.Ct. 2281 (1990).

Bellotti (1978),[80] the U.S. Supreme Court invalidated a Massachusetts statute forbidding business corporations from making contributions or expenditures " 'for the purpose of * * * influencing or affecting the vote on any question submitted to the voters, other than one materially affecting the property, business, or assets of the corporation.' " That statute provided that a corporation violating its provisions could be fined $50,000 and that its officers could be fined up to $10,000, imprisoned for up to one year, or both.

The bank wanted to spend money to publicize its views on a Massachusetts constitutional amendment being submitted to voters as a ballot question. The amendment would have allowed the legislature to place a graduated tax on individual incomes. Massachusetts Attorney General Francis X. Bellotti told the First National Bank of Boston that he would enforce the statute. The bank responded with an action asking that the statute be declared unconstitutional. The Supreme Judicial Court of Massachusetts upheld the statute as valid.[81]

The U.S. Supreme Court, however, found the Massachusetts statute unconstitutional. Writing for the Court, Justice Lewis Powell declared that the political argument the bank wished to make "is at the heart of the First Amendment's protection." He added, "[t]he question in this case, simply put, is whether the corporate identity of the speaker deprives the proposed speech of what otherwise would be its clear entitlement to protection." [82]

Justice Powell cited the Court's 1970s commercial speech cases—including *Virginia State Board of Pharmacy*—as illustrating "that the First Amendment goes beyond protection of the press and the self-expression of individuals to prohibit government from limiting the stock of information from which members of the public may draw." Thus corporations' political speech was entitled to First Amendment protection.[83]

Justice Byron White dissented, and was joined by Justices Brennan and Marshall. He argued that the Massachusetts statute did not infringe on First Amendment interests, but instead protected them. Corporations that had amassed great wealth should thus be prevented from having "an unfair advantage in the political process." White wrote: [84]

[80] First National Bank of Boston v. Bellotti, 435 U.S. 765, 98 S.Ct. 1407 (1978).

[81] First National Bank of Boston v. Attorney General, 371 Mass. 773, 359 N.E.2d 1262 at 1268 (1977).

[82] First National Bank of Boston v. Bellotti, 435 U.S. 765, 778, 98 S.Ct. 1407, 1416 (1978).

[83] First National Bank of Boston v. Bellotti, 435 U.S. 765, 783, 98 S.Ct. 1407, 1409 (1978).

[84] First National Bank of Boston v. Bellotti, 435 U.S. 765, 809, 98 S.Ct. 1407, 1433 (1978).

Indeed, what some have considered to be the principal function of the First Amendment, the use of communication as a means of self-expression, self-realization, and self-fulfillment, is not at all furthered by corporate speech.

Freedom of expression for *self-fulfillment* is an important First Amendment value to many theorists. Other scholars hold that the First Amendment's true role is mainly *utilitarian,* to provide sufficient freedom of expression to enable citizens to participate fully and effectively in self-government. However, neither the proponents of self-fulfillment nor the adherents of a utilitarian theory of the First Amendment tend to look kindly on expanding freedom in the area of commercial speech.[85]

In sum, as Justice White suggested in his dissent, the decision in *Virginia State Board of Pharmacy* sent mixed messages. The Court, without firmly grounding its majority opinion in a defensible theory of the First Amendment, wobbled understandably when trying to define commercial messages which have public interest and those which do not. The Court said, rather lamely, that it could detect "commonsense differences" between commercial speech and, say, political speech.[86] If, indeed, Virginia State Board of Pharmacy is to be the all-time highwater mark for commercial speech, then advertising will continue to be the unwelcome passenger in the First Amendment's lifeboat.

Central Hudson (1980) and the Four–Part Test

In 1980, the Supreme Court of the United States created an important test to try to outline just when advertising might be deemed worthy of constitutional protection. This case, Central Hudson Gas & Electric Corp. v. Public Service Commission of New York, involved a commission order that the utility stop promoting consumption of electricity. This order was promulgated during an energy shortage, under the assumption that cutting Central Hudson's "buy appliances" advertising might assist in energy conservation. The U.S. Supreme Court, however, invalidated New York's ban on promotional advertising by electric utilities. Justice Powell, writing for an 8–1 Court, laid out a four-part test: [87]

In commercial speech cases, then, a four-part analysis has developed. At the outset, we must determine [1] whether the expression is protected by the First Amendment. For

[85] For discussion of such First Amendment values, see Kaplar, op. cit., pp. 38–40, and Steven Shiffrin, "The First Amendment and Economic Regulation: Away from a General Theory of the First Amendment," 78 Northwestern U.L.Rev. 1212 (1983, at pp. 1223–1251).

[86] Footnote 24 in Virginia Pharmacy case, discussed in Kaplar, op. cit., at p. 52.

[87] Central Hudson Gas & Electric Corp. v. Public Service Com'n of New York, 447 U.S. 557, 100 S.Ct. 2343 (1980).

commercial speech to come within that provision, it at least must concern lawful activity and not be misleading. [2] Next, we ask whether the asserted governmental interest is substantial. If both inquiries yield positive answers, we must determine [3] whether the regulation directly advances the governmental interest asserted, and [4] whether it is not more extensive than necessary to serve that interest.

Because advertising promoting use of electricity was seen as protected by the First Amendment, and because the ad was neither misleading nor "unlawful," the New York regulation was overturned as unconstitutional. Although the state had a substantial interest in energy conservation, the state's regulation was more extensive than necessary. No demonstration was made that the state's interest in energy conservation could not have been served adequately by a more limited restriction on the content of promotional advertisements.[88]

Narrowing Constitutional Protection: Posadas de Puerto Rico v. Tourism Company (1986)

For eleven years deciding the abortion advertising case of Bigelow v. Virginia (1975),[89] the U.S. Supreme Court held that if a product or service was legal and was the subject of public or corporate interest, truthful ads for that product or service had First Amendment protection.[90] As noted earlier in this Section, this protection covered ads for abortion referral services, prices of prescription drugs, eyeglasses, lawyers, banks' political stances, promotions by a public utility, even during an energy shortage.

This expansiveness came to a halt in July, 1986, when the Supreme Court ruled that government may forbid truthful ads for some products or services, even though they are legal for sale. Not surprisingly, this 1986 case—involving Puerto Rico's regulations against local ads promoting gambling in Puerto Rico's legal casinos—alarmed the tobacco and liquor industries in the United

---

[88] Central Hudson Gas & Elec. Corp. v. Public Service Com'n, 447 U.S. 557, 100 S.Ct. 2343 (1980). See also a related case, Consolidated Edison Co. of New York, Inc. v. Public Service Commission of New York, 447 U.S. 530, 100 S.Ct. 2326 (1980), 6 Med.L.Rptr. 1518. There, the Court struck down an order forbidding the utility's including in mailings statements of "Con Ed's" views on public policy controversies. Powell, quoting First National Bank of Boston v. Bellotti, 435 U.S. 765, 98 S.Ct. 1407 (1978), wrote for the Court that the Commission's censorship attempt "strikes at the heart of the freedom to speak."

[89] 421 U.S. 809, 95 S.Ct. 2222 (1975).

[90] See also New York Times Co. v. Sullivan, 376 U.S. 254, 84 S.Ct. 710 (1964), the pivotal libel case extending First Amendment protection to ads dealing with major social or political concerns.

States.[91]

The Puerto Rico Legislature, when it legalized regulated casino gambling in 1948, also provided that " '[n]o gambling room shall be permitted to advertise ... to the public of Puerto Rico.' "[92] The Tourism Company of Puerto Rico, a governmental agency, created regulations to implement the no-advertising-in-Puerto Rico ban called for by the statute.

When a hotel-casino challenged the advertising regulations as unconstitutional, it did seem to have plenty to complain about. The regulations were sweepingly broad. For example, consider this Tourism Company memo: [93]

> "This prohibition includes the use of the word 'casino' in matchbooks, lighters, envelopes, inter-office and/or external correspondence, invoices, napkins, brochures, menus, elevators, glasses, plates, lobbies, banners, flyers, paper holders, pencils, telephone books, directories, bulletin boards or in any hotel dependency or object which may be accessible to the public in Puerto Rico."

When the case reached the U.S. Supreme Court, Justice (subsequently Chief Justice) William H. Rehnquist wrote for the Court's five member majority. He said the issue was whether the Puerto Rico statute and regulations "impermissibly suppressed commercial speech in violation of the First Amendment and the equal protection and due process guarantees of the United States Constitution." [94]

Justice Rehnquist said that this case involved " * * * the restriction of pure commercial speech which does 'no more than propose a commercial transaction.' " [95] That meant, he wrote, that First Amendment discussion of this case was controlled by the four-part analysis set forth in the Central Hudson Gas & Electric Corp. case discussed earlier in this Section. Recall that the *Central Hudson* test of whether commercial speech qualified for First Amendment protection involved four questions:

(1) Does ad concern a lawful activity?, and is *not* fraudulent or misleading?

(2) Does government have a substantial interest in restricting this commercial speech?

[91] Stuart Taylor, Jr., "High Court, 5–4, Sharply Limits Constitutional Protection for Ads," The New York Times, July 2, 1986, p. 2 (National Edition).

[92] Posadas de Puerto Rico Associates v. Tourism Co. of Puerto Rico, 478 U.S. 328, 332, 106 S.Ct. 2968, 2972 (1986), 13 Med.L.Rptr. 1033, 1035.

[93] 478 U.S. at 333, 106 S.Ct. at 2873, 13 Med.L.Rptr. at 1035.

[94] 478 U.S. at 328, 106 S.Ct. at 2971, 13 Med.L.Rptr. at 1034.

[95] 478 U.S. at 340, 106 S.Ct. at 2976, 13 Med.L.Rptr. at 1038–1039.

(3) Does the regulation directly advance that governmental interest?

(4) Is the regulation more extensive than necessary to serve that governmental interest?

The Court's majority opinion concluded that advertising of casino gambling in Puerto Rico "concerns a lawful activity and is not misleading or fraudulent, at least in the abstract." [96] Even so, Justice Rehnquist's majority opinion deferred to Puerto Rico's legislative judgment: It was not an unreasonable policy choice to believe that excessive casino gambling by Puerto Rico's residents would produce great harm to citizens welfare. The Court's majority concluded that the hotel/casino's First Amendment claims had been rejected properly.

He wrote acidly that even though products or activities including cigarettes, alcoholic beverages, and prostitution had been legalized for sale in some jurisdictions did not mean that their advertising could not be limited.[97]

In dissent, Justice Brennan (joined by Justices Blackmun and Marshall) depicted the Court's majority as encroaching substantially on free expression. He conceded that government may regulate the content of commercial speech to stop dissemination of false, deceptive, or misleading information. Brennan noted that for a decade before *Posadas* was decided, the U.S. Supreme Court consistently invalidated restrictions which would deprive consumers of accurate information about products and services legally offered for sale. Justice John Paul Stevens also dissented, calling the Puerto Rico ad prohibitions a regime of prior restraint articulating a hopelessly vague and unpredictable standard.[98]

The extent of the fall-out from *Posadas* in shriveling gains toward admittedly limited First Amendment protection for advertising remains to be seen. It might be argued that the Court bowed too low in the direction of federalism, of letting various states or jurisdictions create their own rules legislatively without federal judicial interference. What, however, was the net effect in Puerto Rico? Citizens of that Commonwealth surely know the casinos are there in various hotels. After all, they work in the casinos, and may gamble there if they choose, whether or not those gaming establishments are advertised locally in addition to in northern American cities to attract *turista* dollars.

More significantly, the Posadas decision makes it far more difficult to overturn State laws that constrain commercial free

[96] 478 U.S. at 340–341, 106 S.Ct. at 2975, 13 Med.L.Rptr. at 1039.

[97] 478 U.S. at 346, 106 S.Ct. at 2977.

[98] 478 U.S. at 361, 106 S.Ct. at 2988.

speech. The Central Hudson test Justice Rehnquist claimed to be applying in the Posadas case had permitted States to use only the "least restrictive means" available in regulating advertising messages. In fact, however, Posadas simply requires a State to demonstrate that any advertising laws it adopts are "reasonable" ones.[99]

Banning All Tobacco Ads?

In any event, the interplay of the *Posadas* decision with efforts to get rid of tobacco advertising truly had the attention of cigarette manufacturers in the late 1980s and early 1990s. Back in 1972, of course, the U.S. Supreme Court affirmed—with no explanation—an Act of Congress barring cigarette ads from radio and television. And, in the 1980s, the American Medical Association, among others, urged a ban on all cigarette advertising, including newspapers, magazines, and billboards. Complaints rose from the tobacco and liquor interests that such a ban on print advertising would be unconstitutional. Voices raised in such protests included the American Tobacco Institute and the American Civil Liberties Union.[1]

The growing chorus of concern about interrelationships between tobacco and health may indeed mean that the banning of cigarette ads from radio and television may be only the first wave of control. Starting in 1986, Rep. Michael Synar (D–Okla.) repeatedly introduced legislation calling for banning "consumer sales promotion" of all tobacco products. That meant all forms of tobacco intended for human consumption: cigarettes, little cigars, pipe or loose rolling tobacco, chewing tobacco, snuff, and so on.

Tobacco use has been targeted by virtually all doctors as the largest preventable cause of death in the United States, and is assailed as associated with the unnecessary deaths of more than 300,000 Americans annually.

Unsurprisingly, this has led to multiple efforts to pass legislation to silence the messenger, to put a stop to advertising of tobacco products. For example, consider Rep. Synar's 1986 bill to outlaw "commercial sales promotion" of tobacco products. "Commercial sales promotion" included not only radio and TV commercials but also newspaper and magazine ads. That Synar bill also proposed forbidding of premiums and samples, and of sponsorship of athletic, artistic, or other events under the registered brand name of tobacco

[99] See Denise M. Trauth and John L. Huffman, "The Commercial Speech Doctrine: Posadas Revisionism," Communication and the Law (Feb. 1988), pp. 43–56.

[1] See "Smoking, Smoke and Free Speech," New York Times editorial, Aug. 15, 1986, p. 22; "Free speech under assault," Mobil Oil Corp. ad, The New York Times, Dec. 18, 1986.

products.[2]

Regulatory proposals have not been received tamely by the tobacco industry. In the 1980s and 1990s, the tobacco industry wrapped itself in the American flag and the Bill of Rights, barraging mailboxes with freedom-invoking arguments. Regulatory rollbacks favored by the Republican majority in Congress elected in 1994 may mean less pressure to stop tobacco advertising.

Strengthening Government Ad Regulation: State University of New York v. Fox (1989).

Greater willingness by the Supreme Court to allow state regulation of commercial messages showed in 1990 in a decision seemingly based on a trivial fact situation. The U.S. Supreme Court treated the facts of the case as if "Tupperware Parties" had been held in a State University of New York (SUNY) dormitory. This sales technique—a presentation made by students in this instance representing American Future Systems (AFS)—violated a regulation forbidding private commercial enterprises from operating on New York State university campuses.

Salesperson Todd Fox was arrested by SUNY–Cortland campus police while conducting a demonstration in a dorm. Ultimately, after a trial, a federal district court held that SUNY dormitories were not a public forum and that the regulation was reasonable in view of a dormitory's purpose.[3] The student salespersons' claim that their First Amendment rights were abridged by the university, however, was upheld by the U.S. Court of Appeals for the Second Circuit.[4] The Second Circuit court turned to Part Four of the *Central Hudson* test, holding that the regulation applied by SUNY–Cortland was defective in that it did not apply the least restrictive means of regulating commercial speech.[5]

The U.S. Supreme Court, however, overturned the Court of Appeals, thus upholding the university regulation of commercial activity in dormitories. Writing for a Court divided 6–3, Justice Antonin Scalia again diluted Central Hudson's fourth part (commercial speech regulations should be accomplished by the "least restrictive means").[6] With Justice Scalia's wording, the regulation

---

[2] H.R. 1272, 100th Congress, 1st Sess. (Feb. 25, 1987). See also "Advertising of Tobacco Products," Hearings before the Subcommittee on Health and the Environment, House of Representatives, 99th Congress, 2nd Sess., July 18 and Aug. 1, 1986. For a discussion of 1989 and 1990 bills to curtail tobacco and alcohol ads, see Kaplar, op. cit., pp. 6–8.

[3] Board of Trustees of the State University of New York v. Fox, 492 U.S. 469, 109 S.Ct. 3028 (1989).

[4] Ibid., at 471, 109 S.Ct. at 3030.

[5] Ibid., at 473, 109 S.Ct. at 3022–3033.

[6] Ibid., at 475, 109 S.Ct. at 3035.

of commercial speech should represent "not necessarily the least restrictive means but * * * a means narrowly tailored to achieve the desired objective." [7]

Scalia argued it was essential for the Court to maintain clear distinctions between commercial and non-commercial expression in order to protect traditional free speech rights from being eroded by those restraints States might lawfully impose on advertising messages. Yet, as Justice Blackmun, joined by Justices Marshall and Brennan, pointed out, to achieve this objective Scalia appeared to be indulging in the same type of judicial activism that conservative jurists had criticized so vehemently in the past.[8]

Cincinnati v. Discovery Network, Inc. (1993)

A city has an interest in keeping litter off its streets, but can it regulate distribution of free-circulation magazines that get taken from newsracks and thrown about?

Discovery Network, Inc. had permission from Cincinnati to place its newsracks on public property to distribute free-circulation magazines consisting mostly of advertising. In 1990, evidently because of littering around the newsracks, the city revoked permission, stating that the magazines were "commercial handbills." A pre-existing Cincinnati ordinance forbade distribution of commercial handbills.[9]

A U.S. District Court held that although the city may regulate newsracks for safety and esthetics, its regulations had to meet a standard set by the U.S. Supreme Court in State University of New York v. Fox (1989).[10] That standard said the regulation of speech "should be accomplished by a means narrowly tailored to achieve the desired objective." So under that decision, a government entity regulating commercial speech bears the burden of establishing a "reasonable fit" between the ends and the means chosen to achieve those ends.[11]

When this case reached the U.S. Supreme Court, Justice Stevens declared for a 6–3 majority that although the city's interest in preventing litter had some validity, it was not enough to discriminate against the free circulation of these magazines that were predominantly advertising. Justice Stevens wrote: [12]

[7] Ibid., at 475, 109 S.Ct. at 3035.

[8] Ibid., at 479, 109 S.Ct. at 3038.

[9] Cincinnati v. Discovery Network, Inc., 113 S.Ct. 1505 (1993), 21 Med.L.Rptr. 1161, 1162.

[10] Board of Trustees of State University of New York v. Fox, 492 U.S. 469, 109 S.Ct. 3028 (1989).

[11] Cincinnati v. Discovery Network, Inc., 113 S.Ct. 1505 (1993), 21 Med.L.Rptr. 1161, 1163.

[12] Ibid., 1165.

In our view, the city's argument attaches more importance to the distinction between commercial speech than our cases warrant and seriously underestimates the value of commercial speech.

Concurring, Justice Blackmun likened unresolved issues remaining form the Central Hudson decision of 1980 (see discussion earlier in this section) to chickens coming home to roost. He wrote: " ... I continue to believe that the commercial speech analysis set forth in Central Hudson and as refined in Fox [Board of Trustees v. State University of New York v. Fox] affords insufficient protection for truthful, non-coercive commercial speech concerning lawful activities." [13]

Dissenting, Chief Justice Rehnquist—joined by Justices White and Thomas—complained that the Cincinnati newsracks decision will "unduly hamper our cities' efforts to come to grips with the unique problems posed by the dissemination of commercial speech." [14]

Austin v. Michigan Chamber of Commerce (1990)

Although the Supreme Court found constitutional support for corporate political advertising in First National Bank of Boston v. Bellotti (1978), a 1990 decision marked a retreat in that area. In Austin v. Michigan Chamber of Commerce, the Supreme Court voted 6–3 to uphold a Michigan statute forbidding corporations from using their general treasury funds for "independent expenditures" to support or oppose political candidates seeking state offices.[15] In other words, corporate political ad expenditures concerning candidates had to be made from separate funds used only for political purposes.

In essence, this decision simply permitted a State to prevent wealthy private organizations from financing a political campaign directly from their own general resources. Even so, it can be seen as diminishing to some extent those broad guarantees of corporate free speech granted by the Court in the Central Hudson case.[16]

Despite this post-Posadas tendency of the Court to recognize a more extensive role for State law in the field of commercial speech regulation, it seems unlikely that those Constitutional protections given this type of expression during the 1970s will be greatly

[13] Ibid., p. 1170.

[14] Ibid., 1173.

[15] Austin v. Michigan Chamber of Commerce, 494 U.S. 652, 110 S.Ct. 1391 (1990).

[16] Central Hudson Gas & Elec. Corp. v. Public Service Com'n of New York, 447 U.S. 557, 100 S.Ct. 2343 (1980).

lessened.[17]   Instead, it is more likely that the Court simply will permit States to begin exercising broader regulatory control over the advertising of certain specific products such as tobacco or liquor, where the public policy interests of the State are most clearly evident, and where social values of those products being marketed are most difficult to defend.

[17] For a review of recent federal judicial decisions applying the Posadas test, see Roxanne Hovland and Ronald E. Taylor, "Advertising and Commercial Speech Since the 1986 Posadas Case," Journalism Quarterly (Winter, 1990), pp. 1083–1089.

Chapter 12

COPYRIGHT: PROTECTION AND CONSTRAINT

SEC. 71. THE RATIONALE OF COPYRIGHT LAW

Copyright law provides a financial incentive for creativity while ensuring that the public will eventually gain full access to the copyrighted work.

Copyright poses a real dilemma for anyone who believes in freedom of expression. Copyright laws empower the owner of a copyrighted work to restrict its distribution, its duplication or even the dissemination of other works too closely similar to that of the copyright owner. In reality, then, copyright inhibits the free flow of ideas.

But, if copyright protection didn't exist, there would be no financial incentive for anyone to write a novel, compose a song or produce a feature film. If the law did not recognize a right to own and control the use of intellectual property, authors or composers would have no way to prevent anyone from taking their work without permission and exploiting it without compensating them for its use.

From the standpoint of the marketplace of ideas, then, the ideal copyright act should offer those who create intellectual property a carefully balanced trade-off; sufficient legal protection to encourage and reward their efforts, in return for the broadest possible public access to their property once this period of protection has ended. Unfortunately, this is much easier to describe than to do.

Because copyrights are generally enforced by preventing the unauthorized *use* of intellectual property, every *new form* of *use* that emerges after a copyright act is enacted is likely to fall outside the protection of law. Take, for example, the Copyright Act of

517

1909, that would serve as the only federal protection of intellectual property in the United States until a new Copyright Act took effect on January 1, 1978.

Adopted at a time when radio was still a curiosity and television beyond anyone's wildest dreams, the Act of 1909 was designed to control only those uses of which its drafters were then aware; uses such as Vaudeville, the gramophone, the player piano, the silent film. In essence, then, *use* meant some form of *performance* in 1909, and so as Chapter 10 has described, when CATV systems began to take copyrighted television programs from a broadcast station and distribute them to their cable subscribers, the Supreme Court held they were not in violation of the Act of 1909 because CATV simply relayed rather than *performed* these programs.[1]

It took Congress 15 years to complete the task of enacting a new copyright law to replace the antiquated Act of 1909, a massive struggle that illustrates another major problem involved in efforts to develop effective copyright legislation. Although everyone agreed that the Act of 1909 needed to be replaced, each industry group that participated in the process had very different ideas about how the new Act should be structured.[2]

Clashes among the rival industries—Program Syndicators v. Cable TV Owners, Music Producers v. Electronic Suppliers, Publishers v. Educational Institutions, Music Licensing Organizations v. Juke Box Operators, etc.—stalemated session after session of Congress until the weary combatants finally realized that it was more difficult to continue to operate under an out-dated law than virtually any new Act that Congress might adopt.[3] Although these incessant lobbying pressures resulted in the Copyright Act of 1976 being riddled with awkward exemptions and exceptions, its passage seemed at least to have brought all modern means of communication within its control.

Unfortunately, no one in 1976 could foresee that the VCR revolution lurked just around the corner, launching a home video rental business and providing the public with a means of recording or duplicating television programs and films that copyright owners only intended them to view. Once again technology was moving beyond the boundaries of intellectual property law, a movement that has actually accelerated recently as emerging personal comput-

---

[1] Fortnightly v. United Artists Television Inc., 392 U.S. 390, 88 St.Ct. 2084 (1968).

[2] One of the more useful sources in studying these rival positions and their effect on the legislation ultimately adopted is House of Representatives Report No. 94–1476, "Copyright Law Revision." Title 17, United States Code, "Copyrights," was amended in its entirety by Public Law 94–553, 94th Congress, 94 Stat. 2541 (1976).

[3] For a view of efforts to resolve such disputes, see H.R. Report No. 94–1476, "Copyright Law Revision," pp. 66–70. The guidelines there were later approved by the Senate–House conference committee which hammered out the final bill.

er applications demand new definitions for copyright principles still based on traditional methods of publication and distribution.

And so the process continues, as law attempts to extend the rights of those who create intellectual property to include uses of that property that were unknown at the time the law was adopted. But however copyright law is altered, its underlying principle remains constant; to stimulate creativity without unduly restricting the free flow of ideas and information.

This principle is expressed in Article I, Section 8 of the United States Constitution.

> The Congress shall have power * * * to promote the Progress of Science and useful Arts by securing for limited Times to Authors and Inventors the exclusive Right to their respective Writings and Discoveries.

Passage of the first federal copyright statute as early as 1790 indicates that America's Revolutionary generation had a lively concern about the need for copyright protection. Additional copyright statutes were enacted during the 19th century.[4]

History of Copyright

Underlying the words of Article I, Section 8 of the Constitution was the principle of copyright, which had been recognized by law for several centuries. It is known, for example, that the Republic of Venice in 1469 granted John of Speyer the exclusive right to print the letters of Pliny and Cicero for a period of five years.[5]

The development of printing increased the need for some form of copyright. Although printing from movable type began in 1451 and was introduced in England by 1476, the first copyright law was not passed in England until 1790 in the "Statute of 8 Anne." Before this time, the printing business was influenced in two distinct ways.

First, printing gave royalty and government in England the opportunity to reward favored individuals with exclusive printing monopolies. Second, those in power recognized that printing, unless strictly controlled, tended to endanger their rule.

Hoping to control the output of the printing presses, Queen Mary I granted a charter to the Stationers Company in 1556. This guild of printers was thus given a monopoly over book printing in England. Simultaneously these printers were given the authority to burn prohibited books and to jail the persons who published

---

[4] Thorvald Solberg, Copyright Enactments of the United States, 1783–1906. Washington, 1906.

[5] R.C. DeWolf, Outline of Copyright Law (Boston: John W. Luce, 1925) p. 2.

them.[6] The Stationers Company acted zealously against printers of unauthorized works, making use of terrifying powers of search and seizure.   Tactics paralleling those of the Inquisition were used defending the doctrines of the Catholic Church against the burgeoning Reformation movement.[7]

The Stationers Company remained powerful into the seventeenth century, with its authority augmented by licensing statutes. The Act of 1662, for example, confined printing to 59 master printer members of the Stationers Company then practicing in London, and to the printers at Oxford and Cambridge Universities. The privileged position of the Stationers Company in England during the sixteenth and seventeenth centuries underlies the development of the law of copyright of more recent times.   Printers who were officially sanctioned to print by virtue of membership in the Stationers Company complained when their works were issued in pirated editions by unauthorized printers.[8]

In time, the guild printers who belonged to the Stationers Company began to recognize a principle now known as "common law copyright."   They began to assume that there was a common law right, *in perpetuity,* to literary property.   That is, if a man printed a book, duly approved by government authority, the right to profit from its distribution remained with that man, or his heirs, forever.[9]

Authors, like England's printers, came to believe that they also had some rights to profit from their works.   Authors joined printers in the latter half of the seventeenth century in seeking Parliamentary legislation to establish the existence of copyright.   In 1709, Parliament passed the *Statute of 8 Anne,* believed to have been drafted, in part, by two famed authors of that period, Joseph Addison and Jonathan Swift.   This statute recognized the authors' rights, giving them—or their heirs or persons to whom they might sell their rights—exclusive powers to publish the book for 14 years after its first printing.   If the author were still alive after those 14 years, that person could renew copyright for an additional 14 years.[10]

This limitation of copyright to a total of 28 years displeased both authors and printers.   They complained for many years that they should have copyright in perpetuity under the common law.

[6] Philip Wittenberg, The Law of Literary Property (New York: World Publishing Co., 1957), pp. 25–26; Fredrick S. Siebert, Freedom of the Press in England, 1476–1776 (Urbana: University of Illinois Press, 1952) pp. 22, 65, 249.

[7] Siebert, op. cit., pp. 82–86; Mrs. Edward S. Lazowska, "Photocopying, Copyright, and the Librarian," American Documentation (April, 1968) pp. 123–130.

[8] Siebert, pp. 74–77, 239.

[9] Wittenberg, op. cit., pp. 45–46.

[10] Siebert, op. cit., p. 249; Wittenberg, Ibid., pp. 47–48.

In 1774, the House of Lords, acting in its capacity of a court of the highest appeal, decided the case of Donaldson v. Beckett.

Common Law and Statutory Copyright

This 1774 decision was of enormous importance to the history of American law, because it outlined the two categories of copyrights, *statutory copyright* and *common law copyright*. The House of Lords ruled that the Statute of 8 Anne, providing a limited 28 year term of copyright protection, had superseded the common law protection for *published* works. Only *unpublished* works, therefore, could receive common law copyright protection in perpetuity. An author was to have automatic, limitless common law copyright protection for his creations only as long as they remained unpublished.

But once publication occurred, the author or publisher could have exclusive right to publish and profit from his works for only a limited period of time as decreed by legislative authority. The Statute 8 Anne, as upheld by the House of Lords in Donaldson v. Beckett, is the ancestor of modern copyright legislation in the United States.[11]

When the first federal copyright statute was adopted in the United States in 1790, implementing Article I, Section 8 of the Constitution, it gave the federal government *statutory* authority to administer copyrights. Since there was no common law authority for federal courts, questions involving *common law* copyright remained to be adjudicated in state courts.[12] In the 1834 case of Wheaton v. Peters, the Supreme Court of the United States enunciated the doctrine of common law copyright in America: [13]

> That an author at common law has a property right in his manuscript, and may obtain redress against any one who endeavors to realize a profit by its publication, cannot be doubted; but this is a very different right from that which asserts a perpetual and exclusive property in the future publication of the work, after the author shall have published it to the world.

Congress tried to do away with state authority over common law copyrights, phasing them out of existence with Sec. 301 of the Copyright Act of 1976. Of course, there would have to be a transitional period: Sec. 301 specifically preserved common law

[11] Burr. 2408 (1774); Lazowska, op. cit., p. 124.

[12] Wheaton v. Peters, 33 U.S. (8 Pet.) 591 (1834); W.W. Willoughby, Constitutional Law of the United States, p. 446.

[13] 33 U.S. (8 Pet.) 591 (1834); Hirsch v. Twentieth Century–Fox Film Corp., 207 Misc. 750, 144 N.Y.S.2d 38, 105 U.S.P.Q. 253 (1955).

copyrights which were in effect before January 1, 1978—the effective date of the 1976 Copyright Act.

In point of fact, state laws affecting copyrights continue to have real effects. For example, Bette Midler, "The Divine Miss M," won $400,000 from the Ford Motor Company for using a singer imitating her voice in a series of TV commercials.

The Young and Rubicam advertising agency tried to attract young urban professionals with songs evoking memories of when the Yuppies were in college. The ad agency first attempted to get the original performers who had made songs famous. Failing in that effort, the agency then had ten songs recorded by "sound alikes"—including an imitation of Ms. Midler's rendition of the 1973 song hit, "Do You Want to Dance?".

Ms. Midler sued Ford Motor Company and Young and Rubicam for wrongful use of her singing voice without her consent. The U.S. Court of Appeals, 9th Circuit, held that although "a voice is not copyrightable," when a famous professional singer's distinctive voice is deliberately imitated in order to sell a product, that may be held to be a tort under California law.[14]

Common law copyright had both advantages and disadvantages. Its advantages were that it was automatic and perpetual so long as a manuscript or creation was not published. An author could circulate a manuscript among friends, could use it in class for experimental teaching materials, or, perhaps, could send it to several publishing houses without publication in the technical, legal sense. In general, as long as the manuscript was not offered to the general public, common law copyright protection remained intact.

Published works, however, had to have a copyright notice—for example, © John Steinbeck, 1941—in a specified place on a book or manuscript or other copyrightable item or the work would fall into the public domain. Once "in the public domain" a work no longer has copyright protection, and may be freely republished by others for their own profit.[15]

The Copyright Act of 1976 was intended to allow the federal government to supersede entirely the states' authority to deal with copyright. The federal statute's language certainly sounds preemptive: " * * * no person is entitled to any such [copy] right or equivalent right in any such work under the common law or statutes of any State." [16] Yet despite the best efforts of Congress,

[14] Midler v. Ford Motor Co., 849 F.2d 460, 462 (9th Cir.1988), 15 Med.L.Rptr. 1620, 1623, citing 17 U.S.C.A. § 102(a) for the principle that a voice is not copyrightable because sounds are not "fixed." See "Supreme Court Roundup," The New York Times (Nat'l. Ed.), March 3, 1992, p. A10.

[15] 17 U.S.C.A. § 102.

[16] H.R. Report No. 94–1476, pp. 146–149.

state law continues to exert a significant influence on copyright controversies.

As one authority in this field has pointed out, the vaguely defined tort of "misappropriation" as dealt with in state courts has led to a chaotic situation in conflict with Sec. 301 of the 1976 Copyright Act.[17] So, is unauthorized copying still a misappropriation ("wrongful taking") under the laws of various states, or is only an infringement of copyright under the federal Copyright Act of 1976?

If anything, § 301 [of the 1976 Copyright Act] has frustrated congressional intent to create "a single Federal system" and proliferated the "vague borderline areas between State and Federal protection" which Congress so sincerely yet so artlessly sought to avoid.

The Nature of Copyright

Copyright is an exclusive, legally recognizable claim to literary or pictorial property. It is a right, extended by federal statute, to entitle originators to ownership of the literary or artistic products of their minds. Before launching into more detailed discussion of provisions of the copyright statute now in force, consider the following three principles:

(1) *Facts or ideas cannot be copyrighted.* Copyright applies only to the literary style of an article, news story, book, or other intellectual creation. It does *not* apply to the themes, ideas, or facts contained in the copyrighted material. Anyone may write about any subject. Copyright's protection extends only to the particular manner or style of expression. What is "copyrightable" in the print media, for example, is the order and selection of words, phrases, clauses, sentences, and the arrangement of paragraphs.[18]

(2) *Copyright is both a protection for and a restriction of the communications media.* Copyright protects the media by preventing the wholesale taking of the form of materials, without permission, from one person or unit of the media for publication by another person or unit of the media. Despite the guaranty of freedom of the press, newspapers and other communications media must acquire permission to publish

---

[17] Howard B. Abrams, "Copyright, Misappropriation, and Preemption: Constitutional and Statutory Limits of State Law Protection," pp. 75–147 in David Goldberg, Chairman, Current Developments in Copyright Law, 1985 (New York: Practising Law Institute), at p. 147, quoting H.R. Report No. 94–1476 (1976), at p. 130. See also Abrams' pp. 83ff, for discussion of state cases endeavoring to deal with copying of sound recordings.

[18] Kaeser & Blair, Inc. v. Merchants' Ass'n, Inc., 64 F.2d 575, 577 (6th Cir.1933); Eisenschiml v. Fawcett Publications, Inc., 246 F.2d 598 (7th Cir.1957).

material that is protected by copyright.[19]

(3) *As a form of literary property, copyright belongs to that class of personal property including patents, trade-marks, trade names, trade secrets, good will, unpublished lectures, musical compositions, and letters.*

   (a) Copyright, it must be emphasized, is quite different from a patent. Copyright covers purely composition, style of expression or rhetoric, while a patent is the right given to protect a novel idea which may be expressed physically in a machine, a design, or a process.

   (b) Copyright may be distinguished from a trade-mark in that copyright protects a particular literary style while a trade-mark protects the sign or brand under which a particular product is made or distributed.

   (c) When someone sends you a letter, you do not have the right to publish that letter. You may keep the letter, or throw it away; indeed, you can do anything you wish with the letter but publish it. Although the recipient of a letter gets physical possession of it—of the paper it is written upon—the copyright ownership remains with the sender.[20]

SEC. 72.   SECURING A COPYRIGHT

Essentials in acquiring a copyright include notice of copyright, application, deposit of copies in the Library of Congress, and payment of the required fee.

What May Be Copyrighted

Reflecting awareness that new technologies will emerge and that human ingenuity will devise new forms of expression, the language of the new copyright statute is sweeping in defining what may be copyrighted. Section 102 says: [21]

(a) Copyright protection subsists * * * in original works of authorship fixed in any tangible medium of expression, now known or later developed, from which they can be perceived, reproduced, or otherwise communicated, either directly or with the aid of a machine or device. Works of authorship include the following categories:

   (1) literary works;

[19] Cf. Chicago Record–Herald Co. v. Tribute Ass'n, 275 Fed. 797 (7th Cir.1921).

[20] Baker v. Libbie, 210 Mass. 599, 97 N.E. 109 (1912); Ipswich Mills v. Dillon, 260 Mass. 453, 157 N.E. 604 (1927). See also Alan Lee Zegas, "Personal Letters: A Dilemma for Copyright and Privacy Law," 33 Rutgers Law Review (1980) pp. 134–164. Writers who seek relief for unauthorized publication may sue for recovery under both copyright and privacy theories, although the author suggests that those areas of law offer writers inadequate protection.

[21] 17 U.S.C.A. § 102.

    (2) musical works, including any accompanying words;

    (3) dramatic works, including any accompanying music;

    (4) pantomimes and choreographic works;

    (5) pictorial, graphic, and sculptural works;

    (6) motion pictures and other audiovisual works; and

    (7) sound recordings.

(b) In no case does copyright protection for an original work of authorship extend to any idea, procedure, process, system, method of operation, concept, principle, or discovery, regardless of the form in which it is described, explained, illustrated, or embodied in such work.

The Copyright Notice

Under the 1976 statute, once something has been published the omission of a copyright notice or an error in that notice does not destroy the author or creator's protection.[22] Section 405 gives a copyright owner up to five years to register a work with the Register of Copyrights, Library of Congress, Washington, D.C., even if that work has been published without notice.[23] In 1989, when the United States joined the Berne Copyright Union, this provision was further liberalized to provide full protection beyond this five year period to a copyrighted work without a proper notice.[24]

Section 401 makes the following general requirement about placing copyright notices on "visually perceptible copies." [25]

Whenever a work protected under this title [Title 17, United States Code, the copyright statute] is published in the United States or elsewhere by authority of the copyright owner, a notice of copyright in this section shall be placed on all publicly distributed copies from which the work can be visually perceived, either directly or with the aid of a machine or device.

The copyright notice shall consist of these three elements: [26]

    (1) the symbol © (the letter C in a circle), or the word "Copyright" or the abbreviation "Copr."; and

    (2) the year of first publication of the work; in the case of compilations or derivative works incorporating previously

---

[22] 17 U.S.C.A. §§ 405, 406.

[23] Formerly, under the 1909 statute, publication without notice could mean that the authors lost any copyrights in their works if a defective notice—or no notice at all—appeared on the work. Leon H. Amdur, Copyright Law and Practice (New York: Clark Boardman Co., 1936), pp. 64–65; Holmes v. Hurst, 174 U.S. 82, 19 S.Ct. 606 (1899).

[24] U.S.C.A. ¶ 405

[25] 17 U.S.C.A. § 401(a).

[26] 17 U.S.C.A. § 401(b).

published material, the year date of the first publication of the compilation or derivative work is sufficient. The year date may be omitted where a pictorial, graphic, or sculptural work, with accompanying text matter, if any, is reproduced in or on greeting cards, postcards, stationery, jewelry, dolls, toys, or any useful articles; and

(3) the name of the owner of copyright abbreviation by which the name can be recognized or a generally known alternative designation of the owner.

If a sound recording is being copyrighted, the notice takes a different form. The notice shall consist of the following three elements: [27]

(1) The symbol CIRP (the letter P in a circle); and

(2) the year of first publication of the sound recording; and

(3) the name of the owner of copyright in the sound recording, or an abbreviation by which the name can be recognized, or a generally known alternative designation of the owner; if the producer of the sound recording is named on the phonorecord labels or containers, and if no other name appears in conjunction with the notice, the producer's name shall be considered a part of the notice.

The copyright statute adopts one of the former law's basic principles: in the case of works made for hire, the employer is considered the author of the work (and therefore the initial copyright owner) unless there has been an agreement to the contrary. The statute requires that any agreement under which the employee will own rights be in writing and signed by both the employee and the employer.[28]

The copyright notice shall be placed on the copies "in such manner and location as to give reasonable notice of the claim of copyright." Special methods of this "affixation" of the copyright notice and positions for notices on various kinds of works will be prescribed by regulations to be issued by the Register of Copyrights.[29]

Even though the lack of a proper copyright notice no longer bars a claim for copyright infringement, it is still extremely important to provide proper notice in order to prevent someone who has used a copyrighted work without permission from escaping statutory penalties by claiming to be unaware that the work was copyrighted.

[27] 17 U.S.C.A. § 402(b), (c).

[28] 17 U.S.C.A. § 201(b); see discussion of this section in House of Representatives Report No. 94–1476, "Copyright Law Revision."

[29] 17 U.S.C.A. § 401(c).

Duration of Copyright

A most welcome change under the Act of 1976 set copyright duration at the life of the owner plus 50 years. This replaced the fouled-up and complicated system of the 1909 statute of an initial period of 28 years plus a renewal period of another 28 years.

Under the old Act, renewals had to be applied for, and if unwary copyright owners waited a full 28 years to apply for their second term, they had waited too long and their works became part of the public domain—everybody's property. Also, the U.S. system was badly out of step with a great majority of the world's nations which had adopted a copyright term of the author's life plus 50 years. As noted in the legislative commentary accompanying the 1976 statute,[30]

> * * * American authors are frequently protected longer in foreign countries than in the United States ... [This] disparity in the duration of copyright has provoked * * * some proposals of retaliatory legislation. * * * The need to conform the duration of U.S. copyright to that prevalent throughout the rest of the world is increasingly pressing in order to provide certainty and simplicity in international business dealings. Even more important, a change in the basis of our copyright term would place the United States in the forefront of the international copyright community. Without this change, the possibility of future United States adherence to the Berne Copyright Union would evaporate, but with it would come a great and immediate improvement in our copyright relations.

Existing works already under statutory copyright protection at the time of passage of the new copyright statute have had their copyright duration increased to 75 years. Works now in their first 28-year copyright under the old system must be renewed if they are in their 28th year, but the second term will be expanded to 47 years to provide a total of 75 years' protection. For copyrighted works in their renewal term, 19 years will be added so that copyright on such works will exist for a total of 75 years.[31] Congress repeatedly extended the terms of expiring copyrights from 1964 to 1975, in anticipation of the enactment of copyright revision.[32]

Copyright Registration and Deposit

Copyright registration is accomplished by filling out a form obtainable from:

[30] H.R. Report No. 94–1476, p. 135, discussing 17 U.S.C.A. § 302.

[31] 17 U.S.C.A. § 304.

[32] See H.R. Report No. 94–1476, p. 140.

Register of Copyrights

Library of Congress

Washington, D.C. 20559

In addition, corresponding with the Publications Division of the Copyright Office can yield much helpful information. Information Package 109 contains sample forms, and Copyright Office Packet R–1, "Copyright Basics," provides a clear, concise description of the Act and its major provisions. The Copyright Office information service—as of 1995—was available by calling (202) 707–3000 weekdays between 8:30 a.m. and 5 p.m. A copyright hotline is provided for ordering specific forms: (202) 707–9100.

The Register of Copyrights will require (with some exceptions specified by the Copyright Office), that material deposited for registration shall include two complete copies of the best edition.[33] These copies are to be deposited within three months after publication, along with a completed form as prescribed by the Register of Copyrights.[34] A fee of $10 must be paid for most items being copyrighted.[35] It should be noted that registration is required before any action for copyright infringement can be started.[36]

If an individual attempts a "bluff copyright"—that is, places a copyright notice on a work at the time of publication without bothering to register it and deposit copies as outlined above, that person could have some real difficulties with the Register of Copyrights. The Register of Copyrights may demand deposit of such unregistered works. Unless deposit is made within three months, an individual may be liable to pay a fine of up to $250. If a person "willfully or repeatedly" refuses to comply with such demand, a fine of $2,500 may be imposed.[37]

Authors and the Copyright Act of 1976

The sweeping copyright revision which went into effect in 1978—compared to its 1909 predecessor—is truly the author's friend. As Professor Kent R. Middleton has pointed out, authors' ownership of rights under the old statute was precarious indeed. "One change," Middleton wrote, "which makes copyright divisible, gives the author greater flexibility in selling his work to different

[33] 17 U.S.C.A. § 407. Other useful circulars available in 1989 from the Publications Division of the Copyright include Circular Ric, Copyright Registration Procedures; Circular R22, How to Investigate the Copyright Status of a Work, and Circular R21, Reproduction of Copyrighted Works by Educators and Librarians.

[34] 17 U.S.C.A. § 407.

[35] Payment of fees is specified by 17 U.S.C.A. § 708.

[36] 17 U.S.C.A. § 411; see also 17 U.S.C.A. § 205.

[37] 17 U.S.C.A. § 407(d).

media. The other, vesting initial ownership with the creator of a work, makes the author's title more secure." [38]

Under the 1909 statute, a *single* legal title was held by a "proprietor" to any writing or artistic creation. Typically if an author sold the right to publish a work, it meant that *all* rights then belonged to the purchaser.[39] Under the revised statute, authors can sell *some* rights or *all* rights as they wish. In that way, a writer may sell "one-time rights"—for use of the work only once—and then will keep other rights to re-sell the same work. For example, a magazine article—such as "The Urban Cowboy," published in *Esquire Magazine*—became the basis for a smash motion picture of the same name. Under § 201 of the revised copyright act, an author retains ownership in anything that author has written unless those rights are *expressly* granted to a publisher.[40]

Free-lance journalists should beware of the phrase "work made for hire." Under both the old and new laws, a work produced while working for an employer constituted a "work made for hire," and all rights in that work belong to the employer. As Professor Middleton has warned, "a free-lancer's commissioned work may also be considered a work made for hire if a publisher can get a free lancer to agree." [41]

Journalists should also pay attention to what kinds of rights they are selling. If you sell "all rights," your financial stake in a piece of work is at an end. Perhaps it would be better for you to sell "first serial rights"—which will allow, for example, a magazine to publish your writing one time anywhere in the world. Then, the rights to that work revert to you, the author. Or, you might sell first North American rights, which would allow publication of your work one time in this part of the world, but not anywhere else.[42]

SEC. 73.　ORIGINALITY

The concept of originality means that authors or artists have done their own work, and that their work is not copied from or grossly imitative of others' literary or artistic property.

Originality is a fundamental principle of copyright; originality implies that the author or artist created the work through his own

[38] Kent R. Middleton, "Copyright and the Journalist: New Powers for the Free–Lancer," Journalism Quarterly 56:1 (Spring, 1979), p. 39.

[39] Harry G. Henn, "Ownership of Copyright, Transfer of Ownership," in James C. Goodale, chairman, Communications Law 1979 (New York: Practising Law Institute, 1979), pp. 709–711.

[40] 17 U.S.C.A. § 201.

[41] Middleton, op. cit., p. 40.

[42] The Writer's Market.

skill, labor, and judgment.[43] The concept of originality means that the particular work must be firsthand, pristine; not copied or imitated. Originality, however, does not mean that the work must be necessarily novel or unique, or that it have any value as literature or art. What constitutes originality was explained in an old but frequently quoted case, Emerson v. Davies. The famed Justice Joseph Story of Massachusetts wrote in 1845: [44]

> In truth, in literature, in science and in art, there are, and can be, few, if any, things, which, in an abstract sense, are strictly new and original throughout. Every book in literature, science, and art, borrows, and must necessarily borrow, and use much which was well known and used before.

The question of originality seems clear in concept but this quality of composition is not always easy to separate and identify in particular cases. This is true especially when different authors have conceived like expressions or based their compositions upon commonly accepted ideas, terms, or descriptions in sequence. It must be borne in mind that *an idea* as such cannot be the subject of copyright; to be eligible for copyright, ideas must have particular physical expressions, as signs, symbols, or words. As was stated in Kaeser & Blair, Inc. v. Merchants' Association, Inc., "copyright law does not afford protection against the use of an idea, but only as to the means by which the idea is expressed." [45]

Similarly, a recent Supreme decision has held that no amount of "sweat of the brow" labor ever merits copyright protection in itself unless accompanied by some degree of originality.[46] Rural Telephone, a small Kansas phone company, had invested a substantial amount of time compiling a directory that listed the names and addresses of its subscribers in several different communities.

When Feist Publications sought to publish a regional phone directory, Rural refused to give Feist permission to include Rural's copyrighted white pages in this directory. Feist proceeded to incorporate the Rural listings in its regional telephone directory without permission, altering some of the information to conform to its own directory format, but publishing many of the listings exactly as they appeared in the Rural telephone directory.

[43] American Code Co. v. Bensinger, et al., 282 Fed. 829 (2d Cir.1922).

[44] 8 Fed.Cas. 615, No. 4,436 (C.C.Mass.1845).

[45] 64 F.2d 575, 577 (6th Cir.1933). See also, Holmes v. Hurst, 174 U.S. 82, 19 S.Ct. 606 (1899); Eisenschiml v. Fawcett Publications, Inc., 246 F.2d 598, 114 U.S.P.Q. 199 (7th Cir.1957).

[46] Feist Publications, Inc. v. Rural Telephone Service Co., Inc., 499 U.S. 340, 111 S.Ct. 1282 (1991).

Justice O'Connor, speaking for the Court, explained that although both the Copyright Act of 1909 and 1976 recognized the right of a compiler to claim copyright protection for a collection of facts, a subsequent compiler was free to use those same facts in preparing a competing work so long as the new work did not follow exactly the same selection and arrangement of those facts.

Here the Court found that although Rural had devoted sufficient effort to make its white pages useful, it had not done so in a sufficiently creative way to make the work original. As the Court itself had explained this crucial distinction between effort and originality almost a century ago,

> The right secured by copyright is not the right to forbid the use of certain words or facts or ideas by others; it is a right to that arrangement of words which the author has selected to express his ideas which the law protects.[47]

SEC. 74. INFRINGEMENT AND REMEDIES

Violation of copyright includes such use or copying of an author's work that his possibility of profit is lessened.

Anyone who violates any of the exclusive rights spelled out by Sections 106 through 108 of the copyright statute is an infringer. Section 106 provides that copyright owners have the exclusive rights to do and to authorize any of the following: [48]

(1) to reproduce the copyrighted work in copies or phono records;

(2) to prepare derivative works based upon the copyrighted work;

(3) to distribute copies or phonorecords of the copyrighted work to the public by sale or other transfer of ownership, or by rental, lease or lending;

(4) in the case of literary, musical, dramatic, and choreographic works, to perform the copyrighted work publicly, and

(5) in the case of literary, musical, dramatic and choreographic works, pantomimes, and motion pictures and other audiovi-

[47] Holmes v. Hurst, 174 U.S. 82, 19 S.Ct. 606 (1899); Van Rensselaer v. General Motors Corp., 324 F.2d 354 (6th Cir.1963).

[48] 17 U.S.C.A. § 106. Note, however, that these "exclusive rights" are subject to limitations as spelled out in §§ 107, "Fair Use"; 108 "Reproduction by Libraries and Archives,"; 109, "Effect of transfer of a particular copy or phonorecord"; and 110, "Exemption of certain performances and displays"; as by instructors or pupils in teaching activities in non-profit educational institutions. See, also, §§ 111–118, dealing with secondary transmissions by cable TV systems, ephemeral recordings, pictorial, sculptural and graphic works, sound recordings, plays, juke boxes, computers and information systems, and certain works' use in non-commercial broadcasting.

sual works, including the individual images of a motion picture or other audiovisual work, to display the copyrighted work publicly.

However, Section 107 imposes limitations on each of these "exclusive rights" in terms of the judicially created doctrine of *fair use,* a legal concept will be discussed in detail later in this chapter.

It should be kept in mind that copyright law is now analogous to old wine in a new bottle. The "bottle" which holds this area of law together, so to speak, is the new statute. But its provisions, by and large, will be interpreted to a considerable extent in terms of copyright cases—some decided many years ago.

In order to win a lawsuit for copyright infringement, a plaintiff must establish two separate facts, as the late Circuit Judge Jerome N. Frank wrote some years ago: "(a) that the alleged infringer copied from plaintiff's work, and (b) that, if copying is proved, it was so 'material' or substantial as to constitute unlawful appropriation." [49]

Even so, the material copied need not be extensive or "lengthy" in order to be infringement. "In an appropriate case," Judge Frank noted, "copyright infringement might be demonstrated, with no proof or weak proof of access, by showing that a simple brief phrase, contained in both pieces, was so idiosyncratic in its treatment as to preclude coincidence." [50] Judge Frank also noted that even a great, famous author or artist might be found guilty of copyright infringement. He wrote, "we do not accept the aphorism, when a great composer steals, he is 'influenced'; when an unknown steals, he is 'infringing'." [51]

Infringement occurs even though an unauthorized user does not profit directly from the copyrighted material he is using. The ruling case here is Herbert v. Shanley Co. (1917), where a restaurant owned by the defendant Shanley employed musicians to play at mealtimes. Victor Herbert's song "Sweethearts," was performed, but no arrangement had been made with Herbert or his representatives to use the song. Defendant Shanley argued that he had not infringed upon Herbert's copyright because he did not charge customers for the music they heard. The Supreme Court of the United States disagreed, finding that Shanley had benefited at least indirectly from the music he provided because it attracted diners to his place of business .[52]

[49] Heim v. Universal Pictures Co., 154 F.2d 480, 487 (2d Cir.1946).

[50] Ibid., p. 488.

[51] Ibid.

[52] 242 U.S. 591, 37 S.Ct. 232 (1917).

As under the former statute, a court may, in its discretion, award full court costs plus a "reasonable attorney's fee" to the winning party in a copyright lawsuit.[53] A plaintiff in an infringement suit also may opt to ask for "statutory damages" rather than actual damage and profits: [54]

(1) * * * the copyright owner may elect, at any time before final judgment is rendered, to recover, instead of actual damages and profits, an award of statutory damages for all infringements involved in the action, with respect to any one work, for which any one infringer is liable individually, or for which any two or more infringers are liable jointly and severally, in a sum of not less than $250 or more than $10,000 as the court considers just. * * *

(2) In a case where the copyright owner sustains the burden of proving, and the court finds, that infringement was committed willfully, the court in its discretion may increase the award of statutory damages to a sum of not more than $50,000. In a case where the infringer sustains the burden of proving, and the court finds, that such infringer was not aware and had no reason to believe that his acts constituted an infringement of copyright, the court in its discretion may reduce the award of statutory damages to a sum of not less than $100.

If you own a copyright and it is infringed upon, you have an impressive arsenal of remedies or weapons under the 1976 copyright statute.

For openers, if you know that someone is infringing on your copyright or you can prove is about to do so, a federal court has the power to issue temporary and final injunctions "on such terms as it may deem reasonable to prevent or restrain injunctions." [55] Furthermore, this injunction may be served on the suspected copyright infringer anywhere in the United States.[56] That's a form, in other words, of prior restraint at the disposal of an affronted copyright owner.

A copyright owner may also apply to a federal court to get an order to impound "on such terms as it may deem reasonable, * * * all copies or phonorecords claimed to have been made or used in

[53] 17 U.S.C.A. § 505.

[54] 17 U.S.C.A. § 504(c)(1), (2).

[55] 17 U.S.C.A. § 502(a). For an example of an unsuccessful attempt to get an injunction, see Belushi v. Woodward, 598 F.Supp. 36 (D.D.C.1984), 10 Med.L.Rptr. 1870. The case involved widow of actor John Belushi asking that author Bob Woodward and publisher Simon & Schuster be enjoined from publishing book because of allegedly unauthorized use of her copyrighted photo.

[56] 17 U.S.C.A. § 502(b).

violation of the copyright owner's exclusive rights."[57]   And, if a court orders it as part of a final judgment or decree, the articles made in violation of the copyright owner's exclusive rights may be destroyed or otherwise disposed of.[58]

A copyright infringer, generally speaking, is liable for either of two things: (1) the copyright owner's actual damages and any additional profits of the infringer * * * or (2) statutory damages.[59]

Actual Damages and Profits

Consider the statute's language on "actual damages and profits":[60]

> The copyright owner is entitled to recover the actual damages suffered by him or her as a result of the infringement, and any profits of the infringer that are attributable to the infringement and are not taken into account in computing actual damages. In establishing the infringer's profits, the copyright owner is required to present proof only of the infringer's gross revenue, and the infringer is required to prove his or her deductible expenses and the elements of profit attributable to factors other than the copyrighted work.

"Damages are awarded to compensate the copyright owner for losses from the infringement, and profits are awarded to prevent the infringer from unfairly benefiting from a wrongful act."[61]

In seeking to recover profits from a copyright infringer, the burden of proof falls upon the plaintiff to show the gross sales or profits arising from the infringement. The copyright infringer is permitted to deduct any legitimate costs or expenses which he can prove were incurred during publication of the stolen work. The winner of a suit to recover profits under copyright law can receive only the *net profits* resulting from an infringement. As the Supreme Court of the United States has declared,"The infringer is liable for actual, not for possible, gains."[62]

Net profits can run to a great deal of money, especially when the work is a commercial success as a book or motion picture. Edward Sheldon sued Metro–Goldwyn Pictures Corp. and others for infringing on his play, "Dishonored Lady" through the production of the Metro–Goldwyn film, "Letty Lynton." A federal district

[57] 17 U.S.C.A. § 503(a).

[58] 17 U.S.C.A. § 503(b).

[59] 17 U.S.C.A. § 504(a).

[60] 17 U.S.C.A. § 504(b).

[61] H.R.Rep. No. 94–1476 (Sept. 3, 1976), "Copyright Law Revision," p. 161.

[62] Sheldon v. Metro–Goldwyn Pictures Corp., 309 U.S. 390, 400–401, 60 S.Ct. 681, 683 (1940); Golding v. R.K.O. Pictures, Inc., 35 Cal.2d 690, 221 P.2d 95 (1950).

court, after an accounting had been ordered, found that Metro–Goldwyn had received net profits of $585,604.37 from their exhibitions of the motion picture.[63]

Mr. Sheldon did not get *all* of Metro–Goldwyn's net profits from the movie, however. On appeal, it was held that Sheldon should not benefit from the profits that motion picture stars had made for the picture by their talent and box-office appeal. Sheldon, after his case had been heard by both a United States Court of Appeals and the Supreme Court of the United States, came out with only 20 per cent of the net profits, or roughly $118,000. It still would have been much cheaper for Metro–Goldwyn simply to have bought Sheldon's script. Negotiations with Sheldon for his play had been started by Metro–Goldwyn, but were never completed. The asking price for movie rights to the Sheldon play was evidently to be about $30,000, or slightly more than one-fourth of the amount the courts awarded to the playwright.[64]

Copyright cases involving music have proved to be difficult. The evidence in such cases is largely circumstantial, resting upon similarities between songs. The issue in such a case, as one court expressed it, is whether "so much of what is pleasing to the ears of lay listeners, who comprise the audience for whom such popular music is composed, that defendant wrongfully appropriated something which belongs to the plaintiff." [65]

More than "lay listeners" often get involved in such cases, however. Expert witnesses sometimes testify in copyright infringement cases involving music. But it can happen that the plaintiff who feels that his musical composition has been stolen, and the defendant as well, will *both* bring their own expert witnesses into court, where these witnesses expertly disagree with each other.[66]

In proving a case of copyright infringement—and not just for those cases dealing with music—it is often useful if plaintiffs can show that the alleged infringement had "access" to the original work from which the copy was supposed to have been made. Such "access" needs to be proved by the plaintiff, if only by the circumstantial evidence of similarity between two works.

During the 1940s, songwriter Ira B. Arnstein tried to show that the noted composer, Cole Porter, not only had access to his work, but that Porter had taken freely from Arnstein. The courts declared that Porter had not infringed upon any common law or

---

[63] Sheldon v. Metro–Goldwyn Pictures Corp., 26 F.Supp. 134, 136 (S.D.N.Y.1938), 81 F.2d 49 (2d Cir.1936), 106 F.2d 45 (2d Cir.1939).

[64] 309 U.S. 390, 398, 407, 60 S.Ct. 681, 683, 687 (1940); see Nimmer, op. cit., § 14.03 fn. 30 (1988).

[65] Arnstein v. Porter, 154 F.2d 464, 473 (2d Cir.1946).

[66] Ibid.

statutory copyrights held by Arnstein. Porter's victory in the courts was hard-won, however.

Arnstein began a copyright infringement lawsuit against Cole Porter in a federal district court. Arnstein charged that Porter's "Begin the Beguine" was a plagiarism from Arnstein's "the Lord is My Shepherd" and "A Mother's Prayer." He also claimed that Porter's "My Heart Belongs to Daddy" had been lifted from Arnstein's "A Mother's Prayer."

On the question of access, plaintiff Arnstein testified that his apartment had been burglarized and accused Porter of receiving the stolen manuscripts from the burglars. Arnstein declared that Porter's "Night and Day" had been stolen from Arnstein's "I Love You Madly," which had never been published but which had been performed once over the radio. Technically, this meant that Arnstein's "I Love You Madly" had never been published.

In reply, Porter swore that he had never seen or heard any of Arnstein's compositions, and that he did not know the persons said to have stolen them. Even so, Arnstein's lawsuit asked for a judgment against Porter of "at least one million dollars out of the millions this defendant has earned and is earning out of all the plagiarism." [67]

At the original trial, the district court directed the jury to bring in a summary verdict in favor of Porter. Arnstein then appealed to a U.S. Circuit Court of Appeals, where Judge Jerome Frank explained what the appellate court had done. The Circuit Court of Appeals had listened to phonograph records of Cole Porter's songs and compared them to records of Arnstein's songs. As he sent the case back to a district court jury, Judge Frank wrote:

> * * * we find similarities, but we hold that unquestionably, standing alone, they do not compel the conclusion, or permit the inference, that defendant copied. The similarities, however, are sufficient so that, if there is enough evidence of access to permit the case to go to the jury, the jury may properly infer that the similarities did not result from coincidence.

The jury then found that Cole Porter's "Begin the Beguine" had indeed been written by Cole Porter.

Similarly, the U.S. Court of Appeals, Second Circuit ruled that A.A. Hoehling could not collect damages from Universal City Studios in a dispute involving the motion picture, *The Hindenburg*. Back in 1962, Hoehling—after substantial research—published a copyrighted book, *Who Destroyed the Hindenburg?* That book

[67] Ibid., 474.

advanced the theory that a disgruntled crew member of The Graf Zeppelin had planted a crude bomb in one of its gas cells.

Ten years later, after consulting Hoehling's book plus many other sources, Michael MacDonald Mooney published his own book, *The Hindenburg*. Mooney's book put forward a similar cause for the airship's destruction, but there was also evidence that other authors before Hoehling had suggested the same cause for the explosion. Circuit Judge Kaufman said for the court: [68]

> All of Hoehling's allegations of copying, therefore, encompass material that is non-copyrightable as a matter of law * * *.

* * *

> * * * in granting * * * summary judgment for defendants, courts should assure themselves that the works before them are not virtually identical. In this case, it is clear that all three authors relate the story of the Hindenburg differently.

> In works devoted to historical subjects, it is our view that a second author may make significant use of prior work, so long as he does not bodily appropriate the expression of another. *Rosemont Enterprises, Inc.*, 366 F.2d at 310. This principle is justified by the fundamental policy undergirding the copyright laws—the encouragement of contributions to recorded knowledge * * * Knowledge is expanded as well, by granting new authors of historical works a relatively free hand to build upon the work of their predecessors.

In Litchfield v. Spielberg, the U.S. Court of Appeals for the Ninth Circuit decided in 1984 that a copyright infringement/unfair competition lawsuit involving the movie *E.T.—The Extraterrestrial* was—if not out of this world—at least legally insupportable. Lisa Litchfield claimed that her copyrighted one-act musical play, Lokey from Maldemar, had been infringed upon by *E.T.*, the box-office smash hit. As the appeals court put it, the issue, in addition to that of infringement, was whether the lower court had acted properly in granting defendants a summary judgment.[69]

After independently reviewing the facts, the Court of Appeals held: [70]

---

[68] Hoehling v. Universal City Studios, Inc., 618 F.2d 972, 979–980 (2d Cir.1980), 6 Med.L.Rptr. 1053, 1057–1058.

[69] Litchfield v. Spielberg; MCA, Inc., Universal City Studios, Inc., Extra–terrestrial Productions, Kennedy, Tanen, and Mathison, 736 F.2d 1352 (9th Cir.1984) 10 Med.L.Rptr. 2101, 2102–2103.

[70] 736 F.2d 1352, 1355 (9th Cir.1984), 10 Med.L.Rptr. 2102, at 2105–2106.

> There is no substantial similarity * * * between the se-
> quences of events, mood, dialogue and characters of the
> two works. Any similarities in plot exist only at the
> general level for which plaintiff cannot claim copyright
> protection. * * *

* * *

> As is too often the case, Litchfield's action was prem-
> ised "partly upon a wholly erroneous understanding of the
> extent of copyright protection; and partly upon that obses-
> sive conviction, so common among authors and composers,
> that all similarities between their works and any others to
> appear later must be ascribed to plagiarism." Dellar v.
> Samuel Goldwyn, Inc., 150 F.2d 612 (2d Cir.1945).

As noted earlier in this chapter, facts or ideas are not copyrightable, only the style in which they are expressed. An additional
gloss was put on this by a 1978 case, Miller v. Universal City
Studios, which raised the question whether the research effort put
into gathering facts is copyrightable.

Pulitzer Prize-winning reporter Gene Miller of The Miami
Herald collaborated on writing a book with Barbara Mackle about
her ordeal in a famous kidnapping incident. Ms. Mackle was held
for ransom while literally buried alive in a box with seven days' life-
sustaining capacity. She was rescued from the box on the fifth day.
Miller worked an estimated 2500 hours in researching and writing
this book.

A Universal Studios executive, William Frye, then offered Miller $15,000 for rights to use the Miller–Mackle account in a
television "docudrama." Miller refused, asking for $200,000. At
this point, negotiations between Miller and the studio collapsed, but
the studio proceeded to produce and air a docudrama titled "The
Longest Night." This production had obvious similarities to the
Miller–Mackle book, and Miller sued for copyright infringement.[71]

The script writer had proceeded to write "The Longest Night"
on the assumption that his studios had closed a deal with Miller for
rights to the book and that he could proceed to write the script on
that basis. Even so, Universal City Studios argued that no matter
how hard Miller had worked to research the facts in the Mackle
kidnapping case, he "may not monopolize those facts because they
are historical facts and everyone has the right to write about them
and communicate them to the public." The court disagreed with
Universal City Studios' argument, saying: [72]

[71] Miller v. Universal City Studios, Inc., 460 F.Supp. 984, 985–986 (S.D.Fla.1978).

[72] Ibid., p. 987 n. 988.

To this court it doesn't square with reason or common sense to believe that Gene Miller would have undertaken the research involved in writing of *83 Hours Till Dawn* (or to cite a more famous example, that Truman Capote would have undertaken the research required to write *In Cold Blood*) if the author thought that upon completion of the book a movie producer or television network could simply come along and take the profits of the books and his research from him.

On appeal, however, Universal City Studios won a reversal of the judgment. The U.S. Court of Appeals, Fifth Circuit, ruled that Universal should have a new trial " * * * because the case was presented and argued to the jury on a false premise: that the labor of research by an author is protected by copyright." The Court of Appeals added that its decision was difficult to reach because there was " * * * sufficient evidence to support a finding of infringement * * * under correct theories of copyright law." In sum, the Court of Appeals did not believe that *research* itself is copyrightable, only the manner in which it is *presented.* "It is well settled that copyright protection extends only to an author's expression of facts and not to the facts themselves." [73]

Sometimes, in dealing with a major Hollywood film studio, establishing infringement is actually less difficult than forcing the studio to make an honest disclosure of a film's earnings. Humorist Art Buchwald sold a screen *treatment* (a story outline) to Paramount in 1983 for a movie featuring Eddie Murphy. Paramount subsequently made the movie, "Coming To America" that followed the general plot line of Buchwald's treatment, but refused to honor its contract to pay Buchwald the $250,000 and 19% of the film's net profits specified by the agreement.

Although Paramount contended that the Buchwald screen treatment was only one of several the studio had used in preparing a shooting script, and that three other writers were claiming similar rights in the picture, the Court found that a substantial number of obvious parallels between Buchwald's treatment and the actual screen play justified a holding that the movie was based primarily upon his work.[74]

However, when Buchwald sought to claim his share of the film's profits, Paramount's accountants maintained that even though the film had grossed more than $125 million in all media sales worldwide, there were no profits to share with him because the studio's account books still showed a net loss for the film of $18

[73] Miller v. Universal City Studios, Inc., 650 F.2d 1365, 1368 (5th Cir.1981).
[74] Buchwald v. Paramount Pictures Corp. (Cal.1990), 17 Med.L.Rptr. 1257.

million.[75] The judge was not impressed by studio bookkeeping that appeared to be far more creative than the film itself, and insisted on an independent analysis of the accounting procedures employed by Paramount before making his final award to Buchwald. On the basis of that analysis, the Court awarded Buchwald a $900,000 judgement but Paramount's appeal is still being considered by the Court as this book goes to press.[76]

Alex Haley, author of the best-seller *Roots,* was sued for both copyright infringement and unfair competition by Margaret Walker Alexander. Ms. Alexander claimed that Haley's book, published in 1976, was drawn substantially from her novel, *Jubilee,* published in 1966, and a pamphlet, *How I Wrote Jubilee,* published in 1972. A federal district court granted Haley a summary judgment, finding that no copyright infringement had occurred. The court said: [77]

> Many of the claimed similarities are based on matters of historical or contemporary fact. No claim of copyright protection can arise from the fact that plaintiff has written about such historical and factual items, even if we were to assume that Haley was alerted to the facts in question by reading *Jubilee.* * * *

> Another major category of items consists of material traceable to common sources, the public domain, or folk custom. Thus, a number of claimed infringements are embodiments of the cultural history of black Americans, or of both black and white Americans planning out the cruel tragedy of white-imposed slavery. Where common sources exist for the alleged similarities, or the material that is similar is otherwise not original with the plaintiff, there is no infringement. * * * This group of asserted infringements can no more be the subject of copyright protection than the cause of a date or the name of a president or a more conventional piece of historical information.

Criminal Penalties

There can be *criminal* penalties for copyright infringement. The new statute ups the ante where phonorecord or movie pirates are concerned. Section 506 provides: [78]

---

[75] "Par to Buchwald; We're $18–Mil in Hole," *Variety* February 28, 1990, p. 5.

[76] Dan Cox, "Paramount Finally Files Buchwald Appeal," Variety, April 11, 1994, p. 32.

[77] Alexander v. Haley, 460 F.Supp. 40, 44–45 (S.D.N.Y.1978).

[78] 17 U.S.C.A. § 506. See also § 507, which orders a three-year statute of limitations for both criminal prosecutions and civil proceedings under the Copyright Statute.

(a) CRIMINAL INFRINGEMENT.—Any person who infringes a copyright willfully and for purposes of commercial advantage or private financial gain shall be fined not more than $10,000 or imprisoned for not more than one year, or both: *Provided, however,* That any person who infringes willfully and for purposes of commercial advantage or private financial gain the copyright in a sound recording shall be fined not more than $25,000 or imprisoned for not more than one year, or both, for the first such offense and shall be fined not more than $50,000 or imprisoned for not more than two years, or both, for any subsequent offense.

Criminal penalties—fines of up to $2,500—await any person who, "with fraudulent intent," places on any article a notice of copyright that is known to be false. Similar fines may be levied against individuals who fraudulently remove a copyright notice, or who knowingly make misstatements in copyright applications or related written statements.[79]

SEC. 75. COPYRIGHT, UNFAIR COMPETITION, AND THE NEWS

The news element of a story is not subject to copyright, although the style in which an individual story is written may be protected from infringement. Reporters, in short, should do their own reporting.

Any unauthorized and unfair use of a copyrighted news story constitutes an infringement which will support either lawsuits for damages or an action in equity to get an injunction against further publication. Although a news story—or even an entire issue of a newspaper—may be copyrighted, the *news element* in a newspaper story is not subject to copyright. News is *publici juris*—the history of the day—as was well said by Justice Mahlon Pitney in the important 1918 case of International News Service v. Associated Press. Justice Pitney wrote: [80]

> A News article, as a literary production, is the subject of copyright. But the news element—the information respecting current events in the literary production, is not the creation of the writer, but is a report of matters that ordinarily are publici juris; it is the history of the day. It is not to be supposed that the framers of the Constitution, when they empowered Congress to promote the progress of science and useful arts, by securing for limited times to authors and inventors the exclusive rights to their respec-

[79] 17 U.S.C.A. § 506(c), (d) and (e).
[80] 248 U.S. 215, 39 S.Ct. 68, 71 (1918).

tive writings and discoveries (Const. Art. 1, § 8, par. 8), intended to confer upon one who might happen to be first to report an historic event the exclusive right for any period to spread the knowledge of it.

The Associated Press had complained of news pirating by a rival news-gathering agency, International News Service. The Supreme Court granted the Associated Press an injunction against the appropriation, by INS, of non-copyrighted AP stories while the news was still fresh enough to be salable. This was true even though in that era, and until the Copyright Act of 1976, material was not copyrighted unless it carried the © symbol and notice at the time of publication. "The peculiar value of news," Justice Pitney declared, "is in the spreading of it while it is fresh; and it is evident that a valuable property interest in the news, as news, cannot be maintained by keeping it secret."

Justice Pitney also denounced the taking, by INS, of AP stories, either by quoting or paraphrasing. Justice Pitney wrote that INS, "in appropriating * * * news and selling it as its own is endeavoring to reap where it has not sown, and by disposing of it to newspapers that are competitors * * * of AP members is appropriating to itself the harvest of those who have sown." [81]

What, then, can a newspaper or other communications medium do when it has been "beaten" to a story by its competition? It must be emphasized that the historic case of International News Service v. Associated Press did *not* say that the "beaten" news medium must sit idly by. "Pirating" news, of course, is to be avoided: pirating has been defined as "the bodily appropriation of a statement of fact or a news article, with or without rewriting, but without independent investigation or expense." [82]

However, first-published news items may be used as "tips." When one newspaper discovers an event, such as the arrest of a kidnaper, its particular news presentation of the facts may be protected by copyright. Even so, such a first story may serve as a tip for other newspapers or press associations. After the first edition by the copyrighting news organization, other organizations may independently investigate and present their own stories about the arrest of the kidnaper. In such a case, the time element between the appearance of the first edition of the copyrighting newspaper and the appearance of a second or third edition by a competing newspaper might be negligible as far as the general public is concerned; only a few hours. If other newspapers or press associations make their own investigations and obtain their own stories, they do not violate copyright.

[81] 248 U.S. 215, 239–240, 39 S.Ct. 68, 71–72 (1918).
[82] 248 U.S. 215, 243, 39 S.Ct. 68, 74 (1918).

But, to copy a copyrighted news story—or to copy or paraphrase substantially from the original story—may lead to court action, as shown in the 1921 case of Chicago Record–Herald Co. v. Tribune Association. This case arose when the *New York Tribune* copyrighted a special news story on Germany's reliance upon submarines. This story, printed in the *New York Tribune* on Feb. 3, 1917, was offered for sale for exclusive publication in the *Chicago Herald*. The *Herald* declined this opportunity, and the *Chicago Daily News* then purchased the Chicago rights to the story.

With full knowledge that the *Tribune's* story on the German submarine campaign was copyrighted, the *Herald* nevertheless ran a version of the same story featuring identical paragraph after identical paragraph on the morning of Feb. 3.

The *Chicago Daily News* then refused to publish the story or to pay the *New York Tribune* for it. The *Daily News,* having agreed to purchase an exclusive story, had the right to refuse a story already published in its market. The publishers of the *New York Tribune* successfully sued the *Chicago Herald* for infringement.

The judge declared that the *New York Tribune's* original story "involves authorship and literary quality and style, apart from the bare recital of the facts or statement of news." So, although facts are not copyrightable, the style in which they are expressed is protected by law.

As noted in International News Service v. Associated Press (1918), the AP won its case despite the fact that the news stories it telegraphed to its members were not copyrighted. There, the Supreme Court of the United States held that the AP had a "quasi property" right in the news stories it produced, even after their publication. Once the Supreme Court found that such a "quasi property" right existed, it then declared that appropriation of such stories by INS amounted to unfair competition and could be stopped by a court-issued injunction against INS.[83]

More recently, a newspaper—the Pottstown, Pa., *Mercury*—won an unfair competition suit against a Pottstown radio station, WPAZ, getting an injunction which prevented WPAZ, "from any further appropriation of the newspaper's local news without its permission or authorization." [84]

Adopting the rather cynical view that news coverage was simply a function newspapers and broadcasters employed to attract advertisers, the Pennsylvania Supreme Court held that the radio

[83] See reference to this case at footnote 82, above. The case of International News Service v. Associated Press was cited as important by the more recent case of Pottstown Daily News Pub. Co. v. Pottstown Broadcasting Co., 411 Pa. 383, 192 A.2d 657, 662 (1963).

[84] Ibid.

station had unfairly competed with the *Mercury* for these advertisers through its unauthorized taking of the newspaper's new stories. The court said: [85]

> * * * for the purpose of an action of unfair competition the specialized treatment of news items as a service the newspaper provides for advertisers gives the News Company [publishers of the Pottstown *Mercury*]a limited property right which the law will guard and protect against wrongful invasion by a competitor * * *

The limited property right in news is to some extent waived by member organizations of the Associated Press. All A.P. members are entitled to all *spontaneous* news from areas served by other A.P. member newspapers or broadcasting stations. Membership in the Associated Press includes agreement to follow this condition as stated in Article VII of the A.P. bylaws:

> Sec. 3. Each member shall promptly furnish to the [A.P.] Corporation all the news of such member's district, the area of which shall be determined by the Board of Directors. No news furnished to the Corporation by a member shall be furnished by the Corporation to any other member within such member's district.

> Sec. 4. The news which a member shall furnish to the Corporation shall be all news that is spontaneous in origin, but shall not include news that is not spontaneous in its origin, or which has originated through deliberate and individual enterprise on the part of such member.

A.P. member newspapers or broadcasting stations are expected to furnish spontaneous or "spot" news stories to the Associated Press for dissemination to other members throughout the nation. However, Section 3 of the A.P. By–Laws (above) will protect the news medium originating such a story within its district.

Even if a newspaper copyrights a spot news story, other A.P. members could use the story despite the copyright. By signing the A.P. By–Laws, the originating newspaper has given its consent in advance for all A.P. members to use news stories of *spontaneous* origin. On the other hand, if a newspaper copyrights a story based on that newspaper's individual enterprise and initiative, the other A.P. members could not use the story without permission from the copyrighting newspaper.

Roy Export Company v. CBS

Eagerness to present the news as effectively as possible in pressure situations may sometimes lead to disregard of ownership

---

[85] 411 Pa. 383, 192 A.2d 657, 663–664 (1963).

rights. Evident lack of concern about such rights cost the Columbia Broadcasting System $717,000 [86] in copyright and unfair competition damages for missteps making a documentary on the occasion of the death of film legend Charlie Chaplin.

In 1977, CBS broadcast a film biography of Chaplin, including film clips from six Chaplin-motion pictures. Exclusive rights in those films were held by several parties, including the first-named plaintiff in this case, Roy Export Company Establishment of Vaduz, Liechtenstein.[87]

The events leading to this lawsuit are traceable to 1972, when the Academy of Motion Picture Arts and Sciences (AMPAS) arranged to have a film tribute made from highlights of Chaplin's films. This tribute was broadcast by NBC–TV in connection with an appearance by Chaplin at the 1972 Academy Awards ceremonies. It was understood that excerpts compiled in that tribute were to be used only on that one occasion.[88]

In 1973, CBS started work on a retrospective of Chaplin's life, to be used as a broadcast obituary when Chaplin died. CBS made repeated requests for permission to use excerpts from Chaplin's films, but was rebuffed. CBS was told that the copyright owners were involved in producing their own film biography of Chaplin titled "The Gentleman Tramp." That production used some of the same footage used in the Academy Awards show compilation, but did not use that compilation itself. CBS, meanwhile, made a "rough cut" of a Chaplin obituary/biography. The network was offered a chance to purchase rights to show "The Gentleman Tramp" in 1976 and 1977, but did not do so.

Chaplin died on Christmas day, 1977. CBS had its "rough cut" biography ready to use, but instead used a copy of the 1972 Academy Award show compilation which CBS had obtained from NBC. CBS put together a new biography, depending heavily "on what CBS knew to be copyrighted material." This hastily assembled new biography was broadcast on December 26, 1977.[89]

[86] Roy Export Co. Establishment of Vaduz, Liechtenstein v. CBS, 672 F.2d 1095, 1097 (2d Cir.1982), 8 Med.L.Rptr. 1637, 1639. See footnote 6: "Of the compensatory total, $7,280 was for statutory copyright infringement, $1 was for common-law copyright infringement, and $300,000 was for unfair competition. The punitive damages were divided between the common-law claims: $300,000 for common-law copyright infringement and $110,000 for unfair competition."

[87] 672 F.2d 1095 (2d Cir.1982), 8 Med.L.Rptr. 1637, cert. denied 459 U.S. 826, 103 S.Ct. 60 (1982). This case was complicated, Circuit Judge Newman said, by troublesome questions coming from pre–1978 common law protection for intellectual property, plus challenges to statutory copyrights, "on the ground that the work lost its common copyright prior to January 1, 1978, entered the public domain, and therefore was not eligible for statutory copyright." Judge Newman cited M. Nimmer, Nimmer on Copyright, Sec. 4.01 [B].

[88] 672 F.2d at 1098 (2d Cir.1982), 10 Med.L.Rptr. at 1639.

[89] Ibid.

Roy Export Company and other copyright owners of Chaplin films then sued CBS for copyright infringement and for unfair competition. The latter claim said the CBS broadcast competed unfairly with the copyright owners' own Chaplin retrospective, "The Gentleman Tramp." A jury trial in a U.S. district court found CBS liable to the plaintiffs for $307,281 compensatory and $410,000 punitive damages.

In its appeal, CBS asserted that the First Amendment provides a general privilege to report newsworthy events such as Chaplin's death, and that this privilege shielded the network from liability. CBS claimed that the main reason for Chaplin's fame was his films, and that it would be meaningless to try to provide a full account of his life without making use of his films. Circuit Judge Newman summed up the network's First Amendment argument: [90]

> In CBS's view, the 1972 Academy Awards ceremony, at which the Compilation received its single public showing, was an "irreducible single news event" to which the showing of the Compilation was integral. The significance of the ceremony, CBS contends, was not simply that Chaplin appeared after a twenty-year exile provoked by Senator [Joseph] McCarthy's investigations, but that a collection of his work was shown, thereby bringing home to the American people both what they had been deprived of by McCarthyism and how ludicrous had been the attempt to find subversion and political innuendo in Chaplin's films. CBS concludes that the plaintiff's claims for infringement of the copyright in the films and the compilation must give way to an asserted First Amendment news-reporting privilege.

The Court of Appeals found CBS's First Amendment arguments "unpersuasive," resting on a theory that someday, some way, there might be an inseparability of news value and copyrighted work to the extent that copyright would have to yield. Judge Newman wrote, however: "No Circuit that has considered the question * * * has ever held that the First Amendment provides a privilege in the copyright field distinct from the accommodation embodied in the 'fair use' doctrine." And in a footnote he added,[91]

> Fair use balances the public interest in the free flow of ideas and information with the copyright holder's interest in exclusive proprietary control of his work. It permits use of the copyrighted matter 'in a reasonable manner without [the copyright owner's] consent, notwithstanding the monopoly granted to the owner.' Rosemont Enterprises, Inc., v. Random House, Inc., 366 F.2d 303 (2d Cir.

[90] 672 F.2d 1095, 1099 (2d Cir.1982), 10 Med.L.Rptr. 1637, 1640.
[91] 672 F.2d 1095, 1099 (2d Cir.1982), 10 Med.L.Rptr. 1637, 1640.

1966), cert. denied 385 U.S. 1009, 87 S.Ct. 714 * * * (1967) * * *.

The Roy Export case and Unfair Competition

CBS also argued that the plaintiffs could not maintain a claim that the network's December 26, 1977, broadcast unfairly competed with the plaintiffs' rights in "The Gentleman Tramp." CBS asserted the unfair competition claim rested on "misappropriation" of films under New York state law, " * * * and that a state law claim based on misappropriation of federally copyrighted materials is pre-empted * * * " [92] The Court of Appeals replied:

> An unfair competition claim involving misappropriation usually concerns the taking and use of the plaintiff's property to compete against the plaintiff's use of the same property, e.g. International News Service v. Associated Press * * * [248 U.S. 215, 39 S.Ct. 68 (1918)]. By contrast, in this case the Compilation was taken and used to compete unfairly with a different property, "The Gentleman Tramp." Despite the unusual facts, we are satisfied that the plaintiffs have established an unfair competition tort under New York law.

> * * *

> CBS unquestionably appropriated the "skill, expenditures and labor" of the plaintiffs to its own commercial advantage. Its actions, in apparent violation of its own and the industry's guidelines, were arguably a form of "commercial immorality." We are confident that the New York courts would call that conduct unfair competition.

The Court of Appeals ruled that the damages of more than $700,000 against CBS should stand, including the punitive damage awards totaling $410,000. Judge Newman wrote, "The deterrent potential of an award of $410,000 must be measured by its likely effect on a national television network with 1977 earnings of some $217,000,000 * * * " [93]

Computer Image Piracy

In one of the first legal disputes over the permissible limits of computerized image manipulation, FPG, a stock photo company has sued *Newsweek* magazine for using parts of two FPG copyrighted photo images without permission.[94] In its $1.4 million copyright

---

[92] 697 F.2d at 1104–1105 (2d Cir.1982), 10 Med.L.Rptr. at 1644–1645.

[93] 697 F.2d at 1107 (2d Cir.1982), 10 Med.L.Rptr. at 1646.

[94] George Garneau, "Lawsuit Alleges 'Photographic Piracy'," Editor & Publisher, February 26, 1994, p. 8.

infringement suit, FPG claims that the magazine scanned two photos from FPG's catalog into a computer and then used them to create a "derivative" computer-driven illustration which *Newsweek* subsequently used in an article it published about the "virtual reality" of computer networks.

FPG said it took the unusual step of suing one of its major customer in order to challenge what it described as "the widespread larceny of printed photos by unauthorized digital scanning". According to a FPG spokesperson, magazine editors who would never publish a copyrighted article without permission seem to have no similar concern about using photos that are also copyrighted in creating their magazine's computer generated images.

If this case should eventually go to trial, it will raise fascinating questions not only about basic intellectual property rights in digitally scanned photographs, but also about the process of altering of these images, and when they have been altered sufficiently to invoke the copyright infringement defense discussed in the following section; that of "fair use."

SEC. 76.   THE DEFENSE OF FAIR USE

The fair use doctrine—invented by courts to allow some use of others' works—was made explicit by the Copyright Act of 1976.   Major cases—such as *Sony* and *The Nation* magazine—continue to add to the definition of fair use in a piecemeal fashion.

The copyright law phrase "fair use" made a good deal of news during the mid–1980s.   Its growth in importance is quite remarkable, stemming as it does from judicial wriggling many years ago. Its growth may be understood as being fueled, in a major way, by onrushing technological changes.   Recent examples of important fair use cases decided by the Supreme Court—and which are taken up later in this Section—are Sony Corporation of America v. Universal City Studios, Inc.,[95] and Harper & Row Publishers, Inc. v. Nation Enterprises.[96]

The old 1909 copyright statute gave each copyright holder an exclusive right to "print, reprint, publish, copy and vend the copyrighted * * *."   As stated in that Act, it was an *absolute* right; the wording was put in terms so absolute that even pencil-and-paper copying was a violation of the U.S. Copyright Act.[97]   Because

[95] 464 U.S. 417, 104 S.Ct. 774 (1984).

[96] 471 U.S. 539, 105 S.Ct. 2218 (1985).

[97] See 17 U.S.C.A. § 10 of the statute which preceded the Copyright Statute of 1976: Verner W. Clapp, "Library Photocopying and Copyright: Recent Developments," Law Library Journal 55:1 (Feb., 1962) p. 12.

the 1909 statute's terms were so stringent, if enforced to the letter, it could have prevented anyone except the copyright holder from making any copy of any copyrighted work.

Such a statute was clearly against public policy favoring dissemination of information and knowledge and was plainly unenforceable. As a result, courts responded by developing the doctrine called "fair use."

American courts assumed—in creating a judge-made exception to the absolute language of the 1909 copyright statute—that "the law implies the consent of the copyright owner to a fair use of his publication for the advancement of science or art." [98] The fair use doctrine, although a rather elastic yardstick, was a needed improvement. The 1976 copyright statute has distilled the old common law copyright doctrine into some statutory guidelines. Factors to be considered by courts in determining whether the use made of a work in any particular case is a fair use include: [99]

(1) the purpose and character of the use, including whether such use is of a commercial nature or is for nonprofit educational purposes;

(2) the nature of the copyrighted work;

(3) the amount and substantiality of the portion used in relation to the copyrighted work as a whole; and

(4) the effect of the use upon the potential market for or value of the copyrighted work.

What, then, is fair use? In 1964, one expert asserted that fair use of someone's copyrightable materials exists "somewhere in the hinterlands between the broad avenue of independent creation and the jungle of unmitigated plagiarism." [1] No easy or automatic formula can be presented which will draw a safe line between fair use and infringement. Fifty words taken from a magazine article might be held to be fair use, while taking one line from a short poem might be labeled infringement by a court. The House of Representatives Committee on the Judiciary said this in its report on the 1976 copyright statute: [2]

General intention behind the provision

The statement of the fair use doctrine in section 107 offers some guidance to users in determining when the principles of the doctrine apply. However, the endless

[98] Wittenberg, op. cit., p. 148, offers a good non-technical description of fair use before it was expanded in 1967.

[99] U.S.C.A. § 107.

[1] Arthur N. Bishop, "Fair Use of Copyrighted Books," Houston Law Review, 2:2 (Fall, 1964) at p. 207.

[2] H.R. Report No. 94–1476, discussing the fair use provisions of 17 U.S.C.A. § 107.

variety of situations and combinations of circumstances that can rise in particular cases precludes the formulation of exact rules in the statute. The bill endorses the purpose and general scope of the judicial doctrine of fair use, but there is no disposition to freeze the doctrine in the statute, especially during a period of rapid technological change. Beyond a very broad statutory explanation of what fair use is and some of the criteria applicable to it, the courts must be free to adapt the doctrine to particular situations on a case-by-case basis. Section 107 is intended to restate the present judicial doctrine of fair use, not to change, narrow, or enlarge it in any way.

Generally speaking, courts have been quite lenient with quotations used in scholarly works or critical reviews. However, courts have been less friendly toward use of copyrighted materials for commercial purposes, or in works which compete with the original copyrighted piece.[3] The problems surrounding the phrase "fair use" have often arisen in connection with scientific, legal, or scholarly materials. With such works, it is to be expected that there will be similar treatment given to similar subject matters.[4] A crucial question, obviously, is whether the writer makes use of an earlier writer's work without doing substantial independent work.

Wholesale copying is *not* fair use.[5] Even if a writer had no intention of making unfair use of someone else's work, that writer still could be found liable for copyright infringement.[6] The idea of independent investigation is of great importance here. Copyrighted materials may be used as a *guide* for the purpose of gathering information, provided that the researcher then performs an original investigation and expresses the results of such work in the researcher's own language.[7]

Fair Use and Public Interest

Although many earlier cases expressed a narrow, restrictive view of the doctrine of fair use, some important decisions since the mid–1960s have emphasized the idea of *public* interest. This changed approach is of great importance to journalists and scholars,

[3] Eisenschiml v. Fawcett Publications, Inc., 246 F.2d 598 (7th Cir.1957); Benny v. Loew's Inc., 239 F.2d 532 (9th Cir.1956), affirmed 356 U.S. 43, 78 S.Ct. 667 (1958), rehearing denied 356 U.S. 934, 78 S.Ct. 770 (1958); Pilpel and Zavin, op. cit., pp. 160–161.

[4] Eisenschiml v. Fawcett Publications, Inc., 246 F.2d 598 (7th Cir.1957), certiorari denied 355 U.S. 907, 78 S.Ct. 334 (1957).

[5] Benny v. Loew's Inc., 239 F.2d 532 (9th Cir.1956), affirmed 356 U.S. 43, 78 S.Ct. 667 (1958), rehearing denied 356 U.S. 934, 78 S.Ct. 770 (1958).

[6] Wihtol v. Crow, 309 F.2d 777 (8th Cir.1962).

[7] Jeweler's Circular Pub. Co. v. Keystone Pub. Co., 281 Fed. 83 (2d Cir.1922), certiorari denied 259 U.S. 581, 42 S.Ct. 464 (1922).

for where there are matters which are newsworthy or otherwise of interest to the public, courts will consider such factors in determining whether a fair use was made of copyrighted materials.

A key case here is the 1967 decision known as Rosemont Enterprises, Inc. v. Random House, Inc. and John Keats. This case arose because Howard Hughes, a giant in America's aviation, oil and motion picture industries had a passionate desire to remain anonymously out of the public eye. A brief chronology will illustrate how this copyright infringement action came about:

• January and February, 1954: *Look* magazine, owned by Cowles Communications, Inc., published a series of three articles by Stanley White, titled "The Howard Hughes Story."

• In 1962, Random House, Inc., hired Thomas Thompson, a journalist employed by *Life* magazine, to prepare a book-length biography of Hughes. Later, either Hughes or his attorneys learned of the forthcoming Random House book. An attorney employed by Hughes warned Random House that Hughes did not want this biography and "would make trouble if the book was published." Thompson resigned from the project, and Random House then hired John Keats to complete the biography.

• Rosemont Enterprises, Inc., was organized in September, 1965 by Hughes' attorney and by two officers of his wholly-owned Hughes Tool Company.

• On May 20, 1966, Rosemont Enterprises purchased copyrights to the *Look* articles, advised Random House of this, and five days later brought a copyright infringement suit in New York. Attorneys for Rosemont somehow had gained possession of Random House galley proofs of the Random House biography of Hughes then being published: "Howard Hughes: a Biography by John Keats." [8]

Rosemont Enterprises sought an injunction to restrain Random House from selling, publishing, or distributing copies of its biography of Hughes because the book amounted to a prima facie case of copyright infringement. With his five-day-old ownership of the copyrights for the 1954 Look magazine articles, Hughes was indeed in a position to "cause trouble" for Random House.

The trial court agreed with the Rosemont Enterprises argument that infringement had occurred, and granted the injunction against Random House, holding up distribution of the book. The trial court rejected Random House's claims of fair use of the Look articles, saying that the privilege of fair use was confined to "materials used for purposes of criticism or comment or in scholar-

[8] Rosemont Enterprises, Inc. v. Random House, Inc. and John Keats, 366 F.2d 303, 304–305 (2d Cir.1966).

ly works of scientific or educational value." This district court took the view that if something was published "for commercial purposes"—that is, if it was designed for the popular market—the doctrine of fair use could not be employed to lessen the severity of the copyright law.[9] The district court found that the Hughes biography by Keats was for the popular market and therefore the fair use privilege could not be invoked by Random House.[10]

Circuit Judge Leonard P. Moore, speaking for the Circuit Court of Appeals, took another view. First of all, he noted that the three *Look* articles, taken together, totalled only 13,500 words, or between 35 and 39 pages if published in book form. Keats' 1966 biography on the other hand, had 166,000 words, or 304 pages in book form. Furthermore, Judge Moore stated that the *Look* articles did not purport to be a biography, but were merely accounts of a number of interesting incidents in Hughes' life. Judge Moore declared: [11]

> * * * there can be little doubt that portions of the *Look* article were copied. Two direct quotations and one eight-line paraphrase were attributed to Stephen White, the author of the articles. A mere reading of the *Look* articles, however, indicates that there is considerable doubt as to whether the copied and paraphrased matter constitutes a material and substantial portion of those articles.

> Furthermore, while the mode of expression employed by White is entitled to copyright protection, he could not acquire by copyright a monopoly in the narration of historical events.

In any case, the Keats book should fall within the doctrine of fair use. Quoting a treatise on copyright, Judge Moore stated: "Fair use is a privilege in others than the owner of a copyright to use the copyrighted material in a reasonable manner without his consent, notwithstanding the monopoly granted to the owner * * * ." [12]

Judge Moore demanded that public interest considerations—the public's interest in knowing about prominent and powerful men—be taken into account. He wrote that "public interest should prevail over possible damage to the copyright owner." He complained that the district court's preliminary injunction against Random House deprived the public of the opportunity to become acquainted with the life of a man of extraordinary talents in a

---

[9] Ibid., p. 304, citing the trial court, 256 F.Supp. 55 (S.D.N.Y.1966).

[10] Ibid.

[11] Ibid., pp. 306–307, certiorari denied 385 U.S. 1009, 87 S.Ct. 714 (1967).

[12] Ibid., p. 306, quoting Ball, Copyright and Literary Property, p. 260 (1944).

number of fields: "A narration of Hughes' initiative, ingenuity, determination and tireless work to achieve his concept of perfection in whatever he did ought to be available to a reading public." [13]

The Zapruder Case

A stunning event—the assassination of President John F. Kennedy—gave rise to a copyright case which added luster to the defense of fair use in infringement actions. On November 22, 1963, dress manufacturer Abraham Zapruder of Dallas stationed himself along the route of the President's motorcade, planning to take home movie pictures with his 8 millimeter camera. As the procession came into sight, Zapruder started his camera. Seconds later, the assassin's shots fatally wounded the President and Zapruder's color film caught the reactions of those in the President's car.

On that same day, Zapruder had his film developed and three color copies were made from the original film. He turned over two copies to the Secret Service, stipulating that these were strictly for governmental use and not to be shown to newspapers or magazines because Zapruder expected to sell the film.

Three days later, Zapruder negotiated a written agreement with *Life* magazine, which bought the original and all three copies of the film (including the two in possession of the Secret Service). Under that agreement, Zapruder was to be paid $150,000, in yearly installments of $25,000. *Life,* in its November 29, 1963, issue then featured thirty of Zapruder's frames. *Life* subsequently ran more of the Zapruder pictures. *Life* gave the Commission appointed by President Lyndon B. Johnson to investigate the killing of President Kennedy permission to use the Zapruder film and to reproduce it in the report.[14]

In May of 1967, *Life* registered the entire Zapruder film in the Copyright office as an unpublished "motion picture other than a photoplay." Three issues of *Life* magazine in which the Zapruder frames had been published had earlier been registered in the Copyright office as periodicals.[15] This meant that *Life* had a valid copyright in the Zapruder pictures when Bernard Geis Associates sought permission from *Life* magazine to publish the pictures in Josiah Thompson's book, *Six Seconds in Dallas,* a serious, thoughtful study of the assassination. The firm of Bernard Geis Associates

[13] Ibid., p. 309. And, at p. 311, Judge Moore discussed Rosemont's claim that it was planning to publish a book: "One can only speculate when, if ever, Rosemont will produce Hughes' authorized biography."

[14] Time Inc. v. Bernard Geis Associates, 293 F.Supp. 130, 131–134 (S.D.N.Y.1968). Although the Commission received permission from Time, Inc. to reproduce the photos, the Commission was told that it was expected to give the usual copyright notice. That proviso evidently was disregarded by the Commission.

[15] Ibid., p. 137.

offered to pay *Life* a royalty equal to the profits from publication of the book in return for permission to use specified Zapruder frames in the book. *Life* refused this offer.

Having failed to secure permission from *Life* to use the Zapruder pictures, author Josiah Thompson and his publisher decided to copy certain frames anyway. They did not reproduce the Zapruder frames photographically, but instead paid an artist $1,550 to make charcoal sketch copies. Thompson's book was then published, relying heavily on the sketches, in mid-November of 1967. Significant parts of 22 copyrighted frames were reproduced in the book.[16]

The court ruled that *Life* had a valid copyright in the Zapruder film, and added that "the so-called 'sketches' in the book are in fact copies of the copyrighted film. That they were done by an 'artist' is of no moment." The Court then quoted copyright expert Melville B. Nimmer: [17]

> "It is of course, fundamental, that copyright in a work protects against unauthorized copying not only in the original medium in which the work was produced, but also in any other medium as well. Thus copyright in a photograph will preclude unauthorized copying by drawing or in any other form, as well as by photographic reproduction."

The court then ruled that the use of the photos in Thompson's book was a copyright infringement, "unless the use of the copyrighted material in the Book is a 'fair use' outside the limits of copyright protection." [18] This led the court to a consideration of fair use, the issue which is " 'the most troublesome in the whole law of copyright.' " [19] The court then found in favor of Bernard Geis Associates and author Thompson, holding that the utilization of the Zapruder pictures was a "fair use." [20] The court said:

> There is an initial reluctance to find any fair use by defendants because of the conduct of Thompson in making his copies and because of the deliberate appropriation in the Book, in defiance of the copyright owner. Fair use presupposes "good faith and fair dealing." * * * On the other hand, it was not the nighttime activities of Thompson which enabled defendants to reproduce copies of Zapruder frames in the Book. They could have secured such frames from the National Archives, or they could have used the reproductions in the Warren Report [on the assassination of President Kennedy] or in the issues of *Life*

[16] Ibid., pp. 138–139.

[17] Ibid., p. 144, citing Nimmer on Copyright, p. 98.

[18] Ibid., p. 144.

[19] Ibid., quoting from Dellar v. Samuel Goldwyn, Inc., 104 F.2d 661 (2d Cir.1939).

[20] Ibid., p. 146.

itself.　Moreover, while hope by a defendant for commercial gain is not a significant factor in this Circuit, there is a strong point for defendants in their offer to surrender to *Life* all profits of Associates from the Book as royalty payment for a license to use the copyrighted Zapruder frames.　It is also a fair inference from the facts that defendants acted with the advice of counsel.

In determining the issue of fair use, the balance seems to be in favor of defendants.

There is a public interest in having the fullest information available on the murder of President Kennedy. Thompson did serious work on the subject and has a theory entitled to public consideration.　While doubtless the theory could be explained with sketches * * * [not copied from copyrighted pictures] * * * the explanation actually made in the Book with copies [of the Zapruder pictures] is easier to understand.　The Book is not bought because it contained the Zapruder pictures; the Book is bought because of the theory of Thompson and its explanation, supported by the Zapruder pictures.

There seems little, if any, injury to plaintiff, the copyright owner.　There is no competition between plaintiff and defendants.　Plaintiff does not sell the Zapruder pictures as such and no market for the copyrighted work appears to be affected.　Defendants do not publish a magazine.　There are projects for use by plaintiff of the film in the future as a motion picture or in books, but the effect of the use of certain frames in the Book on such projects is speculative.　It seems more reasonable to speculate that the Book would, if anything, enhance the value of the copyrighted work; it is difficult to see any decrease in its value.

Harper & Row v. Nation Enterprises (1985)

The defense of fair use, often helpful in fending off lawsuits for copyright infringement, can be pushed too far.　The Supreme Court of the United States served notice in 1985 that the fair use doctrine at times may not prevent liability for unauthorized publishing, even if the material involved is highly newsworthy.

Nation Magazine—reputedly America's longest continuously published weekly magazine—in 1979 received an unauthorized copy of former President Gerald R. Ford's memoirs.　Nation Editor Victor Navasky received the draft from an undisclosed source; this writing was the result of a collaboration between Ford and Trevor Armbrister, a senior editor of Reader's Digest.[21]

Nation Magazine carried an article developed by Navasky from the unauthorized copy, published in its issue of April 3, 1979, and was just over 2,000 words long. Harper & Row and The Reader's Digest Association, Inc., sued for copyright infringement. At the trial court level, U.S. District Judge Owen found that Navasky knew that the memoirs were soon to be published in book form by Harper & Row and Reader's Digest, with some advance publication rights assigned to Time Magazine. Judge Owen wrote: [22]

> However, believing that the draft contained "a real hot news story" concerning Ford's pardon of President Nixon * * * Navasky spent overnight or perhaps the next twenty-four hour period quoting and paraphrasing from a number of sections of the memoirs. Navasky added no comment of his own. He did not check the material. As he later testified, "I wasn't reporting on the truth or falsity of the account; I was reporting the fact that Ford reported this * * *." Part of Navasky's rush apparently was caused by the fact that he had to get the draft back to his "source" with some speed.

The Nation's article was about 2,250 words long, of which 300 to 400 words were taken from the Ford memoirs manuscript. Nation's publication may be said to have skimmed some of the more newsworthy aspects from the manuscript, which Harper & Row and Reader's Digest Association, as copyright holders, were preparing to market. For one thing, the copyright owners had negotiated a pre-publication agreement in which Time Magazine agreed to pay $25,000 ($12,500 in advance and the balance at the time of publication) for rights to excerpt 7,500 words from Mr. Ford's story of his pardon of President Nixon.

The Supreme Court of the United States said that The Nation had timed its publication to "scoop" Time Magazine's planned article. As a result of Nation's publication, Time cancelled its article and refused to pay the remaining $12,500 to Harper & Row and to Reader's Digest Association.[23] Writing for the Court, Justice Sandra Day O'Connor found that Nation's publication was not covered by the fair use defense: [24]

[21] Harper & Row Publishers, Inc. and Reader's Digest Ass'n, Inc. v. Nation Enterprises and Nation Associates, 557 F.Supp. 1067, 1069 (S.D.N.Y.1983), 9 Med. L.Rptr. 1229.

[22] Ibid.

[23] Harper & Row Publishers, Inc. v. Nation Enterprises, 471 U.S. 539, 105 S.Ct. 2218 (1985), 11 Med.L.Rptr. 1969, 1971.

[24] 471 U.S. 539, 105 S.Ct. 2218, 2225 (1985), 11 Med.L.Rptr. 1969, 1973.

* * * The Nation has admitted to lifting verbatim quotes of the author's original language totalling between 300 and 400 words and constituting some 13% of The Nation article. In using generous verbatim excerpts of Mr. Ford's unpublished manuscript to lend authenticity to its account of the forthcoming memoirs, The Nation effectively arrogated to itself the right of first publication, an important marketable subsidiary right. * * * [W]e find that use of the copyrighted manuscript, even stripped to the verbatim quotes conceded by The Nation to be copyrightable expression, was not a fair use within the meaning of the Copyright Act.

Justice O'Connor examined the tension between racing to publish news first and copyright: [25]

In our haste to disseminate news, it should not be forgotten that the Framers intended copyright itself to be the engine of free expression. By establishing a marketable right to the use of one's expression, copyright supplies the economic incentive to create and disseminate ideas.

Further, she held that a writer's public figure status did not create a waiver of the copyright laws: [26]

In view of the First Amendment protections already embodied in the Copyright Act's distinction between copyrightable expression and uncopyrightable facts and ideas, and the latitude for scholarship and comment traditionally afforded by fair use, we see no warrant for expanding the doctrine of fair use to create what amounts to a public figure exception to copyright. Whether verbatim copying from a public figure's manuscript in a given case is or is not fair must be judged according to the traditional equities of fair use.

The Court's majority opinion marched through the Copyright Statute's list of four factors to be considered in determining whether a use is "fair":

(1) *The Nature and Purpose of the Use*—Justice O'Connor said the general purpose of The Nation's use was "general reporting." Part of this, however, was The Nation's stated purpose of scooping the forthcoming hardcover books and the excerpts to be published in Time Magazine. This, Justice O'Connor said, had " * * * the intended purpose of

[25] 471 U.S. 539, 105 S.Ct. 2218, 2230 (1985), 11 Med.L.Rptr. 1969, 1978.
[26] 471 U.S. 539, 105 S.Ct. 2218, 2230–2231 (1985), 11 Med.L.Rptr. 1969, 1978.

supplanting the copyright holder's commercially valuable right of first publication." [27]

(2) *Nature of the Copyrighted Work*—Justice O'Connor wrote that President Ford's narrative, "A Time to Heal" was "an unpublished historical narrative or autobiography." She said the unpublished nature of the work was critical to considering whether use of it by The Nation was fair. Although substantial quotes might qualify as fair use in a review or discussion of a published work, "the author's right to control the first public appearance of his expression weighs against such use of the work before its release." [28]

(3) *Amount and Substantiality of the Copying*—"Stripped of the verbatim quotes, the direct takings from the unpublished manuscript constitute at least 13% of the infringing article. * * * The Nation article is structured around the quoted excerpts which serve as its dramatic focal points."

(4) *Effect on the Market*—Noting that Time Magazine had cancelled its projected serialization of the Ford memoirs and had refused to pay $12,500, Justice O'Connor said those occurrences were direct results from the infringement. "Rarely will a case of copyright infringement present such clear cut evidence of damage." [29]

Thus a six-member majority concluded that The Nation's use of the Ford memoirs was not a fair use. This meant that a Court of Appeals finding that The Nation's publication was overturned, and that The Nation was liable to pay the $12,500 in damages, matching the amount which Time Magazine had refused to pay the copyright holders after the unauthorized publication.

Justice William J. Brennan, Jr.—who was joined by Justices Byron White and Thurgood Marshall—dissented. "The Court holds that The Nation's quotation of 300 words from the unpublished 200,000–word manuscript of President Gerald R. Ford infringed the copyright," wrote Brennan. He said the Court's majority reached this finding even though the quotations related to a historical event of undoubted significance—the resignation and pardon of President Richard M. Nixon. Brennan added that "this zealous defense of the copyright owner's prerogative will, I fear, stifle the broad dissemination of ideas and information copyright is intended to nurture." [30]

[27] 471 U.S. 539, 105 S.Ct. 2218, 2232 (1985), 11 Med.L.Rptr. 1969, 1978.
[28] 471 U.S. 539, 105 S.Ct. 2218, 2232 (1985), 11 Med.L.Rptr. 1969, 1980.
[29] 471 U.S. 539, 105 S.Ct. 2218, 2233 (1985), 11 Med.L.Rptr. 1969, 1981.
[30] 471 U.S. 539, 105 S.Ct. 2218, 2240 (1985), 11 Med.L.Rptr. 1969, 1983.

Brennan concluded,[31]

The Court's exceedingly narrow approach to fair use permits Harper & Row to monopolize information. This holding "effect[s] an important extension of property rights and a corresponding curtailment in the free use of knowledge and of ideas." International News Service v. Associated Press, 248 U.S. at 263 (Brandeis, J., dissenting). The Court has perhaps advanced the ability of the historian—or at least the public official who has recently left office—to capture the full economic value of information in his or her possession. But the Court does so only by "risking the robust debate of public issues * * *."

Publication of Another's Private
Letters Held Not a "Fair Use."

J.D. Salinger is a highly regarded novelist and short story writer, best known for his novel, "The Catcher in the Rye". His last work was published in 1965, and since that time he has been trying to avoid any publicity about himself, refusing to grant interviews or to respond to any inquiries about his private life. Ian Hamilton, a respected literary critic for *The London Sunday Times,* contacted the reclusive author in 1983 to tell him that he intended to write a biography about Salinger to be published by Random House. Although Salinger responded that he did not want to have his biography written during his lifetime, Hamilton spent the next three years completing the work, titled "J.D. Salinger: A Writing Life."

Lacking any cooperation from Salinger himself, Hamilton relied heavily upon information contained in letters Salinger had written to various friends during his early years as a writer. These letters had been donated by their recipients to several university libraries, but Salinger was apparently unaware that they would be available to Hamilton.

When Salinger read the galley proofs of the book Random House planned to publish, he notified the publisher that he would attempt to block its publication unless all direct quotations from these private letters he had written his friends were deleted.

Responding to these objections, Hamilton revised his work, omitting most of the direct quotations from Salinger's letters, but still paraphrasing very closely some 59 passages from this correspondence. As Random House was about to publish this revised version of the biography, Salinger sued to prevent publication, claiming among other things that such extensive reliance upon

[31] 471 U.S. 539, 105 S.Ct. 2218, 2254 (1985), 11 Med.L.Rptr. 1969, 1994–1995.

passages from his unpublished letters exceeded the reasonable bounds of fair use.

After originally granting Salinger's request for a preliminary injunction, a lower federal court had decided to lift the injunction and allow publication when a U.S. Court of Appeals intervened, ordering that this ban on publication be made permanent.[32] In its attempt to follow the Supreme Court's concept of fair use as defined in the Harper & Row case, this Court of Appeals decision placed special emphasis upon the fact these letters of Salinger's were unpublished.

That Supreme Court opinion had declared that "the scope of fair use is narrower with respect to unpublished works." Following this argument, the court found that because an author's privilege to incorporate unpublished material of another in his own work was a relatively limited one, and because Hamilton had relied so heavily upon the unpublished letters of Salinger in his biography, he had clearly exceeded the reasonable boundaries of permissible fair use.

In essence, then, the "nature of the copyrighted work" and "the amount and substantiality of the portion used" were the two elements of the Harper & Row decision that this court emphasized in finding that Hamilton's biography of Salinger had abused this legal privilege.

In Craft v. Kobler, the material to be used was from several copyrighted works but the result was exactly the same.[33] In this case an author completing a biography of Igor Stravinsky sought to include in his manuscript passages from the copyrighted works of the composer's personal assistant. Here again the problem was one of excessive usage of the work of others, because the passages to be taken from these copyrighted works of the plaintiff represented nearly three percent of the total biography, and included many richly descriptive paragraphs about Stravinsky based upon the assistant's special knowledge of him.

Technology and Fair Use: The Sony "Betamax" Decision (1984)

When videocassette recorders became available to the general public in the early 1980s, it was clear that technology was once

---

[32] 811 F.2d 90 (2d Cir.1987), 13 Med.L.Rptr. 1954. The Supreme Court has declined to review this decision, so the ban on the publication of the book remains permanent. "Supreme Court Refuses to Review Salinger Ruling," New York Times, October 6, 1987, p. 11. On the other hand, in Maheu v. CBS, 201 Cal.App.3d 662, 247 Cal.Rptr. 304 (1988), 15 Med.L.Rptr. 1548, a California court refused to allow an action for copyright infringement by an assistant of Howard Hughes for the unauthorized use of correspondence he received from Hughes because of his failure to obtain copyright protection for this unpublished correspondence that was copyrightable.

[33] Craft v. Kobler, 667 F.Supp. 120 (S.D.N.Y.1987), 14 Med.L.Rptr. 1617.

again moving beyond the scope of existing copyright law. The public had rejected RCA's efforts to market a videodisc player with no ability to record video programs, but was eager to buy Sony's new Betamax machines that allowed them to record and duplicate those broadcast programs and films that copyright owners had only expected them to view off-air.[34]

Because Congress proved itself incapable of amending the Copyright Act of 1976 to establish what rights copyright owners had to prevent such unauthorized copying of their works, the courts were soon forced to interpret an already out-dated Act in some manner that would bring this new form of usage within its provisions.

In January, 1984, the Supreme Court decided 5–4 that video recorders are legal for sale and home use under the Copyright Statute and the doctrine of fair use.[35] This case arose when Universal City Studios and Walt Disney productions sued Sony, claiming that use of Sony Betamax VCRs in homes by private individuals constituted copyright infringement.

In 1979, a federal district court held off-the-air copying for private, non-commercial use to be a "fair use." Plaintiffs had not proved to the court's satisfaction that harm to copyrighted properties was being done by such taping.[36] But in 1981, the United States Court of Appeals for the Ninth Circuit overturned that ruling, holding that makers and distributors of home video recorders were liable for damages if the machines were used to tape programs broadcast over-the-air.[37]

The Supreme Court, after granting certiorari, agreed in mid–1982 to hear Sony's appeal from the Court of Appeals holding. The Court, however, held the case over into a second term, and had it argued a second time in October, 1983.[38] Writing for a five-Justice majority, Justice John Paul Stevens said that most people use a VCR principally to record a program they cannot see as it is being telecast, and then use the home recording to watch the program at

[34] For a concise description of both RCA's marketing failure and Sony's marketing success, see,"RCA Calls It Quits With Videodisks," Broadcasting, April 4, 1984, p. 39. By the time the Supreme Court decided the Sony case in 1984, more than 13 million VCRs had already been sold. "3–d Quarter VCR U.S. Population Pegged at 13 Mil," Variety, October 23, 1984, p. 1.

[35] Sony Corporation of America v. Universal City Studios, Inc., 464 U.S. 417, 104 S.Ct. 774 (1984). Ironically, although Sony had won this legal battle, its "Beta" format lost out in the marketing war to its "VHS" format competitors. By 1988 Sony was abandoning "Beta" and producing its own VHS format VCRs. See, "Sony Adds VHS to VCR Format," Variety, January 12, 1988, p. 1.

[36] 480 F.Supp. 429, 452–453 (D.Cal.1979).

[37] 659 F.2d 963 (9th Cir.1981).

[38] 464 U.S. 417, 104 S.Ct. 774, 777 (1984); Wermeil, loc. cit.

another time. This "time-shifting" practice, Justice Stevens said, enlarges the viewing audience: [39]

> * * * [A] significant amount of television programming may be used in this manner without objection from the owners of the copyrights on the programs. For the same reason, even the two respondents in this case, who do assert objections to time-shifting * * * were unable to prove that the practice has impaired the commercial value of their copyrights * * *

Justice Stevens noted that Universal and Disney studios were not seeking damages from individual Betamax users whom they claimed infringed their copyrights. Instead, they charged Sony with "contributory infringement." To prevail, this required them to prove that Sony encouraged those who purchased its Betamax machines to unlawfully copy feature films produced by studios such as Universal and Disney. [40] Justice Stevens added,[41]

> If vicarious liability is to be imposed on * * * [Sony] * * *, it must rest on the fact that they have sold equipment with constructive knowledge of the fact that their consumers may use that equipment to make unauthorized copies of copyrighted material. There is no precedent in the law of copyright for the imposition of vicarious liability on such a theory.

The Betamax decision was limited to noncommercial home uses. "If the Betamax were used to make copies for a commercial or profit-making purpose, such use would be presumptively unfair," Justice Stevens said.[42] Thus the Sony case is clearly distinguishable from a situation where off-the-air taping is being done for commercial reasons.[43]

Importantly, Justice Stevens concluded that the home use of VCRs for noncommercial purposes was a fair use.[44]

> * * * [To] the extent that time-shifting expands public access to freely broadcast television programs, it yields societal benefits. Earlier this year, in Community Televi-

[39] 464 U.S. 417, 104 S.Ct. 774, 778 (1984).

[40] 464 U.S. 417, 104 S.Ct. 774, at 785 (1984).

[41] 464 U.S. 417, 104 S.Ct. 774, at 787 (1984).

[42] 464 U.S. 417, 104 S.Ct. 774, 792 (1984).

[43] Melville B. Nimmer, Nimmer on Copyright, Vol. 3, § 13.5[F] (New York: Matthew Bender, 1963, 1980), citing Elektra Records Co. v. Gem Electronic Distributors, Inc., 360 F.Supp. 821 (E.D.N.Y.1973) (taping of copyrighted records for commercial redistribution ruled infringing) and Walt Disney Productions v. Alaska Television Network, Inc., 310 F.Supp. 1073 (W.D.Wash.1969) (videotaping for commercial use).

[44] 464 U.S. 417, 104 S.Ct. 774, 795 (1984).

sion of Southern California v. Gottfried, 103 S.Ct. 885, 891–892, 74 L.Ed.2d 705 (1983), we acknowledged the public interest in making television broadcasting more available. Concededly, that interest is not unlimited. But it supports an interpretation of the concept of "fair use" that requires the copyright holder to demonstrate some likelihood of harm before he may condemn a private act of time-shifting as a violation of federal law.

Justice Stevens concluded the opinion of the Court with a summary of findings and with an invitation to Congress to provide legislative guidance in this case: [45]

> In summary, the record and findings of the District Court lead us to two conclusions. First, Sony demonstrated a significant likelihood that substantial numbers of copyright holders who license their works for broadcast on free television would not object to having their broadcasts time-shifted by private viewers. And second, respondents failed to demonstrate that time-shifting would cause any likelihood of nominal harm to the potential market for, or the value of, their copyrighted works. The Betamax is, therefore, capable of substantial noninfringing uses. Sony's sale of such equipment to the general public does not constitute contributory infringement of respondent's copyrights.

> * * *

> One may search the copyright act in vain for any sign that the elected representatives of the millions of people who watch television every day have made it unlawful to copy a program for later viewing at home, or have enacted a flat prohibition against the sale of machines that make such copying possible.

> It may well be that Congress will take a fresh look at this new technology, just as it so often has examined other innovations in the past. But it is not our job to apply laws that have not yet been written. Applying the copyright statute, as it now reads, to the facts as they have been developed in this case, the judgment of the Court of Appeals must be reversed.

Justice Blackmun, joined by Justices Marshall, Powell, and Rehnquist, dissented.[46]

> It is apparent from the record and from the findings of the District Court that time-shifting does have a substan-

---

[45] 464 U.S. 417, 104 S.Ct. 774, 796 (1984).

[46] 464 U.S. 417, 104 S.Ct. 774, 811 (1984).

tial adverse effect upon the "potential market for" the Studios' copyrighted works. Accordingly, even under the formulation of the fair use doctrine advanced by Sony, time-shifting cannot be deemed a fair use.

Justice Blackmun added that the case should have been sent back to District Court for additional findings of fact on the matter of infringement and contributory infringement.[47]

Parody and Fair Use

Can a parody be fair use? The "Saturday Night Live" television program did a skit poking fun at New York City's public relations campaign and its theme song. In this four-minute skit, the town fathers of Sodom discussed a plan to improve their city's image. This satire ended with the singing of "I Love Sodom" to the tune of "I Love New York." In a per curiam opinion, the U.S. Court of Appeals, Second Circuit rejected the complaint of Elsmere Record Co., owner of copyright to "I Love New York." "Believing that, in today's world of often unrelieved solemnity, copyright law should be hospitable to the humor of parody," the Court of Appeals approved District Judge Goettel's decision granting the defendant National Broadcasting Company a summary judgment on ground that the parody was a fair use.[48]

Judge Goettel's opinion said, in words useful for understanding both the concept of fair use and its application to parodies charged with copyright infringement: [49]

> In its entirety, the original song "I Love New York" is composed of a 45 word lyric and 100 measures. Of this only four notes, D C D E (in that sequence), and the words "I Love" were taken in the Saturday Night Live sketch (although they were repeated 3 or 4 times). As a result, the defendant now argues that the use it made was insufficient to constitute copyright infringement.
>
> This court does not agree. Although it is clear that, on its face, the taking involved in this action is relatively slight, on closer examination it becomes apparent that this portion of the piece, the musical phrase that the lyrics "I Love New York" accompanies, is the heart of the composition. * * * Accordingly, such taking is capable of rising to the level of a copyright infringement.
>
> Having so determined, the Court must next address the question of whether the defendant's copying of the

---

[47] 464 U.S. 417, 104 S.Ct. 774, 815 (1984).

[48] Elsmere Music, Inc. v. NBC, 623 F.2d 252 (2d Cir.1980), 6 Med.L.Rptr. 1457.

[49] Elsmere Music, Inc. v. NBC, 482 F.Supp. 741, 742 (S.D.N.Y.1980), 5 Med. L.Rptr. 2455, 2456.

plaintiff's jingle constituted a fair use which would exempt it from liability under the Copyright Act. Fair use has been defined as a "privilege in others than the owner of the copyright to use the copyrighted material in a reasonable manner without his consent, notwithstanding the monopoly granted to the owner of the copyright".

Judge Goettel then reviewed the four criteria set out by the 1976 copyright revision, 17 U.S.C.A. § 107 [quoted at the beginning of this Section], and compared those criteria to relevant cases on the fair use doctrine. He quoted copyright specialist Melville B. Nimmer, who has said, "short of * * * [a] complete identity of content, the disparity of functions between a serious work and a satire based upon it, may justify the defense of fair use even where substantial similarity exists." [50]

Plaintiff Elsmere Records argued that "I Love Sodom" was not a valid parody of "I Love New York." Elsmere pointed to two raunchy cases in which copyright infringement was found because use of copyrighted material was not parodying the material itself, but was instead using someone's intellectual property, without permission, to make statements essentially irrelevant to the original work.[51] Elsmere Records cited MCA, Inc. v. Wilson, in which the song "Cunnilingus Champion of Company C" was held to infringe the copyright of "Boogie Woogie Bugle Boy of Company B." [52] And in Walt Disney Productions v. Mature Pictures Corporation, the court held that using the copyrighted "Mickey Mouse March" as background for a teen-age group sex scene in a "Happy Hooker" movie was not fair use.[53]

However, Judge Goettel found that the Saturday Night Live sketch validly parodied the plaintiff's jingle and the "I Love New York" ad campaign. Also, he ruled that the parody did not interfere with the marketability of a copyrighted work. Therefore, he held that the sketch was a fair use, and that no copyright violation had occurred.

Campbell aka Skyywalker v. Acuff–Rose Music, Inc.

In 1992 Acuff–Rose Music, Inc. sued 2 Live Crew, contending that the Crew's song "Pretty Woman" infringed the Acuff–Rose

[50] Nimmer on Copyright, § 13.05[C], at 13–60–61 (1979), quoted by Judge Goettel at 482 F.Supp. 741 at 745 (S.D.N.Y.1980), 5 Med.L.Rptr. 2455, 2457.

[51] 482 F.Supp. 741, 745 (S.D.N.Y.1980), 5 Med.L.Rptr. 2455, 2457.

[52] MCA, Inc. v. Wilson, 425 F.Supp. 443 (S.D.N.Y.1976).

[53] 389 F.Supp. 1397 (S.D.N.Y.1975). Similarly, in Fisher v. Dees, 794 F.2d 432 (9th Cir.1986), 13 Med.L.Rptr. 1167, a U.S. Court of Appeals Court found that a parody of the plaintiff composers' song "When Sunny Gets Blue," performed as "When Sunny Sniffs Glue," took no more from the copyrighted song than was necessary to reasonably accomplish its purpose. It was neither obscene nor immoral in nature, and was parody entitled to fair use protection.

copyright of Roy Orbison's rock ballad, "Oh Pretty Woman." The District Court granted summary judgement for 2 Live Crew, holding that its song was a parody that made *fair use* of the original ballad.[54]

The Court of Appeals overturned the lower court decision, deciding that the parody's commercial nature, coupled with what the court found as a matter of law to be its too extensive use of the original song in the parody, presented issues that could result in a finding of copyright infringement against 2 Live Crew.[55]

A unanimous Supreme Court reversed the Court of Appeals.[56] Justice Souter, speaking for the Court, stated that the key in determining whether the parody of a copyrighted work infringes on the original is not its commercial or non-commercial nature, but the extent it alters the original through new expression, message or meaning. Thus, as Souter expressed it, the more "transformative" the parody, the less significant the other factors—(the commercial/non-commercial nature of the use; the amount used; its impact on the market value of the original).

The Court of Appeals had erred, according to Souter, both in finding the borrowing from the original to be too extensive, and in presuming without adequate evidence that market harm would result from the parody.

In essence, then, this decision indicates that the Supreme Court, in cases of parody of copyrighted materials, will place greatest emphasis on the first of the four elements of the fair use defense, not in terms of whether the parody is commercial or non-commercial, but whether it alters substantially the message or meaning of the original. The more "original" the parody, then, the less likely it is to be found to have infringed the copyrighted work.

SEC. 77. BROADCAST MUSIC LICENSING RIGHTS

Electronic media must obtain copyright clearance for the music they use through private agreements with organizations that represent the composers and publishers of this music.

In 1923 the National Association of Broadcasters (NAB) was founded primarily to negotiate an agreement with the American Society of Composers and Publishers (ASCAP) to allow radio stations to broadcast the copyrighted music of the society's composers and music publishers.

---

[54] Acuff–Rose Music, Inc. v. Luther Skyywalker et al., 754 F.Supp. 1150 (M.D.Tenn.1991).

[55] Acuff–Rose Music, Inc. v. Campbell, aka Skyywalker, 972 F.2d 1429 (6th Cir.1992).

[56] Campbell v. Acuff–Rose Music, Inc., 114 S.Ct. 1164 (1994).

ASCAP had been formed in 1914 as a performing rights, copyright licensing agency for a group of music publishers and their composers whose works were being performed in music halls and in Vaudeville theaters without permission or payment.[57] When radio stations began broadcasting recorded music of ASCAP's composers and publishers during the early 1920s, the organization demanded copyright royalties for this program use.

During this pioneering era of broadcasting, stations were not yet permitted to sell commercial time and so until the early 1930s these radio station music licensing payments were little more than token contributions. By 1932, however, as radio was emerging as one of the few profitable industries during the Great Depression, ASCAP suddenly demanded a 300 percent increase in its broadcast music licensing fees.

For a time the NAB was able to convince its member stations to fill their schedules with the few public domain compositions they had on record, but when ASCAP offered a lower rate to newspaper owned stations, opposition collapsed and broadcasters agreed to this massive rate hike.

In 1937 the broadcast industry attempted to dilute ASCAP's absolute power over broadcast music rights by encouraging the formation of a rival group, Broadcast Music Incorporated (BMI), hoping that competition for broadcast business would force ASCAP to reduce its fees. The tactic worked for a short time, but soon BMI began bargaining as aggressively as ASCAP during each renegotiation of its licensing agreements.

When television began to emerge during the 1950s as the dominant electronic medium in the United States, the "blanket license" approach that both ASCAP and BMI used to grant broadcast use of their music was challenged by the television industry. Most radio stations had been willing to accept this type of license that granted them full broadcast use of music from ASCAP and BMI composers in return for a payment of less than one percent of their annual advertising revenues. For television stations, however, with their far larger advertising revenues, and their far less extensive use of music, neither the blanket license nor the per-use alternative offered by ASCAP or BMI seemed reasonably related to the actual value a station owner received from such music usage.

Beginning in 1950, the All–Industry Television Station Music License Committee, negotiating on behalf of its member stations, sought some other type of arrangement with the music licensing

---

[57] During this era, sheet music was still the primary source of income for the music industry. Publishing companies would either hire composers and lyricists to write the songs that would be published and sold to the public or purchase songs from established composers. Today a music publisher simply promotes and produces musical recordings.

groups that would reflect more accurately the minimal benefits the blanket license offered television stations. Although each new round of negotiations resulted in a further reduction of the percentage of advertising revenues to be charged during the subsequent license period, neither ASCAP nor BMI was willing to abandon a licensing structure that by 1970 was providing an estimated 20–25 percent of their annual music rights revenue.[58]

After failing to reach agreement with the music licensing organizations on a satisfactory alternative to the blanket license, CBS, acting on behalf of the television networks, began an antitrust action against ASCAP and BMI in 1969. CBS alleged that these organizations had acted in concert to prevent the composers and publishers they represented from dealing directly with the television networks or its producers who sought to purchase broadcast music rights from the parties who held title to them, in restraint of trade and in direct violation of section 1 of the Sherman Antitrust Laws.[59]

In 1981, the U.S. Supreme Court held that the blanket license was not a per se violation of the Act, and on remand the Court of Appeals then dismissed the action.[60] In 1978 a group of local television stations began their own antitrust action against ASCAP and BMI, alleging the same type of anticompetitive practices. Unlike CBS, however, these local stations were successful in convincing a lower court that the blanket music licensing agreements did constitute an illegal restraint of trade.[61]

According to the opinion, what made the conduct of ASCAP and BMI anti-competitive was their concerted effort to discourage program producers from obtaining directly from composers complete copyright clearance for broadcast usage of the programs they produced. The court found that, unlike the television networks, individual stations did not have sufficient bargaining power to force music licensing organizations to alter their practices, and therefore they required the protection the law provided in order to be capable of bargaining with ASCAP and BMI on equal footing.

ASCAP and BMI challenged this federal trial court decision, and a federal appeals court reversed the lower court holding, finding that the difference in the degree of bargaining power exercised by the stations and the networks was not substantial enough to require a finding that the music licensing organizations were acting in restraint of trade.[62]

[58] "Broadcasters Press On Against ASCAP, BMI," *Variety* January 8, 1986, p. 209.

[59] CBS v. ASCAP, 620 F.2d 930 (2d Cir.1980).

[60] BMI v. CBS, 441 U.S. 1, 99 S.Ct. 1551 (1979).

[61] Buffalo Broadcasting Co. v. ASCAP, 546 F.Supp. 274 (S.D.N.Y.1982).

[62] Buffalo Broadcasting Co. v. ASCAP, 744 F.2d 917 (2d Cir.1984).

When the U.S. Supreme Court refused to review this appellate court decision, broadcasting turned immediately to Congress to obtain through legislation what it had been unable to gain through litigation. During recent years the NAB has been attempting during each session of Congress to obtain passage of a law that would legally obligate every television producer to acquire full musical broadcast performance rights to all programs to be distributed for television broadcast. Although none of these "source licensing" bills have been adopted by Congress, the NAB continues in its lobbying efforts because it believes that such "source licensing" would clear at least 90 percent of the musical content now broadcast by television stations throughout the United States, making it possible for networks and most television stations to avoid the need of a "blanket" music license from ASCAP or BMI.

In 1990, the cable industry charged these music licensing organizations with anti-competitive practices under the Sherman antitrust act, challenging the refusal of these groups to offer cable TV networks a blanket music license. The industry eventually prevailed, obtaining agreements from both organizations to accept license payments from each cable network and a single annual fee from each cable system.[63]

Because payment arrangements for electronic media usage of copyrighted music are not established by the statutory provisions of the Copyright Act, all terms and conditions of usage must be negotiated between the music licensing organizations and representatives of electronic media. Considering the amount of money involved, it is not surprising that so many of these efforts have ended up in litigation, requiring the courts to define for the parties the reasonable value of the music rights involved.

Recently, pay-TV organizations have begun to have their day in court. Early in 1991, HBO negotiated an interim settlement with BMI, agreeing to pay the broadcast music performing rights organization a monthly fee for use of BMI music until a federal court determines whether BMI can rightfully demand music rights payments both from a pay-TV service that is providing programming and each cable system that is distributing it.[64] One week later ASCAP, the other major broadcast music licensing organization, negotiated a similar interim settlement with Showtime.[65]

[63] National Cable Television Assn. v. Broadcast Music Inc., 772 F.Supp. 614 (D.C.C., 1991). U.S. v. American Society of Composers, Authors and Publishers (ASCAP), 782 F.Supp. 778 (S.D.N.Y.1991) affirmed per curiam 956 F.2d 21 (2d Cir., 1992), cert. denied 112 S.Ct. 1950 (1992).

[64] "BMI Makes Deal with HBO; Lawsuit Dropped," Variety, January 14, 1991, p. 121.

[65] "ASCAP, Showtime Settle on Fees," Variety, January 21, 1991, p. 90.

This entire electronic media music performing rights controversy is yet another illustration of technology complicating the process of effectively compensating the creative artist for the use of that individual's intellectual property. Paying some arbitrarily determined amount of money to a licensing organization to be divided in almost as arbitrarily a fashion among that group of artists it represents is certainly far less efficient or cost effective than direct negotiations between the purchaser and the artist.[66]

Unfortunately, though, such direct negotiations for the use of music are seldom possible in this modern era. At the beginning of the twentieth century a vaudeville or music hall producer could purchase from a publisher the performing rights to a complete musical score for a stage show that might run for several years. Today, however, it would be virtually impossible for the typical radio station to negotiate for the rights to each of fifteen to twenty different musical compositions it schedules on each hour's playlist.

[66] Cable TV's compulsory license to allow it to pay a percentage of its subscriber revenues into a pool to compensate those who own the TV programs the system has imported from a distant broadcast market operates in basically the same fashion as the broadcast music licensing agreement, but in cable TV's situation the pooling arrangement is created by federal law.

Part IV

FACT GATHERING AND CITIZENS' RIGHTS

Chapter 13

SHIELDING INFORMATION FROM DISCLOSURE

SEC. 78. THE GOVERNMENT CONTEMPT POWER

Persons who disobey the orders of courts may be cited, tried and convicted for contempt of court, the coercive power that underlies the courts' authority. The legislative branch has similar power. Journalists most often have come in conflict with the contempt power when they have refused court orders to disclose confidential information.

The common law has long provided that relationships between certain people are so personal that their confidences deserve protection against legally compelled disclosure. The clergyman and penitent, the physician and patient, the attorney and client, the husband and wife all share information that in some circumstances warrants unbroken confidentiality. The law has resisted expanding the protection to other interpersonal relationships, and even in the few listed above it has carefully avoided establishing any never-failing or absolute protection against the general rule. When government requires a citizen's testimony in furthering its legitimate ends such as ensuring fair judicial process or making laws, it is the citizen's duty to appear and testify.[1]

Printers of the American colonial period universally provided many contributors with anonymity, and occasionally resisted demands of the legislative branch to reveal their names. Early in nationhood, journalists continued to refuse demands of Congress

---

[1] 8 J. Wigmore, Evidence, 2286, 2290, 2394 (J. McNaughton Rev.Ed.1961).

571

and legislatures to break confidences, and as the Nineteenth Century progressed, sought expansion of the common law's protection to their own setting. They argued that journalistic ethics and their own professional livelihood required that they keep confidences. Especially in reporting corruption in government, they added, the public interest required that the news be told and that sometimes the news could be told only if they promised their source confidentiality. Their success was modest indeed, but by the end of the century, a start was made toward legal protection when the State of Maryland passed the nation's first "shield law" for journalists—a law that recognized a journalist's privilege to not reveal confidential sources. Within the next three or four decades, a few more states joined Maryland in establishing journalists' privilege by statute.[2] Broad protection, however, did not emerge until the 1970s, when some expansive readings of the First Amendment, increased numbers of state statutes, and the federal common law were brought to bear on problems of confidentiality.

The authority of government to compel testimony and to respond to persons'—including journalists'—refusal to break confidences is its contempt power. Government may declare that refusals to testify are contempt of authority, and may punish the person in contempt with imprisonment. It was a student journalist in Oregon who showed professional journalists that contests over compelled testimony is a real issue that should concern them.

Annette Buchanan wrote a story for her college newspaper, the University of Oregon *Daily Emerald,* about the use of marijuana among students at the University. She said that seven students, whom she did not name, gave her information. And when the district attorney asked her to name the sources of information to a grand jury that was investigating drug use, and subsequently a judge directed her to do so, she refused. A reporter should be privileged not to reveal her sources, she said, and not to break confidences. To betray a pledge of secrecy to a source, Buchanan added, would be a signal to many sources to "dry up." The judge, and upon appeal the Oregon Supreme Court, found her in contempt of court for refusing to obey the judge's order, and she was sentenced to a brief jail term.[3]

Buchanan's situation was a case of "direct" contempt. It took place in the presence of the judge. Goss, a television personality,

---

[2] The history of journalists' privilege not to reveal information is best told by A. David Gordon, "Protection of News Sources: the History and Legal Status of the Newsman's Privilege," Ph.D. dissertation, unpublished (Univ. of Wis., 1970). See also Thomas H. Kaminski, "Congress, Correspondents and Confidentiality in the 19th Century: a Preliminary Study," Journalism History, 4:3, Autumn 1977, pp. 83–87. For a recent overview, see The News Media & The Law, Fall, 1989.

[3] State v. Buchanan, 250 Or. 244, 436 P.2d 729 (1968), certiorari denied 392 U.S. 905, 88 S.Ct. 2055 (1968).

was not within shouting distance of the court when on his program he attacked witnesses in a divorce case in which he was accused of adultery with the wife. For his attempt to prevent witnesses from giving testimony unfavorable to him by vilifying them, he was convicted of contempt which takes place away from the court, by publication, called indirect or "constructive" contempt.[4] On appeal, his conviction was overruled, the court holding that his broadcasts were no real danger to justice because while the targets might have been angered by his words, they had no reason to feel threatened in their testimony by them.[5]

In the *Goss* case of contempt by publication as in the *Buchanan* case of direct contempt, a judge ruled initially that the reporter's acts interfered with the administration of justice—that the acts were contemptuous of court. In each case, the judge convicted the reporter under a judge's inherent power to punish for the interference, punishment for contempt being the basis of all legal procedure and the means of courts' enforcing their judgments and orders.[6]

The cases diverged in their results, Buchanan failing in her appeal, Goss succeeding in his. Indeed, the outcomes illustrate the varying fortunes of reporters in recent years in similar circumstances. Direct contempt is a current, serious problem for the press. Indirect or "constructive" contempt has almost vanished, as we saw in Chapter 2, Sec. 10, and needs no further treatment in this chapter.

"Summary" procedure is the ordinary procedure in contempt. In a summary proceeding, a judge accuses, tries, and sentences in his or her own case without resort to trial by jury. It is often justified by reference to the British legal writer of the 18th Century, Sir William Blackstone, who declared that rude or "contumelious" [insolent] behavior in front of a judge, or lying, or "any wilful disturbance whatever" in court could be grounds for punishment for contempt. Also punishable, to Blackstone, were: [7]

> disobeying or treating with disrespect the king's writ, or the rules of process of the court; by perverting such writ or process to the purposes of private malice, extortion, or injustice * * *
>
> The process of attachment for these and the like contempts must necessarily be as ancient as the laws themselves * * *.

[4] People v. Goss, 10 Ill.2d 533, 141 N.E.2d 385, 390 (1957).

[5] Goss v. State of Illinois, 204 F.Supp. 268 (N.D.Ill.1962), reversed on other grounds 312 F.2d 257 (7th Cir.1963).

[6] Sir John C. Fox, History of Contempt of Court (Oxford, 1927), p. 1.

[7] Blackstone, pp. 284, 285.

In the United States, an act establishing the law of contempt in the federal courts, passed in 1831, is the basis of contempt proceedings before federal judges. State courts likewise possess the power to punish for contempt, under authority of a judicially proclaimed inherent power, by a statute, or both.[8] State courts have ignored or denied acts by state legislatures to limit this power.[9] For example, in State v. Morrill (1855) an Arkansas court was faced with a state statute limiting contempt proceedings to specified acts not including out-of-court publications. The court ruled that the statute was not binding upon the judiciary, for it must have power to enforce its own process, and the contempt power which provides this springs into existence upon the creation of the courts.[10] Without this authority, courts would be powerless to enforce their orders.

Attempts by Congress and state legislatures to limit contempt to certain specific classifications have not been universally successful. The legislative and judicial branches of government are equal in importance under the "separation of powers" doctrine that gives each branch of government autonomy. While the legislative branch of any governmental unit has the power to make the law, the judicial branch has inherent rights to enforce its orders, rules, writs, or decrees. Even in states where there is a strict definition of what constitutes contempt, under special circumstances there is precedent for courts' to consider their own inherent power as superior to a legislative enactment.[11]

Some headway has been made by those who pose a more general challenge to the contempt power of courts, and who assert that jury trials should be substituted for a judge's summary proceeding. It is sometimes objected by these that American traditions are violated where a judge may sit as accuser, prosecutor, and judge in his own or a fellow judge's case: "It is abhorrent to Anglo–Saxon justice as applied in this country that one man, however lofty his station * * *, should have the power of taking another man's liberty from him."[12] There are flaws in the Blackstonian position that summary procedure is an "immemorial power" of judges in all contempt cases.[13] The United States Supreme Court addressed itself to that flawed argument in 1968 and said that the old rule did

[8] Act of Mar. 2, 1831, c. 99, 4 Stat. 487.

[9] State v. Morrill, 16 Ark. 384 (1855) is an influential case mimicked by courts elsewhere to protect their "inherent" contempt powers from legislative limitations.

[10] Ibid., 384, 407.

[11] Farr v. Superior Court of Los Angeles County, 22 Cal.App.3d 60, 99 Cal.Rptr. 342, 348 (1971).

[12] Ballantyne v. The United States, 237 F.2d 657, 667 (5th Cir.1956); J. Edward Gerald, The Press and the Constitution, pp. 30–31.

[13] Walter Nelles and Carol Weiss King, "Contempt by Publication in the United States," 28 Columbia L.Rev. 408 (1928).

not justify denying defendants a jury trial in serious contempt cases. The Court ruled in Bloom v. Illinois that "If the right to a jury trial is a fundamental matter in other criminal cases, * * * it must also be extended to criminal contempt cases." Bloom's jail sentence for contempt was two years, which the Court found to be a "serious" penalty.[14]

Legislative Contempt and the Press

In addition to courts, legislative bodies are protective of their power to cite for contempt. Congressional and state legislative investigating committees sometimes seek the testimony of reporters who have special knowledge about subjects under the committees' official inquiry. Citations for contempt have occurred when reporters have refused to answer lawmakers' questions, and occasionally, over the last two centuries, journalists have been convicted.

The legislative power to cite for contempt derives its force from the power possessed by the English Parliament, on which both the legislatures and the Congress were modeled.[15] No limitations are imposed upon Congress in its punishment for either disorderly conduct or contempt, but in Marshall v. Gordon,[16] it was held that the punishment imposed could not be extended beyond the session in which the contempt occurs.

The Supreme Court has conceded to Congress the power to punish nonmembers for contempt when there occurs "either physical obstruction of the legislative body in the discharge of its duties, or physical assault upon its members, for action taken or words spoken in the body, or obstruction of its officers in the performance of their official duties, or the prevention of members from attending so that their duties might be performed, or finally, for refusing with contumacy to obey orders, to produce documents or to give testimony which there was a right to compel." [17]

Seldom has a reporter gone to jail for refusing to reveal a source of information to Congress. One of the cases involved Z.L. White and Hiram J. Ramsdell, Washington correspondents of the *New York Tribune*. They published what they claimed was the "Treaty of Washington," a document being studied by the Senate in a closed session. They refused to say from whom they got the copy, were tried and convicted of contempt by the Senate, and were committed to the custody of the Sergeant at Arms until the end of

---

[14] Bloom v. Illinois, 391 U.S. 194, 88 S.Ct. 1477, 1485 (1968).

[15] Max Radin, Anglo American Legal History, pp. 63, 64.

[16] 243 U.S. 521, 37 S.Ct. 448, L.R.A.1917F, 279, Ann.Cas.1918B, 371 (1917).

[17] Ibid.

the Session.[18]

Congress has not in many decades chosen to try and convict for contempt. Instead, it has cited for contempt and certified the persons cited to the district attorney of the District of Columbia for prosecution under a law that gives the courts power to try such cases.[19]

It is uncertain how far the principles of freedom of the press protect a reporter from contempt charges if he refuses to answer the questions of a Congressional committee. Journalists have argued that the First Amendment sharply limits Congress in questioning and investigating the press: Congress may investigate only the matters on which it may legislate, they point out, and the First Amendment says that "Congress shall make no law * * * abridging freedom of * * * the press."

"The Selling of the Pentagon"

In 1971, a prize-winning television documentary by CBS, "The Selling of the Pentagon," raised a storm of protest against alleged bias in the film's portrayal of the American military's public information programs. Selective editing for the documentary, the military charged, distorted the intent, management and messages of the military. The House of Representatives Commerce Committee, under its chairman Rep. Harley O. Staggers, undertook an investigation of the matter, and CBS president Frank Stanton refused to furnish the committee parts of film edited out of the final version. In response to the subpoena ordering him to appear with the materials, he appeared but declared that furnishing materials would amount to a violation of freedom of the press. The Committee voted 25 to 13 to recommend to Congress a contempt citation. The House, however, turned down the recommendation, Rep. Emanuel Celler declaring that "The First Amendment towers over these proceedings like a colossus. No tenderness of one member for another should cause us to topple over this monument to our liberties." [20]

Daniel Schorr and Congress

In the 1970s, newsman Daniel Schorr, then of CBS, came under protracted investigation by Congress, and heavy fire from a segment of the media, for his refusal to testify. Schorr had obtained a copy of the Pike Committee (House Intelligence Com-

[18] U.S. Senate, Subcommittee on Administrative Practice and Procedure of Committee on the Judiciary, The Newsman's Privilege, 89 Cong., 2 Sess., Oct. 1966, pp. 57–61. Nineteenth century investigations of news media and reporters were not rare according to Kaminski, op.cit., p. 85.

[19] 2 U.S.C.A. §§ 192, 194.

[20] Congressional Record, 117:107, July 13, 1971, p. 6643.

mittee) report on operations of the Central Intelligence Agency, which the House of Representatives had voted should be kept secret after heavy pressure not to disclose it from the federal administration. National security, the administration said, was at stake. Schorr broadcast some of the contents; passed the report to the *Village Voice* which published much of it; was investigated for several months during which he was suspended by CBS; and finally came before the House Ethics Committee.[21] Under a congressman's solemn admonition against publishers' taking it "upon themselves to publish secret and classified information against the will of Congress and the people," [22] Schorr illuminated the rationale for a journalist's refusing to reveal sources, saying in part: [23]

> For a journalist, the most crucial kind of confidence is the identity of a source of information. To betray a confidential source would mean to dry up many future sources for many future reporters. The reporter and the news organization would be the immediate losers. The ultimate losers would be the American people and their free institutions.
>
> But, beyond all that, to betray a source would be to betray myself, my career, and my life. It is not as simple as saying that I refuse to do it. I cannot do it.

Unlike the committee that recommended on Stanton, the Ethics Committee did not recommend to the full House that Schorr be cited for contempt. He was released from subpoena without revealing his source.

The courts have not decided contempt of Congress cases on First Amendment grounds, one of them saying, "We shrink from this awesome task" of drawing lines between the investigative power of Congress and the First Amendment rights of a member of the press. Instead, the courts have found other reasons for reversing convictions of newsmen—such as faulty indictments—who were found in contempt of Congress for refusing to answer questions.[24]

Deja vu set in early in 1992, when reporters Nina Totenberg (National Public Radio) and Timothy Phelps (Newsday) balked at answering Senate questions. They faced subpoenas to reveal the

[21] See Daniel Schorr, Clearing the Air (New York: Houghton Mifflin, 1977), passim; "The Daniel Schorr Investigation," Freedom of Information Center Report, # 361, Oct. 1976.

[22] Anthony Lewis, "Congress Shall Make No Law * * *," New York Times, Sept. 16, 1976, p. 39.

[23] I. William Hill, "Schorr Sticks to His Refusal to Name Source," Editor & Publisher, Sept. 25, 1976, p. 14.

[24] Shelton v. United States, 117 U.S.App.D.C. 155, 327 F.2d 601 (1963); 89 Editor & Publisher 12, July 7, 1956. Russell v. United States, 369 U.S. 749, 767, 82 S.Ct. 1038, 1049 (1962).

sources of their reports of Professor Anita Hill's charges of sexual harassment against Supreme Court nominee—and ultimately Supreme Court Justice—Clarence Thomas.[25]   The Senate soon dropped the inquiry.

SEC. 79. REFUSING TO TESTIFY ABOUT SOURCES AND INFORMATION

Journalists' clashes with courts for refusing to testify as to sources and information were infrequent until the 1970s when the incidence multiplied manyfold. Protection has developed under the First Amendment, the common law, and state statutes.

Reporters' refusal to testify before grand juries and courts about confidential sources has become a familiar phenomenon of since the 1970s. Subpoenas to appear and testify were for decades only an occasional problem for journalists whose stories suggested to officials that the reporters had information of use to government. There were probably fewer than 40 reported contempt cases before 1965 for refusal to testify when subpoenaed. But in 1969 and 1970 the sometime trickle of subpoenas changed to a flood, and across the nation hundreds of reporters faced demands that they appear and testify. No one was able to track down every subpoena issued during the early 1970s. But in a 2½ year segment of this period, 121 subpoenas for news material were said to have gone to CBS and NBC alone, and in three years, more than 30 to Field Enterprises newspapers.[26]

In particular demand were reporters who had been reporting widespread social and political turmoil of the 1970s. Grand juries wanted these journalists to reveal their confidential sources as well as to surrender their unpublished notes and records, unused photographs, tape recordings and television film "outtakes." To much of this, reporters responded "no" with intensity and solidarity.[27] Their unwritten code of ethics stood in the way of breaking confidences, they said. Even more important, if they broke confidences they would become known as untrustworthy and their sources would dry up, thereby harming or destroying their usefulness as

[25] Neil A. Lewis, "Constitutional Test Is Seen in Inquiry in Leak to Press," The New York Times, Feb. 3, 1992, p. A9.

[26] House of Rep. Committee on the Judiciary, Subcommittee No. 3, 92 Cong., 2d sess., "Newsmen's Privilege," Hearings, Oct. 4, 1972, p. 204; Sept. 27, 1972, p. 134.

[27] S.Res. 3552, 91 Cong., 2d Sess., 116 Cong.Rec. 4123–31, 1970; Noyes & Newbold, "The Subpoena Problem Today," Am.Soc. Newspaper Editors Bull., Sept. 1970, pp. 7–8; Editor & Publisher, Feb. 7, 1970, p. 12. For several journalists' positions, see U.S. Congress, Senate, Committee on the Judiciary, Newsmen's Privilege Hearings Before the Subcommittee on Constitutional Rights, 93rd Cong., 1st Sess., 1973, passim.

news gatherers for the public, and their own status as professionals would be damaged. Moreover, some argued, compelling them to disclose their news sources was tantamount to making them agents of government investigation.

As for turning over unused film, files, photos and notes, some media adopted the policy of early destruction of unpublished materials after *Time, Life, Newsweek,* the *Chicago Sun–Times,* CBS, NBC and others were called by subpoena, or in the name of cooperation with government, to deliver large quantities of news materials.[28] According to Attorney General John Mitchell, who served under President Nixon, journalists' willingness to accept contempt convictions and jail terms rather than reveal confidences, along with their unyielding protests to government, made the controversy "one of the most difficult issues I have faced * * *."[29] The storm of objection to subpoenas issuing from the Department of Justice led attorneys general to issue "Guidelines for Subpoenas to the News Media"—a set of instructions to Justice Department attorneys across the nation—that sought to resolve testimonial questions with reporters through negotiating rather than through subpoenas except in the last resort.[30]

From the mid–1970s through the 1980s, there was growing protection shielding journalists from being compelled to testify about sources or otherwise to reveal confidences. The pattern was by no means uniform nationally, however, and there were indications in the 1990s that those hard-won, if spotty, protections are being whittled away.

The Constitutional Protection

Journalists who assumed or asserted that the First Amendment guarantee of freedom of the press has protected the craft historically against compelling testimony did not understand the course of court decisions. Privilege cases were adjudicated for most of a century under the common law or state statutes without the Constitution even entering the picture. Not until 1958, in Garland v. Torre,[31] was the first claim to First Amendment protection an issue in the reported cases.

Marie Torre, columnist for the *New York Herald Tribune,* attributed to an unnamed executive of a broadcasting company, certain statements which actress Judy Garland said libeled her. In the libel suit, Torre refused to name the executive, asserting

[28] Columbia Journalism Rev., Spring 1970, pp. 2–3.

[29] Editor & Publisher, Aug. 15, 1970, pp. 9–10.

[30] Department of Justice, Memo No. 692, Sept. 2, 1970. The guidelines were adjusted and developed by subsequent attorneys general. See "Guidelines on News Media Subpoenas," 6 Med.L.Rptr. 2153 (11/5/80) for more recent guidelines.

[31] 259 F.2d 545 (2d Cir.1958), certiorari denied 358 U.S. 910, 79 S.Ct. 237 (1958).

privilege under the First Amendment. She was cited for contempt and convicted, and the appeals court upheld the conviction. "The concept that it is the duty of a witness to testify in a court of law," the Second Circuit Court of Appeals said, "has roots fully as deep in our history as does the guarantee of a free press." It added that if freedom of the press was involved here, "we do not hesitate to conclude that it too must give place under the Constitution to a paramount public interest in the fair administration of justice." [32] Subsequent claims to constitutional protection also were denied in other cases.[33]

The Branzburg Case (1972)

The United States Supreme Court in 1972 ruled for the first time on whether the First Amendment protects journalists from testifying about their confidential sources and information. The cases of three newsmen who had refused to testify before grand juries during 1970 and 1971 were decided together in Branzburg v. Hayes.[34] Paul Branzburg, a reporter for the *Louisville Courier-Journal*, had observed two people synthesizing hashish from marijuana and written about that and drug use, and had refused to answer the grand jury's questions about the matters. Paul Pappas, a television reporter of New Bedford, Mass., had visited Black Panther headquarters during civil turmoil in July 1970, and refused to tell a grand jury what he had seen there. Earl Caldwell, a black reporter for the *New York Times* in San Francisco, who had covered Black Panther activities regularly for some years, was called by a federal grand jury and had refused to appear or testify.

Only Caldwell received protection from the lower courts. The federal district court of California and the Ninth Circuit Court of Appeals ruled that the First Amendment provided a qualified privilege to newsmen and that it applied to Caldwell.[35] The Kentucky Court of Appeals refused Branzburg protection under either the Kentucky privilege statute, or the First Amendment interpretation of the Caldwell case.[36] And the Supreme Judicial Court of Massachusetts, where no privilege statute existed, rejected the idea of a First Amendment privilege.[37]

[32] Ibid., at 548–549.

[33] In re Goodfader's Appeal, 45 Hawaii 317, 367 P.2d 472 (1961); In re Taylor, 412 Pa. 32, 193 A.2d 181 (1963); State v. Buchanan, 250 Or. 244, 436 P.2d 729 (1968), certiorari denied 392 U.S. 905, 88 S.Ct. 2055 (1968).

[34] Branzburg v. Hayes, 408 U.S. 665, 92 S.Ct. 2646 (1972).

[35] Application of Caldwell, 311 F.Supp. 358 (N.D.Cal.1970); Caldwell v. United States, 434 F.2d 1081 (9th Cir.1970).

[36] Branzburg v. Pound, 461 S.W.2d 345 (Ky.1970); Branzburg v. Hayes, 408 U.S. 665, 92 S.Ct. 2646 (1972).

[37] In re Pappas, 358 Mass. 604, 266 N.E.2d 297 (1971).

The Supreme Court of the United States found that none of the three men warranted First Amendment protection. It reversed the Caldwell decision of the lower federal court and upheld the Kentucky and Massachusetts decisions, in a 5–4 decision.[38] It said that the First Amendment would protect a reporter if grand jury investigations were not conducted in good faith, or if there were harassment of the press by officials who sought to disrupt a reporter's relationship with his news sources.[39] But it found neither of these conditions present here. The journalist's obligation is to respond to grand jury subpoenas as other citizens do and to answer questions relevant to commission of crime, it said.

The Caldwell decisions in lower courts had focused on the need of recognition for First Amendment protection for the news gathering process; the Supreme Court said "It has generally been held that the first Amendment does not guarantee the press a constitutional right of special access to information not available to the public generally * * *," and "Despite the fact that news gathering may be hampered, the press is regularly excluded from grand jury proceedings, our own conferences, the meetings of other official bodies gathered in executive session * * *." [40]

The reporters had asserted that the First Amendment should take precedence over the grand jury's power of inquiry. The Supreme Court said that at common law, courts consistently refused to recognize a privilege in journalists to refuse to reveal confidential information, and that the First Amendment claim to privilege had been turned down uniformly in earlier cases, the courts having concluded "that the First Amendment interest asserted by the newsman was outweighed by the general obligation of a citizen to appear before a grand jury or at trial, pursuant to a subpoena, and give what information he possesses." [41] It said that the only constitutional privilege for unofficial witnesses before grand juries is the Fifth Amendment privilege against compelled self-incrimination, and the Court declined to create another.

The reporters argued that the flow of news would be diminished by compelling testimony from them. The Supreme Court said it was unconvinced, and "the evidence fails to demonstrate that there would be a significant constriction of the flow of news to the public if the Court reaffirms the prior common law and constitutional rule regarding the testimonial obligations of newsmen." [42]

[38] Branzburg v. Hayes, 408 U.S. 665, 92 S.Ct. 2646 (1972).

[39] Ibid., at 706–709, 92 S.Ct. at 2669–2670.

[40] Ibid., at 682, 684, 92 S.Ct. at 2657, 2658.

[41] Ibid., at 684, 686, 92 S.Ct. at 2658, 2659.

[42] Ibid., at 692, 92 S.Ct. at 2662.

The reporters said the freedom of the press would be undermined. The Court said this is not the lesson that history teaches, for the press had operated and thrived without common law or constitutional privilege since the beginning of the nation.[43]

The Supreme Court said that while the Constitution did not provide the privilege sought, Congress and the state legislatures were free to fashion standards and rules protecting journalists from testifying by passing legislation.

Concurring, Justice Lewis F. Powell, Jr., expanded, in general terms, the possibilities for first Amendment protection for journalists subpoenaed to testify. "The Court," he said, "does not hold that newsmen * * * are without constitutional rights with respect to the gathering of news or in safe-guarding their sources. * * * the courts will be available to newsmen under circumstances where legitimate First Amendment interests require protection." And where they claim protection, Powell said, "The asserted claim to privilege should be judged on its facts by the striking of a proper balance between freedom of the press and the obligation of all citizens to give relevant testimony * * *."[44] His opinion was to become central to many subsequent cases.

The dissenting justices wrote two opinions. One was that of Justice William O. Douglas, who said that a reporter's immunity from testifying is "quite complete" under the First Amendment and a journalist "has an absolute right not to appear before a grand jury * * *."[45]

Concurring for himself and two others, Justice Potter Stewart argued for a qualified privilege. He called the majority's opinion a "crabbed view of the First Amendment" that reflected a disturbing insensitivity to the critical role of an independent press. And he said that in denying the protection, "The Court * * * invites state and federal authorities to undermine the historic independence of the press by attempting to annex the journalistic profession as an investigative arm of government." Justice Stewart said the protection was essential, not "for the purely private interests of the newsman or his informant, nor even, at bottom, for the First Amendment interests of either partner in the news-gathering relationship."[46]

> Rather it functions to insure nothing less than democratic decisionmaking through the free flow of information to the public, and it serves, thereby, to honor the "profound national commitment to the principle that debate on

---

[43] Ibid., at 698, 92 S.Ct. at 2665.

[44] Ibid., at 708, 710, 92 S.Ct. at 2670, 2671.

[45] United States v. Caldwell, 408 U.S. 665, 719, 92 S.Ct. 2686, 2691 (1972).

[46] Branzburg v. Hayes, 408 U.S. 665, 737, 92 S.Ct. 2646, 2678 (1972).

public issues should be uninhibited, robust, and wide-open."

Stewart indicated what he felt the government should be required to do in overriding a constitutional privilege for the reporter: [47]

> * * * it is an essential prerequisite to the validity of an investigation which intrudes into the area of constitutionally protected rights of speech, press, association and petition that the State *show a substantial relation between the information sought and a subject of overriding and compelling state interest.*
>
> * * *
>
> Government officials must, therefore, demonstrate that the information sought is *clearly* relevant to a *precisely* defined subject of governmental inquiry. * * * They must demonstrate that it is reasonable to think the witness in question has that information. * * * And they must show that there is not any means of obtaining the information less destructive of First Amendment liberties.

These were essentially the requirements placed upon government by the lower courts in holding that Caldwell had been protected by the First Amendment, and Stewart endorsed that decision. He would have upheld the protection for Caldwell, and vacated and remanded the Branzburg and Pappas judgments.

Largely innocent of the history of the shield, reporters and editors expressed shock and dismay that the First Amendment did not protect the reporters in the Supreme Court's *Branzburg* decision.[48] A few years later, William H. Hornby wrote that the decision had "beclouded what American newsmen had come to assume was a traditional privilege—to refuse to testify either as to the source or the content of information received under confidential circumstances." [49]

After the *Branzburg* decision, many journalists predicted doom for press freedom. Those predictions were premature: buried within *Branzburg* were statements which said the First Amendment was still around and could be used in confidentiality cases. There was Justice White's plurality opinion, which said that journalists would be protected against the harassment of bad-faith

[47] Ibid., at 739–742, 92 S.Ct. at 2679–2680.

[48] See generally Columbia Journalism Review, 10:3, Sept.–Oct. 1972, for articles by Norman E. Isaacs, Benno C. Schmidt, Jr., and Fred W. Friendly. The only extensive history of journalists' privilege is Gordon, op.cit.

[49] William H. Hornby, "Journalists Split in Shield Law Imbroglio," IPI Report, 25:3, March 1976, p. 8.

investigations. Justice Powell's concurrence said that courts would protect journalists "where legitimate First Amendment interests require protection." And Justice Stewart's dissent, as matters turned out, contained concepts that courts quickly came to use in subsequent cases to protect journalists. (See discussion following page 560.)

Then only months after *Branzburg* was decided, the U.S. Court of Appeals, Second Circuit, gave the doom-predictors a most welcome surprise. That court said that journalist Alfred Balk was *protected* by the First Amendment in his refusal to name a source. Balk had once written an article on discriminatory real estate practices—"block busting" for the Saturday Evening Post. Civil rights advocates, in a court action, sought to have Balk reveal the identity of one of his confidential sources ("Vitchek," a pseudonym). Balk refused, on grounds that Vitchek gave him the information in confidence. The trial court ruled in Balk's favor, and the appeals court affirmed. The decision stood because the Supreme Court of the United States—for whatever reason—refused to grant certiorari.[50]

The court found that the identity of Vitchek did not go to the heart of the appellants' case, and that, anyway, there were other available sources that the appellants could have tried to reach and that might have disclosed Vitchek's identity (*vide* Stewart, dissent in *Branzburg*). It said that the majority in *Branzburg* had applied traditional First Amendment doctrine, which teaches that First Amendment rights cannot be infringed absent a "compelling" or "paramount" state interest (once more, Stewart).[51]

> Even though the *Branzburg* majority emphasized public interest in grand jury investigation of crimes, this case found that "there are circumstances, at the very least in civil cases, in which the public interest in non-disclosure of a journalist's confidential sources outweighs the public and private interest in compelled testimony. The case before us is one where the First Amendment protection does not yield."

Here was a line of reasoning (one which took its departure from the widely damned *Branzburg* decision) that was to prove a protection for the journalist in the court-room faceup in which his testimony was being demanded with increasing and truly disturbing frequency. In civil cases, the public's interest was likely to weigh with the journalist's refusal to name his sources, and thus

[50] Baker v. F & F Investment Co., 470 F.2d 778 (2d Cir.1972), certiorari denied 411 U.S. 966, 93 S.Ct. 2147 (1973).

[51] Ibid., 783–785. See also United States v. Orsini, 424 F.Supp. 229 (E.D.N.Y. 1976).

the journalist's position would outweigh the private litigant's demand for disclosure. It was the start of courts' using *Branzburg* in both civil and criminal cases to establish a qualified privilege under the First Amendment for journalists who claimed protection not to reveal sources.

Quickly other courts brought the privilege into play.[52] In a case decided in 1973, the District Court for the District of Columbia ruled on a demand of the Committee for the Re–Election of the President (Nixon) for news materials.[53] The Committee was party to civil actions arising out of the break-in at the Watergate offices of the Democratic National Committee. It had obtained subpoenas for reporters or management of the *New York Times,* the *Washington Post,* the *Washington Star–News,* and *Time* magazine to appear and bring all papers and documents they had relating to the break-in. The media asked the court to quash the subpoenas.

Judge Richey defined the issue: Were the subpoenas valid under the First Amendment? He distinguished this case from *Branzburg,* noting that the re-election committee was not involved in criminal cases, but civil contempts. He declared, furthermore, that the cases were of staggering import: " * * * unprecedented in the annals of legal history." "What is ultimately involved in these cases * * * is the very integrity of the judicial and executive branches of our Government and our political processes in this country." [54]

Not only did the civil nature of the cases involving the re-election committee weigh for the media in Richey's opinion. He saw a chilling effect in the enforcement of the subpoenas upon the flow of information about Watergate to the press and thus to the public: [55]

> This court stands convinced that if it allows the discouragement of investigative reporting into the highest levels of Government no amount of legal theorizing could allay the public suspicions engendered by its actions and by the matters alleged in these lawsuits.

Then Richey tried to balance competing interests. As Justice Powell had instructed in *Branzburg,* a reporter's claim to privilege should be judged " * * * 'on its facts by the striking of a proper balance between freedom of the press and the obligation of all citizens to give relevant testimony.' " Richey said that here, "The scales are heavily weighted in the ... [media's] favor." For the

---

[52] See Press Censorship Newsletter, IX, April–May 1976, pp. 46, 48–9; Loadholtz v. Fields, 389 F.Supp. 1299 (D.Fla.1975).

[53] Democratic National Committee v. McCord, 356 F.Supp. 1394 (D.D.C.1973).

[54] Ibid., 1395–1397.

[55] Ibid., 1397.

Committee for the Re–Election of the President had made no showing that "alternative sources of information have been exhausted or even approached. Nor has there been any positive showing of the materiality of the documents and other materials sought by the subpoenas [i.e., that the materials sought 'go to the heart of the claim']." [56]

Even the legal proceeding which the lead opinion in *Branzburg* was so concerned to elevate above reporter's privilege—namely, the grand jury investigation—could in some circumstances give way to the journalist's claim.

This happened in the case of Lucy Ware Morgan, who for three years fought a 90–day contempt sentence for refusing to disclose her source, and finally won.[57] Her story in the St. Petersburg, Fla., *Times* brought two actions against her to compel her to say who told her of a grand jury's secret criticism of Police Chief Nixon. The Florida Supreme Court found the story innocuous. It overruled the lower court which had found that the mere preservation of secrecy in grand jury proceedings outweighed any First Amendment considerations. The high state court said "A nonspecific interest, even in keeping the inner workings of the Pentagon secret, has been held insufficient to override certain First Amendment values." [58] It found further that the proceedings against Morgan had an improper purpose—namely, "to force a newspaper reporter to disclose the source of published information, so that the authorities could silence the source." Then it called on the leading case in precedent: [59]

> The present case falls squarely within this language in the *Branzburg* plurality opinion: "Official harassment of the press undertaken not for purposes of law enforcement but to disrupt a reporter's relationship with his news sources would have no justification."

Thus with *Branzburg* supporting, First Amendment protection for the reporter's shield was being discovered.[60] No court conceded that the privilege under the First Amendment was an "absolute" protective shield for the journalist in all conceivable circumstances.

---

[56] Ibid., 1398. On exhausting the sources of information, see also Connecticut State Board of Labor Relations v. Fagin, 33 Conn.Sup. 204, 370 A.2d 1095 (1976), 2 Med.L.Rptr. 1765, 1766; Altemose Const. Co. v. Building Trades Council of Philadelphia and Vicinity, 443 F.Supp. 489 (E.D.Pa.1977), 2 Med.L.Rptr. 1878.

[57] Morgan v. State, 337 So.2d 951 (Fla.1976).

[58] Ibid., 955.

[59] Ibid., 956.

[60] Gora, p. 28. Gora's handbook, prepared for the American Civil Liberties Union, despite being dated, should be available to every reporter and editor. It covers true-to-life, practical problems in several fields of law that involve journalists, using a "Q" and "A" approach.

In applying the First Amendment, courts widely started with Justice Powell's instruction in *Branzburg* ("striking a proper balance between freedom of the press and the obligation of all citizens to give relevant testimony"), and then used criteria such as those advocated by Justice Stewart in his *Branzburg* dissent (whether the testimony sought from reporters was clearly relevant, whether the subject was one of overriding state interest, whether all other means of obtaining the sought-after information had first been exhausted). In most cases in which the First Amendment was employed, the procedure worked out to provide protection.[61]

But the First Amendment shield sometimes dropped. For one thing, in balancing the journalist's right to a shield against the need of the state or a plaintiff, as Powell instructed, courts sometimes found that the hurdles such as Stewart's criteria were surmounted by those seeking testimony, and the balance tipped against the journalist. This could happen at trial, or in pre-trial discovery procedure (see Chap. 5, Sec. 30) in which plaintiffs were attempting to obtain from journalists certain facts that would help them establish their cases. Also, some courts interpreted *Branzburg* to deny a First Amendment shield of any kind.

First, consider the hurdles which the state in criminal cases, or the plaintiff in civil cases, would have to clear before overcoming the journalist's First Amendment qualified privilege. These have been expressed in several ways. The most-used rules [62] are that the party seeking the information from the journalist must show:

• That the information sought can be obtained from no other source or by means less destructive of First Amendment interests:

• That the information is centrally relevant to the party's case ("goes to the heart of the claim," or is information for which the party has a "compelling need").

• That the subject is one of "overriding and compelling state interest."

As we saw on the preceding pages, the journalist won because the plaintiffs failed to show that the materials sought "went to the

[61] United States v. Hubbard, 493 F.Supp. 202, 206, 209 (D.D.C.1979), 5 Med. L.Rptr. 1719; Montezuma Realty Corp. v. Occidental Petroleum Corp., 494 F.Supp. 780 (S.D.N.Y.1980), 6 Med.L.Rptr. 1571; Application of Consumers Union of United States, Inc., 495 F.Supp. 582 (S.D.N.Y.1980), 6 Med.L.Rptr. 1681; Hart v. Playboy Enterprises (D.Kan.1978), 4 Med.L.Rptr. 1616; United States v. DePalma, 466 F.Supp. 917 (S.D.N.Y.1979), 4 Med.L.Rptr. 2499; Zelenka v. State, 83 Wis.2d 601, 266 N.W.2d 279 (1978).

[62] Others have included: Plaintiff must show that the information "is necessary to prevent a miscarriage of justice" Florida v. Taylor (Fla.Cir.Ct.1982), 9 Med.L.Rptr. 1551; there is "reasonable possibility that information sought would affect the verdict" State v. Rinaldo, 36 Wash.App. 86, 673 P.2d 614 (1983), 9 Med.L.Rptr. 1419; the action is not "facially frivolous or patently without merit" Winegard v. Oxberger, 258 N.W.2d 847, 852 (Iowa 1977).

heart of their claim," or that the information might not be available from an alternative source, other parties seeking information have been more successful in piercing the shield of the First Amendment. That was the case in Winegard v. Oxberger,[63] decided by the Iowa Supreme Court in 1977.

Winegard v. Oxberger (1977)

Diane Graham, a reporter for the *Des Moines Register,* wrote articles about legal proceedings brought by Sally Ann Winegard to dissolve her claimed common-law marriage to John Winegard. The articles quoted Sally's attorney extensively. John, who denied that there had been a marriage, brought a libel suit and invasion of privacy action against the attorney, who had told John that he had spoken with reporter Graham, but who denied saying the alleged libel. Then John sought, through discovery proceedings before the trial, to obtain from Graham or the Register any information they had in connection with the preparation of the articles.

Graham was subpoenaed, and refused to answer questions about conversations with her sources or their identity, and about preparation and editing of the articles. She said that the First Amendment and the Iowa Constitution protected her. She and the Register applied to the court for an order quashing the subpoena; John Winegard moved to compel discovery; and Judge Oxberger ruled for Graham and the Register, saying that a qualified privilege under the First Amendment protected Graham.

Winegard appealed to the Iowa Supreme Court, which reversed the trial court and said that Judge Oxberger had erred in denying John's motion to compel discovery by reporter Graham. The Supreme Court said that a First Amendment qualified privilege existed, but was lost to Graham upon the application of the Court's "three-pronged standard." [64]

First, it said that John's basic discovery objective "is necessary and critical to his cause of action" against the attorney; John "needs to know what was said to Graham and by whom." Second, the Court said, John's questioning of Sally's attorney resulted in the attorney's denying "having made statements attributed to him by Graham's articles. Under these circumstances we find Winegard did reasonably exercise and exhaust other plausible avenues of information," and that "Graham is apparently the only remaining person who could conceivably provide the information essential to Winegard's invasion of privacy and defamation action." And as for the last of the "three-prong standard," the Court said there was

---

[63] 258 N.W.2d 847 (Iowa 1977), certiorari denied 436 U.S. 905, 98 S.Ct. 2234 (1978), 3 Med.L.Rptr. 2409. See also Goldfeld v. Post Pub. Co. (Conn.Sup.1978), 4 Med.L.Rptr. 1167; In re Powers (Vt.Dist.1978), 4 Med.L.Rptr. 1600.

[64] Winegard v. Oxberger, 258 N.W.2d 847, 852 (Iowa 1977).

nothing in the record to suggest that John's action against the attorney was frivolous or without merit. For good measure, the unanimous opinion said that the Court found no cause to hold that John was abusing judicial process to force a "wholesale disclosure of a newspaper's confidential sources of news," nor that John was embarked upon a course "designed to annoy," embarrass or oppress Graham.[65] John won the case for compelled disclosure.

Some courts have denied or doubted that any First Amendment protection exists. The Massachusetts Supreme Judicial Court did so in the case of Paul Pappas,[66] and reaffirmed that position in 1982.[67] A Connecticut Superior Court has said that the First Amendment gives no greater protection to the electronic media "than the same action by any other citizen," nor "any privilege to refuse to reveal information solely because the writers deem it confidential." [68] Idaho's Supreme Court once read Branzburg v. Hayes, the leading case,[69] to mean that "no newsman's privilege against disclosure of confidential sources exists * * *." [70] In 1985, however, the Idaho Supreme Court recognized a reporter's right to protect source confidentiality in both criminal and civil cases.[71]

For journalists, the best defense against subpoenas probably is a "good offense." That is, if a news organization is known to judges and prosecuting attorneys as one willing to fight against subpoenas—even to the point of having reporters and editors go to jail to resist yielding up confidential sources or information—chances of subpoenas being served doubtless are lessened.

In re Farber (1978)

A shield case which arose in New Jersey cost its media principals more than any other in the 1970s. It was the famous case

[65] The Iowa Court relied directly on the first of the shield cases in which a reporter claimed a First Amendment protection—Garland v. Torre, 259 F.2d 545 (2d Cir.1958), which continues to carry weight with courts in frequent citations. An example is Silkwood v. Kerr–McGee Corp., 563 F.2d 433 (10th Cir.1977), 3 Med. L.Rptr. 1087, 1091.

[66] In the Matter of Paul Pappas, 358 Mass. 604, 266 N.E.2d 297 (1971).

[67] Corsetti v. Massachusetts, 458 U.S. 1306, 103 S.Ct. 3 (1982), 8 Med.L.Rptr. 2117 and reporter's jail term for contempt commuted in 1982, 8 Med.L.Rptr. # 28, 9/14/82, News Notes. In 1984, the Massachusetts Supreme Judicial Court was asked by a governor's task force to promulgate rules about journalists' privilege, and recommended details for protection of journalists asserting such, the Court having denied until then any recognition of privilege: 10 Med.L.Rptr. # 41, 10/16/84, News Notes.

[68] Rubera v. Post–Newsweek (1982), 8 Med.L.Rptr. 2293, 2295.

[69] 408 U.S. 665, 92 S.Ct. 2646 (1972), 1 Med.L.Rptr. 2617.

[70] Caldero v. Tribune Pub. Co., 98 Idaho 288, 562 P.2d 791 (1977), 2 Med.L.Rptr. 1490, 1495.

[71] In re Contempt of Wright, 108 Idaho 418, 700 P.2d 40 (1985).

called In re Farber.[72]   Before it had run its course, in fines alone it had cost the *New York Times* approximately $285,000, at the rate of $5,000 per day in civil contempts plus a flat $101,000 in criminal contempts. Reporter Myron Farber was jailed for 40 days.   Farber had written lengthy articles about deaths at a New Jersey hospital, and their possible connection with drugs.   A grand jury probe of the matter resulted in the indictment of Dr. Mario Jascalevich for murder, and after he went to trial, Farber and the Times were subpoenaed to bring thousands of documents to the court for *in camera* inspection.   The Times and Farber demanded a hearing before turning over materials.   But the trial judge refused a hearing, saying he would have to examine the documents before deciding whether the shield law would protect them against disclosure to Jascalevich.   Facing contempt citations, the Times and Farber appealed unsuccessfully; the contempt findings went into effect, with jail for Farber and the $5,000–a-day fine against the Times pending its bringing forth the materials.

Appealing once more, the newspaper and reporter reached the New Jersey Supreme Court.   That court denied that the First Amendment provided any privilege to remain silent, interpreting Branzburg v. Hayes to be a flat rejection of that notion.   In response to the journalists' claim to privilege, the New Jersey court said that U.S. Supreme Court Justice White, had "stated the issue and gave the Court's answer in the first paragraph of his opinion": [73]

> "The issue in these cases is whether requiring newsmen to appear and testify before state or federal grand juries abridges the freedom of speech and press guaranteed by the First Amendment.   We hold that it does not."

* * *

> Our conclusion that appellants cannot derive the protection they seek from the First Amendment rests upon the fact that the ruling in *Branzburg* is binding upon us and we interpret it as applicable to, and clearly including, the particular issue framed here.   It follows that the obligation to appear at a criminal trial on behalf of a defendant who is enforcing his Sixth Amendment rights is

[72] In re Farber, 78 N.J. 259, 394 A.2d 330 (1978), 4 Med.L.Rptr. 1360, 1362;   see also Anon., "Lets Stand Contempts Against New York Times," News Media & the Law, Jan. 1979, 4–5.   For a step-by-step account of the complex process applied to the Times and Farber, see Anon., "Reporter Jailed; N.Y.Times Fined," Ibid., Oct. 1978, 2–4.   Farber and the Times were ultimately pardoned of the criminal contempt conviction by the Governor of New Jersey, and the $101,000 criminal contempt fine was returned: 7 Med.L.Rptr. # 42, 2/2/82, News Notes.

[73] In re Farber, 78 N.J. 259, 394 A.2d 330 (1978), 4 Med.L.Rptr. 1360, 1362.

at least as compelling as the duty to appear before a grand jury.

Having settled the First Amendment issue for New Jersey, the court went on to say that the Times and Farber of course deserved a hearing such as they sought, but that they had aborted it by refusing to submit the material subpoenaed for the court to examine in private—and that such an examination is no invasion of the New Jersey shield statute. "Rather, it is a preliminary step to determine whether, and if so to what extent, the statutory privilege must yield to the defendant's constitutional rights."

It added, however, that in future similar cases there should be a preliminary determination before being compelled to submit materials to a trial judge—in which the party seeking the materials would show the relevancy of them to his defense, and that the information could not be obtained from any less intrusive source. This, it said, did not stem from any First Amendment right, but rather, it would seem necessary from the legislature's "very positively expressed" intent, in passing the shield law, to protect confidentiality of media sources.

Farber was released from jail in October 1978, following the acquittal of Jascalevich by a jury at the end of an eight-month trial. The New Jersey legislature began work on a bill to prevent a recurrence of the Farber incident, and on Feb. 28, 1981, Governor Byrne signed a law saying that a criminal defendant would have to prove at a subpoenaed journalist's hearing that the material sought was relevant and unavailable elsewhere, and that the hearing would be held before the start of the criminal trial.[74]

It should be clear that despite the language of shield laws or of court precedent erecting some sort of a "shield" for journalists, such shields often turn out to be of little help at crunch time. First Amendment attorney James C. Goodale, for example, looked at the Farber case and exclaimed about the persistent ineffectiveness of New Jersey's shield statute. He complained that Farber had been shipped off to jail without a hearing, even though there was a statute stating that Farber was totally protected against requests for confidential sources and even though there are scores of decisions upholding claims of privilege even in states where there is no shield statute.

Journalists need to keep up with the kaleidoscopically shifting patterns of shield protection. One way of managing this is to subscribe to The News Media & the Law, published four times a year by the Reporters Committee for Freedom of the Press, and

[74] New York Times, Feb. 28, 1981, p. 25. Maressa v. New Jersey Monthly, 89 N.J. 176, 445 A.2d 376 (1982), 8 Med.L.Rptr. 1473, 1475–1476.

which puts out periodic guides on the status of shield laws from jurisdiction to jurisdiction.[75]

Confidentiality Under the Federal Common Law

Even as journalists' successes in asserting a First Amendment privilege not to testify were proving about as frequent as were their failures, in 1979 the United States Third Circuit Court of Appeals discovered and applied an added basis of privilege for journalists to rely on in refusing to divulge sources: the federal common law. In 1979, Judge Sloviter wrote that the Court of Appeals, Third Circuit, had concluded "that journalists have a federal common law privilege, albeit qualified, to refuse to divulge their sources."

Riley v. Chester (1979)

That case began when Policeman Riley of Chester, Pa., a candidate for mayor, alleged that Mayor Battle and Police Chief Owens had violated his constitutional right to freedom to conduct his campaign, by surveillance of his activity, by conducting investigations of his performance as a policeman, and by public announcements of the investigations. He sought a preliminary injunction from federal court to restrain them from continued activities of this kind. Reporter Geraldine Oliver was called as a witness concerning her news story which reported that Riley had been suspended as a policeman, docked, and officially reprimanded, and that he had been investigated on several occasions during his 13 years as a policeman. She refused to give the source of her information and under an order by the trial judge was cited for civil contempt. She appealed, and the Third Circuit Court reversed the contempt citation.[76]

The Court found that Riley had not first exhausted other sources of information that might have "leaked," including other reporters, Battle, and Owens. Nor had Riley shown that the information sought to be disclosed was more than marginally relevant to his case—a matter "of most significance." Criteria such as these were applicable to the case of anyone seeking disclosure, the Court said, under any standard. And with that, it applied the standard of the federal common law, emerging from Rule 501 of the Federal Rules of Evidence and the legislative history of the Rule. The importance of the decision for journalists' privilege

---

[75] "Reporters Have Rights, Too," The Nation, Nov. 3, 1979, pp. 435–436; The Reporters Committee for Freedom of the Press, Suite 504, 1735 Eye Street, N.W., Washington, D.C. 20006. The Reporters Committee has an all-day, every-day libel and freedom of information hotline, including emergency legal aid on subpoena questions: Toll free 800–F–FOI–AID. In Washington, D.C., area, (202) 466–6313.

[76] Riley v. Chester, 612 F.2d 708 (3d Cir.1979). For a state decision bottomed explicitly on common law as providing privilege, see Senear v. Daily Journal–American, 97 Wash.2d 148, 641 P.2d 1180 (1982), 8 Med.L.Rptr. 1151, 1152.

emerges not so much in the finding for Oliver as for the general matter of journalists' privilege.[77]

The Court then added:

> The strong public policy which supports the unfettered communication to the public of information, comment and opinion and the Constitutional dimension of that policy, expressly recognized in Branzburg v. Hayes, lead us to conclude that journalists have a federal common law privilege, albeit qualified, to refuse to divulge their sources.

In two later federal common law cases in the Third Circuit, the reporter's shield was denied. One, concerning a newspaper reporter's refusal to say whether she had conversations with a U.S. attorney in the "Abscam" prosecutions, ruled that the information was crucial to the defendant's case and that it could be obtained only from the reporter. The court followed standard judicial procedure in choosing to decide the case on common law instead of a First Amendment standard: " ' ... [W]e ought not to pass on questions of constitutionality * * * unless such adjudication is unavoidable * * *.' " [78]

In the other case, a television network was ordered by a court to submit to a pre-trial, *in camera* [in private, in the judge's chambers] proceeding. In that proceeding film, audio tapes, and written transcripts were to be revealed concerning persons whom the government intended to call as witnesses in a trial. The TV network refused and appealed the order. But the order was upheld so far as it applied to the named persons whom the government intended to call, but was overturned as to other people, whose testimony was not relevant.[79]

Confidentiality Under State Statutes and in State Courts

The mixed results for confidentiality under the First Amendment and the federal common law, meanwhile, were characteristic of developments under state shield statutes and state court decisions. Media Attorney Robert Sack has said that shield laws are like insurance policies, in that "they cover absolutely everything except what happens to you." [80] If, as attorney Joel Gora had said in the journalistic climate of discouragement under *Branzburg,* "the situation is far from bleak," there were nonetheless more than enough jailings to warrant confusion and anger among journalists. Probably more reporters were going to jail in the 1970s for refusal to reveal sources, than for any offense since 1798–1800 and the

[77] Ibid., 713, 714.

[78] United States v. Criden, 633 F.2d 346, 349 (3d Cir.1980).

[79] United States v. Cuthbertson, 630 F.2d 139 (3d Cir.1980), 6 Med.L.Rptr. 1545.

[80] 9 Med.L.Rptr. # 7, 3/15/83, News Notes.

Alien and Sedition Acts.[81] The interpretations of the legitimacy of journalists' privilege under state laws and rulings contributed heavily to this unlovely fact. Yet it was plain by the 1980s that the large majority of state (and federal) jurisdictions had recognized qualified shield protection. Further, the number of actions by the mid 1980s was declining; media Attorney James C. Goodale found state shield laws increasingly effective.[82] Into the mid–1990s, however, it appeared that subpoenas again were on the increase.

State Shield Laws

The Supreme Court in *Branzburg* made it plain that either Congress or the states or both might pass laws providing a shield. Attempts in state legislatures to adopt shield laws (15 preceded *Branzburg*) were sometimes successful in following years, the total of old and new reaching 28—27 states plus the District of Columbia by 1990. In addition, 16 other states' courts had adopted a qualified privilege in case decisions by that year, while a few rejected the privilege.[83] Some statutes provided a privilege that appeared "absolute," while others qualified the protection in various ways. Alabama's, passed in 1935 and amended in 1949, was one of those that, on the surface, seemed absolute—as long as a person could claim to be with a journalistic organization: [84]

> No person engaged in, connected with, or employed on any newspaper, or radio broadcasting station or television station, while engaged in a news gathering capacity shall be compelled to disclose in any legal proceeding or trial, before any court or before a grand jury of any court, before the presiding officer of any tribunal or his agent or agents or before any committee of the legislature or elsewhere the sources of any information procured or obtained by him and published in the newspaper, broadcast by any broadcasting station or televised by any television station on which he is engaged, connected with or employed.

[81] Quill, 61:1, Jan. 1973, p. 28.

[82] Note, "Developments in the News Media Privilege: the Qualified Constitutional Approach Becoming Common Law," 33 Maine L.Rev. 372, 441 (1981); 10 Med. L.Rptr. # 47, 11/27/84, News Notes.

[83] The News Media & the Law, Fall 1987, special section on source confidentiality; see also Henry R. Kaufman, ed., LDRC (Libel Defense Resource Center), 50–State Survey 1994–95 (New York: LDRC, 1988), *passim.* See also "Confidential Sources and Information," 1990 guide for reporters, The Reporters Committee for Freedom of the Press, and Appendix 3, pp. 867–901 in Robert D. Sack and Sandra S. Baron, Libel, Slander and Related Problems, 2nd ed. (New York: Practising Law Institute, 1994).

[84] Ala.Code § 12–21–142 (Cum.Supp.1988). See Jacqueline L. Jackson, "Shield Laws Vary Widely," Presstime, May 1981, p. 14; See also New Jersey's, Maressa v. New Jersey Monthly, 89 N.J. 176, 445 A.2d 376 (1982), 8 Med.L.Rptr. 1473.

Among states that hedged the privilege, Illinois, for example, said that a person seeking the reporter's information could apply for an order divesting the reporter of the privilege. The application would have to state the specific information sought, its relevancy to the proceedings, and a specific public interest which would be adversely affected if the information sought were not disclosed. And the court would have to find, before taking away the privilege, that all other available sources of information had been exhausted and that disclosure of the information was essential to the protection of the public interest involved.[85]

But absolute or qualified, state laws might contain loopholes through which under certain conditions, journalists could lose the privilege. Branzburg, before seeking constitutional protection, had failed to receive protection under Kentucky's statute. The statute gave him a firm shield, as a newspaper employee, against disclosing before a court or grand jury, the source of information procured by him and published in a newspaper. But the Kentucky court held that he himself was the source of information for a story reporting his observation of the manufacture of hashish by others. He would have to give the identity of the manufacturer—to identify those whom he saw breaking the law. It was contempt for him to refuse to do so.[86]

New York's shield law is termed "absolute" in its protection, and even protects a journalist against testifying before a grand jury.[87] But it applies only to information obtained under the "cloak of confidentiality," and did not protect CBS against producing, under subpoena, video and audio takes and outtakes not made under promises of confidentiality.[88] California's constitution immunizes against contempt convictions for refusing to testify, but not against various other sanctions[89] nor does it protect certain free-lance authors. California's shield statute protects unpublished or "out-take" materials.[90] Ohio's shield law protects against disclosure only of the source of the information, not against disclosure

---

[85] Ill.Legis.H.Bill 1756, 1971, Gen. Assembly.

[86] Branzburg v. Pound, 461 S.W.2d 345 (Ky.1970). For a similar position under New York's statute, see People v. Dupree, 88 Misc.2d 791, 388 N.Y.S.2d 1000 (1976); for Texas, Ex parte Grothe, 687 S.W.2d 736 (Tex.Cr.App.1984), 10 Med.L.Rptr. 2009.

[87] Beach v. Shanley, 62 N.Y.2d 241, 476 N.Y.S.2d 765, 465 N.E.2d 304 (1984), 10 Med.L.Rptr. 1753.

[88] People v. Korkala, 99 A.D.2d 161, 472 N.Y.S.2d 310 (1984), 10 Med.L.Rptr. 1355; see also Knight–Ridder Broadcasting, Inc. v. Greenberg, 70 N.Y.2d 151, 518 N.Y.S.2d 595, 511 N.E.2d 1116 (1987), 14 Med.L.Rptr. 1299.

[89] KSDO v. Superior Court Riverside County, 136 Cal.App.3d 375, 186 Cal.Rptr. 211 (1982), 8 Med.L.Rptr. 2360. Also New York: Oak Beach Inn Corp. v. Babylon Beacon, 62 N.Y.2d 158, 476 N.Y.S.2d 269, 464 N.E.2d 967 (1984), 10 Med.L.Rptr. 1761; see Calif. Constitution Art. I, § 2, subd. (b).

[90] In re Van Ness (Cal.3d 1982), 8 Med.L.Rptr. 2563; Evidence Code of Calif. (§ 1070).

of information in notes, tapes, and records from the source.[91]
Under Tennessee's statute, both confidential and nonconfidential
information is protected, which has the effect of shielding notes,
tapes, or video out-takes from courts or grand juries.[92]

The William Farr Case

A case whose permutations enmeshed a reporter for eight years
was that of William Farr, reporter for the *Los Angeles Herald
Examiner* and later the *Los Angeles Times*. Reporting the murder
trial of Charles Manson, Farr learned that a Mrs. Virginia Graham
had given a statement to a district attorney in the case, claiming
that a Manson "family" member, Susan Atkins, had confessed
taking part in the multiple crimes and told of the group's plans for
other murders. The judge in the case had ordered attorneys,
witnesses and court employees not to release for public dissemination, any content or nature of testimony that might be given at the
trial; but Farr obtained copies of the Graham statement, according
to him from two attorneys in the case. The court learned that he
had the statement. Farr refused to tell the court the names of the
sources, and published a story carrying sensational details. Later,
he identified a group of six attorneys as including the two. The
judge queried them, and all denied being the source. Once more
the court asked Farr for his sources, and he continued to refuse
under the California reporters' privilege law.[93] The court denied
him protection under the statute and he appealed.

The appeals court upheld the conviction for contempt, essentially under the doctrine of the "inherent power" of courts to
regulate judicial proceedings without interference from other government branches—a principle, as we have seen, reaching far back
in the history of contempt. It said that courts' power of contempt
is inherent in their constitutional status, and no legislative act
could declare that certain acts do not constitute a contempt. If
Farr were immunized from liability, it would violate the principle of
separation of powers among the three branches of government; it
would mean that the legislative branch could interfere with the
judicial branch's power to control its own officers:[94]

[91] Ohio v. Geis, 2 Ohio App.3d 258, 441 N.E.2d 803 (1981), 7 Med.L.Rptr. 1675.

[92] Dorothy A. Bowles, Media Law in Tennessee (Stillwater, OK: New Forums
Press, 1993, at pp. 106–107, discussing Tennessee Code Ann. 24–1–208, and Austin
v. Memphis Pub. Co., 655 S.W.2d 146 (Tenn. 1983), and State ex rel. Gerbitz v.
Curriden, 738 S.W.2d 192 (Tenn. 1987).

[93] West's Ann.Cal.Evidence Code § 1070 (1966).

[94] Farr v. Superior Court of Los Angeles County, 22 Cal.App.3d 60, 99 Cal.Rptr.
342, 348 (1971). New Mexico's Supreme Court ruled similarly that that state's
shield law was without effect where testimony before courts was concerned: Ammer-
man v. Hubbard Broadcasting, Inc., 89 N.M. 307, 551 P.2d 1354 (1976).

Farr served 46 days in jail before he was released pending a further appeal, and in his uncertain freedom lived with the possibility of indeterminate, unlimited imprisonment if his appeal failed and he persisted in refusing to reveal his sources. That "coercive" sentence was later ruled by the courts to have no further purpose, as there was no likelihood that continuing it would induce Farr to testify. It was still possible, however, that he might have to serve a further "punitive" sentence for his contempt. Five years after the opening of the case against Farr—on Dec. 6, 1976—he was finally freed from the latter possibility by ruling of the California Court of Appeal, Second District.[95] He had served the longest jail term on record in the United States for refusing to reveal news sources, and his case had lasted longer than any other.

But his ordeal was not over. Two of the six attorneys whom he had identified brought a libel suit for $24 million against him. The trial court and the California Appellate Court ruled that the shield law did not protect him from answering questions in the case.[96] The long contest ended in April 1979. The libel plaintiffs had missed the five-year statute of limitations for bringing an action, and Farr's attorney convinced the trial court that their failure was a result of insufficient effort to bring the case to trial. At long last, the judge dismissed the suit.[97]

Sixteen months later, Californians voted to elevate the state's shield for journalists to a better-fortified position than that of a statute; they passed Proposition 5, which placed the shield directly into the State Constitution.[98]

In 1982, one test demonstrating the limitation of the new California shield came when Riverside (Calif.) policemen brought a libel suit against KSDO radio and its reporter, Hal Brown, for a story that implicated police in drug traffic. They demanded Brown's notes and memoranda.[99] And while the journalists won in their refusal to yield the material, they did so under *First Amendment* protection, said the court of appeal: the police had failed to show that the information was not available from any other source, or that the desired material went to the heart of their case.[1]

[95] In re Farr, 64 Cal.App.3d 605, 134 Cal.Rptr. 595 (1976); Milwaukee Journal, Dec. 7, 1976.

[96] 64 Cal.App.3d 605, 134 Cal.Rptr. 595 (1976). See also Quill, Nov. 1977, p. 14.

[97] Anon., "William Farr's Seven [sic] Year Fight to Protect Sources Is Victorious," News Media & the Law, Aug./Sept. 1979, 22.

[98] Anon., "Californians Vote to Include a Newsmen's Shield in the State Constitution," Quill, July/August 1980, 9; Calif.Const. § 2, subd. (b).

[99] KSDO v. Superior Court of Riverside County, 136 Cal.App.3d 375, 186 Cal.Rptr. 211 (1982), 8 Med.L.Rptr. 2360.

[1] Ibid., at 216, 8 Med.L.Rptr. at 2366.

But so far as California's constitutional shield was concerned, said the court, decades of assumptions about its protective reach were mistaken: All it does is protect a journalist from contempt conviction. It does not stop courts from taking other actions in a libel case, as here, where journalists themselves are defendants: Their refusal to testify about information needed by the plaintiff could result in the court's striking their defense, or even awarding the plaintiff a default judgment. The court said that the shield law [2]

> * * * does not create a privilege for newspeople, rather, it provides an immunity from being adjudged in contempt. This rather basic distinction has been misstated and apparently misunderstood by members of the news media and our courts as well.

Though vulnerable under any law journalists occasionally got more protection from their states' courts than the statutes suggested might be available. One loophole in several "absolute" statutes was the lack of provision protecting the reporter from revealing *information* that he had gathered, even though it protected him from revealing the *source* of that information. Robert L. Taylor, president and general manager, and Earl Selby, city editor of the *Philadelphia Bulletin,* were convicted of contempt of court for refusing to produce documents in a grand jury investigation of possible corruption in city government. Both were fined $1,000 and given five-day prison terms. They appealed, relying on the Pennsylvania statute stating that no newsman could be "required to disclose the source of any information" that he had obtained. "Source" they said, means "documents" as well as "personal informants." The Pennsylvania Supreme Court, reversing the conviction, agreed. The court said that the legislature, in passing the act, declared the gathering of news and protection of the source of news as of greater importance to the public interest than the disclosure of the alleged crime or criminal.[3]

Shield Laws and Libel

Finally, there is the frequent case of whether a shield against testifying is justified where a newspaper and reporter are sued for libel. If a reporter refuses to reveal an unnamed source who had allegedly libeled the plaintiff, may the plaintiff be foreclosed from discovering and confronting his accuser? Who, besides the reporter, can identify the accuser? Conversely, if the sources must be revealed, then is it not possible "for someone to file a libel suit as a

[2] Ibid., at 213, 8 Med.L.Rptr. at 2362.

[3] In re Taylor, 412 Pa. 32, 193 A.2d 181, 185 (1963). The Reporters Committee 1990 Guide, "Confidential Sources of Information," lists "absolute" and "qualified privilege" states as to both confidential sources *and* information.

pretext to discover the reporters' sources and subject them to harassment"?[4]   This line of actions, of course, produced the suit which, perhaps more than any other, alerted the news world to the possibilities of danger in required testimony—Garland v. Torre, of 1958.   As Marie Torre in that case, most other reporters since then who have been sued for libel have argued fruitlessly that they should not be required to name the source.

Shield statutes of Oregon, Rhode Island, and Tennessee provide expressly that the privilege is not available to persons sued for libel.[5]   Supreme Courts of Massachusetts[6] and Idaho, which have no shield statutes, reject reporters' claims that there is an alternative First Amendment protection against the requiring of testimony—including testimony about sources of alleged libel.   An Idaho decision, in which certiorari was denied by the United States Supreme Court, confirmed a 30–day jail sentence for reporter-editor Jay Shelledy.[7]   He had quoted a "police expert" as criticizing state narcotics agent Michael Caldero who had been involved in a shooting incident.   He was sued for libel by the agent, and, refusing to reveal the name of the expert, was held in contempt.   The trial judge decided not to press the contempt citation, however, finding that another course of action would be more helpful to Caldero: The court would treat Shelledy's failure to identify the police expert "as an admission by the defendant Shelledy that no such 'police expert' exists, and the jury shall be so instructed."[8]   The trial proceeded; the jury was instructed, and in place of the shield that his now-spent effort had hoped to raise, the jury served as armor: It brought in the verdict that Shelledy's article was not libelous.

The Caldero trial judge's ruling that Shelledy "had no source" was unusual but not unique.   Only months before, one case in precedent had used the move—a decision by the New Hampshire Supreme Court.   A former police chief sued for libel after a newspaper cast doubt on his truthfulness, alleging that he had failed polygraph tests.   Its staff refused to reveal the sources of the accusation.   The court, after determining that the sought-after testimony was "essential to the material issue in dispute," and "not available from any source other than the press," granted the chief's motion to compel disclosure.   The newspaper appealed, and the New Hampshire Supreme Court felt that there was a better

---

[4] Gora, p. 40.

[5] Gora, p. 247. See Kaufman, op. cit., at footnote 84, above, *passim*, for comments on state shield statutes.

[6] Dow Jones & Co., Inc. v. Superior Court, 364 Mass. 317, 303 N.E.2d 847 (1973).

[7] Caldero v. Tribune Pub. Co., 98 Idaho 288, 562 P.2d 791 (1977), certiorari denied 434 U.S. 930, 98 S.Ct. 418 (1977).

[8] Anon., "Lewiston reporter Wins Jury Verdict in Libel Case," News Media & the Law, Oct./Nov.1980, 10–11, Downing v. Monitor Pub. Co. Inc., 120 N.H. 383, 415 A.2d 683 (1980), 6 Med.L.Rptr. 1193.

way to enforce the trial court's order than by holding the newspaper in contempt.[9]

> We are aware * * * that most media personnel have refused to obey court orders to disclose, electing to go to jail instead. Confining newsmen to jail in no way aids the plaintiff in proving his case. Although we do not say that contempt power should not be exercised, we do say that something more is required to protect the rights of a libel plaintiff. Therefore, we hold that when a defendant in a libel action, brought by a plaintiff who is required to prove actual malice under *New York Times,* refuses to disclose his sources of information upon a valid order of the court, there shall arise a presumption that the defendant had no source. The presumption may be removed by a disclosure of the sources a reasonable time before trial.

Successful Shield Claims

Nonetheless, the frequent success of the claim to the shield (usually where plaintiffs fail to show necessity, relevancy, and unavailability of the information) occasionally can extend to the libel situation, where the reporter is so likely to be vulnerable because he is the only source of the information sought. Before Marie Torre ever pleaded for protection in a libel case, a decision under the shield law of Alabama had furnished it to a reporter who refused to reveal sources of a story on prison conditions.[10] New York, New Jersey, and Pennsylvania protect, in varying degree, confidentiality in libel cases.[11]

Even in Idaho (which has no shield law and whose Supreme Court has interpreted *Branzburg* to provide no First Amendment protection), the appeal process has brought relief to journalists who fruitlessly sought a shield in discovery proceedings in a libel case. Sierra Life Insurance Co. demanded the names of confidential

---

[9] Downing v. Monitor Pub. Co. Inc., 120 N.H. 383, 415 A.2d 683, 686 (1980), 6 Med.L.Rptr. 1193, 1195; see also Sprague v. Walter, 518 Pa. 425, 543 A.2d 1078, 1086 (1988), in which the Pennsylvania Supreme Court held that a reporter-defendant in a libel case could invoke the state's shield law to protect the identity of sources. And the jury was to draw *"no inference either favorable or adverse "* from the invoking of the shield law as to the reliability of an unidentified source.

[10] Ex parte Sparrow, 14 F.R.D. 351 (N.D.Ala.1953). Federal courts have provided protection in some libel cases also: Mize v. McGraw–Hill, Inc., 82 F.R.D. 475 (S.D.Tex.1979), 5 Med.L.Rptr. 1156; Bruno & Stillman, Inc. v. Globe Newspaper Co., 633 F.2d 583 (1st Cir.1980), 6 Med.L.Rptr. 2057.

[11] Respectively, Oak Beach Inn Corp. v. Babylon Beacon, Inc., 62 N.Y.2d 158, 476 N.Y.S.2d 269, 464 N.E.2d 967 (1984), 10 Med.L.Rptr. 1761; Maressa v. New Jersey Monthly, 89 N.J. 176, 445 A.2d 376 (1982), 8 Med.L.Rptr. 1473; D'Alfonso v. A.S. Abell Co., 765 F.2d 138 (4th Cir.1985), 11 Med.L.Rptr. 2117; and Hatchard v. Westinghouse Broadcasting Co., 516 Pa. 184, 532 A.2d 346 (1987): Reporters have to yield up evidence in a libel suit when it does not reveal identify of sources of confidential information.

sources for a series of stories about the firm's financial difficulties, written by reporters for the *Twin Falls Times–News*.[12]   Through complex legal processes, the reporters and the newspaper alleged that their stories were true and refused to name sources.   In response, the trial judge ruled that Idaho provided no protection for them, struck all their defenses, and entered a "default" judgment against them for $1.9 million.

But the Idaho Supreme Court reversed the trial court.   It did not feel that the refusal to testify should stand in the way of the newspaper's employing defenses—truth and lack of a connection between the stories and the damages suffered.   Striking defenses in this case, it agreed, amounted to unwarranted punishment of the newspaper.   And it said that Sierra had failed to show that its inability to discover the sources damaged its ability to prove the news stories false, which would be necessary to its case.   It remanded the case, with "guidance" to the trial judge which included the Supreme Court's suggestion that the confidential sources' identity might not be relevant.[13]

Summarizing Issues in Confidentiality

The *Branzburg* decision having hedged the constitutional protection that the news world sought, the media turned to lobbying for statutes at the state and federal levels, and to strengthening existing state statutes.   The number of states with statutes reached 28 by 1990,[14] about half of them passed during the 1960s and 1970s.

At the federal level, the major news organizations tried periodically for passage of a federal shield law, with—as of early 1989—no success.   They found strong support and strong opposition among congressmen.   It was estimated back in 1973 that more than 50 bills offering a shield had been introduced,[15] and more appeared in subsequent years.   Whatever the level of government, the issues were similar.

(1) What are the competing social values in granting or denying journalists an immunity from testifying?   The reporter's ethic of not betraying sources, and his property right in not losing his effectiveness and value as a reporter through losing his sources, had long been asserted unsuccessfully in cases under the common law.   Now he was grounding his claim in society's loss of his service if he lost his sources through betraying them.

[12] Sierra Life Insurance Co. v. Magic Valley Newspapers, Inc., 101 Idaho 795, 623 P.2d 103, (1980), 6 Mcd.L.Rptr. 1769.

[13] Ibid., at 109, 6 Med.L.Rptr. at 1773.

[14] Reporters Committee 1990 guide, "Confidential Sources of Information."

[15] Thomas Collins, "Congress Grapples with Press Bill," Milwaukee Journal, March 25, 1973, p. 16.

Earl Caldwell was one of a tiny number of reporters who had gained the confidence of the Black Panthers at a time when society had a real need to know about this alienated group. The Ninth Circuit Court of Appeals accepted Caldwell's argument that he would lose the Panthers' confidence if he even entered the secret grand jury chambers, for this extremely sensitive group would not know what he might say under the compulsion of the legal agency.[16] And if Caldwell could not report the Panthers, society was the real loser. This situation illustrated the difference between the values served in the case of privilege for the journalist and that for the doctor, lawyer, or clergyman: [17]

> " * * * the doctor-patient privilege is there to make it possible for patients to get better medical care. A journalist's privilege should be there not only to make it possible for a journalist to get better stories, but to contribute to the public's right to know. So in that sense it is a more critical privilege than some of these other privileges, which are based primarily on the relationship between two people."

Asserting an equal service in the cause of the "public's right to know" was the position that in many circumstances, government-as-the-public sought information from reporters vital to the public welfare. In State v. Knops,[18] an "underground" newspaper editor refused to tell a grand jury the names of people to whom he had talked about the bombing of a university building that killed a researcher, and about alleged arson of another university building. "[T]he appellant's information could lead to the apprehension and conviction of the person or persons who committed a major criminal offense resulting in the death of an innocent person," said the Wisconsin Supreme Court in denying privilege to editor Mark Knops.[19] Here government was saying that the journalist was practicing secrecy similar to that which he so often criticized in government, and that government was trying to serve the public's right to know about a major crime.

The Janet Cooke Debacle

A few reporters, meanwhile, rejected the notion that the privilege was either needed by or appropriate to the journalist. They said that most journalists of the nation had done their work for decades without a shield. And they worried about unethical reporters using a shield law to hide behind in dishonest reporting.

[16] Caldwell v. United States, 434 F.2d 1081, 1088 (9th Cir.1970).

[17] House of Rep. Committee on the Judiciary, Subcommittee No. 3, 92 Cong., 2d Sess., "Newsmen's Privilege," Hearings, Testimony of Victor Navasky, Oct. 5, 1972, p. 236.

[18] State v. Knops, 49 Wis.2d 647, 183 N.W.2d 93 (1971).

[19] Ibid., at 99.

In point was the episode—dismaying to journalists every-where—of the fabricated story of rookie reporter Janet Cooke of the *Washington Post* in 1981. Her account of an unnamed eight-year-old heroin addict, whose identity she refused to disclose to her editors out of alleged fear of death from the child's "supplier," was awarded a Pulitzer Prize. But the award was scarcely announced when a standing challenge to the story's accuracy by city officials (resisted by Post editors who had insisted on shielding their report-er from disclosure of her sources), took strength from the revelation that Cooke had falsified her biographical resumé in applying for a position at the Post. Faced with the dual challenge, she confessed that she had made up the story and resigned. The Post returned the Pulitzer Award with agonized apologies to readers, the city, and the field of journalism. No law court, no threat of contempt was involved, but the parallels were too close for comfort. The integrity of a shield claimed by a reporter and afforded by editors had been shattered; and so, too, in some measure, had that of a great newspaper, and the fact-gathering principle of special treatment—privilege—for the journalist.[20]

(2) Can the news gathering function be protected by a quali-fied immunity, or must it be absolute? Hard positions for absolute shields were taken by many journalists and their organizations including the directors of the American Newspaper Publishers Association and those of the American Society of Newspaper Edi-tors.[21]

Yet "absolute" protection was an illusion, as we have seen in the previous section.[22] And a federal statute of any kind became a more and more remote possibility as years of drafting, committee work, and lobbying failed.[23]

(3) Also at issue was the question: Who deserves the shield? and following that: Would not defining "reporter" in effect be to license journalists and thus bring them under state control? The United States Supreme Court in denying Paul Branzburg protec-tion summarized the question and found that deciding it would bring practical and conceptual difficulties of a high order: [24]

> Sooner or later, it would be necessary to define those
> categories of newsmen who qualified for the privilege, a

---

[20] Jerry Chaney, "Level With Us, Just How Sacred Is Your Source?", Quill, March 1979, 28; Quill, 61:4, April 1973, 38. Paul Magnusson, "Reporter's Lies Undermine Paper, Profession," Wisconsin State Journal, April 19, 1981, Sec. 4, p. 6; Robert H. Spiegel, "Notes from Pulitzer Juror," Wisconsin State Journal, April 21, 1981, Sec. 1, p. 6.

[21] Quill, 61:1, Jan. 1973, 29.

[22] AP Log, Sept. 3–9, 1973, pp. 1, 4.

[23] Press Censorship Newsletter No. IX, April–May 1976, p. 53.

[24] Branzburg v. Hayes, 408 U.S. 665, 702, 92 S.Ct. 2646, 2668 (1972).

questionable procedure in light of the traditional doctrine that liberty of the press is the right of the lonely pamphleteer who uses carbon paper or a mimeograph just as much as of the large metropolitan publisher who utilizes the latest photo-composition methods.... Freedom of the press is a "fundamental personal right" which "is not confined to newspapers and periodicals." It necessarily embraces pamphlets and leaflets.... Almost any author may quite accurately assert that he is contributing to the flow of information to the public, that he relies on confidential sources of information, and that these sources will be silenced if he is forced to make disclosures before a grand jury.

Troubling as the question was, it did not deter states as they adopted statutes from 1970 onward. New York's 1970 law defined "professional journalist" and "newscaster" in its law that protected only those agencies normally considered "mass media"—newspaper, magazine, news agency, press association, wire service, radio or television transmission station or network.[25] Illinois, in its 1971 statute, defined "reporter" as one who worked for similar media.[26] Neither included books among the media immunized; neither included scholars and researchers among the persons immunized. In two cases, courts have ruled that state statutes which gave protection specifically to newspapers did not protect magazines.[27] But in late 1977, the U.S. Court of Appeals, Tenth Circuit, ruled that Arthur (Buzz) Hirsch, a film maker engaged in preparing a documentary on Karen Silkwood who had died mysteriously in a puzzling auto accident in Oklahoma, was indeed protected by the First Amendment in refusing to disclose confidential information concerning his investigation. This was the case despite the fact that the Oklahoma shield law gave protection only to those "regularly engaged in obtaining, writing, reviewing, editing or otherwise preparing news."[28]

9th Circuit Provides Investigative Authors With a Qualified Shield

A wealthy family's internal struggles for control over the U–Haul Co. are part of the background for a defamation/author's

[25] McKinney's N.Y.Civ.Rights Law § 79–h (Supp.1971). In People v. LeGrand, 67 A.D.2d 446, 415 N.Y.S.2d 252 (1979), 4 Med.L.Rptr. 2524, the law was held not to apply to a book author, because the law specifies that only professional journalists and newscasters are shielded.

[26] Ill.Legis.H.Bill 1756, 1971 Gen.Assembly.

[27] Cepeda v. Cohane, 233 F.Supp. 465 (S.D.N.Y.1964); Deltec, Inc. v. Dun & Bradstreet, Inc., 187 F.Supp. 788 (N.D.Ohio 1960).

[28] Silkwood v. Kerr–McGee, see "Court Protects Film Maker's Sources," News Media & the Law, 1:1 (Oct.1977), p. 26.

privilege action known as Shoen v. Shoen.   Leonard Shoen, a major owner of U–Haul, cooperated with investigative author Ronald Watkins, helping him to write a book titled *Birthright*.   This book dealt with members of the family jousting for control of the company.

In 1990, the wife of Shoen's oldest son, Sam, was the victim of an unsolved murder.   In interviews with the news media, Leonard Shoen said he suspected two other sons, Mark and Edward Shoen, of having some indirect ties to the murder.[29]

Mark and Edward Shoen sued their father for defamation. Seeking information for their lawsuit, they subpoenaed book author Watkins to give a deposition and to produce any information he had about the murdered woman, Eva Berg Shoen.   District Court Judge Roger C. Strand refused Watkins' order for a protective order to protect him from a subpoena on grounds that a state court had interpreted Arizona's state law as excluding book authors.[30]

Held in contempt for refusing to testify, Watkins appealed to the U.S. Court of Appeals for thee Ninth Circuit.   Watkins contended that a First Amendment privilege should be available to protect not only regularly employed establishment journalists but also independent authors such as himself.   He also argued that if forced to testify, that would discourage his sources from providing information.   Perhaps most telling, the point was made that the persons subpoenaing Watkins had not exhausted other sources.[31]

The Ninth Circuit held that Watkins, as an investigative journalist, could invoke the shield privilege: "The journalist's privilege is designed to protect investigative reporting, regardless of the medium used to report news to the public.* * *   What makes journalism is not its format but its content."   Further, even if Watkins did not gain access to his material under a confidentiality agreement, the shield privilege still should protect him.

The Court of Appeals said a key showing to be made when a subpoena is sought against a journalist is whether efforts were made to get the information from another source.   Further, for authorities to break the shield, they would have to show that the information sought was "relevant, material, non-cumulative, and crucial to . . . the Shoens' claims." [32]

These issues and questions run deep.   They are not likely to be resolved for all sides soon.   For the journalists who will live with

[29] Shoen v. Shoen, 5 F.3d 1289 (9th Cir.1993), 21 Med.L.Rptr. 1961; News Media & the Law, Fall, 1993, pp. 28–29.

[30] News Media & The Law, Fall, 1993, p. 28.

[31] Shoen v. Shoen, 5 F.3d 1289 (9th Cir.1993), 21 Med.L.Rptr. p. 1961.

[32] Ibid.,. p. 1964.

them and who may find them coming to bear personally in their professional work, a veteran investigative reporter—the late Clark R. Mollenhoff, a Pulitzer Prize-winner, had a key piece of advice: "You'd better know what you're getting into." [33]   In other words, journalists should be reluctant to pledge confidentiality. They may find that if they wish to stay "on the record," sources often will talk to them anyhow. And if confidentiality is pledged, for how long? Until the moon no longer shines? Or for some lesser period? Promises of confidentiality are not to be entered lightly.

Is a Reporter's Confidentiality Pledge a Contract? Cohen v. Cowles Media (1991)

Ethically, if a reporter promises to protect the identity of a source, that sounds relatively simple. Unless the journalist is released from that pledge by the source, then the journalist—if ordered to testify before a grand jury or in court—must choose between ethically keeping the confidence or refusing to testify and being fined or jailed for contempt. That is a hard choice, to be sure, but the rules seem understandable.

But matters are not that simple. Refer back to unfortunate Janet Cooke, discussed earlier in this chapter at page 578? She turned in a brilliant story to the Washington Post about an 8–year-old heroin addict, and said that her source was confidential. The Washington Post backed her, and—perhaps due to its own success with "confidentially sourced" stories by Bob Woodward and Carl Bernstein [34]—did not learn who her source was.

Ever since 1981, when it was seen that Ms. Cooke had made up the entire story and had caused the mortified Washington Post to hand back a Pulitzer Prize, most editors have insisted upon knowing the source's identity. This makes sense because if a paper (or broadcaster) is going to stake its reputation on a story, it is essential to have a good idea of the source's veracity and reliability. With some editors, also, it is an additional protection for a reporter. As John Seigenthaler of the Nashville Tennessean instructed his staff before his retirement in 1991, he insisted on knowing the identity of a confidential source so he could evaluate both source and information. (Then, if a judge wants to put a reporter in jail for not testifying, the judge may also have to jail the editor).[35]

The case of Cohen v. Cowles Media illustrates a situation in which editors decided—over the reporters' objections—that a confidential source's identity should be edited into a story. Its lesson—

[33] Quill, March 1979, p. 27, for Mollenhoff's rules.

[34] Cf. Woodward and Bernstein's All the President's Men (New York: Simon & Schuster, 1974).

[35] Seigenthaler comments on July 26, 1988, edition of MacNeil–Lehrer News Hour.

as handed down by the Supreme Court of the United States in June of 1991—is that a reporter's oral promise of source confidentiality amounts to a contract. Breaking such a contract may expose the reporter's employing organization to financial liability.

Dan Cohen, a former Minneapolis alderman, had been working as a political consultant to a Republican candidate for governor. Cohen found his candidate trailing badly in the polls late in October of 1982, only weeks before the election. Cohen arranged meetings with reporters from Twin Cities news organizations, including the Minneapolis Star and Tribune, the St. Paul Pioneer Press, and WCCO–TV.

Cohen offered to provide information that a candidate for state-wide election had been convicted of a misdemeanor. (The candidate involved was Marlene Johnson, the Democratic–Farmer–Labor [DFL] candidate for lieutenant governor; the DFL was then far ahead of Republicans in the governor's race. The misdemeanor was for shop-lifting merchandise worth $6 a dozen years earlier.) [36]

Reporters for both the Star Tribune and the Pioneer Press promised to keep Cohen's identity anonymous, and Cohen then gave the reporters two court documents showing that Marlene Johnson had been "charged in 1969 with three counts of unlawful assembly, and the second that she had been convicted in 1970 of petty theft." (The unlawful assembly charges stemmed from Ms. Johnson engaging in a protest against claimed failure to hire minority workers in city construction, and those charges were dismissed. The shoplifting conviction involved leaving a store without paying for $6 worth of sewing materials. That incident apparently happened, the Supreme Court noted, at a time when Ms. Johnson was emotionally distraught, "and the conviction was later vacated.")

Evidently not liking being caught by Dan Cohen's political dirty trick, reporters for the newspapers interviewed Marlene Johnson to get her comments. Both the Minneapolis and the St. Paul newspapers decided independently to use Dan Cohen's name as the source of their last-minute-before-the-election stories about Johnson.[37]

> In their stories, both papers identified Cohen as the source of the court records, indicated his connection with the Whitney [Republican candidate for governor] campaign, and included denials by Whitney campaign officials

[36] Cohen v. Cowles Media Co. (1987), 14 Med.L.Rptr. 1460; News Media & the Law, Summer, 1988, p. 349; Andrew Radolf, "Anonymous Sources," Editor & Publisher, Aug. 27, 1988.

[37] Cohen v. Cowles Media Co., 501 U.S. 663, 664, 111 S.Ct. 2513, 2516 (1991), 18 Med.L.Rptr. 2273, 2274.

of any role in the matter. The same day the stories appeared, Cohen was fired by his employer.

(At least one newsman, David Nimmer of WCCO–TV, listened to Cohen's proposition and refused to use the information. It was "no story," Nimmer said: "A conviction when she was 18 years old for shoplifting needles and thread.") [38]

Tim McGuire, managing editor of the Star Tribune, said that "* * * disclosure of an 11th–hour dirty trick [in the political campaign] was at least as important as the 12–year–old shoplifting record which Cohen was revealing." [39]

The trial court rejected the newspapers' contentions that the First Amendment erected a barrier to Dan Cohen's lawsuit alleging fraudulent misrepresentation and breach of contract. By a 5–1 margin, a jury awarded Cohen $200,000 in compensatory damages and $500,000 in punitive damages. [40] In a split decision, however, the Minnesota Court of Appeals overturned the punitive damages award after concluding that Cohen had not established a fraud claim which would support a punitive damage award. That court, however, left standing the $200,000 compensatory damages award. [41]

The Supreme Court of the United States held that the First Amendment does not prohibit a plaintiff from collecting damages for a newspaper's breaking of a promise of confidentiality in exchange for information. Liability could be assessed under Minnesota's "doctrine of promissory estoppel." [42] Justice Byron White wrote for the Court's 5–member majority:

> * * * "[G]enerally applicable laws do not offend the First Amendment simply because their enforcement against the press has incidental effects on its ability to gather and report the news. * * * [T]ruthful information sought to be published must have been lawfully acquired. The press may not with impunity break and enter an office or dwelling to gather news."

The U.S. Supreme Court declared that the Minnesota Supreme Court's "incorrect conclusion that the First Amendment barred Cohen's claim may well have truncated its consideration of whether

[38] MacNeil–Lehrer News Hour, July 26, 1988.

[39] "Verdict on news sources distresses journalists," Associated Press report in Milwaukee Journal, July 23, 1988.

[40] News Media & the Law, Summer, 1988, p. 49.

[41] Ibid., at 50, 18 Med.L.Rptr. at 2276.

[42] Ibid. Black's Law Dictionary says: "*Estoppel.* A man's own act or acceptance stops or closes his mouth to allege or plead the truth." With *promissory estoppel,* "* * * such promise is binding if injustice can be avoided only by enforcement of [the] promise."

a promissory estoppel claim had otherwise been established under Minnesota law and whether Cohen's claim could be upheld on a promissory estoppel basis." [43]   Or, Justice White wrote, perhaps the Minnesota Constitution might be construed to protect the press from such a promissory estoppel action.

In dissent, Justice Blackmun (joined by Justices Marshall and Souter) argued that a damage claim for promissory estoppel should not be used to punish reporting of truthful information about a political campaign.[44]   Justice Souter's dissenting opinion (joined by Marshall, Blackmun, and O'Connor) took the tack that the higher value to be served is an informed public, not a promise kept by a newspaper: [45]

> The importance of this public interest [the information provided by the press necessary to self-government] is integral to the balance that should be struck in this case. There can be no doubt that the fact of Cohen's identity expanded the universe of information relevant to the choice faced by Minnesota voters in that State's 1982 gubernatorial election, the publication of which was thus of the sort quintessentially subject to strict First Amendment protection.

Justice Souter summarized his dissent, arguing that "the State's interest in enforcing a newspaper's promise of confidentiality [is] insufficient to outweigh the interest in unfettered publication of the information revealed in this case * * *."

Whatever else Cohen v. Cowles Media means, the way it was argued by the newspapers ought to be a tremendous embarrassment to the journalistic world.   Journalists have long argued that because they serve the public, they are somehow special and do not have to testify—like ordinary mortals—about the sources of their information.   "We gave our word to protect our confidential sources, and courts should respect that."   But in the Cohen case, the newspapers wanted it both ways; they wound up appearing to want to be free to give promises to get information, and also to have the luxury of reneging on promises when convenient.

But what of Dan Cohen?   This political operative wanted to be a paid political consultant—anonymously—while lobbing bricks over a wall at an opposition candidate.   But was he harmed $200,000 worth (the amount of compensatory damages left standing by the Minnesota Supreme Court)?   Cohen, who lost a $35,000–a–

---

[43] Ibid., 670–673, 111 S.Ct. at 2519–2520, 18 Med.L.Rptr. at 2277.

[44] Ibid., 673, 111 S.Ct. at 2520, 18 Med.L.Rptr. at 2279.

[45] Ibid., 678, 111 S.Ct. at 2523, 18 Med.L.Rptr. at 2280.

year job in public relations in '1982 the day the story was published, by 1987 had his own PR firm and earned $97,000.[46]

Ironically, the Minneapolis Star Tribune was twice burned in 1988 on the issue of confidential sources. A second controversy over naming a source resulted in the newspaper halting circulation of its Sunday magazine for July 24, 1988. The New York Times reported that the Star Tribune could not ascertain whether a story to appear in its magazine had breached a secrecy agreement between a source (who is a lawyer) and the author, a freelance journalist.[47] That magazine issue was withheld.

Ruzicka v. Conde–Nast and Claudia Dreyfus (1992)

This case raises the **legal** question about how precise a journalist's promise needs to be to incur liability when broken. (**Ethical** concerns here might take up the question of making sure journalists and their sources understand each other's ground rules about confidentiality, etc.)

A 1988 issue of Glamour magazine contained an article by Claudia Dreyfus on sexual abuse by therapists. In researching the article, Ms. Dreyfus interviewed Jill Ruzicka, who told of being victimized by a psychiatrist. Ms. Ruzicka contended in her lawsuit against the magazine that she agreed to the interview only on condition that she not be identified. Ms. Dreyfus, on the other hand, recalled only that Ms. Ruzicka had casually asked for "some kind of masking."

The article used the first name "Jill" but did use a fictitious last name. But Ms. Ruzicka argued that the article identified her in other ways. (The article said "Jill" had filed a complaint against the therapist with the state medical examiners, had filed suit against him, and had gone to law school, become an attorney, and served on a state task force on sexual abuse by therapists—all accomplishments of the real-life Ms. Ruzicka.) She sued Conde–Nast and Ms. Dreyfus for breach of contract (promissory estoppel), fraudulent misrepresentation, invasion of privacy, intentional infliction of emotional distress, and unjust enrichment.[48]

A federal district court in Minnesota granted summary judgment to the defendants on all claims, and the Eighth Circuit Court of Appeals affirmed the summary judgments but sent the case back to the district court to consider the promissory estoppel issue as

---

[46] "2 Newspapers Lose Suit for Disclosing a Source," Associated Press story in New York Times, July 23, 1988. Early in 1992, the State's Supreme Court upheld the $200,000 jury award. The News Media & The Law, Winter, 1992, p. 2.

[47] Charles J. Lewis, Trading News for Anonymity, The Bulletin of the American Society of Newspaper Editors, April 1988, p. 3.

[48] Ruzicka v. Conde–Nast, 794 F.Supp. 303, 304–305 (D.Minn.1992), 20 Med. L.Rptr. 1233, 1234.

involved in Cohen v. Cowles media, discussed above. (Promissory estoppel is a doctrine which holds that if a person relies on a clear, unambiguous promise to his or her detriment, he or she may ask compensation for harm caused by the broken promise.) [49]

The federal district court held that Ms. Ruzicka's promissory estoppel claim failed because media coverage of her lawsuit against the psychiatrist before the magazine article appeared had increased the possibility that she would be identifiable from the magazine article. Second, the district court distinguished Ms. Ruzicka's lawsuit from the Cohen case because in her case, neither the promise nor the breach was clear. In the Cohen situation, the defendants simply decided to break a promise not to name him; in the Ruzicka case, defendants made an effort (however unsuccessful) to mask her identity.[50]

Some Ethical Concerns on Attribution

These problems surfaced in a time when journalists were worrying about their ethical standards. Charles J. Lewis, Washington bureau chief of the Associated Press, expressed concern about misuse of confidential sources eroding media credibility.

How can readers evaluate stories when sources are not known? For example, news from the State Department tends to follow certain rules: "on the record" means use names and information, but much news called "background" means that information can be used, but only vaguely attributed, as to "U.S. Officials" or "State Department sources." "Deep Background" means no specific attribution, and "off the record" means reporters can't use what they're told except for background.

Bureau Chief Lewis noted that the Associated Press has developed a three-part test which has helped to cut down the number of unattributed stories sent by the wire service.[51]

(1) The information should be newsworthy.

(2) We couldn't get the information elsewhere with attribution.

(3) The information is arguably factual rather than opinion or judgmental.

Beyond that, some sources discover that they have been quoted after they thought they had an agreement that their names would not be used.[52] Sometimes, releasing a source's name is necessary, as when the source has lied. For example, Lt. Colonel Oliver North

---

[49] 794 F.Supp. at 308, 20 Med.L.Rptr. at 1236.

[50] 794 F.Supp. at 312, 20 Med.L.Rptr. at 1240.

[51] Ibid., p. 5.

[52] Monica Langley and Lee Levine, Broken Promises, Columbia Journalism Review July/August 1986, p. 21.

complained about "leaks" which had led to a story in Newsweek about interception of an Egyptian plane carrying hijackers. Understandably, Newsweek published the rejoinder that the Colonel had failed to mention that he was the source of the leaks.

The Wall Street Journal distinguishes "anonymous sources" from "confidential sources." A memo circulated by managing editor Norman Pearlstine says that anonymous sources are those whose names the Journal has agreed to leave out of the paper but whose identity may later be disclosed, as in defending against a libel suit. A confidential source, on the other hand, is one whose identity the paper has promised to keep secret, even it means losing a lawsuit or going to jail.[53]

Source confidentiality, then, is serious business. Secrecy agreements with sources are not to be entered lightly. Especially worrisome are situations in which reporters' pledges are broken, either by reporters themselves or by their editors.

The basic question is whether the press is to be trusted and credible. Editors wishing to avoid difficulties would do well to emulate John Seigenthaler, former editor of the Nashville Tennessean: He says the only conceivable time to name a source pledged confidentiality would be if it turns out that the source has provided false information.[54]

SEC. 80.   PROTECTING NEWSROOMS FROM SEARCH AND TELEPHONE RECORDS FROM DISCLOSURE

Courts have not granted First Amendment protection against officials' searches of newsrooms, but Congress and several states have passed laws providing protection. Confidentiality of journalists' telephone-call records that are on file at telephone companies has not been recognized.

When the United States Supreme Court rejects a claim to First Amendment protection, Congress and state legislatures may be able to furnish protection by passing laws. The news world's drive for a statutory privilege against revealing sources—after the Supreme Court in Branzburg v. Hayes seemed to journalists to restrict protection under the First Amendment to a shadow—succeeded in a few states by dint of long, hard work, and failed in others. The effort to get a law through Congress ground to a frustrated halt in 1976 and 1977 as we saw above.

---

[53] Ibid., p. 23.

[54] MacNeil–Lehrer News Hour, July 26, 1988. In 1991, Mr. Seigenthaler became chairman of the Freedom Forum First Amendment Center at Vanderbilt University.

But another aspect of confidentiality denied First Amendment protection by the Supreme Court—shielding news rooms and offices against official searches and seizures of news material—got an early remedy in the form of state legislation and a national law—the Privacy Protection Act of 1980.[55] It was passed less than three years after a Supreme Court decision of May 1978 sent the news media into a reaction of alarm and denunciation; the very security of their news rooms and files was at stake. Journalists' outrage over the decision was widespread at what they saw as the Court's approval of a "right to rummage" in their offices, a breach of custom and understanding.

By a 5–3 margin, the Court said in 1978's Zurcher v. Stanford Daily that newspapers (and all citizens, for that matter) may be the subjects of unannounced searches as long as those searches are approved beforehand by a court's issuance of a search warrant.[56] They need not be suspected of any crime themselves; but as "third parties" who may hold information helpful to law enforcement, their property may be searched. A particular issue in this case was a question of how to interpret the words of the Fourth Amendment to the Constitution. That amendment says:

> The right of the people to be secure in their persons, houses, papers, and effects, against unreasonable searches and seizures, shall not be violated, and no Warrants shall issue, but upon probable cause, supported by Oath or affirmation, and particularly describing the place to be searched, and the persons or things to be seized.

The *Zurcher* case arose during violent demonstrations at Stanford University on April 9, 1971. Two days later, the *Stanford Daily* carried articles and photographs about the clash between demonstrators and police. It appeared to authorities from that coverage that a Daily photographer had been in a position to photograph fighting between students and police. As a result, a search warrant was secured from a municipal court. The warrant was issued [57]

> on a finding of "just, probable and reasonable cause for believing that: Negatives and photographs and films, evidence material and relevant to the identification of the perpetrators of felonies, to wit, Battery on a Peace Officer, and Assault with a Deadly Weapon, will be located [on the premises of the Daily]."

[55] Pub.Law # 96–440, 94 Stat. 1879, approved Oct. 13, 1980, 6 Med.L.Rptr. 2255. For summary and discussion of the law and the state actions, see Anon., "Newsroom Searches," News Media & the Law, Oct./Nov. 1980, 3–5.

[56] 436 U.S. 547, 98 S.Ct. 1970 (1978).

[57] Ibid., at 551, 98 S.Ct. at 1974.

Later that day, the newspaper office was searched by four police officers, with some newspaper staffers present. The search turned up only the photographs already published in the Daily, so no materials were removed from the newspaper's office. In May of 1971, the Daily and some of its staffers sued James Zurcher, the Palo Alto chief of police, the officers who conducted the search, and the county's district attorney.

A federal district court held that the search was illegal. It declared that the Fourth and Fourteenth Amendments forbade the issuance of a warrant to search for materials in possession of a person not suspected of a crime unless there was probable cause to believe, based on a sworn affidavit, that a subpoena *duces tecum* would be impractical.

Some translation is needed here. As *New York Times* reporter Warren Weaver, Jr. noted, a subpoena *duces tecum* (that's Latin for "bring it with you") "can be enforced by a judge only after a hearing in which the holder of the evidence has the opportunity to present arguments why the material should not be given to the government." That process means, of course, that the holder of the documents sought would have some warning and perhaps even a chance to "clean up" files. (But if one does tamper with evidence under subpoena—and if that tampering is revealed, it is surely punishable as contempt.) If investigators have a search warrant, on the other hand, the holder of the documents "has no more warning than a knock on the door." [58] In finding in favor of the Stanford Daily, District Judge Robert F. Peckham wrote: [59]

> It should be apparent that means less drastic than a search warrant do exist for obtaining materials from a third party. A subpoena duces tecum, obviously, is much less intrusive than a search warrant: the police do not go rummaging through one's house, office, or desk armed only with a subpoena. And, perhaps equally important, there is no opportunity to challenge the search warrant prior to the intrusion, whereas one can always move to quash the subpoena before producing the sought-after materials. * * * In view of the difference in degree of intrusion and the opportunity to challenge possible mistakes, the subpoena should always be preferred to the search warrant, for non-suspects.

The Daily's lawsuit thus was upheld by a U.S. district court and, five years later, by a U.S. Court of Appeals.[60] The Supreme

[58] Warren Weaver, Jr., "High Court Bars Newspaper Plea Against Search," New York Times, June 1, 1978, pp. Al ff, at p. B6.

[59] Stanford Daily v. Zurcher, 353 F.Supp. 124, 130 (N.D.Cal.1972).

[60] 550 F.2d 464 (9th Cir.1977).

Court of the United States, however, in a decision announced by
Justice White, declared that newspapers are subject to such unan-
nounced "third party" searches as the one involving the *Stanford
Daily*. Justice White's majority opinion said: [61]

> It is an understatement to say that there is no direct
> authority in this or any other federal court for the District
> Court's sweeping revision of the Fourth Amendment. Un-
> der existing law, valid warrants may be issued to search
> *any* property, whether or not occupied by a third party, at
> which there is probable reason to believe that fruits,
> instrumentalities, or evidence of a crime will be found.
>
> * * *
>
> The critical element in a reasonable search is not that
> the owner of the property is suspected of a crime but that
> there is reasonable cause to believe that the specific
> "things" to be searched for and seized are located on the
> property to which entry is sought.

The Court enumerated—and rejected—the following arguments that additional First Amendment factors would forbid use of
search warrants and permit only the subpoena *duces tecum*—
arguments which held that searches of newspaper offices for evidence of crime would threaten the ability of the press to do its job.[62]

> This is said to be true for several reasons: first,
> searches will be physically disruptive to such an extent
> that timely publication will be impeded. Second, confiden-
> tial sources of information will dry up, and the press will
> also lose opportunities to cover various events because of
> fears of the participants that press files will be readily
> available to the authorities. Third, reporters will be de-
> terred from recording and preserving their recollections for
> future use if such information is subject to seizure.
> Fourth, the processing of news and its dissemination will
> be chilled by the prospects that searches will disclose
> internal editorial deliberations. Fifth, the press will resort
> to self-censorship to conceal its possession of information
> of potential interest to the police.

Justice White's majority opinion brushed aside such arguments
and expressed confidence that judges could guard against searches
which would be so intrusive as to interfere with publishing newspapers.

[61] Zurcher v. Stanford Daily, 436 U.S. 547, 554–556, 98 S.Ct. 1970, 1975–1977
(1978).

[62] Ibid., at 561–566, 98 S.Ct. at 1977–1982.

Justice Potter Stewart, joined by Justice Thurgood Marshall, dissented, arguing that in place of the unannounced "knock-on-the-door" intrusion, "a subpoena would afford the newspaper itself an opportunity to locate whatever material might be requested and produce it." Then, as did his dissent in Branzburg v. Hayes, his argument hammered at society's need for confidentiality of the journalist's information, and for its constitutional protection.[63]

> Perhaps as a matter of abstract policy a newspaper office should receive no more protection from unannounced police searches than, say, the office of a doctor or the office of a bank. But we are here to uphold a Constitution. And our Constitution does not explicitly protect the practice of medicine or the business of banking from all abridgment by government. It does explicitly protect the freedom of the press.

Justice John Paul Stevens' dissent focused not on First Amendment matters, but on the justification needed to issue a search warrant without running afoul of the Fourth Amendment. Stevens wrote that every private citizen—not only the media—should be protected.[64]

> Students of the problem questioned Justice White's reliance on "neutral magistrates" to protect media from harassment, and to issue warrants only upon reasonable requests whose propriety they could gauge on the basis of probable cause to believe that evidence would be found on the premises to be searched. For one thing, between the 1971 raid on the *Stanford Daily* offices and the Supreme Court decision in 1978, there were at least 14 other searches of media properties. And in addition: [65]

> Journalists should perhaps be forgiven if they regard the protection of "neutral magistrates" as illusory. First, most, if not all, journalists tend to believe the folklore item about police walking around with fill-in-the-blank search warrants already signed by a complacent magistrate. Even if that is rankest slander of the judiciary, statistics on the issuance of search warrants compel the belief that the preconditions for warrant issuance are often improperly administered. "From 1969 through 1976, police sought 5,563 applications for search warrants under the 1968 Omnibus Crime Control Act. Only 15 of these applications were denied." Bluntly, the general rule seems to be

[63] Ibid., at 572, 576, 98 S.Ct. at 1985, 1987.

[64] Ibid., at 582–583, 98 S.Ct. at 1990.

[65] Dwight L. Teeter and Singer, S.Griffin, Search Warrants in Newsrooms, 67 Ky.L.Journ. 847, 858 (1978–79).

that a search warrant sought equals a search warrant granted.

The legislation that Congress passed in 1980 in reaction to the *Zurcher* decision took effect in 1981. It provides a subpoena procedure, and a hearing for those subpoenaed. It prohibits "knock-on-the-door," search-warrant raids of news media offices and those of authors and researchers, by federal, state, and local law enforcement agencies, except in three unusual circumstances. These are: where there is cause to believe that the reporter himself is involved in a crime, where the information sought relates to the national defense or classified information, or where there is reason to believe that immediate action through search warrant is needed to prevent bodily harm or death to a human being.[66] *News Media & the Law* found that at least nine states had adopted their own laws along the same lines, some extending the protection to all private citizens, not only those in the field of writing. While the federal law avoids that reach, it requires the Justice Department to work out guidelines for federal searches that will take into account personal privacy interests of the person to be searched.[67]

Journalists' Telephone Records

Searches of newsrooms slowed after adoption of the Privacy Protection Act of 1980, but—as discussed at the end of this chapter—occasional police or FBI searches (of dubious legality) may occur.[68] And there are other intrusions. In 1976, the Reporters Committee for Freedom of the Press and other journalists lost a case in federal district court to compel AT & T to inform media when government subpoenas were issued for media phone records. The court of appeals also turned down the media, saying that no right of privacy under the First Amendment existed because the records belonged to the telephone company and not the media.[69] In an unsuccessful appeal to the United States Supreme Court to review the decision, the journalists stated the heart of their case for protection of their telephone records: [70]

> The impact of the ruling below cannot be minimized
> * * *. When government investigators obtain a reporter's

[66] Pub.Law 96–440, 94 Stat. 1879; 6 Med.L.Rptr. 2255, 2256 (1981). And see "Carter Signs Newsroom Raid Ban," News Media & the Law, Oct./Nov. 1980, 3–5.

[67] Attorney General's Guidelines for Litigation to Enforce Obligations to Submit Materials for Predissemination Review, 6 Med.L.Rptr. 2261 (1981), dated 12/9/80, and published 1/2/81.

[68] "Police Raid Newspaper Printing Office," News Media & the Law, Aug./Sept. 1980, 25.

[69] Reporters Committee for Freedom of Press v. American Tel. & Tel. Co., 593 F.2d 1030 (D.C.Cir.1978), certiorari denied 440 U.S. 949, 99 S.Ct. 1431 (1979), 4 Med.L.Rptr. 2536.

[70] News Media & the Law, Oct./Nov. 1980, p. 6.

toll records * * * they learn the identity of (his) sources. And they also learn * * * much about the pattern of his investigative activities—whom he called, when and in what order he makes calls to develop his leads, what subjects he is looking into and how actively he is exploring these subjects.

In the fall of 1980, it was reported that phone records of the Atlanta bureau of the *New York Times,* as well as those of its bureau chief, Howell Raines, had been subpoenaed in June by the Justice Department. The telephone company had waited 90 days, at the request of the Justice Department, before telling the Times. Shortly thereafter, attorney General Benjamin Civiletti announced new rules for issuing subpoenas for phone records—essentially, that no subpoena is to be issued to media people for their toll phone records without "express authorization" of the Attorney General.[71] This was the extent of protection that the media found.

Thus in one more setting, journalists were asserting that secrecy—anathema when employed by the government—was essential to the highest performance of their own craft. And once again, it was clear that deep values in the journalist's work—the "watch-dogging" of government and other powerful institutions, and informing the members of an open society about their world—would be overshadowed in some contests where other values sometimes would take precedence.

Newsroom Confidentiality: A Continuing Struggle

Despite passage of the federal Privacy Act of 1980, aimed at protecting newsrooms from searches under most circumstances,[72] the late 1980s saw a number of efforts to search newsrooms. The searches showed that law is not self-executing, and that reporters need a working understanding of the law—with preparation from knowledgeable attorneys—when a search is attempted. Searches became sufficiently bothersome in 1988 that the National Association of Broadcasters (NAB) issued a memo urging broadcast stations to review procedures with their attorneys for fending off a search.[73]

When a police department or sheriff asks a judge for a search warrant, there is some likelihood that the judge won't know that

[71] New York Times, Nov. 13, 1980, A30; 28 C.F.R. § 50.10.

[72] See discussion at footnote 58, above. Those limited occasions in which a federal or state judge may issue a warrant for a newsroom search include a reasonable showing that newsroom personnel are involved in commission of a crime, in possession of contraband or classified or national defense information, or where there is reason to believe that information in a newsroom is needed by authorities to protect human life.

[73] Jane E. Kirtley, Counsel Memo: "Dealing With Newsroom Searches," N.A.B. Info–Pak, October/November, 1988.

the Privacy Protection Act of 1980 forbids searches of newsrooms except in limited situations as noted above, at footnote 59. Despite this statute and despite similar legislation in at least nine states, occasional searches have continued. The News Media & The Law reported in the fall of 1988 that four newsroom searches had taken place between December, 1986, and mid-August of 1988, in Minneapolis and Golden Valley, Minnesota, and in Palm Springs and Los Angeles, California.

The News Media & The Law emphasized that the Privacy Protection Act of 1980 made it illegal for the seizure of either the "work product" or "documentary materials" from persons who are creating newspapers, books or broadcasts.[74] That magazine recommends:

First, journalists in the newsroom should object to the search and, if possible, should stall long enough for the company's lawyer and upper-level management to arrive.

Second, journalists should not interfere with the search, but they do not have to assist in it. The search should be limited by the terms of the warrant to certain areas and to specific materials.

Third, News Media & The Law recommends that a videotape or photographic record be made if the search proceeds.

Finally, once a search has taken place, a lawyer should be consulted about the possibility of suing the governmental agency carrying out the search. If the search is deemed found illegal under the terms of the Privacy Protection Act of 1980, the journalist whose office was searched can collect $1,000 in damages (plus reimbursement for any actual harm done in the search) plus lawyer's fees.[75] It should be apparent that most search warrants issued against newsrooms are illegal and invalid, and journalists should be prepared to fight back. Lawsuits are not the only weapons, however. Publicity about governmental units acting illegally may be the media's strongest weapon in protecting newsrooms from searches.

Obviously, journalists must remain vigilant, ready to contend—by all lawful means—against newsroom subpoenas or searches. While the threat of searches may have abated considerably, newsroom subpoenas seem to be alive and well. In 1991, for example, the Reporters Committee on Freedom of the Press released a study of 4,400 subpoenas asking for notes, tapes, or testimony served on 1,042 news operations during 1989. Significant details included: [76]

[74] News Media & The Law, Fall, 1988, pp. 4–5.

[75] Ibid., p. 6; See also Kirtley, op. cit.

[76] Anna America, "News Media Under Legal Siege," Presstime, March, 1991, page 34.

— Television stations are far more likely than newspapers to be subpoenaed, and are more likely to comply with subpoenas.

— Responding news organizations (about half of the 2,127 surveyed) indicated that only about 8 percent of the subpoenas were challenged in court.   But nearly half of the subpoenas sought material that had actually been published or broadcast.

— News organizations' courtroom challenges to subpoenas were successful more than 75 percent of the time.

Chapter 14

LEGAL PROBLEMS IN REPORTING LEGISLATIVE AND EXECUTIVE BRANCHES OF GOVERNMENT

SEC. 81. THE PROBLEM OF SECRECY IN GOVERNMENT

Following World War II, obtaining access to information at various levels of government became an acute problem in American journalism.

Government accountability requires an informed public. Self-government depends on citizens' knowledge of what public officials are doing in the name of the public and with the public's money. Some thoughtful historians of the mass media, however, suggest that more and more power to control information has been amassed by governments and by private centers of wealth and power closely linked to government. For example, Norman L. Rosenberg and others have suggested that "the media's attention to social problems in the 1950s and 1960s [and arguably into the 1990s] primarily ebbed and flowed in relationship to nonlegal pressures within the communications industry itself ... and to the complex links between the Fourth Estate and other powerful institutions...."[1]

If such a state of affairs exists, what have journalists been doing about it? Not enough, if one believes Robert M. Entman's gloomy contentions:[2]

> Restricted by the limited tastes of the audience and reliant upon political elites for most information, journalists participate in an interdependent news system, not a free

---

[1] Norman L. Rosenberg, Protecting the Best Men (Chapel Hill: Univ. of North Carolina Press, 1986), p. 265; for a discussion of problems of access to information about great concentrations of wealth and power involving stock market scandals, see James B. Stewart, Den of Thieves (New York: Simon and Schuster, 1991).

[2] Robert M. Entman, Democracy Without Citizens: Media and the Decay of American Politics (New York: Oxford University Press, 1989) p. 8.

market of ideas. In practice ... the news media fall far short of the ideal version of a free press as civic educator and guardian of democracy.

The news media can do only so much in reporting on private power. Much news—especially news which is not favorable to corporate America—comes to reporters via reports from federal, state and local regulatory agencies. Since 1980, especially, the federal government has pruned regulatory activities over business, so that less is learned about private concentrations of power until too late for the news media to serve as an effective sentinel. Then, when a scandal such as the estimated $500 billion savings and loan debacle occurs, disaster strikes, showing government regulators and the news media too often impotent and irrelevant. With newspapers, broadcasting stations and cable TV companies generally owned by corporate conglomerates, it is not only the conspiracy buff who wonders whether news media have sufficient independence.

Cataclysmic changes now taking place in communications industries, however, may make media concentration only a short-run problem. "Demassification" is occurring and accelerating, which may mean that individuals interconnected via communications networks someday may begin to overshadow mass media units—including newspapers, broadcast stations, and cable television—in societal importance. The late Ithiel de Sola Pool, a most important communication theorist, expressed the hope that as new communications networks emerge, they will do so under "guidelines that recognize the preferred position of freedom of discourse." [3] Pool also saw that the First Amendment must apply "to the function of communication, not just to the media that existed in the eighteenth century." [4]

Meaningful communication on the brink of the 21st Century requires that the First Amendment now be given expanded meaning where access to government information is concerned. Growth of governmental power has coincided with expanding government secrecy at all levels and with the rapid changeover to computerized records rather than the more easily accessible paper files. The need for computer-literate reporters and citizens is increasingly important as records once freely available in file drawers now require the intervention of a government gatekeeper. Computer searches for information—and finding patterns in that information—can be far more informative to society than yesterday's

[3] Ithiel de Sola Pool, Technologies of Freedom (Cambridge, MA: Belknap Press of Harvard University, 1983) p. 244.

[4] Ibid., p. 246.

paper-chases, but only if citizen access is protected under the Constitution and under supporting statutes.[5] As is discussed in Section 82 of this chapter, the Supreme Court of the United States has viewed the Constitution and the First Amendment as something apart from the concept of "a public's right to know" or a "citizen's right to gather information." In that context, as government grows more powerful and the news media increasingly embrace corporate values, greater efforts are needed to prevent the First Amendment from becoming obsolete.

No segment of the American public has been more concerned about tendencies to secrecy in government than journalists. Some feel that it is the central threat to freedom of expression in Twentieth Century America. Accepting, during World War II, the need for extensive secrecy for an enormous war machine in a government bureaucracy grown gigantic, journalists after the war soon detected a broad pattern of continued secrecy in government operations. Access to meetings was denied; reports, papers, documents at all levels of government seemed less available than before officialdom's habits of secrecy developed in the passion for security during World War II. An intense, insistent campaign for access to government information was launched in the 1950's by editors, publishers, reporters, and news organizations. It went under a banner labeled "Freedom of Information," and under the claim that the press was fighting for the "people's right to know." [6]

To combat what they viewed as a severe increase in denial of access to the public's business, journalists took organized action. "Freedom of Information" committees were established by the American Society of Newspaper Editors (ASNE) and by the Society of Professional Journalists—Sigma Delta Chi. The ASNE commissioned newspaper attorney Harold L. Cross to perform a major study on the law of access to government activity. His book, *The People's Right to Know,* was published in 1953 and served as a central source of information. State and local chapters of professional groups worked for the adoption of state access laws. In 1958, a Freedom of Information Center was opened at the University of Missouri School of Journalism, as a clearing house and research facility for those concerned with the subject. Meanwhile, an early and vigorous ally was found in the House Subcommittee on Government Information under Rep. John E. Moss of California, created to investigate charges of excessive secrecy in the Executive

---

[5] See generally, Sissela Bok, Secrets: On the Ethics of Concealment and Revelation (New York: Pantheon, 1983); for a discussion of computerized aids to reporting, see Elliot G. Jaspin, "Just do it!," ASNE Bulletin, Dec. 1991, p. 4ff.

[6] See Annual Reports, Sigma Delta Chi Advancement of Freedom of Information Committee (Chicago, Sigma Delta Chi).

branch of government.[7]

Journalism had powerful allies also in the scientific community. It found that the advance of knowledge in vast areas of government-sponsored science was being slowed, sometimes crippled for years, in the blockage of the flow of research information between and even within agencies of the federal government. Fear of "leakage" of secrets important to defense in the Cold War with the Soviet Union brought administrative orders that were contrary to the tenets of scientists and researchers. A snarl of regulations, rules and red tape prevented scientists from sharing their findings with others. Their concern about the damage to the advance of knowledge in science paralleled journalists' alarm about damage to the democratic assumption that free institutions rest on an informed public.[8]

Public understanding of the dangers of official secrecy broadened in the exposé of the Executive's abuse of power in the Watergate episode of the mid–1970's. Earl Warren, retired Chief Justice of the United States, crediting the news media with a share in exposing the fraud and deceit, said if we are to learn from "the debacle we are in, we should first strike at secrecy in government wherever it exists, because it is the incubator for corruption."[9] New recruits entered the battle against official secrecy—Common Cause, the Center for National Security Studies, and Ralph Nader among them.

Although citizens of the United States congratulate themselves upon having an open society, that openness seemed to be in increasing peril in the 1990s. It is one thing to have Freedom of Information legislation at the federal and state levels; it is quite another to find that access is truly open.

In his April, 1987 presidential address to the American Society of Newspaper Editors, Michael Gartner laid out a dirty laundry list of information that is not freely obtainable. Just a few of the many items Gartner listed as being unavailable:

— Information that the government keeps secret for purposes of national defense or foreign policy.

— Information on sources or methods of the Central Intelligence Agency.

[7] Rep. John E. Moss, Preface to Replies from Federal Agencies to Questionnaire Submitted by the Special Subcommittee on Government Information of the Committee on Government Operations, 84 Cong. 1 Sess. (Nov. 1, 1955), p. iii.

[8] Science, Education and Communications, 12 Bulletin of Atomic Scientists, 333 (Nov.1956); Walter Gellhorn, Security, Loyalty, and Science (Ithaca: Cornell Univ. Press, 1950).

[9] Governmental Secrecy: Corruption's Ally, 60 ABA Journal 550 (May, 1974).

— Information concerning virtually anything about the National Security Agency.

— Much of the information at the Consumer Product Safety Commission.

— Information on pre-sentencing investigations and parole reports.

The key to reporting of the legislative and executive branches is persistence: stubbornness in asking questions and virtually endless patience that is often needed in filing and re-filing FOIA (Freedom of Information Act) requests. It took a dozen years of struggle, including three lawsuits, to open the first 1.5 million pages of documents from the Administration of President Nixon, and those pages were mostly trivia and represented less than 4 per cent of the total body of papers. From beyond the grave, Nixon seems determined to thwart public knowledge about the inner workings of his presidency. The New York Times reported in 1994 that the Nixon's heirs were continuing the late President's two-decade fight "to control more than 3,000 hours of White House tapes and 150,000 pages of Presidential papers." Professor Stanley Kutler, a University of Wisconsin historian, sued to get access to the papers, saying: " 'We can safely assume that Richard Nixon's tenacity in fighting this for 20 years does not mean that these materials will exonerate him [from enhanced complicity in the Watergate affair].' " [10]

SEC. 82. ACCESS AND THE CONSTITUTION

Courts have given little support to the position that the First Amendment includes a right of access to government information.

In many journalists' view, freedom of speech and press and the First Amendment encompass a right to gather government information as much as they embrace the right to publish and distribute it. Constitutional protection against denial of access seems to them only reasonable. The legal scholar Harold Cross argued that "Freedom of information is the very foundation for all those freedoms that the First Amendment of our Constitution was intended to guarantee." [11]

Famed First Amendment legal scholar Thomas I. Emerson held that "we ought to consider the right to know as an integral part of the system of freedom of expression, embodied in the first amend-

[10] Tim Weiner, "Nixon Heirs Keep Up Fight to Control Papers and Tapes," The New York Times, April 26, 1994, p. A1.

[11] Harold L. Cross, The People's Right to Know (Morningside Heights: Columbia Univ. Press, 1953), pp. xiii–xiv.

ment and entitled to support by legislation or other affirmative government action." He found the argument for "starting from this point * * * overwhelming," and further, that the Supreme Court has in some respects recognized a constitutional right to know.[12]

A Right of Access?

While an occasional lower court or dissenting judge has found reason for the First Amendment to protect a right of access to government information,[13] the Supreme Court of the United States has done so only in the setting of public, criminal trials. [14] Justice Potter Stewart delivered a rationale for the denial of a constitutional right of access to government in a famous 1975 speech: [15]

> So far as the Constitution goes, the autonomous press may publish what it knows, and may seek to learn what it can.
>
> But this autonomy cuts both ways. The press is free to do battle against secrecy and deception in government. But the press cannot expect from the Constitution any guarantee that it will succeed. There is no constitutional right to have access to particular government information, or to require openness from the bureaucracy. The public's interest in knowing about its government is protected by the guarantee of a Free Press, but the protection is indirect. The Constitution itself is neither a Freedom of Information Act nor an Official Secrets Act.
>
> The Constitution, in other words, establishes the contest, not its resolution. Congress may provide a resolution, at least in some instances, through carefully drawn legislation. For the rest, we must rely, as so often in our system we must, on the tug and pull of the political forces in American society.

Justice Stewart's words ring true. The courts have provided scant acknowledgement of a "right of access" under the First Amendment, except for access to public, criminal court trials, declared open as a First Amendment right in a major case of 1980, Richmond Newspapers v. Virginia (detailed in Chap. 15, below). As noted in Chapter 15, some the *Richmond Newspapers'* language is so sweeping that it may be the forerunner of a First Amendment

[12] Legal Foundations of the Right To Know, 1976 Wash.U.L.Quar. 1–3. See also Jacob Scher, "Access to Information: Recent Legal Problems," Journalism Quarterly, 37:1 (1960), p. 41.

[13] Providence Journal Co. et al. v. McCoy et al., 94 F.Supp. 186 (D.R.I.1950); In re Mack, 386 Pa. 251, 126 A.2d 679, 689 (1956); Lyles v. Oklahoma, 330 P.2d 734 (Okl.Crim. 1958).

[14] Richmond Newspapers v. Virginia, 448 U.S. 555, 100 S.Ct. 2814 (1980).

[15] Potter Stewart, "Or of the Press," 26 Hastings L.J. (1975).

right to gather information. Our concern here, however, is news-gathering problems in the legislative and executive/ administrative branches.

A Right to Travel?

Unlike citizens of many other nations, Americans have long been blessed by taking for granted a right to travel freely from state to state without having to show an "identity card." And for the most part, Americans think they can travel anywhere they wish, but reporter William Worthy was thwarted in his attempt—in the 1950s period of the Cold War tensions with the Soviet Union and other Communist states—to travel to China to report. Worthy, of the *Baltimore Afro–American,* in 1956 ignored an order by Secretary of State John Foster Dulles barring American reporters from going to "Red China" to report. When Worthy returned to the United States, the State Department revoked his passport and refused to give him another. Worthy went to court to attempt to regain it. The trial court held, without elaborating, that Dulles' refusal to issue the passport did not violate Worthy's rights to travel under the First Amendment. Worthy appealed, but his argument for First Amendment protection failed, the Court of Appeals holding: [16]

> The right to travel is a part of the right to liberty, and a newspaperman's right to travel is a part of freedom of the press. But these valid generalizations do not support unrestrained conclusions. * * *

> Freedom of the press bears restrictions * * *. Merely because a newsman has a right to travel does not mean he can go anywhere he wishes. He cannot attend conferences of the Supreme Court, or meetings of the President's Cabinet or executive sessions of the Committees of Congress.

In a 1965 case, Zemel argued that a State Department travel ban was a direct interference with the First Amendment rights of citizens to inform themselves at first hand of events abroad. The United States Supreme Court agreed that the Secretary of State's denial rendered "less than wholly free the flow of information concerning that country," but denied that a First Amendment right was involved. "The right to speak and publish does not carry with it the unrestrained right to gather information," [17] the Court said.

---

[16] Worthy v. Herter, 270 F.2d 905 (D.C.Cir.1959), certiorari denied 361 U.S. 918, 80 S.Ct. 255 (1959).

[17] Zemel v. Rusk, 381 U.S. 1, 17–18, 85 S.Ct. 1271, 1281 (1965). See also Trimble v. Johnston, 173 F.Supp. 651 (D.D.C.1959); In re Mack, 386 Pa. 251, 126 A.2d 679 (1956).

On occasion, the U.S. State Department may deny a passport to a person whose foreign travel is thought to create "substantial likelihood of 'serious damage' to national security or foreign policy." The Supreme Court upheld such a passport revocation involving Philip Agee, a dissident former Central Intelligence agent accused of working to expose the cover and sources of CIA employees.[18]

Pell v. Procunier (1974)
Saxbe v. Washington Post Co. (1974)

From restrictions on foreign travel, turn to the question of whether there is a "right" to report on prisoners in American prisons. This is not a minor question; to protect freedom, journalists and other citizens need to be able to inquire into the health of the criminal justice system, from beginning to end. That is, the system needs surveillance: from arrest to arraignment, to preliminary hearings, to plea bargains, or trials, to appeals, to sentencing of convicted criminals, to incarceration on through parole. Are all persons caught up in the criminal justice system treated alike, or are members of minority groups treated more harshly than other people? To gather some of this information may require interviews with specific persons who are in prison.

Pell v. Procunier arose when journalists Eve Pell, Betty Segal, and Paul Jacobs challenged a California prison regulation which barred media interviews with specific, individual inmates.[19] Denied their requests to interview prison inmates Apsin, Bly and Guild, they asserted that the rule limited their news-gathering activity and thus infringed freedom of the press under the First and Fourteenth Amendments. They lost in district court and appealed to the U.S. Supreme Court. Stewart wrote for the majority that the press and public are afforded full opportunities to observe minimum security sections of prisons, to speak about any subject to any inmates they might encounter, to interview inmates selected at random by the corrections officials, to sit in on group meetings of inmates. "The sole limitation on news-gathering in California prisons is the prohibition in [regulation] # 415.071 of interviews with individual inmates specifically designated by representatives of the press." [20]

Before the regulation was adopted, Stewart continued, unrestrained press access to individual prisoners resulted in concentration of press attention on a few inmates, who became virtual "public figures" in prison society and gained great influence. One inmate who advocated non-cooperation with prison regulations had

[18] Haig v. Agee, 453 U.S. 280, 287, 288, 101 S.Ct. 2766, 2771, 2772 (1981).
[19] 417 U.S. 817, 94 S.Ct. 2800 (1974).
[20] Pell v. Procunier, 417 U.S. 817, 94 S.Ct. 2800, 2808 (1974).

extensive press attention, encouraged other inmates in his purpose, and eroded the institution's ability to deal effectively with inmates in general. San Quentin prison authorities concluded that an escape attempt there, resulting in deaths of three staff members and two inmates, flowed in part from an unrestricted press access policy, and regulation # 415.071 was adopted as a result. Stewart wrote: "The Constitution does not * * * require government to accord the press special access to information not shared by members of the public generally." [21]

Dissenting in this case and in a companion case, Saxbe v. Washington Post Co.[22] which involved an unsuccessful challenge to a Federal Bureau of Prisons rule similar to California's, was Justice Powell. He said that "sweeping prohibition of prisoner-press interviews substantially impairs a core value of the First Amendment." In these cases, he argued, society's interest "in preserving free public discussion of governmental affairs" was great and was the value at stake. Since the public is unable to know most news at first hand, "In seeking out the news the press * * * acts as an agent of the public at large. * * * By enabling the public to assert meaningful control over the political process, the press performs a critical function in effecting the societal purpose of the First Amendment."

Houchins v. KQED Inc. (1978)

Much more restrictive access to a jail was at issue when Sheriff Houchins of Alameda Co., Calif., was ordered by injunction to open up his facility to reporters and their cameras and recorders. His rules had limited journalists to regular, once-a-month tours open to the public in general. No cameras or recorders were allowed, nor was access to a part of the jail where violence had reportedly broken out earlier. KQED, which made a practice of covering prisons in the area and wanted access to shoot film and interview prisoners, took Houchins to court, saying its journalistic usefulness was reduced by his tour rules. The sheriff objected that the access sought would infringe the privacy of inmates, create jail "celebrities" and cause attendant difficulties, and disrupt jail operations. He told of other forms of access by which information about the jail could reach the public. The district court agreed with KQED's contentions, and enjoined the sheriff from further blocking of media access "at reasonable times," cameras and recorders included.[23] The California Court of Appeals upheld the injunction, saying

[21] Ibid., at 834, 94 S.Ct. at 2810.

[22] 417 U.S. 843, 94 S.Ct. 2811 (1974). Powell's statements are at 860–874, 94 S.Ct. at 2820–2826.

[23] Houchins v. KQED, Inc., 438 U.S. 1, 98 S.Ct. 2588 (1978), 3 Med.L.Rptr. 2521.

that the U.S. Supreme Court's *Pell* and *Saxbe* decisions were not controlling.

Houchins appealed to the Supreme Court, and it reversed the lower courts, Chief Justice Warren Burger writing that neither of the earlier cases, nor indeed Branzburg v. Hayes (Chapter 13, above), provided a constitutional right to gather news, or a constitutional right of access to government.[24] He agreed that news of prisons is important for the public to have, and that media serve as "eyes and ears" for the public. He said, however, that the Supreme Court had never held that the First Amendment compels anyone, private or public, to supply information. He discussed various ways in which information about prisons reaches the public, and said the legislative branch was free to pass laws opening penal institutions if it wished. But the press, Burger said, enjoys no special privilege of access beyond that which officials grant to the public in general. *Pell* and *Saxbe* would hold, and Houchins' access rules also. Separately, Justice Stewart joined in the decision, differing only to the extent of saying that reporters on tour with the public should be allowed to carry and use their tools of the trade, including cameras and recorders.

Justice Powell, who as we have seen had dissented in *Pell* and *Saxbe,* joined two others in dissenting again, on similar grounds. He and the other dissenters in *Pell* had totaled four, the greatest support that the Supreme Court has furnished for "access to government" as a constitutionally protected principle outside the judicial branch.[25]

SEC. 83. RECORDS AND MEETINGS
OF FEDERAL GOVERNMENT

Access to records and meetings of federal executive and administrative agencies is provided under the "Freedom of Information" and the "Sunshine in Government" Acts; the Privacy Act provides for secrecy of records.

The Freedom of Information Act

On July 4, 1966, Pres. Lyndon B. Johnson signed the Federal Public Records Law, shortly to be known as the federal Freedom of

---

[24] Ibid., at 584–585, 98 S.Ct. at 2523–2524.

[25] Richmond Newspapers v. Virginia, 448 U.S. 555, 100 S.Ct. 2814 (1980), 6 Med.L.Rptr. 1833. For a view that sees the approach of a broad constitutional right of access to government, see Roy V. Leeper, "Richmond Newspapers, Inc. v. Virginia and the Emerging Right of Access," 61 Journ.Quar. 615 (Autumn 1984).

Information (FOI) Act.[26] Providing for the public availability of records of executive and administrative agencies of the government, it sprang, President Johnson said, "from one of our most essential principles: a democracy works best when the people have all the information that the security of the Nation permits." He expressed a "deep sense of pride that the United States is an open society in which the people's right to know is cherished and guarded." [27]

The FOI Act replaced section 3 of the Administrative Procedure Act of 1946, which had permitted secrecy if it was required in the public interest or for "good cause." [28] The new law expressed neither this limitation nor another which had said disclosure was necessary only to "persons properly and directly concerned" with the subject at hand. In the words of Attorney General Ramsey Clark, the FOI Act.[29]

> imposes on the executive branch an affirmative obligation to adopt new standards and practices for publication and availability of information. It leaves no doubt that disclosure is a transcendent goal, yielding only to such compelling considerations as those provided for in the exemptions of the act.

Every federal executive branch agency is required under the FOI Act to publish in the Federal Register its organization plan, and the agency personnel and methods through which the public can get information. Every agency's procedural rules and general policies are to be published. Every agency's manuals and instructions are to be made available for public inspection and copying, as are final opinions in adjudicated cases. Current indexes are to be made available to the public. If records are improperly withheld, the U.S. district court can enjoin the agency from the withholding and order disclosure. And if agency officials fail to comply with the court order, they may be punished for contempt.

Exceptions to that which must be made public are called "exemptions." There are nine of them: [30]

[26] 5 U.S.C.A. § 552, amended by Pub.Law 93–502, 88 Stat. 1561–1564. For history, text, and extensive judicial interpretation of this act, and information on the federal Privacy Act, see Allan Adler and Halperin, M.H., Litigation under the Federal Freedom of Information Act and Privacy Act, 1984 (Washington, 1983).

[27] Public Papers of the Presidents, Lyndon B. Johnson, 1966 II, p. 699.

[28] 5 U.S.C.A. § 1002 (1946).

[29] Foreword, Attorney General's Memorandum on the Public Information Section of the Administrative Procedure Act (1967).

[30] Some of the exemptions were tightened against abuse by agencies after a three-year congressional study which brought about amendments effective Feb. 19, 1975. On the other hand, as reported later (near the end of this section), the FOI Reform Act of 1986 made it more difficult to get information about businesses and about investigatory records of some law enforcement agencies.

1. Records "specifically authorized under criteria established by an Executive order to be kept secret in the interest of national defense or foreign policy" and which are properly classified.

2. Matters related only to "internal personnel rules and practices" of an agency.

3. Matters exempt from disclosure by statute.

4. Trade secrets and commercial or financial information obtained from a person and that are privileged or confidential.

5. Inter-agency or intra-agency communications, such as memoranda showing how policy-makers within an agency feel about various policy options.

6. Personnel, medical and similar files which could not be disclosed without a "clearly unwarranted invasion" of someone's privacy.

7. Investigatory files compiled for law enforcement purposes, if the production of such records would interfere with law enforcement, deprive one of a fair trial, constitute an unwarranted invasion of personal privacy, disclose the identity of a confidential source, disclose investigative techniques, or endanger the life or safety of law enforcement personnel.

8. Reports prepared by or for an agency responsible for the regulation or supervision of financial institutions.

9. Geological and geophysical information and data, including maps, concerning wells—particularly explorations by gas and oil companies.

Long delays, high costs for searching and copying documents, and widespread agency reluctance to comply with the original act's provisions characterized its early history.[31] Not only were several exemptions tightened by the amendments; also, rules were passed requiring agencies to inform persons making requests for information within ten days whether or not access would be granted, and to decide upon requests for appeals within 20 days. Uniform schedules of fees—limited to reasonable standard charges for document search and copying—were also mandated in the amendments.[32]

[31] Wallis McClain, "Implementing the Amended FOI Act," Freedom of Information Center Report No. 343, Sept. 1975, p. 1; U.S. Congress, Freedom of Information Act and Amendments of 1974 (P.L. 93–502) Source Book: Legislative History, Texts, and Other Documents. Joint Committee Print (94th Cong., 1 Sess.), Washington: U.S. Government Printing Office, March 1975.

[32] Anon., "FOI Act Amendments Summarized," FOI Digest, 17:1, Jan.-Feb. 1975, p. 5.

The amendments brought a flood of requests for information, primarily from persons who asked the FBI, the CIA, and the IRS, whether files were kept on them, and, if so, what the files contained. The Justice Department was receiving 2,000 requests per month by August 1975.[33] Media requests mounted under the amendments. One study found more than 400 between 1972 and 1984, but said that was far fewer than the actual total. Another study found that almost 50% of its list came from "public interest" groups, and about one-fourth from media.[34]

Court cases decided under the Act as of mid–1976 totaled 295, half of them less than two years old.[35] The increase suggested the impact of the 1975 amendments. Actions concerning investigatory files (exemption 7) outstripped the pre-amendments leaders, agency memoranda and trade secrets (exemptions 5 and 4). One important change provided for *in camera* review by judges of documents which the Executive Branch might refuse to open on grounds of national defense or foreign policy (exemption 1). Under the original FOI Act, Congress had not provided this, but rather, said Justice Stewart in an acid concurring opinion, had simply chosen "to decree blind acceptance of Executive fiat" that secrecy was called for.[36]

From government's side of the desk, the FOI Act takes too much time and money.

A Congressional study in 1985 showed that in a year's time, the Federal FOI Act drew 248,000 total requests. Although some agencies approved over 90 percent of the FOI requests, the study did not control for delays in providing information or in fee waivers granted. The Department of State granted less than 30 per cent of its more than 3,000 requests for information, according to the House Subcommittee on Government Information.

With the deluge of requests for information came growing complaints from government agencies that it was too costly and too time-consuming to process FOI Act requests. Costs to the Trea-

[33] Anon., "FOI Act: Access Increases, Some Nagging Problems Remain," FOI Digest, 17:4, July–Aug. 1975, p. 5, citing Wall Street Journal, June 27, 1975; John A. Jenkins, "Ask, and You Shall Receive," Quill, July–Aug. 1975, pp. 22, 24.

[34] Ibid., quoting Attorney Ronald Plesser, 22; Anon., Media Use of FOIA Documented in New Study, 10 Med.L.Rptr. # 34, 8/21/84, News Notes, quoting a study done for the House Subcommittee on Government Information, Justice, and Agriculture; Sam Archibald, Use of the FOIA, Freedom of Information Report # 457, May 1982, 3 (Univ. of Mo.).

[35] Anon., "Justice Dept. Indexes Decided FOIA Cases," FOI Digest, 18:5, Sept.-Oct. 1976, p. 5, citing Congressional Record, Senate, Aug. 2, 1976, p. S13028.

[36] Environmental Protection Agency v. Mink, 410 U.S. 73, 136, 93 S.Ct. 827, 718 (1973).

634   FACT GATHERING AND CITIZENS' RIGHTS   Pt. 4

sury Department in 1978 alone totalled more than $6 million,[37] and CIA Director William Casey said that FOIA and Privacy Act (below) requests of the agency required 257,420 man-hours of service at a cost of about $2 million. Agencies complained that the act was used by law firms and commercial competitors to learn trade secrets and government enforcement policies, by foreign agents to gain national security information, and by organized crime to discover and thwart criminal investigations.[38]

Congressional efforts to restrict access to various agencies by amending the FOI Act never stop. The 1980s saw several. With President Ronald Reagan's support, the Central Intelligence Agency was authorized by law in 1984 to exempt its operational files on sources and methods from disclosure. In 1983, the 97th Congress passed six measures authorizing withholding by agencies that deal with trade, consumer product safety, income tax, energy, and health.[39]

President Clinton's 1994 Memo: Reversing the Reagan–Bush "Culture of Secrecy?"

William Jefferson Clinton's first two years in the White House might optimistically be called "embattled." First Lady Hillary Rodham Clinton took heat for her reluctance to make certain meetings and records open while chairing the President's Task Force on Health Care Reform. In fact, a federal district court told Mrs. Clinton that under the Federal Advisory Committee Act (FACA) that she must open information-gathering sessions of the Task Force to the public.[40]

The Clintons already were on the political defensive over charges of covering up their involvement in an Arkansas land development called Whitewater. Also involved were loans from a now-defunct savings and loan. The Clintons' 1994 reluctance to make information as freely available as their critics demanded was disruptive to the Administration.[41]

[37] "Diverse Legislative Efforts To Amend the FOIA Increase," FOI Digest, Jan.-Feb. 1980, 22:1, p. 5. Rod Perlmutter, Proposed FOIA Amendments—2, Freedom of Information Report # 451, Jan. 1982 (Univ. of Mo.).

[38] "Congress, Courts Mutilate FOI Act," News Media & The Law, Aug.-Sept. 1980, 4:3, p. 16.

[39] Anon., CIA Exemption Bill Passed, News Media & the Law, Nov./Dec. 1984; 8 Med.L.Rptr. # 46, 1/25/83, News Notes; Anon., Note, Developments under the Freedom of Information Act 1983, 1984 Duke Law J. 377, 382; News Media & the Law, Sept./Oct. 1983, 24.

[40] Association of American Physicians and Surgeons, Inc. v. Clinton, 813 F.Supp. 82 (D.D.C.1993), 21 Med.L.Rptr. 1225, also holding that that the Task Force could hold secret meetings while forming policy recommendations to go to the President. See also Robert Pear, "Court Rules That the First Lady is a 'De Facto' Federal Official," The New York Times, June 23, 1993, p. A1.

[41] See, e.g., "Whitewater Torture," Newsweek, March 14, 1994, pp. 20ff.

Despite such travails, President Clinton issued an October, 1993, Memorandum on Open Government, countermanding President Ronald Reagan's restrictive 1981 Executive Order. That Reagan Executive Order also had flourished under President George H.W. Bush, and in effect declared that whenever and wherever possible, federal agency records were presumed to be closed.[42]

In what was called the first major step of the Clinton Administration toward greater disclosure, the President and Attorney General Janet Reno demanded a new policy of openness.[43] In his memo, President Clinton urged that federal agencies handle information requests in a "customer-friendly manner," saying that the "existence of unnecessary bureaucratic hurdles" has no place in the implementation of the Freedom of Information Act (FOIA). He called for reduction of information request backlogs, and that federal agencies conform to new guidelines issued in 1994 by Attorney General Reno.

Attorney General Reno's memorandum specifically rescinded the Department of Justice's 1981 guidelines [issued pursuant to President Reagan's 1981 Executive Order]. She stated that the Department of Justice

> * * *will no longer defend an agency's withholding of information merely because there is a "substantial legal basis" for doing so. Rather, in determining whether or not to defend a nondisclosure decision, we will apply a "presumption of disclosure."

Such words had a welcome sound to journalists or other citizens who seek access to federal government information via the FOIA. As a practical matter, however, the Clinton Administration (or its successors) seem to have limited ability to make changes in the federal culture of closure. As Harry Hammitt of Access Reports pointed out in the I R E Journal [Investigative Reporters and Editors], application of exemptions to openness in the Freedom of Information Act (FOIA) no longer is as discretionary as once it was. Hammitt wrote that although some discretion remains,[44]

> * * *that discretion is circumscribed by case law. The case law in the 1980s and 1990s has tilted considerably in

[42] Tim Weiner, "U.S. Plans Secrecy Overhaul to Open Millions of Records," The New York Times, March 18, 1994, p. A1.

[43] "Clinton Memorandum on Administration of the Freedom of Information Act," and the Attorney General's "Memorandum for Heads of Departments and Agencies," Oct. 4, 1993, available from the White House, Office of Press Secretary, (202) 456–2100, or from records available via Internet. Thanks to Professor Dorothy Bowles, University of Tennessee, for capturing this and other key documents.

[44] Harry Hammitt, "Open Government under the Clinton Administration: What can we expect?", The I R E Journal, Jan.-Feb. 1994, p. 6.

favor of the government. What this means in a practical sense is that the parameters of agency discretion to release become narrower.

One example of such narrowing emphasized by Hammitt is the 1989 decision of the U.S. Supreme Court in Department of Justice v. Reporters Committee for Freedom of the Press.[45] In that case, the Reporters Committee's efforts to get criminal history records ran afoul of the Federal Privacy Act. That effort to get FBI criminal identification records—"rap sheets"—was halted by the Court's unanimous [46] decision that releasing such records would violate the FOIA's Exemption 6, constituting a "clearly unwarranted invasion of privacy."

As Hammitt noted, that Supreme Court decision has closed a great deal of information, because the Court made it easier for an agency to refuse to release personnel information or other government files. No longer did the agency have to bear the burden of showing that the files would amount to a "clearly unwarranted invasion of privacy." Instead, because the 1989 decision reversed the standard of proof, the requester received the burden of trying to prove that a record containing personal information ought to be released.[47]

Exemption 1, the national security exemption, temporarily was clarified in an executive order by President Jimmy Carter, effective in 1978, which imposed stricter minimum standards on classification of material. If the disclosure "reasonably could be expected to cause *identifiable* damage to national security," the information was confidential. However, any reasonable doubt should be resolved in favor of declassification, if the public interest in disclosure outweighed the damage to national security that "might be reasonably expected from disclosure." [48] This presumption favoring disclosure was changed by a March, 1981, Executive Order by President Ronald Reagan, in effect telling federal agencies, in effect, to move from President Carter's presumption of openness to a presumption of disclosure.

Exemption 1 was also the target of suits involving the definition of "possession" of records. In Forsham v. Harris, a 1980 Supreme Court decision, Justice Rehnquist stated that written data

[45] Ibid., p. 7; Department of Justice v. Reporters Committee for Freedom of the Press, 489 U.S. 749, 109 S.Ct. 1468 (1989), 16 Med.L.Rptr. 1545.

[46] 489 U.S. 749, 109 S.Ct. 1468 (1989), 16 Med.L.Rptr. 1545. Justice Stevens delivered the opinion of the Court, with Blackmun, with whom Brennan joined, concurring.

[47] Ibid.; see also Hammitt, p. 7.

[48] Alan S. Madens, "Developments Under the Freedom of Information Act—1979," 1980 Duke L.J. 139, 146–147.

held by a private research firm receiving federal grant money from HEW were not "agency records" if the agency providing the funds had not yet obtained possession of the data. The FOI Act provided no direct access to such data; therefore, HEW had not improperly "withheld" the data. The Act applied not to records that could exist, but only to records that did exist.[49]

In Kissinger v. Reporters Committee for Freedom of the Press, the Supreme Court held that the State Department had not "withheld" records of former Secretary of State Henry Kissinger's phone calls by failing to file a lawsuit to recover documents which Kissinger had improperly donated to the Library of Congress, and which would be unavailable to the public for 25 years.[50] A Justice Department suit was considered, and Kissinger later agreed to a new review of documents to determine whether they are needed for departmental files.[51]

In other developments related to national security, a federal district court judge ruled in Hayden v. National Security Agency/Central Security Service that disclosure of the existence of particular records, obtained through NSA monitoring of foreign electromagnetic signals, could be withheld, since the existence of such records might be more sensitive than their substance.[52]

Openness Is Not Self–Executing

No open records or open meetings victory is ever likely to be won, once and for all. It is simply a fact of life that government officials, especially when under pressure or embarrassed because of mistakes within their agencies, tend to "stonewall" when citizens—including members of the news media—come around asking questions.

Although the Freedom of Information Act, as amended, has been useful in opening government files, any skimming of the American Civil Liberties Union's annual compendium, Litigation Under the Freedom of Information Act and Privacy Act, will indicate that the federal commitment to open records is flawed. To a mind-boggling degree, federal courts have supported federal bureaucracies in keeping secret materials which the public ought to

---

[49] "The Supreme Court 1979 Term," 94 Harv.L.Rev. 1, 232–237 (1980); Forsham v. Harris, 445 U.S. 169, 100 S.Ct. 977 (1980).

[50] "The Supreme Court 1979 Term," Harv.L.Rev. 1, 232–235; Kissinger v. Reporters Committee for Freedom of the Press, 445 U.S. 136, 100 S.Ct. 960 (1980), 6 Med.L.Rptr. 1001.

[51] "Nixon Tapes Available to Public: Archives Requests More Materials," FOI Digest, May–June 1980, 22:3, p. 1.

[52] Madens, op. cit., 148.

have available.[53]   Consider the following "parade of issues," looking at some litigation situations which arose under a number of the Exemptions to the federal FOIA.   Federal agencies tried to withhold information under the exemptions for a variety of reasons (some far-fetched), and were quite often supported in such withholding decisions by federal courts.

Exemption 1—National Security Information.   As outlined by the ACLU's guidebook, Litigation Under the Freedom of Information and Privacy Act, it may be seen that "national security" is an almost magical incantation.   For example, the Central Intelligence Agency (CIA) is allowed, under a 1984 amendment to the National Security Act of 1947, to exempt "operational" files from the search and review requirements of the FOIA.[54]   When will the records be available?   (When the operation is "over.")   When will the operation be declared "over?"   (That's a matter for CIA discretion.) The CIA hangs onto secrets: In some cases, the CIA may turn aside a request for information with the response that for national security reasons, it can neither confirm nor deny the existence of the requested records.[55]   For an example of the U.S. Supreme Court's deference to the CIA even in the face of massive wrongdoing by that agency, see the discussion of CIA v. Sims (1985) later in this chapter.[56]

The CIA—one of the United States' spy agencies—has blundered egregiously and tragically for a good many years.   In 1994, while the CIA guarded its warehouses full of secrets in the name of national security, it was revealed that Aldrich H. Ames, a CIA career operative, had sold out his country for money provided by Russian agents.   Even though he lived well beyond his CIA paycheck for a decade, he was not apprehended until years after the Russians "turned" him and after he had compromised 20 CIA operations.   Because of Ames, 10 agents were executed, and presumably were tortured before they died.[57]

Yet even after the end of the Cold War and the fall of the Soviet Union, surveillance is still big business.   The budget for U.S. spy agents is an open secret—it is not published by Congress, but comments in The New York Times and elsewhere estimated the annual budget for 1994 at about $28 billion.   And although the CIA is better known, the even more secretive National Security Agency

[53] See the valuable compendium edited by Allan Robert Adler, ed., Litigation Under the Federal Freedom of Information and Privacy Act, 18th edition (Washington, D.C.: ACLU Foundation, 1993).

[54] Ibid., p. 42.

[55] Ibid., p. 39, citing Phillippi v. CIA, 546 F.2d 1009, 1012–1013 (D.C.Cir.1976).

[56] CIA v. Sims, 471 U.S. 159, 105 S.Ct. 1881 (1985).

[57] "Deadly Mole," Newsweek, March 7, 1994, pp. 24ff.

(NSA), which specializes in electronic spying/satellite intelligence activities, reportedly has a larger budget than the CIA.[58]

And then there's the National Reconnaissance Office (NRO), an organization run jointly by the CIA and the Pentagon, with a budget estimated at $6 billion, or three times that of the U.S. State Department. In the summer of 1994, a furious Senate Intelligence Committee—which oversees American intelligence activities—was grilling CIA officials. How had the NRO managed to have construction well along on a $350 million spy satellite headquarters building outside of Washington, D.C., without the Senate Intelligence Committee knowing the size, location, and cost of the NRO complex? Some intelligence committee Senators seemed to be startled that the project was underway, but then, the existence of the National Reconnaissance Office was a state secret until 1992. As Senate Intelligence Committee member Howard Metzenbaum (D–Ohio) said: "This project is a good example of what happens when * * * the Government does business in the dark." [59]

Exemption 2—Internal Agency Rules. For example, the Internal Revenue Service (IRS) attempted to withhold its auditing manual, on grounds that this was merely of internal concern. A federal court, however, held—sensibly enough—that the auditing rules used by the IRS should be available to public inspection.[60]

Exemption 3—Information Exempted by Other Statutes. Obviously, there are many such statutes which exclude information from disclosure. The label on this exemption may sound harmless, but this exemption has been used to defend failures to release information which the public clearly ought to know.

For example, air-worthiness and crash-worthiness of commercial airliners seems to be, simply and obviously, of public interest. Parties interested in comparative air safety records sued the Federal Aeronautics Authority in the 1970s to get access to "Systems Worthiness Analysis Reports." The FAA refused to release the reports, evidently on grounds that disclosing information would be bad for some air carriers' reputations and thus would not be in the public interest. The U.S. Supreme Court upheld this exercise of FAA "discretion," [61] although Congress later amended Exemption 3 to restrict administrators' loopholes and to allow a bit more information in the public interest.[62]

[58] For an account of the NSA, see James Bamford, The Puzzle Palace: Inside the NSA, America's Most Secret Intelligence Agency (New York: Viking Penguin, 1983).

[59] Tim Weiner, "New CIA Office Draws Heavy Fire," The New York Times, Aug. 9, 1994, p. A1.

[60] Hawkes v. Internal Revenue Service, 467 F.2d 787, 789 (6th Cir.1972).

[61] Administrator, Federal Aviation Administration v. Robertson, 422 U.S. 255, 95 S.Ct. 2140 (1975).

[62] Adler, op. cit., p. 59.

For an example of a Supreme Court decision upholding the Central Intelligence Agency's refusal to reveal names of universities and scientists who had dosed unsuspecting "subjects" with LSD (in the name of national security during the 1950s and 1960s), see CIA v. Sims (1985), discussed in more detail later in this Section. The CIA did not have to reveal identities of operatives or informants or employees under a section of the National Security Act, and thus found refuge in Exemption 3—Information Exempted by Other Statutes.[63]

Similarly, horror stories about experimenting on humans with nuclear radiation—information long held secret under Atomic Secrets legislation—finally surfaced late in 1993. Energy Secretary Hazel O'Leary, saying she was " 'appalled, shocked and deeply saddened,' " helped disclose experiments such as injecting plutonium into unsuspecting human "guinea pigs." Mrs. O'Leary helped bring about this disclosure when she ordered declassifying of millions of pages of documents at Department of Energy sites around the nation.[64]

Exemption 4—Trade Secrets, Commercial/Financial Information. David Vladeck and Allan Adler have written that this exemption is often criticized for its lack of clarity. Trade secrets or commercial and financial information about businesses in possession of the federal government are supposed to be privileged or confidential, and definitions of those terms vary somewhat among courts.[65]

Exemption 5—Inter- and Intra-Agency Memoranda. Allan Adler and co-authors claim this is the most unclear exemption in terms of its definition. It protects "predecisional documents" (presumably, "working papers") from discovery processes. Also, if a government investigation is stalled and no action is taken, the papers attached to that process would be "predecisional." [66]

This exemption was expanded by the U.S. Supreme Court in Federal Open Market Committee of the Federal Reserve Board v. Merrill (1979). There, the Supreme Court upheld an agency's refusal to release monthly policy directives if they contained sensitive information not otherwise available, and if release of the

[63] CIA v. Sims, 471 U.S. 159, 105 S.Ct. 1881 (1985); see also Adler, op. cit., p.65.

[64] Keith Schneider, "Disclosing Radiation Tests Puts Official in Limelight," The New York Times, Jan. 6, 1994, p. A1; "Nuclear Guinea Pigs," editorial in The New York Times, Jan. 5, 1994, p. A10.

[65] See Adler, op. cit., p.77.

[66] See Adler, op. cit., p. 105, citing case involving Inspector General's evaluation of evidence against two military officers; evidence not released because it was "predecisional;" see Providence Journal v. Department of the Army, 981 F.2d 552 (1st Cir.1992).

directives would significantly harm the government's monetary functions or commercial interests.[67]

Exemption 6—The "Privacy Exemption." (Personnel, medical, and similar records which could not be disclosed without a "clearly unwarranted invasion" of privacy.) Privacy is an important value in in the United States, both sociologically and legally. As important as privacy is, there are countervailing—and sometimes more important—virtues in openness.

The phrase "similar records" in this exemption has taken material exempted from disclosure well beyond personnel or medical files. For example, in Department of State v. Washington Post, the newspaper sought to confirm information that officials of Iran's revolutionary government held U.S. passports/visas. The Department of State denied this information on grounds that its release might endanger the Iranians, and the Supreme Court upheld the refusal to release this information.[68]

In New York Times Co. v. NASA, the newspaper asked for a duplicate of the tape recording of the voices of astronauts aboard the Challenger space shuttle at the time of its explosion on January 28, 1986. The National Aeronautics and Space Administration declined to release a copy of the tape, which had been recovered from the ocean floor. The New York Times then filed suit under the FOIA, but the Court of Appeals found that the tape might be a "similar record" to a medical or personnel file, and remanded the case to a district court.[69] The district court then asserted that "[e]xposure to the voice of a beloved family member immediately prior to that family member's death is what would cause the Challenger families pain." The district court held that the families' privacy interest " * * *outweighs the public interest such that release of the tape would constitute a clearly unwarranted invasion of the families' personal privacy." [70]

Exemption 7—Investigatory files compiled for law enforcement purposes. This exemption is quoted at length, because it provides so many loopholes for federal investigatory agencies—most notably the Federal Bureau of Investigation—to withhold information. Exemption 7 says that the FOIA does not apply to information or records

---

[67] Madens, op. cit., p. 155; Federal Open Market Committee of the Federal Reserve Board v. Merrill, 443 U.S. 340, 99 S.Ct. 2800 (1979).

[68] Department of State v. Washington Post, 456 U.S. 595, 102 S.Ct. 1957 (1982).

[69] New York Times Co. v. NASA, 920 F.2d 1002 (D.C.Cir.1990), 18 Med.L.Rptr. 1465.

[70] New York Times Co. v. NASA, 782 F.Supp. 628 (D.D.C.1991), 19 Med.L.Rptr. 1688, 1691, 1693.

* * * compiled for law enforcement purposes, but only to the extent that the production of such law enforcement records or information (A) could reasonably be expected to interfere with enforcement proceedings, (B) would deprive a person of a fair trial or a right to an impartial adjudication, (C) could reasonably be expected to constitute an unwarranted invasion of personal privacy, (D) could reasonably be expected to disclose the identity of a confidential source, including a state, local or foreign agency or authority or any private institution which furnished information on a confidential basis * * * or information compiled by a criminal law enforcement authority * * * or by an agency conducting a lawful national security intelligence investigation, information furnished by a confidential source, (E) would disclose techniques or procedures for law enforcement investigations or prosecutions * * *, or (F) could reasonably be expected to endanger the life or physical safety of any individual.

A key case showing the slipperiness of this exemption for those seeking records access is Federal Bureau of Investigation v. Abramson (1982). Journalist Howard Abramson was investigating President Richard Nixon's use of the FBI to collect information on persons he considered his political "enemies," the better to harass them. Abramson asked for the files on such "enemies" under the FOIA. The FBI rejected the request, calling release of the information an "unwarranted invasion of privacy" under Exemption 7(C) (quoted above), and also under Exemption 6, which also deals with privacy.

In United States v. Landano (1993), however, the Supreme Court may have put a crimp in the FBI blanket use of Exemption 7(D), records or information compiled for law enforcement purposes that could reasonably be expected to disclose the identity of a confidential source.

Convicted cop-killer Vincent Landano argued that his claims of innocence were thwarted because the FBI refused to release sufficiently complete records that could cast doubt on his guilt. The FBI had interpreted Exemption 7(D) as giving it virtually unlimited authority to protect from disclosure confidential sources or the material they provide.[71]

Writing for a unanimous court, Justice Sandra Day O'Connor declared it is unreasonable to assume that all FBI investigative sources are confidential.[72]

[71] U.S. Department of Justice v. Landano, 113 S.Ct. 2014, 2019, 2023 (1993); Linda Greenhouse, "Court Limits Shielding F.B.I. Sources," The New York Times, May 25, 1994, p.A7.

[72] Ibid., pp. 2023–2024.

We think this more particularized approach is consistent with Congress' intent to provide " 'workable rules' " of FOIA disclosure. Department of Justice v. Reporters Committee, 489 U.S. at 779; 16 Med.L.Rptr. 1545, quoting FTC v. Grolier, 462 U.S. 19, 27 (1983); see also EPA v. Mink, 410 U.S. 73, 80, 1 Med.L.Rptr. 2448 (1973). The government does not deny that, when a document is requested, it generally will be possible to establish factors such as the nature of the crime that was investigated and the source's relation to it. Armed with this information, the requester will have a more realistic opportunity to develop an argument that the circumstances do not support an inference of confidentiality.

Using the FOIA

The FOI Service Center, a project of the Reporters Committee on Freedom of the Press, periodically issues updated booklets titled "How to Use the FOI Act." This useful guide summarizes the uses of the FOIA as a news-gathering tool, and also provides thumbnail sketches of the Act's disclosure exemptions. This is truly a "do-it-yourself" guide, and even includes sample FOI Act request letters—and, if needed—sample appeal letters. This material is available from The Reporters Committee, 1101 Wilson Blvd., Suite 1910, Arlington, VA 22209.

The Case of Samuel L. Morison

National security concerns present real dilemmas for the United States. Government secrets and secrecy—in large part a legacy of Cold War tensions between the United States and Communist-bloc countries in the 1950s through the 1980s—now take on a somewhat different glow in the aftermath of the 1991 collapse of the Soviet Union.

Journalists have long complained about excessive secrecy in the United States' defense and intelligence establishments. One way in which journalists were able to combat secrecy, at least to some extent, was by the "leak," where reporters get tipped off to "inside" or confidential information. In 1988, however, the espionage conviction of Samuel Loring Morison worried some journalists lest that conviction might make it more difficult to get news of wrongdoing out of the Pentagon and the defense industry.

Morison was a civilian employee of the U.S. Navy, and also did some "moonlighting" as a freelance correspondent for a weapons industry journal published in Britain, Jane's Fighting Ships. Morison saw some photos stamped "Secret" on a co-worker's desk, photos taken from a U.S. KH–11 spy satellite. The photos showed construction work on a Russian nuclear aircraft carrier.

Morison, violating a Navy security pledge he had signed, sent the photos to another publication, Jane's Defence Weekly, which published them. The photos were republished in the U.S. in some newspapers. Morison, arguing unconvincingly that he had leaked the pictures to alert the world to a growing Soviet threat,[73] was prosecuted and convicted under an Espionage Statute.[74] Early in 1988, a three-judge panel of the Court of Appeals, Fourth Circuit, upheld Morison's conviction.[75] Thirty-one media organizations joined in a friend-of-the-court brief, arguing that if Morison's conviction stood, the flow of needed information to the public would be impeded. The media groups' amicus brief said: " '[F]or the first time, the court has applied the espionage statute to the dissemination of information to press and public.' " [76]

Court of Appeals Judge Donald Stuart Russell took a hard line in announcing the judgment against Morison. This intelligence department employee had taken secret intelligence from government files and had "wilfully transmitted or given it to one 'not entitled to receive it.' " As such, Morison was "not entitled to invoke the First Amendment as a shield to immunize his act of thievery." [77]

The Court of Appeals ruling was allowed to stand by the U.S. Supreme Court, and Morison began serving a jail term in the fall of 1988.[78] This outcome confirmed fears of some media advocates who argued that the Morison case will discourage government employees from providing information—even evidence of wrongdoing—if that information might be construed as falling under the espionage laws. Further, reporters may face subpoenas to reveal sources if their stories show that they have turned up information (from whatever sources) that the government believes to be classified.

Investigating the Death of Karen Silkwood

Attempts by media to open records through court cases commonly run afoul of Exemptions 7 and 5—investigatory files and agency memoranda—source materials which are often expected by media to be relevant to criminal activity. National Public Radio,

[73] Stuart Taylor, Jr., "Court Ruling on Leaks Could Make it a Crime to Talk to the Press," The New York Times, Sec. 4, P. 7, April 10, 1987. On leaks, generally, see Stephen Hess, The Government/Press Connection: Press Officers and Their Offices (Washington, D.C.: Brookings Institution, 1984, pp. 75–79, 92–94).

[74] 18 U.S.C.A. §§ 641, 793(d) and (e).

[75] United States v. Morison, 844 F.2d 1057 (4th Cir.1988).

[76] News Notes, in flyleaves of 14 Med.L.Rptr. No. 22 (Nov. 3, 1987).

[77] United States v. Morison, 844 F.2d 1057, 1069 (4th Cir.1988), 15 Med.L.Rptr. 1369, 1378.

[78] Taylor, loc. cit.

for example, sought disclosure of records compiled by the Justice Department and the FBI about the perplexing death of Karen Silkwood. An employee of a manufacturer of plutonium and uranium fuels for nuclear reactors, Silkwood was reportedly driving to attend a meeting with a union official and a newspaper reporter when she was killed in an auto crash. Uncertain evidence suggested that her car might have been driven off the road by another car, and that a file of documents she was supposedly carrying was not recovered. NPR also sought the record of the agency's investigation of the contamination of Silkwood by plutonium.

The Justice Department furnished NPR with some of the requested materials, but refused others. The parts of the death investigation file withheld were the "closing memoranda"—agency materials prepared during its final deliberations—and about 15 pages of notes and working papers of Justice Department attorneys. The Justice Department said that exemption 5 of the FOI Act— intra-agency memoranda or letters—protected these materials from disclosure. The Federal district court agreed,[79] saying the agency memoranda are protected as "papers which reflect the agency's group thinking in the process of working out its policy and determining what its law shall be." [80] The court rejected NPR's argument that the memoranda were "final" opinions, which under the Supreme Court's interpretation of the FOI Act would have been subject to disclosure.[81]

As for Exemption 7 of the FOI Act, protecting from disclosure matters which are "investigatory records compiled for law enforcement purposes" whose release would "interfere with enforcement proceedings * * *.": This applied to the Justice Department investigation of Silkwood's contamination by plutonium, and the court said that the records of the case suggested law-violation in materials-handling by personnel. It said that Congress' intent in writing Exemption 7 was plainly to prevent harm to a "concrete prospective law enforcement proceeding" that might result from disclosure of information. And though the department's leads in the investigation had currently run out, and want of finances for the moment precluded assignment of an investigator to the case, the case was "active." Disclosure would present "the very real possibility of a criminal learning in alarming detail of the government's investigation of his crime before the government has had the opportunity to bring him to justice," said the court in rejecting NPR's request.[82]

79 National Public Radio et al. v. Bell, 431 F.Supp. 509 (D.D.C.1977), 2 Med. L.Rptr. 1808.

80 Ibid.

81 N.L.R.B. v. Sears, Roebuck & Co., 421 U.S. 132, 95 S.Ct. 1504 (1975).

82 National Public Radio et al. v. Bell, 431 F.Supp. 509 (D.D.C.1977). The investigatory exemption was tightened in lower court cases. Records must be both

Executive Privilege

A power of withholding has always been asserted by the President and his Executive Department heads. This is the power exercised under the doctrine of "executive privilege." President George Washington was asked by Congress to make available documents relating to General St. Clair's defeat by Indians. He responded that "the Executive ought to communicate such papers as the public good would permit, and ought to refuse those, the disclosure of which would injure the public * * *." [83] In this case the records were made available to Congress, but many Presidents since have refused to yield records, as have the heads of executive departments. Their power to do so was upheld early in the nation's history by the United States Supreme Court. The famous decision written by Chief Justice John Marshall was delivered in 1803 in Marbury v. Madison, where Marshall said that the Attorney General (a presidential appointee) did not have to reveal matters which had been communicated to him in confidence.[84]

> By the Constitution of the United States, the president is invested with certain important political powers, in the exercise of which he is to use his own discretion, and is accountable only to the country in his political character and to his own conscience.

Justice Marshall elaborated the principle in the trial of Aaron Burr, accused of treason, saying that "The propriety of withholding * * * must be decided by [the President] himself, not by another for him. Of the weight of the reasons for and against producing it he himself is the judge." [85]

Executive privilege came to be asserted and used increasingly during the government's efforts to maintain security in the cold war with the U.S.S.R. following World War II. Presidents Truman and Eisenhower used the power to issue orders detailing what might and might not be released from the executive departments; both came under heavy attack from Congress and the news media.[86] President Nixon's Executive Order No. 11–652 of March 8, 1972, replaced and modified rules set by President Eisenhower.

investigatory *and* compiled for law enforcement purposes: Pope v. United States, 599 F.2d 1383 (5th Cir.1979). The information must be originally gathered for law enforcement purposes: Gregory v. Federal Deposit Insurance Corp., 470 F.Supp. 1329 (D.D.C.1979), reversed in part 631 F.2d 896 (D.C.Cir.1980). Courts have given mixed reactions to records for "improper" investigations. See Lamont v. Department of Justice, 475 F.Supp. 761 (S.D.N.Y.1979), and Irons v. Bell, 596 F.2d 468 (1st Cir.1979). See also Madens, op. cit., at 162–163.

[83] Francis E. Rourke, Secrecy and Publicity (Baltimore: Johns Hopkins Press, 1961), p. 65. And see Ibid., pp. 64–69, for general discussion of executive privilege.

[84] 5 U.S. (1 Cranch.) 137 (1803).

[85] 1 Burr's Trial 182.

[86] Rourke, pp. 75–83.

One of the most far-reaching directives of this period was issued by President Eisenhower in 1954. A senate subcommittee was investigating a controversy between the Army and Senator Joseph McCarthy of Wisconsin. President Eisenhower sent to Secretary of the Army Robert Stevens a message telling him that his departmental employees were to say nothing about internal communications of the Department.[87]

> Because it is essential to efficient and effective administration that employees of the executive branch be in a position to be completely candid in advising with each other on official matters, and because it is not in the public interest that any of their conversations or communications, or any documents or reproductions, concerning such advice be disclosed, you will instruct employees of your Department that in all of their appearances before the subcommittee of the Senate Committee on Government Operations regarding the inquiry now before it they are not to testify to any such conversations or communications or to produce any such documents or reproductions.

While the directive was aimed at a single situation and a single Executive Department, it soon became used by many other executive and administrative agencies as justification for their own withholding of records concerning internal affairs.[88] While journalists protested the spread of the practice, and while Congressional allies joined them, there was not much legal recourse then apparent.

The President's powers to restrict access are substantial, used extensively by some and little by others. Journalists have widely asserted that President Ronald Reagan employed these powers more vigorously than his predecessors of many terms. In fact, one of President Reagan's directives placed a "lifelong" nondisclosure restriction on many government employees, although it was partially withdrawn. In his 1982 Executive Order 12,356, he tightened declassification rules set by President Jimmy Carter, permitting permanent exemption from disclosure of documents in the realm of national security and foreign policy. In 1981, he submitted proposals to the Senate to give the Attorney General power to exempt some kinds of intelligence files from disclosure. In 1983, the Justice Department, with his support, notably tightened the rules for waiving fees charged to those who seek information from government agencies. Under him as Commander in Chief, journalists were kept uninformed and were excluded from the armed

---

[87] House Report, No. 2947, 84 Cong., 2 Sess., July 27, 1956. "Availability of Information from Federal Departments and Agencies," Dwight D. Eisenhower to Sec. of Defense, May 17, 1954, pp. 64–65.

[88] Rourke, p. 74.

forces' invasion of the Caribbean island of Grenada. Journalists found him and his administration much less accessible than his predecessor, and expert at frustrating reporters, one analyst declaring that "bureaucrats have largely succeeded in undermining the FOI Act at will." [89]

President Nixon and the Watergate Tapes

A head-on confrontation emerged in the Watergate investigations, as President Richard M. Nixon refused to turn over to a grand jury, tape recordings of conversations with his White House aides. Federal Judge John J. Sirica ruled that the tapes must be submitted to him for *in camera* scrutiny and possible forwarding to the grand jury. The President refused, asserting executive privilege, and said he was protecting "the right of himself and his successors to preserve the confidentiality of discussions in which they participate in the course of their constitutional duties." Special prosecutor Archibald Cox argued it was intolerable that "the President would invoke executive privilege to keep the tape recordings from the grand jury but permit his aides to testify fully as to their recollections of the same conversations." The President fired Cox, and the Attorney General resigned and his deputy was fired before the President yielded the tapes (which of course were to prove central to the discrediting of him and his aides) amid a public cry for his impeachment.[90]

The Supreme Court ruled that executive privilege is not absolute, but qualified. The *in camera* court inspection of the tapes that Sirica ordered, it said, would be a minimal intrusion on the President's confidential communications. The President's claim was not based on grounds of national security—that military or diplomatic secrets were threatened—but only on the ground of his "generalized interest in confidentiality." That could not prevail over "the fundamental demands of due process of law in the fair administration of justice." It would have to yield to the "demonstrated, specific need for evidence in a pending criminal trial." [91]

[89] Floyd Abrams, The New Effort to Control Information, New York Times Magazine, Sept. 25, 1983, 23; Government Shuts Up, Columbia Journalism Rev., July/Aug. 1982, 31; Executive Order No. 12356 on National Security Information, April 2, 1982, 8 Med.L.Rptr. 1306; 1984 Duke L.Journ. 377, 387, op. cit.; Anon., Reagan Signs New Secrecy Order to Seal More Public Documents, News Media & the Law, June/July 1982, 22; 8 Med.L.Rptr. # 46, 1/25/83, News Notes; Anon., Coverage Efforts Thwarted, News Media & the Law, Jan.-Feb. 1984, 6; Carl Stepp, Grenada Skirmish over Access Goes On, SPJ/SDX, Freedom of Information 84–'85, Report, 5; Steve Weinberg, Trashing the FOIA, Columbia Journalism Rev., Jan./Feb. 1985, 21, 22; Donna A. Demac, Keeping America Uninformed (N.Y., 1984).

[90] New York Times, Sept. 11, 1973, p. 36; Oct. 24, 1973, p. 1.

[91] United States v. Nixon, 418 U.S. 683, 684–685, 713, 94 S.Ct. 3090, 3095–3096, 3110 (1974).

Subsequent assertions of executive privilege by Nixon involved his post-resignation claim to custody of presidential papers from his term in office—millions of pages of documents and almost 900 tapes—and also his denial of the rights of record companies and networks to copy, sell, and broadcast tapes that had been played at one of the trials arising from Watergate. The Supreme Court ruled in one case that the government should have custody of all but Nixon's private and personal papers,[92] and in the other it granted Nixon's plea to deny networks and record companies the right to copy, sell, or broadcast the tapes.[93]

On July 24, 1979, a U.S. District Court ruled that Nixon's dictabelt "diaries" were not personal and would not be screened for use by archivists. Also, the court ruled that the public should have access to the actual tapes, instead of synopses or transcripts.[94] As of June 1980, National Archives had released 31, or about 12½ hours of conversation, of the 950 tapes, and Nixon was fighting release of another 6,000 hours.[95] Usage of the tapes is restricted: no more than 24 persons may listen at a time, for 45 to 90 minutes depending on the length of the tape played; and listeners are forbidden to make their own recordings of the tapes.[96]

Access to federal officials' papers and claims of executive privilege were active issues during the latter half of the seventies. The Nixon papers cases and the Kissinger "phone calls" case both involved dispute about ownership of executive papers. President Carter signed the Presidential Records Act of 1978, effective January 1981, which clarified ownership of executive branch papers. The National Archives assumes control of presidential papers at the end of a president's last term. Records related to defense and foreign policy, plus presidential appointment records involving trade secrets, may be restricted for 12 years. Papers not restricted become available to the public under the FOI Act as soon as the Archives processes them.[97]

"Reverse FOIA Suits"

The recorded word, in literally billions of pages of government documents, is the focus of the FOI Act, dedicated to dissemination

[92] Nixon v. General Services Administrator, 433 U.S. 425, 97 S.Ct. 2777 (1977).

[93] Nixon v. Warner Communications, Inc., News Media and the Law, 1:1 (Oct. 1977), p. 14. Anon., "High Court Bars Networks' Right To Nixon Tapes," New York Times, April 19, 1978, p. 1.

[94] "Nixon Documents Litigation Reaches Court Settlement," News Media & The Law, March–April 1980, 4:2, p. 50.

[95] "Nixon Tapes Available to Public; Archives Requests More Materials," op. cit. See also, "Anyone Can Hear Nixon Tapes," Wisconsin State Journal, May 29, 1980, p. 12, sec. 1.

[96] Ibid.

[97] Robert Schwaller, "Access to Federal Officials' Papers," FOI Center Report No. 411, October 1979, pp. 7, 8.

of this record. But developments during 1979 and 1980 included two Supreme Court decisions involving "reverse-FOI Act" suits, in which persons or organizations submitting information to a federal agency sought to prevent disclosure in response to FOI Act requests. In Chrysler Corp. v. Brown, the Court banned such suits under the FOI Act, stating that while exempt records could be withheld, the Act did not *require* nondisclosure.[98] However, in GTE Sylvania, Inc. v. Consumers Union, the Consumer Product Safety Act was used successfully to exempt information from release unless its accuracy is verified first.[99]

The FOI Reform Act of 1986

Efforts to "improve" or "reform" the Freedom of Information Act mean different things to different people. The "Freedom of Information Reform Act of 1986" had some good news and some bad news for reporters. Apparently to the good, the Act required the Office of Management and Budget (OMB) to allow up to 100 pages of document copying free to journalists, and to make charges only for duplication on lengthier requests. Also helpful is allowing FOI requests of demonstrable importance to the public—e.g. reporters investigating an environmental hazard—to get speeded-up treatment for such requests.

On the other hand, journalists or citizens seeking information about businesses could face tougher slogging. Under the Reform Act, in order to protect proprietary information for businesses, the businesses named in information requests are to be notified. Then, they have 35 days to oppose disclosure. At the same time, Sen. Orrin Hatch (R–Utah) successfully sponsored an amendment to a drug control bill which provided broader FOI exemptions for investigatory records of law enforcement agencies.[1]

Privacy Act of 1974

"After long years of debate, a comprehensive federal privacy law passed the Congress * * * as a solid legislative decision in favor of individual privacy and the 'right to be let alone'," writes attorney James T. O'Reilly.[2] It is a statute shaped to deal with the federal government's gargantuan systems of secret dossiers on

[98] Madens, op. cit., pp. 141–142. See also Chrysler Corp. v. Brown, 441 U.S. 281, 99 S.Ct. 1705 (1979).

[99] "Safety Data Release Depends On Who Reaches Courtroom First," News Media & The Law, Feb.–March 1981, 5:1, p. 49; GTE Sylvania, Inc. v. Consumers Union, 445 U.S. 375, 100 S.Ct. 1194 (1980); Consumer Product Safety Commission v. GTE Sylvania, Inc., 447 U.S. 102, 100 S.Ct. 2051 (1980).

[1] Public L. No. 99–570; see also News Media & the Law, Fall, 1986, pp. 28–29, and Spring, 1987, pp. 31–32.

[2] "The Privacy Act of 1974," Freedom of Information Report No. 342, Sept. 1975, p. 1.

citizens, to give citizens access to the content of files that may be kept on them, and to provide citizens with a means for correcting inaccurate content of these files. If agencies are not responsive in making changes, civil suits may be brought against them. A crucial element in the law is that no file may be transferred from one agency to another without the individual's consent, except where the purpose squares with the purpose for which the information was collected.

Under the law, a supposedly exhaustive index to all federal government "data banks" or personal information systems on individuals has been published. Also published in the Federal Register are the categories of individuals on whom records are maintained, and where one can learn whether a particular government agency has information about him.[3] No citizen who inquires about himself need give any reason for a request to examine the record, and may obtain a copy. Some exceptions to citizen access are provided, mostly dealing with law enforcement agencies' records, and including, notably, the CIA and the Secret Service.[4] However, foreign nationals working for the government have no access rights to personnel records about themselves under either the FOI Act or the Privacy Act, according to a U.S. Court of Appeals.[5]

Privacy issues intensified during the 1970s and 1980s, as individuals made greater use of the Privacy Act to see records maintained about them and to amend those records or correct inaccuracies.[6] States also were active in protecting privacy of financial, medical, and criminal records.[7]

Recall that privacy issues also are part of the FOIA; as noted at earlier, Exemptions 6 (personnel or medical files) and 7 (law enforcement investigatory files) both list privacy. In Department of Justice v. Reporters Committee for Freedom of the Press, the U.S. Supreme Court held—in part for privacy reasons—that FBI "rap sheets"—records of a person's arrests, charges, and jailings.

[3] Anon., "Citizens' Guide to Privacy Act Available," FOI Digest, 18:2 (March–April 1976), p. 2. For an editor's struggle of more than a year to get a file kept on him by the FBI, see John Seigenthaler, "Publisher Finally Gets His FBI Files, or Some of Them," (Memphis) Tennessean, July 10, 1977. False accusations, the FBI said after finally releasing contents of the file, would be purged.

[4] Anon., "Government Information and the Rights of Citizens," 73 Mich.L.Rev. 971, 1317. This study of more than 370 pages describes, analyzes, and criticizes the FOI Act, state open records and meetings laws, and the Privacy Act of 1974.

[5] Raven v. Panama Canal Co., 583 F.2d 169 (5th Cir.1978), certiorari denied 440 U.S. 980, 99 S.Ct. 1787 (1979). See also, "Allows Personnel Files to be Kept From Alien," News Media & The Law, March–April 1980, 4:2, p. 31.

[6] In 1977, of 1,417,214 requests, 1,355,515 were granted either entirely or in part: "Privacy Roundup: Report Shows Increasing Use of Privacy Act by Individuals," FOI Digest, July–Aug. 1978, 20:4, p. 2.

[7] "Poll Shows Privacy Concerns Rising," FOI Digest, May–June 1979, 21:3, p. 2.

Release of such criminal identification records was held to be a "clearly unwarranted invasion of privacy" under the terms of the FOIA.[8] Most states—all but Wisconsin, Florida, and Oklahoma— follow the federal lead in withholding rap sheets from public inspection.[9]

The additional emphasis on secrecy brought about by the Privacy Act concerns some journalists about loss of inside sources of information in the federal government, and the possibility of tracing "leaks" through the agencies' records of who got access to various files.[10]

Government in the Sunshine Act

As the FOI Act is to federal government records, so the "Sunshine Act" [11] is to federal government meetings. The Act mandates open meetings for regular sessions and quorum gatherings of approximately 50 agencies—all those headed by boards of two or more persons named by the President and confirmed by the Senate. Included are the major regulatory agencies such as the Securities Exchange Commission and the Interstate Commerce Commission—whose meetings always had been secret—and such little-known entities as the National Council on Educational Research and the National Homeownership Foundation board of directors.[12]

All meetings of the named agencies are to be open—with at least one week's public notice—unless agendas take up matters in 10 categories which permit closed sessions. Either a verbatim transcript or detailed minutes of all matters covered in closed sessions is to be kept. And as for the record of open meetings, it is to be kept as minutes and made available to the public at minimal copying cost.

Closed-to-the-public meetings will hardly be rare, whatever strength the Sunshine Act may prove to generate. The ten categories of subject-matter whose discussion warrants closed doors for meetings of the boards and commissions are much like the exemptions to disclosure under the FOI Act. Abbreviated, the ten are:

[8] Department of Justice v. Reporter's Committee on Freedom of the Press, 489 U.S. 749, 109 S.Ct. 1468 (1989), 16 Med.L.Rptr. 1545.

[9] Ibid., 489 U.S. at 750, 109 S.Ct. at 1470, 16 Med.L.Rptr. at 1547.

[10] Lyle Denniston, "A Citizen's Right to Privacy," Quill, 63:4, April 1975, p. 16. See also Editor & Publisher, Jan. 31, 1976, p. 9.

[11] 5 U.S.C.A. § 552b. The FOI Act and the Privacy Act of 1974 are in the federal statutes under the same number, as 5 U.S.C.A. § 552a and 5 U.S.C.A. § 552c respectively.

[12] Editor & Publisher, Feb. 26, 1977, p. 32. This account's details of the Sunshine Act are taken largely from James T. O'Reilly, "Government in the Sunshine," Freedom of Information Center Report 366, Jan. 1977; O'Reilly, p. 2.

1. National defense or foreign policy matters which are properly classified;

2. Internal agency personnel matters;

3. Matters expressly required by law to be held confidential;

4. Confidential commercial or financial information, and trade secrets;

5. Accusations of criminal activity, or of censure, against a person;

6. Matters which if disclosed would be clearly unwarranted invasions of a person's privacy;

7. Law enforcement and criminal investigatory records, subject to the same categories as FOI Act exemption (b)(7);

8. Bank examiners' records;

9. Matters which if disclosed would generate financial speculation (included to protect the Federal Reserve Board Open Market Committee) or which would frustrate agency action which has not been announced;

10. Matters which involve the agency's issuance of a subpoena or participation in hearings or other adjudication-related proceedings.

It may prove significant that the ten exemptions of the Sunshine Act apply to the some 1,300 Advisory Committees spread throughout the Executive Branch of government. These committees of private citizens contribute expertise, advice, and recommendations to government policy making. The members tend to be prominent persons from industries which deal with the agencies they advise.

Ways exist for attacking illegal secrecy under the Sunshine Act. One may seek an injunction in advance to force a pending meeting to be open, and having found one illegal closing of an agency, a court may enjoin the agency from further illegal closings. One may sue, within 60 days after the secret meeting, to require that a transcript be furnished. No financial penalty for illegal meetings may be levied against members themselves, but courts may assign costs or fees against the United States—or against a plaintiff whose suit is found to be "dilatory or frivolous." The range of possibilities for future secrecy or openness is large, and the crystal balls of various observers offer varied forecasts of cheer and gloom.

Attorneys General

Attorneys general have been called on to interpret meetings and records laws in many states. As for meetings, it is occasionally feasible for a reporter to seek "instant action" in the form of an attorney general's opinion, perhaps by placing a phone call even while an illegal secret meeting is in session. Through such maneuvers, enterprising reporters have, on occasion, forced meetings open.

More likely, however, before an opinion can be had, the meeting will have adjourned. Nevertheless, either a formal opinion delivered at the request of a state government agency, or an informal one delivered at the request of a non-official person or entity—such as a reporter or a newspaper—can have a future impact on the behavior of the secretive group or agency. Reporters, of course, should read up on the open-records, open-meetings opinions of attorneys general. The attorney general interprets the law of a state; an "AG's opinion" does not have the force of a court opinion, but it is authoritative until a court has passed on a particular question.[13]

SEC. 84. ACCESS TO "SECURITY" INFORMATION, COVERING WARS

As discussed elsewhere in this text, traditions of openness run afoul of restrictive executive orders, statutes and court decisions in areas where claims of "national security" are raised.

Access in the "Surveillance State"

It is likely that the crucial battle to preserve what journalists have come to see as the central meaning of the First Amendment will be fought in the arena of access to government information. What is talked about here goes beyond the traditional tugging and hauling between reporters and government. Resistance to access by government officials is to be expected: human nature, of course, dictates an unwillingness to look foolish, and government officials— like all of us—dislike revealing mistakes.

Extrapolating from the words of First Amendment historian Norman L. Rosenberg suggests a scary phrase, the "surveillance state." He wrote, "The central free-speech issue of the post-World War II era involved the expansion of a vast surveillance apparatus, the growing power of an increasingly monopolistic communications industry, and the problems of its ties to other private and public centers of power."[14]

Journalists—and all citizens and public officials—would do well to keep the phrase "surveillance state" in mind, for it conjures up a

[13] William Thompson, "FOI and State Attorneys General," Freedom of Information Center Report No. 307, July, 1973, University of Missouri.

[14] Norman L. Rosenberg, Protecting the Best Men: An Interpretive History of Libel (Chapel Hill: University of North Carolina Press, 1986) p. 266.

vision of a society where government watches the people but the people see only what government wants them to see. A surveillance state, in sum, is an old map of hell.

Anyone paying even scant attention to news reports during the late 1980s saw the phrase "national security" often used as a reason why documents could not be released—or used in a federal court—to try Lt. Col. Oliver North on criminal conspiracy charges coming out of the Iran–Contra affair. (North, along with retired Admiral John M. Poindexter, the former National Security Adviser to President Reagan, was the subject of criminal charges relating to illegal sale of arms to Iran and diversion of the proceeds to fund the Nicaraguan Contras.) With those classified documents unavailable, the main charges against North were dropped early in 1989. The Central Intelligence Agency, itself so clandestine that its budget is secret, opposed release of security-classified documents needed to bring North to trial.[15]

The task for reporters or other citizens who try to keep tabs on what government has done or is doing is monumental. In 1988, fourteen years after President Richard M. Nixon resigned in the wake of the Watergate scandal, historian Dan T. Carter complained about difficulties in access to the Nixon Papers as he worked on a biography of former Alabama Governor George Wallace, pursuing tantalizing bits of evidence that Nixon's Republican White House had involved itself strangely in Wallace's Democratic and Third Party political campaigns in the early 1970s.

After Nixon left the White House, he claimed, through his lawyers, that the President had a right to bottle up or even get rid of materials relating to the Presidency. Congress then passed the 1974 Presidential Records Act, declaring Presidential records to be government property and ordering the National Archives to catalog the records, to cull them for national security and privacy-sensitive areas, and to release those records as soon as practicable.

The historian Carter wrote to The New York Times: [16]

Mr. Nixon's lawyers ... sent several representatives-untrained in historical study—or archival management—to conduct their own examination of the 1.5 million documents. In April 1987, less than a month before the scheduled opening of the first batch of papers, Mr. Nixon's

[15] Marianne Means, "Dr. Strangelove's super-CIA scheme," column in Austin American–Statesman, July 18, 1987, p. A14; Stephen Engelberg, "Data Disclosure in Contra Case Fought by U.S.," The New York Times, June 4, 1988 (Nat'l. Ed.), p. 9; "House Sets Secret Sum for Intelligence Groups," A.P. story in The New York Times, June 10, 1987, p. 13.

[16] Dan T. Carter, "The Nixon Cover–Up Goes On," letter to The New York Times, July 25, 1988, p. 23.

lawyers demanded that an additional 150,000 documents be withheld.

It should be obvious that the existence of federal and state freedom of information acts does not mean that information is freely available. Ask any knowledgeable investigative reporter, and you will get a litany of complaints about problems in getting access. For example, James Derk of the Evansville (Ind.) Courier used the federal Freedom of Information Act (FOIA) to report on a regional airline.

Although, as described earlier in this chapter, there are—on paper—just nine broad exemptions to the Federal FOIA, Derk wrote: "I usually run into the unofficial 10th Exemption, known as the 'forget it' exemption." He noted that he received letters saying his requests had been denied for various reasons, or, at times, never got answers at all. "I've been waiting," Derk wrote late in 1988, "for more than two years for a response from the Department of Justice." He added: [17]

> When I get answers, often they are not the answers I sought.

* * *

> In September, I received 1,150 pages of documents from the U.S. Environmental Protection Agency that I had requested in July. The documents were riddled with deletions and I ended up paying 15 cents a page for 118 blank pages, the contents of which were deemed too sensitive for public eyes.

Road-blocks to information often do seem excessive. John Weiner, a history professor reporting the life of former Beatle John Lennon, reported in 1988 that 14–year–old CIA and FBI files about the singer's anti-Vietnam War activities and his work against President Nixon's reelection were withheld. Professor Weiner asked, " 'How can 14–year–old documents on the peaceful activity of a dead rock singer jeopardize national security?' " [18]

Freedom of information requests, however frustrating they may be, can turn up useful results if persistence is maintained. Late in 1988, for example, it was reported by the Durham (N.C.) Morning Herald—which had received more than 2,000 pages in an FOIA request—that the Federal Bureau of Investigation had kept a confidential file on the Supreme Court of the United States from 1932 until at least 1985. That file included evidence that the FBI

---

[17] James Derk, "It takes a lot of persistence to make the Freedom of Information Act pay off, ASNE Bulletin, November, 1988, pp. 10–11.

[18] "Educators Assailing Curbs on Data," The New York Times (Nat'l. Ed.), Sept. 14, 1988, p. 26.

had wiretapped (evidently without warrants!) or monitored conversations involving four men on the Court, Chief Justice Earl Warren and Justices Abe Fortas, Potter Stewart, and William O. Douglas.[19]

CIA v. SIMS (1985)

A case which provides a disturbing symbol of the power of claimed national security exemptions to shield federal agencies from scrutiny is CIA v. Sims (1985). This Orwellian nightmare of a case concerned a Freedom of Information Act lawsuit to get records on the Central Intelligence Agency's research project code-named MKULTRA. This project, started in 1953 when Richard Helms was CIA deputy director for planning, was to counter Chinese and Soviet advances in brainwashing and interrogation. From 1953 to 1965, the CIA contracted with numerous universities to test the efficacy of certain biological and chemical materials in altering human behavior.[20]

Sims and others sued in 1977 to discover which universities and individuals had taken part in this secret research, but were unsuccessful. The Supreme Court of the United States upheld lower court rulings saying that Exemption 3 of the FOIA Act, in concert with the National Security Act of 1947, allowed the Director of the CIA to decide what should or should not be released—in the national interest—to protect intelligence sources and methods from unauthorized disclosure.[21]

Hidden in that judicial/bureaucratic verbiage is a dangerous dilemma for a society which would be self-governing. If CIA v. Sims is put in human terms, it boils down to this: can a society which would be self-governing adopt the methods of totalitarianism (surreptitious administration of drugs such as LSD to unwitting "subjects?") And, when some aspects of those CIA research projects went terribly wrong—including death of at least two persons and the likelihood of impaired health for other "subjects"—the CIA attempted to cover its tracks.[22]

Because CIA budgetary records are secret, there is no way of tracking down the financial costs. But the MKULTRA project was massive: it consisted of some 149 subprojects which the CIA contracted out to various universities and research foundations. At least 80 institutions—including, apparently, major universities in

[19] "FBI Kept Secret File on the Supreme Court," The New York Times, August 21, 1988, p. 13.

[20] CIA v. Sims, 471 U.S. 159, 161, 105 S.Ct. 1881, 1884 (1985), 11 Med.L.Rptr. 2017.

[21] 471 U.S. at 159, 164, 105 S.Ct. 1882, 1885 (1985).

[22] 471 U.S. 159, 162n, 105 S.Ct. 1881, 1884n (1985).

the U.S. and even in Canada—and 185 private researchers took part in MKULTRA.[23]

But try to keep this in human terms: shouldn't the universities participating—and the researchers who took part in these bizarre and dangerous experiments—be identified? Or if you had a relative who had committed suicide after being dosed with LSD without his permission, in an MKULTRA "research project" might not you want to find out more, to confront those responsible?

According to the Supreme Court decision in CIA v. Sims, you'll get that information only if the Director of the CIA decides that its release would not be harmful to national security interests. And because the CIA had promised the researchers and their institutions—including universities—anonymity, the Director of the CIA could "properly" conclude that such information could not be released, in order to protect "intelligence sources."

The Supreme Court, in upholding the CIA Director's authority to withhold information, said: [24]

> We hold that the Director of the Central Intelligence properly invoked § 102(d)(3) of the National Security Act of 1947 to withhold disclosure of the identities of the individual MKULTRA researchers as protected "intelligence sources." We also hold that the FOIA does not require the Director to disclose the institutional affiliations of the exempt researchers in light of the record which supports the Agency's determination of that such disclosure would lead to an unacceptable risk of disclosing the source's identities.

The lesson of CIA v. Sims, is that the Supreme Court gives an enormous benefit of the doubt to government agencies which can claim some kind of "national security" exemption. The MKULTRA project, which brings to mind certain "research" which led to War Crimes trials in the aftermath of World War II, should never be repeated. After it came to light, a Presidential Executive Order forbade that kind of research.[25]

But it should be kept in mind that MKULTRA—hardly the CIA's finest hour—became known despite a determined effort to erase all evidence that it had ever existed. When Richard Helms—who had himself suggested the project as a CIA functionary in 1953—became President Nixon's CIA director in the 1970s, he ordered all evidence of the project wiped out. But some of the financial records of the project "inadvertently survived" and came

---

[23] 471 U.S. at 162, 105 S.Ct. at 1884 (1985).

[24] Ibid., 471 U.S. at 181, 106 S.Ct. at 1894 (1985).

[25] Exec. Order No. 12333, § 2,103 CFR 213 (1982).

to the attention of Admiral Stansfield Turner, CIA Director under President Carter. Turner turned the information over to the Senate Select Committee on Intelligence, resulting in a major Congressional investigation. But even there, the CIA request to treat the names of the MKULTRA researchers as confidential was honored.[26]

Access to Computerized Records

When is electronically stored information "a record?" How can computerized information be identified with sufficient specificity? As Joe Grimm of the Detroit Free Press has said, both state and federal FOI acts can be used to get computer records that some agencies generally have not deemed to be public. Reporters will need to argue that it is the information, not the way of storing it, that is the record, and news organizations will have to fight this out in the courts, in all likelihood.[27]

One answer where electronic records are concerned is that citizens' groups or newsgathering organizations will have to be willing to be assertive. If what used to be an open public record in a file becomes unavailable or discouragingly expensive when stored electronically, it may be time to go to court. In some states, it may be necessary to lobby legislators to get antiquated statutes updated.

The Reporters Committee on Freedom of the Press makes available "Access to Electronic Records: A Guide to Reporting on State & Local Government in the Computer Age." The Reporters Committee says that in general, electronic records—or at least the pieces of information stored electronically—are subject to federal and state open records laws.[28]

One nasty problem gets the copyright interests of records-management firms tangled up in questions of access to information. For example, access to the computer software may be needed in order to make sense of records, especially for a complicated reporting or research project. State agencies, especially those which have purchased or leased software from private suppliers, may try to deny access to software as a kind of "trade secret." [29]

Access to News of Military Operations

One of the true tests of how free a nation is comes when that nation's government is at war. Some of the givens of wartime include:

---

[26] Ibid., 471 U.S. at 160, 105 S.Ct. at 1883. See also Stansfield Turner, Secrecy and Democracy: The CIA in Transition (Boston: Houghton Mifflin, (1985).

[27] ASNE Bulletin, November 1988, p. 9.

[28] Reporters Committee on Freedom of the Press, Access to Electronic Records: A Guide to Reporting on State & Local Government in the Computer Age, Rev. 1991, p. 3.

[29] Ibid., p. 6.

— There can be prior restraint when safety of military forces or civilians is at stake.

— Prior restraint can be imposed over dispatches sent or broadcast from a battle zone.

— Correspondents in a war zone may have both their mobility and their access to channels of communication curtailed.

"The Uncensored War" is the title Daniel C. Hallin chose for his study of the media and the war in Vietnam. A myth has grown up, Hallin contends, that because the media were allowed, quite freely, to send home images of war in 'Nam, that the U.S. media somehow "lost the war."

The late President Richard M. Nixon blamed television for demoralization at home during the latter stages of the Vietnam conflict. Such views of media—particularly, TV—coverage have affected policy. As Hallin noted,[30]

> [I]t was the example of Vietnam, for instance, that motivated the British government to impose tight controls on news coverage of the Falklands crisis [of 1982]. Back at home, the Reagan administration, with Vietnam in mind, excluded the media from the opening phase of the invasion of Grenada.

The excessive secrecy of the 1983 Grenada invasion led to earnest press protests, and to some rueful admissions from military officials that they may have gone too far with their controls.

As a result, "press pools" were organized. A small number of journalists representing largely establishment publications and broadcast operations were selected to keep their bags packed, to be "at the ready" should the United States embark on another military action. This arrangement meant that the small number of journalists selected for the pool would share their stories with the far larger number of correspondents and media outlets not selected. When the United States invaded Panama on December 20, 1989, pool correspondents belatedly were put into place to cover actions involving 25,000 highly trained U.S. troops, plus a large assortment of military hardware—tanks, jet fighters, helicopter gunships and Stealth bombers, all to try to capture and arrest General Manuel Noriega. It turned out that the Panama pool was not the solution; it was part of the problem.

From the standpoint of the news media, there was only one thing wrong with the Panama pool arrangement: It didn't work. As Editor & Publisher reported, Secretary of Defense Dick Cheney

---

[30] Daniel C. Hallin, "The Uncensored War:" The Media and Vietnam (Berkeley: University of California Press, 1986, p. 4; Tom Wicker, "Ghosts of Vietnam," in The New York Times, Jan. 26, 1991, p. 19.

and his press assistant, Pete Williams, were blamed for the inability of the "National Press Pool" to cover the invasion of Panama effectively.[31]

Fred Hoffman, a former Associated Press reporter who also had served as a Pentagon spokesperson, evaluated the Panama pool experience harshly. It should be noted that Hoffman's evaluative report had been requested by Pete Williams himself.

The Hoffman report complained that Cheney was excessively concerned with secrecy, and concluded that was the reason the pool did not get to the scene until the fighting was nearly over. The press pool—16 reporters—Editor & Publisher quoted from the Hoffman report, which said that in practice sessions during the National Press Pool's five-year history and in covering sea and air battles in the Persian Gulf in 1986–87,[32]

"* * * reporters demonstrated they could be trusted to respect essential ground rules, including operational security * * *

"Unless the Defense Department's leaders are prepared to extend that trust in hot-war situations, the pool probably will be of little value."

Long after the Panama invasion, many questions remained. How many civilians were killed? On December 20, 1990—exactly a year after the U.S. invasion—U.S. Representative Charles Rangel (D–NY) published his views in The New York Times. He wrote:[33]

* * * General Manuel Antonio Noriega sits idly in a Miami jail cell, his trial on charges of drug trafficking delayed by the Government's tape recording of his telephone conversations. But few people know that for the past year Government has been withholding another set of tapes— Government-recorded videotapes of the Panama invasion.

The videotapes of the invasion were taken by highly sophisticated gun cameras aboard Apache attack helicopters. What might those tapes show? They could well suggest that far more civilians died than the U.S. count of 202. (Human rights leaders and some Panamanians have charged that thousands died.) Also, Rangel wrote, as many as 60 percent of the 347 American casualties may have been caused by "friendly fire."[34]

[31] George Garneau, "Panning the Pentagon," Editor & Publisher, March 31, 1990, p. 11.

[32] Quoted in Ibid.

[33] Charles B. Rangel, "The Pentagon Pictures," The New York Times (Nat'l.Ed.), Dec. 20, 1990, p. A19.

[34] Ibid.

Covering the Persian Gulf War

When President George Bush said that the Persian Gulf war was not to be "another Vietnam," he seemed to refer to his determination to bring enough military resources into play to assure a swift victory. The desire to avoid the "Vietnam syndrome" obviously had fallout for press coverage of the war in the Persian Gulf. Although camera operators on rooftops got spectacular footage of Nintendo-like displays of rockets and tracer bullets, the result of warfare—corpses—was little seen.

In the main, the American press acquiesced in the pooling arrangements. Daniel Hallin's comments on American news media in Vietnam are worth pondering in light of media's coverage of Persian Gulf warfare. Just how independent are the media? Hallin wrote: [35]

> Structurally the American news media are both highly autonomous from direct political control and, through the routines of the news-gathering process, deeply intertwined in the actual operation of government.

Hallin argued that news people combine suspicion of power with a respect for established order, institutions, and authority. Given this anomalous status, small wonder the press—watched most carefully by suspicious military officials—had severe problems in the Persian Gulf. The distinguished military correspondent Malcolm W. Browne, long known for his steadiness and balanced coverage, wrote in January, 1991, that many [36]

> * * * news correspondents covering the war with Iraq are bridling under a system of conflicting rules and confusing censorship.
>
> For the first time since World War II, correspondents must submit to near-total military supervision of their work.

Military escorts tagged along with reporters, making it highly unlikely that servicemen and women who were interviewed would speak frankly. At times, escorts interrupted interviews, objecting to questions. When an enlisted man told a reporter how he continued to practice his Christian faith in a country where anything but Muslin rites are not legal, a military "information officer" cut off the interview. The reason? "Military ground rules forbid questions about 'things that we don't know about necessari-

[35] Hallin, p. 8.

[36] Malcolm W. Browne, "Conflicting Censorship Upsets Many Journalists," The New York Times, Jan. 21, 1991, p. A8.

ly.' " [37]

Carol Rosenberg of the Miami Herald and Susan Sachs of Newsday were excluded from covering the First Marine Division in the Persian Gulf because they were thought to have asked "rude questions" of Marine officers.[38]

Uneven application of rules seemed particularly frustrating. Officers in the field would clear a dispatch, only to have it held up somewhere up the line. On the other hand, reporters could understand why a battlefield commander would request that the location of an action not be given, only to have the information withheld in the war zone made public by the Pentagon.

Top brass showed fondness for the spotlight. Malcolm Browne observed that "[t]he Pentagon is clearly eager to be the first to report the most newsworthy information." [39] Later in the war, the Pentagon itself was upstaged by briefings given from Saudi Arabia by General "Stormin Norman" Schwarzkopf.

Despite the grumbling by the press, it surrendered quite meekly to what amounted to military rule, with Cable News Network's Peter Arnett's reports from Baghdad being the most obvious nose-thumbing at pooled journalism. The establishmentarian nature of most American news operations may be seen, perhaps, in the scant coverage given to a lawsuit by Pulitzer Prize-winner Sydney Schanberg, a lawsuit challenging the ground rules for covering Operation Desert Shield (which became "Desert Storm" once the fighting started).

In that lawsuit, nine publications and four journalists sued Secretary of Defense Cheney and Assistant Secretary of Defense for Public Affairs Pete Williams (among others), seeking an injunction against what were characterized as unfair policies. One press rule, issued January 9, 1991, decreed that media reports from combat pools had to be reviewed by an on-site military public affairs officer before transmission, an obvious cause of delay (or worse).[40]

Despite the pro-Administration-cheerleading-for-the-Persian Gulf war attitudes permeating most of America's news media, the military evidently viewed reporters with less than enthusiasm, if

[37] Clarence Page, "Gulf between military, media is so wide that truth has been put in choke hold," Milwaukee Sentinel, Jan. 22, 1991, p. 8, Part 1.

[38] Ibid.

[39] Browne, op. cit.

[40] The journalists bringing the suit were Schanberg (Newsday), novelists E.L. Doctorow and William Styron, and Michael Klare (Nation magazine). The New York Times, the Washington Post, and the Associated Press were not involved in the suit, nor were any of the four big broadcast networks. Plaintiff publications included Harper's, The Nation, Mother Jones, Progressive Magazine, In These Times, and The Village Voice.

not suspicion or outright hostility. The military controlled its own image during the Persian Gulf war.

SEC. 85. RECORDS AND MEETINGS IN THE STATES

The extent of access in the states varies under statutes providing what shall be open and what closed in the meetings and records of executive, administrative, and legislative agencies.

All states have laws declaring that public policy demands substantial if not maximum disclosure of official business, both meetings and records. Rarely, however, is it conceded that every act or document of officialdom must be open to public scrutiny. Every branch of government in the United States conducts some of its work or maintains some of its records in secret. There are situations in the states as in the federal government's domain which favor secrecy as protection for the individual's private rights and for government's carrying out its work. But the principle of disclosure and openness is as important to the democratic spirit at the state and local levels as it is at the federal level. Thanks to open government efforts pushed by the press and by public spirited citizens in the 1960s and 1970s, by mid–1974 48 states had open-meetings laws.[41]

The great diversity among state open meetings and open records statutes defies easy generalization or detailed discussion here.[42] Citizens who need to know how to get information out of particular governmental units—including reporters—need to brief themselves on the special provisions of each state's access laws. Ignorance of such provisions leaves the citizen or reporter at the mercy of officials who choose not to live up to open records or open meetings statutes.

Efforts are made periodically to generalize across state openness statutes, and even to "rank" state statutes in terms of "more open" or "less open." If one learns one is in a state with a highly rated statute, however, do not relax. Openness statutes—or court decisions, for that matter—tend to be rather like airline tickets—good for this time and purpose only. Keeping records and meetings

---

[41] All except Miss. and W.Va. by 1974. See John B. Adams, "State Open Meetings Laws: An Overview," Freedom of Information Foundation Series No. 3, July 1974. For another historical treatment, see William R. Henrick, "Public Inspection of State and Municipal Executive Documents," 45 Fordham L.Rev. 1105 (1977). See also "Gaining Access '84," section of the 1985 Freedom of Information Report, Society of Professional Journalists, Sigma Delta Chi.

[42] Of special usefulness is the series Tapping Officials' Secrets: A State Open Government Compendium, a state-by-state project of the Reporters Committee for Freedom of the Press.

open takes real diligence on the part of the news media and concerned citizens' groups.

To begin with records kept by government offices, just because many records are generically termed "public" does not necessarily mean "open to inspection by the public or press." The old common law (judge-made) definition of public record is something like this: A written memorial by an authorized public officer in discharge of a legal duty to make a record of something written, said, or done.[43]

So, the word "public" does not imply a general right of inspection. In the statutes, furthermore, various qualifications in the public's right to inspect "public records" exist: [44]

> Some documents which constitute public records un-
> der * * * an open records statute have been exempted
> from disclosure. There may be available to specified indi-
> viduals [e.g. licensing examination data available only to
> the individual examined, or reports of mental examina-
> tions of school children available only to their parents.]
> * * * Not all state-affiliated organizations will meet the
> definition of "agency" within an open records act [e.g.,
> consulting firms and quasi-public corporations are fre-
> quently outside the terms of an open records act.]

All the states have certain statutes specifically providing for secrecy. One example is a provision in income tax laws mandating that individual income tax returns be protected from disclosure. Frequent exemptions appearing in state open records laws have much the same character as the exemptions in the Federal Freedom of Information Act (discussed earlier at page 632), including person-nel or medical information, intra- or inter-agency memoranda, preliminary draft documents, and trade secrets. Most if not all states also exempt from disclosure a variety of health department records, juvenile and adoption records, licensing examination data, and public assistance or welfare records.

Modern statute-based open records law contains a major im-provement over the old common-law right of inspection. At com-mon law, the right to inspect public records ordinarily depended upon a citizen's having a proper purpose in seeing or copying the record. Relatively few statutes include such a provision. Some states—e.g. Louisiana, Tennessee, Texas—have statutes providing that record custodians may not inquire into a record applicant's

---

[43] Amos v. Gunn, 84 Fla. 285, 94 So. 615, 616 (1922).

[44] Henrick, p. 1112. A qualified right of inspection does exist under common law. Harold L. Cross, The Public's Right to Know (New York: Columbia University Press, 1953), pp. xiii–xiv.

motives.[45]

Opening the Records

Most state open records laws provide legal instruments for the record-seeker to use in trying to overcome denial of access. Usually, the record-seeker may apply to a court for an order to disclose (which may take several forms, such as an injunction against secrecy or a writ of mandamus ordering disclosure). In a number of states, denial of access to a record may be appealed to a state's attorney general, and, in Connecticut and New York, to a special, statutorily established, freedom of information review group. Penalties for illegal denial of access are provided in many statutes, ranging from the rare removal from office or impeachment to the more common fine and/or imprisonment.[46]

Personnel information is often difficult to obtain, and that difficulty is often linked to claims of "privacy." Even when such claims to privacy are not well-founded, smoking out newsworthy records may take major effort and expenditure. For example, a New York court at first upheld Monroe County in denying a Gannett Company newspaper's request for personnel information. Gannett had asked for the names, titles and salaries of 276 Monroe County employees laid off because of budget cuts. The county's regulations provided that each of its agencies should make such information on every officer or employee available to the news media.

In upholding denial of the request, a court held that the 276 fired individuals were no longer public employees but had become private citizens, and that disclosure of information about them would invade their privacy in a damaging way. A New York appellate court, however, approved Gannett's request for information, saying that the information about the laid off employees was not of a personal nature and that any hardship from disclosure had not been documented.[47]

Police Records

Police records are among the most important in all of government, yet rules of states and municipalities about disclosing such records vary tremendously. If citizens and reporters cannot get access to the "blotter" (the police calls log) and the arrest ("booking") log and the jail log on a constant and continuous basis, the possibility of abuse of citizens' rights may tend to become a

---

[45] Ibid., p. 1131, 1163–1196. See also Anon., "Government Information and the Rights of Citizens," 73 Mich.L.Rev. 971, at 1179 (1975).

[46] Ibid., pp. 1135–36.

[47] Gannett Co. v. Monroe County, 59 A.D.2d 309, 399 N.Y.S.2d 534, at 536 (1977), overruling 90 Misc.2d 76, 393 N.Y.S.2d 676 (1977).

probability. According to yet another useful survey by the Reporters Committee on Freedom of the Press, most states have laws allowing sealing of investigatory files.[48] And in some states—as in Alabama, Georgia, Mississippi, Montana and New Mexico (among others)—state statutes are silent about access to law enforcement records.[49]

Just because a state does not spell out access to law enforcement records in statutory form, that does not mean that reporters or citizens are without remedy. Sometimes getting access to law enforcement records will take a willingness to sue under an open records statute—or, on a common law basis if no such statute applies—to try to get the records. Practical reporters will tell you, however, that developing a good working relationship with police probably is as valuable an avenue to access to their records as is reliance on statutes or courts to enforce access.

Access to Campus Police Records

Many colleges and universities in the United States, said to be educating the young for democracy, have unfortunate histories where openness of campus police records is concerned. Part of the problem, in recent years, has been the United States Department of Education, which was threatening universities with loss of federal funding if they violated student privacy by releasing "educational records." Strangely, the Department of Education functionaries argued that campus police incident reports were "educational records" under the Family Educational Rights and Privacy Act ("FERPA").

The issue gained national notoriety in 1989 when Traci Bauer, a campus newspaper editor at Southwest Missouri State University (SMSU) claimed that she was entitled to SMSU Security Office incident reports.

Ultimately, Ms. Bauer sued Paul Kincaid, SMSU's director of university relations, seeking release of SMSU security office records. Triggering the controversy was Ms. Bauer's request to see an incident report about a rape involving a student athlete.[50]

In July, 1989, Kincaid had distributed a policy statement ordering the withholding of SMSU Security Office records, including the verbatim "incident" reports. The SMSU campus is located within the jurisdiction of the Springfield, Mo., police force.

---

[48] A Guide to Police Records, News Media & the Law, following page 20, Summer, 1987.

[49] Ibid. See also Justin D. Franklin and Robert E. Bouchard, Guide to the Freedom of Information and Privacy Acts, 2nd ed. (New York: Clark Boardman, updated 1990). Contains texts of state open records laws.

[50] Bauer v. Kincaid, 759 F.Supp. 575 (W.D.Mo.1991).

Ms. Bauer's suit claimed that she was entitled to the SMSU incident reports, and that those reports—which were to be filed with the Springfield police by the campus Security Office—were sometimes delayed. She charged that this meant that the Springfield police thus were unable, at times, to investigate on-campus crime promptly. She sought access to the SMSU records under the Missouri Open Records or "Sunshine" Act.

SMSU Officials, whether using the Department of Education edict as an excuse or a reason, expressed fear of losing federal funding if the "incident reports" were released to the public and press contrary to the U.S. Department of Education's (DOE) understanding of FERPA. The DOE had urged campus officials to keep confidential police incident reports as "educational records," all in the name of privacy.[51]

U.S. District Judge Russell G. Clark, however, found that there was credible testimony that " * * * in the past SMSU has concealed or destroyed evidence of contraband and failed or refused to release selected criminal investigation and incident reports concerning sex offenses, student athletes, and university personnel." [52]   In addition, Judge Clark noted credible testimony from Mark Goodman, President of the Student Press Law Center, that no federal funds actually had been withheld as the result of disclosure of police information or incident reports.

The judge noted, however, that the U.S. Department of Education had issued warnings to some schools, and that all schools that had been issued warnings voluntarily fell into compliance with the DOE's interpretation of FERPA.

In sum, Judge Clark ruled that campus crime records were not "educational records," and thus could not be withheld under FERPA.[53]

> [T]his Court concludes that defendants' actions in withholding the criminal investigation and incident reports which contain names and other personally identifiable information, is unconstitutional under the equal protection. Judge Clark concluded that the criminal investigation and incident reports of SMSU are not exempt from disclosure under Missouri's Sunshine Law.

Evidently intent on making FERPA into a campus secrets act, the U.S. Department of Education was slow to comply with Judge Clark's ruling. As a result, the SPLC and student editors from the University of Tennessee and the University of Colorado sought—

[51] Ibid., p. 5; Sec. 610.25 of the Missouri Revised Statutes.

[52] Ibid., p. 11.

[53] Ibid., pp. 47–48.

and were granted—an injunction to prevent the Department of Education from interfering with the release of campus crime reports.[54]

But obviously, it is the most troublesome or "sensitive" incidents (e.g. rape allegations against a star athlete, sexual harassment by professors, or some breach of law by an administrator) that tend to stir the human impulse to conceal damaging information. The trouble with "just a little secrecy"—whether on campus or elsewhere—is that what is hidden is likely to be precisely what society needs most to know.

Access to Disaster Scenes

When disasters happen—when airplanes fall from the sky or when industrial plants explode—that may be bad news but it is *news*. Reporters and photographers need to get to the news scene to report, yet police officials and rescue workers argue that they don't need members of the media getting in the way or exposing themselves to danger.

A Milwaukee plane crash provided a case in point. At 3:30 p.m. on September 6, 1985, Midwest Airlines Flight 105 crashed in the City of Oak Creek just after takeoff from Milwaukee's General Mitchell Field.

Just after the crash, a Milwaukee County sheriff's department lieutenant in charge of airport security ordered the crash scene secured. Only emergency personnel and equipment were allowed near the crash site. Roadblocks were set up.

An unmarked sedan carrying four employees of Milwaukee station WTMJ–TV rolled through the roadblock, following an emergency vehicle down the only road providing access to the crash site. A detective left his post at the roadblock and pursued the sedan. When he caught up to the vehicle, the WTMJ–TV employees, including Peter Ah King, were getting cameras out of the trunk. The detective told the four news people they were in a restricted area and would have to leave. One individual then asked if three of the TV news people—excluding the driver—could walk back along the road to the non-restricted area and began to do so.[55]

Cameraman Peter Ah King then left the others, jumped a fence bearing "No Trespassing" signs, and ran to a low hill where he took pictures of the crash site. The detective then ordered Ah King

---

[54] "Judge Orders Release of Campus Crime Reports," The New York Times, March 15, 1991, p. B9, on decision in Student Press Law Center, Lyn D. Schrotgerber (CO), Sam G. Cristy and James C. Brewer, Jr. (TN) v. Lamar Alexander, U.S. Sec. of Education.

[55] City of Oak Creek v. Peter Ah King, 148 Wis.2d 532, 436 N.W.2d 285, 286–287 (1989).

to leave; Ah King replied that he would not leave unless he was arrested. Ah King was then arrested on suspicion of disorderly conduct. He was charged under a disorderly conduct statute which says: [56]

> *Disorderly conduct.* Whoever, in a public or private place, engages in violent, abusive, profane, boisterous, unreasonably loud or otherwise disorderly conduct under circumstances in which the conduct tends to cause or provoke a disturbance in guilty of a Class B misdemeanor.

Because Ah King's conduct was not of the kind listed by the statute, one question in appellate review of the case was whether the statute's catch-all phrase ("or otherwise disorderly conduct") would sustain the conviction of the cameraman.

Writing for the Wisconsin Supreme Court, Justice Louis J. Ceci cited the 1972 U.S. Supreme Court decision in Branzburg v. Hayes: [57]

> "Newsmen have no constitutional right of access to the scenes of crime or disaster when the general public is excluded * * * ""Despite the fact that news gathering may be hampered, the press is regularly excluded from grand jury proceedings, our own [the U.S. Supreme Court's] conferences, the meetings of other official bodies gathered in executive session, and the meetings of private organizations."

In addition, Justice Ceci denied that Richmond Newspapers v. Virginia (1980), a case speaking of the right of the public to attend courtroom proceedings, was inapplicable to the air crash situation under consideration.[58] Further,

> [o]ur interpretation of * * * [relevant] Supreme Court cases leads us to the conclusion that under the first amendment, the appellant has an undoubted right to gather news from any source by means within the law. However, the appellant does not have a first amendment right of access solely because he is a news gatherer, to the scene of this airplane crash when the public reasonably has been excluded.

Justice Ceci said that while Ah King was disobeying the detective's order and entering a restricted area, other news gatherers were meeting in the airport director's office in line with the rules set out in the General Mitchell Field Media Guide. (That guide

[56] Ibid., pp. 1274–1275.

[57] Ibid., pp. 292–293, quoting Branzburg v. Hayes, 408 U.S. 665, 684–685, 92 S.Ct. 2646, 2658–2659 (1972).

[58] Ibid., p. 293.

states that " 'no representative of the media will be permitted to enter non-public/restricted areas of the airport without an authorized escort.' ")

The crash occurred at 3:30 p.m., and at 4:30 p.m. the airport director held a 15–minute briefing, then taking media representatives to the crash site to photograph or film the scene.

Justice Ceci concluded with some caustic remarks to underscore his holding that the disorderly conduct ordinance was not unconstitutionally vague as applied to cameraman Peter Ah King. Further, he declared that Ah King as a news gatherer had no special First Amendment rights of access to the scene of the airplane crash beyond the general public's right of access. Justice Ceci declared that [59]

> * * * the needs and rights of the injured and dying should be recognized by this court as having preference over newly created "rights" that the dissenting justices would give to a "news gatherer" who is simply trying to beat out his competition and make his employer's deadline.

In dissent, Wisconsin Supreme Court Justice Shirley Abrahamson, joined by Justices Nathan A. Heffernan and William A. Bablitch, wrote that Peter Ah King did not interfere with or obstruct emergency personnel. That said, she concluded: [T]he court can and should take into consideration the media's role as the "eyes and ears" of the public at large.[60]

[59] Ibid., pp. 293–294.

[60] Ibid., p. 297.

Chapter 15

LEGAL PROBLEMS IN REPORTING COURTS

SEC. 86. ACCESS TO JUDICIAL PROCEEDINGS

In a free society, judicial processes remain open to public view.

"Knock-knock," said the lawyer.

"Who's there?", the citizen asked.

"O.J.," responded the lawyer.

"O.J. Who?"

"You're on the jury."

That wretched joke sums up one problem embedded in the prosecution of football legend-actor-pitchman-broadcaster Orenthal James Simpson, as he went to trial on charges of the knife-slash slayings of his estranged wife, Nicole Brown Simpson, and her friend, sometime male model Ronald Goldman. With the thunderous, unprecedented publicity focused on "O.J.," how could he get a fair trial? How could the judicial apparatus live up to the Sixth Amendment to the Constitution of the United States? That amendment says, in part:

> In all criminal prosecutions, the accused shall enjoy the right to a speedy and public trial, by an impartial jury of the State and district wherein the crime shall have been committed . . .

A number of trials have been called "The Trial of the Century." This time, the outrageously publicized 1995 murder trial of O.J. Simpson may be the real deal. Consider the following details, familiar to and endlessly discussed by millions of Americans: [1]

- On Sunday, June 12, the bodies of Nicole Simpson and Ronald Goldman were found outside her condominium in the Brentwood area of Los Angeles.

- O.J. Simpson, having flown to Chicago the night of the murders, was called back to Los Angeles by police.

- Although under suspicion for the murders, he attended his wife's funeral, walking hand-in-hand with their children.

- Simpson, called by Time magazine "the most famous double-murder suspect in history," remained out of custody because he had promised to turn himself in to authorities. Despite being under obvious suspicion, his fame clearly kept him free while others would have been in custody. Why? Many replied, "We never thought he would run." Simpson's superstar attorney Robert Shapiro told authorities he was at Simpson's home the morning of Friday, June 17, with Simpson and his boyhood friend, Al Cowlings, when police called to say they were coming to arrest Simpson. O.J. and Cowlings then disappeared.

- Simpson's arrest on suspicion of murder was accomplished only after a surreal Friday evening (June 17) low-speed "chase" seen nation-wide thanks to video images provide from hovering helicopters. This two-hour ride covered 50 miles of the Los Angeles freeway system, with perhaps a dozen police vehicles, lights flashing, providing an escort while much of the nation watched. Simpson's friend, former teammate Cowlings, was at the wheel of his white Ford Bronco, pleading with police to stay back while a presumably suicidal Simpson crouched low in the back of the truck, clutching a telephone, a pistol, and pictures of his children.

- Simpson was the cover-story for both Newsweek and Time on June 27, and clearly was the biggest story of 1994, getting far more ink and air time than the invasion/occupation of Haiti.

---

[1] See, e.g., "He Could Run ... But He Couldn't Hide," Newsweek, June 27, 1994, pp. 15–26; Nancy Gibbs, "End of the Run," Time, June 27, 1994, pp. 29–35 (This issue featured a retouched cover photo making Simpson look darker and more ominous, drawing protests from civil rights groups and an apology from the magazine.); Associated Press coverage for June 18, 1994, as in The Knoxville News–Sentinel, "O.J. Simpson leads police on dramatic journey home," pp. A1, A8; Walter Goodman, "Television, Meet Life, Meet TV," The New York Times, Sunday, June 19, 1994, Sec. 4, pp. 1, 6; Mike Jensen, reporting on NBC's Today Show, Sept. 30, 1994; Gale Holland and Haya El Nasser, "Bedlam at Camp O.J.," USA TODAY, Sept. 27, 1994, p. 3A.], and Kenneth Noble, "Victim's Sister Denounces Halloween Masks," The New York Times, Oct. 18, 1994, p. A13.

- High-profile attorneys involved in the prosecution and defense and the youthful Judge Lance Ito all became national and international media celebrities. Judge Ito struggled with torrents of leaks and rumors, threatening to end TV coverage of the hearings, then relenting.

- The context became increasingly garish. By September, 1994, paperback books selling hundreds of thousands of copies showed up in supermarkets nationwide. O.J. Simpson crime wristwatches were being sold, and NBC's Mike Jensen reported that his name had been registered as a trademark—after the killings of Nicole Simpson and Ronald Goldman. Playboy was peddling an O.J. Simpson exercise video which it had rushed into production. CNN advertised CD–ROMS on the Simpson case for those who needed even more details. And Denise Brown, sister of Nicole Brown Simpson, complained bitterly about profiteers selling Halloween masks depicting both O.J. and Nicole Simpson.

- At least 75 news organizations had employees attending-or trying to get into pre-trial hearings, and scaffolding of wood and steel rose four and five stories in a parking lot across from the court-house to provide perches for TV cameras and reporters. A 45–foot tower carried the banner, "Brokaw's Butte:" NBC anchor Tom Brokaw would do part of the evening news from that aerie. And the cluttered parking lot? It came to be known as "Camp O.J."

It was apparent late in 1994 that covering notorious criminal trials had entered new territory with the carnival-cum-computer game atmosphere accompanying the O.J. Simpson trial. Struggles to deal with prejudicial publicity in famous cases of yesteryear—the Sheppard case, for example—now seem almost quaint by comparison trial. But if there are solutions to dealing with media/multimedia event criminal trials, they must not include secret justice or closed courtrooms. American liberties are too hard-won.

Somehow, despite the media circus and the posturing by attorneys, Judge Ito would have to try to guarantee that Simpson's right to a fair trial would be honored. That was a tough assignment, with multiple leaks and charges and counter-charges about police misconduct and questionable evidence. And what about finding an impartial jury? With a long trial likely, and with the probable sequestering (locking up) the jury for long periods, would anyone be willing to serve? As it turned out, some people actually wanted to be jurors, perhaps because they hoped do to sell their stories.[2]

---

[2] The Associated Press, "Partisans, opportunists threats in Simpson jury selection," in Knoxville News–Sentinel, Sept. 26, 1994, p.A1.

Before jury selection actually began, Judge Ito—angered at a premature if not false report that DNA tests showed Nicole Simpson's blood on socks found in O.J. Simpson's home—threatened to halt electronic coverage, or at least coverage by the offending station, KNBC–TV of Los Angeles. At the same time, Court TV founder Stephen Brill said he thought Judge Ito's threats applied only to KNBC–TV. Court TV, in fact, gave Judge Ito a forum to denounce coverage he considered prejudicial.[3]

As jury selection started, Judge Ito allowed only three pool reporters to be present for the questioning of jury panel members: Andrea Ford of The Los Angeles Times, CNN correspondent Greg La Motte, and Linda Deutsch of The Associated Press.[4] Judges, as will be discussed later in this chapter, are within their rights in banning electronic media coverage from trials. On the other hand, Supreme Court interpretations of the First Amendment indicate that a judge could not bar the public—including reporters——from seeing and reporting on jury selection and the trial.

Given the bloody English heritage of secret Star Chamber trials, secret court proceedings are very much against the American grain. Even so, as recently as 1979, the Supreme Court of the United States—with an eye to protecting the rights of defendants in criminal trials—touched off a firestorm of protests from journalists and civil libertarians by suggesting that in some instances, pretrial hearings (and even trials themselves) could be shut away from public view. That this case was largely shot down by the Supreme Court a year later is of some consolation, true.[5] Even so, it is astonishing that the nation's highest court—as recently as 1979—could in effect call into question the basic right to see and report on the criminal justice process.

SEC. 87. FREE PRESS *VERSUS* FAIR TRIAL

Attorneys, judges and members of the press continue to try to settle long-standing issues in the "free press—fair trial" dispute.

Back in the 1960s, "trial by newspaper" or "trial by mass media" were phrases which were often heard as the bar-press controversy steamed up. Some attorneys blamed the mass media for many of the shortcomings of the American court system.[6] In

[3] David Margolick, "Simpson Judge's Ambiguous Threat," The New York Times, Sept. 24, 1994, p. 7.]

[4] Holland and El Nasser, op. cit.

[5] See Richmond Newspapers v. Virginia, 448 U.S. 555, 100 S.Ct. 2814 (1980).

[6] See, e.g., Advisory Committee on Fair Trial and Free Press, Standards Relating to Fair Trial and Free Press (New York, 1966); see also draft approved Feb. 19,

reply, many journalists went to great lengths in trying to justify questionable actions of the news media in covering criminal trials.[7]

Many of the lawyers' arguments contained the assertion that the media were destroying the rights of defendants by publicizing cases before they got to court.[8] Such publicity, it was said, prejudiced potential jurors to such an extent that a fair trial was not possible. Editors and publishers—and some attorneys, too—retorted that the media were not harmful, and contended with passion if not historical accuracy that the First Amendment's free press guarantees took precedence over other Constitutional provisions, including the Sixth Amendment.[9]

What about prejudicing jurors by media accounts? More than 100 years ago, Mark Twain questioned whether an impartial—in the sense of know-nothing—jury was not a perversion of justice. He wrote that the first 26 graves in Virginia City, Nevada, were occupied by murdered men, and their murderers were never punished.

Twain asserted that when Alfred the Great invented trial by jury, news could not travel fast. Therefore, he could easily find a jury of honest, intelligent men who had not heard of the case they were to try. Mark Twain swore that with newspapers and the telegraph, the jury system "compels us to swear in juries composed of fools and rascals, because the system rigidly excludes honest men and men of brains." [10]

Actually, Mark Twain had the history of the jury system wrong. The jury began in 11th Century England, utilizing a defendant's neighbors who were called to serve both as witnesses and as arbiters of fact. It was not until several centuries later that juries stopped serving as witnesses and served only as triers of fact. In addition, Twain's 19th Century exaggeration does not apply to jury selection procedures in the last quarter of the 20th Century. Jurors need not be absolutely ignorant of—or completely unbiased about—a case which is to go to trial. If jurors can set aside their prejudices and biases, and keep an open mind, that is sufficient.[11]

1968, by delegates to the American Bar Association convention as published in March, 1968.

[7] See, e.g., American Newspaper Publishers Association, Free Press and Fair Trial (New York): American Newspaper Publishers Association, 1967, p. 1 and passim.

[8] See footnote 3, above.

[9] American Newspaper Publishers Association, op. cit., p. 1.

[10] Mark Twain, Roughing It (New York: New American Library, Signet Paperback, 1962) pp. 256–257.

[11] Rita J. Simon, The Jury: Its Role in American Society (Lexington, Mass. D.C. Health and Company, 1980), p. 5; Murphy v. Florida, 421 U.S. 794, 95 S.Ct. 2031 (1975).

During the past four decades, the free press-fair trial controversy took place against a backdrop of several sensational, nationally publicized trials and the assassinations of President John F. Kennedy in 1963 and Senator Robert Kennedy and Martin Luther King in 1968.   Resultant disputes arrayed the media's right to report against defendants' rights to a fair trial, generated new law in the form of several important Supreme Court decisions, and brought forth efforts to make rules to regularize dealings between the media and law enforcement officials.[12]

The assassination of President Kennedy brought problems of "trial by mass media" dramatically to public consciousness.   That fact was underscored by the report of a Presidential Commission headed by Chief Justice Earl Warren.   The Warren Commission was intensely critical of both the Dallas police and the news media for the reports of the news of that event.   The accused assassin, Lee Harvey Oswald, never lived to stand trial, because he himself was assassinated by Jack Ruby in a hallway of Dallas police headquarters.   The hallway was a scene of confusion, clogged with reporters, cameramen, and the curious.[13]

The month after Kennedy's slaying, the American Bar Association charged that "widespread publicizing of Lee Harvey Oswald's alleged guilt, involving statements by officials and public disclosures of the details of 'evidence' would have made it extremely difficult to impanel an unprejudiced jury and afford the accused a fair trial."[14]   Indeed, had Oswald survived to stand trial, he might not have been convicted.   This was so even though the Warren Commission—after the fact—declared that Oswald was in all likelihood Kennedy's killer.   Under American judicial procedures, it seems possible that Oswald could not have received a fair and unprejudiced trial, and that any conviction of him might have been upset on appeal.[15]

The Warren Commission placed first blame on police and prosecutors, but additionally criticized the media for their part in the events following the President's death.   The Commission said that "part of the responsibility for the unfortunate circumstances following the President's death must be borne by the news media * * *."   Journalists were excoriated by Commission members for showing a lack of self-discipline, and a code of professional conduct

[12] See Advisory Committee on Fair Trial and Free Press, op. cit., passim; see also Irvin v. Dowd, 366 U.S. 717, 81 S.Ct. 1639 (1961); Rideau v. Louisiana, 373 U.S. 723, 83 S.Ct. 1417 (1963); Sheppard v. Maxwell, 384 U.S. 333, 86 S.Ct. 1507 (1966).

[13] Report of the President's Commission on the Assassination of President John F. Kennedy (Washington: Government Printing Office, 1964), p. 241.

[14] William A. Hachten, The Supreme Court on Freedom of the Press: Decisions and Dissents (Ames, Iowa: Iowa State University Press, 1968), p. 106.

[15] Ibid.

was called for as evidence that the press was willing to support the Sixth Amendment right to a fair and impartial trial as well as the right of the public to be informed.[16]

If the reporters behaved badly in Dallas, so did the Dallas law enforcement officials, who displayed "evidence" in crowded corridors and released statements about other evidence. Conduct of police and other law enforcement officials, however, has by no means been the only source of prejudicial materials which later appeared in the press to the detriment of defendants' rights. All too often, both defense and prosecution attorneys have released statements to reporters which were clearly at odds with the American Bar Association's Canons of Professional Ethics. Canon 20, adopted more than 50 years earlier, advised lawyers to avoid statements to the press which might prejudice the administration of justice or interfere with a fair trial. In any case, lawyers were not to go beyond quotation from the records and papers on file in courts in making statements about litigation.[17]

Canon 20, in theory, could be used as a weapon to punish lawyers who released statements to the press which harmed a defendant's chances for a fair trial. Although this Canon was adopted by the bar associations of most states, there was rarely a case brought to disbar or discipline an attorney or judge who made prejudicial remarks to the press.[18]

The ABA's Code of Professional Responsibility—which superseded the old ABA Canons—outlined standards of trial conduct for attorneys. Disciplinary Rule DR 7–107 dealt with "Trial Publicity." It says that lawyers who are involved in a criminal matter shall not make "extra-judicial statements" to the news media which go beyond unadorned factual statements.

In 1991, however, the ABA adopted new Standards for Criminal Justice dealing with out-of-court statements by attorneys. If a state or a court jurisdiction accepts these new standards, they will become mandatory in that region.

Lawyers, again, are allowed to make general statements outside of court about "the general nature of the charges against the accused." This approach is new, according to The News Media & The Law, in that it makes it possible for defense lawyers to try to counterbalance harmful pre-trial publicity against their clients.

---

[16] Report of the President's Commission on the Assassination of President John F. Kennedy, p. 241.

[17] Canons of Professional and Judicial Ethics of the American Bar Association, Canon 20.

[18] Donald M. Gillmor, Free Press and Fair Trial (Washington, D.C., Public Affairs Press, 1966) p. 110.

Lawyers, however, must refrain from making statements which are substantially likely to prejudice a criminal proceeding.

Other language of the ABA's 1991 Fair Trial–Free Press rules may have the potential to make it easier to close pre-trial proceedings, changing the suggested standard for closure to "substantial likelihood of harm" from the harder to demonstrate "clear and present danger." Also, the ABA weakened its previous strictures against using the contempt power to punish lawyers who violate a judge's restrictive order by talking to the press.[19]

Reporters are not the only offenders in disrupting trials. A quick skimming of the General Index of a legal encyclopedia, *American Jurisprudence,* adds support for such a generalization. The General Index of "Amjur" contains nearly 1,000 categories under the topic, "New Trial." New trials may be granted because something went awry in the original trial, somehow depriving a defendant of the right to a fair trial under the Sixth Amendment. These categories include such things as persons fainting in the courtroom, hissing, technical mistakes by attorneys, prejudice of judges, and misconduct by jurors: Jurors who read newspapers.[20]

Findings of social scientists lend modest support to assumptions about jurors being prejudiced by the mass media.[21] Much more research, however, remains to be done before assertions can be made confidently that what a juror reads or learns from the mass media will affect the juror's subsequent behavior. On the other hand, it has been argued that lawyers, before casting aspersions at the press, might consider the question of whether their own legal house is in order. Consider what psychologists can tell lawyers about a fair trial. Consider the rules of procedure in a criminal trial in many states as attorneys make their final arguments to a jury. First, the prosecution sums up its case. Then the defense attorney makes the final argument. And last, the prosecuting attorney makes the final statement to the jury. For years, psychologists have been arguing about order of presentation in persuasion. Some evidence has been found that having the first say is most persuasive; there is other evidence that having the last word might be best.[22] But in many jurisdictions, who gets neither

---

[19] American Bar Association, Code of Professional Responsibility and Code of Judicial Conduct (Chicago, ABA, 1976) p. 37C, ABA 1991 Fair Trial–Free Press Rules; see News Media & The Law, Spring, 1991, p. 22.

[20] 3 American Jurisprudence, Gen.Index, New Trial.

[21] See, e.g., Mary Dee Tans and Steven H. Chaffee, "Pretrial Publicity and Juror Prejudice," Journalism Quarterly Vol. 43:4 (Winter, 1966) pp. 647–654, and a list of juror prejudice studies on p. 647, notes 4, 5 and 6. But see Don R. Pember, "Does Pretrial Publicity Really Hurt?" Columbia Journalism Review, Sept./Oct. 1984, p. 16.

[22] See, e.g., Carl I. Hovland, et al., The Order of Presentation in Persuasion, (New Haven: Yale, 1957) passim.

the first say nor the last word during the final arguments before a jury? The defendant.[23]

SEC. 88.   PRE–TRIAL PUBLICITY

Pre-trial publicity which makes it difficult—if not impossible—for a defendant to receive a fair trial was summed up in the Supreme Court cases of Irvin v. Dowd (1961) and Rideau v. Louisiana (1963).

"Pre-trial publicity" is a phrase which is a kind of shorthand expression meaning strain between the press and the courts. The kind of publicity which "tries" a defendant in print or over the air before the real courthouse trial starts—that's the issue here. This section discusses two classic instances of pre-trial publicity, instances in which the news media did not cover themselves with glory: Irvin v. Dowd and Rideau v. Louisiana.

Irvin v. Dowd (1961)

The Irvin case represents the first time that the Supreme Court overturned a state criminal conviction because publicity before the trial had prevented a fair trial before an impartial jury.[24]

The defendant in this murder case, Leslie Irvin, was subjected to a barrage of prejudicial news items in the hysterical wake of six murders which had been committed in the vicinity of Evansville, Indiana. Two of the murders were committed in December, 1954, and four in March, 1955. These crimes were covered extensively by news media in the locality, and created great agitation in Vanderburgh County, where Evansville is located, and in adjoining Gibson County.[25]

Leslie Irvin, a parolee, was arrested in April, 1955, on suspicion of burglary and writing bad checks. Within a few days, the Evansville police and the Vanderburgh County prosecutor issued press releases asserting that "Mad Dog Irvin" had confessed to all six murders, including three members of one family. The news media had what can conservatively be described as a field day with the Irvin case, and were aided in this by law enforcement officials. Many of the accounts published or broadcast before Irvin's trial referred to him as the "confessed slayer of six." Irvin's court-appointed attorney was quoted as saying he had received much criticism for representing Irvin. The media, by way of excusing the

---

[23] The authors are grateful to Professors Jack M. McLeod and Steven H. Chaffee, of the University of Wisconsin Mass Communications Research Center and Stanford University, respectively for this insight.

[24] Gillmor, op. cit., pp. 116–117.

[25] Irvin v. Dowd, 366 U.S. 717, 719, 81 S.Ct. 1639, 1641 (1961).

attorney, noted that he faced disbarment if he refused to represent the suspect.[26]

Irvin was soon indicted by the Vanderburgh County Grand Jury for one of the six murders. Irvin's court-appointed counsel sought—and was granted—a change of venue. However, the venue change, under Indiana law, was made only from Vanderburgh County to adjoining Gibson County, which had received similar prejudicial accounts about "Mad Dog Irvin" from the news media in the Evansville vicinity.[27]

The trial began in November of 1955. Of 430 prospective jurors examined by the prosecution and defense attorneys, 370— nearly 90 per cent—had formed some opinion about Irvin's guilt. These opinions ranged from mere suspicion to absolute certainty.[28] Irvin's attorney had used up all of his 20 peremptory challenges. When 12 jurors were finally seated by the court, the attorney then unsuccessfully challenged all jurors on grounds that they were biased. He complained bitterly that four of the seated jurors had stated that Irvin was guilty.[29] Even so, the trial was held, Irvin was found guilty, and the jury sentenced him to death. Irvin's conviction was upheld by the Indiana Supreme Court, which denied his motions for a new trial.[30] Lengthy appeals brought Irvin's case to the Supreme Court of the United States twice,[31] but his case was not decided on its merits by the nation's highest court until 1961.

Then, in 1961, all nine members of the Supreme Court agreed that Irvin had not received a fair trial. The upshot of this was that Irvin received a new trial, although he was ultimately convicted. This time, however, his sentence was set at life imprisonment.[32]

In his majority opinion, Justice Tom C. Clark—a former attorney general of the United States—concentrated on the effect of prejudicial publicity on a defendant's rights. Clark noted that courts do not require that jurors be totally ignorant of the facts and

[26] 366 U.S. 717, 725–726, 81 S.Ct. 1639, 1641, 1645 (1961); Gillmor, op. cit., p. 11.

[27] 366 U.S. 717, 720, 81 S.Ct. 1639, 1641 (1961).

[28] 366 U.S. 717, 727, 81 S.Ct. 1639, 1945 (1961).

[29] 359 U.S. 394, 398, 79 S.Ct. 825, 828 (1959).

[30] Irvin v. State, 236 Ind. 384, 139 N.E.2d 898 (1957).

[31] Irvin's appeal for a writ of *habeas corpus* to a Federal District Court was denied on the basis that he had not exhausted his opportunities to appeal through the Indiana courts. 153 F.Supp. 531 (N.D.Ind.1957). A United States Court of Appeals affirmed the dismissal of the writ, 251 F.2d 548 (7th Cir.1958). In a 5–4 decision in 1959, the Supreme Court of the United States sent Irvin's case back to the Federal Court of Appeals for reconsideration. 359 U.S. 394, 79 S.Ct. 825 (1959). The Court of Appeals again refused to grant a writ of *habeas corpus* to Irvin, 271 F.2d 552 (7th Cir.1959). Irvin's case was then appealed to the Supreme Court for the second time.

[32] Gillmor, op. cit., pp. 11–12.

issues involved in a criminal trial. It is sufficient if a juror can render a verdict based on the evidence presented in court.[33]

Justice Clark then considered the publicity Irvin had received, and concluded: "Here the build-up of prejudice is clear and convincing." He noted that arguments for Irvin presented evidence that "a barrage of newspaper headlines, articles, cartoons and pictures was unleashed against him during the six or seven months before his trial" in Gibson County, Indiana. Furthermore, "Evansville radio and TV stations, which likewise blanketed the county, also carried extensive newscasts covering the same incidents." [34]

In a concurring opinion, Justice Frankfurter unleashed a bitter denunciation of "trial by newspapers instead of trial in court before a jury." He stated that the Irvin case was not an isolated incident or an atypical miscarriage of justice. Frankfurter wrote: [35]

> Not a term passes without this Court being importuned to review convictions, had in States throughout the country, in which substantial claims are made that a jury trial has been distorted because of inflammatory newspaper accounts—too often, as in this case, with the prosecutor's collaboration—exerting pressures upon potential jurors before trial and even during the course of trial * * *.

Trial by Television: Rideau v. Louisiana (1963)

If Leslie Irvin was mistreated primarily by newspapers during the period before his trial, Wilbert Rideau found that television was the major offender in interfering with his right to a fair trial. Early in 1961, a Lake Charles, La., bank was robbed. The robber kidnaped three of the bank's employees and killed one of them. Several hours later, Wilbert Rideau was arrested by police and held in the Calcasieu Parish jail in Lake Charles. The next morning, a moving picture—complete with a sound track—was made of a 20–minute "interview" between Rideau and the Sheriff of Calcasieu Parish. The Sheriff interrogated the prisoner and elicited admissions that Rideau had committed the bank robbery, the kidnaping, and the murder. Later in the day, this filmed interview was broadcast over television station KLPC in Lake Charles. Over three days' time, the film was televised on three occasions to an estimated total audience of 97,000 persons, as compared to the approximately 150,000 persons then living in Calcasieu Parish.[36]

Rideau's attorneys subsequently sought a change of venue away from Calcasieu Parish. It was argued that it would take away

[33] Irvin v. Dowd, 366 U.S. 717, 723, 81 S.Ct. 1639, 1642–1643 (1961).

[34] 366 U.S. 717, 728, 81 S.Ct. 1939, 1645 (1961).

[35] 366 U.S. 717, 730, 81 S.Ct. 1639, 1646–1647 (1961).

[36] Rideau v. Louisiana, 373 U.S. 723, 724, 83 S.Ct. 1417, 1419 (1963).

Rideau's right to a fair trial if he were tried there after the three television broadcasts of Rideau's "interview" with the sheriff. The motion for change of venue was denied, and Rideau was convicted and sentenced to death on the murder charge in the Calcasieu Parish trial court. The conviction was affirmed by the Louisiana Supreme Court,[37] but the Supreme Court of the United States granted *certiorari*.[38]

Justice Potter Stewart's majority opinion noted that three of the 12 jurors had stated during *voir dire* examination before the trial that they had seen and heard Rideau's "interview" with the Sheriff. Also, two members of the jury were Calcasieu Parish deputy sheriffs. Although Rideau's attorney challenged the deputies, asking that they be removed "for cause," the trial judge denied this request. Since Rideau's lawyers had exhausted his "peremptory challenges"—those for which no reason need be given—the deputies remained on the jury.[39]

Justice Stewart noted that the *Rideau* case did not involve physical brutality. However, he declared that the "kangaroo court proceedings in this case involved a more subtle but no less real deprivation of due process of law." Justice Stewart added:[40]

> . . . In this case the people of Calcasieu Parish saw and heard, not once but three times, a "trial" of Rideau in a jail, presided over by a sheriff, where there was no lawyer to advise Rideau of his right to stand mute.

Rideau's conviction was reversed, and a new trial was ordered by the Supreme Court. He was convicted again, sentenced to life imprisonment, and became well known again, this time as a journalist writing about prison conditions from inside the walls.

SEC. 89. PUBLICITY DURING TRIAL: CAMERAS IN THE COURTROOM

The notorious Lindbergh kidnaping trial of the 1930s and the Estes case of 1965 severely limited still and television cameras in the courtroom. Cameras are returning now in many states, under the Supreme Court's 1981 decision in Chandler v. Florida.

"The Lindbergh Case" and "the trial of Bruno Hauptmann" are phrases heard whenever the free press—fair trial debate heats up. These phrases, of course, refer to the kidnaping in 1932 of the

---

[37] 242 La. 431, 137 So.2d 283 (1962).

[38] 371 U.S. 919, 83 S.Ct. 294 (1962).

[39] 373 U.S. 723, 725, 83 S.Ct. 1417, 1418 (1963).

[40] 373 U.S. 723, 727, 83 S.Ct. 1417, 1419 (1963).

19–month-old son of the aviator famed for the first solo crossing of the Atlantic. The child's kidnaping was front-page news for weeks, long after the child's body was found in a shallow grave not far from the Lindbergh home in New Jersey.

More than two years later, in September, 1934, Bruno Richard Hauptmann was arrested. His trial for the kidnap-murder of the Lindbergh child did not begin until January, 1935. The courtroom where Hauptmann was tried had a press section jammed with 150 reporters. During the Hauptmann trial, which lasted more than a month, there were sometimes more than 700 newsmen in Flemington, N.J., the site of the trial.[41]

Much of the publicity of the Hauptmann trial was prejudicial, and lawyers and newsmen authored statements which were clearly inflammatory. Hauptmann was described in the press, for example, as a "thing lacking in human characteristics." [42] After the trial—and after Hauptmann's execution—a Special Committee on Cooperation Between the Press, Radio, and Bar was established to search for "standards of publicity in judicial proceedings and methods of obtaining an observance of them." In a grim report issued in 1937, the 18–man committee—including lawyers, editors, and publishers—termed Hauptmann's trial "the most spectacular and depressing example of improper publicity and professional misconduct ever presented to the people of the United States in a criminal trial." [43]

One result of the committee's investigation of the Hauptmann trial was the American Bar Association's adoption in 1937 of Canon 35 of its Canons of Professional Ethics. Canon 35 forbade taking photographs in the courtroom, including both actual court sessions and recesses. As updated, Canon 35 declared that broadcasting or televising court proceedings "detract from the essential dignity of the proceedings, distract the participants and witnesses in giving testimony, and create misconceptions * * * and should not be permitted." This was replaced by ABA Canon of Judicial Conduct 3(7): [44]

> A judge should prohibit broadcasting, televising, recording, or taking photographs in the courtroom and areas

[41] John Lofton, Justice and the Press (Boston: Beacon Press, 1966), pp. 103–104.

[42] Lofton, op. cit., p. 124.

[43] American Bar Association, "Report of Special Committee on Cooperation between Press, Radio and Bar," Annual Report, Volume 62, pp. 851–866 (1937), at p. 861. See, also, New Jersey v. Hauptmann, 115 N.J.L. 412, 180 A. 809 (Err. & App.1935), certiorari denied 296 U.S. 649, 56 S.Ct. 310 (1935).

[44] American Bar Association, Code of Professional Responsibility and Code of Judicial Conduct, p. 59C. For Canon 35, see ABA, Annual Report, Vol. 62, at p. 1134; see it as updated by Justice John Marshall Harlan in his concurring opinion in Estes v. Texas, 381 U.S. 532, 601n., 85 S.Ct. 1628, 1669n. (1965).

immediately thereto during sessions of court or recesses between sessions * * *   The only exceptions involved situations when the judge had given permission, or the filming was to be used only for ceremonial or instructional purposes.

Estes v. Texas

Excesses in televising a trial in Texas during the 1960s meant the end of televising virtually all criminal trials for a period of more than a decade.   As is discussed later in this section, however, developments in the late 1970s—capped by the January, 1981 decision of the Supreme Court of the United States in Chandler v. Florida [45]—have seen a substantial movement toward getting both television and still cameras back into state courtrooms.   At this writing, however, federal courtrooms are still off limits.

The crucial case of the 1960s involved the swindling trial of flamboyant Texas financier Billie Sol Estes.   Estes was ultimately convicted, but not until he had received a new trial as a result of the manner in which a judge allowed his original trial to be photographed and televised.   Fallout from the U.S. Supreme Court decision which granted Estes a new trial seemed to rule out cameras in the courtroom.[46]

Estes came before a judicial hearing in Smith County, Texas, in 1962, after a change of venue from Reeves County, some 500 miles west.   The courtroom was packed and about 30 persons stood in the aisles.   A New York Times story described the setting for the pre-trial hearing in this way: [47]

> A television motor van, big as an intercontinental bus, was parked outside the courthouse and the second-floor courtroom was a forest of equipment.   Two television cameras have been set up inside the bar and four more marked cameras were aligned just outside the gates.
>
> * * *
>
> Cables and wires snaked over the floor.

With photographers roaming unchecked about the courtroom, Estes' attorney moved that all cameras be excluded from the courtroom.   As the attorney spoke, a cameraman walked behind the judge's bench and took a picture.[48]

[45] Chandler v. Florida, 449 U.S. 560, 101 S.Ct. 802 (1981).

[46] Estes v. Texas, 381 U.S. 532, 85 S.Ct. 1628 (1965).

[47] Estes v. Texas, 381 U.S. 532, 553, 85 S.Ct. 1628, 1638 (1965), from Chief Justice Warren's concurring opinion, with which Justices Douglas and Goldberg concurred.

[48] 381 U.S. 532, 553, 85 S.Ct. 1628, 1638 (1965).   From concurring opinion by Chief Justice Warren.

After the two-day hearing was completed on September 25, 1962, the judge granted a continuance (delay) to the defense, with the trial to begin on October 22. Meanwhile, the judge established ground rules for television and still photographers. Televising of the trial was allowed, with the exception of live coverage of the interrogation of prospective jurors or the testimony of witnesses. The major television networks, CBS, NBC, and ABC, plus local television station KLTV were each allowed to install one television camera (without sound recording equipment) and film was made available to other television stations on a pooled basis. In addition, through another pool arrangement, only still photographers for the Associated Press, United Press, and from the local newspaper would be permitted in the courtroom.

At its own expense, and with the permission of the court, KLTV built a booth at the back of the courtroom, painted the same color as the courtroom. An opening in the booth permitted all four television cameras to view the proceedings. However, in this small courtroom, the cameras were visible to all.[49]

Despite these limitations the judge placed on television and still photographers, a majority of the Supreme Court held that Estes had been deprived of a fair trial in violation of the due process clause of the Fourteenth Amendment. Chief Justice Warren and Justices Douglas, Goldberg, and Clark asserted that a fair trial could not be had when television is allowed in any criminal trial. Justice Harlan, the fifth member of the majority in this 5–4 decision, voted to overturn Estes' conviction because the case was one of "great notoriety." Even so, it should be noted that Harlan reserved judgment on the televising of more routine cases.

In delivering the opinion of the Court, Mr. Justice Clark wrote: [50]

> We start with the proposition that it is a "public trial" that the Sixth Amendment guarantees to the "accused." The purpose of the requirement of a public trial was to guarantee that the accused would be fairly dealt with and not unjustly condemned. * * *.

Justice Clark then took aim on an assertion that if courts exclude television cameras or microphones, they are discriminating in favor of the print media. Clark retorted, "[t]he news reporter is not permitted to bring his typewriter or printing press." Clark did concede that technical advances might someday make television equipment and cameras quieter and less obtrusive.[51]

---

[49] 381 U.S. 532, 554–555, 85 S.Ct. 1628, 1638–1639 (1965), from Chief Justice Warren's concurring opinion.

[50] 381 U.S. 532, 538–539, 85 S.Ct. 1628, 1631 (1965).

[51] 381 U.S. 532, 540, 85 S.Ct. 1628, 1631 (1965).

In a strongly worded dissent, Justices Stewart, Black, Brennan and White raised constitutional arguments in objecting to the ban on television from courtrooms, at least at that stage of television's development.   Justice Stewart expressed doubt that Estes had been deprived of a fair trial by the limited televising of it.[52]

Brennan argued that the *Estes* decision was *"not* a blanket constitutional prohibition against the televising of state criminal trials." [53]   Television, said Brennan, was barred by the majority side of *Estes* only from "notorious trials."   Nevertheless, from 1965 to 1975, cameras—including television cameras—were kept out of virtually *all* courtrooms.

Cameras in the Courtroom

After 1975, cautious efforts to get cameras back in the courtroom became evident in a number of states.   In 1977, the Associated Press Managing Editors Association published a report titled "Cameras in the Courtroom: How to Get 'Em There."   The report noted that if "you're going to get your Nikon into that courtroom you've got to have more tools than just a camera.   For one thing, you've got to have the clout of your State Supreme Court."

The report described a process, beginning with work with a bench-bar-press committee, through demonstrations and carefully regulated experimental photo and TV coverage of either mock or actual trials.   Then, a demonstration videotape should be made for use before a hearing to be conducted by the state's supreme court. The final step is writing guidelines for court coverage for adoption by the state supreme court.[54]

Tentatively, a number of states began to allow television, radio and photographic coverage of judicial proceedings.   Modern cameras, available-light photography, smaller and quieter television and camera gear: technological advances have helped get cameras back into many courtrooms.   More important, however, has been intelligent negotiation by thoughtful members of bench, bar and press who realize that photography in the courtroom, properly used, can be a valuable tool for educating and informing the public.

By 1979, six states allowed some form of television, radio or photographic coverage on a permanent basis.   By mid–1994, such coverage was allowed in 47 states—all but Indiana, Mississippi, and South Dakota.   Also, camera coverage was not allowed in the

---

[52] 381 U.S. 532, 601–602, 85 S.Ct. 1628, 1669 (1965).

[53] 381 U.S. 532, 615–616, 85 S.Ct. 1628, 1676–1677 (1965).

[54] Freedom of Information Committee, APME, "Cameras in the Courtroom: How to Get 'Em There," 1977 Freedom of Information Report, p. 2.

District of Columbia. [55]

Chandler v. Florida: The Lower Courts

A key case testing admission of cameras to courtrooms is Chandler v. Florida.[56] It raised the issue of whether admitting television cameras to a courtroom, over the objection of a participant in a criminal case, made a fair trial impossible.[57]

The *Chandler* case stated the issue in rather extreme form, because in jurisdictions where coverage is permitted, consent of parties is required in most instances.[58] The Supreme Court of the United States held early in 1981 that television coverage had not denied Chandler a fair trial.[59]

Chandler v. Florida also is important because of its interrelationship with another Florida matter, In re Petition of Post–Newsweek Stations, Florida, Inc., for Change in Code of Judicial Conduct.[60] In that proceeding, the Supreme Court of Florida ruled that electronic media coverage of courtroom proceedings is not in itself a denial of due process of law. However, the court also held that the First and Sixth Amendments do not mandate the electronic media be allowed to cover courtroom proceedings. The Florida Supreme Court then issued a rule to amend 3A(7) of Florida's Code of Judicial Conduct to allow still photography and electronic media coverage of public judicial proceedings in the appellate and trial courts, subject at all times to the authority of the presiding judge.[61]

The *Post-Newsweek Stations* ruling, with its lengthy appendices spelling out the deployment of equipment and personnel, the kind of equipment to be used, and pooling arrangements for coverage to cut down on in court distractions, has been used elsewhere as a primer for drafting petitions to seek changes in state judicial rules.

Chandler v. Florida: The Trial

Chandler v. Florida involved the burglary trial of two Miami Beach policemen, Noel Chandler and Robert Granger. During

---

[55] Petition of Post–Newsweek Stations, Florida, Inc., 370 So.2d 764 (Fla.1979), Appendix 2; Cameras in the Courts, 1994 study by the RTNDA, summarized in The News Media and the Law, Summer, 1994, p. 62.

[56] Chandler v. State, 366 So.2d 64 (Fla.App.1978), certiorari denied 376 So.2d 1157 (1979), probable juris. noted 446 U.S. 907, 100 S.Ct. 1832 (1980).

[57] 366 So.2d 64, 69 (Fla.App.1978).

[58] See Appendix 2, "Television in the Courtroom—Recent Developments," National Center for State Courts, quoted in entirety in Petition of Post–Newsweek Stations, Florida, Inc., 370 So.2d 764 (Fla.1979).

[59] 449 U.S. 560, 101 S.Ct. 802 (1981).

[60] 370 So.2d 764 (Fla.1979).

[61] Ibid., p. 781.

their trial, the defendants raised various objections to Florida's [then] Experimental Canon 3A(7). Under that canon, despite requests from the defendants that live television coverage be excluded, cameras were allowed to televise parts of the trial.[62]

The Supreme Court of Florida denied a petition for a writ of certiorari, asserting a lack of jurisdiction. That court said, "No conflict has been demonstrated, and the question of great public interest has been rendered moot by the decisions in Petition of Post–Newsweek Stations, Florida, Inc., 370 So.2d 764 (Fla.1979)."

The Supreme Court of the United States, however, noted probable jurisdiction in Chandler v. Florida in 1980.[63]

Chandler v. Florida: The Supreme Court

In 1981, the Supreme Court of the United States decided *Chandler* by an 8–0 vote, thus upholding the conviction of two Miami Beach police officers for burglarizing Piccolo's Restaurant. This case—regardless of its outcome—would have been memorable for its fact situation. Officers Noel Chandler and Robert Grander had been chatting with each other via walkie-talkies as they broke into the restaurant; they were overheard by an insomniac ham radio operator who recorded their conversations.[64]

Writing for that unanimous Court, Chief Justice Burger based his decision on the principle of federalism. States may work out their own approaches to allowing photographic and broadcast coverage of trials, as long as the Constitution of the United States is not violated.

Chandler and Granger had argued that the very presence of television cameras violated their rights to a fair trial because cameras were psychologically disruptive.[65] Chief Justice Burger wrote for the Court: [66]

> An absolute Constitutional ban on broadcast coverage of trials cannot be justified simply because there is a danger in some cases that prejudicial broadcast accounts of pretrial and trial proceedings may impair the ability of jurors to decide the issue of guilt or innocence. * * * [T]he risk of juror prejudice does not warrant an absolute Constitutional ban on all broadcast coverage. * * *

After the U.S. Supreme Court decision in *Chandler,* states increasingly experimented with cameras in courtrooms. The ABA

[62] Chandler v. State, 366 So.2d 64, 69 (Fla.App.1978).

[63] 446 U.S. 907, 100 S.Ct. 1832 (1980).

[64] Chandler v. Florida, 449 U.S. 560, 101 S.Ct. 802 (1981).

[65] The News Media & The Law, 5:1 (Feb./Mar.1981) p. 5.

[66] Chandler v. Florida, 449 U.S. 560, 575, 101 S.Ct. 802, 810 (1981).

model code's Section 3A(7) opposing cameras never was mandatory in any state unless adopted formally by a state's highest court. But in 1990, the ABA abandoned Canon 3A(7) completely, removing it from the ABA's model code of judicial conduct.[67] The reason? The American Bar Association backed off on grounds that the canon did not deal with judicial ethics but was more properly an issue to be governed by separate court rules.[68] Note, that states do not have to admit cameras or broadcast equipment: they *may* do so according to their own rules. Further, any judge who finds cameras disruptive may exclude them.

As the Court said in *Chandler,*[69]

> Dangers lurk in this, as in most, experiments, but unless we are to conclude that television coverage under all conditions is prohibited by the Constitution, the states must be free to experiment. * * * The risk of prejudice to particular defendants is ever present and must be examined carefully as cases arise.

The Federal Cameras in Courts Experiment

Even though remarkable gains have been made in getting television and still cameras into state courtrooms, the federal court picture remained unchanged for many years: No cameras in federal courts. With the camera-despising Chief Justice Warren Burger's retirement—and his replacement as "The Chief" by William Rehnquist—a modest experiment in coverage of federal courts began in July, 1991.

Even so, Rule 53 of the Federal Rules of Criminal Procedure (1953) continued in force, and it forbids photographing or making radio broadcasts during a criminal trial. As the Radio–Television News Directors Association (RTNDA) has pointed out, Rule 53 did not explicitly prohibit TV broadcasts, but it might as well, because that's the way courts interpret it.[70]

With mounting pressure from the news media, the U.S. Judicial Conference approved a three-year experiment with microphones and cameras in federal courtrooms, to run from July 1, 1991 to June 30, 1994. The experiment dealt with substantial media

[67] Kate Aschenbrenner Pate, "Restricting Electronic Media Coverage of Child–Witnesses: A Proposed Rule," University of Chicago Legal Forum 1993, pp. 352–353.

[68] Ibid., p. 353, citing Lisa L. Milord, The Development of The ABA Judicial Code, p. 22 (ABA, 1992).

[69] 449 U.S. 560, 581, 101 S.Ct. 802, 813 (1981).

[70] RTNDA, News Media Coverage of Judicial Proceedings With Cameras and Microphones: A Survey ... (Washington, D.C.: RTNDA, 1994).

coverage of civil trials and appeals in selected courts, with coverage of criminal trials and appeals forbidden in this experiment.[71]

The TV camera experiment began with civil trials in six (of 94) Federal District Courts and two (of 13) Federal Courts of Appeals. Reports that these experiments were quite trouble-free led journalists to hope for cameras in federal courts. Traditions die hard, however, and the U.S. Judicial Conference—perhaps alarmed by sensational media coverage of the early maneuvers in the O.J. Simpson murder case—voted in September, 1994, to end its civil trial coverage experiment.[72]

But in March, 1995, the Judicial Conference reversed itself, deciding to allow further experimentation with coverage of *civil* trials in federal courts. The format for such experimentation was not specified.[73] As Linda Greenhouse explained, the 27-member Judicial Conference—which meets in secret—is made up of chief judges of each federal circuit plus district judges from each circuit, and is chaired by the Chief Justice of the United States. The Judicial Conference has the authority to declare trials open to TV cameras in federal civil cases. However, the more controversial matter of TV coverage of criminal trials is governed by the Federal Rules of Criminal Procedure, which can be changed only with permission from the Supreme Court of the United States and from Congress. Perhaps camera coverage of both criminal and civil trials can help to dilute the harm done by supermarket tabloids, which had a field day sensationalizing the O.J. Simpson trial.[74]

SEC. 90. NOTORIOUS CASES: THE SHADOW OF SHEPPARD

The long ordeal of Dr. Samuel Sheppard ended with the reversal of his murder conviction on grounds that pretrial and during-trial publicity had impaired his ability to get a fair trial.

The Trial of Dr. Sam Sheppard

When the free press—fair trial controversy is raised, the case most likely to be mentioned is that *cause celebre* of American jurisprudence, Sheppard v. Maxwell.[75] This case was one of the

[71] RTNDA, News Media Coverage of Judicial Proceedings With Cameras and Microphones: A Survey ... (Washington, D.C., RTNDA, 1991), pp. 9–10. This experimental civil coverage was to occur in six federal district courts and in the U.S. Courts of Appeal for the Second and Ninth Circuits.

[72] Linda Greenhouse, "U.S. Judges Vote Down TV in Courts," The New York Times, Sept. 21, 1994, p. A11.

[73] Greenhouse, "Judicial Conference Rejects More Secrecy in Civil Court: Plan to Make Records Easier to Seal Dies," The New York Times, March 15, 1995, p. A12.

[74] See Greenhouse, note 72, above; "Federal Courts, Back in the Dark," The New York Times, Sept. 22, 1994, p. A18.

[75] 384 S.Ct. 333, 86 S.Ct. 1507 (1966).

most notorious—and most sensationally reported—trials in American history. With perhaps the exception of the Lindbergh kidnaping case of the 1930s, the ordeal of Dr. Sam Sheppard may well
have been the most notorious case of the Twentieth Century.

This case began in the early morning hours of July 4, 1954,
when Dr. Sheppard's pregnant wife, Marilyn, was found dead in the
upstairs bedroom of their home. She had been beaten to death.
Dr. Sheppard, who told authorities he had found his wife dead,
called a neighbor, Bay Village Mayor Spence Houk. Dr. Sheppard
appeared to have been injured, suffering from severe neck pains, a
swollen eye, and shock.

Dr. Sheppard, a Bay Village, Ohio, osteopath, told a rambling
and unconvincing story to officials: that he had dozed off on a
downstairs couch after his wife had gone upstairs to bed. He said
that he heard his wife cry out and ran upstairs. In the dim light
from the hall, he saw a "form" which he later described as a bushy
haired man standing next to his wife's bed. Sheppard said he
grappled with the man and was knocked unconscious by a blow to
the back of his neck.

He said he then went to his young son's room, and found him
unharmed. Hearing a noise, Sheppard then ran downstairs. He
saw a "form" leaving the house and chased it to the lake shore.
Dr. Sheppard declared that he had grappled with the intruder on
the beach, and had been again knocked unconscious.[76]

From the outset, Dr. Sheppard was treated as the prime
suspect in the case. The coroner was reported to have told his
men, " 'Well, it is evident the doctor did this, so let's go get the
confession out of him.' " Sheppard, meanwhile, had been removed
to a nearby clinic operated by his family. While under sedation,
Sheppard was interrogated in his hospital room by the coroner.
Later, on the afternoon of July 4, he was also questioned by Bay
Village police, with one policeman telling Sheppard that lie detector
tests were "infallible." This same policeman told Dr. Sheppard,
" 'I think you killed your wife.' " Later that same afternoon, a
physician sent by the coroner was permitted to make a careful
examination of Sheppard.[77]

As early as July 7—the date of Marilyn Sheppard's funeral—a
newspaper story appeared quoting a prosecuting attorney's criticism of the Sheppard family for refusing to permit his immediate
questioning. On July 9, Sheppard re-enacted his recollection of the
crime at his home at the request of the coroner. This re-enactment
was covered by a group of newsmen which had apparently been
invited by the coroner. Sheppard's performance was reported at

[76] 384 U.S. 333, 335–336, 86 S.Ct. 1507, 1508–1509 (1966).
[77] 384 U.S. 333, 337–338, 86 S.Ct. 1507, 1509–1510 (1966).

length by the news media, including photographs. Front-page headlines also emphasized Sheppard's refusal to take a lie-detector test.[78]

On July 20, 1954, newspapers began a campaign of front-page editorials. One such editorial charged that someone was "getting away with murder." The next day, another front-page editorial asked, "Why No Inquest?" A coroner's inquest was indeed held on that day in a school gymnasium. The inquest was attended by many newsmen and photographers, and was broadcast with live microphones stationed at the coroner's chair and at the witness stand. Sheppard had attorneys present during the three-day inquest, but they were not permitted to participate.[79]

The news media also quoted authorities' versions of the evidence before trial. Some of this "evidence"—such as a detective's assertion that " 'the killer washed off a trail of blood from the murder bedroom to the downstairs section' "—was never produced at the trial. Such a story, of course, contradicted Sheppard's version of what had happened in the early morning hours of July 4, 1954.[80]

The news media's activities also included playing up stories about Sheppard's extramarital love life, suggesting that these affairs were a motive for the murder of his wife. Although the news media repeatedly mentioned his relationship with a number of women, testimony taken at Sheppard's trial never showed that Sheppard had any affairs except the one with Susan Hayes.[81]

The Supreme Court of the United States, in Justice Tom C. Clark's majority opinion in the Sheppard case in 1966, summed up the news accounts in this way: [82]

> The publicity then grew in intensity until his indictment on August 17. Typical of the coverage during this period is a front-page interview entitled: "Dr. Sam: 'I Wish There Was Something I Could Get Off My Chest—but There Isn't.' " Unfavorable publicity included items such as a cartoon of the body of a sphinx with Sheppard's head and the legend below: " 'I Will Do Everything In My Power to Help Solve This Terrible Murder.'—Dr. Sam Sheppard." Headlines announced, *inter alia* [among other things], that: "Doctor Evidence is Ready for Jury," "Corrigan Tactics Stall Quizzing," "Sheppard 'Gay Set' Is Revealed by [Bay Village Mayor Spence] Houk," "Blood Is

[78] 384 U.S. 333, 338, 86 S.Ct. 1507, 1510 (1966).
[79] 384 U.S. 333, 339, 86 S.Ct. 1507, 1510 (1966).
[80] 384 U.S. 333, 340, 86 S.Ct. 1507, 1511 (1966).
[81] 384 U.S. 333, 340–341, 86 S.Ct. 1507, 1511 (1966).
[82] 384 U.S. 333, 341–342, 86 S.Ct. 1507, 1511–1512 (1966).

Found in Garage," "New Murder Evidence Is Found, Police Claim," "Dr. Sam Faces Quiz At Jail on Marilyn's Fear Of Him."

Although the record of Sheppard's trial included no excerpts from radio and television broadcasts, the Court assumed that coverage by the electronic media was equally extensive since space was reserved in the courtroom for representatives of those media.

Justice Clark also noted that the chief prosecutor of Sheppard was a candidate for common pleas judge and that the trial judge, Herbert Blythin, was a candidate for re-election. Furthermore, when 75 persons were called as prospective jurors, all three Cleveland newspapers published their names and addresses. All of the prospective jurors received anonymous letters and telephone calls, plus calls from friends, about the impending Sheppard trial.[83]

During the trial, pictures of the jury appeared more than 40 times in the Cleveland newspapers. And the day before the jury rendered its verdict of guilty against Dr. Sam Sheppard, while the jurors were at lunch in the company of two bailiffs, the jury was separated into two groups to pose for pictures which were published in the newspapers. The jurors, unlike those in the Estes case, were not sequestered ["locked up" under the close supervision of bailiffs]. Instead, the jurors were allowed to do what they pleased outside the courtroom while not taking part in the proceedings.[84]

The intense publicity given the Sheppard case in the news media continued unabated while the trial was actually in progress. Sheppard's attorneys took a "random poll" of persons of the streets asking their opinion about the osteopath's guilt or innocence in an effort to gain evidence for a change of venue. This poll was denounced in one newspaper editorial as smacking of "mass jury tampering" and stated that the bar association should do something about it.

A debate among newspaper reporters broadcast over radio station WHK in Cleveland contained assertions that Sheppard had admitted his guilt by hiring a prominent criminal lawyer. In another broadcast heard over WHK, columnist and radio-TV personality Robert Considine likened Sheppard to a perjurer. When Sheppard's attorneys asked Judge Blythin to question the jurors as to how many had heard the broadcast, Judge Blythin refused to do this. And when the trial was in its seventh week, a Walter Winchell broadcast available in Cleveland over both radio and television asserted that a woman under arrest in New York City for robbery had stated that she had been Sam Sheppard's mistress and had borne him a child. Two jurors admitted in open court that

[83] 384 U.S. 333, 342, 86 S.Ct. 1507, 1512 (1966).
[84] 384 U.S. 333, 345, 353, 86 S.Ct. 1507, 1513, 1517 (1966).

they had heard the broadcast. However, Judge Blythin merely accepted the jurors' statements that the broadcast would have no effect on their judgment and the judge accepted the replies as sufficient.[85]

When the case was submitted to the jury, the jurors were sequestered for their deliberations, which took five days and four nights. But this "sequestration" was not complete. The jurors had been allowed to call their homes every day while they stayed at a hotel during their deliberations. Telephones had been removed from the jurors' hotel rooms, but they were allowed to use phones in the bailiffs' rooms. The calls were placed by the jurors themselves, and no record was kept of the jurors who made calls or of the telephone numbers or of the persons called. The bailiffs could hear only the jurors' end of the telephone conversations.[86]

When Sheppard's case was decided by the Supreme Court of the United States in 1966, Justice Tom C. Clark's majority opinion included this ringing statement of the importance of the news media to the administration of justice.[87]

> The principle that justice cannot survive behind walls of silence has long been reflected in the "Anglo–American distrust for secret trials." A responsible press has always been regarded as the handmaiden of effective judicial administration, especially in the criminal field. Its function in this regard is documented by an impressive record of service over several centuries. The press does not simply publish information about trials but guards against the miscarriage of justice by subjecting the police, prosecutors, and judicial processes to extensive public scrutiny and criticism.

Implicit in some of Justice Clark's other statements in his opinion was deep disapproval of the news media's conduct before and during the Sheppard trial. But the news media were by no means the only culprits who made it impossible for Sheppard to get a fair trial. There was more than enough blame to go around, and Justice Clark distributed that blame among the deserving: news media, police, the coroner, and the trial court. The trial judge, Herbert Blythin, had died in 1960, but Justice Clark nevertheless spelled out what Judge Blythin should have done to protect the defendant.

At the outset of Sheppard's trial, Judge Blythin stated that he did not have the power to control publicity about the trial. Justice Clark declared that Judge Blythin's arrangements with the news

[85] 384 U.S. 333, 346, 348, 86 S.Ct. 1507, 1514–1515 (1966).

[86] 384 U.S. 333, 349, 86 S.Ct. 1507, 1515 (1966).

[87] 384 U.S. 333, 349–350, 86 S.Ct. 1507, 1515–1516 (1966).

media "caused Sheppard to be deprived of that 'judicial serenity and calm to which [he] was entitled.'" Justice Clark added that "bedlam reigned at the courthouse during the trial and newsmen took over practically the entire courtroom hounding most of the participants in the trial, especially Sheppard."[88] Justice Clark asserted:

> The carnival atmosphere at trial could easily have been avoided since the courtroom and courthouse premises are subject to the control of the court. As we stressed in *Estes*, the presence of the press at judicial proceedings must be limited when it is apparent that the accused might otherwise be prejudiced or disadvantaged. Bearing in mind the massive pre-trial publicity, the judge should have adopted stricter rules governing the use of the courtroom by newsmen, as Sheppard's counsel requested. The number of reporters in the courtroom itself could have been limited at the first sign that their presence would disrupt the trial. They certainly should have not been placed inside the bar. Furthermore, the judge should have more closely regulated the conduct of newsmen in the courtroom. For instance, the judge belatedly asked them not to handle and photograph trial exhibits lying on the counsel table during recesses.

In addition, the trial judge should have insulated the jurors and witnesses from the news media, and "should have made some effort to control the release of leads, information, and gossip to the press by police officers, witnesses, and the counsel for both sides."[89] Justice Clark asserted that the trial's "carnival atmosphere" could have been avoided because the judge controls the courtroom and the courthouse. This control could have included "limiting the presence of the press" and more closely regulating reporters' conduct, such as keeping them outside the bar of the courtroom and preventing reporters from handling exhibits.[90]

The Judge's Role

The decision in the Sheppard case left its mark in the recommendations of the American Bar Association's "Reardon Report" discussed later in this chapter. The cases discussed in this chapter—*Irvin, Rideau, Estes,* and *Sheppard*—generated new law and suggested strongly that American courts may insist more and more on tighter controls over the information released to the news media in criminal trials by police, prosecution and defense attorneys, and

[88] 384 U.S. 333, 355, 86 S.Ct. 1507, 1518 (1966).
[89] 384 U.S. 333, 359, 361, 86 S.Ct. 1507, 1521–1522 (1966).
[90] 384 U.S. 333, 358, 86 S.Ct. 1507 (1966).

by other employees under the control of the courts. The primary responsibility, however, for seeing to it that a defendant receives a fair trial, rests with the courts. Judges are expected to remain in control of trials in their courts.

A judge with great respect for the press, Frank W. Wilson of a U.S. District Court in Nashville, Tenn., wrote: "Certain it is that the press coverage of crimes and criminal proceedings make more difficult the job that a judge has of assuring a fair trial. But no one has yet shown that it renders the job impossible. In fact, no one has yet shown, to the satisfaction of any court, an identifiable instance of miscarriage of justice due to press coverage of a trial where the error was not remedied." [91]   Note that Judge Wilson said that it is the *judge's* job to assure a fair trial. Judge Wilson declared, "show me an unfair trial that goes uncorrected and I will show you a judge who has failed in his duty." [92]

Judge Wilson thus placed great—some would argue *too* great— [93] reliance upon the remedies which a judge can use to attempt to set things right for the defendant once he has received what the judge considers to be an undue amount of prejudicial publicity. Some of the most important of these trial-level "remedies" are outlined below:

(1) *Change of venue,* moving the trial to another area in hopes that jurors not prejudiced by mass media publicity or outraged community sentiment can be found. This "remedy," however, requires that a defendant give up his Sixth Amendment right to a trial in the "State and *district* wherein the crime shall have been committed * * *." [94]

(2) *Continuance or postponement.* This is simply a matter of postponing a trial until the publicity or public clamor abates. A problem with this "remedy" is that there is no guarantee that the publicity will not begin anew. It might be well to remember the axiom, "justice delayed is justice denied." A continuance in a case involving a major crime might mean that a defendant—even an innocent defendant—might thus be imprisoned for a lengthy time before

[91] Frank A. Wilson, "A Fair Trial and a Free Press," presented at 33rd Annual convention of the Ohio Newspaper Association, Columbus, Ohio, Feb. 11, 1966.

[92] Ibid.

[93] Don R. Pember, Pretrial Newspaper Publicity in Criminal Proceedings: A Case Study (unpublished M.A. thesis, Michigan State University, East Lansing, Mich.) pp. 12–16.

[94] Constitution, Sixth Amendment, emphasis added; Lawrence E. Edenhofer, "The Impartial Jury—Twentieth Century Dilemma: Some Solutions to the Conflict Between Free Press and Fair Trial," Cornell Law Quarterly Vol. 51 (Winter, 1966) pp. 306, 314.

his trial. A continuance means that a defendant gives up his Sixth amendment right to a *speedy* trial.

(3) *Voir dire* examination of potential jurors. This refers to the procedure by which each potential juror is questioned by opposing attorneys and may be dismissed "for cause" if the juror is shown to be prejudiced. (In addition, attorneys have a limited number of "peremptory challenges" which they can use to remove jurors who may appear troublesome to one side or the other.) Professor Don R. Pember of the University of Washington says that the voir dire examination is an effective tool and one of the best available trial-level remedies.

(4) *Sequestration,* or "locking up" the jury. Judges have the power to isolate a jury, to make sure that community prejudices—either published or broadcast in the mass media or of the person-to-person variety—do not infect a jury with information during trial which might harm a defendant's chances for a fair trial by an impartial jury. As Professor Pember has said, judges are reluctant to do this today because of the complexities in the life of the average person.[95]

(5) *Contempt of Court.* This punitive "remedy" is discussed at length in Chapter 9. Courts have the power to cite for contempt those actions—either in court or out of court—which interfere with the orderly administration of justice. American courts—until the "gag order" controversies of recent years—have been reluctant to use the contempt remedy to punish pre-trial or during-trial publications. (See Section 92 of this chapter, on "restrictive" or "gag" orders.) Some critics of the American mass media would go even further: they would like to see the British system imported. That would mean using contempt of court citations as a weapon to halt media coverage of ongoing or pending criminal cases.

The British system of contempt citations to regulate media activities has worked well, according to some observers. The British press—knowing that the threat of a contempt citation hangs over it for a misstep—cannot quote from a confession (or even reveal its existence); nor can the British publish material—including previous criminal records—which would not be admissible

---

[95] Another trial-level remedy which is more infrequently used is the blue-ribbon jury. When a case has received massive prejudicial publicity, a court may empower either the prosecution or the defense to impanel a special, so-called "blue ribbon" jury. Intelligent jurors are selected through the use of questionnaires and interviews, under the assumption that a more intelligent jury will be more likely to withstand pressures and remain impartial.

evidence. One of the things about the British system which is most offensive to American journalists is the prohibition of a newspaper's making its own investigation and printing the results of it. After the trial is concluded, *then* British newspapers can cover the trial.[96]

The *New York Times'* Anthony Lewis has suggested that the British system of using contempt citations to preclude virtually all comment on criminal cases simply could not work in the United States. While some criminal trials in the United States drag on for years, even trials involving major crimes—including appeals—are usually completed in Britain in less than two months' time.[97] Anthony Lewis has also argued that Britain is a small, more homogeneous nation where police or judicial corruption is virtually unknown. America has not been so fortunate: occasionally corrupt policemen or judges are discovered, and perhaps the media's watchdog function is more needed in reporting on police and courts in this nation than it is in Britain.[98]

SEC. 91. EXTERNAL GUIDELINES AND SELF–REGULATORY EFFORTS

An external regulatory threat—the fair trial reporting guidelines of the "Reardon Committee"—led to press-bar-bench efforts to agree to rules for covering the criminal justice process.

During the middle 1960s, the American Bar Association again got into the act in attempting to regulate prejudicial publicity.[99] As should be evident from preceding sections, there was plenty of pressure on the ABA to do something. First, as noted earlier in Section 87, the Warren Commission investigating the assassination of President Kennedy had some harsh things to say about media coverage of the arrest of suspect Lee Harvey Oswald.[1] Then, there had been a chain of cases involving prejudicial publicity—Irvin v. Dowd (1961),[2] Rideau v. Louisiana (1963),[3] Estes v. Texas (1965)[4]

[96] Harold W. Sullivan, Trial by Newspaper (Hyannis, Mass., Patriot Press, 1961).

[97] New York Times, June 20, 1965.

[98] Ibid.

[99] Advisory Committee on Fair Trial and Free Press, Standards Relating to Fair Trial and Free Press (New York, 1966); see also draft approved Feb. 19, 1968, by delegates to the ABA Convention as published in March, 1968. For earlier ABA involvement in trying to come to terms with prejudicial publicity see ABA, "Report of Special Committee on Cooperation Between [sic] Press, Radio and Bar," Annual Report, Volume 62, pp. 851–866 (1937).

[1] Report of the President's Commission on the Association of President John F. Kennedy (Washington: Government Printing Office, 1964) p. 241.

[2] 366 U.S. 717, 81 S.Ct. 1639 (1961).

[3] 373 U.S. 723, 83 S.Ct. 1417 (1963).

[4] 381 U.S. 532, 85 S.Ct. 1628 (1965).

and Sheppard v. Maxwell (1966).[5]   Although the [Attorney General Nicholas DeB.] Katzenbach Guidelines for federal courts and law enforcement officers had met with considerable approval, the ABA's concern continued.   Early in 1968, the ABA Convention meeting in Chicago approved the "Standards Relating to Fair Trial and Free Press" recommended by the Advisory Committee headed by Massachusetts Supreme Court Justice Paul C. Reardon.[6]   The "Reardon Report," as the document came to be known, was greeted with outraged concern by a large segment of the American media.[7]   This report dealt primarily with things that attorneys and judges were *not* to say lest the rights of defendants be prejudiced.   For example, if a defendant in a murder case had confessed before trial, that confession should not be revealed until duly submitted as evidence during an actual trial.   Most frightening to the media, however, were suggestions that contempt powers be used against the media if they were to publish statements which could affect the outcome of a trial.

The Reardon Report touched off many press-bar meetings, seeking to reach voluntary guidelines on coverage of the criminal arrest, arraignment, hearing and trial process.[8]   More than two dozen states adopted voluntary agreements based on conferences among judges, lawyers, and members of the media.   States with such guidelines include Colorado, Kentucky, Massachusetts, Minnesota, New York, Oregon, Texas, Washington, and Wisconsin.

In such a setting—in the aftermath of the Warren Commission Report on the Kennedy assassination (which called for curtailment of pretrial news)—the *Sheppard* case came along to illustrate once again just how wretchedly prejudicial news coverage of a criminal trial could become.   In that setting, the ABA Advisory Committee on Fair Trial—Free Press (Reardon Committee) was formed.

In many places, a press-bar agreement occurred, leading to construction, by joint press-bar committees in roughly half of the states, of guidelines for the coverage of criminal trials.

Wisconsin Fair Trial and Free Press Principles and Guidelines

In Wisconsin, for example, informal rules titled "Wisconsin Fair Trial and Free Press Principles and Guidelines were drafted by

[5] 384 U.S. 333, 86 S.Ct. 1507 (1966).

[6] Advisory Committee on Fair Trial and Free Press (of the ABA), Approved Draft, op. cit.

[7] See, e.g., American Newspaper Publishers Association, Free Press and Fair Trial (New York: ANPA, 1967) p. 1 and passim.

[8] Advisory Committee on Fair Trial and Free Press, op. cit., 1966 and 1968; "Bar Votes to Strengthen Code on Crime Publicity," Editor & Publisher, Vol. 101 (Feb.24, 1968) p. 9.

a committee of lawyers and journalists in 1969. These guidelines were reworked and reissued in 1979 and in 1987 in response to changes brought about my cases such as Nebraska Press Association Stuart (1976) and pre–1987 free press-fair trial cases discussed earlier in this chapter."

These are *recommended* principles, for voluntary compliance, and the 1987 version emphasized that they are not binding on anyone. Further, and doubtless in some response to a Washington case which would have made voluntary guidelines mandatory as a condition for covering a trial, Wisconsin's 1987 guidelines specify that they are "not to be applied or used against anyone." [9]

The Wisconsin Guidelines, similarly to those of other states, ask for protection of criminal defendants' presumption of innocence as a shared responsibility among the judiciary, attorneys, news media, and law enforcement agencies. Both access to news of court proceedings and defendants' rights to a fair, unprejudiced trial are recognized as vital rights to be protected. The news media, which have a constitutional and statutory right to report on courts (subject to rare exceptions), and should strive for accuracy, balance, fairness and objectivity.

As to release of information in criminal trials, the guidelines say there should be no restraint on making available to the public, in criminal investigations, the following:

— Information in a public record.

— Information indicating that an investigation is in progress.

— Information on the general scope of an investigation, including a description of the offense.

Non-prejudicial information—such as the defendant's name, age, residence, and place of employment—may also be given, and the circumstances of the arrest may be described.

However, prejudicial information such as the existence of a purported confession, or a defendant's performance on tests related to a crime should not be reported.

Federated Publications v. Swedberg (1981)

Voluntary guidelines may become a two-edged sword. In fact, some states reworked their guidelines after the harsh lesson of Federated Publications v. Swedberg as decided by the Supreme Court of the State of Washington. Reworkings of the state guidelines were to re-emphasize their VOLUNTARY nature.

[9] See Wisconsin News Reporter's Legal Handbook, 2nd ed. (1987), prepared by the Media–Law Relations Committee, State Bar of Wisconsin, in cooperation with the Wisconsin Broadcasters Assn. and the Wisconsin Newspaper Assn. The Washington case is Federated Publications v. Swedberg. See below at footnote 15.

Judge Byron L. Swedberg presided over a trial involving charges of attempted murder. The case, in Whatcom County, north of Seattle, had great notoriety. It involved Veronica Lynn Compton, a woman reputedly the girlfriend of Kenneth Bianchi. Bianchi was known regionally and even nationally as the "Hillside Strangler."

Judge Swedberg refused to grant a defense motion in the case of State v. Compton which would have closed a pretrial hearing to the public. However, the judge conditioned media attendance at the trial upon reporters' signing an agreement to abide by the Washington Bench–Bar–Press Guidelines. Federated Publications, publishers of the Bellingham Herald, challenged Judge Swedberg's order.

The Washington guidelines were created as a voluntary document and had no legal force until Judge Swedberg incorporated them in his order. In that situation, the guidelines—if enforced—would, for example, have stopped the media from reporting on the defendant's previous criminal record or on the existence of a pretrial confession. In most cases, journalists will agree that pre-trial confessions should not be reported until officially accepted as evidence in court. However, situations could conceivably arise where the best judgment of journalists would be to include information about the existence of such a confession in pre-trial stories. As journalist Tony Mauro said in a Society of Professional Journalists Freedom of Information report in 1982,

> * * * [I]n a single stroke, Swedberg made suspect all the guidelines, developed in many instances only after years of delicate negotiations. Editors who were wary in the first place of sitting down with judges and lawyers were given new reasons to be suspicious—if we agree to talk about guidelines, the thinking went, someday they'll be used against us, as with Swedberg.

In upholding Judge Swedberg's ruling that members of the press must agree to abide by the Washington guidelines if so ordered by a judge, Justice Rosellini of the State of Washington's Supreme Court concluded that Swedberg's limitation was "reasonable." He compared the Swedberg situation to the Washington Supreme Court's holding in Federated Publications v. Kurtz. In the Kurtz case, the court held that the public has a right under the state and federal constitutions to have access to judicial proceedings, including pretrial hearings.

Justice Rosellini listed alternatives to closing a courtroom (see discussion of a similar list elsewhere this Chapter: Continuance (delay), change of venue, change of venire, voir dire, and so forth). Those alternatives, Justice Rosellini wrote, "all involved some compromise of a right or interest of the accused or the State. None of the suggested alternatives involved the exercise of some restraint on the part of the media." He concluded that since his court had the power to exclude all of the public, including the media, he also had the power to impose reasonable conditions upon the media's attendance at a trial.[10]

SEC. 92. RESTRICTIVE ORDERS AND REPORTING THE JUDICIAL PROCESS

After "gag orders" became a nationwide problem, Nebraska Press Association v. Stuart (1976) halted such prior restraints on the news media.

Bar-press guidelines such as those disclosed in the preceding sections tried to honor both the public's right to know about the judicial process and a defendant's right to a fair trial. Not all was well, however, despite the various meeting-of-minds between press and bar. Another disturbing counter-current was perceived during the late 1960s, starting mainly in California and involving judges issuing "restrictive" or "gag" orders in some cases.[11] In a Los Angeles County Superior Court in 1966, for example, a judge ordered the attorneys in a case, the defendants, the sheriff, chief of police, and members of the Board of Police Commissioners not to talk to the news media about the case in question. The order forbade "[r]eleasing or authorizing the release of any extrajudicial statements for dissemination by any means of public communication relating to the alleged charge or the Accused."

All that could be reported under such an order were the facts and circumstances of the arrest, the substance of the charge against the defendant, and the defendant's name, age, residence, occupation, and family status. If such an arrangement were to be worked out on a voluntary basis between press and bar, that might be one thing. However, the fact of a judge's *order*—a "gag rule"—worried some legal scholars, and with good reason.

In a New York case during 1971, Manhattan Supreme Court Justice George Postel, concerned about possibly prejudicial news accounts, called reporters into his chambers and laid down what he called "Postel's Law." The trial involved Carmine J. Persico, who had been charged with extortion, coercion, criminal usury ("loan

---

[10] Federated Publications, Inc. v. Swedberg, 96 Wash.2d 13, 633 P.2d 74, 75 (1981), 7 Med.L.Rptr. 1865, 1871, citing Federated Publications, Inc. v. Kurtz, 94 Wash.2d 51, 615 P.2d 440 (1980), 6 Med.L.Rptr. 1577. See also Tony Mauro, "Bench-media misunderstanding threatens press access to courts," FOI '82: A Report from the Society of Professional Journalists, p. 3.

[11] Robert S. Warren and Jeffrey M. Abell, "Free Press—Fair Trial: The "Gag Order,' A California Aberration," Southern California Law Review 45:1 (Winter, 1972) pp. 51–99, at pp. 52–53.

sharking") and conspiracy. Justice Postel admonished the reporters not to use Persico's nickname ("The Snake") in their accounts and not to mention Persico's supposed connections with Joseph A. Columbo, Sr., a person said to be a leader of organized crime. The reporters, irked by Postel's declarations, reported what the judge had told them, including references to "The Snake" and to Columbo.

Persico's defense attorney then asked that the trial be closed to the press and to the public, and Judge Postel so ordered. However, the prosecutor—Assistant District Attorney Samuel Yasgur—complained that the order would set an unfortunate and dangerous precedent. For one thing, Yasgur declared, the absence of press coverage might mean that possible witnesses who could become aware of the trial through the media would remain ignorant of the trial and thus could not come forward to testify. Prosecutor Yasgur added: [12]

> But most importantly, Your Honor, as the Court has noted, the purpose of having press and the public allowed and present during the trial of a criminal case is to insure that defendants do receive an honest and a fair trial.

Newsmen appealed Judge Postel's order closing the trial to New York's highest court, the Court of Appeals. Chief Judge Stanley H. Fuld then ruled that the trial should not have been closed.[13]

> "Because of the vital function served by the news media in guarding against the miscarriage of justice by subjecting the police, prosecutors, and the judicial processes to extensive public scrutiny and criticism," the Supreme Court has emphasized that it has been "unwilling to place any direct limitations on the freedom traditionally exercised by the news media for '[w]hat transpires in the court room is public property.' "

Chief Judge Fuld added that courts should meet problems of prejudicial publicity not by declaring mistrials, but by taking careful preventive steps to protect their courts from outside interferences. In most cases, Judge Fuld suggested, a judge's cautioning jurors to avoid exposure to prejudicial publicity, or to disregard prejudicial material they had already seen or heard, would be effective. In extreme situations, he said, a court might find it

[12] *New York Times,* "Trial of Persico Closed to Public," pp. 1, 40, November 16, 1971.

[13] Oliver v. Postel, 30 N.Y.2d 171, 331 N.Y.S.2d 407, 414, 282 N.E.2d 306, 311 (1972).

necessary to sequester ("lock up") a jury for the duration of a trial.[14]

Although reporters were ultimately vindicated in the *Postel* case, a Louisiana case went against the press. This case, United States v. Dickinson, arose when reporters Larry Dickinson and Gibbs Adams of the Baton Rouge *Star Times* and the *Morning Advocate* tried to report on a U.S. District Court hearing involving a VISTA worker who had been indicted by a Louisiana state grand jury on suspicion of conspiring to murder a state official. The District Court hearing was to ascertain whether the state's prosecution was legitimate. In the course of this hearing, District Court Judge E. Gordon West issued this order:

> "And, at this time, –I do want to enter an order in the case, and that is in accordance with this Court's rule in connection with Fair Trial—Free Press provisions, the Rules of this Court.
>
> "It is ordered that no * * * report of the testimony taken in this case today shall be made in any newspaper or by radio or television, or by any other news media."

Reporters Dickinson and Adams ignored that order, and wrote articles for their newspapers summarizing the day's testimony in detail. After a hearing, Dickinson and Adams were found guilty of criminal contempt and were sentenced to pay fines of $300 each. Appealing to the Court of Appeals for the Fifth Circuit, the reporters were told that the District Court judge's gag order was unconstitutional.[15] They were not in the clear, however. The Court of Appeals sent their case back to the District Court so that the judge could reconsider the $300 fines. The judge again fined the reporters $300 apiece, and they again appealed to the Court of Appeals. This time, the contempt fines were upheld. The Fifth Circuit Court declared that the reporters could have asked for a rehearing or appealed against the judge's order not to publish. Once the appeal was decided in their favor, the court evidently reasoned, *then* they could publish.[16]

Attorney James C. Goodale—then vice president of the *New York Times*—was indignant.

> It doesn't take much analysis to see that what the Court has sanctioned is the right of prior restraint subject

[14] Ibid. See, also, People of the State of New York v. Holder, 70 Misc.2d 31, 332 N.Y.S.2d 933 (1972), and Phoenix Newspapers Inc. v. Jennings, Justice of the Peace, 107 Ariz. 557, 490 P.2d 563, 566–567 (1971).

[15] United States v. Dickinson, 465 F.2d 496, 514 (5th Cir.1972).

[16] 476 F.2d 373, 374 (5th Cir.1973); 349 F.Supp. 227 (M.D.La.1972). See also James C. Goodale's "The Press 'Gag' Order Epidemic," Columbia Journalism Review, Sept./Oct. 1973, pp. 49–50.

to later appeal. * * * What this case means, in effect, is that when a judge is disposed to order a newspaper not to report matters that are transpiring in public he may do so, and a newsman's only remedy is to appeal or decide to pay the contempt penalty, be it a fine or imprisonment.

In the fall of 1973, the Supreme Court—evidently not seeing a major issue requiring its attention—refused to grant certiorari, thereby allowing the lower court decision to stand.[17] By 1976, however, the gag issue was an obvious problem. Attorney Jack C. Landau, Supreme Court reporter for the Newhouse News Service and a trustee of the Reporters Committee for Freedom of the Press, came up with some agonizing statistics. From 1966 to 1976, hundreds of restrictive orders were issued by courts against the news media.[18]

Nebraska Press Ass'n v. Stuart (1976)

Although the Supreme Court refused to hear the reporters' appeal in the Dickinson case [19]—thus allowing contempt fines against two reporters to stand—a virtual nationwide epidemic of restrictive orders quickly showed that the Baton Rouge case was no rarity.[20] A ghastly 1976 multiple-murder case in the hamlet of Sutherland, Neb. (population 840) was reported avidly by the mass media. This provided the Supreme Court with the factual setting which led to the Court's clamping down on the indiscriminate issuance of gag orders. The issue was stated succinctly by E. Barrett Prettyman, the attorney who represented the news media in Nebraska Press Association v. Stuart.[21]

> The basic question before the Court is whether it is permissible under the First Amendment for a court to issue direct prior restraint against the press, prohibiting in advance of publication the reporting of information revealed in public court proceedings, in public court records, and from other sources about pending judicial proceedings.

The nightmarish Nebraska case involved the murder of six members of one family, and necrophilia was involved. Police released the description of a suspect, 29–year-old Erwin Charles Simants, an unemployed handyman, to reporters who arrived at the scene of the crime. After a night of hiding, Simants walked into

[17] 414 U.S. 979, 94 S.Ct. 270 (1973), refusing certiorari in 465 F.2d 496 (5th Cir.1972).

[18] Jack C. Landau, "The Challenge of the Communications Media," 62 American Bar Association Journal 55 (January, 1976).

[19] 414 U.S. 979, 94 S.Ct. 270 (1973).

[20] Landau, p. 57.

[21] "Excerpts from the Gag Order Arguments," Editor & Publisher, May 1, 1976, p. 46A.

the house where he lived—next door to the residence where six had been slain—and was arrested.

Three days after the crime, the prosecuting attorney and Simants' attorney jointly asked the Lincoln County Court to enter a restrictive order. On October 22, 1975, the County Court granted a sweeping order prohibiting the release or publication of any "testimony given or evidence adduced * * * ".[22] On October 23, Simants' preliminary hearing was open to the public, but the press was subject to the restrictive order. On that same day, the Nebraska Press Association intervened in the District Court of Lincoln County and asked Judge Hugh Stuart to set aside the County Court's restrictive order. Judge Stuart conducted a hearing and on October 27 issued his own restrictive order, prohibiting the Nebraska Press Association and other organizations and reporters from reporting on five subjects: [23]

> (1) the existence or contents of a confession Simants had made to law enforcement officers, which has been introduced in open court at arraignment; (2) the fact or nature of statements Simants had made to other persons; (3) the contents of a note he had written the night of the crime; (4) certain aspects of the medical testimony at the preliminary hearing; (5) the identity of the victims of the alleged sexual assault and the nature of the assault.

This order also prohibited reporting the exact nature of the restrictive order itself, and—like the County Court's order—incorporated the Nebraska Bar–Press Guidelines.[24]

The Nebraska Press Association and its co-petitioners on October 31 asked the District Court to suspend its restrictive order and also asked that the Nebraska Supreme Court stop the gag order. Early in December, the state's Supreme Court issued a modification of the restrictive order "to accommodate the defendant's right to a fair trial and the petitioners' [i.e., the Nebraska Press Association, other press associations, and individual journalists'] interest in reporting pretrial events." This modified order prohibited reporting of three matters: [25]

> (a) the existence and nature of any confessions or admissions made by the defendant to law enforcement officers; (b) any confessions or admissions made to any third parties, except members of the press, and (c) other facts "strongly implicative" of the accused.

[22] 427 U.S. 539, 542, 96 S.Ct. 2791, 2795 (1976).

[23] 427 U.S. 539, 543–544, 96 S.Ct. 2791, 2795 (1976).

[24] 427 U.S. 539, 545, 96 S.Ct. 2791, 2796 (1976).

[25] 427 U.S. 539, 545, 96 S.Ct. 2791, 2796 (1976).

The Nebraska Supreme Court did not rely on the Nebraska Bar–
Press Guidelines. After interpreting state law to permit closing of
court proceedings to reporters in certain circumstances, the Ne-
braska Supreme Court sent the case back to District Judge Hugh
Stuart for reconsideration of whether pretrial hearings in the
Simants case should be closed to the press and public. The
Supreme Court of the United States granted certiorari.[26]

Writing for a unanimous Supreme Court, Chief Justice Burger
reviewed free press-fair trial cases and prior restraint cases. He
wrote: "None of our decided cases on prior restraint involved
restrictive orders entered to protect a defendant's right to a fair
and impartial jury, but the opinions on prior restraint have a
common thread relevant to this case." The Chief Justice then
quoted from Organization for a Better Austin v. Keefe: [27]

"Any prior restraint on expression comes to this Court
with a 'heavy presumption' against its constitutional validity. * * * Respondent [Keefe] thus carries a heavy burden
of showing justification for the imposition of such a restraint. He has not met that burden. * * * "

Chief Justice Burger noted that the restrictive order at issue in
the Simants case did not prohibit publication but only postponed it.
Some news, he said, can be delayed and often is when responsible
editors call for more fact-checking. "But such delays," he added,
"are normally slight and they are self-imposed. Delays imposed by
governmental authority are a different matter." [28]

The Court then turned to an examination of whether the
threat to a fair trial for Simants was so severe as to overcome the
presumption of unconstitutionality which prior restraints carry
with them. The Chief Justice borrowed Judge Learned Hand's
language (oft criticized by libertarians) from a case involving the
trial of Communists in 1950: whether the "gravity of the evil,"
discounted by its improbability, justifies such invasion of free
speech as is necessary to avoid the danger.[29] The Court's review of
the pretrial record in the Simants case indicated that Judge Stuart
was justified in concluding that there would be intense and pervasive pretrial publicity. The judge could have concluded reasonably
that the publicity might endanger Simants' right to a fair trial.

Even so, the restrictive order by the trial court judge was not
justified in the view of the Supreme Court of the United States.
Alternatives to prior restraint were not tried by the Nebraska trial
court. Those alternatives included a change of venue; postpone-

[26] 423 U.S. 1027, 96 S.Ct. 557 (1975).
[27] 402 U.S. 415, 91 S.Ct. 1575 (1971).
[28] 427 U.S. 539, 560, 96 S.Ct. 2791, 2803 (1976).
[29] 427 U.S. 539, 562, 96 S.Ct. 2791, 2804 (1976).

ment of the trial to allow public furor to subside, and searching questioning of prospective jurors to screen out those who had already made up their minds about Simants' guilt or innocence. Sequestration ("locking up") of jurors would insulate jurors from prejudicial publicity only after they were sworn, but that measure "enhances the likelihood of dissipating the impact of pretrial publicity and emphasizes the elements of the jurors' oaths." The Chief Justice wrote: [30]

> * * * [P]retrial publicity, even if pervasive and concentrated, cannot be regarded as leading automatically and in every kind of criminal case to an unfair trial.

> * * *

> We reaffirm that the guarantees of freedom of expression are not an absolute prohibition under all circumstances, but the barriers to prior restraint remain high and the presumption against its use continues intact. We hold that, with respect to the order entered in this case prohibiting reporting or commentary on judicial proceedings held in public, the barriers have not been overcome; to the extent that this order restrained publication of such material, it is clearly invalid. To the extent that it prohibited publication based on information gained from other sources, we conclude that the heavy burden imposed as a condition to securing prior restraint was not met and the judgment of the Nebraska Supreme Court is therefore *reversed.*

Nebraska Press Association v. Stuart was hailed as a sizable victory for the news media. Nevertheless, some scholars were fretful about that decision's ultimate impact. Benno C. Schmidt, then a Columbia University law professor, found some "disturbing undertones." He expressed the fear that the [31]

> * * * Court may have invited severe controls on the press's access to information about criminal proceedings from principals, witnesses, lawyers, the police, and others; it is even possible that some legal proceedings may be closed completely to the press and public as an indirect result of *Nebraska.*

He also worried that the Supreme Court's decision might encourage trial judges to place increasing reliance on stipulations that parties in a trial—lawyers, witnesses, police, etc.—not provide information in the press.

[30] 427 U.S. 539, 565, 570, 96 S.Ct. 2791, 2804, 2806 (1976).

[31] Schmidt, "The Nebraska Decision," Columbia Journalism Review, November/December, 1976, p. 51.

Schmidt was correct in his gloomy assessment of the Simants case; the so-called victory of the press in Nebraska Press Association was hollow. As former Washington Star editor Newbold Noyes has observed: [32]

> It was Star Chamber, not publicity, that the founding fathers worried about. Defendants were guaranteed a public trial, not a cleared courtroom. The whole thrust of these amendments was—and must remain—that what happens in the courts happens out in the open, in full view of the citizenry, and that therein lies the individual's protection against the possible tyranny of government. There is no possible conflict between this idea and the idea of a free press.

Gagging Everybody But the Press?

Back in 1978, a trend then was discernible: gag news sources related to a judicial proceeding while leaving the press alone. The net result, of course, was much the same: a diminished flow of information about the judicial process. As trial courts close various courtroom proceedings, seal certain records, and decree that witnesses, attorneys and participants in trials do not speak to reporters, all that can be done is for the news media to fight back by going to court themselves. Noted First Amendment attorneys Dan Paul, Richard Ovelmen, James Spaniolo and Steven Kamp wrote late in 1984: "The most troubling trend in the cases decided during the last twelve months has been the use of gag orders on litigants and trial participants in order to block at the source public access to information concerning judicial proceedings." [33] The leading case? Seattle Times v. Rhinehart.[34]

Seattle Times v. Rhinehart (1984)

Keith Milton Rhinehart was the leader of a religious group, the Aquarian Foundation. The Seattle Times had published a number of stories about Rhinehart and the Foundation, a group with fewer than 1,000 members, believers in life after death and the ability to communicate with the dead. Rhinehart was the group's chief spiritual medium.[35] As Justice Powell described articles about

[32] Speech at the University of Oregon, Ruhl Symposium Lectures, November 21, 1975, reprinted in "The Responsibilities of Power," School of Journalism, University of Oregon, June, 1976, pp. 16–17.

[33] Dan Paul, et al., op. cit., pp. 57–58.

[34] Seattle Times Co. v. Rhinehart, 467 U.S. 20, 104 S.Ct. 2199 (1984), 10 Med. L.Rptr. 1705.

[35] 467 U.S. 20, 104 S.Ct. 2199, 2202 (1984), 10 Med.L.Rptr. 1705, 1706.

Rhinehart in the Seattle Times and the Walla Walla Union–Bulletin: [36]

> One article referred to Rhinehart's conviction, later vacated, for sodomy. The four articles that appeared in 1978 concentrated on an "extravaganza" sponsored by Rhinehart at the Walla Walla State Penitentiary. The articles stated that he had treated 1,100 inmates to a 6–hour-long show, during which he gave away between $35,000 and $50,000 in cash and prizes. One article described a "chorus line of girls [who] shed their gowns and bikinis and sang * * *" The two articles that appeared in 1959 referred to a purported connection between Rhinehart and Lou Ferrigno, star of the popular television program, "The Incredible Hulk."

Rhinehart and five of the female members of the Aquarian Society who had taken part in the presentation at the penitentiary sued for libel and invasion of privacy, claiming that the stories were " 'fictional and untrue.' " They asked damages totalling $14.1 million.

As part of the pre-trial discovery proceedings, the defendant newspapers asked for information about the financial affairs of The Aquarian Foundation, including information on donors. The trial court judge issued a protective order [called a "gag order" by journalists] forbidding the Seattle Times from publishing pre-trial discovery information about the Aquarian Foundation's donors, members, and finances.[37]

A unanimous Supreme Court of the United States upheld the gag order preventing release and publication of deposition material. Writing for the Court, Justice Powell said: [38]

> * * * [I]t is necessary to consider whether the "practice in question [furthers] an important or substantial governmental interest unrelated to the suppression of expression" and whether "the limitation of First Amendment freedoms [is] no greater than necessary or essential to the protection of the particular governmental interest involved." Procunier v. Martinez, 415 U.S. 396, 413, 94 S.Ct. 1800, 1811 (1974) * * *.

* * *

> A litigant has no First Amendment right of access to information made available only for purposes of trying his

---

[36] Ibid.

[37] 467 U.S. 20, 104 S.Ct. 2199, 2204 (1984), 10 Med.L.Rptr. at 1707.

[38] 467 U.S. 20, 104 S.Ct. 2199, 2207 (1984), 10 Med.L.Rptr. at 1711.

suit. * * * Moreover, pretrial depositions and interrogatories are not public components of a civil trial.

Attorney Dan Paul and co-authors were unconvinced by that reasoning. They wrote: [39]

> None of these reasons is persuasive. First Amendment cases have uniformly recognized that once the press has information in hand, by whatever lawful means, any prohibition on publication is a prior restraint.

Prior Restraint Revisited: CNN and the Noriega Tapes

The prosecution of Panamanian dictator Manuel Antonio Noriega during 1991 showed that judicial prior restraint still could occur. Although Nebraska Press Association v. Stuart (see text, above) still is regarded as a major bulwark against prior censorship by judges, the bizarre Noriega Tapes case showed that courts, on occasion, still can crack the prior restraint whip.

General Noriega, of course, was a most unusual suspect. Taken into custody after a massive U.S. deployment of armed forces, Noriega took sanctuary in a Vatican consulate. After several days of listening to American rock music played by troops surrounding the Vatican property, General Noriega surrendered. He was then spirited away to a well-appointed jail cell in Florida (outfitted with TV, telephone, and even a paper shredder). (Concerns about a fair trial for a foreign head of state who surrendered after a potent military attack seemed strained: Could a U.S. court *really* find a jury of his peers?)

Suspicion grew that the last thing the U.S. government wanted after Noriega survived the attack on Panama was to get the ex-dictator on the stand where he could sing about his former chums at the Central Intelligence Agency (CIA). In any event, someone got hold of tape recordings of Noriega's Florida jail-cell calls to the office of his attorney, Frank Rubino. The tapes, which Rubino claimed were evidence of a government plot to spy on Noriega's legal defense plans, were given to the Cable News Network (CNN).[40]

After CNN announced that it had the tapes, U.S. District Judge William Hoeveler, on November 8, 1990, granted defense attorneys' request for an injunction to prevent CNN's broadcast of the tapes. Although CNN broadcast no taped excerpts of conversations between the general and his attorneys, excerpts of Noriega's calls to others were broadcast.

---

[39] Dan Paul et al., op. cit., p. 59.

[40] "Tales of the Tape," Newsweek, Dec. 17, 1990, p. 29; "Eavesdropping on Noriega," Newsweek, Nov. 19, 1990.

Judge Hoeveler evidently saw CNN's eagerness to use the tapes as raising two Sixth Amendment questions: Violation of the attorney-client privilege and the possibility of revealing information harmful to Noriega's defense. Even though Judge Hoeveler noted that prior restraints are "presumptively unconstitutional," he held that the barrier laid down by a three-part test in Nebraska Press Association v. Stuart was not insurmountable. The *Nebraska Press* test for justifying prior restraint to prevent prejudicial publicity requires that: [41]

1. Publicity must impair the right to a fair trial.

2. No less restrictive alternative to prior restraint is available or practicable to mitigate effects of the publicity, and

3. A prior restraint would effectively prevent the harm to defendant's rights.

Judge Hoeveler found that in this instance, prior restraint was justifiable, and ordered a temporary injunction against CNN's broadcast of the tapes until the court could review the tapes in CNN's possession. The following day—Nov. 9, 1990—after an emergency appeal by CNN to the Eleventh Circuit Court of Appeals, Judge Hoeveler limited the temporary injunction to ten days. He complained about CNN's refusal to turn over the tapes to him, putting him in the position of having to make rulings without having heard them.

The next day—Nov. 10, 1990—the Court of Appeals ruled that the temporary restraining order should remain in effect. The appellate court upheld Judge Hoeveler's injunction against CNN and his demand for production of the tapes.[42] Meanwhile, CNN indeed had been defiant, for it repeatedly broadcast—on Nov. 9—a taped conversation said to be an interchange between Noriega and a legal secretary working for his attorneys. Noriega's attorneys asked for dismissal of the charges against their client and that CNN be fined $300,000 each time it played one of the tapes.[43]

CNN then withdrew a bit, agreeing on Nov. 12 to halt playing the tapes until the U.S. Supreme Court could rule. Noriega contended that he was being railroaded and was powerless before an unjust legal system.[44]

[41] United States v. Noriega, 752 F.Supp. 1032 (S.D.Fla.1990), 18 Med.L.Rptr. 1348, 1349.

[42] In re Cable News Network, Inc., 917 F.2d 1543 (11th Cir.1990), 18 Med.L.Rptr. 1352, 1358.

[43] "CNN to Delay Playing of Noriega Tapes," The New York Times, Nov. 13, 1990, p. A12.

[44] Ibid.; see also David Johnston, "Noriega Tells Judge He's at Mercy of an Unfair and Unjust System," The New York Times, Nov. 17, 1990, p. 1.

On Nov. 18, 1990, moving swiftly only eight days after the Court of Appeals ruling against CNN, the U.S. Supreme Court allowed the injunction to stand, denying CNN's petition for a writ of certiorari.[45]

After this defeat, CNN handed over the Noriega tapes to a federal magistrate who reported his evaluation of the tapes to U.S. District Judge Hoeveler. Anticlimactically, Judge Hoeveler ruled that CNN could broadcast the taped conversations. CNN, however, decided not to put the tapes on the air ... at least, not immediately.[46] The New York Times confessed to being puzzled by CNN's behavior: Challenging a U.S. district judge, ultimately getting his permission to run the tapes, and then not doing so. A *Times* editorial said: [47]

> The network's actions and news judgments obscure the important feature of its own story. The existence, not the airing, of some tapes requires explanation from the [U.S.] Justice Department. What safeguards [for defendant Noriega] were in place at Miami's Metropolitan Correction Center and how were they violated?

On March 30, 1994, long after CNN's broadcast excerpts of the "Noriega tapes," CNN was charged with criminal contempt for " 'knowingly and wilfully' " disobeying Judge Hocveler's November, 1990, injunction. Lawyers for CNN attended the arraignment proceeding, pleading not guilty before Judge Hoeveler in the cable network's behalf.[48]

In September, 1994, Judge Hoeveler began a non-jury trial, after offering to assign the case to another judge and to empanel and advisory jury to try questions of fact. Neither the Department of Justice, prosecuting, nor CNN, the defendant, accepted those offers.[49]

On November 1, 1994, Judge Hoeveler found CNN guilty as charged of criminal contempt of court, setting the hearing on sanctions to be levied against CNN for December 9, 1994. Judge

[45] Cable News Network, Inc. v. Noriega, 498 U.S. 976, 111 S.Ct. 451 (1990), 18 Med.L.Rptr. 1358, 1359.

[46] David Johnston, "Judge Lifts Ban on Noriega Tapes; No Broadcast is Planned," The New York Times, Nov. 29, 1990, p. A14.

[47] "Odd Behavior in the Noriega Case," The New York Times, Dec. 1, 1990, p. 14.

[48] Associated Press, "CNN charged in airing tape of Noriega's talks to lawyers," The Knoxville News–Sentinel, March 31, 1994, p. A12; Larry Rohter, "CNN Charged With Ignoring Court Order on Noriega Tapes," The New York Times, March 31, 1994, p.A7.

[49] District Judge William M. Hoeveler's decision in United States v. Cable News Network, Inc., 865 F.Supp. 1549 (S.D.Fla.1994).

Hoeveler acknowledged the press's First Amendment responsibility to provide news of government misconduct, and then wrote: [50]

> * * * CNN, however, had already revealed the potential government misconduct. The intense pressure to play the tapes was actually coming from other news organizations, challenging CNN to show them the tapes or "where's the beef?" * * * [Such circumstances] do not justify the action taken by defendant. The 11th Circuit has held that even when a court's order is ultimately deemed to be invalid, the collateral bar rule requires parties to follow that order.

> * * *

> The thin bright line between anarchy and order—the delicate balance which ultimately is the vital protection of the individual and the public generally—is the rampart which litigants and the public have for the law and the orders issued by the courts. Defiance of court orders and, even more so, public display of such defiance cannot be justified or permitted.

Late in December, 1994, CNN complied with an order from Judge Hoeveler, ending the dispute by broadcasting an apology and paying $85,000 to reimburse the special prosecutor's costs.

SEC. 93.   ACCESS TO CRIMINAL TRIALS AND CIVIL MATTERS

Gannett v. DePasquale (1979) declared that *pre-trial* matters could be closed to press and public; Richmond Newspapers v. Virginia (1980) held that there is a First Amendment right to attend *trials*.

The Supreme Court had some good news for the press in 1978, and it came in the decision in Landmark Communications, Inc. v. Virginia. The Virginian Pilot, a daily newspaper owned by Landmark, late in 1975 published an accurate article reporting on a pending investigation by the Virginia Judicial Inquiry and Review Commission. The article named a state judge whose conduct was being investigated. Because such proceedings were required to be confidential by the Constitution of Virginia and by related enabling statutes, a grand jury indicted Landmark for violating Virginia law.

The newspaper's managing editor, Joseph W. Dunn, Jr., testified that he had chosen to publish material about the Judicial Inquiry and Review Commission because he believed the subject was a matter of public importance. Dunn stated that although he

---

[50] Ibid., pp. 35–37, 23 Med.Law Rptr. No. 1, Jan. 3, 1995.

knew it was a misdemeanor for participants in such an action to divulge information from that Commission's proceedings, he did not think that the statute applied to newspaper reports.[51]

Chief Justice Burger, writing for a unanimous Court, said the issue was whether the First Amendment allows criminal punishment of third persons—including news media representatives—who publish truthful information about proceedings of the Judicial Inquiry and Review Commission. The Court concluded that "the publication Virginia seeks to punish under its statute lies near the core of the First Amendment, and the Commonwealth's interests advanced by the imposition of criminal sanctions are insufficient to justify the actual and potential encroachments on freedom of speech and of the press."

Although the Commission was entitled to meet in secret, and could preserve confidentiality of its proceedings and working papers, the press could not be punished for publication of such information once it has obtained it.[52]

Obtaining information about judicial proceedings, of course, implies access by public and press to those proceedings. And then, after the "good news" of *Landmark Communications* (1978), along came one of the Supreme Court's unpleasant surprises for the press: Gannett v. DePasquale.

Gannett v. DePasquale (1979)

Journalists are taught that government should never be given the power of secret arrest, secret confinement, or secret trial. With its decision in Gannett v. DePasquale, the Supreme Court of the United States said, in effect, that two out of three aren't bad. In a badly fragmented 5–4 vote, with a total of five opinions written, the Court held that the public—including the press—has no right to attend pretrial hearings. The issue in *DePasquale* was narrow: the Gannett Company was seeking to overturn a ruling barring its reporter from a pretrial hearing and forbidding the immediate release of a transcript of a secret hearing.

The Court's majority, however, did not restrict itself to pretrial hearings. Justice Potter Stewart's majority opinion also declared that the rights guaranteed by the Sixth Amendment did not extend to the public or to the press. Instead, those rights "are personal to the accused. * * * We hold that members of the public [and thus the press] have no constitutional right to attend criminal trials." Joining Justice Stewart in that view were Justices William Rehnquist and John Paul Stevens.

[51] Landmark Communications, Inc. v. Virginia, 435 U.S. 829, 98 S.Ct. 1535 (1978).
[52] 435 U.S. 829, 838, 98 S.Ct. 1535, 1541 (1978).

Chief Justice Warren E. Burger joined the opinion of the Court, but argued that by definition, a " * * *; hearing on a motion before trial is not a *trial:* it is a *pre*-trial hearing." Mr. Justice Lewis Powell, like the Chief Justice, concurred separately. Justice Powell expressed the belief that the reporter had an interest protected by the First Amendment to attend the pretrial hearing. However, he added that this right of access to courtroom proceedings is not absolute and must be balanced against a defendant's Sixth Amendment fair trial rights. In his concurring opinion, Justice William Rehnquist said that so far as the Constitution is concerned, it is up to the lower courts, "by accommodating competing interests in a judicious manner," to decide whether to open or close a court proceeding.

In a 44–page dissent joined by Justices William Brennan, Byron White, and Thurgood Marshall, Justice Harry Blackmun contended that the Sixth Amendment guarantees the public's right to attend hearings and trials. Justice Blackmun wrote that the Court's majority overreacted to "placid, routine, and innocuous" coverage of a criminal prosecution.

Gannett v. DePasquale arose when 42–year-old former policeman Wayne Clapp did not return from a July, 1976, fishing trip on upstate New York's Lake Seneca. He had been fishing with two men, aged 16 and 21, and those men returned in the boat without Clapp and drove away in Clapp's pickup truck. They were later arrested in Michigan after Clapp's disappearance had been reported and after bullet holes were found in Clapp's boat.

Gannett newspapers, the morning *Democrat & Chronicle* and the evening *Times-Union,* published stories about Clapp's disappearance and reported on police speculations that Clapp had been shot on his own boat and his body dumped overboard. In one story, the *Democrat & Chronicle* reported that the 16–year-old suspect, Kyle Greathouse, had led Michigan police to a place where he had buried Clapp's .357 magnum revolver. Defense attorneys then began taking steps to try to suppress statements made to police, claiming that those statements had been given involuntarily. The defense also tried to suppress evidence turned up in relation to the allegedly involuntary confessions, including the pistol.

During a pretrial hearing, when defense attorneys requested that press and public be excluded, Justice Daniel DePasquale granted the motion, evidently fearing that reporting on the hearing might prejudice defendants' rights in a later trial. Neither the prosecution nor reporter Carol Ritter of the *Democrat & Chronicle* objected to the clearing of the courtroom. On the next day, however, Ritter wrote Judge DePasquale, asserting a right to cover the hearing and asking to be given access to the transcript. The judge, refused to rescind his exclusion order or to grant the press or public immediate access to a transcript of the pre-trial hearing. Judge DePasquale's orders were overturned by an intermediate-level New York appeals court, but were upheld by the state's highest court, the Court of Appeals.[53]   The Supreme Court of the United States subsequently granted certiorari.[54]

Although the issue of covering a pretrial hearing on suppression of evidence is technically narrow, it is important. As James C. Goodale, former vice president of *The New York Times,* has written: [55]

> Only a fraction of the criminal cases brought ever go to trial. The real courtroom for most criminal trials in the United States is the pre-trial hearing, where proceedings of a vital public concern often take place. * * * [A] successful suppression motion will probably mean that an account of the improper methods the police have used to extract a certain confession will be brought out only at the pretrial hearing, and nowhere else. * * * [T]his is information which the public needs to have if its public officers are to be held accountable. Without multiplying examples, we need only remember the shocking trials of Ginzburg and Scharansky behind closed doors in Russia in the summer of 1978 to realize that criminal trials in this country must remain open.

Other constitutional scholars and a variety of publications expressed both shock and outrage at the Supreme Court's decision in *DePasquale.* Fear of secret trials is in the American grain. Even though England's despised secret Court of the Star Chamber was abolished in 1641, it has been remembered as a symbol of persecution ever since. The assumption by both public and press has long been that open trials are needed to make sure that justice is done. Harvard Law Professor Lawrence Tribe, a leading scholar, said after *DePasquale* was decided that there " ' * * * will be no need to gag the press if stories can be choked off at the source.' " Allen Neuharth, chairman of The Gannett Co., Inc., declared that " ' * * * those judges who share the philosophy of secret trials can now run Star Chamber justice.' " [56] In any event, the *DePasquale* holding was far removed from Justice William O. Douglas's words

[53] Gannett Co., Inc. v. De Pasquale, 43 N.Y.2d 370, 401 N.Y.S.2d 756, 372 N.E.2d 544 (1977), reversing the Supreme Court of the State of New York, Appellate Division, Fourth Department's decision in 55 A.D.2d 107, 389 N.Y.S.2d 719 (1976).

[54] 443 U.S. 368, 99 S.Ct. 2898 (1979).

[55] James C. Goodale, "Open Justice: The Threat of *Gannett,*" Communications and the Law, Vol. 1, No. 1 (Winter, 1979) pp. 12–13.

[56] "Slamming the Courtroom Doors," Time, July 16, 1979, p. 66.

in a 1947 contempt of court case, Craig v. Harney: "[w]hat transpires in the court room is public property." [57]

Justice Potter Stewart wrote for the Court: [58]

* * *

Publicity concerning pretrial suppression hearings such as the one involved in the present case poses special risks of unfairness. The whole purpose of such hearings is to screen out unreliable or illegally obtained evidence and insure that this evidence does not become known to the jury. Cf. Jackson v. Denno, 378 U.S. 368, 84 S.Ct. 1774 (1964). Publicity concerning the proceedings at a pretrial hearing, however, could influence public opinion against a defendant and inform potential jurors of inculpatory information wholly inadmissible at the actual trial.

* * *

The Sixth Amendment, applicable to the States through the Fourteenth, surrounds a criminal trial with guarantees such as the rights to notice, confrontation, and compulsory process that have as their overriding purpose the protection of the accused from prosecutorial and judicial abuses. Among the guarantees that the Amendment provides to a person charged with the commission of a criminal offense, and to him alone, is the "right to a speedy and public trial, by an impartial jury." The Constitution nowhere mentioned any right of access to a criminal trial on the part of the public; its guarantee, like the others enumerated, is personal to the accused. See Faretta v. California, 422 U.S. 806, 846, 95 S.Ct. 2525, 2546 (1975) ("[T]he specific guarantees of the Sixth Amendment are personal to the accused.") (Blackmun, J., dissenting).

Our cases have uniformly recognized the public trial guarantee as one created for the benefit of the defendant.

Chief Justice Burger's concurring opinion simply maintained that by definition, a hearing on a motion before trial to suppress evidence is not a *trial,* it is a *pre-trial* hearing. Trials should be open, but pre-trial proceedings are "private to the litigants" and could be closed.

Justice Powell's concurrence argued that the reporter had an interest protected by the First and Fourteenth Amendments in

[57] Craig v. Harney, 331 U.S. 367, 374, 67 S.Ct. 1249, 1254 (1947).

[58] Gannett Co., Inc. v. DePasquale, 443 U.S. 368, 378–381, 99 S.Ct. 2898, 2905–2906 (1979).

being present at the pretrial suppression hearing. He added: [59]

> As I have argued in Saxbe v. Washington Post Co., 417
> U.S. 843, 850, 94 S.Ct. 2811, 2815 (1974) (Powell, J.,
> dissenting), this constitutional protection derives, not from
> any special status of members of the press as such, but
> rather because "[i]n seeking out the news the press * * *
> acts as an agent of the public at large," each individual
> member of which cannot obtain for himself "the informa-
> tion needed for the intelligent discharge of his political
> responsibilities." Id., at 863, 94 S.Ct., at 2821.

Justice Powell then swung into his balancing act, stating that
the right of access to courtroom proceedings is not absolute. It is
limited by both the right of defendants to a fair trial and by needs
of governments to obtain convictions and to maintain the confidentiality of sensitive information and of the identity of informants.
In his view, representatives of the public and the press must be
given an opportunity to protest closure motions. Then it would be
the defendant's burden to offer evidence that the fairness of his
trial would be jeopardized by public and press access to the proceedings. On the other hand, the press and public should have to show
that alternative procedures are available which would take away
dangers to the defendant's chances of receiving a fair trial.[60]

Justice Rehnquist's concurring opinion scoffed that Justice
Powell was advancing the idea " * * * that the First Amendment is
some sort of constitutional 'sunshine law' that requires notice, an
opportunity to be heard and substantial reasons before a governmental proceeding may be closed to public and press." [61]

Justice Blackmun's lengthy dissent was joined by Justices
Brennan, White, and Marshall. Blackmun termed the news coverage of this case "placid, routine, and innocuous" and, indeed,
relatively infrequent. After a long review of Anglo–American historical and constitutional underpinnings for public trials, he pointed to dangers he saw in closing court proceedings.[62]

> I, for one, am unwilling to allow trials and suppression
> hearings to be closed with no way to ensure that the public
> interest is protected. Unlike the other provisions of the
> Sixth Amendment, the public trial interest cannot ade-
> quately be protected by the prosecutor and judge in con-
> junction, or connivance, with the defendant. The specter
> of a trial or suppression hearing where a defendant of the
> same political party as the prosecutor and the judge—both

---

[59] 443 U.S. 368, 397–398, 99 S.Ct. 2898, 2914 (1979).

[60] 443 U.S. 368, 398–399, 99 S.Ct. 2898, 2915 (1979).

[61] 443 U.S. 368, 405, 99 S.Ct. 2898, 2918 (1979).

[62] 443 U.S. 368, 438–439, 448, 99 S.Ct. 2898, 2935–2936, 2940 (1979).

of whom are elected officials perhaps beholden to the very defendant they are to try—obtains closure of the proceeding without any consideration for the substantial public interest at stake is sufficiently real to cause me to reject the Court's suggestion that the parties be given complete discretion to dispose of the public's interest as they see fit. The decision of the parties to close a proceeding in such a circumstance, followed by suppression of vital evidence or acquittal by the bench, destroys the appearance of justice and undermines confidence in the judicial system in a way no subsequent provision of a transcript might remedy. * * *

III

* * *

It has been said that publicity "is the soul of justice." J. Bentham, A Treatise on Judicial Evidence, 67 (1825). And in many ways it is: open judicial processes, especially in the criminal field, protect against judicial, prosecutorial, and police abuse; provide a means for citizens to obtain information about the criminal justice system and the performance of public officials; and safeguard the integrity of the courts. Publicity is essential to the preservation of public confidence in the rule of law and in the operation of courts.

Richmond Newspapers v. Virginia (1980)

On July 2, 1980—exactly one year after the Supreme Court of the United States ruled in Gannett Co., Inc. v. DePasquale [63] that pretrial hearings could be closed—the Court held 7–1 that the public and the press have a First Amendment right to attend criminal trials. The 1980 case, Richmond Newspapers, Inc. v. Virginia, brought joyous responses from the press.

Anthony Lewis of *The New York Times* wrote, "For once a Supreme Court decision deserves that overworked adjective, historic." [64] His newspaper editorialized: "Now the Supreme Court has reasserted the obvious, at least as it pertains to trials. 'A presumption of openness inheres in the very nature of a criminal trial under our system of justice.' " [65] Even though *Richmond Newspapers* did not overrule *Gannett* where pretrial matters are concerned, the

[63] 443 U.S. 368, 99 S.Ct. 2898 (1979).

[64] Anthony Lewis, "A Right To Be Informed," The New York Times, July 3, 1980, p. A–19.

[65] Editorial, "Wiping the Graffiti Off the Courtroom," The New York Times, July 3, 1980, p. A–18.

Court's 1980 reliance on the First Amendment—and not on the Sixth Amendment as in *Gannett*—gave hope to journalists.

Justice John Paul Stevens' concurring opinion likewise saw *Richmond Newspapers* as remarkable: "This is a watershed case." He continued,[66]

> Until today the Court has accorded virtually absolute protection to the dissemination of information or ideas, but never before has it squarely held that the acquisition of newsworthy matter is entitled to any constitutional protection whatsoever.

Lewis said " * * * the Court today established for the first time that the Constitution gives the public a right to learn how public institutions function: a crucial right in a democracy." [67] Attorney James Goodale said the Richmond case would help reporters to see " 'prisons, small-town meetings, the police blotter' " and other places and documents often closed to the news media in the past.

Years ago, Judge Learned Hand described his career on the bench as "shoveling smoke." In 1979, the Supreme Court unlimbered its smoke generator in the infamous *Gannett* case, ruling by a 5–4 margin that the public and the press did not have a right to attend pre-trial proceedings in criminal cases. Some of the Justices' language billowed beyond pre-trial matters. As noted, Justice Potter Stewart's plurality opinion announcing the Court's judgment in *Gannett* declared that rights guaranteed by the Sixth Amendment did not reach to the public or to the press. Those rights, said Stewart, " * * * are personal to the accused. * * * We hold that members of the public [and thus the press] have no constitutional right to attend criminal trials." [68]

Four members of the Court later made public statements professing shock about the way *Gannett* had been "misinterpreted," and that wholesale closings had not been endorsed by a majority of the Court. Howls of protest arose from the media. Goodale, then executive vice president of *The New York Times,* wrote in 1979 that only a small fraction—perhaps 10 per cent—of all criminal cases reach the trial stage. The real courtroom for most criminal proceedings is the pre-trial hearing.[69]

In the wake of *Gannett,* many pretrial *and* trial proceedings were closed. As a study by The Reporters Committee for Freedom of the Press showed, in the 10 months between the *Gannett*

---

[66] Opinion of Mr. Justice Stevens, 448 U.S. 555, 581, 100 S.Ct. 2814, 2830 (1980).

[67] Lewis, loc. cit.

[68] Gannett Co., Inc. v. DePasquale, 443 U.S. 368, 99 S.Ct. 2898 (1979).

[69] Goodale, loc. cit.

decision of July 2, 1979 and April 30, 1980, there were at least 220 attempts to close criminal justice proceedings. More than half were successful. Jack C. Landau, director of The Reporters Committee, wrote that "[j]udges are closing pre-indictment, trial, and post-trial proceedings, in addition to pre-trial proceedings." [70] *Newsweek* reported that in the year after *Gannett,* 155 proceedings were closed, including 30 actual trials. Four hundred attempts were made to close courtrooms between July, 1979, and May, 1981.[71]

The Richmond case arose when Baltimore resident John Paul Stevenson was convicted of second-degree murder in the slaying of a Hanover County, Virginia, motel manager. In late 1977, however, the Virginia Supreme Court reversed Stevenson's conviction, concluding that a bloodstained shirt belonging to Stevenson had been admitted improperly as evidence.[72] Subsequently, two additional jury trials of Stevenson ended in mistrials, one when a juror had to be excused and the other because a prospective juror may have read about the defendant's previous trials and may have told other jurors about the case before the retrial began.

On September 11, 1978, the same court—for the fourth time—attempted to try Stevenson. Reporters Tim Wheeler of the *Richmond Times–Dispatch* and Kevin McCarthy of the *Richmond News–Leader,* along with all other members of the public, were barred from the courtroom by Hanover County Circuit Court Judge Richard H.C. Taylor, after defense counsel said: [73]

> "[T]here was this woman that was with the family of the deceased when we were here before. She had sat in the Courtroom. I would like to ask that everybody be excluded from the Courtroom because I don't want any information being shuffled back and forth when we have a recess as to what—who testified to what."

Trial Judge Taylor had presided after two of the previous three trials of Stevenson. After hearing that the prosecution had no objection to the closure, excluded all parties from the trial except witnesses when they testified.[74] Since no one—including reporters Wheeler and McCarthy—had objected to closure, the order was made. Later that same day, however, the Richmond newspapers

[70] The Reporters Committee for Freedom of the Press, Court Watch Summary, May, 1980; Southern Newspaper Publishers Association Bulletin, Aug. 10, 1981.

[71] Newsweek, July 14, 1980, p. 24.

[72] Stevenson v. Commonwealth, 218 Va. 462, 237 S.E.2d 779 (1977).

[73] Opinion of Chief Justice Burger, Richmond Newspapers, Inc. v. Virginia, 448 U.S. 555, 559, 100 S.Ct. 2814, 2818 (1980).

[74] Virginia Code § 19.2–2.66, which provided that courts may, in their discretion, exclude any persons from the trial whose presence would impair the trial's conduct, provided that the right of an accused to a fair trial shall not be violated.

and their reporters asked for a hearing on a motion to vacate the closure order. Reporters were not allowed to attend the hearing on that order, however, since Judge Taylor ruled that it was a part of the trial. The closure order remained in force.

On the trial's second day, Judge Taylor—after excusing the jury—declared that Stevenson was not guilty of murder, and the defendant was allowed to leave. The Richmond Newspapers then appealed the court closing, unsuccessfully petitioning the Virginia Supreme Court for writs of mandamus and prohibition. The Supreme Court of the United States granted certiorari.

Chief Justice Burger's Opinion

Chief Justice Warren Burger reiterated his view, as stated in Gannett v. DePasquale, that while pre-trial hearings need not be open, trials should be open. In this case, he did not take the Sixth Amendment (right to fair trial) route of the majority in *DePasquale*.[75] Instead, he emphasized that the question in *Richmond Newspapers*[76] was whether the First and Fourteenth Amendments guarantee a right of the public (including the press) to attend trials.

He said that in prior cases, the Court has dealt with questions involving conflicts between publicity and defendants' rights to a fair trial, including Nebraska Press Association v. Stuart,[77] Sheppard v. Maxwell,[78] and Estes v. Texas.[79] But this case, in his view, was a "first:" the Court was asked to decide whether a criminal trial itself may be closed to the public on the defendant's request alone, with no showing that closure is required to protect the right to a fair trial.

After having thus stated the issue, the Chief Justice traced Anglo–American judicial history back to the days before the Norman Conquest and forward through the American colonial experience.[80] In addition to this historical ammunition, Burger quoted Dean Wigmore, who wrote long ago that " '[t]he publicity of a judicial proceeding is a requirement of much broader bearing than its mere effect on the quality of testimony.' " The Chief Justice also found a "significant community therapeutic value" in public trials. He then became expansive about the role of the press as a

---

[75] Gannett Co., Inc. v. DePasquale, 443 U.S. 368, 99 S.Ct. 2898 (1979).

[76] Richmond Newspapers, Inc. v. Virginia, 448 U.S. 555, 564, 100 S.Ct. 2814, 2821 (1980).

[77] 427 U.S. 539, 96 S.Ct. 2791 (1976).

[78] 384 U.S. 333, 86 S.Ct. 1507 (1966).

[79] 381 U.S. 532, 85 S.Ct. 1628 (1965). The Chief Justice also cited Murphy v. Florida, 421 U.S. 794, 95 S.Ct. 2031 (1975), in which Jack (Murph the Surf) Murphy, unsuccessfully pleaded that prejudicial pre-trial publicity had deprived him of a fair day in court.

[80] Richmond Newspapers, Inc. v. Virginia, 448 U.S. 555, 100 S.Ct. 2814 (1980).

stand-in for the public, a role often claimed by the press but one which had received little judicial support.[81]

Looking back, we see that when the ancient "town meeting" form of trial became too cumbersome, twelve members of the community were delegated to act as surrogates, but the community did not surrender its right to observe the conduct of trials. The people retained a "right of visitation" which enabled them to satisfy themselves that justice was in fact being done.

People in an open society do not demand infallibility from their institutions, but it is difficult for them to accept what they are prohibited from observing.

* * *

In earlier times, both in England and America, attendance at court was a common mode of "passing the time." * * * With the press, cinema and electronic media now supplying the representations of reality of the real life drama once available only in the courtroom, attendance at court is no longer a widespread pastime. * * * Instead of acquiring information about trials by firsthand observation or by word of mouth from those who attended, people now acquire it chiefly through the print and electronic media. In a sense, this validates the media claim of functioning as surrogates for the public. While media representatives enjoy the same right of access as the public, they often are provided special seating and priority of entry so that they may report what people in attendance have seen and heard. This "contribute[s] to public understanding of the rule of law and to comprehension of the functioning of the entire criminal justice system. * * * "Nebraska Press Ass'n v. Stuart, 427 U.S. 539, 587, 96 S.Ct. 2791, 2816 (1976) (Brennan, J., concurring).

Burger than disposed of the State of Virginia's arguments that neither the constitution nor the Bill of Rights contains guarantees of a public right to attend trials. He responded that the Court has recognized that "certain unarticulated rights" are implicit in the Bill of Rights, including the rights of association, privacy, and the right to attend criminal trials. He then inserted footnote 17, which may become important in the future: "Whether the public has a right to attend trials of civil cases is a question not by this case, but we note that historically *both civil and criminal trials* have been

[81] 448 U.S. 555, 572–573, 100 S.Ct. 2814, 2354–2355 (1980).

presumptively open." [82]

Despite the sweep of Burger's words, he was not saying that all criminal trials must be open to the press and public. Instead, he criticized the conduct of the court in the murder trial of John Paul Stevenson. There, despite its being the fourth trial of the defendant, the judge " * * * made no findings to support closure; no inquiry was made as to whether alternative solutions [such as sequestration of the jury] would have met the need to insure fairness; there was no recognition of any right under the Constitution for the public or press to attend the trial." He concluded: "Absent an overriding interest articulated in findings, the trial of a criminal case must be open to the public. Accordingly, the judgment under review is reversed." [83]

Note that Justice Powell took no part in the consideration or decision of this case. And remember that Powell declared, concurring in Gannett v. DePasquale, that reporters had a *limited* First Amendment right to attend pre-trial hearings. And Justices Blackmun, Brennan, White, and Marshall all agreed that public and press had a right, either under the First or the Sixth Amendment, to attend both pre-trial hearings and trials. Thus, although the First Amendment is not an absolute, it appears that the breadth of the language in *Richmond Newspapers* about *trials* has once again made attendance at *pre-trial* proceedings an open question.

In his concurring opinion, Justice Stevens said: [84]

> * * * I agree that the First Amendment protects the public and the press from abridgment of their rights of access to information about the operation of their government, including the judicial branch; given the total absence of any record justification for the closure order entered in this case, that order violated the First Amendment.

Justice Brennan, joined by Justice Marshall, presented a marvelously complex concurrence, speaking of the structural value of public access in various circumstances. "But the First Amendment embodies more than a commitment to free expression and communicative interchange for their own sakes; it has a *structural* role to play in securing and fostering our republican form of self-government." He added: [85]

---

[82] 448 U.S. 555, 581, 100 S.Ct. 2814, 2829 (1980), at footnote 17. Emphasis added.

[83] 448 U.S. 555, 581, 100 S.Ct. 2814, 2830 (1980).

[84] 448 U.S. 555, 584, 100 S.Ct. 2814, 2830 (1980).

[85] 448 U.S. 555, 595, 100 S.Ct. 2814, 2833, 2837 (1980).

Open trials assure the public that procedural rights are respected, and that justice is afforded equally. Closed trials breed suspicion of prejudice and arbitrariness, which in turn spawns disrespect for the law. Public access is essential, therefore, if trial adjudication is to achieve the objective of maintaining public confidence in the administration of justice.

Note also that Justice Rehnquist, seeming unconcerned by possible threats of secret judicial proceedings to society, was the only member of the court in both the *Gannett* and *Richmond* cases who could find no support for a right of public and press to attend judicial proceedings under either a Sixth Amendment or First Amendment rationale.[86]

Access Rights Need Defense

Although *Richmond Newspapers* has a much nicer ring than Gannett v. DePasquale, it did leave unanswered questions about the right to cover pre-trial matters, the matters which make up the bulk of our criminal justice process. During the dark days of 1979 and '80, after Gannett v. DePasquale was decided, reporters covering the judicial process began carrying their "Gannett cards." Various organizations made up statements for reporters to read in court when they were about to be ousted from pre-trial or trial proceedings. In fact, a Gannett card—literally from the Gannett organization—said: [87]

> "Your honor, I am _____, a reporter for _____, and I would like to object on behalf of my employer and the public to this proposed closing. Our attorney is prepared to make a number of arguments against closings such as this one, and we respectfully ask the Court for a hearing on those issues. I believe our attorney can be here relatively quickly for the Court's convenience and he will be able to demonstrate that closure in this case will violate the First Amendment, and possibly state statutory and constitutional provisions as well. I cannot make the arguments myself, but our attorney can point out several issues for your consideration. If it pleases the Court, we request the opportunity to be heard through counsel."

Reporters, then, should hang on to their "Gannett Cards" and be ready to read them should a judge decide—on application from counsel—to give them the heave-ho from a judicial (including pre-trial) proceedings. After all, as attorney James C. Goodale has

---

[86] 448 U.S. 555, 605, 100 S.Ct. 2814, 2843 (1980).

[87] Other news organizations, such as Knight–Ridder, had similar cards made for their reporters.

written, even the *Gannett* case required three conditions before closure of a pre-trial hearing: [88]

(1) there would be irreparable damage to the defendant's fair trial rights,

(2) there were no alternative means to deal with the publicity and

(3) the closure would be effective, i.e. no leaks.

If judicial proceedings are to remain open, reporters will have to stand ready to speak up, to protest closures. And their employers, obviously, will have to stand ready to go to court—to expend the money and energy to try to keep court proceedings open. Without protests and court tests, closures will simply occur. And when contested, closures can often be reversed. Reporters in courts—whether they like it or not—must sometimes be a first line of defense against secret court proceedings.[89]

Access to Courts after *Richmond Newspapers*

During the first few years after Richmond Newspapers v. Virginia (1980), the Supreme Court of the United States filled in some of that decision's promising outlines where coverage of the judicial process is concerned. Four key cases are: [90]

1. Globe Newspaper Co. v. Superior Court (1982).

2. Press–Enterprise Co. v. Superior Court (1984). ("Press Enterprise I")

3. Waller v. Georgia (1984).

4. "Press–Enterprise II (1986)."

Globe Newspaper Co. v. Superior Court (1982)

The Boston Globe challenged the constitutionality of a Massachusetts statute providing for the exclusion of the public from trials of certain sex offenses involving victims under the age of 18. Globe reporters had tried unsuccessfully to get access to a rape trial in the Superior Court for the County of Norfolk, Massachusetts. Charges against the defendant in the trial involved forcible rape and forced

---

[88] James C. Goodale, "The Three–Part Open Door Test in Richmond Newspapers Case," The National Law Journal, Sept. 22, 1980, p. 26.

[89] See James D. Spaniolo, Dan Paul, Parker D. Thomson and Richard Ovemlen, "Access After *Richmond Newspapers,*" in James C. Goodale, chairman, Communications Law 1980 (New York: Practising Law Institute, 1980), pp. 385–648, for an intensive discussion of and listing of recent cases involving access to judicial proceedings. See especially pp. 452–456, dealing with access to judicial records.

[90] Globe Newspaper Co. v. Superior Court for Norfolk County, 457 U.S. 596, 102 S.Ct. 2613 (1982), 8 Med.L.Rptr. 1689; Press–Enterprise Co. v. Superior Court of California, 464 U.S. 501, 104 S.Ct. 819 (1984), 10 Med.L.Rptr. 1161; Waller v. Georgia, 467 U.S. 39, 104 S.Ct. 2210 (1984), 10 Med.L.Rptr. 1714.

unnatural rape of three girls who were minors at the time of the trial—two were 16 and one was 17. Writing for the Court, Justice Brennan held that the Massachusetts statute providing for mandatory closure of such cases violated the First Amendment of access to criminal trials. He said: [91]

> The Court's recent decision in Richmond Newspapers firmly established for the first time that the press and the general public have a constitutional right of access to criminal trials. Although there was no opinion of the Court in that case, seven Justices recognized that this right of access is embodied in the First Amendment, and applied to the States through the Fourteenth Amendment.
>
> * * *
>
> * * * [T]he right of access to criminal trials plays a particularly significant role in the functioning of the judicial process and the government as a whole. Public scrutiny of a criminal trial enhances the quality and safeguards the integrity of the factfinding process, with benefits to both the defendant and to society as a whole.
>
> * * *
>
> We agree * * * that the first interest—safeguarding the physical and psychological wellbeing of a minor is a compelling one. But as compelling as that is, it does not justify a mandatory closure rule, for it is clear that the circumstances of the particular case may affect the significance of the interest. A trial court can determine on a case-by-case basis whether closure is necessary to protect the welfare of a minor victim.

Chief Justice Burger and Justice Rehnquist dissented, complaining that Justice Brennan had ignored " * * * a long history of exclusion of the public from trials involving sexual assaults, particularly those against minors." [92]

Press-Enterprise v. Superior Court (1984)

The Riverside (California) Press–Enterprise was trying to cover a rape trial, and wanted its reporters present during the *voir dire* proceedings, the in-depth questioning of prospective jurors. The newspaper moved that the *voir dire* be open to public and press. The State of California opposed the motion, arguing that with the public and press present, jurors' responses would not be candid, and that this would endanger the entire trial.

[91] Globe Newspaper Co. v. Superior Court for Norfolk County, 457 U.S. 596, 102 S.Ct. 2613, 2618–2620 (1982), 8 Med.L.Rptr. 1689, 1692–1694.

[92] 457 U.S. 596, 102 S.Ct. 2613, 2624 (1984), 8 Med.L.Rptr. at 1697.

Writing for a unanimous Supreme Court, Chief Justice Burger wrote that the roots of open trials reach back to the days before the Norman Conquest in England, and related to that was a "presumptive openness" in the jury selection process.[93]   He added:

> No right ranks higher than the right of the accused to a fair trial.   But the primacy of the accused's right is difficult to separate; from the right of everyone in the community to attend the *voir dire* which promotes fairness.

This fact situation was made harsher by the trial judge's keeping six weeks of the *voir dire* proceedings closed (although three days were open).   Media requests for transcripts of the *voir dire* were refused; the California court argued that Sixth Amendment (defendant's right to a fair trial) and juror privacy rights coalesced to support closure of the proceeding.   The Supreme Court disagreed.   Chief Justice Burger wrote: [94]

> The judge at this trial closed an incredible six weeks of *voir dire* without considering alternatives to closure.   Later the court declined to release a transcript of the voir dire even while stating that most of the material in the transcript was "dull and boring." * * * Those parts of the transcript reasonably entitled to privacy could have been sealed without such a sweeping order; a trial judge should explain why the material is entitled to privacy.

Waller v. Georgia (1984)

Waller was a defendant charged with violation of Georgia's Racketeer Influenced and Corrupt Organizations (RICO) Act.   A pre-trial suppression hearing was held, in which Waller and other defendants asked that wiretap evidence and evidence seized during searches be suppressed—that is, disallowed or declared inadmissible.

The prosecuting attorney asked that the suppression hearing be closed, contending that if the evidence were presented in open court and published, it might become "tainted" and therefore unusable, especially in future prosecutions.   The court ordered the suppression hearing closed to all persons except witnesses, the defendants, and lawyers and court personnel.   Defendant Waller, however, wanted the hearings to be open.

Writing for the Court, Justice Lewis Powell cited Press Enterprise I approvingly, noting that even though the suppression hearing had been closed for its entire seven days, there was less than

[93] Press–Enterprise Co. v. Superior Court of California, 464 U.S. 501, 104 S.Ct. 819, 823 (1984), 10 Med.L.Rptr. 1161, 1164.

[94] 464 U.S. 501, 104 S.Ct. 819, 826 (1984), 10 Med.L.Rptr. 1161, 1166.

two and one-half hours worth of wiretap evidence tapes played in the court.[95]

"Press–Enterprise II"
[Press–Enterprise v. Riverside County Superior Court (1986)]

In 1986, the Supreme Court of the United States continued to back away from its much-criticized decision in Gannett v. DePasquale (1979), which held that pre-trial hearings could be closed to press and public. *De Pasquale*, decided under the Sixth (fair trial) amendment, now seems to have been overruled by "Press Enterprise II, decided under the First Amendment."

In that case, Robert Diaz—a nurse suspected of murdering a dozen hospital patients by lethal injections of huge amounts of the heart drug lidocaine—was to have a hearing to see whether there was probable cause to hold him for trial. The magistrate excluded the press from the hearing, which dragged on for 41 days. The magistrate ordered a trial for Diaz.[96]

The California Supreme Court upheld the exclusion order, on the ground that there is no general First Amendment right of access to preliminary hearings, not if a judge found there was "a reasonable likelihood of substantial prejudice." [97]

The U.S. Supreme Court overturned that view, stating that the California rule called for a lesser burden of proof than is required under the First Amendment: there should be a "substantial probability" of prejudice before closure could be allowed.[98]

Chief Justice Burger, writing for a total of seven Justices (Stevens and Rehnquist dissented), declared that the interest of free press and of fair trial are not necessarily inconsistent. He added, "[O]ne of the important means of assuring a fair trial is that the process is open to neutral observers." Finally: [99]

> The considerations that led the Court to apply the First Amendment right of access to criminal trials in *Richmond Newspapers* and the selection of jurors in *Press Enterprise I* lead us to conclude that the right of access applies to preliminary hearings as conducted in California.

Access to Civil Matters

Although civil trial coverage may not appear as important or sexy as criminal trials to journalists and civil libertarians, all of the

---

[95] Waller v. Georgia, 467 U.S. 39, 42, 104 S.Ct. 2210, 2213 (1984).

[96] 478 U.S. 1, 106 S.Ct. 2735 (1986).

[97] Press–Enterprise Company v. Superior Court, 478 U.S. 1, 5, 106 S.Ct. 2735, 2739 (1986).

[98] 478 U.S. 1, 13, 106 S.Ct. 2735, 2743.

[99] 478 U.S. 1, 10, 106 S.Ct. 2735, 2741.

judicial process—criminal or civil, or in law or equity—needs to be open to the public. Public funds pay for the courts and judges, whether the cases involved be criminal or civil. Furthermore, when the judicial process is closed or otherwise hidden from public view, the likelihood is great that private rather than public welfare is being served.

As Professor Bill Loving of the University of Oklahoma has noted, ask Americans about major American auto makers associated with gas-tank fires and the answer will come back: Ford Motor Company and its Pinto. But as Loving pointed out,[1]

> * * * General Motors built cars with designs similar to Ford's and GM cars were involved in numerous accidents in which persons were severely injured or killed because of gas-tank fires and explosions.

> The difference between the publicity the two received lay in General Motors' savvy use of the court system to throw up a shield of secrecy over its legal problems * * *

The problem for the public has assumed these outlines. Suppose that a firm—we'll call it Feckless Industries for purposes of this discussion—is responsible for manufacturing a dangerous product or causing environmental damage through a spill of toxic chemicals. When injured parties become plaintiffs and sue Feckless Industries for damages, then—as long was customary—defendant Feckless could ask the court to issue a secrecy order. Those orders typically take one of these forms: [2]

Protective Orders: This in effect gags persons who receive information from the defendant, thus keeping information damaging to the defendant away from the public, the press, or other litigants.

Confidentiality Agreements: Defendants and plaintiffs often agree to keep details of the lawsuit, including causes of injuries or amounts of settlements, secret.

Sealed Files: When a lawsuit is settled out of court, sealing the files will keep everyone else—the public, environmental health officials, the news media—from knowing just what kind of deal has been cut.

Paul McMasters, Freedom of Information chair for the Society of Professional Journalists in 1990, put the issue of civil litigation

---

[1] Bill Loving, "Media Access to Civil Court Records," paper presented to the Law Division, Association for Education in Journalism and Mass Communication, Boston, MA, Aug. 1991, p.1.

[2] Society of Professional Journalists and Association of Trial Lawyers of America, Keeping Secrets: Justice on Trial: Report of the Conference on Courtroom Secrecy, April 25, 1990, p. 5.

secrecy in sharp focus: [3]

> "We're not talking about irrelevant facts left in the files of
> the litigants. We're talking about documents and deci-
> sions involving unsafe products, dangerous drugs, toxic
> wastes, all with potentially devastating effects on people
> unaware of that danger."

Such records secrecy in civil litigation has long been routine in
most jurisdictions. In Texas, however, Justice Lloyd Doggett of the
Texas Supreme Court led the fight which resulted in a new standard in that state for sealing court records, saying explicitly that
records may not be removed from (civil) court files except as
allowed by statute or court rule. Such records are presumed open,
and may be closed only upon a showing of a substantial interest
outweighing the presumption of openness and any probable adverse
effect that sealing records might have on public health or safety.
This presumption of openness in Texas does include settlement
agreements "that seek to restrict disclosure of information concerning matters that have a probable adverse effect upon general public
health or safety * * *." [4]

Similarly in 1990, Florida passed its Sunshine in Litigation
statute which demands that courts not enter secrecy orders or seal
records which would prevent the public from being informed about
hazardous products or public hazards in general. Nationwide attention is needed to provide public knowledge of **all** trials; information embedded in civil trials can be at least as important to the
public as knowledge of criminal trials.

[3] Quoted at Ibid.
[4] Quoted in Ibid.

Part V

CONVERGING MEDIA AND THE LAW
Chapter 16

MEDIA OWNERSHIP: CONSOLIDATION AND GLOBALIZATION

SEC. 94. INTERNATIONAL DIMENSIONS OF MEDIA OWNERSHIP

Foreign commerce considerations have begun shaping American media ownership policies.

As long as the United States remained preeminent in the arena of world trade, the federal government firmly opposed mergers among major media organizations. Diversity of opinion was the key principle supporting this policy position; to protect the American marketplace of ideas from domination by a small group of giant mass media corporations.

But as this nation's foreign trade deficits began to mount, federal media ownership policy began to change as well. During the past 15 years, the mass media industries have become one of a very few areas of international commerce still providing the United States with a favorable foreign trade balance.[1]

This fact has not gone unnoticed by other powerful industrial nations. Since the mid–1980s, foreign interests have acquired three of America's six major film studios, and two of the nation's three largest music organizations.[2] Only three of the world's ten

---

[1] The annual U.S. foreign trade deficit increased from $20 billion in 1980 to nearly $150 billion in 1993. During that same time, our trade *surplus* from foreign sales of U.S. feature films, television programs, music and video cassettes increased from less than $2 billion in 1980 to more than $7 billion in 1993.

[2] During the past decade Rupert Murdoch's News Corporation has acquired the film studio 20th Century Fox and Metromedia Broadcasting; Sony has purchased Columbia Pictures and Matsushita has taken over MCA, owner of Universal Studios.

734

largest mass media conglomerates are now American owned, and several of the European and Japanese media groups have been expanding at a more rapid pace than their American competitors.[3]

Because of growing concern that many other American mass media corporations might be tempting foreign takeover targets, mergers to strengthen the financial position of domestic mass media properties and enhance their capacity to compete in a global media marketplace are now viewed with much greater sympathy in Washington.

If anyone had expected this policy would be reversed by a Democratic administration, that hope was dashed in January 1994 when the Clinton Justice Department stood aside as Viacom and Paramount merged to become one of the largest media conglomerates in the United States. With the $10 billion Viacom and its partner Blockbuster paid to acquire Paramount, the new media giant will own nine TV stations, 800 motion picture theaters, five cable TV networks, a library of 890 feature films, an 8,500 title syndication library, 3,500 video rental stores, a major television and film production center as well as five regional theme parks, a major wholesale and retail interactive game distribution system and five publishers.[4]

Yet all this attention being given to foreign trade implications of media ownership in the United States should not obscure the fact that permitting domestic mass media organizations to merge reduces the number of mass cultural options available to the American public, diminishing that level of competition essential for a marketplace of ideas to flourish. So, while it is important to understand why our federal government appears at this point to be

Technically, Murdoch's acquisition is no longer "foreign," since he is now an American citizen but the organization he controls is still a global conglomerate. In the field of music, Bertelsmann, a German media conglomerate, has bought RCA Music and Sony had acquired CBS Records. Disney and the newly conglomerated Time–Warner and Viacom–Paramount are the only remaining American owned film studios, and Warner is also the only remaining major music distributor in the United States. Although foreign corporations have been somewhat less interested in acquiring American publishing interests, five of the largest book publishers in the United States are now foreign owned, as well as over 100 magazines, including TV Guide, McCalls, Family Circle and two of America's largest mass media trade magazines, Variety and Broadcasting.

[3] Since its recent merger, Time–Warner has become the largest media conglomerate in the world, generating global annual entertainment revenues of $9 billion. Bertelsmann, the German media conglomerate that also owns RCA Music, Double-day Publishing, Bantom Books and Dell is in second place, and closing rapidly on Time–Warner. In third place is Berlusconi's Italian media organization Fininvest, with an American entity, Capital Cities/ABC in fourth place. Thomson, the Canadian publisher, is the world's fifth largest media corporation while Rupert Murdoch's News Corporation, owner of the Fox Network, TV Guide and Harper & Row, among other American magazines and book publishers, trails Thompson by a small margin.

[4] Adam Sandler, "The Merged Paramount–Viacom Duo", Variety Jan 27, 1994, p. 185.

permitting and even encouraging national media mergers and consolidations, it is at least equally important to understand what adverse effects this policy could have upon the quality of future media service in the United States.

Clear patterns in national media conglomeration are already beginning to emerge. At this point then, there are two significant questions to raise and consider. First, why has the federal government been so firmly opposed to such consolidation in the past, and secondly, are those fears that prompted that opposition still justified today?

SEC. 95. THE TREND TOWARD MEDIA CONCENTRATION

The natural tendency of media organizations has been to combine and thereby reduce competition, a trend that has become more pronounced during the past two decades.

The disappearance of many daily newspapers—particularly independent, locally owned newspapers—is part of the story. Phrases frequently heard include "concentration of newspaper ownership," "problems of bigness and fewness," and "fewer voices in the marketplace of ideas." [5]

But this threat to the daily newspaper is by no means the only area of concern. Professor Bagdikian of the University of California—one of the best-known media critics—is an important voice pointing out that media power is political, and that only a small group of corporations has real opportunities to control most of "what America sees, hears, and reads." Bagdikian wrote that finance capitalism and new technologies have forged [6]

> * * * a new kind of central authority over information—the national and multinational corporation. By the 1980s, the majority of all major American media—newspapers, magazines, radio, television, books, and movies—were controlled by fifty giant corporations. These corporations were interlocked in common financial interest with other massive industries and with a few dominant banks.

Before the 1980s ended, the 50 giant corporations Bagdikian had described in 1982 had already merged into 26 much larger and

[5] Toby J. McIntosh, "Why the Government Can't Stop Press Mergers," Columbia Journalism Review, December, 1980, pp. 48–50; "America's Press: Too Much Power for Too Few?," U.S. News & World Report, Aug. 15, 1977, pp. 27ff; Kevin Phillips, "Busting the Media Trusts," Harper's Magazine, July 1977, pp. 23ff, and Neil Hickey, "Can the Networks Survive," TV Guide, March 21, 1981, pp. 7ff.

[6] Ben H. Bagdikian, The Media Monopoly (Boston: Beacon Press, 1983), book jacket copy, plus quote from p. xv.

more powerful media conglomerates.[7]

Until deregulation became the policy of choice in Washington during the late 1970s, this clear pattern of media consolidation would almost certainly have triggered federal antitrust investigations by the Justice Department. At the moment, however, federal media antitrust actions—the focus of this chapter—are not politically in vogue. Yet, since fads and fashions change in politics as they do in the real world, it's important to be aware of basic concepts in an area of law that may soon become fashionable once more if the trend towards media consolidation should continue at its present pace.

So what is "antitrust?" Black's Law Dictionary says: [8]

> Antitrust acts. Federal and state statutes to protect trade and commerce from unlawful restraints, price discriminations, price fixing, and monopolies. Most states have mini-antitrust acts patterned on the federal acts. The principal federal antitrust acts are: Sherman Act (1890); Clayton Act (1914); Federal Trade Commission Act (1914); Robinson–Patman Act (1936). See Boycott; Combination in restraint of trade; Price fixing; Restraint of trade; * * *

Antitrust law is a term which from time to time causes considerable concern among publishers and broadcasters. For example, the Federal Communications Commission (FCC) proposed in 1970 that broadcast station owners who also owned a newspaper in their coverage area should be forced to sell either their station or their newspaper property. That FCC "proposed rulemaking" was enough to cause a substantial number of cross-ownerships to be split up by their owners.

The FCC backed down from its proposal in 1975, issuing a ruling which "grandfathered"—left in effect—most existing local cross-ownerships of broadcast and newspaper properties. A group calling itself The National Citizens Commission for Broadcasting sued the FCC, demanding that such cross-ownerships be broken up unless positive showings could be made that such patterns served the public interest.[9] In 1978, the Supreme Court held that it was within the FCC's authority to decide that existing cross-media ownerships were in the public interest. That upheld the FCC's

---

[7] Ben Bagdikian, "The 26 Corporations That Own Our Media," Extra, June 1987, p. 1.

[8] Black's Law Dictionary, Fifth Edition (St. Paul, West Pub. Co., Minn., 1979) p. 86.

[9] National Citizens Committee for Broadcasting v. FCC, 555 F.2d 938 (D.C.Cir. 1977).

grandfathering of existing ownership patterns.[10] The FCC, however, made clear it would approve no new local cross-media ownerships.

In certain circumstances, the power of antitrust law over the media can be awesome. The shock wave generated by the *RKO General* case provides one example. The Federal Communications Commission (FCC), claiming (among other things) antitrust law violations by RKO General and its parent company—General Tire and Rubber Company—refused to renew broadcast licenses of three television stations owned by RKO General. With that decision, the FCC tried to take away the license of WNAC–TV, Boston; WOR–TV, New York City, and KHJ–TV, Los Angeles.

RKO General appealed the FCC's decision, setting off lengthy court battles. The antitrust/trade practices complaints were only part of the FCC's proceedings against RKO General. Even though an FCC administrative law judge had found in 1987 that RKO was unfit to hold a broadcast license, the Commission decided against immediate revocation, giving RKO the opportunity to sell its broadcast properties and transfer the station licenses to purchasers the agency had approved.[11]

Also, it should be kept in mind that antitrust law is not exclusively a federal matter. Although this chapter concentrates on federal antitrust activity, State antitrust laws are a formidable thicket. Under the laws of several States, convictions for antitrust violations can result in the forfeiture of a corporation's charter. This would mean that a media corporation could lose the right to operate not only in the State in which it is chartered, but also in any other State which permits it to conduct business as a "foreign" (out of State) corporation.[12]

This chapter will not consider in any detail the entire range of antitrust activity affecting the media. It is aimed, instead, at the increasingly interrelated question of newspaper and broadcast/cable ownership situations. It does not take up such matters as exclusive syndication or newspaper distribution problems, nor does it treat important related questions of ownership of magazines, community newspapers and billboards.[13]

[10] FCC v. National Citizens Committee for Broadcasting, 436 U.S. 775, 98 S.Ct. 2096 (1978).

[11] RKO General, 63 RR 2d 866 (1987). See also, "FCC Gives RKO Green Light to Sell Stations," Broadcasting July 25, 1988, p. 33.

[12] Conrad M. Shumadine and Michael S. Ives, "Selected Antitrust Issues of Interest to the Media," in James C. Goodale, editor, Communications Law 1980, Vol. 2 (New York: Practising Law Institute, 1980) pp. 296–298.

[13] Exclusive syndication problems involve features such as columns or comic strips. Such features are offered to major newspapers under an agreement that no other newspapers within a certain region can publish those particular features. For

Because of the structure of the newspaper industry, the Antitrust Division of the Department of Justice has been unable to make much of an impact on large publishing chains continually acquiring additional newspapers throughout the United States. As long as the expansion of these publishing empires does not diminish the level of *local* newspaper competition, the federal government has generally refused to intervene to prevent such purchases.

The communications media are businesses, and as such, are ringed about by federal and state laws which regulate businesses. Congress has enacted several statutes—most commonly called antitrust laws—which attempt to preserve competition. The most important statements of national antitrust policy are found in the *Sherman*[14] and *Clayton*[15] Acts.

The *Sherman Act of 1890* begins: "Every contract, combination in the form of a trust or otherwise, or conspiracy, in restraint of trade or commerce among the several states, or with foreign nations, is hereby declared to be illegal." [16] Every person who acts to restrain trade, as mentioned generally above, is guilty of a crime.[17] The Sherman Act prohibits "contracts, combinations * * * or conspiracies in restraint of trade or commerce" and makes it illegal to "monopolize, or attempt to monopolize, or combine or conspire * * * to monopolize * * * trade or commerce." [18]

Criminal prosecution—with penalties of fines, imprisonment, or both—is provided for in the Sherman Act. Fines may reach a maximum amount of $100,000 per individual, and imprisonment for up to three years may also be imposed. A corporation may be fined up to $1 million for violating the Sherman Act. The Act also enables the government to seek injunctions against violators of the statute to stop anti-competitive practices. Also, a business that has suffered damages because a competitor has violated the Sherman Act may sue the competitor for *treble damages*.

Treble damages lawsuits work in this way: suppose that the Daily Tribune newspaper has violated the Sherman Act. The United States Department of Justice takes the Daily Tribune to court and gets an order to make it stop monopolistic or trade-restraining practices. An interested spectator, meanwhile, is the Tribune's competitor, the Evening Post. The Post then begins a

a discussion of territorial exclusivity problems and distribution problems involving newspapers, see Marc A. Franklin, et al., The First Amendment and the Fourth Estate (Mineola, N.Y.; Foundation Press, 1977 and later editions).

[14] 26 Stat. 209, 15 U.S.C.A. §§ 1–7; P.L. No. 190, 51st Congress (1890).

[15] 38 Stat. 730, 15 U.S.C.A. § 12ff; P.L. No. 201, 63rd Congress (1914).

[16] 15 U.S.C.A. § 1.

[17] 15 U.S.C.A. § 20.

[18] 15 U.S.C.A. §§ 1, 4.

treble damage antitrust suit, and is able to prove in court that the Daily Tribune's illegal business practices cost the Post $100,000 in business. However, since this would be a *treble damage* lawsuit, the Post would actually collect $300,000 from the competing Tribune company.

The *Clayton Act of 1914* added to the government's antitrust enforcement powers, enumerating many acts as illegal when "they tend to lessen competition or to create a monopoly in any line of commerce." [19]   Section 7 of the Clayton Act—more commonly called the Celler–Kefauver Act of 1950—is the most important section of the Clayton Act where the media are concerned.[20]   The "Celler–Kefauver Act" forbids corporations to acquire stock or assets of a competing corporation "where * * * the effect * * * may be substantially to lessen competition, or tend to create a monopoly."

Upon such vaguely worded provisions of the Sherman and Clayton Acts is built federal antitrust policy. The vagueness of the statutory provisions make antitrust one of the most perplexing branches of public law, especially where newspapers and other units of the communications media are involved.

Increasingly and perhaps inevitably, the business of media is more prominent—and often seems more highly valued—than the social roles of the media. Unfortunately, media theorists who talk about a free press or competition in the marketplace of ideas seem more and more out-of-date. Whatever else they are, the First Amendment rights of speech and press and religion and assembly are supposed to be citizens' rights:

> Congress shall make no law respecting an establishment of religion, or prohibiting the free exercise thereof; or abridging the freedom of speech, or of the press; or the right of the people peaceably to assemble, and to petition the Government for a redress of grievances.

Although it may be true, as historian Leonard W. Levy has argued, that the First Amendment was merely a fortunate political accident, freedom of speech and press are now rights we deeply cherish. It is commonly accepted—or at least given lip service— that the news media provide incalculably valuable services to society.[21]   The media, so the belief goes, create an informed public necessary for meaningful self-government. This is one key reason why the press is shielded by the First Amendment, so that citizens might be informed about government and speak out as necessary.

[19] 15 U.S.C.A. § 18.

[20] 64 Stat. 1125, 15 U.S.C.A. § 18; P.L. 899, 81st Congress (1950).

[21] Leonard W. Levy, Emergence of a Free Press (New York: Oxford University Press, 1985), passim.

Those are the kinds of assumptions ringed about the First Amendment.

Now, however, there is room for skepticism about the First Amendment as a citizens' right. Increasingly, it demands enormously large amounts of capital to own a newspaper or broadcast station, on the one hand, or to defend oneself against a libel or privacy lawsuit, on the other. And as the pace of media mergers accelerates, the number of different voices able to exercise this right continues to diminish with each passing year.

In April 1985, the FCC relaxed its broadcast station ownership restrictions, increasing the number of radio, FM and television properties a licensee could own from 7 to 12 of each type of station.[22] This action set off a massive surge of broadcast industry acquisitions and mergers, resulting in a record-breaking total of $30 billion in broadcast and allied media industry sales transactions occurring before the year ended.[23]

Among the more that 100 separate media purchases that each exceeded $10 million, the acquisition of RCA–NBC by General Electric for $6.3 billion; the purchase of ABC by Capital Cities Broadcasting for $3.5 billion, and Australian media baron Rupert Murdoch's takeover of Metromedia for $2 billion captured the greatest amount of public attention. Through acquiring the Metromedia stations, Murdoch's new Fox Network obtained virtually the same amount of network-owned television station audience coverage as his three major network competitors.[24]

Although the pace of this trading in broadcast properties has slowed to some extent since 1985, more than 1,300 broadcast stations were sold in the year 1987 alone, at a value of $7.5 billion.[25] In addition, during this era—

— Washington Post Co., bought 17 percent of Cowles Media. (The flagship enterprise of Cowles Media is the Minneapolis Star and Tribune.)

— Advance Publications (S.I. Newhouse, chairman) bought New Yorker Magazine for $142 million.

[22] The following FCC rules were amended for the three broadcast services 47 CFR 73.35(a); 47 CFR 43.240(a) 1; 47 CFR 73.636(a) 1–2; and 47 CFR 76.501. Bowing to Congressional pressure, the FCC did limit to 25% the maximum size of the national television audience that any 12 group owned stations could serve.

[23] "Fifth Estate's $30 Billion-plus Year," Broadcasting, December 30, 1985, p. 35.

[24] ABC's owned and operated TV stations reach 24.5% of all American TV households; NBC's O & O stations reach 22.4%; CBS reaches 19.46% and Fox, through its Metromedia holdings, now serves 19.39% of the total TV population. "Television's Top 20," Broadcasting, August 31, 1987, p. 33.

[25] "Broadcasting–$7.5 Billion, Cable–$6 Billion," Broadcasting February 6, 1988, p. 61.

— U.S. News & World Report sold to Mortimer Zuckerman for $164 million.

Small wonder that Newsweek Magazine termed this wave of acquisitiveness a "feeding frenzy." Newsweek added: [26]

> For the American news media, accustomed to thinking of themselves as a Fourth Estate, it has been something of a shock to be treated as Wall Street darlings instead. The pell-mell quest for media properties has bid up their sale prices to heady levels.

And *Variety* commented,

> So small businesses were gobbled up by larger companies and corporations were devoured by still larger corporations. And to all this Washington—the FCC and Justice Dept.—said fine. The era of regulation was at an end.[27]

Many journalists (except for business writers, Wall Street Journal types, and the like) have long had the reputation for being financial illiterates. But when the media became such attractive properties in the 1980s, self-interest began to impel journalists to learn some new terms, such as:

"Leveraged Buyout"—This is a deal in which money is borrowed to buy a corporation. Then, the cash flow from the purchased company is put to work to pay off the interest and principal of the loan.

> The purchase of the ABC Network by Capital Cities is a startling example of a leveraged buyout. A Nebraska financier—Warren Buffett—bought Capital Cities stock to provide $517.5 million of the $3.5 billion "Cap Cities" spent to get control of ABC. Note that Cap Cities was much smaller than ABC—its 1984 revenues amounted to $950 million, compared to $3.7 billion for ABC. "It's a little like the canary eating the cat," said Roone Arledge, president of ABC News and Sports.[28]

> But then, with media companies, cash flow can be great that enormous loans can be paid off. Alex S. Jones reported in The New York Times that "well-run television stations in major markets can generate pre-tax operating income of over 50 percent * * * cash flow can be 60 percent or more of revenues." Further, cash flow for the

[26] Ibid.

[27] "The Year in Review," Variety, January 8, 1986, p. 159.

[28] Peter W. Kaplan, "Takeover's Impact Is Uncertain," The New York Times, March 19, 1985, p. 54.

more profitable newspapers can range as high as 40 percent or more.[29]

"Friendly Takeover"—As the term implies, it is an amicable merger between two corporations. The Capital Cities Communications–ABC merger again provides a good example. ABC's architect and Chairman, 79–year-old Leonard Goldenson, had for some years been the subject of speculation: who would replace him at the 214–station network? Cap Cities Chairman Thomas Murphy talked with the ABC Executive Vice President, and they agreed that if the FCC ever liberalized its "7–7–7 rule" to permit one corporation to own a larger number of television stations, the two companies would be a "natural fit." After the FCC changed to its "12–12–12" rule on April 1, 1985, the merger took place.[30]

Similarly, General Electric's purchase of NBC in December of 1985 for $6.3 billion was also a friendly merger. The management of NBC's parent company RCA, had taken defensive measures against a hostile take-over, but was still concerned about its long term vulnerability. The merger, creating the second largest industrial corporation in the nation (excluding the auto industry) provided NBC with a massive infusion of capital, while GE gained re-entry into a field with the strong profit base the company saw as being essential to support its worldwide manufacturing and marketing activities.[31]

"Hostile Takeover"—There had been rumors that ABC was being stalked for a hostile takeover—a situation in which entrepreneurs buy up a controlling interest in a company's stock, thus gaining effective ownership. The rumors mentioned potential takeover bidders as the Bass brothers of Fort Worth, Texas, and Ted Turner, the feisty and aggressive owner of Atlanta "super-station" WTBS, Cable News Network, the Atlanta Braves baseball team, and so on. But ABC Board Chairman Goldenson said that the network had found no evidence of investors buying up huge blocs of ABC stock, and added that the sale to Capital Cities was not put together to prevent someone less desirable from gaining control of the network.[32]

"Junk Bonds"—A failed hostile takeover, especially one financed with "junk bonds", can sometimes be as damaging for

[29] See Geraldine Fabrikant, "3 TV Stations High Margins," The New York Times, July 1, 1985, p. 25.

[30] Newsweek, April 1, 1985, p. 54.

[31] "RCA + GE: Marriage Made in Takeover Heaven," Broadcasting, December 16, 1985 p. 43. At the time of the merger, GE did own one television property, KCNC–TV Denver that NBC had previously tried to acquire. With the purchase, it became the 6th NBC owned and operated TV station.

[32] Ibid., p. 53; "Network Blockbuster," Time, April 1, 1985, p. 60.

media organizations as a successful takeover. In 1985, Ted Turner, the cable TV magnate, decided he wanted to own CBS. Turner tried, unsuccessfully, to purchase the 67 percent of CBS's common stock required under New York to gain control of the corporation. Since he lacked the $5.4 billion needed to acquire the stock, he attempted to float more than $5 billion of the purchase price in "junk bonds," trying to persuade stockholders to support him by promising them an annual dividend some seven times their current dividend rate.[33]

Although Turner failed in his campaign to take over CBS, the massive expenses the network incurred in fighting off his attack weakened its financial structure, making it much more vulnerable to the next takeover effort by another corporate giant. For a time it seemed that giant might be Coca–Cola, but while CBS executives were guarding their corporate flanks from attack, the actual takeover of CBS was occurring right behind their backs.

"Inside Takeover"—When Lawrence Tisch used the 24.9% of CBS stock he had recently acquired through his Loews Corporation to become acting chief executive officer (CEO) of CBS in September 1986, the FCC accepted the network's argument that Tisch's stock purchase and CEO appointment did not require Commission review because there had been no actual change in the ownership or control of CBS.[34] Before the year 1986 had ended, however, the 500 network employees he had already fired were among those who had reason to question the FCC's determination that Tisch was not in charge of CBS.

For a few brief weeks, Tisch was viewed as a hero at the network, because he had saved CBS from the rumored take-over move by Coca–Cola. But, as *Time* magazine described it, as Tisch continued to direct a "rapid and ruthless austerity program,"

[33] The term "junk bond" is slang for a bond issued by a company that is too poor a credit risk to borrow money in a conventional manner. These bonds can often be purchased for far less than their stated value (e.g. $10,000 face value worth of bonds for $100) because the chance that the company issuing them will ever being able to pay them off is so slight. What usually happens after "junk bonds" have financed the purchase of corporate stock is that the new owner then plunders the assets of the corporate acquired to pay the high rates of return demanded by the bonds tendered to purchase it.

[34] "FCC on CBS: No Change in Control," Broadcasting, October 20, 1986, p. 28. The FCC's concern was not about ownership of the network per se, but about control of those licensed broadcast stations owned by CBS, because the Commission is required by Sec. 310(d) of the Communications Act to determine whether the transfer of control over a broadcast license is in the public interest before authorizing any change in ownership or control.

The September mood of euphoria at CBS suffered accordingly. Says one mid-level executive: "Half the people here curse Tisch." A television producer ... describes employee morale as "pulverized with fear." Staffers soon coined a bitter name for the layoffs; to be fired was to be "tisched".[35]

In January 1987, Tisch assumed complete control of the network, restructuring its organization and selecting his own managerial staff. Thus, while CBS was not taken over by an outside corporation, it was effectively taken over from within.

When all this merger activity is considered—and there is far more of it than a short summary can include—it's clear that the pace of media consolidation in the United States accelerated significantly during the past decade and shows little sign of slowing down during the years ahead. The 50 major media organizations of 1982 that had become only 26 media giants of 1988 are almost certain to continue merging and combining until perhaps only a dozen of them will be dominating every form of American mass culture by the end of this decade.

While reduced competition may mean greater prosperity for the American media conglomerates themselves, it will certainly continue to diminish the vigor of public discourse and discussion totally dependent upon competition for its vitality.

SEC. 96. NEWSPAPER ANTITRUST LAW

Antitrust statutes, as applied to the press, are not in violation of the First Amendment guarantee of freedom of the press.

Until the late 1970s, national rather than international mass media competition was the primary concern of the federal government. During this era the Justice Department was deeply committed to preventing anti-competitive trade practices in the newspaper industry.

Although decided just after the end of World War II, the decision of the Supreme Court of the United States in Associated Press v. United States [36] still ranks as a leading case in antitrust law affecting the media. The Justice Department had brought suit under the Sherman Act [37] to get an injunction preventing the AP from continuing to operate under a restrictive clause in its by-laws.

The Associated Press is a cooperative news-gathering organization. Its by-laws forbade AP member newspapers or broadcast

[35] "A Cut Above the Ordinary," Time, December 22, 1986, p. 53.

[36] 326 U.S. 1, 65 S.Ct. 1416 (1945).

[37] See discussion of the Sherman Act, Section 93, supra, at footnote 15.

stations from selling news to non-members. Other by-law provisions also gave a newspaper which had an AP membership virtual veto power over competing newspapers' attempts to gain AP membership.[38]

Associated Press v. United States (1945)

One of several cases combined under the case name of Associated Press v. United States involved Chicago publisher Marshall Field's efforts to get an AP membership for his Chicago Sun, a new newspaper trying to compete with crusty Col. Robert R. McCormick's Chicago Tribune. The Chicago Tribune protested against the upstart Chicago Sun's AP membership application, trying to prevent the competition from gaining the benefit of the premier news wire service.

Once such a protest was made, the AP by-laws then required a majority vote of ALL members of the Associated Press before the new applicant could be admitted to the club.[39] That majority vote—from publisher members of AP, many of whom enjoyed exclusive use of that wire service in their own publication areas— was most unlikely to occur. Thus Marshall Field's Chicago Sun could not join the AP without Col. McCormick's consent, unless the federal government intervened—in the public interest, of course— to use antitrust laws to force a change in the AP bylaws.

In 1943, the Justice Department charged that the conduct of the AP and the Chicago Tribune constituted "(1) a combination and conspiracy of restraint of trade and commerce in news among the states, and (2) an attempt to monopolize part of that trade." [40] The Associated Press and the Chicago Tribune fought against the Justice Department charges, arguing that the application of the Sherman Act in this case would violate freedom of the press guaranteed by the First Amendment. A majority of the Supreme Court was not impressed by this argument. Writing for the Court, Justice Hugo L. Black said: [41]

> * * * All are alike covered by the Sherman Act. The fact that the publisher handles news while others handle goods does not, as we shall later point out, afford the publisher a peculiar constitutional sanctuary in which he can with impunity violate laws regulating his business practices.

[38] Chafee, op. cit., pp. 542–543; Associated Press v. United States, 326 U.S. 1, 9–10, 65 S.Ct. 1416, 1419 (1945).

[39] Chafee, p. 543; Associated Press v. United States, loc. cit. Another newspaper which like the Chicago Sun had applied for AP membership and had been turned down by a 2–1 vote margin of AP members, was the Washington Times–Herald.

[40] 326 U.S. 1, 7, 65 S.Ct. 1416, 1418 (1945).

[41] 326 U.S. 1, 8–10, 65 S.Ct. 1416, 1419 (1945).

Finally, Justice Black answered the assertion that the Sherman Act's application to the Associated Press abridged the AP's First Amendment freedom. He declared that it would be strange if the concern for press freedom underlying the First Amendment should be read "as a command that the government was without power to protect that freedom." Black continued,[42]

> Freedom to publish means freedom for all and not for some. Freedom to publish is guaranteed by the Commission, but freedom to combine to keep others from publishing is not. Freedom of the press from governmental interference under the First Amendment does not sanction repression of that freedom by private interests. The First Amendment affords not the slightest support for the contention that a combination to restrain trade in news and views has any constitutional immunity.

Justice Frankfurter added other arguments in favor of government action under the Sherman Act to attempt to control media activities which tended to restrain trade. To Frankfurter, the press was a business, but it was also much more: "in addition to being a commercial enterprise, it [the press] has a relation to the public interest unlike that of any other enterprise pursued for profit." Following this premise, Justice Frankfurter then quoted words written by America's most famous United States District Court judge. The oft-quoted words below came from Judge Learned Hand's lower-court opinion in this same case of Associated Press v. United States,[43]

> * * * that [the newspaper] industry serves one of the most vital of all general interests: the dissemination of news from as many different sources, and with as many different facets and colors as is possible. That interest is closely akin to, if indeed it is not the same as, the interest protected by the First Amendment; it presupposes that right conclusions are more likely to be gathered out of a multitude of tongues than through any kind of authoritative selection. To many this is, and always will be, folly; but we have staked upon it our all.

To Frankfurter, the By–Laws of the Associated Press were a clear restriction of commerce. Such a restriction was unreasonable because it subverted the function of a constitutionally guaranteed free press.

[42] 326 U.S. 1, 20, 65 S.Ct. 1416, 1424–1425 (1945).

[43] 326 U.S. 1, 28, 65 S.Ct. 1416, 1428 (1945), quoting Judge Hand, United States v. Associated Press, 52 F.Supp. 362, 372 (S.D.N.Y.1943).

Dissents from Justices Owen J. Roberts and Frank Murphy took a traditional libertarian view: In general, government should leave the press alone.   Justice Murphy wrote: [44]

> Today is * * * the first time that the Sherman Act has been used as a vehicle for affirmative intervention by the Government in the realm of dissemination of information. As the Government states, this is an attempt to remove "barriers erected by private combination against access to reports of world news."   * * *. [The press associations] are engaged in collecting and distributing news and information rather than in manufacturing automobiles, aluminum or gasoline. We cannot avoid that fact. Nor can we escape the fact that governmental action directly aimed at the methods or conditions of such collection or distribution is an interference with the press, however differing in degree it may be from governmental restraints on written or spoken utterances themselves * * *. We should therefore be particularly vigilant in reviewing a case of this nature, a vigilance that apparently is not shared by the Court today.

Lorain Journal Company v. United States (1951)

Media can violate antitrust laws in one of two general ways. The first is by attempting through acquisition, merger or some other type of corporate restructuring to reduce the level of media competition in an unlawful manner. The second, and far more common type of media antitrust violation is to engage is some form of anti-competitive media business practice. The Lorain Journal case presents a clear illustration of the type of anti-competitive practices antitrust law has been designed to prevent.[45]

The paper had tried and failed to obtain a broadcast license to operate a radio station in the city in which it was located, Lorain, Ohio.[46]   Soon afterward, the FCC issued a radio license to an applicant whose station was located in Elyria, Ohio, just eight miles from Lorain.

In an effort to force this competitor out of business, the paper adopted a strict policy of refusing to accept advertising from any local merchants who also purchased any advertising time from the radio station. Because the Lorain Journal reached 99 percent of

[44] 326 U.S. 1, 51–52, 65 S.Ct. 1416, 1439 (1945).

[45] Lorain Journal Co. v. United States, 342 U.S. 143, 72 S.Ct. 181 (1951).

[46] See 92 F.Supp. 794 (N.D.Ohio 1950). See also Mansfield Journal Co. v. FCC, 180 F.2d 28 (D.C.Cir.1950). This refusal of the FCC to grant the license application was based in part on allegations of similar past anti-competitive behavior of the Mansfield Journal, jointly owned with the Lorain Journal, in its advertising practices and its refusal to print the schedules of competing radio stations in its area.

the area's households, local advertisers had little choice but to avoid buying commercial time from the radio station.

The Justice Department brought a civil antitrust suit against the Journal, charging the paper with attempting to monopolize commerce under the Sherman Act. The newspaper responded by claiming that this government action infringed not only on its constitutionally protected right of free speech, but also its right to accept or refuse advertisements from whomever it pleased.

A federal district court found that Lorain Journal had indeed been attempting to illegally monopolize commerce, and issued an injunction to prevent the paper from continuing its anticompetitive trade practices. The Journal appealed to the Supreme Court but to no avail. In a 7–0 decision, the Court upheld the lower court decision and the injunction that issued from it.

The Court, through Mr. Justice Harold Burton, rejected the argument that the newspaper's "bold, relentless and predatory commercial behavior" was in any way sheltered by the First Amendment and also rejected its asserted right to accept or reject advertisements, saying: [47]

> The right claimed by the publisher is neither absolute nor exempt from regulation. [The refusal to accept advertising] * * * as a purposeful means of monopolizing interstate commerce is prohibited by the Sherman Act. The operator of the radio station, equal with the publisher of newspaper, is entitled to the protection of the Act.

Because the findings of fact in a civil or criminal antitrust action brought by the government may be used in a lawsuit for **treble damages** by the injured party, the radio station was later able to sue the Journal and recover three times the damages it actually sustained for advertising revenues lost because of the newspaper's anticompetitive behavior.[48]

Times–Picayune Pub. Co. v. United States (1953)

In this case, the publisher of a morning (Times–Picayune) and an afternoon newspaper (States) in New Orleans would not accept advertising unless a merchant purchased advertising space in both of its newspapers, but did not refuse ads from those who also advertised in a competing afternoon paper (The Item). The Justice Department challenged this advertising practice, claiming that it constituted an anticompetitive "tying agreement"—that is, forcing a customer to buy an unwanted product in order to obtain the one desired.

[47] Lorain Journal Co. v. United States, 342 U.S. 143, 155, 72 S.Ct. 181, 187 (1951).

[48] Elyria–Lorain Broadcasting Co. v. Lorain Journal Co., 298 F.2d 356 (6th Cir.1961).

The government contended that most advertisers desired to place their ads in the morning Times–Picayune, with a circulation of 188,000, but were forced by its unit-buying rule to purchase space in its sister afternoon paper, the States, with a circulation of only 105,000.[49] This, of course, would operate to divert potential advertising revenues away from the independent New Orleans afternoon paper, the Item.

In a 5–4 decision, the Supreme Court disagreed with the Justice Department, finding that there had been no unlawful "tying" because the government had not established that the publisher's morning paper was in fact the desired or "dominant" product or that its afternoon paper the unwanted or "inferior" product for newspaper advertisers. Instead, Justice Tom C. Clark's majority opinion held that the two newspapers—owned by one publisher—were selling identical products: advertising space in a newspaper. But did competition survive? The name of the afternoon paper—after a 1958 merger—is the States–Item.

United States v. Kansas City Star (1957)

In Kansas City, the morning Times and afternoon and Sunday Star were owned by the same publisher, who also owned a local radio and television station. The Kansas City Post, the Star's only former competitor had gone bankrupt and ceased publication.

Readers were forced to subscribe to all three papers, the Times, and both the afternoon and Sunday Star in order to receive service. Advertisers were also forced to place their ads in all three papers, and there was evidence that merchants who did not advertise in the newspaper were not permitted to buy radio or television commercial time from the newspaper's stations.

In prosecuting its case, the government was able to show that the Star's dominant media position in the Kansas City area gave it the power to exclude competition. The government also assembled evidence to demonstrate that this power had been exercised in a ruthless fashion to coerce both readers and advertisers in a manner that would not have been possible in a truly competitive environment.

The Star was found guilty of criminal violations of antitrust law, as the jury rejected the publisher's argument that the morning and afternoon papers were separate entities in competition with one another. Eventually, after a federal appeals court affirmed the conviction, the Star agreed to a consent decree, ending a companion civil suit brought by the government.

[49] 345 U.S. 594, 73 S.Ct. 872 (1953).

This decree, like other consent decrees between an antitrust defendant and the government, was a negotiated settlement. By it terms, the Star agreed, in return for the government ending its civil action, to sell its radio and television stations and never again attempt to purchase any broadcast properties without the prior consent of the government. The decree also prohibited the newspapers from forcing advertisers to buy advertising space in both the Star and the Times in order to have their ads accepted.

Even the consent decree did not end the Star's legal problems. The criminal antitrust conviction was used repeatedly as evidence by would-be competitors who brought treble-damage antitrust suits against the paper. Defending against such lawsuits was an expensive proposition, and a number of such actions were settled out of court.[50]

United States v. Times–Mirror (1967)

Unlike the Lorain Journal, Times–Picayune or Kansas City Star antitrust actions, the Times–Mirror case did not involve anti-competitive conduct, but rather an attempt through merger to reduce competition.[51] The Times–Mirror Corporation had purchased the San Bernardino (California) Sun, a profitable daily newspaper located about 40 miles from Los Angeles for $15 million. The Pulitzer Corporation of St. Louis had offered to pay the same amount for the Sun, but the Sun's owner decided to accept the Times–Mirror offer instead.

Acquisition of the Sun by the Times–Mirror Corporation was challenged by the Antitrust Division of the Justice Department. The government complained that the merger meant that the publisher of California's largest daily newspaper, the Times, had now gained control of the largest independent daily newspaper in Southern California.

The federal trial judge found that the three San Bernardino County newspapers published by the Sun Corporation constituted the only major advertising competition faced by the Times–Mirror in the area and its primary competitor for subscribers in that region of the state.

Based on these findings, the Court ruled that the purchase of the Sun Company by Times–Mirror violated the anti-merger provisions of Section 7 of the Clayton Act. As a result, the Times–Mirror was forced to divest itself of Sun Company stock and

---

[50] See e.g. Goodfriend and Levinson v. Kansas City Star Co., 158 F.Supp. 531 (W.D.Mo.1958); Duff v. Kansas City Star Co., 299 F.2d 320 (8th Cir.1962) and Siegfried v. Kansas City Star Co., 193 F.Supp. 427 (W.D.Mo.1961).

[51] United States v. Times Mirror Co., 274 F.Supp. 606 (W.D.Cal.1967), affirmed by the U.S. Supreme Court without opinion 390 U.S. 712, 88 S.Ct. 1411 (1968).

present a plan for divestiture that provided for the continuation of the Sun Company as a strong and viable organization.

The Antitrust Division of the Department of Justice viewed its victory in the Times–Mirror case as being a significant one. In 1968, the leading antitrust lawyer Charles D. Mahaffie, Jr. wrote that the Antitrust Division was "and will continue to be particularly concerned with mergers which may eliminate the actual and potential competition afforded by the suburban, small-city and community papers." [52] Underlying this statement was a basic philosophy of communication and freedom of expression protected through antitrust law. The idea is that many voices in the marketplace of information and opinion—"diversified, quarrelsome, and competitive"—are; in the public interest.[53]

However, although the Justice Department had been able to prevent the Times–Mirror from acquiring the San Bernardino Sun, the Sun newspapers were eventually acquired by the nation's largest newspaper group, The Gannett Company.

And after one last action during the Reagan administration to block the Orlando Sentinel's acquisition of five competing weekly suburban papers, the Justice Department has stood by passively as major daily newspapers throughout the United States have continued to absorb their suburban competitors.[54]

United States v. Citizen Publishing Co. (1968) and the "Newspaper Preservation Act" of 1970

In 1969, the Supreme Court of the United States decided a case of great importance to the daily newspaper industry: United States v. Citizen Publishing Company, often called "The Tucson Case." That decision declared *joint operating agreements* to be illegal. Such agreements were and are important to the profit margins if not to the very survival of competing newspapers in about two-dozen cities.[55]

[52] Charles D. Mahaffie, Jr., "Mergers and Diversification in the Newspaper, Broadcasting and Information Industries," The Antitrust Bulletin Vol. 13 (Fall 1968) pp. 927–935, at p. 928.

[53] See the classic statement by Judge Learned Hand in United States v. Associated Press, 52 F.Supp. 362, 372 (S.D.N.Y.1943), quoted at 326 U.S. 1, 28, 65 S.Ct. 1416, 1428 (1945), and printed in the text to footnote 52 earlier in this chapter.

[54] In 1989, for example, the Columbus Dispatch, owner of a radio and television station in Columbus, Ohio, bought a chain of five suburban weeklies and three shoppers; in 1990, the Orange County Register, the Los Angeles Times, the Chicago Sun–Times and the Seattle Times each acquired competing suburban papers and in 1992 the Mason City Globe–Gazette purchased its competing Mason City Shopper, all without attracting the attention of the Justice Department.

[55] Editor & Publisher, Jan. 18, 1969, p. 9. Such cities include Tucson; San Francisco; Madison, Wisconsin; El Paso, Texas, and Honolulu.

The Supreme Court's judgment that joint operating agreements were illegal didn't last long. The ruling brought a wave of protests from publishers whose newspapers are involved in joint operating agreements. On March 12, 1969, just two days after the Court's Tucson decision, a number of bills were offered in both the U.S. House of Representatives and the Senate to legalize joint operating agreements between two newspapers. Those bills tied in with lengthy hearings held by the preceding Congress on the so-called "Failing Newspaper Act." [56]

After the Supreme Court's decision in the Tucson Case, the "Failing Newspaper Act" was given the euphemistic label "Newspaper Preservation Act" and was passed by both houses of Congress.[57] President Nixon signed the bill into law on July 24, 1970.

Joint operating agreements work in this fashion. Two competing newspapers in one town combine their printing, advertising, circulation and business operations. The news and editorial operations of the two newspapers, however, retain their separate identities. Then, the two newspapers—one published in the morning and the other in the afternoon—can use the same publishing, business and distribution facilities, resulting in substantial economies in operation.

To say that the Tucson Case obviously worried a number of publishers would be a major understatement. Arguments filed before the Supreme Court in the Tucson Case early in 1969 included an amicus curiae brief filed on behalf of newspaper publishers in 16 cities. In that brief, attorney Robert L. Stern asserted that "a joint operating plant is the only feasible way to preserve competition in cities which cannot support two completely separate newspapers." [58]

The Antitrust Division of the Department of Justice, however, disagreed with the line of thinking argued by attorney Stern. So did a Federal district court, in deciding that the Tucson joint operating agreement was illegal.[59] That joint operating agreement had been in existence since 1940. Then, Citizen Publishing Company (publishers of The Tucson Daily Citizen, an evening paper) and The Star Publishing Company (publishers of The Arizona Daily Star, a morning and Sunday paper) joined forces to form a third corporation: Tucson Newspapers, Inc. Tucson Newspapers, Inc.

[56] See Subcommittee on Antitrust and Monopoly of the Committee on the Judiciary, United States Senate, 90th Congress, First Session, on S. 1312, The Failing Newspaper Act, Part 1, July 12–14, 18–19, 25–26, 1967, at p. 2.

[57] 15 U.S.C.A. §§ 1801–1804.

[58] Editor & Publisher, Dec. 21, 1968, p. 9.

[59] United States v. Citizen Pub. Co., Tucson Newspapers, Inc., Arden Pub. Co. and William A. Small, Jr., 280 F.Supp. 978 (D.Ariz.1968).

took over all departments of the two newspapers except news/editorial.

This joint operating agreement was started because the publishers of the two newspapers later said they believed there could not be successful operation of two competing dailies in a city with a population of less than 100,000.

In the district court decision, Chief Justice James A. Walsh found that the joint operating agreement amounted to illegal "price fixing, profit pooling, and market allocations by the parties to the agreement," a violation of the Sherman Act.

In arguments to the Supreme Court of the United States, the Tucson newspapers contended that joint operating agreements were necessary in a number of cities to allow newspapers to survive while maintaining competing news and editorial voices. There were 22 cities with a total of 44 newspapers involved in joint operating agreements similar to the Tucson situation in the mid–1960s. Thus, it was feared that the Justice Department, should it succeed in the Tucson case, would begin antitrust actions against other newspapers' joint operating agreements. That would mean, to use the example of Arizona, that Tucson Newspapers, Inc., could no longer operate single advertising and circulation departments serving both newspapers.[60]

In March of 1969, the Supreme Court of the United States indeed did find the Tucson joint operating agreement illegal. Writing for the Court, Mr. Justice Douglas ruled that the agreement was for the purpose of ending competition between the two newspapers.

The Supreme Court thus affirmed the orders issued by the U.S. District Court in the Tucson case. This meant that the Tucson newspapers must "submit a plan for divestiture and re-establishment of the Star as an independent competitor and for modification of the joint operating agreement so as to eliminate the price-fixing, market control, and profit pooling provisions."

It should be noted that Douglas emphasized the "failing company doctrine" as he wrote the majority opinion in the Tucson case. Douglas declared the "only real defense of appellants [the Citizen Publishing Company and its co-defendants] was the failing company defense—a judicially created doctrine." The failing company doctrine means that acquisition of a company by a competitor does not illegally lessen competition if the firm which has been purchased is in grave danger of business failure. Justice Douglas, however, found that the Citizen had not been a failing newspaper

---

[60] Ibid. See also Editor & Publisher, Jan. 18, 1969, p. 9.

in 1940 when it entered the joint operating agreement with the Star, despite the fact that the Citizen was then losing money.[61] The Supreme Court, as Justice Douglas put it, found that "beyond peradventure of doubt" the joint operating agreement between Tucson's two daily newspapers violated antitrust laws.

The Newspaper Preservation Act

As noted earlier, the Supreme Court's decision in the Citizen Publishing Company case was promptly legislated out of existence by the Newspaper Preservation Act.[62] This act's purpose was stated to be maintaining—in the public interest—"a newspaper press editorially and reportorially competitive in all parts of the United States" by legalizing such joint operating agreements.

In one sense, this legislation might be viewed as "too little, too late" because by 1969 there were not many cities left with competing, independently owned daily newspapers. In another sense, there is also room for doubt about how truly "independent" newspapers that are bound together by common financial and business interests will be when a choice has to be made between serving the public interest and serving economic self-interest.[63]

The Newspaper Preservation Act of 1970 approved all 22 joint operating agreements then in existence, involving 44 daily papers.[64]

The Act was passed despite strenuous objections from the Antitrust Division of the Department of Justice. The government's attorneys expressed fear that if profit pooling or price fixing laws were relaxed to aid newspapers, "many publishers will opt for that way [joint operating agreements] even though they might be capable of remaining fully independent, or of finding other solutions to the

[61] 394 U.S. 131, 89 S.Ct. 927 (1969); United States Law Week, Vol. 37, pp. 4208–4212 (March 11, 1969); Barry Schweid, "Newspapers Want Congress to Legalize Joint Operation," Associated Press dispatch in Madison, Wis., Capital Times, March 11, 1969; "Publishers seek relief in Congress," Editor & Publisher, March 15, 1969, p. 9ff. See also International Shoe Co. v. Federal Trade Commission, 280 U.S. 291, 302, 50 S.Ct. 89, 93 (1930).

[62] 15 U.S.C.A. §§ 1801–1804.

[63] See Ben H. Bagdikian, The Media Monopoly (Boston: Beacon Press, 1983, pp. 98–103.

[64] Cities with daily newspapers in JOA in 1970 included: Albuquerque, N.M.; Bristol, Tenn.; Charleston, W.Va.; Columbus, Ohio; El Paso, Texas; Evansville, Ind.; Fort Wayne, Ind.; Franklin–Oil City, Pa.; Honolulu; Knoxville, Tenn.; Lincoln, Neb.; Madison, Wis.; Miami, Fla.; Nashville, Tenn.; Pittsburgh, Pa.; Saint Louis, Mo.; Salt Lake City; San Francisco; Shreveport, La.; Tucson, and Tulsa. Since then, Birmingham, Ala.; Cincinnati, Oh.; Chattanooga, Tenn., and Seattle, Washington, have gone into JOAs. Dailies in Anchorage, Alaska, dissolved a JOA after a brief period, and The Derrick, Oil City, Pa., ended its JOA in 1985 by buying its partner, the Franklin News–Herald. The Knoxville, TN, News–Sentinel and the Journal ended their JOA at the end of 1991.

difficulties which preserve competition." [65]   Weekly newspapers, small dailies, and the American Newspaper Guild also strongly and repeatedly urged against passage of the Act, complaining that joint advertising rates provide newspapers in a joint operation situation with a competitive advantage that other newspapers in the area simply could not overcome.[66]

The Newspaper Preservation Act authorizes the creation of a joint operating agreement only when at least one of the two newspapers is "failing," or "in probable danger of financial failure."   In addition, the Act requires that any *new* joint operating agreements must receive written approval in advance from the Attorney General of the United States.   The Act also specifies that the Attorney General cannot approve the agreement without first making a formal determination that at least one of the newspapers applying for joint operation is "failing" or "in probable danger of financial failure."

Despite its initial opposition to the Newspaper Preservation Act, the Justice Department eventually approved each of the seven additional newspaper joint operating agreements (JOA) it reviewed during the next 20 years.[67]   Perhaps the most controversial of these approvals occurred in 1988, when then Attorney General Edwin Meese overruled his own Antitrust Division lawyers to permit a JOA between Knight–Ridder's Detroit Free Press and Gannett's Detroit News.

Several local citizen groups formed a coalition, "Michigan Citizens for a Free Press" to challenge the Justice Department decision in federal court.   They argued that both newspapers had intentionally adopted short-term practices designed to reduce their revenues, creating artificial losses to justify their application for the JOA.   A divided federal court of appeals upheld the JOA but admitted:

> We can envision a perfectly rational different policy, one that would require a showing that the weaker paper was more bloodied before approving a JOA and therefore *might* discourage the sort of competition we saw in Detroit.   Congress, however, delegated to the Attorney General and not to us the delicate and troubling responsibility

[65] Statement of Donald F. Turner, assistant attorney general, Antitrust Division, Department of Justice, before the Senate Judiciary Committee, Subcommittee on Antitrust and Monopoly, on S. 1312, April 1968, p. 18.

[66] See, e.g., The Guild Reporter, Sept. 8, 1967, p. 8; "Failing Newspaper Bill Assailed," Associated Press dispatch in Wisconsin State Journal, Madison, Sec. 1, p. 8, April 17, 1968.

[67] The seven new joint operating agreements were in the cities of Anchorage (1974), Cincinnati (1979), Chattanooga (1980), Seattle (1982), Detroit (1988), York, Pennsylvania (1990) and Las Vegas (1990).

of putting content into the ambiguous phrase "probable danger of financial failure."[68]

Rehearing en banc was denied 5–4. The Supreme Court affirmed without a written opinion, 4–4, Justice White not participating.[69]

Yet, although these two wealthy newspaper chains had managed by the narrowest of margins to claim the benefits of a JOA, their success soon led to disappointment. Instead of achieving the massive increase in profits they anticipated, the consolidation left them instead with diminished advertising revenues and a greatly weakened publishing empire.

In reality, though, the Detroit experience merely confirmed what many other newspaper publishers were already beginning to realize; that JOA arrangements were no longer as financially beneficial as they once might have been. In fact, the major trend among JOA operations during the past decade has been for the stronger local newspaper to absorb its weaker competitor; exactly the result the Newspaper Preservation Act was enacted to prevent.[70] And one expert recently predicted that as many as seven of the remaining 18 cities in which these agreements still remain in effect are likely to lose their second newspaper within the next few years.[71]

Anticompetitive Marketing Practices

Rather than trying to buy out its suburban competitors, a large metropolitan newspaper may decide instead to rely upon its more cost-effective publication and distribution processes to force the competitors out of business. "Total Market Coverage", (TMC) has come to mean expanding a newspaper's advertising revenue base through the creation of separate "suburban" sections or editions of the metropolitan paper, and the delivery of special advertising fliers or weekly shopper inserts throughout the region in which the paper operates.

Obviously, a newspaper has every right to attempt to increase its advertising revenues, but if it pursues this tactic primarily to

[68] Michigan Citizens for an Independent Press v. Thornburgh, 868 F.2d 1285 (D.C.Cir.1989).

[69] 493 U.S. 38 (1989).

[70] This trend began in St. Louis in 1983, when Newhouse, operating under a JOA, closed the Globe–Dispatch. Since that time JOAs have ended in six other cities: Columbus, Ohio; Shreveport, Louisiana; Knoxville, Tennessee; Tulsa, Oklahoma; Miami, Florida; and Pittsburgh, Pennsylvania, leaving each with only one dominant newspaper.

[71] Stephen R. Barnett, "Anything Goes," American Journalism Review October 1993, p. 39. Barnett believes the cities most likely to lose their second newspaper are San Francisco, Nashville, Tucson, Birmingham, Cincinnati, Detroit and Evansville, Indiana.

undercut its rivals, offering potential advertisers unreasonably low rates to destroy its smaller competitors, then it is acting in an anti-competitive manner. The problem, of course, is to determine at what point an aggressive TMC campaign becomes an illegal effort to eliminate competition.

Because the Justice Department has been so reluctant to review the legality of major daily newspaper marketing campaigns, the smaller suburban newspapers have had to challenge these practices themselves in the federal courts. In 1983, in *Advantage Publications v. Daily Press,* a free weekly newspaper shopper in Virginia succeeded in obtaining an injunction to prevent a daily newspaper from distributing a competing shopper that used a combination of artificially low ad rates and secret rebates to control more than 85 percent of the print advertising in the area. [72]

At least 25 private lawsuits during the 1980s zeroed in on daily newspapers efforts to provide total-market-coverage publications, but because most of these cases were eventually settled out of court, no clear judicial guidelines have been established to determine at exactly what point a major newspaper's advertising strategies cease to be effective business practices and take on the characteristics of illegal tactics to damage its competitors.[73]

Consent Decrees

Court decisions, however, are only a part of the antitrust story affecting the communications media. Also available in antitrust law is a court-adjudicated legal instrument known as a consent decree. Consent decrees—also sometimes called consent judgments—are negotiated final legal settlements between the government and a business. Consent decrees have the force of law once they have been approved by a judge. Such consent decree settlements can take place in civil, but not criminal, antitrust cases.[74]

Where a newspaper or broadcasting station is concerned, antitrust consent decrees have been used in the following fashion. First, civil antitrust suit is filed by the Antitrust Division of the Justice Department against the owners of a newspaper or broadcasting station. In the opinion of the Justice Department, the

[72] Advantage Publications v. Daily Press, 9 Media Law Reporter, 1763 (1983).

[73] George Freeman, "Antitrust Actions: At least 25 Lawsuits in the Last Few Years Have Focused on Newspapers' Total Market Coverage Products," Presstime, January 1985, p. 1.

[74] As the late Dr. Lorry Rytting noted, the Justice Department is sensitive to charges that criminal antitrust suits might be filed, in effect, to force the signing of civil consent decrees. Department of Justice policy discourages the use of concurrent criminal and civil antitrust complaints. Rytting, "Antitrust Consent Decrees: A Threat to Freedom of the Press?," unpublished paper, School of Journalism, University of Wisconsin, 1967.

communications medium involved may have been engaging in anti-competitive business practices.

Second, the owners may decide that it will do them no good to fight the antitrust suit. The owners' attorneys may see that a court battle is almost certain to result in defeat. So, in order to avoid a lengthy and expensive trial, lawyers for the owner will sit down to negotiate with attorneys from the Antitrust Division of the Justice Department. Once a consent agreement is worked out, it means that the owners have promised to stop certain business practices or to divest themselves of certain media units. After the agreement is reached, it is made final by being formalized before a federal district judge.

Consent decrees have the advantage of allowing a defendant to settle a suit without admitting a violation of law. An example of this was the sale, late in 1968, of WREX–TV in Rockford, Ill., by the Gannett Company of Rochester, New York. In that year, the Antitrust Division of the Department of Justice filed a civil antitrust suit against the Gannett Company, which owned Rockford television station WREX–TV, and two Rockford newspapers, the Morning Star and the Register–Republic. Gannett had acquired the two newspapers in 1967, and had purchased WREX–TV in 1962. Under the terms of the consent decree Gannett was allowed to sell its television station for almost twice the amount it had paid for it and permitted to retain its two Rockford newspapers.[75]

Earl A. Jinkinson, formerly chief of the Midwest Office of Chicago of the Department of Justice's Antitrust Division, has summarized some of the differing ways consent decrees are viewed.[76]

> To the Government attorneys the consent decree is an act of grace granted in order to give the attorneys and the entire staff more time to attend to other ever-pressing and sometimes more important matters. On the other hand, many defense counsel at least profess to believe, erroneously I might add, that the consent decree is a governmental device for winning cases, thrust upon an unwilling defendant which, to adopt the words of Seth Dabney, is like "Byron's maiden who strove and repented, but ultimately consented." To attorneys for private parties injured because of the violation [of antitrust statutes], the consent decree is an abrogation of the duty of the Department of Justice to protect their client's rights.

[75] The Gannetteer, magazine of the Gannett Co., January 1969, p. 3.

[76] Earl A. Jinkinson, "Negotiation of Consent Decrees," Antitrust Bulletin, Vol. 9: Nos. 5–9 (Sept.-Dec., 1964), pp. 673–690, at pp. 676–677.

Almost a half century ago, Zechariah Chafee warned that consent decrees could increase the danger to press freedom through heavy use of the antitrust laws. Consent decrees are reached without trials, after secret proceedings. Evidence presented in reaching these decrees is not made public. Furthermore, such decrees are as legally binding as the decision of a federal court, and may be enforced with contempt-of-court sanctions if they are not obeyed.[77]

It has been suggested that the government, when it begins—or which has indicated that it soon may begin—an antitrust action is very much in the driver's seat against the defendant, who may feel compelled to "settle" by way of a consent decree. While it is true that a defendant may halt the proceedings and demand a full trial at any time before accepting the settlement, it is also true that a trial is expensive, lengthy, and is likely to involve unfavorable publicity that media owners seek to avoid.[78]

Whether consent decrees are a threat to press freedom or a boon to media owners which allows them to avoid full-dress antitrust trials, the fact remains that such decrees affecting the mass media are a weapon in government's antitrust arsenal.

SEC. 97. ELECTRONIC MEDIA OWNERSHIP POLICIES

Traditional electronic media ownership policies have been altered substantially by greater government reliance on deregulation as the policy of choice.

The FCC's primary broadcast ownership policy, as that of the FRC that preceded it, has often been described as favoring the licensing of locally owned stations to provide broadcast audiences with locally produced, community oriented programming. Yet as most government "policies," local ownership was not a specific objective that either regulatory agency worked systematically to attain, but rather only a vague statement of intention appearing periodically in various regulatory pronouncements.[79]

The FCC's efforts to prevent broadcast networks from exerting too much influence upon local station program decisions have been discussed in Chapter 9 of this text. In addition, the Commission

[77] Chafee, op. cit. Vol. 2, p. 670.

[78] Rytting, op. cit.

[79] As the President's Task Force on Telecommunications: Final Report (Govt. Printing Office, Wash. D.C.1969) pointed out, the concept of a nationwide system of local stations, "produced a relatively large number of individual stations, but relatively few accessible broadcast signals for the individual listener." Chapter 7, p. 12–13. The industry itself evolved towards national network services popular with broadcast audiences, and federal policy was powerless to impose upon this national system the local orientation Congress had once envisioned.

adopted rules that prevented any licensee from owning more than one station in a single broadcast market.[80]   Later, when television and FM services emerged, the FCC prohibited joint ownership of television and either an AM or FM facility in a single market, but "grandfathered" those already owning such broadcast facilities.[81]

In contested license proceedings, the Commission has attempted to broaden the base of broadcast ownership by favoring the candidate without other media holdings. For example, as discussed earlier in this Chapter, the FCC decided in 1975 to adopt rules that prohibited newspaper ownership of any broadcast station within the paper's main service area.[82]   However, in adopting this rule, the FCC managed to avoid antagonizing powerful publishers by "grandfathering" all existing newspaper owned stations except those controlling the only radio or television station in their market.[83]

FCC Minority Ownership Policies

From 1978 onward the Commission began to retreat from vigorous enforcement of its broadcast ownership policies, relying more heavily on a deregulated marketplace to decide how broadcast licenses should be acquired or transferred.[84]   During the same period though, the FCC also began developing new licensing policies to encourage more widespread minority ownership of broadcast stations.

In 1978 the Commission adopted a policy statement offering tax certificates to those selling their broadcast stations to minority owners. These certificates allowed sellers to defer the capital gains tax that otherwise would be imposed on any profits made from the sale. At the same time the agency also authorized anyone whose license renewal had been designated for hearing to avoid possible

[80] 47 CFR § 73.35. It was this rule that lead to the famous NBC case, 319 U.S. 190, 63 S.Ct. 997 (1943) discussed in Chapter 7 of this text.

[81] CFR § 73.240 and CFR § 73.636. To "grandfather" is to enforce a rule only prospectively, allowing those currently in violation of its terms to continue their existing practices without penalty. From an equitable standpoint, grandfathering avoids punishing those who were acting in good faith at a time when their actions were not in violation of law. The greatest drawback of grandfathering, however, is that it creates a privileged class of individuals who are thereafter able to do what all others are prohibited from doing. From a practical point, agencies like the FCC prefer to "grandfather" whenever possible, because in this way they can avoid legal challenges from those who otherwise would be adversely affected by their new rules.

[82] 50 FCC 2d 1046, amended on rehearing by 53 FCC 2d 589 (1975).

[83] This decision to grandfather all other newspaper owners of broadcast stations was sustained by the U.S. Supreme Court in FCC v. National Citizens Committee for Broadcasting, 436 U.S. 775, 98 S.Ct. 2096 (1978).

[84] At the FCC's urging, Congress has even authorized the agency to award licenses by chance through use of a lottery, rather than by hearing, Omnibus Reconciliation Act of 1981, 95 Stat. 736–37, but the Commission has used a lottery only to award LPTV, MMDS and other specialized spectrum services to this point.

loss of license by disposing of the broadcast property to a minority owner for a price not in excess of 75% of its fair market value.[85]

In addition, after having been instructed by the D.C. Court of Appeals in the TV 9 v. FCC case [86] that, "when the minority ownership is likely to increase diversity of content, especially on opinion and viewpoint, merit should be awarded," the agency began granting "enhancement" points to minority applicants in comparative license hearing cases, thus improving their prospects of being awarded the license.

The FCC's efforts to extend the same rights to women as a minority group was struck down by the Court in Steele v. FCC,[87] because Congress had not authorized women to be classified as a minority in awarding these license preferences. When the *Steele* case was remanded to the Commission for further consideration, the agency indicated that it was no longer certain that granting any minority preferences served the public interest.[88]

Alarmed by this apparent change in regulatory attitude, Congress included in its Omnibus Spending Bill of 1987 a provision preventing the agency from repealing or even continuing to reconsider its minority preference policies.[89]

In 1983, Alan Shurberg had filed a license application for television channel 18 in Hartford, Connecticut. Shurberg's application was rejected by the Commission because the current licensee of channel 18, Faith Center, was facing a license revocation hearing. Before the hearing was completed, Faith Center took advantage of the FCC's "distress sale" policy to sell the station to Astroline Communications, an Hispanic partnership qualifying as a minority-owned organization under FCC rules.

[85] Minority Ownership of Broadcast Facilities, 44 RR 2d 1051 (1978).

[86] 495 F.2d 929 (D.C.Cir.1973), cert. denied 419 U.S. 986, 95 S.Ct. 245 (1974).

[87] 770 F.2d 1192 (D.C.Cir.1985).

[88] The FCC had originally launched its regulatory programs to expand minority ownership of broadcast properties because studies indicated that less than 2 percent of all broadcast stations were owned by minorities in the mid 1970s. When the Supreme Court in Wygant v. Jackson Board of Education, 476 U.S. 267, 106 S.Ct. 1842 (1986) held that mere numerical evidence of minimal minority presence in a particular activity is not sufficient in itself to justify government intervention to rectify racial imbalance in the absence of actual evidence of prior discrimination, this holding undercut the entire basis for the Commission's position, because there was no documentation of any discrimination in the issuance or sale of broadcast licenses.

[89] Pub.L. 100–202 (1987). However, in January 1991, while still serving on the D.C. Court of Appeals, now Supreme Court Justice Clarence Thomas wrote the majority opinion for a divided three-judge panel in Lamprecht v. FCC that overturned the FCC female ownership preference policy on the grounds that Congress had not demonstrated previous discrimination against women who sought to acquire broadcast properties. Harry A. Jessell, "Court Overturns FCC Gender Preference," Broadcasting, February 24, 1992, p. 16.

Shurberg, a white applicant, challenged this minority preference policy, and in a 2–1 decision, one panel of D.C. Court of Appeals judges upheld the challenge, deciding that this FCC minority ownership program was "not narrowly tailored to remedy past discriminations or to promote program diversity. Specifically, the program unduly burdens Shurberg, an innocent non-minority, and is not reasonably related to the interest it seeks to vindicate." [90]

Three weeks later a different three judge D.C. Court of Appeals panel in another 2–1 decision upheld the Commission's policy of awarding minority enhancements in comparative hearing situations.[91] In this case Winter Park Communications with 20 percent black ownership and non-minority owned Metro Broadcasting both challenged the FCC's awarding of a new television license in Orlando, Florida to Hispanic-owned Rainbow Broadcasting. In affirming the Commission's decision to grant the license to the Hispanic group the court declared, "the Commission's award of minority enhancements is not a grant of any number of permits to minorities or a denial to qualified non-minorities of the ability freely to compete for permits."

Because the D.C. Court of Appeals was unable to resolve these two conflicting decisions, the Supreme Court agreed to hear both cases, and in June 1990 it rendered its decision.

The Court affirmed, by a 5–4 vote, the constitutionality of both the FCC distress sale and its minority preference policies. The decision to uphold these two Commission affirmative action programs surprised many communication lawyers who had expected only three Justices; Brennan, Marshall and Blackmun to support these measures.[92] This assumption become even more widespread after oral arguments before the Court in which all parties seemed to agree that changing the racial characteristics of broadcast ownership would be unlikely to have any significant effect on the nature of broadcast programming, because programming decisions tended to be dictated primarily by marketplace considerations.

In the end, however, Justices White and Stevens joined the three strongest proponents of minority preference, influenced perhaps by the special circumstances of this particular type of affirmative action. Justice Brennan, writing for the majority, placed great emphasis on broadcasting's status as a unique institution, legitimately subject to a far wider range of Congressional controls than any other medium simply because a scarcity of spectrum space has required the federal government to regulate the privilege of spectrum access.

[90] Shurberg Broadcasting of Hartford, Inc. v. FCC, 876 F.2d 902 (D.C.Cir.1989).

[91] Winter Park Communications, Inc. v. FCC, 873 F.2d 347 (D.C.Cir.1989).

[92] Metro Broadcasting v. FCC, 497 U.S. 547, 110 St. Ct. 2997 (1990).

Under such circumstances, according to Brennan, Congressional intent must be given special recognition, and as he observed, these particular FCC policies, "have been specifically approved—indeed, mandated—by Congress," through riders attached to FCC appropriation bills in 1988, 1989 and 1990, preventing the FCC from spending any portion of its funding to reconsider the validity of its minority preference policies.

Quoting Justice White's *Red Lion* opinion with approval, Brennan pointed out that since no one has a First Amendment right to broadcast, no applicant has the right to expect that a broadcast license will be granted without consideration of such significant public interest factors such as minority ownership.

In essence, then, the majority opinion affirmed those specific FCC ownership preference programs under review because in this particular instance there was clear evidence of Congressional support for such programs to serve the public interest through encouraging broader minority participation in a field where federal authority is paramount. (The issue of broadcast ownership preferences for women was not considered by the court because it was not involved in FCC actions being appealed.)

Justice O'Connor wrote a scathing 30 page dissent, in which Justices Rehnquist, Scalia and Kennedy joined. She charged the FCC with using "race as a proxy for whatever views it believes to be underrepresented in the broadcast spectrum," adding, "The reflexive or unthinking use of a suspect classification is the hallmark of an unconstitutional policy."

Justice Kennedy also wrote a separate dissent, in which Justice Scalia joined. Kennedy said that he could not accept the argument of the majority that, "the Constitution permits the government to discriminate among its citizens on the basis of race in order to serve interests so trivial as 'broadcast diversity' ".

If this case had been considered by the Court just a few months later, after Justice Brennan had retired, those minority broadcast ownership policies it affirmed might well have been rejected, quite possibly by the 6–3 margin the experts had been predicting before Brennan began working both on his opinion and his colleagues.

But even though the FCC's minority ownership policies have finally been affirmed by the Supreme Court, the most crucial test of their value still lies ahead. Will more extensive minority ownership of broadcast properties actually lead to a wider range of broadcast programming designed to meet the special needs of minority viewers and listeners? Perhaps the mere presence of a greater number of minority owners deeply involved in the day-to-day programming decisions of a station will achieve this objective, but if its realization is dependent to any extent upon enlightened guidance and direction from the FCC, then the outlook for such improvement is not particularly promising.

Antitrust and Electronic Media Ownership Practices

In National Broadcasting Company v. United States [93], the Supreme Court had affirmed the power of the FCC to consider federal antitrust implications of broadcast practices in determining whether broadcast licensees were operating in the public interest. In his opinion, Justice Frankfurter quoted with approval the justification the Commission had advanced for adopting regulations designed to prevent this type of abuse of the broadcast license privilege:

> While many of the network practices raise serious questions under the antitrust law, our jurisdiction does not depend on a showing that they do in fact constitute a violation of the antitrust laws. It is not our function to apply the antitrust laws as such. It is our duty, however, to refuse licenses or renewals to any person who engages or proposes to engage in practices which will prevent either himself or other licensees or both from making the fullest use of radio facilities. This is the standard of public interest ... which we must apply to all applications for licenses and renewals.[94]

One casualty of the FCC's decade-long policy of deregulation seems to have been this traditional concern for anti-trust implications of broadcast ownership. As discussed earlier in this chaper, during the 1980s the FCC increased the number of TV, AM and FM stations each licensee could own from 7–7–7 to 12–12–12. In 1992, the Commission raised its ownership limits once again, this time permitting each licensee to own as many as 20 AM and 20 FM stations.[95]

In the same proceeding, however, the agency made another and even more controversial decision, authorizing the creation of local AM and FM *duopolies* by permitting a single licensee to own *two* separate FM or AM stations in markets with less than 15 radio stations; and *two FM and two AM stations* in markets with more than 15 radio outlets. Thus, for the first time in American broad-

---

[93] National Broadcasting Co. v. United States, 319 U.S. 190, 222–223, 63 S.Ct. 997 (1943).

[94] Ibid., at 219–223, 63 S.Ct. at 1011–1012.

[95] Revision of Radio Rules and Policies, 71 R.R. 2d 227 (1992). The Commission established the ownership limit at 18 AM and 18 FM stations per owner in 1992 with the proviso that this number would increase to 20 AM and 20 FM stations in September 1994, unless the agency decided prior to that time not permit this increase to occur.

cast regulatory history, one owner may now operate as many as *four* different stations in the same community.

In 1992 the FCC also relaxed its 22 year ban on television network ownership of cable TV systems, permitting each network to acquire cable systems serving a maximum of 10 percent of all cable homes nationwide and no more than 50 percent of the cable homes in a single market.[96] The networks had been pressing for a complete repeal of the ban arguing that the new rules, with their 50 percent local cable subscriber limitation, will still prevent a network from purchasing any major cable MSO. On the other hand, even this modest gesture angered network affiliate stations who fear that networks will use cable TV to by-pass their affiliates and deliver network programs directly to the viewer.[97]

It is the Justice Department, rather than the FCC, that has primary responsibility for enforcing federal antitrust laws in the field of broadcasting, as in every other area of American commerce.[98] However, the courts have given the FCC far greater latitude than the Justice Department to prevent media practices that are not illegal in terms of anti-trust law, but that might tend to constrain "the development of diverse and antagonistic sources of program service." [99]

During the past 15 years, the Commission had been contending that broadcast ownership restrictions are no longer as necessary to protect this diversity in service, because electronic media audiences have such a wide range of viewing and listening alternatives today that no combination of conglomerates could possibly deny them their free choice of programming.

Unfortunately, this view of electronic mass communication operation completely overlooks the anti-competitive influences that electronic media conglomerates are capable of exerting on those entertainment and information services seeking to reach their audiences. From the beginning, broadcasting has acted primarily as a distribution system for the programming of others, and today, all electronic media remain dependent upon the film and music industries for their most popular features.

Radio began this pattern of dependency, as local stations delegated popular "prime time" programming responsibility to a network that in turn relied upon advertising agencies to produce its

[96] Common Ownership of Cable Television Systems and National Television Networks, 70 R.R. 2d 1531 (1992).

[97] On Reconsideration, 72 R.R.2d 39 (1993).

[98] United States v. RCA, 358 U.S. 334, 79 S.Ct. 457 (1959).

[99] Mount Mansfield Television, Inc. v. FCC, 442 F.2d 470, 480 (2d Cir.1971).

shows.[1] When television program production became too expensive to be underwritten by advertising agency sponsors in the mid 1950s, the network turned to Hollywood film studios to produce their series programs.

Financial Interest Rules

With film audiences dwindling because of television competition, these Hollywood producers were only too eager to accept this new type of financial support. The problem these film producers faced in dealing with the networks, however, was that they were sellers in a market with only three potential buyers who often seemed less interested in obtaining the best program quality than in obtaining the most favorable ownership terms for the programs they agreed to schedule.

When the Justice Department began an anti-trust action against the three networks in 1972, alleging that they used their dominant position in the field of television program distribution to obtain financial advantages from program producers, the FCC enacted *financial interest rules* denying the networks the right to benefit financially from the distribution of any programs they had not produced themselves.[2] Not satisfied either by the scope of these rules or the Commission's commitment to enforce them, the Justice Department continued its anti-trust action until each of the three networks eventually entered into consent agreements to alter their program procurement practices.[3]

In enacting its financial interest rules, the FCC explained quite clearly why it believed these network practices were not only damaging to independent producers, but to the interests of the public as well. As the Commission pointed out, selecting network programs on the basis of price rather than quality artificially deprived television audiences of their best possible viewing opportunities while encouraging those who produced these shows to be more concerned with production costs than production values.

[1] American newspapers tried to prevent radio stations from using press wire services for their newscasts, but after a short period of constraint, broadcasting became as dependent upon the newsgathering capacity of the American press during the 1930s as it was dependent upon the music and entertainment industries for its popular programming. The short-term agreement between the press and broadcasting specifying how wire service stories could be handled on radio is published as "The Biltmore Agreement" in Frank J. Kahn, Documents of American Broadcasting 4th ed. (Englewood Cliffs NY: Prentice Hall 1984) p. 101.

[2] 47 CFR 73.658(j). The Justice Department action was United States v. CBS, Civ.Action # 74–5399 (C.D.Cal.1974).

[3] For details of these settlements, see "NBC Breaks Ranks: Settles with Justice," Broadcasting, November 22, 1976, p. 21; "CBS Settles with Justice," Broadcasting, May 12, 1980, p. 29; "It's Settled; ABC, Justice Come to Terms," Broadcasting, August 25, 1980.

In 1982 the FCC attempted to rescind these rules, but pulled back when program producers rallied enough support in Congress to discourage this effort.[4] During this same period, the Justice Department had indicated its willingness to release the networks from the terms of their consent agreements if the Commission repealed its rules.[5]

In 1988, the networks began a new campaign to be released from these program ownership restraints.[6] As might be expected, they based their plea for release upon the FCC's own argument that there is now such a competitive electronic media environment that marketplace alone should determine how programs are to be financed and distributed.

In January 1990, Fox Broadcasting petitioned the FCC for permission to provide its stations more than 15 hours of weekly programming without thereby becoming a "network" subject to the agency's financial interest rules.[7] Fox contended that granting it an 18 month waiver would allow it to take advantage of its ownership of 20th Century Fox film studios to produce programming during this period that would increase its audience and enable it to compete more effectively with the three major television networks.

Instead of responding directly to the Fox petition, the FCC tried to avoid getting caught in the middle of this controversy by directing the television networks and Hollywood film producers to work out some compromise agreement the Commission could then adopt as its new rules. By June 1990, however, it was clear that no compromise agreement could be reached and the FCC was forced to begin its own deliberations to determine whether the rules should be retained, modified or rescinded.

Hollywood producers claimed that the networks had not been bargaining in good faith, because they were confident that the administration would not be sympathetic to a continuation of restrictions on the marketplace behavior of the television networks. That suspicion seemed to be confirmed when the U.S. Justice

---

[4] 54 RR2d 457 (1983). The Hollywood producers were even successful in enlisting the help of former Actors Guild President Reagan to stop this recision effort. For a more detailed account of this entire financial interest issue, see Don R. Le Duc, Beyond Broadcasting: Patterns in Policy and Law (White Plains NY: Longman, 1987) chapter 5.

[5] "Consent Decree Held Hostage: Justice Department Backs FCC," Variety, February 2, 1983, p. 84.

[6] "Fin–Syn Phoenix Out of the Ashes," Broadcasting July 4, 1988, p. 30.

[7] "Fox Waiver Petition May Be Open Sesame for Fin–Syn Revision." Broadcasting Jan. 29, 1990, p. 19. FCC rules defined a television "network" as an organization that distributed 15 hours or more hours of weekly programs to its affiliated stations. Fox was distributing less than 15 hours a week to its stations to avoid becoming a "network" subject to the Commission's financial interest rules.

Department, the Federal Trade Commission and the President's Chief of Staff all urged the Commission to repeal the rules.[8]

The networks argued that to continue to deny them the right to share in the off-network domestic and international sales revenues of those programs they scheduled unfairly reduced their capacity to survive in the much more competitive electronic media environment of the 1990s.

On the other hand, producers contended that because the networks pay only 75–80 percent of the production costs of those programs they schedule, they have no right to demand a share of those domestic and international syndication revenues producers need to recoup their costs and profit from their own productions. In addition, these producers pointed out that without the protection of the rules, networks would be able to coerce them into granting the networks ownership or monetary concessions because only a very limited number of programs are able to obtain network exposure, and each network can exert a significant influence on a show's popularity by determining where it will be positioned in its schedule, and how heavily it will be promoted.[9]

Obviously, there was no simple, sensible solution to this extremely complex problem and so in April 1991, by a 3–2 vote, a sharply divided Commission adopted new financial syndication rules that as everyone had expected, pleased none of the parties.[10]

The one major benefit these new rules would have offered the networks was immediate entry to the international television program sales market. Limited by the old rules to the sale of only those programs the networks themselves produced, network international program sales had never exceeded $175 million, less than 8 percent of the $2.3 billion earned annually from foreign sales of American television programs.[11] However, counterbalancing this benefit was the restriction the new rules continued to impose on network program ownership, limiting each network to the prime-time scheduling of no more than 40 percent of its own productions.

In November 1992, a federal court overturned these new *financial interest* rules, finding no justification for continuing to impose

---

[8] "Justice Dept. Urges Fin–Syn Repeal in FCC Filing Flood," Variety, June 20, 1990, pg. 47; "White House Sends Loud and Clear Fin–Syn Signal," Broadcasting, Feb. 18, 1991, pg. 27.

[9] The ratings success of a program is vitally important to the TV producer, because the amount of money a producer will earn from the $5.7 billion domestic syndication market and $2.3 billion foreign syndication market is largely dependent on the program's popularity during its network run.

[10] 69 RR2d 341 (1991). This 30 day waiting period has been provided in the rules to give a TV producer who has been coerced by the network into granting it syndication rights adequate opportunity to revoke this permission before the network exercises its right.

[11] "MIP Hip to Net's New Game", Variety, April 22, 1991, p. 1.

any program ownership restrictions on television networks.[12] Soon afterward the court agreed to delay issuing its vacating order for 120 days to give the Commission sufficient time to revise its findings in a manner that would satisfy the court.

As the deadline approached, acting FCC chairman Quello managed to obtain from a deeply divided Commission the approval he needed for a revised report that phased out virtually all limitations on network ownership and syndication of television programming by November 1995.[13] Until that time, the new FCC policy permits networks to acquire financial interests and syndication rights in any programs they air, but does not allow them to domestically syndicate *prime time or first-run* programs, or to withhold any of their own programs from syndication.[14]

In July 1994 the federal court approved these revised Commission financial interest rules, praising the agency for its decision to authorize immediate entry by the three networks into the program syndication business.[15] At this point then, all remaining restrictions are set to expire in November 1995 unless independent program producers are able to convince the Commission before this date that existing restrictions on network domestic program syndication are still essential to protect these producers from unfair competitive practices by the networks.

Ironically, the three major networks could end up losing far more than they gain from the repeal of the financial interest rules. Until now, the Fox network has been providing its affiliate stations less than 15 hours of programming a week to avoid being classified by FCC rules as a *television network* and thereby subject to network financial interest restrictions. When these restraints end in November 1995, Fox will be free to expand its program offerings in order to compete more effectively with ABC, CBS and NBC.

Two other major media powers, Warner and Paramount, both major television program producers, have also been waiting for the financial interest rules to be repealed in order to be able to achieve the greatest financial benefit from the new television networks they are both in the process of creating. So the net result of this victory for the three major networks is likely to be a significant increase in the level of economic competition these networks will be forced to face.

[12] Shurz Communications v. FCC, 982 F 2d 1043 (7th Cir.1992).

[13] Financial Interest Rules, 72 RR2d 1044 (1993); affirmed on reconsideration, 73 RR2d 1452 (1993).

[14] The primary constraints imposed on the three major television networks by the consent decrees they had entered into in the mid 1970s were vacated by a federal district court in United States v. NBC, 74 RR2d 986 (C.C.D. Cal., 1993).

[15] Capital Cities/ABC v. FCC, 29 F.3d 309 (7th Cir.1994).

Prime Time Access Rules (PTAR)

In an allied development, First Media Corporation, owner of a CBS affiliate station in Orlando, Florida, petitioned the FCC in 1990 to rescind the agency's "Prime Time Access Rule." The current version of the rule, adopted in 1975, requires network affiliate television stations in the nation's largest 50 broadcast markets to set aside one hour of their primetime schedules each evening for non-network programming.[16] First Media argued that such sweeping interference in the programming choices of urban television stations no longer was justified by electronic media marketplace conditions, and therefore improperly infringed upon the First Amendment rights of those broadcasters.

The Commission initially appeared ready to ignore the First Media petition, with FCC Chairman Sikes declaring that a review of PTAR was, "certainly not on the front burner." As *Broadcasting* magazine noted editorially,[17]

> If anything remains sacrosanct in this day and age, it is that no one in his right mind will suggest laying a glove on PTAR. It is that most peculiar of regulations: one that apparently benefits everyone. Creation of PTAR cut back the network inventories and made ABC a competitive third network. It almost singlehandedly created a viable syndication industry * * * and it improved the position of the top 50 independents remarkably.

However, after Disney, Bonneville International and a large coalition of ABC and CBS affiliates joined First Media in asking that the rule be re-examined, the FCC came under increasing pressure to hold hearings to evaluate the continuing validity of this 15 year old policy.[18] Those opposing the rule point out that television producers of those "first-run" game and tabloid news programs that now dominate the first hour of affiliate station primetime schedules no longer need to be guaranteed major market exposure to survive economically, because the vast number of new cable TV networks that have emerged since 1975 now furnish such non-network producers a broad range of purchasers for their shows.

In addition, these PTAR opponents argue that the rule unfairly discriminates against producers of network programs, because it denies them the opportunity to recoup their production expenses through subsequent syndication of these shows in major markets during one of the most lucrative periods of the broadcast day.

In June 1994 the FCC agreed to reconsider these rules.

[16] 47 CFR § 73.658(k) 1.
[17] "No Larger Than A Man's Hand," Broadcasting, Dec. 10, 1990, p. 138.
[18] "Bonneville Calls for PTAR Relaxation," Broadcasting, Jan. 21, 1991, p. 44.

Program Standards, Violence and
Anticompetitive Practices

Although program producers constantly claimed during the 1980s that television networks were engaging in anticompetitive practice, the only broadcast-related antitrust action launched by the Justice Department during the decade was against the National Association of Broadcasters' Radio and Television Codes. These Codes the NAB had developed to prevent over-commercialization and encourage good taste in broadcast programs were challenged by the Justice Department in 1981 as being anticompetitive in nature.[19]

Smaller corporations claimed they could not purchase network television advertising time because the NAB Code specified that each commercial should be no less than 30 seconds in length to avoid cluttering each two minute commercial break with too many different messages. The Codes had no legal effect, but the three networks complied with them voluntarily to enhance the image and reputation of the industry. Because of this compliance, these advertisers contended that the networks refused to sell them the less expensive 10–15 seconds segments of network commercial time they could afford.

Charging that the networks and their affiliate stations were acting in concert to prevent these advertisers from being able to place their ads on television, the Justice Department forced the NAB to agree to a consent decree, pledging to abandon all efforts to negotiate further restrictions on broadcast advertising.

This "victory" of the Justice Department over those who dared to try to limit the number of commercials on American television also had another unintended consequence. When the NAB was forced by the government to end its "program practices" activities in 1981, it provided the industry with a perfect excuse for avoiding any further responsibility for the quality of television programming.

From that time onward, industry representatives could simply explain even though they were eager to cooperate with one another in efforts to improve the overall quality of the programs they broadcast, the Justice Department could once again find such a cooperative industry effort to be anticompetitive in nature.

In November 1990, Congress gave the broadcast and the cable industry the protection they had claimed to be so eager to receive, granting both industries a three year exemption from antitrust laws in order to develop program standards capable of reducing the amount of violence and improper sexual behavior portrayed in the

---

[19] United States v. NAB, 536 F.Supp. 149 (D.D.C.1982).

shows they distributed.[20]   The anti-trust exemption granted by Congress in 1990 for "any joint discussion, consideration, review, action or agreement by or among persons in the television industry for the purpose of, and limited to, developing and disseminating voluntary guidelines designed to alleviate the negative impact of violence in telecast material" was to end on December 1, 1993.

However, the Justice Department agreed at the last minute to extend that deadline for an additional two months to provide time for the networks to set up some process for monitoring and controlling the amount of violence portrayed on network TV.[21]   When the networks tried to stand united against what they saw as unwarranted Congressional pressure, the cable industry moved in for a public relations victory, offering to have an independent panel rate each cable program for violence and then encode them so that the "V-chip" proposed by Congressman Markey, a circuit that could be activated by concerned parent, would prevent children from viewing any program with an unacceptable level of violence.[22]

Isolated and exposed to political pressure by this maneuver, television networks are expected to agree eventually to establishing a similar violence monitoring plan.

Although it has been the programming practices of the broadcast networks that have attracted most regulatory attention in the past, some of the competitive tactics of the nation's major cable TV MSOs would seem to deserve similar attention.

In 1980, for example, ATC Home Box Office was the only pay TV service offered by 87 percent of all ATC-owned cable-TV systems.   Warner's "The Movie Channel" was the sole pay-TV service available to 80 percent of Warner's cable system subscribers and Teleprompter's jointly owned "Showtime" was the only pay service provided by 78 percent of Teleprompter's cable systems.[23]

Although market demand forced most systems to add other pay-TV services during the 1980s, the recent example of Manhattan Cable TV suggests quite clearly that the tendency to base program carriage decisions upon participation in the service's profits still

[20] Pub.L. 101–650 (1990). Also see "TV Violence Bill Passed by Congress in 11th Hour," Broadcasting, November 5, 1990, p. 90.

[21] "Justice Dept. Comes Through at 11th Hour", Broadcasting, December 6, 1993, p. 90.

[22] Dennis Wharton, "Cable Tries on a White Hat", Variety, February 7, 1994, p. 30.

[23] Paul Kagan Associates, The Pay TV Census, December 31, 1980. The same survey revealed that only 4% of all ATC systems, and 5% of all Teleprompter and Warner systems offered any competing non-owned pay TV services at the time, and no system offered only the pay TV service of a competing MSO.

exists today, always ready to dictate program choices under the right conditions.[24]

Recently, a disturbing new trend has begun to surface in the cable TV programming field. From 1986 onward, MSO ownership and profit participation in new satellite delivered programming services has become the quid pro quo for choosing one service instead of others in competitive contests to fill the last remaining cable channels in many group owned systems.[25] Here, as in the pay TV field of a decade ago, cable conglomerates are using their dominant power over electronic media distribution to obtain economic advantages from those program channels they agree to deliver, and allowing those financial considerations to dictate which particular communication options they will offer the subscribers they serve.

And yet, while such influence over entertainment programming is unfortunate, an even greater threat to the interests of the public may be posed by the cable industry's control over those information services cable systems are likely to be distributing in the near future. As a recent Congressional report points out, although cable in the United States is still primarily involved in the dissemination of entertainment services, the 1990s are likely to see a significant expansion in cable's role as a distributor of a wide range of information services as well.[26] Its broadband capacity, providing the ability to handle high volumes of electronic traffic, makes cable the ideal network for computer data, electronic mail, videotext, security monitoring, home banking and other interactive services.

Although such "blue sky" claims have been made for cable during the past two decades, a number of recent studies predict that both a saturation point in terms of increased demand for cable delivered entertainment and the competitive challenge posed by telephone companies will motivate major MSOs to become more deeply involved in developing their own cable-distributed information services during the next few years.[27]

[24] In December 1987, Manhattan Cable, owned by ATC, entered into a settlement with a local citizens group, agreeing to add to its ATC owned HBO and Cinemax pay TV services a group of non-owned pay TV channels. See "MCTV Forced to Offer Channels Not Affiliated with HBO or Time," Variety December 9, 1987, p. 34.

[25] For a description of this trend, see "Vertical Integration: The Business Behind the Boom in Cable Programming," Broadcasting November 23, 1987, p. 40. Increasing cable system capacity by compressing the size of each channel may lessen the impact of this vertical integration, but it is more likely that this additional channel space will be used for data and pay-per-view services.

[26] U.S. Congress, Office of Technology Assessment, "Science, Technology and the First Amendment," Special Report. (Washington D.C., GPO 1988) See particularly chapter 3.

[27] See, for example, Yankee Group, "Cable and the Telcos: From Confrontation to Detente," (Cambridge, MA: Yankee Group, 1983) or Walter S. Baer, "Telephone and

Based upon their past performance, there is every reason to believe that during such a "new information age," cable MSOs will continue to follow their old strategy of denying carriage to any videotext, home banking or other interactive service in which they have no ownership interest. Once again, then, the public as well as the supplier of each communication service will be at the mercy of a media distributor who has the power to demand tribute for the privilege of delivery, and who is free to offer the public only those services for which this tribute has been paid.

It's difficult to believe that this is that "media marketplace" to which the FCC has delegated responsibility for all public entertainment or information programming decisions, or that this is the competitive environment the Justice Department will continue to rely upon to protect the interests of the public in these vital areas of mass communication.

And yet, as media mergers continue to consolidate control in the hands of an ever smaller group of media conglomerates, their power to determine what communication services the public will receive solely on the basis of their own financial interest in these services will increase with each passing year.

SEC. 98. THE GLOBALIZATION OF AMERICAN MEDIA

An expanding international market for film and television productions and mergers to prevent foreign acquisitions of American media could both have a significant impact on future media service in the United States.

Foreign corporations currently are not interested in trying to acquire an American television network because the Communications Act prohibits granting a broadcast license to an alien or any corporation organized under the laws of a foreign government.[28] Because the most valuable assets of each of the three major networks are those television stations they own and operate in the nation's largest television markets, a foreign purchaser would be prevented by law from realizing the greatest benefits of such an acquisition.

Recently, however, because tighter credit controls and declining advertising revenues have resulted in a sluggish market for broadcast station sales, lobbying efforts have begun to convince Congress to rescind this section of the Act so that foreign investors

---

Cable Companies: Rivals or Partners," in Eli Noam (ed.) Video Media Competition (New York: Columbia University Press 1985) p. 187.

[28] Title 47, U.S.C.A. § 310(b)1–2. Virtually every nation in the world has a similar citizenship requirement. Rupert Murdoch was not allowed to receive the licenses to those Metromedia television group stations that form the backbone of his Fox television network until he applied for and received American citizenship.

will be able to acquire broadcast properties in the United States.[29] If Congress yields to this pressure, particularly now that the networks have been released from virtually all program ownership restrictions of the old "Financial Interest" rules, it is quite likely that several of the world's largest media conglomerates would be in the market for an American television network.

An even more likely scenario is that one or more of these networks will eventually merge with or be taken over by a Hollywood studio.[30] NBC's General Electric is known to be dissatisfied with its broadcast earnings, and CBS continues to struggle financially. It is reasonable to expect that General Electric eventually will sell its marginally profitable television network to an entertainment conglomerate better equipped to produce and promote its programming, while CBS may have no choice but to turn its operations over to a media giant with financial assets necessary to allow it to stay competitive in a global market beset by constantly escalating production costs.

One question that should concern the American public if one or more of the major networks are taken over either by a foreign or domestic mass entertainment conglomerate is how supportive the new owners will be of that vital national and international broadcast journalism service provided by that network it acquires? Although it is true that the present network owners have pared their news department budgets down substantially during the past few years, it is difficult to believe that entertainment giants such as Warner, Disney, Bertelsmann or Berlusconi will be even as committed as the current owners are to a service that informs rather than entertains, and does so without increasing a conglomerate's bottom line.

But broadcast journalism isn't the only type of American television programming that may be affected by changing patterns in mass media commerce. As broadcast and satellite services continue to expand in Europe, American television producers have become increasingly unwilling to produce programs for the networks that are too "American" in orientation to attract foreign audiences as well. Because these producers depend on sales to foreign broadcast organizations to recoup a significant portion of production costs not covered by network license payments, they have become more reluctant with each passing year to produce dramas or situation comedies reflecting values that are alien to

[29] See, for example, the arguments advanced in "Monday Memo," Broadcasting, April 22, 1991, p. 16.

[30] See, for example. Paul Noglows, "Mergers That Might Be," Variety, July 18, 1994, p. 1 and Jim Benson, "TV's Traumatic Times, "Variety, July 18, 1994, p. 1.

other cultures.[31]

Foreign television audiences find it much easier to understand and enjoy simple and superficial series such as "Baywatch" or "Melrose Place" rather than dialogue-driven, American context shows such as "Murphy Brown" or "Northern Exposure". Similarly, Hollywood studios have begun to analyze foreign audience preferences as carefully as domestic audience interests when deciding which major feature films to produce. For example, Warner studio made the third, fourth and fifth sequels to "Police Academy" even though box office revenues in the United States didn't justify their production, simply because of their continued popularity in foreign nations. On the other hand, several major studios rejected the opportunity to produce the 1989 Oscar winning film, "Driving Miss Daisy" because they doubted that foreign film audiences would be attracted to a story about an elderly Jewish Southern woman and her Afro–American driver.

In addition, the growing involvement of American television networks in hundreds of European and Japanese co-productions projects also tends to result in the creation of generalized, somewhat simplistic action-oriented television films and series, rather than drama reflecting any particular American issues or values.[32]

This increasing desire of the American mass entertainment industry to produce feature films and television series capable of satisfying the tastes of global television and film audiences will not result in these producers totally ignoring the interests of the largest and most prosperous domestic audience in the world. It will, however, cause them to be more cautious in the future about producing films or television series reflecting uniquely American social issues or concerns. In this way then, that global dominance of our mass entertainment industry that some feared would result in shaping foreign mass cultures in America's image may in the end have shaped American mass culture far more significantly than their own.

[31] With the explosive growth of newly authorized private commercial broadcast networks and satellite services, the number of Western European television channels is likely to increase from 74 in 1989 to 97 in 1995, with the 484,000 hours of broadcast time increasing to 602,285 by the end of that period. This should result in Europe alone providing a $2 billion market for US programs, constituting 25% of their total broadcast schedules. See, "Euro TV Boom Seems a Steady Thing," Variety, April 15, 1991, M–2 and "U.S. TV Exports to Rise, Study Says", Variety, February 4, 1991, p. 70. At the same time, 43 percent of the $3.13 billion American film rentals came from foreign countries in 1990, up from only 33 percent in 1985.

[32] For example, CBS now is co-producing films and television series with Antenna 2 (France), ORF (Austria), RAI (Italy) ZDF (Germany), as well as film and broadcast organizations in Switzerland, Spain and the United Kingdom. None of its current co-production projects in production—"Eurocops," "Eureka" and "S.O.S. Disparus" is set in the United States.

At the moment federal policy is so preoccupied with reducing the foreign trade deficit and encouraging economic growth that those mass cultural issues raised by media mergers or international film and television trade practices have been virtually ignored. Yet, are American mass media just another domestic industry, whose value to this society is determined solely by the revenues it generates for the United States in international trade? Arguably, a vigorous marketplace of ideas is more vital to the welfare of any nation than a prosperous marketplace for consumer goods.

Reducing media competition through mergers and conglomerations may offer tangible domestic and international trade benefits, but at what cost in diminishing those reading, listening, and viewing options that provide the American public with access to diverse thoughts and ideas? [33] There are no longer any simple answers to these complex media ownership issues in an era when the globalization of media operations extends the scope of policy considerations far beyond national borders. Yet it is important to keep in mind that many of those concerns of the past about media conglomeration and its tendency to concentrate too much influence over our society in the hands of too few still seem equally valid today.

[33] Media industry representatives are quick to claim that with technology providing a continuous expansion in the number of electronic channels available for distributing entertainment and information services, there is no need for concern about reduced media competition through mergers. This is about as reassuring as a government promising to increase commerce simply by expanding its network of roads. The critical mass of funds available to produce mass entertainment and news is relatively fixed, and increasing the number of channels through which it can be distributed does not operate to increase significantly the amount of content produced. See Le Duc, Beyond Broadcasting: Patterns in Policy and Law, chapter 7.

Chapter 17

DISTRIBUTING MASS COMMUNICATIONS

Sec.
99. Mass Media and the Common Carrier Connection.
100. The Telephone Network Competitor.
101. Communication Law and the Challenge of Change.

SEC. 99. MASS MEDIA AND THE COMMON CARRIER CONNECTION

Common carriers have played a crucial role in the development of mass communications in the United States.

It was the telegraph that transformed the provincial gazette of the early 1800s into the modern newspaper capable of providing comprehensive coverage of national and world events. The steam-driven rotary press may have launched the era of mass news in the 1830s, but not until telegraph lines of the newly formed Western Union spanned the continent from coast to coast in 1861 did reports of major events occurring in San Francisco, New Orleans or Atlanta begin reaching newsrooms in the Northeast in a matter of seconds rather than days or weeks.

Associated Press, the first American wire service, was formed in 1848, and by the end of the Civil War this cooperative newspooling venture of the nation's largest newspapers provided its member publishers with immediate coverage of events anywhere in the United States through telegraphed news dispatches from local AP reporters at the scene.[1]

Less than a decade later, as the first trans-Atlantic submarine cable began operation, this channel of telegraphed dispatches linked American publishers not only with Europe, but through the British news agency Reuters and the French news agency Havas, with

[1] During the 1850s, several of the privately owned telegraph companies tried to form their own news organizations in competition with AP. When many of these companies merged to form Western Union in 1861, AP offered to give the new nationwide telegraph company the exclusive right to carry its news dispatches, in return for priority handling of these dispatches. Western Union agreed, and by 1880, these AP transmissions constituted 11 percent of Western Union's total message traffic. By 1880, the volume in telegraphed news traffic was so heavy that Western Union began dedicating private leased lines solely to AP news dispatches. See Robert Thompson, Wiring A Continent (Princeton: Princeton University Press, 1947). The AP organized in 1848 was later supplanted by the Western AP, which survived when the earlier AP went out of business in 1892.

colonial offices of these agencies located throughout the Middle East, Africa and Asia.

Thus, in less than a half century, the telegraph and those wire services formed to take advantage of this new technology allowed local newspapers in the United States to begin covering the world for their readers. The daily newspaper was no longer isolated from distant events by days or weeks of mail delivery, but connected directly by reports travelling at the speed of light through the wires of the Western Union.

During the late 1920s, it was AT&T, another communications common carrier, whose long distance lines transformed a weak, locally oriented collection of radio stations into a national broadcast medium. In its original license allocation plan, the Federal Radio Commission had established an elaborate system of local and regional broadcast services, but had made no provision for simultaneous nationwide distribution of broadcast programming.

A small group of radio stations had begun to use AT&T lines as early as 1923 to pool programs, but it was not until the late 1920s that NBC's two national networks (its second network would later become ABC) and the newly formed CBS leased AT&T's recently completed nationwide broadcast lines to emerge as the dominant forces in American broadcasting. By using AT&T's lines to distribute programs *directly* to each of its affiliate stations, networks were able avoid the elaborate FRC local licensing system to offer their audiences a nationwide service of polished and professional entertainment that no other medium could rival.

Then, when the FCC attempted to establish a system of community oriented television stations in the early 1950s, it was AT&T's long line systems, now augmented by microwave relays, that once again allowed the networks to by-pass the agency's spectrum licensing regulations to establish *national* programming channels where only local services had been envisioned by government planners.

In a very real sense, then, it is entirely possible that if AT&T and its Bell Systems had not established their nationwide system of telephone networks before broadcasting emerged as a mass medium in the United States during the 1920s, our radio and television services of today might be as provincial in nature as our local newspapers were before the advent of the telegraph.

Then, during the mid–1950s, when "community antenna systems" were simply enhancing the quality of the television picture from one or two nearby television stations, it was AT&T's microwave relay systems that allowed cable TV operators to begin importing from distant markets the programs of television networks with no local affiliates. In time, the FCC began restricting this microwave signal importation to preserve its broadcast market system, but not before the cable TV industry was firmly established in the United States.[2] Without this AT&T microwave network, it is quite likely that "community antenna," dependent solely on local television signals, would have withered away as predicted when more television stations began broadcast service during the late 1950s. In that event, of course, there would have been no cable TV industry to emerge during the 1980s with dozens of new program channels, and viewers in the United States today would still have to be content with only a handful of viewing alternatives.

In 1972, when the FCC announced its "Open Skies" communication satellite policy, no government planner could have foreseen how encouraging new operators to provide nationwide satellite common carrier services in competition with AT&T would alter the competitive relationship between broadcasting and cable TV in the United States, or erode the strength of the American television networks. As discussed in Chapter 3, it was this decision by the Commission that eventually allowed cable TV to become a medium in its own right, able because of lower nationwide video distribution costs, to launch its own unique cable networks.

In addition, these lower video distribution costs also enabled television stations affiliated with a network to become more independent of that network in making their own programming decisions, because they now had the option of using satellites to obtain their own programs directly from feature film, sports or series program syndicators.

In each of these past situations, the communications common carrier has only played a supporting role to the mass medium it has served, providing the distribution function essential for its growth and expansion. But what if a carrier should attempt to take over the medium and become the mass communicator itself?

Until 1982 this would have been an idle question, because federal law prohibited a communications common carrier from offering any service other than its traditional distribution of communication messages. In that year, however, a *consent decree,* negotiated without any serious consideration of its possible implications for mass media, offered AT&T and its former Bell Systems the promise of eventual freedom to move beyond basic telephone service and into the field of mass communications.

SEC. 100. THE TELEPHONE NETWORK COMPETITOR

When local and national telephone networks are released from legal constraints, they could radically transform

[2] For a more detailed account of this era, see Don R. Le Duc, Cable TV v. the FCC: A Crisis in Media Control (Temple University Press: Philadelphia, 1973).

the existing structure of mass media service in the United States.

In 1974 the Justice Department launched a massive antitrust action against AT&T, its manufacturing subsidiary, Western Electric and Bell Laboratory, the research and development facility it owned jointly with its Bell Systems. The suit charged AT&T and its subsidiaries with using their dominant position in the telecommunications market to inhibit competition.

The government wanted AT&T to divest itself of one or more of these subsidiaries to prevent the possibility of the company using revenues from its regulated monopoly telephone networks to subsidize its development and promotion of specialized services in competitive areas of the telecommunications marketplace. In addition, the Justice Department believed that breaking up the AT&T–Bell System would deny AT&T any opportunity to use its monopoly control over its telephone networks in the United States either to discourage the use of non-AT&T equipment on its lines, or block the carriage of rival telecommunication services.

In January 1982 AT&T agreed to the terms of the Justice Department settlement requiring it to divest itself of its 22 Bell Systems, Bell Laboratory and Western Electric in return for the right to enter markets previously denied it because of its regulated common carrier monopoly status. In August of that same year, Federal District Judge Harold Greene indicated he would approve the agreement if certain additional conditions were added. Judge Greene insisted that the agreement prohibit AT&T from offering "electronic publishing" [3] through its own facilities for a minimum period of seven years, and allow the new and independent Regional Bell Operating Companies (RBOCs) formed from the old Bell Systems to produce, publish and distribute telephone directory "yellow pages."

On August 24, 1982, Judge Greene gave final approval to the AT&T divestiture plan.[4] During the next year AT&T spun off its 22 Bell Systems; systems that then reorganized themselves into seven separate Regional Bell Operating Companies.[5]

[3] Judge Greene defined "electronic publishing" in legal context as including "the provision of any information which AT&T or its affiliates has, or has caused to be originated, authored, compiled, collected or edited, or in which it has a direct or indirect financial or proprietary interest and which is disseminated to an unaffiliated person through some electronic means."

[4] United States v. AT&T, 552 F.Supp. 131 (D.D.C.1982), affirmed sub nom. Maryland v. U.S., 460 U.S. 1001, 103 S.Ct. 1240 (1983). Thirteen state regulatory commissions contested the consent agreement on various grounds but since only three Supreme Court Justices voted to accept an appeal from the consent agreement (4 are needed to grant review), no further legal challenge was possible.

[5] These newly formed Regional Bell Operating Companies (RBOCs) were Ameritech, Atlantic, Nynex, Bell South, Pacific Telesis, Southwestern Bell and US West.

In 1984 Greene approved a proposed order filed by the Justice Department to permit these newly formed RBOCs to engage in non-telephonic businesses as long as the estimated net revenues of these activities would not exceed 10 percent of the company's telephone service net revenues. Under this standard, the Justice Department allowed several RBOCs to enter a wide variety of businesses from equipment leasing and real estate management to retail sales and international consulting.[6]

Judge Greene retained authority to approve or disapprove each new non-telephone venture, and to review the agreement every three years to determine whether conditions had changed sufficiently to authorize RBOCs to engage in an even broader range of these activities. However, under the terms of the modified final judgment (MFJ) entered in 1987, he continued to prohibit the RBOCs from providing "information services"—a broad category of activities Judge Greene defined as including everything from videotext to the operation of a cable TV system.

The non-telephone business revenues of these RBOCs increased from a 1986 total of $4.3 billion to $7 billion in 1987, nearly doubling within a single year as their telephone earnings remained relatively stable at $70 billion.[7] To put these industry revenues in perspective, as the seven BOCs were earning this $77 billion in 1987, the entire newspaper industry, including some 1,640 papers, generated combined earnings of $40 billion; some 15,000 broadcast stations earned a total of $24.4 billion, and the nation's 8,800 cable TV systems were sharing revenues of $14 billion.[8]

And none of these RBOC revenues had been generated by those non-telephonic activities that the companies could perform the most effectively; distributing public information, electronic publishing and video services through their telecommunication networks.

At the time of the consent agreement in 1982, the American Newspapers Publishing Association proposed what it called a "diversity principle" to guide future judicial supervision of the RBOCs under the terms of the agreement. To ensure the greatest degree of diversity, the press association urged that telephone companies

Although they are often called "Baby Bells," each of them actually commands sufficient corporate wealth to be listed among the Fortune magazine's largest 500 American corporations.

[6] "Broadening Business Horizons for BOCs," Telecommunications, December 1984, p. 42.

[7] "Putting Out Lines in All Directions," Time, May 5, 1986, p. 49. "Baby Bells Prospering," Telecommunications, March 1988, p. 12.

[8] "Broadcasting versus the Telco Monster," Broadcasting, May 8, 1989, p. 44. In 1987, the combined revenues of just two BOCs, Nytex and Bell South in itself exceeded the combined revenues of the entire cable TV industry.

controlling transmission facilities be prevented from acquiring any interest in or control over the information content flowing through their facilities.

Although Judge Greene did allow the RBOCs to begin offering their customers access to information services in 1987, he did so in a manner consistent with this principle, limiting the companies to the role of a *conduit*, simply furnishing subscribers data bases supplied by others. But in 1991 the D.C. Court of Appeals overturned this decree, directing Judge Greene either to permit RBOCs to provide their own information services, or to make a finding of fact that allowing RBOC entry into this information market would significantly lessen competition in this field.[9] Lacking the evidence required for such a finding, Judge Greene was forced to lift the ban he had imposed.[10]

At this time, though, this right of the Bell Companies to deliver their own information services to their customers has been overshadowed by another right these companies were granted in 1992.

Telco Video Services

In July 1992 the FCC authorized the seven major regional Bell companies to begin providing *video dial tone* services.[11] The decision allowed these telephone carriers to deliver a full range of television programming to their customers, as long as the phone company did not own or exercise editorial control over the programming it distributed.[12]

Chesapeake & Potomac Telephone, a subsidiary of Bell Atlantic and US West each challenged the FCC's authority to prevent them from owning or controlling the video services they provided. In both cases a federal district judge agreed with the telephone carrier position. In the US West case, a federal district judge found the ban to be "unnecessarily severe" and in violation of US West's first amendment rights, while in the Chesapeake and Potomac case, the judge described the ban as directly abridging the telephone carrier's

[9] For Judge Greene's initial review holding see, United States v. Western Electric Co., 673 F.Supp. 525 (D.D.C.1987) and 714 F.Supp. 1 (D.D.C.1988). Reversal by the U.S. Court of Appeals, directing Greene to apply a broader range of criteria than those used in his original decision can be found at United States v. Western Electric Co., 900 F.2d 283 (D.C.Cir.1990).

[10] Unable to do so, Greene was forced to vacate his original decision in United States v. Western Electric, 767 F.Supp. 308 (D.C.C. 1991); review denied sub nom. American Newspaper Publishers Association v. U.S. 112 S.Ct. 336 (1991).

[11] Further Proceedings on Cable Cross–Ownership Rules, 69 RR2d 1613 (1992).

[12] In 1984, Congress had prohibited telephone carriers from operating as cable TV systems in section 533(b)(1) of the Cable Policy section of the Communications Act of 1934. Because of this Congressional ban, the FCC had no choice but to limit the role of these BOCs to that of a passive video delivery system.

"right to express ideas by means of a particular and significant mode of communication-video programming." [13]

However, even though these decisions may strengthen the legal position of telephone carriers challenging federal video program ownership restrictions in other regions of the nation, they apply at the moment *only* to telco video operations in communities within the jurisdiction of these two district courts. As a result, pending further litigation or an affirming decision by a federal appeals court, the impact of these decisions remains limited to those areas surrounding Alexandria, Virginia and Seattle, Washington.

In July 1994 the FCC approved the first of more than 20 telephone carrier applications it had already received, authorizing Bell Atlantic to build a "video dialtone" network to compete directly with local cable TV systems.[14] Bell Atlantic intends to construct a $16 million interactive video system that will be available to some 38,000 homes in Dover Township, New Jersey by 1995.

The National Association of Regulatory Utility Commissioners and the National League of Cities had joined cable TV, broadcast and press groups in lobbying for federal legislation to prevent the FCC from implementing its video dialtone decision.[15] In part, this opposition reflected a concern that efforts to attract new information and video service subscribers would tempt the RBOCs to neglect their special and primary responsibility to the public to provide efficient, economical and technologically advanced telephone service. Certainly the temptation is there, because furnishing local telephone service in a monopoly environment offers no incentives to improve service, while there is every incentive to divert those profit-regulated payments received from telephone subscribers into competitive investments in videotext and cable TV services with no restrictions on profits.[16]

[13] Chesapeake & Potomac Telephone v. United States, 830 F.Supp. 909 (E.D.Va. 1993); U.S. West v. United States, 855 F.Supp. 1184 (W.D.Wash.1994).

[14] Kate Fitzgerald and David Wallace, "The First Baby Bell Gets Green Light," Advertising Age, July 18, 1994, p. 23. See also, Christopher Stern, "Hundt Has Dialtone on Fast Track," Broadcasting, April 18, 1994, p. 6. These local cable TV systems in the areas Bell Atlantic plans to serve have reason to fear this competitive challenge, because this single RBOC posted earnings of more than $12 billion in 1993, revenues ⅔ the size of those earned by the entire cable TV industry.

[15] The opposition of the National League of Cities may have resulted from FCC's decision to allow telcos to provide video service without obtaining a franchise from the community in which they operated. This meant that the revenue each community was currently receiving from its cable franchise fee was likely to be reduced significantly as the local telephone carrier began attracting former cable system subscribers.

[16] A 1989 study commissioned by the National Cable Television Association claimed that despite the constraints of the consent agreement, cross-subsidies between revenues earned from rate-regulated telephone services and non-regulated

But it seems to be "self interest" far more than "public interest" that is motivating the political pressure now being applied by various mass media trade groups to delay, if not prevent more telephone carriers from launching electronic publishing and video distribution operations in the United States. For one thing, they simply fear direct competition from seven corporate giants boasting combined capital assets in excess of $225 billion.[17] But far more significantly, they fear the complex and sophisticated electronic distribution systems these capital assets reflect, and that technological potential they may soon be capable of realizing.

Today's telephone network, unlike the modern cable TV system, is all-switched, virtually all-digital and is rapidly becoming all fiber optic. A *switched* system is one that is totally interactive, permitting each subscriber select any signal or channel available from its switching center, ordering and being charged for that order at the same instant the specific channel chosen is being sent directly to that subscriber. Thus, unlike even the most advanced cable TV system, the telephone switching center is already capable of responding directly and individually to each subscriber request for any type of communication service from pay-per-view (PPV) feature films to international banking transactions, billing the customer automatically as the service is being provided.[18]

All electronic media are attempting to convert from analog to digital transmission as rapidly as possible, because delivering audio or visual information by binary code rather than in a continuous wave of signals reduces distortion significantly while at the same time allowing the transmission to be compressed into a much narrower band of frequencies. What may eventually provide the telephone industry with a distinct advantage in this area of new technology is its continuing commitment to developing *Integrated Service Digital Networks* (ISDN), special broadband communications channels capable of distributing a broad array of different

telecommunication activities were still rampant. "NCTA Attacks Telco Business Practices," Broadcasting, March 20, 1989, p. 72.

[17] "Valuing the Big Three: Telcos Get Bigger," Broadcasting, August 19, 1991, p. 19. All local exchange carrier assets are valued at $300 billion; BOCs account for ¾ of these total assets. In comparison, cable TV assets are currently valued at only $58 billion and broadcast assets at $29 billion. Broadcast industry revenues in 1990 were estimated to be $23 billion; cable TV, $19 billion and telco revenues, $90 billion.

[18] One example of the impressive service capacity of an all-switched network is provided by the "Video-on-Demand" channels developed for the telephone carrier operated test project in Cerritos, California. "Video-on-Demand" not only allows a subscriber to select any movie offered by the system at any time, but also to control the delivery of the movie by being able to "fast forward," "reverse" or stop the movie to view a still frame whenever desired. This is only possible because of the completely interactive qualities of the telephone "switched network."

types of communication services simultaneously within a single network channel.[19]

But the most impressive advantage the telephone carriers appear to have over the cable TV industry is that 1.5 million miles of fiber optic trunk lines that are already in service delivering telephone company voice and data transmissions.[20] A fiber optic circuit is a hair-thin, flexible glass filament that guides pulses of message-delivering light along the length of the narrow fiber. Typical fiber systems carry data at a rate of more than a billion digital bits of information per second, and can transport this data for 20 miles without need of amplification.[21] In contrast, the coaxial cable used by cable TV systems can deliver data at a rate of only 1.5 million bits per second and requires amplification at least once every mile.[22]

Studies indicate that fiber optic circuits have the potential to be at least 30 times more cost effective than coaxial circuits, when operating at full capacity and delivering digital signals. At the moment, though, this potential can't be realized because "full capacity" would require a payload of 500 separate video-sized communication channels during an era when those 50 to 60 video channels now available have access only to analog produced programs.[23]

In other words, today's fiber optic networks are still much faster, larger and more efficient than necessary to carry those video

[19] The primary barrier in the path of ISDN development has been international politics, with various regions of the world clashing over the one universal set of standards that should be adopted for ISDN operation, so that worldwide ISDN service will be possible. Currently, some telcos have been experimenting with ASDL (asymmetrical digital subscriber line), a technique that can use existing copper wire system trunk lines to deliver video programming, but this approach is considered too expensive and ultimately too inefficient to ever be more than a stop-gap approach to video distribution.

[20] In contrast, at the end of 1990, cable TV systems had installed only 1,000 miles of fiber optic trunk lines. "Fiber Optics and the Future of Television," NVR Reports, Winter 1991, p. 4.

[21] In addition, fiber optic performance continues improving. In 1990, for example, each fiber optic filament was capable of delivering 100 times the amount of data it could carry in 1980, as the price of the fiber dropped from $3 dollars to 15 cents a yard. Karen Wright, "The Road to the Global Village," Scientific American, March 1990, p. 92.

[22] Because each time a signal is amplified, distortion is introduced by the amplifier, the fact that fiber optic delivered signal can travel 20 times as far as coaxial cable delivered signal without need of amplification not only significantly reduces equipment, installation and maintenance costs, but also substantially diminishes signal distortion.

[23] Technology already being developed for HDTV and cable TV channel compression will be capable of converting video productions for digital transmission easily and inexpensively, but with the huge channel capacity already available to it, this is unlikely to increase fiber optic cost effectiveness in the foreseeable future. The greater problem for the BOCs is that most of these channels are owned by cable MSOs unlikely to permit fiber optic carriage of their programming.

services available for them to deliver. At this point, then, using an optic network to deliver cable TV service would be much like buying a Concorde jet to travel to work each morning. And, engineers must still solve the "last mile" problem of fiber optic networks, finding some way of reducing the cost of connecting individual homes to the network. Adding subscribers to a coaxial cable system can be accomplished for less than $150 per household, but because there has been no economic inducement as yet to provide fiber optic service to the home, the cost for each hookup is still estimated to be in the range of $1,500–$2,000.[24]

New Federal Regulatory Policies

In 1990, the Bush administration launched the first major federal effort to break down the traditional regulatory barriers that separated broadcast, cable and communication common carrier services. Although Congress rejected each of the administration's legislative proposals, the FCC during this era drew upon all the regulatory authority it could muster to undercut those barriers Congress had erected.

In addition to its video dialtone decision, the Commission, guided by chairman Alfred Sikes, also allocated spectrum space for personal communication service (PCS), a new form of wireless phone and computer terminal network the cable industry is eager to develop.[25] These low-cost PCS systems will enable cable operators to compete directly with existing telephone companies, providing an alternative system for the delivery of point-to-point messages. In essence, then, the FCC was seeking to encourage cable operators to offer telephone services, as it encouraged telephone companies to offer video services, intending to let the marketplace determine which combination of services each could provide most cost-effectively.

Underlying these decisions was the philosophy that rival communication delivery services should be permitted to compete or combine in whatever form they believed they could function most efficiently, with government playing the most limited role possible in deciding how various video, audio or information services actually reach the home. As Sikes once explained it, whether by telephone fiber optic, coaxial cable, satellite or some hybrid combination of the three, the actual distribution system should be *transparent* to the message being delivered, a "seamless" universe of

[24] "Sikes Says Telcos Are Revaluating Fiber to Home," Broadcasting, February 12, 1990, p. 15.

[25] "FCC Releases PCS Spectrum Allocations," Broadcasting September 21, 1992, p. 6. Major cable organizations such as Time Warner, Continental Cablevision, Tele–Communications Inc., and Viacom International, among others, have already received experimental licenses for PCS development.

communication channels in which the specific method of dissemination is irrelevant as long as the entire system functions in the most effective manner possible.[26]

Soon after the Clinton administration assumed power, Vice President Gore launched a policy initiative designed to eliminate every outdated federal regulatory restriction that prevented direct competition among the various telecommunication service providers.[27] This proposal envisioned the development of national fiber optic networks capable of providing a full range of communication services, a concept that soon became known as the *information superhighway*.

In 1994, the House passed two telecommunications bills designed to achieve some of these objectives; legislation to repeal the telco-cable cross-ownership ban, to permit telephone carriers to distribute video programming, to allow cable TV to offer phone services and to authorize regional Bell systems, subject to Justice Department and FCC approval, to provide long distance service and sell telephone equipment.[28]

In the Senate, however, Commerce Committee Chairman Hollings slowed the progress of this RBOC legislation, questioning the need to free RBOCs from all Congressional control and expressing serious concern about the ability of either the FCC or the Justice Department to supervise this radical transformation of American telecommunications policy.[29] As a result, complete regulatory freedom for telephone carriers seems unlikely in the near future as each industry group continues to pressure its own coalition of politicians to obtain the greatest benefits from every proposal under consideration.

It is far easier, of course, to proclaim a visionary policy than it is to achieve it. Whatever long range benefits might be gained from a merging of separate and overlapping broadcast, satellite,

[26] "Subject to Change," Broadcasting, Jan. 28, 1991, p. 82.

[27] Kim McAvoy, "Al Gore: Directing Traffic onto the Superhighway," Broadcasting, January 10, 1994, p. 10.

[28] The Brooks–Dingell bill (H.R. 3626) would have authorized the RBOCs to compete with AT&T and others in the long-distance telephone service market and to manufacture and sell their own telephone equipment. The Markey–Fields bill (H.R. 3636) would have repeal the Congressionally imposed telco-cable cross-ownership ban and would have pre-empted state regulation in order to permit cable operators to provide telephone service everywhere in the United States, despite any State or local law to the contrary. Both bills were passed by an overwhelming margin in the House; H.R. 3626 by a vote of 423 to 5 and H.R. 3636 by a vote of 423 to 4.

[29] Hollings own bill, S.1822, would bar RBOCs from entering long distance service field until they could clearly establish that they no longer monopolized local phone service in their own area and that their entry would create a more competitive telecommunications service market. The bill also provides strict standards the FCC and Justice Department must follow in determining when these conditions have been met.

cable TV and telephone distribution services, it is the short term effects of this policy that will decide how each rival medium will react to it; an impact almost certain to threaten many of each media industry's most fundamental and cherished economic interests.

Yet, even if this particular legislative initiative should fail, the trend towards an ever greater degree of consolidation among previously independent video, audio, informational and personal distribution systems seems destined to continue, simply because every media industry will be able to realize substantial savings from combining with others to permit its messages to be delivered through a single network, rather than continuing to maintain and operate its own distribution facilities.

As all previous "revolutions" in the history of American mass communications, this trend towards consolidation among media delivery systems is likely to occur so gradually and sporadically during this decade and the next that it will again be difficult in the future to point to any specific date when the final form of the new multi-media delivery network was actually determined. But even at this point it is possible to begin considering what effects this tendency is likely to have upon future broadcast, cable TV and newspaper service in the United States and those First Amendment rights now accorded to each of these media by American law.

SEC. 101. COMMUNICATION LAW AND THE CHALLENGE OF CHANGE

Changing the way mass media are distributed in the United States could have a profound effect on those legal rights each medium can now assert.

The nation's telephone carriers appear to be in the best position to emerge as the dominant partners in future media merger ventures. In addition to their greater economic power and more advanced distribution systems, the phone companies also have a significant advantage in being able to underwrite the costs of network operation through their capacity to offer and bill their customers for a far broader range of telecommunications related services than any of their media competitors.[30]

And, in the near future, the 500 video channel capacity of their fiber optic networks that now seems so totally unnecessary could

---

[30] In 1990, for example, telephone carrier local exchange billings in themselves were reported to be in excess of $20 billion, thereby generating 50% of the revenues of the entire newspaper industry, and virtually equalling the earnings of the entire broadcasting industry.

actually be their most significant competitive advantage of all.[31] This vast channel space will not only permit each fiber optic network to carry a large number of "high definition television" (HDTV) channels without reducing its other services, but will also make it an ideal distribution system for "pay-per-view" feature films and other special events.[32]

This extensive network channel capacity could also be used to deliver the daily newspaper by facsimile to each subscriber home. With newsprint, ink and distribution now representing at least 35 percent of the operating expenses of the typical newspaper, the substantially reduced costs offered through electronic transmission could prove very attractive to a number of publishers in the future.[33]

On the other hand, electronic publishing could pose a significant competitive threat to the local newspaper if the system were to decide instead to allow its customers select directly from wire services and other news sources those specific news topics of greatest interest to each subscriber.[34] In this way, a subscriber could create a daily "newspaper" that would much more clearly reflect that reader's own particular interests in business, sports, international or entertainment news by drawing upon the resource of that 90–95 percent of those relevant wire stories in each topic area not selected to be published by the local newspaper.

[31] The cable industry is planning to increase dramatically the number of video channels their systems can carry through digital compression of each video signal. In reality, however, this will not increase the coaxial cable actual frequency capacity, but only allow more signals to be delivered within the same space constraints.

[32] Major film studios have shown great interest in a marketing plan that devotes one network channel to each of a dozen or more of their most popular recent releases that system subscribers could pay to see at any time. In this way they could by-pass pay-TV distribution, where they are generally paid only one license fee by the service for a package of their films, and the video cassette rental market, where because of the "first sale" doctrine, they earn money only from the original sale of a film cassette to the rental store, with all rental proceeds being kept by the store. Because of its "all-switched" configuration, a telco network would allow a viewer to start the film selected at any time, while a cable system could only provide access at certain specific times each day when the film is scheduled to begin.

[33] The 35% figure is derived from Christopher H. Sterling and Timothy Haight, The Mass Media: Aspen Institute Guide to Communication Trends (Praeger, New York, 1976), Table 321–B, p. 166. Industry sources indicate that because of substantial increases in newsprint costs during the 1980s, the actual publishing and distribution costs of the typical daily newspaper may now exceed 40 percent of total operating expenses. In fact, the main reason that no newspaper publisher has attempted electronic distribution is simply that so few American homes are yet equipped to receive facsimile transmissions, and so few cable TV systems serve more than 60 percent of the homes in their market area.

[34] This type of service is already being provided on an experimental basis in New York City, where subscribers may use their phone network to select and print news items arranged by topic from a number of different news sources including USA Today, New York Newsday and some 50 other non-newspaper information providers.

Clearly, a vast majority of a newspaper's subscribers will probably prefer to continue to receive their pre-packaged news and advertising directly from the local publisher, but if the competing electronic service would cause only a 5 to 10 percent reduction in newspaper subscribership, the impact of even this relatively minor drop in circulation on potential advertising revenues could undercut the financial foundation of a significant number of America's daily newspapers.

The competitive threat that this type of media distribution system poses for television broadcasters is even more severe. Because the typical television station operates primarily as a distributor of programs produced by others, it is extremely vulnerable to challenge from rival delivery systems that are capable of delivering these same television programs more efficiently and economically.[35]

In reality, there is no logical reason why each television station should continue to incur operating expenses in excess of a million dollars a year simply to encumber the valuable public resource of spectrum space with retransmissions of programs it receives by microwave or satellite; programs that actually could be viewed with far greater clarity and less distortion if delivered directly to the home through a fiber optic channel. The one unique mass communication role now played by most television stations, the production of local news and other public affairs programs, could continue to be performed, and at a far lower cost by simply delivering these programs through the channels of a wired distribution network.

Cable TV might appear at first glance to be the industry most seriously threatened by a rival media delivery system, but because most corporate cable TV system owners are now almost as deeply involved in the production of entertainment programming as the four major television networks, they seem likely to remain as potential partners in future fiber optic network ventures.[36] In addition, cable TV operators have the advantage of already providing video distribution service in most of the major markets telephone carriers are interested in entering, making it much more

[35] FCC Commissioner Mimi Dawson was aware of this vulnerability of the television station when she predicted in 1987 that within 15 years all communications would be delivered through fiber optic networks, freeing the valuable public resource of spectrum space for other more beneficial uses. Broadcasting, November 30, 1987. This susceptibility to competitive challenge from new media delivery systems was clearly illustrated during the cable TV era of the 1960s, when without FCC repression of cable system growth, a substantial number of television stations seemed unable to survive.

[36] For some examples of recent major cable MSO production efforts, see John Dempsey, "Star-studded Cable Stable," Variety, June 10, 1991, p. 1, "Costs May Make Strange Bedfellows of Broadcasting Cable," Broadcasting, April 29, 1991, p. 27, "ABC Gets Cable Friendlier," Broadcasting, June 17, 1991, p. 45.

sensible for the carriers to attempt to merge with, rather than seek to displace the existing system.

Similarly, it is unlikely that telephone carriers will ever try to undercut local network-affiliate television stations by dealing directly with their networks for local program distribution rights, simply because this tactic would anger a large number of Congressional leaders very sympathetic to the concerns of the broadcast industry.[37]   Instead, these carriers will probably begin simply by offering each local television station the opportunity to lease a channel to program with 24 hour-a-day news, sports or other features capable of generating additional advertising revenue for the station.[38]   The intention, of course, would be to demonstrate to station management the substantial savings that can be realized by abandoning over-the-air transmissions, but should that tactic fail, the carriers would then at least be in a stronger position to launch a public relations campaign creating support for ending the practice of permitting broadcasters to squander the precious public resource of spectrum space on services that could be delivered far more efficiently through a fiber optic network.

As all of this may suggest, the evolution of fiber optic delivery systems in the United States is almost certain to occur in a cautious, tentative manner.   Since this is a game without any known rules, different approaches will be taken to achieve the goal of consolidating all major communication services within a single conduit until one of them seems to work more effectively than any of the others.   For example, one approach would be for a telephone carrier simply to construct a fiber optic network for a cable TV system, and then lease from that cable operator those channels necessary for the telecommunication services the carrier intends to provide.   Another approach would be for a carrier to build and operate the fiber optic network in partnership with some film studio, television network or cable conglomerate, with each partner then managing its own set of communication services.   Still another approach would be for the carrier to build and operate the network itself, choosing and furnishing all the system's telecommu-

[37] As discussed in Chapter 9, this sympathy results largely from the "equal access" requirements federal law imposes on broadcasters, and the favorable rates for advertising time politicans receive because of the Political Spending Act of 1971.

[38] A number of cable TV systems across the country are already carrying such broadcast originated programs.   See, for example, "Cable News Covers Chicago" Variety, April 22, 1991, p. 22, "Allbritton to Launch All News Cable Channel in D.C." Broadcasting, November 19, 1990, p. 21, "Cox Proposes California News Channel," Broadcasting, May 6, 1991, p. 23.   And now that the "mandatory carriage" provisions of the Cable Act of 1992 have been sustained by the courts, the number of broadcasters taking advantage of its provisions to obtain their own local cable channel has increased substantially.

nications, entertainment and news services.[39]

Each of these divergent approaches will obviously raise a different set of legal issues. And yet, because the pace of this trend towards media consolidation will be gradual and tentative, the federal government is almost certain to ignore these developments until, once again, it is unprepared when the time has come to answer those crucial mass communications policies it has been unable to anticipate.

As we have seen, American law has always defined the rights of each medium on the basis of how it has been delivered to the public—through the spectrum, through wire, through cable, through the printed page—but now, as mergers blur these legal distinctions based on mode of distribution, what new principles of law should be established, and what objectives should they be designed to realize?

If telephone companies, for example, are permitted to provide a full range of mass communication and other informational services to the public, should they be restricted to functioning solely as traditional common carriers, prohibited by law from doing anything but distributing the services of others who have leased their channels? Some assert that to restrict telcos only to this "video dial tone" role would be to improperly abridge their constitutionally protected right to communicate.

Others argue, however, that to permit a telephone carrier to exercise total control over what is likely in time to become the only conduit of communication linking each home with the world would be to vest in one corporate entity far too much power over each individual's access to information and entertainment.

And what should be the legal consequences of distributing television programming through privately owned channels rather than through the public resource of spectrum? If scarcity of spectrum space furnishes the only constitutionally acceptable justification for imposing special content constraints on broadcast programming, then distribution by fiber optic network should finally allow broadcasters to be as free of government control as the press. But once this federal regulation has ended, will the public really be content to permit a force as powerful and pervasive as television, the only visual medium readily accessible to children in the home,

[39] All of these approaches presuppose, of course, either that Congress will eventually rescind its ban on telco video distribution or that the Supreme Court will find this ban to impose an unconstitutional burden on telco freedom of expression, as several lower federal courts have already done. In reality, though, even if Congress does not act and the Supreme Court should sustain the constitutionality of this ban, the prohibition is actually less formidable than it appears because of the FCC's willingness to circumvent it by authorizing telco "video dialtone" services on a commercial basis.

to operate free of any legal responsibility for those images it delivers to each American household ? [40]

And what threat, if any, to freedom of the press may emerge from electronic publishing of newspapers and magazines? Will the use of a fiber optic network result, as some fear, in bringing newspapers within the supervisory authority of the FCC's Common Carrier Bureau or a State Public Utility Commission? Is it even possible that federal regulations imposing content controls on video channels could also be found by the courts to be equally applicable to print channels using the same electronic distribution system? [41]

These are just a few illustrations of the many equally important and difficult free speech legal issues that remain to be resolved before additional mergers among various forms of communication and mass media distribution systems have further eroded that conceptual framework of First Amendment rights and obligations that has always in the past been founded upon differences in the ways that media messages are delivered.[42]

Because this chapter has ventured out beyond the safe harbor of established law and into the reef-filled waters of speculation, it is quite possible that some of its assertions about future media developments will prove to be incorrect. However, the one assumption about future media service that has constantly proven to be accurate in the past is that whenever the channel capacity of any communications delivery system expands, ingenious entrepreneurs will eventually develop more services than that system is capable of delivering.[43]

[40] In a perfectly rational realm of law, operating above and beyond political reality, it might be argued because "spectrum scarcity" has been the only justification accepted by the Supreme Court for broadcast regulation, ending the use of spectrum also ends any justification for that regulation. This, however, overlooks the fact that because "spectrum scarcity" has always been conveniently available, the court has never been forced to look beyond it to decide whether other characteristics of broadcasting, and more particularly of television, might continue to justify some degree of federal supervision on other grounds.

[41] These fears seem less justified than those that relate to the economic threat that fiber optic networks may pose for the daily newspaper, but because the Common Law tradition does not permit a judge or Supreme Court Justice to predict in advance how some hypothetical regulatory or constitutional issue will be decided, it is impossible to be certain at this point how broadly governmental regulatory authority could be exercised over electronic publishing without infringing on the constitutionally protected rights of the publisher.

[42] Another kind of major social policy issue will certainly be raised if broadcast television services now freely available to all citizens are restricted in the future only to those able to subscribe to a fiber optic network. However, since the shift from broadcast to fiber optic delivery of electronic media is apt to be quite gradual, there should be ample time for some political solution to this problem.

[43] Examples include the 10,500 commercial broadcast stations in service in the United States today when experts claimed in the mid-1940s that the economy could support no more than those 1,000 commercial stations then in operation; Intelsat's present generation of satellites providing 600 times the international communication

If this continues to hold true in the future, then no matter how these various competing delivery channels do converge in the future, the most significant questions raised by their convergence will be those resulting from fundamental changes in traditional communication functions this intermingling of media systems will cause.

As technology continues to increase the capacity of mass communication distribution systems in the future, that expansion will stimulate the launching of new forms and combinations of media services. That in turn will require a drastic reformulation of mass communication principles derived from our Constitution, but defined by the Congress and the courts during an era when legal distinctions among media that once seemed so logical and reasonable are becoming increasingly illogical and unreasonable.

The last two decades have brought us, among other changes, a substantial reduction in federal regulatory control over broadcasting in the United States; the creation of modern cable TV as a distinct communications medium with its own specialized sports, music and public affairs channels; the establishment of a totally new national newspaper, USA Today, with a distinctive approach and style that has significantly influenced formats and coverages of daily newspapers across the country; the beginnings of 24 hour-a-day national and global television news channels; ENG and remote television news coverage; the emergence of pay-TV and the VCR; the development of a fourth national television network; the eroding of the network television programming power, and the growth of a new international orientation for the entire American mass entertainment industry.

As significant as these changes have been, it is quite likely that the changes occurring during the next two decades will be even more dramatic.

traffic capacity that national telecommunication agencies of the world believed was possible in the mid–1960s, and still not having enough channels to satisfy all demands; America's domestic satellites launched in the mid–1970s at a time when many felt there would never be enough users to make them profitable continue to be launched on a regular basis with long lists of users waiting to lease their transponders; and the cable TV industry, that when required by the FCC to provide 20 channels of service for urban markets in 1972 argued that most of those channels would never be used—that same industry that is now planning band compression for its 50 channel systems to provide as many as 500 channels of service.

Appendix A

ABBREVIATIONS

A. --------------------Atlantic Reporter.
A.2d------------------Atlantic Reporter, Second Series.
A.C. ------------------Appeal Cases.
A.L.R. ----------------American Law Reports.
Aff. Affirmed; affirming.
Ala.--------------------Alabama;—Alabama Supreme Court Reports.
Am.Dec.---------------American Decisions.
Am.Jur. --------------American Jurisprudence, a legal encyclopedia.
Am.Rep. -------------American Reports.
Am.St.Rep.-----------American State Reports.
Ann.Cas. -------------American Annotated Cases.
App.D.C.--------------Court of Appeals, District of Columbia.
App.Div. -------------New York Supreme Court, Appellate Divisions, Reports.
Ariz.--------------------Arizona; Arizona Supreme Court Reports.
Ark. ------------------Arkansas; Arkansas Supreme Court Reports.
Bing. ------------------Bingham, New Cases, Common Pleas (England).
C.D. ------------------Copyright Decision.
C.J.--------------------Corpus Juris, a legal encyclopedia.
C.J.S. ----------------Corpus Juris Secundum, a legal encyclopedia.
Cal.--------------------California; California Supreme Court Reports.
Can.Sup.Ct. ---------Canada Supreme Court Reports.
Cert. ------------------Certiorari, a legal writ by which a cause is removed from an inferior to a superior court.
C.F.R. ----------------Code of Federal Regulations.
Colo. ------------------Colorado; Colorado Supreme Court Reports.
Conn. ------------------Connecticut; Connecticut Supreme Court of Errors Reports.
Cranch ----------------Cranch, United States Supreme Court Reports; United States Circuit Court Reports.
Cush. ------------------Cushing (Massachusetts).
D.C.App.---------------District of Columbia Court of Appeals Reports.
Dall, Dal. ------------Dallas, United States Supreme Court Reports; Pennsylvania Reports.
Del.--------------------Delaware; Delaware Supreme Court Reports.
Edw. ------------------Edward; refers to a particular king of England; which king of that name is indicated by the date; used to identify an act of Parliament.
Eng.Rep. -------------English Reports (reprint).
F. ----------------------Federal Reporter.
F.2d--------------------Federal Reporter, Second Series.
F.C.C. ----------------Federal Communications Commission Reports.

F.R.D. --------------- Federal Rules Decisions.
F.Supp.--------------- Federal Supplement.
Fed.Cas. or
F.Cas. --------------- Reports of United States Circuit and District
                       Courts, 1789–1879.
Fla.------------------ Florida; Florida Supreme Court Reports.
Ga.------------------- Georgia; Georgia Supreme Court Reports.
Ga.App. -------------- Georgia Appeals Reports.
How.St.Tr. ---------- Howell's State Trials.
Hun ------------------ Hun, New York Supreme Court Reports.
Ibid.----------------- Ibidem, the same, in the same volume, or on the
                       same page.
Ill. ------------------ Illinois; Illinois Supreme Court Reports.
Ill.App. -------------- Illinois Appellate Court Reports.
Ind.------------------ Indiana; Indiana Supreme Court Reports.
Ind.App. ------------- Indiana Appellate Court Reports.
Johns.Cas.----------- Johnson's Cases (New York).
K.B. ----------------- King's Bench Reports (England).
Kan.------------------ Kansas; Kansas Supreme Court Reports.
Ky. ------------------ Kentucky; Kentucky Court of Appeals Reports.
L.J.------------------ Law Journal (England).
L.R.Q.B. ------------- Law Reports, Queen's Bench (England).
L.R.A. --------------- Lawyers Reports Annotated.
L.R.A.,N.S.,--------- Lawyers Reports Annotated, New Series.
L.R.Ex. -------------- Law Reports, Exchequer (England).
L.T. ----------------- The Law Times (England).
La.------------------- Louisiana; Louisiana Supreme Court Reports.
La.Ann. -------------- Louisiana Annual Reports.
Mass. ---------------- Massachusetts; Massachusetts Supreme Judicial
                       Court Reports.
Md.------------------- Maryland; Maryland Court of Appeals Reports.
Me.------------------- Maine; Maine Supreme Judicial Court Reports.
Mich.----------------- Michigan; Michigan Supreme Court Reports.
Minn. ---------------- Minnesota; Minnesota Supreme Court Reports.
Miss.----------------- Mississippi; Mississippi Supreme Court Reports.
Mo.------------------- Missouri; Missouri Supreme Court Reports.
Mo.App.-------------- Missouri Appeals Reports.
Mont. ---------------- Montana; Montana Supreme Court Reports.
N.C.------------------ North Carolina; North Carolina Supreme Court
                       Reports.
N.D.------------------ North Dakota; North Dakota Supreme Court Re-
                       ports.
N.E.------------------ Northeastern Reporter.
N.E.2d--------------- Northeastern Reporter, Second Series.
N.H.------------------ New Hampshire; New Hampshire Supreme Court
                       Reports.
N.J. ----------------- New Jersey; New Jersey Court of Errors and
                       Appeals Reports.
N.J.L. --------------- New Jersey Law Reports.
N.M. ----------------- New Mexico; New Mexico Supreme Court Reports.
N.W. ----------------- Northwestern Reporter.

N.W.2d ------------Northwestern Reporter, Second Series.

N.Y. ----------------New York; New York Court of Appeals Reports.

N.Y.S. ---------------New York Supplement Reports.

Neb. -----------------Nebraska; Nebraska Supreme Court Reports.

Nev. -----------------Nevada; Nevada Supreme Court Reports.

Ohio App. ----------Ohio Appeals Reports.

Ohio St. ------------Ohio State Reports.

Okl. -----------------Oklahoma; Oklahoma Supreme Court Reports.

Ops. ----------------Opinions, as of Attorney General of the United States, or a state.

Or., Ore., Oreg. ----Oregon; Oregon Supreme Court Reports.

P. --------------------Pacific Reporter.

P.2d -----------------Pacific Reporter, Second Series.

P.L. & R. -----------Postal Laws and Regulations (1948 ed.).

Pa. -------------------Pennsylvania District and County Court Reports.

Pa.D. & C. ----------Pennsylvania District and County Court Reports.

Pa.Super. -----------Pennsylvania Superior Court Reports.

Paige----------------Paige, New York Chancery Reports.

Phila. (Pa). ---------Philadelphia Reports.

Pick. ----------------Pickering, Massachusetts Reports.

Q.B. -----------------Queen's Bench.

R. --------------------Rex king; regina, queen.

R.C.L. ---------------Ruling Case Law.

R.C.P. ---------------Rules of Civil Procedure.

R.I. ------------------Rhode Island; Rhode Island Supreme Court Reports.

R.R. -----------------Pike & Fisher Radio Regulations.

S.C. ------------------South Carolina; South Carolina Supreme Court Reports.

S.D. -----------------South Dakota; South Dakota Supreme Court Reports.

S.E. -----------------Southeastern Reporter.

S.E.2d ---------------Southeastern Reporter, Second Series.

S.W. -----------------Southwestern Reporter.

S.W.2d---------------Southwestern Reporter, Second Series.

Sandf. ----------------Sandford, New York Superior Court Reports.

Sec. ------------------Section.

So. -------------------Southern Reporter.

So.2d-----------------Southern Reporter, Second Series.

Stark. ----------------Starkie, English Reports.

S.Ct. ----------------Supreme Court Reporter.

T.L.R. ---------------Times Law Reports (England).

Tenn. ----------------Tennessee; Tennessee Supreme Court Reports.

Tex. ------------------Texas; Texas Supreme Court (and the Commission of Appeals) Reports.

Tex.Civ.App. --------Texas Civil Appeals Reports.

Tex.Cr.R. -----------Texas Court of Criminal Appeals Reports.

U.S.C. ---------------United States Code.

U.S.C.A. .... United States Code Annotated.
U.S.P.Q. .... United States Patents Quarterly.
V. .... Volume.
Va. .... Virginia; Virginia Supreme Court of Appeals Re-
                        ports.
Vt. .... Vermont; Vermont Supreme Court Reports.
W.Va. .... West Virginia; West Virginia Supreme Court of
                        Appeals Reports.
Wash. .... Washington; Washington Supreme Court Reports.
Wash.L.Rep. .... Washington Law Reporter, Washington, D.C.
Whart. .... Wharton (Pa.).
Wheat. .... Wheaton (U.S.).
Wis. .... Wisconsin; Wisconsin Supreme Court Reports.
Wyo. .... Wyoming; Wyoming Supreme Court Reports.

Appendix B

SELECTED COURT AND PLEADING TERMS

Action

A formal legal demand of one's rights made in a court of law.

Actionable per quod

Words not actionable in themselves may be defamatory when special damages are proved.

Actionable per se

Words that need no explanation in order to determine their defamatory effect.

Amicus curiae

A friend of the court or one who interposes and volunteers information upon some matter of law.

Answer

The pleading of a defendant against whom a complaint has been filed.

Appeal

An application by an appellant to a higher court to change the order or judgment of the court below.

Appellant

The person or party appealing a decision or judgment to a higher court.

Appellee

The party against whom an appeal is taken.

Bind over

To hold on bail for trial.

Brief

A written or printed document prepared by counsel to file in court, normally providing both facts and law in support of the case.

Cause of action

The particular facts on which an action is based.

Certiorari

A writ commanding judges of a lower court to transfer to a higher court records of a case so that judicial review may take place.

Change of venue

Removing a civil suit or criminal action from one county or district to another county or district for trial.

Civil action (suit, trial)

Court action brought to enforce, redress, or protect private rights, as distinguished from a Criminal action (q.v.).

Code

A compilation or system of laws, arranged into chapters, and promulgated by legislative authority.

Common law

The law of the decided cases, derived from the judgments and decrees of courts. Also called "case law." Originally, meant law which derived its authority from the ancient usages or customs of England.

Complaint

The initial proceeding by a complainant, or plaintiff, in a civil action.

Contempt of court

Any act calculated to embarrass, hinder, or obstruct a court in the administration of justice, or calculated to lessen its dignity or authority.

Courts of record

Those whose proceedings are permanently recorded, and which have the power to fine or imprison for contempt. Courts not of record are those of lesser authority whose proceedings are not permanently recorded.

Criminal action (trial)

An action undertaken to punish a violation of criminal laws, as distinguished from a Civil action (q.v.).

Damages

> Monetary compensation which may be recovered in court by a person who has suffered loss, detriment, or injury to his person, property, rights, or business, through the unlawful or negligent act of another person or party.

De novo

> Anew, afresh. A trial de novo is a retrial of a case.

Dictum (pl. Dicta; also, Obiter Dictum)

> An observation made by a judge, in an opinion on a case, that does not go to the main issue—a saying "by the way".

Discovery

> A party's pre-trial devices used, in preparation for trial, to obtain facts from the other party.

Due process

> Law in its regular course of administration through the courts of justice. The guarantee of due process requires that every person have the protection of a fair trial.

En banc

> A session where the entire membership of a court, instead of one or a few, participates in the decision of an important case. ("Banc" means the judge's "bench" or place to sit.)

Equity

> That system of jurisprudence which gives relief when there is no full, complete and adequate remedy at law; based originally upon the custom of appealing to the King or chancellor when the formality of the common law did not give means for relief.

Estoppel

> An admission which prevents a person from using evidence which proves or tends to prove the contrary.

Executive session

> A meeting of a board or governmental body that is closed to the public.

Ex parte

> By or concerning only one party. This implies an examination in the presence of one party in a proceeding and the absence of the opposing party.

Ex post facto

> After the fact.

Habeas corpus

> Latin for "you have the body." A writ issued to an officer holding a person in detention or under arrest to bring that person before a court to determine the legality of the detention.

In camera

> In the judge's private chambers or in a courtroom from which all spectators have been excluded.

Indictment

> A written accusation of a crime prepared by a prosecuting attorney and presented for the consideration of a grand jury.

Information

> A formal, written accusation of a crime prepared by a competent law officer of the government, such as a district or prosecuting attorney.

Injunction

> A judicial order in equity directed against a person or organization directing that an act be performed or that the person or organization refrain from doing a particular act.

Judgment

> The decision of a court of law.

Jury

> A group of a certain number of persons, selected according to law and sworn to inquire into certain matters of fact, and to declare the truth from evidence brought before them. A *grand jury* hears complaints and accusations in criminal cases, and issues bills of indictment in cases where the jurors believe that there is enough evidence to bring a case to trial. A *petit jury* consists of 12 (or fewer) persons who hear the trial of a civil or criminal case.

Mandamus

> An extraordinary legal writ issued from a court to a corporation or its officers, to a public official, or to an inferior

court commanding the doing of an act which the person, corporation, or lower court is under a duty to perform.

Motion to dismiss

A formal application by a litigant or his counsel addressed to the court for an order to dismiss the case.

Nol pros, nolle prosequi

A formal notification of unwillingness to prosecute which is entered upon the court record.

N.O.V. ("non obstante veredicto")

A judgment by the court in favor of one party notwithstanding a verdict that has been given to the other party.

Per se

In itself or by itself, as in libelous *per se*.

Plaintiff

The person (including an organization or business) who initiates a legal action.

Pleading

The process in which parties to a lawsuit or legal action alternately file with a court written statements of their contentions. By this process of statement and counter-statement, legal issues are framed and narrowed. These statements are often termed "pleadings."

Preliminary hearing, preliminary examination

A person charged with a crime is given a preliminary examination or hearing before a magistrate or judge to determine whether there is sufficient evidence to hold that person for trial.

Prima facie (pron.: prī ma fă shē)

"At first sight" or "on the face of it." So far as can be judged from the first disclosure.

Reply

The pleading of plaintiff in response to the "answer" of the defendant.

Res adjudicata or res judicata

A thing decided.

Respondent

> A party who gives an answer to a bill in equity; also, one who opposes a party who has taken a case to a higher court.

Stare decisis

> To stand by the decisions, or to maintain precedent. This legal doctrine holds that settled points of law will not be disturbed.

Subpoena

> A command to appear at a place and time and to give testimony. "Subpoena-duces tecum" is a command to produce some document or paper at a trial.

Summary

> Connoting "without a full trial." A summary judgment is a judge's rule that one party in a lawsuit wins before the conclusion of a full trial.

Venue

> The particular county, city, or geographical area in which a court with jurisdiction may hear and decide a case.

Verdict

> The decision of a jury as reported to the court.

Voir dire

> Denotes the preliminary examination which the court may make of one presented as a witness or juror, where his competency or interest is objected to.

Writ

> A legal instrument in the judicial process to enforce compliance with orders and sentences of a court.

Appendix C

SOME NOTES ON THE LEGAL PROCESS

During the first chapter of this book you were introduced rather rapidly to a wide assortment of legal terms. At that point, you probably did nothing more than to try to memorize as many of these terms as possible, expecting to find one or more of them lurking somewhere on your mid-term exam.

In reality, though, the most effective way of understanding what each of these legal terms actually means is to see how it operates in an actual case situation. Here, for example, are how the terms "criminal", "civil", "common" and "constitutional" law apply to various elements of a case discussed in Chapter 7 of this text. Although the right of the press to publish public information has been extended to some extent since Cox Broadcasting v. Cohn was decided in 1975, the case still serves as a useful illustration of how the legal process operates.[1]

A. Criminal, Civil and Common Law

In Cox Broadcasting v. Cohn a reporter disclosed the name of a rape victim during a television broadcast. The State of Georgia, where the broadcast originated, had enacted a provision in its criminal code that made it a crime for,

> any news media or other person to print, publish, broadcast, televise or disseminate through any other medium ... the name or identity of any female who may have been raped.

If that official responsible for prosecuting those in that locality violating Georgia's "criminal law", (generally called the "District Attorney") believed that a reporter had violated this statute and thus committed a crime as defined by the criminal code of Georgia, the District Attorney would file a complaint describing the nature of the crime and charging the reporter with having committed it.[2] If the reporter entered a plea of "guilty" to this charge, the

---

[1] Cox Broadcasting v. Cohn, 420 U.S. 469 (1975). This protection was extended to include information gathered from a police report in Florida Star v. B.J.F., 491 U.S. 524 (1989). Also see Smith v. Daily Mail, 443 U.S. 97 (1979).

[2] Criminal law in most states classifies each crime as being either a "misdemeanor" or a "felony". A misdemeanor is a less serious crime, generally providing for a maximum jail term of less than one year, while a felony is a more serious crime, carrying a prison sentence in excess of one year. In this instance, disclosing the name of a rape victim was classified as being a misdemeanor crime.

criminal court judge would then have the authority to impose any penalties provided by the law for this offense. However, if the reporter should enter a plea of "not guilty", the state would be required to prove "beyond a reasonable doubt" that *each* element of the crime had occurred—in this case that (1) that the defendant reporter had knowingly disclosed the name of a woman (2) who may in fact have been a rape victim (3) and that the reporter's disclosure was disseminated by broadcasting or some other communications medium to the general public. Unless the state can establish beyond a reasonable doubt that each element of the criminal charge has taken place, the defendant reporter must be found "not guilty".

Here, for instance, if the District Attorney could not prove that this disclosure had actually been broadcast or disseminated to the public through some other medium, the charge against the defendant would have had to be dismissed "with prejudice", meaning that the State could not try this reporter again for this same offense.

But even if the reporter had been tried and found not guilty of any criminal offense, he could still be required by "civil law" to compensate anyone damaged because of the disclosure. In other words, even though not guilty of violating a criminal law designed to protect society in general, a reporter could still be required by civil law to pay money damages to any specific individual actually injured by this same act.

Civil law actions can be based either upon statutory rights granted individuals by State legislation or upon traditional rights granted by Anglo Saxon "common law". In the *Cox* case the father of the deceased rape victim used a "common law" right of "invasion of privacy" as the basis for a legal action claiming damages from the reporter and his television station employer.[3] Although the state of Georgia had not enacted a law granting an individual the right to sue for invasion of privacy, the Georgia courts did recognize a historic right of privacy developed by past judicial decisions that allowed those damaged by public disclosure of private information to be compensated for their embarrassment or humiliation.[4]

As this civil action to recover damages for invasion of privacy was about to begin, however, an issue of "constitutional law" was raised, delaying the trial until this question could be resolved.

---

[3] Even though the reporter may have been the one primarily responsible for any damages the father of the deceased rape victim sustained, law suits of this type always attempt to include the media organization as a co-defendant, because juries tend to be far more generous in awarding damages when they are taking them from a giant corporation, rather than an individual.

[4] At common law, this type of right is called a "tort", meaning that the law allows a party injured by the act of another to recover damages caused by that act.

The defendant broadcast station claimed that the rape victim's name had already been revealed to the public before it was disclosed during the television news program, because she had been identified by name in the criminal proceedings used to charge her assailants. Under these circumstances, the defendant argued that to compel a broadcast station to pay damages for disclosing a fact that any member of the public could have discovered in the files of the local courthouse improperly penalized a communications medium for exercising its free speech right to disseminate public information.

In essence then, the defendant broadcast station was claiming that no matter how much anguish or embarrassment it might have caused, there should be no civil trial to determine what monetary compensation it should pay for these damages. Instead, the defendant demanded that the case be dismissed immediately without awarding any damages, because to punish a station for reporting information already a matter of public record would improperly inhibit its right of freedom of expression protected by the First and Fourteenth Amendments.

B.   The Judicial Process

The Supreme Court of Georgia rejected this constitutional argument, finding nothing in either the Georgia state constitution or the federal constitution that guaranteed a broadcaster an absolute right to reveal the identity of an individual whose privacy was expressly protected by Georgia law. This decision meant that the civil action to decide whether the defendants were actually liable for damages caused by their news report could now begin.

Here, however, the Supreme Court of the United States intervened to grant *certiorari*, meaning that it would review the Georgia court's decision to determine if the State court had correctly interpreted the constitutionally protected free speech rights of the broadcast medium under these circumstances. Once again, then, the trial had to be postponed until the Supreme Court was able to decide whether the defendant broadcast station could be held liable for invasion of privacy damages without illegally infringing upon its right of freedom of expression.

Eventually, as you may recall, a majority of the Supreme Court Justices joined in a decision that shielded the broadcast defendant from civil liability for any damages caused by the disclosure of information already a matter of public record, finding that to allow a communications medium to be penalized for disseminating facts available to every citizen would "invite timidity and self-censorship and very likely lead to the suppression of many items . . . that should be made available to the public".[5]

Thus in *Cox*, as in many of the other cases discussed in this book, there was never any exciting conflict in open court; no trial with its fascinating array of witnesses, caustic cross examinations, angry objections or eloquent closing statements. Instead, clashes between attorneys representing the embittered family of the rape victim and those protecting the free speech rights of the broadcasters occurred in the hushed atmosphere of an appeals court, defined by carefully researched legal arguments in written documents called "briefs", and explained by these attorneys in polite, precisely reasoned statements to the court.

After considering these briefs and arguments, an appeals court determines how to resolve the issue or issues of law raised by the appeal, writing an opinion to explain the legal basis for this decision, and to point out to those lower trial courts under its authority how they should resolve the same legal issue if it should arise again during any legal proceeding in the future.

But what if the trial in the *Cox* case had already taken place before the defense attorneys raised any questions about its constitutionality, and the jury had found that this news broadcast did invade the privacy of the plaintiff, entering a verdict granting the injured party a massive award of monetary damages? In that case, the attorneys for the defendants would have the right to appeal this verdict, asking the court with review authority over the trial judge to consider any material legal issues the appealing attorney claims were not considered, or were decided erroneously at during the trial, resulting in the appealing party losing the case.

In our *Cox* case example, the reviewing court judge would then accept briefs and hear arguments on only that single issue raised on appeal, determining whether the free speech safeguards of the First and Fourteenth amendments protect a broadcast station from being held liable for monetary damages caused by disclosure of information already a matter of public record.

This appeals court generally has three options available to it after considering the legal issues it has reviewed. The first option is to *affirm* the lower court decision, indicating that the lower court was correct in its interpretation of the legal issue raised on appeal. The second option is to *reverse and remand* with instructions, finding the lower court to be in error and sending the case back for a new trial or "retrial" in which the judge will follow the guidance of the review court to avoid those errors that caused the first trial to be invalid. In this situation, the third option would be to *vacate* the judgement, declaring that law suit should not have been tried

---

[5] Cox Broadcasting v. Cohn, 420 U.S. 469 (1975).

in the first place because the plaintiff had no legal right to bring the action.

Unfortunately, this is seldom the end of the litigation process. The party losing at this appeal court level generally has the right to seek a review of the appeal court decision by a higher level appellate court or the state Supreme Court, and if as in the *Cox* case, an important federal issue has been raised by the litigation, the entire matter can be removed to federal court, where the proceedings begins anew.

A process this slow, expensive and risky is one that provides every incentive for out-of-court settlements and explains why one legal scholar described litigation as being the "pathology" of the law. In reality, then, those appeal court opinions published and discussed in this book can be understood most accurately not as typical cases in communication law, but rather the unusual ones that were considered so important by the parties involved that they were willing to accept the delays, costs and risks of litigation in order to establish that point of law described in the opinion.

C. Administrative Law and the Courts

The FCC is an administrative agency, created by Congress to enforce the provisions of the Communications Act of 1934. As a regulatory body, the Commission has been granted authority by Congress to adopt "administrative law" rules to define more clearly those generalized broadcast public interest standards contained in the Communications Act. In addition, the FCC has been empowered by Congress to hold hearings to determine whether a broadcast licensee may have violated Commission rules, or the provisions of the Communications Act, and to impose penalties upon those licensees not conforming to these regulatory standards.

At the same time, Congress has established the Court of Appeals for the District of Columbia as the federal court responsible for reviewing FCC decisions. In a case such as CBS v. FCC, described in chapter 9 of your text, an administrative law judge held a hearing to determine whether the refusal of CBS to provide air time for the broadcast of a political documentary represented a violation of the reasonable access requirements of section 312(a) of the Communications Act.

As administrative law has been structured by Congress, this hearing is considered to be a "trial court" proceeding, establishing a legal record for the decision that can later be reviewed on appeal by the Court of Appeals for the District of Columbia, and ultimately by the United States Supreme Court if it should decide to accept certiorari.

The finding of the administrative law judge that CBS had violated the access requirements of section 312(a) was reviewed initially within the FCC by review board created expressly for this purpose. When this decision was affirmed by the board, and finally approved by a 4–3 vote of the FCC Commissioners, the network petitioned the D.C. Court of Appeals to review those errors in law alleged to have caused the Commission to improperly interpret the legal requirements of this section of the Act.

As in the *Cox* case, the Court of Appeals had the option of affirming the Commission decision, remanding it for a new hearing on issues it overlooked or improperly decided at the original hearing, or vacating the decision if the appeals court could find no legal basis for the FCC's determination.

In this example, after the appeals court affirmed the FCC decision, the Supreme Court agreed to review the case and eventually also affirmed the Commission's decision by a 6–3 margin, with Justice Burger writing the majority opinion explaining that such a reasonable political access requirement did not improperly infringe upon the free speech rights of the broadcaster because there was "nothing in the First Amendment which prevents Government from requiring a licensee to share his frequency with others ..." [6]

Understanding these basic legal terms in the context of that system of law in which they operate should help you to become more fully aware of the actual legal effects of those communication law decisions contained in this book. But if you'd be interested in finding and actually reading these or other important communication law opinions on your own, no area of study is organized more logically or indexed more effectively than the field of American law.

D. Locating Judicial Source Material

All decisions of the United States Supreme Court are published officially in a series called *US Reports*, and by two commercial publishers in series called *Supreme Court Reporter* (West Publishing) and another called *U.S. Supreme Court Reports, Lawyer's Edition* (Lawyers' Cooperative Publishing Company). Each of these series contains every opinion of the Supreme Court, but West and Lawyers' Cooperative provide additional reference and indexing material as part of their total system of legal publications for lawyers.

Decisions of the federal Courts of Appeal are published in the *Federal Reporter*, and most federal District Court decisions are found in the *Federal Supplement*, both West Publishing series. All reported decisions of state courts are contained in West Publishing's National Reporter System, divided geographically into seven

---

[6] CBS v. FCC, 453 U.S. 367 (1981).

different regional series; the *Atlantic, Pacific, Southern, Southwestern, Southeastern, Northwestern* and *Northeastern.* To locate a particular judicial opinion, all you need to do is to follow the instructions provided by its citation. For example, to find the famous United Church of Christ v. FCC case, cited as 359 F.2d 994, that recognized the right of citizen groups to challenge the renewal of a broadcast license, you would open the 359th volume of the *Federal Reporter*, 2nd series, and turn to page 994 where the opinion begins.

If your university library doesn't have these legal publications among its holdings, they can all be found in the library of your nearest county courthouse. In addition, you should find a service called *Shepard's Citators* there that allows you, by using its various judicial indexing books, to discover whether any later decisions have had any effect upon those legal principles defined by that judicial opinion you've just been reading.

This brief survey of communication law research literature is not intended to do anything more than illustrate how simple the process of legal research can really be. There is no reason to provide a elaborate description of a wide variety of communication law research techniques here, because there are so many excellent books and studies already covering every aspect of this topic in great detail. For further guidance, any of the following books and articles are highly recommended:

1. Cohen, M.L. *How to Find the Law* St. Paul, Minn., West Publishing. (often updated with new editions)

2. Cohen, M.L. *Legal Research in a Nutshell* St. Paul, Minn., West Publishing, (frequently updated).

3. Foley, J.M. "Broadcast Regulation Research: A Primer for Non–Lawyers," *Journal of Broadcasting* 17/2 (Summer 1973) pp. 147–159.

4. Goehlert, R. *Congress and Law Making: Researching the Legislative Process* Santa Barbara, CA Clio Books, 1979.

5. Honigsburg, P.J. *Cluing Into Legal Research* Berkeley, CA Golden Rain Press, 1979.

6. Jacobstein J.M. and R. M. Mersky, *Fundamentals of Legal Research* Mineola, NY Foundation Press, 1992.

7. Le Duc, D.R. "Broadcast Legal Documentation: A Four–Dimensional Guide," *Journal of Broadcasting* 17/2 (Summer 1973) pp. 131–146.

8. Pauwels, C.K, in J.R. Bittner, *Broadcast Law and Regulation* Englewood Cliffs NJ Prentice Hall 1982 pp. 397–411.

9. Price, M.O. and H. Bittner, *Effective Legal Research* Boston Little Brown (1979).

Appendix D

BIBLIOGRAPHY

American Law Institute, Restatement of the Law: Torts. 2d ed. St. Paul, 1977.

Adler, Allan, ed. Litigation Under the Federal Open Government Act, 18th ed., Washington, D.C., 1990.

Adler, Renata, Reckless Disregard, New York, 1986.

Angoff, Charles, Handbook of Libel. New York, 1946.

Bagdikian, Ben, The Media Monopoly. Boston, 1993.

Barnouw, Erik, A History of Broadcasting in the United States, 3 vols. (N.Y., 1966–1972).

Barron, Jerome, Freedom of the Press for Whom? Bloomington, Ind., 1973.

Berns, Walter, The First Amendment and the Future of American Democracy. New York, 1976.

Bezanson, Randall P., Gilbert Cranberg, and John Soloski, Libel Law and The Press: Myth and Reality, New York, 1987.

Blackstone, William, Commentaries on the Law of England, IV, adapted by Robert Malcom Kerr, Boston, 1952.

Blasi, Vincent, The Checking Value in First Amendment Theory, Am.Bar Foundation Research Journal, 1977, # 3.

Bok, Sissela, Secrets. New York, 1983.

Brenner, Daniel L. and William L. Rivers, Free But Regulated: Conflicting Traditions in Media Law. Ames, Iowa, 1982.

Canavan, Francis, Freedom of Expression: Purpose as Limit. Durham, N.C., 1984.

Center for National Security Studies, FOIA Handbook. Washington, D.C., 1979.

Chafee, Zechariah, Jr., Free Speech in the United States. Boston, 1941.

————, Government and Mass Communications, 2 vols. Chicago, 1947.

Bittner, John R., Law and Regulation of Electronic Media (2nd ed.) New Jersey, 1994.

Chamberlin, Bill F., and Charlene Brown, The First Amendment Reconsidered. Chapel Hill, 1981.

Cline, Victor (ed.), Where Do You Draw the Line? Provo, UT, 1974.

Cooley, Thomas M., Constitutional Limitations. (8th ed.). Boston, 1927.

Cooper, Thomas, The Law of Libel and the Liberty of the Press. New York, 1830.

Denniston, Lyle, The Reporter and the Law. New York, 1980.

Devol, Kenneth S., Mass Media and the Supreme Court, 2d ed. New York, 1976.

Duniway, Clyde A., The Development of Freedom of the Press in Massachusetts. Cambridge, 1906.

Emerson, Thomas I., The System of Freedom of Expression. New York, 1970.

Emery, Walter B., Broadcasting and Government: Responsibilities and Regulations. East Lansing, Mich., 1961.

Folkerts, Jean and Dwight L. Teeter, Voices of a Nation: A History of the Media in the United States. New York, 1989.

Fox, Sir John C., The History of Contempt of Court. Oxford, 1927.

Friendly, Fred, Minnesota Rag. New York, 1981.

Gerald, J. Edward, The Press and the Constitution, 1931–1947. Minneapolis, 1948.

Gillmor, Donald M., Free Press and Fair Trial. Washington, D.C., 1966.

Goldfarb, Ronald L., The Contempt Power. New York, 1963.

Goodale, James, C., Communications Law 1984. New York, 1984.

Goodman, Mark, Law of the Student Press (2nd ed.) Washington, D.C., SPLC, 1994.

Gora, Joel M., The Rights of Reporters. New York, 1974.

Hachten, William A., The Supreme Court on Freedom of the Press: Decisions and Dissents. Ames, Iowa, 1968.

Haight, Anne Lyon, Banned Books (rev. 2d ed.). New York, 1955.

Havick, John J., Communications Policy and the Political Process. Westport, Conn., 1983.

Head, Sydney W. and Christopher Sterling, Broadcasting in America. (5th ed.). Boston, 1987.

Hentoff, Nat, History of Freedom of the Press in America. New York, 1980.

Hocking, William E., Freedom of the Press. Chicago, 1947.

Holmes, Oliver Wendell Jr., The Common Law. Boston, 1881.

Hopkins, W. Wat, Mr. Justice Brennan and Freedom of Expression. New York, 1991.

Jolliffe, John, The Constitutional History of Medieval England (2d ed.). London, 1947.

Jones, William, Cases and Materials on Electronic Mass Media. Mineola, N.Y., 1977.

Kahn, F.J., ed., Documents of American Broadcasting, 4th ed. New York, 1984.

Kaufman, Henry R., ed., LDRC 50–State Survey 1984, III. New York, 1984.

Kinsley, Philip, Liberty and the Press. Chicago, 1944.

Konvitz, Milton R., First Amendment Freedoms. Ithaca, 1963.

Le Duc, Don R., Beyond Broadcasting: Patterns in Policy and Law. (New York, 1987).

Levin, Harvey J., Fact and Fancy in Television Regulation. New York, 1980.

Levy, Leonard W., Emergence of a Free Press. New York, 1985.

————, ed., Freedom of the Press from Zenger to Jefferson. Indianapolis, 1966.

————, Legacy of Suppression: Freedom of Speech and Press in Early American History. Cambridge, 1960.

Lewis, Anthony, Make No Law: The Sullivan Case and the First Amendment. New York, 1991.

Lockhart, William B., and Robert C. McClure, Censorship of Obscenity: the Developing Constitutional Standards, 45 Minnesota Law Review 5 (Nov. 1960).

————, Literature, the Law of Obscenity, and the Constitution, 38 Minnesota Law Review (March 1954).

Lofton, John, The Press as a Defender of the First Amendment. Columbia, S.C., 1980.

McCormick, Robert R., The Freedom of the Press. New York, 1936.

Meiklejohn, Alexander, Free Speech and Its Relation to Self Government. New York, 1948.

Miller, Arthur, The Assault on Privacy. Ann Arbor, 1971.

Murphy, Paul, World War I and the Origins of Civil Liberties in the United States. New York, 1979.

Nelson, Harold L., ed., Freedom of the Press from Hamilton to the Warren Court. Indianapolis, 1967.

Nimmer, Melville B., Nimmer on Copyright, 4 vols. New York, 1963–1988.

Odgers, W. Blake, A Digest of the Law of Libel and Slander (6th ed.). London, 1929.

Owen, Bruce M., Economics and Freedom of Expression. Cambridge, 1975.

Parsons, Patrick, Cable Television and the First Amendment. Lexington, MA, 1987.

Paterson, James, Liberty of Press, Speech and Public Worship. London, 1880.

Patterson, Giles J., Free Speech and a Free Press. Boston, 1939.

Paul, James C.N., and Murray L. Schwartz, Federal Censorship: Obscenity in the Mail. New York, 1961.

Pember, Don R., Privacy and the Press. Seattle, 1972.

Peterson, H.C., and Gilbert C. Fite, Opponents of War, 1917–1918. Madison, 1957.

Pilpel, Harriet, and Theodora Zavin, Rights and Writers. New York, 1960.

Powe, Lucas A., Jr., American Broadcasting and the First Amendment, Berkeley, 1987.

————, The Fourth Estate and the Constitution. Berkeley, 1991.

Preston, Ivan, The Tangled Web They Weave: Truth Falsity and Advertisers. Madison, 1994.

Preston, William, Jr., Aliens and Dissenters. Cambridge, 1963.

Prosser, William L., The Law of Torts. 4th ed. St. Paul, 1971.

Rosden, George Eric and Peter Eric, The Law of Advertising, 2 vols. (New York, 1963, 1976, 1988).

Rosenberg, Norman L., Protecting the Best Men: An Interpretive History of Libel, Chapel Hill, 1986.

Rourke, Francis E., Secrecy and Publicity. Baltimore, 1961.

Sack, Robert D., Libel, Slander, and Related Problems. New York, 1980.

Sanford, Bruce, The Law of Libel and the Right of Privacy. New York, 1984.

Schmidt, Benno C., Jr., Freedom of the Press vs. Public Access. New York, 1976.

Seldes, George, Freedom of the Press. Cleveland, 1935.

Shapiro, Martin, Freedom of Speech: The Supreme Court and Judicial Review. Englewood Cliffs, N.J., 1966.

Siebert, Fredrick S., Freedom of the Press in England, 1476–1776. Urbana, 1952.

Simmons, Steven J., The Fairness Doctrine and the Media. Berkeley, 1978.

Simon, Morton J., Public Relations Law. New York, 1969.

Smith, James Morton, Freedom's Fetters: the Alien and Sedition Laws and American Civil Liberties. Ithaca, 1956.

Smolla, Rodney, Jerry Falwell v. Larry Flynt. Urbana, 1988.

————, Suing the Press. New York, 1986.

Stansbury, Arthur J., Report of the Trial of James H. Peck. Boston, 1833.

Starkie, Thomas, The Law of Slander, Libel, Scandalum Magnatum and False Rumors, with the Practise and Pleadings. London, 1813; 4th ed. by Henry C. Folkard, with notes and references to American Cases by Horace G. Wood. New York, 1877.

Sterling, Christopher, and John Michael Kittross, Stay Tuned: An Informal History of American Broadcasting. Belmont, CA, 1978.

Sullivan, Harold W., Contempts by Publication. New Haven, 1940.

Warren, Samuel D., and Louis D. Brandeis, The Right to Privacy, 4 Harvard Law Review 193 (1890).

Westin, Alan, Privacy and Freedom. New York, 1967.

Winfield, Richard N., New York Times v. Sullivan, the Next Twenty Years (New York, Practising Law Institute, 1984).

Wolff, Robert Paul, Barrington Moore and Herbert Marcuse, A Critique of Pure Tolerance. Boston, 1965.

Wortman, Tunis, Treatise Concerning Political Enquiry, and the Liberty of the Press. New York, 1800.

Yudof, Mark G., When Government Speaks. Berkeley, 1983.

Additional Resources

American Digest System, Decennial Digests, valuable for lists of cases and points adjudicated.

American Jurisprudence, a legal encyclopedia.

Annotated Report System, selected reports and annotations, with summaries of arguments of counsel.

Compilations of Laws Affecting Publications, particularly those put out by various states. Consult managers of various state press associations.

Corpus Juris Secundum, a legal encyclopedia.

Freedom of Information Center, University of Missouri, issues frequent Reports, the FOI Digest (bi-monthly newsletter), and occasional studies covering a wide variety of media-and-law-subjects. Invaluable for state laws on meetings and records.

Law Dictionaries, including Black's, Ballentine's, and Bouvier's.

Law Reviews. Among the outstanding law reviews published under the direction of law schools are Columbia Law Review, Cornell Law Quarterly, Harvard Law Review, Illinois Law Review, Michigan Law Review, Texas Law Review, Wisconsin Law Review, and Yale Law Journal.

Libel Defense Resource Center Bulletin. Reports studies and analyses by the Center, many of them wide-sweeping surveys of aspects of libel nationally.

Media Law Reporter. Bureau of National Affairs, Inc., Washington, D.C. This looseleaf service provides up-to-date coverage of court decisions (full texts) and news notes in communication law, beginning in 1976.

National Reporter System, giving texts of appellate court decisions in various jurisdictions of the nation.

News Media and the Law, publication of the Reporters Committee for Freedom of the Press (formerly Press Censorship Newsletter). Washington, D.C.

Words and Phrases, a legal encyclopedia based on definitions of terms as used in statutes and by the courts.

Appendix E

THE SOCIETY OF PROFESSIONAL JOURNALISTS AND ASNE CODES OF ETHICS

THE SOCIETY OF PROFESSIONAL JOURNALISTS CODE OF ETHICS

The Society of Professional Journalists believes the duty of journalists is to serve the truth.

We believe the agencies of mass communication are carriers of public discussion and information, acting on their Constitutional mandate and freedom to learn and report the facts.

We believe in public enlightenment as the forerunner of justice, and in our Constitutional role to seek the truth as part of the public's right to know the truth.

We believe those responsibilities carry obligations that require journalists to perform with intelligence, objectivity, accuracy and fairness.

To these ends, we declare acceptance of the standards of practice here set forth:

I. Responsibility: The public's right to know of events of public importance and interest is the overriding mission of the mass media. The purpose of distributing news and enlightened opinion is to serve the general welfare. Journalists who use their professional status as representatives of the public for selfish or other unworthy motives violate a high trust.

II. Freedom of the Press: Freedom of the press is to be guarded as an inalienable right of people in a free society. It carries with it the freedom and the responsibility to discuss, question and challenge actions and utterances of our government and of our public and private institutions. Journalists uphold the right to speak unpopular opinions and the privilege to agree with the majority.

III. Ethics: Journalists must be free of obligation to any interest other than the public's right to know the truth.

1. Gifts, favors, free travel, special treatment or privileges can compromise the integrity of journalists and their employers. Nothing of value should be accepted.

2. Secondary employment, political involvement, holding public office and service in community organizations should be avoided if it compromises the integrity of journalists and their employers. Journalists and their employers should conduct their personal lives in a manner which protects them from conflict of interest, real or apparent. Their responsibilities to the public are paramount. That is the nature of their profession.

3. So-called news communications from private sources should not be published or broadcast without substantiation of their claims to news value.

4. Journalists will seek news that serves the public interest, despite the obstacles. They will make constant efforts to assure that the public's business is conducted in public and that public records are open to public inspection.

5. Journalists acknowledge the newsman's ethic of protecting confidential sources of information.

IV. Accuracy and Objectivity: Good faith with the public is the foundation of all worthy journalism.

1. Truth is our ultimate goal.

2. Objectivity in reporting the news is another goal, which serves as the mark of an experienced professional. It is a standard of performance toward which we strive. We honor those who achieve it.

3. There is no excuse for inaccuracies or lack of thoroughness.

4. Newspaper headlines should be fully warranted by the contents of the articles they accompany. Photographs and telecasts should give an accurate picture of an event and not highlight an incident out of context.

5. Sound practice makes clear distinction between news reports and expressions of opinion. News reports should be free of opinion or bias and represent all sides of an issue.

6. Partisanship in editorial comment which knowingly departs from the truth violates the spirit of American journalism.

7. Journalists recognize their responsibility for offering informed analysis, comment and editorial opinion on public events and issues. They accept the obligation to present such material by individuals whose competence, experience, and judgment qualify them for it.

8. Special articles or presentations devoted to advocacy or the writer's own conclusions and interpretations should be labeled as such.

V. Fair Play: Journalists at all times will show respect for the dignity, privacy, rights, and well-being of people encountered in the course of gathering and presenting the news.

1. The news media should not communicate unofficial charges affecting reputation or moral character without giving the accused a chance to reply.

2. The news media must guard against invading a person's right to privacy.

3. The media should not pander to morbid curiosity about details of vice and crime.

4. It is the duty of news media to make prompt and complete correction of their errors.

5. Journalists should be accountable to the public for their reports and the public should be encouraged to voice its grievances against the media. Open dialogue with our readers, viewers, and listeners should be fostered.

VI. Pledge: Adherence to this code is intended to preserve and strengthen the bond of mutual trust and respect between American Journalists and the American People.

The Society shall—by programs of education and other means—encourage individual journalists to adhere to these tenets, and shall encourage journalistic publications and broadcasters to recognize their responsibility to frame codes of ethics in concert with their employers to serve as guidelines in furthering these goals.

Adopted by the 1973 national convention; revised 1984, 1987.

ASNE STATEMENT OF PRINCIPLES

PREAMBLE

The First Amendment, protecting freedom of expression from abridgment by any law, guarantees to the people through their press a constitutional right, and thereby places on newspaper people a particular responsibility.

Thus journalism demands of its practitioners not only industry and knowledge but also the pursuit of a standard of integrity proportionate to the journalist's singular obligation.

To this end the American Society of Newspaper Editors sets forth this Statement of Principles as a standard encouraging the highest ethical and professional performance.

ARTICLE I: RESPONSIBILITY

The primary purpose of gathering and distributing news and opinion is to serve the general welfare by informing the people and enabling them to make judgments on the issues of the time. Newspapermen and women who abuse the power of their professional role for selfish motives or unworthy purposes are faithless to that public trust.

The American press was made free not just to inform or just to serve as a forum for debate but also to bring an independent scrutiny to bear on the forces of power in the society, including the conduct of official power at all levels of government.

ARTICLE II: FREEDOM OF THE PRESS

Freedom of the press belongs to the people. It must be defended against encroachment or assault from any quarter, public or private.

Journalists must be constantly alert to see that the public's business is conducted in public. They must be vigilant against all who would exploit the press for selfish purposes.

ARTICLE III: INDEPENDENCE

Journalists must avoid impropriety and the appearance of impropriety as well as any conflict of interest or the appearance of conflict. They should neither accept anything nor pursue any activity that might compromise or seem to compromise their integrity.

ARTICLE IV: TRUTH AND ACCURACY

Good faith with the reader is the foundation of good journalism. Every effort must be made to assure that the news content is accurate, free from bias and in context, and that all sides are presented fairly. Editorials, analytical articles and commentary should be held to the same standards of accuracy with respect to facts as news reports.

Significant errors of fact, as well as errors of omission, should be corrected promptly and prominently.

ARTICLE V: IMPARTIALITY

To be impartial does not require the press to be unquestioning or to refrain from editorial expression. Sound practice, however, demands a clear distinction for the reader between news reports and opinion. Articles that contain opinion or personal interpretation should be clearly identified.

ARTICLE VI: FAIR PLAY

Journalists should respect the rights of people involved in the news, observe the common standards of decency and stand accountable to the public for the fairness and accuracy of their news reports.

Persons publicly accused should be given the earliest opportunity to respond.

Pledges of confidentiality to news sources must be honored at all costs, and therefore should not be given lightly. Unless there is clear and pressing need to maintain confidences, sources of information should be identified.

These principles are intended to preserve, protect and strengthen the bond of trust and respect between American journalists and the American people, a bond that is essential to sustain the grant of freedom entrusted to both by the nation's founders.

Originally adopted in 1922 by the ASNE as the Canons of Journalism, it was revised and renamed the Statement of Principles in October, 1975.

Appendix F

COMMUNICATIONS ACT OF 1934
(MAJOR PROVISIONS)

COMMUNICATIONS ACT OF 1934

48 Stat. 1064 (1934), as amended, 47 U.S.C.A. § 151 et seq.

TITLE I—GENERAL PROVISIONS
PURPOSES OF ACT; CREATION OF FEDERAL
COMMUNICATIONS COMMISSION

Sec. 151

For the purpose of regulating interstate and foreign commerce in communication by wire and radio so as to make available, so far as possible, to all the people of the United States a rapid, efficient, Nationwide, and world-wide wire and radio communication service with adequate facilities at reasonable charges, for the purpose of the national defense, for the purpose of promoting safety of life and property through the use of wire and radio communication, and for the purpose of securing a more effective execution of this policy by centralizing authority heretofore granted by law to several agencies and by granting additional authority with respect to interstate and foreign commerce in wire and radio communication, there is hereby created a commission to be known as the "Federal Communications Commission," which shall be constituted as hereinafter provided, and which shall execute and enforce the provisions of this Act.

* * *

APPLICATION OF ACT

Sec. 152

(a) The provisions of this Act shall apply to all interstate and foreign communication by wire or radio and all interstate and foreign transmission of energy by radio, which originates and/or is received within the United States, and to all persons engaged within the United States in such communication or such transmission of energy by radio, and to the licensing and regulating of all radio stations as hereinafter provided.... The provisions of this Act shall apply with respect to cable service to all persons engaged within the United States in providing such service, and to the

825

facilities of cable operators which relate to such service as provided in title VI.

* * *

TITLE II—COMMON CARRIERS

(omitted)

TITLE III—PROVISIONS RELATING TO RADIO

LICENSE FOR RADIO COMMUNICATION OR TRANSMISSION OF ENERGY

Sec. 301

It is the purpose of this Act, among other things, to maintain the control of the United States over all the channels of interstate and foreign radio transmission; and to provide for the use of such channels, but not the ownership thereof, by persons for limited periods of time, under licenses granted by Federal authority, and no such license shall be construed to create any right, beyond the terms, conditions, and periods of the license. No person shall use or operate any apparatus for the transmission of energy or communications or signals by radio (a) from one place in any Territory or possession of the United States or in the District of Columbia to another place in the same Territory, possession, or district; or (b) from any State, Territory, or possession of the United States, or from the District of Columbia to any other State, Territory, or possession of the United States; or (c) from any place in any State, Territory, or possession of the United States, or in the District of Columbia, to any place in any foreign country or to any vessel; or (d) within any State when the effects of such use extend beyond the borders of said State, or when interference is caused by such use or operation with the transmission of such energy, communications, or signals from within said State to any place beyond its borders, or from any place beyond its borders to any place within said State, or with the transmission or reception of such energy, communications, or signals from and/or to places beyond the borders of said State; or (e) upon any vessel or aircraft of the United States; or (f) upon any other mobile stations within the jurisdiction of the United States, except under and in accordance with this Act and with a license in that behalf granted under the provisions of this Act.

* * *

GENERAL POWERS OF THE COMMISSION

Sec. 303

Except as otherwise provided in this Act, the Commission from time to time, as public convenience, interest, or necessity requires shall:

(a) Classify radio stations;

(b) Prescribe the nature of the service to be rendered by each class of licensed stations and each station within any class;

(c) Assign bands of frequencies to the various classes of stations, and assign frequencies for each individual station and determine the power which each station shall use and the time during which it may operate;

(d) Determine the location of classes of stations or individual stations;

(e) Regulate the kind of apparatus to be used with respect to its external effects and the purity and sharpness of the emissions from each station and from the apparatus therein;

(f) Make such regulations not inconsistent with law as it may deem necessary to prevent interference between stations and to carry out the provisions of this Act: *Provided, however,* That changes in the frequencies, authorized power, or in the times of operation of any station, shall not be made without the consent of the station licensee unless, after a public hearing, the Commission shall determine that such changes will promote public convenience or interest or will serve public necessity, or the provisions of this Act will be more fully complied with;

(g) Study new uses for radio, provide for experimental uses of frequencies, and generally encourage the larger and more effective use of radio in the public interest;

(h) Have authority to establish areas or zones to be served by any station;

(i) Have authority to make special regulations applicable to radio stations engaged in chain broadcasting;

(j) Have authority to make general rules and regulations requiring stations to keep such records of programs, transmissions of energy, communications, or signals as it may deem desirable;

* * *

(m)(1) Have authority to suspend the license of any operator upon proof sufficient to satisfy the Commission that the licensee—

(A) has violated any provision of any Act, treaty, or convention binding on the United States, which the Commission is authorized to administer, or any regulation made by the Commission under any such Act, treaty, or convention; or

* * *

(D) has transmitted superfluous radio communications or signals or communications containing profane or obscene words, language, or meaning. . . .

* * *

(r) Make such rules and regulations and prescribe such restrictions and conditions, not inconsistent with law, as may be necessary to carry out the provisions of this Act, or any international radio or wire communications treaty or convention, or regulations annexed thereto, including any treaty or convention insofar as it relates to the use of radio, to which the United States is or may hereafter become a party.

(s) Have authority to require that apparatus designed to receive television pictures broadcast simultaneously with sound be capable of adequately receiving all frequencies allocated by the Commission to television broadcasting when such apparatus is shipped in interstate commerce, or is imported from any foreign country into the United States, for sale or resale to the public.

* * *

ALLOCATION OF FACILITIES; TERM OF LICENSES

Sec. 307

(a) The Commission, if public convenience, interest, or necessity will be served thereby, subject to the limitations of this Act, shall grant to any applicant therefor a station license provided for by this Act.

(b) In considering applications for licenses, and modifications and renewals thereof, when and insofar as there is demand for the same, the Commission shall make such distribution of licenses, frequencies, hours of operation, and of power among the several States and communities as to provide a fair, efficient, and equitable distribution of radio service to each of the same.

* * *

(d) No license granted for the operation of a television broadcasting station shall be for a term longer than five years . . . and any license granted may be revoked as hereinafter provided. Each license granted for the operation of a radio broadcasting station shall be for a term of not to exceed seven years. Upon the expiration of any license, upon application therefor, a renewal of such license may be granted from time to time for a term of not to exceed five years in the case of television broadcasting licenses, for a term of not to exceed seven years in the case of radio broadcasting station licenses, and for a term of not to exceed five years in the case of other licenses, if the Commission finds that public interest, convenience, and necessity would be served thereby....

(e) No renewal of an existing station license in the broadcast or the common carrier services shall be granted more than thirty days prior to the expiration of the original license.

APPLICATIONS FOR LICENSES ...

Sec. 308

* * *

(b) All applications for station licenses, or modifications or renewals thereof, shall set forth such facts as the Commission by regulation may prescribe as to the citizenship, character, and financial, technical, and other qualifications of the applicant to operate the station; the ownership and location of the proposed station and of the stations, if any, with which it is proposed to communicate; the frequencies and the power desired to be used; the hours of the day or other periods of time during which it is proposed to operate the station; the purposes for which the station is to be used; and such other information as it may require....

ACTION UPON APPLICATIONS; FORM OF AND CONDITIONS ATTACHED TO LICENSES

Sec. 309

(a) Subject to the provisions of this section, the Commission shall determine, in the case of each application filed with it to which section 308 applies, whether the public interest, convenience, and necessity will be served by the granting of such application, and, if the Commission, upon examination of such application and upon consideration of such other matters as the Commission may officially notice, shall find that public interest, convenience, and necessity would be served by the granting thereof, it shall grant such application.

* * *

(d)(1) Any party in interest may file with the Commission a petition to deny any application....

(2) If the Commission finds on the basis of the application, the pleadings filed, or other matters which it may officially

notice that there are no substantial and material questions of fact and that a grant of the application would be consistent with subsection (a), it shall make the grant, deny the petition, and issue a concise statement of the reasons for denying the petition, which statement shall dispose of all substantial issues raised by the petition. If a substantial and material question of fact is presented or if the Commission for any reason is unable to find that grant of the application would be consistent with subsection (a), it shall proceed as provided in subsection (e).

(e) If, in the case of any application to which subsection (a) of this section applies, a substantial and material question of fact is presented or the Commission for any reason is unable to make the finding specified in such subsection, it shall formally designate the application for hearing on the ground or reasons then obtaining and shall forthwith notify the applicant and all other known parties in interest of such action and the grounds and reasons therefor, specifying with particularity the matters and things in issue but not including issues or requirements phrased generally. . . .

* * *

(h) Such station licenses as the Commission may grant shall be in such general form as it may prescribe, but each license shall contain, in addition to other provisions, a statement of the following conditions to which such license shall be subject: (1) The station license shall not vest in the licensee any right to operate the station nor any right in the use of the frequencies designated in the license beyond the term thereof nor in any other manner than authorized therein; (2) neither the license nor the right granted thereunder shall be assigned or otherwise transferred in violation of this Act; (3) every license issued under this Act shall be subject in terms to the right of use or control conferred by section 606 of this Act.*

* * *

LIMITATION ON HOLDING AND TRANSFER OF LICENSES

Sec. 310

(a) The station license required hereby shall not be granted to or held by any foreign government or representative thereof.

(b) No broadcast or common carrier ... license shall be granted to or held by—

(1) Any alien or the representative of any alien;

* [Section 606 grants broad powers to the President to utilize communications facilities during wartime or a national emergency.]

(2) Any corporation organized under the laws of any foreign government;

* * *

(d) No construction permit or station license, or any rights thereunder, shall be transferred, assigned, or disposed of in any manner, voluntarily or involuntarily, directly or indirectly, or by transfer of control of any corporation holding such permit or license, to any person except upon application to the Commission and upon finding by the Commission that the public interest, convenience, and necessity will be served thereby. Any such application shall be disposed of as if the proposed transferee or assignee were making application under section 308 for the permit or license in question; but in acting thereon the Commission may not consider whether the public interest, convenience, and necessity might be served by the transfer, assignment, or disposal of the permit or license to a person other than the proposed transferee or assignee.

SPECIAL REQUIREMENTS WITH RESPECT TO CERTAIN APPLICATIONS IN THE BROADCASTING SERVICE

Sec. 311

* * *

(c)(1) If there are pending before the Commission two or more applications for a permit for construction of a broadcasting station, only one of which can be granted, it shall be unlawful, without approval of the Commission, for the applicants or any of them to effectuate an agreement whereby one or more of such applicants withdraws his or their application or applications.

(2) The request for Commission approval in any such case shall be made in writing jointly by all the parties to the agreement. Such request shall contain or be accompanied by full information with respect to the agreement, set forth in such detail, form, and manner as the Commission shall by rule require.

(3) The Commission shall approve the agreement only if it determines (A) that the agreement is consistent with the public interest, convenience, or necessity; and (B) no party to the agreement filed its application for the purpose of reaching or carrying out such agreement. If the agreement does not contemplate a merger, but contemplates the making of any direct or indirect payment to any party thereto in consideration of his withdrawal of his application, the Commission may determine the agreement to be consistent with the public interest, convenience, or necessity only if the amount or value

of such payment, as determined by the Commission, is not in excess of the aggregate amount determined by the Commission to have been legitimately and prudently expended and to be expended by such applicant in connection with preparing, filing, and advocating the granting of his application.

* * *

ADMINISTRATIVE SANCTIONS

Sec. 312

(a) The Commission may revoke any station license or construction permit—

(1) for false statements knowingly made either in the application or in any statement of fact which may be required pursuant to section 308;

(2) because of conditions coming to the attention of the Commission which would warrant it in refusing to grant a license or permit on an original application;

(3) for willful or repeated failure to operate substantially as set forth in the license;

(4) for willful or repeated violation of, or willful or repeated failure to observe any provision of this Act or any rule or regulation of the Commission authorized by this Act or by a treaty ratified by the United States;

(5) for violation of or failure to observe any final cease and desist order issued by the Commission under this section;

(6) for violation of section 1304, 1343, or 1464 of title 18 of the United States Code; * or

* [Relevant provisions read as follows:

§ 1304.   Broadcasting lottery information

Whoever broadcasts by means of any radio station for which a license is required by any law of the United States, or whoever, operating any such station, knowingly permits the broadcasting of, any advertisement of or information concerning any lottery, gift enterprise, or similar scheme, offering prizes dependent in whole or in part upon lot or chance, or any list of the prizes drawn or awarded by means of any such lottery, gift enterprise, or scheme, whether said list contains any part or all of such prizes, shall be fined not more than $1,000 or imprisoned not more than one year, or both.

§ 1343.   Fraud by wire, radio, or television

Whoever, having devised or intending to devise any scheme or artifice to defraud, or for obtaining money or property by means of false or fraudulent pretenses, representations, or promises, transmits or causes to be transmitted by means of wire, radio, or television communication in interstate or foreign commerce, any writings, signs, signals, pictures, or sounds for the purpose of executing such scheme or artifice, shall be fined not more than $1,000 or imprisoned not more than five years, or both.

(7) for willful or repeated failure to allow reasonable access to or to permit purchase of reasonable amounts of time for the use of a broadcasting station by a legally qualified candidate for Federal elective office on behalf of his candidacy.

(b) Where any person (1) has failed to operate substantially as set forth in a license, (2) has violated or failed to observe any of the provisions of this Act, or section 1304, 1343, or 1464 of title 18 of the United States Code, or (3) has violated or failed to observe any rule or regulation of the Commission authorized by this Act or by a treaty ratified by the United States, the Commission may order such person to cease and desist from such action.

(c) Before revoking a license or permit pursuant to subsection (a), or issuing a cease and desist order pursuant to subsection (b), the Commission shall serve upon the licensee, permittee, or person involved an order to show cause [at a hearing] why an order of revocation or a cease and desist order should not be issued....

(d) In any case where a hearing is conducted pursuant to the provisions of this section, both the burden of proceeding with the introduction of evidence and the burden of proof shall be upon the Commission.

* * *

APPLICATION OF ANTITRUST LAWS; REFUSAL OF LICENSES AND PERMITS IN CERTAIN CASES

Sec. 313

(a) All laws of the United States relating to unlawful restraints and monopolies and to combinations, contracts, or agreements in restraint of trade are hereby declared to be applicable to the manufacture and sale of and to trade in radio apparatus and devices entering into or affecting interstate or foreign commerce and to interstate or foreign radio communications. Whenever in any suit, action, or proceeding, civil or criminal, brought under the provisions of any of said laws or in any proceedings brought to enforce or to review findings and orders of the Federal Trade

§ 1464. Broadcasting obscene language

Whoever utters any obscene, indecent, or profane language by means of radio communications shall be fined not more than $10,000 or imprisoned not more than two years, or both.

§ 1307. State-conducted lotteries

(a) The provisions of sections 1301, 1302, 1303, and 1304 shall not apply to an advertisement, list of prizes, or information concerning a lottery conducted by a State acting under the authority of State law—

(1) contained in a newspaper published in that State, or

(2) broadcast by a radio or television station licensed to a location in that State or an adjacent State which conducts such a lottery....]

Commission or other governmental agency in respect of any matters as to which said Commission or other governmental agency is by law authorized to act, any licensee shall be found guilty of the violation of the provisions of such laws or any of them, the court, in addition to the penalties imposed by said laws, may adjudge, order, and/or decree that the license of such licensee shall, as of the date the decree or judgment becomes finally effective or as of such other date as the said decree shall fix, be revoked and that all rights under such license shall thereupon cease: *Provided, however,* That such licensee shall have the same right of appeal or review, as is provided by law in respect of other decrees and judgments of said court.

(b) The Commission is hereby directed to refuse a station license and/or the permit hereinafter required for the construction of a station to any person (or to any person directly or indirectly controlled by such person) whose license has been revoked by a court under this section.

* * *

FACILITIES FOR CANDIDATES FOR PUBLIC OFFICE

Sec. 315

(a) If any licensee shall permit any person who is a legally qualified candidate for any public office to use a broadcasting station, he shall afford equal opportunities to all other such candidates for that office in the use of such broadcasting station: *Provided,* That such licensee shall have no power of censorship over the material broadcast under the provisions of this section. No obligation is imposed under this subsection upon any licensee to allow the use of its station by any such candidate. Appearance by a legally qualified candidate on any—

(1) Bona fide newscast,

(2) Bona fide news interview,

(3) Bona fide news documentary (if the appearance of the candidate is incidental to the presentation of the subject or subjects covered by the news documentary), or

(4) On-the-spot coverage of bona fide news events (included but not limited to political conventions and activities incidental thereto), shall not be deemed to be use of a broadcasting station within the meaning of this subsection. Nothing in the foregoing sentence shall be construed as relieving broadcasters, in connection with the presentation of newscasts, news interviews, news documentaries, and on-the-spot coverage of news events, from the obligation imposed upon them under this Act

to operate in the public interest and to afford reasonable opportunity for the discussion of conflicting views on issues of public importance.

(b) The charges made for the use of any broadcast station by any person who is a legally qualified candidate for any public office in connection with his campaign for nomination for election, or election, to such office shall not exceed—

(1) During the 45 days preceding the date of a primary or primary runoff election and during the 60 days preceding the date of a general or special election in which such person is a candidate, the lowest unit charge of the station for the same class and amount of time for the same period; and

(2) At any other time, the charges made for comparable use of such station by other users thereof.

(c) For the purposes of this section:

(1) The term "broadcasting station" includes a community antenna television system.

(2) The terms "licensee" and "station licensee" when used with respect to a community antenna television system, mean the operator of such system.

(d) The Commission shall prescribe appropriate rules and regulations to carry out the provisions of this section.

MODIFICATION BY COMMISSION OF CONSTRUCTION PERMITS OR LICENSES

Sec. 316

(a) Any station license or construction permit may be modified by the Commission either for a limited time or for the duration of the term thereof, if in the judgment of the Commission such action will promote the public interest, convenience, and necessity, or the provisions of this Act or of any treaty ratified by the United States will be more fully complied with. No such order of modification shall become final until the holder of the license or permit shall have been notified in writing of the proposed action and the grounds and reasons therefor, and shall have been given reasonable opportunity, in no event less than thirty days, to show cause by public hearing, if requested, why such order of modification should not issue. . . .

(b) In any case where a hearing is conducted pursuant to the provisions of this section, both the burden of proceeding with the introduction of evidence and the burden of proof shall be upon the Commission.

ANNOUNCEMENT WITH RESPECT TO
CERTAIN MATTER BROADCAST

Sec. 317

(a)(1) All matter broadcast by any radio station for which any money, service or other valuable consideration is directly or indirectly paid, or promised to or charged or accepted by, the station so broadcasting, from any person, shall, at the time the same is so broadcast, be announced as paid for or furnished, as the case may be, by such person: *Provided,* That "service or other valuable consideration" shall not include any service or property furnished without charge or at a nominal charge for use on, or in connection with, a broadcast unless it is so furnished in consideration for an identification in a broadcast of any person, product, service, trademark, or brand name beyond an identification which is reasonably related to the use of such service or property on the broadcast.

* * *

CENSORSHIP . . .

Sec. 326

Nothing in this Act shall be understood or construed to give the Commission the power of censorship over the radio communications or signals transmitted by any radio station, and no regulation or condition shall be promulgated or fixed by the Commission which shall interfere with the right of free speech by means of radio communication.

JURISDICTION TO ENFORCE ACT AND
ORDERS OF COMMISSION

Sec. 401

(a) The district courts of the United States shall have jurisdiction, upon application of the Attorney General of the United States at the request of the Commission, alleging a failure to comply with or a violation of any of the provisions of this Act by any person, to issue a writ or writs of mandamus commanding such person to comply with the provisions of this Act.

(b) If any person fails or neglects to obey any order of the Commission other than for the payment of money, while the same is in effect, the Commission or any party injured thereby, or the United States, by its Attorney General, may apply to the appropriate district court of the United States for the enforcement of such order. . . .

Sec. 402

(a) [Provides that any proceeding to review an order of the Commission not appealable under Sec. 402(b) is within the exclusive jurisdiction of the courts of appeal, venue to lie in the circuit in which the filing party resides or has his principal office, or in the D.C. Circuit.]

(b) [Provides that appeals from licensing decisions and cease and desist orders may be taken to the D.C. Circuit Court of Appeals.]

FORFEITURES

Sec. 503

* * *

(b)(1) Any person who is determined by the Commission, in accordance with paragraph (3) or (4) of this subsection, to have—

(A) willfully or repeatedly failed to comply substantially with the terms and conditions of any license, permit, certificate, or other instrument or authorization issued by the Commission;

(B) willfully or repeatedly failed to comply with any of the provisions of this Act or of any rule, regulation, or order issued by the Commission under this Act or under any treaty convention, or other agreement to which the United States is a party and which is binding upon the United States;

(C) violated any provision of section 317(c) or 509(a) of this Act; or

(D) violated any provision of section 1304, 1343, or 1464 of Title 18, United States Code;

shall be liable to the United States for a forfeiture penalty. A forfeiture penalty under this subsection shall be in addition to any other penalty provided for by this Act; except that this subsection shall not apply to any conduct which is subject to forfeiture under ... section 507 of this Act.

(2) The amount of any forfeiture penalty determined under this subsection shall not exceed $25,000 for each violation. Each day of a continuing violation shall constitute a separate offense, but the total forfeiture penalty which may be imposed under this subsection, for acts or omissions described in paragraph (1) of this subsection and set forth in the notice or the notice of apparent liability issued under this subsection, shall not exceed:

(A) $250,000, if the violator is (i) a common carrier subject to the provisions of this Act, (ii) a broadcast station licensee or permittee, or (iii) a cable television operator . . .

The amount of such forfeiture penalty shall be assessed by the Commission, or its designee, by written notice. In determining the amount of such a forfeiture penalty, the Commission or its designee shall take into account the nature, circumstances, extent, and gravity of the prohibited acts committed and, with respect to the violator, the degree of culpability, any history of prior offenses, ability to pay, and such other matters as justice may require.

* * *

TITLE VI—CABLE COMMUNICATIONS
PURPOSES

Sec. 521

The purposes of this title are to

(1) establish a national policy concerning cable communications;

(2) establish franchise procedures and standards which encourage the growth and development of cable systems and which assure that cable systems are responsive to the needs and interests of the local community;

(3) establish guidelines for the exercise of Federal, State, and local authority with respect to the regulation of cable systems;

(4) assure and encourage that cable communications provide and are encouraged to provide the widest possible diversity of information sources and services to the public.

(5) establish an orderly process for franchise renewal which protects cable operators against unfair denials of renewal where the operator's past performance and proposal for future performance meet the standards established by this title; and

(6) promote competition in cable communications and minimize unnecessary regulation that would impose an undue economic burden on cable systems.

* * *

CABLE CHANNELS FOR PUBLIC, EDUCATIONAL OR GOVERNMENTAL USE

Sec. 531

(a) A franchising authority may establish requirements in a franchise with respect to the designation or use of channel capacity for public, educational, or governmental use only to the extent provided in this section.

(b) A franchising authority may in its request for proposals require as part of a franchise, and may require as part of a cable operator's proposal for a franchise renewal, subject to section 626, that channel capacity be designated for public, educational, or governmental use, . . .

(c) A franchising authority may enforce any requirement in any franchise regarding the providing or use of such channel capacity. Such enforcement authority includes the authority to enforce any provisions of the franchise for services, facilities, or equipment proposed by the cable operator, which relate to public, educational, or governmental use of channel capacity, whether or not required by the franchising authority pursuant to subsection (b).

* * *

(e) Subject to section 624(d), a cable operator shall not exercise any editorial control over any public, educational, or governmental use of channel capacity provided pursuant to this section.

* * *

GENERAL FRANCHISE REQUIREMENTS

Sec. 541

(a)(1) A franchising authority may award, in accordance with the provisions of this title, one or more franchises within its jurisdiction.

* * *

(3) In awarding a franchise or franchises, a franchising authority shall assure that access to cable service is not denied to any group of potential residential cable subscribers because of the income of the residents of the local area in which such group resides.

* * *

(c) Any cable system shall not be subject to regulation as a common carrier or utility by reason of providing any cable service.

* * *

FRANCHISE FEES

Sec. 542

(a) Subject to the limitation of subsection (b), any cable operator may be required under the terms of any franchise to pay a franchise fee.

(b) For any 12–month period, the franchise fees paid by a cable operator with respect to any cable system shall not exceed 5 percent of such cable operator's gross revenues derived in such period from the operation of the cable system.

* * *

REGULATION OF RATES

Sec. 543

(a) Any Federal agency or State may not regulate the rates for the provision of cable service except to cable subscribers only to the extent provided under this section. Any franchising authority may regulate the rates for the provision of cable service or any other communications service provided over a cable system to cable subscribers, but only to the extent provided under this section.

(b)(1) Within 180 days after the date of the enactment of this title, the Commission shall prescribe and make effective regulations which authorize a franchising authority to regulate rates for the provision of basic cable service in circumstances in which a cable system is not subject to effective competition. Such regulations may apply to any franchise granted after the effective date of such regulations. Such regulations shall not apply to any rate while such rate is subject to the provisions of subsection (c).

(2) For purposes of rate regulation under this subsection, such regulations shall—

(A) define the circumstances in which a cable system is not subject to effective competition; and

(B) establish standards for such rate regulation.

* * *

(c) In the case of any cable system for which a franchise has been granted on or before the effective date of this title, until the end of the 2–year period beginning on such effective date, the franchising authority may, to the extent provided in a franchise—

(1) regulate the rates for the provision of basic cable service, including multiple tiers of basic cable service;

(2) require the provision of any service tier provided without charge (disregarding any installation or rental charge for equipment necessary for receipt of such tier); or

(3) regulate rates for the initial installation or the rental of one set of the minimum equipment which is necessary for the subscriber's receipt of basic cable service.

* * *

RENEWAL

Sec. 546

(a) During the 6–month period which begins with the 36th month before the franchise expiration, the franchising authority may on its own initiative, and shall at the request of the cable operator, commence proceedings which afford the public in the franchise area appropriate notice and participation for the purpose of—

(1) identifying the future cable-related community needs and interests; and

(2) reviewing the performance of the cable operator under the franchise during the then current franchise term.

(b)(1) Upon completion of a proceeding under subsection (a), a cable operator seeking renewal of a franchise may, on its own initiative or at the request of a franchising authority, submit a proposal for renewal.

(2) Subject to section 624, any such proposal shall contain such material as the franchising authority may require, including proposals for an upgrade of the cable system.

(3) The franchising authority may establish a date by which such proposals shall be submitted.

(c)(1) Upon submittal by a cable operator of a proposal to the franchising authority for the renewal of a franchise, the franchising authority shall provide prompt public notice of such proposal and, during the 4–month period which begins on the completion of any proceedings under subsection (a), renew the franchise or, issue a preliminary assessment that the franchise should not be renewed and, at the request of the operator or on its own initiative, commence an administrative proceeding after providing prompt public notice of such proceeding in accordance with paragraph (2) to consider whether—

(A) the cable operator has substantially complied with the material terms of the existing franchise and with applicable law;

(B) the quality of the operator's service including signal quality, response to consumer complaints, and billing practices, but without regard to the mix, quality, or level of cable services or other services provided over the system, has been reasonable in light of community needs;

(C) the operator has the financial, legal, and technical ability to provide the services, facilities, and equipment as set forth in the operator's proposal; and

(D) the operator's proposal is reasonable to meet the future cable-related community needs and interests, taking into account the cost of meeting such needs and interests.

* * *

(3) At the completion of a proceeding under this subsection, the franchising authority shall issue a written decision granting or denying the proposal for renewal based upon the record of such proceeding, and transmit a copy of such decision to the cable operator. Such decision shall state the reasons therefor.

(d) Any denial of a proposal for renewal shall be based on one or more adverse findings made with respect to the factors described in subparagraphs (A) through (D) of subsection (c)(1)....

* * *

OBSCENE PROGRAMMING

Sec. 559

Whoever transmits over any cable system any matter which is obscene or otherwise unprotected by the Constitution of the United States shall be fined not more than $10,000 or imprisoned not more than two years, or both.

UNAUTHORIZED PUBLICATION OR
USE OF COMMUNICATIONS

Sec. 705

(a) Except as authorized by Chapter 119, Title 18, no person receiving, assisting in receiving, transmitting, or assisting in transmitting, any interstate or foreign communication by wire or radio shall divulge or publish the existence, contents, substance, purport, effect, or meaning thereof, except through authorized channels of transmission or reception, (1) to any person other than the addressee, his agent, or attorney, (2) to a person employed or authorized to forward such communication to its destination, (3) to proper accounting or distributing officers of the various communicating centers over which the communication may be passed, (4) to the master of a ship under whom he is serving, (5) in response to a subpoena issued by a court of competent jurisdiction, or (6) on demand of other lawful authority. No person not being authorized by the sender shall intercept any radio communication and divulge or publish the existence, contents, substance, purport, effect, or meaning of such intercepted communication to any person. No person not being entitled thereto shall receive or assist in receiving any interstate or foreign communication by radio and use such communication (or any information therein contained) for his own benefit or for the benefit of another not entitled thereto. No person having received any intercepted radio communication or having become acquainted with the contents, substance, purport, effect, or meaning of such communication (or any part thereof) knowing that such communication was intercepted, shall divulge or publish the existence, contents, substance, purport, effect, or meaning of such communication (or any part thereof) or use such communication (or any information therein contained) for his own benefit or for the benefit of another not entitled thereto. This section shall not apply to the receiving, divulging, publishing, or utilizing the contents of any radio communication which is transmitted by any station for the use of the general public, which relates to ships, aircraft, vehicles or persons in distress, or which is transmitted by an amateur radio station operator or by a citizens band radio operator.

(b) The provisions of subsection (a) shall not apply to the interception or receipt by any individual, or the assisting (including the manufacture or sale) of such interception or receipt, of any satellite cable programming for private viewing if—

(1) the programming involved is not encrypted; and

(2)(A) a marketing system is not established under which—

(i) an agent or agents have been lawfully designated for the purpose of authorizing private viewing by individuals, and

(ii) such authorization is available to the individual involved from the appropriate agent or agents; or

(B) a marketing system described in subparagraph (A) is established and the individuals receiving such programming have obtained authorization for private viewing under that system.

(c) For purposes of this section—

(1) the term "satellite cable programming" means video programming which is transmitted via satellite and which is primarily intended for the direct receipt by cable operators for their retransmission to cable subscribers;

(2) the term "agent," with respect to any person, includes an employee of such person;

(3) the term "encrypt," when used with respect to satellite cable programming, means to transmit such programming in a form whereby the aural and visual characteristics (or both) are modified or altered for the purpose of preventing the unautho-

rized receipt of such programming by persons without authorized equipment which is designed to eliminate the effects of such modification or alteration;

(4) the term "private viewing" means the viewing for private use in an individual's dwelling unit by means of equipment, owned or operated by such individual, capable of receiving satellite cable programming directly from a satellite; and

(5) the term "private financial gain" shall not include the gain resulting to any individual for the private use in such individual's dwelling unit of any programming for which the individual has not obtained authorization for that use.

(d)(1) Any person who willfully violates subsection (a) shall be fined not more than $1,000 or imprisoned for not more than 6 months or both.

(2) Any person who violates subsection (a) willfully and for purposes of direct or indirect commercial advantage or private financial gain shall be fined not more than $25,000 or imprisoned for not more than 1 year, or both, for the first such conviction and shall be fined not more than $50,000 or imprisoned for not more than 2 years, or both, for any subsequent conviction.

(3)(A) Any person aggrieved by any violation of subsection (a) may bring a civil action in a United States district court or in any other court of competent jurisdiction.

(B) The court may—

(i) grant temporary and final injunctions on such terms as it may deem reasonable to prevent or restrain violations of subsection (a);

(ii) award damages as described in subparagraph (C); and

(iii) direct the recovery of full costs, including awarding reasonable attorneys' fees to an aggrieved party who prevails.

(C)(i) Damages awarded by any court under this section shall be computed, at the election of the aggrieved party, in accordance with either of the following subclauses:

(I) the party aggrieved may recover the actual damages suffered by him as a result of the violation and any profits of the violator that are attributable to the violation which are not taken into account in computing the actual damages; in determining the violator's profits, the party aggrieved shall be required to prove only the violator's gross revenue, and the violator shall be required to prove his deductible expenses and the elements of profit attributable to factors other than the violation; or

(II) the party aggrieved may recover an award of statutory damages for each violation involved in the action in a sum of not less than $250 or more than $10,000, as the court considers just.

(ii) In any case in which the court finds that the violation was committed willfully and for purposes of direct or indirect commercial advantage or private financial gain, the court in its discretion may increase the award of damages, whether actual or statutory, by an amount of not more than $50,000.

(iii) In any case where the court finds that the violator was not aware and had no reason to believe that his acts constituted a violation of this section, the court in its discretion may reduce the award of damages to a sum of not less than $100.

(4) The importation, manufacture, sale, or distribution of equipment by any person with the intent of its use to assist in any activity prohibited by subsection (a) shall be subject to penalties and remedies under this subsection to the same extent and in the same manner as a person who has engaged in such prohibited activity.

(5) The penalties under this subsection shall be in addition to those prescribed under any other provision of this title.

*

TABLE OF CASES

References are to Pages.

847

*

INDEX

References are to Pages

†